The American Bibliography of Slavic and East European Studies for 1993

The American Bibliography of Slavic and East European Studies for 1993

American Association for the Advancement of Slavic Studies

Compiled and edited by

Patt Leonard
and
Rebecca Routh

Prepared at the
University of Illinois at Urbana-Champaign for
The American Associaion for the
Advancement of Slavic Studies

M.E. Sharpe
Armonk, New York
London, England

Table of Contents

Introduction

The American Bibliography of Slavic and East European Studies has been published since 1957 (covering 1956 imprints). Through the volume for 1966 it bore the title *American Bibliography of Russian and East European Studies* and was published under the auspices and with the support of the Russian and East European Institute of Indiana University. Since 1968, the *Bibliography* has been sponsored by the American Association for the Advancement of Slavic Studies. The volumes for 1973 through 1989 were compiled at the Library of Congress. Subsequent volumes have been compiled under the auspices of the Mortenson Center for International Library Programs at the Library of the University of Illinois at Urbana-Champaign.

The *Bibliography* indexes English-language and selected foreign-language materials published in the United States and Canada. It also indexes publications produced by American institutions abroad.

The *Bibliography* lists primarily material in the humanities and social sciences relating to Eastern and East-Central Europe and the former Soviet Union, including Albania, Armenia, Azerbaijan, Belarus, Bulgaria, the Czech Republic, the former East Germany, Estonia, Georgia, Greece and Cyprus (since 1821), Hungary, Kazakhstan, Kyrgyzstan, Latvia, Lithuania, Moldova, Poland, Romania, the Russian Federation, Slovakia, Tajikistan, Turkmenistan, Ukraine, Uzbekistan, and the former Yugoslavia. All items are selected on the basis of their relation to the peoples, cultures, and geography of this region. Works that apply to Communism, for example, but that have no direct reference to the former U.S.S.R. or the countries of Eastern or East-Central Europe were omitted.

The *Bibliography* contains citations of books, journal articles, government and research reports, dissertations, and book reviews published in 1993. Newspapers, digests, translation journals, and nonprint materials such as microfilm, audio recordings, videos, and computer software have been excluded.

For European publications, the reader is advised to consult the *European Bibliography of Slavic and East European Studies*.

■ Notes on Organization

The table of contents lists the main subject categories into which entries are grouped. The chapters on the arts, language and linguistics, literature, and science have topical subdivisions, but within the other chapters, the major division is geographic. Most subjects are divided into "Russia/U.S.S.R./C.I.S." or "Eastern Europe." "Eastern Europe" is understood in its broadest possible meaning: it includes all of the countries from Germany to Russia, and from the Baltics to the Balkans. Some citations on the Baltic states have been classified under "U.S.S.R." while others, when it was more appropriate, have been classified under "Eastern Europe."

In this volume, in contrast to previous editions of the *Bibliography*, chapters from edited collections are not given separate entries, but are cited in the entry for the monograph. The authors and titles of those chapters can be found in the indexes.

The Library of Congress transliteration system was used for sources in the Cyrillic alphabet.

■ Acknowledgments

Publication of *The American Bibliography of Slavic and East European Studies* for 1993 would not have been possible without the cooperation and support of many people and institutions. Work on this volume was funded by a U.S. Department of State Title VIII grant administered through the Social Science Research Council. The University of Illinois at Urbana-Champaign provided a work base, library resources, and staff support. Several University staff members assisted in the production of *ABSEES*; in particular, we would like to thank Pam Lindell and Helen Sullivan. We would also like to thank the members of the AAASS Bibliography and Documentation Committee's Subcommittee on ABSEES: Susan Bronson, Robert H. Burger, Marianna Tax Choldin (Chair), June Pachuta Farris, Robert T. Huber, Roger E. Kanet, and Peter B. Maggs.

Special thanks go to David H. Kraus and Zbigniew Kantorosinski of the European Division of the Library of Congress for their ongoing support of the *Bibliography*, and to Mark Kulikowski (SUNY, Oswego), who has contributed a substantial number of citations.

Dissertation citations were graciously provided by University Microfilms International (UMI, A Bell and Howell Company, 300 North Zeeb Road, Ann Arbor, MI 48106-1346). Copies can be ordered directly from UMI by calling (800) 521-0600 x3781 and speaking with a UMI dissertation order representative.

Indexing for this edition was done primarily by Patt Leonard, Rebecca Routh, Natalia Tolstikova, and Aaron Trehub, with additional contributions from Laura Hjerpe and Magdalena Pietraszek. Proofreading was done by Joy Garling, Laura Hjerpe, Patt Leonard, and Rebecca Routh. Page layout was done by Emilio Millán. Clerical support was provided by Patrick Publow and María Sánchez.

Readers are invited to send reprints and notices concerning relevant publications—particularly those published in journals not regularly screened—to the editor of *ABSEES* at the address below.

■ Ordering *ABSEES*

Some past editions of *ABSEES* are available from the American Association for the Advancement of Slavic Studies:

> AAASS
> 8 Storey Street
> Cambridge, MA 02138
>
> Telephone: (617) 495-0677
> Fax: (617) 495-0680
> E-Mail: aaass@hcs.harvard.edu

Beginning with this edition, *ABSEES* will be available from M.E. Sharpe, Inc.:

> M.E. Sharpe, Inc.
> 80 Business Park Drive
> Armonk, NY 10504
>
> Telephone (Sales): (800) 541-6563
> Fax: (914) 273-2106

■ ABSEES Online

ABSEES Online is a database composed of the citations compiled since the *Bibliography* moved to the University of Illinois in 1991. It currently contains over 26,000 records for material published since the late 1980s. New records are added monthly. Connections to ABSEES Online can be made through the Internet or by direct dial-up to the ABSEES Online host computer.

Access to ABSEES Online is available through an annual subscription. Subscriptions can be made on an institutional or individual basis. The subscription service is administered through the University of Illinois Library. For more information, please contact the editor of *ABSEES*.

Patt Leonard
Editor, *ABSEES*

American Bibliography of Slavic and East European Studies (ABSEES)
246A Library
University of Illinois at Urbana-Champaign
1408 West Gregory Drive
Urbana, IL 61801

Telephone: (217) 244-3899
Fax: (217) 244-3077
E-Mail: pleonard@uiuc.edu

Journals

The following is a list of journals indexed for this edition. All journals are selectively indexed; that is, only those articles, book reviews, and obituaries relevant to the field of Slavic and East European area studies are indexed. Boldface indicates the journals that the ABSEES staff covers every year; plain type indicates other journals that have been included as they came to the editor's attention. Not all of the issues were available to the ABSEES staff for examination. The letter before the title indicates whether the volumes published in 1993 were indexed in full (F), only in part (P), or not at all (N). The number "0" indicates that no issues of the journal were published in 1993.

P **AAASS NewsNet**, 33, nos. 1-3, 5
F **Advances in Librarianship**, no. 17
F **Agricultural History**, 67, nos. 1-4
F **Airpower Journal**, 7, nos. 1-4
N Albanica
F **American Anthropologist**, 95, nos. 1-4
F **American Archivist**, 56, nos. 1-4
N **American Asian Review**
P American Biology Teacher, 55, no. 7
P American Criminal Law Review, 30, no. 4
F **American Defence Annual**, no. 8
F **American Economic Review**, 83, nos. 1-5
P American Educator, 17, nos. 1, 3
P American Enterprise, 4, no. 4
N **American Historical Association Recently Published Articles**
F **American Historical Review**, 98, nos. 1-5
P American Indian Quarterly 17, no. 1
F **American Jewish Archives**, 45, nos. 1-2
F **American Jewish History**, 81, nos. 1-4
F **American Journal of Comparative Law**, 41, nos. 1, 3-4
F **American Journal of International Law**, 87, nos. 1-4
P American Journal of Political Science, 37, nos. 1, 3
F **American Journal of Public Health**, 83, nos.1-12
F **American Journal of Sociology**, 98, nos. 4-6, vol. 99, nos. 1-3
P **American Journalism Review**, 15, nos. 3, 5, 9
F **American Political Science Review**, 87, nos. 1-4
P American Prospect, no. 13
F **American Scholar**, 62, nos. 1-4
F **American Sociological Review**, 58, nos. 1-6
F **American Sociologist**, 24, nos. 1-4
F **American Spectator**, 26, nos. 1-12
P American University Journal of International Law and Policy, 9, no. 1
F **Annals of the American Academy of Political and Social Science**, nos. 525-530
F **Annals of the Association of American Geographers**, 83, nos. 1-4
F **Annals of Tourism Research**, 20, nos. 1-4

F **Anthropological Quarterly**, 66, nos. 1-4
F **Antioch Review**, 51, nos. 1-4
P Appalachian Journal, 20, no. 2
F **Ararat**, 34, nos. 1-4
P Architectural Digest, 50, no. 9
F **Arctic**, 46, nos. 1-4
F **Arctic Anthropology**, 30, nos. 1-2
P Arethusa
P Arizona Journal of International and Comparative Law, 10, no. 2
P **Armed Forces & Society**, 19, no. 2
P **Army**, 43, nos. 2-4, 6-12
P **Art & Antiques**, 15, nos. 1-9
F **Art Criticism**, 8, nos. 1-2
P Art in America, 81, no. 5
P **Artforum**, 31, nos. 5
F **ARTnews**, 92, nos. 1-0
F **Asian Affairs: An American Review**, 19, no. 4, vol. 20, nos. 1-3
F **Asian Survey**, 33, nos. 1-12
F **Asian Thought and Society**, 18, nos. 52-54
P **Atlantic Monthly**, 271, nos. 1-6, vol. 272, nos. 1-5
P Audubon, 95, no. 3
F **Australian Slavonic and East European Studies**, 7, nos. 1-2
F **Austrian History Yearbook**, no. 24
F **Aviation Week and Space Technology**, 138, nos. 1-2, 4-5, 20-23, 25-26, vol. 139, nos. 1, 3, 10-13, 15-20

P Behavioral Science, 38, no. 4
F **Behind the Headlines**, 50, nos. 1-4
F **Berkeley Journal of Sociology**, no. 38
P Biblion: The Bulletin of the New York Public Library, 1, no. 2
P **Book World (Washington Post)**, 23
F **Booklist**, 89, nos. 9-22, vol. 90, nos. 1-8
F **Boston College International and Comparative Law Review**, 16, nos. 1-2
F **Brookings Papers on Economic Activity**, 1993, nos. 1-2
F **Brookings Review**, 11, nos. 1-4
F Brooklyn Journal of International Law, 19, no. 1-3
N **Bulletin of Bibliography**
F **Bulletin of the Atomic Scientists**, 49, nos. 1-10
P **Bulletin of the History of Medicine**, 67, nos. 2, 4
F **Business America**, 114, nos. 1-25
P Business & the Contemporary World, 5, no. 4
N **Business History Review**

P California Western International Law Journal, 23, no. 1
F **Canadian-American Slavic Studies**, 27, nos. 1-4
F **Canadian Geographer = Le Géographie Canadien**, 37, nos. 1-4

F **Canadian Geographic**, 113, nos. 1-6
P **Canadian Historical Review**, 74, nos. 1-2
F **Canadian Journal of History = Annales Canadiennes d'Histoire**, 28, nos. 1-3
F **Canadian Journal of Political Science = Revue canadienne de science politique**, 26, nos. 1-4
P Canadian Journal of Sociology = Cahiers canadiens de sociologie, 18, nos. 2-4
F **Canadian Modern Language Review = La Revue Canadienne des langues vivantes**, 49, nos. 2-4, vol. 50, no. 1
F **Canadian Review of Comparative Literature = Revue Canadienne de Littérature Comparée**, 20, nos. 1-4
F **Canadian Review of Sociology and Anthropology = La Revue Canadienne de Sociologie et d'Anthropologie**, 30, nos. 1-4
F **Canadian Review of Studies in Nationalism = Revue Canadienne des Etudes sur le Nationalisme**, 20, nos. 1-2
F **Canadian Slavonic Papers**, 35, nos. 1-4
P Canadian Woman Studies = Les cahiers de la femme, 13, nos. 2-4, vol. 14, no. 1
F **Canadian Yearbook of International Law = Annuaire Canadien de droit international**, no. 30
P Career Development Quarterly, 41, no. 4
P **Carpatho-Rusyn American**, 16, no. 2
F **Case Western Reserve Journal of International Law**, 25, nos. 1-3
F **Catholic Historical Review**, 79, nos. 1-4
P Cato Journal, 12, no. 3
F **Central Asia Monitor**, nos. 1-6
P **Central European History**, 26, nos. 1-3
P Child Psychiatry and Human Development, 24, no. 2
P Child Welfare, 72, no. 5
F **Chronicle of Higher Education**, 39, nos. 18-49, vol. 40, nos. 1-17
F **Church History**, 62, nos. 1-4
F **Cimarron Review**, nos. 102-105
F **Cinema Journal**, 32, nos. 3-4, vol. 33, nos. 1-2
P Cineaste, 19, no. 4
P Cithara, 32, no. 2
F **Clavier**, 32, nos. 1-10
P Cold War International History Project Bulletin, no. 3
P College & Research Libraries News, 54, no. 8
N **College Literature**
P Columbia Human Rights Law Review, 25, no. 1
F **Columbia Journal of Transnational Law**, 31, nos. 1-3
F **Columbia Journal of World Business**, 28, nos. 1-4
P Columbia Journalism Review, 31, nos. 5-6
N **Combat Fleets of the World**
F **Commentary**, 95, nos. 1-6, vol. 96, nos. 1-6
N **Common Knowledge**
F **Commonweal**, 120, nos. 1-22
F **Communist and Post-Communist Studies**, 26, nos. 1-4
F **Comparatist**, no. 17
F **Comparative Drama**, 27, nos. 1-4
F **Comparative Economic Studies**, 35, nos. 1-4
F **Comparative Education Review**, 37, nos. 1-4
F **Comparative Labor Law Journal**, 14, nos. 2-4, vol. 15, no. 1

F **Comparative Law Yearbook of International Business**, no. 15
F **Comparative Literature Studies**, 30, nos. 1-4
F **Comparative Political Studies**, 25, no. 4, vol. 6, nos. 1-3
F **Comparative Politics**, 25, nos. 2-4, vol. 26, no. 1
F **Comparative Strategy**, 12, nos. 1-4
N **Conflict Quarterly**
F **Congress Monthly**, 60, nos. 1-7
F **Connecticut Journal of International Law**, 8, no. 2, vol. 9, no. 1
P Connecticut Review, 15, no. 2
P Contemporary Family Therapy, 15, no. 1
F **Contemporary Literature**, 34, nos. 1-4
F Contemporary Policy Issues, 11, nos. 1-4
F **Contemporary Sociology**, 22, nos. 1-6
F **Contention: Debates in Society, Culture, and Science**, 2, nos. 2-3, vol. 3, no. 1
F **Cornell International Law Journal**, 26, nos. 1-3
F **Criminal Law Forum**, 4, nos. 1-3
N **Critical Inquiry**
P Counseling Psychologist, 21, no. 4
P Creative Woman, 13, no. 2
P Criminal Law Forum, 4, nos. 1, 3
P Critical Inquiry, 19, no. 2-3
F **Cross Currents: A Yearbook of Central European Culture**, no. 12
F **Cross Currents: Religion & Intellectual Life**, 43, nos. 1-4
P Current Anthropology, 34, nos. 1, 3-5
F **Current History**, 92, nos. 570-578
P Current Psychology, 12, no. 1
P **Czechoslovak and Central European Journal**, 11, no. 2

F **Daedalus**, 122, nos. 1-4
F **Dalhousie Review**, 73, nos. 1-4
F **Dance Chronicle**, 16, nos. 1-3
F **Dance Magazine**, 67, nos. 1-12
P **Denver Journal of International Law and Policy**, 21, no. 2, vol. 22, no. 1
P Diogenes, 41, no. 2
F **Diplomatic History**, 17, nos. 1-4
F **Dissent**, 40, nos. 1-4F
F **Dostoevsky Studies = Dostoevskii: Stat'i i materialy**, 1, nos. 1-2
F **Dumbarton Oaks Papers**, no. 47

0 **East Central Europe = L'Europe du Centre-Est** [none published in 1993]
F **East European Constitutional Review**, 2, nos. 1-4
F **East European Politics and Societies**, 7, nos. 1-3
F **East European Quarterly**, 27, nos. 1-4
F **East/West Education**, 14, nos. 1-2
P Economic Development and Cultural Change, 41, no. 3
F **Educational Studies**, 24, nos. 1-4
F **Emory International Law Review**, 7, nos. 1-2
P Environmental Science & Technology, 27, no. 4
P **Essays in Literature**, 20, nos. 1-2
F **Ethnic Forum**, 13, nos. 1-2
F Ethnic Groups, 10, nos. 1-4

F **Ethnohistory**, 40, nos. 1-4
F **Ethnomusicology**, 37, nos. 1-3
P **Eurasian Reports**, 3, no. 2
P **Explorations in Ethnic Studies**, 16, no. 1, supplement no. 13

P Federal Bar News & Journal, 40, no. 9
N **Field**
F **Film Quarterly**, 46, nos. 3-4, vol. 47, nos. 1-2
F **Fletcher Forum of World Affairs**, 17, no. 1
P **Fordham International Law Journal**, 17, nos. 1
P **Foreign Affairs**, 72, nos. 2-5
P **Foreign Policy**, nos. 91-93
P Foreign Policy Bulletin, 4, no. 2
F Foreign Service Journal, 70, nos. 1-12
P Four Quarters, 7, no. 2
F **Freedom Review**, 24, nos. 1-6
F Future Survey Annual 1993

N **General Linguistics**
F **Geographical Review**, 83, nos. 1-4
F **George Washington Journal of International Law and Economics**, 26, no. 3, vol. 27, nos. 1-3
P Georgia Journal of International and Comparative Law, 23, no. 2
P **German Quarterly**, 66, nos. 2-4
P **German Studies Review**, 16, no. 2
F **Germanic Review**, 68, nos. 1-4
0 **Germano-Slavica** [none published in 1993]
P Global Affairs, 8, nos. 2-3
P **Grand Street**, 12, nos. 1-3
N **Greek Orthodox Theological Review**

F **Harper's**, 286, nos. 1712-1717, 287, nos. 1718-1723
F **Harriman Institute Forum**, 6, nos. 5-12, vol. 7, nos. 1-2
F **Harvard Business Review**, 71, nos. 1-6
P **Harvard International Law Journal**, 34, nos. 1
F **Harvard International Review**, 15, nos. 3-4, vol. 16, no. 1
P Harvard Law Review, 106, no. 8
F **Harvard Library Bulletin**, 4, nos. 1-4
0 **Harvard Ukrainian Studies** [none published in 1993]
F **Hastings International & Comparative Law Review**, 16, nos. 2-4, vol. 17, no. 1
P Hemisphere, 5, no. 2
P Histoire sociale = Social History, 26, no. 51
F **Historian: A Journal of History**, 55, nos. 2-4, vol. 56, no. 1
F **Historical Studies in Physical and Biological Sciences**, 23, no. 2, vol. 24, nos. 1
F **History: Reviews of New Books**, 21, nos. 2-3, vol. 22, no. 1
F **History Teacher**, 26, nos. 2-4, vol. 27, no. 1
F **Holocaust and Genocide Studies**, 7, nos. 1-3
P Housing Policy Debate, 3, no. 4
P Houston Journal of International Law, 15, nos. 2-3
F **Hudson Review**, 45, nos. 1-4
N **Human Rights Internet Reporter**
P Human Rights Law Journal, 14, nos. 5-6, 11-12
F **Human Rights Quarterly**, 15, nos. 1-4

P **Human Rights Tribune**, 1, nos. 4
P Human Studies, 16, no. 3
P Humboldt Journal of Social Relations, 19, no. 2
F **Hungarian Studies Review**, 20, nos. 1-2
N **Industrial and Labor Relations Review**
P Hypatia, 8, nos. 1, 4

P Illinois Historical Journal, 86, no. 4
F In Depth, 3, no. 1-3
F Industrial and Labor Relations Review, 46, nos. 2-4, vol. 47, no. 1
F **International Economic Insights**, 4, nos. 1-6
F **International Economic Review** (U.S. International Trade Commission)
P International Economy, 7, nos. 4-5
F **International Executive**, 35, nos. 1-6
F **International Fiction Review**, 20, nos. 1-2
F **International History Review**, 15, nos. 1-4
F **International Journal**, 48, nos. 2-4, vol. 49, no. 1
F **International Journal of Health Services**, 23, nos. 1-4
P International Journal of Law & Psychiatry, 16, nos. 3/4
F **International Journal of Mental Health**, 22, nos. 1-4
P International Journal of Offender Therapy and Comparative Criminology, 37, no. 1
P **International Labor and Working Class History**, no. 43
F **International Lawyer**, 27, nos. 1-4
P International Legal Perspectives, 5, no. 1
F **International Migration Review**, 27, nos. 1-4
F **International Organization**, 47, nos. 1-4
F **International Poetry Review**, 19, nos. 1-2
P **International Security**, 17, no. 4, vol. 18, nos. 1-2
F **International Social Science Review**, 68, nos. 1-4
P International Sociology, 8, no. 3
P **International Studies Quarterly**, 37, no. 1
F International Tax & Business Lawyer, 10, no. 2, vol. 11, nos. 1-2
F **Isis: History of Science Society**, 84, nos. 1-4
F **Items** (Social Science Research Council), 47, nos. 1-4

P JAMA: Journal of the American Medical Association, 270, no. 5
P Jewish Social Studies, 50, nos. 3-4
F **Journal for the Scientific Study of Religion**, 32, nos. 1-4
F **Journal of Aesthetics and Art Criticism**, 51, nos. 1-4
F **Journal of American Culture**, 16, nos. 1-4
F **Journal of American Ethnic History**, 12, nos. 3-4, 13, nos. 1-2
N **Journal of American Folklore**
P **Journal of American History**, 80, no. 1
F **Journal of Anthropological Research**, 49, nos. 1-4
F **Journal of Baltic Studies**, 24, nos. 1-4
P **Journal of Business Strategy**, 14, nos. 3-6
P Journal of Career Development, 20, no. 1
F **Journal of Church and State**, 35, nos. 1-4
F **Journal of Communication**, 43, nos. 2-4, vol. 43, no. 1
F **Journal of Comparative Economics**, 17, nos. 1-4
P Journal of Creative Behavior, 27, no. 2
F **Journal of Conflict Resolution**, 37, nos. 1-4
P **Journal of Decorative and Propaganda Arts**, no. 19
F **Journal of Democracy**, 4, nos. 1-4

P **New York Times Book Review**
P **New York Times Magazine**
P New York University Journal of International Law and Politics, 25, no. 2
P **New Yorker**, 68, nos. 47-52, vol. 69 nos. 1-21, 23-44
P Newsletter of the Association for Gravestone Studies, 17, no. 3
F **19th Century Music**, 17, nos. 1-3
F **North Carolina Journal of International Law and Commercial Regulation**, 18, nos. 2-3, vol. 19, no. 1
P North Dakota Quarterly, 61, no. 1
F **Notes**, 49, nos. 2-4, vol. 50, no. 1
F **Notre Dame Law Review**, 68, nos. 3-5, vol. 69, nos. 1-2
F **Novel**, 26, nos. 2-3, vol. 27, no. 1
F **Numismatic Literature**, nos. 129-130
F **Numismatist**, 106, nos. 1-12

F **Ocean Development and International Law**, 24, nos. 1-4
P October, no. 64
P Ohio State Law Journal, 54, no. 3
P On the Issues, no. 26
F **Opera Journal**, 26, nos. 1-4
P Oral History Review, 21, nos. 1-2
F **Orbis**, 37, nos. 1-4
P Oregon Law Review, 72, no. 4

F **Pacific Affairs**, 66, nos. 1-4
F **Pacific Historical Review**, 62, nos. 1-4
F **Pacific Northwest Quarterly**, 84, nos. 1-4
P **Papers on Language and Literature**, 29, nos. 1-3
P **Parameters: Journal of the U.S. Army War College**, 23, nos. 1, 3
P **Parnassus** vol. 17, no. 2, vol. 18, no. 1, vol. 19, no. 1
F **Partisan Review**, 60, nos. 1-4
F Patterns of Prejudice, 27, nos. 1-2
F **Peace Magazine**, 9, nos. 1-6
F **Peace Research**, 25, nos. 1-4
N **Pequod**
F **Performing Arts Journal**, 15, nos. 1-3
F **Perspectives of New Music**, 31, nos. 1-2
F **Perspectives on Political Science**, 22, nos. 1-4
P Phi Delta Kappan, 74, no. 9
F **Philosophy and Literature**, 17, nos. 1-2
P **Philosophy and Phenomenological Research**, 53, nos. 1-3
F **Philosophy and Social Criticism**, 19, nos. 1-2
F **Ploughshares**, 19, nos. 1-4
F **Poet Lore**, 88, nos. 1-4
F **Poetics Today**, 14, nos. 1-4
F **Policy Review**, nos. 63-66
F **Policy Studies Journal**, 21, nos. 1-4
F **Polish American Studies**, 50, nos. 1-2
N **Polish Heritage**
N **Polish National Catholic Church Studies**
F **Polish Review**, 38, nos. 1-2
F Political Power and Social Theory, vol. 8
F **Political Psychology**, 14, nos. 1-4
F **Political Research Quarterly**, 46, nos. 1-4
F **Political Science Quarterly**, 108, nos. 1-4

F **Political Theory**, 21, nos. 1-4
F **Politics and Society**, 21, nos. 1-4
F **Polity**, 25, nos. 3-4, vol. 26, nos. 1-2
F **Polyphony**, no. 13
F **Population and Development Review**, 19, nos. 1-4
F **Population Bulletin**, 48, nos. 1-4
F **Post-Soviet Affairs**, 9, nos. 1-4
F **Post-Soviet Geography**, 34, nos. 1-10
P Prism International, 31, no. 2
F **Proceedings of the American Philosophical Society**, 137, nos. 1-4
F **Professional Geographer**, 45, nos. 1-4
F **Progressive**, 57, nos. 1-12
N **Prologue**
F **Prooftexts: A Journal of Jewish Literary History**, 13, nos. 1
F **P.S.** (American Political Science Association), 26, nos. 1-4
F **Psychiatry**, 56, nos. 1-4
P Psychoanalytic Quarterly, 62, no. 2
P Psychoanalytic Review, 80, no. 3
P Psychological Record, 43, no. 3
P Psychological Reports, 73, no. 1
P Psychology of Women Quarterly, 17, no. 4
P Public Adminstration Review, 53, no. 4
P Public Health Reports, 108, no. 2
F **Public Opinion Quarterly**, 57, nos. 1-4
P **Publications of the Modern Language Association**, 108, nos. 2-3, 5-6
P **Publishers Weekly**, 240

P Quarterly Journal of Speech, 79, no. 2

P Radical History Review, no. 57
F **RCDA**, 32, nos. 1-4
F **Reason**, 24, nos. 8-11, vol. 25, nos. 2-5, 7
F **Religion in Eastern Europe**, 13, nos. 1-6
F **Research & Exploration**, 9, nos. 1-4 + special issue
N **Research in Political Sociology**
N **Research in Social Movements, Conflicts and Change**
F **Research on Language and Social Interaction**, 26, nos. 1-4
P Research Technology Management, 36, no. 1
F **Review (Fernand Braudel Center for the Study of Economics, Historical Systems, and Civilizations)**, 16, nos. 1-4
F **Review of Politics**, 55, nos.1- 4
F **Review of Radical Political Economics**, 25, nos. 1-4
N **Reviews in American History**
P **RFE/RL Research Report**, 2, nos. 1-36, 38-50
P Ripon Forum, 29, no. 2
P Rocky Mountain Review of Language and Literature, 47, nos. 1-2
N **Rodziny: The Journal of the Polish Genealogical Society of America**
F **Russian History**, 20, nos. 1-4
F **Russian Language Journal**, 47, nos. 156-158
F **Russian Review**, 52, nos. 1-4

F **SAIS Review**, 13, nos. 1-2 + special issue

F **Salmagundi**, nos. 97-100
F **Science & Society**, 57, nos. 1-4
P **SEEL: Survey of East European Law**, 4, nos. 3
F **Selecta: Journal of the PNCFL**, vol. 14
F **Seminar: A Journal of Germanic Studies**, 29, nos. 1-4
F **Serbian Studies**, 7, nos. 1-2
P Sex Roles, 29, no. 5/6
F **Signs: Journal of Women in Culture and Society**, 18, nos. 2-4, vol. 19, no. 1
N **Simon Wiesenthal Center Annual**
P Simulation & Gaming, 24, nos. 1, 4
N **Slavic and East European Arts**
F **Slavic and East European Journal**, 37, nos. 1-4
P **Slavic and East European Performance**, 13, nos. 1-3
F **Slavic Review**, 52, nos. 1-4
N **Slovakia**
F **Slovene Studies**, 14, nos. 1-2
F **Smithsonian**, 23, nos. 10-12, vol. 24, nos. 1-9
F **Social Education**, 57, nos. 1-7
F **Social Forces**, 71, nos. 3-4, vol. 72, nos. 1-2
P Social Philosophy & Policy, 10, no. 2
P Social Problems, 40, no. 2
P Social Psychology Quarterly, 56, no. 1
F **Social Research**, 60, nos. 1-4
F **Social Science and Medicine**, 36, nos. 1-12, vol. 37, nos. 1-12
F **Social Science Journal**, 30, nos. 1-4
F **Social Science Quarterly**, 74, nos. 1-4
P Social Studies and the Young Learner, 5, no. 4
P Social Theory and Practice, 19, no. 3
0 **Socialism and Democracy** [none published in 1993]
P **Society**, 30, nos. 2-6
P Sociology of Religion, 54, no. 3
N **Soundings**
F **Soundings: An Interdisciplinary Journal**, 76, nos. 1-4
F South Atlantic Review, 58, nos. 1-4
0 **Southeastern Europe** [none published in 1993]
P Southern California Quarterly, 75, no. 1
F **Southern Economic Journal**, 59, nos. 3-4, vol. 60, nos. 1-2
F **Soviet and Post-Soviet Review**, 20, nos. 1-3
N **Soviet Armed Forces Review Annual**
P Stanford Journal of International Law, 29, no. 2
F **Strategic Review**, 21, nos. 1-4
P Studies in Comparative International Development, 28, no. 2
F **Studies in Conflict and Terrorism**, 16, nos. 1-4
F **Studies in East European Thought**, 45, nos. 1-4
F Studies in Religion = Sciences Religieuses, 22, nos. 1-3
F **Studies in Short Fiction**, 30, nos. 1-4
F **Studies in the Humanities**, 20, nos. 1-2
P **Studies in the Novel**, 25, nos. 1
F **Studies in 20th Century Literature**, 17, nos. 1-2
F **Style**, 27, nos. 1-4
P Suffolk Transnational Law Review, 16, no. 2
F **Surviving Together**, 11, nos. 1-4
P Swords and Ploughshares, 7, nos. 3-4
P Symbolic Interaction, 16, no. 4
F **Syracuse Journal of International Law and Commerce**, vol. 19

P **TDR: The Drama Review**, 37, nos. 1-2
P Teaching of Psychology, 20, no. 3
F **Technology and Culture**, 34, nos. 1-4
F **Technology in Society**, 15, nos. 1-4
F **Technology Review**, 96, nos. 1-8
F **Telos**, nos. 96-99
F Temple International and Comparative Law Journal, 7, nos. 1-2
F **Texas International Law Journal**, 28, nos. 1-3
F **Theatre Design & Technology**, 29, nos. 1-4
F **Theatre History Studies**, no. 13
F **Theatre Journal**, 45, nos. 1-4
F **Tikkun**, 8, nos. 1-6
F **Touro Journal of Transnational Law**, vol. 4
P Transition, 4
P **Translation: The Journal of Literary Translation**, no. 28
P **Translation Review**, nos. 41-43
F **Transnational Lawyer**, 6, nos. 1-2
F **TriQuarterly**, nos. 87-89
F **Tulane Law Review**, 67, nos. 3-6, vol. 68, no. 1

P UCLA Women's Law Journal, 4, no. 1
F **Ukrainian Quarterly**, 49, nos. 1-4
P UN Chronicle, 30, no. 1
P **Uncaptive Minds**, 6, nos. 1-3 (nos. 22-24)
F **University of Dayton Review**, 22, nos. 1-2
P University of Louisville Journal of Family Law, 31, no. 2
F **University of Pennsylvania Journal of International Business Law**, 13, vol. 4, vol. 14, nos. 1-3
P Urban Lawyer, 25, no. 2
P **U.S. Naval Institute: Proceedings**, 119, no. 6
N **USA Today**

P **Vanderbilt Journal of Transnational Law**, 26, nos. 1-4
F **Virginia Journal of International Law**, 33, nos. 2-4, vol. 34, no. 1
P Vox Benedictina, 10, no. 1

P War Cry, 113, no. 13
F **Washington Quarterly**, 16, nos. 1-4
F **Washinton Journalism Review**, 15, nos. 1-10
F **Western Historical Quarterly**, 24, nos. 1-4
F **Wilson Quarterly**, 17, nos. 1-4
F **Wisconsin International Law Journal**, 11, no. 2, vol. 12, nos. 1
P **Wisconsin Magazine of History**, 77, nos. 1-2
P Woman and Earth, 2, no. 1
F **Women & Politics**, 13, nos. 1-4
N **Women in German Yearbook**
P **Women's Studies International Forum**, 16, nos. 1, 3-4
F **World & I**, 8, nos. 1-12
F **World Affairs**, 155, nos. 3-4, vol. 156, nos. 1-2
P World Bank Research Observer, 8, no. 2
P World Development, 21, no. 4
F **World Leisure & Recreation**, 35, nos. 1-4
F **World Literature Today**, 67, nos. 1-2
P **World Monitor**, 6, nos. 1-5

F **World Policy Journal**, 10, nos. 1-4
F **World Politics**, 45, nos. 2-4, vol. 46, no. 1
P World Trade, 6
F **World Watch**, 6, nos. 1-6

F **Yale Journal of International Law**, 18, nos. 1-2
P **Yale Law and Policy Review**, 11, nos. 1

P **Yale Review**, 81, nos. 1-2, 4
F **Yearbook for Traditional Music**, vol. 25
N **Yearbook on International Communist Affairs**

N **Zapiski Russkoi Akademicheskoi Gruppy v SShA = Transactions of the Association of Russian-American Scholars in the U.S.A.**

The
American Bibliography
of Slavic and
East European
Studies for 1993

1 General

■ General Collections, Festschrifts, Symposia

1. Clark, Dick, ed. *United States Relations with Central and Eastern Europe: Thirteenth Conference, August 22-27, 1993.* Contributions by Dick Clark, Michael Mandelbaum, Leszek Balcerowicz, Zbigniew Bochniarz, Allen H. Kassof, Ivo Banac, Rita Klimová, Hanna Suchocka, Misha Glenny, and Helmet Schmidt. Queenstown, MD: Aspen Institute, 1993. iii, 68 pp. [Contents: Dick Clark, Michael Mandelbaum, "Conference report"; Leszek Balcerowicz, "The Polish way to the market economy"; Zbigniew Bochniarz, "Environmental concerns in Central and Eastern Europe: Challenges and solutions"; Allen H. Kassof, "Ethnic conflict in Eastern Europe"; Ivo Banac, "Main trends in the current Balkan conflict"; Rita Klimová, "Western policy towards Central and Eastern Europe"; Hanna Suchocka, "Address of the honorable"; Misha Glenny, "Beyond Hades: the wars of Yugoslav succession and the international community"; Helmet Schmidt, "A new European security order."]

2. Costlow, Jane T., Stephanie Sandler, and Judith Vowles, eds. *Sexuality and the Body in Russian Culture.* Contributions by Eve Levin, Judith Vowles, Catriona Kelly, Jane A. Sharp, Elizabeth A. Wood, Cathy Popkin, Svetlana Boym, Diana Lewis Burgin, Helena Goscilo, Jane T. Costlow, Barbara Heldt, and Eric Naiman. Stanford, CA: Stanford University Press, 1993. x, 357 pp. [Chiefly papers from a 1989 symposium. Contents: Jane T. Costlow, Stephanie Sandler and Judith Vowles, "Introduction"; Pt. I. The Cultural History of Sexual Representation. Eve Levin, "Sexual Vocabulary in Medieval Russia"; Judith Vowles, "Marriage *a la russe*"; Catriona Kelly, "A Stick with Two Ends, or, Misogyny in Popular Culture: A Case Study of the Puppet Text 'Petrushka'"; Jane A. Sharp, "Redrawing the Margins of Russian Vanguard Art: Natalia Goncharova's Trial for Pornography in 1910"; Elizabeth A. Wood, "Prostitution Unbound: Representations of Sexual and Political Anxieties in Postrevolutionary Russia"; Pt. II. Literary Versions of Sex and Body. Cathy Popkin, "Kiss and Tell: Narrative Desire and Discretion"; Svetlana Boym, "Loving in Bad Taste: Eroticism and Literary Excess in Marina Tsvetaeva's 'The Tale of Sonechka'"; Diana Lewis Burgin, "Laid Out in Lavender: Perceptions of Lesbian Love in Russian Literature and Criticism of the Silver Age, 1893-1917"; Helena Goscilo, "Monsters Monomaniacal, Marital, and Medical: Tatiana Tolstaya's Regenerative Use of Gender Stereotypes"; Pt. III. The Maternal Body. Jane T. Costlow, "The Pastoral Source: Representations of the Maternal Breast in Nineteenth-Century Russia"; Barbara Heldt, "Motherhood in a Cold Climate: The Poetry and Career of Maria Shkapskaya"; Eric Naiman, "Historectomies: On the Metaphysics of Reproduction in a Utopian Age."]

3. De Soto, Hermine G., and David G. Anderson, eds. *The Curtain Rises: Rethinking Culture, Ideology, and the State in Eastern Europe.* Contributions by Claude Meillassoux, Aidan Southall, David A. Kideckel, David G. Anderson, Christopher Hann, Fahrünnisa E. Kulluk, Dejan Trickovic, Anatoly M. Khazanov, William Graf, William Hansen, Brigitte Schulz, Sam Beck, Laszlo Kürti, Hermine G. De Soto, Oriol Pi-Sunyer, and Tahsin Corat. Atlantic Highlands, NJ: Humanities Press, 1993. xvii, 342 pp. [Contents: David G. Anderson, Hermine G. De Soto, "Introduction," pp. ix-xvii. Pt. I. Setting the Stage: Theoretical Controversies on Eastern Europe. Claude Meillassoux, "Toward a Theory of the 'Social Corps'," trans. Tahsin Corat, pp. 2-42; Aidan Southall, "The Problems of Socialism: A Reappraisal of the Orthodox Texts," pp. 43-60. Pt. II. The Politics of Decollectivization. David A. Kideckel, "Once Again, the Land: Decollectivization and Social Conflict in Rural Romania," pp. 62-75; David G. Anderson, "Civil Society in Siberia: The Institutional Legacy of the Soviet State," pp. 76-98; Christopher Hann, "Property Relations in the New Eastern Europe: The Case of Specialist Cooperatives in Hungary," pp. 99-119. Pt. III. Fractured Socialism and the Rise of Nationalism. Fahrünnisa E. Kulluk, "From the 'National Question' to Autogestion and Perestroika: Controversies in Theoretical and Political Approaches to National(ist) Movements," pp. 122-148; Dejan Trickovic, "Yugoslavia and the Rise of Volkgeist," pp. 149-181; Anatoly M. Khazanov, "Interethnic Relations in the Soviet Union during the First Years of 'Restructuring'," pp. 182-206; William Graf, William Hansen, and Brigitte Schulz, "From *The* People to *One* People: The Social Bases of the East German 'Revolution' and Its Preemption by the West German State," pp. 207-230. Pt. IV. The Transition: Identities, Ideologies, and New Utopias. Sam Beck, "The Struggle for Space and the Development of Civil Society in Romania, June 1990," pp. 232-265; Laszlo Kürti, "The Wingless Eros of Socialism: Nationalism and Sexuality in Hungary," pp. 266-288; Hermine G. De Soto, "Equality/Inequality: Contesting Female Personhood in the Process of Making Civil Society in Eastern Germany," pp. 289-304; Oriol Pi-Sunyer, "The Spanish Route to Democracy: A Model for Eastern Europe in Transition?" pp. 305-333.]

4. International Congress of Slavists (11th: 1993: Bratislava, Slovakia). *American Contributions to the Eleventh International Congress of Slavists, Bratislava, August-September 1993: Literature, Linguistics, Poetics.* Edited by Robert A. Maguire and Alan Timberlake. Columbus, OH: Slavica Publishers, c1993. 459 pp. [Contributions in English, Russian and Serbo-Croatian.]

5. Janos, Andrew C. *The Domestic and Internationational Context of East European Politics.*

Working Paper (University of California, Berkeley. Center for German and European Studies), 5.8. Berkeley, CA: Center for German and European Studies, University of California, [1993]. 30 pp. [Conference on Markets, States and Democracy, February 11-13, 1993.]

6. Kraljic, Matthew A., ed. *The Breakup of Communism: The Soviet Union and Eastern Europe.* Contributions by Zbigniew Brzezinski, Adrian Karatnycky, George Weigel, Richard C. Longworth, Leonid Zagalsky, George J. Church, Eric Hobsbawm, Yelena Bonner, Mark Kramer, Karen LaFollette, Jude Wanniski, Kenneth L. Adelman, Norman R. Augustine, Charles Gati, Gregory F. Treverton, Barbara Bicksler, James Rupert, Tatyana Vorozheikina, Llewellyn D. Howell, and Joseph S. Nye, Jr. Reference Shelf, v. 65, no. 1. New York, NY: H.W. Wilson, 1993. 224 pp. [Reprints of journal articles. Contents: Zbigniew Brzezinski, "The Cold War and its Aftermath," pp. 10-28; Adrian Karatnycky, "Minsk Meet," pp. 28-39; George Weigel, "Death of a Heresy," pp. 39-43; Richard C. Longworth, "Eastern Europe: The Party's Over," pp. 45-51; Leonid Zagalsky, "Social Realism Bites the Dust," pp. 51-59; George J. Church, "Splinter, Splinter Little State," pp. 60-64; Eric Hobsbawm, "The Perils of the New Nationalism," pp. 65-68; Yelena Bonner, "For Every Nationality, A State," pp. 68-71; Mark Kramer, "Eastern Europe Goes to Market," pp. 73-93; Karen LaFollette, "Establishing Free Enterprise in Former Soviet Republics," pp. 93-101; Jude Wanniski, "The Future of Russian Capitalism," pp. 101-110; Kenneth L. Adelman and Norman R. Augustine, "Defense Conversion: Bulldozing the Management," pp. 110-130; Charles Gati, "From Sarajevo to Sarajevo," pp. 132-146; Gregory F. Treverton and Barbara Bicksler, "Germany and the New Europe," pp. 146-161; James Rupert, "Dateline Tashkent: Post-Soviet Central Asia," pp. 161-176; Tatyana Vorozheikina, "Why Not Try Democracy?" pp. 177-181; Llewellyn D. Howell, "Speculations on the New Russia," pp. 181-184; Joseph S. Nye, Jr., "What New World Order?" pp. 184-197.]

7. Nazarov, Bakhtiyar A., and Denis Sinor, eds. *Essays on Uzbek History, Culture, and Language.* Technical editor Devin DeWeese. Contributions by G. A. Abdurakhmanov, Edward Allworth, Devin DeWeese, A. Khaiitmetov, Iristai K. Kuchkartaev, Nizamiddin Mamadalievich Makhmudov, Ruth I. Meserve, A. Nurmanov, A. Shermatov, and Denis Sinor. Uralic and Altaic Series, v. 156. Bloomington, IN: Indiana University, Research Institute for Inner Asian Studies, 1993. 119 pp. [Contents: G. A. Abdurakhmanov, "The Ethnogenesis of the Uzbek People and the Formation of the Uzbek Language," pp. 1-12; Edward Allworth, "A New Ethnic Tone in Writings for the 21st Century," pp. 13-37; Devin DeWeese, "A Neglected Source on Central Asian History: The 17th-Century Yasavi Hagiography *Manaqib al-Akhyar*," pp. 38-50; A. Khaiitmetov, "On the Creative Method of Medieval Uzbek Literature," pp. 51-59; Iristai K. Kuchkartaev, "The Lexico-Semantic Field of Written Language in Old Turkic, Old Uzbek, and Modern Uzbek," pp. 60-68; Nizamiddin Mamadalievich Makhmudov, "The Semantic-Syntactic Mechanism of the Uzbek Comparative Sentence," pp. 69-78; Ruth I. Meserve, "The Latin Source for *Khwarezm*," pp. 79-

94; A. Nurmanov, "The Presuppositional Aspect of the Simple Sentence in Uzbek," pp. 95-100; A. Shermatov, "A New Stage in the Development of Uzbek Dialectology," pp. 101-109; Denis Sinor, "Some Latin Sources on the Khanate of Uzbek," pp. 110-119.]

8. New Hampshire Symposium on the German Democratic Republic (16th: 1990: World Fellowship Center), and New Hampshire Symposium on the German Democratic Republic (17th: 1991: World Fellowship Center). *The End of the GDR and the Problems of Integration: Selected Papers from the Sixteenth and Seventeenth New Hampshire Symposia on the German Democratic Republic.* Edited by Margy Gerber and Roger Woods. Studies in GDR Culture and Society, 11/12. Lanham, MD: University Press of America, c1993. ix, 240 pp.

9. Solomon, Susan Gross, ed. *Beyond Sovietology: Essays in Politics and History.* Contributions by Susan Gross Solomon, Joseph Schull, Mark Saroyan, Joel S. Hellman, Jane I. Dawson, Kathryn Hendley, Michael Smith, Ellen Hamilton, and Edward W. Walker. Contemporary Soviet/Post-Soviet Politics. Armonk, NY: M.E. Sharpe, c1993. ix, 254 pp. [Contents: Susan Gross Solomon, "Beyond Sovietology: Thoughts on Studying Russian Politics after Perestroika," pp. 1-7; Joseph Schull, "The Self-Destruction of Soviet Ideology," pp. 8-22; Mark Saroyan, "Rethinking Islam in the Soviet Union," pp. 23-52; Joel S. Hellman, "Bureaucrats vs. Markets?: Rethinking the Bureaucratic Response to Market Reform in Centrally Planned Economies," pp. 53-93; Jane I. Dawson, "Intellectuals and Anti-Nuclear Protest in the USSR," pp. 94-124; Kathryn Hendley, "The Quest for Rational Labor Allocation within Soviet Entreprises: Internal Transfers before and during Perestroika," pp. 125-158; Michael Smith, "The Eurasian Imperative in Early Soviet Language Planning: Russian Linguists at the Service of the Nationalities," pp. 159-191; Ellen Hamilton, "Social Areas under State Socialism: The Case of Moscow," pp. 192-225; Edward W. Walker, "Sovietology and Perestroika: A Post-Mortem," pp. 226-247.] REV: *Items* (Social Science Research Council) 47, no. 4 (December 1993): 99.

10. Staar, Richard F., ed. *Transition to Democracy in Poland.* Contributions by Raymond Taras, Miroslawa Grabowska, Andrew A. Michta, James F. Hicks, Jr., A. E. Dick Howard, Edward P. Lazear, Lucja Swiatkowski Cannon, Benjamin H. Slay, Michal Rutkowski, Thomas J. Sargent, Bartlomiej Kaminski, Sarah Meiklejohn Terry, and Arthur R. Rachwald. New York: St. Martin's Press, c1993. xiv, 271 pp. [Published in cooperation with the Hoover Institution on War, Revolution and Peace, Stanford University. Contents: Richard F. Staar, "Introduction: The Future of Poland," pp. 1-13; Raymond Taras, "Voters, Parties, and Leaders," pp. 15-39; Miroslawa Grabowska, "Political Activation of Social Groups," pp. 41-55; Andrew A. Michta, "The Presidential-Parliamentary System," pp. 57-76; James F. Hicks, Jr., and Bartolomiej Kaminski, "Local Government Reform," pp. 77-96; A. E. Dick Howard, "Constitutional Reform," pp. 97-110; Edward P. Lazear, "Interaction between Political and Economic Freedom," pp. 111-122;

Lucja Swiatkowski Cannon, "Privatization Strategy and Its Political Context," pp. 123-143; Benjamin H. Slay and Michal Rutkowski, "Product and Labor Markets," pp. 145-166; Thomas J. Sargent, "The Role of Monetary Policy in Market Economies," pp. 167-180; Bartlomiej Kaminski, "Emerging Patterns of Foreign Trade," pp. 181-201; Sarah Meiklejohn Terry, "Prospects for Regional Cooperation," pp. 203-233; Arthur R. Rachwald, "National Security Relations," pp. 235-255.]

■ Bibliographies, Reference Works, Sources

11. *The American Bibliography of Slavic and East European Studies for 1991.* Compiled and edited by Aaron Trehub and Magdalena Pietraszek. Stanford, CA: American Association for the Advancement of Slavic Studies, 1993. xix, 411 pp.

12. Batalden, Stephen K., and Sandra L. Batalden. *The Newly Independent States of Eurasia: Handbook of Former Soviet Republics.* Phoenix, AZ: Oryx, 1993. xvi, 205 pp. [Partial contents: Sergei A. Arutiunov, "Foreword"; Pt. 1. Russian Federation — pt. 2. Belarus, Moldova, and Ukraine — pt. 3. Transcaucasia — pt. 4. Central Asia.]

13. Boiko, Maksym, comp. and ed. *Bibliohrafiia Volynoznavstva v Pivnichnii Ameritsi 1949-1993, z Prychynkamy = Bibliography of Knowledge of Volhyniana in North America (1949-1993).* Bloomington, IN: Volhynian Bibliographic Centre, 1993. 143 pp.

14. ———. *Three Landmarks of Ukrainian Bibliography: 1073-1832.* Editorial assistance by Ihor H. Boyko. Bloomington, IN: Volhynian Bibliographic Centre, 1993. 85 pp.

15. Buttolo, Franca. "Commentary: Slovenia in the 1990s: The *Slovenski biografski leksikon*—Once Again from the Beginning, But How?" *Slovene Studies* 14, no. 2 (1992, published September 1994): 217-222. Translated by Tom Priestly. [Translation of "Slovenski biografski leksikon—kako se enkrat od zacetka?" *Delo* (October 14, 1993), in the supplement *Knizevni listi*.]

16. Citizens Democracy Corps. *NIS E-Mail Directory: A Listing of E-Mail Addresses in the Former Soviet Union and the Baltics.* Washington, DC: CDC Clearinghouse, [1993]. vi, 120 pp.

17. Croucher, Murlin, comp. and ed. *Slavic Studies: A Guide to Bibliographies, Encyclopedias, and Handbooks.* Wilmington, DE: Scholarly Resources, 1993. 2 vols.

18. Diller, Daniel C., ed. *Russia and the Independent States.* Washington, DC: Congressional Quarterly, c1993. vi, 342 pp. REV: *Booklist* 90, no. 2 (September 15, 1993): 187-188.

19. Friedman, Francine, comp. and ed. *Yugoslavia: A Comprehensive English-Language Bibliography.* Wilmington, DE: Scholarly Resources, 1993. xv, 547 pp.

20. Gates-Coon, Rebecca, comp. *Eastern Europe Bibliography.* Scarecrow Area Bibliographies, no. 2.

Metuchen, NJ: Scarecrow Press, 1993. ix, 175 pp.

21. Geron, Leonard, and Alex Pravda, eds. *Who's Who in Russia and the New States.* Rev. ed. London; New York: I.B. Tauris, c1993. 1 vol. [Updated version of the 1989 publication. Contents: Pt. 1. Governments — pt. 2. Biographical Entries.]

22. Kubijovyc, Volodymyr, and Danylo Husar Struk, ed. *Encyclopedia of Ukraine.* Toronto; Buffalo, NY: University of Toronto Press, c1984-c1993. 5 vols. [Translation of *Entsyklopediia ukrainoznavstva.* Published by the University of Toronto Press for the Canadian Institute of Ukrainian Studies, University of Alberta, the Shevchenko Scientific Society, Sarcelles, France, and the Canadian Foundation for Ukrainian Studies. Vols. 1-2 edited by Kubijovyc, vols. 3-5 edited by Struk. Contents: Vol. 1. A-F — v. 2. G-K — v. 3. L-Pf — v. 4. Ph-Sr — v. 5. St-Z.]

23. Kuharets, Irina A. "Russian Books." *Booklist* 89, no. 18 (May 15, 1993): 1679. [Books recently published in the Russian Federation.]

24. McIntosh, Jack, and Connie Wawruck-Hemmett. "Canadian Publications on the Former Soviet Union and Eastern Europe for 1992." *Canadian Slavonic Papers* 35, nos. 3-4 (September-December 1993): 345-384.

25. Nersessian, Vrej Nerses, comp. *Armenia.* World Bibliographical Series, v. 163. Oxford; Santa Barbara, CA: Clio Press, c1993. xxiii, 304 pp.

26. Paxton, John. *Encyclopedia of Russian History: From the Christianization of Kiev to the Break-up of the U.S.S.R.* Santa Barbara, CA: ABC-CLIO, c1993. x, 483 pp. [Rev. ed. of: Companion to Russian History (1983).]

27. Shoemaker, M. Wesley. *Russia, Eurasian States and Eastern Europe, 1993.* 24th annual ed. World Today Series. Washington, DC: Stryker-Post Publications, c1993. vi, 340 pp. [First appearing as *The Soviet Union and Eastern Europe 1970*; revised annually.]

28. Smith, Inese A., and Marita V. Grunts, comps. *The Baltic States: Estonia, Latvia, Lithuania.* World Bibliographical Series, v. 161. Oxford; Santa Barbara, CA: Clio, c1993. lxxvii, 199 pp.

29. Wertsman, Vladimir. "Romanian Books." *Booklist* 89, no. 10 (January 15, 1993): 883. [Books recently published in Romania.]

30. Wieczynski, Joseph L., ed. *The Gorbachev Encyclopedia: Gorbachev, the Man and His Times, March 11, 1985-December 25, 1991.* Salt Lake City, UT: C. Schlacks, Jr., c1993. xxii, 437 pp.

31. ———, ed. *The Gorbachev Reader.* Los Angeles, CA: C. Schlacks, Jr., c1993. x, 187 pp.

32. World Bank. Europe and Central Asia Region. Country Department III, and World Bank. Europe and Central Asia Region. Country Department IV. *Statistical Handbook 1993: States of the Former USSR.* Studies of Economies in Transformation, no. 8. Washington, DC: World Bank, 1993. xii, 778 pp. [Handbook was compiled under the supervision of Misha V. Belkindas and Rosalinda C. Dacumos. Principal contributors were Misha V. Belkindas, Rosalinda C. Dacumos, Timothy E. Heleniak, and Gregory V. Kisunko. Includes macroeconomic data, information on the labor force, foreign trade, monetary statistics and government finance, agriculture, industry, prices and wages, and capital investment. Partial contents: Country Tables. Armenia, pp. 25-72; Azerbaijan, pp. 73-120; Belarus, pp. 121-168; Estonia, pp. 169-216; Georgia, pp. 217-264; Kazakhstan, pp. 265-312; Kyrgyzstan, pp. 313-360; Latvia, pp. 361-408; Lithuania, pp. 409-456; Moldova, pp. 457-504; Russian Federation, pp. 505-552; Tajikistan, pp. 553-600; Turkmenistan, pp. 601-648; Ukraine, pp. 649-696; Uzbekistan, pp. 697-744; Technical Notes, pp. 745-758; Country Notes, pp. 759-773; Bibliography, pp. 775-778.]

33. Wynar, Bohdan S. *The International Writings of Bohdan S. Wynar, 1949-1992: A Chronological Bibliography*. Foreword by Yaroslav Isajevych. Englewood, CO: Ukrainian Academic Press of Libraries Unlimited, 1993. 265 pp.

■ Bibliology and the History of Printing

34. Brockett, Clyde, Jr. "A Previously Unknown *Ordo Prophetarum* in a Manuscript Fragment in Zagreb." *Comparative Drama* 27, no. 1 (Spring 1993): 114-127. [*Ordo Prophetarum*, a medieval music and drama manuscript from Metropolitanski Archive in Zagreb, dates from the late 12th or early 13th century.]

35. Compton, Susan P. *Russian Avant-Garde Books, 1917-34*. 1st MIT Press ed. Cambridge, MA: MIT Press, 1993, c1992. 175 pp. [Contents: 1. The 1920s and 1930s: an introduction; 2. Writers and Designers: new partnerships; 3. Medium and Message: design, technique and content; 4. Theatre: a revolution in design; 5. Utopian Ideas in Art and Architecture.]

36. Der Nersessian, Sirarpie. *Miniature Painting in the Armenian Kingdom of Cilicia from the Twelfth to the Fourteenth Century*. Jointly prepared for publication with Sylvia Agemian. Introduction by Annemarie Weyl Carr. Dumbarton Oaks Studies, 31. Washington, DC: Dumbarton Oaks Research Library and Collection, c1993. 2 vols.

37. Herzog-August-Bibliothek, and S. Katalin Nemeth. *Ungarische Drucke und Hungarica 1480-1720: Katalog der Herzog August Bibliothek Wolfenbuttel = Magyar es Magyar Vonatkozasu Nyomtatvanyok 1480-1720: A Wolfenbutteli Herzog August Konyvtar Katalogusa*. Munchen; New York: Saur, 1993. 3 vols. [In German and Hungarian. Contents: t. 1. A-H; t. 2. I-R; t. 3. S-Z.]

38. Polak, Emil J. *Medieval and Renaissance Letter Treatises and Form Letters: A Census of Manuscripts Found in Eastern Europe and the Former U.S.S.R.* Davis Medieval Texts and Studies, v. 8. Leiden; New York: E.J. Brill, 1993. xxii, 324 pp.

■ Biography and Autobiography

Russia/U.S.S.R./C.I.S.

39. Birt, Raymond. "Personality and Foreign Policy: The Case of Stalin." *Political Psychology* 14, no. 4 (December 1993): 607-625.

40. Bloomberg, Marty, and Buckley Barry Barrett. *Stalin: An Annotated Guide to Books in English*. Edited by Michael Burgess and Paul David Seldis. 1st ed. Borgo Reference Guides, no. 1. San Bernardino, CA: Borgo Press, c1993. 128 pp.

41. Bonet, Pilar. *Figures in a Red Landscape*. Translated from the Spanish by Norman Thomas Di Giovanni, and Susan Ashe. Washington, DC: Woodrow Wilson Center Press; Baltimore, MD: Johns Hopkins University Press, c1993. xv, 148 pp. [Translation of: *Imagenes sobre fondo rojo*. Author is a Spanish journalist who reported from Moscow from 1984 to 1991.] REV: Gary Lee, *Book World* 23, no. 35 (August 29, 1993): 4. Robert Legvold, *Foreign Affairs* 72, no. 5 (November-December 1993): 174-175. Peter Reddaway, *New York Review of Books* 40, no. 20 (December 2, 1993): 16ff.

42. Bonner, Elena. "Mothers and Daughters." *Ararat* 34, no. 2 (no. 134) (Spring 1993): 14-17. [Excerpt from author's autobiography of the same title (NY: 1992).]

43. Bullock, Alan. *Hitler and Stalin: Parallel Lives*. 1st Vintage Books ed. New York: Vintage Books, 1993. xxv, 1089 pp. [Originally published: (London: HarperCollins, 1991).] REV: Joseph Shattan, *American Spectator* 26, no. 1 (January 1993): 85-87.

44. Chuev, Feliks Ivanovich, and Viacheslav Molotov. *Molotov Remembers: Inside Kremlin Politics: Conversations with Felix Chuev*. Edited and with an introduction and notes by Albert Resis. Chicago, IL: I.R. Dee, 1993. xxiii, 438 pp. [Translation of *Sto sorok besed s Molotovym* [One Hundred Forty Talks with Molotov]. Contents: Pt. 1. International Affairs. Pt. 2. With Lenin. Pt. 3. With Stalin. Pt. 4. Since Stalin.] REV: David Remnick, *New York Review of Books* 40, no. 6 (March 25, 1993): 33-38.

45. Clemens, Walter C., Jr. "Privileged Sources: Insider Accounts of Soviet Politics at Home and Abroad." *Soviet and Post-Soviet Review* 20, nos. 2-3 (1993): 233-239. [Review article on Sergei Khrushchev, *Khrushchev on Khrushchev: An Inside Account of the Man and His Era*, ed. and trans. William Taubman (Boston: 1990); Andrei Gromyko, *Memoirs*, trans. Harold Shukman (New York: 1990); and A. A. Gromyko, *Pamiatnoe* (Moscow: 1988).]

46. Cracraft, James. "Great Catherine." *Slavic Review* 52, no. 1 (Spring 1993): 107-115. [Review article on John T. Alexander, *Catherine the Great: Life and Legend* (NY: 1989).]

47. Cutler, Robert M. "A Rediscovered Source on Bakunin in 1861: The Diary of F.P. Koe and [Excerpts from the Diary of F.P. Koe]." *Canadian Slavonic Papers* 35, nos.

1-2 (March-June 1993): 121-130.

48. Dune, Eduard M. *Notes of a Red Guard.*
Translated and edited by Diane P. Koenker and S. A. Smith.
Urbana, IL: University of Illinois Press, c1993. xxxvi, 285
pp. [Translated from Russian. Contents: Pt. 1. The Red
Guard. 1. To Moscow; 2. The February Revolution; 3.
Workers' Power; 4. Rob the Robbers; 5. The Russian Vendee
— Pt. 2. The Red Army. 6. Soviet Power in 1918; 7. On the
Don Again; 8. Retreat; 9. Prisoner of the Volunteer Army;
10. In the Novorossiisk Underground; 11. On My Own
Again; 12. Rebellion in Dagestan.]

49. Hunt, Priscilla. "Ivan IV's Personal Mythology
of Kingship." *Slavic Review* 52, no. 4 (Winter 1993): 769-
809.

50. Lee, Stephen J. *Peter the Great.* Lancaster
Pamphlets. London; New York: Routledge, 1993. x, 78 pp.

51. Ligachev, Yegor. *Inside Gorbachev's Kremlin:
the Memoirs of Yegor Ligachev.* Introduction by Stephen F.
Cohen. Translated from the Russian by Catherine A.
Fitzpatrick, Michele A. Berdy, and Dobrochna Dyrcz-
Freeman. 1st American ed. New York: Pantheon Books,
c1993. xxxix, 369 pp. [Russian edition is titled *Zagadka
Gorbacheva* [The Riddle of Gorbachev]. Contents: Stephen
F. Cohen, "Introduction: Ligachev and the Tragedy of Soviet
Conservatism"; A Note to American Readers — 1. Inside the
Kremlin and Old Square. A Late-Night Call. Andropov. The
Leader's Health. Favoring Political Ambitions. Making the
Connection. What Will the New Day Bring? — 2. The
Gorbachev Enigma: In the Trap of Radicalism. Shock
Therapy. *Eminence Grise.* The Khrushchev Syndrome — 3.
Harbinger of Disaster — 4. The Tbilisi Affair. A Political
Typhoon. The Secret Is Out. Why Did Shevardnadze
Disobey Gorbachev? The Tragedy of Perestroika. Sobchak's
Move — 5. Gdlyan and Others. A Stab in the Back.
Rashidov. Counterattack. Tactic or Strategy? "Ligachev vs.
Gdlyan"? — 6. Ghosts of the Past. The Kolpashevo Incident.
The Closed Circle. We Got Things Done! — 7. Witch Hunt.
The Rift. Nina Andreyeva's Letter — 8. Our Own Path.
Successes and Errors. The Fateful Error.] REV: Robert
Legvold, *Foreign Affairs* 72, no. 3 (Summer 1993): 205. Lars
T. Lih, *Political Science Quarterly* 108, no. 3 (Fall 1993):
584-585. Arch Puddington, *American Spectator* 26, no. 6
(June 1993): 68-69. David Remnick, *New York Review of
Books* 40, no. 6 (March 25, 1993): 33-38. Serge Schmemann,
New York Times Book Review 98, no. 8 (February 21, 1993):
7. David K. Shipler, *Nation* 256, no. 15 (April 19, 1993):
528-530. Adam B. Ulam, *Book World* 23, no. 8 (February
21, 1993): 7.

52. Nazároff, Paul. *Hunted through Central Asia.*
Translated by Malcolm Burr. Oxford; New York: Oxford
University Press, 1993. xii, 335 pp. [Translated from
Russian. Originally published: (Edinburgh; London: Wm.
Blackwood & Sons, 1932).]

53. Ferro, Marc. *Nicholas II: The Last of the Tsars.*
Translated by Brian Pearce. New York: Oxford University
Press, 1993. x, 305 pp.

54. Niditch, B. Z. "Lenin." *Literary Review* 36, no. 2
(Winter 1993): 186. [Poem.]

55. Nordlander, David. "Khrushchev's Image in the
Light of Glasnost and Perestroika." *Russian Review* 52, no.
2 (April 1993): 248-264. [Earlier version of this article was
presented at the Southern Conference on Slavic Studies at
Savannah, GA, on March 22, 1991.]

56. Radzinsky, Edvard. *The Last Tsar: The Life and
Death of Nicholas II.* Translated from the Russian by
Marian Schwartz. 1st Anchor Books ed. New York: Anchor
Books: Doubleday, 1993. vi, 475 pp. [Translation of *Zhizn i
smert Nikolaia II.*]

57. Ravindranathan, T. R. "The Stalinist Enigma:
A Review Article." *Canadian Journal of History = Annales
canadiennes d'histoire* 28, no. 3 (December 1993): 545-559.
[Review article on Dmitri Volkogonov, *Stalin: Triumph and
Tragedy* (NY: 1991); Robert C. Tucker, *Stalin in Power: The
Revolution From Above, 1928-1941* (NY: 1990); Robert
Conquest, *Stalin: Breaker of Nations* (London: 1991); and
Robert Conquest, *The Great Terror: A Reassessment*
(Edmonton, Alberta: 1990).]

58. Shattan, Joseph. [Book Review]. *American
Spectator* 26, no. 1 (January 1993): 85-87. [Review article
on Alan Bullock, *Hitler and Stalin: Parallel Lives* (NY:
Knopf, 1992).]

59. Spahr, William J. *Zhukov: The Rise and Fall of
a Great Captain.* Novato, CA: Presidio Press, c1993. xiv, 290
pp. [Contents: Early Years, 1896-1918; In the Red Army
during the Civil War, 1918-1921; The Peacetime Army,
1922-1936; The Purges, 1937-1938; Halhin Gol, 1939; In the
High Command, 1940-1941; Chief of the General Staff;
Stalin and the Chief of the General Staff; The Initial
Operations, 1941; Savior of Leningrad and Moscow, 1941-
1942; Counterattacks Become a Counteroffensive; The
Stalingrad Campaign, 1942-1943; The Battle of the Kursk
Salient, 1943; The Battle for the Ukraine, 1943; The 1944
Campaigns; The Belorussian and Ukrainian Campaigns of
1944; Return to Front Command, 1944; From the Vistula to
the Oder, 1945; The Capture of Berlin, 1945; The Allied
Control Council for Germany; Commander in Chief, Soviet
Occupation Forces, Germany, 1945-1946; Commander of
Secondary Military Districts, 1946-1953; Return to Moscow,
1953; The Year 1957: Zenith and Nadir of a Career; The
October Plenum—the Secret Reprisals; The Last Exile,
1957-1974; Conclusion.]

60. Zelnik, Reginald E. "Before Class: The Foster-
ing of A Worker Revolutionary, The Construction of His
Memoir." *Russian History* 20, nos. 1-4 (1993): 61-80. [Vasilii
Gerasimov.]

Eastern Europe

61. Borsanyi, Gyorgy. *The Life of a Communist
Revolutionary, Béla Kun.* Translated from the Hungarian
original by Mario D. Fenyo. Atlantic Studies on Society in
Change, no. 75. East European Monographs, no. 263.
Boulder, CO: Social Science Monographs; New York:

Distributed by Columbia University Press, 1993. xiii, 520 pp. [Translation of *Kun Bela*. Contents: Childhood; The Journalist; Combat and Captivity; The Founder of the Communist Party of Hungary; Consolidating the Revolution; In Exile; The Reorganization of the Hungarian Communist Party; Member of the Presidium.]

62. Dubcek, Alexander. *Hope Dies Last: The Autobiography of Alexander Dubcek.* Edited and translated by Jirí Hochman. New York: Kodansha International, 1993. 354 pp. REV: Robert Legvold, *Foreign Affairs* 72, no. 4 (September-October 1993): 168. Karl E. Meyer, *New York Times Book Review* 98, no. 26 (June 27, 1993): 11-12. Tad Szulc, *Book World* 23, no. 21 (May 23, 1993): 4-5. Paul Wilson, *New York Review of Books* 40, no. 15 (September 23, 1993): 41-45.

63. Groberg, Kristi A. "The Life and Influence of Simon Dubnov (1860-1941): An Appreciation." *Modern Judaism* 13, no. 1 (February 1993): 71-93.

64. Kriseová, Eda. *Václav Havel: The Authorized Biography.* Translated by Caleb Crain. 1st ed. New York: St. Martin's Press, 1993. xvi, 297 pp. REV: Michael T. Kaufman, *New York Times Book Review* 98, no. 43 (October 24, 1993): 33. Tina Rosenberg, *Book World* 23, no. 38 (September 19, 1993): 1ff.

65. Perry, Duncan M. *Stefan Stambolov and the Emergence of Modern Bulgaria, 1870-1895.* Durham: Duke University Press, 1993. xiv, 308 pp. [Contents: 1. The Days Before Liberation; 2. A Statesman Emerges; 3. Union, War, Abduction, and Abdication; 4. The Regency; 5. Bulgaria Finds a Prince; 6. The Church, thc Panitsa Plot, and the Matter of Stabilty; 7. The Transformation; 8. Opposition Solidifies; 9. The Last Days; Stambolov in Retrospect.]

66. Rosenberg, Tina. [Book Review]. *Book World (Washington Post)* 23, no. 38 (September 19, 1993): 1ff. [Review article on Eda Kriseová, *Václav Havel: The Authorized Biography* (NY: 1993).]

67. Warren, Wini. "The Search for Copernicus in History and Fiction." *Soundings* 76, nos. 2-3 (Summer/Fall 1993): 383-406.

68. Wilson, Paul. "Unlikely Hero." *New York Review of Books* 40, no. 15 (September 23, 1993): 41-45. [Review article on Alexander Dubcek, *Hope Dies Last: The Autobiography of Alexander Dubcek* (NY: 1993).]

69. Zawadzki, W. H. *A Man of Honour: Adam Czartoryski As a Statesman of Russia and Poland, 1795-1831.* Oxford: Clarendon Press; New York: Oxford University Press, 1993. xvi, 374 pp.

■ Communications and the Media

General

70. Burns, David. "30 Million Know His Voice—You Don't." *World Monitor* 6, no. 2 (February 1993): 14-16. [Profile of Willis Conover of the Voice of America.]

71. Hachten, William. "The Triumph of Western News Communication." *Fletcher Forum of World Affairs* 17, no. 1 (Winter 1993): 17-34.

72. Hester, Al, and L. Earle Reybold, eds. *Revolutions for Freedom: The Mass Media in Eastern and Central Europe.* Contributions by Richard Schwarzlose, Frank L. Kaplan, James E. Fletcher, Kehrt Reyher, Peggy Simpson, Elli Lester-Massman, Johnston M. Mitchell, Roland Page, Jill Dianne Swenson, W. Ronald Lane, Otto W. Smith, and Al Hester. Athens, GA: James M. Cox, Jr. Center for International Mass Communication Training and Research, Henry W. Grady College of Journalism and Mass Communication, University of Georgia, 1993. x, 242 pp. [Contents: Al Hester, "The Incredible Demise of Communism," pp. 1-12; Richard Schwarzlose, "Press Freedom in Bulgaria and Yugoslavia: A Tale of Two Nations," pp. 13-29; Frank L. Kaplan, "Czechoslovakia's Press Law: Shaping the Media's Future," pp. 31-58; James E. Fletcher, "Eastern Europe: Public Opinion Polling Practices and Organizations" [title on p. 59: "Eastern and Central Europe: Public Opinion Polling Practices and Organizations"], pp. 59-78; Kehrt Reyher, "Prospects for a Commerical Press in Post-Communist Poland," pp. 79-87; Peggy Simpson, "Magazines in Eastern Europe: A Time of Dynamic Change" [title on p. 89: "Magazines in Eastern Europe: A Time of Dramatic Change"], pp. 89-113; Elli Lester-Massman, "Without the Wall: Women's Communication in Berlin," pp. 115-129; Johnston M. Mitchell, "The Evolution of a Free Press in Hungary: 1986-1990," pp. 131-170; Roland Page, "Back to the Future: How Public Relations Is Helping to Build a New Czechoslovakia," pp. 171-180; Jill Dianne Swenson, "Communications and Rural Development in Former East Germany" [title on p. 181: "Communications and Rural Development in Germany"], pp. 181-209; W. Ronald Lane and Otto W. Smith, "A Perspective for Advertising / Marketing / Media Research in the Emerging Eastern European Countries" [title on p. 211: "A Perspective of Advertising / Marketing / Media Research"], pp. 211-227.]

73. Hester, Al, and Kristina White, eds. *Creating a Free Press in Eastern Europe.* Contributions by Al Hester, Owen V. Johnson, Marguerite Moritz, Cathy Packer, Eric Mark Kramer, Barbara Köpplová, Jan Jirák, Frank L. Kaplan, Marty Tharp, Michele Kayal, Elli Lester, April Orcutt, Milan Smid, Peggy Simpson, Kent R. Middleton, and Johnston Mitchell. Athens, GA: James M. Cox, Jr. Center for International Mass Communication Training and Research, Henry W. Grady College of Journalism and Mass Communication, University of Georgia, c1993. xiii, 487 pp. [Contents: Al Hester, "Introduction," pp. xi-xiii; Owen V. Johnson, "Whose Voice? Freedom of Speech and the Media in Central Europe," pp. 1-51; Marguerite Moritz, "After the Wall: Women and News Media Practices in the Context of Political Change," pp. 53-80; Cathy Packer, "The Emergence of the Free Press in Albania," pp. 83-109; Eric Mark Kramer, "Investigative Journalism in Bulgaria: A Postponed Renaissance," pp. 111-158; Eric Mark Kramer, "Reversal of Fortunes: Rehabilitations and Counter-Purges in Bulgaria," pp. 161-190; Barbara Köpplová, Jan Jirák and Frank L. Kaplan, "Major Trends in the Czech Mass Media after November, 1989," pp. 193-228; Marty Tharp, "The New Papers in the Czech Republic: Growing Pains," pp. 231-255; Michele Kayal, "The Unfinished Revolution: The Czech Republic's Press in Transition," pp. 257-280; Elli Lester, "The English-Language Press in Prague, the Czech Republic," pp. 283-308; April Orcutt, "Optimism, Pessimism and Paradox: Broadcast Press Freedom in Slovakia," pp. 311-339; Frank L. Kaplan, Jan Jirák, and Milan Smid, "The Broadcasting Law: First Step in Defining a Media Policy for the Czech Republic," pp. 341-372; Peggy Simpson, "Poland Gets a Crash Course in Advertising," pp. 375-402; Kent R. Middleton, "Applying Europe's 'First Amendment' to Romanian Libel and Access Law," pp. 405-429; Johnston Mitchell, "FIEJ and the Forming of Newspaper Publishers' Associations in Central and Eastern Europe," pp. 431-446; Johnston Mitchell, "Print Media Privatization: Ownership, Distribution and Production: The Baltic States and Bulgaria," pp. 449-464; Johnston Mitchell, "Moving Forward with the Free Press in Central and Eastern Europe," pp. 479-476.]

74. Horvat, Janos, and Andras Szanto. *The Crucial Facts: Misleading Cues in the News of Central and Eastern Europe During Communism's Collapse.* Occasional Paper (Freedom Forum Media Studies Center), no. 9. New York: Freedom Forum Media Studies Center, 1993. 27 pp.

75. "Interview: USIA Director Joseph Duffey." *Foreign Service Journal* 70, no. 8 (August 1993): 42-45.

76. Jakubowicz, Karel. "Freedom vs. Equality." *East European Constitutional Review* 2, no. 3 (Summer 1993): 42-48. ["Dissidents in Eastern Europe used to dream about creating open, democratic media organizations. Now that they are in power, have they changed channels?"]

77. Johnson, Owen V. "Half Slave-Half Free: The Crisis of the Russian and East European Press." *AAASS Newsletter* 33, no. 2 (March 1993): 1ff.

78. Kirschten, Dick. "Radio Wars." *National Journal* 25, no. 15 (April 10, 1993): 865-867. [On the Clinton Administration's plan to phase out Radio Free Europe and Radio Liberty.]

79. Koven, Ronald. "Media Laws: The Meddler's Itch." *Uncaptive Minds* 6, no. 2 (23) (Summer 1993): 103-114. [Part of a special survey on the media in Eastern Europe.]

80. Krishnaiah, Jothik, Nancy Signorielli, and Douglas M. McLeod. "The Evil Empire Revisited: *New York Times* Coverage of the Soviet Intervention in and Withdrawal from Afghanistan." *Journalism Quarterly* 70, no. 3 (Autumn 1993): 647-655.

81. Medvedev, Grigori. *No Breathing Room: The Aftermath of Chernobyl.* Translated from the Russian by Evelyn Rossiter. Introduction by David R. Marples. New York, NY: Basic Books, 1993. 213 pp. [Translation of *Bez kisloroda.*] REV: Felicity Barringer, *New York Times Book Review* 98, no. 22 (May 30 1993): 12. Andrew M. Davis, *JAMA* 270, no. 5 (August 4, 1993): 647-649. David Holloway, *New York Review of Books* 40, no. 11 (June 10,

1993): 36-38. Robert Legvold, *Foreign Affairs* 72, no. 3 (Summer 1993): 207.

82. Raghavan, Sudarsan V., Stephen S. Johnson, and Kristi K. Bahrenburg. "Sending Cross-Border Static: On the Fate of Radio Free Europe and the Influence of International Broadcasting." *Journal of International Affairs* 47, no. 1 (Summer 1993): 73-87. [Interview with Malcom S. Forbes, Jr.]

83. Roberts, Walter R. "The Voices of America." *World & I* 8, no. 11 (November 1993): 102-107.

84. Tuch, Hans N. "Speaking Out." *Foreign Service Journal* 70, no. 5 (May 1993): 11-14. [On Voice of America, Radio Free Europe and Radio Liberty.]

85. United States. Congress. House. Committee on Foreign Affairs, and Subcommittee on International Operations. *The Audience for U.S. Government International Broadcasting: Hearing before the Subcommittee on International Operations of the Committee on Foreign Affairs, House of Representatives, One Hundred Second Congress, Second Session, September 23, 1992.* Washington: U.S. G.P.O., 1993. iii, 79 pp.

86. Wooster, Martin Morse. "Magazines: The Post-Soviet Sphere." *Reason* 24, no. 8 (January 1993): 47-48. [Survey of Western media coverage of events in Russia, Hungary, and the former Yugoslavia.]

Russia/U.S.S.R./C.I.S.

87. Anderson, Jim. "My Dinner with Boris." *American Journalism Review* 15, no. 3 (April 1993): 37-38. ["A veteran journalist remembers his encounters with the KGB."]

88. Azhgikhina, Nadezhda. "High culture meets trash TV." *Bulletin of the Atomic Scientists* 49, no. 1 (January-February 1993): 42-46.

89. Baker, John F. "Crisis in Russian Publishing." *Publishers Weekly* 240, no. 12 (March 22, 1993): 10ff. [On a conference at the Library of Congress, March 9-10, 1993.]

90. Bonnell, Victoria E., and Gregory Freidin. "*Televorot*: The Role of Television Coverage in Russia's August 1991 Coup." *Slavic Review* 52, no. 4 (Winter 1993): 810-838.

91. Borisov, Vadim, and Vladimir Potapov. "Letter from the Friends of *Novyi Mir*." *World Literature Today* 67, no. 1 (Winter 1993): 24. [Prepared for release to the *Times Literary Supplement* (London) and to other Western literary periodicals.]

92. Coetzee, J. M. "Emerging from Censorship." *Salmagundi*, no. 100 (Fall 1993): 36-50. [Includes discussion of the Soviet Union and Osip Mandelshtam.]

93. Daniloff, Nicholas. "Will Russia's Free Press Survive?" *Fletcher Forum of World Affairs* 17, no. 1 (Winter 1993): 35-48.

94. Eribo, Festus. "Coverage of Africa South of the Sahara by *Pravda, Izvestia, Trud,* and *Selskaya Zhizn,* 1979-1987: A Content Analysis." *Journalism Quarterly* 70, no. 1 (Spring 1993): 51-57.

95. Gambrell, Jamey. "Moscow: Storm Over the Press." *New York Review of Books* 40, no. 21 (December 16, 1993): 69-74.

96. Gutiontov, Pavel. "Suppressing a rising press." *Bulletin of the Atomic Scientists* 49, no. 1 (January-February 1993): 39-41. [On Ruslan Khasbulatov's attempt to close the Russian newspaper *Izvestiia.*]

97. Harsch, Jonathan. "Robert Rodale (1930-1990): Mission Accomplished." *World & I* 8, no. 7 (July 1993): 234. [On the periodical *Novyi fermer.*]

98. Helvey, Laura Roselle. "Legitimizing Policy Shifts: Leadership Television Strategies in the Cases of American Withdrawal from Vietnam and Soviet Withdrawal from Afghanistan." Ph.D. diss., Stanford University, 1993. [UMI order no: AAC 9326485.]

99. Hyrych, Ihor. "The Ukrainian Historian Turns Thirty (1963-1993)." *Ethnic Forum* 13, no. 2; v. 14, no. 2 (1993-1994): 81-87. Translated from Ukrainian by Luba Gawur.

100. Jensen, Linda. "The Press and Power in the Russian Federation." *Journal of International Affairs* 47, no. 1 (Summer 1993): 97-125.

101. Koven, Ronald. "Waiting It Out." *Uncaptive Minds* 6, no. 3 (24) (Fall 1993): 129-132. [Part of a survey on the mass media in Eastern Europe.]

102. Lowe, David A. "The Book Business in Postcommunist Russia: Moscow, Year One (1992)." *Harriman Institute Forum* 6, no. 5 (January 1993): 1-8.

103. "The Media in the Countries of the Former Soviet Union." *RFE/RL Research Report* 2, no. 27 (July 2, 1993): 1-15. Contributions by Vera Tolz, Bohdan Nahaylo, Alexander Lukashuk, Vladimir Socor, Elizabeth Fuller, Bess Brown, Dzintra Bungs, and Saulius Girnius. [Includes articles by Vera Tolz, "Russia," pp. 3-5; Bohdan Nahaylo, "Ukraine," pp. 5-6; Alexander Lukashuk, "Belarus," pp. 6-8; Vladimir Socor, "Moldova," pp. 8-9; Elizabeth Fuller, "Transcaucasia," pp. 9-10; Bess Brown, "Central Asia," pp. 10-11; Dzintra Bungs, "Latvia," pp. 13-14; and Saulius Girnius, "Lithuania," pp. 14-15.]

104. Morgan, Lyndall. "*Pravda* and the Putsch." *Australian Slavonic and East European Studies* 7, no. 2 (1993): 85-114.

105. Naby, Eden. "Publishing in Central Asia." *Central Asia Monitor*, no. 1 (1993): 27-30.

106. Pavlova, Elena. "Consumed by Inflation? A Russian Magazine Struggles to Survive." *World & I* 8, no. 6 (June 1993): 230-239.

107. Rhodes, Mark. "The Newspaper in Russia Today." *RFE/RL Research Report* 2, no. 45 (November 12, 1993): 39-42.

108. ———. "Russians and Television." *RFE/RL Research Report* 2, no. 39 (October 1, 1993): 54-56.

109. Sterling, Claire. "The Press: Source-Greasing." *New Republic* 209, no. 20 (November 15, 1993): 11.

110. Tadjbakhsh, Shahrbanou. "The 'Tajik Spring of 1992.'" *Central Asia Monitor*, no. 2 (1993): 21-29.

111. Thomas, Cathy Lynn. "A Comparison of the Rhetorical Visions of Ronald Reagan: First Term Versus Second Term." Ph.D. diss., Ohio University, 1993. [UMI order no: AAC 9412452.]

112. Tolz, Vera. "The Russian Media in the Power Struggle between the President and the Congress." *RFE/RL Research Report* 2, no. 13 (March 26, 1993): 5.

113. Uspensky, Gleb, and Peter B. Kaufman. "Russia Passes Copyright Law: Anti-Piracy Task Force Formed." *Publishers Weekly* 240, no. 32 (August 9, 1993): 7.

114. Von Hippel, Frank. "Russia's new censorship." *Bulletin of the Atomic Scientists* 49, no. 2 (March 1993): 7-8. [On an article about chemical weapons tests in the Soviet Union that was published in *Moscow News* in 1992.]

115. Ware, Ruth Winchester. "The Effect of the Gorbachev Era (1985-1991) on *Newsweek*'s Photo Coverage and Image of the Soviet Union." Ph.D. diss., University of Tennessee, 1993. [UMI order no: AAC 9331738.]

116. Wishnevsky, Julia. "Media Still Far From Free." *RFE/RL Research Report* 2, no. 20 (May 14, 1993): 86-91.

117. Young, Cathy. "Russian Presswatch: In the Name of Humanity." *American Spectator* 26, no. 4 (April 1993): 52-53.

118. ———. "Russian Presswatch: Prophet Sharing." *American Spectator* 26, no. 9 (September 1993): 68-69.

119. Yurkovsky, Andrew. "His 'Ministry of Truth': Can Yeltsin Tame the Press?" *Nation* 256, no. 11 (March 22, 1993): 379-380.

Eastern Europe

120. Bailin, Iris. "A Hungarian Publisher Takes Home Some Tips." *American Journalism Review* 15, no. 9 (November 1993): 16.

121. Bass, Gary J. "Swing Kids." *New Republic* 208, no. 14 (April 5, 1993): 17-18. [Survey of the editorial positions of American magazines on the war in the former Yugoslavia.]

122. Buikema, Rosemarie. "Dialogue with a Many-Voiced Past: Milena Jesenska and Her Biographers." *Women's Studies International Forum* 16, no. 4 (July-August 1993): 339-346. [On the Czech journalist Jeŝenska.]

123. Gotovska-Popova, Teodorichka, and Kjell Engelbrekt. "The Tortuous Reform of Bulgarian Television." *RFE/RL Research Report* 2, no. 38 (September 24, 1993): 45-49.

124. Grudzinska Gross, Irena. "Broadcasting Values." *East European Constitutional Review* 2, no. 3 (Summer 1993): 51-53. [On the media law and Catholic values in Poland.]

125. Herrmann, Peter. "Social Goals for Media Endorsed by Poles." *RFE/RL Research Report* 2, no. 10 (March 5, 1993): 58-59.

126. Holmes, Stephen. "Focus: Media in Eastern Europe: Introduction." *East European Constitutional Review* 2, no. 3 (Summer 1993): 41. [Introduces articles by Jakubowicz, Kolarova, Dimitrov and Grudzinska Gross, versions of which were presented at the Central European University in Budapest, June 1993, at a conference on the mass media in Eastern Europe, organized by Andras Sajo and CEU's Legal Studies Program.]

127. Ingram, Judith. "The Media War." *Uncaptive Minds* 6, no. 1 (22) (Winter-Spring 1993): 45-50.

128. Jastrzebski, Marek. "Avoiding censorship: The 'second circulation' of books in Poland." *Journal of Reading* 36, no. 6 (March 1993): 470-473. Translated by Ewa Krysiak.

129. Kaplan, Morton A. "The *New Yorker*'s 'Sieg Heil' to Herr Honecker." *World & I* 8, no. 4 (April 1993): 110-113.

130. Kayal, Michele. "Former Communist Frees Party Paper." *American Journalism Review* 15, no. 3 (April 1993): 14. [On the re-opening of *Rude Pravo* in the Czech Republic.]

131. Kesic, Vesna. "The Press in War, The War in the Press: The Press in Croatia." *Uncaptive Minds* 6, no. 2 (23) (Summer 1993): 75-79. [Part of a special survey on the media in Eastern Europe.]

132. Kolarova, Rumyana, and Dimitr Dimitrov. "Media Wars in Sofia." *East European Constitutional Review* 2, no. 3 (Summer 1993): 48-51.

133. Man, Liviu. "The Independent Press in Romania: Against the Grain." *Uncaptive Minds* 6, no. 2 (23) (Summer 1993): 89-96. [Part of a special survey on the media in Eastern Europe.]

134. "The Media in Eastern Europe." *RFE/RL Research Report* 2, no. 19 (May 7, 1993): 22-35. Contributions by Jiri Pehe, Louis Zanga, Kjell Engelbrekt, Patrick Moore, Edith Oltay, Duncan M. Perry, Anna Sabbat-Swidlicka, Dan Ionescu, Jan Obrman, and Milan Andrejevich. [Includes articles by Jiri Pehe, pp. 22-23; Louis Zanga, "Albania," pp. 23-24; Kjell Engelbrekt, "Bulgaria," pp. 24-25; Patrick Moore, "Croatia," pp. 25-26; Jiri Pehe, "Czech Republic," pp. 26-27; Edith Oltay, "Hungary," pp. 27-28; Duncan M. Perry, "Macedonia," pp. 28-29; Anna Sabbat-Swidlicka, "Poland," pp. 29-30; Dan Ionescu, "Romania," pp. 30-32; Jan Obrman, "Slovakia," pp. 32-33; Milan Andrejevich, "Slovenia," pp. 33-34; Milan Andrejevich, "Serbia and Montenegro," pp. 34-35; and Louis Zanga, "Kosovo," p. 35.]

135. Obrman, Jan. "The Slovak Government versus the Media." *RFE/RL Research Report* 2, no. 6 (February 5, 1993): 26-30.

136. Oltay, Edith. "The Hungarian Press Struggles to Survive." *RFE/RL Research Report* 2, no. 39 (October 1, 1993): 50-53.

137. ———. "Hungarian Radio and Television under Fire." *RFE/RL Research Report* 2, no. 38 (September 24, 1993): 40-44.

138. Pataki, Judith. "Power Struggle over Broadcasting in Hungary." *RFE/RL Research Report* 2, no. 11 (March 12, 1993): 16-20.

139. Pehe, Jiri. "Czech Republic: Furor over Independent Radio and Television." *RFE/RL Research Report* 2, no. 15 (April 9, 1993): 23-27.

140. Ricchiardi, Sherry. "Exposing Genocide... For What?" *American Journalism Review* 15, no. 5 (June 1993): 32-36. ["*Newsday*'s Roy Gutman won a Pulitzer for his coverage of carnage in the former Yugoslavia. But he is outraged by how long it has taken the world to do something about it."]

141. Sever, Mjusa. "The Power of Images: The Media in Slovenia, The Media in Yugoslavia." *Uncaptive Minds* 6, no. 2 (23) (Summer 1993): 65-73. [Part of a special survey on the media in Eastern Europe.]

142. Sustrova, Petruska. "Pitfalls of the Independent Press in the Czech Republic." *Uncaptive Minds* 6, no. 2 (23) (Summer 1993): 97-101. [Part of a special survey on the media in Eastern Europe.]

143. Urban, Rob, and Laura Zelenko. "Here Comes the New Boss, Worse Than the Old Boss." *Columbia Journalism Review* 31, no. 6 (March-April 1993): 45-47. [Discusses freedom of the press in Slovakia.]

144. Zanga, Louis. "Two New Journalistic Ventures in Albania." *RFE/RL Research Report* 2, no. 24 (June 11, 1993): 41-43.

■ Emigres, Refugees, Diaspora

General

145. Avery, Donald, Marco Carynnyk, N. Fred Dreisziger, Mykola Hrynchyshyn, Bohdan Kordan, and Desmond Morton. "Divided Loyalties? Homeland Ties in Times of Crisis." *Polyphony*, no. 13 (1993): 29-54. [Includes Chairman's Remarks (p. 29), Commentary (pp. 47-49), and Discussion (pp. 50-54).]

146. Brym, Robert J., William Shaffir, and Morton Weinfeld, eds. *The Jews in Canada*. Toronto: Oxford University Press, 1993. x, 435 pp. [Contains 24 articles and is divided into seven sections: the history of Canadian Jewry; anti-Semitism; culture and religious observance; relations with other communities, including Ukrainian

Canadians; politics; women and the family; and minorities such as small-town Jews, Soviet Jewish émigrés, and the Jewish poor.] REV: Henry Srebrnik, *Canadian Journal of Political Science = Revue canadienne de science politique* 26, no. 4 (December 1993): 806-807.

147. Clayton, Jacklyn Blake. "Your Land, My Land: The Process of Acculturation for Four International Students in an Elementary School Setting in the United States." Ed.D. diss., Boston University, 1993. [UMI order no: AAC 9318535.]

148. Fisher, Sharon. "Romanies in Slovakia." *RFE/RL Research Report* 2, no. 42 (October 22, 1993): 54-59.

149. Fletcher, Holly. "A Patriotic Glow." *World & I* 8, no. 7 (July 1993): 266-277. [On Moravian-Americans in Pennsylvania.]

150. Hoerder, Dirk. "The Traffic of Emigration via Bremen/Bremerhaven: Merchants' Interests, Protective Legislation, and Migrants' Experiences." *Journal of American Ethnic History* 13, no. 1 (Fall 1993): 68-101.

151. Isajiw, Wsevolod W., Aysan Sev'er, and Leo Driedger. "Ethnic identity and social mobility: A test of the 'drawback model.'" *Canadian Journal of Sociology = Cahiers canadiens de sociologie* 18, no. 2 (Spring 1993): 177-196. [Includes discussion of German, Jewish and Ukrainian emigration to and assimilation in Canada.]

152. Kloberdanz, Timothy J., and Rosalinda Kloberdanz. *Thunder on the Steppe: Volga German Folklife in a Changing Russia*. 1st ed. Lincoln, NE: American Historical Society of Germans from Russia, 1993. xvi, 302 pp.

153. Klusmeyer, Douglas B. "Aliens, Immigrants, and Citizens: The Politics of Inclusion in the Federal Republic of Germany." *Daedalus* 122, no. 3 (Summer 1993): 81-114.

154. Loewen, Royden K. *Family, Church, and Market: A Mennonite Community in the Old and the New Worlds, 1850-1930*. Statue of Liberty-Ellis Island Centennial Series. Urbana, IL: University of Illinois Press, c1993. xi, 370 p.

155. Magocsi, Paul Robert, ed. *The Persistence of Regional Cultures: Rusyns and Ukrainians in Their Carpathian Homeland and Abroad*. Includes contributions by Oleksa V. Mysanyc, Mykola Musynka, Olena Duc'-Fajfer, István Udvari, Ljubomir Medjesi, Paul Robert Magocsi, Petro Trochanovskij, Wieslaw Witkowski, Paul Robert Magocsi, and Andrzej A. Zieba. Classics of Carpatho-Rusyn Scholarship, 5. East European Monographs, no. 365. Fairview, NJ: Carpatho-Rusyn Research Center; New York: Distributed by Columbia University Press, 1993. ix, 218, ix, 220 pp. [Essays and commentaries published both in English translation (first section) and in the authors' languages (second section). Ukrainian title page: *Tryvalist' rehional'nykh kul'tur: rusyny i ukraintsi na ikhnii karpats'kii bat'kivshchyni ta za kordonom*. Partial contents: Oleksa V. Mysanyc, "From Subcarpathian Rusyns to

Transcarpathian Ukrainians," pp. 7-52 (in Ukrainian, second section, pp. 7-49); Mykola Musynka, "The Postwar Development of the Regional Culture of the Rusyn-Ukrainians of Czechoslovakia," pp. 53-82 (in Ukrainian, pp. 50-79); Olena Duc'-Fajfer, "The Lemkos in Poland," pp. 83-103 (in Lemko Rusyn, pp. 80-102); István Udvari, "Rusyns in Hungary and the Hungarian Kingdom," pp. 103-138 (in Russian, pp. 103-139); Ljubomir Medjesi, "The Problem of Cultural Borders in the History of Ethnic Groups: The Yugoslav Rusyns," pp. 139-162 (in Vojvodinian Rusyn, pp. 141-165); Paul Robert Magocsi, "Made or Re-Made in America? Nationality and Identity Formation Among Carpatho-Rusyn Immigrants and Their Descendants," pp. 163-178 (in Ukrainian, pp. 166-181); Petro Trochanovskij, "Commentary," pp. 179-186 (in Polish, pp. 182-189); Wieslaw Witkowski, "Commentary," pp. 187-190 (in Polish, pp. 190-193); Paul Robert Magocsi "Commentary," pp. 191-202 (in Ukrainian, pp. 194-205); Andrzej A. Zieba, "Commentary" pp. 203-217 (in Polish, pp. 206-220).]

156. Mavratsas, Caesar V. "Ethnic Entrepreneurialism, Social Mobility, and Embourgeoisement. The Formation and Intergenerational Evolution of Greek-American Economic Culture." Ph.D. diss., Boston University, 1993. [UMI order no: AAC 9311117.]

157. Neckermann, Peter. "Germany's Refugee Crisis." *World & I* 8, no. 2 (February 1993): 82-87.

158. Range, Peter Ross. "Europe Faces an Immigrant Tide." *National Geographic* 183, no. 5 (May 1993): 94-124. ["Fleeing poverty and persecution, millions of immigrants from Africa, the Middle East, and Eastern Europe seek refuge in the West. But resentment and even violence make for an often bitter welcome."]

159. Rothbart, Ron. "The Ethnic Saloon as a Form of Immigrant Enterprise." *International Migration Review* 27, no. 2 (Summer 1993): 332-358. [Discusses entrepreneurial activity of Lithuanian, Polish, Jewish, and German immigrants in Shenandoah, Pennsylvania, between 1880 and World War I.]

160. Said, Edward W. "Intellectual Exile: Expatriates and Marginals." *Grand Street* 12, no. 3 (no. 47) (1993): 112-124.

161. Schmid, Gerhard. "Immigration in Europe: How Much 'Other' Is Too Much?" *Social Education* 57, no. 4 (April-May 1993): 181-183. [Part of a special section entitled "United Germany in a Uniting Europe, Part 1."]

162. Schwartz, Lee. "Refugee Flows and Capacities for Their Accommodation." *Post-Soviet Geography* 34, no. 4 (April 1993): 239-249. [Edited version of the Proceedings of the Fifth Theodore Shabad Memorial Roundtable on the Geography of the (former) USSR, held in conjunction with the 1993 Annual Meeting of the Association of American Geographers in Atlanta, GA.]

163. Slajchrt, Viktor. "A Song Is All That's Left of Them." *RCDA* 32, no. 4 (1993-1994): 72-74. [On Gypsies. Abridgement of article from *Respekt* (Prague) no. 23 (1994).]

164. Straumanis, Andris. " 'This Sudden Spasm of Newspaper Hostility': Stereotyping of Latvian Immigrants in Boston Newspapers, 1980." *Ethnic Forum* 13, no. 2; v. 14, no. 2 (1993-1994): 88-107.

165. Tucker, Aviezer. "The New Jews." *Telos*, no. 98-99 (Winter 1993-Fall 1994): 209-215. [On Gypsies in Eastern Europe and the former Soviet Union.]

166. Winland, Daphne Naomi. "The quest for Mennonite peoplehood: ethno-religious identity and the dilemma of definitions." *Canadian Review of Sociology and Anthropology* 30, no. 1 (February 1993): 110-138.

167. Wolkovich-Valkavicius, William. "The Lithuanian Angle in a Hollywood Movie: An Analysis of *Once Around*." *Lituanus* 39, no. 3 (Fall 1993): 44-56.

Armenians

168. Accomando, Claire Hsu. "Father of the Bride." *Ararat* 34, no. 1 (Winter 1993): 28-30. [Armenians in France.]

169. ———. "Marguerite Babian." *Ararat* 34, no. 1 (Winter 1993): 62-64. [Armenians in France.]

170. "Armenians of Auvergne." *Ararat* 34, no. 1 (Winter 1993): 6. [Armenians in France; reprinted from the journal *La Montagne*.]

171. Asadourian, Hagop. "Van Cortlandt Park." *Ararat* 34, no. 2 (no. 134) (Spring 1993): 18-19. [An excerpt from *Gardens of Our City*.]

172. Bakalian, Anny. *Armenian-Americans: From Being to Feeling Armenian*. New Brunswick, NJ: Transaction Publishers, c1993. xii, 511 pp.

173. Balakian, Peter. *Sad Days of Light: Poems*. Pittsburgh, PA: Carnegie Mellon University Press, 1993. 79 pp.

174. Boudakian, Max M. "The Serendipitous Mystery of Christoforo the Armenian." *Ararat* 34, no. 2 (no. 134) (Spring 1993): 46-47.

175. Bricout, Jacques. "9th Century Church." *Ararat* 34, no. 1 (Winter 1993): 10. [Armenians in France.]

176. Chantikian, Kosrof. "Grandmother Maria Marna." *Ararat* 34, no. 3 (no. 135) (Summer 1993): 47.

177. Cholakian, Rouben. "An Armenian-American in Paris." *Ararat* 34, no. 1 (Winter 1993): 76-79.

178. Darvishian, Dan. "A Crowded Place." *Ararat* 34, no. 2 (no. 134) (Spring 1993): 22-23.

179. Delwasse, Lilliane. "Shoes by Armenia." *Ararat* 34, no. 1 (Winter 1993): 74. Translated by A. J. Hacikyan. [Armenians in France.]

180. Dorian, Peter H. "An Armenian in the Mogul Court." *Ararat* 34, no. 3 (no. 135) (Summer 1993): 22-23. [Accompanied by "Old Calcuttans," a reprint from *The Statesman* (September 10, 1992).]

181. Eisen, Christine. "Poetry: Ode to My Armenian Grandmother." *Ararat* 34, no. 1 (Winter 1993): 11.

182. Guroian, Vigen. "Is the Armenian Family Alive and Well?" *Ararat* 34, no. 2 (no. 134) (Spring 1993): 41-45.

183. Heboyan-DeVries, Esther. "Leon of Lusignan." *Ararat* 34, no. 1 (Winter 1993): 7-9. [Armenians in France.]

184. Hovanessian, Diana Der. "Lecture (For Philip Ketchian)." *Ararat* 34, no. 3 (no. 135) (Summer 1993): 47.

185. Kaprielian-Churchill, Isabel. "Armenian Refugee Women: The Picture Brides, 1920-1930." *Journal of American Ethnic History* 12, no. 3 (Spring 1993): 3-29.

186. Kebabjian, Jean-Claude. "Paris of the Armenians." *Ararat* 34, no. 1 (Winter 1993): 38-47.

187. Manoukian, Agopik. "Diaspora of the Mind: A Conversation with Herman Vahramian." *Ararat* 34, no. 2 (no. 134) (Spring 1993): 37-40.

188. Minassian, Yvonne. "Beginning to Grow Up Armenian." *Ararat* 34, no. 2 (no. 134) (Spring 1993): 24-26.

189. Nourikhan, P. Minas. "Napoleon and the Mekhitarists." *Ararat* 34, no. 1 (Winter 1993): 12-16. Translated from the French by Marjorie Appel. [Armenians in France.]

190. Ohanian, Bernard. "A Fine Sense of Survival." *Ararat* 34, no. 2 (no. 134) (Spring 1993): 27-30. [Article reprinted from *The Los Angeles Times*.]

191. Ophuls, Marcel. "Mitterrand's Red Scare." *Ararat* 34, no. 1 (Winter 1993): 20-24. [Armenians in France.]

192. Roditi, Edouard. "40, rue Armenie, Lyons." *Ararat* 34, no. 1 (Winter 1993): 10-11. [Armenians in France.]

193. ———. "Collector's Item." *Ararat* 34, no. 1 (Winter 1993): 80.

194. ———. "Poetry from the Left." *Ararat* 34, no. 1 (Winter 1993): 31.

195. ———. "Up from the Slums." *Ararat* 34, no. 1 (Winter 1993): 65-66. [On Martin Melkonian.]

196. Schwarcz, Vera. "Sabrina, A Tale of Transference." *Ararat* 34, no. 2 (no. 134) (Spring 1993): 20-21.

197. Tchakmakian, Pascal, and Felix Leo. "Renaissance in France." *Ararat* 34, no. 1 (Winter 1993): 2-5. [Armenians in France.]

198. Tekian, Vehanoush. "Story of a Peach Tree and a Potato." *Ararat* 34, no. 3 (no. 135) (Summer 1993): 7-8.

199. Torgomian, Haig. "With the Free French in Sudan." *Ararat* 34, no. 1 (Winter 1993): 17-19. [Armenians in France and French North Africa during World War II.]

200. Trendle, Giles. "Report from Lebanon." *Ararat* 34, no. 2 (no. 134) (Spring 1993): 50.

201. Vassilian, Hamo B., ed. *The Armenians: A Colossal Bibliographic Guide to Books Published in the English Language.* 1st ed. Glendale, CA: Armenian Reference Books Co., c1993. 206 pp.

202. Verneuil, Henri. "Mayrig." *Ararat* 34, no. 1 (Winter 1993): 50-59. Translated by Elise Antreassian and Esther Heboyan-DeVries.

Carpatho-Rusyns (Ruthenians)

203. Magocsi, Paul R. "Carpatho-Rusyns: A Tortuous Quest for Identity." *Cross Currents: A Yearbook of Central European Culture*, no. 12 (1993): 147-159.

204. ———. "Carpatho-Rusyns: Their Current Status and Future Perspectives." *Carpatho-Rusyn American* 16, no. 2 (1993): 4-9.

205. Stefka, Joseph, ed. *Kalendár-Almanac National Slovak Society of the USA for the Year 1993.* Includes contribution by Paul Magocsi. Pittsburgh, PA: 1993. [Partial contents: Paul Magocsi, "Carpatho-Rusyns: A New or Revived People?" pp. 38-45.]

Czechs and Slovaks

206. Garver, Bruce. "Americans of Czech and Slovak Ancestry in the History of Czechoslovakia." *Czechoslovak and Central European Journal* 11, no. 2 (Winter 1993): 1-14.

207. Stolarik, M. Mark. "The Slovak Search for Identity in the United States, 1880-1918." *Canadian Review of Studies in Nationalism = Revue Canadienne des Etudes sur le Nationalisme* 20, nos. 1-2 (1993): 45-55.

208. Stone, Gregory Martin. "Ethnicity, Class, and Politics Among Czechs in Cleveland,1870-1940." Ph.D. diss., Rutgers University, 1993. [UMI order no: AAC 9412687.]

209. Tibbetts, John C. "An Abiding Legacy: The Spillville Centennial Celebrates Dvorák's Retreat." *World & I* 8, no. 8 (August 1993): 246-257.

Hungarians

210. Bisztray, George. "Image or Self Image? Reports on Hungarian Canadians in Hungarian Publications of the 1980s." *East European Quarterly* 27, no. 1 (Spring 1993): 65-77.

211. Dreisziger, Kalman. "Hungarian Community Folkdance Groups in Canada." *Hungarian Studies Review* 20, nos. 1-2 (Spring-Fall 1993): 71-82.

212. Dreisziger, N. F. "The 1956 Hungarian Student Movement in Exile: An Introduction." *Hungarian Studies Review* 20, nos. 1-2 (Spring-Fall 1993): 93-116.

213. Oltay, Edith. "Hungarians under Political Pressure in Vojvodina." *RFE/RL Research Report* 2, no. 48 (December 3, 1993): 43-48.

214. Szanton, Andrew. "Shaping an Uncertain Future." *World & I* 8, no. 6 (June 1993): 206-213.

215. Teleky, Richard. "The Archives of St. Elizabeth of Hungary." *Ethnic Forum* 13, no. 1 (1993): 53-64. [Describes Hungarica in the library of a Catholic church in Cleveland, Ohio.]

216. Vardy, Steven Bela. "Hungarian National Consciousness and the Question of Dual and Multiple Identity." *Hungarian Studies Review* 20, nos. 1-2 (Spring-Fall 1993): 53-70.

Jews

217. Abrams, Sylvia F. "Meeting the Educational and Cultural Needs of Soviet Newcomers." *Religious Education* 88, no. 2 (Spring 1993): 315-323.

218. Al-Haj, Majid. "Ethnicity and Immigration: The Case of Soviet Immigration to Israel." *Humboldt Journal of Social Relations* 19, no. 2 (1993): 279-305.

219. Applebaum, Terry L., and Patricia Vile. "Resettling Russian Musicians: From Emigre to Artist-Entrepreneur." *Journal of Jewish Communal Service* 69, nos. 2-3 (Winter-Spring 1993): 117-124.

220. Chiswick, Barry R. "Soviet Jews in the United States: An Analysis of Their Linguistic and Economic Adjustment." *International Migration Review* 27, no. 2 (Summer 1993): 260-285.

221. Cohen, Stephen Z. "Issues in Absorbing Aged Russian Jewish Immigrants: Observations from the Current Israel Experience." *Journal of Jewish Communal Service* 69, no. 4 (Summer 1993): 30-37.

222. Diner, Hasia. "A Time for Gathering: The Second Migration." *American Jewish History* 81, no. 1 (Autumn 1993): 22-33.

223. Hiebert, Daniel. "Jewish Immigrants and the Garment Industry of Toronto, 1901-1931: A Study of Ethnic and Class Relations." *Annals of the Association of American Geographers* 83, no. 2 (June 1993): 243-271.

224. Isserman, Maurice. "Erlich and Alter." *Dissent* 40, no. 2 (Spring 1993): 239-241.

225. Kabakoff, Jacob. "Rethinking the American Jewish Experience: Some East European Letters on Emigration." *American Jewish Archives* 45, no. 1 (Spring-Summer 1993): 73-80.

226. Klier, John D. "The Russian Jewish Intelligentsia and the Concept of *Sliianie*." *Ethnic Groups* 10, nos. 1-3 (1993): 157-174. [Part of special issue devoted to "Pre-Modern and Modern National Identity in Russia and Eastern Europe."]

227. Kozulin, Alex, and Alex Venger. "Psychological and Learning Problems of Immigrant Children from the Former Soviet Union." *Journal of Jewish Communal Service* 70, no. 1 (Fall 1993): 64-72.

228. Markowitz, Fran. *A Community in Spite of Itself: Soviet Jewish Emigres in New York.* Smithsonian Series in Ethnographic Inquiry. Washington, DC: Smithsonian Institution Press, 1993. xvi, 317 pp.

229. Matlin, Vladimir. "Culture Shocks." *Commentary* 96, no. 4 (October 1993): 44-49. [On Jewish immigrants in the United States.]

230. Rockaway, Robert A. " 'I Feel as if Newly Born': Immigrant Letters to the Industrial Removal Office." *American Jewish Archives* 45, no. 2 (Fall/Winter 1993): 159-192.

231. Siegel, Lee. "Russian Jews and African Americans." *Dissent* 40, no. 3 (Summer 1993): 369-371.

232. Solomon, Deborah. "The Rashomon Coat Tale." *Lilith* 18, no. 1 (Winter 1993): 17-19.

233. Sorin, Gerald. "Mutual Contempt, Mutual Benefit: The Strained Encounter Between German and Eastern European Jews in America, 1880-1920." *American Jewish History* 81, no. 1 (Autumn 1993): 34-59.

234. Stavans, Ilan. "Lost in Translation." *Massachusetts Review* 34, no. 4 (Winter 1993-1994): 489-502. [Concerns Jews in Mexico who are of Russian and East European ancestry.]

235. Tress, Madeleine. "Germany's New 'Jewish Question' or German-Jewry's 'Russian Question'?" *New Political Science*, no. 24/25 (Spring-Summer 1993): 75-86.

236. Wexler, Paul. *The Ashkenazic Jews: A Slavo-Turkic People in Search of a Jewish Identity.* Columbus, Ohio: Slavica Publishers, c1993. 306 pp.

237. Wingfield, Nancy M. "Czechoslovak Jewish Immigration to the United States, 1938-1945." *Czechoslovak and Central European Journal* 11, no. 2 (Winter 1993): 38-48.

238. Wissolik, Richard David, Michelle Howatineck, and Erica Wissolik. *The Jewish Community of Westmoreland County, Pennsylvania: A Collection of Oral Histories, 1991-1992.* Latrobe, PA: Saint Vincent College Center for Northern Appalachian Studies/Oral History Program in cooperation with the Westmoreland Jewish Community Council of the United Jewish Federation, 1993-. vols.

239. Zicht, Gloria. "The Effects of Emigration on Soviet Children: Latency to Adolescence." *Journal of Jewish Communal Service* 70, no. 1 (Fall 1993): 57-63.

240. ———. "Working with Interpreters: An Experience in Soviet Resettlement." *Journal of Jewish Communal Service* 69, nos. 2/3 (Winter-Spring 1993): 111-116.

Poles

241. Blejwas, Stanislaus A. "Stanislaw Osada: Immigrant Nationalist." *Polish American Studies* 50, no. 1 (Spring 1993): 23-50.

242. Bukowczyk, John J. " 'Harness for Posterity the Values of a Nation': Fifty Years of the Polish American Historical Association and *Polish American Studies*." *Polish American Studies* 50, no. 2 (Autumn 1993): 5-100.

243. Cienciala, Anna M. "Foundations of Polish-American Scholarship: Karol Wachtl." *Polish American Studies* 50, no. 1 (Spring 1993): 51-73.

244. Harnish, Glen C. "Immigration and Naturalization Law: Deportation and Denaturalization: *Petkiewytsch v. Immigration and Naturalization Service*." *Suffolk Transnational Law Review* 16, no. 2 (Spring 1993): 750-760.

245. Hoffmann, Roald, and Vivian Torrence. " 'Marie Curie Still Makes Him Cry': The Seeds of a Career in Science." *Chronicle of Higher Education* 39, no. 45 (July 14, 1993): B36. [Excerpt from Roald Hoffmann and Vivian Torrence, *Chemistry Imagined: Reflections on Science* (Washington, DC: Smithsonian Institution Press, 1993).]

246. Mostwin, Danuta. "Thomas and Znaniecki's *The Polish Peasant in Europe and America*: Survival of the Book." *Polish American Studies* 50, no. 1 (Spring 1993): 75-84.

247. Orzechowski, Emil, and Kazimierz Braun. *Madame Modjeska, Countess Bozenta. Emigre Queen. Krolowa Emigrantka.* Buffalo, NY: Council on International Studies and Programs, State University of New York at Buffalo, 1993. viii, 124 pp. [Contents: "American poets in honor of Madame Modjeska = Amerykanscy poeci ku czci Heleny Modrzejewskiej," compiled and edited by Emil Orzechowski; Kazimierz Braun, "Emigre queen = Krolowa emigrantka: a soliloquy."]

248. Szymczak, Robert. "The Pioneer Days: Mieczyslaw Haiman and Polish American Historiography." *Polish American Studies* 50, no. 1 (Spring 1993): 7-21.

249. Ubriaco, Robert D., Jr. "The Yalta Conference and Its Impact on the Chicago Congressional Elections of 1946." *Illinois Historical Journal* 86, no. 4 (Winter 1993): 225-244.

250. Warwick, Ioanna-Veronika. "In the Mirror." *Poet Lore* 88, no. 4 (Winter 1993-1994): 29.

251. Zubrzycki, Jerzy. "Whither *Emigracja*? The Future of the Polish Community in Great Britain." *Polish Review* 38, no. 4 (1993): 391-406. [Describes in part research themes of the M. B. Grabowski Polish Migration Project of the School of Slavonic and East European Studies, University of London.]

Romanians

252. Carter, Sarah T. "One Foot in Each Culture: A Romanian Community in Ohio." *World & I* 8, no. 1 (January 1993): 680-691.

253. Patterson, G. James, and Paul Petrescu. "The Romanian Language Press in America." *East European Quarterly* 27, no. 2 (Summer 1993): 261-270.

Russians

254. Brandt, Nat. *Con Brio: Four Russians Called the Budapest String Quartet.* New York: Oxford University Press, 1993. xvi, 272 pp. REV: James R. Oestreich, *New York Times Book Review* 98, no. 38 (September 19, 1993): 35. *New Yorker* 69, no. 22 (July 19, 1993): 87.

255. Tanton, John, and Wayne Lutton. "Immigration and Criminality in the U.S.A." *Journal of Social, Political and Economic Studies* 18, no. 2 (Summer 1993): 217-234. [Includes section "Russian Emigres," pp. 224-225.]

256. Taylor, Keith. "Resurrection." *Michigan Quarterly Review* 32, no. 1 (Winter 1993): 74-75. [On the Dukhobors.]

Ukrainians

257. Gregorovich, John B. "The Ukrainian Canadian Congress: Some Thoughts on Its Past, Present, and Future." *Polyphony*, no. 13 (1993): 79-81.

258. Hryniuk, Stella, and Lubomyr Luciuk. "Multiculturalism and Ukrainian Canadians: Identity, Homeland Ties, and the Community's Future: Introduction." *Polyphony*, no. 13 (1993): 1-3. [Issue based largely on papers presented at a symposium organized by the Ukrainian Canadian Centennial Commission and held in Toronto on November 30, 1991.]

259. Isajiw, Wsevolod W. "The Ukrainian Canadian Community at a Historic Turning Point: Its Goals Revisited." *Polyphony*, no. 13 (1993): 82-89.

260. Isajiw, Wsevolod, Peter Galadza, Stanford Lucyk, Ihor W. Bardyn, and Ostap Skrypnyk. "A New Commons? The Viability of Ukrainian-Canadian Organizational Structures in the 1990s and Beyond." *Polyphony*, no. 13 (1993): 55-73. [On the Ukrainian Orthodox Church in Canada, and the role of the clergy in the Ukrainian-Canadian community. Includes Chairman's Remarks (p. 55) and Commentaries (pp. 65-68, 69-73).]

261. Lukianenko, Levko. "After Words." *Polyphony*, no. 13 (1993): 77-78. Translated by Bohdan Tkachenko. [Excerpts from a speech given to the Seventeenth Congress of Ukrainian Canadians, which was held in Winnipeg, Manitoba, October 6-11, 1992.]

262. Lupul, Manoly R. "A Question of Identity: Canada's Ukrainians and Multiculturalism." *Polyphony*, no. 13 (1993): 8-13.

263. Mulroney, Brian. "After Words." *Polyphony*, no. 13 (1993): 74-76. [Partial transcript of address to the Seventeenth Congress of Ukrainian Canadians, which was held in Winnipeg, Manitoba, October 6-11, 1992.]

264. Stern, Steven. "From the Annals of the Kabakoffs." *Tikkun* 8, no. 5 (September-October 1993): 72-80. [Fiction.]

265. Swyripa, Frances. *Wedded to the Cause: Ukrainian-Canadian Women and Ethnic Identity, 1891-1991.* Toronto; Buffalo: University of Toronto Press, 1993.

xii, 330 pp. [Contents: Introduction: Queen Elizabeth the Ukrainian; 1. Failing to Measure Up: The Peasant Immigrant; 2. Jeopardizing the Future: Alienated and Rebellious Daughters; 3. Models for Their Sex: Princess Olha and the Cossack Mother; 4. Putting the Models to Work: Organizational Propaganda and Programs; 5. Canadianizing a Legacy: Women's Organizations after the Second World War; 6. Rehabilitating the Peasant Immigrant: Baba and the Canadianized Heroine; Conclusion: Baba Meets the Queen.] REV: Ihor V. Zielyk, *Canadian Journal of Sociology* 18, no. 4 (Fall 1993): 463-465.

(Former) Yugoslavs

266. Cebulj-Sajko, Breda. "The Religious Life of Slovenes in Australia." *Slovene Studies* 14, no. 2 (1992, published September 1994): 185-203. [Paper presented at a panel entitled "The Catholic Church and Slovene Immigrants," AAASS Convention, Honolulu, HI, November 1993.]

267. Corsellis, John. "Yugoslav Refugees in Camps in Egypt and Austria 1944-47." *North Dakota Quarterly* 61, no. 1 (Winter 1993): 40-54.

268. Drnovsek, Marjan. "The Attitude of the Slovene Catholic Church to Emigration to the United States of America Before 1924." *Slovene Studies* 14, no. 2 (1992, published September 1994): 169-184. [Paper presented at a panel entitled "The Catholic Church and Slovene Immigrants," AAASS Convention, Honolulu, HI, November 1993.]

269. Fris, Darko. "A Brief Survey of the Activities of the Catholic Church Among Slovene Immigrants in the USA (1871-1941)." *Slovene Studies* 14, no. 2 (1992, published September 1994): 205-216. [Paper presented at a panel entitled "The Catholic Church and Slovene Immigrants," AAASS Convention, Honolulu, HI, November 1993.]

270. Jancar, Drago. "Slovene Exile." *Nationalities Papers* 21, no. 1 (Spring 1993): 91-105.

271. Novakovich, Josip. "Writing in Tongues." *Four Quarters* 7, no. 2 (Fall 1993): 37-43.

■ Genealogy

272. Bell, George E. *The Pancios from Galicia: The Pancio Family History.* Ontario, NY: Wayne & Ridge Pub, 1993. 1 vol.

273. Denissoff, Basile A. *The Denissoffs: Cossacks of the Don and Members of the Russian Nobility.* Big Flats, NY: B.A. Denissoff, 1993. xx, 117 pp.

274. Miloradovich, Petro Mikolaevich. *Miloradovich.* [United States]: Published by his three sons, c1993. 58, 71 pp. ["Myloradovychy." English and Ukrainian.]

275. Schlyter, Daniel M. *Essentials in Polish Genealogical Research.* Chicago, IL: Polish Genealogical Society of America, [c1993]. 12 pp.

■ Libraries and Library Science

276. Bellows, Heather E. "The Challenge of Informationalization in Post-Communist Societies." *Communist and Post-Communist Studies* 26, no. 2 (June 1993): 144-164.

277. Browder, George C. "Update on the Captured Documents in the Former Osoby Archive, Moscow." *Central European History* 26, no. 3 (1993): 335-342. [Includes corrections to author's "Scholarly Note: Captured German and Other Nations' Documents in the Osoby (Special) Archive, Moscow," *Central European History* 24, no. 4 (1991): 424-445.]

278. Crayne, Janet Irene. "Library News." *AAASS Newsletter* 33, no. 2 (March 1993): 19. [University of Texas acquires Jakobson collection on Czech and Slovak culture; Columbia University periodicals collection; New York Public Library receives Papanek, Broucek, and Hinian collections, and purchases Brozek collection; Radio Free Europe/Radio Liberty Research Institute processes Russian samizdat and continues its WEBNET (World East European Bibliographic Network) participation.]

279. ———. "Library News." *AAASS Newsletter* 33, no. 3 (May 1993): 11. [Proposed budget cuts for Radio Free Europe/Radio Liberty may affect Imagelink and WEBNET; request to GLOSAS/USA to help establish IDENET, a U.S.-Russian electronic distance education system; University of Illinois at Urbana-Champaign hosting Third Annual Slavic Librarians' Workshop, June 1993; ABSEES Online available over the Internet.]

280. ———. "Library News." *AAASS NewsNet* 33, no. 5 (November 1993): 8. [SOVLIT Project, a textbase of Soviet literary journals of the 1920s and 1930s, initiated by Thomas Lahusen, Fred Choate and computer specialists in Moscow. IREX announces competition for Special Projects in Library and Information Science.]

281. Fink, Carole. "Resolution by the AHA Council." *Slavic Review* 52, no. 1 (Spring 1993): 105-106.

282. Getty, J. Arch. "Commercialization of Scholarship: Do We Need a Code of Behavior?" *Slavic Review* 52, no. 1 (Spring 1993): 101-104.

283. Grimsted, Patricia Kennedy. "Russian Archives in Transition: Caught Between Political Crossfire and Economic Crisis." *American Archivist* 56, no. 4 (Fall 1993): 614-662.

284. Johnson, Eric A. *Central Asia: A Survey of Libraries and Publishing in the Region*. Washington, DC: IREX, International Research & Exchanges Board, [1993]. 9, [11] leaves.

285. Keller, Dean H., ed. *Academic Libraries in Greece: The Present Situation and Future Prospects*. Contributions by Don L. Tolliver, Nancy Birk, Dimitris Karageorgiou, Cacouris Mersini Moreleli, Michael Kreyche, George D. Bokos, Stella Korobili, Bouki Vicki Syroglou, James Krikelas, Michael Tzekakis, Peter D. Haikalis, Nicolaos Dimitriou Dimitrios Alexandrou, Tod Alex Noel, Martha Kyrillidou, Thomas Marion Davis, and Athena Salaba. New York: Haworth Press, c1993. xiv, 226 p. [Contents: Don L. Tolliver, "International interlibrary cooperation: exchanging goals, values, and culture exchange between Kent State University and Aristotle University, Thessaloniki," pp. 3-7; "Academic libraries in Greece with emphasis on Aristotle University," reprinted from *International Library Review* (July 1984), pp. 9-22; Nancy Birk and Dimitris Karageorgiou, "Academic libraries in Greece: a new profile," reprinted from *Libri* (June 1988), pp. 23-38; Cacouris Mersini Moreleli, "Library education in Greece," pp. 39-53; Michael Kreyche, "Library Automation in Greece: a visitor's perspective at the University of Crete and Aristotle University of Thessaloniki," pp. 55-67; George D. Bokos, "Automation of the National Library of Greece," pp. 69-79; Stella Korobili, "Collection Development and interlibrary loan in Greek academic libraries," pp. 81-92; Bouki Vicki Syroglou, "The American Center Library in Thessaloniki, Greece," pp. 93-95; James Krikelas and Michael Tzekakis, "Automation and the University of Crete," pp. 97-107; Peter D. Haikalis, "Academic libraries in transition: A Case study of the library at the University of Crete in Rethymnon," pp. 109-26; Nicolaos Dimitriou Dimitrios Alexandrou, "The library of Aristotle University of Thessaloniki: organization, operation, and perspectives," pp. 127-128; Tod Alex Noel, "The library of the Department of English Language and Literature at the Aristotle University of Thessaloniki, Greece," pp. 129-150; Martha Kyrillidou, "A user survey of the English Department Library at Aristotle," pp. 151-196; Thomas Marion Davis, "Kent State University, Kent, Ohio, and Aristotle University, Thessaloniki, Greece: An exchange program," pp. 197-204; Athena Salaba, "A Greek librarian in America: personal reflections on an eight-month practicum at the Kent State University Libraries," pp. 205-213.]

286. Knight, Amy. "The Fate of the KGB Archives." *Slavic Review* 52, no. 3 (Fall 1993): 583-586.

287. Kramer, Mark. "Archival Research in Moscow: Progress and Pitfalls." *Cold War International History Project Bulletin*, no. 3 (Fall 1993): 1ff. [A detailed look at archival developments in the Soviet Union and the Russian Federation, with particular attention to CPSU, KGB, and Foreign Ministry archives, access issues, publishing joint ventures, and Stephen Morris' discovery of materials concerning American prisoners of war in Vietnam.]

288. Little, Martha C. "Limited Access to Documents on Gorbachev's Foreign Policy Found in Foreign Ministry Archives." *Cold War International History Project Bulletin*, no. 3 (Fall 1993): 27ff.

289. Mickiewicz, Ellen. "The Commercialization of Scholarship in the Former Soviet Union." *Slavic Review* 52, no. 1 (Spring 1993): 90-95.

290. Mironov, Boris N. "Much Ado About Nothing?" *Slavic Review* 52, no. 3 (Fall 1993): 579-581. Translated by Sergei Pershman and Lesley Rimmel. [Response to essays by Mossman, Mickiewicz, von Hagen, and Getty in vol. 52, no. 1 (Spring 1993): 87-104.]

291. Mossman, Elliott. "On Russian Archives: An Interview with Sergei V. Mironenko." *Slavic Review* 52, no. 4 (Winter 1993): 839-846. Translated by Vitaly Chernetsky. [Interview conducted October 27, 1993 in New Haven, CT.]

292. ———. "Research, Ethics and the Marketplace: The Case of the Russian Archives." *Slavic Review* 52, no. 1 (Spring 1993): 87-89. [Introduces essays which follow by Mickiewicz, von Hagen, Getty and Fink.]

293. Mossman, Elliott, and Dar'ia Khubova. "The Case of the Russian Archives: An Interview with Iurii N. Afanas'ev." *Slavic Review* 52, no. 2 (Summer 1993): 338-352. Translated by Vitaly Chernetsky. [Interview was conducted on April 16, 1993 by Mossman and transcribed and edited by Khubova.]

294. *Revelations from the Russian Archives: A Report from the Library of Congress.* Washington, DC: Library of Congress, 1993. 64 pp.

295. Sokolov, Vladimir V., and Sven G. Holtsmark. "Note on the Foreign Policy Archive of the Russian Federation." *Cold War International History Project Bulletin*, no. 3 (Fall 1993): 26ff.

296. Tering, Arvo. "The Tartu University Library and Its Use at the End of the Seventeenth and the Beginning of the Eighteenth Century." *Libraries & Culture* 28, no. 1 (Winter 1993): 44-54.

297. Trebse-Stolfa, Milica. "ARHIVI [Journal of the Society of Slovene Archivists]." *American Archivist* 56, no. 1 (Winter 1993): 143-145. [Review article on journal *ARHIVI* [The Archives] (Ljubljana: Arkhivsko drustvo Slovenije, Jugoslavija, 1978-).]

298. Von Hagen, Mark. "The Archival Gold Rush and Historical Agendas in the Post-Soviet Era." *Slavic Review* 52, no. 1 (Spring 1993): 96-100.

299. Wheaton, Elizabeth. "Prague's library of banned books." *Progressive* 57, no. 8 (August 1993): 39-40.

300. Woodard, Colin. "American, Russian Scholars Gather Materials on Jewish Culture in the Former Soviet Union." *Chronicle of Higher Education* 39, no. 33 (April 21, 1993): A41ff.

301. Wynar, Lubomyr R. "Guides to Ethnic Archival and Library Collections in the United States and Canada." *Ethnic Forum* 13, no. 1 (1993): 69-73. [Review article on Suzanna Moody and Joel Wurl, comps. and eds., *A Guide to Collections* (NY: 1991); and Nick G. Forte, comp., and Gabrielle Scardellato, ed., *A Guide to the Collections of the Multicultural History Society of Ontario* (Toronto: 1992).]

■ Numismatics and Philately

302. "De La Rue Cashes in on Collapse of Communism." *Numismatist* 106, no. 6 (June 1993): 751. [De La Rue PLC is printing legal tender for newly independent states of the former Soviet Union.]

303. "Eastern Europe and the Balkans." *Numismatic Literature*, no. 129 (March 1993): 66-68.

304. "Eastern Europe and the Balkans." *Numismatic Literature*, no. 130 (September 1993): 78-80.

305. Friedberg, Arthur. "A Tribute to Those Who Fought Back." *Numismatist* 106, no. 11 (November 1993): 1517-1523. [Commemorating the Warsaw Ghetto uprising.]

306. "General." *Numismatic Literature*, no. 130 (September 1993): 1-6. [Includes East Germany, Romania, and Poland.]

307. Gluschenko, Nick. "Russian Friend Offers Glimpse of Old and New Currency." *Numismatist* 106, no. 7 (July 1993): 879-881.

308. "Greek." *Numismatic Literature*, no. 129 (March 1993): 7-15.

309. "Greek." *Numismatic Literature*, no. 130 (September 1993): 7-12.

310. Hochfield, Sylvia. "Whose Gold Is It?" *ARTnews* 92, no. 8 (October 1993): 68-69. [On a dispute over a collection of gold coins that is claimed by both Turkey and Germany and is located in the Pushkin Museum in Moscow.]

311. Hoge, Robert W. "A 3 Roubles of Nicholas I." *Numismatist* February 106, no. 2 (1993): 279.

312. "Hungary: Political Change Shows Up in Pockets." *Numismatist* 106, no. 12 (December 1993): 1669-1670.

313. Marshall, Dan. "A Rebirth for Russian Collectors." *Numismatist* 106, no. 9 (September 1993): 1248ff.

314. "Medals and Decorations." *Numismatic Literature*, no. 130 (September 1993): 86-90. [Includes Hungary and the Habsburg Empire.]

315. "Paper Money." *Numismatic Literature*, no. 129 (March 1993): 81-83. [Includes Eastern Europe, Estonia, Hungary, and Russia.]

316. "Paper Money." *Numismatic Literature*, no. 130 (September 1993): 90-95. [Includes Russia, East Germany, and Yugoslavia.]

317. "A Place of Remembrance." *Numismatist* 106, no. 11 (November 1993): 1518. [U.S. Holocaust Memorial Museum.]

318. "Poland: Commemorative Coin Recalls Jewish Uprising." *Numismatist* 106, no. 11 (November 1993): 1501-1502.

319. Robins, Trevor D. "Imperial Russia's Sestroretsk Ruble." *Numismatist* 106, no. 9 (September 1993): 1253ff.

320. "Tokens and Jetons." *Numismatic Literature*, no. 130 (September 1993): 95-96. [Includes Hungary.]

321. Urban, William. "Medieval Livonian Numismatics." *Journal of Baltic Studies* 24, no. 1 (Spring 1993): 37-52.

322. "Western and Central Europe." *Numismatic Literature*, no. 130 (September 1993): 68-78. [Includes Russia and Poland.]

■ Slavic and East European Studies in the West

323. "AAASS Awards." *AAASS Newsletter* 33, no. 1 (January 1993): 9. [Awards granted by the American Association for the Advancement of Slavic Studies at their convention, November 20, 1992 in Phoenix, AZ.]

324. Abramson, Henry. "Electronic Mail for the Technologically Timid." *AAASS Newsletter* 33, no. 2 (March 1993): 21.

325. Altstadt, Audrey L. "Events in the Field: Fifth International Conference on Central Asia." *Central Asia Monitor*, no. 3 (1993): 38. [Report on the "Democratization in Central Asia" conference, held in Madison, WI, April 15-18, 1993.]

326. Armstrong, John A. "New Essays in Sovietological Introspection." *Post-Soviet Affairs* 9, no. 2 (April-June 1993): 171-175. [Commentary on an analysis of Sovietology published in v. 8, no. 3 (1992): 175-269.]

327. Atkinson, Dorothy. "1992: *Plus ça change...*" *AAASS Newsletter* 33, no. 1 (January 1993): 5.

328. "Awards Offered in 1993." *Items* (Social Science Research Council) 47, no. 2-3 (June-September 1993): 52-67. ["Predissertation and Dissertation Fellowships for Area and Comparative Training and Research: Eastern Europe; Soviet Union and Successor States," pp. 55-56, 59-60; "Advanced Grants for Area and Comparative Research and Training: Eastern Europe; Soviet Union and its Successor States," pp. 61, 63-64.]

329. Braley, Russ. [Letter to the Editor]. *National Interest*, no. 32 (Summer 1993): 108. [Response to articles in issue no. 31 (Spring 1993).]

330. "Chronicle of the Polish Institute: Annual Meeting Program, May 28 and 29, 1993." *Polish Review* 38, no. 3 (1993): 349-384. [Includes: Jan Krzysztof Frackowiak, "Science and Scientific Policy in Post-Communist Poland," pp. 355-358; Feliks Gross, "President's Annual Report," pp. 359-361; Thaddeus V. Gromada, "Annual Report: June 1992-May 1993," pp. 362-375; and Krystyna Baron, "The Alfred Jurzykowski Memorial Library," pp. 376-377.]

331. Conquest, Robert. "Academe and the Soviet Myth." *National Interest*, no. 31 (Spring 1993): 91-98.

332. Daniels, Robert V. "The State of the Field." *AAASS Newsletter* 33, no. 1 (January 1993): 1-3. [Abridged version of presidential address delivered November 20, 1992, at the American Association for the Advancement of Slavic Studies convention in Phoenix, AZ.]

333. DeCoker, Gary, Christi Dunfee, and Stacy Grebeck. "Teaching About the Former Soviet Union: Activities and Resources." *Social Studies and the Young Learner* 5, no. 4 (March-April 1993): 1-4.

334. Dobriansky, Paula J., and David B. Rivkin. [Letter to the Editor]. *National Interest*, no. 33 (Fall 1993): 111-112. [Response to articles in issue no. 31 (Spring 1993).]

335. Fairbanks, Charles H., Jr. "Introduction." *National Interest*, no. 31 (Spring 1993): 5-8.

336. Fleron, Frederic J., Jr. "Comparative Politics and Lessons for the Present." *Harriman Institute Forum* 6, nos. 6-7 (February-March 1993): 3-13. [Paper from a workshop held at the Harriman Institute, December 4, 1992.]

337. Fukuyama, Francis. "The Modernizing Imperative: The USSR as an Ordinary Country." *National Interest*, no. 31 (Spring 1993): 10-18.

338. "The Future of Research on the Former Soviet Union." *Items* (Social Science Research Council) 47, no. 4 (December 1993): 94-95.

339. Goldstone, Jack A. "Predicting Revolution: Why We Could (And Should) Have Foreseen the Revolutions of 1989-1991 in the U.S.S.R. and Eastern Europe." *Contention: Debates in Society, Culture and Science* 2, no. 2 (Winter 1993): 127-152. [Followed by replies from Said Amir Arjomand (pp. 171-183) and Nikki R. Keddie (pp. 159-170), and Goldstone's response to Keddie (pp. 185-189).]

340. Heckman, Dale. "Studying 'East Russia.'" *AAASS NewsNet* 33, no. 5 (November 1993): 3.

341. Hoffman, Erik P. "Nuturing Post-Sovietology: Some Practical Suggestions." *Harriman Institute Forum* 6, nos. 6-7 (February-March 1993): 14-23. [Paper from a workshop held at the Harriman Institute, December 4, 1992.]

342. Huttenbach, Henry R. "Editorial Note: And Then There Were...(None?): An SOS to the AAASS." *Nationalities Papers* 21, no. 2 (Fall 1993): 7-8. [On support for scholarly publishing.]

343. "Institutional News." *AAASS Newsletter* 33, no. 1 (January 1993): 8. [American Council of Teachers of Russian exchange program; Florida State University undergraduate major; Hoover Institution advisors in Russia; Joselyn Director of International Research and Exchanges Board Moscow office; Stanford University plans Moscow center.]

344. Kasinec, Edward. "Nicholas V. Riasanovsky: A Biographical Sketch." *Russian History* 20, nos. 1-4 (1993): 3-4. [Revised version of the introduction to Molly Molloy's "Nicholas V. Riasanovsky: A Bibliography," *Russian Review* 43, no. 1 (January 1984): 55-72.]

345. Klenbort, Daniel. [Letter to the Editor]. *National Interest*, no. 32 (Summer 1993): 107. [Response to articles in issue no. 31 (Spring 1993).]

346. Korbonski, Andrzej, and Luigi Graziano. "Introduction." *Communist and Post-Communist Studies* 26, no. 4 (December 1993): 339-340. [Introduction to special issue which features selected papers from the conference "The Emergence of Pluralism in East Central Europe," held at the University of California, Los Angeles, CA, September 10-12, 1992.]

347. Kurland, Jordan E. "Keeping Tabs on Our Slavic Scholars: McCarthyism Endured." *Slavic Review* 52, no. 1 (Spring 1993): 116-121. [Review article on Sigmund Diamond, *Compromised Campus: The Collaboration of Universities with the Intelligence Community, 1945-1955* (NY: 1992).]

348. Laqueur, Walter. "Intelligence and Secrecy: Sovietology Redux." *Society* 30, no. 2 (January-February 1993): 6-13.

349. ———. [Letter to the Editor]. *National Interest*, no. 32 (Summer 1993): 105. [Response to articles by William Odom and Martin Malia in issue no. 31 (Spring 1993). Followed with replies in issue no. 33 (Fall 1993) from Malia (p. 112) and Odom (p. 113).]

350. Lee, William T. [Letter to the Editor]. *National Interest*, no. 32 (Summer 1993): 106. [Response to articles in issue no. 31 (Spring 1993).]

351. Lichenstein, Charles. [Letter to the Editor]. *National Interest*, no. 32 (Summer 1993): 106-107. [Response to articles in issue no. 31 (Spring 1993).]

352. Malia, Martin. "A Fatal Logic." *National Interest*, no. 31 (Spring 1993): 80-90.

353. ———. [Letter to the Editor]. *National Interest*, no. 33 (Fall 1993): 112. [Reply to letter to the editor by Walter Laqueur in issue no. 32 (Summer 1993): p. 105.]

354. Marker, Gary. "Editor's Introduction." *Russian History* 20, nos. 1-4 (1993): 1-2. [Introduction to Festschrift in Commemoration of the Seventieth Birthday of Nicholas Valentine Riasanovsky.]

355. Markiw, Michael. "Internet for Russian and East European studies." *College & Research Libraries News* 54, no. 8 (September 1993): 444ff.

356. McKinnon, Mike. "How to Encourage Studying Germany and Europe in the Classroom." *Social Education* 57, no. 5 (September 1993): 231-232. [Part of special section entitled "The Case of Germany, Part 2," edited by Dagmar Kraemer and Manfred Stassen.]

357. ———. "Why Study Germany and Europe Now?" *Social Education* 57, no. 4 (April-May 1993): 168-170. [Part of a special section entitled "United Germany in a Uniting Europe, Part 1."]

358. Monaghan, Peter. "Preparing Students to Work and Study in the New Republics of Central Asia." *Chronicle of Higher Education* 39, no. 49 (August 11, 1993): A31-A32. [University of Washington.]

359. Moss, Kevin. "A Russian Culture Course Based on a Semiotic Pattern." *Russian Language Journal* 47, nos. 156-158 (Winter-Spring-Fall 1993): 3-15.

360. Mossman, Elliott. "From the Editor." *Slavic Review* 52, no. 1 (Spring 1993): vii-x. [Includes dicussion of access to Soviet historical material in the Russian Federation.]

361. Natov, Nadine. "The Eighth International Symposium." *Dostoevsky Studies = Dostoevskii: stat'i i materialy* 1, no. 2 (1993): 267-272.

362. "New Look at Imperial Russia." *Items* (Social Science Research Council) 47, no. 4 (December 1993): 95.

363. "1992 National Council for Soviet and East European Research Contracts." *AAASS Newsletter* 33, no. 3 (May 1993): 10.

364. Odom, William. [Letter to the Editor]. *National Interest*, no. 33 (Fall 1993): 113. [Reply to letter to the editor by Walter Laqueur in issue no. 32 (Summer 1993): p. 105.]

365. ———. "The Pluralist Mirage." *National Interest*, no. 31 (Spring 1993): 99-108.

366. Perlmutter, Amos. [Letter to the Editor]. *National Interest*, no. 32 (Summer 1993): 107-108. [Response to articles in issue no. 31 (Spring 1993).]

367. Pipes, Richard. "1917 and the Revisionists." *National Interest*, no. 31 (Spring 1993): 68-79.

368. "Preliminary Program, 25th National Convention, Hilton Hawaiian Village, Honolulu, Hawaii, November 19-22, 1993." *AAASS Newsletter* 33, no. 3 (May 1993): 23-55.

369. Raun, Toivo U. "The Baltic States: A Brief Guide to Sources." *AAASS NewsNet* 33, no. 5 (November 1993): 5.

370. Reddaway, Peter. "Research on Soviet Decline." *Post-Soviet Affairs* 9, no. 2 (April-June 1993): 176-181. [Commentary on an analysis of sovietology published in vol. 8, no. 3 (1992): 175-269.]

371. ———. "Sovietology and Dissent: New Sources on Protest." *RFE/RL Research Report* 2, no. 5 (January 29, 1993): 12-16.

372. "Research in Progress: Russian, Eurasian, and East European Studies: Fall 1993." *AAASS NewsNet* 33, no. 5 (November 1993): 17-42.

373. "Resources." *Social Education* 57, no. 4 (April-May 1993): 192. [Part of a special section entitled "United Germany in a Uniting Europe, Part 1."]

374. "Resources." *Social Education* 57, no. 5 (September 1993): 258. [Part of special section entitled "The Case of Germany, Part 2," edited by Dagmar Kraemer and Manfred Stassen.]

375. Rockwell, Llewellyn H., Jr. "Mrs. Tyson's Fried Economics." *National Review* 45, no. 2 (February 1,

1993): 48. [On Laura D'Andrea Tyson's work on Eastern Europe.]

376. Rutland, Peter. "Sovietology: Notes for a Post-Mortem." *National Interest*, no. 31 (Spring 1993): 109-122.

377. Sayan, Erdinc. "Notes and Comments: Is Marxist Philosophy Withering Away?" *Studies in East European Thought* 45, no. 4 (December 1993): 313-315. [Author notes a decline from 1981 to 1992 in published material on the study of Marx and Marxism.]

378. Sharlet, Robert. "Teaching Soviet Studies: The Role of Law in Teaching Soviet/Russian Politics." *AAASS NewsNet* 33, no. 5 (November 1993): 7.

379. Shlapentokh, Vladimir. "The American Vision of the World: The Tendency to Find Nice Things." *AAASS Newsletter* 33, no. 3 (May 1993): 5ff.

380. Solomon, Peter H., Jr. "Against Premature Closure." *Post-Soviet Affairs* 9, no. 3 (July-September 1993): 278-280.

381. Suny, Ronald G. "A Second Look at Sovietology and the National Question." *AAASS Newsletter* 33, no. 3 (May 1993): 1-2.

382. "Useful Addresses." *Social Education* 57, no. 4 (April-May 1993): 191. [Part of a special section entitled "United Germany in a Uniting Europe, Part 1."]

383. "Useful Addresses." *Social Education* 57, no. 5 (September 1993): 256-257.

384. Ustinova, L. I. "Assotsiativnyi eksperiment kak metodicheskii podkhod v prepodavanii russkogo iazyka v Amerike." *Russian Language Journal* 47, nos. 156-158 (Winter-Spring-Fall 1993): 35-42.

385. Walker, Edward W. "Post-Sovietology, Area Studies, and the Social Sciences." *Harriman Institute Forum* 6, nos. 6-7 (February-March 1993): 24-28. [Paper from a workshop held at the Harriman Institute, December 4, 1992.]

386. Whitesell, Robert S. "Teaching Slavic Studies: Teaching About the Former Soviet Economy." *AAASS Newsletter* 33, no. 1 (January 1993): 15.

387. Wildman, Allan. "The Age of the Democratic Revolution and the Transvaluation of Russian Historiography." *Russian Review* 52, no. 4 (October 1993): vi-vii.

388. ———. "Is a Social History of Stalinist Russia Possible?" *Russian Review* 52, no. 3 (July 1993): v-vi.

389. Williams, Joanna Radwanska. "Integrating Polish Studies into the Liberal Arts Curriculum." *Polish Review* 38, no. 1 (1993): 85-91.

390. Youngblood, Denise J. "Teaching Slavic Studies: Teaching Soviet History Through Film." *AAASS Newsletter* 33, no. 2 (March 1993): 6.

■ Travel and Description

General

391. De Weck, Christine. *Siberia, Outer Mongolia, Central Asia: Crossroads of Civilization*. 1st ed. New York, NY: Vantage Press, c1993. xiii, 235 pp.

392. Severin, Tim. *In Search of Genghis Khan*. Photograpy by Paul Harris. 1st Collier Books ed. New York: Collier Books: Maxwell Macmillan International, 1993. xii, 141 pp. [Originally published (New York: Atheneum, 1992).] REV: Denys J. Voaden, *Mongolian Studies* 16 (1993): 101.

Russia/U.S.S.R./C.I.S.

393. Christie, Ian R. *The Benthams in Russia, 1780-1791*. Anglo-Russian Affinities Series. Oxford, UK; Providence, RI: Berg, 1993. xiii, 264 pp.

394. Cunningham, Mark. "To Russia with Love." *National Review* 45, no. 18 (September 20, 1993): 30-32.

395. Edwards, Mike. "A Broken Empire: Kazakhstan." *National Geographic* 183, no. 3 (March 1993): 22-37.

396. ———. "A Broken Empire: Russia." *National Geographic* 183, no. 3 (March 1993): 4-21.

397. ———. "A Broken Empire: Ukraine." *National Geographic* 183, no. 3 (March 1993): 38-53.

398. Elon, Amos. "The Nowhere City." *New York Review of Books* 40, no. 9 (May 13, 1993): 28-33. [Kaliningrad (Königsberg).]

399. Fisher, Lois. *Survival in Russia: Chaos and Hope in Everyday Life*. Boulder, CO: Westview Press, 1993. vii, 187 pp. [Originally published as *Überleben in Russland: Chaos und Hoffnung im Alltag* (Hamburg: Hoffmann und Campe Verlag, 1991). Contents: Introduction; My Friend, the Black Marketeer; The Adventurer; Miss Perestroika; Masha and the Forgotten; Babushka Natasha; The Soldiers Are Not Homesick; The Lonely Fighter; The Last Communist; The Striking Democrats; One Year After the Putsch.]

400. Kopkind, Andrew. "What Is to Be Done? From Russia with Love and Squalor." *Nation* 256, no. 2 (January 18, 1993): 44-62.

401. Lydon, Christopher. "Russia: Agent of Influence." *Atlantic* 271, no. 2 (February 1993): 28ff. ["A brisk journey with the historian Suzanne Massie through the streets of St. Petersburg."]

402. Raymer, Steve. "St. Petersburg, Capital of the Tsars." *National Geographic* 184, no. 6 (December 1993): 96-119.

403. Richardson, William. *To the World of the Future: Mexican Visitors to the USSR, 1920-1940*. The Carl Beck Papers in Russian and East European Studies, no. 1002. Pittsburgh, PA: Center for Russian and East European Studies, 1993. 54 pp.

404. Shapiro, Bess. "Three Vignettes from Visits to the U.S.S.R. in the '50s and '60s." *The Creative Woman* 13, no. 2 (Summer 1993): 46-48.

405. Twining, David T. *Guide to the Republics of the Former Soviet Union.* Westport, CT: Greenwood Press, 1993. xxi, 213 pp. [Also published in paperback under title *The New Eurasia.*] REV: Sean Patrick Murphy, *Current History* 92, no. 576 (October 1993): 347. *Booklist* 90, no. 2 (September 15, 1993): 187-188.

406. ———. *The New Eurasia: A Guide to the Republics of the Former Soviet Union.* Westport, CT: Praeger, 1993. xxi, 213 pp. [Also published in hard cover under title *Guide to the Republics of the Former Soviet Union.*]

407. Zinkevych, Osyp, and Volodymyr Hula, comps. *Ukraina: Putivnyk.* Kyiv; Baltimore, MD: Smoloskyp, 1993. 450 pp.

408. ———. *Ukraine: A Tourist Guide.* Translated and edited by Marta D. Olynyk. Kyiv; Baltimore, MD: Smoloskyp, 1993. 440 pp.

Eastern Europe

409. Arana-Ward, Marie. [Book Review]. *Book World (Washington Post)* 23, no. 50 (December 12, 1993): 2. [Review article on Eva Hoffman, *Exit into History: A Journey Through the New Eastern Europe* (NY: Viking, 1993).]

410. Balamaci, Nicholas S. "Albania in the 1990s: A Travel Memoir and Oral History." *Journal of the Hellenic Diaspora* 19, no. 2 (1993): 121-148.

411. Bammesberger, Alfred. "Homage to Lithuania: My Trip to Vilnius and Kaunas." *Lituanus* 39, no. 3 (Fall 1993): 26-43.

412. Biddle, Nicholas. *Nicholas Biddle in Greece: The Journals and Letters of 1806.* Edited by R. A. McNeal. University Park, PA: Pennsylvania State University Press, c1993. viii, 243 pp.

413. Carter, Rowlinson. *Eastern Europe.* Editorial director Brian Bell. Created and directed by Hans Hoefer.

1st ed. Insight Guides. [Hong Kong]: APA Publications; Boston: Distributed in the U.S. by Houghton Mifflin, c1993. 390 pp.

414. Demetz, Peter. "A Difficult Return to Prague." *Cross Currents: A Yearbook of Central European Culture,* no. 12 (1993): 25-35. Translated from the German by Harry Zohn.

415. Hoffman, Eva. *Exit Into History: A Journey Through the New Eastern Europe.* New York, NY: Viking, 1993. xvii, 410 pp. [Contents: Poland I; Poland II; Czechoslovakia; Hungary; Romania; Bulgaria.] REV: Marie Arana-Ward, *Book World* 23, no. 50 (December 12, 1993): 2. Robert D. Kaplan, *New York Times Book Review* 98, no. 47 (November 21, 1993): 3ff. Halle Shilling, *Washington Monthly* 25, no. 12 (December 1993): 56-57.

416. Kurzweil, Edith. "Once Again Prague." *Partisan Review* 60, no. 1 (Winter 1993): 10-13.

417. Murphy, Dervla. *Transylvania and Beyond: A Travel Memoir.* 1st ed. Woodstock, NY: Overlook Press, 1993, 1992. xv, 239 pp.

418. Newberry, Jon. "Cincinnati on the Vltava." *American Spectator* 26, no. 5 (May 1993): 57.

419. Nitecki, Alicia. "Recovered Land." *Massachusetts Review* 34, no. 1 (Spring 1993): 7-30. [Travel in the western part of Poland.]

420. Slapsak, Svetlana. "Yugoslav Memoir: Trains, Times Lost Forever." *Nation* 256, no. 21 (May 31, 1993): 738-740.

421. United States. Dept. of State. *Background Notes, Hungary.* Department of State Publication. Background Notes Series, 7915. [Washington, DC: U.S. Dept. of State, Bureau of Public Affairs, Office of Public Communication, 1993]. 6 pp.

422. Von Flotow, Luise. "Many Returns to the East." *Cross Currents: A Yearbook of Central European Culture,* no. 12 (1993): 218-228. [Describes visits to a small town in eastern Germany before and after reunification.]

2 Anthropology, Ethnology, Archaeology

■ General

423. Bakunas, Patricia. *The Decorated Egg: An Ethnic Folk Art Tradition*. Chicago, IL: Balzekas Museum of Lithuanian Culture, 1993. 54 pp.

424. Chapman, John, and Pavel Dolukhanov, eds. *Cultural Transformations and Interactions in Eastern Europe*. Contributions by John Chapman, Pavel Dolukhanov, Clive Gamble, Marcel Otte, Olga Soffer, John Chapman, Marek Zvelebil, Anthony F. Harding, Janusz Ostoja-Zagórski, Brian B. Shefton, Michel Kazanski, and Evgeny N. Nosov. Worldwide Archaeology Series, 6. Monograph (Centre for the Archaeology of Central and Eastern Europe), 1. Aldershot; Brookfield, VT: Avebury, c1993. xiv, 256 pp. [Papers presented at a conference, held April 13-14, 1990, in the Dept. of Archaeology, University of Newcastle upon Tyne. Contents: John Chapman and Pavel Dolukhanov, "Cultural Transformations and Interactions in Eastern Europe: Theory and Terminology," pp. 1-36; Clive Gamble, "People on the Move: Interpretations of Regional Variation in Palæolithic Europe," pp. 37-55; Marcel Otte, "Upper Palæolithic Relations between Central and Eastern Europe," pp. 56-64; Olga Soffer, "Migration vs Interaction in Upper Palæolithic Europe," pp. 65-70; John Chapman, "Social Power in the Iron Gates Mesolithic," pp. 71-121; Pavel M. Dolukhanov, "Foraging and Farming Groups in North-Eastern and North-Western Europe: Identity and Interaction," pp. 122-145; Marek Zvelebil, "Hunters or Farmers? The Neolithic and Bronze Age Societies of North-East Europe," pp. 146-162; Anthony F. Harding and Janusz Ostoja-Zagórski, "The Lausitz Culture and the Beginning and End of Bronze Age Fortifications," pp. 163-177; Brian B. Shefton, "The White Lotus, Rogozen and Colchis: The Fate of a Motif," pp. 178-209; Michel Kazanski, "The Sedentary Élite in the 'Empire' of the Huns and its Impact on Material Civilisation in Southern Russia during the Early Middle Ages (5th-7th Centuries AD)," pp. 211-232; Evgeny N. Nosov, "The Problem of the Emergence of Early Urban Centres in Northern Russia," pp. 236-256.]

425. Milovsky, Alexander S. "The Death of Winter." *Natural History* 102, no. 1 (January 1993): 34-38.

426. Moss, Joyce, and George Wilson. *Peoples of the World. Eastern Europe and the Post-Soviet Republics: The Culture, Geographical Setting, and Historical Background of 34 Eastern European Peoples*. 1st ed. Detroit, MI: Gale Research, c1993. 415 pp.

427. Sigmon, Becky A., ed. *Before the Wall Fell: The Science of Man in Socialist Europe*. Contributions by B. A. Sigmon, A. G. Kozintsev, M. L. Butovskaya, R. I. Sukernik, M. H. Crawford, V. Leonovicová, J. Slípka, L. Kordos, H. Ullrich, A. B. Fistani, and J. Piontek. Toronto: Canadian Scholars' Press, 1993. xx, 204 pp. [Papers presented at the Symposium on East and Central European Physical Anthropology, held in Toronto in October 1991. Contents: B.A. Sigmon, "The Effects of Socialism on the Science of Man," pp. 1-18; A.G. Kozintsev, "Current Developments in Soviet Physical Anthropology," pp. 19-37; M.L. Butovskaya, "Non-Human Primate Research in the USSR," pp. 39-54; R.I. Sukernik and M.H. Crawford, "Genetic Adaptation Studies in the Soviet Union: Malaise and Cure," pp. 55-73; V. Leonovicová, "Sociobiological Aspects of Human Evolution and Comparisons of Sociobiological Approaches in the USSR and Czechoslovakia," pp. 75-84; J. Slípka, "Human Evolution in Microcosm," pp. 85-100; L. Kordos, "Paleoanthropology in Hungary," pp. 101-121; H. Ullrich, "Interdisciplinary Studies in the Project *Menschwerdung*," pp. 123-139; A.B. Fistani, "Human Evolution in Albania for the Quaternary Period," pp. 141-178; J. Piontek, "Physical Anthropology in Poland: Past, Present and Future Directions," pp. 179-198; B.A. Sigmon, "Epilogue: Future Prospects," pp. 199-200.]

428. Treister, Michael J., and Yuri G. Vinogradov. "Archaeology on the Northern Coast of the Black Sea." *American Journal of Archaeology* 97, no. 3 (July 1993): 521-563.

429. Tringham, Ruth. *Nationalism and Internationalism in Writing the Prehistory of the New East Europe*. Working Paper (University of California, Berkeley. Center for German and European Studies), 3.10. Berkeley, CA: Center for German and European Studies, University of California, [1993]. 20 pp.

■ The Baltics

430. Mugurevics, Evalds. "A Historical Survey and Present Problems of Archaeological Science in the Baltic States." *Journal of Baltic Studies* 24, no. 3 (Fall 1993): 283-294.

431. Spitz, Douglas R., and William Urban. "A Hindu Nationalist View of Baltic History." *Journal of Baltic Studies* 24, no. 3 (Fall 1993): 295-298.

432. Urtans, Juris. "About a Destroyed Stone with Signs on the Daugava River." *Journal of Baltic Studies* 24, no. 4 (Winter 1993): 385-388.

■ Central Asia and the Caucasus

433. Downing, Charles, ed. and trans. *Armenian Folk-Tales and Fables*. Illustrated by William Papas. Oxford Myths and Legends. Oxford; New York: Oxford University Press, c1993. xiii, 217 pp.

434. Goldstein, Darra. *The Georgian Feast: The Vibrant Culture and Savory Food of the Republic of Georgia*. Paintings by Niko Pirosmani. 1st ed. New York, NY: HarperCollins, c1993. xxv, 229 pp.

435. Hostler, Charles Warren. *The Turks of Central Asia*. Westport, CT: Praeger Press, 1993. xi, 237 pp. [Rev., updated ed. of *Turkism and the Soviets* (London: Allen & Unwin, 1957).] REV: Daniel Newberry, *Foreign Service Journal* 70, no. 10 (October 1993): 53-54.

■ **Eastern Europe**

436. Bogucki, Peter, and Ryszard Grygiel. "The First Farmers of Central Europe: A Survey Article." *Journal of Field Archaeology* 20, no. 4 (Winter 1993): 399-426.

437. Botev, Nikolai Vassilev. "Essays on Nuptiality and Fertility in South-Eastern Europe." Ph.D. diss., University of Pennsylvania, 1993. [UMI order no: AAC 9413805.]

438. Chang, Claudia. "Pastoral Transhumance in the Southern Balkans as a Social Ideology: Ethno-archeological Research in Northern Greece." *American Anthropologist* 95, no. 3 (September 1993): 687-703.

439. Jovanovic, Borislav. "Silver in the Yamna (Pit-Grave) Culture in the Balkans." *Journal of Indo-European Studies* 21, nos. 3 & 4 (Fall/Winter 1993): 207-214.

440. Mackley, Lesley. *The Book of Greek Cooking*. Los Angeles, CA: HPBooks, c1993. 120 pp.

441. Roth, Klaus, and Gabriele Wolf, comp. and ed. *South Slavic Folk Culture: A Bibliography of Literature in English, German, and French on Bosnian-Hercegovinian, Bulgarian, Macedonian, Montenegrin and Serbian Folk Culture = Sudslavische Volkskultur: Bibliographie zur Literatur in englischer, deutscher und französischer Sprache zur bosnisch-herzegowinischen, bulgarischen, mazedonischen, montenegrinischen und serbischen Volkskultur*. Compiled with the cooperation of Tomislav Helebrant. Columbus, OH: Slavic Publishers, c1993. 553 pp.

442. *Serbo-Croatian Heroic Poems: Epics from Bihac, Cazin and Kulen Vakuf*. Translated and annotated by David E. Bynum. Collected by Milman Parry, Albert B. Lord, and David E. Bynum. Milman Parry Studies in Oral Tradition. New York: Garland, 1993. 832 pp. [Additional translations by Mary P. Coote and John F. Loud.]

443. Shennan, Stephen J. "Settlement and Social Change in Central Europe, 3500-1500 BC." *Journal of World Prehistory* 7, no. 2 (June 1993): 121-161.

■ **Russia/U.S.S.R./C.I.S.**

444. "Buryatia at a Glance." *Surviving Together* 11, no. 3 (Fall 1993): 38-39. [Primarily photographs.]

445. Goebel, Ted, Anatoli P. Derevianko, and Valerii T. Petrin. "Dating the Middle-to-Upper-Paleolithic Transition at Kara-Bom." *Current Anthropology* 34, no. 4 (August-October 1993): 452-458.

446. Jacobson, Esther. [Review Article]. *Mongolian Studies*, no. 16 (1993): 65-81. [Review article on Anatoly I. Martynov, *The Ancient Art of Northern Asia* (Urbana, IL: 1991).]

447. Konakov, N. D. "Ecological Adaptation of Komi Resettled Groups." *Arctic Anthropology* 30, no. 2 (1993): 92-102. Translated by Lydia T. Black.

448. Krupnik, Igor I. "Prehistoric Eskimo Whaling in the Arctic: Slaughter of Calves or Fortuitous Ecology?" *Arctic Anthropology* 30, no. 1 (1993): 1-12.

449. Leibovich, Anna. "The Russian and His Work: Suffering, Drama, and Tradition in the 1890s-1930s." Ph.D. diss., New York University, 1993. [UMI order no: AAC 9423000.]

450. Lofstedt, Torsten Martin Gustaf. "Russian Legends About Forest Spirits in the Context of Northern European Mythology." Ph.D. diss., University of California, Berkeley, 1993. [UMI order no: AAC 9408050.]

451. Mayer, Fred, photographer. *The Forgotten Peoples of Siberia*. Edited by Gunther Doeker-Mach. Includes contributions by James Forsyth, Gunther Doeker-Mach, and Fred Mayer. 1st ed. Zurich; New York: Scalo Publishers, c1993. 207 pp.

452. Mochanov, Yuri A. "The Most Ancient Paleolithic of the Diring and the Problem of a Nontropical Origin for Humanity." *Arctic Anthropology* 30, no. 1 (1993): 22-53. Translated by Richard L. Bland.

453. Pavlova, Elena. "A *Chum* Alone: A Day among Siberia's Reindeer Breeders." *World & I* 8, no. 11 (November 1993): 248-255.

454. Pitul'ko, Vladimir V. "An Early Holocene Site in the Siberian High Arctic." *Arctic Anthropology* 30, no. 1 (1993): 13-21.

455. Reeder, Roberta, trans. and ed. *Russian Folk Lyrics*. Introductory essay by V. J. Propp. Bloomington, IN: Indiana University Press, c1993. xvi, 189 pp. [Rev. and enl. ed. of *Down along the Mother Volga* (1975). Essay by Propp is a new translation of "O russkoi liricheskoi pesne," which was originally published in *Narodnye liricheskie peseni* (1961).] REV: Natalie Kononenko, *Slavic Review* 52, no. 4 (Winter 1993): 865-866.

456. Tirado, Isabel A. *The Village Voice: Women's Views of Themselves and Their World in Russian Chastushki of the 1920's*. The Carl Beck Papers in Russian and East European Studies, no. 1008. Pittsburgh, PA: Center for Russian & East European Studies, University of Pittsburgh, c1993. 69 pp.

457. Tishkov, V. A. "On the Crisis in Soviet Ethnography: Reply to Comments." *Current Anthropology* 34, no. 3 (June 1993): 275-279.

458. Tolstaya, Tatyana. "The Age of Innocence." *New York Review of Books* 40, no. 17 (October 21, 1993): 24-26. Translated by Jamey Gambrell. [Review article on

Classic Russian Cooking: Elena Molokhovets' "A Gift to Young Housewives" trans. and ed. Joyce Toomre (Bloomington, IN: 1992).]

459. Vasil'ev, Sergei A. "The Upper Palæolithic of Northern Asia." *Current Anthropology* 34, no. 1 (February 1993): 82-92.

460. Vasil'ev, Sergey A., and Vladimir A. Semenov. "Prehistory of the Upper Yenisei Area (Southern Siberia)." *Journal of World Prehistory* 7, no. 2 (June 1993): 213-242.

461. Yovino-Young, Marjorie. *Pagan Ritual and Myth in Russian Magic Tales: A Study of Patterns.* Lewiston: E. Mellen Press, c1993. iv, 130 pp.

462. Yekelchyk, Serhy. "The Body and National Myth: Motifs from the Ukrainian National Revival in the Nineteenth Century." *Australian Slavonic and East European Studies* 7, no. 2 (1993): 31-59.

3 Culture and the Arts

■ General

463. Arlt, Herbert, and Ulrike Bischof, Hrsg. *Mir ist in den 80er Jahren kein DDR-Theater bekannt.* Frankfurt am Main; New York: P. Lang, c1993. xix, 321 pp.

464. Dziemidok, Bohdan. "Artistic Formalism: Its Achievements and Weaknesses." *Journal of Aesthetics and Art Criticism* 51, no. 2 (Spring 1993): 185-193.

465. Edelman, Robert. "The Icon and the Sax: Stites in Bright Lights." *Slavic Review* 52, no. 3 (Fall 1993): 568-578. [Review article on Richard Stites, *Revolutionary Dreams: Utopian Vision and Experimental Life in the Russian Revolution* (NY: 1989); and Richard Stites, *Russian Popular Culture: Entertainment and Society since 1900* (NY: 1992).]

466. Harriman, Helga H. "Women Writers and Artists in *Fin-de-Siècle* Vienna." *Modern Austrian Literature* 26, no. 1 (1993): 1-18.

467. Hart, Joan. "Erwin Panofsky and Karl Mannheim: A Dialogue on Interpretation." *Critical Inquiry* 19, no. 3 (Spring 1993): 534-566.

468. Klíma, Ivan. "The European Cultural Tradition and the Limits of Growth." *Philosophy and Literature* 17, no. 1 (April 1993): 77-83.

469. Meisel, Maude Frances. "Russian Performers' Memoirs." Ph.D. diss., Columbia University, 1993. [UMI order no: AAC 9412813.]

470. Working Group for the Study of Contemporary Russian Culture. *Russian Culture in Transition: Selected Papers of the Working Group for the Study of Contemporary Russian Culture, 1990-1991 = Transformatsiia russkoi kul'tury: Izbrannye doklady Rabochei Gruppy po Izucheniiu Sovremennoi Russkoi Kul'tury, 1990-1991 g.* Edited by Gregory Freidin. Stanford Slavic Studies, v. 7. Stanford, CA: Dept. of Slavic Languages and Literatures, Stanford University; Oakland, CA: Distributed by Berkeley Slavic Specialties, 1993. 323 pp. [Papers are based on the originals presented at the first two meetings of the International Working Group.] REV: *Items* (Social Science Research Council) 47, no. 4 (December 1993): 101.

■ Culture and Politics

471. Akinsha, Konstantin. "Buy, but don't export." *ARTnews* 92, no. 5 (May 1993): 37. [On art and foreign trade in Ukraine.]

472. ————. "From Russia, with a License." *ARTnews* 92, no. 5 (May 1993): 37. [On the export of cultural objects from Russia.]

473. ————. " 'Irina Shchukina versus Vladimir Lenin.' " *ARTnews* 92, no. 6 (Summer 1993): 71-72.

474. Bonnell, Victoria E. "The Peasant Woman in Stalinist Political Art of the 1930s." *American Historical Review* 98, no. 1 (February 1993): 55-82.

475. Calinescu, Matei. "Romania's 1930's Revisited." *Salmagundi*, no. 97 (Winter 1993): 133-151.

476. Dietrich, Gerd. *Politik und Kultur in der sowjetischen Besatzungszone Deutschlands (SBZ) 1945-1949: mit einem Dokumentenanhang.* Bern; New York: P. Lang, c1993. 474 pp.

477. Djumaev, Alexander. "Power Structures, Culture Policy, and Traditional Music in Soviet Central Asia." *Yearbook for Traditional Music* 25 (1993): 43-49.

478. Dornberg, John. " 'Things Are Moving.' " *ARTnews* 92, no. 8 (October 1993): 134-136. [On art galleries in Germany.]

479. Emery, Douglas B. "Self, Creativity, Political Resistance." *Political Psychology* 14, no. 2 (June 1993): 347-362.

480. Erlick, June Carolyn. "Knocking Down the Invisible Wall." *ARTnews* 92, no. 8 (October 1993): 137. [On an art exhibition in Berlin portraying Germany's Communist and Nazi past.]

481. Freidin, Gregory. "By the Walls of Church and State: Literature's Authority in Russia's Modern Tradition." *Russian Review* 52, no. 2 (April 1993): 149-165.

482. Groys, Boris. "On the Ethics of the Avant-Garde." *Art in America* 81, no. 5 (May 1993): 110-113. [Discusses the role of artists in the Russian revolution.]

483. Havel, Václav, and Miroslav Kusy. "Conversation: In the Realm of Culture." *Uncaptive Minds* 6, no. 1 (22) (Winter-Spring 1993): 63-66. [Conversation published in *Mosty* (October 27, 1992).]

484. Howard, Jennifer. "Budapest Coffeehouse Culture Revisited: Cafe New-York, 1992." *East European Quarterly* 27, no. 2 (Summer 1993): 223-230.

485. Jedlicki, Jerzy. "Poland's Perpetual Return to Europe." *Cross Currents: A Yearbook of Central European Culture*, no. 12 (1993): 78-88.

486. Komar, Vitaly, and Alexander Melamid. "Stalin in Jersey." *New Yorker* 69, no. 30 (September 20, 1993): 124-125.

487. Lahusen, Thomas, ed. *Late Soviet Culture: From Perestroika to Novostroika.* Edited with Gene Kuperman. Contributions by Mikhail Kuraev, Boris

Kagarlitsky, Sidney Monas, Paul Debreczeny, Renata Galtseva, Irina Rodnyanskaya, Maya Turovskaya, Evgeny Dobrenko, Thomas Lahusen, Michael Holquist, Valery Leibin, Valery Podoroga, Helena Goscilo, Mikhail Epstein, Katerina Clark, and Donald Raleigh. Post-Contemporary Interventions. Durham, NC: Duke University Press, 1993. vi, 338 pp. [Includes essays written for an international symposium held at Duke University (Durham, NC) in March 1990. Contents: Mikhail Kuraev, "Perestroika: The Restructuring of the Past or the Invention of the Future?" pp. 13-20; Boris Kagarlitsky, "A Step to the Left, a Step to the Right," pp. 21-34; Sidney Monas, "Perestroika in Reverse Perspective; The Reforms of the 1860s," pp. 35-46; Paul Debreczeny, " 'Zhitie Aleksandra Boldinskogo': Pushkin's Elevation to Sainthood in Soviet Culture," pp. 47-68; Renata Galtseva and Irina Rodnyanskaya, "The Obstacle: The Human Being, or the Twentieth Century in the Mirror of Dystopia," pp. 69-94; Maya Turovskaya, "The Tastes of Soviet Moviegoers during the 1930s," pp. 95-107; Evgeny Dobrenko, "The Literature of the Zhdanov Era: Mentality, Mythology, Lexicon," pp. 109-137; Thomas Lahusen, "The Mystery of the River Adun: Reconstruction of a Story," pp. 139-154; Michael Holquist, "Dialogism and Aesthetics," pp. 155-176; Valery Leibin, "Freudianism, or the 'Trotskiite Contraband': Soviet Psychoanalysis in the 1920s and 1930s," pp. 177-186; Valery Podoroga, "The Eunuch of the Soul: Positions of Reading and the World of Platonov," pp. 187-231; Helena Goscilo, "Domostroika or Perestroika? The Construction of Womanhood in Soviet Culture under Glasnost," pp. 233-255; Mikhail Epstein, "After the Future: On the New Consciousness in Literature," pp. 257-287; Katerina Clark, "Changing Historical Paradigms in Soviet Culture," pp. 289-306; Donald Raleigh, "Beyond Moscow and St. Petersburg: Some Reflections on the August Revolution, Provincial Russia, and Novostroika," pp. 289-321.] REV: Harold N. Ingle, *Canadian Slavonic Papers* 35, nos. 3-4 (September-December 1993): 422-423.

488. Laqueur, Walter. "Le Carré in Russian Eyes." *Commentary* 96, no. 3 (September 1993): 54-55. [Review article on John Le Carré, *The Russia House* (NY: 1989) and *The Night Manager* (NY: 1993).]

489. Levin, Theodore. "The Reterritorization of Culture in the New Central Asian States: A Report from Uzbekistan." *Yearbook for Traditional Music* 25 (1993): 51-59.

490. Manea, Norman. "Empty Theaters?" *World Policy Journal* 10, no. 1 (Spring 1993): 79-82. Translated from the Romanian by Adriana Parau.

491. Marga, Andrei. "Cultural and Political Trends in Romania before and after 1989." *East European Politics and Societies* 7, no. 1 (Winter 1993): 14-32. [Paper was contributed to the JCEE conference on Intellectual Trends, Institutional Changes and Scholarly Needs in Eastern Europe.]

492. Miljan, Toivo. "In Spite of Everything: Literacy is the Cultural Foundation of Estonian Independence." *World & I* 8, no. 2 (February 1993): 678-391.

493. Nelson, Amy. "Music and the Politics of Culture in Revolutionary Russia, 1921-1930." Ph.D. diss., University of Michigan, 1993. [UMI order no: AAC 9409774.]

494. Neumann, Victor. *The Temptation of Homo Europaeus*. Translated by Dana Miu. East European Monographs, 384. Boulder, CO: East European Monographs; New York: Distributed by Columbia University Press, 1993. 269 pp. [Translation of: *Tentatia lui homo-europaeus*.]

495. Notley, Margaret. "Brahms as Liberal: Genre, Style, and Politics in Late Nineteenth-Century Vienna." *19th Century Music* 17, no. 2 (Fall 1993): 107-123.

496. Paperny, Zinovy. "Today and Always: The Role of Jokes in Russian Humor." *World & I* 8, no. 1 (January 1993): 652-663.

497. Paternost, Joseph. "Symbols, Slogans and Identity in the Slovene Search for Sovereignty, 1987-1991." *Slovene Studies* 14, no. 1 (1992, published March 1994): 51-68.

498. Poshyvanyk, Motria. "Lions of the Dniester Combine Culture and Conservation." *Surviving Together* 11, no. 4 (Winter 1993): 18-19.

499. Ragsdale, Hugh. "The Constraints of Russian Culture." *National Interest*, no. 33 (Fall 1993): 68-72. [Followed with letter to the editor by David Brooks in issue no. 34 (Winter 1993-1994): 107-108, and response by Ragsdale, p. 108.]

500. Richardson, Rick. "A Russian Thaw?" *ARTnews* 92, no. 10 (December 1993): 47. [On Polish art works confiscated by the Soviet Union during World War II.]

501. Shanahan, Daniel. "The Last Time I Saw Zadar." *North Dakota Quarterly* 61, no. 1 (Winter 1993): 171-173.

502. Sieg, Katrin. "The Revolution Has Been Televised: Reconfiguring History and Identity in Post-Wall Germany." *Theatre Journal* 45, no. 1 (March 1993): 35-48.

503. Sloan, Kay. "Presleystroika." *Michigan Quarterly Review* 32, no. 1 (Winter 1993): 77-90.

504. Soljan, Antun. "The Mannheim Story." *North Dakota Quarterly* 61, no. 1 (Winter 1993): 182-185. Translated by Ellen Elias-Bursac.

505. Syberberg, Hans Jürgen. "Germany's New Nostalgia: How Benign?" *Harper's* 286, no. 1714 (March 1993): 18-23. [Excerpt from an interview with Hans Jürgen Syberberg in *New Perspectives Quarterly* (Winter 1993).]

506. "Taking art into the streets of Eastern and Central Europe." *Smithsonian* 24, no. 1 (April 1993): 118-123. [Describes the exhibit "Art as Activist: Revolutionary Posters from Central and Eastern Europe," based on the collections of the Moravian Gallery in Brno, Czech Republic.]

507. Ugresic, Dubravka. "*Yugo-Americana.*" *Cross Currents: A Yearbook of Central European Culture*, no. 12 (1993): 182-188. Translated from the Croatian by Mark Baskin.

508. Valgemäe, Mardi. "Text and Context in Recent Estonian Drama." *Journal of Baltic Studies* 24, no. 1 (Spring 1993): 67-72.

509. Voinovich, Vladimir. "Letter from Moscow." *Book World (Washington Post)* 23, no. 10 (March 7, 1993): 1ff. [On the Russian Writer's Union.]

510. Von Geldern, James. *Bolshevik Festivals, 1917-1920.* Studies on the History of Society and Culture, 15. Berkeley, CA: University of California Press, c1993. xiv, 316 pp. [Contents: 1. The Precursors: Tsars, Socialists, and Poets; 2. Revolution and Festivity; 3. The Politics of Meaning and Style; 4. New Uses for Popular Culture; 5. Transformation by Festival: Mass Festivals as Performance; 6. Marking the Center: Festivals and Legitimacy.]

511. Wartofsky, Marx W. "The Politics of Art: The Domination of Style and the Crisis in Contemporary Art." *Journal of Aesthetics and Art Criticism* 51, no. 2 (Spring 1993): 217-225.

512. Weschler, Lawrence. "Slight Modification." *New Yorker* 69, no. 21 (July 12, 1993): 59-65. ["What is to be done with the monuments of the former Soviet Union? Artists from around the world offer their solutions."]

■ Architecture

513. Brumfield, William Craft. *A History of Russian Architecture.* Cambridge; New York: Cambridge University Press, 1993. 644 pp. [Contents: Pt. I. Early Medieval Architecture. 1. Kiev and Chernigov. 2. Novgorod and Pskov: Eleventh to Thirteenth Centuries. 3. Vladimir and Suzdal Before the Mongol Invasion. 4. The Revival of Architecture in Novgorod and Pskov — Pt. II. The Muscovite Period. 5. Moscow: Architectural Beginnings. 6. The Ascent of Architecture in Muscovy. 7. The Seventeenth Century: From Ornamentalism to the New Age — Pt. III. The Turn to Western Forms. 8. The Foundations of the Baroque in Saint Petersburg. 9. The Late Baroque in Russia: The Age of Rastrelli. 10. Neoclassicism in Petersburg: The Age of Catherine the Great. 11. Eighteenth-Century Neoclassicism in Moscow and the Provinces. 12. The Early Nineteenth Century: Alexandrine Neoclassicism — Pt. IV. The Formation of Modern Russian Architecture. 13. Nineteenth-Century Historicism and Eclecticism. 14. Modernism During the Early Twentieth Century. 15. Revolution and Reaction in Soviet Architecture — Appendix I. Russian Wooden Architecture.] REV: Suzanne Massie, *New York Times Book Review* 98, no. 44 (October 31, 1993): 31ff.

514. Brumfield, William Craft, and Blair A. Ruble, eds. *Russian Housing in the Modern Age: Design and Social*

History. Contributions by Robert Edelman, William Craft Brumfield, Milka Bliznakov, Vladimir Paperny, Stephen Kotkin, Judith Pallot, Blair A. Ruble, and Aleksandr Vysokovskii. Woodrow Wilson Center Series. Washington, DC: Woodrow Wilson Center Press; Cambridge; New York: Cambridge University Press, 1993. xiv, 322 pp. [Contents: Robert Edelman, "Everybody's got to be someplace: organizing space in the Russian peasant house, 1880 to 1930"; William Craft Brumfield, "Redesigning the Russian house, 1895 to 1917; Building for comfort and profit: the new apartment house"; Milka Bliznakov, "Soviet housing during the experimental years, 1918 to 1933"; Vladimir Paperny, "Men, women, and the living space"; Stephen Kotkin, "Shelter subjectivity in the Stalin period : a case study of Magnitogorsk"; Judith Pallot, "Living in the Soviet countryside"; Blair A. Ruble, "From *khrushcheby* to *korobki*"; Aleksandr Vysokovskii, "Will domesticity return?"]

515. Danta, Darrick. "Ceausescu's Bucharest." *Geographical Review* 83, no. 2 (April 1993): 170-182.

516. McCord, Olga Alexandra. "Nationalism and Its Expression in Architecture: The Czech National Theater and Its Legacy." Ph.D. diss., University of California, Berkeley, 1993. [UMI order no: AAC 9430600.]

517. Soloukhin, Vladimir. *A Time to Gather Stones: Essays.* Translated and with an introduction by Valerie Z. Nollan. Evanston, IL: Northwestern University Press, c1993. xxi, 251 pp. [Translation of: *Vremia sobirat' kamni.* First published (Moscow: Sovremennik, 1980). On literary landmarks and cultural monuments of Russia.]

518. Vachou, Michael. "Bucharest: The House of the People." *World Policy Journal* 10, no. 4 (Winter 1993-1994): 59-63. [Description of Ceausescu's Casa Poporului (House of the People).]

■ Dance

519. Alovert, Nina. " 'The Return of the Firebird.' " *Dance Magazine* 67, no. 6 (June 1993): 70-71. [Review of "The Return of the Firebird", a ballet performed at the Mariinskii Theater, St. Petersburg.]

520. Corn, Alfred. "Balanchine's *Western Symphony*." *New Republic* 209, no. 20 (November 15, 1993): 38. [Poem.]

521. Croce, Arlene. "The Balanchine Show." *New Yorker* 69, no. 16 (June 7, 1993): 99-103.

522. ———. "George Balanchine's *The Nutcracker*." *New Yorker* 69, no. 44 (December 27, 1993-January 3, 1994): 141-144.

523. Daniel, David. "In Mr. B.'s Steps." *New Yorker* 69, no. 13 (May 17, 1993): 56-59. ["Why has New York City Ballet's Balanchine retrospective slighted Suzanne Farrell, his quintessential interpreter?"]

524. "Family Ties: A Photo Essay." *Dance Magazine* 67, no. 5 (May 1993): 54-56. [Photos from the family albums of Fokine, Liepa, Massine, Youskevitch, and Petipa.]

525. Garafola, Lynn. "Ten Years After: Peter Martins on Preserving Balanchine's Legacy." *Dance Magazine* 67, no. 5 (May 1993): 38-42. [On the New York City Ballet.]

526. Gruen, John. "In His Words." *Dance Magazine* 67, no. 4 (April 1993): 39. ["Excerpts from interviews conducted by John Gruen with Rudolf Nureyev over fifteen years."]

527. ———. "Natalia Makarova: Off Her Toes." *Dance Magazine* 67, no. 1 (January 1993): 48-52.

528. ———. "Rosemary Dunleavy: A Teacher to the Corps." *Dance Magazine* 67, no. 5 (May 1993): 34-37. [On Rosemary Dunleavy and the Balanchine repertoire at the New York City Ballet.]

529. Hardy, Camille. "Where Angels Tread: Honoring the Tradition of George Balanchine." *World & I* 8, no. 11 (November 1993): 109-113.

530. Horosko, Marian. "Vail's Global Workshop." *Dance Magazine* 67, no. 11 (November 1993): 76-79. [Followed by an interview with Sophia N. Golovkina, Director of the Bolshoi Ballet Academy.]

531. Hunt, Marilyn. "Balanchine's Democratic Aristocracy." *Dance Magazine* 67, no. 5 (May 1993): 43-44.

532. Johnson, Robert. "Igor Zelensky: A Tiger on the Loose." *Dance Magazine* 67, no. 1 (January 1993): 70-75.

533. Kendall, Elizabeth. "Communiqué: St. Petersburg." *Dance Magazine* 67, no. 6 (June 1993): 30-32.

534. Roca, Octavio. "Cutting Up with Tharp and Baryshnikov." *World & I* 8, no. 5 (May 1993): 105-109.

535. Ruddy, Jeanne. "Durham on the Moscow: The American Dance Festival in Russia." *Dance Magazine* 67, no. 1 (January 1993): 54-57.

536. Taper, Bernard, and Richard Avedon. "A Festival for Mr. B." *New Yorker* 69, no. 12 (May 10, 1993): 74. ["The New York City Ballet remembers George Balanchine ten years after his death."]

537. Thom, Rose Anne. "Nureyev, Documented." *Dance Magazine* 67, no. 7 (July 1993): 50-51. [Review of television documentary on Nureyev.]

538. "VBA's Yelena Vinogradova." *Dance Magazine* 67, no. 2 (February 1993): 66-68. [On the Vaganova Ballet Academy (St. Petersburg, Russian Federation).]

539. Willis, Margaret. "Bolshoi Ballet." *Dance Magazine* 67, no. 6 (June 1993): 71-72. [Review of performances by the Bolshoi Ballet at the Royal Albert Hall (London), January 9-February 14, 1993.]

540. Windreich, Leland. "On Toe, Nowhere to Go: Dance in Vienna, Budapest, and Prague." *World & I* 8, no. 3 (March 1993): 107-113.

541. Zuck, Barbara. "Together Again: Tharp and Baryshnikov in Ohio." *Dance Magazine* 67, no. 3 (March 1993): 36-38.

■ Decorative Arts

542. Guliayev, Vladimir. *The Fine Art of Russian Lacquered Miniatures*. Translated by Sergei Volynets. San Francisco, CA: Chronicle Books, 1993, c1989. 287 pp.

543. Hochfield, Sylvia. "Reviews: Russian and Soviet Design; The Great Experiment; Liberation of the Aesthetic." *ARTnews* 92, no. 1 (January 1993): 138.

544. Johnson, Robert. "Theatre in Revolution: An Exhibition and a Catalogue." *Dance Chronicle* 16, no. 1 (1993): 121-127. [Review article on Nancy Van Norman Baer et al., *Theatre in Revolution: Russian Avant-Garde Stage Design, 1913-1935* (NY: 1991).]

545. Kezys, Algimantas. "The Art of Albinas Elskus." *Lituanus* 39, no. 1 (Spring 1993): 53-66. [Excerpt from author's *Lithuanian Artists in North America* (Stickney, IL: Galerija, forthcoming). Text, pp. 53-55; photographs of Elskus' stained glass works, pp. 4, 56-66.]

546. Shandler, Jeffrey. "Status Symbol: Before Fur Coats, There Was the *Shterntikhl*." *Lilith* 18, no. 1 (Winter 1993): 19.

547. Simakov, N. *Islamic Designs in Color*. Dover Pictorial Archive Series. New York: Dover Publications, c1993. 68 pp. [Reproductions from the portfolio *Iskusstvo Srednei Azii... = L'art de l'Asie Centrale...* (St. Petersburg: Imperatorskie Obscestvo Pooscreniya Khudozestv, 1883).]

548. Slesin, Suzanne. "Design: The Nutcracker Suite." *New York Times Magazine* (September 26, 1993): 54-59. [On the Nureyev home.]

549. Sljivic-Simsic, Biljana. "Savka Subotic (1834-1918): 'The Mother of Serbian Women's Culture.'" *Serbian Studies* 7, no. 1 (Spring 1993): 69-86.

550. Snowman, A. Kenneth. *Fabergé, Lost and Found: The Recently Discovered Jewelry Designs from the St. Petersburg Archives*. New York: H. N. Abrams, 1993. 176 pp.

551. Veritale, A. "The image of the cat in the works of Koshkin." *Columbia Pottery Annual*, no. 2 (1993): 7-21.

■ Music

General

552. Bellman, Jonathan. *The Style Hongrois in the Music of Western Europe*. Boston, MA: Northeastern University Press, c1993. viii, 261 pp. [Partial contents: 1. Provenance and Musical Origins; 2. The Magyars, the Turks, the Siege of Vienna, and the Turkish Style; 3. The Emergence of the Style Hongrois; 4. Stereotypes: The Gypsies in Literature and Popular Culture; 5. A Lexicon for the Style Hongrois; 6. Weber; 7. Schubert; 8. Liszt; 9. Brahms; 10. Decline and Disappearance.]

553. Prial, Frank. "A Story, A Passion, A Life of Song." *Ararat* 34, no. 1 (Winter 1993): 25-27. [Profile of Charles Aznavour.]

Russia/U.S.S.R./C.I.S.

554. Dilanchian, Noric. "Musical Cousins." *Ararat* 34, no. 3 (no. 135) (Summer 1993): 56-60.

555. Ferenc, Anna. "Investigating Russian Musical Modernism: Nikolai Roslavets and His New System of Tone Organization." Ph.D. diss., University of Michigan, 1993. [UMI order no: AAC 9319524.]

556. Hacikyan, A. H. "Quatra: Twenty Years of Devotion." *Ararat* 34, no. 1 (Winter 1993): 48-49.

557. Matyakubov, Otanazar. "A Traditional Musician in Modern Society: A Case Study of Turgun Alimatov's Art." *Yearbook for Traditional Music* 25 (1993): 60-66.

558. Melikyan, Sevan. "The Double Life of Armine." *Ararat* 34, no. 2 (no. 134) (Spring 1993): 48-49.

559. Montparker, Carol. "Evgeny Kissin Comes of Age." *Clavier* 32, no. 7 (September 1993): 16-19.

560. Roberts, Peter Deane. *Modernism in Russian Piano Music: Skriabin, Prokofiev, and Their Russian Contemporaries*. Russian Music Studies (Bloomington, IN). Bloomington, IN: Indiana University Press, c1993. 2 vols. [Vol. 2 consists of musical examples.]

561. Seaman, Gerald R. [Book Review]. *Notes* 49, no. 3 (March 1993): 1013-1016. [Review article on Alexandra Orlova, comp., *Tchaikovsky: A Self-Portrait*, trans. R.M. Davison (Oxford, England: 1990); and Alexander Poznansky, *Tchaikovsky: The Quest for the Inner Man* (NY: 1991).]

562. Tumanov, Alexander N. "Correspondence of Literary Text and Musical Phraseology in Shostakovich's Opera *The Nose* and Gogol's Fantastic Tale." *Russian Review* 52, no. 3 (July 1993): 397-414.

563. Walker, James, comp. and trans. *Classical Essays on the Development of the Russian Art Song, and Twenty-Seven Outstanding Russian Romances of the Eighteenth- and Nineteenth-Centuries*. [Nerstrand, MN (14995 Lamb Ave., Nerstrand, 55053)]: James Walker, c1993. 115, 98, 102 pp. [Essays translated from Russian by James Walker. Includes scores of 27 romances with Russian words. Partial contents: Cesar Cui, "Essays: The Russian romance"; Nikolay Findeisen, "The Russian art song (romance)". Includes essays by F. Dietz, I. Kozlowsky, Mikhail Glinka, Aleksandr Dargomyzhsky, Anton Rubinstein, Nikolay Rimsky-Korsakov, Modest Musorgsky, Aleksandr Borodin, and Peter Chaikovsky.]

Eastern Europe

564. Brown, Stephen. "Four Greek Miniatures." *Clavier* 32, no. 10 (December 1993): 35-39. [Text by Brown, p. 35; musical score by Constantinidis, pp. 36-39.]

565. Clendinning, Jane Piper. "The Pattern-Meccanico Compositions of György Ligeti." *Perspectives of New Music* 31, no. 1 (Winter 1993): 192-234.

566. Cortright, Cynthia Susan. "Gyorgy Sebok: A Profile As Revealed Through Interviews with the Artist, His Colleagues and His Students." D.M.A. diss., University of Oklahoma, 1993. [UMI order no: AAC 9332266.]

567. Dohnányi, Ernst von. "Dohnányi's Etude No. 12 in A flat." *Clavier* 32, no. 2 (February 1993): 34-39. [Piano étude from "12 Short Studies for the Advanced Pianist"; musical score.]

568. Elder, Dean. "Edward Kilenyi Remembers Dohnányi." *Clavier* 32, no. 2 (February 1993): 16-17.

569. Griffiths, Paul. "The Excursions of Mr. Janácek." *New Yorker* 68, no. 49 (January 25, 1993): 98-100.

570. ———. "Musical Events: The European Mystics." *New Yorker* 69, no. 40 (November 29, 1993): 152-157.

571. Hicks, Michael. "Interval and Form in Ligeti's *Continuum* and *Coulée*." *Perspectives of New Music* 31, no. 1 (Winter 1993): 172-190.

572. Holt, Dorma Earl. "Interpretive Suggestions for Selected Czech, Swedish, and American Secular Organ Works Published, 1977-1988." D.M.A. diss., Arizona State University, 1993. [UMI order no: AAC 9410976.]

573. Koo, Jae-Hyang. "A Study of Four Representative Piano Quintets by Major Composers of the Nineteenth Century: Schumann, Brahms, Dvorak and Franck." D.M.A. diss., University of Cincinnati, 1993. [UMI order no: AAC 9424588.]

574. Lebic, Lojze. "From Generation to Generation the Spirit Seeks the Way: Slovene Musical Creativity in the Past and Today." *Nationalities Papers* 21, no. 1 (Spring 1993): 145-155.

575. Ligeti, György. "States, Events, Transformations." *Perspectives of New Music* 31, no. 1 (Winter 1993): 164-171. [Previously published "Zustände, Ereignisse, Wandlungen," *Melos* 34 (1967): 165-69; reprinted from *Bilder und Blätter* 11 (1960), where the article had the subtitle "Bemerkungen zu meinem Orchesterstück *Apparitions*."]

576. Niewiadomska-Bugaj, M., and S. Zeranska-Kominek. "Musical Self-Image and Cultural Change: Lithuanian Minority in Poland Case Study." *Behavioral Science* 38, no. 4 (October 1993): 273-292.

577. Papandreou, Nicholas. "Mikis and Manos: A Tale of Two Composers." *Journal of the Hellenic Diaspora* 19, no. 1 (1993): 113-131.

578. Pniewski, Tom. "Penderecki at Sixty: Poland's Global Voice." *World & I* 8, no. 11 (November 1993): 114-119.

579. Schwartz, Elliot. "1992 Warsaw ISCM." *Perspectives of New Music* 31, no. 1 (Winter 1993): 316-322. [Description of "World Music Days," sponsored by the

International Society for Contemporary Music, and held in Warsaw in May 1992.]

580. Serra, Marie-Hélène. "Stochastic Composition and Stochastic Timbre: *Gendy3* by Iannis Xenakis." *Perspectives of New Music* 31, no. 1 (Winter 1993): 236-257.

581. Vuza, Dan Tudor. "Supplementary Sets and Regular Complementary Unending Canons (Part Four)." *Perspectives of New Music* 31, no. 1 (Winter 1993): 270-305.

582. Webb, Charles. "Premiere." *Poet Lore* 88, no. 4 (Winter 1993-1994): 39-40.

Composers

Bartók

583. Bartók, Bela. "Second Dance in Bulgarian Rhythm." *Clavier* 32, no. 8 (October 1993): 31-33. [Musical score.]

584. Lust-Cobb, Jo Ellen. "Training the Hands with Bartók's *Mikrokosmos.*" *Clavier* 32, no. 8 (October 1993): 29-30.

585. Stevens, Halsey. *The Life and Music of Bela Bartok.* Prepared by Malcolm Gillies. 3rd ed. Oxford: Clarendon Press; New York: Oxford University Press, 1993. xxii, 358 pp. ["Chronological list of works," pp. [321]-341.]

Mussorgsky

586. Taruskin, Richard. *Musorgsky: Eight Essays and an Epilogue.* Princeton, NJ: Princeton University Press, c1993. xxxiv, 415 pp. [Contents: Caryl Emerson, "Foreword"; Pronouncing the Name: A Pronouncing Glossary of Selected Russian Names and Titles; What Is A *Kuchka*?; Introduction: Who Speaks for Musorgsky?; 1. "Little Star": An Etude in the Folk Style; 2. Handel, Shakespeare, and Musorgsky: The Sources and Limits of Russian Musical Realism; 3. Serov and Musorgsky; 4. The Present in the Past: Russian Opera and Russian Historiography, circa 1870; 5. Musorgsky versus Musorgsky: The Versions of *Boris Godunov*; Appendix: Folk Texts in *Boris Godunov*; 6. Slava!; 7. The Power of the Black Earth: Notes on *Khovanshchina*; Appendix: The *Khovanshchina* Manuscripts; 8. *Sorochintsi Fair* Revisited; Epilogue: Musorgsky in the Age of Glasnost'.] REV: Laurel E. Fay, *Russian History = Histoire russe* 20, nos. 1-4 (1993): 301-303. Donal Henahan, *New York Times Book Review* 98, no. 5 (January 31, 1993): 31. Robert A. Maguire, *Slavic Review* 52, no. 4 (Winter 1993): 847. Patrick J. Smith, *Opera News* 57, no. 12 (February 27, 1993): 44.

Prokofiev

587. Fay, Laurel E. [Book Review]. *Notes* 49, no. 2 (June 1993): 1417-1419. [Review article on Hermann Danuser, et al., eds., *Sergej Prokofjew: Beiträge zum Thema, Dokumente, Interpretationen, Programme, Das Werke* (1990); and Oleg Prokofiev, trans. and ed., and Christopher Palmer, associate ed., *Sergei Prokofiev: Soviet Diary 1927 and Other Writings* (London: 1991).]

588. Thibodeau, Michael James. "An Analysis of Selected Piano Works by Sergey Prokofiev Using the Theories of B. L. Yavorsky." Ph.D. diss., Florida State University, 1993. [UMI order no: AAC 9318528.]

Rachmaninoff

589. Elder, Dean. "Recent Recordings: The Art of Sergei Rachmaninoff." *Clavier* 32, no. 3 (March 1993): 30-32.

590. Martyn, Barrie. "The Legacy of Rachmaninoff." *Clavier* 32, no. 3 (March 1993): 15-17.

591. Matushevski, Voytek. "Rachmaninoff's Last Tour." *Clavier* 32, no. 3 (March 1993): 18ff.

592. Meza, Esequiel, Jr. "External Influences on Rachmaninov's Early Piano Works as Exemplified in the 'Morceaux De Salon', Opus 10 and 'Moments Musicaux', Opus 16." D.M.A. diss., University of Arizona, 1993. [UMI order no: AAC 9328606.]

593. Rachmaninoff, Sergei. "Oriental Sketch." *Clavier* 32, no. 3 (March 1993): 26-29. [Musical score.]

594. Sokasits, Jonathan F. "The Keyboard Style of Sergei Rachmaninoff As Seen Through His Transcriptions for Piano Solo." D.M.A. diss., University of Wisconsin-Madison, 1993. [UMI order no: AAC 9318643.]

595. Tibbetts, John C. "Rachmaninoff's Piano Legacy." *World & I* 8, no. 3 (March 1993): 114-121.

Stravinsky

596. Horgan, Paul. *Tracings: A Book of Partial Portraits.* New York: Farrar Straus Giroux, c1993. 260 pp. [Includes an account of the last days of Stravinsky.] REV: *New Yorker* 69, no. 36 (November 1, 1993): 131.

597. Wallis, William. "Act III, Scene iii of Stravinsky's *The Rake's Progress.*" *Opera Journal* 26, no. 4 (December 1993): 3-18.

■ Painting, Sculpture, Graphic Arts

General

598. Bowlt, John E., and Nicoletta Misler. *Twentieth-Century Russian and East European Painting.* London: Zwemmer; New York: Distributed in the USA and Canada by Rizzoli International Publications, 1993. 329 pp. [The Thyssen-Bornemisza Collection.]

599. Cerwinske, Laura. "An Emigré's Life on Safari." *Art & Antiques* 15, no. 5 (May 1993): 62-67.

600. Cohen, Jean Lawlor. "Reviews: Theme and Improvisation: Kandinsky and the American Avant-Garde, 1912-1959." *ARTnews* 92, no. 3 (March 1993): 139. [Review of exhibit at the Phillips Collection in Washington, DC.]

601. Heboyan-DeVries, Esther. "Painter from Paris." *Ararat* 34, no. 1 (Winter 1993): 32-37. [Richard Jeranian, artist of Armenian origin.]

602. Kaplan, Morton A. "Armen Kankanian: Beyond the Eye." *World & I* 8, no. 12 (December 1993): 146-155. [Text, pp. 147-149; pictures, pp. 148-155.]

603. Kezys, Algimantas. "The Art of Vytautas Kasuba." *Lituanus* 39, no. 2 (Summer 1993): 36-50. [Text, pp. 36-38; photographs of Kasuba's sculpture, pp. 4, 39-50.]

604. ———. "Otis Tamasauskas: Printmaking." *Lituanus* 39, no. 3 (Fall 1993): 16-25. [Statement by Tamasauskas, pp. 16-18; text by Kezys, p. 18; reproductions of prints by Tamasauskas, pp. 4, 19-25.]

605. Krzyzanowski, Jerzy R. "Canadian Art Critics on Rafal Malczewski." *Polish Review* 38, no. 2 (1993): 191-201.

606. Leo, Felix. "A Man for All Seasons." *Ararat* 34, no. 1 (Winter 1993): 75. [Pascal Tchakmakian, artist of Armenian origin.]

607. Mueller, Megan. "Zoran Music." *ARTnews* 92, no. 2 (February 1993): 107-108. [Review of a show at Jan Krugier (New York) by Yugoslav-born artist Zoran Music; includes images drawn from Music's days as a prisoner at Dachau (1944-1945).]

608. Roditi, Edouard. "Ardash." *Ararat* 34, no. 1 (Winter 1993): 76. [Ardash Kakafian, artist of Armenian origin.]

609. ———. "Assadour." *Ararat* 34, no. 1 (Winter 1993): 28. [Artist of Armenian origin.]

610. "Talking to Philippe Ouzounian." *Ararat* 34, no. 1 (Winter 1993): 68-69. Translated by A. J. Hacikyan. [Artist of Armenian origin.]

611. Tepelian, Bernard. "Adelina von Furstenberg." *Ararat* 34, no. 1 (Winter 1993): 67.

Russia/U.S.S.R./C.I.S.

612. Akinsha, Konstantin. "Ukraine: The Martinchiki." *ARTnews* 92, no. 5 (May 1993): 118.

613. Barooshian, Vahan D. *V.V. Vereshchagin, Artist at War.* Gainesville, FL: University Press of Florida, c1993. xvii, 216 pp.

614. Blessing, Jennifer. "The upside-down world of Marc Chagall." *ARTnews* 92, no. 3 (March 1993): 100-105. [Pictures from a traveling exhibition of the artist's murals done for the Moscow State Jewish Chamber Theater in 1920.]

615. Bowlt, John E. "Utopia revisited." *Art in America* 81, no. 5 (May 1993): 98-105. [Comments on the exhibit "The Great Utopia: The Russian and Soviet Avant-Garde, 1915-1932" held at the Guggenheim Museum in 1993.]

616. Dickinson, Carol V. "Reviews: Tengiz." *ARTnews* 92, no. 5 (May 1993): 146. [Review of the show "Kremlin Mysteries: Theater of the Absurd," by the Georgian-born Tengiz at the Sloan Gallery (Denver, CO).]

617. Esterow, Milton. "Sergei Gitman's 'Mad Invention.'" *ARTnews* 92, no. 3 (March 1993): 43-44.

618. Farrell, Dianne E. "Shamanic Elements in Some Early Eighteenth Century Russian Woodcuts." *Slavic Review* 52, no. 4 (Winter 1993): 725-744.

619. Fattal, Laura. "Collections of Russian and Soviet Art." *Russian Review* 52, no. 1 (January 1993): 91-92. [Zimmerli Art Museum acquires the George Riabov Collection of Russian Art (16th-20th centuries) and the Norton and Nancy Dodge Collection of Nonconformist Art from the Soviet Union (1956-1986).]

620. Fauchereau, Serge, and Kazimir Severinovich Malevich. *Malevich.* Translated by Alan Swan. New York: Rizzoli, 1993. 128 pp. [Contents: The Man and the Black Square; The Early Years; From Symbolism to Cezannism; Neo-Primitivism; Cubo-Futurism; Victory Over the Sun, Alogism; Suprematism and the Black Quadrangle; Suprematism and the Revolution; Unovis; Architektons and GINKhUK; Suprematism Contested; The Return to Painting; Death and Transfiguration; Plates.]

621. Gambrell, Jamey. "Art and the Great Utopia." *New York Review of Books* 40, no. 8 (April 22, 1993): 52-59. [Review article on Elizabeth Kridl Valkenier, *Ilya Repin and the World of Russian Art* (NY: 1990); Peter Noever, ed., *Aleksandr M. Rodchenko/Varvara Stepanova: The Future Is Our Only Goal* (NY: 1991); Dmitri V. Sarabianov and Natalia L. Adaskina, eds., *Popova* (NY: 1990); *The Great Utopia: The Russian and Soviet Avant-Garde, 1915-1932* (NY: 1992); Vladimir Tolstoy et al., eds., *Street Art of the Revolution: Festivals and Celebrations in Russia 1918-33* (NY: 1990).]

622. Henkin, Stephen. "'Psychological Portraits' of the CIS: The Photography of Anatoly Petrenko." *World & I* 8, no. 7 (July 1993): 160-165.

623. Hochfield, Sylvia. "The Malevich Legacy: Heirs vs. Museums." *ARTnews* 92, no. 9 (November 1993): 65-60.

624. ———. "Reviews: Suprematism." *ARTnews* 92, no. 1 (January 1993): 138. [On Leonard Hutton's show of Russian Suprematism.]

625. ———. "Under a Russian sofa: 101 looted treasures." *ARTnews* 92, no. 4 (April 1993): 120-125. [On the discovery of art stolen from Germany during World War II by a Red Army officer.]

626. Kiaer, Christina. "Photographs for a Russian Future." *Art in America* 81, no. 5 (May 1993): 51-55.

627. Nochlin, Linda. "'Matisse' and Its Other." *Art in America* 81, no. 5 (May 1993): 88-97. [Comments on the exhibit "The Great Utopia: The Russian and Soviet Avant-Garde, 1915-1932" held at the Guggenheim Museum in 1993.]

628. Norman, Geraldine. "International Report: Russia Rising." *Art & Antiques* 15, no. 5 (May 1993): 86-87.

629. Parton, Anthony. *Mikhail Larionov and the Russian Avant-garde.* Princeton, NJ: Princeton University

Press, c1993. xxiv, 254 pp. [Contents: 1. Tiraspol to Myasnitskaya Ulitsa 1881-1908; 2. The Golden Fleece 1908-1910; 3. The Jack of Diamonds and Donkey's Tail 1910-1912; 4. The Futurists Take Command 1913-1914; 5. Russian Folk Art and the Sources of Neo-Primitivism; 6. Antiquity and the Buryat Shaman; 7. The Cubist and Futurist Roots of Rayism; 8. The Modern Prometheus: Ouspensky's Four-Dimensional Superman; 9. Towards an Avant-Garde Theatre 1914-1917; 10. Up and Coming in Paris and London 1917-1919; 11. Montparnasse Bienvenue 1919-1929; 12. Zhizn' Prokhodit, Lyubov' Net 1930-1964; Principal Exhibitions and Catalogues.]

630. Richardson, William. "Alexandre Benois and the Imperial Russian Past." *Russian History* 20, nos. 1-4 (1993): 213-235.

631. Riley, Charles A., II. "Armand Hammered." *Art & Antiques* 15, no. 3 (March 1993): 98ff.

632. Salys, Rimgaila. "Leonid Pasternak's *Moi Proizvedenija*: Text and Commentary." *Russian Language Journal* 47, nos. 156-158 (Winter-Spring-Fall 1993): 159-322. ["Introduction," pp. 159-174; "Explanatory Notes," pp. 174-178; "Exhibitions," pp. 178-190; "Catalogue Raisonné," pp. 190-205; "Illustrations," pp. 295-322.]

633. Salzberg, Joel. "The 'Loathly Landlady,' Chagallian Unions, and Malamudian Parody: 'The Girl of My Dreams' Revisited." *Studies in Short Fiction* 30, no. 4 (Fall 1993): 543-554. [Includes section on Chagall's painting in relation to Malamud's fiction, pp. 552-553.]

634. Solomon, Andrew, and Josif Bakshteyn. "A Riddle Wrapped in a Mystery inside an Enigma: The Art of S.Y. Kochelev." *Artforum* 31, no. 5 (January 1993): 68-71.

635. Tupitsyn, Margarita, guest curator. *After Perestroika: Kitchenmaids or Stateswomen*. Essays by Margarita Tupitsyn and Martha Rosler. New York: Independent Curators, [1993]. 63 pp. [A traveling exhibition organized and circulated by Independent Curators Incorporated, New York.]

636. Virshup, Amy. "Russian Lessons." *ARTnews* 92, no. 5 (May 1993): 27. [On Ilya Kabakov.]

637. Weber, Nicholas Fox. "Russian Constructivism: Dynamic Aesthetic of a Revolutionary Era." *Architectural Digest* 50, no. 9 (September 1993): 162ff.

638. Weinberg, Helen. "Chagall Restored." *Congress Monthly* 60, no. 1 (January 1993): 16-17.

639. Weiss, Evelyn, Stephan Diederich, and Josef-Haubrich-Kunsthalle Köln. *Russische Avantgarde im 20. Jahrhundert: von Malewitsch bis Kabakov: [Ausstellung] die Sammlung Ludwig*. München; New York: Prestel, c1993. 279 p. [Issued in connection with an exhibition held October 16, 1993-January 2, 1994 in the Josef-Haubrich-Kunsthalle, Cologne.]

640. Williamson, Anne. "Paradoxes of Victory." *Art & Antiques* 15, no. 5 (May 1993): 68-77. [On Soviet photography of World War II.]

Eastern Europe

641. Anderson, Geneva J. "Sofia: A New Noah's Ark." *ARTnews* 92, no. 1 (January 1993): 45-47.

642. Batorska, Danuta. "Economic and Other Changes in the Fine Arts World in Post-1989 Poland." *Polish Review* 38, no. 2 (1993): 213-220.

643. Brejc, Tomaz. "Slovene Images." *Nationalities Papers* 21, no. 1 (Spring 1993): 139-144.

644. Bronstein, Léo. *Romantic Homage to Greece and Spain: My Fable, Their Art*. New Brunswick, NJ: Transaction Publishers, c1993. xv, 301 pp.

645. Corbett, Jacqueline. "Bratislava: Clashing with the Czechs." *ARTnews* 92, no. 5 (May 1993): 53-54.

646. Georgievska-Shine, Aneta. "Annunciations out of the Dark: A View of Macedonian Art Today." *Cross Currents: A Yearbook of Central European Culture*, no. 12 (1993): 172-181.

647. Haus, Mary. "The Bombs on the building walls." *ARTnews* 92, no. 8 (October 1993): 154-155. [On the art of Krzysztof Wodiczko.]

648. Husarska, Anna. "Boom Town." *New Republic* 209, no. 7 (August 16, 1993): 14-15. ["Sarajevo's thriving art world."]

649. Kiel, Mark W. "Roman Vishniac: Beyond Nostalgia." *Congress Monthly* 60, no. 4 (May-June 1993): 16-17.

650. Kotalík, Jirí. "The Baroque Meets the Present." *Cross Currents: A Yearbook of Central European Culture*, no. 12 (1993): 15-24. Translated by Zdenka Brodská and Mary Hrabík Sámal.

651. Livas, Haris. *Contemporary Greek Artists*. 1st ed. New York: Vantage Press, c1993. 569 pp.

652. Melrod, George. "Reviews: Xawery Wolski." *ARTnews* 92, no. 1 (January 1993): 137-138. [Review of the first New York exhibit of Wolski's sculpture.]

653. Millie, Elena, and Zbigniew Kantorosinski. *The Polish Poster: From Young Poland through the Second World War: Holdings in the Prints and Photographs Division, Library of Congress*. Washington, DC: Library of Congress, 1993. 104 pp.

654. Popovich, Ljubica D. "Formal and Thematical Manifestations of Medievalism in Compositions: Selected Examples of Serbian Lithographs and Paintings of the 19th and 20th Centuries." *Serbian Studies* 7, no. 2 (Fall 1993, published in 1995): 49-71. [Contains illustrations.]

655. Struth, Thomas. "Photographs from Germany, East." *October*, no. 64 (Spring 1993): 32-55.

656. "Tomasz Zydler: Nature's Palette." *World & I* 8, no. 5 (May 1993): 132-141. [Text, p. 132; photographs, pp. 133-141.]

657. Vishniac, Roman. *To Give Them Light: The Legacy of Roman Vishniac.* Edited by Marion Wiesel. Preface by Elie Wiesel. New York: Simon & Schuster, c1993. 158 pp. [Contents: Cornell Capa, "Appreciation"; Marion Wiesel, "Editor's Note"; Elie Wiesel, "Preface"; "Bratislava"; "Carpathian Ruthenia"; "Warsaw"; "Lodz"; "Lublin"; "Slonim"; "Galicia"; "Vilna"; Mara Vishniac Kohn, "Biographical Note."] REV: Anna Husarska, *New York Times Book Review* 98, no. 14 (April 4, 1993): 35.

■ Theater and Cinema

General

658. Avakian, Florence. "Angry Young Actor from Paris." *Ararat* 34, no. 1 (Winter 1993): 70-73. [Simon Abkarian, actor of Armenian origin.]

659. Brown, Jeffrey A. "Bullets, Buddies, and Bad Guys: The 'Action Cop' Genre." *Journal of Popular Film & Television* 21, no. 2 (Summer 1993): 79-87. [Includes discussion of the film *Red Heat* (1988) in which Schwarzenegger plays a Soviet police officer.]

660. Caulfield, Carl. "*Moscow Gold* and Reassessing History." *Modern Drama* 36, no. 4 (1993): 490-498. [Review of a play by Howard Brenton and Tariq Ali, directed by Barry Kyle in September 1990.]

661. Cohen, Roger. "Holland Without a Country." *New York Times Magazine* (August 8, 1993): 28-32. [On Agnieszka Holland.]

662. Corman, Linda, and Charles A. Carpenter. "Modern Drama Studies: An Annual Bibliography." *Modern Drama* 36, no. 2 (June 1993): 316-336. With the assistance of Rebecca Cameron. [Includes "Section K: Eastern European (Russian, Polish, Czech, Hungarian, Balkan, Baltic)," pp. 316-336.]

663. Freedman, John. "The First Anton Chekhov International Theater Festival." *Slavic and East European Performance* 13, no. 1 (Spring 1993): 28-39. [Festival held in Moscow, October 4-27, 1992. Article critiques productions of various playwrights, staged by companies from Russia, Germany, Ukraine, Armenia, Turkmenistan, Greece, Tajikistan, Czechoslovakia, and Romania.]

664. Herer, Lisbeth. "Events." *Slavic and East European Performance* 13, no. 3 (Fall 1993): 7-11. [Includes Russian and East European theater and cinema.]

665. Martin, Matthew. "Stephen Poliakoff's Drama for the Post-Scientific Age." *Theatre Journal* 45, no. 2 (May 1993): 197-211.

666. Mitchell, Tony. "Caryl Churchill's *Mad Forest:* Polyphonic Representations of Southeastern Europe." *Modern Drama* 36, no. 4 (1993): 499-511.

667. Plum, Jay. "Events." *Slavic and East European Performance* 13, no. 1 (Spring 1993): 6-12. [Includes Russian, C.I.S., and East European theater and cinema.]

668. Plum, Jay, and Patrick Hennedy. "Events." *Slavic and East European Performance* 13, no. 2 (Summer 1993): 6-9. [Includes Russian, Soviet, and East European theater and cinema.]

669. Sharrett, Christopher. "The Horror Film in Neoconservative Culture." *Journal of Popular Film & Television* 21, no. 3 (Fall 1993): 100-110. [Includes analysis of Francis Ford Coppola's *Bram Stoker's Dracula* (1992).]

670. Shepard, Jim. "Nosferatu." *TriQuaterly*, no. 87 (Spring-Summer 1993): 88ff. [The vampire film *Nosferatu, A Symphony of Horrors* was directed by Albin Grau in Oravsky Zamok, a castle in Slovakia.]

Russia/U.S.S.R./C.I.S.

671. Adams, Brooks. "Chagall Onstage." *Art in America* 81, no. 5 (May 1993): 106-109.

672. Ananian, Jirair. "Taxi, Taxi." *Ararat* 34, no. 3 (no. 135) (Summer 1993): 52-54. Translated by Nishan Parlakian.

673. Bordwell, David. *The Cinema of Eisenstein.* Cambridge, MA: Harvard University Press, 1993. xv, 316 pp. [Contents: 1. A Life in Cinema. From Theatre to Cinema. The Silent Films. Europe, Hollywood, and Mexico. Projects and Problems. Triumph and Decline. The Particularities of Method — 2. Monumental Heroics: The Silent Films. Toward Plotless Cinema. Strike. Potemkin. October. Old and New. A Note on Versions of Eisenstein's Silent Films — 3. Seizing the Spectator: Film Theory in the Silent Era. Between Theory and Practice. Agitation as Excitation. Montage in Theatre and Film. Film Language and Intellectual Cinema. Film Form as Dialectics. The Eclectic Modernist — 4. Practical Aesthetics: Pedagogy. Structure and Style: The Episode. Structure and Style: From Episode to Work. Assaulting the Eye — 5. Cinema as Synthesis: Film Theory, 1930-1948. From Agitprop Formalism to Socialist Realism. Conceptions of Psychological Activity. Film Form: Organic Unity. Montage: The Musical Analogy Revisited. Pathos and Ecstasy. A Mature Poetics — 6. History and Tragedy: The Late Films. Alexander Nevsky. Ivan the Terrible. The Making and Remaking of Sergei Eisenstein. Legend in Life. The Assimilation into Orthodoxy. The Exemplary Modernist. Eisenstein Our Contemporary; Filmography, pp. 279-281.]

674. Brandesky, Joe. "Boris Anisfeld: Portrait of an Emigré Artist." *Theatre Design & Technology* 29, no. 3 (Summer 1993): 17-21.

675. Carnicke, Sharon Marie. "Stanislavsky: Uncensored and Unabridged." *TDR: The Drama Review* 37, no. 1 (Spring 1993): 22-37.

676. Farber, Vreneli. "Kiev Season: Autumn 1991." *Slavic and East European Performance* 13, no. 2 (Summer 1993): 10-18.

677. Field, Edward. "A Toast to Vera Soloviova." *Michigan Quarterly Review* 32, no. 2 (Spring 1993): 263-272.

678. Freedman, John. "A Glimpse into Anatoly Vasilyev's School of Dramatic Art." *Slavic and East European Performance* 13, no. 2 (Summer 1993): 19-22.

679. ———. "The Year of the Actor in Moscow." *Slavic and East European Performance* 13, no. 3 (Fall 1993): 14-26.

680. Frodon, Jean-Michel. "A Language Before Babel." *Ararat* 34, no. 1 (Winter 1993): 60-62. Translated by A. J. Hacikyan. [Interview with Arthur Peleshian, film director of Armenian origin.]

681. Goodwin, James. *Eisenstein, Cinema, and History*. Urbana, IL: University of Illinois Press, c1993. x, 262 pp. [Contents: 1. Revolutionary Beginnings: From Theater to Cinema; 2. Strike: The Beginnings of Revolution; 3. Battleship Potemkin: Pathos and Politics; 4. October: History and Genesis; 5. Old and New: History and Utopia; 6. Dislocation: Projects, 1929-32; 7. Disjunction: Projects, 1932-37; 8. Alexander Nevsky: The Great Man in History; 9. Ivan the Terrible: An Inversion of History.] REV: Denise J. Youngblood, *Slavic Review* 52, no. 4 (Winter 1993): 863-864. Robert C. Williams, *Russian History = Histoire russe* 20, nos. 1-4 (1993): 361-363.

682. Gordon, Mel. "Mikhail Chekhov's *The Castle Awakens*." *Slavic and East European Performance* 13, no. 2 (Summer 1993): 45-47.

683. Greer, Herb. "Fearful Eye on the West: A Russian Views the McCarthy Years." *World & I* 8, no. 11 (November 1993): 120-125.

683a. Horton, Andrew, ed. *Inside Soviet Film Satire: Laughter with a Lash*. Contributions by Kirill Razlogov, Andrew Horton, Valentin Tolstykh, Kevin Moss, Denise J. Youngblood, Peter Christensen, Michael Brashinsky, Vlada Petric, Maya Turovskaya, Andrew Andreyev, Moira Ratchford, Olga Reizen, Vida T. Johnson, Julie Christensen, Greta N. Slobin, Svetlana Boym, and Andrei Codrescu. Cambridge Studies in Film. Cambridge; New York, NY: Cambridge University Press, 1993. xi, 171 pp. [Papers from the Conference on the Spirit of Satire in Soviet Cinema held at Loyola University, New Orleans, in October 1990. Contents: Kirill Razlogov, "Foreword: If life itself is a satire...," p. vii; Andrew Horton, "Introduction: Carnival versus lashing laughter in Soviet cinema," pp. 1-13. Pt. 1. The long view: Soviet satire in context. Valentin Tolstykh, trans. from the Russian by Andrew Andreyev, "Soviet film satire yesterday and today," pp. 17-19; Kevin Moss, "A Russian Munchausen: Aesopian translation," pp. 20-35; Denise J. Youngblood, " 'We don't know what to laugh at': Comedy and satire in Soviet cinema (from *The Miracle Worker* to *St. Jorgen's Feast Day)*," pp. 36-47; Peter Christensen, "An ambivalent NEP satire of bourgeois aspirations: *The Kiss* of Mary Pickford," pp. 48-57; Michael Brashinsky, "Closely watched drains: Notes by a dilettante on the Soviet absurdist film," pp. 58-62. Pt. 2. Middle-distance shots: The individual satire considered. Vlada Petric, "A subtextual reading of Kuleshov's satire *The Extraordinary Adventures of Mr. West in the Land of the Bolsheviks* (1924)," pp. 65-74; Maya Turovskaya, trans.

from the Russian by Andrew Andreyev, "The strange case of the making of *Volga, Volga*," pp. 75-82; Moira Ratchford, "*Circus* of 1936: Ideology and entertainment under the big top," pp. 83-93; Olga Reizen, "Black humor in Soviet cinema," pp. 94-97; Vida T. Johnson, "Laughter beyond the mirror: Humor and satire in the cinema of Andrei Tarkovsky," pp. 98-104; Julie Christensen, "The films of Eldar Shengelaya: From subtle humor to biting satire," pp. 105-113. Pt. 3. Close-ups: Glasnost and Soviet satire. Greta N. Slobin, "A forgotten flute and remembered popular tradition," pp. 117-124; Svetlana Boym, "Perestroika of kitsch: Sergei Soloviev's *Black Rose, Red Rose*," pp. 125-137; Andrew Horton, "Carnivals bright, dark, and grotesque in the glasnost satires of Mamin, Mustafayev, and Shakhnazarov," pp. 138-148; Andrei Codrescu, "Quick takes on Yuri Mamin's *Fountain* from the perspective of a Romanian," pp. 149-153; Andrew Horton, "One should begin with zero': A discussion with satiric filmmaker Yuri Mamin," pp. 154-156; "Filmography," pp. 157-164.]

684. House, Jane. "Reviews: Chekhov at the Festival du Théâtre des Amériques, Montreal, May/June 1993." *Slavic and East European Performance* 13, no. 3 (Fall 1993): 54-57. [Review of Théâtre de l'Opsis' adapation of "Platonov" (Comédie russe) and Theatre of Moscow's adaptation of "Three Sisters."]

685. Hughes, R. I. G. "Tolstoy, Stanislavski, and the Art of Acting." *Journal of Aesthetics and Art Criticism* 51, no. 1 (Winter 1993): 39-48.

686. Ignatieva, Maria, and Joseph Brandesky. "The Wheel of Misfortune: *Intrigue and Love* at the Bolshoi Dramatic Theatre, St. Petersburg." *Slavic and East European Performance* 13, no. 3 (Fall 1993): 37-39.

687. Law, Alma. "Yuri Lyubimov Directs in Helsinki." *Slavic and East European Performance* 13, no. 1 (Spring 1993): 13-27.

688. Mally, Lynn. "Autonomous Theater and the Origins of Socialist Realism: The 1932 Olympiad of Autonomous Art." *Russian Review* 52, no. 2 (April 1993): 198-212.

689. Menashe, Louis. "Festivals: Documentary Films in St. Petersburg." *Soviet and Post-Soviet Review* 20, no. 2-3 (1993): 241-244. [Account of the St. Petersburg International Documentary Film Festival in February 1993.]

690. Parlakian, Nishan. "Armenian/American (AR/ AM) Playwriting." *Ararat* 34, no. 4 (no. 136) (Autumn 1993): 2-3.

691. ———. "Theatre in Armenia: An Update." *Ararat* 34, no. 3 (no. 135) (Summer 1993): 48-51.

692. Schuler, Catherine. "Female Theatrical Entrepreneurs in the Silver Age: A Prerevolutionary Revolution." *Theatre History Studies* 13 (1993): 79-94. [Discusses the efforts of Komissarzhevskaya (The Dramaticheski Theatre), Brenko (The Pushkin Theatre) and other Russian actresses to create and manage new theaters.]

693. Shlapentokh, Dmitry, and Vladimir Shlapentokh. *Soviet Cinematography, 1918-1991: Ideological Conflict and Social Reality*. Communication and Social Order. New York: A. de Gruyter, 1993. xv, 278 pp. [Filmography: pp. 257-266. Contents: Pt. I. Theoretical and Historical Introduction. 1. Social Reality and Ideology in Interaction. 2. State, Ideology, and Film in Soviet History — Pt. II. Soviet Movies in the Revolutionary Period (1918-1928): Cordial Acceptance of Official Ideology. 3. Soviet Movies in the Aftermath of the October Revolution: The Civil War. 4. The Partial Restoration of Capitalism (1921-1929) — Pt. III. Movies During Stalin's Time: Total Submission to the Official Ideology. 5. Stalin and Soviet Movies. 6. Industrialization and Collectivization (1929-1934). 7. Time of Mass Terror (1934-1941). 8. The Great Patriotic War. 9. Stalin's Postwar Years — Pt. IV. The Game with Official Ideology. 10. Movies during the First Thaw (1954-1968): Timid Challenges to Official Ideology. 11. Movies in the Period of Conservatism (1968-1985): The Use of Diversified Official Ideology for Social Critique — Pt. V. Soviet Cinematographers Reject Official Ideology: Cinema during the Last Years of the Soviet Empire. The First Years of Freedom: The Beginning of the Offensive against Official Ideology. 13. Movie Heroes 1986-1989. 14. Total Freedom from Totalitarianism and Its Ideology. 15. Russian Movies After the Fall of the Empire.]

694. Shvydkoi, Mikhail. "Nostalgia for Soviet Theatre—Is There Hope for the Future?" *Performing Arts Journal* 15, no. 1 (no. 43) (January 1993): 111-119. Translated by Elise Thoran.

695. Stanislavsky, Konstantin. "From *The Actor: Work on Oneself*." *TDR: The Drama Review* 37, no. 1 (Spring 1993): 38-42. Translated by Jean Benedetti.

696. Stephens, Jeff. [Performance Review]. *Theatre Journal* 45, no. 2 (May 1993): 250-251. [Review of director Otar Djangisherashvili's production of "The Suicide" by Nikolai Erdman, performed at the Cleveland Play House by the New Experimental Theater of Volgograd, Russia, and sponsored by the Cleveland Play House's International Theatre Exchange, June 13-21, 1992.]

697. Swain, Elizabeth. "*Ivanov and Others*." *Slavic and East European Performance* 13, no. 3 (Fall 1993): 44-48. [Review of a Moscow Youth Theatre production of an adaptation of Chekhov's works, directed by Yanovskaya.]

698. Tarkovsky, Andrey. *Time within Time: The Diaries, 1970-1986*. Translated from the Russian by Kitty Hunter-Blair. London; New York: Verso, 1993, c1991. viii, 392 pp. [Diary of a Russian film director.]

699. Taubman, Jane. "The Cinema of Kira Muratova." *Russian Review* 52, no. 3 (July 1993): 367-381.

700. Trauth, Suzanne. "Theatre-On-Podol: Kiev, Ukraine Repertoire and Performance Style." *Slavic and East European Performance* 13, no. 1 (Spring 1993): 40-43.

701. Vlasov, Slava, and Serge Roshal. "Let's Taking a Meeting." *Harper's* 287, no. 1719 (August 1993): 20-21. [Excerpt from a proposal for a lesbian film sent to Western

film companies by a Russian production company.]

702. Woolgar, Claudia. "St. Petersburg: A Tale of Two Theaters." *World & I* 8, no. 6 (June 1993): 120-125.

703. ———. "Staged Anarchy: Moscow Theater Mirrors the Chaos." *World & I* 8, no. 10 (October 1993): 107-111.

Eastern Europe

704. Aronson, Arnold. "The 1991 Prague Quadrennial." *TDR: The Drama Review* 37, no. 1 (Spring 1993): 61-73.

705. Bassin, Joel. "Reviews: Mrozek's *Tango* by the Independent Theatre Co." *Slavic and East European Performance* 13, no. 2 (Summer 1993): 48-50.

706. Biro, Yvette. "Within and Without the Walls: Film in Eastern Europe." *Dissent* 40, no. 1 (Winter 1993): 105-109. Translated from the French by John Savage.

707. Bischoff, Peter. "*Limonádovy Joe*; or, The Western in Czechoslovakia." *Journal of Popular Culture* 27, no. 1 (Summer 1993): 23-27.

708. Braun, Kazimierz. "The Underground Theater in Poland under Martial Law during the Last Years of Communism (1981-1989)." *Polish Review* 38, no. 2 (1993): 159-186.

709. Bren, Paulina. "Privatizing Czechoslovakia's Barrandov Film Studios." *RFE/RL Research Report* 2, no. 2 (January 8, 1993): 54-57.

710. Burian, J. M. "Grossman, Machácek, Schorm: The Loss of Three Major Czech Directors of the Late Twentieth Century." *Slavic and East European Performance* 13, no. 3 (Fall 1993): 27-30.

711. Callaghan, David. "Reviews: Stanislaw Ignacy Witkiewicz's *The Water Hen* Performed at the Playground Theatre." *Slavic and East European Performance* 13, no. 1 (Spring 1993): 53-54. [Review of production.]

712. Cornell, Katharine F. "After the Wall: Eastern European Cinema Since 1989." *Cineaste* 19, no. 4 (1993): 43-46.

713. ———. "Paradise Redrawn: Film and Transition in Eastern Europe." *World Policy Journal* 10, no. 2 (Summer 1993): 57-65.

714. Dowell, Pat. "An Interview with Andrzej Wajda." *Cineaste* 19, no. 4 (1993): 51-53.

715. Feidler, Manfred. "Theatre in Berlin Before and After Unification." *Theatre Design & Technology* 29, no. 3 (Summer 1993): 31-34. ["A German theatre technician talks of life before and after the fall of the Wall."]

716. Findlay, Robert. "Grotowski at Fifty-Nine: The Ten-Day Conference at Irvine (August 1992) and the Six-Day Mini-Course at NYU (February 1993)." *Slavic and East European Performance* 13, no. 2 (Summer 1993): 23-30.

717. Gerould, Daniel. "Zygmunt Hübner's Letter to Václav Havel." *Slavic and East European Performance* 13, no. 1 (Spring 1993): 48-49.

717a. Goldfarb, David A. "Reviews: Cinema in Transition: Recent Films from East and Central Europe: Symposium." *Slavic and East European Performance* 13, no. 2 (Summer 1993): 51-54. [Symposium at the New School for Social Research in New York, part of the "Cinema in Transition: Recent Films from East and Central Europe" festival, April 17-28, 1993.]

718. Greer, Herb. "After the Velvet Revolution." *World & I* 8, no. 9 (September 1993): 132-137.

719. Grossman, Elwira M. "Jerzy Grzegorzewski: The Power of Images." *Slavic and East European Performance* 13, no. 3 (Fall 1993): 31-36.

720. Gyorgyey, Clara, ed. and trans. *A Mirror to the Cage: Three Contemporary Hungarian Plays.* Introduction by Ervin C. Brody. Plays by Istvan Orkeny, Gyorgy Spiro, and Mihaly Kornis. Fayetteville: University of Arkansas Press, c1993. ix, 245 pp. [Translated from the Hungarian. Contents: Istvan Orkeny, "Stevie in the Bloodbath: A Grotesque Play in Two Parts"; Gyorgy Spiro, "The Impostor"; Mihaly Kornis, "Kozma: A Tragedy."]

721. Hennedy, Patrick. "Reviews: Iztok Kovac's Slovenian Performance Art: How I Caught A Falcon." *Slavic and East European Performance* 13, no. 1 (Spring 1993): 55-57. [Review of production.]

722. Horínek, Zdenek. "HaDivadlo: An Author's Workshop." *Czechoslovak and Central European Journal* 11, no. 2 (Winter 1993): 110-115.

723. Horton, Andrew. "The Moving Image in the Post-Yugoslav Republics." *Cineaste* 19, no. 4 (1993): 54-57.

724. House, Jane. "Reviews: *No Conductor* and *In Shadow*." *Slavic and East European Performance* 13, no. 1 (Spring 1993): 50-52. [Review of production; play by Gezá Páskándi, director Pamela Billig.]

725. Kantor, Tadeusz. *A Journey Through Other Spaces: Essays and Manifestos, 1944-1990.* Edited and translated by Michal Kobialka. Berkeley, CA: University of California Press, 1993. xxi, 430 pp. [Contents: Pt. I. Further on, Nothing... Chronology. A. A Selection of Tadeusz Kantor's Essays and Manifestos. My Work—My Journey (Excerpts) (1988). Credo (1942-44). The Autonomous Theatre (1956/63). The Informel Theatre (1961). The Informel Theatre: Definitions (Undated). The Zero Theatre (1963). Annexed Reality (1963). Emballages (1957-65). Theatre Happening (1967). The Impossible Theatre (1969-73). The Theatre of Death (1975). Reality of the Lowest Rank (1980). The Work of Art and the Process (1976). The Situation of an Artist (1977). Where Are the Snows of Yesteryear? (Cricotage) (1978). New Theatrical S p a c e . Where F i c t i o n Appears (1980). The Room. Maybe a New Phase (1980). The Infamous Transition from the World of the Dead into the World of the Living: Fiction and Reality (1980). Prison (1985). Reflection (1985). Memory (1988). The Real "I" (1988). To Save from Oblivion (1988). Silent Night (Cricotage) (1990). A Painting (1990). From the Beginning, in My Credo Was... (1990). B. The Milano Lessons (1986). Lesson 1. Lesson 2. Lesson 3. Lesson 4. Lesson 5. Lesson 6. Lesson 7. Lessons 8, 9, 10, and 11. Lesson 12 — Pt. 2. The Quest for the Self/Other: A Critical Study of Tadeusz Kantor's Theatre. The Quest for the Self: Thresholds and Transformations. The Quest for the Other: Space/Memory. Found Reality — Writings by Tadeusz Kantor — Selected Writings About Tadeusz Kantor, Cricot 2 Theatre, and Their Productions.]

726. Kaufmann, Stanley. "On Films: Of Human Bondage." *New Republic* 208, no. 6 (February 8, 1993): 24-25. [Film review of Lucian Pintile's *The Oak*, a "Romanian black comedy."]

727. Koch, Gertrud. "On the Disappearance of the Dead Among the Living—The Holocaust and the Confusion of Identities in the Films of Konrad Wolf." *New German Critique*, no. 60 (Fall 1993): 57-75. Translated by Jeremy Gaines.

728. Kornatowska, Maria. "Polish Cinema." *Cineaste* 19, no. 4 (1993): 47-50.

729. Kott, Jan. "Antigone Hangs Herself in Tompkins Square Park." *Slavic and East European Performance* 13, no. 1 (Spring 1993): 44-47. Translated by Jadwiga Kosicka.

730. Law, Alma. "Grotowski Visits Moscow." *Slavic and East European Performance* 13, no. 2 (Summer 1993): 35-44. [Introduction, p. 35; photographs, pp. 35-44.]

731. Liehm, Antonin J. "Czech and Slovak Cinema." *Cineaste* 19, no. 4 (1993): 62.

732. Petrut, Tudor. "An Overview of the Romanian Theatre." *Slavic and East European Performance* 13, no. 2 (Summer 1993): 31-34.

733. Portuges, Catherine. *Screen Memories: The Hungarian Cinema of Marta Meszaros.* Women Artists in Film. Bloomington, IL: Indiana University Press, 1993. ix, 190 pp. [Filmography: pp. [171]-175.] REV: Marek Haltof, *Canadian Slavonic Papers* 35, nos. 3-4 (September-December 1993): 424-425. Kevin Moss, *Slavic Review* 52, no. 4 (Winter 1993): 862-863.

734. Quart, Barbara. "A Few Short Takes on Eastern European Film." *Cineaste* 19, no. 4 (1993): 63-64.

735. ———. "Three Central European Women Directors Revisited." *Cineaste* 19, no. 4 (1993): 58-61.

736. Robinson, Homer. "Bulgarian Cinema: Freedom Gained but Funding Lost." *RFE/RL Research Report* 2, no. 2 (January 8, 1993): 58-61.

737. Rouse, John. "Heine Müller and the Politics of Memory." *Theatre Journal* 45, no. 1 (March 1993): 65-74.

738. Schölling, Traute. "On with the Show? The Transition to Post-Socialist Theater in Eastern Germany." *Theatre Journal* 45, no. 1 (March 1993): 21-34. Translated by Marc Silberman.

739. Silberman, Marc. "A Postmodernized Brecht?" *Theatre Journal* 45, no. 1 (March 1993): 1-20.

740. Sohlich, Wolfgang. "The Dialectic of Mimesis and Representation in Brecht's *Life of Galileo.*" *Theatre Journal* 45, no. 1 (March 1993): 49-64.

741. Sontag, Susan. "Godot Comes to Sarajevo." *New York Review of Books* 40, no. 17 (October 21, 1993): 52-59.

742. Stein, Elliot. "CineMythology." *World & I* 8, no. 8 (August 1993): 148-153. [On Greek cinema.]

743. Stone, Judy. "Jurai Jakubisko, A Slovak Filmmaker." *Cross Currents: A Yearbook of Central European Culture*, no. 12 (1993): 36-41.

744. Svoboda, Josef. *The Secret of Theatrical Space: The Memoirs of Josef Svoboda.* Edied and translated by J. M. Burian. New York, NY: Applause Theatre Books, c1993. 144 pp. [Translation of *Tajemstvi divadelniho prostoru.*] REV: W. Joseph Stell, *TD&T: Theatre Design & Technology* 29, no. 5 (Fall 1993): 54.

745. Tesich, Nadja. "Belgrade: Theater of War." *Nation* 256, no. 5 (February 8, 1993): 174-176.

746. Troy, Shari. "Reviews: *Pinokio*, Theatre Drak (Czechoslovakia) at the Joseph Papp Public Theatre, New York." *Slavic and East European Performance* 13, no. 3 (Fall 1993): 51-53. [Review of production at the First New York International Festival of Puppet Theatre. Play directed by Josef Krofta. A version of this review was published in the American Alliance for Theatre and Education's *Youth Journal* 7 (1993).]

747. Tyszka, Juliusz. "Polish Theatre." *TDR: The Drama Review* 37, no. 1 (Spring 1993): 18. [Letter to the editor concerning the article by Halina Filipowicz, "Theatre after Solidarity," 36, no. 1 (Spring 1992).]

748. Unruh, Delbert. "The Theatre is a Dream: The Paintings of Jan Vancura." *Theatre Design & Technology* 29, no. 1 (Winter 1993): 17-25.

749. Weber, Carl. "Crossing the Footbridge Again, Or: A Semi-Sentimental Journey." *Theatre Journal* 45, no. 1 (March 1993): 75-89.

750. Woolgar, Claudia. "Poland's Theatrical Vision." *World & I* 8, no. 3 (March 1993): 122-127.

751. ———. "Romania Looks Back in Anger." *World & I* 8, no. 2 (February 1993): 166-171.

4 Economics and Foreign Trade

■ General

753. Abrams, Richard K., and Hernan Cortes-Douglas. *Introduction of a New National Currency: Policy, Institutional, and Technical Issues.* IMF Working Paper, WP/93/49. [Washington, DC]: International Monetary Fund, c1993. iii, 33 pp.

754. Adam, Jan. *Planning and Market in Soviet and East European Thought, 1960s-1992.* New York, NY: St. Martin's Press, 1993. xviii, 320 pp.

755. Adams, Walter, and James W. Brock. *Adam Smith Goes to Moscow: A Dialogue on Radical Reform.* Princeton, NJ: Princeton University Press, c1993. xxiii, 156 pp. REV: Alice H. G. Phillips, *Current History* 92, no. 576 (October 1993): 347. Leonard Solomon Silk, *New Leader* 76, no. 12 (October 4-18, 1993): 17-18. Martin C. Spechler, *Comparative Economic Studies* 35, no. 3 (Fall 1993): 68-70.

756. Althaus, Rickert R., and Dean L. Yarwood. "Policy/Program Interactions: Organizational Domain Overlap with Cooperative Outcomes: The Departments of Agriculture and State and International Agricultural Policy During the Carter Administration." *Public Adminstration Review* 53, no. 4 (July-August 1993): 357-367. [Discusses the PL 480 allocations to Egypt, Commodity Credit Corporation export credits to Poland, and the Soviet grain embargo.]

757. Artisien, Patrick, Matija Rojec, and Marjan Svetlicic, eds. *Foreign Investment in Central and Eastern Europe.* Foreword by Peter J. Buckley. Contributions by Patrick Artisien, Matija Rojec, Marjan Svetlicic, John H. Dunning, Carl H. McMillan, Patrick Gutman, Yuri Adjubei, David G. Young, Zbigniew Bochniarz, Wladyslaw Jermakowicz, Cecelia Drazek, John Pinder, and William Crisp. New York, NY: St. Martin's Press, 1993. xiv, 206 pp. [Contents: Peter J. Buckley, "Foreword," pp. xiii-xiv. Pt. I. Contextual and Thematic Aspects; Marjan Svetlicic, Patrick Artisien, and Matija Rojec, "Foreign Direct Investment in Central and Eastern Europe: An Overview," pp. 3-15; John H. Dunning, "The Prospects for Foreign Direct Investment in Eastern Europe," pp. 16-33; Patrick Artisien and Carl H. McMillan, "Some Contextual and Thematic Aspects of East-West Industrial Cooperation, with Special Reference to Yugoslav Multinationals," pp. 34-53; Patrick Gutman, "Joint Ventures in Eastern Europe and the Dynamics of Reciprocal Flows in East-West Direct Investments: Some New Perspectives," pp. 54-81; Part II. Empirical Country Studies; Yuri Adjubei, "Foreign Investment in the Commonwealth of Independent States: Growth, Operations and Problems," pp. 85-108; David G. Young, "Foreign Direct Investment in Hungary," pp. 109-122; Zbigniew Bochniarz and Wladyslaw Jermakowicz, "Foreign Direct Investment in Poland: 1986-90," pp. 123-132; Matija Rojec, "Foreign Direct Investment in the Newly-Independent Republic of Slovenia: Experiences and Policy Options," pp. 133-148; Wladyslaw Jermakowicz and Cecelia Drazek, "Joint Venture Laws in Eastern Europe: A Comparative Assessment," pp. 149-168. Pt. III. Current and Future Trends; John Pinder, "The European Community and Investment in Central and Eastern Europe," pp. 171-191; William Crisp, "Appendix: The Practicalities of Establishing a Joint Venture in the Commonwealth of Independent States," pp. 192-194.]

758. Baldassarri, Mario, Luigi Paganetto, and Edmund S. Phelps, eds. *Privatization Processes in Eastern Europe: Theoretical Foundations and Empirical Results.* Contributions by Lamberto Dini, Kenneth J. Arrow, Edmund S. Phelps, Carlo Boffito, Roman Frydman, Andrzej Rapaczynski, Rosario Bonavoglia, John Vickers, Luigi Paganetto, Pasquale Lucio Scandizzo, Joseph E. Stiglitz, Bruno Jossa, Dominick Salvatore, Martin L. Weitzman, and Edmund S. Phelps. Central Issues in Contemporary Economic Theory and Policy. New York, NY: St. Martin's Press in association with Rivista di Politica Economica, SIPI, Rome and CEIS, University "Tor Vergata", Rome, 1993. 281 pp. [Translation of: *Privatizzazioni nell'Est europeo.* Contents: Lamberto Dini, "Privatization processes in Eastern Europe: theoretical foundations and empirical results"; Kenneth J. Arrow and Edmund S. Phelps, "Proposed reforms of the economic system of information and decision in the USSR: commentary and advice"; Carlo Boffito, "Privatization in Central Europe and the Soviet Union"; Roman Frydman and Andrzej Rapaczynski, "Evolution and design in the East European transition"; Rosario Bonavoglia, "Evolution and design in Eastern European transition: comment"; John Vickers, "Privatization and the risk of expropriation"; Luigi Paganetto and Pasquale Lucio Scandizzo, "Privatization and competitive behavior: endogenous objectives, efficiency and growth"; Joseph E. Stiglitz, "Some theoretical aspects of the privatization: applications to Eastern Europe"; Bruno Jossa, "Is there an option to the denationalization of Eastern European enterprises?"; Dominick Salvatore, "Foreign trade, foreign direct investments and privatization in Eastern Europe"; Martin L. Weitzman, "How not to privatize"; Edmund S. Phelps, "Concluding remarks."]

759. Belous, Richard S., and Sheila M. Cavanagh, eds. *The Former Soviet Republics and Eastern Europe: Struggling for Solutions.* Contributions by Richard S. Belous, Marshall I. Goldman, Richard Sterling Surrey, Alexander C. Tomlinson, and Thibaut de Saint-Phalle. Walter Sterling Surrey Memorial Series. NPA Report, 269. Washington, DC: National Planning Association, c1993. vii, 40 pp. [Contents: Richard S. Belous, "From Communism to Capitalism: Struggling for Solutions," pp. 1-6; Marshall I. Goldman, "Why Economic Reforms in the Former Soviet

Republics Have Not Worked Thus Far," pp. 7-16; Richard Sterling Surrey, "The Czech Republic's 'Velvet' Transition," pp. 17-23; Alexander C. Tomlinson, "Hungary's Ongoing Transition to a Free Market Economy," pp. 24-30; Thibaut de Saint-Phalle, "Private Sector Technical Assistance in the Former Soviet Republics: The Experience of One American Organization," pp. 31-35.]

760. Berkowitz, Daniel. "A Simple Model of an Oligopolistic Parallel Market." *Journal of Comparative Economics* 17, no. 1 (March 1993): 92-112.

761. Blackshaw, Philip W., and Louis S. Thompson. *Railway Reform in the Central and Eastern European (CEE) Economies.* Policy Research Working Papers, WPS 1137. [Washington, DC]: World Bank, [1993]. 18 pp. [Prepared by the Transport, Water, and Urban Development Dept. and the Technical Dept., Europe and Central Asia Regional Office of the World Bank.]

762. Blanchard, Olivier et al. *Post-Communist Reform: Pain and Progress.* Cambridge, MA: MIT Press, c1993. viii, 183 pp. [Contents: 1. Overview; 2. Stabilization versus Reform? Russia's First Year; 3. The Politics of Russian Privatization; 4. Payments Arrangements among the Republics; 5. The Progress of Restructuring in Poland; Statistical Appendix on Russia.]

763. Blejer, Mario I., Guillermo A. Calvo, Fabrizio Coricelli, and Alan H. Gelb, ed. *Eastern Europe in Transition: From Recession to Growth? Proceedings of a Conference on the Macroeconomic Aspects of Adjustment, Co-sponsored by the International Monetary Fund and the World Bank.* Contributions by Mario Blejer, Alan H. Gelb, Richard Portes, Michael Bruno, Andrew Berg, Dani Rodrik, Gábor Oblath, Guillermo A. Calvo, Fabrizio Coricelli, Mark Gertler, Josef Tosovsky, Saul Estrin, Mark E. Schaffer, Inderjit Singh, E. R. Borensztein, D. G. Demekas, J. D. Ostry, Simon Commander, Fabrizio Coricelli, Roman Frydman, Gyorgy Suranyi, and Malcolm Knight. World Bank Discussion Papers, 196. Washington, DC: World Bank, 1993. vi, 210 pp. [Contents: Mario I. Blejer and Alan H. Gelb, "The contraction of Eastern Europe's economies: introduction to the conference," pp. 1-7; Richard Portes, "Comment," pp. 8-11; Michael Bruno, "Stabilization and reform in Eastern Europe: preliminary evaluation," pp. 12-38; Andrew Berg, "Measurement and mismeasurement of economic activity during transition to the market," pp. 39-63; Dani Rodrik, "Making sense of the Soviet trade shock in Eastern Europe: a framework and some estimates," pp. 64-85; Gábor Oblath, "Comment," pp. 86-89; Dani Rodrik, "Rejoinder to Comment," pp. 90-91; Guillermo A. Calvo and Fabrizio Coricelli, "Output collapse in Eastern Europe: the role of credit," pp. 92-105; Mark Gertler, "Comment," pp. 106-107; Josef Tosovsky, "Comment," pp. 108-110; Saul Estrin, Mark E. Schaffer and Inderjit Singh, "Enterprise adjustment in transition economies: Czechoslovakia, Hungary, and Poland," pp. 111-136; E.R. Borensztein, D.G. Demekas and J. D. Ostry, "Output decline in the aftermath of reform: the cases of Bulgaria, Czechoslovakia, and Romania," pp. 137-167; Simon Commander and Fabrizio Coricelli, "Output decline in Hungary and Poland in 1990/

1991: structural change and aggregate shocks," pp. 168-198; Roman Frydman, "Comment," pp. 199-202; Gyorgy Suranyi, "Comment," pp. 203-205; Malcolm Knight, "Rapporteur's comments," pp. 206-210.]

764. Bollen, Kenneth A., and Stephen J. Appold. "National Industrial Structure and the Global System." *American Sociological Review* 58, no. 2 (April 1993): 283-301.

765. Braverman, Avishay, Karen M. Brooks, and Csaba Csaki, eds. *The Agricultural Transition in Central and Eastern Europe and the Former U.S.S.R.* Contributions by D. Gale Johnson, Joseph E. Stiglitz, G. Edward Schuh, Stanley R. Johnson, Stefan Tangermann, Andras Inotai, Karen M. Brooks, Michael Marrese, Charles W. Calomiris, Wlodzimierz Rembisz, Dariusz K. Rosati, Marton Tardos, Csaba Csaki, Gyula Varga, Balazs Szelenyi, Ivan Szelenyi, Vladimir Stipetic, Karl-Eugen Wädekin, Viktor Nazarenko, Yoav Kislev, Justin Yifu Lin, Richard Burcroff II, and Gerson Feder. A World Bank Symposium. Washington, DC: World Bank, 1993. ix, 314 pp. [Contents: Part I. Background and Concepts. D. Gale Johnson, "Historical Experience of Eastern and Central European and Soviet Agriculture," pp. 11-26; Joseph E. Stiglitz, "Incentives, Organizational Structures, and Contractural Choice in the Reform of Socialist Agriculture," pp. 27-46. Part II. The International Environnment. G. Edward Schuh, "The Role of Government in Agriculture in Developed Market Economies," pp. 49-64; Stanley R. Johnson, "Trends and Developments in Agricultural Commodity Markets," pp. 65-91; Stefan Tangermann, "United Western Europe and the Agriculture of Central and Eastern Europe and the USSR," pp. 92-112; Andras Inotai, "The Central and Eastern European and Soviet Intra-Regional Agricultural Market," pp. 113-122. Part III. The Policy Framework: Ownership, Pricing, and Finance. Karen M. Brooks, "Property Rights in Land," pp. 125-136; Michael Marrese, "Agricultural Price Reform: Effect on Real Incomes and the Inflationary Process," pp. 137-156; Charles W. Calomiris, "Agricultural Capital Markets," pp. 157-181. Part IV. Regional Case Studies. Wlodzimierz Rembisz and Dariusz K. Rosati, "Poland," pp. 184-198; Marton Tardos, "Hungary: A Brief Review of the Inherited Agricultural System and Issues of the Transition," pp. 199-203; Csaba Csaki and Gyula Varga, "Economic Dimensions," pp. 204-218; Balazs Szelenyi and Ivan Szelenyi, "The Social Effects of Agrarian Reform," pp. 219-229; Vladimir Stipetic, "Yugoslavia," pp. 230-243; Karl-Eugen Wädekin, "Bulgaria, Czechoslovakia, and the GDR," pp. 244-264; Viktor Nazarenko, "The USSR," pp. 265-275. Part V. Relevant Experiences in Other Regions. Yoav Kislev, "Structure and Reform of Agriculture in Israel," pp. 278-291; Justin Yifu Lin, Richard Burcroff II, and Gerson Feder, "Agricultural Reform in a Socialist Economy: The Experience of China," pp. 292-300.] REV: Daniel Brower, *Agricultural History* 67, no. 3 (Summer 1993): 105-106.

766. Buchanan, James M. "Asymmetrical Reciprocity in Market Exchange: Implications for Economies in Transition." *Social Philosophy & Policy* 10, no. 2 (Summer 1993): 51-64. [Essay builds on arguments in *Tacit Presup-

positions of Political Economy: Implications for Societies in Transition (Fairfax, VA: George Mason University, Center for the Study of Public Choice, 1991).]

767. "Building Business Ties with Russia/NIS/ Eastern Europe." *Business America* 114, no. 6 (March 22, 1993): 2-7.

768. Burkett, Paul, and Richard Lotspeich. "Financial Liberalization, Development, and Marketization: A Review of McKinnon's *The Order of Economic Liberalization: Financial Control in the Transition to a Market Economy* (1991)." *Comparative Economic Studies* 35, no. 1 (Spring 1993): 59-84. [Review article on Ronald I. McKinnon, *The Order of Economic Liberalization: Financial Control in the Transition to a Market Economy* (Baltimore, MD: 1991).]

769. Carter, F. W., and David Turnock, eds. *Environmental Problems in Eastern Europe.* Contributions by F. W. Carter, D. Turnock, Derek R. Hall, Don Hinrichsen, Istvan Láng, and Barbara Jancar-Webster. Routledge Natural Environment: Problems and Management Series. London; New York: Routledge, 1993. xiv, 249 pp. [Contents: Francis W. Carter and David Turnock, "Introduction," pp. 1-6; Derek R. Hall, "Albania," pp. 7-37; Francis W. Carter, "Bulgaria," pp. 38-62; Francis W. Carter, "Czechoslovakia," pp. 63-88; Don Hinrichsen and Istvan Láng, "Hungary," pp. 89-106; Francis W. Carter, "Poland," pp. 107-134; David Turnock, "Romania," pp. 135-163; Barbara Jancar-Webster, "Former Yugoslavia," pp. 164-187; Francis W. Carter and David Turnock, "Problems of the Pollution Scenario," pp. 188-219; "Bibliography," pp. 220-243.]

770. Crawford, Beverly. *Markets, States and Democracy: A Framework for Analysis of the Political Economy of Post-Communist Transformation.* Working Paper (University of California, Berkeley. Center for German and European Studies), 2.6. Berkeley, CA: Center for German and European Studies, University of California, [1993]. 47 pp.

771. De Weydenthal, Jan B. "Troubled Polish-Russian Economic Relations." *RFE/RL Research Report* 2, no. 27 (July 2, 1993): 31-33.

772. Dorn, James A. "Introduction: Monetary Reform in Ex-Communist Countries." *Cato Journal* 12, no. 3 (Winter 1993): 509-525. [Part of special issue devoted to "Monetary Reform in Ex-Communist Countries."]

773. Dowd, Kevin. "Money and the Market: What Role for Government?" *Cato Journal* 12, no. 3 (Winter 1993): 557-576. [Part of special issue devoted to "Monetary Reform in Ex-Communist Countries."]

774. Dyker, David A. "Free Trade and Fair Trade with Eastern Europe." *RFE/RL Research Report* 2, no. 26 (June 25, 1993): 39-42.

775. Earle, John S., Roman Frydman, and Andrzej Rapaczynski, eds. *Privatization in the Transition to a Market Economy: Studies of Preconditions and Policies in Eastern Europe.* Contributions by László Szakadát, Michal Mejstrik, Jiří Hlávacek, Jan Szomburg, Éva Voszka, László Urbán, Jan Mladek, John S. Earle, Dana Sapatoru, Piotr Tamowicz, Kálmán Mészáros, and Tivadár Faur. New York, NY: St. Martin's Press, 1993. vi, 221 pp. [Published in association with the Central European University. Contents: John S. Earle, Roman Frydman, and Andrzej Rapaczynski, "Introduction," pp. 1-13. Part I: Preconditions. László Szakadát, "Property rights in a socialist economy: the case of Hungary," pp. 17-45; Michal Mejstrik and Jiří Hlávacek, "Preconditions for privatization in Czechoslovakia in 1990-92," pp. 46-74; Jan Szomburg, "The decision-making structure of Polish privatization," pp. 75-85. Part II: Privatization plans, policies, and results. Éva Voszka, "Spontaneous privatization in Hungary," pp. 89-107; László Urbán, "The role and impact of the legislature in Hungary's privatization," pp. 108-120; Jan Mladek, "The different paths of privatization: Czechoslovakia, 1990-?" pp. 121-146; John S. Earle and Dana Sapatoru, "Privatization in a hypercentralized economy: the case of Romania," pp. 147-170; Piotr Tamowicz, "Small privatization in Poland: an inside view," pp. 171-183. Part III: The stock market and foreign capital: some evidence from Hungary. Kálmán Mészáros, "Evolution of the Hungarian capital market: the Budapest Stock Exchange," pp. 187-202; Tivadár Faur, "Foreign capital in Hungary's privatization," pp. 203-214.]

776. "East/West aerospace ventures on the rise." *Aviation Week & Space Technology* 139, no. 8 (August 23, 1993): 51. [Includes table of international joint ventures.]

777. Ellman, Michael, Egor T. Gaidar, and Grzegorz W. Kolodko. *Economic Transition in Eastern Europe.* Edited by P. H. Admiraal. De Vries Lectures in Economics. Oxford, UK; Cambridge, MA: Blackwell, 1993. ix, 99 pp. [Collection of essays from the F. de Vries seminar held at the Erasmus University in the autumn of 1991. Contents: P. H. Admiraal, "Introduction," pp. vii-ix; Michael Ellman, "General Aspects of Transition," pp. 1-42; Grzegorz W. Kolodko, "Recession and Growth during Transition to a Market Economy," pp. 43-61; Egor T. Gaidar, "Inflationary Pressures and Economic Reform in the Soviet Union," pp. 63-90.]

778. "Europe." *Business America* 114, no. 8 (April 19, 1993): 14-32. Contributions by Ann Corro, Christine Lucyk, Timothy J. Smith, Pamela Feodoroff, R. Scott Marshall, Jeremy Keller, Pam Green, Lynn Fabrizio, Audrey Zuck, Brian Toohey, and Mark J. Mowrey. [Section includes: Ann Corro, "Greece: Major Infrastructure Projects Boost U.S. Export Potential," p. 25; "Newly Independent States," p. 26; Timothy J. Smith, "Russia: U.S. Companies Will Find Growing Opportunities in '93," pp. 26-27; Christine Lucyk, "Ukraine: Economic Reform Is Key," p. 27; Christine Lucyk, "Belarus: Market to Open Gradually," pp. 27-28; Pamela Feodoroff, "Central Asia: Trade Channels Are Opening," p. 28; R. Scott Marshall, "Caucasus, Moldova: Future Depends on Reform," p. 28; Pam Green, "Baltic States: Do Business Here Now!" p. 29; Jeremy Keller, "Slovenia/Croatia: Don't Overlook Opportunities," p. 29; Lynn Fabrizio, "Bulgaria: Government Sets Sights On

Economic Change," p. 30; Audrey Zuck, "Poland: U.S. Business Expands As Economic Outlook Brightens," p. 30-31; Brian Toohey, "Hungary: Trade Should Expand As Economy Recovers," p. 31; Lynn Fabrizio, "Romania: Improved Business Climate Offered to U.S. Firms," p. 31; Mark J. Mowrey, "Czech Republic/Slovak Republic: Birth of New Nations Should Yield Opportunities," p. 32; Lynn Fabrizio, "Albania: Economic Engine Shifts Into Second Gear," p. 32.]

779. Fender, John, and Derek Laing. "A Macro Model of Queuing and Resale in a Transition Economy." *Comparative Economic Studies* 35, no. 2 (Summer 1993): 1-17.

780. Ferguson, William J. "The Emerging Role of Global Corporations in Restructuring Eastern Europe." *Connecticut Review* 15, no. 2 (Fall 1993): 51-58.

781. Fischer, Stanley. "Socialist Economic Reform: Lessons of the First Three Years." *American Economic Review* 83, no. 2 (May 1993): 390-395.

782. Frenkel, William G. "Eastern European Purchasing Power." *Journal of European Business* 4, no. 6 (July-August 1993): 33-39. [Guidelines for doing business in Eastern Europe and the C.I.S.]

783. Frydman, Roman, Andrzej Rapaczynski, John S. Earle et al. *The Privatization Process in Central Europe: Economic Environment, Legal and Ownership Structure, Institutions for State Regulation, Overview of Privatization Programs, Initial Transformation of Enterprises.* CEU Privatization Reports, v. 1. Budapest; New York: Central European University Press, 1993. xiii, 262 pp. [Contents: Bulgaria; Hungary; Poland; Romania.] REV: Gundar J. King, *Journal of Baltic Studies* 24, no. 4 (Winter 1993): 395-402. Heidi Kroll, *Slavic Review* 52, no. 4 (Winter 1993): 894-895.

784. ———. *The Privatization Process in Russia, Ukraine, and the Baltic States: Economic Environment, Legal and Ownership Structure, Institutions for State Regulation, Overview of Privatization Programs, Initial Transformation of Enterprises.* CEU Privatization Reports, v. 2. Budapest; New York: Central European University Press, 1993. xiii, 276 pp.

785. Goldin, Ian, ed. *Economic Reform, Trade and Agricultural Development.* Includes contributions by Csaba Csaki and Kym Anderson. New York: St. Martin's Press in association with the OECD Development Centre, c1993. xv, 338 pp. [Partial contents: Csaba Csaki, "Agricultural Policy Reforms in Eastern Europe and the Former USSR: A Note on the Implications for International Trade in Agricultural Products," pp. 279-290; Kym Anderson, "Intersectoral Changes in Former Socialist Economies: Distinguishing Initital from Longer-Term Responses," pp. 291-321.]

786. Guerrieri, Paolo. *Trade Integration of Eastern Europe and the Former Soviet Union into the World Economy: A Structuralist Approach.* Working Paper (University of California, Berkeley. Center for German and European Studies), 5.7. Berkeley, CA: Center for German and European Studies, University of California, [1993]. 24 pp. [Conference on Markets, States and Democracy, February 11-13, 1993.]

787. Heath, John, ed. *Revitalizing Socialist Enterprise: A Race Against Time.* Includes contributions by John Heath, Elena Veduta, Konstantin Kagalovsky, Serik A. Akhanov, Pawel Bozyk, Michal Mejstrík, James L. Burger, Robert Bischof, Gottfried von Bismarck, Wendy Carlin, and R. Jayashankar. London; New York: Routledge, 1993. xiv, 263 pp. [Partial contents: John Heath, "Survey of Contributors," pp. 3-36; Elena Veduta, "The Soviet System and Its Aftermath in Russia," pp. 39-54; Konstantin Kagalovsky, "Revitalizing the Russian Economy—Catching Up," pp. 55-75; Serik A. Akhanov, "Reconstruction in Central Asia: Kazakhstan," pp. 76-89; Pawel Bozyk, "Poland—The 'Big Bang'," pp. 90-102; Michal Mejstrík and James L. Burger, "The Czechoslovak 'Large Privatization'," pp. 103-125; Robert Bischof, Gottfried von Bismarck and Wendy Carlin, "East Germany: Scaling Down," pp. 126-143; R. Jayashankar, "Reforming 'Self-Managed' Enterprises in Slovenia," pp. 144-161.]

788. Hesse, Joachim Jens, ed. *Administrative Transformation in Central and Eastern Europe: Towards Public Sector Reform in Post-Communist Societies.* Contributions by Janusz Letowski, Wojciech Taras, Michael Kulesza, Dusan Hendrych, Richard Pomanac, Olga Vidláková, István Balázs, Gábor Szabó, Imre Verebélyi, Michael Lesage, Klaus König, Theo A. J. Toonen, Jon Elster, and Joachim Jens Hesse. Oxford; Cambridge, MA: Blackwell Publishers, 1993. viii, 263 pp. [Contents: Joachim Jens Hesse, "Introduction," pp. v-viii; Janusz Letowski, "Polish public administration between crisis and renewal," pp. 1-11; Wojciech Taras, "Changes in Polish public administration 1989-1992," pp. 13-32; Michael Kulesza, "Options for administrative reform in Poland," pp. 33-40; Dusan Hendrych, "Transforming Czechoslovakian public administration: traditions and new challenges," pp. 41-54; Richard Pomanac, "Administrative modernization in Czechoslovakia between constitutional and economic reform," pp. 55-63; Olga Vidláková, "Options of administrative reform in the Czech Republic," pp. 65-74; István Balázs, "The transformation of Hungarian public administration," pp. 75-88; Gábor Szabó, "Administrative transition in a Post-Communist society: the case of Hungary," pp. 89-103; Imre Verebélyi, "Options for administrative reform in Hungary," pp. 105-120; Michael Lesage, "The crisis of public administration in Russia," pp. 121-133; Klaus König, "Administrative transformation in Eastern Germany," pp. 135-149; Theo A. J. Toonen, "Analysing institutional change and administrative transformation: a comparative view," pp. 151-168; Jon Elster, "Constitution-making in Eastern Europe: rebuilding the boat in the open sea," pp. 109-217; Joachim Jens Hesse, "From transformation to modernization: administrative change in Central and Eastern Europe," pp. 219-257.]

789. Hill, Malcolm R., and Caroline M. Hay. *Trade, Industrial Co-operation and Technology Transfer: Continuity and Change in a New Era of East-West Relations.* Aldershot, Hants; Brookfield, VT: USA Avebury, c1993. viii, 123 pp.

790. Houpt, Amy Elizabeth. "Restructuring." *International Economic Insights* 4, no. 2 (March/April 1993): 34-35. [Review article on articles in *Economic Policy* 15 (October 1992): Patrick Bolton and Gerard Roland, "Privatization in Central and Eastern Europe"; Wendy Carlin and Colin Mayer, "Enterprise Restructuring"; and Claudia Senik-Leygonie and Gordon Hughes, "The Break-Up of the Soviet Union."]

791. International Labour Organisation, and United Nations. Economic Commission for Europe. *Management Development in East-West Joint Ventures: A Guide for Managers in the Economies in Transition.* New York, NY: United Nations, 1993. iv, 128 pp.

792. Islam, Shafiqul, and Michael Mandelbaum, eds. *Making Markets: Economic Transformation in Eastern Europe and the Post-Soviet States.* Contributions by Robert Hormats, Michael Mandelbaum, Richard Portes, Paul Marer, Robert W. Campbell, Jeffrey Sachs, and Shafiqul Islam. New York: Council on Foreign Relations Press, c1993. ix, 238 pp. [Chapters were first presented at a symposium on "Making Markets: Economic Transformation in Eastern Europe and the Post-Soviet Republics," held in New York, February 12-13, 1994, and sponsored by the International Economics and Finance Program and the Project on East-West Relations. Contents: Robert D. Hormats, "Foreword," pp. vii-viii; Michael Mandelbaum, "Introduction," pp. 1-15; Richard Portes, "From Central Planning to a Market Economy," pp. 16-52; Paul Marer, "Economic Transformation in Central and Eastern Europe," pp. 53-98; Robert W. Campbell, "Economic Reform in the USSR and its Successor States," pp. 99-142; Jeffrey Sachs, "Western Financial Assistance and Russia's Reforms," pp. 143-175; "Appendix to Chapter 4: A Note on G-7 Assistance Extended to the Soviet Union," pp. 176-181; Shafiqul Islam, "Conclusion: Problems of Planning a Market Economy," pp. 182-215.] REV: Richard Carson, *International Journal* 49, no. 1 (Winter 1993-1994): 167-168. Gundar J. King, *Journal of Baltic Studies* 24, no. 4 (Winter 1993): 395-402. Peter Rona, *International Economic Insights* 4, no. 4 (July-August 1993): 39-40.

793. Jordan, Jerry L. "Getting the Rules Right." *Cato Journal* 12, no. 3 (Winter 1993): 585-591. [Comment on Kevin Dowd, "Money and the Market: What Role for Government?" pp. 557-576. Part of special issue devoted to "Monetary Reform in Ex-Communist Countries."]

794. Kahan, Arcadius. *Studies and Essays on the Soviet and Eastern European Economies.* Edited by Peter B. Brown. Newtonville, MA: Oriental Research Partners, 1991-1994. 2 vols. [Contents: Vol. 1. Published Works on the Soviet Economy — v. 2. Unpublished Works on the Soviet and Eastern European Economies.] REV: Peter Gatrell, *Slavic Review* 52, no. 4 (Winter 1993): 898. Robert C. Stuart, *Russian Review* 52, no. 3 (July 1993): 435-436.

795. King, Gundar J., and David O. Porter. "Moving to Markets: A Review Essay." *Journal of Baltic Studies* 24, no. 4 (Winter 1993): 395-402. [Review article on George Soros, *Nationalist Dictatorships versus Open Society* (NY: 1993); Arne Jon Isachsen, Carl B. Hamilton, and Thorvaldur Gylfason, *Understanding the Market Economy* (NY: 1992); Roman Frydman, Andrzej Rapaczynski, and John S. Earle et al., *The Privatization Process in Central Europe* (London: 1993); and Shafiqul Islam and Michael Mandelbaum, eds., *Making Markets: Economic Transformation in Eastern Europe and the Post-Soviet States* (NY: 1993).]

796. Kolodko, Grzegorz W. "From Recession to Growth in Post-Communist Economies: Expectations versus Reality." *Communist and Post-Communist Studies* 26, no. 2 (June 1993): 123-143.

797. Kozminski, Andrzej K. *Catching Up? Organizational and Management Change in the Ex-Socialist Block.* SUNY Series in International Management. Albany, NY: State University of New York Press, c1993. viii, 236 pp.

798. Lipschutz, Ronnie, and Ken Conca, eds. *The State and Social Power in Global Environmental Politics.* Includes contribution by Barbara Jancar. New Direction in World Politics. New York: Columbia University Press, c1993. xviii, 363 pp. [Partial contents: Barbara Jancar, "The Environmental Attractor in the Former USSR: Ecology and Regional Change."]

799. Martino, Antonio. "A Monetary Constitution for Ex-Communist Countries." *Cato Journal* 12, no. 3 (Winter 1993): 533-555. [Part of special issue devoted to "Monetary Reform in Ex-Communist Countries."]

800. Maruyama, Magoroh, ed. *Management Reform in Eastern and Central Europe: Use of Pre-Communist Cultures.* Contributions by Alexei V. Zagorsky, Adam Podgórecki, Milan Zeleny, Maria Los, Reuven Brenner, Jone Pearce, Imre Branyiczki, Gyula Bakacsi, and Magoroh Maruyama. 1st ed. Aldershot, Hants; Brookfield, VT: Dartmouth Publishing Co., c1993. x, 180 pp. [Contents: Magoroh Maruyama, "Introduction," pp. 1-2; Alexei V. Zagorsky, "Cultural Impact of the Post-Perestroika Period on Russian Economic Reforms," pp. 3-12; Adam Podgórecki, "Polish Traditions and Perspectives of Post-socialist Reforms," pp. 13-43; Milan Zeleny, "Reforms in Czechoslovakia: Traditions or Cosmopolitanism?" pp. 45-64; Maria Los, "Crimes of the Functionaries: Bribery, Extortion and Favouritism," pp. 65-79; Reuven Brenner, "The Long Road from Serfdom and How to Shorten It," pp. 81-109; Jone Pearce, "From Socialism to Capitalism: The Effects of Hungarian Human Resources Practices," pp. 111-131; Jone Pearce, Imre Branyiczki and Gyula Bakacsi, "Person-Based Reward Systems: Reward Practices in Reform-Communist Organizations," pp. 133-162; Magoroh Maruyama, "Survival, Adaptive and Maladaptive Strategies, and Pitfalls in Management Transfer: Lessons from Other Parts of the World and Their Use in Management Reforms in Central and Eastern Europe," pp. 163-173.]

801. McIntyre, Robert. "Collective Agriculture in Eastern Europe and the Former Soviet Union." *Monthly*

Review 45, no. 7 (December 1993): 1-15.

802. McKinnon, Ronald I. *The Order of Economic Liberalization: Financial Control in the Transition to a Market Economy.* 2nd ed. Johns Hopkins Studies in Development. Baltimore, MD: Johns Hopkins University Press, c1993. xii, 242 pp. [Contents: 1. Introduction: The Order of Economic Liberalization; 2. Financial Repression and the Productivity of Capital: Empirical Findings on Interest Rates and Exchange Rates; 3. High Real Interest Rates: Japan and Taiwan versus Chile; 4. Instruments of Financial Repression; 5. Inflation Tax, Monetary Control, and Reserve Requirements on Commercial Banks; 6. Macroeconomic Control during Disinflation: Chile versus South Korea; 7. Macroeconomic Instability and Moral Hazard in Banking; 8. Protectionism in Foreign Trade: Quotas versus Tariffs; 9. Exchange-Rate Policy in Repressed and Open Economies; 10. The International Capital Market and Economic Liberalization: The Overborrowing Syndrome; 11. Stabilizing the Ruble: Financial Control during the Transition from a Centrally Planned to a Market Economy; 12. Foreign Trade, Protection, and Negative Value-Added in a Liberalizing Socialist Economy. 13. Financial Growth and Macroeconomic Stability in China, 1978-1992: Implications for Russia and Eastern Europe; 14. Gradual versus Rapid Liberalization in Socialist Foreign Trade: Concluding Notes on Alternative Models.]

803. Meigs, A. James. "Eurodollars: A Transition Currency." *Cato Journal* 12, no. 3 (Winter 1993): 711-727. [Part of special issue devoted to "Monetary Reform in Ex-Communist Countries."]

804. Milanovic, Branko. *Cash Social Transfers, Direct Taxes, and Income Distribution in Late Socialism.* Policy Research Working Papers, WPS 1176. Washington, DC: Policy Research Dept., World Bank, [1993]. 33 pp.

805. Mininberg, Mark, Iveta Hodková, and Diane Bellantoni. "Promoting Economic Growth and Environmental Protection: The Institute for Sustainable Development." *Connecticut Journal of International Law* 9, no. 1 (Fall 1993): 69-86.

806. Murrell, Peter. "What Is Shock Therapy? What Did It Do in Poland and Russia?" *Post-Soviet Affairs* 9, no. 2 (April-June 1993): 111-140.

807. Murrell, Peter, and Yijiang Wang. "When Privatization Should Be Delayed: The Effect of Communist Legacies on Organizational and Institutional Reforms." *Journal of Comparative Economics* 17, no. 2 (June 1993): 385-406.

808. National Economic Research Associates, and Commission of the European Communities Directorate-General for Regional Policy. *Trade and Foreign Investment in the Community's Regions: The Impact of Economic Reform in Central and Eastern Europe.* Regional Development Studies. Brussels: Commission of the European Communities; Lanham, MD: UNIPUB [distributor], 1993. 157 pp. [At head of title: Commission of the European Communities, Directorate-General for Regional Policies.]

809. National Planning Association. Board of Trustees. *An Economic Rehabilitation Corps for the Former Soviet Republics and Eastern Europe: A Policy Statement.* NPA Report, 262. Washington, DC: National Planning Association, c1993. 12 pp.

810. Niskanen, William A. "Monetary Institutions During the Transition to a Market Economy." *Cato Journal* 12, no. 3 (Winter 1993): 729-730. [Comment on A. James Meigs, "Eurodollars: A Transition Currency," pp. 711-727. Part of special issue devoted to "Monetary Reform in Ex-Communist Countries."]

811. Organisation for Economic Co-operation and Development. *Economic Integration: OECD Economies, Dynamic Asian Economies, and Central and Eastern European Countries.* Includes contributions by André Barsony, John West, Eduard Hochreiter, Tan Sri Zainal Abidin Sulong, Wisarn Pupphavesa, K. Y. Tang, Béla Szentmáry, Anna Wziatek Kubiak, Blanka Kalinova, John A. Martens, Rolf Alter, and Vlastimil Gejdos. Paris: Organisation for Economic Co-operation and Development; Washington, DC: OECD Publications and Information Centre [distributor], c1993. 118 pp. [Includes a summary of discussions and a selection of the papers from a workshop held in June 1992. Partial contents: André Barsony and John West, "Economic Integration of OECD Economies, Dynamic Asian Economies and Central and Eastern European Countries: Main Issues and Summary of Discussions," pp. 7-16; Eduard Hochreiter, "Lessons for the CEECs from the DAE Experience," pp. 67-69; John West, "Recent Developments and Impediments to DAE/CEEC Economic Integration," pp. 73-84; Tan Sri Zainal Abidin Sulong, "Economic Integration of Malaysia and the CEECs," pp. 85-88; Wisarn Pupphavesa, "Trade Between Thailand and the CEECs," pp. 89-91; K. Y. Tang, "Transition to a Market Economy—A DAE Perspective," pp. 93-94; Béla Szentmáry, "Economic Linkages Between Hungary and the DAEs," pp. 95-97; Anna Wziatek Kubiak, "Economic Co-operation Between Poland and the DAEs: Prospects and Barriers," pp. 99-102; Blanka Kalinova and John A. Martens, "Integration of CEECs and NIS Into the World Economy," pp. 105-112; Rolf Alter, "CEEC Foreign Direct Investment (FDI) Regimes and Trends," pp. 113-115; Vlastimil Gejdos, "Recent Developments in the CSFR Economy," pp. 117-118.]

812. ———. *Policy Issues in Insurance = Aspects fondamentaux des assurances.* Paris: Organisation for Economic Co-operation and Development; Washington, DC: OECD Publications and Information Centre, Distributor, 1993. 301 pp. [Material for this publication was assembled for a workshop on insurance policy issues in Central and Eastern European Countries (CEEC), held in Paris on 2-3 July 1992.]

813. Organisation for Economic Co-operation and Development, and OECD. Centre for Co-operation with European Economies in Transition. *Valuation and Privatisation.* Paris: [Washington, DC: Organisation for Economic Co-operation and Development: Centre for Co-operation with the European Economies in Transition; OECD Publications and Information Centre, Distributor], c1993. 118 pp. [Various contributors; edited by Enery Quinones.]

814. Ostry, Sylvia. *The Threat of Managed Trade to Transforming Economies.* Occasional Paper (Group of Thirty), no. 41. Washington, DC: Group of Thirty, 1993. 47 pp.

815. PA Cambridge Economic Consultants, and Commission of the European Communities. Directorate-General XXIII. Tourism Unit. *Tourism Resources in Eastern Europe: Problems and Prospects for Cooperation.* Document. Studies (Commission of the European Communities, Directorate-General), XXIII. Luxembourg: Office for Official Publications of the European Communities; Lanham, MD: UNIPUB [distributor], 1993. 2 vols. [At head of title: Commission of the European Communities, D.G. XXIII, Tourism Unit. Contents: Vol. 1. Issues and recommendations — v. 2. Country profiles.]

816. Parker, Richard. "Delusions of 'Shock Therapy': Western Economists, Eastern Economies." *Dissent* 40, no. 1 (Winter 1993): 72-80.

817. Patterson, Perry L., ed. *Capitalist Goals, Socialist Past: The Rise of the Private Sector in Command Economies.* Contributions by Perry L. Patterson, Ben Slay, John E. Tedstrom, Catherine Sokil-Milnikiewicz, Dennis A. Rondinelli, Evan Kraft, Michael A. Murphy, and David L. Bartlett. Boulder, CO: Westview Press, 1993. vii, 225 pp. [Contents: Perry L. Patterson, "Overview: The Return of the Private and Cooperative Sectors in Eastern Europe and the Soviet Union," pp. 1-16; Part One: The Development of Small-Scale Enterprise in Former Command Economies; Ben Slay, "The Indigenous Private Sector in Poland," pp. 19-39; John E. Tedstrom, "Privatization in Post-Soviet Russia: The Politics and Psychology of Reform," pp. 41-66; Catherine Sokil-Milnikiewicz, "Struggles over a Growing Private Sector: The Case of Hungary," pp. 67-87; Dennis A. Rondinelli, "Private Enterprise Development and the Transition to a Market Economy in the Czech and Slovak Republics," pp. 89-115; Evan Kraft, "The Growth of Small Enterprise and the Private Sector in Yugoslavia," pp. 117-143; Part Two: The Environment for Private Enterprise; Michael A. Murphy, "Competition Under the Laws Governing Soviet Producer Cooperatives During Perestroika," pp. 147-167; David L. Bartlett, "Banking and Financial Reform in a Mixed Economy: The Case of Hungary," pp. 169-192; Ben Slay, "The Perils of Privatizing State Property: The Polish Case," pp. 193-214; Perry L. Patterson, "Afterword: On the Future of Private Entrepreneurship in Former Command Economies," pp. 215-217.]

818. Paul, Ellen Frankel, Fred D. Miller, Jr., and Jeffrey Paul, eds. *Liberalism and the Economic Order.* Includes contributions by Norman Barry, John Gray, James M. Buchanan, Svetozar Pejovich, William H. Riker, and David L. Weimer. Cambridge; New York, NY: Cambridge University Press, 1993. xv, 319 pp. [Essays also published in Social Philosophy & Policy 10, no. 2. Partial contents Norman Barry, "The Social Market Economy," pp. 1-25;

John Gray, "From Post-Communism to Civil Society: The Reemergence of History and the Decline of the Western Model," pp. 26-50; James M. Buchanan, "Asymmetrical Reciprocity in Market Exchange: Implications for Economies in Transition," pp. 51-64; Svetozar Pejovich, "Institutions, Nationalism, and the Transition Process in Eastern Europe," pp. 65-78; William H. Riker and David L. Weimer, "The Economic and Political Liberalization of Socialism: The Fundamental Problem of Property Rights," pp. 79-102.]

819. Pogany, Peter. "Central and East Europe's oil and gas imports from former Soviet republics: Concerns and hopes." *International Economic Review* (May 1993): 15-19.

820. Raiszadeh, Farhad M. E., Marilyn M. Helms, and Michael C. Varner. "How Can Eastern Europe Help American Manufacturers?" *International Executive* 35, no. 4 (July-August 1993): 357-365.

821. Ramanadham, V. V., ed. *Privatization: A Global Perspective.* Includes contributions by William H. Draper III, Spiros K. Lioukas, Ekaterina A. Kouprianova, Gregory T. Jedrzejczak, Zoltan Roman, Michal Mejstrik, Volkhart Vincentz, Christo Dalkalachev, Matija Skof, Branko Vukmir, and V. V. Ramanadham. London; New York: Routledge, 1993. xxvi, 610 pp. [Partial contents: William H. Draper III, "Foreword"; Spiros K. Lioukas, "Privatization in Greece"; Ekaterina A. Kouprianova, "Privatization in the USSR"; Gregory T. Jedrzejczak, "Privatization in Poland"; Zoltan Roman, "Privatization in Hungary: regulatory reform and public enterprise performance"; Michal Mejstrik, "Privatization in Czechoslovakia"; Volkhart Vincentz, "Privatization in East Germany: regulatory reform and public enterprise performance"; Christo Dalkalachev, "Privatization in Bulgaria"; Matija Skof and Branko Vukmir, "Privatization in Yugoslavia"; V. V. Ramanadham, "Concluding review."]

822. RAND/DIW/IFO Conference on the European Challenge and the Role of the USA (1992: Dusseldorf, Germany). *The RAND/DIW/IFO Conference on the European Challenge and the Role of the USA: Conference Proceedings.* Contributions by Heiner Flassbeck, Wolfgang Gerstenberger, Charles Cooper, and Robert Levine. Santa Monica, CA: RAND, 1993. v, 56 pp. [Three papers from a workshop/conference jointly sponsored by RAND, DIW and IFO. The meeting took place in Duesseldorf, November 23-24, 1992. Contents: Conference summary; Participants; Heiner Flassbeck, "The economic situation in Russia and White Russia"; Wolfgang Gerstenberger, "The Role of government in restructuring East German industry"; Charles Cooper and Robert Levine, "The United States and Germany in the world economy."]

823. Rausser, G. C., and S. R. Johnson. "State-Market-Civil Institutions: The Case of Eastern Europe and the Soviet Republics." *World Development* 21, no. 4 (April 1993): 675-689.

824. Riker, William H., and David L. Weimer. "The Economic and Political Liberalization of Socialism: The Fundamental Problem of Property Rights." *Social Philosophy & Policy* 10, no. 2 (Summer 1993): 79-102.

825. Rona, Peter. "Whose Markets?" *International Economic Insights* 4, no. 4 (July-August 1993): 39-40. [Review article on Shafiqul Islam and Michael Mandelbaum, eds., *Making Markets: Economic Transformation in Eastern Europe and the Post-Soviet States* (NY: 1993).]

826. Rose, Andrew K., and Lars Svensson. *European Exchange Rate Credibility before the Fall.* Working Paper (University of California, Berkeley. Center for German and European Studies), 1.17. Berkeley, CA: Center for German and European Studies, University of California, [1993]. 36 pp.

827. Rose, Richard, and Yevgeniy Tikhomirov. "Who Grows Food in Russia and Eastern Europe?" *Post-Soviet Geography* 34, no. 2 (February 1993): 111-126.

828. Sanders, Jerry, and Ivo Ptyr. *Environmental Cooperation and Conflict; Dangers and Opportunities in the New Europe.* Working Paper (University of California, Berkeley. Center for German and European Studies), 2.16. Berkeley, CA: Center for German and European Studies, University of California, [1993]. 35 pp.

829. Sandler, Gregory. "Where Experts Are the Exports." *Journal of European Business* 5, no. 1 (September-October 1993): 12-15. [The International Executive Service Corps is offering American executives to advise on economic issues in post-communist Eastern Europe and Russia.]

830. Saunders, Christopher T., ed. *The Role of Competition in Economic Transition.* Includes contributions by Stanislav Belehrádek, Miroslav Hrncîr, Imrich Flassik, Péter Pogácsás, János Stadler, Ruben Yevstigneyev, Rikard Lang, Dragomir Vojnic, András Inotai, David G. Mayes, Alain Bienaymé, János Gács, and Nobuko Inagawa. European Economic Interaction and Integration Workshop Papers, 14. New York, NY: St. Martin's Press in association with the Vienna Institute for Comparative Economic Studies, 1993. ix, 245 pp. [Based on the Workshop on East-West European Economic Interaction (14th: 1992: Marianske Lazne, Czech Republic). Partial contents: Stanislav Belehrádek, "Competition policy and privatisation in Czechoslovakia," pp. 49-54; Miroslav Hrncîr, "The roles of foreign competition and of financial intermediation in revitalising the Czechoslovak economy," pp. 55-72; Imrich Flassik, "Priorities of the Czechoslovak anti-trust office," pp. 73-77; Péter Pogácsás and János Stadler, "Promoting competition in Hungary," pp. 78-89; Ruben Yevstigneyev, "Creating a competitive environment in Russia," pp. 90-100; Rikard Lang and Dragomir Vojnic, "Privatisation, market structure and competition: a progress report on Croatia," pp. 101-123; András Inotai, David G. Mayes, Alain Bienaymé, and János Gács, "Comments on Part II," pp. 124-130; Nobuko Inagawa, "Japan's post-war industrial policy (1945-1970) as a model for East European countries," pp. 149-178.]

831. Stone, Randall Warren. "Pursuit of Interest: The Politics of Subsidized Trade in the Soviet Bloc." Ph.D. diss., Harvard University, 1993. [UMI order no: AAC 9412397.]

832. Tanzi, Vito. *Fiscal Policy and the Economic Restructuring of Economies in Transition.* IMF Working Paper, WP/93/22. Washington, DC: International Monetary Fund, 1993. iii, 33 pp.

833. ———, ed. *Transition to Market: Studies in Fiscal Reform.* Includes contributions by Vito Tanzi, Sheetal K. Chand, Henri R. Lorie, Jim Prust, George Kopits, Ved P. Gandhi, Leif Mutén, Adrienne Cheasty, Ehtisham Ahmad, Ke-young Chu, George Kopits, Dubravko Mihaljek, Dieter Bös, Gerd Schwartz, and Parthasarathi Shome. Washington, DC: International Monetary Fund, 1993. ix, 387 pp. [Partial contents: Vito Tanzi, "Financial Markets and Public Finance in the Transformation Process," pp. 1-28; Sheetal K. Chand and Henri R. Lorie, "Bulgaria's Transition to a Market Economy: Fiscal Aspects," pp. 31-48; Jim Prust, "The Czech and Slovak Federal Republic: Government Finances in a Period of Transition," pp. 49-64; George Kopits, "Hungary: A Case of Gradual Fiscal Reform," pp. 65-90; Ved P. Gandhi, "Fundamental Fiscal Reform in Poland: Issues of Design and Implementation," pp. 91-107; Ved P. Gandhi and Leif Mutén, "Romania: Assessment of Turnover and Income Taxes," pp. 108-121; Adrienne Cheasty, "The Realized Net Present Value of the Soviet Union," pp. 125-134; Ehtisham Ahmad and Ke-young Chu, "Russian Federation: Economic Reform and Policy Options for Social Protection," pp. 135-154; George Kopits and Dubravko Mihaljek, "Fiscal Federalism and the New Independent States," pp. 155-176; Dubravko Mihaljek, "Intergovernmental Fiscal Relations in Yugoslavia, 1972-90," pp. 177-201; Dieter Bös, "Privatization in East Germany," pp. 202-223; Gerd Schwartz, "Privatization: Trade-Offs, Experience, and Policy Lessons from Eastern European Countries," pp. 224-249; Jacques Baldet and Geoffrey Walton, "Mongolia: Opportunities for Simplicity in Tax Policy Design and Implementation," pp. 292-304; Parthasarathi Shome, "Transition and Transformation: Fiscal Sector Issues in Kazakhstan," pp. 305-321.]

834. United Nations. Economic Commission for Europe. *Housing Policy Guidelines: The Experience of ECE with Special Reference to Countries in Transition.* Prepared by L. Kieffer et al. New York: United Nations, 1993. v, 48 pp.

835. United Nations Economic Commission for Europe, and International Labour Organisation. *Management development in East-West joint ventures: a guide for managers in the economics in transition.* New York: United Nations, 1993. iv, 128 pp.

836. Vari, Anna, and Pal Tamas, eds. *Environment and Democratic Transition: Policy and Politics in Central and Eastern Europe.* Contributions by Richard N. L. Andrews, Stanley J. Kabala, Kristalina Georgieva, Stephen Stec, Oleg Yanitsky, Viktoria Szirmai, Bernd Baumgartl, Judit Galambos, Judit Juhasz, Anna Vari, Janos Tolgyesi, Boris Z. Doktorov, Boris M. Firsov, Viatcheslav V. Safronov, and Nikolai Genov. Technology, Risk, and Society, v. 7. Dordrecht; Boston: Kluwer Academic Publishers, c1993. x, 283 pp. [Contents: Anna Vari and Pal Tamas, "Environmental Policy and Politics in Central and Eastern Europe:

Introduction and Overview," pp. 1-4; Richard N.L. Andrews, "Environmental Policy in the Czech and Slovak Republic," pp. 5-48; Stanley J. Kabala, "Environmental Affairs and the Emergence of Pluralism in Poland: A Case of Political Symbiosis," pp. 49-66; Kristalina Georgieva, "Environmental Policy in a Transition Economy: The Bulgarian Example," pp. 67-87; Stephen Stec, "Public Participation Laws, Regulations and Practices in Seven Countries in Central and Eastern Europe: An Analysis Emphasizing Impacts on the Development Decision-Making Process," pp. 88-119; Oleg Yanitsky, "Environmental Initiatives in Russia: East-West Comparisons," pp. 120-145; Viktoria Szirmai, "The Structural Mechanisms of the Organization of Ecological-Social Movements in Hungary," pp. 146-156; Bernd Baumgartl, "Environmental Protest as a Vehicle for Transition: The Case of Ekoglasnost in Bulgaria," pp. 157-175; Judit Galambos, "An International Environmental Conflict on the Danube: The Gabcikovo-Nagymaros Dams," pp. 176-226; Judit Juhasz, Anna Vari, and Janos Tolgyesi, "Environmental Conflict and Political Change: Public Perception on Low-Level Radioactive Waste Management in Hungary," pp. 227-248; Boris Z. Doktorov, Boris M. Firsov, and Viatcheslav V. Safronov, "Ecological Consciousness in the USSR: Entering the 1990s," pp. 249-267; Nikolai Genov, "Environmental Risks in a Society in Transition: Perceptions and Reactions," pp. 268-278.]

837. Waters, Anne D. "Trade, Intellectual Property, and the Development of Central and Eastern Europe: Filling the GATT Gap." *Vanderbilt Journal of Transnational Law* 26, no. 4 (November 1993): 927-974.

■ Russia/U.S.S.R.

General

838. Berkowitz, Daniel M., Joseph S. Berliner, Paul R. Gregory, Susan J. Linz, and James R. Millar. "An Evaluation of the CIA's Analysis of Soviet Economic Performance, 1970-90." *Comparative Economic Studies* 35, no. 2 (Summer 1993): 33-57. [Paper was prepared in 1991 in response to an instruction to the CIA by the House Permanent Select Committee on Intelligence (HPSCI) to establish a panel of outside reviewers to evaluate CIA estimates of Soviet economic performance.]

839. Boettke, Peter J. *Why Perestroika Failed: The Politics and Economics of Socialist Transformation.* London; New York: Routledge, 1993. viii, 199 pp. [Contents: Introduction; The road to nowhere; The theoretical problems of socialism; The nature of the Soviet-type system; The logic of politics and the logic of reform; Credibility in Soviet reforms; Charting a new course; Conclusion.]

840. Moskoff, William. *Hard Times: Impoverishment and Protest in the Perestroika Years: The Soviet Union 1985-1991.* Armonk, NY: M.E. Sharpe, c1993. xi, 243 pp.

841. Pokorny, Dusan. *Efficiency and Justice in the Industrial World.* Armonk, NY: M.E. Sharpe, c1993-. vols. [Contents: Vol. 1. The failure of the Soviet experiment.]

842. Rosenberg, William G., and Lewis H. Siegelbaum, eds. *Social Dimensions of Soviet Industrialization.* Contributions by Ronald G. Suny, Sheila Fitzpatrick, Stephen Merl, Stephen Kotkin, R. W. Davies, Don K. Rowney, Hiroaki Kuromiya, Lewis H. Siegelbaum, David Shearer, Peter Solomon, Jr., Katerina Clark, Geoff Eley, Moshe Lewin, and Steven Coe. Indiana-Michigan Series in Russian and East European Studies. Bloomington, IN: Indiana University Press, c1993. xix, 296 pp. [Papers from a seminar sponsored by the Social Science Research Council on Twentieth-Century Russian and Soviet Social History, held at the University of Michigan, Ann Arbor, in April 1988. Contents: William G. Rosenberg and Lewis H. Siegelbaum, "Introduction"; Lewis H. Siegelbaum and Ronald G. Suny, "Conceptualizing the Command Economy: Western Historians on Soviet Industrialization"; Sheila Fitzpatrick, "The Great Departure: Rural-Urban Migration in the Soviet Union, 1929-33"; Stephen Merl, "Social Mobility in the Countryside"; Stephen Kotkin, "Peopling Magnitostroi: The Politics of Demography"; R.W. Davies, "The Management of Soviet Industry, 1928-41"; Don K. Rowney, "The Scope, Authority, and Personnel of the New Industrial Commissariats in Historical Context"; Hiroaki Kuromiya, "The Commander and the Rank and File: Managing the Soviet Coal-Mining Industry, 1928-33"; Lewis H. Siegelbaum, "Masters of the Shop Floor: Foremen and Soviet Industrialization"; David Shearer, "Factories Within Factories: Changes in the Structure of Work and Management in Soviet Machine-Building Factories, 1926-34"; Peter Solomon, Jr., "Criminal Justice and the Industrial Front"; Katerina Clark, "Engineers of Human Souls in an Age of Industrialization: Changing Cultural Models, 1929-41"; Geoff Eley, "Soviet Industrialization from a European Perspective"; Moshe Lewin, "On Soviet Industrialization"; Steven Coe, "Guide to Further Reading."]

843. Treyvish, Andrey I., Kavita K. Pandit, and Andrew R. Bond. "Post-Industrial Transformation in the European Regions of the Former USSR, 1959-1985." *Post-Soviet Geography* 34, no. 10 (December 1993): 613-630.

844. Wolf, Charles, Jr. *Economic Transformation and the Changing International Economic Environment.* Santa Monica, CA: RAND Corporation, 1993. vii, 83 pp. [Collection of essays published between November 1990 and April 1993.]

Agriculture

845. Shend, Jaclyn Y., and United States. Dept. of Agriculture. Economic Research Service. *Agricultural Statistics of the Former USSR Republics and the Baltic States.* Statistical Bulletin (United States. Dept. of Agriculture), no. 863. Washington, DC: U.S. Dept. of Agriculture, Economic Research Service; Herndon, VA: ERS-NASS [distributor, 1993]. viii, 239 pp.

Foreign Economic Relations

846. Alam, Ghazi Mohammad Shahidul. "Transfer of Dual-Use Technology from the United States to the USSR: The Tradeoff Between National Security and

Economic Benefits, or, Klitgaard's Dilemma Revisited in the Gorbachev Era." Ph.D. diss., Boston University, 1993. [UMI order no: AAC 9317445.]

History

847. Chandler, Alfred D., Jr. "Organizational Capabilities and Industrial Restructuring: A Historical Analysis." *Journal of Comparative Economics* 17, no. 2 (June 1993): 309-337.

848. Graham, Loren R. "Palchinsky's Travels: A Russian Engineer's Adventures Among Gigantic Projects and Small Minds." *Technology Review* 96, no. 8 (November-December 1993): 22-31. [Includes sidebar by Graham, "Red Elephants," pp. 27-28.]

849. Siegel, Katherine A. S. "Technology and Trade: Russia's Pursuit of American Investment, 1917-1929." *Diplomatic History* 17, no. 3 (Summer 1993): 375-398.

Industry and Transportation

850. Nourzad, Farrokh, and Peter G. Toumanoff. "The Effects of the Defense Sector on the Productivity of Civilian Industry in the United States and the USSR." *Journal of Comparative Economics* 17, no. 4 (December 1993): 768-785.

851. Whitefield, Stephen. *Industrial Power and the Soviet State.* Oxford: Clarendon Press; New York: Oxford University Press, 1993. 279 pp.

Labor

852. Christensen, Paul Thomas. "Industrial Russia under the New Regimes: Labor Relations and Democratization, 1985-1993." Ph.D. diss., Princeton University, 1993. [UMI order no: AAC 9407076.]

853. Cook, Linda J. *The Soviet Social Contract and Why it Failed: Welfare Policy and Workers' Politics from Brezhnev to Yeltsin.* Russian Research Center Studies, 86. Cambridge, MA: Harvard University Press, 1993. xiii, 272 pp.

854. Corneo, Giacomo G. "Job Rights and Labor Productivity in a Soviet-Type Economy." *Journal of Comparative Economics* 17, no. 1 (March 1993): 113-128.

855. Siegelbaum, Lewis H. [Book Review]. *International Labor and Working Class History*, no. 43 (Spring 1993): 135-138. [Review article on Stephen Kotkin, *Steeltown, USSR: Soviet Society in the Gorbachev Era* (Berkeley, CA: University of California Press, 1991); and Walter D. Connor, *The Accidental Proletariat: Workers, Politics, and Crisis in Gorbachev's Russia* (Princeton, NJ: Princeton University Press, 1991).]

Natural Resources and Ecology

856. Golubchikov, Sergei. "Whither the Whale? A Riddle for Modern-Day Chukotka." *Surviving Together* 11, no. 3 (Fall 1993): 11-12. Translated by Eric Sievers.

857. Gore, Albert. *Earth in the Balance: Ecology and the Human Spirit.* New York, NY: Plume, c1993. xx, 407 pp. [Includes discussion of the destruction of the Aral Sea.]

858. Khotuleva, Marina V., Vladimir A. Chechetkin, and Nicolay A. Melnichenko. "Radioactive Contamination of Russia's Techa River." *Environmental Science & Technology* 27, no. 4 (April 1993): 606-607.

859. Peterson, D. J. *Troubled Lands: The Legacy of Soviet Environmental Destruction.* RAND Research Study. Boulder, CO: Westview Press, 1993. xviii, 276 pp. REV: Richard Cooper, *Foreign Affairs* 72, no. 4 (September-October 1993): 158. William Moskoff, *Slavic Review* 52, no. 3 (Fall 1993): 649-650. *Journal of Forestry* 91, no. 7 (July 1993): 49. *Orbis* 37, no. 4 (Fall 1993).

860. Rozdzynski, Jan. "A Remnant of the Dalstroy." *Uncaptive Minds* 6, no. 1 (22) (Winter-Spring 1993): 95-99. [On the pollution at the site of a prison camp in the Kolyma region.]

861. Suokko, Kristen, and Dan Reicher. "Radioactive Waste and Contamination." *Environmental Science & Technology* 27, no. 4 (April 1993): 602-604.

Standard of Living

862. Flakierski, Henryk. *Income Inequalities in the Former Soviet Union and Its Republics.* Armonk, NY: M.E. Sharpe, 1993. 87 pp. [Published simultaneously as *International Journal of Sociology* 22, no. 3.]

863. Sedik, David J. "A Note on Soviet Per Capita Meat Consumption." *Comparative Economic Studies* 35, no. 3 (Fall 1993): 39-48. [Earlier version of this paper published in *Economies in Transition Agriculture Report* 5, no. 4 (1992): 11-15.]

Theory, Planning, Management

864. Blaney, John, and Mike Gfoeller. "Lessons from the Failure of Perestroika." *Political Science Quarterly* 108, no. 3 (Fall 1993): 481-496.

865. Keren, Michael. "Optimal Tautness and the Economics of Incentives in Bureaucracies." *Comparative Economic Studies* 35, no. 1 (Spring 1993): 85-117. [Revised version of a paper prepared for the Hunter Conference, Haverford, PA, March 1989.]

866. Kontorovich, Vladimir. "The Economic Fallacy." *National Interest*, no. 31 (Spring 1993): 35-45.

867. Krueger, Gary. "*Goszakazy* and the Soviet Economic Collapse." *Comparative Economic Studies* 35, no. 3 (Fall 1993): 1-18.

868. ———. "Priorities in Central Planning." *Journal of Comparative Economics* 17, no. 3 (September 1993): 646-662.

869. Mandel, William M. "Socialism: Feasibility and Reality." *Science & Society* 57, no. 3 (Fall 1993): 349-355.

870. Moltz, James Clay. "Divergent Learning and the Failed Politics of Soviet Economic Reform." *World Politics* 45, no. 2 (January 1993): 301-325.

871. Puffer, Sheila M., and Daniel J. McCarthy. "Decision-Making Authority of Former Soviet and American Managers: Not So Different After All?" *International Executive* 35, no. 6 (November-December 1993): 497-512.

872. Rutland, Peter. *The Politics of Economic Stagnation in the Soviet Union: The Role of Local Party Organs in Economic Management.* Soviet and East European Studies, 88. Cambridge; New York, NY: Cambridge University Press, 1993. xv, 297 pp. REV: Stephen K. Wegren, *Soviet and Post-Soviet Review* 20, nos. 2-3 (1993): 254-255.

873. Turgeon, Lynn. "The Transformation of Soviet Economics." *Monthly Review* 44, no. 8 (January 1993): 49-57. [Review article on Stanislav Menshikov, *Catastrophe or Catharsis? The Soviet Economy* (London: 1991).]

■ C.I.S.

General

874. Afrasiabi, Kaveh L. "The Economic Cooperation Organization (ECO): Problems & Prospects." *Central Asia Monitor*, no. 4 (1993): 28-30. [The Economic Cooperation Organization was established by Iran, Turkey and Pakistan; the five Central Asian republics were accepted as members in 1992.]

875. Anderson, Annelise. "The Ruble Problem: A Competitive Solution." *Cato Journal* 12, no. 3 (Winter 1993): 633-649. [Part of special issue devoted to "Monetary Reform in Ex-Communist Countries."]

876. Åslund, Anders, and Richard Layard, eds. *Changing the Economic System in Russia.* Contributions by Marek Dabrowski, Anders Åslund, Michael Ellam, Richard Layard, Alexei V. Mozhin, Sergei A. Vasiliev, Anatoly B. Chubais, Maria Vishnevskaya, Maxim Boycko, Andrei Shleifer, Boris G. Fedorov, Jeffrey D. Sachs, David Lipton, Ardo H. Hansson, Simon Johnson, Heidi Kroll, Mark Horton, and Peter Boone. New York, NY: St. Martin's Press, 1993. xviii, 237 pp. [Papers in book were commissioned by the Stockholm Institute of East European Economics, and were discussed at a conference held at the Stockholm School of Economics, June 15-16, 1992. Contents: Anders Åslund and Richard Layard, "Introduction," pp. xi-xviii. Part I. Assessment of the Initial Reforms. Marek Dabrowski, "The First Half Year of Russian Transformation," pp. 1-18; Anders Åslund, "The Gradual Nature of Economic Change in Russia," pp. 19-38; Michael Ellam and Richard Layard, "Prices, Incomes, and Hardship," pp. 39-61. Part II. Government Strategies. Alexei V. Mozhin, "Russia's Negotiations with the IMF," pp. 65-71; Sergei A. Vasiliev, "Economic Reform in Russia: Social, Political and Institutional Aspects," pp. 72-86. Part III. Privatisation. Anatoly B. Chubais and Maria Vishnevskaya, "Main Issues of Privatisation in Russia," pp. 89-99; Maxim Boycko and

Andrei Shleifer, "The Voucher Programme for Russia," pp. 100-111; Boris G. Fedorov, "Privatisation with Foreign Participation," pp. 112-124. Part IV. Money and Foreign Trade. Jeffrey D. Sachs and David Lipton, "Remaining Steps to a Market-Based Monetary System in Russia," pp. 127-162; Ardo H. Hansson, "The Trouble with the Ruble: Monetary Reform in the Former Soviet Union," pp. 163-182; Simon Johnson, Heidi Kroll and Mark Horton, "New Banks in the Former Soviet Union: How Do They Operate?" pp. 183-209; Peter Boone, "Russia's Balance of Payments Prospects," pp. 210-229.]

877. Bass, Ilya, and Leslie Dienes. "Defense Industry Legacies and Conversion in the Post-Soviet Realm." *Post-Soviet Geography* 34, no. 5 (May 1993): 302-317.

878. Bim, Alexander S., Derek C. Jones, and Thomas E. Weisskopf. "Hybrid Forms of Enterprise Organization in the Former USSR and the Russian Federation." *Comparative Economic Studies* 35, no. 1 (Spring 1993): 1-37. [Revised version of a paper presented at an ACES panel at the ASSA meetings in Anaheim, CA, January 1993.]

879. Blecher, Beryl Cohen. "Doing Business in the Newly Independent States: A Step-by-Step Guide for American Companies." *Business America* 114, no. 19 (September 20, 1993): 5-9.

880. Boettke, Peter J. "Credibility, the Monetary Regime, and Economic Reform in the Former Soviet Union." *Cato Journal* 12, no. 3 (Winter 1993): 577-584. [Comment on Kevin Dowd, "Money and the Market: What Role for Government?" pp. 557-576. Part of special issue devoted to "Monetary Reform in Ex-Communist Countries."]

881. Bond, Andrew R., and Richard M. Levine. "Antimony and Mercury Processing in Russia and Tajikistan." *Post-Soviet Geography* 34, no. 7 (September 1993): 467-474.

882. Brada, Josef C. "The Transformation from Communism to Capitalism: How Far? How Fast?" *Post-Soviet Affairs* 9, no. 2 (April-June 1993): 87-110.

883. "Central Asia: A New Business Frontier." *Business America* 114, no. 18 (September 6, 1993): 2-7. Contributions by Eric T. Bruder, Kathleen A. Scanlan, Rashmi Nehra, Patricia K. Vhay, and Kelly L. Knight. [Section includes: Eric T. Bruder and Kathleen A. Scanlan, "Central Asia: A New Business Frontier," pp. 2-3; Rashmi Nehra, "Kazakhstan Has An Abundance of Oil and Other Resources," p. 4; Kathleen A. Scanlan, "Kyrgyzstan Offers a Wealth of Untapped Mineral Reserves," p. 5; Patricia K. Vhay, "Uzbekistan Looking to Develop Mineral and Cotton Industries," pp. 5-6; Kelly L. Knight, "Turkmenistan's Gas and Oil Reserves Worth a Close Look," p. 6; Kathleen A. Scanlan, "Tajikistan Emerges from Year-Long Civil War With Hydroelectric and Mineral Resource Opportunities," p. 7.]

884. Christophorou, Yianna. "Programs and Personnel Expand to Help U.S. Firms in Russia and NIS." *Business America* 114, nos. 15/16 (July 26, 1993/August 9,

1993): 22.

885. Clark, Dick, ed. *Russia, Ukraine and the U.S. Response: Twelfth Conference, January 9-14, 1993.* Contributions by Gail W. Lapidus, Anders Åslund, Roman Szporluk, William J. Perry, Robert Legvold, Serhiy Holowaty, and Valery A. Tishkov. Queenstown, MD: Aspen Institute, 1993. iii, 76 pp. [Contents: Gail W. Lapidus, "Political developments in Russia: the first year"; Anders Aslund, "Economic developments in Russia"; Roman Szporluk, "Independent Ukraine"; William J. Perry, "Demilitarization in Russia and the United States"; Robert Legvold, "Designing U.S. policy toward the new states of the former Soviet Union"; Serhiy Holowaty, "Ukraine: one year of independence"; Valery A. Tishkov, "Governing post-Soviet ethnicity: ethnic states or plural societies?"]

886. Claudon, Michael. "Shock Therapy: Too Much Shock, Too Little Therapy." *Surviving Together* 11, no. 2 (Summer 1993): 54-46. [Reprinted from *Geonomics Newsletter* (January-February 1993).]

887. Claudon, Michael P., and Kathryn Wittneben, eds. *After the Cold War: Russian-American Defense Conversion for Economic Renewal.* Contributions by Michael P. Claudon, Kathryn Wittneben, John P. Hardt, Aleksei K. Ponomarev, Sergei Y. Glaziev, Ivan S. Materov, Andrei O. Gorbachev, Sergei G. Chevardov, Boris D. Yurlov, Evgenii A. Rogovskii, Valerian M. Sobolev, Sergei V. Kortunov, Vasilii P. Bakhar, Valerii V. Filippov, Sergei I. Kovalev, Aleksandr F. Kononenko, and Jeffrey Moore. Geonomics Institute for International Economic Advancement Series. New York: New York University Press, c1993. xvii, 133 pp. [Papers presented at a Geonomics seminar, October 15-18, 1992. Contents: Michael P. Claudon, "The Bread Loaf Charter: An Action Plan for American-Russian Partnership in Defense Conversion," pp. ix-xiv; I. Defense Conversion: An Overview. Kathryn Wittneben, "Defense Conversion: An Overview," pp. 1-8; John P. Hardt, "Achieving U.S.-Russian Business Cooperation for an Orderly Build-down and Economic Renewal," pp. 9-19; Aleksei K. Ponomarev, "Prospects for Russian-American Cooperation in Defense Conversion," pp. 20-25; Sergei Y. Glaziev, "Russian Foreign Economic Policy and Defense Conversion," pp. 26-28; Ivan S. Materov, "Economic Reform Strategies and the Problems of Conversion," pp. 29-31. II. The View from the Ministries. Andrei O. Gorbachev, "Defense Conversion: Problems and Solutions," pp. 36-39; Sergei G. Chevardov, "Western Involvement in Defense Conversion," pp. 40-42; Boris D. Yurlov, "Technology Transfer and Conversion," pp. 43-49; Evgenii A. Rogovskii, "High-Technology Exports and Economic Restructuring," pp. 50-54; Valerian M. Sobolev, "A Regional Approach to Conversion," pp. 55-56; Sergei V. Kortunov, "Defense Conversion in Russia: The Need for Multilateral Support," pp. 57-66. III. The View from the Enterprises. Vasilii P. Bakhar and Valerii V. Filippov, "The Managers' Perspective: Star Wars to High-Tech Consumer Goods," pp. 71-76; Sergei I. Kovalev and Aleksandr F. Kononenko, "Officer Retraining and Conversion," pp. 77-78. IV. The View from American Business. Kathryn Wittneben, "Perspectives and the Role of U.S. Business in Russian Defense Conversion," pp. 81-106; Jeffrey Moore, "Defense Conversion in Russia: A U.S. Business Perspective," pp. 107-113. Appendix 1. Text: Joint Russian-U.S. Declaration on Defense Conversion, June 17, 1992 Summit, pp. 114-115; Appendix 2. Text: Law, On Conversion of the Defense Industry in the Russian Federation, March 1992, pp. 116-123; Appendix 3. Text: Supreme Soviet Resolution, Law on Conversion, pp. 124-125.]

888. Cohen, Stephen S., and Andrew Schwartz. "Privatization in the Former Soviet Empire: The Tunnel at the End of the Light." *American Prospect*, no. 13 (Spring 1993): 99-108.

889. Commonwealth of Independent States. Statistical Committee, and OECD. Centre for Co-operation with Economies in Transition. *Short-Term Economic Statistics, Commonwealth of Independent States: 1980-1993 = Statistiques Economiques a Court Terme, Communaute des Etats Independants: 1980-1993.* Paris: OECD = OCDE, c1993. 176 pp. [English and French.]

890. Cosman, Catherine. "Labor Issues in Post-Soviet Society." *Central Asia Monitor*, no. 3 (1993): 11-16.

891. Dean, Richard N. *The Implications of Economic and Legal Reforms on Doing a Deal in Russia and Ukraine.* New York, NY: Practising Law Institute, c1993. 584 pp. [Prepared for distribution at a program with the same title, March 22-23, 1993, New York, NY.]

892. Dienes, Leslie. "Economic Geographic Relations in the Post-Soviet Republics." *Post-Soviet Geography* 34, no. 8 (October 1993): 497-529.

893. Duch, Raymond M. "Tolerating Economic Reform: Popular Support for Transition to a Free Market in the Former Soviet Union." *American Political Science Review* 87, no. 3 (September 1993): 590-608.

894. "Economic News." *Central Asia Monitor*, no. 1 (1993): 3-4.

895. "Economic News." *Central Asia Monitor*, no. 2 (1993): 2.

896. "Economic News." *Central Asia Monitor*, no. 3 (1993): 7-9.

897. "Economic News." *Central Asia Monitor*, no. 4 (1993): 5-8.

898. "Economic News." *Central Asia Monitor*, no. 5 (1993): 8-11.

899. "Economic News." *Central Asia Monitor*, no. 6 (1993): 6-8.

900. Filatotchev, Igor, Trevor Buck, and Mike Wright. "Soviet All-Union Enterprises as New Multinationals of the CIS." *International Executive* 35, no. 6 (November-December 1993): 525-538. [On the restructuring of the former Soviet economy with emphasis on former All-Union enterprises.]

901. Forbes, Malcolm S., Jr. "Sound Money and a Liberal Market Order." *Cato Journal* 12, no. 3 (Winter 1993): 731-734. [Part of special issue devoted to "Monetary Reform in Ex-Communist Countries."]

902. Freeman, William E. "Environmental Assistance to the Newly Independent States." *Environmental Science & Technology* 27, no. 4 (April 1993): 608-609.

903. Frenkel, William G., and Michael Y. Sukhman. "New Foreign Investment Regimes of Russia and other Republics of the Former U.S.S.R.: A Legislative Analysis and Historical Perspective." *Boston College International and Comparative Law Review* 16, no. 2 (Summer 1993): 321-423.

904. Galazy, Grigory, Valerian Vikulov, and Tatyana Strizova. "Views from Ecologists of the Lake Baikal Region." *Surviving Together* 11, no. 4 (Winter 1993): 39-42.

905. Goldberg, Linda S., Barry Ickes, and Randi Ryterman. *Departures from the Ruble Area: The Political Economy of Adopting Independent Currencies.* Working Paper (University of California, Berkeley. Center for German and European Studies), 5.13. Berkeley, CA: Center for German and European Studies, University of California, [1993]. 28 pp. [Conference on Markets, States and Democracy, February 11-13, 1993.]

906. Golitsyn, Georgii S. "Ecological Problems in the CIS during the Transitional Period." *RFE/RL Research Report* 2, no. 2 (January 8, 1993): 33-42.

907. Green, Michael J. B., comp. *Nature Reserves of the Himalaya and the Mountains of Central Asia.* Oxford; New York: IUCN—World Conservation Union; Oxford University Press, 1993. xxiii, 471 pp.

908. Halperin, Jonathan. "Learning to Do Business in the Former Soviet Union." *Surviving Together* 11, no. 2 (Summer 1993): 52-53. [Reprinted from *Christian Science Monitor* (February 24, 1993).]

909. Hanke, Steve H., and Kurt Schuler. "Currency Boards and Currency Convertibility." *Cato Journal* 12, no. 3 (Winter 1993): 687-705. [Part of special issue devoted to "Monetary Reform in Ex-Communist Countries."]

910. Hardt, John P., Richard F. Kaufman, and United States. Congress. Joint Economic Committee. *The Former Soviet Union in Transition: Study Papers.* S. Print, 103-11. Washington: U.S. G.P.O., 1993. 2 vols. [103d Congress, 1st session. The study was planned, directed, and edited by John P. Hardt and Richard F. Kaufman.]

911. Heleniak, Tim. "Labor Shedding and Unemployment." *Post-Soviet Geography* 34, no. 4 (April 1993): 252-258. [Edited version of the Proceedings of the Fifth Theodore Shabad Memorial Roundtable on the Geography of the (former) USSR, held in conjunction with the 1993 Annual Meeting of the Association of American Geographers in Atlanta, GA.]

912. Hoyer, Steny H., United States. Congress. Commission on Security and Cooperation in Europe, and United States. Congress. House. Committee on Ways and Means. Subcommittee on Trade. *Statement by Steny H. Hoyer Co-Chairman, Helsinki Commission, before the Subcommittee on Trade, Committee on Ways and Means, June 15, 1993.* [Washington, DC?: s.n., 1993?]. 6 pp.

913. Ivanova, Natasha. "Quiet Revolution Among Consumers." *Surviving Together* 11, no. 1 (Spring 1993): 46-47. [Reprinted from *Consuming Interest* (July 1992).]

914. Johnson, Simon, and Oleg Ustenko. "Ukraine Slips into Hyperinflation." *RFE/RL Research Report* 2, no. 26 (June 25, 1993): 24-32.

915. Kaminski, Bartlomiej, and Alexander Yeats. *OECD Trade Barriers Faced by the Successor States of the Soviet Union.* Policy Research Working Papers, WPS 1175. Washington, DC: International Economics Dept., World Bank, [1993]. 30 pp.

916. Kirschten, Dick. "Greetings, Comrades!" *National Journal* 25, no. 37 (September 11, 1993): 2188-2192. [On the opportunities for Western lawyers, lobbyists, consultants and others in the newly independent states.]

917. Laird, Roy D. *The Soviet Legacy.* Westport, CT: Praeger, 1993. xi, 223 pp.

918. Lee, Catherine. "Economic Union Signals Hope for New CIS Cooperation." *Surviving Together* 11, no. 4 (Winter 1993): 45-46.

919. Leijonhufvud, Axel. "Privatization Is No Panacea." *Surviving Together* 11, no. 3 (Fall 1993): 59-61. [Adapted from the article "Depression in Russia," *New Left Review*, no. 199 (1993).]

920. Lenorovitz, Jeffrey M. "Former Soviet Union expands air safety ties with West." *Aviation Week & Space Technology* 138, no. 4 (January 25, 1993): 57-60.

921. Lewis, Robert A. "Working-Age Population and Society in the Former USSR." *Post-Soviet Geography* 34, no. 4 (April 1993): 223-228. [Edited version of the Proceedings of the Fifth Theodore Shabad Memorial Roundtable on the Geography of the (former) USSR, held in conjunction with the 1993 Annual Meeting of the Association of American Geographers in Atlanta, GA.]

922. Mandel, David. *Rabotyagi: perestroika and after viewed from below: interviews with workers in the former Soviet Union.* New York: Monthly Review Press, 1993. 286 pp.

923. Marples, David R. "The Post-Soviet Nuclear Power Program." *Post-Soviet Geography* 34, no. 3 (March 1993): 172-184.

924. ———. "Ukraine, Belarus, and the Energy Dilemma." *RFE/RL Research Report* 2, no. 27 (July 2, 1993): 39-44.

925. Meltzer, Allan H. "The Benefits and Costs of Currency Boards." *Cato Journal* 12, no. 3 (Winter 1993): 707-710. [Comment on Steve H. Hanks and Kurt Schuler, "Currency Boards and Currency Convertibility," pp. 687-

705. Part of special issue devoted to "Monetary Reform in Ex-Communist Countries."]

926. Michalopoulos, Constantine. *Trade Issues in the New Independent States*. Studies of Economies in Transformation, paper no. 7. Washington, DC: World Bank, c1993. vii, 32 pp.

927. Moffitt, Gregory J. "Events in the Field: Georgetown Conference." *Central Asia Monitor*, no. 2 (1993): 35-37. [Report on the Conference of the American Council for the Study of Islamic Societies, held at Georgetown University, March 5-6, 1993.]

928. Molkner, Keith. "A Comparison of the Legal Regimes for Foreign Investment in Russia, Kazakhstan, and Kyrgyzstan." *International Tax & Business Lawyer* 11, no. 1 (1993): 71-101.

929. Muller, Friedemann. "Polluted Potential: Ecology and the Economy in Central Asia." *Harvard International Review* 15, no. 3 (Spring 1993): 22ff.

930. "National Currencies." *Central Asia Monitor*, no. 4 (1993): 8-9.

931. Noren, James H. "The FSU Economies: First Year of Transition." *Post-Soviet Geography* 34, no. 7 (September 1993): 419-452.

932. Nove, Alec. *Economics of Transition: Some Gaps and Illusions*. Working Paper (University of California, Berkeley. Center for German and European Studies), 5.6. Berkeley, CA: Center for German and European Studies, University of California, [1993]. 30 pp. [Conference on Markets, States, and Democracy, February 11-13, 1993.]

933. OECD. Centre for Co-operation with European Economies in Transition, and Commonwealth of Independent States. Statistical Committee. *National Accounts for the Former Soviet Union: Sources, Methods, and Estimates = Comptes nationaux de l'ex-Union Soviétique*. Paris: Organisation for Economic Co-operation and Development; [Washington, DC: OECD Publications and Information Centre, Distributor], 1993. 152 pp.

934. Peterson, D. J. "Environmental Movement Must Find Alternatives to Status Quo." *Surviving Together* 11, no. 2 (Summer 1993): 15-17. [Excerpts from *Troubled Lands: The Legacy of Soviet Environmental Destruction*, (Boulder, CO: Westview Press, 1993).]

935. Poe, Richard. *How to Profit from the Coming Russian Boom: The Insider's Guide to Business Opportunities and Survival on the Frontiers of Capitalism*. New York: McGraw-Hill, 1993. xxvi, 305 pp. REV: Robert E. Weigand, *Columbia Journal of World Business* 28, no. 4 (Winter 1993): 93-94.

936. Ponomarev, Vitalii. "The Nuclear Industry in Kazakhstan and Kyrgyzstan (Conclusion)." *Central Asia Monitor*, no. 3 (1993): 31-37.

937. Russia (Federation). Academy of Sciences, and University of Pittsburgh. School of Law, comps. and eds. *Trade & Commercial Laws of the Russian Federation: Official Codification & Commentary*. [Dobbs Ferry, NY]: Oceana Publications, c1993-. vols. [Compiled and edited by: the Academy of Jurisprudence of the Ministry of Justice of the Russian Federation, the Institute of Economic Problems of the Transitional Period of the Academy of Sciences of the Russian Federation, in association with Dickie McCamey & Chilcote, P.C., and Emmanuel Zeltser. Commentaries by University of Pittsburgh School of Law faculty. Translated by Anna Reid, Alexander Fishkin. Translated from Russian.]

938. Sagers, Matthew J. "The Energy Industries of the Former USSR: A Mid-Year Survey." *Post-Soviet Geography* 34, no. 6 (June 1993): 341-418.

939. ———. "Government-Enterprise Management-Labor Relations in the Republics." *Post-Soviet Geography* 34, no. 4 (April 1993): 250-252. [Edited version of the Proceedings of the Fifth Theodore Shabad Memorial Roundtable on the Geography of the (former) USSR, held in conjunction with the 1993 Annual Meeting of the Association of American Geographers in Atlanta, GA.]

940. ———. "The Iron and Steel Industry in the Former USSR in 1992 and Thereafter." *Post-Soviet Geography* 34, no. 7 (September 1993): 453-466.

941. ———. "News Notes: Background and Analysis: Inter-republican Coal Trade in Sharp Decline." *Post-Soviet Geography* 34, no. 10 (December 1993): 661-670.

942. Selgin, George A. "Currency Reform: Is Freedom Enough?" *Cato Journal* 12, no. 3 (Winter 1993): 651-655. [Comment on Annelise Anderson, "The Ruble Problem: A Competitive Solution," pp. 633-649. Part of special issue devoted to "Monetary Reform in Ex-Communist Countries."]

943. Shaw, Denis J. B. "Housing Privatization in Urban Areas." *Post-Soviet Geography* 34, no. 4 (April 1993): 268-273. [Edited version of the Proceedings of the Fifth Theodore Shabad Memorial Roundtable on the Geography of the (former) USSR, held in conjunction with the 1993 Annual Meeting of the Association of American Geographers in Atlanta, GA.]

944. Simonov, Eugene. "An Open Letter to Western Organizations Offering Assistance in the Former Soviet Union." *Surviving Together* 11, no. 2 (Summer 1993): 4-8.

945. Skorikov, Vladimir, and Fred W. Vondracek. "Career Development in the Commonwealth of Independent States." *Career Development Quarterly* 41, no. 4 (June 1993): 314-329.

946. Sparaco, Pierre. "Europe's CIS market expands, business aviation slows." *Aviation Week & Space Technology* 139, no. 12 (September 20, 1993): 56-57.

947. Starr, Robert. "Structuring Investments in the C.I.S." *Columbia Journal of World Business* 28, no. 3 (Fall 1993): 12-19.

948. Tourevski, Mark, and Eileen Morgan. *Cutting the Red Tape: How Western Companies Can Profit in the*

New Russia. New York: Free Press; Toronto: Maxwell Macmillan Canada; New York: Maxwell Macmillan International, c1993. xxiii, 310 pp. [Contents: 1. The Human Dimension of Doing Business: A Key to Success in the Former Soviet Union; 2. Ten Advantages of Doing Business in the Russian Federation and Other Former Soviet Republics; 3. Ten Obstacles to Developing Business in the Former Soviet Union; 4. Potential Opportunities in Trade and Investment Activities for American Companies in the Former Soviet Republics; 5. Important Sociocultural Dynamics of Doing Business; 6. Discrepancies between Law and Reality; 7. Categories of Soviet Organizations and Business People as Partners of American Companies; 8. Negotiating with Soviet Business People; Appendix: Natural Resources and Industries of the Republics of the Former Soviet Union and Contact Addresses and Phone Numbers: A Short Guide.]

949. Treyvish, Andrey I., Kavita K. Pandit, and Andrew R. Bond. "Macrostructural Employment Shifts and Urbanization in the Former USSR: An International Perspective." *Post-Soviet Geography* 34, no. 3 (March 1993): 157-171.

950. Tsigelny, Igor. *Business Strategies For the Ex-USSR: Business Guide.* La Jolla, CA: International University Line, c1993. xix, 227 pp.

951. United Nations. Economic Commission for Europe. *Directory of Chemical Producers and Products.* 1st ed. New York: United Nations, 1993-. vols. [Partial contents: Vol. 1, pt. 1. Chemical enterprises in central and eastern Europe — v. 3. Chemical manufacturers' associations and related organizations.]

952. United States. Congress. House. Committee on Ways and Means. Subcommittee on Trade. *Cold War Trade Statutes Affecting U.S. Trade and Commercial Relations with Russia and Other Successor States of the Former Soviet Union: Hearing before the Subcommittee on Trade of the Committee on Ways and Means, House of Representatives, One Hundred Third Congress, First Session, June 15, 1993.* Washington: U.S. G.P.O., 1993. iii, 113 pp.

953. United States. Congress. Joint Economic Committee. *The Former Soviet Union in Transition.* Edited by Richard F. Kaufman and John P. Hardt. Contributions by Steven J. Woehrel, James Noren, Laurie Kurtzweg, James R. Millar, Gertrude E. Schroeder, Douglas Diamond, Gregory Kisunko, Jozef M. van Brabant, Stuart S. Brown, Misha V. Belkindas, Anders Åslund, James A. Duran, Jr., John E. Tedstrom, Joseph S. Berliner, Marvin Jackson, Sandra Hughes, Scot Butler, Philip Hanson, Elizabeth Teague, Lillian Liu, Lawrence E. Modisett, George D. Holliday, Marie Lavigne, Heinrich Vogel, Shirley A. Kan, Patricia A. Wertman, Daniel L. Bond, Franklyn D. Holzman, William H. Cooper, Philip J. Kaiser, Joseph P. Riva, Jr., Jeffrey W. Schneider, William M. Liefert, Allan Mustard, Christopher E. Goldthwait, Barbara S. Severin, Remy Jurenas, Philip R. Pryde, Murray Feshbach, Holland Hunter, William C. Boesman, Marica S. Smith, Genevieve J. Knezo, Katlijn Malfliet, Richard F. Kaufman, Mary C.

FitzGerald, Martin C. Spechler, Nicholas Forte, Shelley Deutch, Ronald L. Davis, John R. Thomas, Steven W. Popper, Donald Creacey, James Voorhees, W. Ward Kingkade, Christopher Mark Davis, Michael Alexeev, Harley Balzer, Jim Nichol, David C. Johnson, Gail Albergo, Donald Green, Jay K. Mitchell, Vadim Myachin, Matthew Sagers, Elizabeth M. Sellers, Jan Vanous, Keith Bush, Steven J. Woehrel, Bess Brown, Elizabeth Fuller, Sergiu Verona, Kathleen Mihalisko, John Dunlop, Marc Rubin, Lee Schwartz, and David Zaslow. Armonk, NY: M.E. Sharpe, c1993. xxiv, 1222 pp. [Contents: John P. Hardt and Richard F. Kaufman, "Introduction," pp. xi-xxiv; Volume 1. I. The Transition to Market Economies. Steven J. Woehrel, "Overview," pp. 1-7; James Noren and Laurie Kurtzweg, "The Soviet Economy Unravels: 1985-91," pp. 8-33; James R. Millar, "The Economies of the CIS: Reformation, Revolution, or Restoration?" pp. 34-56; Gertrude E. Schroeder, "Post-Soviet Economic Reforms in Perspective," pp. 57-80; Douglas Diamond and Gregory Kisunko, "Industrial Growth by Republic in the Former U.S.S.R., 1981-90," pp. 81-120; Gertrude E. Schroeder, "Regional Economic Disparities, Gorbachev's Policies, and the Disintegration of the Soviet Union," pp. 121-145; Jozef M. van Brabant, "The New East and Its Preferred Trade Regime—The Impact of Soviet Disintegration," pp. 146-162; Stuart S. Brown and Misha V. Belkindas, "Who's Feeding Whom? An Analysis of Soviet Interrepublic Trade," pp. 163-183; Anders Åslund, "Heritage of the Gorbachev Era," pp. 184-195; James A. Duran, Jr., "Russian Fiscal and Monetary Stabilization: A Tough Road Ahead," pp. 196-217; John E. Tedstrom, "Problems of Fiscal Policy Reform During the Transition: A Baltic Case Study," pp. 218-239; Joseph S. Berliner, "The Gains from Privatization," pp. 240-254; Marvin Jackson, "Large-Scale Privatization in the CIS Republics: Some Comparisons with Central Europe," pp. 255-272; Sandra Hughes and Scot Butler, "Measuring the 'Private Sector' in Russia," pp. 273-289; Philip Hanson and Elizabeth Teague, "The Political Economy of Unemployment Benefits and Indexation in the Russian Federation," pp. 290-310; Lillian Liu, "Social Security in Transition in the Soviet Union (1985-1991) and in the Russian Federation (1992)," pp. 311-329; Lawrence E. Modisett, "The Cultural Dimension: Is There a Basis for Free Enterprise?" pp. 330-339. II. Integration into the World Economy. George D. Holliday, "Overview," pp. 341-344; Marie Lavigne, "Prospects for Commerce—A French Perspective," pp. 345-352; Heinrich Vogel, "Prospects for Commerce—A German Perspective," pp. 353-359; Shirley A. Kan and Patricia A. Wertman, "International Financial Institutions and the Restructuring of the Soviet Successor States," pp. 360-376; Daniel L. Bond, "The Role of Export Credit Agencies in the 'New East,'" pp. 377-388; Patricia A. Wertman, "The External Financial Position of the Former Soviet Union: From Riches to Rags?" pp. 389-404; Franklyn D. Holzman, "The Soviet-Russian Ruble: The Past, Present and Future of Convertibility," pp. 405-421; Jozef M. van Brabant, "Ruble Convertibility and External and Internal Equilibrium," pp. 422-438; William H. Cooper, "U.S. Commercial Relations with Russia and the Other Successor States: Opportunities and Obstacles," pp. 439-454. Volume 2. III. Key Sectoral Developments. Philip J. Kaiser,

"Overview," pp. 455-460; A. Energy. Joseph P. Riva, Jr., "The Petroleum Resources of Russia and the Commonwealth of Independent States," pp. 461-476; Jeffrey W. Schneider, "Republic Energy Sectors and Inter-State Dependencies of the Commonwealth of Independent States and Georgia," pp. 477-489; B. Agriculture. William M. Liefert, "Distribution Problems in the Food Economy of the Former Soviet Union," pp. 491-505; Allan Mustard and Christopher E. Goldthwait, "Food Availability in the Former Soviet Union: A Summary Report of Three Missions Led by the U.S. Department of Agriculture," pp. 506-513; Barbara S. Severin, "Differences in Food Production and Food Consumption Among the Republics of the Former Soviet Union," pp. 514-540; Remy Jurenas, "U.S. Agricultural Exports and Assistance to the Former Soviet Union," pp. 541-565; C. Environment. Philip R. Pryde, "The Environmental Implications of the Dissolution of the U.S.S.R.," pp. 567-576; Murray Feshbach, "Environmental Calamities: Widespread and Costly," pp. 577-596; D. Science and Transportation. Holland Hunter, "Transport in the Commonwealth of Independent States: An Aging Circulatory System," pp. 597-609; William C. Boesman, "Science and Technology in the Former Soviet Union: Capabilities and Needs," pp. 610-628; Marica S. Smith, "The Post-Soviet Space Program," pp. 629-647; Genevieve J. Knezo, "Scientific and Technical Collaboration with Former Soviet Countries," pp. 648-664; Katlijn Malfliet, "Toward a CIS Protection System for Inventions," pp. 665-680; IV. Defense and Conversion. Richard F. Kaufman, "Overview," pp. 681-685; Mary C. FitzGerald, "Russian Military Doctrine: Program for the 1990s and Beyond," pp. 686-703; Richard F. Kaufman, "Problems of Downsizing and Dissolution: Russian Defense Policy After the Breakup," pp. 704-716; Martin C. Spechler, "Conversion of Military Industries in the Successor States of the Former Soviet Union," pp. 717-729; Nicholas Forte and Shelley Deutch, "Defense Conversion in the Former U.S.S.R.: The Challenge Facing Plant Managers," pp. 730-738; Ronald L. Davis, "China's Unheralded Defense Conversion," pp. 739-753; John R. Thomas, "Russian Defense Conversion Under Old Management," pp. 754-766; Steven W. Popper, "Conversion, Regional Economies, and Direct Foreign Investment in Russia," pp. 767-782; Donald Creacey, "The Defense Industries of the Newly Independent States of Eurasia," pp. 783-790; V. Human Resources Affecting the Economy. James Voorhees, "Overview," pp. 791-794; W. Ward Kingkade, "Demographic Prospects in the Republics of the Former Soviet Union," pp. 795-819; Steven W. Popper, "A Note on the Emigration of Russia's Technical Intelligentsia," pp. 820-839; Murray Feshbach, "Continuing Negative Health Trends in the Former U.S.S.R.," pp. 840-851; Christopher Mark Davis, "The Health Sector in the Soviet and Russian Economies: From Reform to Fragmentation to Transition," pp. 852-872; Michael Alexeev, "The Current Conditions and Reform in the Housing Sector of the Former Soviet Union," pp. 873-888; Harley Balzer, "Science, Technology, and Education in the Former U.S.S.R.," pp. 889-908; VI. Political-Economic Profiles. Jim Nichol, "Overview," pp. 909-912; David C. Johnson, Gail Albergo, Donald Green, Jay K. Mitchell, Vadim Myachin, Matthew Sagers, Elizabeth M. Sellers, and

Jan Vanous, "Recent Economic Developments in the 15 Former Soviet Republics," pp. 913-949; Keith Bush, "Political-Economic Assessments: Russia," pp. 950-960; Steven J. Woehrel, "Political-Economic Assessments: Ukraine," pp. 961-970; Bess Brown, "Political-Economic Assessments: The Central Asian States," pp. 971-978; Elizabeth Fuller, "Political-Economic Assessments: The Transcaucasus," pp. 979-989; Sergiu Verona, "Political-Economic Assessments: Moldova," pp. 990-1002; Kathleen Mihalisko, "Political-Economic Assessments: Belarus," pp. 1003-1018; John Dunlop, Marc Rubin, Lee Schwartz, and David Zaslow, "Profiles of the Newly Independent States: Economic, Social and Demographic Conditions," pp. 1019-1187.]

954. United States. Congress. Joint Economic Committee. Subcommittee on Technology and National Security. *Global Economic and Technological Change: Former Soviet Union and Eastern Europe, and China: Hearing before the Subcommittee on Technology and National Security of the Joint Economic Committee, Congress of the United States, One Hundred Second Congress, Second Session.* United States. Congress. Senate S. hrg., 102-586. Washington: U.S. G.P.O., 1993-. vols.

955. United States. International Trade Commission. *Ferrosilicon from Kazakhstan and Ukraine: Determinations of the Commission in Investigations nos. 731-TA-566 and 569 (Preliminary) under the Tariff Act of 1930, Together with the Information Obtained in the Investigations.* USITC Publication, 2616. Washington, DC: U.S. International Trade Commission, [1993]. 34, 5, 8 pp.

956. ———. *Trade and Investment Patterns in the Crude Petroleum and Natural Gas Sectors of the Energy-Producing States of the Former Soviet Union.* USITC Publication, 2656. Washington, DC: U.S. International Trade Commission, [1993]. 1 vol.

957. Villanueva, Delano. *Options For Monetary and Exchange Arrangements in Transition Economies.* IMF Paper on Policy Analysis and Assessment, PPAA/93/12. [Washington, DC]: International Monetary Fund, c1993. 20 pp.

958. Wasyliw, Mary E. "New Coal-Burning Process Promises Cleaner Air for Ukraine and Russia." *Surviving Together* 11, no. 3 (Fall 1993): 16-17.

959. Whitlock, Erik. "The CIS Economy." *RFE/RL Research Report* 2, no. 1 (January 1, 1993): 46-49.

960. ———. "Obstacles to CIS Economic Integration." *RFE/RL Research Report* 2, no. 27 (July 2, 1993): 34-38.

961. ———. "Ukrainian-Russian Trade: The Economics of Dependency." *RFE/RL Research Report* 2, no. 43 (October 29, 1993): 38-42.

962. Williamson, John, ed. *Economic Consequences of Soviet Disintegration.* Contributions by C. Fred Bergsten, John Williamson, Maria Schaumayer, Evgeni Yasin, Nikolai Petrakov, Alexander Granberg, Daniel Gros, Boris Fedorov, Andrey Vavilov, Oleg Vjugin, Tim Snyder, Dmitri Subbotin,

Andreas Wörgötter, Assaf Razin, Sergey Alexashenko, Georg Winckler, John Williamson, Sergei A. Vasiliev, Stanislav Bogdankiewicz, Michael Marrese, Alexander Granberg, Alexander Ovsyannikov, Beisenbay Izteleuov, Surén Karapetyan, Korkhmaz Imanov, Rustam Narzikulov, Donna Bahry, Peter Havlik, David T. Onoprishvili, Mamuka Tsereteli, Inna Shteinbuka, Peter Nyberg, Mikhail Bronshtein, Adalbert Knöbl, Boris Fedorov, Bernhard Felderer, Lajos Bokros, W. E. Butler, and John Williamson. Washington, DC: Institute for International Economics, c1993. xiii, 637 pp. [Proceedings of a conference cosponsored by the Institute of International Economics and the Austrian National Bank, held in Vienna in April 1992. Partial contents: C. Fred Bergsten, "Preface," pp. vii-viii. I. Introduction. John Williamson, "Introduction," pp. 3-6; Maria Schaumayer, "Reform and Responsibility: The Role of Western Assistance in the Transition from Socialism," pp. 7-9. II. Disintegration and Reintegration. Evgeni Yasin, "The Economic Space of the Former Soviet Union, Past and Present," pp. 13-37; Nikolai Petrakov, "Political Prospects for Preservation of the Single Economic Space," pp. 38-46; Alexander Granberg, "The Economic Interdependence of the Former Soviet Republics," pp. 47-77; Daniel Gros, "Comment," pp. 78-83; Boris Fedorov, "Comment," pp. 84-87; "Discussion," pp. 88-96. III. Patterns of Trade and Industrial Organization. Andrey Vavilov and Oleg Vjugin, "Trade Patterns After Integration Into the World Economy," pp. 99-174; Tim Snyder, "Soviet Monopoly," pp. 175-243; Dmitri Subbotin, "Comment," pp. 244-248; Andreas Wörgötter, "Comment," pp. 249-251; Assaf Razin, "Comment," pp. 252-255; "Discussion," pp. 256-257. IV. Post-Soviet Macroeconomic Policy. Sergey Alexashenko, "Macroeconomic Stabilization in the Former Soviet Republics: Dream or Reality?" pp. 261-302; Georg Winckler, "Comment," pp. 303-306; John Williamson, "Comment," pp. 307-311; "Discussion," pp. 312-319. V. Russia and Belarus. Sergei A. Vasiliev, "Russia," pp. 323-333; Stanislav Bogdankiewicz, "Belarus," pp. 334-353; Michael Marrese, "Comment," pp. 354-357; Alexander Granberg, "Comment," pp. 358-361; Alexander Ovsyannikov, "Comment," pp. 362-364; "Discussion," pp. 365-366. VI. Kazakhstan, The Caucasus, and Central Asia. Beisenbay Izteleuov, "Kazakhstan," pp. 369-388; Surén Karapetyan, "Armenia," pp. 389-414; Korkhmaz Imanov, "Azerbaijan," pp. 415-428; Rustam Narzikulov, "The Central Asian Republics," pp. 429-453; Donna Bahry, "Comment," pp. 454-457; Peter Havlik, "Comment," pp. 458-461; "Discussion," pp. 462-464. VII. The Non-CIS Republics. David T. Onoprishvili and Mamuka Tsereteli, "Georgia," pp. 467-481; Inna Shteinbuka, "The Baltics," pp. 482-509; Peter Nyberg, "Comment," pp. 510-512; Mikhail Bronshtein, "Comment," pp. 513-515. VIII. Summary. Adalbert Knöbl, Boris Fedorov, Bernhard Felderer, and Lajos Bokros, "Panel Discussion," pp. 519-535; "Discussion," pp. 536-549; W.E. Butler, "The Russian Federation and State Succession," pp. 550-557; John Williamson, "Trade and Payments After Soviet Disintegration," pp. 558-629.]

963. Winston, Victor. "Geography of Human Resources: Implications for Policy." *Post-Soviet Geography* 34, no. 4 (April 1993): 273-277. [Edited version of the Proceedings of the Fifth Theodore Shabad Memorial Roundtable on the Geography of the (former) USSR, held in conjunction with the 1993 Annual Meeting of the Association of American Geographers in Atlanta, GA.]

Armenia

964. Armenia (Republic), United States. President (1993- : Clinton), and United States. Congress. Senate. Committee on Foreign Relations. *Investment Treaty with the Republic of Armenia: Message from the President of the United States Transmitting the Treaty Between the United States of America and the Republic of Armenia Concerning the Reciprocal Encouragement and Protection of Investment, Signed at Washington on September 23, 1992.* Washington: U.S. G.P.O., 1993. xiv, 26 pp.

965. Donovan, Donal et al. *Armenia.* Prepared under the direction of John C. Odling-Smee. IMF Economic Reviews, 1 (1993). Washington, DC: International Monetary Fund, 1993. vii, 104 pp.

966. Kelegian, Peter. "Paradise Suspended: The Challenge to Armenia's Nature Preserves." *Surviving Together* 11, no. 2 (Summer 1993): 12-13. [Reprinted from *AIM* (March 1993).]

967. United States. Congress. Senate. Committee on Foreign Relations. *Treaty with the Republic of Armenia Concerning the Reciprocal Encouragement and Protection of Investment: Report (To Accompany Treaty Doc. 103-11).* [Washington, DC?: U.S. G.P.O., 1993]. 5 pp.

968. Vodopivec, Milan, and Wayne Vroman. *The Armenian Labor Market in Transition: Issues and Options.* Policy Research Working Papers, WPS 1193. Washington, DC: Policy Research Department, World Bank, [1993]. i, 34 pp.

Azerbaijan

969. "Azerbaijan's Manat: Ticket to Renewal Or Toy Money?" *Surviving Together* 11, no. 1 (Spring 1993): 40-41. [Reprinted from *Armenian General Benevolent Union News* (December 1992).]

970. Carpenter, Mary, and Lynn Richards. "The Azerbaijan Green Movement: A Snapshot." *Surviving Together* 11, no. 2 (Summer 1993): 14-15.

971. Gurgen, Emine et al. *Azerbaijan.* Prepared under the direction of John C. Odling-Smee. IMF Economic Reviews, 3 (1993). Washington, DC: International Monetary Fund, c1993. vii, 112 pp.

972. Hussein-Zadeh, Nigar. "Help Us Heal the Caspian Sea." *Surviving Together* 11, no. 2 (Summer 1993): 14.

973. World Bank. *Azerbaijan: From Crisis to Sustained Growth.* World Bank Country Study. Washington, DC: World Bank, c1993. xxii, 223 pp. [Report is based on the work of two economic missions led by Zeynep Taymas, which visited Azerbaijan in July and October 1992.]

Belarus

974. "Nukes or Negawatts?" *Surviving Together* 11, no. 4 (Winter 1993): 49-50. [Reprinted from *Rocky Mountain Institute Newsletter* (Summer 1993).]

975. Spencer, Grant H. et al. *Belarus*. Prepared under the direction of John C. Odling-Smee. IMF Economic Reviews, 11 (1993). Washington, DC: International Monetary Fund, [1993]. vii, 125 pp.

Georgia

976. Donovan, Donal et al. *Georgia*. Prepared under the direction of John C. Odling-Smee. IMF Economic Reviews, 9 (1993). Washington, DC: International Monetary Fund, c1993. vii, 91 pp.

977. World Bank. *Georgia: A Blueprint For Reforms*. A World Bank Country Study. Washington, DC: World Bank, c1993. ix, 140 pp.

Kazakhstan

978. Bedell, J. M., D. Horowitz, and C. A. Nordberg, Jr. "Strangers in a New Land: U.S. Tax Lawyers Come to Kazakhstan." *Journal of International Taxation* 4, no. 7 (July 1993): 301-307.

979. Bell, Helen et al. *Kazakhstan: The Golden Road to Oil and Gas in Central Asia*. New York, NY: Petroleum Intelligence Weekly, [1993]. 63 pp. [With special contributions from Geoinformmark and Mayer, Brown & Platt. Partial contents: "Appendix I: Excerpts from the Draft Oil Law," pp. 56-59.]

980. Dosmukhamedov, Erzhan K. "Legal Aspects of Doing Business in the Republic of Kazakhstan." *International Legal Perspectives* 5, no. 1 (Spring 1993): 93-107.

981. Grzesiak, Christine M. "The Denationalization of Kazakhstan." *Denver Journal of International Law and Policy* 21, no. 2 (Winter 1993): 441-454.

982. Kapur, Ishan et al. *Kazakhstan*. Prepared under the direction of John C. Odling-Smee. IMF Economic Reviews, 5 (1993). Washington, DC: International Monetary Fund, c1993. vii, 121 pp.

983. Kazakhstan, United States. President (1993- : Clinton), and United States. Congress. Senate. Committee on Foreign Relations. *Investment Treaty with the Republic of Kazakhstan: Message from the President of the United States Transmitting the Treaty between the United States of America and the Republic of Kazakhstan Concerning the Reciprocal Encouragement and Protection of Investment, Signed at Washington on May 19, 1992*. Treaty doc., 103-12. Washington, DC: U.S. G.P.O., 1993. xiv, 26 pp.

984. Kuratov, Sergei. "The Kazakhstan Green Movement." *Surviving Together* 11, no. 3 (Fall 1993): 20-21.

985. Library of Congress. Documents Expediting Project, and National Technical Information Service (U.S.).

Kazakhstan: An Economic Profile. Washington, DC: Document Expediting (DOCEX) Project, Exchange and Gift Division, Library of Congress; Springfield, VA: National Technical Information Service, [1993]. vi, 36 pp.

986. Sievers, Eric. "The Legacy of Industrialization: Environmental Degradation in Northern Kazakhstan." *Surviving Together* 11, no. 3 (Fall 1993): 17-19.

987. United States. Congress. Senate. Committee on Foreign Relations. *Treaty with the Republic of Kazakhstan Concerning the Reciprocal Encouragement and Protection of Investment: Report (To Accompany Treaty Doc. 103-12)*. United States. Congress. Senate Executive Report, 103-11. [Washington, DC?: U.S. G.P.O., 1993]. 6 pp.

988. Ustiugov, Mikhail. "Big Oil Moves In." *Bulletin of the Atomic Scientists* 49, no. 8 (October 1993): 44-47.

989. ———. "Gold and Diamonds." *Bulletin of the Atomic Scientists* 49, no. 8 (October 1993): 51.

990. ———. "Imaginary Billions." *Bulletin of the Atomic Scientists* 49, no. 8 (October 1993): 50.

991. World Bank. *Kazakhstan: The Transition to a Market Economy*. A World Bank Country Study. Washington, DC: World Bank, 1993. x, 234 pp.

Kyrgyzstan

992. Henderson, Carol. "Grass Roots Aspects of Agricultural Privatization in Kyrgyzstan." *Central Asia Monitor*, no. 5 (1993): 29-35.

993. Huskey, Eugene. "Kyrgyzstan Leaves the Ruble Zone." *RFE/RL Research Report* 2, no. 35 (September 3, 1993): 38-43.

994. Keller, Peter et al. *Kyrgyz Republic*. Prepared under the direction of John C. Odling-Smee. Economic Review (Washington, DC), 12 (1993). Washington, DC: International Monetary Fund, c1993. vii, 98 pp.

995. Richards, Lynn. "The Greens of Kyrgyszstan." *Surviving Together* 11, no. 3 (Fall 1993): 21-22.

996. World Bank. *Kyrgyzstan: Social Protection in a Reforming Economy*. A World Bank Country Study. Washington, DC: World Bank, c1993. xviii, 160 pp. [Based on the findings of a mission which worked in Kyrgyzstan from August 14 to September 2, 1992.]

997. ———. *Kyrgyzstan: The Transition to a Market Economy*. A World Bank Country Study. Washington, DC: World Bank, c1993. xviii, 230 pp. [Based on the work of an economic mission that visited Kyrgyzstan.]

Moldova

998. Moldova, United States. President (1993- : Clinton), and United States. Congress. Senate. Committee on Foreign Relations. *Investment Treaty with the Republic of Moldova: Message from the President of the United States*

Transmitting the Treaty between the United States of America and the Republic of Moldova Concerning the Encouragement and Reciprocal Protection of Investment, with Protocol and Related Exchange of Letters, Signed at Washington on April 21 1993. Treaty doc., 103-14. Washington: U.S. G.P.O., 1993. xv, 34 pp.

999. Ouanes, Abdessatar et al. *Moldova.* Prepared under the direction of John C. Odling-Smee. IMF Economic Reviews, 2 (1993). Washington, DC: International Monetary Fund, c1993. vii, 99 pp.

1000. United States. Congress. Senate. Committee on Foreign Relations. *Treaty with the Republic of Moldova Concerning the Encouragement and Reciprocal Protection of Investment: Report (To Accompany Treaty Doc. 103-14).* United States. Congress. Senate Executive Report, 103-13. [Washington, DC?: U.S. G.P.O., 1993]. 6 pp.

Russian Federation

General

1001. Alexeev, Michael, Clifford Gaddy, and Jim Leitzel. "Russia's Black Market Bulwark: How Economic Crime Prods Market Reform." *World & I* 8, no. 10 (October 1993): 420-439.

1002. Belyanova, Elena, and Sergei Aukutsenek. "Russia's Economic Decline: State Manufacturers Suffer Less." *RFE/RL Research Report* 2, no. 4 (January 22, 1993): 41-44.

1003. Berger, Mikhail. "The Economy: Disintegrating." *Bulletin of the Atomic Scientists* 49, no. 1 (January-February 1993): 32-35.

1004. Bernstein, Jonas. "The Moscow Spectator: A Land of Individualists." *American Spectator* 26, no. 6 (June 1993): 48-49.

1005. Bienen, Henry, and Mansur Sunyaev. "Adjustment and Reform in Russia." *SAIS Review* 13, no. 1 (Winter-Spring 1993): 29-44.

1006. Boycko, Maxim, Andrei Shleifer, and Robert Vishny. "Privatizing Russia." *Brookings Papers on Economic Activity*, no. 2 (1993): 139-192. [Followed by a discussion with Jeffrey D. Sachs, Stanley Fisher and others.]

1007. Bush, Keith. "Conversion and Unemployment in Russia." *RFE/RL Research Report* 2, no. 2 (January 8, 1993): 29-32.

1008. ———. "Light at the End of the Tunnel?" *RFE/RL Research Report* 2, no. 20 (May 14, 1993): 61-67.

1009. Commander, Simon et al. *The Behaviour of Russian Firms in 1992: Evidence from a Survey.* Policy Research Working Papers, WPS 1166. Washington, DC: Economic Development Institute, World Bank, [1993]. 46 pp.

1010. Dyson, Esther. "Remaking Russia, By Computer." *New York Times Magazine* (October 10, 1993): 26ff.

1011. Edwards, Mike. "Playing by New Rules." *National Geographic* 183, no. 3 (March 1993): 4-20.

1012. Elliott, John E., and Abu F. Dowlah. "Transition Crises in the Post-Soviet Era." *Journal of Economic Issues* 27, no. 2 (June 1993): 527-536.

1013. Ericson, Richard E. "Self-Evident Truths: The Challenge of Marketization." *Harriman Institute Forum* 7, nos. 1-2 (September-October 1993): 3-6. [Paper from the Fifth Annual Workshop on Post-Soviet Nations, held at the Harriman Institute, April 30, 1993.]

1014. Gimpelson, Vladimir. "Russia's New Independent Entrepreneurs." *RFE/RL Research Report* 2, no. 36 (September 10, 1993): 44-48.

1015. Goldman, Marshall I. "The Chinese Model: The Solution to Russia's Economic Ills?" *Current History* 92, no. 576 (October 1993): 320-324.

1016. Grossman, Gregory. "The Underground Economy in Russia." *International Economic Insights* 4, no. 6 (November-December 1993): 14-17.

1017. Hernandez-Cata, Ernesto et al. *Russian Federation.* Prepared under the direction of John C. Odling-Smee. IMF Economic Reviews, 8 (1993). Washington, DC: International Monetary Fund, [1993]. ix, 140 pp.

1018. Hough, Jerry. "On the Road to Paradise Again?" *Brookings Review* 11, no. 1 (Winter 1993): 12-17.

1019. Islam, Shafiqul. "Moscow's Rough Road to Capitalism." *Foreign Affairs* 72, no. 2 (Spring 1993): 57-66.

1020. Malkov, Leonid P., and Peter B. Maggs. "Protecting Intellectual Property in Russia." *Research Technology Management* 36, no. 1 (January-February 1993): 15-16.

1021. Mihalisko, Kathleen. "Market Reforms and the Russian Leadership." *RFE/RL Research Report* 2, no. 26 (June 25, 1993): 48-50.

1022. Odling-Smee, John C., and Henri Lorie. *The Economic Reform Process in Russia.* IMF Working Paper, WP/93/55. [Washington, DC]: International Monetary Fund, c1993. iii, 8 pp.

1023. Rhodes, Mark. "A Renewal of Public Confidence in the Russian Economy?" *RFE/RL Research Report* 2, no. 35 (September 3, 1993): 59-61.

1024. Rose, Richard. "The Russian Response to Privatization." *RFE/RL Research Report* 2, no. 47 (November 26, 1993): 50-55.

1025. Russia (Federation). *Business and Commercial Laws of Russia: Translations with Expert Commentary.* General editor John P. Hupp. Translations By Russica Information, Inc. Colorado Springs, CO: Shepard's/McGraw-Hill, c1993-. vols. [Translated from Russian. Contents: Vol. 1. Business enterprises, privatization, commercial trade — v. 2. Taxation.]

1026. ——. *The Commercial Code of Russia: An Adaptive Translation of the Laws of the Russian Federation Relating to Domestic and Foreign Commerce.* Edited by Nellie V. Romanovskaya and Robert G. Allen. Manassas, VA: AMH Publications, c1993-. vols.

1027. "Russian Economic Reform." *International Economic Insights* 4, no. 1 (January-February 1993): 33-34.

1028. Sagers, Matthew J., Judith Pallot, and Denis J. B. Shaw. "News Notes: Background and Analysis." *Post-Soviet Geography* 34, no. 3 (March 1993): 204-218. [Off-shore Gas Project in Barents Sea Taken from Western Consortium and Turned Over to Russian Industrial Group; Russian Crude Oil Exports in 1992: Who Exported Russian Oil?; Update on Russian Federation Land Reform; Progress in Housing Privatization.]

1029. Schillinger, Liesl. "The Yupskies are Coming." *New York* 26, no. 30 (August 2, 1993): 34-40. [Profiles of ten Americans who have moved to Moscow.]

1030. Sorokin, Konstantin E. "Conversion in Russia: The Need for a Balanced Strategy." *Journal of Political and Military Sociology* 21, no. 2 (Winter 1993): 163-179.

1031. Stevenson, Matthew. "Dealing in Russia." *American Scholar* 62, no. 4 (Autumn 1993): 497-512.

1032. Stuttaford, Andrew. "Springtime in Moscow." *National Review* 45, no. 8 (April 26, 1993): 21-22.

1033. Whiting, Bruce G. "The Creative Business Challenges of Russia." *Journal of Creative Behavior* 27, no. 2 (Second Quarter 1993): 143-146.

1034. Whitlock, Erik. "Defense Conversion and Privatization in St. Petersburg." *RFE/RL Research Report* 2, no. 24 (June 11, 1993): 21-25. [On a seminar on conversion and privatization sponsored by RFE/RL Research Institute and the St. Petersburg University of Economics and Finance, held in St. Petersburg, Russia, on May 7, 1993.]

1035. Wolf, Charles, Jr. "Russia: Reasons for Hope." *World Monitor* 6, no. 1 (January 1993): 48-50.

1036. Young, Cathy. "Russia: Trip to the Market." *Reason* 25, no. 4 (August-September 1993): 52-53.

1037. ——. "Russia Watch: Evil Emperors." *American Spectator* 26, no. 2 (February 1993): 52-54.

Agriculture

1038. DeVault, George. "Farming's Real Rewards." *Surviving Together* 11, no. 1 (Spring 1993): 25-27. [Excerpted from *The New Farm* (February 1993).]

1039. Goldstein, Walter. "Ecological Agriculture." *Surviving Together* 11, no. 1 (Spring 1993): 21-22.

1040. Haberern, John. "Ready for Sustainability." *Surviving Together* 11, no. 1 (Spring 1993): 20-21.

1041. Johnson, D. Gale. "Trade Effects of Dismantling the Socialized Agriculture of the Former Soviet Union." *Comparative Economic Studies* 35, no. 4 (Winter 1993): 21-31. [Earlier version of this paper was prepared for presentation at the International Agricultural Trade Research Consortium, December 1992.]

1042. Liefert, William M., Robert B. Koopman, and Edward C. Cook. "Agricultural Reform in the Former USSR." *Comparative Economic Studies* 35, no. 4 (Winter 1993): 49-68.

1043. Marnie, Sheila. "The Unresolved Question of Land Reform in Russia." *RFE/RL Research Report* 2, no. 7 (February 12, 1993): 35-37.

1044. Marshall, Daniel W. "Who Is Tending the Hive? Beekeeping's Unique Role in Russian Society." *World & I* 8, no. 9 (September 1993): 235-245.

1045. Moran, Mike, and Carmen Censky. "US Volunteers Earn Good Credit with Russian Farmers." *Surviving Together* 11, no. 3 (Fall 1993): 32-34.

1046. Tangermann, Stefan. "Economic Reform and World Agricultural Markets." *Comparative Economic Studies* 35, no. 4 (Winter 1993): 33-47. [Earlier version of this paper was prepared for presentation at International Agricultural Trade Research Consortium, December 1992.]

1047. United States. Congress. House. Committee on Agriculture. Subcommittee on Foreign Agriculture and Hunger. *Current Agricultural Situation in Russia: Hearings before the Subcommittee on Foreign Agriculture and Hunger of the Committee on Agriculture, House of Representatives, One Hundred Third Congress, First Session, March 30, 31, and April 1, 1993.* Washington: U.S. G.P.O., 1993. iv, 291 pp.

1048. Van Atta, Don, ed. *The "Farmer Threat": The Political Economy of Agrarian Reform in Post-Soviet Russia.* Contributions by Don Van Atta, William M. Liefert, Werner Hahn, David A. J. Macey, Stephen K. Wegren, Roy L. Prosterman, and Timothy Hanstad. Boulder, CO: Westview Press, 1993. xiii, 221 pp. [Contents: Don Van Atta, "Introduction," pp. 1-8; Part One: The Political Economy of Agriculture and Food Supplies; Don Van Atta, "Russian Agriculture Between Plan and Market," pp. 9-24; William M. Liefert, "The Food Problem in the Republics of the Former USSR," pp. 25-42; Werner Hahn, "The Farms' Revolt and Grain Shortages in 1991," pp. 43-54; Don Van Atta, "Russian Food Supplies in 1992," pp. 55-67. Part Two: The Post-Soviet Agrarian Reforms; Don Van Atta, "The Return of Individual Farming in Russia," pp. 71-95; David A.J. Macey, "Stolypin Is Risen! The Ideology of Agrarian Reform in Contemporary Russia," pp. 97-120; Stephen K. Wegren, "Political Institutions and Agrarian Reform in Russia," pp. 121-147; Roy L. Prosterman and Timothy Hanstad, "A Fieldwork-Based Appraisal of Individual Peasant Farming in Russia," pp. 149-189; Part Three: The Agrarian Reforms and Russia's Future; Don Van Atta, "Agrarian Interests and the Politics of Reform in Post-Soviet Russia," pp. 193-212.]

1049. ———. "The Human Dimension of Agrarian Reform in Russia." *Post-Soviet Geography* 34, no. 4 (April 1993): 258-268. [Edited version of the Proceedings of the Fifth Theodore Shabad Memorial Roundtable on the Geography of the (former) USSR, held in conjunction with the 1993 Annual Meeting of the Association of American Geographers in Atlanta, GA.]

1050. ———. "The Second Congress of the Russian Agrarian Union." *RFE/RL Research Report* 2, no. 31 (July 30, 1993): 42-49.

1051. Wegren, Stephen K. "Rural Reform in Russia." *RFE/RL Research Report* 2, no. 43 (October 29, 1993): 43-53.

1052. ———. "Trends in Russian Agrarian Reform." *RFE/RL Research Report* 2, no. 13 (March 26, 1993): 46-57.

Finance

1053. Angell, Wayne D. "A Gold-Based Monetary Policy for Russia." *Cato Journal* 12, no. 3 (Winter 1993): 677-682. [Comment on Alan Reynolds, "Monetary Reform in Russia: The Case for Gold," pp. 657-676. Part of special issue devoted to "Monetary Reform in Ex-Communist Countries."]

1054. Aukutsenek, Sergei, and Elena Belyanova. "Russian Credit Markets Remain Distorted." *RFE/RL Research Report* 2, no. 4 (January 22, 1993): 37-40.

1055. Bogdanovicz-Bindert, Christine A., and Charles E. Ryan. "The Privatization Program of the City of St. Petersburg." *Columbia Journal of World Business* 28, no. 1 (Spring 1993): 150-156.

1056. Bogomolov, Oleg. "Is Russia Threatened with Hyperinflation?" *Cato Journal* 12, no. 3 (Winter 1993): 593-602. [Part of special issue devoted to "Monetary Reform in Ex-Communist Countries."]

1057. Delyagin, Mikhail, and Lev Freinkman. "Extrabudgetary Funds in Russian Public Finance." *RFE/RL Research Report* 2, no. 48 (December 3, 1993): 49-54.

1058. Hanke, Steve H., Lars Jonung, and Kurt Schuler. *Russian Currency and Finance: A Currency Board Approach to Reform.* London; New York: Routledge, 1993. xvi, 222 pp.

1059. Hellman, Joel Scott. "Breaking the Bank: Bureaucrats and the Creation of Markets in a Transitional Economy." Ph.D. diss., Columbia University, 1993. [UMI order no: AAC 9412768.]

1060. Ickes, Barry W., and Randi Ryterman. "Roadblock to Economic Reform: Inter-Enterprise Debt and the Transition to Markets." *Post-Soviet Affairs* 9, no. 3 (July-September 1993): 231-252.

1061. Lambroza, Sam. "Rubles and Sense." *Journal of European Business* 5, no. 2 (November-December 1993): 14-15.

1062. Lieberman, Edward H. "Russia Modernizes Its Tax System, But Ghosts of the USSR Still Haunt." *Journal of International Taxation* 4, no. 1 (January 1993): 32-36.

1063. Petrakov, Nikolai. "Monetary Stabilization in Russia: What Is to Be Done?" *Cato Journal* 12, no. 3 (Winter 1993): 607-615. [Part of special issue devoted to "Monetary Reform in Ex-Communist Countries."]

1064. Reynolds, Alan. "Monetary Reform in Russia: The Case for Gold." *Cato Journal* 12, no. 3 (Winter 1993): 657-676. [Part of special issue devoted to "Monetary Reform in Ex-Communist Countries."]

1065. Roberts, Paul Craig. "Russia's Informal Revolution." *Cato Journal* 12, no. 3 (Winter 1993): 603-606. [Comment on Oleg Bogomolov, "Is Russia Threatened with Hyperinflation?" pp. 593-602. Part of special issue devoted to "Monetary Reform in Ex-Communist Countries."]

1066. Schwartz, Anna J. "A Commodity Standard for Russia." *Cato Journal* 12, no. 3 (Winter 1993): 683-686. [Comment on Alan Reynolds, "Monetary Reform in Russia: The Case for Gold," pp. 657-676. Part of special issue devoted to "Monetary Reform in Ex-Communist Countries."]

1067. Schwartz, Pedro. "A Market Approach to Monetary Perestroika." *Cato Journal* 12, no. 3 (Winter 1993): 621-632. [Part of special issue devoted to "Monetary Reform in Ex-Communist Countries."]

1068. Shelton, Judy. "What Went Wrong?" *Cato Journal* 12, no. 3 (Winter 1993): 617-620. [Comment on Nikolai Petrakov, "Monetary Stabilization in Russia: What Is to Be Done?" pp. 607-615. Part of special issue devoted to "Monetary Reform in Ex-Communist Countries."]

1069. Streng, William P. "Introduction to Tax and Fiscal Documents." *Houston Journal of International Law* 15, no. 3 (Winter-Spring 1993): 853-854.

1070. ———. "Russian Federation Tax Legislation Impacting Russia Based Oil and Gas Operations: Endless (?) Transition." *Houston Journal of International Law* 15, no. 2 (Winter-Spring 1993): 553-631.

1071. Streng, William P., Ray Jones, and Richard Gordon. "Executive Summary: Fundamental Issues Concerning Russian Oil and Gas Tax Legislation." *Houston Journal of International Law* 15, no. 3 (Winter-Spring 1993): 869-870.

1072. Viehe, Karl William, Richard P. Bernard, Allan Roth, and Yan Melkumov. "The Russian Federation Law on Regulation of the Securities Market." *Transnational Lawyer* 6, no. 1 (Spring 1993): 81-107.

1073. Vysman, Inna. "The New Banking Legislation in Russia: Theoretical Adequacy, Practical Difficulties, and Potential Solutions." *Fordham Law Review* 62, no. 1 (October 1993): 265-286.

1074. Whitlock, Erik. "The Return of the Ruble." *RFE/RL Research Report* 2, no. 35 (September 3, 1993): 34-37.

1075. ———. "The Russian Government, the Central Bank, and the Resolution on Constitutional Reform." *RFE/RL Research Report* 2, no. 13 (March 26, 1993): 3.

1076. World Bank. *Russia: The Banking System During Transition.* Prepared by Ruben Lamdany. A World Bank Country Study. Washington, DC: World Bank, c1993. x, 61 p. [Report is based on the work of two World Bank missions.]

1077. Yakovlev, Andrei. "Commodity Exchanges and the Russian Government." *RFE/RL Research Report* 2, no. 45 (November 12, 1993): 24-28.

1078. Zhurek, Stefan. "Commodity Exchanges in Russia: Success or Failure?" *RFE/RL Research Report* 2, no. 6 (February 5, 1993): 41-44.

Foreign Economic Relations

1079. Basi, Rajpreet. "Foreign Investment in the Russian Oil and Gas Industry: A Time for Reckoning." *International Legal Perspectives* 5, no. 1 (Spring 1993): 33-64.

1080. Bertovich, Jayne, and Joanne Guth. "The EC Commission negotiates toward a new agreement with Russia." *International Economic Review* (June 1993): 12-13.

1081. Bruder, Eric T. "Vancouver Summit Initiatives Generate Business Opportunities in Russia." *Business America* 114, no. 10 (May 17, 1993): 7-8.

1082. Buchanan, Thompson R. "Helping Russia Reform." *Foreign Service Journal* 70, no. 4 (April 1993): 31-39.

1083. Burke, Justin. "Russia Gets Taste of 'Caring Capitalism.'" *Surviving Together* 11, no. 2 (Summer 1993): 51. [Reprinted from *Christian Science Monitor* (March 5, 1993).]

1084. Corn, David. "Sawyer, Miller Goes to Moscow: Propagandists to Power." *Nation* 257, no. 4 (July 26, 1993): 139-140.

1085. Dorian, James P., David Fridley, and Kristin Tressler. "Multilateral Resource Cooperation among Northeast Asian Countries: Energy and Mineral Joint Venture Prospects." *Journal of Northeast Asian Studies* 12, no. 1 (Spring 1993): 3-34.

1086. Fabrizio, Lynn. "New U.S.-Russia Commission Pushes Commercial Cooperation in Energy and Space." *Business America* 114, no. 19 (September 20, 1993): 2.

1087. Gunn, Trevor J. "Racing to Enter the Russian Far East Market." *Business America* 114, no. 17 (August 23, 1993): 2-5.

1088. Hughes, David. "Russian avionics ventures making rapid progress." *Aviation Week & Space Technology* 139, no. 9 (August 30, 1993): 54-55.

1089. Imse, Ann. "American Know-How and Russian Oil." *New York Times Magazine* (March 7, 1993):

28ff. ["A case study of why capitalism and bureaucracy don't mix."]

1090. Isaacs, John. "House OK's Russian Aid." *Bulletin of the Atomic Scientists* 49, no. 7 (September 1993): 3-4.

1091. Kvint, Vladimir, and Natalia Darialova. *The Barefoot Shoemaker: Capitalizing on the New Russia.* 1st ed. New York: Arcade Pub.: Distributed by Little, Brown, c1993. xii, 234 pp. REV: Peter Koster, *Canadian Business* 66, no. 10 (October 1993): 130-131. Koeleman Hans van Wouw, *Across the Board* 30, no. 9 (November-December 1993): 59-60.

1092. LaFollette, Karen. *Soft Assistance for Hard Russian Reform.* Foreign Policy Briefing, no. 25 (June 3, 1993). Washington, DC: Cato Institute, 1993. 17 pp.

1093. Lawrence, Paul, and Charalambos Vlachoutsicos. "Joint Ventures in Russia: Put the Locals in Charge." *Harvard Business Review* 71, no. 1 (January-February 1993): 44ff.

1094. O'Connor, Robert. "Risky Business." *Journal of European Business* 4, no. 6 (July-August 1993): 24-31.

1095. "Open for Business: Russia's Return to the Global Economy." *International Economic Insights* 4, no. 1 (January-February 1993): 34-35.

1096. Osakwe, Christopher. "Navigating the Minefields of Russian Joint Venture Law and Tax Regulation: A Procedural Compass." *Vanderbilt Journal of Transnational Law* 25, no. 5 (1993): 799-880.

1097. Platkovsky, Alexander. "North Korean Agents Searching for Escaped Lumberjacks." *RCDA* 32, no. 1 (1993-1994): 18. [Translation of excerpt from *Izvestiia* (March 4, 1994).]

1098. Reznik, Boris. "Top Secret Korean Establishments in the Russian Taiga." *RCDA* 32, no. 1 (1993-1994): 15-17. [Translation of an article from *Izvestiia* (March 26, 1994).]

1099. Ring, Mary Ann. "Countertrade Business Opportunities in Russia." *Business America* 114, no. 1 (January 11, 1993): 15-16.

1100. Rybak, Boris. "Aviaexport joins Bravia for global Tu-204 sales." *Aviation Week & Space Technology* 139, no. 2 (July 12, 1993): 34-35.

1101. Sachs, Jeffrey. "Strengthening Western Support for Russia." *International Economic Insights* 4, no. 1 (January-February 1993): 10-13.

1102. Smith, Alan. *Russia and the World Economy: Problems of Integration.* London; New York: Routledge, 1993. x, 253 pp.

1103. Suokko, Kristen. "US Assistance to the Russian Energy Sector Needs Long-term Goals." *Surviving Together* 11, no. 2 (Summer 1993): 26-27.

1104. United States. Congress. House. Committee on Foreign Affairs. Subcommittee on Economic Policy, Trade and Environment. *Agricultural Export Credit Guarantees: Hearing before the Subcommittee on Economic Policy, Trade, and Environment of the Committee on Foreign Affairs, House of Representatives, One Hundred Third Congress, First Session, May 6, 1993.* Washington, DC: U.S. G.P.O., 1993. iii, 62 pp.

1105. "U.S., Russia settle export disagreement." *Aviation Week & Space Technology* 139, no. 4 (July 26, 1993): 27. [On rocket technology.]

1106. Yancik, Joseph, and Marianne Vanatta. "U.S.-Russian Oil and Gas Officials Establish Close Links for Future." *Business America* 114, no. 11 (May 31, 1993): 10-11.

Industry and Transportation

1107. "Aeroflot, Perot in cargo talks." *Aviation Week & Space Technology* 138, no. 20 (May 17, 1993): 37-38.

1108. Berman, Sheila. "Pioneering Printmakers Collaborate with Russian Artists." *Surviving Together* 11, no. 3 (Fall 1993): 52-53.

1109. Bush, Keith. "Industrial Privatization in Russia: A Progress Report." *RFE/RL Research Report* 2, no. 7 (February 12, 1993): 32-34.

1110. Covault, Craig. "Russia revamping aerospace identity." *Aviation Week & Space Technology* 138, no. 23 (June 7, 1993): 58-61.

1111. ———. "Yeltsin to review Russian aerospace plea." *Aviation Week & Space Technology* 138, no. 21 (May 24, 1993): 22-23.

1112. Fortescue, Stephen. "Organization in Russian Industry: Beyond Decentralization." *RFE/RL Research Report* 2, no. 50 (December 17, 1993): 35-39.

1113. Hughes, David. "U.S.-Russian firm creating low-cost glass cockpits." *Aviation Week & Space Technology* 139, no. 3 (July 19, 1993): 37.

1114. Kachalin, Vladimir V. "Defense Industry Conversion in the Russian Federation: A Case Study of Kaluga Region." *Harriman Institute Forum* 6, no. 10 (June 1993): 1-12.

1115. Komlev, Sergei, and Daniel Satinsky. "Developing a Dial Tone: Russia's Telecommunications Challenge." *Surviving Together* 11, no. 1 (Spring 1993): 41-42. [Excerpt from *Geonomics Newsletter* (November-December 1992).]

1116. Lenorovitz, Jeffrey M., and Boris Rybak. "Volga-Dnepr cargo airline seeks major global role." *Aviation Week & Space Technology* 139, no. 16 (October 18, 1993): 47.

1117. McFaul, Michael, and Stanford University Center for International Security and Arms Control Russian Defense Conversion Project. *Can the Russian Military-Industrial Complex Be Privatized? Evaluating the Experiment in Employee Ownership at the Saratov Aviation Plant.* Stanford, CA: Stanford University, c1993. 60 pp. [A report of the Russian Defense Conversion Project, Center for International Security and Arms Control.]

1118. McKenna, James T. "Mil signs Hungarian firm to service helicopters." *Aviation Week & Space Technology* 138, no. 12 (March 22, 1993): 47-48.

1119. Proctor, Paul. "Russians, U.S. drill for rescue." *Aviation Week & Space Technology* 139, no. 17 (October 25, 1993): 31.

1120. Rybak, Boris. "Russian shows attract broad participation." *Aviation Week & Space Technology* 139, no. 8 (August 23, 1993): 49-50.

1121. ———. "Russians advance privatization plans." *Aviation Week & Space Technology* 138, no. 13 (March 29, 1993): 60.

1122. Sagers, Matthew J. "Destruction of Russia's Largest Manufacturing Facility for Diesel Truck Engines." *Post-Soviet Geography* 34, no. 7 (September 1993): 474-477.

1123. Sagers, Matthew J., and Valeriy Kryukov. "The Hydrocarbon Processing Industry in West Siberia." *Post-Soviet Geography* 34, no. 2 (February 1993): 127-152.

1124. Sparaco, Pierre. "Ilyushin Il-96M debuts to uncertain market." *Aviation Week & Space Technology* 138, no. 14 (April 5, 1993): 33-34.

1125. Sturino, John. "SoapBerry Combines Conservation and Cosmetics." *Surviving Together* 11, no. 3 (Fall 1993): 56.

1126. Webster, Leila, and Joshua Charap. *The Emergence of Private Sector Manufacturing in St. Petersburg: A Survey of Firms.* World Bank Technical Paper, no. 228. Washington, DC: World Bank, 1993. vii, 105 pp.

1127. Whitlock, Erik. "Industrial Policy in Russia." *RFE/RL Research Report* 2, no. 9 (February 26, 1993): 44-48.

Labor

1128. Brown, Annette N. "A Note on Industrial Adjustment and Regional Labor Markets in Russia." *Comparative Economic Studies* 35, no. 4 (Winter 1993): 147-157.

1129. Clarke, Simon et al., comps. *What About the Workers? Workers and the Transition to Capitalism in Russia.* London; New York: Verso, 1993. 248 pp.

1130. Commander, Simon, and Richard Jackman. *Providing Social Benefits in Russia: Redefining the Roles of Firms and Government.* Policy Research Working Papers, WSP 1184. Washington, DC: National Economic Management Division, Economic Development Institute, World Bank, [1993]. 41 pp.

1131. Commander, Simon, Leonid Liberman, and Ruslan Yemtsov. *Unemployment and Labour Market*

Dynamics in Russia. Policy Research Working Papers, WPS 1167. Washington, DC: Economic Development Institute, World Bank, [1993]. 46 pp.

1132. Crowley, Stephen. "From Coal to Steel: The Formation of an Independent Workers' Movement in the Soviet Union, 1989-1991." Ph.D. diss., University of Michigan, 1993. [UMI order no: AAC 9409669.]

1133. Gendler, Grigorii, and Marina Gildingersh. "Labor Exchanges in St. Petersburg." *RFE/RL Research Report* 2, no. 33 (August 20, 1993): 43-48.

1134. Gimpelson, Vladimir. "Changing Work Attitudes in Russia's New Private Sector." *RFE/RL Research Report* 2, no. 6 (February 5, 1993): 37-40.

1135. Marnie, Sheila. "Who and Where Are the Russian Unemployed?" *RFE/RL Research Report* 2, no. 33 (August 20, 1993): 36-42. [Includes sidebar: "Recent Legislation on Employment," p. 39.]

1136. Silverman, Bertram, Robert Vogt, and Murray Yanowitch, eds. *Double Shift: Transforming Work in Postsocialist and Postindustrial Societies: A U.S.-Post Soviet Dialogue*. Contributions by Leonid A. Gordon, Vladimir Iadov, Vladimir Gimpelson, Boris Rakitskii, Galina Rakitskaia, Ovsei Shkaratan, Natalia Rimashevskaia, Richard B. Freeman, Thomas E. Weisskopf, Murray Yanowitch, Ray Marshall, Harry C. Katz, Sarosh Kuruvilla, Lowell Turner, George T. Milkovich, Ruth Milkman, David Brody, Alice Kessler-Harris, and Bertram Silverman. U.S.-Post-Soviet Dialogues. Armonk, NY: M.E. Sharpe, c1993. xxvi, 281 pp. [Revised versions of papers presented at two symposia held in Moscow, June 2-8, 1991, and in New York, March 12-15, 1992, and jointly organized by Hofstra University's Center for the Study of Work and Leisure and the Russian Institute of Sociology, the Institute of Employment Problems and the Academy of Labor and Social Relations. Contents: Bertram Silverman and Murray Yanowitch, "Introduction: The Transformation of Work in Postsocialist and Postindustrial Societies." Pt. 1. The Emergence of Post-Soviet Labor Relations: Russian Views. Leonid A. Gordon, "Russia on the Road to New Industrial Relations: From Unipartite Commands to Tripartite Partnership via Bipartite Conflicts and Bargaining"; Vladimir Iadov, "The Formation of Working-Class Consciousness Under Conditions of Social Crisis and the Developing Market Economy in Russia"; Vladimir Gimpelson, "Economic Consciousness and Reform of the Employment Sphere"; Boris Rakitskii, "New Buyers and New Sellers in Russia's Labor Markets"; Galina Rakitskaia, "The Struggle for Property Is a Struggle for Power in the Economy"; Ovsei Shkaratan, "The Old and the New Masters of Russia: From Power Relations to Proprietary Relations"; Natalia Rimashevskaia, "Changes in Social Policy and Labor Legislation: The Gender Aspect." Pt. 2. Postsocialist Marketization and Privatization: Western Views. Richard B. Freeman, "What Direction for Labor-Market Institutions in Eastern and Central Europe?"; Thomas E. Weisskopf, "Democratic Self-management: An Alternative Approach to Economic Transformation in the Former Soviet Union";

Murray Yanowitch, "The Problem of 'Egalitarianism': Continuity and Change in Soviet Attitudes." Pt. 3. Labor Strategies in a Postindustrial Society, Ray Marshall, "High-Performance Production Systems in a More Competitive, Knowledge-Intensive World Economy"; Harry C. Katz, Sarosh Kuruvilla and Lowell Turner, "Trade Unions and Collective Bargaining: Suggestions for Emerging Democracies in Eastern Europe and the Former Soviet Union"; George T. Milkovich, "Restructuring Human Resource Management in the United States"; Ruth Milkman, "The Impact of Foreign Investment on U.S. Industrial Relations: The Case of Japan"; David Brody, "The Enduring Labor Movement: A Job-Conscious Perspective"; Alice Kessler-Harris and Bertram Silverman, "Beyond Industrial Unionism."]

1137. Sinder, Riley M. "Protection for Mobilizing Improvements in the Workplace: The United States and Russia." *American University Journal of International Law and Policy* 9, no. 1 (Fall 1993): 309-356.

1138. Teague, Elizabeth. "Organized Labor in Russia in 1992." *RFE/RL Research Report* 2, no. 5 (January 29, 1993): 38-41.

1139. Tidmarsh, Kyril. "Russia's Work Ethic." *Foreign Affairs* 72, no. 2 (Spring 1993): 67-77.

Natural Resources and Ecology

1140. Adibi, Jennifer. "Volga Greens Mount Protest Action To Protect Samarskaya Luka." *Surviving Together* 11, no. 3 (Fall 1993): 14-15.

1141. Archibald, George. "The Lily of Birds: The Elegant Siberian Crane." *Surviving Together* 11, no. 4 (Winter 1993): 14-15.

1142. Bentham, Richard W. "A Petroleum Regime: Background and Legalities." *Houston Journal of International Law* 15, no. 2 (Winter-Spring 1993): 489-497.

1143. Bobylev, Sergei. "An Ecological Approach to Russian Agriculture." *Surviving Together* 11, no. 3 (Fall 1993): 31-32.

1144. Bond, Andrew R., and Richard M. Levine. "The Manganese Shortfall in Russia." *Post-Soviet Geography* 34, no. 5 (May 1993): 293-301.

1145. Bothe, Michael, Thomas Kurzidem, and Christian Schmidt. *Amazonia and Siberia: Legal Aspects of the Preservation of the Environment and Development in the Last Open Spaces*. International Environmental Law and Policy Series. London; Boston: Graham & Trotman/M. Nijhoff, 1993. xvi, 356 pp.

1146. Broekhoff, Derick. "The Forest or the Trees? The Case for Sustainable Forestry in Siberia." *Surviving Together* 11, no. 4 (Winter 1993): 16-18. [Excerpt from *Prout Journal* v. 6, no. 3.]

1147. Conine, Gary B. "Petroleum Licensing: Formulating an Approach for the New Russia." *Houston Journal of International Law* 15, no. 2 (Winter-Spring

1993): 317-461.

1148. Davis, G. Gordon. "Looking at Long-Term Solutions for Lake Baikal." *Surviving Together* 11, no. 4 (Winter 1993): 35-38.

1149. Dienes, Leslie. "Prospects for Russian Oil in the 1990s: Reserves and Costs." *Post-Soviet Geography* 34, no. 2 (February 1993): 79-110.

1150. Gregory, Paul R. "Creating a Legislative Framework for a Market in Energy Resources: An Economist's View." *Houston Journal of International Law* 15, no. 2 (Winter-Spring 1993): 539-552.

1151. Hardy, George W., III. "The University of Houston Russian Petroleum Legislation Project: A Brief Perspective." *Houston Journal of International Law* 15, no. 2 (Winter-Spring 1993): 263-269.

1152. Hiatt, Fred. "Russian Government Approves Plan for Massive Nuclear Reactor Constructions." *Surviving Together* 11, no. 1 (Spring 1993): 31. [Reprinted from *Washington Post* (January 13, 1993).]

1153. Knauss, Robert L. "University of Houston Russian Petroleum Legislation Project." *Houston Journal of International Law* 15, no. 3 (Winter-Spring 1993): 633-639.

1154. Kritkausky, Randy. "Recycling vs. Incineration: Americans Help Moscow Consider Indigenous Choices." *Surviving Together* 11, no. 1 (Spring 1993): 29-31.

1155. Levin, Julia. "Siberia for Sale." *Surviving Together* 11, no. 2 (Summer 1993): 17-19. [Excerpt from *Audubon* 95, no. 3 (May-June 1993): 20ff.]

1156. ———. "Siberia for Sale." *Audubon* 95, no. 3 (May-June 1993): 20ff.

1157. Maloney-Dunn, Kathleen M. "Russia's Nuclear Waste Law: A Response to the Legacy of Environmental Abuse in the Former Soviet Union." *Arizona Journal of International and Comparative Law* 10, no. 2 (Fall 1993): 364-430.

1158. Martin, Patrick H. "The Proposed Russian Petroleum Conservation and Environmental Protection Law of 1992." *Houston Journal of International Law* 15, no. 2 (Winter-Spring 1993): 499-523.

1159. Martin, Patrick H., John McMahon, and Jacqueline Lang Weaver. "Commentary on the Proposed Petroleum Conservation and Environmental Protection Act for the Russian Federation." *Houston Journal of International Law* 15, no. 3 (Winter-Spring 1993): 765-808.

1160. Matthiessen, Peter. "The Last Cranes of Siberia." *New Yorker* 69, no. 11 (May 3, 1993): 76-86. ["As the breeding grounds of the endangered Asian cranes are being destroyed in a frenzy of post-*perestroika* development, conservationists fight to establish an international wildlife reserve."]

1161. McMahon, John. "Environmental Protection for Exploration and Production Activities in Russia." *Houston Journal of International Law* 15, no. 2 (Winter-

Spring 1993): 525-537.

1162. Medvedev, Yuri. "Alternative Prospects for Power: Considering the Options for Russia." *Surviving Together* 11, no. 4 (Winter 1993): 50-51. [Reprinted from *Moscow News* (July 9, 1993).]

1163. "Memorandum: University of Houston Law Center Russian Petroleum Legislation Project; Russian Oil & Gas Tax Provisions: 'Supertax' Summary." *Houston Journal of International Law* 15, no. 3 (Winter-Spring 1993): 855-868.

1164. Morrison, Lois. "Joining Efforts in Conservation on the Tyosha and Seryosha Rivers." *Surviving Together* 11, no. 4 (Winter 1993): 15-16.

1165. Peterson, D. J. "Chelyabinsk: Environmental Affairs in a Russian City." *Environmental Science & Technology* 27, no. 4 (April 1993): 596-600.

1166. ———. "The Environment in the Post-Soviet Era." *RFE/RL Research Report* 2, no. 2 (January 8, 1993): 43-46.

1167. Ponamarenko, Elena, and Sergei Ponamarenko. "Green Wall of Russia: Ancient Defense System Offers Answer to Modern Ecological Problems." *Surviving Together* 11, no. 3 (Fall 1993): 13-14. [Adapted from article in *Priroda* no. 6 (1992).]

1168. Popova, Lydia. "Russia's Nuclear Elite on the Rampage." *Surviving Together* 11, no. 2 (Summer 1993): 23-25. [Reprinted from *Bulletin of Atomic Scientists* 49, no. 3 (April 1993): 14ff.]

1169. "Proposed Petroleum Code of the Russian Federation." *Houston Journal of International Law* 15, no. 3 (Winter-Spring 1993): 641ff. ["Part I: Licenses," pp. 641-704; "Part II: Conservation and Environmental Protection," pp. 705-764; "Part III: Oil Pipeline Transportation," pp. 809-852.]

1170. Quigley, Howard B. "Saving Siberia's Tigers." *National Geographic* 184, no. 1 (July 1993): 38-47.

1171. Sagers, Matthew J. "News Notes: Background and Analysis." *Post-Soviet Geography* 34, no. 2 (February 1993): 153-156. [International Tender for Udokan Copper Deposit: Awarded to Russian Consortium.]

1172. Schucker, Rachel. "Homeland of the Crane: The Making of a Nature Reserve." *Surviving Together* 11, no. 4 (Winter 1993): 12-14.

1173. Seifulmulukov, Iskander, and Erik Whitlock. "Deregulation in the Russian Oil Industry." *RFE/RL Research Report* 2, no. 34 (August 27, 1993): 58-63.

1174. Shapkhaev, Sergei. "Can the International Community Help Save Baikal?" *Surviving Together* 11, no. 4 (Winter 1993): 43.

1175. Skelton, James W., Jr. "Drafting the Russian Law on Oil and Gas: An Industry Lawyer's Perspective." *Houston Journal of International Law* 15, no. 2 (Winter-Spring 1993): 463-488.

1176. Stanislaw, Joseph, and Daniel Yergin. "Oil: Reopening the Door." *Foreign Affairs* 72, no. 4 (September-October 1993): 81-93.

1177. Streng, William P., Ray Jones, and Richard Gordon. "Memorandum Identifying Fundamental Russian Oil & Gas Considerations." *Houston Journal of International Law* 15, no. 3 (Winter-Spring 1993): 871-876.

1178. Weaver, Jacqueline Lang. "The History and Organization of the Russian Petroleum Legislation Project at the University of Houston Law Center." *Houston Journal of International Law* 15, no. 2 (Winter-Spring 1993): 271-315.

1179. Winestock, Geoff. "Russian Supreme Court Rules Against Hyundai Logging Operation." *Surviving Together* 11, no. 1 (Spring 1993): 32. [Reprinted from *Moscow Times* (November 30, 1992).]

Regional and Urban Development

1180. Hoff, Magdalene, and Heinz Timmermann. "Kaliningrad: Russia's Future Gateway to Europe?" *RFE/RL Research Report* 2, no. 36 (September 10, 1993): 37-43.

1181. Ivanov, Vladimir. "Federation on the Pacific: Does the Crisis Lead to Collapse?" *Eurasian Reports* 3, no. 2 (Winter 1993): 65-82. [Part of special issue devoted to "What Is Russia?"]

1182. Neff, Charles B. "Russia's Booming Far East Frontier." *Surviving Together* 11, no. 4 (Winter 1993): 5-7. [Reprinted from *Washington Post* (August 27, 1993).]

1183. Teague, Randal, and Maxim Brataevskii. "Working with NGOs in Russia." *Surviving Together* 11, no. 1 (Spring 1993): 51-52. [Adapted from article in *Initiatives in the New Independent States* (Winter 1992).]

Standard of Living

1184. Gardner, Bruce, and Karen M. Brooks. *How Retail Food Markets Responded to Price Liberalization in Russia after January 1992.* Policy Research Working Papers, WPS 1140. Washington, DC: Agriculture and Rural Dept., World Bank, [1993]. 66 pp.

1185. Husarska, Anna. "Cottage Cheese." *New Republic* 208, nos. 1 & 2 (January 4 & 11, 1993): 18. ["Why Russians cannot afford it anymore."]

1186. Koen, Vincent, and Steven Phillips. *Price Liberalization in Russia: Behavior of Prices, Household Incomes, and Consumption During the First Year.* IMF Occasional Paper, no. 104. Washington, DC: International Monetary Fund, c1993. vii, 51 pp. REV: Jim Leitzel, *International Economic Insights* 4, no. 6 (November-December 1993): 39-40.

1187. Marnie, Sheila. "Economic Reform and Poverty in Russia." *RFE/RL Research Report* 2, no. 6 (February 5, 1993): 31-36.

1188. Nehf, James P. "Empowering the Russian Consumer in a Market Economy." *Michigan Journal of International Law* 14, no. 4 (Summer 1993): 739-826.

1189. Van Atta, Don. "Declining Soviet/Russian Per Capita Meat Consumption : A Comment." *Comparative Economic Studies* 35, no. 4 (Winter 1993): 69-71.

Theory, Planning, Management

1190. Bogomolov, Oleg. "Who Will Own 'Nobody's Property'?: The Perils of Russian Privatization" *Dissent* 40, no. 2 (Spring 1993): 201-208. Translated from Russian by Peggy McInerny.

1191. Burbach, Roger. "Russia's Upheaval." *Monthly Review* 44, no. 9 (February 1993): 11-24.

1192. Bush, Keith. "Chernomyrdin's Price Control Decree Is Revoked." *RFE/RL Research Report* 2, no. 5 (January 29, 1993): 35-37.

1193. Ellman, Michael. "Russia: The Economic Program of the Civic Union." *RFE/RL Research Report* 2, no. 11 (March 12, 1993): 34-45.

1194. Guardiano, John R. "A Free Market Revolution." *World & I* 8, no. 8 (August 1993): 30-39. [Part of the special report "Russia: Is Reform Still Possible?"]

1195. Kaffenberger, Wilfried E. "Privatization in Russia." *International Economic Insights* 4, no. 3 (May-June 1993): 44-47.

1196. Kotz, David M. "Shock Therapy in Russia: The Cure That Could Kill." *Nation* 256, no. 15 (April 19, 1993): 514-516.

1197. Luthans, Fred, Dianne H. B. Welsh, and Stuart A. Rosenkrantz. "What Do Russian Managers Really Do? An Observational Study with Comparisons to U.S. Managers." *Journal of International Business Studies* 24, no. 4 (1993): 741-761.

1198. Oborotova, Ludmila V., and Alexander Y. Tsapin. *The Privatization Process in Russia: An Optimistic Color in the Picture of Reform.* Edited by Kimberly Marten Zisk. Occasional Paper (Ohio State University. Mershon Center). Columbus, OH: Mershon Center at the Ohio State University, [1993]. 23 pp. [An occasional paper from the Mershon Center project entitled "Assessing alternative futures for the United States and Post-Soviet relations."]

1199. Passell, Peter. "Dr. Jeffrey Sachs, Shock Therapist." *New York Times Magazine* (June 27, 1993): 20ff.

1200. Sachs, Jeffrey. "Moscow Meltdown." *New Republic* 209, nos. 8 & 9 (August 23 & 30, 1993): 26.

1201. Shlapentokh, Vladimir. "Privatization Debates in Russia: 1989-1992." *Comparative Economic Studies* 35, no. 2 (Summer 1993): 19-32.

1202. Whitlock, Erik. "New Russian Government to Continue Economic Reform?" *RFE/RL Research Report* 2, no. 3 (January 15, 1993): 23-27.

Turkmenistan

1203. United States, and Central Intelligence Agency. *Turkmenistan: An Economic Profile.* [Washington, DC?: U.S. Central Intelligence Agency, 1993]. vi, 31 pp.

1204. Zatoka, Andrei. "Animals in the Headlights: The Vanishing Wildlife of Turkmenistan." *Surviving Together* 11, no. 1 (Spring 1993): 33-35.

Ukraine

1205. Bej, Emil. "Market Structure and Indicative Planning in the Post-Collectivist Societies." *Ukrainian Quarterly* 49, no. 4 (Winter 1993): 362-384.

1206. Dackiw, Borys Y. "Voucher Privatization in Ukraine." *SEEL: Survey of East European Law* 4, no. 3 (April 1993): 3.

1207. Gogek, Daniel, and Mary E. Hartnett. "Foreign Investment in Ukraine: New Laws, Opportunities, and Issues." *International Lawyer* 27, no. 1 (Spring 1993): 189-209.

1207a. Hole, Peter et al. *Ukraine.* Prepared under the direction of John C. Odling-Smee. IMF Economic Reviews, 10 (1993). Washington, DC: International Monetary Fund, 1993. vii, 129 pp.

1208. Huntwork, James R. "Legal Reform and Economic Freedom in Ukraine." *Ukrainian Quarterly* 49, no. 2 (Summer 1993): 184-194.

1209. Lenorovitz, Jeffrey M. "Ukrainian firms seek Western ties." *Aviation Week & Space Technology* 139, no. 11 (September 13, 1993): 98.

1210. Matlack, Carol. "As Moscow Burned." *National Journal* 25, no. 42 (October 16, 1993): 2490. ["While Russia erupted in abortive revolution, Ukrainians were more concerned about their own serious economic problems."]

1211. "New Process Turns Waste into Profit." *Surviving Together* 11, no. 1 (Spring 1993): 43. [Reprinted from *Commersant* (November 17, 1992).]

1212. Ottoboni, Gina. "Capturing the Wind in Crimea." *Surviving Together* 11, no. 2 (Summer 1993): 27.

1213. Sherman, Karen. "The Development of NGOs in Ukraine." *Surviving Together* 11, no. 3 (Fall 1993): 51-52.

1214. World Bank. *Ukraine: The Social Sectors During Transition.* World Bank Country Study. Washington, DC: World Bank, c1993. ix, 223 pp.

Uzbekistan

1215. Akchurin, Marat. "Uzbekistan: The Quest for Economic Independence: A Conversation with Professor Nurislam Tukhliyev." *Central Asia Monitor*, no. 2 (1993): 12-15.

1216. [omitted]

1217. International Monetary Fund. *Uzbekistan: An Economic Profile.* [Washington, DC: International Monetary Fund; Springfield, VA: National Technical Information Service [distributor], 1993]. vi, 34 pp.

1218. Sharipov, Alisher. "The Undiscovered Country: Economic Prospects in Uzbekistan." *Harvard International Review* 15, no. 3 (Spring 1993): 26-29.

1219. Sievers, Eric. "Uzbek NGOs Await a Brighter Future." *Surviving Together* 11, no. 2 (Summer 1993): 34.

1220. Van Atta, Don. "The Current State of Agrarian Reform in Uzbekistan." *Post-Soviet Geography* 34, no. 9 (November 1993): 598-606.

1221. World Bank. *Uzbekistan: An Agenda for Economic Reform.* World Bank Country Study. Washington, DC: World Bank, c1993. xxii, 318 pp. [Report is based on the findings of two economic missions to Uzbekistan in June and September-October 1992, led by Silvina Vatnick.]

■ Eastern Europe

General

1222. Acs, Zoltan J., and David B. Audretsch, eds. *Small Firms and Entrepreneurship: An East-West Perspective.* Includes contributions by Zoltan J. Acs, David B. Audretsch, Gerald A. McDermott, Michal Mejstrik, Hans-Gerd Bannasch, Simon Johnson, Gary Loveman, and Hans-Peter Brunner. Cambridge; New York, NY: Cambridge University Press, 1993. xvi, 240 pp. [Papers presented at a conference held July 6-7, 1990 in Berlin. Partial contents: Zoltan J. Acs and David B. Audretsch, "Introduction"; Gerald A. McDermott and Michal Mejstrik, "The role of small firms in Czechoslovak manufacturing"; Hans-Gerd Bannasch, "The evolution of small business in East Germany"; Simon Johnson and Gary Loveman, "The implications of the Polish economic reform for small business: evidence from Gdansk"; Hans-Peter Brunner, "The development experience and government policies: lessons for Eastern Europe?"; Zoltan J. Acs and David B. Audretsch, "Conclusion."]

1223. Amsden, Alice H. "Beyond Shock Therapy: Why Eastern Europe's Recovery Starts in Washington." *American Prospect*, no. 13 (Spring 1993): 87-98.

1224. Arbess, Daniel J., and James B. Varanese. "On the Frontier: What Your Lawyer Brings to Privatization in Eastern and Central Europe." *Columbia Journal of World Business* 28, no. 1 (Spring 1993): 212-218.

1225. Arne Ryde Symposium (13th: 1992: Rungsted, Denmark). *The Political Economy of the Transition Process in Eastern Europe: Proceeding of the 13th Arne Ryde Symposium, Rungsted Kyst, 11-12 June 1992.* Edited by Laszlo Somogyi. Contributions by John Williamson, Domenico Mario Nuti, Thorvaldur Gylfason, László Csaba, György Szapáry, Michael L. Wyzan, Dragomir Vojnic, Paul H. Rubin, Dominique Redor, Alastair McAuley, Laszlo Somogyi, Adam Török, Éva Voszka, Frederic L. Pryor, Jozef M. van Brabant, Axel Leijonhufvud, Ingemar Ståhl, Christopher Lingle, and Hans Aage. Aldershot, Hants; Brookfield,

VT: E. Elgar, c1993. x, 375 pp. [Contents: Laszlo Somogyi, "Introduction," pp. 1-24; John Williamson, "Why Did Output Fall in Eastern Europe?" pp. 25-39; Domenico Mario Nuti, "Lessons from the Stabilisation Programmes of Central and Eastern European Countries, 1989-1991," pp. 40-66; Thorvaldur Gylfason, "Output Gains from Economic Liberalisation: A Simple Formula," pp. 67-87; László Csaba, "After the Shock. Some Lessons from Transition Policies in Eastern Europe," pp. 88-107; György Szapáry, "Transition Issues as Seen through the Experience of Hungary: There is No Cookbook to Go By," pp. 108-123; Michael L. Wyzan, "Stabilisation Policy in Post-Communist Bulgaria," pp. 124-145; Dragomir Vojnic, "Some Issues on Macro-Economic Stabilisation Policy in the Economies in Transition," pp. 146-157; Paul H. Rubin, "Private Mechanisms for the Creation of Efficient Institutions for Market Economies," pp. 158-170; Dominique Redor, "Employment Issues in a Period of Systemic Mutation," pp. 171-188; Alastair McAuley, "The Political Economy of Privatisation," pp. 189-207; Laszlo Somogyi and Adam Török, "Property Rights, Competition Policy, and Privatisation in the Transition from Socialism to Market Economy," pp. 208-226; Éva Voszka, "Escaping from the State—Escaping to the State: Managerial Motivation and Strategies in Changing the Ownership Structure in Hungary," pp. 227-239; Frederic L. Pryor, "Problems of Decollectivisation with Special Attention to East Germany," pp. 240-259; Jozef M. van Brabant, "The New East, Preferred Trade Regimes, and Designing the Transition," pp. 260-288; Axel Leijonhufvud, "Problems of Socialist Transformation: Kazakhstan 1991," pp. 289-311; Ingemar Ståhl, "A Coasean Journey through Estonia—A Study in Property Rights and Transaction Costs," pp. 312-326; Christopher Lingle, "Ethnic Nationalism and Post-Communist Transition Problems," pp. 327-339; Hans Aage, "Sustainable Transition," pp. 340-362.]

1226. Baldassarri, Mario, and Robert Mundell, eds. *Building the New Europe.* Central Issues in Contemporary Economic Theory and Policy. New York: St. Martin's Press in association with Rivista di Politica Economica, SIPI, Rome, 1993. 2 vols. [Contents: Vol. 1. The Single Market and Monetary Unification — v. 2. Eastern Europe's Transition to a Market Economy.]

1227. Baldassarri, Mario, Robert Mundell, and John McCallum, eds. *Debt, Deficit, and Economic Performance.* Includes contribution by Yannis A. Stournaras. Central Issues in Contemporary Economic Theory and Policy. Basingstoke, Hampshire: MacMillan Press; New York: St. Martin's Press, 1993. 486 pp. [Published in association with Rivista di Politica Economica, SIPI, Rome. Partial contents: Yannis A. Stournaras, "Public sector debt and deficit in Greece: the experience of the 1980s and future prospects."]

1228. Balfour, Michele, and Cameron Crise. "A Privatization Test: The Czech Republic, Slovakia and Poland." *Fordham International Law Journal* 17, no. 1 (1993): 84-125.

1229. Barry, Norman. "The Social Market Economy." *Social Philosophy & Policy* 10, no. 2 (Summer

1993): 1-25.

1230. Berend, Ivan. *Alternatives of Transition?— Choices and Determinants: East Central Europe in the 1990's.* Working Paper (University of California, Berkeley. Center for German and European Studies), 5.16. Berkeley, CA: Center for German and European Studies, University of California, [1993]. 31 pp. [Conference on Markets, States, and Democracy, February 11-13, 1993.]

1231. Bird, Richard, and Christine Wallich. *Fiscal Decentralization and Intergovernmental Relations in Transition Economies: Toward a Systemic Framework of Analysis.* Policy Research Working Papers. Washington, DC: Policy Research Dept., World Bank, [1993]. ii, 85 pp.

1232. Boeri, Tito, and P. Garonna, eds. *Employment and Unemployment in Economies in Transition: Conceptual and Measurement Issues.* Paris: Organisation for Economic Co-operation and Development; Washington, DC: OECD Publications and Information Centre, c1993. 129 pp. [Centre for Co-operation with European Economies in Transition.]

1233. Bogetic, Zeljko, and Louise Fox. "Incomes Policy During Stabilization: A Review and Lessons from Bulgaria and Romania." *Comparative Economic Studies* 35, no. 1 (Spring 1993): 39-57.

1234. Bonin, John P. "On the Way to Privatizing Commercial Banks: Poland and Hungary Take Different Roads." *Comparative Economic Studies* 35, no. 4 (Winter 1993): 103-119.

1235. Bookman, Milica Zarkovic. *The Economics of Secession.* New York: St. Martin's Press, 1993. 262 pp. REV: Daniel Berkowitz, *Comparative Economic Studies* 35, no. 3 (Fall 1993): 65-67.

1236. Borensztein, Eduardo. *The Strategy of Reform in the Previously Centrally-Planned Economies of Eastern Europe: Lessons and Challenges.* IMF Paper on Policy Analysis and Assessment, PPAA/93/6. [Washington, DC]: International Monetary Fund, c1993. ii, 20 pp.

1237. Boric, Tomislav, and Willibald Posch. *Privatisierung in Ungarn, Kroatien und Slowenien im Rechtsvergleich: Gesetzestexte mit Erlauternden Beitragen, Stand 16. Juni 1993.* Wien; New York: Springer-Verlag, c1993. viii, 278 pp.

1238. Brabant, Jozef M. van. *Industrial Policy in Eastern Europe: Governing in Transition.* International Studies in Economics and Econometrics, v. 31. Dordrecht; Boston: Kluwer Academic Publishers, c1993. xiv, 358 pp.

1239. ———. "Lessons from the Wholesale Transformations in the East." *Comparative Economic Studies* 35, no. 4 (Winter 1993): 73-102.

1240. ———, ed. *The New Eastern Europe and the World Economy.* Eastern Europe after Communism. Boulder, CO: Westview Press, 1993. xii, 219 pp.

1241. Brada, Josef C. "Enterprise Behavior and Economic Reforms in Central and Eastern Europe: A World

Bank Project." *AAASS Newsletter* 33, no. 2 (March 1993): 3.

1242. Brunner, Hans-Peter. "Entrepreneurship in Eastern Europe: Neither Magic nor Mirage. A Preliminary Investigation." *Journal of Economic Issues* 27, no. 2 (June 1993): 505-513.

1243. Calvo, Guillermo, Manmohan S. Kumar, Eduardo Borensztein, and Paul R. Masson. *Financial Sector Reforms and Exchange Arrangements in Eastern Europe.* Occasional Paper (International Monetary Fund), no. 102. Washington, DC: International Monetary Fund, 1993. vii, 59 pp. [Pt. I by Guillermo A. Calvo and Manmohan S. Kumar; Pt. II by Eduardo Borensztein and Paul R. Masson. Contents: Pt. I. Financial Markets and Intermediation. II. Recent Developments and the Role of the Financial Sector. Recent Economic Developments. Role of the Financial Sector. III. Development of the Financial Sector. Prereform Financial System. Reforms and the Two-Tier Banking System. IV. Performance of the Banking Sector. Quality of Loan Portfolios. Enterprise Restructuring and Credit Allocation. Competition in the Banking Sector. V. Privatization and Capital Markets. Equity Markets. Banks and the Privatization Process. VI. Financial Sector Reforms and Stabilization Policies. Monetary Policy. Fiscal Policy. Exchange Rate Policy and Convertibility. VII. Credibility and Prudential Supervision. Confidence Building. Deposit Protection Schemes; Appendix. Corporate Financing Patterns: Some Illustrative Evidence. Pt. II. Exchange Arrangements of Previously Centrally Planned Economies. II. Currency Convertibility. Current Account Convertibility. Capital Account Convertibility. Speed of the Move to Convertibility and Preconditions for Its Success. III. The Desirable Degree of Exchange Rate Flexibility. Advantages of Exchange Rate Stability. A Currency Board. Implementing Exchange Rate Stability. Implementing a Floating Rate. Dual Exchange Rates. Conclusions. IV. The Experience of Eastern European Countries. Convertibility. Exchange Arrangements and Domestic Stabilization. Exchange Arrangements and International Competitiveness. CMEA Trade and Payments. Lessons from the Eastern European Experience.]

1244. Chaudhry, Kiren Aziz. "The Myths of the Market and the Common History of Late Developers." *Politics & Society* 21, no. 3 (September 1993): 245-274.

1245. Chin, Seung-Kwon. "Privatization of State Enterprises in Former State Socialist Countries in Eastern Europe: Privatization Modes and Ownership Transfer Patterns in Hungary, Poland, and the Czech and Slovak Republic." Ph.D. diss., Yale University, 1993. [UMI order no: AAC 9331307.]

1246. Cirulli, Carol. "U.S. Retailers Develop Aggressive Expansion Plans." *Journal of European Business* 4, no. 3 (January-February 1993): 55-59.

1247. Cochrane, Nancy et al. *Agricultural Policies and Performance in Central and Eastern Europe, 1989-92.* Foreign Agricultural Economic Report, no. 247. Washington, DC: U.S. Dept. of Agriculture; [Herndon, VA: Economic Research Service; ERS-NASS, Distributor, 1993]. iv, 72 pp.

1248. Cohen, S. I., ed. *Patterns of Economic Restructuring for Eastern Europe.* Contributions by Fred Lafeber, Hans Tuyl, Solomon Cohen, Leszek Zienkowski, Tamás Révész, Ernö Zalai, Rini Braber, Zbigniew Zólkiewski, Harry de Haan, and Adam Czyzewski. Aldershot, Hants: Avebury: Brookfield, VT; Ashgate Pub. Co., c1993. 205 pp. [Contents: S.I. Cohen, "Preface," pp. ix-xi; Part I: SAM-Based Comparative Patterns; F.N. Lafeber and J.M.C. Tuyl, "Comparative Social Accounting Matrices for Eastern and Western European Countries: Description, Construction, and Structural Differences," pp. 1-31; S.I. Cohen, F.N. Lafeber, J.M.C. Tuyl, and L. Zienkowski, "Prospective Structures for Eastern Europe: A Comparative Social Accounting Approach," pp. 32-49; S.I. Cohen, F.N. Lafeber, and L. Zienkowski, "A Comparative Analysis of the Economic System of Poland within a SAM Framework," pp. 50-75; T. Révész and E. Zalai, "An Analysis of the Economic System of Hungary within a SAM Framework," pp. 76-92; Part II: The Modelling of Transitional Policies; M.C. Braber, S.I. Cohen, T. Révész and Z. Zólkiewski, "Policy Simulations for Poland and Hungary under Fixed and Flexible Price Regimes: A SAM-CGE Confrontation," pp. 93-126; H. de Haan, "Supply versus Demand Constraints: A Post-Kaleckian CGE Model of the Polish Economy," pp. 127-152; S.I. Cohen and A.B. Czyzewski, "A Simple Model of a Privatization Transaction," pp. 153-167; E. Zalai, "Modelling the Restructuring of Foreign Trade, Hungarian Applications," pp. 168-189.]

1249. Coricelli, Fabrizio, and Timothy D. Lane. "Wage Controls During the Transition from Central Planning to a Market Economy." *World Bank Research Observer* 8, no. 2 (July 1993): 195-210.

1250. Crum, Roy L. *Managing the Enterprise in Transition while Coping with Inflation.* Washington, DC: World Bank, c1993. v, 36 pp. [Edited versions of lectures presented on July 11, 1992, at a conference held at the French Management Training Center in Warsaw.]

1251. Dawson, Andrew H. *A Geography of European Integration.* London; New York: Belhaven Press; New York, NY: Halsted Press, 1993. ix, 225 pp.

1252. Dowall, David E. "From Central Planning to Market Systems: Implications of Economic Reforms for the Construction and Building Industries." *Housing Policy Debate* 3, no. 4 (1993): 977-994.

1253. Eastern Europe Business Information Center (U.S.). *U.S. Trade with Eastern Europe: 1988-1992 Highlights and Outlook for 1993.* [Washington, DC?]: U.S. Dept. of Commerce, International Trade Administration, Eastern Europe Business Information Center, [1993]. [42] pp. [Originally published in *Business America* (April 19, 1993).]

1254. Ely, Michael E. C. "Euro-Expansion." *International Economic Insights* 4, no. 2 (March/April 1993): 33-34. [Review article on *CEPR Annual Report Is Bigger Better? The Economics of EC Enlargement. Monitoring European Integration 3* (London: 1992).]

1255. Estrin, Saul, and Martin Cave, eds. *Competition and Competition Policy: A Comparative Analysis of Central and Eastern Europe.* Contributions by Saul Estrin, Martin Cave, Ferenc Vissi, Anna Fornalczyk, Lina Takla, Paul Hare, Jan Korenovsky, Eugen Jurzyca, Mark E. Schaffer, Philippe Aghion, Kurt Stockmann, Jean-Patrice de la Laurencie, and Sally J. Van Siclen. London: Pinter; New York, NY: Distributed in the USA and Canada by St. Martin's Press, 1993. ix, 143 pp. [Published as a result of the reactions to a conference held at the London Business School on June 7-8, 1992 on "Competition Policy and the Regulation of Utilities During Transition." Contents: Martin Cave and Saul Estrin, "Introduction," pp. 1-19; Ferenc Vissi, "Hungary's Experience of Competition Policy," pp. 20-27; Anna Fornalczyk, "Competition Policy in the Polish Economy in Transition," pp. 28-43; Saul Estrin and Lina Takla, "Competition and Competition Policy in the Czech and Slovak Republics," pp. 44-61; Paul Hare, "Comments on the Development of Competition Policy in the CSFR," pp. 62-64; Jan Korenovsky and Eugen Jurzyca, "The Development of Competition Policy in the Slovak Republic," pp. 65-73; Mark E. Schaffer, "Regulation, Competition Policy and Economic Growth in Transition Economies," pp. 74-78; Philippe Aghion, "Some Issues in Competition and Competition Policy in Transition," pp. 79-82; Kurt Stockmann, "Competition Policy in Transition: The Issues," pp. 83-92; Jean-Patrice de la Laurencie, "A European Perspective on the Development of Competition Policy in Transition," pp. 95-108; Sally J. Van Siclen, "Restructuring for Competition," pp. 109-199; Saul Estrin and Martin Cave, "Conclusions," pp. 130-138.]

1256. Ewing, Andrew, Barbara W. Lee, and Roger Leeds. "Accelerating Privatization in Ex-Socialist Economies." *Columbia Journal of World Business* 28, no. 1 (Spring 1993): 158-167.

1257. Feltenstein, Andrew, and Jiming Ha. *An Analysis of Repressed Inflation in Three Transition Economies.* Policy Research Working Papers, WPS 1132. Washington, DC: International Economics Dept., World Bank, [1993]. 32 pp. [A product of the Socio-Economic Data Division, International Economics Department.]

1258. Fischer, Georg, and Guy Standing, eds. *Structural Change in Central and Eastern Europe: Labour Market and Social Policy Implications.* Paris: Organisation for Economic Co-operation and Development; Washington, DC: OCED Publication and Information Centre, c1993. 288 pp. [Centre for Co-operation with the Economies in Transition. A selection of papers presented at the High-Level Conference on Labour and Social Implications of Structural Change in Central and Eastern Europe in Sept. 1991, jointly organized by OECD's Directorate for Education, Employment, Labour and Social Affairs and the ILO.]

1259. Gehrig, Gerhard, and Wladyslaw Welfe, eds. *Economies in Transition: A System of Models and Forecasts for Germany and Poland.* Contributions to Economics. Heidelberg: Physica-Verlag; New York: Springer-Verlag Co., [1993]. ix, 293 pp.

1260. Gelpern, Anna. "The Laws and Politics of Reprivatization in East-Central Europe: A Comparison." *University of Pennsylvania Journal of International Business Law* 14, no. 3 (Fall 1993): 315-372.

1261. Goodrich, Monica Michejda. "Construction Market Booms in Eastern Europe." *Business America* 114, no. 18 (September 6, 1993): 11-12.

1262. Gray, Cheryl W. et al. *Evolving Legal Frameworks for Private Sector Development in Central and Eastern Europe.* World Bank Discussion Papers, 209. Washington, DC: World Bank, c1993. ix, 153 pp.

1263. Gray, Cheryl W., and Rebecca J. Hanson. *Corporate Governance in Central and Eastern Europe: Lessons from Advanced Market Economies.* Policy Research Working Papers, WPS 1182. Washington, DC: Policy Research Dept., World Bank, [1993]. 29 pp.

1264. Gray, Cheryl W., and William Jarosz. *Foreign Investment Law in Central and Eastern Europe.* Policy Research Working Papers, WPS 1111. Washington, DC: Policy Research Dept., World Bank, [1993]. 21 pp. [A product of the Transition and Macro-Adjustment Division, Policy Research Department.]

1265. Green, Edward J. "Privatization, the Enterpreneurial Sector, and Growth in Post-Comecon Economies." *Journal of Comparative Economics* 17, no. 2 (June 1993): 407-417.

1266. Hall, Derek R., ed. *Transport and Economic Development in the New Central and Eastern Europe.* Contributions by Wieslaw Michalak, Richard Gibb, David Pinder, Bridget Simmonds, Leslie Symons, Jan Kowalski, István Prileszky, Zbigniew Taylor, Zofia Sawiczewska, Anu Kull, David Turnock, Colin Thomas, and Derek Hall. London; New York: Belhaven Press; New York: Co-published in the Americas by Halsted Press, 1993. xxiii, 253 pp. [Edited on behalf of the Transport Geography Study Group of the Institute of British Geographers. Contents: Derek Hall and Jan Kowalski, "Introduction and overview," pp. 1-33; Wieslaw Michalak and Richard Gibb, "Development of the transport system: prospects for East-West integration," pp. 34-48; David Pinder and Bridget Simmonds, "Oil transport: pipelines, ports and the new political climate," pp. 49-66; Leslie Symons, "Airlines in transition to the market economy," pp. 67-81; Jan Kowalski, "Transport implications of German unification," pp. 82-92; István Prileszky, "Transport restructuring in Hungary," pp. 93-107; Zbigniew Taylor, "Recent transport development and economic change in Poland," pp. 108-134; Zofia Sawiczewska, "The impact of economic and political change on Polish sea transport," pp. 135-148; Anu Kull, "Transport decentralization in the Baltic states; the case of Estonia," pp. 149-160; David Turnock, "The role of transport in the development of rural Romania," pp. 161-182; Colin Thomas, "Geopolitics, transport and regional development in the south Slav lands," pp. 183-205; Derek Hall, "Transport implications of tourism development," pp. 206-225; Derek Hall, "Key themes and agendas," pp. 226-236.]

1267. Hamilton, Carl B. "Growing Pains." *International Economic Insights* 4, no. 5 (September-October 1993): 27-29. [Review article on L. Alan Winters, *The European Community: A Case of Successful Integration* (London: 1993); and Richard Baldwin, *An Eastern Enlargement of EFTA: Why the East Europeans Should Join and the EFTAns Should Want Them* (Geneva: 1992).]

1268. Harris, Robert L. "Goin' Down the Road Feeling Bad: U.S. Trade Laws' Discriminatory Treatment of the East European Economies in Transition to Capitalism." *Columbia Journal of Transnational Law* 31, no. 2 (1993): 403-446.

1269. Hartnell, Helen E. "Central/Eastern Europe: The Long and Winding Road toward European Union." *Comparative Law Yearbook of International Business* 15 (1993): 179-229.

1270. Havrylyshyn, Oleh. "Importing Credibility." *International Economic Insights* 4, no. 4 (July-August 1993): 41-42. [Review article on Holger Schmieding, *Lending Stability to Europe's Emerging Market Economies* (Kiel: 1992).]

1271. Holmes, Carol A. "Eastern Europe Is a Smashing Success." *International Economy* 7, no. 4 (July-August 1993): 41ff.

1272. Ingram, Leah. "Bloc Party." *World Trade* 6 (November 1993): 106ff.

1273. International Bar Association. Regional Conference (1992: Budapest, Hungary). *Butterworths Trade and Finance in Central and Eastern Europe: A Collection of Papers Delivered at the International Bar Association Regional Conference, Budapest, Hungary, 21-24 June 1992.* Edited by Stephen A. Rayner. London: Butterworths; Austin, TX: Butterworths Legal Publishers, 1993. xiv, 200 pp.

1274. Iseman, Ellen. "Testing the Waters in Eastern Europe." *Journal of European Business* 4, no. 3 (January-February 1993): 53-54. ["U.S. firms eager to dip into the pool of investment opportunities in Eastern Europe are literally testing the waters with environmental cost assessments."]

1275. Jancar-Webster, Barbara, ed. *Environmental Action in Eastern Europe: Responses to Crisis.* Contributions by Barbara Jancar-Webster, Jakub Szacki, Irmina Glowacka, Anna Liro, Barbara Szulczewska, Sandor Peter, Eva Adamova, Michael Kozeltsev, Evaldas Vebra, Duncan Fisher, Stanley J. Kabala, Miklos Persanyi, Leo Seserko, Evgenii A. Shvarts, and Irina Prochozova. Armonk, NY: M.E. Sharpe, c1993. 238 pp. [Contents: Barbara Jancar-Webster, "Introduction," pp. 1-8. Part I. Problems and Changes in Environmental Management. Jakub Szacki, Irmina Glowacka, Anna Liro, and Barbara Szulczewska, "Political and Social Changes in Poland: An Environmental Perspective," pp. 11-27; Sandor Peter, "New Directions in Environmental Management in Hungary," pp. 28-41; Eva Adamova, "Environmental Management in Czecho-Slovakia," pp. 42-57; Michael Kozeltsev, "Old and New in the Environmental Policy of the Former Soviet Union: What

Has Already Occurred and What Is To Be Done," pp. 58-72; Evaldas Vebra, "New Directions in Environmental Protection Management in the Baltic States," pp. 73-85; Part II. The Influence of Environmental Movements. Duncan Fisher, "The Emergence of the Environmental Movement in Eastern Europe and Its Role in the Revolutions of 1989," pp. 89-113; Stanley J. Kabala, "The History of Environmental Protection in Poland and the Growth of Awareness and Activism," pp. 114-133; Miklos Persanyi, "Red Pollution, Green Evolution, Revolution in Hungary: Environmentalists and Societal Transition," pp. 134-157; Leo Seserko, "Ecology in Slovenia," pp. 158-175; Evgenii A. Shvarts and Irina Prochozova, "Soviet Greens: Who Are They? The View from Inside," pp. 176-191; Barbara Jancar-Webster, "The East European Environmental Movement and the Transformation of East European Society," pp. 192-219; Barbara Jancar-Webster, "Conclusion," pp. 220-225.]

1276. Jeffries, Ian. *Socialist Economies and the Transition to the Market: A Guide.* London; New York: Routledge, 1993. x, 562 pp.

1277. Kaminski, Bartlomiej. *How the Market Transition Affected Export Performance in the Central European Economies.* Policy Research Working Papers, WPS 1179. Washington, DC: International Economics Dept., World Bank, [1993]. 38 pp.

1278. Kelley, Jonathan, and M. D. R. Evans. "The Legitimation of Inequality: Occupational Earnings in Nine Nations." *American Journal of Sociology* 99, no. 1 (July 1993): 75-125. [Includes Hungary and Poland.]

1279. Kendall, Maryanne B., and United States. International Trade Administration. *European Trade Fairs: A Key to the World for U.S. Exporters.* [Washington, D.C.?]: U.S. Dept. of Commerce, International Trade Administration, [1993]. 83 pp.

1280. Ketch, David R. *Economic Realignments Affecting Trade: EC Agreements with EFTA and Eastern Europe.* Agriculture Information Bulletin, no. 664-3. [Washington, DC?]: U.S. Dept. of Agriculture, Economic Research Service, [1993]. [2] pp.

1281. Klaus, Vaclav. "Creating a Stable Monetary Order." *Cato Journal* 12, no. 3 (Winter 1993): 527-531. [Paper is based on an address at the Cato Institute's Tenth Annual Monetary Conference on March 5, 1992. Part of special issue devoted to "Monetary Reform in Ex-Communist Countries."]

1282. Kraft, Evan. "Recasting Finance in Eastern Europe: Options and Possibilities." *Review of Radical Political Economics* 25, no. 3 (September 1993): 17-25.

1283. Laban, Raul, and Holger C. Wolf. "Large-Scale Privatization in Transition Economies." *American Economic Review* 83, no. 5 (December 1993): 1199-1210.

1284. Langwick, John J. *Eastern European Technological Business Opportunities: An Executive Report.* Lilburn, GA.: Fairmont Press; Englewood Cliffs, NJ: Distributed by PTR Prentice-Hall, c1993. 298 pp.

1285. Lassanyi, Mary E. *Central and Eastern Europe: Going Global.* Special Reference Briefs, NAL-SRB. 93-10. Beltsville, MD: National Agricultural Library, [1993]. 95 pp. [Updates SRB 92-01.]

1286. Lieberman, Ira W. "Privatization: The Theme of the 1990s: An Overview." *Columbia Journal of World Business* 28, no. 1 (Spring 1993): 8-17.

1287. Major, Ivan. *Privatization in Eastern Europe: A Critical Approach.* Studies of Communism in Transition. Aldershot, Hants; Brookfield, VT: E. Elgar, c1993. xi, 164 pp.

1288. Mann, Catherine L., Stephanie Lenway, and Derek Utter. *Political and Economic Consequences of Alternative Privatization Schemes.* Working Paper (University of California, Berkeley. Center for German and European Studies), 5.14. Berkeley, CA: Center for German and European Studies, University of California, [1993]. 31 pp. [Conference on Markets, States and Democracy, February 11-13, 1993.]

1289. Manser, Roger. *Failed Transitions: The Eastern European Economy and Environment Since the Fall of Communism.* New York: New Press, c1993. ix, 195 pp.

1290. Marko, David Everett. "A Critical Review of Market Access in Central and Eastern Europe: The European Community's Role." *Maryland Journal of International Law and Trade* 17, no. 1 (Spring 1993): 1-29.

1291. Mastalir, Roger W. "Regulation of Competition in the 'New' Free Markets of Eastern Europe: A Comparative Study of Antitrust Laws in Poland, Hungary, Czech and Slovak Republics, and Their Models." *North Carolina Journal of International Law and Commercial Regulation* 19, no. 1 (Fall 1993): 61-89.

1292. Maticic, Brane. "Agricultural Research and Development in Eastern European Countries: Challenges and Needs." *Technology in Society* 15, no. 1 (1993): 111-129. [Part of special issue on science and technology in Eastern Europe.]

1293. Mihaly, Zoltan M. "Tax Reforms Roll Out a Red Carpet for Investors Looking at Central Europe." *Journal of International Taxation* 4, no. 4 (April 1993): 156-163.

1294. Minovi, Maziar. "A Comparison of the National Privatization Strategies of Medium-to-Large Industrial Enterprises in Hungary and Poland: 1989-1992." Ph.D. diss., George Washington University, 1993. [UMI order no: AAC 9417667.]

1295. Mizsei, Kálmán. *Bankruptcy and the Post-Communist Economies of East Central Europe.* New York: Institute for EastWest Studies, 1993. 54 pp.

1296. ———. "Bankruptcy Laws in the Post-Communist Economies." *International Economic Insights* 4, no. 1 (January-February 1993): 43-44.

1297. Myant, Martin. *Transforming Socialist Economies: The Case of Poland and Czechoslovakia.* Studies of Communism in Transition. Aldershot, Hants; Brookfield, VT: E. Elgar, c1993. xii, 297 pp.

1298. Nasierowski, Wojciech, and Phillip C. Wright. "Perceptions of Needs: How Cross-Cultural Differences Can Affect Market Penetration into Central Europe." *International Executive* 35, no. 6 (November-December 1993): 513-524.

1299. Nelson, Joan M. "The Politics of Economic Transformation: Is Third World Experience Relevant in Eastern Europe?" *World Politics* 45, no. 3 (April 1993): 433-463.

1300. OECD. Centre for Co-operation with European Economies in Transition. *Short-Term Economic Indicators, Central and Eastern Europe: Sources & Definitions = Indicateurs Economiques a Court Terme, Europe Centrale et Orientale.* Paris: Organisation for Economic Co-operation and Development: Centre for Co-operation with the European Economies in Transition; Washington, DC: OECD Publications and Information Centre [distributor], c1993. 127 pp. [Volume provides information on the sources and definitions underlying the indicators published in *Short-Term Economic Indicators: Central and Eastern Europe.*]

1301. OECD. Centre for Co-operation with the Economies in Transition. *Road Strengthening in Central and Eastern European Countries: Report.* Paris: Organisation for Economic Co-operation and Development; Washington, DC: OECD Publications and Information Centre [Distributor], c1993. 150 pp. [Published in French under the title: *Renforcement des chausses dans les pays d'Europe Centrale et Orientale.*]

1302. Okolicsanyi, Karoly. "Trade between East Central Europe and the EC Moving Forward." *RFE/RL Research Report* 2, no. 35 (September 3, 1993): 44-47.

1303. ———. "Visegrad Banking Systems Stunt Economic Growth." *RFE/RL Research Report* 2, no. 42 (October 22, 1993): 33-37.

1304. ———. "The Visegrad Triangle's Free-Trade Zone." *RFE/RL Research Report* 2, no. 3 (January 15, 1993): 19-22.

1305. Ost, David. *Labor in Post Communist Transformations.* Working Paper (University of California, Berkeley. Center for German and European Studies), 5.17. Berkeley, CA: Center for German and European Studies, University of California, [1993]. 45 pp. [Conference on Marketing, States and Democracy, February 11-13, 1993.]

1306. Pereira, Luiz Carlos Bresser, Jose Maria Maravall, and Adam Przeworski. *Economic Reforms in New Democracies: A Social-Democratic Approach.* Cambridge; New York, NY: Cambridge University Press, 1993. vii, 227 pp. [Partial contents: Jose Maria Maravall, "Politics and policy: economic reforms in Southern Europe". Adam Przeworski, "Economic reforms, public opinion, and political institutions: Poland in the Eastern European perspective."]

1307. PlanEcon, Inc. *How to Invest in Eastern Europe*. Arlington, VA: Pasha Publications, c1993. xvi, 254 pp.

1308. Pogany, Peter. "Achievements and prospects in U.S. economic relations with Central and Eastern Europe." *International Economic Review* (January 1993): 8-9.

1309. ———. "Central European Countries conclude free-trade agreement." *International Economic Review* (February 1993): 6-7. ["The Governments of the Czech Republic, Hungary, Poland, and Slovakia agreed to eliminate tariffs and all other restrictions of trade among themselves in eight years."]

1310. ———. "Central European Free Trade Agreement starts smoothly." *International Economic Review* (August 1993): 13-14.

1311. ———. "U.S. trade with the countries of the Central European Free Trade Agreement expands." *International Economic Review* (October 1993): 9-11.

1312. Polak, Jacques J. "Europe: East and West." *International Economic Insights* 4, no. 2 (March/April 1993): 40-42.

1313. Poznanski, Kazimierz. *Divestment of Public Capital in Eastern Europe: Political Implications of Economic Choices*. Working Paper (University of California, Berkeley. Center for German and European Studies), 5.12. Berkeley, CA: Center for German and European Studies, University of California, [1993]. 27 pp. [Conference on Markets, States, and Democracy, February 11-13, 1993.]

1314. Ramanadham, V. V., ed. *Constraints and Impacts of Privatization*. Includes contributions by V. V. Ramanadham, Dieter Bös, Gusztáv Báger, Jersy Cieslik, Olivier Bouin, John Howell, Andrew D. Cao, and Tony Bennett. London; New York: Routledge, 1993. xv, 378 pp. [Partial contents: V.V. Ramanadham, "Privatization: Constraints and Impacts," pp. 1-63; Dieter Bös, "Privatization in East Germany," pp. 81-92; Gusztáv Báger, "Privatization in Hungary," pp. 93-101; Jersy Cieslik, "Privatization in Poland," pp. 102-114; Olivier Bouin, "Privatization in Czechoslovakia," pp. 115-138; John Howell, "Privatization in Central and Eastern Europe," pp. 139-147; Andrew D. Cao, "Privatization of State-Owned Enterprises: A Framework for Impact Analysis," pp. 313-327; Tony Bennett, "Accounting Aspects of Privatization," pp. 328-341; V.V. Ramanadham, "Concluding Review," pp. 342-363.]

1315. Reardon, Jack, and Paulis Lazda. "The Development of the Market System in the Baltic Republics." *Journal of Economic Issues* 27, no. 2 (June 1993): 537-545.

1316. *Report of the Delegation to the Czech & Slovak Federal Republics and Hungary: Legal Challenges in Central Europe*. Edited by Elizabeth Ballantine. ILEX Briefing Monograph Series, #6. Chicago, IL: American Bar Association; Washington, DC: ABA Section of International Law and Practice, International Legal Exchange Committee, c1993. ii, 74 pp. [ABA International Legal Exchange Committee (ILEX) Delegation to Czechoslovakia and Hungary, September 13-23, 1992. Delegation chair: Gerold W. Libby; delegation leader: Marcia Wiss; section chair: Louis B. Sohn.]

1317. Richter, Stefan. *Die Assoziierung Osteuropaischer Staaten Durch die Europaischen Gemeinschaften: Eine Untersuchung der Rechtlichen Grundlagen der Vertragsgestaltung Zwischen den Europaischen Gemeinschaften und Polen, Ungarn und der Tschechoslowakei: Recht der Europaischen Gemeinschaften und GATT = The Association of the Eastern European Countries with the European Communities*. Beitrage zum Auslandischen Offentlichen Recht und Volkerrecht, Bd. 107. Berlin; New York: Springer, c1993. xix, 285 pp. [Summary in English. Originally presented as the author's thesis (doctoral)—Universitat Heidelberg, Wintersemester 1991-1992.]

1318. Riemer, Jeremiah. "The ECU as the 'Mark' of Unity: Europe between Monetary Integration and Monetary Union." *Social Education* 57, no. 4 (April-May 1993): 184-186. [Part of special section entitled "United Germany in a Uniting Europe, Part 1."]

1319. Sacklén, Mats. "Managing Environmental Risks in Eastern Europe: The Framework for Negotiated Solutions." *International Lawyer* 27, no. 3 (Fall 1993): 783-793.

1320. Samonis, Valdas, and Csilla Hunyadi. *Big Bang and Acceleration: Models for the Postcommunist Economic Transformation*. Commack, NY: Nova Science Publishers, 1993. 58 pp.

1321. Schmidt, Klaus M., and Monika Schnitzer. "Privatization and Management Incentives in the Transition Period in Eastern Europe." *Journal of Comparative Economics* 17, no. 2 (June 1993): 264-287.

1322. Sereghyova, Jana, Benjamin Bastida Vila et al. *Entrepreneurship in Central East Europe: Conditions, Opportunities, Strategies*. Heidelberg; New York: Physica-Verlag, c1993. xi, 279 pp.

1323. Shen, Raphael. *Economic Reform in Poland and Czechoslovakia: Lessons in Systemic Transformation*. Westport, CT: Praeger, 1993. xiv, 268 pp.

1324. Slay, Ben. "The East European Economies." *RFE/RL Research Report* 2, no. 1 (January 1, 1993): 113-118.

1325. ———. "The Postcommunist Economic Transitions: Barriers and Progress." *RFE/RL Research Report* 2, no. 39 (October 1, 1993): 35-44.

1326. ———. "Roundtable: Privatization in Eastern Europe." *RFE/RL Research Report* 2, no. 32 (August 13, 1993): 47-57. Louisa Vinton, Franz-Lothar Altmann, Karoly Okolicsanyi, Dan Ionescu, Kjell Engelbrekt, Christoph Royen, Wolfgang Quaisser, and Klaus Schroeder, participants. [Roundtable held June 21, 1993 at the RFE/RL Research Institute (Munich, Germany).]

1327. Starrels, John M. *The Baltic States in Transition.* Washington, DC: International Monetary Fund, 1993. 18 pp.

1328. Stiglitz, Joseph E. *Financial Systems for Eastern Europe's Emerging Democracies.* Occasional Papers (International Center for Economic Growth), no. 38. San Francisco, CA: ICS Press in collaboration with the Institute for Policy Reform, c1993. 39 pp.

1329. Stokes, Gale. "Is It Possible To Be Optimistic About Eastern Europe?" *Social Research* 60, no. 4 (Winter 1993): 685-704.

1330. Strasser, Kurt A. "Pollution Control in an Era of Economic Redevelopment: An Overview." *Connecticut Journal of International Law* 8, no. 2 (Spring 1993): 425-437. [Paper from the symposium, "Human Rights in Theory and Practice: A Time of Change and Development in Central and Eastern Europe," held in Budapest, March 19-20, 1993.]

1331. Thomas, Scott. "The Politics and Economics of Privatization in Central and Eastern Europe." *Columbia Journal of World Business* 28, no. 1 (Spring 1993): 168-178.

1332. Thorne, Alfredo. *Eastern Europe's Experience with Banking Reform: Is There a Role for Banks in the Transition?* Policy Research Working Papers, WPS 1235. Washington, DC: World Bank, Europe and Central Asia, and Middle East and North Africa Regions Technical Dept., Private Sector and Finance Team, [1993]. 38 pp.

1333. United States. Congress. Office of Technology Assessment. *Energy Efficiency Technologies for Central and Eastern Europe.* Washington, DC: Office of Technology Assessment, Congress of the U.S.: [Supt. of Docs., U.S. G.P.O., Distributor, 1993]. ix, 129 pp.

1334. United States. Dept. of Energy. *The Baltics: Regional Energy Profiles.* Eastern European Series Country Report. Washington, DC: Springfield, VA: Office of International Affairs, U.S. Dept. of Energy; Available from National Technical Information Service, U.S. Dept. of Commerce, [1993]. viii, 58 pp.

1335. Vaughn, Gerald F. "Comment on Koslowski's 'Market Institutions, East European Reform, and Economic Theory.'" *Journal of Economic Issues* 27, no. 4 (December 1993): 1273-1275. [Koslowski's article published in vol. 26, no. 3 (September 1992).]

1336. Wagener, Hans-Jurgen, ed. *On the Theory and Policy of Systemic Change.* Studies in Contemporary Economics. Heidelberg; New York: Physica-Verlag, c1993. viii, 234 pp.

1337. Walden, Gene. "Not Ready for Prime Time." *World Trade* 6 (November 1993): 94ff.

1338. Welch, Jonathan B. "Investing in Eastern Europe: Perspectives of Chief Financial Officers." *International Executive* 35, no. 1 (January/Feburary 1993): 45-56.

1339. Wijnbergen, Sweder van. *Enterprise Reform in Eastern Europe.* Policy Research Working Papers, WPS 1068. Washington, DC: Europe and Central Asia Dept., [1993]. 36 pp.

1340. Wilson, Ernest J., III. "A Mesolevel Comparative Approach to Maxi and Mini Strategies of Public Enterprise Reform." *Studies in Comparative International Development* 28, no. 2 (Summer 1993): 22-60.

1341. Winiecki, Jan. *Post-Soviet-Type Economies in Transition.* Prepared in collaboration with Centre for Research into Communist Economies. Aldershot, Hants; Brookfield, VT: Avebury, c1993. v, 199 pp.

1342. Winiecki, Jan, and Andrzej Kondratowicz, eds. *The Macroeconomics of Transition: Developments in East Central Europe.* London; New York: Routledge, 1993. ix, 154 pp. [Prepared in collaboration with the Adam Smith Research Centre, Warsaw.]

1343. Wisner, Robert. "A Socialist Shortcut to Capitalism? The Role of Worker Ownership in Eastern Europe's Mass Privatizations." *North Carolina Journal of International Law and Commercial Regulation* 19, no. 1 (Fall 1993): 123-142.

1344. Zoethout, Tseard. "Financing Eastern Europe's Capital Requirements." *RFE/RL Research Report* 2, no. 7 (February 12, 1993): 38-43.

Albania

1345. Mikelsons, Maris. *An Initial Assessment of the Albanian Housing Sector.* Consultants Ira S. Lowry and Carol Rabenhorst. Washington, DC: The Urban Institute, [1993]. 1 vol. [Prepared for the East European Regional Housing Project, Housing Finance Component.]

1346. Weech, William. "Postcard from Abroad: Albanian Vignettes." *Foreign Service Journal* 70, no. 11 (November 1993): 60.

1347. Zanga, Louis. "The Albanian Economy: Progress Despite Massive Problems." *RFE/RL Research Report* 2, no. 46 (November 19, 1993): 40-43.

1348. ———. "The Prospects of the Albanian Oil Industry." *RFE/RL Research Report* 2, no. 45 (November 12, 1993): 35-38.

Bulgaria

1349. Gotovska-Popova, Teodorichka. "Bulgaria's Troubled Social Security System." *RFE/RL Research Report* 2, no. 26 (June 25, 1993): 43-47.

1350. Harrison, David. "Bulgarian Tourism: A State of Uncertainty." *Annals of Tourism Research* 20, no. 3 (1993): 519-534.

1351. Schlack, Robert F. "Going to Market in Bulgaria: Uphill on a Knife Edge." *Journal of Economic Issues* 27, no. 2 (June 1993): 515-526.

1352. Trachtman, Joel P., Jay Gladis, William G. Martin, Norman S. Poser, David Reid, Edward J. Waitzer, William J. Williams, and Christopher J. Zinski. "American Bar Association Central and East European Law Initiative (CEELI): A Concept Paper on Securities Regulation for Bulgaria." *International Lawyer* 27, no. 3 (Fall 1993): 837-854.

1353. United States. Congress. Senate. Committee on Foreign Relations. *Treaty with the Republic of Bulgaria Concerning the Encouragement and Reciprocal Protection of Investment: Report (To Accompany Treaty Doc. 103-3).* United States. Congress. Senate Executive Report, 103-12. [Washington, DC?: U.S. G.P.O., 1993]. 6 pp.

1354. Valchev, Rumen. "An Examination of Industrial Conflict in a Post-Communist Society." *Mediation Quarterly* 10, no. 3 (Spring 1993): 265-272.

(Former) Czechoslovakia

1355. Brada, Josef C. "Take Two: The Czech Republic." *International Economic Insights* 4, no. 3 (May-June 1993): 13-16.

1356. Ham, John, Jan Svejnar, and Katherine Terrell. "The Emergence of Unemployment in the Czech and Slovak Republics." *Comparative Economic Studies* 35, no. 4 (Winter 1993): 121-134.

1357. Leeds, Eva Marikova. "Voucher Privatization in Czechoslovakia." *Comparative Economic Studies* 35, no. 3 (Fall 1993): 19-37.

1358. Pehe, Jiri. "The Czech-Slovak Currency Split." *RFE/RL Research Report* 2, no. 10 (March 5, 1993): 27-32.

1359. Pogany, Peter. "Data on trade with the Czech and Slovak Republics are available, but beware!" *International Economic Review* (June 1993): 7-8.

1360. Vidláková, Olga. "Environmental Law in Czechoslovakia." *Czechoslovak and Central European Journal* 11, no. 2 (Winter 1993): 49-59.

1361. Webster, Leila, and Dan Swanson. *The Emergence of Private Sector Manufacturing in Former Czech and Slovak Federal Republic: A Survey of Firms.* World Bank Technical Paper, no. 230. Washington, DC: World Bank, 1993. viii, 93 p.

1362. Wood, Barry D. "Privatization in the Czech Republic and Slovakia." *International Economic Insights* 4, no. 2 (March/April 1993): 47-48.

Czech Republic

1363. Bakes, Milan. "New Czech Tax System Aims at Harmonization with EC." *Journal of International Taxation* 4, no. 6 (June 1993): 281-283.

1364. Klaus, Vaclav. *Interplay of Political and Economic Reform Measures in the Transformation of Postcommunist Countries.* Heritage Lectures, 470. Washington, DC: Heritage Foundation, 1993. 5 pp. [Address by the Prime Minister of the Czech Republic followed by questions and answers.]

1365. ———. *Ten Commandments of Systematic Reform.* Occasional Paper (Group of Thirty), 43. Washington, DC: Group of Thirty, 1993. 14 pp.

1366. ———. "The Ten Commandments Revisited." *International Economy* 7, no. 5 (September-October 1993): 36ff.

1367. Sacks, Paul M. "Privatization in the Czech Republic." *Columbia Journal of World Business* 28, no. 1 (Spring 1993): 188-194.

1368. Williams, Christopher. "New Rules for a New World: Privatization of the Czech Cement Industry." *Columbia Journal of World Business* 28, no. 1 (Spring 1993): 62-68.

Slovakia

1369. Fisher, Sharon. "Economic Developments in the Newly Independent Slovakia." *RFE/RL Research Report* 2, no. 30 (July 23, 1993): 42-48.

1370. ———. "The Slovak Arms Industry." *RFE/RL Research Report* 2, no. 38 (September 24, 1993): 34-39.

Eastern Germany

1371. Autenrieth, Christine. "Impact of System Culture on West and East German Managers: A New Topic of Intercultural Management Research." *International Executive* 35, no. 1 (January/Feburary 1993): 73-88.

1372. Bechtolf, Uwe. *Möglichkeiten einer rechtlich und ökonomisch operationalen Optimierung im treuhandgesetzlichen Privatisierunsprozess: Ein interdisziplinaerer Ansatz.* Wirtschaftsrecht und Wirtschaftsverfassung, Bd. 14. Frankfurt am Main; New York: P. Lang, c1993. 313 pp. [Originally presented as the author's thesis (Dr. rer. pol.—Universitat-GH-Siegen, 1993).]

1373. "Business Outlook Abroad: Germany: Here As Well As in Surrounding Countries." *Business America* 114, no. 12 (June 14, 1993): 13-15.

1374. Cantwell, John. "All Change." *International Economic Insights* 4, no. 2 (March/April 1993): 32-33. [Review article on Karel Cool, Damien J. Neven, and Ingo Walter, eds., *European Industrial Restructuring in the 1990s* (NY: 1992).]

1375. Dennis, Mike. *Social and Economic Modernization in Eastern Germany from Honecker to Kohl.* The New Germany Series. London: New York: Pinter Publishers; St. Martin's Press, 1993. viii, 252 pp.

1376. Dinan, Desmond. "The Economic Development of Postwar Germany." *Social Education* 57, no. 4

(April-May 1993): 176-181. [Part of special section entitled "United Germany in a Uniting Europe, Part 1."]

1377. Drost, Helmar. "The Great Depression in East Germany: The Effects of Unification on East Germany's Economy." *East European Politics and Societies* 7, no. 3 (Fall 1993): 452-481.

1378. East Germany, and United States. Dept. of State. *Fisheries: Agreement between the United States of America and the German Democratic Republic, Amending and Extending the Agreement of April 13, 1983, Effected by Exchange of Notes Dated at Washington January 14 and April 12, 1988.* United States Treaties, etc. (Treaties and Other International Acts Series), 11579. Washington, DC: Dept. of State, [1993?]. 5 pp.

1379. Heilemann, Ullrich, and Reimut Jochimsen. *Christmas in July? The Political Economy of German Unification Reconsidered.* Brookings Occasional Papers. Washington, DC: Brookings Institution, c1993. 82 pp. [Expanded and updated version of the authors' presentations at a Brookings Institution workshop, September 8-11, 1991, in Rottach-Etgern, Germany.]

1380. Heitger, Bernhard, and Leonard Waverman, eds. *German Unification and the International Economy.* Contributions by Heidemarie C. Sherman, Dieter Duwendag, Karlhans Sauernheimer, Bernhard Heitger, Roland Döhrn, Ullrich Heilemann, Dieter Schumacher, Uta Möbius, Peter Pauly, Albert Berry, Rogelio Ramirez de la O, Frank D. Weiss, Guy Kirsch, and Sylvia Ostry. London; New York: Routledge, 1993. xx, 294 pp. [Contents: Part I. Developments in Eastern Europe. Heidemarie C. Sherman, "The economics of German unification," pp. 3-20; Dieter Duwendag, "Recent developments of world savings and investment," pp. 21-33; Karlhans Sauernheimer, "Causes and consequences of the expected shift in savings-investment balance in Europe: the case of German unification," pp. 34-64; Bernhard Heitger, "Comparative Economic growth: East and West," pp. 65-82; Roland Döhrn and Ullrich Heilemann, "Structural change in Eastern Europe," pp. 83-112; Dieter Schumacher and Uta Möbius, "Eastern Europe and the EC—trade relations and trade policy with regard to industrial products," pp. 113-175. Pt. II. Spillovers. Peter Pauly, "Global investment and savings flows: macroeconomic scenarios," pp. 179-202; Albert Berry, "Implications of changes in global investment flows for the less developed countries (LDCs)," pp. 203-219; Rogelio Ramirez de la O, "Macroeconomic outlook for Mexico and economic policy," pp. 220-237; Frank D. Weiss, "Prospects for the Uruguay Round," pp. 241-253; Guy Kirsch, "The nationstate—much ado about (almost) nothing?" pp. 254-274; Sylvia Ostry, "Beyond the Uruguay Round means beyond the border," pp. 275-284.]

1381. Hitchens, D. M. W. N., Karin Wagner, and J. E. Birnie. *East German Productivity and the Transition to the Market Economy: Comparisons with West Germany and Northern Ireland.* Aldershot, Hants: Avebury; Brookfield, VT: Ashgate Pub. Co., c1993. xv, 126 pp. [Contents: 1.

Comparative industrial productivity in East Germany: An overview; 2. Methods and descriptions of the sample; 3. Comparative company performance; 4. Prospects for the future; 5. Explanations of comparative performance: Machinery; 6. Explanations of comparative performance: Management and labour force; 7. Other explanatory factors: Environment, premises and business services; 8. Policy and the competitiveness of East Germany: Comparisons with Western and Eastern Europe; 9. Comparisons of East and West Germany and Northern Ireland.]

1382. Johnson, Denise M., and Scott D. Johnson. "One Germany... But Is There a Common German Consumer? East-West Differences for Marketers to Consider." *International Executive* 35, no. 3 (May-June 1993): 211-228.

1383. Jürgens, Ulrich, Larissa Klinzing, and Lowell Turner. "The Transformation of Industrial Relations in Eastern Germany." *Industrial and Labor Relations Review* 46, no. 2 (January 1993): 229-244.

1384. Niethammer, Lutz. "The Structuring and Restructuring of the German Working Classes after 1945 and after 1990." *Oral History Review* 21, no. 2 (Winter 1993): 9-18.

1385. Schlesinger, Helmut. "Banking on the Mark: Germany in the European and World Economies." *Harvard International Review* 15, no. 4 (Summer 1993): 20ff.

1386. "A Unified Germany Welcomes U.S. Business." *Business America* 114, nos. 15/16 (July 26, 1993/ August 9, 1993): 2-19. [Section includes: James L. Joy, "Business Opportunities in the New German States," pp. 5-6; Birgit Lehne, "Leipzig: A Magnet for U.S. Business in Eastern Germany," pp. 6-7; John A. Larsen with contributions by Patricia Adler, "Massive Environmental 'Clean-Up' Required in Eastern Germany," pp. 8-9.]

Estonia

1387. Barr, Donald Adams. "Medical Professionals in Estonia: The Interaction of Professional Knowledge, Organizational Setting, and Personal Characteristics in Affecting Status and Rewards." Ph.D. diss., Stanford University, 1993. [UMI order no: AAC 9326423.]

1388. Brown, William S. "Economic Transition in Estonia." *Journal of Economic Issues* 27, no. 2 (June 1993): 493-503.

1389. Cannon, Lucia Swiatkowski. "Estonia Draws up Reformers' Blueprint." *Surviving Together* 11, no. 3 (Fall 1993): 57-58. [Excerpt from the *Financial Times* (July 13, 1993).]

1390. "Diary of the Estonian Dairy Industry." *Surviving Together* 11, no. 3 (Fall 1993): 34-35. [Excerpt from *Geonomics* (May-June 1993).]

1391. Estonia Vabariigi Suursaatkond (U.S.). *Investment Opportunity Estonia.* Washington, DC: Embassy of Estonia, [1993]. 1 vol.

1392. Knöbl, Adalbert et al. *Estonia*. Prepared under the direction of John C. Odling-Smee. IMF Economic Reviews, 4 (1993). Washington, DC: International Monetary Fund, c1993. vii, 84 pp.

1393. Sepp, Urmas. "Some Comments on 'Economic Transition in Estonia.'" *Journal of Economic Issues* 27, no. 4 (December 1993): 1270-1272. [On William S. Brown, "Economic Transition in Estonia," *Journal of Economic Issues* 27, no. 2 (June 1993).]

1394. World Bank. *Estonia: The Transition to a Market Economy*. A World Bank Country Study. Washington, DC: World Bank, 1993. xxxi, 330 pp.

Greece and Cyprus (Since 1821)

1395. DeWalle, F. B., M. Nikolopoulou-Tamvakli, and W. J. Heinen, eds. *Environmental Condition of the Mediterranean Sea: European Community Countries*. With major contributions from V. Silano et al. Environment & Assessment, v. 5. Dordrecht; Boston: Kluwer Academic Publishers, c1993. xii, 524 pp.

1396. "Greece Undertakes 75 Major Projects for Infrastructure and Development." *Business America* 114, no. 10 (May 17, 1993): 17.

1397. Harlaftis, Gelina. *Greek Shipowners and Greece, 1945-1975: From Separate Development to Mutual Interdependence*. London: Atlantic Highlands, NJ: Athlone Press, 1993. xv, 243 pp.

1398. Ioakimoglou, Elias, and John Milios. "Capital Accumulation and Over-Accumulation Crisis: The Case of Greece (1960-1989)." *Review of Radical Political Economics* 25, no. 2 (June 1993): 81-107.

1399. Kotsires, Lampros E. *Greek Company Law*. 2nd ed. Athens, Greece: Ant. N. Sakkoulas; Cambridge, MA: Distributed in the U.S.A. and Canada [by] Kluwer Law and Taxation Publishers, 1993. 183 pp.

1400. "The Labors of Mitsotakis." *Journal of European Business* 4, no. 4 (March/April 1993): 13-16. [On Prime Minister Mitsotakis and the Greek economy.]

1401. Lianos, Theodore P., and Vassilis Droucopoulos. "Convergence and Hierarchy of Industrial Profit Rates: The Case of Greek Manufacturing." *Review of Radical Political Economics* 25, no. 2 (June 1993): 67-80.

1402. Matziorinis, Kenneth. "Greek Economy at a Turning Point: Recent Performance, Current Challenges and Future Prospects." *Journal of the Hellenic Diaspora* 19, no. 2 (1993): 57-83. [Presented at a seminar on "Greece, the Balkans and the Eastern Mediterranean," at Dawson College in November 1992.]

1403. Moschonas, A., and V. Droucopoulos. "Small and Medium-Scale Industry Greece: Oasis of Dynamism or Symptom of Malaise?" *Review of Radical Political Economics* 25, no. 2 (June 1993): 108-131.

1404. Philopoulos, Ioannis. "Perspectives économiques dans les Balkans; Le cas de la Grèce dans une région en pleine mutation." *Journal of the Hellenic Diaspora* 19, no. 2 (1993): 85-108. [Presented at a seminar on "Greece, the Balkans and the Eastern Mediterranean," at Dawson College in November 1992.]

Hungary

1405. Agócs, Peter, and Sándor Agócs. "Entrepreneurship in Post-Communist Hungary." *Journal of Social, Political and Economic Studies* 18, no. 2 (Summer 1993): 159-179.

1406. Andorka, Rudolf. "The Socialist System and its Collapse in Hungary: An Interpretation in Terms of Modernisation Theory." *International Sociology* 8, no. 3 (September 1993): 317-337.

1407. Bandi, Gyula. "The Right to Environment in Theory and Practice: The Hungarian Experience." *Connecticut Journal of International Law* 8, no. 2 (Spring 1993): 439-465. [Paper from the symposium, "Human Rights in Theory and Practice: A Time of Change and Development in Central and Eastern Europe," held in Budapest, March 19-20, 1993.]

1408. Bangert, David C., and Jozef Poór. "The Evolution of Multinational Participation in Eastern Europe." *International Executive* 35, no. 2 (March/April 1993): 161-172.

1409. Chang, Valerie J., and Catherine L. Mann. *Industry Restructuring and Export Performance: Evidence on the Transition in Hungary*. International Finance Discussion Papers, no. 445. Washington, DC: Board of Governors of the Federal Reserve System, [1993]. 36 pp.

1410. Comisso, Ellen. *Legacies of the Past vs. New Institutions: Restitution and Agricultural Reform in Hungary*. Working Paper (University of California, Berkeley. Center for German and European Studies), 2.11. Berkeley, CA: Center for German and European Studies, University of California, [1993]. 37 pp.

1411. Copeland, Henry. "Mr. Greed." *New Republic* 208, no. 15 (April 12, 1993): 14-16. ["Meet Marc Holtzman, the new version of foreign aid."]

1412. Feick, Lawrence F., Robin A. Higie, and Linda L. Price. *Consumer Search and Decision Problems in a Transitional Economy: Hungary, 1989-1992*. Report (Marketing Science Institute), no. 93-113. Cambridge, MA: Marketing Science Institute, c1993. 55 pp.

1413. Gray, Cheryl W., Rebecca J. Hanson, and Michael Heller. "Hungarian Legal Reform for the Private Sector." *George Washington Journal of International Law and Economics* 26, no. 2 (1993): 293-354.

1414. "Hungary: An Update for U.S. Companies." *Business America* 114, no. 13 (June 28, 1993): 6-10. [Reprints of articles published in *Eastern Europe Business Bulletin*: Monika Michejda Goodrich, "Privatization Progess," pp. 6-7; "Commercial Contacts for Hungary," p. 6; "Hungarian Trade Fairs Attract Foreign Firms," p. 7; Monika Michejda Goodrich, "World Expo '96," p. 8; Patrick

Hughes, "Telecommunications," pp. 8-9; "Opportunties Outside Budapest," pp. 9-10; "Franchising Catches On in Eastern Europe," p. 10.]

1415. Hungary, and United States. Dept. of State. *Aviation, Transport Services: Agreement between the United States of America and Hungary, Extending the Agreement of July 12, 1989, Effected by Exchange of Notes, Dated at Budapest June 24 and July 10, 1992.* United States Treaties, etc. (Treaties and Other International Acts Series), 11868. Washington, DC: Dept. of State, [1993?]. 3 pp.

1416. ———. *Aviation, Transport Services: Agreement between the United States of America and the Hungarian People's Republic, Extending the Agreement of May 30, 1972, as Amended and Extended, Effected by Exchange of Notes, Dated at Budapest December 20, 1984, and April 5, 1985.* United States Treaties, etc. (Treaties and Other International Acts Series). Washington, DC: Dept. of State, [1993?]. 3 pp.

1417. ———. *Employment: Agreement between the United States of America and Hungary, Effected by Exchange of Notes, Dated at Budapest November 18, 1991, and January 16, 1992.* United States Treaties, etc. (Treaties and Other International Acts Series), 11841. Washington, DC: Dept. of State, [1993?]. 7 pp.

1418. Jun, Meeka. "New Capital Markets and Securities Regulations in Hungary: A Comparative Analysis of Insider Trading Regulations in Hungary and the United States." *Brooklyn Journal of International Law* 19, no. 3 (1993): 1047-1100.

1419. Kalleberg, Arne L., and David Stark. "Career Strategies in Capitalism and Socialism: Work Values and Job Rewards in the United States and Hungary." *Social Forces* 72, no. 1 (September 1993): 181-198.

1420. Knuepfer, Robert C., Jr., and Patrick N. Z. Rona. "Hungary May Eliminate Tax Incentives for Foreigners." *Journal of International Taxation* 4, no. 12 (December 1993): 562-567.

1421. Kurucz, Mihály. "Land Protection, Property Rights and Environmental Preferences (Land Use Control and Land Development)." *Connecticut Journal of International Law* 8, no. 2 (Spring 1993): 467-485. [Paper from the symposium, "Human Rights in Theory and Practice: A Time of Change and Development in Central and Eastern Europe," held in Budapest, March 19-20, 1993.]

1422. Laki, Mihály. "The Chances for the Acceleration of Transition: The Case of the Hungarian Privatization." *East European Politics and Societies* 7, no. 3 (Fall 1993): 440-451.

1423. Lewis, Michael. "Budapest Postcard: My Friend Tony." *New Republic* 209, no. 23 (December 6, 1993): 16-18.

1424. Libertiny, Karen S. "Cause for Cautious Celebration: Hungarian Post-Communist Environmental

Reform." *Michigan Journal of International Law* 14, no. 3 (Spring 1993): 518-552.

1425. Lipschutz, Ronnie. *Environmentalism in One Country? The Case of Hungary.* Working Paper (University of California, Berkeley. Center for German and European Studies), 2.15. Berkeley, CA: Center for German and European Studies, University of California, [1993]. 33 pp.

1426. Morkre, Morris E., and David G. Tarr. *Reforming Hungarian Agricultural Trade Policy: A Quantitative Evaluation.* Policy Research Working Papers, WPS 1185. Washington, DC: Trade Policy Division, Policy Research Dept., World Bank, [1993]. 28 pp.

1427. Murphy, Brendan. "Finance: The Unifying Theme." *Atlantic* 272, no. 1 (July 1993): 25ff. [On George Soros and investment in Hungary.]

1428. Okolicsanyi, Karoly. "Hungarian Agricultural Production Declines." *RFE/RL Research Report* 2, no. 44 (November 5, 1993): 46-49.

1429. ———. "Hungary Plans to Introduce Voucher-Type Privatization." *RFE/RL Research Report* 2, no. 17 (April 23, 1993): 37-40.

1430. ———. "Hungary's Foreign Trade in Transition." *RFE/RL Research Report* 2, no. 29 (July 16, 1993): 32-36.

1431. ———. "Private Sector Gains Little from High Hungarian Savings." *RFE/RL Research Report* 2, no. 15 (April 9, 1993): 49-51.

1432. Ritook, Magda. "Career Development in Hungary at the Beginning of the 90's." *Journal of Career Development* 20, no. 1 (Fall 1993): 33-40.

1433. Rondinelli, Dennis A., and Martin R. Fellenz. "Privatization and Private Enterprise Development in Hungary: An Assessment of Market-Reform Policies." *Business & the Contemporary World* 5, no. 4 (Autumn 1993): 75-80.

1434. Solimano, Andres, and David E. Yuravlivker. *Price Formation, Nominal Anchors, and Stabilization Policies in Hungary: An Empirical Analysis.* Policy Research Working Papers, WPS 1234. Washington, DC: World Bank, [1993]. 36 pp.

1435. Székely, István P., and David M. G. Newbery, eds. *Hungary: An Economy in Transition.* Contributions by Mario Sarcinelli, David M. G. Newbery, László Csaba, Kálmán Mizsei, László Halpern, István P. Székely, Renzo Daviddi, Zsigmond Járai, Péter Mihályi, János Stadler, John P. Bonin, Rumen Dobrinsky, Paul Seabright, Júlia Király, Éva Várhegyi, Lucian Ionescu, Colin Mayer, Gábor Oblath, Werner Riecke, L. Alan Winters, Richard Portes, Tamás Sárközy, Jenő Koltay, Athar Hussain, János Köllö, Mária Augusztinovics, David Winter, István Abel, David Begg, Robert E. Rowthorn, and

Adam Ridley. Cambridge; New York, NY: Cambridge University Press, 1993. xxvii, 360 pp. [Proceedings of the conference organised by the Centre for Economic Policy Research and held in London on February 7-8, 1992. Contents: István P. Székely and David M.G. Newbery, "Preface," p. xvii; Mario Sarcinelli, "Foreword," pp. xix-xxiii; István P. Székely and David M.G. Newbery, "Introduction," pp. 1-23. Pt. One: Foreign trade; László Csaba, "Economic consequences of Soviet disintegration for Hungary," pp. 27-43; Kálmán Mizsei, "Regional cooperation in East-Central Europe," pp. 44-50; László Halpern and István P. Székely, "Export supply and import demand in Hungary: an econometric analysis for 1968-89," pp. 51-70; Renzo Daviddi, "Discussion of Part One," pp. 70-74. Pt. Two: Privatisation and competition policy; Zsigmond Járai, "10 per cent already sold: privatisation in Hungary," pp. 77-83; Péter Mihályi, "Hungary: a unique approach to privatisation—past, present and future," pp. 84-117; János Stadler, "Competition policy in transition," pp. 118-125; John P. Bonin, Rumen Dobrinsky and Paul Seabright, "Discussion of Part Two," pp. 125-134. Pt. Three: The financial system and private savings; Júlia Király, "A short-run money market model of Hungary," pp. 137-148; Éva Várhegyi, "The modernisation of the Hungarian banking sector," pp. 149-162; István Ábel and István P. Székely, "Changing structure of household portfolios in emerging market economies: the case of Hungary, 1970-89," pp. 163-180; John P. Bonin, Lucian Ionescu and Colin Mayer, "Discussion of Part Three," pp. 180-190. Pt. Four: Foreign debt and monetary policy; Gábor Oblath, "Hungary's foreign debt: controversies and macroeconomic problems," pp. 193-223; Werner Riecke, "Managing foreign debts and monetary policy during transformation," pp. 224-230; L. Alan Winters and Richard Portes, "Discussion of Part Four," pp. 231-235. Pt. Five: Legislative and tax reform; Tamás Sárközy, "A legal framework for the Hungarian transition, 1989-91," pp. 239-248; Jenö Koltay, "Tax reform in Hungary," pp. 249-270; Athar Hussain, "Discussion of Part Five," pp. 270-274. Pt. Six: Labour markets, unemployment and social security; János Köllö, "The transformation of shop floor bargaining in Hungarian industry," pp. 277-295; Mária Augusztinovics, "The social security crisis in Hungary," pp. 296-320; David M.G. Newbery and David Winter, "Discussion of Part Six," pp. 321-325. Pt. Seven: State desertion; István Ábel and John P. Bonin, "State desertion and convertibility: the case of Hungary," pp. 329-341; David Begg and Robert E. Rowthorn, "Discussion of Part Seven," pp. 341-346; Adam Ridley, "Conclusion," pp. 342-352.]

1436. Török, Adam. "Trends and Motives of Organizational Change in Hungarian Industry—A Synchronic View." *Journal of Comparative Economics* 17, no. 2 (June 1993): 366-384.

1437. United Nations. Industrial Development Organization. *Hungary: Progressing Towards a Market Economy*. Industrial Development Review Series. Oxford, UK; Cambridge, MA: Published by Blackwell for the United Nations Industrial Development Organization, 1993. xxiv, 220 pp.

1438. Webster, Leila M. *The Emergence of Private Sector Manufacturing in Hungary: A Survey of Firms*. World Bank Technical Paper, no. 229. Washington, DC: World Bank, 1993. vii, 99 pp.

Latvia

1439. Grigorievs, Alexi. "High Dive into the Market." *Uncaptive Minds* 6, no. 1 (22) (Winter-Spring 1993): 83-86.

1440. Hansen, Leif et al. *Latvia*. Prepared under the direction of John C. Odling-Smee. IMF Economic Reviews, 6 (1993). Washington, DC: International Monetary Fund, c1993. vii, 91 pp.

1441. Knöbl, Adalbert et al. *Lithuania*. Prepared under the direction of John C. Odling-Smee. IMF Economic Reviews, 7 (1993). Washington, DC: International Monetary Fund, 1993. vii, 102 pp.

1442. Latvia, United States. President (1993- : Clinton), and United States. Congress. House. Committee on Merchant Marine and Fisheries. *Fishing Agreement with the Republic of Latvia: Message from the President of the United States Transmitting a Copy of an Agreement between the United States Government and the Government of the Republic of Latvia Concerning Fisheries off the Coasts of the United States, with Annex, Signed at Washington on April 8, 1993, Pursuant to 16 U.S.C. 1823(A)*. House Document (United States. Congress. House), 103-102. Washington, DC: U.S. G.P.O., 1993. 21 pp.

1443. World Bank. *Latvia: The Transition to a Market Economy*. A World Bank Country Study. Washington, DC: World Bank, c1993. xxiv, 305 pp.

Lithuania

1444. Lithuania, United States. President (1989-1993: Bush), and United States. Congress. House. Committee on Merchant Marine and Fisheries. *Governing International Fishery Agreement between the United States and the Republic of Lithuania: Communication from the President of the United States Transmitting an Agreement between the Government of the United States and the Government of the Republic of Lithuania Concerning Fisheries off the Coasts of the United States, Pursuant to 16 U.S.C. 1823(A)*. House Document (United States. Congress. House), 103-38. Washington, DC: U.S. G.P.O., 1993. iii, 39 pp.

1445. Odling-Smee, John C., and Adalbert Knöbl. *Lithuania*. Washington, DC: International Monetary Fund, c1993. vii, 102 pp.

1446. Povilanskas, Ramunas. "Oil—At What Price?" *Surviving Together* 11, no. 4 (Winter 1993): 48-49. [Reprinted from *WWF Baltic Bulletin* (March 1993).]

1447. World Bank. *Lithuania: The Transition to a Market Economy*. World Bank Country Study. Washington, DC: World Bank, 1993. xxix, 397 pp.

Poland

1448. Anderson, Sheldon R. *A Dollar to Poland Is a Dollar to Russia: U.S. Economic Policy toward Poland, 1945-1952.* Foreign Economic Policy of the United States. New York: Garland Pub., 1993. xxiii, 242 pp. [Originally presented as the author's thesis (Ph. D.). Contents: 1. Obstacles to Economic Cooperation, 1945-1946; 2. Negotiations for American Loans, 1945-1946; 3. The Suspension of the Loan Agreement, 1946; 4. The Change in U.S. Aid Policy, 1946-1947; 5. The Denial of U.S. Relief Aid for Poland, 1947; 6. Poland and the Marshall Plan, 1947-1948; 7. The Strategic Embargo of Poland, 1948-1949; 8. Polish Foreign Economic Policy, 1949-1950; 9. The Impact of Economic Warfare on the Polish Economy, 1949-1952.]

1449. Barford, Charlotte, Jesse Norman, and Lawrence Weschler. *Breaking the Habits of a Lifetime: Poland's First Steps toward the Market: Field Studies.* Ipswich, MA: Ipswich Press, c1993. iii, 223 pp.

1450. Bielecki, Jan Krzysztof. "Poland and the European Community: Toward Full Integration." *Hastings International and Comparative Law Review* 16, no. 4 (1993): 619-635.

1451. Brzezinski, Carolyn. "The EC-Poland Association Agreement: Harmonization of an Aspiring Member State's Company Law." *Harvard International Law Journal* 34, no. 1 (Winter 1993): 105-148.

1452. Byrnes, Timothy A. "One leap forward, one step back." *Commonweal* 120, no. 20 (November 19, 1993): 29-30. [Review article on Jeffrey Sachs, *Poland's Jump to the Market Economy* (Cambridge, MA: MIT Press, 1993).]

1453. Cultice, Curtice K. " 'American Showhouse' in Warsaw Shows Poles the Advantages of U.S. Housing Technology." *Business America* 114, no. 19 (September 20, 1993): 11-13.

1454. Cummings, Susan S. "Polish Environmental Regulation: The State of Poland's Environment, Governmental Authorities and Policy." *Suffolk Transnational Law Review* 16, no. 2 (Spring 1993): 379-404.

1455. Dobek, Mariusz Mark. *The Political Logic of Privatization: Lessons from Great Britain and Poland.* Westport, CT: Praeger, 1993. xiii, 162 pp.

1456. Estrin, Saul, and Xavier Richet. "Industrial Restructuring and Microeconomic Adjustment in Poland: A Cross-Sectoral Approach." *Comparative Economic Studies* 35, no. 4 (Winter 1993): 1-19.

1457. Hoshi, Takeo, Anil Kashyap, and Gary Loveman. *Lessons from the Japanese Main Bank System for Financial System Reform in Poland.* Research Report (University of California, San Diego. Graduate School of International Relations and Pacific Studies), 93-01. La Jolla, CA: Graduate School of International Relations and Pacific Studies, University of California, San Diego, [1993]. 67 pp.

1458. Hunter, Richard J., and John Northrop. "Management, Legal and Accounting Perspectives: Privatization in Poland." *Polish Review* 38, no. 4 (1993): 407-420.

1459. Kalecki, Michal. *Socialism: Economic Growth and Efficiency of Investment.* Edited by Jerzy Osiatynski. Translated by Bohdan Jung. Collected Works of Michal Kalecki, v. 4. Oxford: Clarendon; New York: Oxford University Press, 1993. xiii, 369 pp.

1460. Kaminski, Bartlomiej. *The Foreign Trade Dimension of the Market Transition in Poland: The Surprising Export Performance and Its Sustainability.* Policy Research Working Papers, WPS 1144. Washington, DC: International Economics Dept., World Bank, [1993]. 27 pp.

1461. Kierzkowski, Henryk, Marek Okolski, and Stanislaw Wellisz, eds. *Stabilization and Structural Adjustment in Poland.* Contributions by Andrzej Kondratowicz, Marek Okolski, Stanislaw Wellisz, Henryk Kierzkowski, Ryszard Kokoszczynski, Peter Mieszkowski, Izabela Bolkowiak, Donald Lubick, Hanna Sochacka-Krysiak, Jan Jakub Michalek, Mieczyslaw W. Socha, Urszula Sztanderska, Janusz A. Ordover, Maciej Iwanek, Marek Bednarski, Andrzej Lubbe, Andrzej Kwiecinski, Antoni Leopold, Katarzyna Tymowska, Marian Wisniewski, Tomasz Zylicz, Dariusz Olszewski, Grazyna Pruban, Monika Pawlica, Piotr Nojszewski, and Miroslawa Sibilska. London; New York: Routledge, 1993. xi, 314 pp. [Contents: Andrzej Kondratowicz and Marek Okolski, "The Polish Economy on the Eve of the Solidarity Take-Over," pp. 7-28; Stanislaw Wellisz, Henryk Kierzkowski and Marek Okolski, "The Polish Economy 1989-1991," pp. 29-63; Ryszard Kokoszczynski and Andrzej Kondratowicz, "Banking, Credit and Monetary Policy," pp. 67-91; Peter Mieszkowski, Izabela Bolkowiak, Donald Lubick and Hanna Sochacka-Krysiak, "Tax Reform," pp. 92-111; Jan Jakub Michalek, "The Opening Up of the Polish Economy," pp. 112-127; Mieczyslaw W. Socha and Urszula Sztanderska, "The Labour Market," pp. 131-152; Maciej Iwanek and Janusz A. Ordover, "Transition to a Market Economy: Some Industrial Organizational Issues," pp. 153-170; Stanislaw Wellisz, Maciej Iwanek and Marek Bednarski, "Privatization," pp. 171-187; Andrzej Lubbe, "Transforming Poland's Industry," pp. 188-205; Andrzej Kwiecinski and Antoni Leopold, "Polish Agriculture during the Transition Period," pp. 206-216; Katarzyna Tymowska and Marian Wisniewski, "Public Health and Social Security," pp. 219-242; Tomasz Zylicz, "Problems of the Environment," pp. 243-254; Dariusz Olszewski, Grazyna Pruban, Monika Pawlica, Piotr Nojszewski and Miroslawa Sibilska, "Appendix I: Chronology of Economic and Political Events 1989-91," pp. 255-291; "Appendix II: Basic Statistics," pp. 292-306.]

1462. Kowalik, Tadeusz. "Can Poland Afford the Swedish Model?" *Dissent* 40, no. 1 (Winter 1993): 88-96. Translated from the Polish by Jane Cave.

1463. Krawczyk, Marek, and Jose A. Lopez-Lopez. "The Role of Government in Poland's Economic Transition: Ideas and Experience from the Recent Past." *Columbia Journal of World Business* 28, no. 1 (Spring 1993): 180-187.

1464. Kulig, Jan, and Adam Lipowski. "Polish Economists Lag Behind Changes in the Economy." *Social Research* 60, no. 4 (Winter 1993): 835-852. Translated by Jerzy B. Warman. [With an introduction by Jacek Kochanowicz.]

1465. Leven, Bozena. "Short-term Effects of Economic Transition on Inequality and Poverty: The Polish Case." *Journal of Economic Issues* 27, no. 1 (March 1993): 237-243.

1466. ———. "Unemployment Among Polish Women." *Comparative Economic Studies* 35, no. 4 (Winter 1993): 135-145.

1467. McDonald, Kevin R. "Why Privatization Is Not Enough." *Harvard Business Review* 71, no. 3 (May-June 1993): 49ff.

1468. Meaney, Constance Squires. *Privatization and the Ministry of Privatization in Poland: Outsiders As Political Assets and Political Liabilities.* Working Paper (University of California, Berkeley. Center for German and European Studies), 2.13. Berkeley, CA: Center for German and European Studies, University of California, [1993]. 32 pp.

1469. Milanovic, Branko. *Social Costs of Transition to Capitalism: Poland 1990-91.* Policy Research Working Papers, WPS 1165. Washington, DC: Policy Research Department, World Bank, [1993]. 29 pp.

1470. Pinto, Brian, Marek Belka, and Stefan Krajewski. "Transforming State Enterprises in Poland: Evidence on Adjustment by Manufacturing Firms. Comments and Discussion." *Brookings Papers on Economic Activity*, no. 1 (1993): 213-270. [Followed by discussion with Andrei Schleifer and others.]

1471. ———. *Transforming State Enterprises in Poland: Microeconomic Evidence on Adjustment.* Policy Research Working Papers, WPS 1101. Washington, DC: Poland Resident Mission, Country Dept. II, Europe and Central Asia Region, World Bank, [1993]. 43 pp.

1472. Poznanski, Kazimierz Z. "Restructuring of Property Rights in Poland: A Study in Evolutionary Economics." *East European Politics and Societies* 7, no. 3 (Fall 1993): 395-421.

1473. ———, ed. *Stabilization and Privatization in Poland: An Economic Evaluation of the Shock Therapy Program.* Contributions by Kazimierz Z. Poznanski, Branko Milanovic, Keith Crane, Dariusz K. Rosati, Jozef M. van Brabant, Ronald I. McKinnon, Wojciech W. Charemza, Przemyslaw T. Gajdeczka, Jeffrey Sachs, Peter Murrell, Jacek Kochanowicz, Josef C. Brada, and Arthur E. King. International Studies in Economics and Econometrics, v. 29. Boston, MA: Kluwer Academic Publishers, c1993. vi, 269 pp. [Volume is a by-product of the U.S.-Polish Economic Roundtable, jointly sponsored on an annual basis by the Henry Jackson School of International Studies at the University of Washington and the Economics Department of Warsaw University. Contents: Kazimierz Z. Poznanski, "Introduction," pp. 1-11; Kazimierz Z. Poznanski, "Poland's Transition to Capitalism: Shock and Therapy," pp. 15-42; Branko Milanovic, "Poland's Quest for Economic Stabilization, 1988-1991: Interaction of Political Economy and Economics," pp. 43-62; Keith Crane, "Taking Stock of the 'Big Bang,'" pp. 63-83; Dariusz K. Rosati, "The CMEA Demise, Trade Restructuring, and Trade Destruction in Eastern Europe: Initial Assesssment," pp. 87-104; Jozef M. van Brabant, "The New East and Old Trade and Payment Problems," pp. 105-123; Ronald I. McKinnon, "Liberalizing Foreign Trade in a Socialist Economy: The Problem of Negative Value Added," pp. 125-147; Wojciech W. Charemza, "East European Transformation: The Supply Side," pp. 151-171; Przemyslaw T. Gajdeczka, "Inflation Tax, Household Wealth, and Privatization in Poland," pp. 173-195; Jeffrey Sachs, "The Economic Transformation of Eastern Europe; The Case of Poland," pp. 197-212; Peter Murrell, "Evolutionary and Radical Approaches to Economic Reform," pp. 215-231; Jacek Kochanowicz, "Transition to Market in a Comparative Perspective: A Historian's Point of View," pp. 233-250; Josef C. Brada and Arthur E. King, "Is There a J-Curve for the Economic Transition from Socialism to Capitalism?" pp. 251-269.]

1474. Ruff, Jackie. "Job Security in Poland: Economic Privatization Policy and Workplace Protections." *Temple International and Comparative Law Journal* 7, no. 1 (Spring 1993): 1-28.

1475. Sachs, Jeffrey D. *Poland's Jump to the Market Economy.* The Lionel Robbins Lectures. Cambridge, MA: MIT Press, c1993. xv, 126 pp. [Contents: 1. What Is To Be Done NOW?; 2. Poland's Big Bang; 3. The Return to Europe.] REV: Timothy A. Byrnes, *Commonweal* 120, no. 20 (November 19, 1993): 29-30. Richard Cooper, *Foreign Affairs* 72, no. 5 (November-December 1993): 161.

1476. Slay, Ben. "Evolution of Industrial Policy in Poland since 1989." *RFE/RL Research Report* 2, no. 2 (January 8, 1993): 21-28.

1477. ———. "Poland: The Role of Managers in Privatization." *RFE/RL Research Report* 2, no. 12 (March 19, 1993): 52-56.

1478. Stulberg, Joseph B. "Cultural Diversity and Democratic Institutions: What Role for Negotiations?" *Mediation Quarterly* 10, no. 3 (Spring 1993): 249-263.

1479. Taylor, Robert F., and Zbigniew Marek Czarny. "Poland Joins the Queue to European Integration." *Transnational Lawyer* 6, no. 1 (Spring 1993): 169-180.

1480. United States. International Trade Administration, and United States. Bureau of Mines. *A Cost comparison of selected U.S. and Polish coal mines.* Washington, DC: Bureau of Mines: International Trade Administration, 1993. xxi, 108 pp.

1481. Vinton, Louisa. "Political Brinkmanship: Polish Coalition Wins Budget Vote." *RFE/RL Research Report* 2, no. 11 (March 12, 1993): 7-15.

1482. ———. "Privatization in Poland: A Statistical Picture." *RFE/RL Research Report* 2, no. 32 (August 13, 1993): 58-62.

1483. Webster, Leila M. *The Emergence of Private Sector Manufacturing in Poland: A Survey of Firms.* World Bank Technical Paper, no. 237. Washington, DC: World Bank, 1993. vii, 94 pp.

1484. Wilson, Gavin. "The Privatization of Swarzedz Furniture Company (SFM)." *Columbia Journal of World Business* 28, no. 1 (Spring 1993): 18-35. ["Lessons from Poland's first underwritten public offering."]

1485. World Bank. *Poland: Income Support and the Social Safety Net During the Transition.* Compiled by Nicholas Barr. A World Bank Country Study. Washington, DC: World Bank, c1993. xviii, 144 pp. [Based on the findings of missions that visited Poland between 1989 and 1992.]

1486. Wyznikiewicz, Bohdan, Brian Pinto, and Maciej Grabowski. *Coping with Capitalism: The New Polish Entrepreneurs.* Discussion Paper (International Finance Corporation), no. 18. Washington, DC: World Bank, c1993. v, 35 pp. REV: *International Economic Insights* 4, no. 6 (November-December 1993): 34-35.

1487. Zarembka, Paul. "Poland: The Deepening Crisis in the Summer of 1992." *Monthly Review* 44, no. 8 (January 1993): 21-29.

Romania

1488. Bush, Larry S. "Collective Labor Disputes in Post-Ceausescu Romania." *Cornell International Law Journal* 26, no. 2 (Spring 1993): 373-420.

1489. Grama, Mihaela, and Nicholas S. Hammond. "Romania's Tax System Evolves with the Free Market Economy." *Journal of International Taxation* 4, no. 6 (June 1993): 276-280.

1490. Ionescu, Dan. "Between Two Price Shocks: Social Unrest in Romania." *RFE/RL Research Report* 2, no. 26 (June 25, 1993): 13-18.

1491. ———. "Romania's Cabinet in Search of an Economic Strategy." *RFE/RL Research Report* 2, no. 4 (January 22, 1993): 45-49.

1492. ———. "Romania's Currency Plummeting." *RFE/RL Research Report* 2, no. 49 (December 10, 1993): 43-48.

1493. ———. "Romania's Winter of Shortages." *RFE/RL Research Report* 2, no. 6 (February 5, 1993): 45-48.

1494. Lane, Charles. "Cluj Postcard: Ubi Caritas." *New Republic* 209, no. 19 (November 8, 1993): 9-10. ["Capitalism comes to Romania."]

1495. Romania, and United States. Dept. of State. *Aviation: Transport Services: Agreement between the United States of America and Romania, Amending and Extending the Agreement of December 4, 1973, As Amended and Extended, Effected by Exchange of Notes, Signed at Bucharest Mar. 19, 1990.* United States Treaties, etc. (Treaties and Other International Acts Series), 11730. Washington, DC: Dept. of State, [1993?]. 7 pp.

1496. ———. *Aviation, Transport Services: Agreement between the United States of America and Romania, Extending the Agreement of December 4, 1973, As Amended and Extended, Effected by Exchange of Notes, Signed at Bucharest January 16 and 24, 1992.* United States Treaties, etc. (Treaties and Other International Acts Series), 11840. Washington, DC: Dept. of State, [1993?]. 3 pp.

1497. ———. *Aviation, Transport Services: Agreement between the United States of America and the Socialist Republic of Romania, Extending the Agreement of December 4, 1973, As Amended and Extended, Effected by Exchange of Notes, Dated at Bucharest January 23 and 30 and February 18, 1989, and Exchange of Notes Dated at Bucharest August 10 and 11, 1989.* United States Treaties, etc. (Treaties and Other International Acts Series), 11691. Washington, DC: Dept. of State, [1993?]. 9 pp.

1498. Shafir, Michael. "The Caritas Affair: A Transylvanian 'Eldorado.'" *RFE/RL Research Report* 2, no. 38 (September 24, 1993): 23-27.

1499. United States. *Joint Resolution to Approve the Extension of Nondiscriminatory Treatment with Respect to the Products of Romania.* [Washington, DC?: U.S. G.P.O., 1993]. [1] leaf.

1500. United States. Congress. House. Committee on Ways and Means. *Extension of Nondiscriminatory Treatment with Respect to the Products of Romania: Report (To Accompany H.J. Res. 228) (Including Cost Estimate of the Congressional Budget Office).* United States. Congress. House Report, 103-279. [Washington, DC?: U.S. G.P.O., 1993]. 8 pp.

1501. United States. Congress. Senate. Committee on Finance. *Approving the Extension of Nondiscriminatory Treatment (Most-Favored-Nation Treatment) to the Products of Romania: Report (To Accompany S.J. Res. 110).* United

States. Congress. Senate Report, 103-159. [Washington, DC?: U.S. G.P.O., 1993]. 11 pp.

1502. United States. Congress. Senate. Committee on Foreign Relations. *Treaty with the Government of Romania Concerning the Reciprocal Encouragement and Protection of Investment: Report (To Accompany Treaty Doc. 102-36).* United States. Congress. Senate Executive Report, 103-7. [Washington, DC?: U.S. G.P.O., 1993]. 6 pp.

1503. United States. President (1993- : Clinton), and United States. Congress. House. Committee on Ways and Means. *Nondiscriminatory Treatment to the Products of Romania: Communication from the President of the United States Transmitting a Copy of the "Agreement on Trade Relations Between the Government of the United States and the Government of Romania" Will Promote the Purposes of the Trade Act of 1974 and Is in the National Interests, Pursuant to 19 U.S.C. 2437(A).* House Document (United States. Congress. House), 103-112. Washington, DC: U.S. G.P.O., 1993. 46 pp.

1504. U.S. Congress. House of Representatives. Subcommittee on Trade of the Committee on Ways and Means. *Written Comments on a Trade Agreement between the United States and Romania.* Washington, DC: U.S. G.P.O., 1993. vi, 189 pp. [At head of title: 103d Congress, 1st session. Committee print. WMCP: 103-20.]

(Former) Yugoslavia

1505. Cvikl, Milan, Evan Kraft, and Milan Vodopivec. *Costs and Benefits of Independence: Slovenia.* Policy Research Working Papers, WPS 1126. Washington, DC: Policy Research Dept., World Bank, [1993]. 36 pp.

1506. Dyker, David A. "Rump Yugoslavia's New Economic Policy Package." *RFE/RL Research Report* 2, no. 41 (October 15, 1993): 33-36.

1507. Estrin, Saul, and Jan Svejnar. "Wage Determination in Labor-Managed Firms under Market-Oriented Reforms: Estimates of Static and Dynamic Models." *Journal of Comparative Economics* 17, no. 3 (September 1993): 687-700.

1508. Gapinski, James H. *The Economic Structure and Failure of Yugoslavia.* Westport, CT: Praeger, 1993. xviii, 212 pp. [Contents: 1. A Sketch of Facts. 1.1. A History Through Tito. 1.2. The Final Months and Beyond. 1.3. An Economic Record. 1.4. Inflation and Money Growth; 2. Theory and Practice. 2.1. Limits to Theory. 2.2. Illyrian Theory. 2.3. Beyond Illyrian Theory. 2.4. Thoughts from Orthodoxy and Heterodoxy. 2.5. Implications for Modeling Yugoslavia; 3. Quantity Relationships. 3.1. Consumption. 3.2. Investment. 3.3. Capital Stock. 3.4. Output: Capacity and Actual. 3.5. Labor. 3.6. Fiscal Factors. 3.7. Volumes of Exports and Imports; 4. Prices and Values. 4.1. Sectoral Wage Inflation. 4.2. Sectoral Price Inflation. 4.3. The Inflation Network. 4.4. Counterfactual Policy Implications.

4.5. Bridging to the Mark. 4.6. Consumer Price Inflation. 4.7. Further Reflections on Price Indices. 4.8. Balance of Payments; 5. Domestic Counterfactual Scenarios. 5.1. Price and Wage Adjustments. 5.2. Increased Output Growth. 5.3. Investment Reallocation. 5.4. Reallocations from Government Activities to Investment. 5.5. Credit Contraction; 6. International Counterfactual Maneuvers. 6.1. Accelerated Dinar Depreciation. 6.2. Hard Currency Incentives. 6.3. Equipment and Technology Transfers; 7. Conclusions from a Broader Perspective. 7.1. Comprehensive Restructuring. 7.2. Sectoral and Regional Implications. 7.3. A Lesson from Eastern Europe. 7.4. A Preventable Failure?; Appendix A: The EIZFSU Mark 4.0: Selected Equations and Glossary; Appendix B: Comparing the Marks.]

1509. Horvat, Branko. "Requiem for the Yugoslav Economy." *Dissent* 40, no. 3 (Summer 1993): 333-339.

1510. Isanlar Avcisoy, Hayriye Gulderen. "The Effects of National and International Economic Policies on Regional Disparities: The Case of Yugoslavia." Ph.D. diss., Cornell University, 1993. [UMI order no: AAC 9406119.]

1511. Madzar, Ljubomir. "Rump Yugoslavia Mired in Economic Problems." *RFE/RL Research Report* 2, no. 39 (October 1, 1993): 45-49.

1512. Pogany, Peter. "U.S. Government and business continue to develop ties with republics of former Yugoslavia." *International Economic Review* (November 1993): 6-7.

1513. Vodopivec, Milan. "Determination of Earnings in Yugoslavia Firms: Can It Be Squared with Labor Management?" *Economic Development and Cultural Change* 41, no. 3 (April 1993): 623-632.

1514. Yugoslavia, and United States. Dept. of State. *Aviation, Transport Services: Agreement between the United States of America and the Socialist Federal Republic of Yugoslavia, Amending the Agreements of September 27, 1973 and December 15, 1977 and Extending the Memorandums of Understanding of March 17 and May 19, 1982, As Amended and Extended, Effected by Exchange of Notes, Dated at Belgrade January 15 and July 6, 1987.* United States Treaties, etc. (Treaties and Other International Acts Series), 11547. Washington, DC: Dept. of State, [1993?]. 8 pp.

1515. ———. *Aviation, Transport Services: Memorandum of Understanding between the United States of America and the Socialist Federal Republic of Yugoslavia, Signed at Belgrade, June 28, 1989.* United States Treaties, etc. (Treaties and Other International Acts Series), 11666. Washington, DC: Dept. of State, [1993?]. 5 pp.

Croatia

1516. Bicanic, Ivo. "Croatians Struggle to Make Ends Meet." *RFE/RL Research Report* 2, no. 45 (November

12, 1993): 29-34.

1517. ———. "Privatization in Croatia." *East European Politics and Societies* 7, no. 3 (Fall 1993): 422-439.

1518. Bicanic, Ivo, and Iva Dominis. "The Croatian Economy: Achievements and Prospects." *RFE/RL Research Report* 2, no. 26 (June 25, 1993): 33-38.

Macedonia

1519. Petkovski, Mihail, Goce Petreski, and Trajko Slaveski. "Stabilization Efforts in the Republic of Macedonia." *RFE/RL Research Report* 2, no. 3 (January 15, 1993): 34-37.

Serbia

1520. Minic, Jelica. "The Black Economy in Serbia: Transition from Socialism?" *RFE/RL Research Report* 2, no. 34 (August 27, 1993): 26-29.

Slovenia

1521. Gray, Cheryl W., and Franjo D. Stiblar. "The Evolving Legal Framework for Private Sector Activity in Slovenia." *University of Pennsylvania Journal of International Business Law* 14, no. 2 (Spring 1993): 119-167. [Article is part of a research project in the World Bank studying legal frameworks in Eastern Europe.]

1522. Mencinger, Joze. "The Slovene Economy." *Nationalities Papers* 21, no. 1 (Spring 1993): 81-89.

5 Education and Scholarship

◼ General

1523. Anweiler, Oskar. "Educational Problems of Post-Communist Societies: A Challenge for Public Policy, Research and Practical Action." *East/West Education* 14, no. 1 (Spring 1993): 1-12. Translated by Clayton Gray, Jr. [Article published in *Bildung und Erziehung* 45, no. 3 (September 1992): 251-263.]

1524. Kohn, Melvin L. "Doing Social Research Under Conditions of Radical Social Change: The Biography of an Ongoing Research Project." *Social Psychology Quarterly* 56, no. 1 (March 1993): 4-20.

1525. Woodard, Colin. "Rapid Academic Growth in Eastern Europe Brings Calls for Regulation." *Chronicle of Higher Education* 39, no. 39 (June 2, 1993): A29ff.

◼ Russia/U.S.S.R./C.I.S.

1526. Clark, Charles E. "The Russian 'Down with Illiteracy' Society, 1923-1927." *East/West Education* 14, no. 1 (Spring 1993): 35-50.

1527. David, Sheri. "Teaching in Minsk: The Experience of a Fulbright Scholar." *East/West Education* 14, no. 2 (Fall 1993): 163-170.

1528. Dneprov, Edvard Dmitrievich. "Reform of Education in Russia and Government Policy in the Sphere of Education." *East/West Education* 14, no. 1 (Spring 1993): 13-34.

1529. Dushenkov, Vjacheslav M. "Biological Olympiads in the USSR." *American Biology Teacher* 55, no. 7 (October 1993): 399-404.

1530. Eklof, Ben, and Edward Dneprov, eds. *Democracy in the Russian School: The Reform Movement in Education Since 1984.* Contributions by Ben Eklof, Edward Dneprov, Oleg Matiatin, G. Shalaev, M. Dmukhovsky, I. Prelovskaia, Olga Marinicheva, Adam Petrovsky, Boris Yeltsin, V. S. Lazarev, and V. S. Sobkin. Boulder, CO: Westview Press, 1993. vi, 269 pp. [Contents: Ben Eklof, "Democracy in the Russian School: Education Reform since 1984," pp. 1-33; Teachers' Gazette Editor, "Here's Wishing You Well, Comrade Minister," pp. 34-35; Part One. The Educational System Under Fire. Edward Dneprov, "Bureaucratic Tyranny (Must Be Eliminated from the School)," pp. 36-41; Edward Dneprov, "Faith in the Teacher: The Energy of Renewal for the School," pp. 42-46; Edward Dneprov, "Learning to Teach," pp. 47-52; Edward Dneprov, "The Yardstick of History," pp. 53-58; Edward Dneprov, "Who Will Restructure the Academy of Pedagogical Sciences, and in What Direction?" pp. 59-64; Part Two. The VNIK Program. Edward Dneprov, "The Fourth Reform: Polemical Notes on a History of the Present," pp. 65-76; Edward Dneprov, "A Concept of General (Secondary) Education," pp. 77-103; Oleg Matiatin, "You Won't Get Anywhere on the Sidelines," pp. 104-108; Edward Dneprov, "Vseobuch: A General Secondary Education for All—From Illusion to Reality," pp. 109-113; G. Shalaev and M. Dmukhovsky, "Dneprov's Principles," pp. 114-118; I. Prelovskaia, "The Russian School: A New Era?" pp. 119-121; Edward Dneprov, "One Hundred Days, and a Lifetime," pp. 122-127; Olga Marinicheva, "Power Was Dumped in Our Laps: What Happens to the Former Opposition When It Ends up in the Corridors of Power," pp. 128-133; Part Three: The Opposition in Power. Adam Petrovsky, "The Attack on the Minister," pp. 134-138; Boris Yeltsin, "Decree No. 1 of the President of the Russian Federation: On Priority Measures to Promote Education," pp. 139-141; Edward Dneprov, "Al'ternativa," pp. 142-147; E.D. Dneprov, V.S. Lazarev, and V.S. Sobkin, "The State of Education in Russia Today," pp. 148-220; Edward Dneprov, "The Educational System of the Russian Federation," pp. 221-235; "The Law of the Russian Federation on Education (Draft)," pp. 236-259.]

1531. Fox, Michael S. "Political Culture, Purges, and Proletarianization at the Institute of Red Professors, 1921-1929." *Russian Review* 52, no. 1 (January 1993): 20-42.

1532. Fox, Michael Sheldon. "The Higher Party Schools: Education, Politics and the Transformation of Intellectual Life in the Soviet Union, 1921-1929." Ph.D. diss., Yale University, 1993. [UMI order no: AAC 9400623.]

1533. Gershunsky, Boris S. *Russia in Darkness: On Education and the Future: An Open Letter to President Yeltsin.* San Francisco, CA: Caddo Gap Press, 1993. xix, 82 pp. REV: Patrick L. Alston, *East/West Education* 14, no. 2 (Fall 1993): 171-174.

1534. Granik, Lisa A. "Legal Education in Post-Soviet Russia and Ukraine." *Oregon Law Review* 72, no. 4 (1993): 963-976.

1535. Gransden, Gregory. "Moscow State U. Strives to Navigate Its Country's Turbulent Transition." *Chronicle of Higher Education* 39, no. 34 (April 28, 1993): A37ff.

1536. ———. "Once-Secret Institutes in Russia Now Court Foreign Students." *Chronicle of Higher Education* 40, no. 2 (September 1, 1993): A50ff.

1537. ———. "Russians Flock to New Business Schools as Marxism Yields to Study of Capitalism." *Chronicle of Higher Education* 39, no. 27 (March 10, 1993): A33ff.

1538. Hemesath, Michael. "Reflections on the Impact of Soviet Ideology on Post-Soviet Higher Education."

East/West Education 14, no. 2 (Fall 1993): 156-162. [Based on two semesters (Fall 1991 and Fall 1993) of teaching Russian students in the economics department at Kuban State University in Krasnodar, Russia.]

1539. Holmes, Larry E. "The Oral Record and Historical Objectivity (Moscow's Model School No. 25, 1931-1937)." *East/West Education* 14, no. 1 (Spring 1993): 66-68.

1540. Kanevskaya, Marina. "Nikolai Pavlovich Antsiferov: 'Teacher of Human Science.' " *East/West Education* 14, no. 2 (Fall 1993): 139-155.

1541. Kirschenbaum, Lisa. "Socialism in the Soviet Kindergarten, 1921-1928." *East/West Education* 14, no. 2 (Fall 1993): 126-138.

1542. Konecny, Peter. "The Unwanted: Students in the Factories During the First Five-Year Plan." *East/West Education* 14, no. 2 (Fall 1993): 87-112.

1543. Kuebart, Friedrich. "Perspectives on the Emergence of Tsarist Russia's Vocational Education System." *East/West Education* 14, no. 2 (Fall 1993): 113-125.

1544. Marker, Gary. "Who Rules the Word? Public School Education and the Fate of Universality in Russia, 1782-1803." *Russian History* 20, nos. 1-4 (1993): 15-34.

1545. Petherbridge-Hernandez, Patricia, and Rosalind Latiner Raby. "Twentieth-Century Transformations in Catalonia and the Ukraine: Ethnic Implications in Education." *Comparative Education Review* 37, no. 1 (February 1993): 31-49.

1546. Recknagel, Charles. "American University Beats the Odds to Stay Open During Blockade by Armenia's Hostile Neighbors." *Chronicle of Higher Education* 39, no. 48 (August 4, 1993): A32.

1547. Ruane, Christine. "Divergent Discourses: The Image of the Russian Woman Schoolteacher in Post-Reform Russia." *Russian History* 20, nos. 1-4 (1993): 109-123.

1548. Tomusk, Voldemar, and Anu Tomusk. "Teaching Psychology in Estonia, USSR Revisited." *Teaching of Psychology* 20, no. 3 (October 1993): 175-177. [Response to article by R. Sommer and B.A. Sommer, "Teaching Psychology in Estonia, USSR," *Teaching of Psychology* vol. 18 (1991): 105-107.]

1549. Toom, Andrei. "A Russian Teacher in America." *Journal of Mathematical Behavior* 12, no. 2 (June 1993): 117-139.

1550. ———. "A Russian Teacher in America." *American Educator* 17, no. 3 (Fall 1993): 9ff. [Article is adapted from author's "A Russian Teacher in America," *Journal of Mathematical Behavior* 12, no. 2 (June 1993): 117-139.]

1551. Tucker, Jan L. "Global Lessons from Siberia." *Social Education* 57, no. 3 (March 1993): 101-103.

1552. Ulymzhiev, D. "Dorzhi Banzarov: The First Buryat Scholar." *Mongolian Studies*, no. 16 (1993): 55-57.

1553. Valkenier, Elizabeth Kridl. "Teaching History in Post-Communist Russia." *Harriman Institute Forum* 6, no. 8 (April 1993): 1-10.

1554. Watkins, Beverly T. "Reporters Notebook: Russians Hope to Woo Americans." *Chronicle of Higher Education* 40, no. 13 (November 17, 1993): A48.

1555. Wolfe, Joseph. "A History of Business Teaching Games in English-Speaking and Post-Socialist Countries: The Origination and Diffusion of a Management Education and Development Technology." *Simulation & Gaming* 24, no. 4 (December 1993): 446-463.

1556. ———. "A Report on Two Gaming Conferences in Russia and Ukraine." *Simulation & Gaming* 24, no. 1 (March 1993): 106-109. [Description of the "18th International Seminar on Gaming-Simulation in Education and Scientific Research," held in Kiev, September 17-21, 1991, sponsored by the East European Simulation and Gaming Association, and of "White Nights '92," held in St. Petersburg, June 23-26, 1992, sponsored by the Social Simulation Game Modeling Designer's Association.]

1557. Woodard, Colin. "Humanities and Social Sciences Hit Hard by Russia's Financial Crisis." *Chronicle of Higher Education* 39, no. 47 (July 28, 1993): A37.

1558. World Congress for Soviet and East European Studies (4th: 1990: Harrogate, England). *School and Society in Tsarist and Soviet Russia: Selected Papers from the Fourth World Congress for Soviet and East European Studies, Harrogate, 1990.* Edited by Ben Eklof. Contributions by Charles E. Timberlake, Elliott Mossman, Gary Thurston, Ben Eklof, Scott J. Seregny, Larry E. Holmes, Feliks Aronovich Fradkin, Klas-Goran Karlsson, and Howard D. Mehlinger. New York, NY: St. Martin's Press, 1993. xii, 254 pp. [World Congress for Soviet and East European Studies (4th: 1990: Harrogate, England). Contents: Charles E. Timberlake, "N.A. Korf (1834-83): designer of the Russian elementary school classroom"; Elliott Mossman, "Tolstoi and peasant learning in the era of the great reforms"; Gary Thurston, "Theatre in the village school: the Bunakovs' discoveries"; Ben Eklof, "Worlds in conflict: patriarchal authority, discipline and the Russian school, 1861-1914"; Scott J. Seregny, "Teachers, politics and the peasant community in Russia, 1895-1918"; Larry E. Holmes, "Shatsky: reformer and realist (introductory remarks to F.A. Fradkin's 'Shatsky's last years')"; Feliks Aronovich Fradkin, "Soviet experimentalism routed: S.T. Shatsky's last years"; Larry E. Holmes, "Legitimizing the Soviet regime: School no. 25, 1931-1937"; Klas-Goran Karlsson, "History teaching in twentieth-century Russia and the Soviet Union: classicism and its alternatives"; Howard D. Mehlinger, "School textbooks: weapons for the Cold War."]

1559. Zdravkovska, Smilka, and Peter Duren, eds. *Golden Years of Moscow Mathematics.* History of Mathematics, v. 6. Providence, RI: American Mathematical Society;

London: London Mathematical Society, 1993. ix, 271 pp.

■ Eastern Europe

1560. Andorka, Rudolf. "Institutional Changes and Intellectual Trends in Some Hungarian Social Sciences." *East European Politics and Societies* 7, no. 1 (Winter 1993): 74-108. [Paper was contributed to the JCEE conference on Intellectual Trends, Institutional Changes and Scholarly Needs in Eastern Europe.]

1561. Baumgart, Karl. "Interview with an East German Teacher about the Effects of German Unification on Schools in the 'New Federal States.'" *Social Education* 57, no. 5 (September 1993): 249-250. Adapted and translated by Dagmar Kraemer, and Manfred Stassen. [Interview with Marita Knauf, conducted November 18, 1992, in East Berlin. Part of special section entitled "The Case of Germany, Part 2," edited by Dagmar Kraemer and Manfred Stassen.]

1562. Bollag, Burton. "All Czech Professors Required to Reapply for Their Jobs." *Chronicle of Higher Education* 40, no. 4 (September 15, 1993): A43.

1563. ———. "East Europe's Universities Struggle to Cope as Aid Dwindles." *Chronicle of Higher Education* 39, no. 46 (July 21, 1993): A33-A35.

1564. ———. "Ethnic Strife in Macedonia Threatens to Destroy Higher-Education System." *Chronicle of Higher Education* 39, no. 49 (August 11, 1993): A35-A36.

1565. ———. "Hopes for Campus Reform in East Europe Frustrated by Inertia and Conservatism." *Chronicle of Higher Education* 39, no. 30 (March 31, 1993): A32ff.

1566. ———. "Lithuanian Academics Expect to Continue Campus Reforms." *Chronicle of Higher Education* 39, no. 19 (January 13, 1993): A39.

1567. ———. "Researchers at Central Europe's New University Focus on Tough Issues: Privatization, Legislative Policies, and the Raw Nerve of Nationalism." *Chronicle of Higher Education* 40, no. 8 (October 13, 1993): A47.

1568. ———. "Return of a Lost Generation." *Chronicle of Higher Education* 40, no. 11 (November 3, 1993): A41-A42. ["Czech scholars who were purged in Communist era strive to resume their careers."]

1569. Bula, Inese. "Der Rigaer Deutsch-Baltische Mathematiker Piers Bohl (1865-1921)." *Journal of Baltic Studies* 24, no. 4 (Winter 1993): 319-326.

1570. Burns, Richard. "A Living Embroidery: English Teaching and Cultural Contacts in Yugoslavia." *North Dakota Quarterly* 61, no. 1 (Winter 1993): 4-11.

1571. Doder, Dusko. "Belgrade Professor Who Fought Tito Now Scorned as a Serb Leader." *Chronicle of Higher Education* 39, no. 31 (April 7, 1993): A37-A38.

1572. ———. "Economic Sanctions, Fighting in Bosnia Prompt Scholars to Flee Yugoslavia." *Chronicle of Higher Education* 39, no. 35 (May 5, 1993): A41ff.

1573. ———. "Government Thwarted in Effort to Replace Rector at U. of Belgrade." *Chronicle of Higher Education* 39, no. 20 (January 20, 1993): A47.

1574. ———. "Professors at U. of Belgrade Become Targets of Government Efforts to Silence Opposition." *Chronicle of Higher Education* 39, no. 25 (February 24, 1993): A39-A40.

1575. Dorn, David N. "A War against Children." *American Educator* 17, no. 1 (Spring 1993): 36-41.

1576. Duff, Patricia Ann. "Changing Times, Changing Minds: Language Socialization in Hungarian-English Schools." Ph.D. diss., University of California, Los Angeles, 1993. [Ph. D. dissertation. UMI order no: AAC 9317902.]

1577. Gabor, Francis A. "Legal Education in Hungary." *Oregon Law Review* 72, no. 4 (1993): 957-962.

1578. Gostynski, Zbigniew, and Alan Garfield. "Taking the Other Road: Polish Legal Education During the Past Thirty Years." *Temple International and Comparative Law Journal* 7, no. 2 (Fall 1993): 243-286.

1579. Gotchev, Atanas. "Education and Research in the Social Sciences: Transition Dilemmas in Bulgaria." *East European Politics and Societies* 7, no. 1 (Winter 1993): 43-58. [Paper was contributed to the JCEE conference on Intellectual Trends, Institutional Changes and Scholarly Needs in Eastern Europe.]

1580. Gustaff, Leona T. "A Promise Fulfilled." *Lituanus* 39, no. 4 (Winter 1993): 84-83. [Teaching English in Lithuania.]

1581. Gustaff, Leona T., and Albert J. Gustaff. "Observations in Lithuania in 1992." *Lituanus* 39, no. 4 (Winter 1993): 79-83. [Teaching English in Lithuania.]

1582. Kalniczky, Adele. "Academic Freedom in Slovakia: The Case of Trnava University." *RFE/RL Research Report* 2, no. 11 (March 12, 1993): 53-56.

1583. Kollath, Katalin, and Robert Laurence. "Teaching Abroad, Or, 'What Would That Be in Hungarian?'" *Journal of Legal Education* 43, no. 1 (March 1993): 85-95.

1584. Kowalski, Kazimierz. "The Polish Academy of Arts and Sciences in the Past, Present and Future." *Polish Review* 38, no. 2 (1993): 149-158.

1585. Kraemer, Dagmar. "The Dual System of Vocational Training in Germany." *Social Education* 57, no. 5 (September 1993): 245-247. [Part of special section entitled "The Case of Germany, Part 2," edited by Dagmar Kraemer and Manfred Stassen.]

1586. Kyriakopoulos, Irene. "Education without Borders: Greek Policy in a Pan-European Setting." *Mediterranean Quarterly* 4, no. 3 (Summer 1993): 81-95.

1587. Lörincz, Judit. "The Sociology of reading: A comparison of novel reading in Hungary and Finland in the 1980s." *Journal of Reading* 36, no. 8 (May 1993): 642-646. [Discusses "a joint Hungarian-Finnish study which compared how readers in the two countries approach selected novels, and the different roles that fiction reading plays in the two societies."]

1588. Musil, Jiří. "Education and Research in the Czech Republic: Burden of the Past and Hope for the Future." *East European Politics and Societies* 7, no. 1 (Winter 1993): 59-73. [Paper was contributed to the JCEE conference on Intellectual Trends, Institutional Changes and Scholarly Needs in Eastern Europe.]

1589. Nixon, Nora. "Designing an English Curriculum for Hungarian Teachers of Math and Science." *Hungarian Studies Review* 20, nos. 1-2 (Spring-Fall 1993): 83-92.

1590. Pataki, Judith. "Political Controversy over Hungarian Church School." *RFE/RL Research Report* 2, no. 47 (November 26, 1993): 56-59.

1591. Plut-Pregelj, Leopoldina. "Changes in the Slovene Educational System, 1990-1992." *East/West Education* 14, no. 1 (Spring 1993): 51-65.

1592. Pusic, Vesna. "Intellectual Trends, Institutional Changes and Scholarly Needs in Eastern Europe: A New Agenda for the Social Sciences." *East European Politics and Societies* 7, no. 1 (Winter 1993): 1-13. [Introduces papers by Marga, Tarifa, Gotchev, Musil, and Andorka, which were contributed to the JCEE conference on Intellectual Trends, Institutional Changes and Scholarly Needs in Eastern Europe.]

1593. Ricchiardi, Sherry. "Journalism Students in Zagreb Look to Free Press as Weapon in the Struggle for Croatian Democracy." *Chronicle of Higher Education* 39, no. 43 (June 30, 1993): A33.

1594. Rodden, John. "Repairing the Red Schoolhouse: Report Card from East Germany." *Four Quarters* 7, no. 2 (Fall 1993): 7-12.

1595. Sadlak, Jan. "Legacy and Change—Higher Education and Restoration of Academic Work in Romania." *Technology in Society* 15, no. 1 (1993): 75-100. [Part of special issue on science and technology in Eastern Europe.]

1596. Simpson, Peggy. "Poland Struggles to Help Industry Make Better Use of Universities." *Chronicle of Higher Education* 39, no. 20 (January 20, 1993): A48.

1597. Tarifa, Fatos. "Is There a Future for the Social Sciences in Albania?" *East European Politics and Societies* 7, no. 1 (Winter 1993): 33-42. [Paper was contributed to the JCEE conference on Intellectual Trends, Institutional Changes and Scholarly Needs in Eastern Europe.]

1598. Woodard, Colin. "$230-Million Gift to Central European U. Expected to Enlarge Its Role in Region." *Chronicle of Higher Education* 40, no. 8 (October 13, 1993): A46.

1599. ———. "The Cream of Bulgaria." *Chronicle of Higher Education* 40, no. 10 (October 27, 1993): A37ff.

1600. ———. "Restructuring of Croatian Universities Sparks Concern for Their Autonomy." *Chronicle of Higher Education* 39, no. 43 (June 30, 1993): A31ff.

1601. ———. "University to Close Prague Campus After Losing Czech Government Aid." *Chronicle of Higher Education* 39, no. 22 (February 3, 1993): A36.

6 Geography and Demography

■ General

1602. Coleman, David A. "Contrasting Age Structures of Western Europe and of Eastern Europe and the Former Soviet Union: Demographic Curiosity or Labor Resource?" *Population and Development Review* 19, no. 3 (September 1993): 523-555.

1603. Facts on File, Inc. *CIS and Eastern Europe on File*. New York: Facts on File, c1993. 1 vol.

1604. Menefee, Samuel Pyeatt. " 'The Oar of Odysseus': Landlocked and 'Geographically Disadvantaged' States in Historical Perspective." *California Western International Law Journal* 23, no. 1 (1992-1993): 1-65.

1605. Velkoff, Victoria A., and Kevin Kinsella. *Aging in Eastern Europe and the Former Soviet Union*. International Population Reports, Series P-95; no. 93-1. Washington, DC: U.S. Dept. of Commerce, Economics and Statistics Administration, Bureau of the Census, [1993]. 1 vol. [Overview of the populations in Eastern Europe and the former Soviet republics: the size and trends of the elderly portion of these populations; the factors determining the rates at which populations are aging; health indicators and social characteristics of the elderly; and the economic implications of aging populations.]

■ Russia/U.S.S.R./C.I.S.

1606. Bond, Andrew R. "Geography of Human Resources: An Introduction." *Post-Soviet Geography* 34, no. 4 (April 1993): 219-223. [Edited version of the Proceedings of the Fifth Theodore Shabad Memorial Roundtable on the Geography of the (former) USSR, held in conjunction with the 1993 Annual Meeting of the Association of American Geographers in Atlanta, GA.]

1607. Clem, Ralph S. "Interethnic Relations at the Republic Level: The Example of Kazakhstan." *Post-Soviet Geography* 34, no. 4 (April 1993): 229-232. [Edited version of the Proceedings of the Fifth Theodore Shabad Memorial Roundtable on the Geography of the (former) USSR, held in conjunction with the 1993 Annual Meeting of the Association of American Geographers in Atlanta, GA.]

1608. Clingermayer, James C. "Different Countries, Different Cities, Different Answers to the Same Policy Questions." *Policy Studies Journal* 21, no. 1 (Spring 1993): 144-148. [Review article on five monographs, including Blair A. Ruble, *Leningrad: Shaping a Soviet City* (Berkeley, CA: 1990).]

1609. Dunlop, John B. "Will a Large-Scale Migration of Russians to the Russian Republic Take Place Over the Current Decade?" *International Migration Review* 27, no. 3 (Fall 1993): 605-629. [Revised version of a paper presented at a workshop on "The New Russian Diaspora," sponsored by the Institute of History of the Latvian Academy of Sciences and the University of Oslo, held in Lielupe, Jurmala, Latvia, November 13-15, 1992.]

1610. Gachechiladze, Revaz, and Michael J. Bradshaw. "News Notes: Background and Analysis: Civil Unrest and Net Migration Balance in Tbilisi, 1989-1993." *Post-Soviet Geography* 34, no. 8 (October 1993): 541-542.

1611. Gaston, Greg G. "A Procedure for Estimating the Carbon Budget of Terrestrial Ecosystems in the Former Soviet Union by Geographic Information System Analysis and Classification of AVHRR Derived Global Vegetation Index." Ph.D. diss., Oregon State University, 1993. [UMI order no: AAC 9413716.]

1612. Gilbert, Martin. *Atlas of Russian history*. 2nd ed. New York: Oxford University Press, 1993. 161 pp. [Rev. ed. of: *Russian History Atlas*. First published in Great Britain by the Orion Publishing Group, 1972.]

1613. Harris, Chauncy D. "Ethnic Tensions in Areas of the Russian Diaspora." *Post-Soviet Geography* 34, no. 4 (April 1993): 233-239. [Edited version of the Proceedings of the Fifth Theodore Shabad Memorial Roundtable on the Geography of the (former) USSR, held in conjunction with the 1993 Annual Meeting of the Association of American Geographers in Atlanta, GA.]

1614. ———. "A Geographic Analysis of Non-Russian Minorities in Russia and Its Ethnic Homelands." *Post-Soviet Geography* 34, no. 9 (November 1993): 543-544.

1615. ———. "The New Russian Minorities: A Statistical Overview." *Post-Soviet Geography* 34, no. 1 (January 1993): 1-27.

1616. Harris, Godfrey, and Sergei A. Diakonov. *Mapping Russia and Its Neighbors, The New Atlas of the Changed Geographical Face of the former Soviet Union*. 1st ed. Los Angeles, CA: Americas Group, 1993. 1 atlas.

1617. Ilyin, Pavel. "Renaming of Soviet Cities after Exceptional People: A Historical Perspective on Toponymy." *Post-Soviet Geography* 34, no. 10 (December 1993): 631-660.

1618. Matthews, Mervyn. *The Passport Society: Controlling Movement in Russia and the USSR*. Boulder, CO: Westview Press, 1993. xiv, 118 pp. [Contents: 1. Passports Under the Tsars. The Origins of the System. Tsarist Control at Its Zenith. Crossing the Imperial Frontier. The Liberalisation Decrees; 2. Early Bolshevik Policies. Controls Through the Labour Book. Freedoms in the Mid-and Late Twenties. Arrangements for Travel Abroad; 3. Stalin's Passport System. Other Legislation in the Thirties.

Developments from September, 1940 to July, 1974. The 1974 Passport Statute. Some Legal Comment. Foreign Travel Under Khrushchev and Brezhnev; 4. Long-Standing Social Problems. Daily Uses of the Passport in the Eighties. Homelessness and Vagrancy. The Plight of Ex-Convicts. Employment, Training and Housing Difficulties. Fictitious Marriages. Public Opinion and Response; 5. The Bureaucratic Morass. Mainstream Registration Procedures. Deregistration (Vypiska). Propiska. The Bureaucratic Workload. The Size and Nature of the Bureaucracy. Housing Office Clerks. The Militia. The Assessment of Efficiency; 6. Liberalisation After Communism. Some Minor Adjustments. Absence for Employment Purposes. Young Marrieds in Hostels. Internal Passports and Frontier Crossing. Identity Cards for Rationing. Military Documentation and Labour Books. Changes in Moscow. More Flexibility for Pensioners? More Glasnost', Relief Ex-Convicts. Constitutional Proposals. Attempts at Administrative Change. Post-Communist Legislation. Towards Open Frontiers; 7. Regional Dimensions. Policies in the Non-Russian Republics. The Baltic States. The Chinese Experience. The States of the Former Soviet Bloc.]

1619. Mitchneck, Beth. "Panel on Social Dimensions of Interdependence in the States of the Former USSR." *Post-Soviet Geography* 34, no. 1 (January 1993): 28-51. Participants: Ralph S. Clem, Timothy Heleniak, Robert J. Kaiser, Michael Paul Sacks, and Lee Schwartz. [Based on a panel at the Annual Meeting of the American Association for the Advancement of Slavic Studies, November 21, 1992, Phoenix, AZ.]

1620. Monyak, Robert. "Geographic Perspectives on Soviet Central Asia." *Nationalities Papers* 21, no. 2 (Fall 1993): 150-153. Report of a talk by Robert A. Lewis. [Notes from the Harriman Institute Seminar on Soviet Republics and Regional Issues, December 7, 1990. Presentation based largely on Robert A. Lewis, ed., *Geographic Perspectives on Soviet Central Asia* (London: 1991).]

1621. ———. "Post-1985 Internal Migration: Spatial Patterns and Issues." *Nationalities Papers* 21, no. 2 (Fall 1993): 154-156. Report of a talk by Beth Mitchneck. [Notes from the Harriman Institute Seminar on Soviet Republics and Regional Issues, January 25, 1991.]

1622. Pika, Alexander. "The Spatial-Temporal Dynamic of Violent Death among the Native Peoples of Northern Russia." *Arctic Anthropology* 30, no. 2 (1993): 61-76. Translated by Eugenia W. Davis. [Edited by Igor I. Krupnik.]

1623. Rudelson, Justin Jon. "The Uighurs in the Future of Central Asia." *Central Asia Monitor*, no. 6 (1993): 16-25.

1624. Sagers, Matthew J., Andrew R. Bond, and Denis J. B. Shaw. "News Notes: Background and Analysis." *Post-Soviet Geography* 34, no. 1 (January 1993): 52-78. [Regional Differences in the Russian Federation: Social Tensions and Quality of Life (based on work of N.V. Petrov,

S.S. Mikheyev, and L.V. Smirnyagin); Russia's Regional Associations in Decline; Long-Term Plans for Oil and Gas Sector in Kazakhstan; Ukraine's Troubled Oil Trade with Russia: Impact on Ukrainian Refineries; Nationalization of Resort Complexes by Crimea; Restoration of Don Cossacks: Opposition and Support; Environmental Disruption During Economic Downturn: "White Book" Report.]

1625. Shaw, Denis J. B., Philip R. Pryde, Andrew R. Bond, and Philip P. Micklin. "News Notes: Background and Analysis." *Post-Soviet Geography* 34, no. 5 (May 1993): 318-336. [Integrity of Science City Threatened by Housing; Financial Crisis on the Baykal-Amur Mainline; Bids for Autonomy by Northern Regions of the Russian Federation; Expansion of Collective Gardening and Vegetable Growing; Russia's Division into "Rich" and "Poor" Regions; Commerical Ring Road for St. Petersburg?; The St. Petersburg Flood Barrier: Update; Issyk-Kul' Resort Zone Under Environmental Pressure; Small Town Initiative Gains Momentum in Moscow's White House; Krasnoyarsk Kray's Refusal to Accept Ukrainian Nuclear Waste; Russia Coping with "Cotton Crisis"; Political Aspects of Concern Over Russia's Forests.]

■ Eastern Europe

1626. Balteanu, Dan, and National Geophysical Data Center. *Environmental Hazards and Mud Volcanoes in Romania.* Boulder, CO: U.S. Dept. of Commerce, National Oceanic and Atmospheric Administration, National Geophysical Data Center, [1993?]. 6 pp.

1627. Bungs, Dzintra. "Recent Demographic Changes in Latvia." *RFE/RL Research Report* 2, no. 50 (December 17, 1993): 44-50.

1628. Gams, Ivan. "Slovenia: Geographic Constants of the New State." *Nationalities Papers* 21, no. 1 (Spring 1993): 15-30.

1629. Hooz, Istvan. "Nationality Statistics and the Possibilities of Reforming Them." *East European Quarterly* 27, no. 4 (Winter 1993): 417-436.

1630. Kushner, James A. "A Tale of Three Cities: Land Development and Planning for Growth in Stockholm, Berlin, and Los Angeles." *Urban Lawyer* 25, no. 2 (Spring 1993): 197-221.

1631. Magocsi, Paul Robert. *Historical Atlas of East Central Europe.* Cartographic design by Geoffrey J. Matthews. A History of East Central Europe, v. 1. Seattle, WA: University of Washington Press, 1993. xiii, 218 pp. [Covers "the lands between the linguistic frontier of German- and Italian-speaking peoples on the west and the political boundaries of the former Soviet Union on the east ... from about 400 C.E. (common era) to the present." Treated in depth are the Poles, Czechs, Slovaks, Hungarians, Romanians, Yugoslav peoples, Albanians, Bulgarians, and Greeks.] REV: Edward B. Cone, *Library Journal* 108, no. 19 (1993): 74. *Booklist* 90, no. 8 (December 15, 1993): 777-778.

1632. Nikolaev, Rada. "Bulgaria's 1992 Census: Results, Problems, and Implications." *RFE/RL Research Report* 2, no. 6 (February 5, 1993): 58-62.

1633. Sunstein, Cass R. "Information, Please." *East European Constitutional Review* 2, no. 3 (Summer 1993): 54-58. [Proposes a "Human Development Index."]

7 Government, Law, Politics

■ General

1634. Bauer, Yehuda. "Antisemitism as a European and World Problem." *Patterns of Prejudice* 27, no. 1 (July 1993): 15-24.

1635. Benz, Wolfgang. "Traditional and Rediscoverd Prejudices in the New Europe: Antisemitism, Xenophobia, Discrimination Against Minorities." *Patterns of Prejudice* 27, no. 1 (July 1993): 3-13.

1636. "Constitution Watch." *East European Constitutional Review* 2, no. 1 (Winter 1993): 2-11.

1637. "Constitution Watch." *East European Constitutional Review* 2, no. 4/vol. 3, no. 1 (Fall 1993-Winter 1994): 2-22.

1638. "Constitution Watch." *East European Constitutional Review* 2, no. 2 (Spring 1993): 2-14.

1639. "Constitution Watch." *East European Constitutional Review* 2, no. 3 (Summer 1993): 2-19.

1640. Cuthbertson, Ian M., and Jane Leibowitz, eds. *Minorities: The New Europe's Old Issue.* Foreword by Joseph S. Nye, Jr. Contributions by Iván Gyurcsík, Robert W. Mickey, Adam Smith Albion, André W. M. Gerrits, Ivanka Nedeva, Alexander A. Konovalov, Dmitri Evstafiev, Nicolai N. Petro, Andrzej Karkoszka, Richard Allan, Koen Koch, István Ijgyártó, and Konrad J. Huber. Prague; New York: Institute for EastWest Studies: Boulder, CO: Distributed by Westview Press, c1993. xii, 322 pp. [Contents: Ian M. Cuthbertson and Jane Leibowitz, "Introduction," pp. 1-15; Iván Gyurcsík, "New Legal Ramifications of the Question of National Minorities," pp. 19-50; Robert W. Mickey and Adam Smith Albion, "Success in the Balkans? A Case Study of Ethnic Relations in the Republic of Macedonia," pp. 53-98; André W.M. Gerrits, "Paradox of Freedom: The 'Jewish Question' in Postcommunist East Central Europe," pp. 99-121; Ivanka Nedeva, "Democracy Building in Ethnically Diverse Societies: The Cases of Bulgaria and Romania," pp. 123-155; Alexander A. Konovalov and Dmitri Evstafiev, "The Problem of Ethnic Minority Rights Protection in the Newly Independent States," pp. 157-181; Nicolai N. Petro, "Can Decentralization Solve Russia's Ethnic Problems?" pp. 185-206; Andrzej Karkoszka, "A Call for Confidence-Building Measures for Minorities in Eastern Europe," pp. 209-225; Richard Allan, "The Failure to Recognize Minority Rights and Claims: Political Violence/Terrorism in the East and West," pp. 227-250; Koen Koch, "The International Community and Forms of Intervention in the Field of Minority Rights Protection," pp. 253-272; István Ijgyártó, "Codification of Minority Rights," pp. 273-284; Konrad J. Huber, "Preventing Ethnic Conflict in the New Europe: The CSCE High Commissioner on National Minorities," pp. 285-310.]

1641. Darski, Jozef. "Decommunization in Eastern Europe." *Uncaptive Minds* 6, no. 1 (22) (Winter-Spring 1993): 73-81.

1642. Diamond, Larry, and Marc F. Plattner, eds. *Capitalism, Socialism and Democracy Revisted.* Baltimore, MD: Johns Hopkins University Press, c1993. xii, 137 pp. [Chapter 13 originally published in *Journal of Democracy* (April 1993); remainder of volume appeared in a special issue of *Journal of Democracy* (July 1992).]

1643. ———, eds. *The Global Resurgence of Democracy.* Includes contributions by Marc F. Plattner, Ken Jowitt, Giuseppe Di Palma, Leszek Kolakowski, and Charles H. Fairbanks, Jr. Baltimore, MD: Johns Hopkins University Press, c1993. xxvi, 336 pp. [Essays originally published in *Journal of Democracy* (1990-1991). Partial contents: Marc F. Plattner, "The Democratic Moment," pp. 26-38; Ken Jowitt, "The New World Disorder," pp. 247-256; Giuseppe Di Palma, "Why Democracy Can Work in Eastern Europe," pp. 257-267; Leszek Kolakowski, "The Postrevolutionary Hangover," pp. 268-272; Charles H. Fairbanks, Jr., "After the Moscow Coup," pp. 273-280.] REV: Francis Fukuyama, *Foreign Affairs* 72, no. 5 (November-December 1993): 158-159. Juliana Geran Pilon, *Freedom Review* 24, no. 6 (November-December 1993): 47-48.

1644. Drakulic, Slavenka. *How We Survived Communism and Even Laughed.* 1st HarperPerennial ed. New York: HarperPerennial, 1993. xvii, 197 pp. [Originally published: (New York: W.W. Norton, 1992). With a new epilogue by the author.]

1645. Forsythe, David P. [Review Article]. *Contemporary Sociology* 22, no. 3 (May 1993): 360-362. [Review article on Abdullahi Ahmed An-Na'im, ed., *Human Rights in Cross-Cultural Perspectives: A Quest for Consensus* (Philadelphia, PA: 1992); Helen Fein, ed., *Genocide Watch* (New Haven, CT: 1992); and Thomas B. Jabine and Richard P. Claude, eds., *Human Rights and Statistics: Getting the Record Straight* (Philadelphia, PA: 1992).]

1646. Fowkes, Ben. *The Rise and Fall of Communism in Eastern Europe.* Houndmills, Hampshire: Macmillan Press; New York: St. Martin's Press, 1993. xv, 228 pp.

1647. Frentzel-Zagórska, Janina, ed. *From a One-Party State to Democracy: Transition in Eastern Europe.* Contributions by Zygmunt Bauman, Leslie Holmes, Leszek Nowak, Jan Pakulski, Adam Czarnota, Martin Krygier, Maté Szabó, Edmund Mokrzycki, Janina Frentzel-Zagórska, and Robert F. Miller. Poznan Studies in the Philosophy of the Sciences and the Humanities, v. 32. Amsterdam;

Atlanta, GA: Rodopi, 1993. xiii, 224 pp. [Contents: Janina Frentzel-Zagórska, "Introduction," pp. ix-xiii; Zygmunt Bauman, "A Post-modern Revolution?" pp. 3-19; Leslie Holmes, "On Communism, Post-communism, Modernity and Post-Modernity," pp. 21-43; Leszek Nowak, "The Totalitarian Approach and the History of Socialism," pp. 45-66; Jan Pakulski, "East European Revolutions and 'Legitimacy Crisis,' " pp. 67-87; Adam Czarnota and Martin Krygier, "From State to Legal Traditions? Prospects for the Rule of Law after Communism," pp. 91-112; Maté Szabó, "Social Protest in a Post-communist Democracy: The Taxi Drivers' Demonstration in Hungary," pp. 113-137; Zygmunt Bauman, "Dismantling a Patronage State," pp. 139-154; Edmund Mokrzycki, "Between Reform and Revolution: Eastern Europe Two Years after the Fall of Communism," pp. 155-164; Janina Frentzel-Zagórska, "The Road to a Democratic Political System in Post-communist Eastern Europe," pp. 165-193; Robert F. Miller, "Yugoslavia: The End of the Experiment," pp. 195-219.]

1648. Gottlieb, Gidon. *Nation Against State: A New Approach to Ethnic Conflicts and the Decline of Sovereignty.* New York: Council on Foreign Relations Press, c1993. xiii, 148 pp.

1649. Graubard, Stephen R., ed. *Exit From Communism.* New Brunswick, NJ: Transaction Publishers, c1993. xii, 292 pp. [Augmented version of a special issue of *Daedalus* (Spring 1992).]

1650. Hall, John. *The Vacuum.* Working Paper (University of California, Berkeley. Center for German and European Studies), 5.10. Berkeley, CA: Center for German and European Studies, University of California, [1993]. 35 pp. [Conference on Markets, States and Democracy, February 11-13, 1993.]

1651. Hannum, Hurst. "Rethinking Self-Determination." *Virginia Journal of International Law* 34, no. 1 (Fall 1993): 1-69.

1652. Hockenos, Paul. *Free to Hate: The Rise of the Right in Post-Communist Eastern Europe.* New York: Routledge, c1993. x, 332 pp. [Contents: 1. Germany: One People, One Right — 2. East Germany: Fascism in the Anti-Fascist State — 3. Hungary: The Ghosts of Conservatism Past — 4. Hungary: Black in the Land of the Magyars — 5. Romania: Ceausescu's Revenge — 6. The Czech Republic: Skinheads Who Cry — 7. Poland: Christ of Nations — 8. Anti-Semitism without Jews.]

1653. Holmes, Stephen. *Conceptions of Democracy in the Draft Constitutions of Post-Communist Countries.* Working Paper (University of California, Berkeley. Center for German and European Studies), 5.11. Berkeley, CA: Center for German and European Studies, University of California, [1993]. 19 pp. [Conference on Markets, States and Democracy, February 11-13, 1993.]

1654. Irwin-Zarecka, Iwona. "In Search of Usable Pasts." *Society* 30, no. 2 (January-February 1993): 32-36.

1655. Johnson, Hank. "Religio-Nationalist Subcultures under the Communists: Comparisons from the Baltics, Transcaucasia and Ukraine." *Sociology of Religion* 54, no. 3 (Fall 1993): 237-255.

1656. Karatnycky, Adrian, and George Zarycky. "Return of the Communists? The Post-Soviet Bloc." *Freedom Review* 24, no. 6 (November-December 1993): 13-14.

1657. Kasza, Gregory J. "Parties, Interest Groups, and Administered Mass Organizations." *Comparative Political Studies* 26, no. 1 (April 1993): 81-110.

1658. Katz, Mark N. "The Legacy of Empire in International Relations." *Comparative Strategy* 12, no. 4 (October-December 1993): 365-383.

1659. Kim, Ilpyong, and Jane Shapiro Zacek, eds. *Establishing Democratic Rule: The Reemergence of Local Governments in Post-Authoritarian Systems.* Includes contributions by Tamara J. Resler, Roger E. Kanet, and Brian V. Souders. Washington, DC: In Depth Books, c1993. v, 329 pp. [Partial contents: Tamara J. Resler and Roger E. Kanet, "Democratization: The National-Subnational Linkage," pp. 17-34; Roger E. Kanet and Brian V. Souders, "Democratization and Local Government in Poland," pp. 77-100.]

1660. Krooth, Richard, and Boris Vladimirovitz. *Quest for Freedom: The Transformation of Eastern Europe in the 1990s.* Jefferson, NC: McFarland, c1993. xviii, 390 pp.

1661. Levin, Bernard. "One Who Got It Right." *National Interest*, no. 31 (Spring 1993): 64-65. [Essay originally published in *The Times* (London), (August 1977).]

1662. Lucky, Christian. "A Comparative Chart of Presidential Powers in Eastern Europe." *East European Constitutional Review* 2, no. 4/vol. 3, no. 1 (Fall 1993-Winter 1994): 81-94.

1663. Ludwikowski, Rett R. "Constitution Making in the Countries of the Former Soviet Dominace: Current Development." *Georgia Journal of International and Comparative Law* 23, no. 2 (Summer 1993): 155-267.

1664. Merkl, Peter H., and Leonard Weinberg, eds. *Encounters with the Contemporary Radical Right.* Includes contributions by Trond Gilberg and Vladislav Krasnov. New Directions in Comparative Politics. Boulder, CO: Westview Press, 1993. x, 277 pp. [Partial contents: Part Two: Eastern Europe and Israel. Trond Gilberg, "Ethnochauvanism, Agrarian Populism, and Neofascism in Romania and the Balkans," pp. 95-110; Vladislav Krasnov, "Pamiat: Russian Right-Wing Radicalism," pp. 111-131.] REV: Francis Fukuyama, *Foreign Affairs* 72, no. 5 (November-December 1993): 156-157.

1665. Mullerson, Rein. "New Developments in the Former USSR and Yugoslavia." *Virginia Journal of International Law* 33, no. 2 (Winter 1993): 299-322.

1666. Offe, Claus. "Disqualification, Retribution, Restitution: Dilemmas of Justice in Post-Communist Transitions." *Journal of Political Philosophy* 1, no. 1 (March 1993): 17-44.

1667. O'Loughlin, John, and Herman van der Wusten, eds. *The New Political Geography of Eastern Europe.* Contributions by Jirí Musil, Jan Nijman, Herman van der Wusten, John O'Loughlin, Janet E. Kodras, Simon Dalby, Petr Dostál, Snjezana Mrdjen, Kveta Kalibova, Tomas Haisman, Jitka Gjuricova, Leo Paul, John Pickles, Bourgas Group, Vladimir Kolossov, Joanna Regulska, Petr Jehlicka, Tomás Kostelecky, Ludek Sykora, and Zoltán Kovacs. London; New York: Belhaven; New York: Halsted, 1993. x, 280 pp. [Contents: John O'Loughlin and Herman van der Wusten, "The new political geography of Eastern Europe," pp. 1-8; Jiri Musil, "The transition to democracy," pp. 9-12; Jan Nijman and Herman van der Wusten, "Breaking the Cold War mould in Europe: a geopolitical tale of gradual change and sharp snaps," pp. 15-30; John O'Loughlin, "Precursor of crisis: political and economic relations of the Soviet Union, 1960-90," pp. 31-52; Janet E. Kodras, "Geopolitical transitions in agriculture: the changing role of American food policy in Eastern Europe, 1955-91," pp. 53-70; Simon Dalby, "Post-Cold War security in the new Europe," pp. 73-85; Petr Dostál, "Ethno-national aspirations in the Soviet Union and its sucessor regimes: juggling with options," pp. 89-114; Snjezana Mrdjen, "Pluralist mobilization as a catalyst for the dismemberment of Yugoslavia," pp. 115-131; Kveta Kalibova, Tomas Haisman and Jitka Gjuricova, "Gypsies in Czechoslovakia: demographic developments and policy perspectives," pp. 133-144; Leo Paul, "The stolen revolution: minorities in Romania after Ceausescu," pp. 145-165; John Pickles and the Bourgas Group, "Environmental politics, democracy and economic restructuring in Bulgaria," pp. 167-185; Vladimir Kolossov, "The electoral geography of the former Soviet Union, 1989-91: retrospective comparisons and theoretical issues," pp. 189-215; Joanna Regulska, "Democratic elections and political restructuring in Poland, 1989-91," pp. 217-234; Petr Jehlicka, Tomás Kostelecky and Ludek Sykora, "Czechoslovak parliamentary elections 1990: old patterns, new trends and lots of surprises," pp. 235-254; Zoltán Kovacs, "The political geography of Hungarian parliamentary elections, 1989," pp. 255-273.]

1668. Park, Andrus. "Ideological Dimension of the Post-Communist Domestic Conflicts." *Communist and Post-Communist Studies* 26, no. 3 (September 1993): 265-276.

1669. Pejovich, Svetozar. "Institutions, Nationalism, and the Transition Process in Eastern Europe." *Social Philosophy & Policy* 10, no. 2 (Summer 1993): 65-78. [Earlier version of this essay was presented at the Einaudi Foundation seminar in Rome on June 25, 1992.]

1670. Radu, Michael. "Life After Death." *Society* 30, no. 2 (January-February 1993): 23-31.

1671. Resler, Tamara J., and Roger E. Kanet. "Democratization: The National-Subnational Linkage." *In Depth* 3, no. 1 (Winter 1993): 5-22.

1672. Schöpflin, George. *Politics in Eastern Europe, 1945-1992.* Oxford, UK: Cambridge, MA: Blackwell, 1993. 327 pp.

1673. Schwartz, Herman. "The New Courts: An Overview." *East European Constitutional Review* 2, no. 2 (Spring 1993): 28-32.

1674. Shonholtz, Raymond. "Editor's Notes." *Mediation Quarterly* 10, no. 3 (Spring 1993): 225-229. [Notes for a special issue on "Developing Mediating Processes in the New Democracies."]

1675. Shugart, Matthew S. "Of Presidents and Parliaments." *East European Constitutional Review* 2, no. 1 (Winter 1993): 30-32.

1676. Stokes, Gale. *The Walls Came Tumbling Down: The Collapse of Communism in Eastern Europe.* New York; Oxford: Oxford University Press, 1993. viii, 319 pp. [Contents: 1. The New Opposition: Antipolitics and Solidarity; 2. The Gang of Four and Their Nemesis; 3. The Momentum of Change in Hungary; 4. Solidarity: The Return of the Repressed in Poland; 5. The Glorious Revolutions of 1989; 6. 1990 and 1991: The First Two Years of a Long Time; 7. The Devil's Finger: The Disintegration of Yugoslavia; 8. Epilogue and Prologue: The New Pluralism.] REV: Abraham Brumberg, *New York Times Book Review* 98, no. 41 (October 10, 1993): 22.

1677. Stone, Norman. "1849: The Morning After." *National Interest*, no. 34 (Winter 1993-1994): 91-95. [Review article on David Remnick, *Lenin's Tomb: The Last Days of the Soviet Empire* (NY: 1993); John B. Dunlop, *The Rise of Russia and the Fall of the Soviet Empire* (Princeton, NJ: 1993); Anatol Lieven, *The Baltic Revolution: Estonia, Latvia, Lithuania and the Path to Independence* (New Haven, CT: 1993); and Andrew Nagorski, *The Birth of Freedom: Shaping Lives and Societies in the New Eastern Europe* (NY: 1993).]

1678. Summy, Ralph. "The Efficacy of Nonviolence: Examining 'the Worst Case Scenario.'" *Peace Research* 25, no. 2 (May 1993): 1-19.

1679. Tamir, Yael. *Liberal Nationalism.* Studies in Moral, Political and Legal Philosophy. Princeton, NJ: Princeton University Press, c1993. xi, 194 pp. REV: Michael Ignatieff, *New Republic* 209 (November 1, 1993): 36-39. David McCabe, *Commonweal* 120 (May 21, 1993): 28-29. Conor Cruise O'Brien, *Foreign Affairs* 72, no. 5 (November-December 1993): 142-149.

1680. Terry, Sarah Meiklejohn. "Thinking About Post-Communist Transitions: How Different Are They?" *Slavic Review* 52, no. 2 (Summer 1993): 333-337.

1681. Walker, Rachel. *Six Years That Shook the World: Perestroika—The Impossible Project.* Manchester; New York: Manchester University Press: Distributed by St. Martin's Press, c1993. viii, 312 pp.

1682. Waller, Michael. *The End of the Communist Power Monopoly.* Manchester; New York: Manchester University Press; New York, NY: Distributed in the USA and Canada by St. Martin's Press, c1993. vii, 287 pp.

1683. Wang, Qin. "Political Democratization of Communist Systems: An Empirical Study of the Developmental Approach." Ph.D. diss., Southern Illinois University at Carbondale, 1993. [UMI order no: AAC 9505372.]

1684. Whitefield, Stephen, ed. *The New Institutional Architecture of Eastern Europe.* Contributions by Gordon Smith, Richard Crampton, Judy Batt, Karen Henderson, Bill Lomax, George Kolankiewicz, Jonathan Eyal, Stephen Whitefield, David Dyker, and George Schöpflin. Studies in Russia and East Europe. New York, NY: St. Martin's Press, 1993. ix, 204 pp. [Contents: Gordon Smith, "Transitions to Liberal Democracy," pp. 1-13; Richard Crampton, "Bulgaria," pp. 14-34; Judy Batt, "Czechoslovakia," pp. 35-55; Karen Henderson, "The East German Legacy," pp. 56-78; Bill Lomax, "Hungary," pp. 79-98; George Kolankiewicz, "Poland," pp. 99-120; Jonathan Eyal, "Romania," pp. 121-142; Stephen Whitefield, "Russia," pp. 143-161; David Dyker, "Yugoslavia," pp. 162-182; George Schöpflin, "The Road from Post-Communism," pp. 183-200.]

1685. Williamson, Edwin D., and John E. Osborn. "A U.S. Perspective on Treaty Succession and Related Issues in the Wake of the Breakup of the USSR and Yugoslavia." *Virginia Journal of International Law* 33, no. 2 (Winter 1993): 261-274.

1686. Zacek, Jane Shapiro. "Prospects for Democratic Rule." *In Depth* 3, no. 1 (Winter 1993): 257-277.

1687. Zhang, Baohui. "Institutional Aspects of Reforms and the Democratization of Communist Regimes." *Communist and Post-Communist Studies* 26, no. 2 (June 1993): 165-181.

■ U.S.S.R.

General

1688. Adler, Nanci. *Victims of Soviet Terror: The Story of the Memorial Movement.* Foreword by Jonathan Sanders. Westport, CT: Praeger, 1993. xviii, 155 pp. [Contents: Jonathan Sanders, "Foreword". Pt. I. Memorial: History as Moral Imperative; The Formation of the Soviet System; Stalinism: Inheritance and Legacy; The Rediscovery of Soviet History. Pt. II. The Emergence and Evolution of Memorial; 1987-1988: Gaining Support; 1988-1989: Toward the Founding Conference; 1989-1990: Memorial Branches Out. Pt. III. Memorial Actualizes Itself, History as Dissidence; Memorial in Action; The Politics of Memorial; Epilogue: "Today We Are Historians of Dissidence, and Not Dissidents."]

1689. Bardos, Gordon. "Federation, Confederation, or Disintegration?" *Nationalities Papers* 21, no. 2 (Fall 1993): 163-165. Report of a talk by Michael Rywkin. [Notes from the Harriman Institute Seminar on Soviet Republics and Regional Issues, April 5, 1991.]

1690. Bayley, John. "Comrades." *New York Review of Books* 40, no. 14 (August 12, 1993): 3-4. [Review article on David Remnick, *Lenin's Tomb: The Last Days of the Soviet Empire* (NY: 1993).]

1691. Black, J. L., ed. *Disintegration of the USSR.* USSR Documents Annual, 1991. Gulf Breeze, FL: Academic International Press, c1993-. vols.

1692. Blacker, Coit D. *Hostage to Revolution: Gorbachev and Soviet Security Policy, 1985-1991.* New York: Council on Foreign Relations Press, c1993. xviii, 239 pp. [Contents: 1. The Brezhnev Legacy; 2. Military Doctrine and the Restructuring of the Armed Forces; 3. Arms Control and Regional Security; 4. Perestroika and the Soviet Military; 5. Gorbachev, Security Policy, and the Soviet Collapse.] REV: Robert Legvold, *Foreign Affairs* 72, no. 4 (September-October 1993): 170. Robert A. Vitas, *Journal of Baltic Studies* 24, no. 3 (Fall 1993): 314-315.

1693. Bowers, Stephen R. "Soviet and Post-Soviet Environmental Problems." *Journal of Social, Political and Economic Studies* 18, no. 2 (Summer 1993): 131-158.

1694. Brooker, David Cortland. "The Institutional Autonomy of Soviet Political Groups: A Komsomol Case Study." Ph.D. diss., Miami University, 1993. [UMI order no: AAC 9424061.]

1695. Carrère d'Encausse, Hélène. *The End of the Soviet Empire: The Triumph of the Nations.* Translated by Franklin Philip. New York: BasicBooks, c1993. xii, 292 pp. [Translation of *Gloire des nations*.] REV: Roger Brubaker, *Contemporary Sociology* 22, no. 4 (July 1993): 514-517. Glenn Chafetz, *Political Science Quarterly* 108, no. 2 (Summer 1993): 358-359. Robert Legvold, *Foreign Affairs* 72, no. 2 (Spring 1993): 178.

1696. Chiesa, Giulietto, and Douglas Taylor Northrop. *Transition to Democracy: Political Change in the Soviet Union, 1987-1991.* Nelson A. Rockefeller Series in Social Science and Public Policy. Hanover, NH: Dartmouth College, University Press of New England, c1993. xiv, 304 pp. [Contents: 1. Two Hundred Years Later; 2. Soviet Democracy's First Model; 3. Compromise, Constitutional Change, and New Electoral Law; 4. The Electoral Campaign; 5. A Political Geography of the First Congress; 6. Different Paths to Political Pluralism; 7. Main Features of the Political Geography; 8. The National Dimension; 9. The First Congress; 10. Gorbachev's Tactics; 11. The First Congress: Political Forces and Behaviors; 12. The Supreme Soviet's First Two Sessions; 13. Pluralism or Conflagration? 14. The Second Congress: Debates; 15. The Second Congress: Changes in the Political Geography; 16. Power Struggle, Party Crisis: The Third Congress Debates; 17. The Third Congress: Changes in the Political Geography; 18. Reflections and Provisional Conclusions.]

1697. Daniels, Robert V. *The End of the Communist Revolution.* London; New York: Routledge, 1993. viii, 222 pp. REV: Abraham Brumberg, *Book World* 23, no. 34 (August 22, 1993): 11. Robert Legvold, *Foreign Affairs* 72, no. 5 (November-December 1993): 174.

1698. Davidow, Mike. *Perestroika: Its Rise and Fall.* New York: International Publishers, 1993. ix, 182 pp.

1699. Dawson, Jane Irons. "Social Mobilization in Post-Leninist Societies: The Rise and Fall of the Anti-

Nuclear Power Movement in the USSR." Ph.D. diss., University of California, Berkeley, 1993. [UMI order no: AAC 9407926.]

1700. Duffy, Gloria. "Transformation in the USSR—The Role of Track-Two Diplomacy." *Surviving Together* 11, no. 1 (Spring 1993): 3-5. [Reprinted from *Nuclear Times* (Autumn-Winter 1992).]

1701. Dunlop, John B. *The Rise of Russia and the Fall of the Soviet Empire*. Princeton, NJ: Princeton University Press, c1993. xi, 360 pp. [Contents: 1. Gorbachev and Russia; 2. Yeltsin and Russia; 3. The "Democrats"; 4. The Statists; 5. Anatomy of a Failed Coup; 6. From the Failed Putsch to the Founding of CIS.] REV: Celestine Bohlen, *New York Times Book Review* 98, no. 47 (November 21, 1993): 13. Michael Mandelbaum, *World Policy Journal* 10, no. 3 (Fall 1993): 97-109. Peter Reddaway, *New York Review of Books* 40, no. 20 (December 2, 1993): 16ff. Norman Stone, *National Interest*, no. 34 (Winter 1993-1994): 91-95. John F. Young, *Canadian Slavonic Papers* 35, nos. 3-4 (September-December 1993): 414-415.

1702. Fairbanks, Charles H., Jr. "The Nature of the Beast." *National Interest*, no. 31 (Spring 1993): 46-56.

1703. Fish, Michael Steven. "Democracy from Scratch: Opposition and Regime in Russia during the Gorbachev Period." Ph.D. diss., Stanford University, 1993. [UMI order no: AAC 9326468.]

1704. Foster, Frances H. "Procedure as a Guarantee of Democracy: The Legacy of the Perestroika Parliament." *Vanderbilt Journal of Transnational Law* 26, no. 1 (April 1993): 1-109.

1705. Hahn, Jeffrey. "Attitudes Toward Reform Among Provincial Russian Politicians." *Post-Soviet Affairs* 9, no. 1 (January-March 1993): 66-85.

1706. Hendley, Kathryn Ann. "Trying to Make Law Matter: Legal Reform and Labor Law in the Soviet Union." Ph.D. diss., University of California, Berkeley, 1993. [UMI order no: AAC 9430526.]

1707. Khasbulatov, Ruslan. *The Struggle for Russia: Power and Change in the Democratic Revolution*. Edited by Richard Sakwa. London; New York: Routledge, 1993. xviii, 270 pp. [Translated from Russian. Contents: Richard Sakwa, "Introduction"; Pt. I. On the eve. 1. Personal. 2. Russia, Socialism and the Transition. 3. In Politics and Government. 4. Remaking the State. The Union Treaty. The Federal Treaty. The Constitution of the Federation. In the community of the Union. 5. Economic Transformation. Russia and the economic crisis. The '500 days' plan and beyond. Land reform. Privatisation and the market. Economic reform and the world. 6. Beyond Communism. Politics before the coup. Rebuilding Russia; Appendix: Union Treaty (drafted in August 1990); Pt. II. The coup. 7. Day One: 19 August 1991. Democracy in danger. The deputies: organisers of the defence. 8. Day Two: 20 August 1991. The ultimatum. 9. Day Three: 21 August 1991. A tragic night. The session of the Supreme Soviet. 10. 23 August 1991: Gorbachev in Parliament. 11. The Origins of

the Conspiracy. Questions, questions. The role of the miltary. The military-industrial complex. The dirty work of Kryuchkov's KGB. 12. The Fate of Freedom. On the verge of ruin. The bankruptcy of the doomed; Pt. III. Power. 13. On Power. Thoughts of the Speaker. 14. The Separation of Powers and Russia's Crisis. The separation of powers. Dictatorship and democracy. Economic and political power. The CIS: the collapse of a great empire and post-Union cooperation. 15. Power and Russia. The search for common sense. Parliamentarianism, parliament and democracy. Parliament and opposition. Parliament and the market economy. The professionalism of parliament. The vertical and horizontal separation of power. Parliament in civil society. Parliament and the government. Presidential and parliamentary forms of government. 16. Federalism and Democracy. Russia and modern federalism. Federalism as a method of resolving ethnic disputes. Federalism and the problem of sovereignty. Federalism and the decentralisation of administration. Federalism, democracy and the treaty process. Federation and the defence of its principles. Federalism as a basis of national unity. Interaction of President and parliament.] REV: Gary Lee, *Book World* 23, no. 35 (August 29, 1993): 4. S.P.M. [Sean Patrick Murphy], *Current History* 92, no. 576 (October 1993): 347. Peter Reddaway, *New York Review of Books* 40, no. 20 (December 2, 1993): 16ff. *Orbis* 37, no. 4 (Fall 1993).

1708. Kiernan, Brendan. *The End of Soviet Politics: Elections, Legislatures, and the Demise of the Communist Party*. Boulder, CO: Westview Press, 1993. xii, 241 pp. REV: Jeffrey W. Hahn, *Slavic Review* 52, no. 4 (Winter 1993): 850-851.

1709. Mandelbaum, Michael. "The Fall of the House of Lenin." *World Policy Journal* 10, no. 3 (Fall 1993): 97-109. [Review article on David Remnick, *Lenin's Tomb: Russia and the Fall of Communism* (NY: 1993); Nadia Diuk and Adrian Karatnycky, *New Nations Rising* (NY: 1993); John B. Dunlop, *The Rise of Russia and the Fall of the Soviet Empire* (Princeton, NJ: 1993); Don Oberdorfer, *The Turn: From the Cold War to a New Era* (NY: 1992); and Michael R. Beschloss and Strobe Talbott, *At the Highest Levels: The Inside Story of the End of the Cold War* (Boston, MA: 1993).]

1710. Miller, John. *Mikhail Gorbachev and the End of Soviet Power*. New York, NY: St. Martin's Press, 1993. xviii, 267 pp.

1711. Nichols, Thomas M. *The Sacred Cause: Civil-Military Conflict over Soviet National Security, 1917-1992*. Cornell Studies in Security Affairs. Ithaca, NY: Cornell University Press, 1993. xiii, 259 pp. [Contents: Introduction: "Our National and Sacred Cause"; 1. Bureaucrats or Bonapartes? Western Views of the Soviet Military; 2. Setting the Stage: Stalin and the Military; 3. Khrushchev's Revolution: Stalinism Without Stalin?; 4. The "Golden Age" and After: Brezhnev's Retreat and Military Ascendance; 5. Reform and Resistance: Gorbachev and the Military, 1985-1986; 6. Abandoning Pretenses: Gorbachev and the Military, 1987-1988; 7. The End of an Era: The Soviet Armed Forces and the "Political Struggle"; 8. Rethinking Soviet Civil-

Military Relations: Prospects for the 1990s.] REV: Robert Legvold, *Foreign Affairs* 72, no. 4 (September-October 1993): 169.

1712. Ponomaryov, Lev. "Power to the Russian People." *Freedom Review* 24, no. 3 (May-June 1993): 1.

1713. Puddington, Arch. [Book Review]. *American Spectator* 26, no. 1 (January 1993): 89-90. [Review article on Georgi Arbatov, *The System: An Insider's Life in Soviet Politics* (NY: Times Books, 1992).]

1714. Rahr, Alexander. "Kryuchkov, the KGB, and the 1991 Putsch." *RFE/RL Research Report* 2, no. 31 (July 30, 1993): 16-23.

1715. Raleigh, Donald J. "Mikhail Sergeevich Gorbachev and the Moral Revolution." *Soviet and Post-Soviet Review* 20, no. 1 (1993): 1-10.

1716. Reddaway, Peter. "The Role of Popular Discontent." *National Interest*, no. 31 (Spring 1993): 57-63.

1717. Remnick, David. "The Counterrevolution." *New York Review of Books* 40, no. 6 (March 25, 1993): 33-38. [Review article on Feliks Chuyev, *Sto sorok besed s Molotovym (One Hundred Forty Talks with Molotov)* (Moscow: 1991); and Yegor Ligachev, *Inside Gorbachev's Kremlin: The Memoirs of Yegor Ligachev* (NY: 1993).]

1718. ————. *Lenin's Tomb: The Last Days of the Soviet Empire.* 1st ed. New York: Random House, c1993. xii, 576 pp. REV: John Bayley, *New York Review of Books* 40, no. 14 (August 12, 1993): 3-4. Arnold Beichman, *National Review* 45, no. 15 (August 9, 1993): 64. Francine du Plessix Gray, *Book World* 23, no. 24 (June 13, 1993): 1ff. Robert Legvold, *Foreign Affairs* 72, no. 4 (September-October 1993): 167. John Lloyd, *New York Times Book Review* 98, no. 22 (May 30, 1993): 1ff. Michael Mandelbaum, *World Policy Journal* 10, no. 3 (Fall 1993): 97-109. Richard Pipes, *Commentary* 96, no. 6 (December 1993): 53-54. Norman Stone, *National Interest*, no. 34 (Winter 1993-1994): 91-95. *New York Times Book Review* 98, no. 49 (December 5, 1993): 83. *New Yorker* 69, no. 44 (December 27, 1993-January 3, 1994): 161. *Wilson Quarterly* 17, no. 4 (Autumn 1993): 82-83.

1719. Roeder, Philip G. *Red Sunset: The Failure of Soviet Politics.* Princeton, NJ: Princeton University Press, c1993. xii, 317 pp.

1720. Rosser, Marina Vcherashnaya. "The External Dimension of Systematic Transformation: The Case of the Former Soviet Union." *Journal of Economic Issues* 27, no. 3 (September 1993): 813-824.

1721. Rush, Myron. "Fortune and Fate." *National Interest*, no. 31 (Spring 1993): 19-25.

1722. Sallis, Dorit. "Democratic Social Movements of St. Petersburg and Their Transitional Ideologies, 1987-1991." Ph.D. diss., New School for Social Research, 1993. [UMI order no: AAC 9420279.]

1723. Shlapentokh, Vladimir, and Neil F. O'Donnell. *The Last Years of the Soviet Empire: Snapshots from 1985-1991.* Westport, CT: Praeger, 1993. xvi, 223 pp. [Contents: 1. 1985-1986: Initial Steps Toward Modernizarion. Gorbachev's Reforms: Ritual or Reality? June 1985. Is the KGB on the Rise in Moscow? August 1985. In the Soviet Union, the Myth is the Message. September 1985. The Poor Soviet Apparatchik. December 1985. How Firm is Gorbachev's War on Deceit? March 1986. Soviets Must Revise Ideas on Property. March 1986. Goodbye to an Old Soviet Dream: Catching Up to the West. April 1986. Fewer Rubles Under the Table. June 1986. Gorbachev's Still Lauding the Collective. August 1986. Seeing Through the New Soviet Image. November 1986. Russia's New Interest in Religion. November 1986. The Unfamiliar Side of Mikhail Gorbachev: The Dissident at the Top. December 1986 — 2. 1987: The Beginnings of Real Change—and Real Unrest. Ethnic Tensions Smolder in Russia. January 1987. Glasnost Holds No Meaning for Soviet Jews. April 1987. Can Gorbachev Cope with the Privatization of Soviet Society? May 1987. Gorbachev's Glasnost: The Lesson for American Media. May 1987. Glasnost Stirs the Dustbin of History. May 1987. Soviets Head for Showdown on Reforms. July 1987. Will the Ethnic Bomb Destroy Gorbachev? August 1987. Melons, Rubles, and the Comrades' Work Ethic. August 1987. Soviet Consumers Still Have No Voice. October 1987 — 3. 1988: Political Progress, Economic Decline, and Increasing Tension. Fighting to Warm Up the Cold Soviet Heart. April 1988. Reagan Will Face a Russia in Deep Internal Conflict. May 1988. A Nation of Discontent: Political Gains Can't Hide a Burdensome, Empty Material Life. June 1988. Is the USSR Headed Toward Bloom or Doom? July 1988. The Soviet Empire Continues Its Move Toward Decentralization. August 1988. Soviet Private Business: Boon or Blight for Gorbachev's Russia? August 1988. Who is the Third Force in the Kremlin? October 1988. Gorbachev's Pyrrhic Victory. October 1988. Technological Retardation in the Soviet Union: Gorbachev's Strongest Ally. December 1988 — 4. 1989: The Masses Speak Out. Gorbachev's Retreat: Tactical or Strategic? January 1989. Gorbachev's Globalism: The World Revolution in Reverse. February 1989. The Election—A Warning Signal to the Party. April 1989. The Ruble on the Verge of Collapse. July 1989. The Apocalyptic Mood of the Soviet People. July 1989. A Simmering Threat to the Jews? August 1989. The KGB—The Current Guarantor of Gorbachev's Reforms. September 1989. The Moscow Mass Media Calls Down Curses. September 1989. Watch the Soviet Working Class. October 1989. All-Out Dissension in the Soviet Union. December 1989 — 5. 1990: The Battle Over the Empire. Religion Fills the USSR's Ideological Vacuum. January 1990. Gorbachev's Presidency: An Attempt to Maintain Order? March 1990. Soviets Indifferent to Foreign Affairs. May 1990. Not All Russians Want the Empire. May 1990. A Drama for Two Players: The Gorbachev-Yeltsin Confrontation, Act I. June 1990. Gorbachev's Brilliant and Bitter Victory. July 1990. Competence: A Soviet Resource in Short Supply. September 1990. Bumper Crop: An Unwelcome Gift in Russia. September 1990. Bread, Cake, and Flowers in Moscow. September 1990. Gorbachev's Gordian Knot. November 1990. A Drama for Two Players: The Gorbachev-Yeltsin Confrontation, Act II. November 1990. A Society Without Myths. December

1990 — 6. 1991: The End of the Empire. The Gulf War and the Political Struggle in the USSR. March 1991. Yeltsin in a Different Perspective. March 1991. Gorbachev as Yeltsin's Best Friend. April 1991. The Continuing Duel Between Two Soviet Leaders. April 1991. The Difficult Decisions of President Gorbachev and King John: England, 1215 Revisited. May 1991. Russia Again at a Crossroads: Military Coup or Loose Confederation? June 1991. Focus on Human Rights in the Soviet National Republics. July 1991. Gorbachev: The World's Most Important Hostage. August 1991. The Most Bourgeois Revolution in History. August 1991. The End of the Coup Spells the End of the Empire. August 1991. Emperor Francis-Joseph: Ten Heads of State Are Not Viable. September 1991.]

1724. Solnick, Steven Lee. "Growing Pains: Youth Policies and Institutional Collapse in the Former Soviet Union." Ph.D. diss., Harvard University, 1993. [UMI order no: AAC 9331033.]

1725. Soviet Union. S"ezd Narodnykh Deputatov. *First Congress of People's Deputies of the USSR, 25 May-9 June 1989: The Stenographic Record.* Edited by Patrick J. Rollins. Translated by United States. Foreign Broadcast Information Service. [Gulf Breeze, FL]: Academic International Press, 1993-. vols. [Records first appeared in *Izvestiya*; were translated and printed by the Foreign Broadcast Information Service.]

1726. Sullivan, Paige. "Russian Democracy: Year One." *Freedom Review* 24, no. 1 (January-February 1993): 58-62.

1727. Theen, Rolf H. W. "Russia at the Grassroots: Reform at the Local and Regional Levels." *In Depth* 3, no. 1 (Winter 1993): 53-90.

1728. Toffler, Alvin. "Dark Colonel, the Sequel." *World Monitor* 6, no. 4 (April 1993): 24-28. [Interview with Victor Alksnis.]

1729. Tolz, Vera, and Melanie Newton, eds. *The USSR in 1991: A Record of Events.* Foreword by Iain Elliot. Boulder, CO: Westview Press, 1993. vii, 997 pp. [Published in cooperation with Radio Free Europe/Radio Liberty.]

1730. Urban, George R., ed. *End of Empire: The Demise of the Soviet Union.* Contributions by George R. Urban, Sidney Hook, Hugh Trevor-Roper, Elie Kedourie, Otto von Habsburg, Adam B. Ulam, Milovan Djilas, and Karl Popper. Washington, DC: American University Press, c1993. xxxiii, 238 pp. ["G.R. Urban in conversation with leading thinkers of our time." Contents: G.R. Urban, "Introduction: the Cold War in perspective"; Sidney Hook, "End of an era of political faiths"; Hugh Trevor-Roper (Lord Dacre), "Aftermaths of empire"; Elie Kedourie, "Nationalism and the balance of power"; Otto von Habsburg, "A tale of two empires"; Adam B. Ulam, "What is 'Soviet'—what is 'Russian'?"; Milovan Djilas, "End of the Bolshevik Utopia"; Karl Popper, "The best world we have yet had."] REV: Robert Legvold, *Foreign Affairs* 72, no. 3 (Summer 1993): 207. Theodore H. Von Laue, *Slavic Review* 52, no. 4 (Winter 1993): 912-913.

1731. Vanden Heuvel, Katrina, and Stephen Kotkin. [Letters to the Editor.] *Russian Review* 52, no. 3 (July 1993): 444-445. [Letter by vanden Heuvel objecting to a footnote by Kotkin in "Interview with Dmitri Iurasov" (April 1992), challenging the way Kotkin described an article by vanden Heuvel and Kevin Coogan in *The Nation* (1988). Letter followed by Kotkin's reply and vanden Heuvel's response to that reply.]

1732. Vogt-Downey, Marilyn, ed. *The USSR 1987-1991: Marxist Perspectives.* Revolutionary Studies. Atlantic Highlands, NJ: Humanities Press, 1993. xvi, 544 pp. [Volume is a collection of Marxist analyses of recent Soviet history; includes articles from Soviet, European and American Marxist journals.]

1733. White, Stephen. *After Gorbachev.* 4th ed. Cambridge Soviet Paperbacks, 3. Cambridge; New York: Cambridge University Press, 1993. xi, 357 pp. [Rev. ed. of: *Gorbachev and After* (1992) and *Gorbachev in Power* (1990).]

1734. White, Stephen, Rita Di Leo, and Ottorino Cappelli, eds. *The Soviet Transition: From Gorbachev to Yeltsin.* London; Portland, OR: Frank Cass, 1993. 241 pp. [Studies first appeared in a special issue of *Journal of Communist Studies* 9, no. 1.]

1735. "Why Did Soviet Communism Fail? A Survey of Recent Articles." *Wilson Quarterly* 17, no. 3 (Summer 1993): 123-124.

1736. Yegorov, Vladimir K. *Out of a Dead End, Into the Unknown: Notes on Gorbachev's Perestroika.* Translated by David Floyd. Chicago, IL: Edition q, c1993. xiii, 159 pp. [Translation of *Aus der Sackgasse in die Ungewissheit.* Contents: 1. Designs in the Arras; 2. Was Perestroika Really Necessary?; 3. Why Gorbachev?; 4. The Philosophy of Renewal; 5. Gorbachev and Public History; 6. Evolution, Revolutionary Evolution, Revolution; 7. What Happened in the Perestroika Years?; 8. Gorbachev's Algorithm.]

1737. Young, Ralph, Chris Binns, Martin Burch, Douglas Jaenicke, and Michael Moran, eds. *Introducing Government: A Reader.* Includes contributions by Chris Binns, Sheila Fitzpatrick, Robert C. Tucker, Seweryn Bialer, Bohdan Harasymiw, Alec Nove, Victor Zaslavsky, Robert J. Brym, Jeremy R. Azrael, John A. Armstrong, David Lane, Moshe Lewin, Mikhail Gorbachev, and Stephen White. Manchester, UK; New York, NY: Manchester University Press; New York, NY: Distributed by St. Martin's Press, c1993. ix, 386 pp. [Partial contents: Part Four. The Soviet political system in perspective. Chris Binns, "Introduction," pp. 243-245; Sheila Fitzpatrick, "Background to revolution," pp. 246-256; Sheila Fitzpatrick, "The Russian revolutions of 1917: from February to October," pp. 256-268; Robert C. Tucker, "Stalinism as revolution from above," pp. 268-281; Seweryn Bialer, "The mature Stalinist system," pp. 282-293; Bohdan Harasymiw, "The nomenklatura: the Soviet Communist Party's personnel control system," pp. 293-296; Alec Nove, "Is there a ruling class in the USSR?" pp. 296-307; Victor Zaslavsky and Robert J. Brym, "The functions of Soviet elections," pp. 307-

310; Jeremy R. Azrael, "Soviet nationality problems in the 1970s," pp. 310-318; John A. Armstrong, "Soviet nationalities: recent trends," pp. 318-328; David Lane, "Totalitarianism and industrialism," pp. 328-336; Moshe Lewin, "The urban revolution in the USSR," pp. 336-348; Mikhail Gorbachev, "Perestroika: the challenge of radical reform," pp. 348-358; Stephen White, "Democratizing the political system," pp. 358-372; Stephen White, "The August 1991 coup," pp. 373-375.]

Law and Police

1738. Burrage, Michael. "Russian Advocates: Before, During and after Perestroika." *Law and Social Inquiry: Journal of the American Bar Foundation* 18, no. 3 (Summer 1993): 573-592. [Review article on Robert Rand, *Comrade Lawyer: Inside Soviet Justice in an Era of Reform* (Boulder, CO: 1991).]

1739. Clark, William A. *Crime and Punishment in Soviet Officialdom: Combating Corruption in the Political Elite, 1965-1990.* Contemporary Soviet/Post-Soviet Politics. Armonk, NY: M.E. Sharp, c1993. xi, 242 pp. [Contents: 1. Introduction: Corruption, Politics, and Soviet Society. Conceptualizing Corruption. Conceptualizing Corruption in Comparative Perspective. Corruption and Soviet Society; 2. Public Administration and the Structure of Corruption in Soviet Officialdom. Bureaucratic Organization and Bureaucratic Behavior. Historical Influences. Soviet-Specific Influences; 3. Corruption in the Political Elite, 1965-1990. Officialdom, Corruption, and the Soviet Criminal Code. Data and Methodology. Findings. An Informal Criminology of System Maintenance; 4. Combating Corruption in Soviet Society. The Control Organs. Soviet Whistleblowers and the Control Function. The Cadres Weapon and the Control of Officialdom; 5. The Politics of Corruption and Anti-Corruption in the Soviet System. Andropov's Rise to Power. The Decline of Brezhnev and the Politics of Succession. The Politics of Anti-Corruption After Brezhnev; 6. Official Corruption, the Soft State, and the Future of Reform. The Soviet Soft State: Past and Future. A Balance Sheet. Official Corruption, Perestroika, and Beyond.]

1740. Cullen, Robert. *The Killer Department: Detective Viktor Burakov's Eight-Year Hunt for the Most Savage Serial Killer in Russian History.* 1st ed. New York: Ivy Books, 1993. 278 pp.

1741. ———. *The Killer Department: Detective Viktor Burakov's Eight-Year Hunt for the Most Savage Serial Killer in Russian History.* 1st ed. New York: Pantheon Books, 1993. 258 pp. REV: M. D. Carnegie, *American Spectator,* 26, no. 6 (June 1993): 66-68. Valerie Gladstone, *Publishers Weekly* 240 (February 8, 1993): 22-23. Julian Symons, *New York Times Book Review* 98, no. 11 (March 14, 1993): 6-7.

1742. Gladstone, Valerie. "Chikatilo Times Three." *Publishers Weekly* 240, no. 6 (February 8, 1993): 22-23. [Review article on Mikhail Krivich and Ol'gert Ol'gin, *Comrade Chikatilo: The Psychopathology of Russia's Notorious Serial Killer* (Fort Lee, NJ: 1993); Robert Cullen,

The Killer Department: Detective Viktor Burakov's Eight-Year Hunt for the Most Savage Serial Killer in Russian History (NY: Pantheon, 1993); Richard Lourie, *Hunting the Devil: The Pursuit, Capture and Confession of the Most Savage Serial Killer in History* (NY: HarperCollins, 1993).]

1743. Jakobson, Michael. *Origins of the Gulag: The Soviet Prison Camp System, 1917-1934.* Lexington, KY: University Press of Kentucky, c1993. 176 pp.

1744. Krivich, Mikhail, and Ol'gert Ol'gin. *Comrade Chikatilo: The Psychopathology of Russia's Notorious Serial Killer.* Translated from the Russian by Todd P. Bludeau. Edited by Sandi Gelles-Cole. Fort Lee, NJ: Barricade Books; Emeryville, CA: Distributed by Publishers Group West, c1993. 287 pp. REV: Valerie Gladstone, *Publishers Weekly* 240 (February 8, 1993): 22-23. Julian Symons, *New York Times Book Review* 98, no. 11 (March 14, 1993): 6-7.

1745. Lourie, Richard. *Hunting the Devil.* 1st ed. New York: HarperCollins, c1993. xxii, 263 p. REV: M. D. Carnegie, *American Spectator* 26, no. 6 (June 1993): 66-68. Valerie Gladstone, *Publishers Weekly* 240 (February 8, 1993): 22-23. Ann Rule, *Book World* 23, no. 14 (April 4, 1993): 6. Julian Symons, *New York Times Book Review* 98, no. 11 (March 14, 1993): 6-7. *Orbis,* 37, no. 4 (Fall 1993).

1746. Nikiforov, Alexander S. "Organized Crime in the West and in the Former USSR: An Attempted Comparison." *International Journal of Offender Therapy and Comparative Criminology* 37, no. 1 (Spring 1993): 5-15. [Reprinted from *Journal of State and Law* (Moscow), April 1991.]

1747. Quigley, John. "Government Corruption in the Soviet Union." *Criminal Law Forum* 4, no. 3 (1993): 567-572. [Review article on Arkady Vaksberg, translated by John Roberts and Elizabeth Roberts, *The Soviet Mafia* (New York: St. Martin's Press, 1991).]

1748. Sharlet, Robert. "The Russian Constitutional Court: The First Term." *Post-Soviet Affairs* 9, no. 1 (January-March 1993): 1-39.

1749. Tumanov, Oleg. *Tumanov: Confessions of a KGB Agent.* Chicago, IL: Edition Q, c1993. x, 187 pp. [Translated from an unpublished manuscript. Also published in German under title: *Geständnisse eines KGB-Agenten.*]

Nationalities, Ethnic Relations, Regions

1750. Atkin, Muriel. "The Islamic Revolution that Overthrew the Soviet State." *Contention: Debates in Society, Culture and Science* 2, no. 2 (Winter 1993): 89-106. [Review article on A. Bennigsen and M. Broxup, *The Islamic Threat to the Soviet State* (NY: 1983); A. Taheri, *Crescent in a Red Sky* (London: 1989); and M. Rywkin, *Moscow's Muslim Challenge* (NY: 1990).]

1751. Boldyrev, Petr. *Uroki Rossii: Dnevnik rossiiskogo separatista: tematicheskii sbornik statei = Russia's Lessons.* Tenafly, NJ: Ermitazh, c1993. xvi, 248 pp.

[Summary in English.]

1752. Dailey, Erika. "Current Developments in the Jewish Community in the USSR." *Nationalities Papers* 21, no. 2 (Fall 1993): 147-150. Report of a talk by Mordechai Altshuler. [Notes from the Harriman Institute Seminar on Soviet Republics and Regional Issues, November 9, 1990.]

1753. Derluguian, Georgi M. "Rouge et Noire: Contradictions of the Soviet Collapse." *Telos*, no. 96 (Summer 1993): 13-25.

1754. Dunlop, John B. "Russia: Confronting a Loss of Empire,1987-1991." *Political Science Quarterly* 108, no. 4 (Winter 1993-1994): 603-634.

1755. Gerner, Kristian, and Stefan Hedlund. *The Baltic States and the End of the Soviet Empire*. London; New York: Routledge, 1993. x, 211 pp.

1756. Gleason, Gregory. "Nationalism and Its Discontents." *Russian Review* 52, no. 1 (January 1993): 79-90. [Review article on Vasilii V. Markhinin, *Osnovnye zakonomernosti protsessa internatsionalizatsii obshchestvennoi zhizni* (Novosibirsk: 1989); Ivan P. Tsamerian, *Natsional'nye otnosheniia v SSSR* (Moscow: 1987); Adkham M. Yunusov, *Internatsional'noe i natsional'noe v razvitii dukhovnykh tsennostei sovetskogo naroda* (Tashkent: 1987); Vladimir A. Zamlinskii, Ivan F. Kuras, and Larisa A. Nagornaia, *Osushchestvlenie leniniskoi natsional'noi politiki* (Kiev: 1987); and Salyk Z. Zimanov and Ivan K. Reitor, *Teoreticheskie voprosy sovetskogo natsional'no-gosudarstvennogo stroitel'stva* (Alma-Ata: 1987).]

1757. Hajda, Lubomyr. "Ethnic Politics and Ethnic Conflict in the USSR and the Post-Soviet States." *Humboldt Journal of Social Relations* 19, no. 2 (1993): 193-278.

1758. Mongush, Mergen. " 'Ethnic' Disturbances in Tannu-Tuva in 1990." *Nationalities Papers* 21, no. 2 (Fall 1993): 171-178.

1759. Monyak, Robert. "Contemporary Relations Among Nationalities in Ukraine." *Nationalities Papers* 21, no. 2 (Fall 1993): 160-162. Report of a talk by Valentin Sazhin. [Notes from the Harriman Institute Seminar on Soviet Republics and Regional Issues, March 8, 1991.]

1760. ———. "The Current Political and Cultural Situation in Belorussia." *Nationalities Papers* 21, no. 2 (Fall 1993): 157-160. Report of a talk by Jan Zaprudnik. [Notes from the Harriman Institute Seminar on Soviet Republics and Regional Issues, February 8, 1991.]

1761. ———. "Human Rights and the Quest for Peace in the Transcaucasus." *Nationalities Papers* 21, no. 2 (Fall 1993): 168-170. Report of a talk by Nadir Mekhtiev. [Notes from the Harriman Institute Seminar on Soviet Republics and Regional Issues, October 25, 1991.]

1762. ———. "Russian Nationalism: Social Movement?" *Nationalities Papers* 21, no. 2 (Fall 1993): 145-147. Report of a talk by Yitzhak Brudny. [Notes from the Harriman Institute Seminar on Soviet Republics and Regional Issues, October 5, 1990.]

1763. ———. "Soviet Ethnic Issues and Their Implications for National Security." *Nationalities Papers* 21, no. 2 (Fall 1993): 165-167. Report of a talk by Jack Snyder. [Notes from the Harriman Institute Seminar on Soviet Republics and Regional Issues, September 27, 1991.]

1764. Muiznieks, Nils Raymond. "The Baltic Popular Movements and the Disintegration of the Soviet Union." Ph.D. diss., University of California, Berkeley, 1993. [UMI order no: AAC 9430621.]

1765. Suny, Ronald Grigor. *The Revenge of the Past: Nationalism, Revolution, and the Collapse of the Soviet Union*. Stanford, CA: Stanford University Press, c1993. xix, 200 pp. [Contents: Norman M. Naimark, "Foreword"; 1. Rethinking Social Identities: Class and Nationality; 2. National Revolutions and Civil War in Russia; 3. State-Building and Nation-Making: The Soviet Experience; 4. Nationalism and Nation-States: Gorbachev's Dilemmas.]

1766. Yukhneva, Natalia. "Political and Popular Antisemitism in Russia in the Period of Perestroika." *Patterns of Prejudice* 27, no. 1 (July 1993): 65-70.

Political Parties

1767. Armstrong, John A. "Persistent Patterns of the Ukrainian Apparatus." *Soviet and Post-Soviet Review* 20, nos. 2-3 (1993): 213-231.

1768. Brudny, Yitzhak M. "The Dynamics of 'Democratic Russia,' 1990-1993." *Post-Soviet Affairs* 9, no. 2 (April-June 1993): 141-176.

1769. Harris, Jonathan. *Adrift in Turbulent Seas: The Political and Ideological Struggles of Ivan Kuz'mich Polozkov*. The Carl Beck Papers in Russian and East European Studies, no. 1005. Pittsburgh, PA: REES, Center for Russian and East European Studies, University of Pittsburgh, c1993. 38 pp.

1770. ———. *Ligachev on Glasnost and Perestroika*. The Carl Beck Papers in Russian and East European Studies, no. 706. Pittsburgh, PA: University of Pittsburgh Center for Russian and East European Studies, c1993. 57 pp.

1771. Neimanis, George J. "The View from Inside: A Review Essay." *Journal of Baltic Studies* 24, no. 2 (Summer 1993): 201-206. [Review article on Janis Aboltins, *Biju biedrs, tagad kungs* [I was a Comrade, Now I am Mister] (Riga: 1992); and Georgi Arbatov, *The System: An Insider's Life in Soviet Politics* (NY: 1992).]

1772. Peck, Laurence Freeman. "Social Power: Its Nature, Function, and Context." Ph.D. diss., University of Colorado at Boulder, 1993. [UMI order no: AAC 9320466.]

1773. Puddington, Arch. [Book Review]. *American Spectator* 26, no. 6 (June 1993): 68-69. [Review article on Yegor Ligachev, *Inside Gorbachev's Kremlin* (New York: Pantheon Books, 1993).]

1774. Sherlock, Thomas Dean. "Myth and History in Transitions from Nondemocratic Rule: The Role of Historical Glasnost in the Collapse of the Soviet Union." Ph.D. diss., Columbia University, 1993. [UMI order no: AAC 9412843.]

■ C.I.S.

General

1775. Adams, Jan S. "CIS: The Interparliamentary Assembly and Khasbulatov." *RFE/RL Research Report* 2, no. 26 (June 25, 1993): 19-23.

1776. Allworth, Edward. "The Cultural Identity of Central Asian Leaders: The Problem of Affinity with Followers." *Central Asia Monitor*, no. 6 (1993): 25-32. [An expanded version of this paper will appear in a new edition of *Central Asia: A Century of Russian Rule*, ed. by Allworth (Durham, NC: expected 1994).]

1777. Barylski, Robert V. "The Caucasus, Central Asia and the Near-Abroad Syndrome (Conclusion)." *Central Asia Monitor*, no. 5 (1993): 21-28. [Part I in issue 4 (1993).]

1778. ———. "The Caucasus, Central Asia, and the Near-Abroad Syndrome (Part I)." *Central Asia Monitor*, no. 4 (1993): 31-37. [Conclusion in issue 5 (1993).]

1779. Bremmer, Ian, and Ray Taras, eds. *Nation and Politics in the Soviet Successor States*. Contributions by Robert Conquest, Ian Bremmer, Victor Zaslavsky, John Dunlop, Bohdan Krawchenko, Michael Urban, Jan Zaprudnik, Daria Fane, Richard Krickus, Nils Muiznieks, Cynthia Kaplan, Shireen T. Hunter, Nora Dudwick, Stephen F. Jones, Martha Brill Olcott, Gregory Gleason, Muriel Atkin, David Nissman, Gene Huskey, Ron Wixman, Jane Ormrod, Gail A. Fondahl, Ray Taras, Siobhán Fisher, and Daria Fane. Cambridge; New York, NY: Cambridge University Press, 1993. xxvii, 577 pp. [Cover title: Nations and Politics in the Soviet Successor States. Contents: Robert Conquest, "Foreword," pp. xvii-xviii; Ian Bremmer and Ray Taras, "Preface," pp. xix-xxvii; Part I. Introduction. Ian Bremmer, "Reassessing Soviet nationalities theory," pp. 3-26. Pt. II. The Center. Victor Zaslavsky, "Success and collapse: traditional Soviet nationality policy," pp. 29-42; John Dunlop, "Russia: confronting a loss of empire," pp. 43-72. Pt. III. The "new" Eastern Europe. Bohdan Krawchenko, "Ukraine: the politics of independence," pp. 75-98; Michael Urban and Jan Zaprudnik, "Belarus: a long road to nationhood," pp. 99-120; Daria Fane, "Moldova: breaking loose from Moscow," pp. 121-153. Pt. IV. The Baltics. Richard Krickus, "Lithuania: nationalism in the modern era," pp. 157-181; Nils Muiznieks, "Latvia: origins, evolution, and triumph," pp. 182-205; Cynthia Kaplan, "Estonia: a plural society on the road to independence," pp. 206-221. Pt. V. The Transcaucasus. Shireen T. Hunter, "Azerbaijan: search for identity and new partners" [misprinted on p. 225 as "Azerbaijan: search for industry and new partners"], pp. 225-260; Nora Dudwick, "Armenia: the nation awakens," pp. 261-287; Stephen F. Jones, "Georgia: a failed democratic transition," pp. 288-310. Pt. VI. Central

Asia. Martha Brill Olcott, "Kazakhstan: a republic of minorities," pp. 313-330; Gregory Gleason, "Uzbekistan: from statehood to nationhood?" pp. 331-360; Muriel Atkin, "Tajikistan: ancient heritage, new politics," pp. 361-383; David Nissman, "Turkmenistan: searching for a national identity," pp. 384-397; Gene Huskey, "Kyrgyzstan: the politics of demographic and economic frustration," pp. 398-418. Pt. VII. Nations without States. Ron Wixman, "The Middle Volga: ethnic archipelago in a Russian sea," pp. 421-447; Jane Ormrod, "The North Caucasus: fragmentation or federation?" pp. 448-476; Gail A. Fondahl, "Siberia: Native peoples and newcomers in collision," pp. 477-510. Pt. VIII. Conclusion. Ray Taras, "Making sense of matrioshka nationalism," pp. 513-538; Siobhán Fisher, comp., "Appendix A: Chronology of ethnic unrest in the USSR, 1985-1991" pp. 539-549; Daria Fane, comp. "Appendix B: Soviet census data, union republic and ASSR, 1989," pp. 550-560; "Further reading," pp. 561-565.]

1780. Brown, Bess. "Central Asia: The First Year of Unexpected Statehood." *RFE/RL Research Report* 2, no. 1 (January 1, 1993): 25-36.

1781. ———. "Regional Cooperation in Central Asia?" *RFE/RL Research Report* 2, no. 5 (January 29, 1993): 32-34.

1782. Carley, Patricia M. "Conference in Bishkek on Human Rights." *Central Asia Monitor*, no. 1 (1993): 14-18. [Report on the symposium "Human Rights and the Fate of Nations: An International Conference on the Problems of Central Asia," held in Bishkek, Kyrgyzstan, December 6-7, 1992.]

1783. Clemens, Walter C., Jr. "Soviet Centrifugalism: Republics as Independent Actors." *Nationalities Papers* 21, no. 2 (Fall 1993): 9-24.

1784. Cullen, Robert. "Human Rights After the Cold War." *Harper's* 286, no. 1715 (April 1993): 26-29. [Excerpt from author's "Human Rights Quandary" *Foreign Affairs* (Winter 1992-1993).]

1785. Diuk, Nadia, and Adrian Karatnycky. *New Nations Rising: The Fall of the Soviets and the Challenge of Independence*. New York: John Wiley & Sons, c1993. vii, 292 pp. [Contents: Nationalism and the Fall of the Soviets; The Rulers and the Ruled: The Economics of Inequality; Ukraine: The Pivotal Nation; The Baltic States: Vanguard of Independence; The Caucasus: Region of Conflict; Central Asia: The Muslim Factor and the Turkic Continuum; Russians: Democracy or Empire?; The New States: Prospect and Policy.] REV: Gary Lee, *Book World* 23, no. 35 (August 29, 1993): 4. Michael Mandelbaum, *World Policy Journal* 10, no. 3 (Fall 1993): 97-109.

1786. Dorsey, James, and Yoav Karny. "New Players in the Middle East." *American Spectator* 26, no. 4 (April 1993): 24-27. [On politics in the Caucasus.]

1787. Fondahl, Gail. "Mending Cultural Fences." *Surviving Together* 11, no. 1 (Spring 1993): 16-17. [Excerpt from article in *Earthwatch* (January-February 1993).]

1788. Fuller, Elizabeth. "Transcaucasia: Ethnic Strife Threatens Democratization." *RFE/RL Research Report* 2, no. 1 (January 1, 1993): 17-24.

1789. Gleason, Gregory. "Central Asia: Land Reform and the Ethnic Factor." *RFE/RL Research Report* 2, no. 3 (January 15, 1993): 28-33.

1790. Gleason, Gregory W., and Susan J. Buck. "Decolonization in the Former Soviet Borderlands: Politics in Search of Principles." *PS: Political Science & Politics* 26, no. 3 (September 1993): 522-525.

1791. Hazard, John N. "Prospects for a Rule of Law State." *Harriman Institute Forum* 7, nos. 1-2 (September-October 1993): 12-16. [Paper from the Fifth Annual Workshop on Post-Soviet Nations, held at the Harriman Institute, April 30, 1993.]

1792. Huttenbach, Henry R. "Post-*Raspad* Collapse in Caucasia (1992-1993)." *Harriman Institute Forum* 7, nos. 1-2 (September-October 1993): 22-26. [Paper from the Fifth Annual Workshop on Post-Soviet Nations, held at the Harriman Institute, April 30, 1993.]

1793. Juviler, Peter. "The Twilight of Democracy?" *Harriman Institute Forum* 7, nos. 1-2 (September-October 1993): 7-11. [Paper from the Fifth Annual Workshop on Post-Soviet Nations, held at the Harriman Institute, April 30, 1993.]

1794. Karasik, Theodore. *Azerbaijan, Central Asia, and Future Persian Gulf Security.* RAND Note, N-3579-AF/A. Santa Monica, CA: RAND, 1993. xv, 63 pp. [Prepared for the United States Air Force, United States Army.]

1795. Karatnycky, Adrian. "Time of Troubles." *American Spectator* 26, no. 7 (July 1993): 28-29. ["Washington take note: Russian revanchism is being countered by Ukraine's democratic evolution."]

1796. Khodakov, Alexander G. "The Commonwealth of Independent States as a Legal Phenomenon." *Emory International Law Review* 7, no. 1 (Spring 1993): 13-34.

1797. Kiselyov, Sergei. "Nothing in common, no wealth." *Bulletin of the Atomic Scientists* 49, no. 1 (January-February 1993): 12-13.

1798. Kortunov, Andrei. "Relations Between the Former Soviet Republics." *Society* 30, no. 3 (March/April 1993): 36-48.

1799. Miller, Arthur H., William M. Reisinger, and Vicki L. Hesli, eds. *Public Opinion and Regime Change: The New Politics of Post-Soviet Societies.* Contributions by Arthur H. Miller, Vicki L. Hesli, Elena I. Bashkirova, Jeffrey W. Hahn, Michael Paul Sacks, Andrei Yu. Melville, James L. Gibson, Raymond M. Duch, Joel D. Barkan, Cynthia S. Kaplan, Alexander I. Nikitin, Thomas F. Remington, John P. Willerton, Lee Sigelman, Gennady M. Denisovsky, Polina M. Kozyreva, Mikhail S. Matskovsky, Lois W. Sayrs, James M. Lindsay, William Zimmerman, and William M. Reisinger. Boulder, CO: Westview Press, 1993.

viii, 310 pp. [Contents: Arthur H. Miller and Vicki L. Hesli, "Introduction," pp. 1-13. Pt. 1. Conducting Public Opinion Research in the Soviet Union. Elena I. Bashkirova and Vicki L. Hesli, "Polling and Perestroika," pp. 17-36; Jeffrey W. Hahn, "Public Opinion Research in the Soviet Union: Problems and Possibilities," pp. 37-47. Pt. 2. How Citizens Relate to Politics: Individuals, Groups, and the Political System. Michael Paul Sacks, "Foreword to Part Two: Social Change and Soviet Public Opinion," pp. 51-55; Andrei Yu. Melville, "An Emerging Civic Culture? Ideology, Public Attitudes, and Political Culture in the Early 1990s," pp. 56-68; James L. Gibson and Raymond M. Duch, "Emerging Democratic Values in Soviet Political Culture," pp. 69-94; Arthur H. Miller, "In Search of Regime Legitimacy," pp. 95-123; Vicki L. Hesli and Joel D. Barkan, "The Center-Periphery Debate: Pressures for Devolution within the Republics," pp. 124-152; Cynthia S. Kaplan, "New Forms of Political Participation," pp. 153-167; William M. Reisinger and Alexander I. Nikitin, "Public Opinion and the Emergence of a Multi-Party System," pp. 168-196; Thomas F. Remington, "Afterword to Part Two: Agendas—Researching the Emerging Political Cultures," pp. 197-202. Pt. 3. Public Opinion and the Economy. John P. Willerton and Lee Sigelman, "Perestroika and the Public: Citizens' Views of the 'Fruits' of Economic Reform," pp. 205-223; Gennady M. Denisovsky, Polina M. Kozyreva, and Mikhail S. Matskovsky, "Twelve Percent of Hope: Economic Consciousness and a Market Economy," pp. 224-238. Pt. 4. Public Opinion and Foreign Policy. Lois W. Sayrs and James M. Lindsay, "Threat Perceptions," pp. 241-258; William Zimmerman, "Intergenerational Differences in Attitudes Toward Foreign Policy," pp. 259-270; William M. Reisinger, "Conclusions: Mass Public Opinion and the Study of Post-Soviet Societies," pp. 271-277; "Appendix," pp. 279-291; "References," pp. 292-305.]

1800. Moffitt, Gregory J. "Diverging Paths: The Popular Front Movements in Uzbekistan and Azerbaijan." *Central Asia Monitor*, no. 3 (1993): 24-30.

1801. Mooradian, Moorad. "Spotlight on Nagorno-Karabakh: Resolving the Karabakh Conflict." *Surviving Together* 11, no. 1 (Spring 1993): 13-14.

1802. Naftalin, Micah. "Bishkek Conference Addresses Fragile Human Rights in Central Asia." *Surviving Together* 11, no. 1 (Spring 1993): 48-49. [Adapted from a report by the author published in *RFE/RL Daily Report* (January 29, 1993).]

1803. Nalle, David. "Columbia Conference on the Emergence of New States." *Central Asia Monitor*, no. 6 (1993): 33-35. [Report on the conference "The Emergence of a New State System in Central Asia" held at Columbia University, December 3-4, 1993.]

1804. "News and Comments." *Central Asia Monitor*, no. 2 (1993): 1-2.

1805. "News and Comments." *Central Asia Monitor*, no. 3 (1993): 1-9. [Diary of Events (pp. 1-2); New Constitution of the Kyrgyz Republic (pp. 2-3); Uzbek Military Exercises in the Kyrgyz Republic (p. 3); Radioactive

Waste in Kazakhstan (pp. 3-4); Pressure on Opposition Leaders in Uzbekistan (p. 4); Events in Tajikistan (pp. 4-9).]

1806. "News and Comments." *Central Asia Monitor*, no. 4 (1993): 1-5. [Diary of Events (pp. 1-3); Slavic Economic Agreement (pp. 3-4); Rioting at the Baikonur Space Center (p. 4); Public Life (p. 5).]

1807. "News and Comments (August-September)." *Central Asia Monitor*, no. 5 (1993): 1-8. [Public Life (pp. 3-4); Tajik Diary (pp. 5-8).]

1808. "News and Comments (December 1992-January 1993)." *Central Asia Monitor*, no. 1 (1993): 1-3.

1809. "News and Comments (October-November)." *Central Asia Monitor*, no. 6 (1993): 1-6. [Tajikistan Update (pp. 3-4); Public Life (pp. 4-5); Rafsanjani's Visit (pp. 5-6); Ambassador Defected (p. 6).]

1810. Olcott, Martha Brill. "Central Asia on Its Own." *Journal of Democracy* 4, no. 1 (January 1993): 92-103.

1811. "Other Events." *Central Asia Monitor*, no. 6 (1993): 35-36. [Refugees International held "Tajikistan Open Forum," December 13, 1993, in Washington, DC; Voice of America, Central Asian Division, held roundtable on "Water Resources in Central Asia: Policies and Politics," December 15, 1993.]

1812. Otunbayeva, Roza. "Leap of Faith: Central Asia's Plunge into Democracy." *Harvard International Review* 15, no. 3 (Spring 1993): 16ff.

1813. Rumer, Boris Z. "Central Asia's Gathering Storm." *Orbis* 37, no. 1 (Winter 1993): 89-105.

1814. Sakwa, Richard. *Russian Politics and Society*. London; New York: Routledge, 1993. x, 506 pp.

1815. Sheehy, Ann. "The CIS: A Shaky Edifice." *RFE/RL Research Report* 2, no. 1 (January 1, 1993): 37-40.

1816. ———. "The CIS Charter." *RFE/RL Research Report* 2, no. 12 (March 19, 1993): 23-27.

1817. ———. "Seven States Sign Charter Strengthening CIS." *RFE/RL Research Report* 2, no. 9 (February 26, 1993): 10-14.

1818. Sneider, Daniel. "The Mountain Jews of Azerbaijan and Russia." *Surviving Together* 11, no. 2 (Summer 1993): 36-37. [Reprinted from *Christian Science Monitor* (November 27, 1992).]

1819. Solchanyk, Roman. "Russia, Ukraine, and the Imperial Legacy." *Post-Soviet Affairs* 9, no. 4 (October-December 1993): 337-365.

1820. ———. "Ukraine and the CIS: A Troubled Relationship." *RFE/RL Research Report* 2, no. 7 (February 12, 1993): 23-27.

1821. Sturino, John. "Spotlight on Nagorno-Karabakh: Nagorno-Karabakh: The Roots of Conflict." *Surviving Together* 11, no. 1 (Spring 1993): 10-13.

1822. Szporluk, Roman. "Belarus', Ukraine, and the Russian Question: A Comment." *Post-Soviet Affairs* 9, no. 4 (October-December 1993): 366-374.

1823. United States. Congress. Commission on Security and Cooperation in Europe. *Implementation of the Helsinki Accords: Hearing before the Commission on Security and Cooperation in Europe, One Hundred Third Congress, First Session: The Countries of Central Asia, Problems in the Transition to Independence and the Implications for the United States, March 25, 1993.* Washington: U.S. G.P.O., 1993. iii, 115 pp. [CSCE 103-1-6.]

1824. Walker, Edward W. "The Nationality Problem and Center-Periphery Relations in Russia." *Harriman Institute Forum* 7, nos. 1-2 (September-October 1993): 32-35. [Paper from the Fifth Annual Workshop on Post-Soviet Nations, the Harriman Institute, April 30, 1993.]

1825. ———. "The Neglected Dimension: Russian Federalism and its Implications for Constitution-Making." *East European Constitutional Review* 2, no. 2 (Spring 1993): 24-27.

1826. Waller, David Vincent. "From Sovereignty to State Breakdown: Geopolitics and Ethnic Mobilization in the Former Soviet Union." Ph.D. diss., University of California, Riverside, 1993. [UMI order no: AAC 9402376.]

1827. Weaver, Russell L., and John C. Knechtle. "Constitutional Drafting in the Former Soviet Union: The Kyrghyzstan and Belarus Constitutions." *Wisconsin International Law Journal* 12, no. 1 (Fall 1993): 29-57.

1828. White, Stephen, Graeme Gill, and Darrell Slider. *The Politics of Transition: Shaping a Post-Soviet Future.* Cambridge; New York: Cambridge University Press, 1993. x, 277 pp.

1829. Wilson, Andrew. "Crimea's Political Cauldron." *RFE/RL Research Report* 2, no. 45 (November 12, 1993): 1-8.

Armenia

1830. "Key Officials in Armenia." *RFE/RL Research Report* 2, no. 12 (March 19, 1993): 49.

Azerbaijan

1831. Atabaki, Touraj. *Azerbaijan: Ethnicity and Autonomy in Twentieth-Century Iran.* London; New York: British Academy Press; New York: In the United States of America and Canada, distributed by St Martin's Press, 1993. xiv, 238 pp.

1832. Fuller, Elizabeth. "Azerbaijan: Geidar Aliev's Political Comeback." *RFE/RL Research Report* 2, no. 5 (January 29, 1993): 6-11.

1833. ———. "Azerbaijan's June Revolution." *RFE/RL Research Report* 2, no. 32 (August 13, 1993): 24-29.

1834. "NDI Survey Mission to Azerbaijan." *Central Asia Monitor*, no. 2 (1993): 3.

1835. Sunley, Jonathan. "Back in the USSR." *National Review* 45, no. 25 (December 27, 1993): 22-24.

1836. Swietochowski, Tadeusz. "The Spirit of Baku, Summer 1993." *Central Asia Monitor*, no. 4 (1993): 18-20.

1837. Uhlig, Mark A. "The Karabakh War." *World Policy Journal* 10, no. 4 (Winter 1993-1994): 47-52.

Belarus

1838. Lukashuk, Alexander. "Belarus: A Year on a Treadmill." *RFE/RL Research Report* 2, no. 1 (January 1, 1993): 64-68.

1839. ———. "The New Draft Constitution of Belarus: A Shaky Step Toward the Rule of Law." *East European Constitutional Review* 2, no. 1 (Winter 1993): 17-20.

1840. ———. "Survey of Presidential Powers in Eastern Europe: Belarus." *East European Constitutional Review* 2, no. 4/vol. 3, no. 1 (Fall 1993-Winter 1994): 58-60.

1841. Markus, Ustina. "Belarus a 'Weak Link' in Eastern Europe?" *RFE/RL Research Report* 2, no. 49 (December 10, 1993): 21-27.

1842. Marples, David R. "Belarus: The Illusion of Stability." *Post-Soviet Affairs* 9, no. 3 (July-September 1993): 253-277.

1843. Mihalisko, Kathleen. "Belarusian Leader on First Year of Statehood." *RFE/RL Research Report* 2, no. 3 (January 15, 1993): 8-13. [Interview with Stanislau Shushkevich.]

1844. ———. "Politics and Public Opinion in Belarus." *RFE/RL Research Report* 2, no. 41 (October 15, 1993): 47-55.

1845. Stevenson, Gail. "Changing Patterns of Fiscal Interdependence: Social Financing and Expenditure in Belarus'." *Post-Soviet Geography* 34, no. 3 (March 1993): 185-203.

Georgia

1846. Allison, Lincoln. "The Other Georgia on My Mind." *World & I* 8, no. 7 (July 1993): 478-489.

1847. Amnesty International. *Georgia: Alleged Human Rights Violations During the Conflict in Abkhazia.* New York, NY: Amnesty International U.S.A., [1993]. 11 pp.

1848. Dale, Catherine. "Turmoil in Abkhazia: Russian Responses." *RFE/RL Research Report* 2, no. 34 (August 27, 1993): 48-57.

1849. Doroszewska, Urszula. "Who Is Fighting Whom?" *Uncaptive Minds* 6, no. 1 (22) (Winter-Spring 1993): 101-112. [On the Abkhazia-Georgia conflict.]

1850. Fuller, Elizabeth. "Aslan Abashidze: Georgia's Next Leader?" *RFE/RL Research Report* 2, no. 44 (November 5, 1993): 23-26.

1851. ———. "Eduard Shevardnadze's Via Dolorosa." *RFE/RL Research Report* 2, no. 43 (October 29, 1993): 17-23.

1852. ———. "Georgia since Independence: Plus Ça Change..." *Current History* 92, no. 576 (October 1993): 342-346.

1853. Jones, Stephen F. "Georgia's Power Structures." *RFE/RL Research Report* 2, no. 39 (October 1, 1993): 5-9. [Includes sidebar: "Key Officials in Georgia," p. 6.]

1854. Montefiore, Simon Sebag. "Eduard Shevardnadze." *New York Times Magazine* (December 26, 1993): 16-19.

1855. United States. Congress. Commission on Security and Cooperation in Europe. *Current Situation in Georgia and Implications for U.S. Policy.* Implementation of the Helsinki Accords. Washington, DC: The Commission, [1993]. iii, 18 pp.

Kazakhstan

1856. "Appendix: The Constitution of the Republic of Kazakhstan." *International Legal Perspectives* 5, no. 1 (Spring 1993): 109-132. [Passed on January 28, 1993.]

1857. Ardaev, Vladimir. "AWOL." *Bulletin of the Atomic Scientists* 49, no. 8 (October 1993): 36.

1858. ———. "Bridging East and West." *Bulletin of the Atomic Scientists* 49, no. 8 (October 1993): 24-29.

1859. ———. "Don't Blame Moscow." *Bulletin of the Atomic Scientists* 49, no. 8 (October 1993): 52.

1860. Edwards, Mike. "Facing the Nightmare." *National Geographic* 183, no. 3 (March 1993): 22-36. [Facing the consequences of Soviet nuclear testing.]

1861. Gillette, Philip S. "Ethnic Balance and Imbalance in Kazakhstan's Regions." *Central Asia Monitor*, no. 3 (1993): 17-23.

1862. Kanter, Stephen. "Constitution Making in Kazakhstan." *International Legal Perspectives* 5, no. 1 (Spring 1993): 65-91. [Article is adapted from a speech given by Dean Kanter to the International Law Society of Northwestern School of Law of Lewis and Clark College on March 12, 1993.]

1863. Moore, Mike. "Beyond the yurt." *Bulletin of the Atomic Scientists* 49, no. 8 (October 1993): 2. [Editorial introducing a special issue on Kazakhstan.]

1864. Nougmanov, Assan. "Kazakhstan's Challenges: The Case of a Central Asian Nation in Transition." *Harvard International Review* 15, no. 3 (Spring 1993): 10ff.

1865. Puzanov, Oleg. "Quiet tensions." *Bulletin of the Atomic Scientists* 49, no. 8 (October 1993): 30-32. [On relations between Kazakhs and Russians.]

1866. Rudenshiold, Eric. "Endangered Species: Political Parties in Kazakhstan." *Surviving Together* 11, no. 2 (Summer 1993): 39.

1867. "Survey of Political Parties in Kazakhstan." *Surviving Together* 11, no. 2 (Summer 1993): 40-42. Compiled by Eric Rudenshiold.

1868. Ustiugov, Mikhail. "A 'Temporarily Nuclear State.'" *Bulletin of the Atomic Scientists* 49, no. 8 (October 1993): 33-36.

1869. Zagalsky, Leonid. "Finding its own way." *Bulletin of the Atomic Scientists* 49, no. 8 (October 1993): 14-22.

Moldova

1870. Dailey, Erika. *Human Rights in Moldova: The Turbulent Dniester*. Edited by Jeri Laber, and Lois Whitman. New York, NY: Helsinki Watch, c1993. vii, 69 pp. [Helsinki Watch, a division of Human Rights Watch.]

1871. Socor, Vladimir. "Isolated Moldova Being Pulled into Russian Orbit." *RFE/RL Research Report* 2, no. 50 (December 17, 1993): 9-15. [Includes sidebar: "Key Officials in the Republic of Moldova," p. 10.]

1872. ———. "Moldova: Another Major Setback for Pro-Romanian Forces." *RFE/RL Research Report* 2, no. 9 (February 26, 1993): 15-21.

1873. ———. "Moldova's 'Dniester' Ulcer." *RFE/RL Research Report* 2, no. 1 (January 1, 1993): 12-16.

Russian Federation

General

1874. Andreyev, Nikolai. "From 'nyet' to 'don't know.'" *Bulletin of the Atomic Scientists* 49, no. 1 (January-February 1993): 21-25.

1875. Aron, Leon. "The Morass in Moscow I: Boris Yeltsin and Russia's Four Crises." *Journal of Democracy* 4, no. 2 (April 1993): 4-16.

1876. Barrie, Jeffrey, Vladimir Mikheyev, and Gordon Feller. "Kremlin Kingmaker." *World Monitor* 6, no. 3 (March 1993): 30-34. [On Arkady Volsky.]

1877. "Behind the Russian Crisis: Politics and Medicine in the New Russia." *Freedom Review* 24, no. 6 (November-December 1993): 17.

1878. Belyaeva, Nina. "Russian Democracy: Crisis as Progress." *Washington Quarterly* 16, no. 2 (Spring 1993): 5-17.

1879. Belyaeva, Nina, and Vera Tolz. "Crisis as a Form of Political Development." *RFE/RL Research Report* 2, no. 20 (May 14, 1993): 4-8.

1880. Bernstein, Jonas. "Moscow Bulletin: Bolshie Ballet." *American Spectator* 26, no. 11 (November 1993): 83-84.

1881. ———. "The Moscow Spectator: Horsing Around." *American Spectator* 26, no. 3 (March 1993): 52-53.

1882. "The Black House." *New Republic* 209, no. 17 (October 25, 1993): 7. ["Yeltsin's violent defense of democracy."]

1883. Blankenagel, Alexander. "Where Has All the Power Gone?" *East European Constitutional Review* 2, no. 1 (Winter 1993): 26-29.

1884. Bonner, Elena. "Yeltsin and Russia: Two Views." *New York Review of Books* 40, no. 8 (April 22, 1993): 16-19. [Elena Bonner's reply to Peter Reddaway's article (January 28, 1993).]

1885. "Boris Alone." *New Yorker* 69, no. 34 (October 18, 1993): 4-6.

1886. Breslauer, George W. "The Roots of Polarization: A Comment." *Post-Soviet Affairs* 9, no. 3 (July-September 1993): 223-230.

1887. Brookings Institution, and Gruter Institute for Law and Behavioral Research. *Law and Democracy in the New Russia*. Edited by Bruce L. R. Smith and Gennady M. Danilenko. Contributions by Bruce L. R. Smith, Wolfgang Fikentscher, Vasily A. Vlasihin, Robert D. Cooter, Gordon P. Getty, Robert E. Litan, Gennady M. Danilenko, and E. Donald Elliott. Brookings Dialogues on Public Policy. Washington, DC: Brookings Institution, c1993. ix, 118 pp. [Volume grew out of a January 1993 conference held in Washington, DC, and jointly sponsored by Brookings and the Gruter Institute for Law and Behavioral Research. Contents: Bruce L. R. Smith, "Constitutionalism in the New Russia," pp. 1-23; Wolfgang Fikentscher, "From a Centrally Planned Government System to a Rule-of-Law Democracy," pp. 24-42; Vasily A. Vlasihin, "Toward a Rule of Law and a Bill of Rights for Russia," pp. 43-52; Robert D. Cooter, "Organizational Property and Privatization in Russia," pp. 53-72; Gordon P. Getty, "Fertile Money," pp. 73-88; Robert E. Litan, "Fertile Money and Banks in Russia: A Comment," pp. 89-95; Gennady M. Danilenko, "International Law and the Future of the *Rechtsstaat* in Russia," pp. 96-106; E. Donald Elliott, "Environmental Protection and the Development of Free Markets in Russia," pp. 107-115.]

1888. Brown, Archie. "The October Crisis of 1993: Context and Implications." *Post-Soviet Affairs* 9, no. 3 (July-September 1993): 183-195.

1889. Brown, Kathryn. "Nizhnii Novgorod: A Regional Solution to National Problems?" *RFE/RL Research Report* 2, no. 5 (January 29, 1993): 17-23.

1890. Brumberg, Abraham. [Book Review]. *Book World (Washington Post)* 23, no. 34 (August 22, 1993): 11. [Review article on Robert V. Daniels, *The End of the Communist Revolution* (NY: Routledge, 1993).]

1891. Bukovsky, Vladimir. "Boris Yeltsin's Hollow Victory." *Commentary* 95, no. 6 (June 1993): 31-36.

1892. Calabresi, Massimo. "Two Steps Back." *National Review* 45, no. 1 (January 18, 1993): 22-24.

1893. Campbell, Adrian. "Local Government Policymaking and Management in Russia: The Case of St.

Petersburg (Leningrad)." *Policy Studies Journal* 21, no. 1 (Spring 1993): 133-142.

1894. Chugaev, Sergei. "Khasbulatov & Co." *Bulletin of the Atomic Scientists* 49, no. 1 (January-February 1993): 26-31.

1895. Clem, Ralph S., and Peter R. Craumer. "The Geography of the April 25 (1993) Russian Referendum." *Post-Soviet Geography* 34, no. 8 (October 1993): 481-496.

1896. Cline, Mary, Amy Corning, and Mark Rhodes. "The Showdown in Moscow: Tracking Public Opinion." *RFE/RL Research Report* 2, no. 43 (October 29, 1993): 11-16.

1897. Cohen, Ariel. "Comparing Russia's Constitutional Drafts." *Eurasian Reports* 3, no. 2 (Winter 1993): 27-38. [Part of special issue devoted to "What Is Russia?"]

1898. ———. "Competing Visions: Russian Constitutional Drafts and Beyond." *RFE/RL Research Report* 2, no. 38 (September 24, 1993): 50-56.

1899. Colby, Gale. "Fabricating Guilt." *Surviving Together* 11, no. 4 (Winter 1993): 55-57. [Reprinted from the *Bulletin of the Atomic Scientists* (October 1993).]

1900. "The Continuing Crisis." *New Republic* 208, no. 15 (April 12, 1993): 7.

1901. Corning, Amy. "Public Opinion and the Russian Parliamentary Elections." *RFE/RL Research Report* 2, no. 48 (December 3, 1993): 16-23.

1902. ———. "The Russian Referendum: An Analysis of Exit Poll Results." *RFE/RL Research Report* 2, no. 19 (May 7, 1993): 6-9.

1903. Crow, Suzanne. "Ambartsumov's Influence on Russian Foreign Policy." *RFE/RL Research Report* 2, no. 19 (May 7, 1993): 36-41. [Includes sidebar: "Evgenii Arshakovich Ambartsumov," p. 37.]

1904. ———. "Processes and Policies." *RFE/RL Research Report* 2, no. 20 (May 14, 1993): 47-52. [Includes sidebar: "The Russian Federation Security Council: Legal Provisions," p. 51.]

1905. Crozier, Brian. "Gorbachev, Foundation Man." *National Review* 45, no. 14 (July 18, 1993): 25-26.

1906. Daniels, Robert V. "The Riddle of Russian Reforms." *Dissent* 40, no. 4 (Fall 1993): 489-496.

1907. Darski, Jozef. "Did Yeltsin Save Russia for Democracy?" *Uncaptive Minds* 6, no. 3 (24) (Fall 1993): 13-17.

1908. Dobbs, Michael. "Yeltsin's Coup: The Undoing of Democracy?" *Surviving Together* 11, no. 4 (Winter 1993): 3-5.

1909. Elliot, Iain. "Russia in Search of an Identity." *RFE/RL Research Report* 2, no. 20 (May 14, 1993): 1-3.

1910. Feldbrugge, F. J. M. *Russian Law: The End of the Soviet System and the Role of Law.* Law in Eastern Europe, no. 45. Dordrecht; Boston, MA: M. Nijhoff, c1993. xii, 486 pp. [Contents: The Purpose of this Work. Russian Law in Transition: The Time Factor; The Soviet System. Totalitarianism. The Political Form of Soviet Totalitarianism. The Economic Structure. Society. The Role of Ideology: From Dream to Meal-Ticket. The International Position of the USSR. Law in a Totalitarian System. The Russian Heritage. The Multinational Soviet State. The Failure of Soviet Totalitarianism. Perestroika as a Learning Process. The Progress of Perestroika. The Role of Law in Perestroika; The Legal System. Russian Law Before the October Revolution: Introduction. The History of Russian Law until Peter the Great. From Peter the Great to the October Revolution. Soviet Law and the Soviet State from 1917 to Brezhnev. The October Revolution of 1917 and the Era of War Communism. The Making of the Federal System. The Stalin Era. From Khrushchev to Brezhnev. The Constitutional Order: From the USSR to the Commonwealth of Independent States. The Party-State: Party Statute and Constitution. The Organization of the Communist Party. The Party Leads the State. The Decline of Party Influence Under Perestroika. The Soviet Federal System Until 1990. The 1990 Reforms and the Crisis of the Federal System. The Emergence of the Commonwealth of Independent States. Russia and the USSR. The Central State Agencies of the Soviet Union. The Soviet Parliament: Congress of People's Deputies and Supreme Soviet. The Presidium of the Supreme Soviet of the USSR. The President of the USSR and His Councils. The Government of the USSR. The Committee of Constitutional Supervision of the USSR. The Organization of the Russian State. The Russian Parliament: Congress of People's Deputies and Supreme Soviet. The President of Russia. The Government (Council of Ministers) of Russia. The Constitutional Court of Russia. Provincial and Local Government. Legislation of the USSR and Russia. Administration of Justice. The Organization of the Courts. The Prokuratura. The Legal Profession. Civil Procedure and Arbitration. Law Enforcement (including Armed Forces). Fundamental Rights: Historical Overview. The Socialist Concept of Fundamental Rights. Equality. Citizenship. Social Rights. Political Rights. Personal Rights. The Declarations of the Rights and Freedoms of Man. The Economic System: From Plan to Market. Ownership. Privatization. Soviet Land Law. Russian Land Law. From Economic Planning to Commercial Law. Enterprises. Cooperatives. The Lease System. Foreign Economic Relations. Legal Form of Involvement in Foreign Economic Activities. The Conduct of Foreign Economic Activities. Taxation of Foreign Economic Activities. Contracts and Torts (Obligations). Industrial and Intellectual Ownership. Labour Law. Taxation in the USSR. Taxation in the Russian Federation. Public Finance. The Environment. The Social System. The Legal Framework of Private Life. Marriage and Family Law. Inheritance Law. Housing. Health and Social Welfare. Education. Associations. Criminal Law. Criminal Procedure. Legislation. Constitution (Fundamental Law) of the USSR. Agreement on the Creation of a Commonwealth of Independent States. Constitution (Fundamental Law) of the Russian Federation—Russia. Federative Treaty. USSR Legislation from the Perestroika Era. Russian Legislation after 27 October 1989.] REV: Peter B. Maggs, *American Journal of Comparative Law* 41, no. 3 (Summer 1993): 513-514.

1911. Fleishman, Lana C. "The Empire Strikes Back: The Influence of the United States Motion Picture Industry on Russian Copyright Law." *Cornell International Law Journal* 26, no. 1 (Winter 1993): 189-238.

1912. Foster, Frances H. "*Izvestiia* As a Mirror of the Russian Legal Reform: Press, Law, and Crisis in the Post-Soviet Era." *Vanderbilt Journal of Transnational Law* 26, no. 4 (November 1993): 675-748.

1913. Foye, Stephen. "Confrontation in Moscow: The Army Backs Yeltsin, for Now." *RFE/RL Research Report* 2, no. 42 (October 22, 1993): 10-15.

1914. ———. "The Defense Ministry and the New Military 'Opposition.'" *RFE/RL Research Report* 2, no. 20 (May 14, 1993): 68-73.

1915. Gevorkian, Natalia. "The KGB: 'They still need us.'" *Bulletin of the Atomic Scientists* 49, no. 1 (January-February 1993): 36-38.

1916. Gray, John. "From Post-Communism to Civil Society: The Reemergence of History and the Decline of the Western Model." *Social Philosophy & Policy* 10, no. 2 (Summer 1993): 26-50.

1917. Gualtieri, Dominic. "Russian Parliament Renews Power Struggle with Yeltsin." *RFE/RL Research Report* 2, no. 32 (August 13, 1993): 30-33.

1918. ———. "Russia's New 'War of Laws.'" *RFE/RL Research Report* 2, no. 35 (September 3, 1993): 10-15.

1919. Gubman, Boris L. "Contemporary Russia: Alternatives of the Future Development." *International Social Science Review* 68, no. 2 (Spring 1993): 78-82.

1920. Herbert, Douglas J. "Russian Thugs." *Freedom Review* 24, no. 3 (May-June 1993): 6-8.

1921. Hoge, James F., Jr. "Who is to Rule Russia?" *Foreign Affairs* 72, no. 2 (Spring 1993): ix-xi.

1922. Holmes, Stephen. "Superpresidentialism and its Problems." *East European Constitutional Review* 2, no. 4/vol. 3, no. 1 (Fall 1993-Winter 1994): 123-126.

1923. ———. "Yeltsin's Constitutional Proposal." *East European Constitutional Review* 2, no. 2 (Spring 1993): 22-23. [Includes translation of Chapter 6 of the Alekseev draft.]

1924. Holmes, Stephen, and Christian Lucky. "Storm over Compatibility." *East European Constitutional Review* 2, no. 4/vol. 3, no. 1 (Fall 1993-Winter 1994): 120-123.

1925. Hsuan, Abraham B., and Judith L. Church. "The Russian Parliament Tackles Intellectual Property Rights." *Journal of European Business* 4, no. 4 (March/April 1993): 10-12.

1926. Huttenbach, Henry R. "Can the Russian Federation Survive?" *Surviving Together* 11, no. 3 (Fall 1993): 8-10. [Adapted from the article, "Whither the Russian Federation," *Analysis of Current Events* (February 1993).]

1927. Jakobson, Max. "What To Do About Russia." *World Monitor* 6, no. 5 (May 1993): 44-49.

1928. Kagarlitsky, Boris. "Witness to Yeltsin's Coup." *Progressive* 57, no. 12 (December 1993): 27-31.

1929. Kagarlitsky, Boris, Alexandr Likhotal, and Daniel Singer. "Yeltsin's Elections: Make Them Truly Democratic." *Nation* 257, no. 19 (December 6, 1993): 688-693.

1930. Kaplan, Morton A. "Russia: Is Reform Still Possible?" *World & I* 8, no. 8 (August 1993): 22-23.

1931. Kass, Ilana. "View from Russia: Whither Russia?" *Comparative Strategy* 12, no. 2 (April/June 1993): 233-237.

1932. "Key Officials in the Russian Federation: Executive Branch." *RFE/RL Research Report* 2, no. 6 (February 5, 1993): 6-9.

1933. Kirschten, Dick. "Bumpy Ride." *National Journal* 25, nos. 51-52 (December 18, 1993): 3003-3004. [On the Russian elections and American support for President Yeltsin.]

1934. ———. "Rescuing Russia." *National Journal* 25, no. 12 (March 20, 1993): 723.

1935. Laqueur, Walter. *Black Hundred: The Rise of the Extreme Right in Russia.* 1st ed. New York: Harper Collins Publishers, c1993. xvii, 317 pp. [Contents: Pt. 1. Before the Revolution. 1. The Russian Idea and Manifest Destiny. 2. The Black Hundred and the Emergence of the Russian Right. 3. The Appearance of the Protocols and the Great Masonic Plot. 4. Damn Thee, Black Devil: The Orthodox Church and the Radical Right. Pt. 2. Communism and Nationalism, 1917-1987. 5. Soviet Patriotism. 6. Fascism and the Russian Emigration. 7. The Russian Party and National Bolshevism. 8. Judaism Without a Mask. 9. Neopaganism and the Myth of the Golden Age. Pt. 3. Villains Galore—The Postcommunist Age. 10. The Ideology of the New Right (1). 11. The Ideology of the New Right (2). Pt. 4. The Struggle for Power 1987- . 12. Tsars and Cossacks. 13. Pamyat. 14. The Revival of the Orthodox Church. 15. The New Nationalist Establishment: Literary Manifestos and Political Initiatives. 16. Conclusion: Russian Nationalism Today and Tomorrow.] REV: Paul A. Goble, *National Interest*, no. 33 (Fall 1993): 93-96. Gary Lee, *Book World* 23, no. 35 (August 29, 1993): 4. Robert Legvold, *Foreign Affairs* 72, no. 4 (September-October 1993): 168. Richard Pipes, *National Review* 45, no. 15 (August 9, 1993): 58-60. Joshua Rubenstein, *New York Times Book Review* 98, no. 24 (June 13, 1993): 9. Victor Williams, *American Journal of Comparative Law* 41, no. 4 (Fall 1993): 678-685. *Wilson Quarterly* 17, no. 4 (Autumn 1993): 82-83.

1936. Lawyers Committee for Human Rights (U.S.). *Human Rights and Legal Reform in the Russian Federation*. New York: Lawyers Committee for Human Rights, c1993. vi, 119 pp. [On cover: "Emerging Concertion of Rights [and] Selected Laws and Institutions". Researched and written by Mary Holland; edited by Michael Posner and William O'Neill.] REV: *Human Rights Quarterly* 15, no. 4 (November 1993): 784-785.

1937. "Leadership Update: Key Officials in the Russian Federation." *RFE/RL Research Report* 2, no. 20 (May 14, 1993): 112-119. ["Executive Branch," pp. 112-116; "Legislative Branch," pp. 117-119.]

1938. "Lenin without Leninism." *New Yorker* 69, no. 32 (October 4, 1993): 8-10. [On the new Russian constitution proposed by Yeltsin.]

1939. Linden, Carl. "Can Russia Be Founded Anew?" *Eurasian Reports* 3, no. 2 (Winter 1993): 3-12. [Part of special issue devoted to "What Is Russia?"]

1940. Lorrain, Pierre. "The Bolsheviks' Last Stand." *Freedom Review* 24, no. 6 (November-December 1993): 17-18.

1941. Lough, John. "Defining Russia's Role in Relations with Neighboring States." *RFE/RL Research Report* 2, no. 20 (May 14, 1993): 53-60.

1942. Malia, Martin. "Apocalypse Not." *New Republic* 208, no. 8 (February 22, 1993): 21ff.

1943. ———. "The End." *New Republic* 209, no. 16 (October 18, 1993): 16-20. ["Yeltsin's final gambit against remnants of the Soviet Union should have come earlier, but now it's here. A chronology of the president's strategy, and of his clandestine alliance with the Russian regions."]

1944. ———. "The Soft Coup." *New Republic* 208, no. 16 (April 19, 1993): 18-20. ["Boris Yeltsin's latest revolution."]

1945. Mandelbaum, Michael. "By a Thread." *New Republic* 208, no. 14 (April 5, 1993): 18-23. ["Yeltsin survives—but only just. Here's how we can help him, and what the real consequences will be if we don't."]

1946. McElvoy, Anne. "Plastic Carnations." *New Republic* 209, nos. 8 & 9 (August 23 & 30, 1993): 27. [On Yeltsin's governing style.]

1947. ———. "Raging Bull." *New Republic* 208, nos. 1 & 2 (January 4 & 11, 1993): 17ff. ["A glimpse of Yeltsin—through opera glasses."]

1948. McFaul, Michael, and Sergei Markov. *The Troubled Birth of Russian Democracy: Parties, Personalities, and Programs*. Hoover Institution Press Publication, no. 415. Stanford, CA: Hoover Institution Press, c1993. xiv, 317 pp. [Consists chiefly of interviews with various Russian personalities. Contents: The Origins of Party Formation in Revolutionary Russia, 1985-1992; The Democratic Union; Interview with Victor Kuzin; Document: Declaration of the Democratic Union Party; Pamyat'; Interview with Dmitrii Vasiliev; The Democratic Party of Russia; Interview with Nikolai Travkin; Document: Declaration of Narodnoe Soglasie (Popular Accord); The Social-Democratic Party of Russia; Interview with Oleg Rumyantsev; The Republican Party of Russia; Interview with Vladimir Lysenko; Documents: Statement by the Founding Congress of the Republican Party of Russia, Declaration of the Republican Party of Russia; The Russian Christian-Democratic Movement of Russia (RXDD); Interview with Victor Aksiuchits; The Democratic Russia Movement; Interview with Mikhail Schneider; Interview with Victor Dmitriev; Strike Committees and the Independent Union of Miners; Interview with Anatoly Malykhin. Interview with Pavel Shuspanov; Documents; The Neo-Communists; Interview with Richard Kosolapov; Interview with Igor Malyarov; Document: The Motherland Is Sick. How Can She Be Aided? Platform of United Workers' Front; Soyuz; Interview with Colonel Victor Alksnis; The Liberal-Democratic Party of the USSR; Interview with Vladimir Zhirinovsky; The Movement for Democratic Reform; Interview with Eduard Shevardnadze.]

1949. Miller, Stephen, and Nicolai N. Petro. "How Benign is Russia's Vice-President?" *Orbis* 37, no. 2 (Spring 1993): 289-292. [On Alexander Rutskoi. Miller replies (pp. 289-290) to article, "The Rising Star of Russia's Vice-President," in vol. 37, no. 1 (Winter 1993): 107-122; Petro responds (pp. 291-292).]

1950. Mitchell, R. Judson. "Leadership, Legitimacy, and Institutions in Post-Soviet Russia." *Mediterranean Quarterly* 4, no. 2 (Spring 1993): 90-107.

1951. Myers, Nancy. "Rediscovering Russia." *Bulletin of the Atomic Scientists* 49, no. 1 (January-February 1993): 2. [Introductory editorial to special issue on Russia.]

1952. Olcott, Martha Brill. "Russia's Place in the CIS." *Current History* 92, no. 576 (October 1993): 314-319.

1953. Osherov, Vladimir. *No vechnyi vyshe vas zakon: bor'ba za amerikanskuiu konstitutsiiu = But the Eternal Law Is Above You*. Tenafly, NJ: Ermitazh, c1993. 173 pp.

1954. Peterson, D. J. "Norilsk in the Nineties." *RFE/RL Research Report* 2, no. 5 (January 29, 1993): 24-28.

1955. ———. "The Post-Soviet Challenge: Creating Effective Government Agencies." *Surviving Together* 11, no. 4 (Winter 1993): 21-22. [First of two articles considering the environmental regulatory system in Russia.]

1956. Petro, Nicolai N. "The Rising Star of Russia's Vice President." *Orbis* 37, no. 1 (Winter 1993): 107-122. [On Alexander Rutskoi.]

1957. Rahr, Alexander. "The First Year of Russian Independence." *RFE/RL Research Report* 2, no. 1 (January 1, 1993): 50-57.

1958. ———. "The Future of the Russian Democrats." *RFE/RL Research Report* 2, no. 39 (October 1, 1993): 1-4.

108

GOVERNMENT, LAW, POLITICS: C.I.S.

1959. ——. "The October Revolt: Mass Unrest or Putsch?" *RFE/RL Research Report* 2, no. 44 (November 5, 1993): 1-4.

1960. ——. " 'Power Ministries' Support Yeltsin." *RFE/RL Research Report* 2, no. 40 (October 8, 1993): 8-11. [On the relations between Yeltsin and the three "power ministries" (Defense, Security, and Internal Affairs).]

1961. ——. "Preparations for the Parliamentary Elections in Russia." *RFE/RL Research Report* 2, no. 47 (November 26, 1993): 1-6.

1962. ——. "Profiles of Fifteen Leaders." *RFE/RL Research Report* 2, no. 20 (May 14, 1993): 96-111.

1963. ——. "The Rise and Fall of Ruslan Khasbulatov." *RFE/RL Research Report* 2, no. 24 (June 11, 1993): 12-16.

1964. ——. "The Roots of the Power Struggle." *RFE/RL Research Report* 2, no. 20 (May 14, 1993): 9-15. [Includes sidebars: "Constitutional Court Judges," pp. 12-13, and Julia Wishnevsky, "The Constitutional Court," p. 14.]

1965. ——. "Russia: The Struggle for Power Continues." *RFE/RL Research Report* 2, no. 6 (February 5, 1993): 1-5.

1966. ——. "Yeltsin and Khasbulatov: Anatomy of a Power Struggle." *RFE/RL Research Report* 2, no. 12 (March 19, 1993): 18-22.

1967. ——. "Yeltsin and New Elections." *RFE/RL Research Report* 2, no. 34 (August 27, 1993): 1-6.

1968. Reddaway, Peter. "On the Eve." *New York Review of Books* 40, no. 20 (December 2, 1993): 16-21. [Review article on Pilar Bonet, *Figures in a Red Landscape*, trans. Norman Thomas di Giovanni and Susan Ashe (Washington, DC: 1993); John B. Dunlop, *The Rise of Russia and the Fall of the Soviet Empire* (Princeton, NJ: 1993); Ruslan Khasbulatov, *The Struggle for Russia: Power and Change in the Democratic Revolution* (London and NY: 1993); Vladimir A. Zviglyanich, *The Morphology of Russian Mentality: A Philosophical Inquiry into Conservatism and Pragmatism* (Lewiston, NY: 1993).]

1969. ——. "Russia on the Brink?" *New York Review of Books* 40, no. 3 (January 28, 1993): 30-35.

1970. Reddaway, Peter, Gail W. Lapidus, Gertrude E. Schroeder, Jeffrey Hahn, Victor Winston, and George Breslauer. "Two Years After the Collapse of the USSR: A Panel of Specialists." *Post-Soviet Affairs* 9, no. 4 (October-December 1993): 281-313.

1971. Rubinfien, Elisabeth. "The Chelovek in the Street." *National Review* 45, no. 21 (November 1, 1993): 48.

1972. "Rump Roast." *Nation* 257, no. 12 (October 18, 1993): 411-412.

1973. Russia (Federation). "An Excerpt from Yeltsin's Constitution." *East European Constitutional Review* 2, no. 4/vol. 3, no. 1 (Fall 1993-Winter 1994): 114-116. Translated by Zaza Namoradze and Stephen Holmes. [Translation of the final section of the new Russian constitution with introduction by Stephen Holmes.]

1974. Satter, David. "Yeltsin: Shadow of a Doubt." *National Interest*, no. 34 (Winter 1993-1994): 52-57.

1975. Schneider, William. "Political Pulse." *National Journal* 25, no. 13 (March 27, 1993): 790.

1976. ——. "Political Pulse." *National Journal* 25, no. 18 (May 1, 1993): 1086. ["The Yeltsin vote of confidence was driven by Russians' experiences of the discredited past."]

1977. Semler, Dwight. "The End of the First Russian Republic." *East European Constitutional Review* 2, no. 4/vol. 3, no. 1 (Fall 1993-Winter 1994): 107-114.

1978. ——. "Meeting of the Russian Congress Produces Turmoil, But Little Progress in Dividing Up State Authority." *East European Constitutional Review* 2, no. 1 (Winter 1993): 12-14.

1979. ——. "Summer in Russia Brings No Real Political Progress; Federative Issues Dominate Constitutional Discussions." *East European Constitutional Review* 2, no. 3 (Summer 1993): 20-23.

1980. Semler, Dwight, Andrei Kortunov, and Sergei Parkhomenko. "Crisis in Russia." *East European Constitutional Review* 2, no. 2 (Spring 1993): 15-22. ["Dwight Semler on the events leading up to the April referendum; viewpoints on the vote and its significance from Andrei Kortunov, Sergei Parkhomenko and others."]

1981. Sergeyev, Victor, and Nikolai Biryukov. *Russia's Road to Democracy: Parliament, Communism, and Traditional Culture.* Studies of Communism in Transition. Aldershot, Hants; Brookfield, VT: E. Elgar, c1993. xi, 227 pp.

1982. Sharlet, Robert. "Russia: Chief Justice as Judicial Politician." *East European Constitutional Review* 2, no. 2 (Spring 1993): 32-37. [On Valery Zorkin.]

1983. ——. "Russian Constitutional Crisis: Law and Politics Under Yel'tsin." *Post-Soviet Affairs* 9, no. 4 (October-December 1993): 314-336.

1984. Sherr, James. "To the Abyss and Back." *National Review* 45, no. 21 (November 1, 1993): 44ff. [On Yeltsin and the Russian parliament.]

1985. ——. "Yeltsin Rolls the Dice." *National Review* 45, no. 7 (April 12, 1993): 36-40.

1986. Shipler, David K. "Four Futures for Russia." *New York Times Magazine* (April 4, 1993): 28ff. ["New Coup? Civil War? Muddling Through? Happy Ending?"]

1987. Singer, Daniel. "Letter from Europe: Our Man in Moscow." *Nation* 256, no. 18 (May 10, 1993): 622-624.

1988. ———. "Letter from Europe: Yeltsin in Dubious Battle." *Nation* 257, no. 11 (October 11, 1993): 381-384.

1989. ———. "Putsch in Moscow." *Nation* 257, no. 13 (October 25, 1993): 448-449.

1990. ———. "Yeltsin's Round." *Nation* 256, no. 19 (May 17, 1993): 652.

1991. Slater, Wendy. "The Church's Attempts to Mediate in the Russian Crisis." *RFE/RL Research Report* 2, no. 43 (October 29, 1993): 6-10.

1992. ———. "Head of Russian Constitutional Court under Fire." *RFE/RL Research Report* 2, no. 26 (June 25, 1993): 1-5.

1993. ———. "Moscow City Politics Reflect National Issues." *RFE/RL Research Report* 2, no. 10 (March 5, 1993): 5-10.

1994. Slater, Wendy, and Vera Tolz. "Yeltsin Wins in Moscow but May Lose to the Regions." *RFE/RL Research Report* 2, no. 40 (October 8, 1993): 1-7.

1995. Sneider, Daniel, and Elisabeth Rubinfien. "Yeltsin's Rubicon." *National Review* 45, no. 20 (October 18, 1993): 24-26. ["How Russia is responding to the latest power struggle."]

1996. Socor, Vladimir. "Dniester Involvement in the Moscow Rebellion." *RFE/RL Research Report* 2, no. 46 (November 19, 1993): 25-32.

1997. Soler-Sala, Paul. "One Woman's Road to Environmental Activism in Ryazan." *Surviving Together* 11, no. 1 (Spring 1993): 28-29.

1998. Stavrakis, Peter J. "Government Bureaucracies: Transition or Disintegration?" *RFE/RL Research Report* 2, no. 20 (May 14, 1993): 26-33.

1999. ———. *State Building in Post-Soviet Russia: The Chicago Boys and the Decline of Administrative Capacity.* Occasional Paper (Kennan Institute for Advanced Russian Studies), no. 254. Washington, DC: Kennan Institute for Advanced Russian Studies, The Wilson Center, [c1993]. 60 pp.

2000. Stephan, John J. "The Russian Far East." *Current History* 92, no. 576 (October 1993): 331-336.

2001. Stokes, Bruce. "Russian Roulette." *National Journal* 25, no. 13 (March 27, 1993): 758-759.

2002. Teague, Elizabeth. "Yeltsin Disbands the Soviets." *RFE/RL Research Report* 2, no. 43 (October 29, 1993): 1-5.

2003. ———. "Yeltsin's Difficult Road toward Elections." *RFE/RL Research Report* 2, no. 41 (October 15, 1993): 1-4.

2004. Thorne, Ludmilla. "The Nomenklatura Today." *Freedom Review* 24, no. 3 (May-June 1993): 9-11.

2005. Thorson, Carla. "The Battle for Central Authority in Russia: A Presidential or Parliamentary System?" *Eurasian Reports* 3, no. 2 (Winter 1993): 13-26. [Part of special issue devoted to "What Is Russia?"]

2006. ———. "Russia's Draft Constitution." *RFE/RL Research Report* 2, no. 48 (December 3, 1993): 9-15.

2007. Tolz, Vera. "The Moscow Crisis and the Future of Democracy in Russia." *RFE/RL Research Report* 2, no. 42 (October 22, 1993): 1-9.

2008. ———. "Thorny Road toward Federalism in Russia." *RFE/RL Research Report* 2, no. 48 (December 3, 1993): 1-8.

2009. Tolz, Vera, and Julia Wishnevsky. "Russia after the Referendum." *RFE/RL Research Report* 2, no. 19 (May 7, 1993): 1-5.

2010. ———. "The Russian Media and the Political Crisis in Moscow." *RFE/RL Research Report* 2, no. 40 (October 8, 1993): 12-15.

2011. United States. Central Intelligence Agency. Directorate of Intelligence. *Top Officials in Russia.* [Washington, DC]: Central Intelligence Agency, Directorate of Intelligence, [1993]. v, 71 pp.

2012. United States. Congress. Commission on Security and Cooperation in Europe. *Report on the April 25, 1993, Referendum in Russia: Moscow, Ivangorod and Environs, and Narva, Estonia: A Report.* Washington, DC: The Commission, 1993. 15 pp.

2013. Van Atta, Don. "Rutskoi Loses Responsibility for Agriculture." *RFE/RL Research Report* 2, no. 18 (April 30, 1993): 11-16. [Includes sidebar: "Aleksandr Vladimirovich Rutskoi," pp. 12-13.]

2014. ———. "Yeltsin Decree Finally Ends 'Second Serfdom' in Russia." *RFE/RL Research Report* 2, no. 46 (November 19, 1993): 33-39.

2015. Viechtbauer, Volker. "Arbitration in Russia." *Stanford Journal of International Law* 29, no. 2 (Summer 1993): 355-457.

2016. Vlasihin, Vasily A. "Towards a Bill of Rights for Russia: Progress and Roadblocks." *Nova Law Review* 17, no. 4 (Spring 1993): 1201-1212.

2017. Walker, Edward W. "The Politics of Blame and Presidential Powers in Russia's New Constitution." *East European Constitutional Review* 2, no. 4/vol. 3, no. 1 (Fall 1993-Winter 1994): 116-119.

2018. Weir, Fred. "Moscow Night." *Nation* 257, no. 14 (November 1, 1993): 485ff.

2019. White, Stephen. "Russia: Yeltsin's Kingdom or Parliament's Playground?" *Current History* 92, no. 576 (October 1993): 309-313.

2020. Wishnevsky, Julia. "Constitutional Crisis Deepens after Russian Congress." *RFE/RL Research Report* 2, no. 13 (March 26, 1993): 1-7.

2021. ———. "Liberal Opposition Emerging in Russia?" *RFE/RL Research Report* 2, no. 44 (November 5, 1993): 5-11.

2022. ———. "The Role of Media in the Parliamentary Election Campaign." *RFE/RL Research Report* 2, no. 46 (November 19, 1993): 8-12.

2023. Yakovlev, Alexander. "Russia: The Struggle for a Constitution." *Emory International Law Review* 7, no. 2 (Fall 1993): 277-292.

2024. Yasmann, Victor. "Corruption in Russia: A Threat to Democracy?" *RFE/RL Research Report* 2, no. 10 (March 5, 1993): 15-18.

2025. ———. "Legislation on Screening and State Security in Russia." *RFE/RL Research Report* 2, no. 32 (August 13, 1993): 11-16. [Includes sidebar: "Recent Legislation on Foreign Intelligence, State Security, and Related Matters," p. 12.]

2026. ———. "New Russian Copyright Laws Protect Computer Software." *RFE/RL Research Report* 2, no. 11 (March 12, 1993): 46-48.

2027. Young, Cathy. "Scattered Opposition." *Reason* 24, no. 10 (March 1993): 18-24.

2028. Zagalsky, Leonid. "Concerto for democrats with orchestra." *Bulletin of the Atomic Scientists* 49, no. 1 (January-February 1993): 14-20.

2029. Zarycky, George. "Letter from Perm: Shadows of the Past, Hopes for the Future." *Freedom Review* 24, no. 4 (July-August 1993): 24-26.

2030. Zaslavsky, Victor. "Russia and the Problem of Democratic Transition." *Telos*, no. 96 (Summer 1993): 26-52.

Law and Police

2031. Azrael, Jeremy R., and Alexander G. Rahr. *The Formation and Development of the Russian KGB, 1991-1994.* RAND Library Collection, MR-355-USDP. Santa Monica, CA: RAND, 1993. viii, 21 pp. [Prepared for the Under Secretary of Defense for Policy.]

2032. Handelman, Stephen. "Inside Russia's Gangster Economy." *New York Times Magazine* (January 24, 1993): 12ff.

2033. Jennings, Andrew. "The Free-Market Mafia: Oil, Money and Murder in Chechnia." *Nation* 257, no. 8 (September 20, 1993): 265ff.

2034. Knight, Amy. "Russian Security Services Under Yel'tsin." *Post-Soviet Affairs* 9, no. 1 (January-March 1993): 40-65.

2035. Kushen, Robert A. "The Death Penalty and the Crisis of Criminal Justice in Russia." *Brooklyn Journal of International Law* 19, no. 2 (1993): 523-581.

2036. Marnie, Sheila, and Albert Motivans. "Rising Crime Rates: Perceptions and Reality." *RFE/RL Research Report* 2, no. 20 (May 14, 1993): 80-85.

2037. Mirzayanov, Vil. "Letter to Amnesty International." *RCDA* 32, no. 3 (1993-1994): 47-48. [Translation of letter published in *Izvestiia* (June 26, 1993).]

2038. Rahr, Alexander. "The Revival of a Strong KGB." *RFE/RL Research Report* 2, no. 20 (May 14, 1993): 74-79.

2039. Slater, Wendy. "The Trial of the Leaders of Russia's August 1991 Coup." *RFE/RL Research Report* 2, no. 48 (December 3, 1993): 24-30.

2040. Waller, J. Michael. "The KGB and Its Successors under Gorbachev and Yeltsin: Russian State Security and Elusive Civil Controls." Ph.D. diss., Boston University, 1993. [UMI order no: AAC 9330153.]

2041. Way, Lucan. "In the K.G.B. Files: Exhuming the Buried Past." *Nation* 256, no. 8 (March 1, 1993): 267-268. [On Victoria Dubnowa's struggle to discover the fate of her uncle, Henryk Erlich.]

2042. Wishnevsky, Julia. "Russian Constitutional Court: A Third Branch of Government?" *RFE/RL Research Report* 2, no. 7 (February 12, 1993): 1-8.

2043. Yasmann, Victor. "The Role of Security Agencies in the October Uprising." *RFE/RL Research Report* 2, no. 44 (November 5, 1993): 12-18.

2044. ———. "Where Has the KGB Gone?" *RFE/RL Research Report* 2, no. 2 (January 8, 1993): 17-20.

Nationalities, Ethnic Relations, Regions

2045. Binder, Ellen. "The Sound of Cossack Thunder." *New York Times Magazine* (October 31, 1993): 72-77. Text by Kyle Crichton. [Photo essay.]

2046. Brodsky, Peter. "Are Russian Jews in Danger?" *Commentary* 95, no. 5 (May 1993): 37-40.

2047. Brym, Robert J., and Andrei Degtyarev. "Anti-Semitism in Moscow: Results of an October 1992 Survey." *Slavic Review* 52, no. 1 (Spring 1993): 1-12.

2048. Cullen, Robert. "Nationalism Explodes: Russia Confronts Its 'Near Abroad.'" *Nation* 257, no. 8 (September 20, 1993): 274-278.

2049. Goble, Paul A. "Russia's Extreme Right." *National Interest*, no. 33 (Fall 1993): 93-96. [Review article on Walter Laqueur, *Black Hundred: The Rise of the Extreme Right in Russia* (NY: 1993).]

2050. Kreitor, Nikolai-Klaus von. "Elements of the New Russian Nationalism." *Telos*, no. 96 (Summer 1993): 61-64.

2051. Lee, Gary. [Book Review]. *Book World (Washington Post)* 23, no. 35 (August 29, 1993): 4. [Review article on Walter Laqueur, *Black Hundred: The Rise of the Extreme Right in Russia* (NY: HarperCollins, 1993); Ruslan Khasbulatov, *The Struggle for Russia: Power and Change in the Democratic Revolution* (NY: Routledge, 1993); Pilar Bonet, *Figures in a Red Landscape* (Baltimore, MD: 1993); and Nadia Diuk and Adrian Karatnycky, *New Nations*

Rising: The Fall of the Soviets and the Challenge of the Independence (NY: Wiley, 1993).]

2052. Malik, Hafeez. "Tatarstan: A Kremlin of Islam in the Russian Federation." *Journal of South Asian and Middle Eastern Studies* 17, no. 1 (Fall 1993): 1-27.

2053. McMullen, Ronald K. "Ethnic Conflict in Russia: Implications for the United States." *Studies in Conflict and Terrorism* 16, no. 3 (July-September 1993): 201-218.

2054. "Native Peoples Gain Power." *Surviving Together* 11, no. 1 (Spring 1993): 19. [Reprinted from *Russian Far East Update* (1992).]

2055. Naumkin, Vitaly. "Active Leadership: Russia's Role in Central Asia." *Harvard International Review* 15, no. 3 (Spring 1993): 14ff.

2056. Sharlet, Robert. "Russia's 'Ethnic' Republics and Constitutional Politics." *Eurasian Reports* 3, no. 2 (Winter 1993): 39-46. [Part of special issue devoted to "What Is Russia?"]

2057. Sheehy, Ann. "Russia's Republics: A Threat to Its Territorial Integrity?" *RFE/RL Research Report* 2, no. 20 (May 14, 1993): 34-40.

2058. Smith, Raymond A. "The Kaliningrad Region: Applications of the Civic and Ethnic Models of Nationalism." *Journal of Baltic Studies* 24, no. 3 (Fall 1993): 233-246.

2059. Starovoitova, Galina. "Politics After Communism II: Weimar Russia?" *Journal of Democracy* 4, no. 3 (July 1993): 106-109.

2060. Teague, Elizabeth. "North-South Divide: Yeltsin and Russia's Provincial Leaders." *RFE/RL Research Report* 2, no. 47 (November 26, 1993): 7-23. [Correction for article appears in vol. 2, no. 49 (December 1993): 8.]

2061. Tolz, Vera. "The Burden of the Imperial Legacy in Russia." *RFE/RL Research Report* 2, no. 20 (May 14, 1993): 41-46.

2062. ———. "Regionalism in Russia: The Case of Siberia." *RFE/RL Research Report* 2, no. 9 (February 26, 1993): 1-9.

2063. ———. "The Role of the Republics and Regions." *RFE/RL Research Report* 2, no. 15 (April 9, 1993): 8-13.

2064. Walker, Edward W. "Moscow and the Provinces: Economic and Political Dimensions of Russian Regionalism." *Eurasian Reports* 3, no. 2 (Winter 1993): 47-64. [Part of special issue devoted to "What Is Russia?"]

Political Parties

2065. Corning, Amy. "How Russians View Yeltsin and Rutskoi." *RFE/RL Research Report* 2, no. 12 (March 19, 1993): 57-59.

2066. Dallin, Alexander, ed. *Political Parties in Russia.* Contributions by Michael McFaul, Philippe C. Schmitter, Steven Fish, Lilia Shevtsova, Nikolai V. Zlobin, and Alexander Dallin. Research Series (University of California, Berkeley. International and Area Studies), no. 88. [Berkeley, CA]: International and Area Studies, University of California at Berkeley, c1993. x, 102 pp. [Articles from a workshop which met at Stanford University, April 30 to May 2, 1992. Contents: Alexander Dallin, "Introduction," pp. 1-6; Michael McFaul, "Party Formation after Revolutionary Transitions: The Russian Case," pp. 7-28; Philippe C. Schmitter, "Reflections on Revolutionary and Evolutionary Transitions: The Russian Case in Comparative Perspective," pp. 29-33; Steven Fish, "Who Shall Speak for Whom? Democracy and Interest Representation in Post-Soviet Russia," pp. 34-48; Lilia Shevtsova, "Political Pluralism in Post-Communist Russia," pp. 49-62; Nikolai V. Zlobin, "The Political Spectrum," pp. 63-79; Alexander Dallin, "Alternative Forms of Political Representation and Advocacy," pp. 80-88; Alexander Dallin, "Conclusions: The Prospects for Multiparty Democracy in Russia," pp. 89-93.]

2067. "Every Man a Tsar." *New Yorker* 69, no. 44 (December 27, 1993-January 3, 1994): 8-10. ["In the Russian election, populism took the form of fascism."]

2068. Hughes, James. "Yeltsin's Siberian Opposition." *RFE/RL Research Report* 2, no. 50 (December 17, 1993): 29-34.

2069. Linden, Carl. "The Desire for Democracy." *World & I* 8, no. 8 (August 1993): 24-29. [Part of the special report "Russia: Is Reform Still Possible?"]

2070. Matlock, Jack F., Jr. "The Most Important Struggle." *World & I* 8, no. 8 (August 1993): 46-49. [Part of the special report "Russia: Is Reform Still Possible?"]

2071. McFaul, Michael. "The Morass in Moscow II: The Democrats in Disarray." *Journal of Democracy* 4, no. 2 (April 1993): 17-29.

2072. ———. *Post-Communist Politics: Democratic Prospects in Russia and Eastern Europe.* Foreword by Stephen Sestanovich. Significant Issues Series: Creating the Post-Communist Order, v. 15, no. 3. Washington, DC: Center for Strategic and International Studies, c1993. xix, 132 pp.

2073. ———. "Russian Centrism and Revolutionary Transitions." *Post-Soviet Affairs* 9, no. 3 (July-September 1993): 196-222.

2074. Oates, Sarah. "Elected Officials, Political Groups, and Voting in Russia." *RFE/RL Research Report* 2, no. 33 (August 20, 1993): 62-64.

2075. Podrabinek, Alexander. "Between Defeat and Victory." *Uncaptive Minds* 6, no. 3 (24) (Fall 1993): 5-12. [Article published in *Ekspress-Khronika* (October 8, 1993).]

2076. Remnick, David. "Letter From Moscow: The Hangover." *New Yorker* 69, no. 39 (November 22, 1993): 51-65. ["Boris Yeltsin is walking a line between creating a democracy and becoming an autocrat."]

2077. ———. "Yeltsin's Tightrope." *New Yorker* 69, no. 12 (May 10, 1993): 76-82.

2078. Rittersporn, Gábor T. "Buying Intellectual Pre-Fabs." *Telos*, no. 96 (Summer 1993): 53-60.

2079. Sakwa, Richard. "Parties and the Multiparty System in Russia." *RFE/RL Research Report* 2, no. 31 (July 30, 1993): 7-15.

2080. Schillinger, Liesl. "Moscow Postcard: *Oora! Oora!*" *New Republic* 209, no. 17 (October 25, 1993): 9-11.

2081. Schneider, William. "Political Pulse." *National Journal* 25, nos. 51-52 (December 18, 1993): 3032. ["Centrist voters support Yeltsin's constitution and economic reforms but have doubts about Yeltsin himself."]

2082. ———. "Surviving the New Era of Populism." *National Journal* 25, no. 15 (April 10, 1993): 902.

2083. Slater, Wendy. "The Center Right in Russia." *RFE/RL Research Report* 2, no. 34 (August 27, 1993): 7-14.

2084. ———. "Russian Communists Seek Salvation in Nationalist Alliance." *RFE/RL Research Report* 2, no. 13 (March 26, 1993): 8-13.

2085. ———. "Russia's National Salvation Front 'on the Offensive.'" *RFE/RL Research Report* 2, no. 38 (September 24, 1993): 1-6.

2086. Thorson, Carla. "A Loss of Direction for Russia's Movement for Democratic Reforms." *RFE/RL Research Report* 2, no. 10 (March 5, 1993): 11-14.

2087. Tolz, Vera, Wendy Slater, and Alexander Rahr. "Profiles of the Main Political Blocs." *RFE/RL Research Report* 2, no. 20 (May 14, 1993): 16-25. [Includes sidebars: Nina Belyaeva and Vladimir Lepekhin, "Factions, Groups, and Blocs in the Russian Parliament," pp. 18-19, and "The Main Political Parties and Movements at a Glance," pp. 21-22.]

2088. Vanden Heuvel, Katrina. "Russia's Veep." *Nation* 256, no. 14 (April 12, 1993): 473.

2089. Webb, John Charles. "The Regional Russian Leadership Formation Process, 1987-1993: Four Case Studies." Ph.D. diss., Georgetown University, 1993. [UMI order no: AAC 9424497.]

2090. Weir, Fred. "Review of the Month: An Interview with Roy Medvedev." *Monthly Review* 44, no. 9 (February 1993): 1-10.

2091. Young, Cathy. "Russia Votes Yes." *American Spectator* 26, no. 7 (July 1993): 26ff.

2092. Zagalsky, Leonid. "The guns of October." *Bulletin of the Atomic Scientists* 49, no. 10 (December 1993): 16-20.

Tajikistan

2093. Akchurin, Marat. "Tajikistan: Another Bosnia in the Making?" *Central Asia Monitor*, no. 3 (1993): 9-10.

2094. Brown, Bess. "Tajikistan: The Conservatives Triumph." *RFE/RL Research Report* 2, no. 7 (February 12, 1993): 9-12.

2095. Denber, Rachel, and Barnett R. Rubin. *Human Rights in Tajikistan: In the Wake of Civil War.* Edited by Jeri Laber. [New York]: Helsinki Watch, c1993. xxiii, 64 pp. [Based on a mission conducted by the Memorial Human Rights Center (Memorial HRC) and Human Rights Watch/Helsinki Watch in Tajikistan from May 26 through June 8, 1993.]

2096. Doroszewska, Urszula. "The Forgotten War." *Uncaptive Minds* 6, no. 3 (24) (Fall 1993): 25-35.

2097. Dubnov, Arkadi. "The Forgotten Country." *Uncaptive Minds* 6, no. 3 (24) (Fall 1993): 19-24. [Article published in *Novoe Vremya* no. 4 (April 1993).]

2098. "Events in Tajikistan." *Central Asia Monitor*, no. 2 (1993): 2-3.

2099. "Events in Tajikistan." *Central Asia Monitor*, no. 4 (1993): 9-16.

2100. "Tajikistan: End of the Civil War? Diary of Events." *Central Asia Monitor*, no. 1 (1993): 5-8.

2101. "Tajikistan: End of the Civil War? Statements of the Government." *Central Asia Monitor*, no. 1 (1993): 8-9. ["Statement by the Government of Tajikstan (21 December 1992) as delivered to the United Nations," p. 8; and "Statement of Emomali Rakhmonov, Chairman of the Supreme Soviet, as delivered to the United Nations," pp. 8-9.]

2102. Grossman, Leanne. "Small Groups Make Valiant Efforts to Turn the Tide in Tajikistan." *Surviving Together* 11, no. 3 (Fall 1993): 45-47.

2103. Martin, Keith. "Tajikistan: Civil War without End?" *RFE/RL Research Report* 2, no. 33 (August 20, 1993): 18-29. [Includes sidebars: "Imomali Rakhmonov," p. 20; "Ali Akbar Turadzhonzoda," p. 21; "Abdumalik Abdullodzhanov," p. 22; and "Aleksandr Shishlyannikov," p. 23.]

2104. Maynard, Kim. "Tajikistan: Will We Heed the Warning?" *Central Asia Monitor*, no. 5 (1993): 11-16.

2105. Tadjbakhsh, Shahrbanou. "The Bloody Path of Change: The Case of Post-Soviet Tajikistan." *Harriman Institute Forum* 6, no. 11 (July 1993): 1-10.

2106. ———. "Causes and Consequences of the Civil War." *Central Asia Monitor*, no. 1 (1993): 10-14.

Turkmenistan

2107. Coon, Jane A. "Impressions from Turkmenistan." *Central Asia Monitor*, no. 4 (1993): 16-18.

2108. Dailey, Erika. *Human rights in Turkmenistan.* Edited by Jeri Laber and Alexander Petrov. New York, NY: Helsinki Watch, c1993. x, 46 pp.

2109. Laber, Jeri. "The Dictatorship Returns." *New York Review of Books* 40, no. 13 (July 15, 1993): 42-44.

2110. Panico, Christopher J. "Turkmenistan Unaffected by Winds of Democratic Change." *RFE/RL Research Report* 2, no. 4 (January 22, 1993): 6-10.

Ukraine

2111. Arel, Dominique. "Language and the Politics of Ethnicity: The Case of Ukraine." Ph.D. diss., University of Illinois at Urbana-Champaign, 1993. [UMI order no: AAC 9411556.]

2112. Bilinsky, Yaroslav. "Ukraine: The Multiple Challenges to Independence." *Harriman Institute Forum* 7, nos. 1-2 (September-October 1993): 27-31. [Paper from the Fifth Annual Workshop on Post-Soviet Nations, held at the Harriman Institute, April 30, 1993.]

2113. Bremmer, Ian. "Ethnic Issues in Crimea." *RFE/RL Research Report* 2, no. 18 (April 30, 1993): 24-28.

2114. "Chronicle of Events: January 3, 1993-February 25, 1993." *Ukrainian Quarterly* 49, no. 1 (Spring 1993): 93-106.

2115. Edwards, Mike. "Running on Empty." *National Geographic* 183, no. 3 (March 1993): 38-53. ["Fiercely nationalistic, Ukraine warily eyes its worrisome neighbor, Russia, even as the two share remnants of Soviet military might."]

2116. Futey, Bohdan A. "Ukraine's Draft Constitution Meets Political Reality." *East European Constitutional Review* 2, no. 1 (Winter 1993): 14-16.

2117. Holovaty, Serhiy. "Politics after Communism III: Ukraine: A View from Within." *Journal of Democracy* 4, no. 3 (July 1993): 110-113.

2118. "An Interview with Ukrainian Prime Minister Leonid Kuchma." *Ukrainian Quarterly* 49, no. 1 (Spring 1993): 5-13. Translated by R. K. Stojko-Lozynski.

2119. Jarosewich, Irene, and Volodymyr Skachko. "Rukh: To Be or Not To Be?" *Surviving Together* 11, no. 1 (Spring 1993): 17-18. [Reprinted from *Ukrainian Weekly* (November 29, 1992).]

2120. Lapychak, Chrystyna. "Ukraine's Troubled Rebirth." *Current History* 92, no. 576 (October 1993): 337-341.

2121. Markov, Ihor. "The Role of the President in the Ukrainian Political System." *RFE/RL Research Report* 2, no. 48 (December 3, 1993): 31-35.

2122. Marples, David R. " 'After the Putsch': Prospects for Independent Ukraine." *Nationalities Papers* 21, no. 2 (Fall 1993): 35-46.

2123. Martyniuk, Jaroslaw. "The Demographics of Party Support in Ukraine." *RFE/RL Research Report* 2, no. 48 (December 3, 1993): 36-42. [Includes sidebar: "A Brief Guide to the Major Political Parties," pp. 40-41.]

2124. Mihalisko, Kathleen. "Ukrainians and Their Leaders at a Time of Crisis." *RFE/RL Research Report* 2, no. 31 (July 30, 1993): 54-62.

2125. Naboka, Serhiy. "A Lack of Everything." *Uncaptive Minds* 6, no. 3 (24) (Fall 1993): 139-143. [Part of a survey on the mass media in Eastern Europe.]

2126. Solchanyk, Roman. "The Politics of Language in Ukraine." *RFE/RL Research Report* 2, no. 10 (March 5, 1993): 1-4.

2127. ———. "Ukraine: A Year of Transition." *RFE/RL Research Report* 2, no. 1 (January 1, 1993): 58-63.

2128. Solchanyk, Roman, and Taras Kuzio. "Democratic Political Blocs in Ukraine." *RFE/RL Research Report* 2, no. 16 (April 16, 1993): 14-17.

2129. Stewart, Susan. "Ukraine's Policy toward Its Ethnic Minorities." *RFE/RL Research Report* 2, no. 36 (September 10, 1993): 55-62.

2130. United States. Central Intelligence Agency. Directorate of Intelligence. *Top Officials in Ukraine.* [Washington, DC]: Central Intelligence Agency, Directorate of Intelligence: Purchase from Photoduplication Service, Library of Congress, [1993]. v, 24 pp.

2131. Wilson, Andrew. "The Growing Challenge to Kiev from the Donbas." *RFE/RL Research Report* 2, no. 33 (August 20, 1993): 8-13.

Uzbekistan

2132. Brown, Bess. "Tajik Civil War Prompts Crackdown in Uzbekistan." *RFE/RL Research Report* 2, no. 11 (March 12, 1993): 1-6.

2133. Critchlow, James. "Uzbekistan and the West: Time for a New Departure." *Central Asia Monitor*, no. 5 (1993): 17-21.

2134. Dailey, Erika. *Human Rights in Uzbekistan.* Edited by Jeri Laber. New York, NY: Helsinki Watch, c1993. vii, 61 pp.

2135. Gretsky, Sergei. "NDI Talks with Former Uzbek Ambassador Babur Malikov." *Central Asia Monitor*, no. 6 (1993): 9-10.

2136. Hanks, Reuel Ross. "Glasnost, Islam and Nationalism: Uzbekistan in the Gorbachev and Post-Soviet Eras." Ph.D. diss., University of Kansas, 1993. [UMI order no: AAC 9425915.]

2137. Levison, Joanna. "Bread? Democracy? Or Both?" *Surviving Together* 11, no. 2 (Summer 1993): 32-34.

2138. Motyl, Alexander J. *Dilemmas of Independence: Ukraine after Totalitarianism.* New York: Council on Foreign Relations Press, c1993. xv, 217 pp. [Contents: Preface: Premises, Consequences, Biases; Introduction: Dilemmas for Ukraine; Historical Perspectives on Ukraine's Independence; Overcoming the Legacies of Empire and Totalitarianism; Forging a New National Identity; Engaging a Post-totalitarian Russia; Transforming a Dependent

Economy; Fashioning a Postcolonial Elite; Conclusion: Dilemmas for the West.] REV: Robert Legvold, *Foreign Affairs* 72, no. 3 (Summer 1993): 206.

2139. Nalle, David. "Legal Development: Testimony of Uzbek Human Rights Activist." *Central Asia Monitor*, no. 2 (1993): 4. [Report of U.S. Commission for Security and Cooperation in Europe hearing before the U.S. Congress, March 25, 1993. Includes testimony of Abdumanob Pulatov and Micah Naftalin.]

2140. Panico, Christopher. "Uzbekistan: Past and Present." *Surviving Together* 11, no. 2 (Summer 1993): 28-30.

2141. Pulatov, Abdumannob. "A Call to the West: Stop Aid to the Uzbek Government." *Surviving Together* 11, no. 2 (Summer 1993): 31.

2142. Tokgozoglu, Yalcin. "Uzbek Government Continues to Stifle Dissent." *RFE/RL Research Report* 2, no. 39 (October 1, 1993): 10-15.

■ **Eastern Europe**

General

2143. Arato, Andrew. "Interpreting 1989." *Social Research* 60, no. 3 (Fall 1993): 609-646.

2144. Attali, Jacques. "An Age of Yugoslavia." *Harper's* 286, no. 1712 (January 1993): 20-22. [An excerpt from "Europe's Descent Into Tribalism" by Jacques Attali, part of a collection of essays on Europe entitled "After the Nation-State" in *New Perspectives Quarterly* (Fall 1992).]

2145. Baranczak, Stanislaw. [Book Review]. *Book World (Washington Post)* 23, no. 38 (September 19, 1993): 1ff. [Review article on Andrew Nagorski, *The Birth of Freedom: Shaping Lives and Societies in the New Eastern Europe* (NY: Simon & Schuster, 1993).]

2146. Benomar, Jamal. "Confronting the Past I: Justice After Transitions." *Journal of Democracy* 4, no. 1 (January 1993): 3-14. [Includes section "The Postcommunist Experience," pp. 6-8, on Eastern Europe, as well as sections on South America and Africa.]

2147. Berentsen, William H. "A Geopolitical Overview of Europe." *Social Education* 57, no. 4 (April-May 1993): 170-176. [Part of a special section entitled "United Germany in a Uniting Europe, Part 1."]

2148. Berman, Nathaniel. " 'But the Alternative is Despair': Nationalism and the Modernist Renewal of International Law." *Harvard Law Review* 106, no. 8 (June 1993): 1792-1903.

2149. Bernhard, Michael. "Civil Society and Democratic Transition in East Central Europe." *Political Science Quarterly* 108, no. 2 (Summer 1993): 307-326.

2150. Borsody, Stephen. *The New Central Europe.* East European Monographs, no. 366. Boulder, CO: East European Monographs; New York: Distributed by Columbia University Press, 1993. xiv, 321 pp. [Originally appeared in shorter versions under the titles: *The Triumph of Tyranny*, and *The Tragedy of Central Europe*. Contents: Introduction: From Habsburgs to Soviets—and Beyond. Pt. 1. The Tragedy of Central Europe. 1. The New Europe That Failed. 2. Federalist Experiments. 3. The Revisionist Challenge. 4. Czechs and Hungarians. 5. Collapse in Central Europe. 6. Munich: Tragedy of Appeasement. 7. From Munich to Moscow. 8. Hitler's New Order. 9. Federalist Interlude. 10. Europe's Coming Partition. Pt. 2. From Partition to European Union. 11. Churchill's Bargain. 12. Yalta: Tragedy of Liberation. 13. Stalin's New Order. 14. From Potsdam to Prague. 15. Benes and the Russians. 16. The Iron Curtain and the Cold War. 17. Cold War Becomes Detente. 18. Epilogue Becomes Prologue. 19. The Collapse of Eastern Europe. 20. Central Europe and the European Union.]

2151. Brown, J. F. "Eastern Europe: The Revolution So Far." *RFE/RL Research Report* 2, no. 1 (January 1, 1993): 69-74.

2152. Bugajski, J. "The Fate of Minorities in Eastern Europe." *Journal of Democracy* 4, no. 4 (October 1993): 85-99.

2153. Bugajski, Janusz. *Nations in Turmoil: Conflict and Cooperation in Eastern Europe.* Boulder, CO: Westview Press, 1993. ix, 260 pp.

2154. "Bulletin of Electoral Statistics and Public Opinion Research Data." *East European Politics and Societies* 7, no. 3 (Fall 1993): 555-576.

2155. Bungs, Dzintra. "Elections and Restoring Democracy in the Baltic States." *RFE/RL Research Report* 2, no. 38 (September 24, 1993): 12-16.

2156. Burg, Steven L. "Nationalism Redux: Through the Glass of the Post-Communist States Darkly." *Current History* 92, no. 573 (April 1993): 162-166.

2157. Campeanu, Pavel, and Stefana Steriade. "The Revolution: The Beginning of the Transition." *Social Research* 60, no. 4 (Winter 1993): 915-932. Translated by Ronald Radzai.

2158. Chirot, Daniel. *National Liberations and Nationalist Nightmares: The Consequences of the End of Empires in Eastern Europe in the 20th Century.* Working Paper (University of California, Berkeley. Center for German and European Studies), 5.9. Berkeley, CA: Center for German and European Studies, University of California, [1993]. 45 pp. [Conference on Markets, States, and Democracy, February 11-13, 1993.]

2159. Curry, Jane L. "Pluralism in Eastern Europe: Not Will It Last But What Is It?" *Communist and Post-Communist Studies* 26, no. 4 (December 1993): 446-461.

2160. Darski, Jozef. "Baltic Politics." *Uncaptive Minds* 6, no. 3 (24) (Fall 1993): 37-48.

2161. Desruisseaux, Paul. "Championing the Rights and Freedoms of Academics Who Face Persecution."

Chronicle of Higher Education 39, no. 38 (May 26, 1993): A35ff.

2162. Elster, Jon. "Bargaining over the Presidency: Myopic bargains among the framers in Poland, Hungary and Bulgaria." *East European Constitutional Review* 2, no. 4/vol. 3, no. 1 (Fall 1993-Winter 1994): 95-98.

2163. Francisco, Ronald A. "Theories of Protest and the Revolutions of 1989." *American Journal of Political Science* 37, no. 3 (August 1993): 663-680.

2164. Friedheim, Daniel V. "Bringing Society Back into Democratic Transition Theory after 1989: Pact Making and Regime Collapse." *East European Politics and Societies* 7, no. 3 (Fall 1993): 482-512.

2165. Gabriel, Oscar W., and Klaus G. Troitzsch, eds. *Wahlen in Zeiten des Umbruchs*. Empirische und Methodologische Beitrage zur Sozialwissenschaft, Bd. 12. Frankfurt am Main; New York: P. Lang, c1993. xi, 518 pp.

2166. Geremek, Bronislaw. "Politics After Communism I: A Horizon of Hope and Fear." *Journal of Democracy* 4, no. 3 (July 1993): 100-105.

2167. Glynn, Patrick. "The Age of Balkanization." *Commentary* 96, no. 1 (July 1993): 21-24.

2168. Gotovska-Popova, Teodoritchka. "Nationalism in Post-Communist Eastern Europe." *East European Quarterly* 27, no. 2 (Summer 1993): 171-186.

2169. Held, Joseph, ed. *Democracy and Right-Wing Politics in Eastern Europe in the 1990s*. Contributions by Andrzej Korbonski, Sarah M. Terry, Sharon Wolchik, Otto Ulc, Ivan T. Berend, Joseph Held, Michael Shafir, Ivan Siber, Luan Troxel, Elez Biberaj, and Iván Völgyes. East European Monographs, no. 376. Boulder, CO: East European Monographs; New York: Distributed by Columbia University Press, 1993. vi, 232 pp. [Proceedings from a conference held April 1992. Contents: Stephen Fischer-Galati, "The Political Right in Eastern Europe in Historical Perspective," pp. 1-12; Andrzej Korbonski, "The Revival of the Political Right in Post-Communist Poland: Historical Roots," pp. 13-31; Sarah M. Terry, "What's Right, What's Left, and What's Wrong in Polish Politics?" pp. 33-60; Sharon Wolchik, "The Right in Czech-Slovakia," pp. 61-87; Otto Ulc, "The Role of the Political Right in Post-Communist Czech-Slovakia," pp. 89-103; Ivan T. Berend, "Jobbra Át! [Right Face!]: Right-Wing Trends in Post-Communist Hungary," pp. 105-134; Joseph Held, "Building Civil Society in Post-Communist Hungary," pp. 135-152; Michael Shafir, "The Revival of the Political Right in Post-Communist Romania," pp. 153-174; Ivan Siber, "Strengthening of the Right and Social Changes in Croatia and Yugoslavia," pp. 175-189; Luan Troxel, "The Political Spectrum in Post-Communist Bulgaria," pp. 191-202; Elez Biberaj, "Albania," pp. 203-222; Iván Völgyes, "Concluding Thoughts on the Revival of the Political Right in Eastern Europe," pp. 223-232.]

2170. Heydt, Barbara von der. *Candles Behind the Wall: Heroes of the Peaceful Revolution That Shattered Communism*. Grand Rapids, MI: William B. Eerdmans, c1993. xxi, 266 pp.

2171. Hollander, Paul. "Why Communism Collapsed in Eastern Europe." *Society* 30, no. 2 (January-February 1993): 43-51. [Followed with letter to the editor by Karl Friedrich Smith, "Whose Socialism Collapsed?" in vol. 30, no. 5 (July-August 1993): 5, and Hollander's reply, pp. 5-6.]

2172. Holmes, Stephen. "Back to the Drawing Board: An Argument for Constitutional Postponement in Eastern Europe." *East European Constitutional Review* 2, no. 1 (Winter 1993): 21-25.

2173. ———. "The Postcommunist Presidency." *East European Constitutional Review* 2, no. 4/vol. 3, no. 1 (Fall 1993-Winter 1994): 36-39.

2174. Howard, A. E. Dick, ed. *Constitution Making in Eastern Europe*. Contributions by A. E. Dick Howard, Péter Paczolay, Katarina Mathernova, Andrzej Rapaczynski, Joanna Regulska, and Herman Schwartz. Woodrow Wilson Center Special Studies. Washington, DC: Woodrow Wilson Center Press; Baltimore, MD: Distributed by the Johns Hopkins University Press, c1993. viii, 215 pp. [Contents: A.E. Dick Howard, "Introduction," pp. 1-7; A.E. Dick Howard, "How Ideas Travel: Rights at Home and Abroad," pp. 9-20; Péter Paczolay, "The New Hungarian Constitutional State: Challenges and Perspectives," pp. 21-55; Katarina Mathernova, "Czecho?Slovakia: Constitutional Disappointments," pp. 57-92; Andrzej Rapaczynski, "Constitutional Politics in Poland: A Report on the Constitutional Committee of the Polish Parliament," pp. 93-131; Joanna Regulska, "Self-Governance or Central Control? Rewriting Constitutions in Central and Eastern Europe," pp. 133-161; Herman Schwartz, "The New East European Constitutional Courts," pp. 163-207.]

2175. Ivekovic, Rada. "Women, Nationalism, and War: 'Make Love Not War.'" *Hypatia* 8, no. 4 (Fall 1993): 113-126.

2176. Karklins, Rasma, and Roger Petersen. "Decision Calculus of Protesters and Regimes: Eastern Europe 1989." *Journal of Politics* 55, no. 3 (August 1993): 588-614.

2177. Karpinski, Jakub. "Postcommunist Difficulties." *Uncaptive Minds* 6, no. 2 (23) (Summer 1993): 5-13. [Article is adapted from a lecture given at Charles University in Prague, in April 1993.]

2178. Kovács, Dezsö, and Sally Ward Maggard. "The Human Face of Political, Economic, and Social Change in Eastern Europe." *East European Quarterly* 27, no. 3 (Fall 1993): 317-349.

2179. Kurth, James. "Eastern Question, Western Answer." *National Interest*, no. 34 (Winter 1993-1994): 96-101. [Review article on William Pfaff, *The Wrath of Nations: Civilization and the Fury of Nationalism* (NY: 1993).]

2180. Larrabee, F. Stephen. *East European Security after the Cold War*. Santa Monica, CA: RAND,

1993. xxxi, 195 pp. [Contents: Eastern Europe's Changing Security Environment; NATO and Eastern Europe; The European Community and Eastern Europe; Regional and Subregional Cooperation: Germany and Eastern Europe; France and Eastern Europe; Russia, Ukraine, and Eastern Europe; Implications for U.S. Policy; The Need for U.S. Leadership.]

2181. McGregor, James. "How Electoral Laws Shape Eastern Europe's Parliaments." *RFE/RL Research Report* 2, no. 4 (January 22, 1993): 11-18.

2182. Mestrovic, Stjepan G., Miroslav Goreta, and Slaven Letica. *The Road from Paradise: Prospects for Democracy in Eastern Europe.* Lexington, KY: University Press of Kentucky, c1993. xx, 204 pp. REV: Ivo Banac, *Political Science Quarterly* 108, no. 3 (Fall 1993): 550-551. Patrick H. Mooney, *Rural Sociology* 58, no. 4 (Winter 1993): 643-645. *Orbis* 37, no. 4 (Fall 1993).

2183. Mestrovic, Stjepan G., Slaven Letica, and Miroslav Goreta. *Habits of the Balkan Heart: Social Character and the Fall of Communism.* 1st ed. College Station, TX: Texas A&M University Press, c1993. xiv, 181 pp. [Contents: 1. The Collapse of Communism and Its Cultural Nemesis; 2. The Fifth Yugoslavia and the New World Order; 3. The Aristocratic Temperament in the Balkans; 4. Veblen and Spengler on Barbarism within Modernity; 5. Explaining War in the Land of Medjugorje; 6. Conclusions.]

2184. Michnik, Adam, and Václav Havel. "Confronting the Past III: Justice or Revenge?" *Journal of Democracy* 4, no. 1 (January 1993): 20-27. Translated from the Polish by Magdalena Potocka. [Excerpt from a longer dialogue published in *Gazeta Wyborcza* (November 30, 1991).]

2185. Milosz, Czeslaw. "Swing Shift in the Baltics." *New York Review of Books* 40, no. 18 (November 4, 1993): 12-16. [Review article on Anatol Lieven, *The Baltic Revolution: Estonia, Latvia, Lithuania and the Path to Independence* (New Haven, CT: 1993).]

2186. Murphy, Brian C. "A Progress Report on the Democracy Development Initiative." *Federal Bar News & Journal* 40, no. 9 (October 1993): 579-580.

2187. Nankin, Kenneth S. "The Future of the Democracy Development Initiative." *Federal Bar News & Journal* 40, no. 9 (October 1993): 581-583.

2188. Nedzi, Lucien N. "Institutionalization of New Democracies: A Fresh Approach to Security." *Mediterranean Quarterly* 4, no. 3 (Summer 1993): 1-9.

2189. O'Brien, Conor Cruise. "The Wrath of Ages." *Foreign Affairs* 72, no. 5 (November-December 1993): 142-149. [Review article on William Pfaff, *The Wrath of Nations: Civilization and the Fury of Nationalism* (NY: 1993) and Yael Tamir, *Liberal Nationalism* (Princeton, NJ: 1993).]

2190. Offe, Claus, Frank Bönker, Stephen Holmes, Shlomo Avineri, George Sher, and Ulrich Preuss. "A Forum on Restitution." *East European Constitutional Review* 2, no. 3 (Summer 1993): 30-40. [Workshop organized by the

Center for the Study of Constitutionalism in Eastern Europe, held June 18-19, 1993, at the Central European University in Budapest, on the political, economic and legal problems surrounding the restitution of confiscated property in post-Communist societies.]

2191. Ondrusek, Dusan. "The Mediator's Role in National Conflicts in Post-Communist Central Europe." *Mediation Quarterly* 10, no. 3 (Spring 1993): 243-248.

2192. Pesic, Vesna. "The Challenge of Ethnic Conflict VI: The Cruel Face of Nationalism." *Journal of Democracy* 4, no. 4 (October 1993): 100-103. [Based on remarks the author delivered at the Fourth World Conference of the National Endowment for Democracy in Washington, DC, on April 27, 1993.]

2193. Poznanski, Kazimierz. "An Interpretation of Communist Decay: The Role of Evolutionary Mechanisms." *Communist and Post-Communist Studies* 26, no. 1 (March 1993): 3-24.

2194. Reiterer, Albert F. "Minorities in Austria." *Patterns of Prejudice* 27, no. 2 (October 1993): 49-62.

2195. Roemer, John, and Jon Elster. "A Third Way? Constitutional Issues in Market Socialism." *East European Constitutional Review* 2, no. 1 (Winter 1993): 38-39.

2196. Singer, Daniel. "Letter from Europe: The Emperors Are Naked." *Nation* 257, no. 6 (August 23-30, 1993): 208-210.

2197. Sunstein, Cass. "Against Positive Rights." *East European Constitutional Review* 2, no. 1 (Winter 1993): 35-38. ["Why social and economic rights don't belong in the new constitutions."]

2198. Swain, Geoffrey, and Nigel Swain. *Eastern Europe since 1945.* New York: St. Martin's Press, 1993. xiv, 255 pp.

2199. Tanchev, Evgeni. "Parliamentarism Rationalized." *East European Constitutional Review* 2, no. 1 (Winter 1993): 33-35.

2200. Tismaneanu, Vladimir. "Public Enemies." *Society* 30, no. 2 (January-February 1993): 37-42.

2201. Utter, Robert F., and David C. Lundsgaard. "Judicial Review in the New Nations of Central and Eastern Europe: Some Thoughts from a Comparative Perspective." *Ohio State Law Journal* 54, no. 3 (1993): 559-606.

2202. Varga, Csaba. "Transformation to Rule of Law from No-Law: Societal Contexture of the Democratic Transition in Central and Eastern Europe." *Connecticut Journal of International Law* 8, no. 2 (Spring 1993): 487-505. [Paper from the symposium, "Human Rights in Theory and Practice: A Time of Change and Development in Central and Eastern Europe," held in Budapest, March 19-20, 1993.]

2203. Webster, Alexander F. C. "Kingdoms of God in the Balkans?" *East European Quarterly* 27, no. 4 (Winter 1993): 437-451.

2204. White, Stephen, Judy Batt, and Paul G. Lewis, eds. *Developments in East European Politics.* Contributions by Stephen White, Judy Batt, Paul G. Lewis, George Schöpflin, David S. Mason, Gordon Wightman, Nigel Swain, John D. Bell, Jim Seroka, Krzysztof Jasiewicz, Jan Åke Dellenbrant, Ray Taras, Chris Corrin, Judy Batt, Bob Deacon, Daniel N. Nelson, Paul G. Lewis, and Judy Dempsey. Durham, NC: Duke University Press, 1993. xiii, 304 pp. [Contents: Stephen White, Judy Batt, and Paul G. Lewis, "Preface," pp. ix-x. Pt. One: Perspectives on Eastern Europe; Stephen White, "Eastern Europe after Communism," pp. 2-15; George Schöpflin, "Culture and Identity in Post-Communist Europe," pp. 16-34. Pt. Two: Models of Transition in Eastern Europe; David S. Mason, "Poland," pp. 36-50; Gordon Wightman, "The Czech and Slovak Republics," pp. 51-65; Nigel Swain, "Hungary," pp. 66-82; John D. Bell, "Bulgaria," pp. 83-97; Jim Seroka, "Yugoslavia and Its Successor States," pp. 98-121. Pt. Three: Patterns of Politics in Post-Communist Eastern Europe; Krzysztof Jasiewicz, "Structures of Representation," pp. 124-146; Jan Åke Dellenbrant, "Parties and Party Systems in Eastern Europe," pp. 147-162; Ray Taras, "Leaderships and Executives," pp. 163-185; Chris Corrin, "People and Politics," pp. 186-204; Judy Batt, "The Politics of Economic Transition," pp. 205-224; Bob Deacon, "Social Change, Social Problems and Social Policy," pp. 225-239. Pt. Four: Eastern Europe and Political Science; Daniel N. Nelson, "The Comparative Politics of Eastern Europe," pp. 242-261; Paul G. Lewis, "History, Europe and the Politics of the East," pp. 262-279; Judy Dempsey, "East European Voices," pp. 280-288; "Further Reading," pp. 289-291; "Bibliography," pp. 292-301.]

2205. Wiggins, Charles B. "Exporting Process Technology: Transplanting North American Public Interest Mediation to Central Europe." *Mediation Quarterly* 10, no. 3 (Spring 1993): 273-289.

2206. Zhelev, Zhelyu. "Personal Reflection on a Changing Eastern Europe: Comments on What Has Happened and What Should Be Done in the Future." *Federal Bar News & Journal* 40, no. 9 (October 1993): 570-572.

Nationalities, Ethnic Relations, Regions

2207. Bell-Fialkoff, Andrew. "A Brief History of Ethnic Cleansing." *Foreign Affairs* 72, no. 3 (Summer 1993): 110-121.

2208. Bonte-Friedheim, Robert. "Hungarians Abroad: Next up for Ethnic Cleansing?" *Freedom Review* 24, no. 2 (March-April 1993): 22-24.

2209. Bugajski, Janusz. "The Challenge of Ethnic Conflict V: The Fate of Minorities in Eastern Europe." *Journal of Democracy* 4, no. 4 (October 1993): 85-99.

2210. "Ethnic Conflicts Worldwide." *Current History* 92, no. 573 (April 1993): 167-168.

2211. Gurr, Ted. *Minorities at Risk: A Global View of Ethnopolitical Conflicts.* Includes contribution by Monty G. Marshall. Washington, DC: United States Institute of Peace Press, 1993. xii, 427 pp. [Partial contents: Monty G. Marshall, "States at risk: ethnopolitics in the multinational states of Eastern Europe."]

2212. Harris, Chauncy D. "New European Countries and Their Minorities." *Geographical Review* 83, no. 3 (July 1993): 301-320.

2213. Karpinski, Jakub. "The South Slavs." *Uncaptive Minds* 6, no. 1 (22) (Winter-Spring 1993): 5-8.

2214. Kirch, Aksel, Marika Kirch, and Tarmo Tuisk. "Russians in the Baltic States: To Be or Not to Be?" *Journal of Baltic Studies* 24, no. 2 (Summer 1993): 173-188.

2215. Lerman, Antony. "Introduction." *Patterns of Prejudice* 27, no. 1 (July 1993): 1-2. [Introduction to special issue on "Antisemitism in Europe: I". Issue features selected papers from an international conference organized by the Zentrum für Antisemitismusforschung, Technische Universität Berlin, in association with the Institute of Jewish Affairs, London, and the Vidal Sassoon International Center for the Study of Antisemitism, the Hebrew University, Jerusalem, held September 21-23, 1992, in Berlin.]

2216. Lingle, Christopher. "Authoritarian Socialism, Interest Group Formation and Ethnic Nationalism." *Canadian Review of Studies in Nationalism = Revue Canadienne des Etudes sur le Nationalisme* 20, nos. 1-2 (1993): 7-11.

2217. Malcolm, Noel. "Seeing Ghosts." *National Interest*, no. 32 (Summer 1993): 83-88. [Review article on Robert D. Kaplan, *Balkan Ghosts: A Journey through History* (NY: 1993). Followed with letter to the editor by Kaplan in issue no. 33 (Fall 1993): 109-110, and response by Malcolm, pp. 110-111.]

2218. Raphael, Phyllis. "Tri-City Travels." *Congress Monthly* 60, no. 6 (September-October 1993): 12-14. [Observations on Jewish culture in Budapest, Vienna and Prague.]

2219. Seiler, Daniel-Louis. "Inter-Ethnic Relations in East Central Europe: The Quest for a Pattern of Accommodation." *Communist and Post-Communist Studies* 26, no. 4 (December 1993): 352-366.

2220. Shonholtz, Raymond. "The Role of Minorities in Establishing Mediating Norms and Institutions in the New Democracies." *Mediation Quarterly* 10, no. 3 (Spring 1993): 231-241.

2221. Soiefer, Ronald M. "A Promise Fulfilled." *Congress Monthly* 60, no. 3 (March/April 1993): 11-13.

2222. Szayna, Thomas S. "Ultra-Nationalism in Central Europe." *Orbis* 37, no. 4 (Fall 1993): 527-550.

2223. Todorova, Maria. "Ethnicity, Nationalism and the Communist Legacy in Eastern Europe." *East European Politics and Societies* 7, no. 1 (Winter 1993): 135-154. [Extended version of a paper presented at the conference on the Social Legacy of Communism, in Washington, DC, February 1992.]

2224. Urban, William. "Ethnic Tensions in the Baltics." *Lituanus* 39, no. 1 (Spring 1993): 67-76.

2225. Zarycky, George. "East-Central Europe: Post-Communist Blues." *Freedom Review* 24, no. 1 (January-February 1993): 48-52.

Political Parties

2226. Ishiyama, John T. "Founding Elections and the Development of Transitional Parties: The Cases of Estonia and Latvia, 1990-1992." *Communist and Post-Communist Studies* 26, no. 3 (September 1993): 277-299.

2227. Roskin, Michael G. "The Emerging Party Systems of Central and Eastern Europe." *East European Quarterly* 27, no. 1 (Spring 1993): 47-63.

Albania

2228. Austin, Robert. "What Albania Adds to the Balkan Stew." *Orbis* 37, no. 2 (Spring 1993): 259-279.

2229. Biberaj, Elez. "Albania's Road to Democracy." *Current History* 92, no. 577 (November 1993): 381-385.

2230. Bransten, Jeremy. "Letter from Albania: Tirana Blues." *Freedom Review* 24, no. 6 (November-December 1993): 22-23.

2231. Gage, Nicholas. "The Forgotten Minority in the Balkans: The Greeks of Northern Epirus." *Mediterranean Quarterly* 4, no. 3 (Summer 1993): 10-29.

2232. Imholz, Kathleen. "A Landmark Constitutional Court Decision in Albania." *East European Constitutional Review* 2, no. 3 (Summer 1993): 22-25.

2233. Jones, John Paul. "Albania: The Tribunal in Tirana." *East European Constitutional Review* 2, no. 2 (Spring 1993): 51-53.

2234. Jones, Lloyd. "After the Gatekeepers Fled." *Grand Street* 12, no. 3 (1993): 10-25.

2235. Laber, Jeri. "Albania: Slouching Toward Democracy." *New York Review of Books* 40, nos. 1-2 (January 14, 1993): 24-27.

2236. Van Heuven, Marten. *Albania Opens Up: But to What Future?* Santa Monica, CA: RAND, 1993. iii, 8 pp.

2237. Zanga, Louis. "Albania: Democratic Revival and Social Upheaval." *RFE/RL Research Report* 2, no. 1 (January 1, 1993): 75-77.

2238. ———. "Cabinet Changes in Albania." *RFE/RL Research Report* 2, no. 19 (May 7, 1993): 14-16. [Includes sidebar: "Key Officials in Albania," p. 15.]

2239. Zanga, Louis, and Robert Austin. "Albania's Growing Political Instability." *RFE/RL Research Report* 2, no. 36 (September 10, 1993): 27-32.

Bulgaria

2240. Anson, Jon et al., ed. *Ethnicity and Politics in Bulgaria and Israel*. Aldershot; Brookfield, VT: Avebury,

c1993. xi, 259 pp. [Edited papers from the First Bulgarian-Israeli Sociology Seminar, held at Simeonovo Lodge, Bulgaria, in August-September 1991.]

2241. Chin, Jill. "Political Attitudes in Bulgaria." *RFE/RL Research Report* 2, no. 18 (April 30, 1993): 39-41.

2242. Curtis, Glenn E., ed. *Bulgaria: A Country Study.* Contributions by Glenn E. Curtis, Pamela Mitova, William Marsteller, and Karl Wheeler Soper. 2nd ed. Area Handbook Series, DA Pam 550-168. Washington, DC: Library of Congress. Federal Research Division, 1993. xlvi, 328 pp. [Supercedes *Area Handbook for Bulgaria* (1974). Partial contents: "Table A. Chronology of Important Events," pp. xv-xx; "Country Profile," pp. xxi-xxvi; Glenn E. Curtis, "Introduction," pp. xxix-xlvi; Glenn E. Curtis, "Historical Setting," pp. 1-57; Pamela Mitova, "The Society and Its Environment," pp. 59-114; William Marsteller, "The Economy," pp. 115-169; Glenn E. Curtis, "Government and Politics," pp. 171-223; Karl Wheeler Soper, "National Security," pp. 225-273; "Bibliography," pp. 287-295.]

2243. Darski, Jozef. "The Strange Case of Bulgaria." *Uncaptive Minds* 6, no. 2 (23) (Summer 1993): 15-25.

2244. Engelbrekt, Kjell. "Bulgaria: The Weakening of Postcommunist Illusions." *RFE/RL Research Report* 2, no. 1 (January 1, 1993): 78-83.

2245. ———. "Reinventing the Bulgarian Secret Services." *RFE/RL Research Report* 2, no. 47 (November 26, 1993): 41-49.

2246. ———. "Technocrats Dominate New Bulgarian Government." *RFE/RL Research Report* 2, no. 4 (January 22, 1993): 1-5.

2247. Ganev, Venelin. "Survey of Presidential Powers in Eastern Europe: Bulgaria II." *East European Constitutional Review* 2, no. 4/vol. 3, no. 1 (Fall 1993-Winter 1994): 62-64.

2248. Gray, Cheryl W., and Peter G. Ianachkov. "Bulgaria's Evolving Legal Framework for Private Sector Development." *International Lawyer* 27, no. 4 (Winter 1993): 1091-1110.

2249. Ilchev, Ivan, and Duncan M. Perry. "Bulgarian Ethnic Groups: Politics and Perceptions." *RFE/RL Research Report* 2, no. 12 (March 19, 1993): 35-41.

2250. "Key Officials in Bulgaria." *RFE/RL Research Report* 2, no. 4 (January 22, 1993): 3.

2251. Kolarova, Rumyana. "Bulgaria: A Self-Restricting Court." *East European Constitutional Review* 2, no. 2 (Spring 1993): 48-50.

2252. Nikolaev, Rada. "Bulgaria and Its Emigrants: Past and Present." *RFE/RL Research Report* 2, no. 27 (July 2, 1993): 50-56.

2253. Poshtov, Georgi. "Survey of Presidential Powers in Eastern Europe: Bulgaria I." *East European Constitutional Review* 2, no. 4/vol. 3, no. 1 (Fall 1993-Winter 1994): 61-62.

2254. Todorov, Nikolay. "Politics and Contemporary Bulgaria." *Journal of the Hellenic Diaspora* 19, no. 2 (1993): 109-120.

2255. Troxel, Luan. "Bulgaria: Stable Ground in the Balkans?" *Current History* 92, no. 577 (November 1993): 386-389.

2256. United States. Congress. Commission on Security and Cooperation in Europe. *Human Rights and Democratization in Bulgaria.* Implementation of the Helsinki Accords. Washington, DC: The Commission, [1993]. v, 25 pp.

(Former) Czechoslovakia

2257. Abercrombie, Thomas J. "Czechoslovakia: The Velvet Divorce." *National Geographic* 184, no. 3 (September 1993): 2ff.

2258. "After the Velvet Divorce: A Survey of Recent Articles." *Wilson Quarterly* 17, no. 2 (Spring 1993): 147-149.

2259. Baker, Stephanie, and Jen Nessel. "The Velvet Split: Czechs, Slovaks Go It Alone." *Nation* 256, no. 5 (February 8, 1993): 157-160.

2260. Bren, Paulina. "Lustration in the Czech and Slovak Republics." *RFE/RL Research Report* 2, no. 29 (July 16, 1993): 16-22.

2261. Draper, Theodore. "The End of Czechoslovakia." *New York Review of Books* 40, no. 3 (January 28, 1993): 20-26. [Followed with response by Rita Klimová and reply by Draper, vol. 40, no. 7 (April 8, 1993): 50-52.]

2262. ———. "A New History of the Velvet Revolution." *New York Review of Books* 40, nos. 1-2 (January 14, 1993): 14-20.

2263. Fenic, Fero. "Breaking Up Isn't So Hard to Do." *Harper's* 286, no. 1712 (January 1993): 22. [Excerpt from a letter by Fenic, the head of Febio, an independent television production company in Czechoslovakia, to several advertising agencies based in Prague.]

2264. Jílek, Dalibor. "Human Rights Treaties and the New Constitution." *Connecticut Journal of International Law* 8, no. 2 (Spring 1993): 407-419. [Paper from the symposium, "Human Rights in Theory and Practice: A Time of Change and Development in Central and Eastern Europe," held in Budapest, March 19-20, 1993.]

2265. Kalvoda, Joseph. "The Breakup of Czechoslovakia." *Ukrainian Quarterly* 49, no. 1 (Spring 1993): 44-67.

2266. Knoll, Erwin. "The Poet as President." *Progressive* 57, no. 4 (April 1993): 40-43. [Review article on Václav Havel, *Open Letters: Selected Writings, 1965-1990* (NY: Knopf, 1991); Václav Havel, *Summer Meditations* (NY: Knopf, 1992); and Jan Vladislav, ed., *Václav Havel: Living in Truth* (London: Faber and Faber, 1989).]

2267. Komarik, Emil. "Vestiges of Communism and the Dissolution of Czechoslovakia." *Uncaptive Minds* 6, no. 1 (22) (Winter-Spring 1993): 55-58.

2268. Mates, Pavel. "Drug Abuse and Trafficking in the Czech and Slovak Republics." *RFE/RL Research Report* 2, no. 4 (January 22, 1993): 55-58.

2269. Michnik, Adam. "An Embarrassing Anniversary." *New York Review of Books* 40, no. 11 (June 10, 1993): 19-21. [On the 25th anniversary of Prague Spring.]

2270. Obrman, Jan. "The Czech and Slovak Presidential Elections." *RFE/RL Research Report* 2, no. 7 (February 12, 1993): 13-17.

2271. Olson, David M. "Dissolution of the State: Political Parties and the 1992 Election in Czechoslovakia." *Communist and Post-Communist Studies* 26, no. 3 (September 1993): 301-314.

2272. Ort, Thomas. "The Far Right in the Czech Republic." *Uncaptive Minds* 6, no. 1 (22) (Winter-Spring 1993): 67-72. [On the Association for the Republic-The Republican Party of Czechoslovakia.]

2273. Pehe, Jiri. "Czechoslovakia: Toward Dissolution." *RFE/RL Research Report* 2, no. 1 (January 1, 1993): 84-88.

2274. Pithart, Petr. "Intellectuals in Politics: Double Dissent in the Past, Double Disappointment Today." *Social Research* 60, no. 4 (Winter 1993): 751-761.

2275. Radicova, Iveta. "The Velvet Divorce." *Uncaptive Minds* 6, no. 1 (22) (Winter-Spring 1993): 51-53.

2276. Reshova, Jana. *Injustice of the Past, Fairness of the Present?* Working Paper (University of California, Berkeley. Center for German and European Studies), 2.12. Berkeley, CA: Center for German and European Studies, University of California, [1993]. 21, 27 pp. [Includes "Restitution Laws in Czecho-Slovakia," p. 3 and "Constitution of the Czech Republic," pp. 1-27 [2nd group].]

2277. Schmidt-Hartmann, Eva. "The Enlightenment that Failed: Antisemitism in Czech Political Culture." *Patterns of Prejudice* 27, no. 2 (October 1993): 119-128.

2278. Szomolnyiova, Sona. "The Inevitable Breakup?" *Uncaptive Minds* 6, no. 1 (22) (Winter-Spring 1993): 59-62. [Adapted from a paper prepared for a conference held at the University of California, Berkeley.]

2279. Vidláková, Olga. "Local Decisionmaking and Management in Czechoslovakia: 1990-1992." *Policy Studies Journal* 21, no. 1 (Spring 1993): 126-132.

2280. Wilson, Paul. "Unlikely Hero." *New York Review of Books* 40, no. 15 (September 23, 1993): 41-45. [Review article on Alexander Dubcek, *Hope Dies Last: The Autobiography of Alexander Dubcek*, ed. and trans. Jiří Hochman (NY: Kodansha International, 1993).]

2281. Wolchik, Sharon. "The Repluralization of Politics in Czechoslovakia." *Communist and Post-Communist Studies* 26, no. 4 (December 1993): 412-431.

Czech Republic

2282. Bollag, Burton. "Professor Survives a Broken Career, Isolation, and Fear of Arrest to Triumph Over a Communist Purge." *Chronicle of Higher Education* 40, no. 11 (November 3, 1993): A42.

2283. Cepl, Vojtech, and David Franklin. "Senate, Anyone?" *East European Constitutional Review* 2, no. 2 (Spring 1993): 58-60.

2284. Cepl, Vojtech, and Mark Gillis. "Survey of Presidential Powers in Eastern Europe: Czech Republic." *East European Constitutional Review* 2, no. 4/vol. 3, no. 1 (Fall 1993-Winter 1994): 64-68.

2285. Gray, Cheryl W. "The Legal Framework for Private Sector Activity in the Czech Republic." *Vanderbilt Journal of Transnational Law* 26, no. 2 (May 1993): 271-299.

2286. Havel, Václav. "The Post-Communist Nightmare." *New York Review of Books* 40, no. 10 (May 27, 1993): 8-10. [Speech given on April 22, 1993 at George Washington University in Washington, DC.]

2287. Mates, Pavel. "The Czech Constitution." *RFE/RL Research Report* 2, no. 10 (March 5, 1993): 53-57.

2288. McCarthy, Tim. "Growing up or selling out?" *Commonweal* 120, no. 16 (September 24, 1993): 13-16.

2289. Obrman, Jan. "Czech Opposition Parties in Disarray." *RFE/RL Research Report* 2, no. 16 (April 16, 1993): 1-6.

2290. ———. "Czech Parliament Declares Former Communist Regime Illegal." *RFE/RL Research Report* 2, no. 32 (August 13, 1993): 6-10.

2291. Pehe, Jiri. "Constitutional Imbroglio in the Czech Republic." *RFE/RL Research Report* 2, no. 5 (January 29, 1993): 1-5.

2292. ———. "Law on Romanies Causes Uproar in Czech Republic." *RFE/RL Research Report* 2, no. 7 (February 12, 1993): 18-22.

2293. ———. "Spying Scandal in the Czech Republic." *RFE/RL Research Report* 2, no. 32 (August 13, 1993): 1-5.

2294. ———. "The Waning Popularity of the Czech Parliament." *RFE/RL Research Report* 2, no. 45 (November 12, 1993): 9-13.

2295. Pratt, Greta. "Y(oung) A(mericans in) P(rague)." *New York Times Magazine* (December 12, 1993): 70-73.

2296. Spencer, Metta. "Helsinki Citizens Assembly." *Peace Magazine* 9, no. 6 (November-December 1993): 21. [Account of the September 1993 meeting of the Assembly near Prague.]

Slovakia

2297. Bollag, Burton. "Third-World Students in Slovakia Fearful After Skinheads Attack Their Dormitory." *Chronicle of Higher Education* 39, no. 18 (January 6, 1993): A48.

2298. Bútora, Martin, and Zora Bútorová. "Slovakia After the Split." *Journal of Democracy* 4, no. 2 (April 1993): 71-83.

2299. ———. "Slovakia: The Identity Challenges of the Newly Born State." *Social Research* 60, no. 4 (Winter 1993): 705-736.

2300. Bútorová, Zora, and Martin Bútora. "A Democratic Road for Slovakia?" *Uncaptive Minds* 6, no. 2 (23) (Summer 1993): 51-62.

2301. Fisher, Sharon. "Church Restitution Law Passed in Slovakia." *RFE/RL Research Report* 2, no. 46 (November 19, 1993): 51-55.

2302. ———. "Is Slovakia Headed for New Elections?" *RFE/RL Research Report* 2, no. 32 (August 13, 1993): 34-41. [Includes sidebar: "Key Officials in Slovakia," p. 37.]

2303. ———. "Slovakia's Foreign Policy Since Independence." *RFE/RL Research Report* 2, no. 49 (December 10, 1993): 28-34.

2304. Hrib, Stefan. "The Advantages of Slovakia's Independence." *RCDA* 32, no. 2 (1993-1994): 32-33. [Translation of article from *Lidove Noviny* (December 8, 1992).]

2305. Kalniczky, Adele. "The Slovak Government's First Six Months in Office." *RFE/RL Research Report* 2, no. 6 (February 5, 1993): 18-25.

2306. Kurlansky, Mark. "Letter from Slovakia." *Partisan Review* 60, no. 2 (Spring 1993): 201-206.

2307. Langerova, Viera. "Facing the Masses." *Uncaptive Minds* 6, no. 3 (24) (Fall 1993): 133-137. [Part of a survey on the mass media in Eastern Europe.]

2308. Morrison, David C. "On Their Own." *National Journal* 25, no. 4 (January 23, 1993): 202-204.

2309. Nic, Milan, Jan Obrman, and Sharon Fisher. "New Slovak Government: More Stability?" *RFE/RL Research Report* 2, no. 47 (November 26, 1993): 24-30. [Includes sidebars: "Key Officials in Slovakia," p. 28; and "Background of New Cabinet Members," p. 29.]

2310. Obrman, Jan. "Internal Disputes Shake Slovak Government." *RFE/RL Research Report* 2, no. 14 (April 2, 1993): 13-17.

2311. ———. "Polls Reveal Gloomy Mood among Slovaks." *RFE/RL Research Report* 2, no. 19 (May 7, 1993): 51-54.

2312. Reisch, Alfred A. "Slovakia's Minority Policy under International Scrutiny." *RFE/RL Research Report* 2, no. 49 (December 10, 1993): 35-42.

Eastern Germany

2313. Adams, Kif Augustine. "What is Just? The Rule of Law and Natural Law in the Trials of Former East German Border Guards." *Stanford Journal of International Law* 29, no. 2 (Summer 1993): 271-314.

2314. Bergmann, Werner. "Antisemitism in (East and West) German Public Opinion, 1987-1992." *Patterns of Prejudice* 27, no. 2 (October 1993): 21-28.

2315. Bredow, Wilfried von. "Post-post-nationalism in Germany." *International Journal* 48, no. 3 (Summer 1993): 413-433.

2316. Brockmann, Stephen. "Living where the wall was: What still divides the Germans?" *Commonweal* 120, no. 16 (September 24, 1993): 16-19.

2317. Burgess, John P. [Book Review]. *Religion in Eastern Europe* 13, no. 6 (December 1993): 46-47. [Review article on Mark Jantzen, *The Wrong Side of the Wall: An American in East Berlin During the Peaceful Revolution* (Beatrice, NE: Evangel Press, 1993).]

2318. Conradt, David P. *The German Polity.* 5th ed. New York: Longman, c1993. xiii, 257 pp.

2319. Cooper, Rand Richards. "It isn't Weimar all over again." *Commonweal* 120, no. 9 (May 7, 1993): 11-13.

2320. Engelbrekt, Kjell. "The *Stasi* Revisited." *RFE/RL Research Report* 2, no. 46 (November 19, 1993): 19-24.

2321. Erb, Rainer. "Jews and Other Minorities in Germany since the 1990s." *Patterns of Prejudice* 27, no. 2 (October 1993): 13-19.

2322. Evers, Tilman. "Popular Sovereignty in Germany: Anti-Absolutism and its Democratic Recycling." *Telos* 26, no. 3 (no. 97) (Fall 1993): 41-51.

2323. Gedmin, Jeffrey. "The German Left and Democracy." *World Affairs* 156, no. 1 (Summer 1993): 46-51.

2324. Geipel, Gary L., ed. *Germany in a New Era.* Indianapolis, IN: Hudson Institute, 1993. x, 311 pp. REV: Michael Rühle, *Comparative Strategy* 12, no. 4 (1993): 475-477.

2325. Grass, Günter. "On Loss: The Condition of Germany." *Dissent* 40, no. 2 (Spring 1993): 178-188. Translated from the German by Krishna Winston.

2326. Hirschman, Albert O. "Exit, Voice, and the Fate of the German Democratic Republic: An Essay in Conceptual History." *World Politics* 45, no. 2 (January 1993): 173-202.

2327. Jantzen, Mark. *The Wrong Side of the Wall: An American in East Berlin during the Peaceful Revolution.* Beatrice, NE: Evangel Press; Distributed by Henry and Gretl Jantzen, 1993. [Author describes three years in East Germany as a theological student at Humboldt University.] REV: John P. Burgess, *Religion in Eastern Europe* 13, no. 6 (December 1993): 46-47.

2328. Jones, Merrill E. "Origins of the East German Environmental Movement." *German Studies Review* 16, no. 2 (May 1993): 235-264.

2329. Kinzer, Stephen. "A Climate for Demagogues." *Atlantic Monthly* 273, no. 2 (February 1993): 21ff. [Discusses the political consequences of German reunification.]

2330. Kirschten, Dick. "Gloomy Giant." *National Journal* 25, no. 47 (November 20, 1993): 2771-2775.

2331. ———. "Rebuilding." *National Journal* 25, no. 45 (November 6, 1993): 2668-2670. ["Dresden is typical of the problems unification has brought to the former East Germany."]

2332. Koch, Burkhard. "Post-Totalitarianism in Eastern Germany and German Democracy." *World Affairs* 156, no. 1 (Summer 1993): 26-54.

2333. Kramer, Jane. "Neo-Nazis: A Chaos in the Head." *New Yorker* 69, no. 17 (June 14, 1993): 52-70.

2334. Lankowski, Carl. "Germany's Social Movement Sector, the Greens, and the European Community." *Social Education* 57, no. 5 (September 1993): 242-245. [Part of special section entitled "The Case of Germany, Part 2," edited by Dagmar Kraemer and Manfred Stassen.]

2335. Lasky, Melvin J. "Before the Breakdown and After." *Society* 30, no. 2 (January-February 1993): 14-22.

2336. ———. "The Trial of Erich Honecker." *National Review* 45, no. 6 (March 29, 1993): 23-25.

2337. Lee, Martin A. "Hitler's Offspring." *Progressive* 57, no. 3 (March 1993): 28-31.

2338. Marcuse, Peter. "Moral Indignation and Politics: The Debate Over the Stasi." *New Political Science*, nos. 24/25 (Spring-Summer 1993): 9-18.

2339. Markovits, Andrei. "Political Parties in Germany: Agents of Stability in a Sea of Change." *Social Education* 57, no. 5 (September 1993): 239-242. [Part of special section entitled "The Case of Germany, Part 2," edited by Dagmar Kraemer and Manfred Stassen.]

2340. Minkenberg, Michael. "The Wall after the Wall: On the Continuing Division of Germany and the Remaking of Political Culture." *Comparative Politics* 26, no. 1 (October 1993): 53-68.

2341. Neaman, Elliot. "The Escalation of Terror in Germany." *Tikkun* 8, no. 1 (January-February 1993): 32ff. [On the Neo-Nazi threat.]

2342. Neaman, Elliot, and Hajo Funke. "Germany: The Nationalism Backlash." *Dissent* 40, no. 1 (Winter 1993): 11-15.

2343. Neckermann, Peter. "Germany's Reunification Woes." *World & I* 8, no. 10 (October 1993): 76-81.

2344. O'Brien, Conor Cruise. "Germany Resurgent." *Harper's* 286, no. 1714 (March 1993): 15-17. [Excerpt from author's "The Future of 'The West,'" *National Interest*

(Winter 1992-1993).]

2345. Opp, Karl-Dieter, and Christiane Gern. "Dissident Groups, Personal Networks, and Spontaneous Cooperation: The East German Revolution of 1989." *American Sociological Review* 58, no. 5 (October 1993): 659-680.

2346. Pluchinsky, Dennis A. "Germany's Red Army Faction: An Obituary." *Studies in Conflict and Terrorism* 16, no. 2 (April-June 1993): 135-157.

2347. "The Politics of German Pessimism." *Harper's* 287, no. 1720 (September 1993): 15. [From an internal memo prepared by the German Free Democratic Party (FDP).]

2348. Raufer, Xavier. "The Red Brigades: Farewell to Arms." *Studies in Conflict and Terrorism* 16, no. 4 (October-December 1993): 315-325.

2349. Schneider, Peter. "Neo-Nazi Violence: Stop It Now, Explain It Later." *Harper's* 286, no. 1717 (June 1993): 20-22. [Excerpt from "Marginalizing the Victim" in Peter Schneider, *Deutsche Zustande* [The German Situation], a book of essays published by Rowohlt Verlag (Hamburg: 1993).]

2350. Stassen, Donna. "A United Germany in a Uniting Europe." *Social Education* 57, no. 4 (April-May 1993): 187-190. [Includes photographs provided by the German Information Center, New York City. Part of a special section entitled "United Germany in a Uniting Europe, Part 1."]

2351. Stassen, Manfred, and Dagmar Kraemer. "Europe's New Center." *Social Education* 57, no. 4 (April-May 1993): 166-167. [Part of a special section entitled "United Germany in a Uniting Europe, Part 1."]

2352. Stern, Fritz. "Freedom and Its Discontents." *Foreign Affairs* 72, no. 4 (September-October 1993): 108-125. ["After 40 years of division, the two former halves of Germany are discovering the psychological stress of unity."]

2353. Stokes, Bruce. "Germany in a Jam." *National Journal* 25, no. 26 (June 26, 1993): 1637-1641. [Includes discussion of the financial burden of reunification.]

2354. Thaysen, Uwe. "A New Constitution for a New Germany?" *German Studies Review* 16, no. 2 (May 1993): 299-310.

2355. Toro, Taryn. "Anti-Foreign Violence Leaves Its Legacy on a German Campus." *Chronicle of Higher Education* 39, no. 26 (March 3, 1993): A41-A42.

2356. Ward, James J. "*Was bleibt?* (What's Left?) Antifascism as Historical Experience and Contemporary Politics in Post-Marxist (East) Germany." *New Political Science*, nos. 24/25 (Spring-Summer 1993): 39-57.

2357. Whitney, Craig R. "Spy Trader." *New York Times Magazine* (May 23, 1993): 36-40. [On Wolfgang Vogel.]

Estonia

2358. Clemens, Walter C., Jr. "*Eesti Redux*." *Harriman Institute Forum* 7, nos. 1-2 (September-October 1993): 17-21. [Paper from the Fifth Annual Workshop on Post-Soviet Nations, held at the Harriman Institute, April 30, 1993.]

2359. Doroszewska, Urszula. "A Bashkir in Estonia." *Uncaptive Minds* 6, no. 3 (24) (Fall 1993): 55-59.

2360. Hanson, Philip. "Estonia's Narva Problem, Narva's Estonian Problem." *RFE/RL Research Report* 2, no. 18 (April 30, 1993): 17-23.

2361. Herbert, Douglas J. "Letter from Tallinn: Baltic Trailblazer." *Freedom Review* 24, no. 6 (November-December 1993): 20-21.

2362. Kionka, Riina. "Estonia: A Difficult Transition." *RFE/RL Research Report* 2, no. 1 (January 1, 1993): 89-91.

2363. Laitin, David D. "The Russian-Speaking Nationality in Estonia: Two Quasi-Constitutional Elections." *East European Constitutional Review* 2, no. 4/vol. 3, no. 1 (Fall 1993-Winter 1994): 23-27.

2364. Pettai, Vello A. "Estonia: Old Maps and New Roads." *Journal of Democracy* 4, no. 1 (January 1993): 117-125.

2365. Sheehy, Ann. "The Estonian Law on Aliens." *RFE/RL Research Report* 2, no. 38 (September 24, 1993): 7-11.

2366. Stuttaford, Andrew. "Back to Normal." *National Review* 45, no. 21 (November 1, 1993): 22-24.

2367. Taagepera, Rein. "Running for President of Estonia: A Political Scientist in Politics." *PS: Political Science & Politics* 26, no. 2 (June 1993): 302-304.

2368. United States. Congress. Commission on Security and Cooperation in Europe. *Human Rights and Democratization in Estonia*. Implementation of the Helsinki Accords. Washington, DC: The Commission, [1993]. v, 23 pp.

2369. Yelesyeyenko, Valentin. "Problems on Problems." *Uncaptive Minds* 6, no. 3 (24) (Fall 1993): 49-53. [Interview with Lagle Parek, minister of internal affairs for the Estonian Government.]

Greece and Cyprus (Since 1821)

2370. Clogg, Richard. *Greece, 1981-89: The Populist Decade*. New York, NY: St. Martin's Press, 1993. xiv, 194 pp.

2371. Karakasidou, Anastasia. "Fellow Travelers, Separate Roads: The KKE and the Macedonian Question." *East European Quarterly* 27, no. 4 (Winter 1993): 453-477.

2372. Kerameus, Konstantinos D., and Phaedon J. Kozyris. *Introduction to Greek Law*. 2nd rev. ed. Deventer; Boston, MA: Kluwer Law and Taxation Publishers, c1993. xxviii, 448 pp.

2373. Prodromou, Elizabeth H. "Democracy, Religion and Identity in Socialist Greece: Church-State Relations under Pasok, 1981-1989." Ph.D. diss., Massachusetts Institute of Technology, 1993.

2374. Samatas, Minas. "The Populist Phase of an Underdeveloped Surveillance Society: Political Surveillance in Post-Dictatorial Greece." *Journal of the Hellenic Diaspora* 19, no. 1 (1993): 31-70.

2375. Szulc, Tad. "Cyprus: A Time of Reckoning." *National Geographic* 184, no. 1 (July 1993): 104-130.

Hungary

2376. Agh, Attila. "The Premature Senility of the New Democracies: The Hungarian Experience." *PS: Political Science & Politics* 26, no. 2 (June 1993): 305-307.

2377. Agócs, Sándor. "The Collapse of the Communist Ideology in Hungary—November 1988 to February 1989." *East European Quarterly* 27, no. 2 (Summer 1993): 187-211.

2378. Bozóki, András. "Hungary's Road to Systematic Change: The Opposition Roundtable." *East European Politics and Societies* 7, no. 2 (Spring 1993): 276-308. Translated by József Böröcz.

2379. Bunce, Valerie, and Mária Csanádi. "Uncertainty in the Transition: Post-Communism in Hungary." *East European Politics and Societies* 7, no. 2 (Spring 1993): 240-275.

2380. Cooper, Leland R., and Andrea Kenesei. *Hungarians in Transition: Interviews with Citizens of the Nineties.* Jefferson, NC: McFarland & Co., c1993. xiv, 206 pp.

2381. Feher, Gyorgy. *Struggling for Ethnic Identity: The Gypsies of Hungary.* Edited by Holly Cartner and Lois Whitman. New York: Human Rights Watch, [c1993]. viii, 72 pp. [Based on a mission conducted by Feher in January of 1993.]

2382. Herczegh, Geza. "The Evolution of Human Rights Law in Central and Eastern Europe: One Jurist's Response to the Distinguished Panelists." *Connecticut Journal of International Law* 8, no. 2 (Spring 1993): 323-325. [Paper from the symposium, "Human Rights in Theory and Practice: A Time of Change and Development in Central and Eastern Europe," held in Budapest, March 19-20, 1993.]

2383. Ingram, Judith. "The Party's Just Begun." *Uncaptive Minds* 6, no. 2 (23) (Summer 1993): 27-31.

2384. Kardos, Gábor. "Freedom of Speech in the Time of Transition." *Connecticut Journal of International Law* 8, no. 2 (Spring 1993): 529-545. [Paper from the symposium, "Human Rights in Theory and Practice: A Time of Change and Development in Central and Eastern Europe," held in Budapest, March 19-20, 1993.]

2385. "Key Officials in Hungary." *RFE/RL Research Report* 2, no. 12 (March 19, 1993): 45.

2386. Klingsberg, Ethan. "Hungary: Safeguarding the Transition." *East European Constitutional Review* 2, no. 2 (Spring 1993): 44-48.

2387. Kovacs, Andras. "Antisemitism in Post-Communist Hungary." *Patterns of Prejudice* 27, no. 2 (October 1993): 95-101.

2388. McDonald, Jason. "Transition to Utopia: A Reinterpretation of Economics, Ideas, and Politics in Hungary, 1984-1990." *East European Politics and Societies* 7, no. 2 (Spring 1993): 203-239.

2389. Mink, Andras. "Survey of Presidential Powers in Eastern Europe: Hungary." *East European Constitutional Review* 2, no. 4/vol. 3, no. 1 (Fall 1993-Winter 1994): 68-71.

2390. Morvai, Krisztina. "Retroactive Justice based on International Law: A Recent Decision by the Hungarian Constitutional Court." *East European Constitutional Review* 2, no. 4/vol. 3, no. 1 (Fall 1993-Winter 1994): 32-34.

2391. Okolicsanyi, Karoly. "Hungarian Compensation Programs off to a Slow Start." *RFE/RL Research Report* 2, no. 11 (March 12, 1993): 49-52.

2392. ———. "Hungary's Political Front-Runners Outline Economic Programs." *RFE/RL Research Report* 2, no. 50 (December 17, 1993): 40-43.

2393. Oltay, Edith. "Controversy over Restitution of Church Property in Hungary." *RFE/RL Research Report* 2, no. 6 (February 5, 1993): 54-57.

2394. ———. "Horthy's Reburial Sparks Controversy in Hungary." *RFE/RL Research Report* 2, no. 43 (October 29, 1993): 33-37.

2395. ———. "Hungarian Democratic Forum Expels Radical Leader." *RFE/RL Research Report* 2, no. 31 (July 30, 1993): 24-29.

2396. ———. "Hungarian Democratic Forum Opts for Centrist Policy." *RFE/RL Research Report* 2, no. 9 (February 26, 1993): 22-26.

2397. ———. "Hungary Attempts to Deal with Its Past." *RFE/RL Research Report* 2, no. 18 (April 30, 1993): 6-10.

2398. ———. "Hungary: Csurka Launches 'National Movement.'" *RFE/RL Research Report* 2, no. 13 (March 26, 1993): 25-31.

2399. ———. "Hungary Passes Law on Minority Rights." *RFE/RL Research Report* 2, no. 33 (August 20, 1993): 57-61.

2400. ———. "Hungary Reforms Its Police Force." *RFE/RL Research Report* 2, no. 4 (January 22, 1993): 50-54.

2401. Paczolay, Péter. "Constitutional Transition and Legal Continuity." *Connecticut Journal of International Law* 8, no. 2 (Spring 1993): 559-574. [Paper from the symposium, "Human Rights in Theory and Practice: A Time of Change and Development in Central and Eastern

Europe," held in Budapest, March 19-20, 1993.]

2402. Pataki, Judith. "The Hungarian Cabinet Reshuffle." *RFE/RL Research Report* 2, no. 12 (March 19, 1993): 42-46.

2403. ————. "Hungarian Government Signs Social Contract with Unions." *RFE/RL Research Report* 2, no. 5 (January 29, 1993): 42-45.

2404. ————. "Hungary: Domestic Political Stalemate." *RFE/RL Research Report* 2, no. 1 (January 1, 1993): 92-95.

2405. ————. "Hungary Tightens Up Its Citizenship Law." *RFE/RL Research Report* 2, no. 32 (August 13, 1993): 42-46.

2406. ————. "Hungary's Leading Opposition Party Torn by Dissension." *RFE/RL Research Report* 2, no. 50 (December 17, 1993): 24-28.

2407. ————. "A New Era in Hungary's Social Security Administration." *RFE/RL Research Report* 2, no. 27 (July 2, 1993): 57-60.

2408. ————. "The Possible Newcomers to Hungary's Parliament." *RFE/RL Research Report* 2, no. 15 (April 9, 1993): 19-22.

2409. ————. "The Szarszo Conference and Its Political Implications." *RFE/RL Research Report* 2, no. 41 (October 15, 1993): 11-16.

2410. Plachy, Sylvia. "Graveyard of the Statues." *New York Times Magazine* (May 2, 1993): 46-49. ["Communist heroes, in perspective."]

2411. Sajo, Andras. "The Judiciary in Contemporary Society: Hungary." *Case Western Reserve Journal of International Law* 25, no. 2 (Spring 1993): 293-301.

2412. ————. "The Role of Lawyers in Social Change: Hungary." *Case Western Reserve Journal of International Law* 25, no. 2 (Spring 1993): 137-146.

2413. Simon, Janos. "Post-paternalist Political Culture in Hungary: Relationship between Citizens and Politics during and after the 'Melancholic Revolution' (1989-1991)." *Communist and Post-Communist Studies* 26, no. 2 (June 1993): 226-238.

2414. Susskind, Jack. "Hungary: A Nation in Transition." *Social Education* 57, no. 6 (October 1993): 280-281.

2415. United States. Congress. Commission on Security and Cooperation in Europe. *Human Rights and Democratization in Hungary.* Implementation of the Helsinki Accords. Washington, DC: Commission on Security and Cooperation in Europe, [1993]. vi, 25 pp.

2416. Vámos, Miklós. "Hungary's Media Apparatchiks." *Nation* 257, no. 20 (December 13, 1993): 725-729.

2417. "What Went Right in Hungary." *Uncaptive Minds* 6, no. 3 (24) (Fall 1993): 107-117. [Interview with

Balint Magyar, campaign director for the Alliance of Free Democrats (SzDSz).]

Latvia

2418. Boyle, Patrick. "Did *Life* Magazine Hype Antisemitism in Latvia?" *American Journalism Review* 15, no. 3 (April 1993): 10.

2419. Bungs, Dzintra. "Latvia: Toward Full Independence." *RFE/RL Research Report* 2, no. 1 (January 1, 1993): 96-98.

2420. ————. "The New Latvian Government." *RFE/RL Research Report* 2, no. 33 (August 20, 1993): 14-17. [Includes sidebars: "Key Officials in Latvia," p. 15; "Valdis Birkavs," p. 16; and "Guntis Ulmanis," p. 17.]

2421. ————. "The Shifting Political Landscape in Latvia." *RFE/RL Research Report* 2, no. 12 (March 19, 1993): 28-34.

2422. ————. "Twenty-three Groups Vie for Seats in the Latvian Parliament." *RFE/RL Research Report* 2, no. 23 (June 4, 1993): 44-49.

2423. Grigorievs, Alexei. "Letter from Latvia: The Ghosts." *Freedom Review* 24, no. 3 (May-June 1993): 12-14. [Followed with letter to the editor by Vilis Varsbergs, and response by Grigorievs, in vol. 24, no. 5 (September-October 1993): 3-4.]

2424. Krickus, Richard J. "Latvia's 'Russian Question.'" *RFE/RL Research Report* 2, no. 18 (April 30, 1993): 29-34.

2425. United States. Congress. Commission on Security and Cooperation in Europe. *Human Rights and Democratization in Latvia.* Implementation of the Helsinki Accords. Washington, DC: The Commission, [1993]. v, 30 pp.

Lithuania

2426. Chelminski, Rudolph. "Vytautas Landsbergis: Lithuania's Freedom Fighter." *Freedom Review* 24, no. 2 (March-April 1993): 34-38.

2427. Clark, Terry D. "Coalition Realignment in the Supreme Council of the Republic of Lithuania and the Fall of the Vangorius Government." *Journal of Baltic Studies* 24, no. 1 (Spring 1993): 53-66.

2428. Girnius, Saulius. "Crime Rate in Lithuania Rises Sharply." *RFE/RL Research Report* 2, no. 31 (July 30, 1993): 50-53.

2429. ————. "Lithuania: Former Communists Return to Power." *RFE/RL Research Report* 2, no. 1 (January 1, 1993): 99-101.

2430. ————. "Lithuanian Democratic Labor Party in Trouble." *RFE/RL Research Report* 2, no. 24 (June 11, 1993): 17-20.

2431. ————. "Lithuanian Politics Seven Months after the Elections." *RFE/RL Research Report* 2, no. 27 (July 2, 1993): 16-21. [Includes sidebar: "Key Officials in

Lithuania," p. 17.]

2432. ———. "A Weary Lithuania Elects Brazauskas." *RFE/RL Research Report* 2, no. 10 (March 5, 1993): 19-22.

2433. Gordon, Ellen J. "Legislating Identity: Language, Citizenship, and Education in Lithuania." Ph.D. diss., University of Michigan, 1993. [UMI order no: AAC 9319531.]

2434. Klimas, Tadas. "A Comparison of the Struggles for Independence of the United States and Lithuania." *Lituanus* 39, no. 3 (Fall 1993): 5-15.

2435. Levin, Dov. "Lithuanian Attitudes toward the Jewish Minority in the Aftermath of the Holocaust: The Lithuanian Press, 1991-1992." *Holocaust and Genocide Studies* 7, no. 2 (Fall 1993): 247-262.

2436. Lithuania. "Constitution of the Republic of Lithuania." *Lituanus* 39, no. 1 (Spring 1993): 5-52. [Text of constitution adopted by referendum October 25, 1992. Translation provided by the Lithuanian Embassy in Washington, DC.]

2437. Scammon, Richard M. "International Election Notes: Lithuania." *World Affairs* 156, no. 2 (Fall 1993): 108.

2438. Senn, Alfred, and Violeta Motulaite. "The Lithuanian Concept of Statehood." *Nationalities Papers* 21, no. 2 (Fall 1993): 25-34.

2439. Tuckus, Andrius. "A View from Lithuania." *Uncaptive Minds* 6, no. 3 (24) (Fall 1993): 61-63. [Interview with Vytautas Landsbergis on the Balkan War.]

2440. Viesulas, Romas Tauras. "Party Formation in Lithuania: Prospects for Multiparty Democracy." *Lituanus* 39, no. 2 (Summer 1993): 5-35.

2441. Vitas, Robert A. "The Recognition of Lithuania: The Completion of the Legal Circle." *Journal of Baltic Studies* 24, no. 3 (Fall 1993): 247-262.

Poland

2442. Albright, Michael. "Poland's 1991 Labor Statutes: A Refinement of Earlier Legislation Rather Than a Liberalization of Union Rights and Powers." *Case Western Reserve Journal of International Law* 25, no. 3 (Summer 1993): 571-617.

2443. Artman, Boguslaw. "Poland: Turning Back the Clock?" *Freedom Review* 24, no. 6 (November-December 1993): 15-16.

2444. Balcerowicz, Leszek. "Lessons and Consequences of the Left's Victory in Poland." *Transition* 4 (October-November 1993): 1-3.

2445. Baranczak, Stanislaw. "Eastern Europe: Grand Disillusion (Part 3)." *Salmagundi*, nos. 98-99 (Spring-Summer 1993): 18-27.

2446. Brzezinski, Mark F. "The Emergence of Judicial Review in Eastern Europe: The Case of Poland." *American Journal of Comparative Law* 41, no. 2 (Spring 1993): 153-200.

2447. ———. "Poland: Constitutionalism within Limits." *East European Constitutional Review* 2, no. 2 (Spring 1993): 38-43.

2448. Cala, Alina. "Antisemitism in Poland Today." *Patterns of Prejudice* 27, no. 1 (July 1993): 121-126.

2449. Cirtautas, Arista Maria, and Edmund Mokrzycki. "The Articulation and Institutionalization of Democracy in Poland." *Social Research* 60, no. 4 (Winter 1993): 787-819.

2450. Cline, Mary. "The Demographics of Party Support in Poland." *RFE/RL Research Report* 2, no. 36 (September 10, 1993): 17-21.

2451. Coughlan, Elizabeth P. "Martial Law in Poland: The Dynamics of Military Involvement in Politics." Ph.D. diss., Indiana University, 1993. [UMI order no: AAC 9323237.]

2452. Darnton, John. "Enormous Changes at the Last Minute." *New York Times Magazine* (June 13, 1993): 24ff.

2453. De Weydenthal, Jan B. "Polish Foreign Policy after the Elections." *RFE/RL Research Report* 2, no. 41 (October 15, 1993): 17-20.

2454. Dixon, Michael. "Fault Lines in Warsaw." *East European Constitutional Review* 2, no. 2 (Spring 1993): 54-57.

2455. Duffy, Diane M., John L. Sullivan, and Leonard A. Polakiewicz. "Patriotic Perspectives in Contemporary Poland: Conflict or Consensus?" *Polish Review* 38, no. 3 (1993): 259-298.

2456. Engelberg, Stephen. "Her Year of Living Dangerously." *New York Times Magazine* (September 12, 1993): 38ff. [On Prime Minister Hanna Suchocka.]

2457. Greer, Herb. "Eastern Europe Renascent: An Interview with Radek Sikorski." *World & I* 8, no. 12 (December 1993): 426-439.

2458. Jasiewicz, Krzysztof. "Polish Politics on the Eve of the 1993 Elections: Toward Fragmentation or Pluralism?" *Communist and Post-Communist Studies* 26, no. 4 (December 1993): 387-411.

2459. Kanet, Roger E., and Brian V. Souders. "Democratization and Local Government in Poland." *In Depth* 3, no. 1 (Winter 1993): 91-113.

2460. Karabel, Jerome. "Polish Intellectuals and the Origins of Solidarity: The Making of an Oppositional Alliance." *Communist and Post-Communist Studies* 26, no. 1 (March 1993): 25-46.

2461. Karpinski, Jakub. "Towards a Left Victory." *Uncaptive Minds* 6, no. 3 (24) (Fall 1993): 119-128.

2462. Kochanowicz, Jacek. "The Disappearing State: Poland's Three Years of Transition." *Social Research* 60, no. 4 (Winter 1993): 821-834.

2463. Krzeminski, Ireneusz. "Antisemitism in Today's Poland: Research Hypotheses." *Patterns of Prejudice* 27, no. 1 (July 1993): 127-135.

2464. Kurczewski, Jacek. *The Resurrection of Rights in Poland.* Oxford: Clarendon Press; New York: Oxford University Press, 1993. xix, 462 pp.

2465. Miklaszewska, Marta. "The Myth Factory." *Uncaptive Minds* 6, no. 2 (23) (Summer 1993): 37-42. [Article published in *Tygodnik Solidarnosc* no. 17 (April 23, 1993).]

2466. Nowak, Leszek. " 'Post-Communist Society'? An Attempt at a Theoretical Analysis." *Social Theory and Practice* 19, no. 3 (Fall 1993): 249-273.

2467. Olson, David M. "Compartmentalized Competition: The Managed Transitional Election System of Poland." *Journal of Politics* 55, no. 2 (May 1993): 415-441.

2468. Olszanska, Justyna, Robert Olszanski, and Jacek Wozniak. "Do Peaceful Conflict Management Methods Pose Problems in Posttotalitarian Poland?" *Mediation Quarterly* 10, no. 3 (Spring 1993): 291-302. Written in cooperation with Nela Szyszko-Oniszek, Yvonne Odrowaz-Pieniazek, and Rafael Stefanski.

2469. Osiatynski, Wiktor. "Lech Walesa: Profile and Interview." *East European Constitutional Review* 2, no. 4/vol. 3, no. 1 (Fall 1993-Winter 1994): 40-46. Interview translated by Krzysztof Moscicki. [Interview conducted October 12, 1993.]

2470. ———. "Wojciech Jaruzelski: Note and Interview." *East European Constitutional Review* 2, no. 4/vol. 3, no. 1 (Fall 1993-Winter 1994): 47-50. Interview translated by Krzysztof Moscicki. [Interview conducted October 7, 1993 in Warsaw.]

2471. Peretz, Martin. "Warsaw Diarist: Ghetto Politics." *New Republic* 208, no. 19 (May 10, 1993): 58.

2472. Rosenberg, Tina. "Meet the New Boss, Same As the Old Boss." *Harper's* 286, no. 1716 (May 1993): 47-53. ["How Poland's nomenklatura learned to love capitalism."]

2473. Rzeplinski, Andrzej. "The Polish Bill of Rights and Freedoms: A case study of constitution-making in Poland." *East European Constitutional Review* 2, no. 3 (Summer 1993): 26-29.

2474. ———. "Survey of Presidential Powers in Eastern Europe: Poland." *East European Constitutional Review* 2, no. 4/vol. 3, no. 1 (Fall 1993-Winter 1994): 71-75.

2475. Sabbat-Swidlicka, Anna. "Crisis in the Polish Justice Ministry." *RFE/RL Research Report* 2, no. 15 (April 9, 1993): 14-18. [Includes sidebar: "Jan Piatkowski," p. 18.]

2476. ———. "The Legacy of Poland's 'Solidarity' Governments." *RFE/RL Research Report* 2, no. 44 (November 5, 1993): 19-22.

2477. ———. "Pawlak to Head Poland's 'Postcommunist' Government." *RFE/RL Research Report* 2, no. 43 (October 29, 1993): 24-32.

2478. ———. "Poland: A Year of Three Governments." *RFE/RL Research Report* 2, no. 1 (January 1, 1993): 102-107.

2479. ———. "Poland's Agriculture Minister Resigns." *RFE/RL Research Report* 2, no. 19 (May 7, 1993): 10-13.

2480. ———. "The Polish Elections: The Church, the Right, and the Left." *RFE/RL Research Report* 2, no. 40 (October 8, 1993): 24-30.

2481. ———. "Questions about the Polish Security Police." *RFE/RL Research Report* 2, no. 39 (October 1, 1993): 16-20.

2482. ———. "Solidarity Parts Company with Walesa." *RFE/RL Research Report* 2, no. 31 (July 30, 1993): 1-6.

2483. Sikorski, Radek. "Lack of Solidarity." *National Review* 45, no. 20 (October 18, 1993): 28-30.

2484. Singer, Daniel. "Letter from Europe: Of Lobsters and Poles." *Nation* 257, no. 21 (December 20, 1993): 764-766.

2485. Stanosz, Barbara. "Emerging Democracy or Religious State?" *Uncaptive Minds* 6, no. 2 (23) (Summer 1993): 33-36.

2486. Sterbenz, Jolanta. "Modern Development of Polish Unemployment Law." *Comparative Labor Law Journal* 14, no. 2 (Winter 1993): 163-184.

2487. Tymowski, Andrzej. "The Unwanted Social Revolution: Poland in 1989." *East European Politics and Societies* 7, no. 2 (Spring 1993): 169-202.

2488. Vinton, Louisa. "Correcting Pilsudski: Walesa's Nonparty Bloc to Support Reform." *RFE/RL Research Report* 2, no. 35 (September 3, 1993): 1-9.

2489. ———. "Dissonance: Poland on the Eve of New Elections." *RFE/RL Research Report* 2, no. 33 (August 20, 1993): 1-7.

2490. ———. "Poland Goes Left." *RFE/RL Research Report* 2, no. 40 (October 8, 1993): 21-23.

2491. ———. "Poland: Governing without Parliament." *RFE/RL Research Report* 2, no. 26 (June 25, 1993): 6-12.

2492. ———. "Poland: Pawlak Builds a Cabinet, Kwasniewski Builds a Future." *RFE/RL Research Report* 2, no. 47 (November 26, 1993): 31-40. [Includes sidebars: "Key Officials in Poland," p. 33; and "Leszek Miller: A Political Profile," pp. 38-39.]

2493. ———. "Poland's New Election Law: Fewer Parties, Same Impasse?" *RFE/RL Research Report* 2, no. 28 (July 9, 1993): 7-17.

2494. ———. "Poland's New Government: Continuity or Reversal?" *RFE/RL Research Report* 2, no. 46 (November 19, 1993): 1-7.

2495. ———. "Poland's Political Spectrum on the Eve of the Elections." *RFE/RL Research Report* 2, no. 36 (September 10, 1993): 1-16.

2496. ———. "Walesa and the Collaboration Issue." *RFE/RL Research Report* 2, no. 6 (February 5, 1993): 10-17.

2497. ———. "Walesa Applies Political Shock Therapy." *RFE/RL Research Report* 2, no. 24 (June 11, 1993): 1-11.

2498. Walesa, Lech. "Poland's Great Communicator." *Harper's* 287, no. 1720 (September 1993): 16. [From an exchange published in *Gazeta Wyborcza* (March 26).]

2499. Zubek, Voytek. "The Fragmentation of Poland's Political Party System." *Communist and Post-Communist Studies* 26, no. 1 (March 1993): 47-71.

2500. Zuzowski, Robert. "Political Culture and Dissent: Why Were There Organizations like KOR in Poland?" *East European Quarterly* 27, no. 4 (Winter 1993): 503-522.

Romania

2501. Amnesty International. *Romania, Continuing Violations of Human Rights*. New York, NY: Amnesty International USA, [1993]. 12 pp.

2502. Blenesi, Eva. "Violence Breeds Violence." *Uncaptive Minds* 6, no. 1 (22) (Winter-Spring 1993): 41-44.

2503. Cartner, Holly. *Struggling for Ethnic Identity: Ethnic Hungarians in Post-Ceausescu Romania*. Edited by Lois Whitman. New York, NY: Human Rights Watch, 1993. vii, 142 pp. [Based on a series of missions that Helsinki Watch has conducted since January 1990.]

2504. Gallagher, Tom. "Ethnic Tension in Cluj." *RFE/RL Research Report* 2, no. 9 (February 26, 1993): 27-33.

2505. Harsanyi, Doina, and Nicolae Harsanyi. "Romania: Democracy and the Intellectuals." *East European Quarterly* 27, no. 2 (Summer 1993): 243-260.

2506. Ionescu, Dan. "Has Romania's Ruling Party Become Stronger or Weaker?" *RFE/RL Research Report* 2, no. 34 (August 27, 1993): 15-20.

2507. ———. "Romania Admitted to the Council of Europe." *RFE/RL Research Report* 2, no. 44 (November 5, 1993): 40-45.

2508. ———. "Romania's Liberals." *RFE/RL Research Report* 2, no. 22 (May 28, 1993): 22-27.

2509. ———. "Romania's Trade Unions Unite." *RFE/RL Research Report* 2, no. 28 (July 9, 1993): 56-59.

2510. "Key Officials in Romania." *RFE/RL Research Report* 2, no. 4 (January 22, 1993): 47.

2511. Maturo, Mike. "Communism's Staying Power in Romania." *World & I* 8, no. 5 (May 1993): 78-85.

2512. Mihok, Brigitte. "Minorities and Minority Policies in Romania since 1945." *Patterns of Prejudice* 27, no. 2 (October 1993): 81-93.

2513. "Minority Rights in Romania: A Roundtable Discussion." *Uncaptive Minds* 6, no. 1 (22) (Winter-Spring 1993): 23-38. [Featuring representatives of the UDMR; highlights are taken from the transcription published in *22* (November 12-18).]

2514. Montefiore, Simon Sebag. "Bucharest Postcard: Vampire City." *New Republic* 208, no. 12 (March 22, 1993): 14-15.

2515. Ratesh, Nestor. "Romania: Slamming on the Brakes." *Current History* 92, no. 577 (November 1993): 390-395.

2516. Shafir, Michael. " 'A Future for Romania' Group: Fish or Foul?" *RFE/RL Research Report* 2, no. 49 (December 10, 1993): 9-14.

2517. ———. "Best-Selling Spy Novels Seek to Rehabilitate Romanian *Securitate*." *RFE/RL Research Report* 2, no. 45 (November 12, 1993): 14-18.

2518. ———. "Growing Political Extremism in Romania." *RFE/RL Research Report* 2, no. 16 (April 16, 1993): 18-25.

2519. ———. "The HDFR Congress: Confrontations Postponed." *RFE/RL Research Report* 2, no. 9 (February 26, 1993): 34-39.

2520. ———. "Minorities Council Raises Questions." *RFE/RL Research Report* 2, no. 24 (June 11, 1993): 35-40.

2521. ———. "Romania: The Rechristening of the National Salvation Front." *RFE/RL Research Report* 2, no. 27 (July 2, 1993): 22-26.

2522. ———. "Romanian Prime Minister Announces Cabinet Changes." *RFE/RL Research Report* 2, no. 38 (September 24, 1993): 17-22. [Includes sidebar: "Key Officials in Romania," p. 18.]

2523. ———. "Romanians and the Transition to Democracy." *RFE/RL Research Report* 2, no. 18 (April 30, 1993): 42-48.

2524. ———. "Romania's Party of Civic Alliance in Disarray." *RFE/RL Research Report* 2, no. 35 (September 3, 1993): 16-22.

2525. Shafir, Michael, and Dan Ionescu. "Romania: Political Change and Economic Malaise." *RFE/RL Research Report* 2, no. 1 (January 1, 1993): 108-112.

2526. Stefoi, Elena. "Ion Iliescu: Profile and Interview." *East European Constitutional Review* 2, no. 4/ vol. 3, no. 1 (Fall 1993-Winter 1994): 51-58. [Interview conducted November 23, 1993 in Bucharest.]

2527. Tismaneanu, Vladimir. "The Quasi-Revolution and its Discontents: Emerging Political Pluralism in Post-Ceausescu Romania." *East European Politics and Societies* 7, no. 2 (Spring 1993): 309-348.

2528. Tismaneanu, Vladimir, and Dorin Tudoran. "The Bucharest Syndrome." *Journal of Democracy* 4, no. 1 (January 1993): 41-52.

2529. Vago, Raphael. "The Traditions of Antisemitism in Romania." *Patterns of Prejudice* 27, no. 1 (July 1993): 107-119.

2530. Verdery, Katherine. "Nationalism and National Sentiment in Post-Socialist Romania." *Slavic Review* 52, no. 2 (Summer 1993): 179-203.

(Former) Yugoslavia

2531. Ajami, Fouad. "The Summoning." *Foreign Affairs* 72, no. 4 (September-October 1993): 2-9.

2532. Bernstein, Alvin H. "Ethnicity and Imperial Break-up: Ancient and Modern." *SAIS Review* 13, no. 1 (Winter-Spring 1993): 121-132.

2533. Binder, David. "Where Did the Yugoslav Experiment Go Wrong?" *Mediterranean Quarterly* 4, no. 3 (Summer 1993): 30-40.

2534. Burg, Steven L. "Why Yugoslavia Fell Apart." *Current History* 92, no. 577 (November 1993): 357-363.

2535. Butler, Thomas. "Yugoslavia Mon Amour." *Wilson Quarterly* 17, no. 1 (Winter 1993): 118-125.

2536. Cohen, Lenard J. "Yugoslavia's Pluralist Revolution: The Democratic Prelude to Civil War." *In Depth* 3, no. 1 (Winter 1993): 115-149.

2537. Critchley, W. Harriet. "The failure of federalism in Yugoslavia." *International Journal* 48, no. 3 (Summer 1993): 434-447.

2538. Garvey, John. "Between Dracula & Bovary." *Commonweal* 120, no. 10 (May 21, 1993): 7-8. [On Yugoslavian nationalism.]

2539. Kull, Steve. *U.S. Public Opinion on Intervention in Bosnia*. College Park, MD: Program on International Policy Attitudes, University of Maryland, 1993. 26 pp.

2540. Magas, Branka. *The Destruction of Yugoslavia: Tracking the Break-up, 1980-92*. London; New York: Verso, 1993. xxv, 366 pp. REV: Ivo Banac, *Foreign Policy*, no. 93 (December 1993-1994): 173-182. W.W. F. [William W. Finan, Jr.], *Current History* 92, no. 577 (November 1993): 396. Michael Ignatieff, *New York Review of Books* 40, no. 9 (May 13, 1993): 3-5. Michael Scammell, *Book World* 23, no. 17 (April 25, 1993): 6.

2541. Markotich, Stan. "Vojvodina: A Potential Powder Keg." *RFE/RL Research Report* 2, no. 46 (November 19, 1993): 13-18.

2542. Necak, Dusan. "A Chronology of the Decay of Tito's Yugoslavia, 1980-1991." *Nationalities Papers* 21, no. 1 (Spring 1993): 173-187.

2543. Schmidt, Fabian. "Kosovo: The Time Bomb That Has Not Gone Off." *RFE/RL Research Report* 2, no. 39 (October 1, 1993): 21-29.

2544. Sekelj, Laslo. "Antisemitism and Nationalist Conflicts in the Former Yugoslavia." *Patterns of Prejudice* 27, no. 2 (October 1993): 63-80.

2545. Tupurkovski, Vasil. "The Dissolution of Yugoslavia: An Insider's View." *Mediterranean Quarterly* 4, no. 2 (Spring 1993): 14-25.

2546. Varady, Tibor, and Nenad Dimitrijevic. "Survey of Presidential Powers in Eastern Europe: Ex-Yugoslavia." *East European Constitutional Review* 2, no. 4/ vol. 3, no. 1 (Fall 1993-Winter 1994): 75-81.

Bosnia and Herzegovina

2547. Andrejevich, Milan. "The Bosnian Muslim Leader Fikret Abdic." *RFE/RL Research Report* 2, no. 40 (October 8, 1993): 16-20.

2548. Glenny, Misha. "The Godfather of Bihac." *New York Review of Books* 40, no. 14 (August 12, 1993): 18-19.

2549. Remington, Robin Alison. "Bosnia: The Tangled Web." *Current History* 92, no. 577 (November 1993): 364-369.

Croatia

2550. Bicanic, Ivo, and Iva Dominis. "The Multiparty Elections in Croatia: Round Two." *RFE/RL Research Report* 2, no. 19 (May 7, 1993): 17-21. [Includes sidebar: "Key Officials in the Republic of Croatia," p. 18.]

2551. Bjorken, Johanna. "Opposition in Wartime." *Uncaptive Minds* 6, no. 3 (24) (Fall 1993): 71-79. [Interview with Drazen Budisa, president of the Croatian Social Liberal Party (HSLS), the largest opposition party in Croatia.]

2552. Budisa, Drazen. "Opposition in Wartime." *Uncaptive Minds* 6, no. 3 (24) (Fall 1993): 71-79.

2553. Cviic, Christopher. "Croatia's Violent Birth." *Current History* 92, no. 577 (November 1993): 370-375.

2554. Drakulic, Slavenka. "Falling Down." *New Republic* 209, no. 24 (December 13, 1993): 14-15.

2555. ———. "Letter from Croatia." *Partisan Review* 60, no. 3 (Summer 1993): 377-386.

2556. ———. "Nazis Among Us." *New York Review of Books* 40, no. 10 (May 27, 1993): 21-22. [On the renaming of streets in Zagreb, Croatia.]

2557. Markotich, Stan. "Istria Seeks Autonomy." *RFE/RL Research Report* 2, no. 36 (September 10, 1993): 22-26.

2558. Plestina, Dijana. *Politics, Economics and War: Problems of Transition in Contemporary Croatia.* Working Paper (University of California, Berkeley. Center for German and European Studies), 5.15. Berkeley, CA: Center for German and European Studies, University of California, [1993]. 27 pp. [Conference on Markets, States, and Democracy, February 11-13, 1993.]

2559. Rieff, David. "Croatia: A Crisis of Meaning." *World Policy Journal* 10, no. 2 (Summer 1993): 41-45.

2560. Smerdel, Branko. "Extraconstitutional Developments in the Republic of Croatia." *East European Constitutional Review* 2, no. 4/vol. 3, no. 1 (Fall 1993-Winter 1994): 34-35. [Describes program of the Croatian Democratic Community's general convention in Zagreb, October 15-16, 1993.]

2561. United States. Congress. Commission on Security and Cooperation in Europe. *Human Rights and Democratization in Croatia.* Implementation of the Helsinki Accords. Washington, DC: The Commission, [1993]. vi, 26 pp.

Macedonia

2562. "Macedonia Must Be Free." *Uncaptive Minds* 6, no. 3 (24) (Fall 1993): 81-89. [Interview with Ljupco Georgievski, president of the VMRO-Democratic Party for Macedonian National Unity, the largest Macedonian opposition party.]

2563. Perry, Duncan M. "Politics in the Republic of Macedonia: Issues and Parties." *RFE/RL Research Report* 2, no. 23 (June 4, 1993): 31-37.

2564. Poulton, Hugh. "The Republic of Macedonia after UN Recognition." *RFE/RL Research Report* 2, no. 23 (June 4, 1993): 22-30.

2565. ———. "The Roma in Macedonia: A Balkan Success Story?" *RFE/RL Research Report* 2, no. 19 (May 7, 1993): 42-45.

Serbia

2566. Andrejevich, Milan. "The Radicalization of Serbian Politics." *RFE/RL Research Report* 2, no. 13 (March 26, 1993): 14-24.

2567. Canak, Branislav. "The Power and the Powerless: The Media in Serbia." *Uncaptive Minds* 6, no. 2 (23) (Summer 1993): 81-87. [Part of a special survey on the media in Eastern Europe.]

2568. Djilas, Aleksa. "A Profile of Slobodan Milosevic." *Foreign Affairs* 72, no. 3 (Summer 1993): 81-96.

2569. "Documents on Democracy." *Journal of Democracy* 4, no. 3 (July 1993): 134-139. [Includes excerpts from acceptance speech of Vesna Pesic, receiving the National Endowment for Democracy's Democracy Award, in a ceremony April 27, 1993, in Washington, DC (pp. 135-137).]

2570. Hall, Brian. "A Holy War in Waiting." *New York Times Magazine* (May 9, 1993): 22ff. ["The Serbs view Kosovo as their Jerusalem. How long before it becomes their next target?"]

2571. Inic, Slobodan. "Serbia's Historic Defeat." *New Politics* 4, no. 3 (Summer 1993): 161-166.

2572. Kesic, Obrad. "Serbia: The Politics of Despair." *Current History* 92, no. 577 (November 1993): 376-380.

2573. "Key Officials in the Republic of Serbia." *RFE/RL Research Report* 2, no. 13 (March 26, 1993): 19.

2574. Markotich, Stan. "Serbia Prepares for Elections." *RFE/RL Research Report* 2, no. 49 (December 10, 1993): 15-20.

2575. Matic, Veran, and Ivo Skoric. "B92: Struggling for Air." *Uncaptive Minds* 6, no. 3 (24) (Fall 1993): 95-105. [Conversation between Matic of B92, an independent radio station in Belgrade, and Skoric, his former colleague.]

2576. Nincic, Roksanda. "The Toothless Second Serbia." *Uncaptive Minds* 6, no. 3 (24) (Fall 1993): 91-93. [Article published in *Vreme* (Belgrad) (August 23).]

2577. Rosenberger, Chandler. "Serbian Tightrope." *National Review* 45, no. 2 (February 1, 1993): 22ff.

2578. Schoen, Douglas E. "How Milosevic Stole the Election." *New York Times Magazine* (February 14, 1993): 32ff.

Slovenia

2579. Balkovec, Bojan. "Political Parties in Slovenia." *Nationalities Papers* 21, no. 1 (Spring 1993): 189-192.

2580. Bibic, Adolf. "The Emergence of Pluralism in Slovenia." *Communist and Post-Communist Studies* 26, no. 4 (December 1993): 367-386.

2581. Cohen, Lenard J. "Slovenia: A New Equilibrium." *In Depth* 3 (Winter 1993): 120-125. [From author's *Yugoslavia's Pluralist Revolution: The Democratic Prelude to Civil War.*]

2582. Hribar, Valentin. "Slovene Statehood." *Nationalities Papers* 21, no. 1 (Spring 1993): 43-49.

2583. Huttenbach, Henry R. "Editorial Note: *Quo Vadis* Slovenia? 'The (Re)Birth of a Nation' (Re)Imagined." *Nationalities Papers* 21, no. 1 (Spring 1993): 3-4.

2584. "Key Officials in the Federal Republic of Yugoslavia." *RFE/RL Research Report* 2, no. 13 (March 26, 1993): 22.

2585. Klemencic, Matjaz. "Slovenia at the Crossroads of the Nineties: From the First Multiparty Elections and Declaration of Independence to Membership in the Council of Europe." *Slovene Studies* 14, no. 1 (1992, published March 1994): 9-34.

2586. Rupel, Dimitrij. "Slovenia in Post-Modern Europe." *Nationalities Papers* 21, no. 1 (Spring 1993): 51-59.

2587. Tos, Niko. "Democratization Processes in Slovenia, 1980-1990." *Nationalities Papers* 21, no. 1 (Spring 1993): 61-69.

8 History

■ General

2588. Brody, Ervin C. "Early Echoes of Panslavism in Lope de Vega's *El Gran Duque de Moscovia y Emperador Perseguido*." *Polish Review* 38, no. 4 (1993): 421-439.

2589. Hagen, William. *Before the "Final Solution": Toward a Comparative Analysis of Political Anti-Semitism in Interwar Germany and Poland*. Working Paper (University of California, Berkeley. Center for German and European Studies), 3.7. Berkeley, CA: Center for German and European Studies, University of California, [1993]. 44 pp.

2590. Hertzberg, Arthur. "Is Anti-Semitism Dying Out?" *New York Review of Books* 40, no. 12 (June 24, 1993): 51-57. [Review article on Robert S. Wistrich, *Anti-Semitism: The Longest Hatred* (NY: 1991); Leon Poliakov, *The History of Anti-Semitism* (London: 1974-1985); Joel Carmichael, *The Satanizing of the Jews: Origin and Development of Mystical Anti-Semitism* (NY: 1992); "*Foreigners Out*": *Xenophobia and Right-wing Violence in Germany* (NY: 1992); *Highlights from an Anti-Defamation League Survey on Anti-Semitism and Prejudice in America* (1992); Jennifer L. Golub, *What Do We Know About Black Anti-Semitism?* (NY: 1990); Renae Cohen and Jennifer L. Golub, *Attitudes Toward Jews in Poland, Hungary, and Czechoslovakia* (NY: 1991); and Lev Gudkov and Alex Levinson, *Attitudes Toward Jews in the Soviet Union: Public Opinion in Ten Republics* (NY: 1992).]

2591. Hryniuk, Stella. "Polish Lords and Ukrainian Peasants: Conflict, Deference, and Accommodation in Eastern Galicia in the Late Nineteenth Century." *Austrian History Yearbook*, no. 24 (1993): 119-132.

2592. Lieven, Dominic. *The Aristocracy in Europe, 1815-1914*. New York: Columbia University Press, 1993. xxiv, 308 pp.

2593. Lukacs, John. "The End of the Twentieth Century." *Harper's* 286, no. 1712 (January 1993): 39-58. ["Historical reflections on a misunderstood epoch."]

2594. ———. *The End of the Twentieth Century and the End of the Modern Age*. New York: Ticknor & Fields, 1993. 291 pp. REV: John B. Judis, *Book World* 23, no. 13 (March 28, 1993): 1. Charles E. Clark, *History Teacher* 27, no. 1 (November 1993): 95-96. Ronald Hamowy, *Canadian Journal of History = Annales canadienne d'histoire* 28, no. 2 (August 1993): 391.

2595. Rothschild, Joseph. *Return to Diversity: A Political History of East Central Europe Since World War II*. 2nd ed. New York: Oxford University Press, 1993. xii, 299 pp. [Chapter 6 has been revised; Chapter 7 and the Epilogue are new. Contents: 1. The Interwar Background; 2. World War II; 3. The Communists Come to Power; 4. The Dialectics of Stalinism and Titoism; 5. The Revenge of the Repressed: East Central Europe Reasserts Itself; 6. A Precarious Stalemate; 7. The Various Endgames; 8. Epilogue.]

2596. Simpson, Christopher. *The Splendid Blond Beast: Money, Law, and Genocide in the Twentieth Century*. 1st ed. New York: Grove Press, 1993. x, 399 pp. [Contents: 1. The Splendid Blond Beast; 2. "The Immediate Demands of Justice"; 3. Young Turks; 4. Bankers, Lawyers, and Linkage Groups; 5. The Profits of Persecution; 6. "Who Still Talks of the Armenians?"; 7. No Action Required; 8. Katyn; 9. Silk Stocking Rebel; 10. "The Present Ruling Class of Germany"; 11. The Trials Begin; 12. Morgenthau's Plan; 13. "This Needs to Be Dragged Out into the Open"; 14. Sunrise; 15. White Lists; 16. Prisoner Transfers; 17. Double-Think on Denazification; 18. "It Would Be Undesirable If This Became Publicly Known"; 19. The End of the War Crimes Commission; 20. Money, Law, and Genocide.] REV: Andrew J. Pierre, *Foreign Affairs* 72, no. 3 (Summer 1993): 194.

2597. Spencer, Thomas T. [Book Review]. *History Teacher* 26, no. 3 (May 1993): 389-391. [Review article on Stephen Padgett and William Patterson, *A History of Social Democracy in Postwar Europe* (NY: 1991); and Peter Calvocoressi, *Resilient Europe: A Study of the Years 1870-2000* (NY: 1991).]

■ Historiography

2598. Bassin, Mark. "Turner, Solov'ev, and the 'Frontier Hypothesis': The Nationalist Signification of Open Spaces." *Journal of Modern History* 65, no. 3 (September 1993): 473-511.

2599. Bess, Michael D. "E. P. Thompson: The Historian as Activist." *American Historical Review* 98, no. 1 (February 1993): 18-38.

2600. Burbank, Jane. "Revisioning Imperial Russia." *Slavic Review* 52, no. 3 (Fall 1993): 555-567. [Report of the workshop "Reconstructing the History of Imperial Russia," held at the University of Iowa in November 1991.]

2601. Byrnes, Robert F. "Kliuchevskii's View of the Flow of Russian History." *Review of Politics* 55, no. 4 (Fall 1993): 565-591.

2602. Friedländer, Saul. *Memory, History, and the Extermination of the Jews of Europe*. Bloomington, IN: Indiana University Press, c1993. xiv, 142 p. [Contents: German Struggles with Memory; A Conflict of Memories? The New German Debates about the "Final Solution"; The Shoah in Present Historical Consciousness; Reflections on the Historicization of National Socialism; Martin Broszat and the Historicization of National Socialism; The "Final Solution": On the Unease in Historical Interpretation; Trauma and Transference.]

2603. Gleason, William. "The Second Annual Seminar of Russian and American Historians: A Report." *East/West Education* 14, no. 1 (Spring 1993): 69-73.

2604. Kozicki, Henry, ed. *Western and Russian Historiography: Recent Views.* Introduced by Sidney Monas. Contributions by Sidney Monas, Ernst A. Breisach, B. G. Mogilnitsky, Geoffrey Elton, Peter Munz, A. I. Rakitov, A. V. Margulis, Yuri K. Pletnikov, V. N. Sagatovsky, Nikolai N. Bolkhovitinov, A. N. Sakharov, and Juhan Kahk. New York: St. Martin's Press, 1993. x, 218 pp. [Contents: Sidney Monas, "Introduction: History Problems," pp. 1-22; Ernst A. Breisach, "The American Quest for a New History: Observations on Developments and Trends," pp. 25-44; B. G. Mogilnitsky, "Some Tendencies in the Development of Contemporary Bourgeois Historical Thought," pp. 45-70; Geoffrey Elton, "Comment on B. G. Mogilnitsky," pp. 71-79; Peter Munz, "A Reasoned Reply to Professor Mogilnitsky's Moves," pp. 80-105; A. I. Rakitov, "Historical Process and Truth in History," pp. 109-123; A. V. Margulis, "The Subject of the Historical Process," pp. 124-137; Yuri K. Pletnikov, "A Philosophical Interpretation of the Historical Process: An Instance of Substantiantion of the Marxist Approach," pp. 138-157; V. N. Sagatovsky, "The Whole-Interactive Approach to Philosophy of History: A Criticism of Reductional Monism and Asystem Pluralism," pp. 158-175; Nikolai N. Bolkhovitinov, "New Thinking and the Study of American History in the USSR," [title on p. 179: "New Thinking and the Study of the History of the United States in the USSR"] pp. 179-190; A. N. Sakharov, "Soviet Historiography: Modern Trends," pp. 191-205; Juhan Kahk, "The 'Neutral Territory' of Mathematical Models: Collaboration between Soviet and American Historians," pp. 206-213.]

2605. Krauss, H. Alexander. *Die Rolle Preussens in Der DDR-Historiographie: zur Thematisierung und Interpretation der preussischen Geschichte durch die ostdeutsche Geschichtswissenschaft.* Mit Einem Geleitwort von Dieter Stievermann. Europäische Hochschulschriften. Reihe III, Geschichte und ihre Hilfswissenschaften = European University Studies. Series III, History and Allied Studies, 544. Frankfurt am Main; New York: P. Lang, c1993. 155 pp.

2606. Marples, David R. "New Interpretations of Ukrainian History." *RFE/RL Research Report* 2, no. 11 (March 12, 1993): 57-61.

2607. McClarnand, Elaine. "The Debate Continues: Views on Stalinism from the Former Soviet Union." *Soviet and Post-Soviet Review* 20, no. 1 (1993): 11-34.

2608. Nothnagle, Alan. "From Buchenwald to Bismarck: Historical Myth-Building in the German Democratic Republic, 1945-1989." *Central European History* 26, no. 1 (1993): 91-113.

2609. Pearson, Raymond. "Fact, Fantasy, Fraud: Perceptions and Projections of National Revival." *Ethnic*

Groups 10, nos. 1-3 (1993): 43-64. [Part of special issue devoted to "Pre-Modern and Modern National Identity in Russia and Eastern Europe."]

2610. Siegelbaum, Lewis, and Ronald Grigor Suny. "Making the Command Economy: Western Historians on Soviet Industrialization." *International Labor and Working Class History*, no. 43 (Spring 1993): 65-76.

2611. Valkenier, Elizabeth Kridl. "Stalinizing Polish Historiography: What Soviet Archives Disclose." *East European Politics and Societies* 7, no. 1 (Winter 1993): 109-134.

2612. Velychenko, Stephen. *Shaping Identity in Eastern Europe and Russia: Soviet-Russian and Polish Accounts of Ukrainian History, 1914-1991.* New York: St. Martin's Press, 1993. 266 pp. [Contents: Pt. I. Background and Context. 1. Nations, States, and History. 2. The Institutions and the Ideology. 3. Delineating the Past — Pt. II. Polish Historiography. 4. Neoromanticism and Positivism (1914-1944). 5. The Imposed Continuity (1944-1982). 6. Monographs and Articles on Ukrainian Subjects — Pt. III. Soviet-Russian Historiography. 7. Degrees of Inclusion, Exclusion, and Affinity. 8. The History of the Ukrainian SSR (1948-1982). 9. Deductivist Discourse and Research — Appendix: Perestroika and Interpretation.]

■ Byzantine Empire

2613. Knysh, George. "The Crimean Roots of Ancient Ukrainian Statehood." *Ukrainian Quarterly* 49, no. 3 (Fall 1993): 294-317.

2614. Meyendorff, John. "Continuities and Discontinuities in Byzantine Religious Thought." *Dumbarton Oak Papers*, no. 47 (1993): 69-81.

■ Ottoman Empire

2615. Amirian, Thomas T. "The Epochal Defense of Van." *Ararat* 34, no. 2 (no. 134) (Spring 1993): 2-10.

2616. Blaum, Paul A. "The Coming of the Turks." *Ararat* 34, no. 3 (no. 135) (Summer 1993): 9-21.

2617. Dadrian, Vahakn N. "The Secret Young Turk Ittihadist Conference and the Decision for the World War I Genocide of the Armenians." *Holocaust and Genocide Studies* 7, no. 2 (Fall 1993): 173-201. [Article presents and analyzes a Turkish World War I document regarding the genocide of the Armenians in the Ottoman Empire.]

2618. Gounaris, Basil C. "Salonica." *Review* (Fernand Braudel Center) 16, no. 4 (Fall 1993): 499-518. [Part of special issue devoted to "Port-Cities of the Eastern Mediterranean 1800-1914."]

2619. Hupchick, Dennis P. *The Bulgarians in the Seventeenth Century: Slavic Orthodox Society and Culture under Ottoman Rule.* Jefferson, NC: McFarland, c1993. xxvii, 314 pp.

2620. Katchadourian, Stina. *Efronia: An Armenian Love Story*. Translated by Herant Katchadourian. Women's Life Writings from Around the World. Boston, MA: Northeastern University Press, c1993. xviii, 221 pp. [Based on an unpublished memoir by Efronia Katchadourian translated by Herant Katchadourian.]

2621. Keyder, Caglar, Y. Eyüp Ozveren, and Donald Quataert. "Port-Cities in the Ottoman Empire: Some Theoretical and Historical Perspectives." *Review* (Fernand Braudel Center) 16, no. 4 (Fall 1993): 519-558. [Part of special issue devoted to "Port-Cities of the Eastern Mediterranean 1800-1914."]

2622. Miller, Donald E., and Lorna Touryan Miller. *Survivors: An Oral History of the Armenian Genocide*. Berkeley, CA: University of California Press, c1993. xii, 242 pp. [Contents: Pt. I. Historical Background. 1. Remembrances of a Forgotten Genocide. 2. The Historical and Political Context of the Genocide. Pt. II. Survivor Accounts. 3. Life and Politics Before the Deportations. 4. The Deportation Marches. 5. The Experience of Women and Children. 6. Orphanage Life and Family Reunions. 7. Emigration and Resettlement. Pt. III. Analysis. 8. Survivor Responses to the Genocide. 9. Moral Reflections on the Genocide; Appendix A: Methodology; Appendix B: Interview Guide; Appendix C: Survivors Interviewed.] REV: Eileen Barker, *Journal for the Scientific Study of Religion* 32, no. 4 (December 1993): 422. Joseph W. Constance, Jr., *Library Journal* 118, no. 8 (May 1, 1993): 100. Firuz Kazemzadeh, *New York Times Book Review* 98, no. 17 (April 25, 1993): 13-14.

2623. Salt, Jeremy. *Imperialism, Evangelism, and the Ottoman Armenians, 1878-1896*. London; Portland, OR: F. Cass, 1993. 188 pp.

2624. Salzmann, Ariel. "An *Ancien Regime* Revisited: 'Privatization' and Political Economy in the Eighteenth-Century Ottoman Empire." *Politics & Society* 21, no. 4 (December 1993): 393-423.

2625. Todorova, Maria N. *Balkan Family Structure and the European Pattern: Demographic Developments in Ottoman Bulgaria*. Washington, DC: American University Press; Lanham, MD: University Pub. Associates, c1993. xii, 251 pp. [Contents: I. Introduction: Rethinking the Unknown; II. Population Structure. Age Structure. Sex Structure; III. Marriage and Nuptiality. The Marriage Ritual and Seasonal Patterns of Marriage. Age at Marriage. Remarriage, Cross-Kin Marriages, and Other Characteristics; IV. Birth and Fertility. Births, Baptisms, and Their Registration. Measurements of Fertility. Twins in a Closed Population; V. Death and Mortality. Gender and Age-Specific Mortality. Seasonal Patterns of Mortality and Causes of Death; VI. Family and Household Size and Structure. Family and Household Structure. Family and Household Size. Inheritance Patterns; VII. The Problem of the South Slav Zadruga. Distribution and Development of the Zadruga in the Balkans. An Alternative Explanation; VIII. Conclusion: A Hypothesis of Converging Theories; App. I. The Sources; App. II. The Liber Status Animarum of

Seldzhikovo; App. III. Note on the Plague; App. IV. A Marriage Contract.]

■ The Holocaust

2626. Alexander, Edward. "What the Holocaust Does *Not* Teach." *Commentary* 95, no. 2 (February 1993): 32-36. [Review article on Lucy S. Dawidowicz, *What is the Use of Jewish History? Essays* (NY: 1992); Christopher R. Browning, *Ordinary Men: Reserve Police Battalion 101 and the Final Solution in Poland* (NY: 1992); and Raul Hilberg, *The Destruction of the European Jews* (Chicago, IL: 1961) and Raul Hilberg, *Perpetrators, Victims, Bystanders: The Jewish Catastrophe, 1933-1945* (NY: 1992).]

2627. Amishai-Maisels, Ziva. *Depiction and Interpretation: The Influence of the Holocaust on the Visual Arts*. 1st ed. Holocaust Series. Oxford; New York: Pergamon Press, 1993. xxxiii, 567 pp., [144] pp. of plates. [Partial contents: Pt. I. Depiction. 1. I Am a Camera. 2. On the Run. 3. Mass Murder into Art. 4. The Six Million. 5. Resistance and Liberation; Intermezzo: From Depiction to Interpretation. Pt. II. Interpretation. 1. Primary Holocaust Symbols. 2. Biblical Imagery. 3. The Crucified Jew. 4. Of Myths and Monsters. 5. Distance through Abstraction. 6. Jewish Identity. 7. Conclusions in the Aftermath.]

2628. Ancel, Jean. "The 'Christian' Regimes of Romania and the Jews, 1940-1942." *Holocaust and Genocide Studies* 7, no. 1 (Spring 1993): 14-29.

2629. Angele, E. D., comp. *Remembering the Past: National Socialism in Germany and the Holocaust: A Selective Bibliography of Books, Articles, and Audio-Visual Materials*. Chicago, IL: Goethe-Institute Chicago Library, c1993. 126 pp.

2630. Aronsfeld, C. C. "A German Neo-Nazi." *Congress Monthly* 60, no. 7 (November-December 1993): 11.

2631. Baider, Lea, Tamar Peretz, and Atara Kaplan De-Nour. "Holocaust Cancer Patients: A Comparative Study." *Psychiatry* 56, no. 4 (November 1993): 349-355.

2632. Bar-On, Dan. "First Encounter Between Children of Survivors and Children of Perpetrators of the Holocaust." *Journal of Humanistic Psychology* 33, no. 4 (Fall 1993): 6-14. [Description of workshop held in Wuppertal, Germany, June 18-21, 1992.]

2633. Baum, Phil. "The Demjanjuk Decision of the U.S. Court of Appeals." *Congress Monthly* 60, no. 6 (September-October 1993): 4.

2634. Berenbaum, Michael. *The World Must Know: The History of the Holocaust As Told in the United States Holocaust Memorial Museum*. Photograph editor Arnold Kramer. 1st ed. Boston: Little, Brown, c1993. xv, 240 pp.

2635. Berkley, George E. *Hitler's Gift: The Story of Theresienstadt*. Boston, MA: Branden Books, c1993. 308 pp.

2636. Birnbaum, Meyer, and Yonason Rosenblum. *Lieutenant Birnbaum: A Soldier's Story: Growing up Jewish in America, Liberating the D.P. Camps, and a New Home in

Jerusalem. 1st ed. ArtScroll History Series. Brooklyn, NY: Mesorah Publications, c1993. xiv, 263 pp.

2637. Blondo, Richard A., and Wynell Burroughs Schamel. "Teaching with Documents: Correspondence Urging Bombing of Auschwitz during World War II." *Social Education* 57, no. 4 (April-May 1993): 150-155.

2638. Blum, Debra E. "A Holocaust Survivor Breathes Life into a Destroyed Past." *Chronicle of Higher Education* 39, no. 34 (April 28, 1993): A5.

2639. B'nai B'rith. Anti-Defamation League. *Hitler's Apologists: The Anti-Semitic Propaganda of Holocaust "Revisionism"*. New York: Anti-Defamation League, 1993. 86 pp.

2640. Bolchover, Richard. *British Jewry and the Holocaust*. Cambridge; New York: Cambridge University Press, 1993. xi, 208 pp.

2641. Borch, Fred L. "The Anatomy of the Nuremberg Trials [Book Review]." *Military Law Review*, no. 142 (Fall 1993): 191-193. [Review article on Telford Taylor, *The Anatomy of the Nuremberg Trials* (New York: Alfred Knopf, 1992).]

2642. Borin, Jacqueline. "Embers of the Soul: The Destruction of Jewish Books and Libraries in Poland during World War II." *Libraries & Culture* 28, no. 4 (Fall 1993): 445-460.

2643. Breznitz, Shlomo. *Memory Fields*. 1st ed. New York: Knopf, 1993. x, 179 pp. [Issued in Hebrew as: *Sedot ha-zikaron*.] REV: Wendy Smith, *Book World* 23, no. 1 (January 3, 1993): 4. *New Yorker* 68, no. 9 (April 19, 1993): 119.

2644. Burns, Richard. "A Grove of Trees and a Grove of Stones." *North Dakota Quarterly* 61, no. 1 (Winter 1993): 36-39.

2645. Bush, Jonathan A. "Nuremberg: The Modern Law of War and its Limitations." *Columbia Law Review* 93, no. 8 (December 1993): 2022-2085. [Review article on Telford Taylor, *The Anatomy of the Nuremberg Trials: A Personal Memoir* (New York: Alfred Knopf, 1992).]

2646. Butnaru, I. C. *Waiting for Jerusalem: Surviving the Holocaust in Romania*. Contributions to the Study of World History, no. 37. Westport, CT: Greenwood Press, 1993. xiii, 264 pp.

2647. Cargas, Harry James. *Voices from the Holocaust*. Interviews with Arnost Lusting, Simon Wiesenthal, Yitzhak Arad, Mordecai Paldiel, Jan Karski, Marion Pritchard, Leon Wells, Whitney Harris, Leo Eitinger, Dorothee Soelle, Emil Fackenheim, and Elie Wiesel. Lexington, KY: University Press of Kentucky, c1993. xix, 164 pp.

2648. Cole, Diane. "A Sudden Spate of Women's Holocaust Memoirs." *Lilith* 18, no. 1 (Winter 1993): 26-28. [Review article on Liana Millu, *Smoke over Birkenau* (Philadelphia, PA: 1991); Adina Blady Szwajger, *I Remember Nothing More: The Warsaw Children's Hospital and the Jewish Resistance* (NY: 1992); and Annette Kahn, *Why My Father Died: A Daughter Confronts Her Family's Past at the Trial of Klaus Barbie* (NY: 1992).]

2649. Colombat, Andre Pierre. *The Holocaust in French Film*. Filmmakers Series, no. 33. Metuchen, NJ: Scarecrow Press, 1993. xx, 435 pp. [Contents: Pt. I. The Evolution of the Representation of the Holocaust. 1. Persecution in the "Golden Age" of French Cinema, 1940-1945. 2. Deportation, Resistance and Betrayal, 1946-1961. 3. Nazis, Collaborators and the Holocaust, 1961-1970. 4. The Struggle for Accuracy, 1971-1985. 5. Facing the Future; Fighting Oblivion, 1983-present. Pt. II. Cinematographic Studies. 6. Alain Resnais' Night and Fog. a. Images to Be Seen. b. Words to Be Heard. c. The Art of Alain Resnais. 7. Marcel Ophuls. a. The Sorrow and the Pity. A Chronicle. Disjunctions, Distortions and Irony. The Art of Marcel Ophuls. b. The Memory of Justice. c. Hotel Terminus. How to Tell the Life of a Nazi. Irony and the Official Story. 8. Ambiguity and Mastery in Three Renowned Fiction Films. a. Louis Malle's Lacombe Lucien and Goodbye Children. b. Joseph Losey's Mr. Klein. 9. Claude Lanzmann's Shoah. a. This Is the Place. b. To Know and to See. 10. Pierre Sauvage's Weapons of the Spirit; Appendix: An Interview with Pierre Sauvage; Filmography: pp. 389-395.]

2650. David ben Majer. *They Say It Never Happened*. 1st ed. Harrison, NY: Koegel Enterprises, 1993. xii, 340 pp.

2651. Deák, István. "Misjudgment in Nuremberg." *New York Review of Books* 40, no. 16 (October 7, 1993): 46-52. [Review article on Telford Taylor, *The Anatomy of the Nuremberg Trials: A Personal Memoir* (NY: 1992); Edward Alexander, *A Crime of Vengeance: An Armenian Struggle for Justice* (NY: 1991); Stephen A. Garrett, *Ethics and Airpower in World War II: The British Bombing of German Cities* (NY: 1993); and Alain Finkielkraut, *Remembering in Vain: The Klaus Barbie Trial and Crimes Against Humanity* (NY: 1992).]

2652. Dobroszycki, Lucjan, and Jeffrey S. Gurock, eds. *The Holocaust in the Soviet Union: Studies and Sources on the Destruction of the Jews in the Nazi-Occupied Territories of the USSR, 1941-1945*. Foreword by Richard Pipes. Contributions by Zvi Gitelman, Lukasz Hirszowicz, William Korey, Mordechai Altshuler, Rafael Medoff, David Engel, Dalia Ofer, Jan Gross, Andrzej Zbikowski, Gertrude Schneider, Zvi Kolitz, Sergei Maksudov, Lucjan Dobroszycki, Robert Moses Shapiro, and Simon Schochet. Armonk, NY: M.E. Sharpe, c1993. xii, 260 pp. [Contents: Richard Pipes, "Foreword," pp. vii-viii. Pt. 1. The Holocaust in the Soviet Union. Zvi Gitelman, "Soviet Reactions to the Holocaust, 1945-1991," pp. 3-27; Lukasz Hirszowicz, "The Holocaust in the Soviet Mirror," pp. 29-59; William Korey, "A Monument Over Babi Yar?" pp. 61-74. Pt. 2. Soviet Policies During the Holocaust. Mordechai Altshuler, "Escape and Evacuation of Soviet Jews at the Time of the Nazi Invasion: Policies and Realities," pp. 77-104; Rafael Medoff, "A Soviet View of Palestine on the Eve of the Holocaust," pp. 105-109; David Engel, "Soviet Jewry in the Thinking of the Yishuv Leadership, 1939-1943: Some

Preliminary Observations," pp. 111-129. Pt. 3. Regional Studies. Dalia Ofer, "The Holocaust in Transnistria: A Special Case of Genocide," pp. 133-154; Jan Gross, "The Jewish Community in the Soviet-Annexed Territories on the Eve of the Holocaust: A Social Scientist's View," pp. 155-171; Andrzej Zbikowski, "Local Anti-Jewish Pogroms in the Occupied Territories of Eastern Poland, June-July 1941," pp. 173-179; Gertrude Schneider, "The Two Ghettos in Riga, Latvia, 1941-1943," pp. 181-193; Zvi Kolitz, "The Physical and Metaphysical Dimensions of the Extermination of the Jews in Lithuania," pp. 195-204. Pt. 4. Sources for the Study of the Holocaust in the Soviet Union. Sergei Maksudov, "The Jewish Population Losses of the USSR from the Holocaust: A Demographic Approach," pp. 207-213; Lucjan Dobroszycki, "Captured Nazi Documents on the Destruction of Jews in the Soviet Union," pp. 215-221; Robert Moses Shapiro, " 'Yizker-Bikher' as Sources on Jewish Communities in Soviet Belorussia and Soviet Ukraine During the Holocaust," pp. 223-236; Simon Schochet, "Polish Jewish Officers Who Were Killed in Katyn: An Ongoing Investigation in Light of Documents Recently Released by the USSR," pp. 237-247.]

2653. Eckardt, Alice L., ed. *Burning Memory: Times of Testing and Reckoning.* Includes contributions by Alice L. Eckardt, Nechama Tec, Mordecai Paldiel, Susan Zuccotti, Frieda W. Aaron, Karl A. Plank, Iwona Irwin-Zarecka, Richard L. Rubenstein, and Gabrielle Tyrnauer. 1st ed. Holocaust Series. Oxford; New York: Pergamon, 1993. xi, 340 pp. [Includes papers from the 16th Annual and the 18th Annual Scholars Conference on the Church Struggle and the Holocaust. Partial contents: Alice L. Eckardt, "Memory: Blessing, Burden, or Curse? The Shoah as a Burning Memory," pp. 1-17; Nechama Tec, "How Did We Survive?" pp. 109-116; Mordecai Paldiel, "The Rescue of Jewish Children in Poland and the Netherlands," pp. 119-139; Susan Zuccotti, "The Italians' Role in the Rescue of Jews," pp. 141-152; Frieda W. Aaron, "A Handful of Memories: Two Levels of Recollection," pp. 169-184; Karl A. Plank, "The Survivor's Return: Reflections on Memory and Place," pp. 185-202; Iwona Irwin-Zarecka, "Catholics and Jews in Poland Today," pp. 241-261; Richard L. Rubenstein, "Waldheim, the Pope and the Holocaust," pp. 263-279; Gabreille Tyrnauer, "Holocaust History and the Gypsies," pp. 283-295.]

2654. Edelheit, Abraham J., and Hershel Edelheit. *Bibliography on Holocaust Literature. Supplement, Volume 2.* Boulder, CO: Westview Press, c1993. xxvi, 564 pp.

2655. Elon, Amos. "The Politics of Memory." *New York Review of Books* 40, no. 16 (October 7, 1993): 3-5.

2656. Epstein, Leslie. [Book Review]. *Book World (Washington Post)* 23, no. 15 (April 11, 1993): 1ff. [Review article on Yitzhak Zuckerman, *A Surplus of Memory: Chronicle of the Warsaw Ghetto Uprising* (NY: 1993) and Willy Georg, *In the Warsaw Ghetto: Summer 1941* (NY: Aperature, 1993).]

2657. Fackenheim, Emil L. "The Criminals Hijack the Law: Two Nights of Nazi Terror." *Congress Monthly* 60,

no. 4 (May-June 1993): 11-14.

2658. Fittko, Lisa. *Solidarity and Treason: Resistance and Exile, 1933-1940.* Translated in collaboration with the author by Roslyn Theobald. Evanston, IL: Northwestern University Press, c1993. 160 pp. [Translation of: *Solidaritat unerwunscht.*]

2659. Fleischner, Eva. "Interfaith Journey to Poland." *Journal of Ecumenical Studies* 30, no. 2 (Spring 1993): 304-305.

2660. *Forever in the Shadow of Hitler? Original Documents of the Historikerstreit, the Controversy Concerning the Singularity of the Holocaust.* Translated by James Knowlton and Truett Cates. Atlantic Highlands, NJ: Humanities Press, 1993. xii, 282 pp. [Translation of: *Historikerstreit.*] REV: Rod Stackelberg, *Central European History* 26, no. 2 (1993): 250. Rolf Berghahn-Volker, *New York Times Book Review* 98, no. 16 (April 18, 1993): 3ff.

2661. Friedman, Saul S., ed. *Holocaust Literature: A Handbook of Critical, Historical, and Literary Writings.* Foreword by Dennis Klein. Includes contributions by Dennis Klein, Annette El-Hayek, Charles W. Sydnor, Jr., Leon W. Wells, Bea Stadtler, Shmuel Krakowski, Asher Cohen, Saul S. Friedman, Sol Littman, Alexander Kitroeef, Laurence Kutler, Gloria Young, and Saul S. Friedman. Westport, CT: Greenwood Press, 1993. xxx, 677 pp. [Partial contents: Dennis Klein, "Foreword: The Fate of Holocaust Literature," pp. xiii-xvii. Part I: Conceptual Approaches to the Holocaust. Annette El-Hayek, "The Major Texts of the Holocaust," pp. 3-20; Charles W. Sydnor, Jr., "The Concentration Camps and Killing Centers of the Third Reich," pp. 74-105; Leon W. Wells, "The Righteous Gentiles," pp. 140-160; Bea Stadtler, "Jewish Women in the Holocaust Resistance," pp. 176-193. Part II: Holocaust Area Studies. Shmuel Krakowski, "Relations Between Jews and Poles During the Holocaust: New and Old Approaches in Polish Historiography," pp. 203-215; Asher Cohen, "The Last Tragedy of the Shoah: The Jews of Hungary," pp. 216-248; Saul S. Friedman, "The Holocaust in Czechoslovakia: A Survey of the Literature," pp. 249-278; Sol Littman, "The Ukrainian Halychyna Division: A Case Study of Historical Revisionism," pp. 279-300; Alexander Kitroeef, "Approaches to the Study of the Holocaust in the Balkans," pp. 301-320. Pt. III. The Holocaust in Education and the Arts. Laurence Kutler, "Holocaust Diaries and Memoirs," pp. 521-532; Gloria Young, "The Poetry of the Holocaust," pp. 547-574; Saul S. Friedman, "Resources for Holocaust Study," pp. 623-632.] REV: *Booklist* 90, no. 3 (October 1, 1993): 384-385.

2662. Fromer, Rebecca Camhi. *The Holocaust Odyssey of Daniel Bennahmias, Sonderkommando.* Introduction by Steven B. Bowman. Judaic Studies Series. Tuscaloosa, AL: University of Alabama Press, c1993. xxviii, 151 pp. [Contents: Steven B. Bowman, "Introduction: The Greeks in Auschwitz"; The Shock of Recognition; The Absence of Light; The Unfolding Debacle; The First Incarcerations; The Withdrawal; The Selection; The Process of Annihilation; The Smile; The Questions; The Revolt; The Death March; The Reunion; The Return.]

2663. Fung, Annie. "The Extradition of John Demjanjuk as 'Ivan the Terrible.'" *New York Law School Journal of International and Comparative Law* 14, nos. 2 & 3 (1993): 471-502.

2664. Garlinski, Józef. *Fighting Auschwitz: The Resistance Movement in the Concentration Camp.* Classics of World War II. The Secret War. [Alexandria, VA]: Time Life, [1993]. xi, 327 pp. [Translation of *Oswiecim walczacy.* Originally published: (London: Julian Friedmann, 1975 and Greenwich, CT: Fawcettt, 1975).]

2665. Gediman, Paul. "This Museum is Not a Metaphor: Confronting the Hard Facts of the Holocaust." *Commonweal* 120, no. 11 (June 4, 1993): 13-15. [On the U.S. Holocaust Memorial Museum.]

2666. Gefen, Aba. *Defying the Holocaust: A Diplomat's Report.* Edited by Nathan Kravetz. 1st ed. Studies in Judaica and the Holocaust, no. 11. San Bernardino, CA: Borgo Press, 1993. 248 pp. [On the Holocaust in Lithuania.]

2667. "Genocide or Holocaust? Gypsies and Jews." *History Teacher* 26, no. 3 (May 1993): 385-386. [Editors' summary of exchange between Yehuda Bauer and Sybil Milton, concerning use of the term "Holocaust" for the genocide perpetrated against the Gypsies by Nazi Germany, written in response to Milton's article in the August 1992 issue (pp. 515-521).]

2668. Georg, Willy, photographer. *In the Warsaw Ghetto: Summer 1941.* Passages from Warsaw Ghetto diaries compiled and with an afterword by Rafael F. Scharf. 1st ed. New York: Aperture, c1993. 111 pp. REV: Leslie Epstein, *Book World* 23, no. 15 (April 11, 1993): 1ff. Anna Husarska, *New York Times Book Review* 98, no. 14 (April 4, 1993): 35.

2669. Gilbert, Martin. *Atlas of the Holocaust.* 1st U.S. ed. New York: William Morrow and Company, c1993. 1 atlas (282 pp.). [First published by (Macmillan, 1982), and later by (New York: Pergamon, 1988).] REV: *Booklist* 90, no. 6 (November 15, 1993): 645.

2670. Gilson, Estelle. "Americanizing the Holocaust: The Museum in Washington." *Congress Monthly* 60, no. 6 (September-October 1993): 3-6.

2671. Ginsburg, Bernard L. *A Wayfarer in a World in Upheaval.* Edited and introduction by Nathan Kravetz. Studies in Judaica and the Holocaust, no. 12. San Bernardino, CA: Borgo Press, c1993. 128 pp.

2672. Goldreich, Gloria. "A Trio of Lonely Voices." *Congress Monthly* 60, no. 6 (September-October 1993): 20-21. [Review article on Melvin Jules Bukiet, *Stories of an Imaginary Childhood* (Evanston, IL: 1992); Rebecca Goldstein, *Strange Attractors* (NY: 1993); and Shulamith Hareven, *Twilight and Other Stories* (San Francisco, CA: 1992).]

2673. Gourevitch, Philip. "Behold Now Behemoth." *Harper's* 287, no. 1718 (July 1993): 55-62. [On the U.S. Holocaust Memorial Museum.]

2674. Grobman, Alex, and Judah L. Magnes Memorial Museum. *Rekindling the Flame: American Jewish Chaplains and the Survivors of European Jewry, 1944-1948.* Detroit, MI: Wayne State University Press, c1993. xii, 259 pp. [Published in cooperation with the Judah L. Magnes Museum, Berkeley, CA.]

2675. Grossman, Ibolya. "A Mother's Kiss From the Grave." *Canadian Woman Studies = Les cahiers de la femme* 14, no. 1 (Fall 1993): 25-26.

2676. Hallie, Philip Paul. *Rescue & Goodness: Reflections on the Holocaust.* [Washington, DC]: U.S. Holocaust Memorial Museum, [1993]. 9 pp.

2677. Harris, Lis. "The Jewish Resistance." *World Policy Journal* 10, no. 2 (Summer 1993): 83-87. [Review article on Yitzhak Zuckerman, *A Surplus of Memory: Chronicle of the Warsaw Ghetto Uprising* (Berkeley, CA: 1993).]

2678. Heller, Fanya Gottesfeld. *Strange and Unexpected Love: A Teenage Girl's Holocaust Memoirs.* Foreword by Irving Greenberg. Hoboken, NJ: Ktav Pub. House, c1993. xvi, 279 pp.

2679. Herczl, Moshe Y. *Christianity and the Holocaust of Hungarian Jewry.* Translated by Joel Lerner. New York: New York University Press, c1993. ix, 299 pp. [Translation from the Hebrew. Partial contents: 1. The Preparatory Years. Background. The Blood Libel of Tisza Eszlar. The Catholic People's Party. The Revolutions and the White Terror. The Catholic Press. The 'Numerus Clausus' Law. The Consolidation of the Twenties and the Christian Antisemitism of the Thirties. Popular Antisemitism of the Thirties. Cross Movements and the Arrow-Cross Party — 2. Anti-Jewish Legislation. The First Anti-Jewish Act. The Eucharistic Convention. In the Wake of the Act's Adoption. The Second Anti-Jewish Act. The Debate in the Upper House: The Stand of Church Leaders. Extraparliamentary Activity during and after the Debate on the Second Anti-Jewish Act. The Demand for Additional Anti-Jewish Legislation. The Third Anti-Jewish Act. The Labor Battalions Act. The Jewish Religion Status-Lowering Act. The Jewish Estates Expropriation Act. The Kallay Proposal for the Expulsion of the Jews from Hungary — 3. 1944. The Expulsion. Who Carried Out the Expulsion? Priestly Activity. The Shepherds' Epistles. A Quarter of a Million Budapest Jews—Trapped. Hungarian Initiatives.]

2680. Jackel, Eberhard. *David Irving's Hitler: A Faulty History Dissected: Two Essays.* Translation and comments by H. David Kirk. Foreword by Robert Fulford. Port Angeles, WA; Brentwood Bay, B.C.: Ben-Simon Publications, c1993. 58 pp. [Originally appeared in German as part of: *Im Kreuzfeuer, der Fernsehfilm "Holocaust,"* 1979. Translated from the German.]

2681. Jacobs, Steven L., ed. *Contemporary Christian Religious Responses to the Shoah.* Includes contributions by Harry James Cargas, Eugene J. Fisher, Thomas A. Idinopolos, and John K. Roth. Studies in the *Shoah,* v. 6. Lanham, MD: University Press of America, c1993. 289 pp.

[Partial contents: Harry James Cargas, "Revisionism and Theology; Two Sides of the Same Coin?" pp. 2-14; Eugene J. Fisher, "*Mysterium Tremendum*: Catholic Grapplings with the *Shoah* and Its Theological Implications," pp. 60-84; Thomas A. Idinopolos, "How the *Shoah* Affects Christian Belief," pp. 110-122; John K. Roth, "Asking and Listening, Understanding and Doing," pp. 196-212.]

2682. ———, ed. *Contemporary Jewish Religious Response to the Shoah*. Studies in the *Shoah*, v. 5. Lanham, MD: University Press of America, c1993. 247 pp.

2683. Johnson, Paul. [Book Review]. *Book World (Washington Post)* 23, no. 28 (July 11, 1993): 1ff. [Review article on Deborah E. Lipstadt, *Denying the Holocaust: The Growing Assault on Truth and Memory* (NY: Free Press, 1993).]

2684. Kape, Salomea. "On the Autopsy Table in Lodz...Biebow from Bremen." *Lilith* 18, no. 3 (Summer 1993): 24-26.

2685. Katz, Steven T. *The Holocaust and Comparative History*. Leo Baeck Memorial Lecture, 37. New York: Leo Baeck Institute, 1993. 32 pp.

2686. Keneally, Thomas. *Schindler's List*. Touchstone ed. New York: Simon and Schuster, 1993, c1982. 398 pp.

2687. Kernan, Michael. "A National monument bears witness to the tragedy of the Holocaust." *Smithsonian* 24, no. 1 (April 1993): 50ff. [On the U.S. Holocaust Memorial Museum. Followed with letters to the editor by Kazimierz Dziewanowski, John W. McKenna, and Richard Lockhart in vol. 24, no. 3 (June 1993): 10.]

2688. Knoll, Erwin. "Crime Against Humanity." *Progressive* 57, no. 1 (January 1993): 36-37. [Review article on Telford Taylor, *The Anatomy of the Nuremberg Trials: A Personal Memoir* (NY: Knopf, 1992).]

2689. Kozinski, Alex. "Sanhedrin II." *New Republic* 209, no. 11 (September 13, 1993): 16-18. [Discusses the Israeli Supreme Court's conduct of the Ivan Demjanjuk trial.]

2690. Kurzman, Dan. *The Bravest Battle: The Twenty-Eight Days of the Warsaw Ghetto Uprising*. 1st Da Capo Press ed. New York: Da Capo Press, 1993. 386 pp. [Originally published: (New York: Putman, 1976).]

2691. Langer, Lawrence L. "A Tainted Legacy: Remembering the Warsaw Ghetto." *Tikkun* 8, no. 3 (May-June 1993): 37ff.

2692. Lerner, Motti. "Kastner." *Modern International Drama* 27, no. 1 (Fall 1993): 33-93. Translated from the Hebrew by Imre Goldstein. [Play awarded the Aharon Meskin Prize of the Israel Centre of the I.T.I. from the decision of the 1985/1986 Meskin Prize Jury.]

2693. Levi, Primo. *The Reawakening*. Translated from the Italian by Stuart Woolf. New York: Macmillan; Toronto: Maxwell Macmillan Canada; New York: Maxwell Macmillan International, 1993. 231 pp. [Translation of *Tregua*. Originally published: (London: Bodley Head, 1965).]

Companion vol. to: *Survival in Auschwitz*.]

2694. Lieberg, Alice. *Remembrance of Things Past*. Dedham, MA (150 Court St., Dedham 02026-4343): Sylvester Press, 1993. vii, 175, xxv pp.

2695. Linden, R. Ruth. *Making Stories, Making Selves: Feminist Reflections on the Holocaust*. A Helen Hooven Santmyer Prize Winner. Columbus, OH: Ohio State University Press, c1993. xv, 191 pp. REV: Katherine Bischoping, *Contemporary Sociology* 22, no. 6 (November 1993): 884-885.

2696. Linenthal, Edward T. "In the Service of Memory." *World & I* 8, no. 5 (May 1993): 158-167. [On the U.S. Holocaust Memorial Museum.]

2697. Lippman, Matthew. "The Nazi Doctors Trial and the International Prohibition on Medical Involvement in Torture." *Loyola of Los Angeles International and Comparative Law Journal* 15, no. 2 (February 1993): 395-441.

2698. Lipstadt, Deborah E. "Academe Must Not Legitimize Denials of the Holocaust." *Chronicle of Higher Education* 39, no. 47 (July 28, 1993): B1-B2.

2699. ———. *Denying the Holocaust: The Growing Assault on Truth and Memory*. New York: Free Press; Toronto: Maxwell Macmillan Canada; New York: Maxwell Macmillan International, c1993. ix, 278 pp. [Contents: 1. Canaries in the Mine: Holocaust Denial and the Limited Power of Reason; 2. The Antecedents: History, Conspiracy, and Fantasy; 3. In the Shadow of World War II: Denial's Initial Steps; 4. The First Stirrings of Denial in America; 5. Austin J. App: The World of Immoral Equivalencies; 6. Denial: A Tool of the Radical Right; 7. Entering the Mainstream: The Case of Arthur Butz; 8. The Institute for Historical Review; 9. The Gas Chamber Controversy; 10. The Battle for the Campus; 11. Watching on the Rhine: The Future Course of Holocaust Denial; Appendix: Twisting the Truth: Zyklon-B, the Gas Chambers, and the *Diary of Anne Frank*.] REV: Edward Alexander, *Commentary* 96, no. 5 (November 1993): 54-56. Paul Johnson, *Book World* 23, no. 28 (July 11, 1993): 1ff. Alan J. Levine, *World & I* (December 1993): 316ff. Walter Reich, *New York Times Book Review* 98, no. 28 (July 11, 1993): 1ff. Fritz Stern, *Foreign Affairs* 72, no. 5 (November-December 1993): 168-169.

2700. Loker, Zvi. "Documentation: The Testimony of Dr. Edo Neufeld: The Italians and the Jews of Croatia." *Holocaust and Genocide Studies* 7, no. 1 (Spring 1993): 67-76. [Holocaust survivor testimony describing atrocities against the Jews and Serbs commited at Gospic, Jadovno, Pag Island, Susak, and Pristina.]

2701. Maltiel-Gerstenfeld, Jacob. *My Private War: One Man's Struggle to Survive the Soviets and the Nazis*. Library of Holocaust Testimonies. London; Portland, OR: Vallentine Mitchell, 1993. xxii, 313 pp.

2702. Marks, Jane. *The Hidden Children: The Secret Survivors of the Holocaust*. New York: Ballantine Books, c1993. xxvii, 307 pp.

2703. McCloskey, Liz Leibold. "No Ordinary Museum." *Commonweal* 120, no. 11 (June 4, 1993): 10-11. [On the U.S. Holocaust Memorial Museum.]

2704. Megged, Aharon. "Hanna Senesh." *Modern International Drama* 27, no. 1 (Fall 1993): 95-134. Translated from the Hebrew by Michael Taub.

2705. Michel, Ernest W. *Promises to Keep.* Foreword by Leon Uris. New York: Barricade Books; Emeryville, CA: Distributed by Publishers Group West, c1993. xvii, 298 pp.

2706. Michman, Dan. "Jewish religious life under Nazi domination: Nazi attitudes and Jewish problems." *Studies in Religion* 22, no. 2 (Spring 1993): 147-165.

2707. Milchman, Alan, and Alan Rosenberg. "The Unlearned Lessons of the Holocaust." *Modern Judaism* 13, no. 2 (May 1993): 177-190.

2708. Milfull, John, ed. *Why Germany? National Socialist Anti-semitism and the European Context.* Contributions by Silke Beinssen-Hesse, Gunter Hartung, Tony Barta, Carole Elizabeth Adams, Konrad Kwiet, Wolfgang Benz, John Milfull, Mira Crouch, Alan Chamberlain, Margaret Sampson, Jacques Adler, Jenny Wajsenberg, Peter Lawrence, Sophie Caplan, and Claudio Segre. Providence: Berg, 1993. vi, 257 pp. [Contents: Silke Beinssen-Hesse, "Weininger and the time-honored analogy between the inferiority of women and Jews"; Gunter Hartung, "Pre-planners of the Holocaust: the case of Theodor Fritsch"; Tony Barta, "Living in Dachau: Bavarian Catholics and the fate of the Jews, 1893-1943"; Carole Elizabeth Adams, "Anti-Semitism in the political culture of Wihelmine Germany: the case of white-collar workers"; Konrad Kwiet, "From the diary of a killing unit"; Wolfgang Benz, "The persecution and extermination of the Jews in the German consciousness"; John Milfull, "Imagining Jew(esse)s. Gregor von Rezzori's *Memoirs of an Anti-Semite*: an etiology of 'German' anti-Semitism"; Mira Crouch, "Jews, other Jews and 'the others': some marginal considerations concerning the limits of tolerance"; Alan Chamberlain, "*Vous, les jutifs*: Jewish characters in four French literary texts"; Margaret Sampson, "Jewish anti-Semitism? The attitudes of the Jewish community in Britain toward refugees from Nazi Germany: *The Jewish Chronicle*, March 1933-September 1938"; Jacques Adler, "The changing attitude of the 'by-standers' toward the Jews in France, 1940-1943"; Jenny Wajsenberg, "Toward an interpretation of ghetto: Bialystok, a case study"; Peter Lawrence, "Why Lithuania? a study of active and passive collaboration in mass murder in a Lithuanian village, 1941"; Sophie Caplan, "Polish and German anti-Semitism"; Claudio Segre, "Primo Levi, witness of the Holocaust"; John Milfull, "The subject of responsibility."]

2709. Milivojevic, Dragan. "What Revolutions Don't Change." *World & I* 8, no. 9 (September 1993): 355-359. [Review article on Mark Kharitonov, *Linii sud'by ili sunduchok Milashevicha* (Moscow: 1992).]

2710. Milton, Sybil. "Re-Examining Scholarship on the Holocaust." *Chronicle of Higher Education* 39, no. 33 (April 21, 1993): A52.

2711. Mirkovic, Damir. "Victims and Perpetrators in the Yugoslav Genocide of 1941-1945: Some Preliminary Observations." *Holocaust and Genocide Studies* 7, no. 3 (Winter 1993): 317-332. [Article identifies three genocides in Yugoslavia during World War II: (1) against the Serbs, Jews, and Gypsies in Croatia, committed by Croatian nationalists (Ustasa); (2) against Moslems in Bosnia and Herzegovina, committed by Serbian royalists (Chetniks); and (3) against the collaborationist forces ("politicide" of POWs) committed by Tito's partisans (People's Liberation Army).]

2712. Morsink, Johannes. "World War Two and the Universal Declaration." *Human Rights Quarterly* 15, no. 2 (May 1993): 357-405.

2713. Neusner, Jacob, ed. *In the Aftermath of the Holocaust.* Contributions by Edward Alexander, Salo W. Baron, Michael Berenbaum, Eliezer Berkovits, Seymour Cain, Alice Eckardt, Roy Eckardt, Jerome Eckstein, Emil L. Fackenheim, Lewis S. Feuer, Maurice Friedman, Jacob Neusner, Richard L. Rubenstein, Harold M. Schulweis, Stephen J. Whitfield, and Michael Wyschogrod. Judaism in Cold War America, 1945-1990, v. 2. New York: Garland, 1993. x, 263 pp. [Reprints of articles published 1962-1989. Contents: Edward Alexander, "The Holocaust in American-Jewish Fiction: A Slow Awakening," pp. 2-12; Edward Alexander, "Stealing the Holocaust," pp. 14-19; Salo W. Baron, "European Jewry Before and After Hitler," pp. 21-71; Michael Berenbaum, "The Nativization of the Holocaust," pp. 73-83; Eliezer Berkovits, "Approaching the Holocaust," pp. 84-86; Seymour Cain, "The Question and the Answers After Auschwitz," pp. 87-102; Alice and Roy Eckardt, "Studying the Holocaust's Impact Today: Some Dilemmas of Language and Method," pp. 104-114; Jerome Eckstein, "The Holocaust and Jewish Theology," pp. 116-125; Emil L. Fackenheim, "The Human Condition After Auschwitz; A Jewish Testimony a Generation After," pp. 126-143; Emil L. Fackenheim, "The Holocaust and Future Jewish Thought," pp. 144-148; Lewis S. Feuer, "The Reasoning of Holocaust Theology," pp. 150-162; Maurice Friedman, "Elie Wiesel's Messianism of the Unredeemed," pp. 164-319; Jacob Neusner, "A 'Holocaust' Primer," pp. 175-179; Jacob Neusner, "The Implications of the Holocaust," pp. 181-196; Jacob Neusner, "Judaism in a Time of Crisis: Four Responses to the Destruction of the Second Temple," pp. 197-327; Richard L. Rubenstein, "Journey to Poland," pp. 212-220; Richard L. Rubenstein and Jacob Neusner, "Germany and the Jews: Two Views," pp. 221-237; Harold M. Schulweis, "A Jewish Theology for Post-Holocaust Healing," pp. 238-240; Stephen J. Whitfield, "The Holocaust and the American Jewish Intellectual," pp. 241-251; Michael Wyschogrod, "Faith and the Holocaust," pp. 252-260.]

2714. Norden, Edward. "Yes and No to the Holocaust Museums." *Commentary* 96, no. 2 (August 1993): 23-32. [Followed with letters to the editor in vol. 96 (December 1993): 13.]

2715. Nyiszli, Miklos. *Auschwitz: A Doctor's Eyewitness Account.* Translated by Tibere Kremer, and Richard Seaver. Foreword by Bruno Bettelheim. 1st Arcade paperback ed. New York: Arcade Pub.; [Boston]: Distributed by Little, Brown, and Co., 1993. xviii, 222 pp. [Originally published: (New York: F. Fell, c1960).]

2716. Paldiel, Mordecai. *The Path of the Righteous: Gentile Rescuers of Jews During the Holocaust.* Foreword by Harold M. Schulweis. Afterword by Abraham H. Foxman. Hoboken, NJ: Ktav, c1993. xix, 401 pp. [Published in association with the Jewish Foundation for Christian Rescuers/ADL, New York, NY. Contents: Introduction; France; Belgium; The Netherlands; Germany; Poland; Lithuania & Latvia; Ukraine & Byelorussia; Czechoslovakia; Hungary; Yugoslavia; Greece; Italy; Norway & Denmark; Concluding words.]

2717. Panstwowe Muzeum w Oswiecimiu, and Dokumentations- und Kulturzentrum Deutscher Sinti und Roma. *Memorial Book: The Gypsies at Auschwitz-Birkenau = Ksiega pamieci: cyganie w obozie koncentracyjnym Auschwitz-Birkenau = Gedenkbuch: Die sinti und roma im Konzentrationslager Auschwitz-Birkenau.* Edited by State Museum of Auschwitz-Birkenau, and Documentary and Cultural Centre of German Sintis and Roms. Munchen; New York: Saur, 1993. 2 vols.

2718. Pawlikowski, John T. "Warsaw Conference Remembers Polish Righteous." *Journal of Ecumenical Studies* 30, nos. 3-4 (Summer-Fall 1993): 492-493.

2719. Pelican, Fred. *From Dachau to Dunkirk.* The Library of Holocaust Testimonies. London; Portland, OR: Vallentine Mitchell, 1993. vii, 208 pp.

2720. Porat, Dina. "The Jewish Councils of the Main Ghettos of Lithuania: A Comparison." *Modern Judaism* 13, no. 2 (May 1993): 149-163.

2721. Radzilowski, John. "Remembering the Ghetto Uprising at the U.S. Holocaust Museum." *Historian* 55, no. 4 (Summer 1993): 635-640. [Text, p. 635; photographs, pp. 636-640.]

2722. Rittner, Carol, and John K. Roth, eds. *Different Voices: Women and the Holocaust.* Contributions by Ida Fink, Etty Hillesum, Charlotte Delbo, Isabella Leitner, Olga Lengyel, Livia E. Bitton Jackson, Pelagia Lewinska, Gisella Perl, Anna Heilman, Rose Meth, Sara Nomberg-Przytyk, Vera Laska, Gitta Sereny, Irena Klepfisz, Rachel Altman, and Joan Ringelheim. 1st ed. New York, NY: Paragon House, 1993. xiv, 435 pp. [Partial contents: "Prologue: Women and the Holocaust," pp. 1-19; "General Suggestions for Further Reading," pp. 20-21; "Chronology," pp. 22-32. Part One: Voices of Experience. Ida Fink, "A Scrap of Time," pp. 40-45; Etty Hillesum, "A Letter from Westerbork," pp. 46-57; Charlotte Delbo, "Arrivals, Departures," pp. 58-64; Isabella Leitner, "Fragments of Isabella," pp. 65-68; Olga Lengyel, "The Arrival," pp. 69-72; Livia E. Bitton Jackson, "Coming of Age," pp. 73-83; Pelagia Lewinska, "Twenty Months at Auschwitz," pp. 84-98; Charlotte Delbo, "Lulu," pp. 99-103; Gisella Perl, "A Doctor

in Auschwitz," pp. 104-118; Olga Lengyel, "Scientific Experiments," pp. 119-129; Anna Heilman and Rose Meth, "Resistance," pp. 130-142; Sara Nomberg-Przytyk, "The Camp Blanket," pp. 143-148; "Suggestions for Further Reading," pp. 149-151. Part Two. Voices of Interpretation. Vera Laska, "Women in the Resistance and in the Holocaust," pp. 250-269; Gitta Sereny, "Into that darkness," pp. 270-286; "Suggestions for Further Reading," pp. 317-318. Part Three. Voices of Reflection. Irena Klepfisz, "A Few Words In the Mother Tongue," pp. 324-327; Charlotte Delbo, "Days and Memory," pp. 328-331; Ida Fink, "The Table," pp. 332-348; Rachel Altman, "Fragments of a Broken Past," pp. 363-372; Joan Ringelheim, "Women and the Holocaust: a Reconsideration of Research," pp. 373-418; "Suggestions for Further Reading," pp. 419-420; "Epilogue: Different Voices," pp. 421-426.] REV: Rochelle G. Saidel, *Lilith* 18, no. 4 (Fall 1993): 32.

2723. Rosen, Sara. *My Lost World: A Survivor's Tale.* Library of Holocaust Testimonies. London; Portland, OR: Vallentine Mitchell, 1993. vii, 299 pp.

2724. Rosenberg, Blanca. *To Tell at Last: Survival under False Identity, 1941-45.* Urbana, IL: University of Illinois Press, c1993. xv, 178 pp.

2725. Rovit, Rebecca. "Emerging from the Ashes: The Akko Theater Center Opens the Gates to Auschwitz." *TDR: The Drama Review* 37, no. 2 (Summer 1993): 161-173. [In the Akko Theater Center, second-generation Israelis attempt to come to terms with the Holocaust trauma of their parents.]

2726. Ryback, Timothy W. "Between Art and Atrocity." *ARTnews* 92, no. 10 (December 1993): 116-121. [On the artistic community in Dachau.]

2727. ———. "Evidence of Evil." *New Yorker* 69, no. 38 (November 15, 1993): 68-81. [On the preservation of Holocaust evidence at the Auschwitz Museum (Poland).]

2728. Sack, John. *An Eye for an Eye.* New York, NY: BasicBooks, c1993. xii, 252 pp.

2729. Scheindlin, Raymond P. "Museum of Life, Museum of Death." *Tikkun* 8, no. 6 (November-December 1993): 85-87. [On the U.S. Holocaust Memorial Museum and the Jewish Museum.]

2730. Schoefer, Christine. *The Politics of Commemoration: The Concentration Camp Memorial Sites in the Former GDR.* Working Paper (University of California, Berkeley. Center for German and European Studies), 3.9. Berkeley, CA: Center for German and European Studies, University of California, 1993. 28 pp.

2731. Segev, Tom. *The Seventh Million: The Israelis and the Holocaust.* Translated by Haim Watzman. 1st ed. New York: Hill and Wang, 1993. ix, 593 pp. [Translation of: *ha-Milyon ha-shevi'i.* Contents: Prologue: Ka-Tzetnik's Trip — Pt. I. Hitler: The Yekkes Are Coming. 1. The Streets Are Paved with Money; 2. A Son of Europe — Pt. II. Holocaust: It Was in the Papers. 3. Rommel, Rommel, How Are You?; 4. Happy Is the Match; 5. A Warm Jewish

Heart — Pt. III. Israel: The Last Jews. 6. At First I Thought They Were Animals; 7. A Certain Distance; 8. Six Million Germans; 9. A Barrier of Blood and Silence — Pt. IV. Restitution: How Much Will We Get for Grandma and Grandpa? 10. Add a Few Moral Arguments; 11. Gas against Jews; 12. The Baby Went for Free — Pt. V. Politics: The Kastner Affair. 13. It Is Hard for Us, the Judges of Israel; 14. His Soul to the Devil; 15. The Walls Are Beginning to Crack; 16. Jeremiah the Prophet, for Example; 17. There Is No Certainty That Our Children Will Remain Alive — Pt. VI. Trial: Eichmann in Jerusalem. 18. Let Them Hate, and Let Them Go to Hell; 19. Six Million Times No! 20. Gloom Shall Not Prevail — Pt. VII. Growing Up: From War to War. 21. Everyone Thought about It; 22. Hitler Is Already Dead, Mr. Prime Ministers; 23. Deep in Our Souls — Pt. VIII. Memory: The Struggle to Shape the Past. 24. Holocaust and Heroism; 25. The Rest of Your Life with Monik and Frieda; 26. What Is There to Understand? They Died and That's It; 27. When You See a Graveyard; 28. What Does it Do to Me?] REV: Norman Birnbaum, *Nation* 257, no. 4 (July 26, 1993-August 2, 1993): 142-145. Benjamin Frankel, *Book World* 23, no. 18 (May 2, 1993): 5.

2732. Shapiro, Edward S. "Holocaust Revisionism: Denying the Undeniable." *Congress Monthly* 60, no. 7 (November-December 1993): 9ff.

2733. Shaw, Stanford J. *Turkey and the Holocaust: Turkey's Role in Rescuing Turkish and European Jewry from Nazi Persecution, 1933-1945.* New York: New York University Press, 1993. xiii, 423 pp.

2734. Steinlauf, Michael. "Fifty Years Later: The Warsaw Ghetto Uprising." *Tikkun* 8, no. 2 (March/April 1993): 29-32.

2735. Stern, Kenneth S. *Holocaust Denial.* New York: American Jewish Committee, c1993. xii, 193 pp.

2736. Strand, John. "The Storyteller: Jeshajahu Weinberg of the U.S. Holocaust Memorial Museum." *Museum News* 72, no. 2 (March/April 1993): 40ff.

2737. Swiebocka, Teresa, comp. and ed. *Auschwitz: A History in Photographs.* English edition prepared by Jonathan Webber and Connie Wilsack. Contributions by Kazimierz Smolén, Teresa Swiebocka, Renata Boguslawska-Swiebocka, and Jonathan Webber. Bloomington, IN: Published for the Auschwitz-Birkenau State Museum, Oswiecim, by Indiana University Press and Ksiazka i Wiedza, Warsaw, c1993. 295 pp. [First published in Polish in 1990 by the Panstwowe Muzeum Oswiecim-Brzezinka under the title: *Auschwitz: Zbrodnia przeciwko ludzkosci* (Auschwitz: Crime against Humanity). Contents: Kazimierz Smolén, "Auschwitz: The Nazi Murder Camp," pp. 13-27; Teresa Swiebocka and Renata Boguslawska-Swiebocka, "Auschwitz in Documentary Photographs," pp. 33-215; Kazimierz Smolén, "The Art Inspired by Auschwitz," pp. 217-257; Kazimierz Smolén, "Auschwitz Today: The Auschwitz-Birkenau State Museum," pp. 259-280; Jonathan Webber, "Personal Reflections on Auschwitz Today," p. 281-291.]

2738. Taylor, Telford. *The Anatomy of the Nuremberg Trials: A Personal Memoir.* 1rst paperback ed. Boston, MA: Back Bay Books, 1993. xii, 703 pp.

2739. Thomas, Laurence Mordekhai. *Vessels of Evil: American Slavery and the Holocaust.* Philadelphia, PA: Temple University Press, 1993. xvii, 211 pp. [Contents: Pt. I. On Becoming an Evil Self. 1. Two Faces of Evil: An Introduction. 2. The Human Condition. 1. Good and Bad. 2. Immoral Rapprochement. 3. Understanding Obedience to Authority. 4. Obeying Authority and Becoming Morally Sullied. 3. The Moral Community. 5. Common-Sense Morality. 6. Moral Drift. 7. The People of Le Chambon. 4. Characterizing Evil. 8. Acts of Evil. 5. The Psychology Of Doubling. 9. The Problem. 10. Doubling and Multiple Personality Disorder. 11. The Psychology of Doubling. 12. Moral Disassociation — Pt. II. The Institutions. 6. American Slavery and the Holocaust. 13. The Conception of the Victims. 14. The Institutions. 7. Murderous Extermination and Natal Alienation. 15. Doing Justice to the Difference. 16. Ultimates in Evil: Alienation and Extermination. 17. Self-Hatred — Pt. III. Surviving into the Future. 8. After the Ashes. 18. Jews. 19. Blacks. 20. Historical Contexts. 21. Group Autonomy. 9. The Fate of Blacks and Jews. 22. The General Problem of Cooperation. 23. Neither Coercive nor Affirming Cooperation. 24. Cooperation and Having a Narrative. 25. Blacks and Jews.]

2740. United States. *Joint Resolution Concerning the Dedication of the United States Holocaust Memorial Museum.* [Washington, DC: U.S. G.P.O., 1993]. [2] pp. [H.J. Res. 156. 107 Stat. 47. Public Law 103-15.]

2741. U.S. Holocaust Memorial Museum. *Annotated Bibliography.* Washington, DC: U.S. Holocaust Memorial Museum, c1993. 32 pp.

2742. ———. *Annotated Videography.* Washington, DC: U.S. Holocaust Memorial Museum, c1993. 13 pp.

2743. ———. *Days of Remembrance, April 18-25, 1993: Fifty Years Ago: Revolt Amid the Darkness: Planning Guide for Commemorative Programs.* Washington, DC: U.S. Holocaust Memorial Museum, [1993]. xiii, 411 pp. [Prepared by the Days of Remembrance Committee, United States Holocaust Memorial Council. Filmography: pp. 387-395.]

2744. ———. *Fifty Years Ago: Revolt Amid the Darkness: Days of Remembrance 1993 Lesson Plans.* Washington, DC: U.S. Holocaust Memorial Museum, 1993. 20, 21 pp. [Lesson plans for grades seven through twelve. Developed by the Educational Department, United States Holocaust Memorial Council. Primary authors, William R. Fernekes and David G. Klevan.]

2745. ———. *Guidelines for Teaching about the Holocaust.* Washington, DC: U.S. Holocaust Memorial Museum, c1993. 16 pp.

2746. ———. *Resistance.* Washington, DC: U.S. Holocaust Memorial Museum, c1993. 16 pp.

2747. Volavkov, Hana, ed. *I Never Saw Another Butterfly: Children's Drawing and Poems from Terezin Concentration Camp, 1942-1944.* Foreword by Chaim Potok. Afterword by Václav Havel. expanded 2nd ed. New York: Schocken Books, 1993. xxii, 106 pp. [Translation of *Detske kresby na zastavce k smrti, Terezin, 1942-1944.* Translated into English by Jeanne Nemcova; revised and expanded by the U.S. Holocaust Memorial Council.]

2748. Wermuth, Henry. *Breathe Deeply, My Son.* The Library of Holocaust Testimonies. Portland, OR: Vallentine Mitchell, c1993. 210 pp.

2749. Whiteman, Dorit Bader. *The Uprooted: A Hitler Legacy: Voices of Those Who Escaped before the "Final Solution".* Foreword by William B. Helmreich. New York: Insight Books, c1993. xv, 446 pp.

2750. Wieseltier, Leon. "After Memory." *New Republic* 208, no. 18 (May 3, 1993): 16ff. [On the U.S. Holocaust Memorial Museum.]

2751. Wise, Michael Z. "Diplomacy: Reparations." *Atlantic* 272, no. 4 (October 1993): 32ff. [On reparations from Germany to Holocaust victims.]

2752. Wolffsohn, Michael. *Eternal Guilt? Forty Years of German-Jewish-Israeli Relations.* Translated by Douglas Bokovoy. New York: Columbia University Press, 1993. xii, 225 pp. [Contents: Archives; 1. Without Hitler—No Israel? 2. *Geschichtspolitik*: Phases of German-Jewish-Israeli Relations; 3. German-Israeli *Geschichtspolitik*: The Political Function of the Holocaust; 4. German-Israeli Role Reversal: Or, The Legend of the Hair-Shirt; 5. German-Israeli Language Problems: Different Meanings for the Same Terms; 6. Public Opinion: A Mirror of Generational Change; 7. Public Behavior: Tourism as an Indicator?; 8. Personalities; 9. Institutions and Organizations; 10. Triangular Relationships; 11. Images as a Source of Information and Danger: Or, Germans and Jews in Search of Reality; 12. Relaxation but No Relief?]

2753. Wyden, Peter. *Stella.* 1st Anchor Books ed. New York: Anchor Books, 1993. 382 pp. [Originally published: (New York: Simon & Schuster, c1992). With additional material.]

2754. Young, James E. "A Holocaust Rorschach Test." *New York Times Magazine* (April 25, 1993): 36-38.

2755. ———. *The Texture of Memory: Holocaust Memorials and Meaning.* New Haven, CT: Yale University Press, c1993. xvii, 398 pp. [Contents: Introduction: The Texture of Memory — Pt. I. Germany: The Ambiguity of Memory; The Countermonument: Memory against Itself in Germany; The Sites of Destruction; The Gestapo-Gelande: Topography of Unfinished Memory; Austria's Ambivalent Memory — Pt. II. Poland: The Ruins of Memory; The Rhetoric of Ruins: The Memorial Camps at Majdanek and Auschwitz; The Biography of a Memorial Icon: Nathan Rapoport's Warsaw Ghetto Monument; Broken Tablets and Jewish Memory in Poland — Pt. III. Israel: Holocaust, Heroism, and National Redemption; Israel's Memorial Landscape: Forests, Monuments, and Kibbutzim; Yad Vashem: Israel's Memorial Authority; When a Day Remembers: A Performative History of Yom Hashoah — Pt. IV. America: Memory and the Politics of Identity; The Plural Faces of Holocaust Memory in America; Memory and the Politics of Identity: Boston and Washington, D.C.] REV: Nathan Glazer, *New Leader* 76 (May 17-31, 1993): 15-16. Joanne Jacobson, *Nation* 257 (October 18, 1993): 431-432. Mark Lilla, *New York Times Book Review* 98, no. 38 (September 19, 1993): 31-32.

2756. Zuckerman, Yitzhak. *A Surplus of Memory: Chronicle of the Warsaw Ghetto Uprising.* Translated and edited by Barbara Harshav. Berkeley, CA: University of California Press, c1993. xviii, 702 pp. [Translation of *Sheva' ha-shanim ha-hen.* Contents: On Jewish Parties and Youth Movements; The War; Underground in the Soviet Zone; To the German Hell; A Week in a Labor Camp; The Tidings of Job; The Struggle for the Jewish Fighting Organization; The January Uprising and Its Lesson; The Ghetto Uprising; Underground in "Aryan" Warsaw; On the Edge of the Abyss; The Polish Uprising; The Longed-For Liberation: The Central Committee of the Jews in Poland and the Beginning of Brikha; London Conference: Split in the Movement and Its Restoration; Argument about Our Image; The Pogroms in Kielce and the Great Brikha: Departure from Poland.] REV: Christopher R. Browning, *New York Times Book Review* 98, no. 21 (May 23, 1993): 22-23. Leslie Epstein, *Book World* 23, no. 15 (April 11, 1993): 1ff. Lis Harris, *World Policy Journal* 10, no. 2 (Summer 1993): 83-87. Irving Howe, *New Republic* 208, no. 18 (May 3, 1993): 29-36. Michael Robert Marrus, *New Leader* 76, no. 7 (May 17-31, 1993): 17-19.

■ Russia/U.S.S.R.

General

2757. Bunce, Valerie. "Domestic Reform and International Change: The Gorbachev Reforms in Historical Perspective." *International Organization* 47, no. 1 (Winter 1993): 107-138.

2758. Engelstein, Laura. "Combined Underdevelopment: Discipline and the Law in Imperial and Soviet Russia." *American Historical Review* 98, no. 2 (April 1993): 338-353. [Followed with responses from Rudy Koshar ("Foucault and Social History," pp. 354-363) and Jan Goldstein ("Framing Discipline with Law: Problems and Promises of the Liberal State," pp. 364-375), and a reply from Engelstein (pp. 376-381).]

2759. Green, William C. "The Historic Russian Drive for a Warm Water Port: Anatomy of a Geopolitical Myth." *Naval War College Review* 46, no. 2 (Spring 1993): 80-102.

2760. Hosking, Geoffrey A. *Empire and Nation in Russian History.* 1st ed. Charles Edmondson Historical Lectures, 14th. Waco, TX: Markham Press Fund, Baylor University Press, 1993. 38 pp.

2761. Kappeler, Andreas. "Some Remarks on Russian National Identities (Sixteenth to Nineteenth Centuries)." *Ethnic Groups* 10, nos. 1-3 (1993): 147-155. [Part of special issue devoted to "Pre-Modern and Modern National Identity in Russia and Eastern Europe."]

2762. Lawrence, John. *A History of Russia.* 7th rev. ed. New York: Meridian, 1993. xiii, 364 pp.

2763. Molloy, Molly. "Nicholas V. Riasanovsky: An Updated and Revised Bibliography." *Russian History* 20, nos. 1-4 (1993): 237-263. [Earlier version published in *Russian Review* 43, no. 1 (January 1984).]

2764. Riasanovsky, Nicholas V. *A History of Russia.* 5th ed. New York: Oxford University Press, 1993. xx, 711 pp.

2765. Westwood, J. N. *Endurance and Endeavour: Russian History 1812-1992.* 4th ed. The Short Oxford History of the Modern World. Oxford; New York: Oxford University Press, 1993. xi, 624 pp. [Contents: Eighteen Twelve and After; The Russia of Nicholas I; Tsar and Serf; Thaw; From Bombs to Pogroms; Russia in Asia; 1905; On the Eve; The Empire's Last War; 1917; The Civil War; Disputes and Decisions; The Thirties; The Great Patriotic War; Consolidation or Ossification?; The Khruschchev Revival; The Brezhnev Regime; Infirmity; From Red Flag to Double-headed Eagle.]

2766. Zaprudnik, Jan. *Belarus: At a Crossroads in History.* Westview Series on the Post-Soviet Republics. Boulder, CO: Westview Press, c1993. xxi, 278 pp.

Medieval Rus' and Muscovy

2767. Keenan, Edward. "Ivan IV and the 'Kings Evil': *Ni maka li to budet?*" *Russian History* 20, nos. 1-4 (1993): 5-13.

2768. Kivelson, Valerie A. "The Devil Stole His Mind: The Tsar and the 1648 Moscow Uprising." *American Historical Review* 98, no. 3 (June 1993): 733-756.

2769. Mason, Richard Andrew Edward. "The Mongol Mission and Kyivan Rus'." *Ukrainian Quarterly* 49, no. 4 (Winter 1993): 385-402.

2770. Miller, David B. "The Cult of Saint Sergius of Radonezh and Its Political Uses." *Slavic Review* 52, no. 4 (Winter 1993): 680-699.

2771. Obolensky, Alexander P. "From First to Third Millennium: The Social Christianity of St. Vladimir of Kiev." *Cross Currents* 43, no. 2 (Summer 1993): 203-211.

2772. Weickhardt, George G. "The Pre-Petrine Law of Property." *Slavic Review* 52, no. 4 (Winter 1993): 663-679.

2773. World Congress for Soviet and East European Studies (4th: 1990: Harrogate, England). *New Perspectives on Muscovite History: Selected Papers from the Fourth World Congress for Soviet and East European Studies, Harrogate, 1990.* Edited by Lindsey Hughes. New York: St. Martin's Press, 1993. xvii, 197 pp. [Published in association with the International Council for Soviet and East European Studies.]

Imperial Period: (1725-1917)

2774. Anisimov, Evgenii V. *The Reforms of Peter the Great: Progress through Coercion in Russia.* Translated and with an introduction by John T. Alexander. New Russian History. Armonk, NY: M.E. Sharpe, c1993. xi, 327 pp.

2775. Austin, Paul Britten. *1812: The March on Moscow.* London: Greenhill Books; Mechanicsburg, PA: Stackpole Books, c1993. 416 pp.

2776. Bormanshinov, Arash. "The *Buzava* (Don Kalmyk) Princes Revisited." *Mongolian Studies*, no. 16 (1993): 59-63. [Follow-up to author's "Prolegomena to a History of the Kalmyk *Noyons* (Princes). I. The *Buzava* (Don Kalmyk) Princes," *Mongolian Studies* 14 (1991): 41-80.]

2777. Bushnell, John. "Did Serf Owners Control Serf Marriage? Orlov Serfs and Their Neighbors, 1773-1861." *Slavic Review* 52, no. 3 (Fall 1993): 419-445.

2778. Cross, Anthony Glenn. *Anglo-Russica: Aspects of Cultural Relations between Great Britain and Russia in the Eighteenth and Early Nineteenth Centuries: Selected Essays.* Anglo-Russian Affinities Series. New York: St. Martin's Press, 1993. x, 269 pp. [First published in Great Britain (Berg: 1992).]

2779. Engel, Barbara Alpern. "Russian Peasant Views of City Life, 1861-1914." *Slavic Review* 52, no. 3 (Fall 1993): 446-459.

2780. Greenfeld, Liah. "The Crisis of the Aristocracy and the Emergence of Russian National Identity." *Ethnic Groups* 10, nos. 1-3 (1993): 125-145. [Part of special issue devoted to "Pre-Modern and Modern National Identity in Russia and Eastern Europe."]

2781. Kohls, Winfred A. "Chapters in the History of Foreign Colonization in Russia: The Sarepta Crisis in Its Historical Context." *Russian History* 20, nos. 1-4 (1993): 35-60.

2782. Lindenmeyr, Adele. "Public Life, Private Virtues: Women in Russian Charity, 1762-1914." *Signs* 18, no. 3 (Spring 1993): 562-591.

2783. Löwe, Heinz-Dietrich. "Government Policies and the Tradition of Russian Antisemitism, 1772-1917." *Patterns of Prejudice* 27, no. 1 (July 1993): 47-63.

2784. ———. *The Tsars and the Jews: Reform, Reaction, and Anti-Semitism in Imperial Russia, 1772-1917.* Chur, Switzerland; New York: Harwood Academic Publishers, c1993. x, 455 pp. [Originally published in German as *Antisemitismus und reaktionare Utopie* (Hamburg: Hoffmann und Campe Verlag, 1978).]

2785. Lutski, Joseph Solomon ben Moses. *Karaite Separatism in Nineteenth-Century Russia: Joseph Solomon Lutski's Epistle of Israel's Deliverance.* Edited by Philip E. Miller. Monographs of the Hebrew Union College, no. 16.

Cincinnati, OH: Hebrew Union College Press, c1993. xix, 252 pp. [English and Hebrew. Includes annotated text and translation of *Igeret Teshu'at Yisra'el*.]

2786. Pomper, Philip. *The Russian Revolutionary Intelligentsia*. 2nd ed. European History Series (Arlington Heights, IL). Arlington Heights, IL: H. Davidson, c1993. x, 241 pp.

2787. Ragsdale, Hugh, ed. and trans. *Imperial Russian Foreign Policy*. Assistant editor Valerii Nikolaevich Ponomarev. Includes contributions by Hugh Ragsdale, E. V. Anisimov, Hans Bagger, Robert E. Jones, David M. Goldfrank, V. N. Vinogradov, V. N. Ponomarev, N. N. Bolkhovitinov, David MacKenzie, A. V. Ignat'ev, David M. McDonald, and Alfred J. Rieber. Woodrow Wilson Center Series. [Washington, DC]: Woodrow Wilson Center Press; Cambridge; New York: Cambridge University Press, 1993. xv, 457 pp. [Some contributions translated from Russian. Partial contents: Hugh Ragsdale, "Introduction: the traditions of Imperial Russian foreign policy: problems of the present, agenda for the future"; E. V. Anisimov, "The imperial heritage of Peter the Great in the foreign policy of his early successors"; Hans Bagger, "The role of the Baltic in Russian foreign policy, 1721-1773"; Hugh Ragsdale "Russian projects of conquest in the eighteenth century"; Robert E. Jones, "Runaway peasants and Russian motives for the partitions of Poland"; David M. Goldfrank, "Policy traditions and the Menshikov mission of 1853"; V. N. Vinogradov, "The personal responsibility of Emperor Nicholas I for the coming of the Crimean War: an episode in the diplomatic struggle in the Eastern Question"; V. N. Ponomarev, "Russian policy and the United States during the Crimean War"; N. N. Bolkhovitinov, "The sale of Alaska in the context of Russo-American relations in the nineteenth century"; David MacKenzie, "Russia's Balkan policies under Alexander II, 1855-1881"; A. V. Ignat'ev, "The foreign policy of Russia in the Far East at the turn of the nineteenth and twentieth centuries"; David M. McDonald, "A lever without a fulcrum: domestic factors and Russian foreign policy, 1905-1914"; Alfred J. Rieber, "Persistent factors in Russian foreign policy: an interpretive essay"; Alfred J. Rieber, "The historiography of Imperial Russian foreign policy: a critical survey"; Hugh Ragsdale, "Afterword."]

2788. Rothstein, Morton, and Daniel Field, eds. *Quantitative Studies in Agrarian History*. Contributions by Morton Rothstein, Daniel Field, Juhan Kahk, O. G. Bukhovets, L. V. Milov, I. M. Garskova, I. D. Koval'chenko, L. I. Borodkin, and N. B. Selunskaia. 1st ed. Ames, IA: Iowa State University Press, 1993. xii, 275 pp. [Contains essays for a conference held in Tallinn, Estonian S.S.R., in 1987. The Soviet papers appeared in *Russian Review* 47, no. 4 (October 1988), and the American contributions in *Agricultural History* 62, no. 3 (Summer 1988). Partial contents: Daniel Field, Morton Rothstein, "Introduction," pp. vii-xii. Part I. American Scholars. Juhan Kahk, 2. "The Spread of Agricultural Machines in Estonia from 1860 to 1880," pp. 30-41 — Part II. Russian Scholars. O. G. Bukhovets, 9. "The Political Consciousness of the Russian Peasantry in the Revolution of 1905-1907: Sources, Meth-

ods, and Some Results," pp. 209-226; L. V. Milov and I. M. Garskova, 10. "A Typology of Feudal Estates in Russia in the First Half of the Seventeenth Century (Factor Analysis)," pp. 227-142; I. D. Koval'chenko and L. I. Borodkin, 11. "Two Paths of Bourgeois Agrarian Evolution in European Russia: An Essay in Multivariate Analysis," pp. 243-260; N. B. Selunskaia, 12. "Levels of Technology and the Use of Hired Labor in the Peasant and Manorial Economy of European Russia in 1917," pp. 261-275.]

Eighteenth Century

2789. Leonard, Carol S. *Reform and Regicide: The Reign of Peter III of Russia*. Indiana-Michigan Series in Russian and East European Studies. Bloomington, IN: Indiana University Press, c1993. 232 pp. [Contents: Introduction: Interpreting the Reign of Peter III; Origins of Reform; Emancipation of the Russian Nobility; Secularization of the Ecclesiastical Estates; National Revenues; Foreign Policy; Why the Coup?; Conclusion: Russian Autocracy at Mid-Century.] REV: Marc Raeff, *American Historical Review* 98, no. 4 (October 1993): 1143-1155.

2790. Raeff, Marc. "Autocracy Tempered by Reform or by Regicide?" *American Historical Review* 98, no. 4 (October 1993): 1143-1155. [Review article on Carol S. Leonard, *Reform and Regicide: The Reign of Peter III of Russia* (Bloomington, IN: 1993); John T. Alexander, *Catherine the Great: Life and Legend* (NY: 1989); and Roderick E. McGrew, *Paul I of Russia, 1754-1801* (Oxford: 1992).]

2791. Walker, James. *Engraved in the Memory: James Walker, Engraver to the Empress Catherine the Great, and His Russian Anecdotes*. Edited and introduced by Anthony Cross. Anglo-Russian Affinities Series. Oxford; Providence, RI: Berg, 1993. vii, 192 pp.

Nineteenth Century

2792. Downey, James. "Civil Society and the Campaign against Corporal Punishment in Late Imperial Russia, 1863-1904." Ph.D. diss., Indiana University, 1993. [UMI order no: AAC 9418788.]

2793. Engel'gardt, Aleksandr Nikolaevich. *Aleksandr Nikolaevich Engelgardt's Letters from the Country, 1872-1887*. Translated and edited by Cathy A. Frierson. New York: Oxford University Press, 1993. xiii, 272 pp. [Consists of 12 separate letters which first appeared in the Russian journals *Notes of the Fatherland* and *Herald of Europe*. Translated and abridged version of: *Iz derevni*. Contents: Cathy A. Frierson, "Introduction," pp. 3-20 — "Letter I" Daily Life with the Peasants on My Estate. Village Poverty and Charity: Crusts of Bread. My Natural Healer: The "Old Woman". Village Justice, pp. 21-35 — "Letter II" The Peasants' Poverty and Dependence on Local Gentry Landowners. The Peasant Thief Kostik and the Volost Court. The Question of Public Health in the Countryside. The Rural Clergy. My Trip to the Zemstvo Elections", pp. 36-50 — "Letter III" Work Done "Out of Respect". Trespassing and the Peasants' Sense of Private Property.

Peasant Fatalism and Attitudes toward Agricultural Innovation. The Subsistence Nature of Russian Agriculture, pp. 51-78 — "Letter IV" "Rogues Exist to Teach Fools to Be on Guard". Honesty and Industry of the Russian Peasant. Individualism in Peasant Farming. A Visit to the Local Agricultural Exhibition, pp. 79-101 — "Letter V" Old Lyska. The Role of Peasant Women in the Rural Economy. Peasant Individualism in Labor. Peasants as Skilled Laborers. Intelligence of the Russian Peasant, pp. 102-133 — "Letter VI" Rural Responses to the Russo-Turkish War, pp. 134-155 — "Letter VII" The Diggers' Artel as a Model of Collective Labor. Extended Peasant Households, Collective Labor, and Prosperity. Individualism of the Peasant Woman. The Futility of Legislation for the Village. The Peasant Economy in Post-Emancipation Russia, pp. 156-183 — "Letter VIII" New District Officials. Persecution of Local Jews. Bureaucratic Measures to Prevent Plague. My Descent into Alcoholism, pp. 184-202 — "Letter IX" The Economics of Seasonal Labor for the Peasant, pp. 203-209 — "Letter X" Prospering Peasants in the "Happy Little Corner" The Peasant Exploiter: The Kulak, pp. 210-227 — "Letter XI" Peasants' Rumors about the Land, pp. 228-238 — "Letter XII" Peasant Land Purchases and Local Farming. The Promise of Phosphorite Fertilizer for Russian Agriculture, pp. 245-255 — Bibliography of Related Works, pp. 269-272.]

2794. Longhofer, Jeffrey. "Specifying the Commons: Mennonites, Intensive Agriculture, and Landlessness in Nineteenth-Century Russia." *Ethnohistory* 40, no. 3 (Summer 1993): 384-409.

2795. Martin, Alexander M. "Defenders of the Old Regime: Russian Conservatives in the Age of Napoleon and the Holy Alliance." Ph.D. diss., University of Pennsylvania, 1993. [UMI order no: AAC 9321439.]

2796. Melton, Edgar. "Household Economies and Communal Conflicts on a Russian Serf Estate, 1800-1817." *Journal of Social History* 26, no. 3 (Spring 1993): 559-585.

2797. Mironov, Boris. "Bureaucratic- or Self-Government: The Early Nineteenth Century Russian City." *Slavic Review* 52, no. 2 (Summer 1993): 233-255. Translated by Vitaly Chernetsky and Lesley Rimmel.

2798. Ofek, Adina. "Cantonists: Jewish Children as Soldiers in Tsar Nicholas's Army." *Modern Judaism* 13, no. 3 (October 1993): 277-308.

2799. Pomeranz, William E. "Justice from Underground: The History of the Underground *Advokatura*." *Russian Review* 52, no. 3 (July 1993): 321-340.

2800. Semyonova Tian-Shanskaia, Olga. *Village Life in Late Tsarist Russia*. Edited by David L. Ransel. Translated by David L. Ransel and Michael Levine. Indiana-Michigan Series in Russian and East European Studies. Bloomington, IN: Indiana University Press, c1993. xxx, 175 pp. [Translated from the Russian. Contents: Ivan's Parents; Childbirth, Christening, Wife Beating; Childhood; Courtship and Sexual Relations; Ivan Prepares for Marriage; Pledging the Bride, the Bride-Show, and Marriage; Infanticide, Emotion, Sexual Disorder, Drink and Food; Housing, Property, Trades, Budgets, and Religious Belief; Peasant Ideals, Work Habits, and Causes of Poverty; Court Cases and Political Structure.] REV: Abraham Rzepkowicz, *Canadian Slavonic Papers* 35, nos. 3-4 (September-December 1993): 429-430.

2801. Senn, Alfred E. *The Russian Revolutionary Movement of the Nineteenth Century as Contemporary History*. Occasional Paper (Kennan Institute for Advanced Russian Studies), no. 250. Washington, DC: Kennan Institute for Advanced Russian Studies, The Wilson Center, [c1993]. 31 pp.

2802. Sunderland, Willard. "Peasants on the Move: State Peasant Resettlement in Imperial Russia, 1805-1830s." *Russian Review* 52, no. 4 (October 1993): 472-485.

Late Empire, War, Revolution (1894-1917)

2803. Avrus, A. I., and E. V. Kostyayev. "Rossiiskaia sotsial-demokratiia i russko-iaponskaia voina 1904-1905 godov." *Australian Slavonic and East European Studies* 7, no. 2 (1993): 115-141.

2804. Bortnevski, Viktor G. "White Administration and White Terror (The Denikin Period)." *Russian Review* 52, no. 3 (July 1993): 354-366.

2805. Bowman, Linda. "Russia's First Income Taxes: The Effects of Modernized Taxes on Commerce and Industry, 1885-1914." *Slavic Review* 52, no. 2 (Summer 1993): 256-282.

2806. Foran, John. "Revolutionizing Theory/ Theorizing Revolutions: State, Culture, and Society in Recent Works on Revolution." *Contention: Debates in Society, Culture and Science* 2, no. 2 (Winter 1993): 65-88. [Review article on Jack A. Goldstone, *Revolution and Rebellion in the Early Modern World* (Berkeley, CA: 1991); Tim McDaniel, *Autocracy, Modernization and Revolution in Russia and Iran* (Princeton, NJ: 1991); and Timothy P. Wickham-Crowley, *Guerrillas and Revolution in Latin America. A Comparative Study of Insurgents and Regimes Since 1956* (Princeton, NJ: 1992).]

2807. Fox, Martyna Agata. "The Eastern Question in Russian Politics: Interplay of Diplomacy, Opinion and Interest, 1905-1917." Ph.D. diss., Yale University, 1993. [UMI order no: AAC 9418527.]

2808. Geifman, Anna. *Thou Shalt Kill: Revolutionary Terrorism in Russia, 1894-1917*. Princeton, NJ: Princeton University Press, c1993. xii, 376 pp. [Contents: Revolutionary Terrorism in the Empire: Background, Extent, and Impact; The Party of Socialists—Revolutionaries and Terror; The Social Democrats and Terror; Terrorists of a New Type: The Anarchists and the Obscure Extremist Groups; The "Seamy Side" of the Revolution: The Criminal Element, the Psychologically Unbalanced, and Juveniles; The United Front: Interparty Connections and Cooperation; The Kadets and Terror; The End of Revolutionary Terrorism in Russia.]

2809. Henriksson, Anders. "Nationalism, Assimilation and Identity in Late Imperial Russia: The St. Petersburg Germans, 1906-1914." *Russian Review* 52, no. 3 (July 1993): 341-353.

2810. Hogan, Heather. *Forging Revolution: Metalworkers, Managers, and the State in St. Petersburg, 1890-1914.* Indiana-Michigan Series in Russian and East European Studies. Studies of the Harriman Institute. Bloomington, IN: Indiana University Press, c1993. xiv, 319 pp. [Contents: Petersburg's Metalworking Industry in the Post-Emancipation Era; The Industrialization of the 1890s; The Emerging Crisis, 1900-1904; Labor-Management Conflict in the Revolution of 1905; Rethinking Labor Relations "From Above": State Managers and the Entrepreneurial Elite in 1906; The Changing Nature of Metalworker Activism in 1906-1907; Financiers, Employers, and Engineers: Confronting the Imperatives of Economic Modernization; Rationalizing the Metalworking Industry; The Uneven Struggle in the Years before Lena; Labor and Management in Conflict, 1912-1914.]

2811. Horsbrugh-Porter, Anna, ed. *Memories of Revolution: Russian Women Remember.* Interviews by Elena Snow and Frances Welch. London; New York: Routledge, 1993. ix, 138 pp. [Contents: Anna Horsbrugh-Porter, "Introduction," pp. 1-7; Anya Troup, pp. 8-12; Tatiana Vladimirovna Toporkova, pp. 13-25; Princess Sophia Wacznadze, pp. 26-38; Dorothy Russell, pp. 39-46; Irina Sergevna Tidmarsh, pp. 47-69; Ludmila Mathias, pp. 70-82; Marie Allan, pp. 83-95; Olga Lawrence, pp. 96-104; Eugenia Peacock, pp. 120-119; Ada Nikolskaya, pp. 120-127.]

2812. Jahn, Hubertus F. "Aspects of Patriotic Culture in Russia During World War I." *Ethnic Groups* 10, nos. 1-3 (1993): 187-200. [Part of special issue devoted to "Pre-Modern and Modern National Identity in Russia and Eastern Europe."]

2813. Korros, Alexandra Shecket. "Activist Politics in a Conservative Institution: The Formation of Factions in the Russian Imperial State Council, 1906-1907." *Russian Review* 52, no. 1 (January 1993): 1-19.

2814. Leikin, Ezekiel, trans. and ed. *The Beilis Transcripts: The Anti-Semitic Trial that Shook the World.* Northvale, NJ: Jason Aronson, 1993. xxvi, 241 pp.

2815. Lindenmeyr, Adele. "Maternalism and Child Welfare in Late Imperial Russia." *Journal of Women's History* 5, no. 2 (Fall 1993): 114-125.

2816. Maxwell, Margaret. "The Lady and the Tsar: The Courageous Life of Maria Tsebrikova." *Woman and Earth* 2, no. 1 (December 10, 1993): 35-37.

2817. McReynolds, Louise. "Mobilizing Petrograd's Lower Classes to Fight the Great War: Patriotism as a Counterweight to Working-Class Consciousness in *Gazeta kopeika*." *Radical History Review*, no. 57 (Fall 1993): 160-180.

2818. Melançon, Michael. "The Syntax of Soviet Power: The Resolutions of Local Soviets and Other Institu-

tions, March-October 1917." *Russian Review* 52, no. 4 (October 1993): 486-505.

2819. Neuberger, Joan. *Hooliganism: Crime, Culture, and Power in St. Petersburg, 1900-1914.* Studies on the History of Society and Culture, 19. Berkeley, CA: University of California Press, c1993. xiv, 324 pp. [Based on the author's thesis. Contents: Introduction. Crime and Culture; 1. The Boulevard Press Discovers a New Crime; 2. From Under Every Rock: Hooligans in Revolution, 1905-1907; 3. Ripples Spread: To the Village, the Law, and the Arts; 4. Nobody's Children: Juvenile Crime, Youth Culture, and the Roots of Hooliganism; 5. Violence and Poverty in a City Divided.]

2820. Pearl, Deborah L. "Tsar and Religion in Russian Revolutionary Propaganda." *Russian History* 20, nos. 1-4 (1993): 81-107.

2821. Ruud, Charles A. "A. A. Lopukhin, Police Insubordination and the Rule of Law." *Russian History* 20, nos. 1-4 (1993): 147-162.

2822. Surh, Gerald D. "A Matter of Life or Death: Politics, Profession, and Public Health in St. Petersburg before 1914." *Russian History* 20, nos. 1-4 (1993): 125-146.

2823. Weeks, Charles J., Jr. *An American Naval Diplomat in Revolutionary Russia: The Life and Times of Vice Admiral Newton A. McCully.* Annapolis, MD: Naval Institute Press, c1993. xii, 348 pp. [Contents: Prologue: A Magician in Russia; 1. From Anderson to Port Arthur; 2. Marching with a Beaten Army; 3. A Journey to the Eastern Front; 4. The Fall of Kings: The Russian Revolution; 5. Mission in Murmansk and Archangelsk; 6. The Cry of the Humble; 7. Last Mission to Russia; 8. Crimean Twilight; 9. The End of a Journey.]

2824. Weinberg, Robert. *The Revolution of 1905 in Odessa: Blood on the Steps.* Indiana-Michigan Series in Russian and East European Studies. Studies of the Harriman Institute. Bloomington, IN: Indiana University Press, c1993. xvi, 302 pp. [Contents: 1. Odessa on the Eve of 1905: The Russian El Dorado? 2. Workers in Odessa on the Eve of 1905; 3. Labor Organizations and Politics before 1905; 4. First Stirrings: The Workers' Movement from January to May; 5. First Confrontation: Popular Unrest in May and June; 6. Breathing Spell and Renewed Confrontation; 7. Politics and Pogrom; 8. Final Confrontation.]

2825. Wood, Alan. *The Origins of the Russian Revolution, 1861-1917.* 2nd ed. Lancaster Pamphlets. London; New York: Routledge, 1993. xix, 59 pp.

Soviet Period (1917-1991)

2826. Daniels, Robert V. "Was Stalin Really a Communist?" *Soviet and Post-Soviet Review* 20, nos. 2-3 (1993): 169-175. [Followed with response by Allen Lynch (pp. 177-182).]

2827. Daniels, Robert Vincent, ed. *A Documentary History of Communism in Russia: From Lenin to Gorbachev.* Introduction, notes, and original translations by Robert

Vincent Daniels. 3rd, revised and updated ed. Hanover, NH: University of Vermont; Published by University Press of New England, 1993. xxxv, 392 pp. [Contents: Leninism and the Bolshevik Party, to 1917; The Bolshevik Revolution, 1917-1921; Soviet Communism: The Era of Controversy, 1922-1929; The Transformation Under Stalin, 1929-1953; The Interval of Reform, 1953-1964; The Era of Stagnation; Perestroika and the End of Communism, 1985-1991.]

2828. Dziewanowski, M. K. *A History of Soviet Russia*. 4th ed. Englewood Cliffs, NJ: Prentice Hall, c1993. xvi, 425 pp.

2829. Hosking, Geoffrey A. *The First Socialist Society: A History of the Soviet Union from Within*. 2nd enl. ed. Cambridge, MA: Harvard University Press, 1993. 570 pp.

2830. Knight, Amy. *Beria: Stalin's First Lieutenant*. Princeton, NJ: Princeton University Press, c1993. xvi, 312 pp. [Contents: Map of Georgia, 1991; Chronology of Beria's Life; Early Life and Career; Service in the Georgian Political Police; Leader of Georgia and Transcaucasia: 1931-1936; The Purges in Georgia; Master of the Lubianka; The War Years; Kremlin Politics after the War; Beria under Fire: 1950-1953; The Downfall of Beria; The Aftermath; Beria Reconsidered.] REV: Robert Legvold, *Foreign Affairs* 72, no. 5 (November-December 1993): 173-174. David Pryce-Jones, *National Review* 45, no. 23 (November 29, 1993): 64ff.

2831. Kort, Michael. *The Soviet Colossus: The Rise and Fall of the USSR*. 3rd ed. Armonk, NY: M.E. Sharpe, c1993. xii, 365 pp. [Partial contents: The Fundamentals of Russian History; The End of the Old Order; Lenin's Russia; Steeling the Revolution; The Socialist Superpower.]

2832. Lynch, Allen. "Comments on Robert V. Daniel's Paper." *Soviet and Post-Soviet Review* 20, nos. 2-3 (1993): 177-182. [Response to "Was Stalin Really a Communist?" (pp. 169-175).]

2833. Mäkinen, Ilkka. "Libraries in Hell: Cultural Activities in Soviet Prisons and Labor Camps from the 1930s to the 1950s." *Libraries & Culture* 28, no. 2 (Spring 1993): 117-142.

2834. McCauley, Martin. *The Soviet Union: 1917-1991*. 2nd ed. Longman History of Russia. London; New York: Longman, 1993. xvii, 422 pp.

2835. Nove, Alec. *The Soviet System in Retrospect: An Obituary Notice*. Annual W. Averell Harriman Lecture, 4th. New York, NY: Harriman Institute, Columbia University, c1993. 32 pp.

2836. ———, ed. *The Stalin Phenomenon*. Contributions by Alec Nove, R. W. Davies, Sheila Fitzpatrick, J. Arch Getty, and Sergo Mikoyan. New York: St. Martin's Press, 1993. vi, 216 pp. [Contents: Alec Nove, "Stalin and Stalinism: some introductory thoughts"; R.W. Davies, "Economic aspects of Stalinism"; Sheila Fitzpatrick, "Constructing Stalinism: changing Western and Soviet perspectives"; J. Arch Getty, "The politics of Stalinism"; Sergo Mikoyan, "Stalinism as I saw it"; Alec Nove, "Stalin and

Stalinism: some afterthoughts."]

2837. Riordan, James. *Russia and the Commonwealth of Independent States*. 2nd rev. ed. Silver Burdett Countries. Morristown, NJ: Silver Burdett, 1993. 48 pp. [Rev. ed. of: *Soviet Union*. 1987, c1986.]

2838. Shaw, Denis J. B. "Geographic and Historical Observations on the Future of a Federal Russia." *Post-Soviet Geography* 34, no. 8 (October 1993): 530-540.

2839. Von Laue, Theodore H. *Why Lenin? Why Stalin? Why Gorbachev? The Rise and Fall of the Soviet System*. 3rd ed. Critical Periods of History. New York, NY: HarperCollins College Publishers, c1993. xii, 194 pp. [Rev. ed. of: *Why Lenin? Why Stalin?* 2nd ed. c1971.]

2840. Ward, Chris. *Stalin's Russia*. Reading History. London; New York: Edward Arnold: Distributed in the USA by Routledge, Chapman and Hall, 1993. xxii, 241 pp.

1917 through 1938

2841. Argenbright, Robert. "Bolsheviks, Baggers and Railroaders: Political Power and Social Space, 1917-1921." *Russian Review* 52, no. 4 (October 1993): 506-527.

2842. Ball, Alan. "State Children: Soviet Russia's *Besprizornye* and the New Socialist Generation." *Russian Review* 52, no. 2 (April 1993): 228-247.

2843. Conquest, Robert. " 'The Evil of This Time.' " *New York Review of Books* 40, no. 15 (September 23, 1993): 24-27. [Review article on Anna Larina, *This I Cannot Forget: The Memoirs of Nikolai Bukharin's Widow*, trans. Gary Kern (NY: Norton, 1993).]

2844. Fitzpatrick, Sheila. "Ascribing Class: The Construction of Social Identity in Soviet Russia." *Journal of Modern History* 65, no. 4 (December 1993): 745-770. [Previous versions of this article were presented at the University of Chicago, Johns Hopkins University, and the first Midwestern Workshop of Russian Historians in Ann Arbor.]

2845. ———. "How the Mice Buried the Cat: Scenes from the Great Purges of 1937 in the Russian Provinces." *Russian Review* 52, no. 3 (July 1993): 299-320.

2846. Getty, J. Arch, and Roberta T. Manning, eds. *Stalinist Terror: New Perspectives*. Contributions by Boris A. Starkov, J. Arch Getty, Lynne Viola, Gábor T. Rittersporn, Robert Thurston, David L. Hoffman, Roberta T. Manning, Roger R. Reese, William Chase, Sheila Fitzpatrick, Alec Nove, and Stephen G. Wheatcroft. Cambridge; New York: Cambridge University Press, 1993. viii, 294 pp. [Contents: J. Arch Getty and Roberta T. Manning, "Introduction," pp. 1-20 — Pt. I. Persons and Politics. Boris A. Starkov, "Narkom Ezhov," pp. 21-39; J. Arch Getty, "The Politics of Repression Revisited," pp. 40-62 — Pt. II. Backgrounds. Lynne Viola, "The Second Coming: Class Enemies in the Soviet Countryside, 1927-1935," pp. 65-98; Gábor T. Rittersporn, "The Omnipresent Conspiracy: On Soviet Imagery of Politics and Social Relations in the 1930s," pp. 99-115; Roberta T. Manning, "The Soviet Economic Crisis of

1936-1940 and the Great Purges," pp. 116-141; Robert Thurston, "The Stakhanovite Movement: The Background to the Great Terror in the Factories, 1935-1938," pp. 142-160 — Pt. III. Case Studies. David L. Hoffman, "The Great Terror on the Local Level: Purges in Moscow Factories, 1936-1938," pp. 163-167; Roberta T. Manning, "The Great Purges in a Rural District: Belyi Raion Revisited," pp. 168-197; Roger R. Reese, "The Red Army and the Great Purges," pp. 198-214; Hiroaki Kuromiya, "Stalinist Terror in the Donbas: A Note," pp. 215-222 — Pt. IV. Impact and Incidence. J. Arch Getty and William Chase, "Patterns of Repression Among the Soviet Elite in the Late 1930s: A Biographical Approach," pp. 225-246; Sheila Fitzpatrick, "The Impact of the Great Purges on Soviet Elites: A Case Study from Moscow and Leningrad Telephone Directories of the 1930s," pp. 247-260; Alec Nove, "Victims of Stalinism: How Many?" pp. 261-274; Stephen G. Wheatcroft, "More Light on the Scale of Repression and Excess Mortality in the Soviet Union in the 1930s," pp. 275-290.]

2847. Getty, J. Arch, Gábor T. Rittersporn, and Viktor N. Zemskov. "Victims of the Soviet Penal System in the Pre-War Years: A First Approach on the Basis of Archival Evidence." *American Historical Review* 98, no. 4 (October 1993): 1017-1049.

2848. Heinzen, James Warren. "Politics, Administration and Specialization in the Russian People's Commissariat of Agriculture, 1917-1927." Ph.D. diss., University of Pennsylvania, 1993. [UMI order no: AAC 9413845.]

2849. Hochschild, Adam. "The Secret of a Siberian River Bank." *New York Times Magazine* (March 28, 1993): 28ff. [On the discovery of skeletons of NKVD victims.]

2850. Kirschenbaum, Lisa Ann. "Raising Young Russia: The Family, the State, and the Preschool Child, 1917-1931." Ph.D. diss., University of California, Berkeley, 1993. [UMI order no: AAC 9408033.]

2851. Livi-Bacci, Massimo. "On the Human Costs of Collectivization in the Soviet Union." *Population and Development Review* 19, no. 4 (December 1993): 743-766.

2852. Pipes, Richard. *Russia Under the Bolshevik Regime.* 1st ed. New York: A.A. Knopf, 1993. xviii, 587 pp.

2853. Tirado, Isabel A. "The Komsomol and Young Peasants: The Dilemma of Rural Expansion, 1921-1925." *Slavic Review* 52, no. 3 (Fall 1993): 460-476.

2854. Weinberg, Robert. "Purge and Politics in the Periphery: Birobidzhan in 1937." *Slavic Review* 52, no. 1 (Spring 1993): 13-27.

1939 through 1945

2855. Hoyt, Edwin P. *199 Days: The Battle for Stalingrad.* 1st ed. New York: Tor, 1993. 304 pp. REV: Jonathan M. House, *Army* 43, no. 3 (March 1993): 59.

2856. Knappe, Siegfried, and Ted Brusaw. *Soldat: Reflections of a German Soldier, 1936-1949.* New York: Dell Books, 1993. xvii, 430 pp.

2857. Tec, Nechama. *Defiance: The Bielski Partisans.* New York: Oxford University Press, 1993. xiii, 276 pp. [Contents: 1. Before the War; 2. The Russian Occupation; 3. The German Invasion; 4. The Beginning of the Bielski Otriad; 5. Escapes from the Ghetto; 6. The Partisan Network; 7. Rescue or Resistance; 8. Eluding the Enemy; 9. The "Big Hunt"; 10. Building a Forest Community; 11. The Emergence of New Social Arrangements; 12. The Fate of Women; 13. Keeping Order; 14. The End of the Otriad; 15. From Self-Preservation to Rescue; Organization of the Bielski Otriad.]

2858. Westad, Odd Arne. *Cold War and Revolution: Soviet-American Rivalry and the Origins of the Chinese Civil War, 1944-1946.* New York: Columbia University Press, 1993. x, 260 pp. [Contents: 1. Yalta and the Search for Stability; 2. The Jiang-Stalin Pact and the Collapse of Great Power Cooperation; 3. The Seventh Party Congress and the Origins of CCP Foreign Policy; 4. The Race to Shenyang: Chinese Politics and the Soviet Occupation of the Northeast; 5. Allies and Enemies: Mao, Jiang, and the U.S. Intervention in North China; 6. The Origins of the Marshall Mission; 7. The Soviet Withdrawal and the Coming of the Civil War; Conclusion: Revolt, Intervention, and Cold War; A Word on Chinese Archives and Materials.] REV: Donald Zagoria, *Foreign Affairs* 72, no. 4 (September-October 1993): 176.

2859. Woll, Josephine. "An Epic Endurance." *Atlantic* 272, no. 1 (July 1993): 113-116. [Review article on John Garrard and Carol Garrard, eds., *World War II and the Soviet People* (NY: 1993).]

2860. World Congress for Soviet and East European Studies (4th: 1990: Harrogate, England). *World War 2 and the Soviet People.* Edited by John Garrard and Carol Garrard. New York, NY: St. Martin's Press, 1993. xxix, 268 pp. [Edited for the International Council for Soviet and East European Studies by Stephen White.] REV: Josephine Woll, *Atlantic* 272, no. 1 (July 1993): 113-116.

1946 through 1964

2861. Goncharov, Sergei N., John W. Lewis, and Litai Xue. *Uncertain Partners: Stalin, Mao, and the Korean War.* Studies in International Security and Arms Control. Stanford, CA: Stanford University Press, c1993. xi, 393 pp. [Contents: 1. Stalin, Mao, and the Chinese Civil War, 1945-1948; 2. Prelude to Negotiations; 3. The Making of the Alliance; 4. End Game; 5. The Decision for War in Korea; 6. China Enters the Korean War; 7. Summing Up; Appendix: Documents on the Sino-Soviet Alliance and the Korean War.]

2862. Klusáková, Jana. "Who Was Lavrenty Beria?" *RCDA* 32, no. 2 (1993-1994): 37-39. [Abbreviated from *Slovenské Listy* no. 3 (1994).]

2863. Park, Soo-Heon. "Party Reform and 'Volunteer Principle' under Khrushchev in Historical Perspective." Ph.D. diss., Columbia University, 1993. [UMI order no: AAC 9412828.]

2864. Weiner, Douglas. "Three Men in a Boat: The All-Russian Society for the Protection of Nature (VOOP) in the Early 1960s." *Soviet and Post-Soviet Review* 20, nos. 2-3 (1993): 195-212. [Article is part of a larger study, entitled *The Citizen's Movement that Refused to Die: Conservation and the Struggle for Civic Dignity in the Soviet Union from Stalin to Gorbachev* (Bloomington: Indiana University Press, forthcoming).]

1965 through 1985

2865. Alexeyeva, Ludmilla, and Paul Goldberg. *The Thaw Generation: Coming of Age in the Post-Stalin Era.* Paperback ed. Pittsburgh, PA: University of Pittsburgh Press, 1993. x, 339 pp.

2866. Morris, Stephen J. "The '1205 Document': A Story of American Prisoners, Vietnamese Agents, Soviet Archives, Washington Bureaucrats, and the Media." *National Interest*, no. 33 (Fall 1993): 28-42.

Territories and Adjacent States

General

2867. McDougall, Walter A. *Let the Sea Make a Noise: A History of the North Pacific from Magellan to MacArthur.* New York, NY: Basic Books, 1993. ix, 793 pp. REV: *Wilson Quarterly* 17, no. 4 (Autumn 1993): 68-71.

Alaska and Russian America

2868. Frost, O. W. "Vitus Bering Resurrected: Recent Forensic Analysis and the Documentary Record." *Pacific Northwest Quarterly* 84, no. 3 (July 1993): 91-97.

2869. Grinev, Andrei V. "On the Banks of the Copper River: The Ahtna Indians and the Russians, 1783-1867." *Arctic Anthropology* 30, no. 1 (1993): 54-66.

2870. Lightfoot, Kent G., Thomas A. Wake, and Ann M. Schiff. "Native Responses to the Russian Mercantile Colony of Fort Ross, Northern California." *Journal of Field Archaeology* 20, no. 2 (Summer 1993): 159-175.

2871. Schabelski, Achille. "Visit of the Russian Warship *Apollo* to California in 1822-1823." *Southern California Quarterly* 75, no. 1 (Spring 1993): 1-13. Translated and edited by Glenn Farris. [Excerpt from *Voyage aux colonies russes de l'Amérique, fait à bord du sloop de guerre, l'Apollon, pendant les années 1821, 1822, et 1823* (St. Petersburg: 1826).]

2872. Sears, David. "Of Venerable Bones and Intrigue: Discovering a Discoverer, the Great Vitus Jonassen Bering." *World & I* 8, no. 8 (August 1993): 155-163.

Caucasus and Central Asia

2873. Adshead, S. A. M. *Central Asia in World History.* New York: St. Martin's Press, 1993. vii, 291 pp.

2874. Bergholz, Fred W. *The Partition of the Steppe: The Struggle of the Russians, Manchus, and the Zunghar Mongols for Empire in Central Asia, 1619-1758: A Study in Power Politics.* American University Studies. Series IX, History, vol. 109. New York: Peter Lang, 1993. vi, 522 pp.

2875. Bournoutian, George A. *A History of the Armenian People.* Costa Mesa, CA: Mazda Publishers, c1993-. vols. [Contents: Vol. 1. Pre-history to 1500 A.D.]

2876. Khalid, Adeeb. "The Politics of Muslim Cultural Reform: Jadidism in Tsarist Central Asia." Ph.D. diss., University of Wisconsin-Madison, 1993. [UMI order no: AAC 9320907.]

2877. Matthew, of Edessa, and Erets' Grifor. *Armenia and the Crusades: Tenth to Twelfth Centuries: The Chronicle of Matthew of Edessa.* Translated from the original Armenian with a commentary and introduction by Ara Edmond Dostourian. Foreword by Krikor H. Maksoudian. Armenian Heritage Series. [Belmont, MA?]: National Association for Armenian Studies and Research; Lanham, MD: University Press of America, c1993. xiii, 375 pp. [By Matthew of Edessa, continued by Grigor Erets'.]

2878. Minassian, Michael. "Uncle Minas." *Ararat* 34, no. 3 (no. 135) (Summer 1993): 43.

2879. Shahrani, Nazif. "The Lessons and Uses of History." *Central Asia Monitor*, no. 1 (1993): 24-27. [Excerpts from an address by Shahrani at the Third Annual Nava'i Lecture in Central Asian Studies, held at Georgetown University, November 10, 1992.]

2880. Suny, Ronald Grigor. *Looking toward Ararat: Armenia in Modern History.* Bloomington, IN: Indiana University Press, c1993. xi, 289 pp. [Contents: Introduction: From National Character to National Tradition. Pt. 1. Imagining Armenia. 1. Armenia and Its Rulers; 2. Images of the Armenians in the Russian Empire; 3. The Emergence of the Armenian Patriotic Intelligentsia in Russia; 4. Populism, Nationalism, and Marxism among Russia's Armenians; 5. Labor and Socialism among Armenians in Transcaucasia; 6. Rethinking the Unthinkable: Toward an Understanding of the Armenian Genocide. Pt. 2. State, Nation, Diaspora; 7. Armenia and the Russian Revolution; 8. Building a Socialist Nation; 9. Stalin and the Armenians; 10. Return to Ararat: Armenia in the Cold War; 11. The New Nationalism in Armenia; 12. Nationalism and Democracy: The Case of Karabagh; 13. Looking toward Ararat: The Diaspora and the "Homeland"; 14. Armenia on the Road to Independence, Again; Bibliography of Books and Articles in Western Languages on Modern Armenian History.]

Siberia and the Russian Far East

2881. Gehrmann, Udo. "Kazachestvo vostochnykh regionov Rossii v osveshchenii nemetskikh istochnikov 18-go veka." *Australian Slavonic and East European Studies* 7, no. 1 (1993): 91-110.

2882. Mongush, Mergen. "The Annexation of Tannu-Tuva and the Formation of the Tuvinskaya ASSR." *Nationalities Papers* 21, no. 2 (Fall 1993): 47-52.

2883. Pereira, N. G. O. "The Idea of Siberian Regionalism in Late Imperial and Revolutionary Russia." *Russian History* 20, nos. 1-4 (1993): 163-178.

Ukraine

2884. Beauplan, Guillaume Le Vasseur. *A Description of Ukraine*. Introduction, translation, and notes by Andrew B. Pernal and Dennis F. Essar. Harvard Series in Ukrainian Studies. Ukraina v mizhnarodnykh zv'iazkakh: khroniky, memuary, shchodennyky. [Cambridge, MA]: Distributed by the Harvard University Press for the Harvard Ukrainian Research Institute, 1993. cxiii, 242 pp. [Translation of: *Description d'Ukranie*.]

2885. Clinton, Bill. "President Clinton's Statement on the Sixtieth Anniversary of the Ukrainian Famine-Genocide." *Ukrainian Quarterly* 49, no. 2 (Summer 1993): 213.

2886. Dmitriev, Mikhail V. "Ukraine and Russia." *Canadian Slavonic Papers* 35, nos. 1-2 (March-June 1993): 131-147. Translated from the Russian by Eva DeMarco. [Review article on P.J. Potichnyj, Marc Raeff, Jaroslaw Pelenski and Gleb N. Zekulin, eds., *Ukraine and Russia in Their Historical Encounter* (Edmonton: 1992).]

2887. Drach, Ivan. "To the Famine-Genocide of 1933." *Ukrainian Quarterly* 49, no. 4 (Winter 1993): 357-361. Translated by R. K. Stojko-Lozynskyj. [Address read at the Sixtieth Anniversary Commemoration of the Famine-Genocide held at Kyiv, September 9, 1993.]

2888. Hamm, Michael F. *Kiev: A Portrait, 1800-1917*. Princeton, NJ: Princeton University Press, c1993. xvii, 304 pp. [Contents: The Early History of Kiev; The Growth of Metropolitan Kiev; Polish Kiev; Ukrainians in Russian Kiev; Jewish Kiev; Recreation, the Arts, and Popular Culture in Kiev; The Promise of Change: Kiev in 1905; The Promise Shattered: The October Pogrom; The Final Years of Romanov Kiev.] REV: Bohdan Klid, *Canadian Slavonic Papers* 35, nos. 3-4 (September-December 1993): 418-420.

2889. Kosyk, Wolodymyr. *The Third Reich and Ukraine*. Translated by Irene Ievins Rudnytzky. Studies in Modern European History, vol. 8. New York: P. Lang, c1993. xvi, 669 pp.

2890. Kulchytsky, George P. "Western Relief Efforts during the 'Stalin Famine.' " *Ukrainian Quarterly* 49, no. 2 (Summer 1993): 152-164.

2891. Mace, James E. "How Ukraine Was Permitted to Remember." *Ukrainian Quarterly* 49, no. 2 (Summer 1993): 121-151.

2892. Plokhy, Serhii M. "Ukraine and Russia in their Historical Encounter." *Canadian Slavonic Papers* 35, nos. 3-4 (September-December 1993): 335-344. [Response to Mikhail Dmitriev's book review in vol. 35, nos. 1-2 (March-June 1993): 131-147.]

2893. Saunders, David. "What Makes a Nation a Nation? Ukrainians since 1600." *Ethnic Groups* 10, nos. 1-3 (1993): 101-124. [Part of special issue devoted to "Pre-

Modern and Modern National Identity in Russia and Eastern Europe."]

2894. Silberfarb, Moses. *The Jewish Ministry and Jewish National Autonomy in Ukraine*. Translated by David Lincoln. New York: Aleph Press, 1993. xi, 115 pp. [Translation of the 1918 Yiddish-language memoir.] REV: Henry Abramson, *Canadian Slavonic Papers* 35, nos. 1-2 (March-June 1993): 197-198.

2895. Slavutych, Yar. "The Famine of 1932-1933 in the Ukrainian Literature Abroad." *Ukrainian Quarterly* 49, no. 2 (Summer 1993): 165-183.

2896. Stojko, Wolodymyr. "On the Sixtieth Anniversary of the Famine-Genocide in Ukraine." *Ukrainian Quarterly* 49, no. 2 (Summer 1993): 117-120.

2897. Ukrains'ka narodnia respublika. *Derzhavnyi tsentr Ukrains'koi narodn'oi respubliky v ekzyli: statti i materiialy*. Zredahuvaly Liubomyr R. Vynar, and Nataliia Pazuniak. Kyiv: Vyd-vo "Veselka"; Filadel'fiia: Fundatsiia im. S. Petliury v SShA; Vashington: Fundatsiia Rodyny Feshchenko-Chopivs'kykh, 1993. 493 pp. [Title on added t.p.: *Ukrainian National Republic Government in Exile*. At head of title: Instytut doslidzhennia modernoi istorii Ukrainy.]

2898. World Congress for Soviet and East European Studies (4th: 1990: Harrogate, England). *Ukrainian Past, Ukrainian Present*. Edited by Bohdan Krawchenko. Contributions by Orest Pelech, Catherine B. Clay, Alexis E. Pogorelskin, Ihor Stebelsky, Rex A. Wade, Serhii Pirozhkov, Taras Hunczak, Taras Kuzio, and Peter J. Potichnyj. New York: St. Martin's Press, 1993. xii, 137 pp. [Selected papers from the World Congress for Soviet and East European Studies (4th: 1990: Harrogate, England). Contents: Orest Pelech, "The State and the Ukrainian Triumvirate in the Russian Empire, 1831-47," pp. 1-17; Catherine B. Clay, "From Savage Ukrainian Steppe to Quiet Russian Field: Ukrainian Ethnographers and Imperial Russia in the Reform Era," pp. 18-34; Alexis E. Pogorelskin, "A. N. Pypin's Defence of Ukraine: Sources and Motivation," pp. 35-54; Ihor Stebelsky, "Ukrainian Migration to Siberia before 1917: The Process and Problems of Losses and Survival Rates," pp. 55-69; Rex A. Wade, "Ukrainian Nationalism and 'Soviet Power': Kharkiv, 1917," pp. 70-83; Serhii Pirozhkov, "Population Loss in Ukraine in the 1930s and 1940s," pp. 84-96; Taras Hunczak, "Between Two Leviathans: Ukraine during the Second World War," pp. 97-106; Taras Kuzio, "Restructuring from Below: Informal Groups in Ukraine under Gorbachev, 1985-89," pp. 107-122; Peter J. Potichnyj, "The March 1990 Elections in Ukraine," pp. 123-133.]

■ Eastern Europe

General

2899. Banac, Ivo. "The Insignia of Identity: Heraldry and the Growth of National Ideologies Among the South Slavs." *Ethnic Groups* 10, no. 1-3 (1993): 215-237.

[Part of special issue devoted to "Pre-Modern and Modern National Identity in Russia and Eastern Europe."]

2900. Bowman, Shearer Davis. *Masters & Lords: Mid-19th-Century U.S. Planters and Prussian Junkers.* New York: Oxford University Press, 1993. ix, 357 pp. [Contents: Prussia 1848-49. The South 1860-61, Secession; 1. Landed Autocrats, Gentlemen Farmers, and British Influences; 2. Agrarian Entrepreneurs; 3. Contentious Concepts; 4. Planter Republicanism versus Junker Monarchism; 5. Patriarchy and Paternalism; 6. Planter and Junker Conservatism.]

2901. Dornbusch, Rudiger, Wilhelm Nölling, and Richard Layard, eds. *Postwar Economic Reconstruction and Lessons for the East Today.* Includes contributions by Jouko Paunio, Koichi Hamada, Munehisa Kasuya, J. Bradford De Long, Barry Eichengreen, Olivier Blanchard, Wilhelm Nölling, and Richard Portes. Cambridge, MA: MIT Press, c1993. xiv, 249 pp. [Essays from a conference organized by the Centre for Economic Policy Performance of the London School of Economics. Partial contents: "Introduction," pp. vii-xii; Jouko Paunio, "A Perspective on Postwar Reconstruction in Finland," pp. 139-153; Koichi Hamada and Munehisa Kasuya, "The Reconstruction and Stabilization of the Postwar Japanese Economy: Possible Lessons for Eastern Europe?" pp. 155-187; J. Bradford De Long and Barry Eichengreen, "The Marshall Plan: History's Most Successful Structural Adjustment Program," pp. 189-230; Olivier Blanchard, Wilhelm Nölling, Richard Portes, "Panel Discussion: Lessons for Eastern Europe Today," pp. 231-241.] REV: Richard Cooper, *Foreign Affairs* 72, no. 5 (November-December 1993): 161.

2902. Fromkin, David. "Dimitrios Returns: Macedonia and the Balkan Question in the Shadow of History." *World Policy Journal* 10, no. 2 (Summer 1993): 67-71.

2903. Gorski, Philip S. "The Protestant Ethic Revisited: Disciplinary Revolution and State Formation in Holland and Prussia." *American Journal of Sociology* 99, no. 2 (September 1993): 265-316.

2904. Hobsbawm, Eric. "The New Threat to History." *New York Review of Books* 40, no. 21 (December 16, 1993): 62-64. [Lecture given by author at the Central European University (Budapest).]

2905. Korbonski, Andrzej. "The Decline and Rise of Pluralism in East Central Europe, 1949-1989, or How Not to See the Forest for the Trees." *Communist and Post-Communist Studies* 26, no. 4 (December 1993): 432-445.

2906. Magocsi, Paul Robert. "The Ukrainian Question Between Poland and Czechoslovakia: The Lemko Rusyn Republic (1918-1920) and Political Thought in Western Rus'-Ukraine." *Nationalities Papers* 21, no. 2 (Fall 1993): 95-105.

2907. Maier, Charles S. "Austria Between Memory and Obsolescence." *Society* 30, no. 4 (May-June 1993): 65-70.

2908. Milojkovic-Djuric, Jelena. "Pan-Slavic Aspirations and the First Pan-Slavic Congress: Images of the Self and Others." *Serbian Studies* 7, no. 1 (Spring 1993): 3-17.

2909. Nagorski, Andrew. *The Birth of Freedom: Shaping Lives and Societies in the New Eastern Europe.* New York: Simon & Schuster, c1993. 319 pp. [Contents: 1. Resistance, Rebellion, and Life; 2. The Communist Afterlife; 3. Outsiders as Insiders; 4. To Market; 5. Poisoned Air, Poisoned Bodies; 6. Life Without Censors; 7. God and the Devil; 8. Neighbors.] REV: Stanislaw Baranczak, *Book World* 23, no. 38 (September 19, 1993): 1ff. Abraham Brumberg, *New York Times Book Review* 98, no. 41 (October 10, 1993): 22. Norman Stone, *National Interest*, no. 34 (Winter 1993-1994): 91-95.

2910. Rathmann, Janos. *Historizität in der deutschen Aufklarung.* Daedalus (Frankfurt am Main, Germany), Bd. 3. Frankfurt am Main; New York: P. Lang, c1993. iii, 175 pp.

2911. Simons, Thomas W., Jr. *Eastern Europe in the Postwar World.* 2nd ed. New York: St. Martin's Press, 1993. xiii, 282 pp. [Contents: The Roots; Independence and Destruction, 1918-1941; The War and the Victors, 1939-1948: Trial by Fire; High Stalinism: Trial by Ice; De-Stalinization, 1953-1956; The Iron Ring, 1956-1968; Interlude: The Personality of the Old Regime; Goulash Communism, 1968-1980; The Return to Politics, 1980-1987; The Road to 1989; Afterword: Post-Communist Eastern Europe in Historical Perspective; Appendix: Leaders of Eastern Europe Since 1945.]

2912. Tismaneanu, Vladimir. *Reinventing Politics: Eastern Europe from Stalin to Havel.* 1st free Press paperback ed., with a new afterword. New York: Free Press, c1993. xvii, 330 pp.

2913. Tzvetkov, Plamen S. *A History of the Balkans: A Regional Overview from a Bulgarian Perspective.* San Francisco, CA: EM Text; Lewiston, NY: Order fulfillment, E. Mellen Press, c1993. 2 vols.

2914. Weisbrod, Carol. "Minorities and Diversities: The 'Remarkable Experiment' of the League of Nations." *Connecticut Journal of International Law* 8, no. 2 (Spring 1993): 359-406. [Paper from the symposium "Human Rights in Theory and Practice: A Time of Change and Development in Central and Eastern Europe," held in Budapest, March 19-20, 1993.]

Habsburg Empire

2915. Albrecht, Catherine. "Pride in Production: The Jubilee Exhibition of 1891 and Economic Competition between Czechs and Germans in Bohemia." *Austrian History Yearbook*, no. 24 (1993): 101-118.

2916. Glant, Tibor. "The War for Wilson's Ear: Austria-Hungary in Wartime American Propaganda." *Hungarian Studies Review* 20, nos. 1-2 (Spring-Fall 1993): 25-51.

2917. Himka, John-Paul. "The Galician Triangle: Poles, Ukrainians, and Jews under Austrian Rule." *Cross Currents: A Yearbook of Central European Culture*, no. 12 (1993): 125-146.

2918. Pajakowski, Philip. "The Polish Club, Badeni, and the Austrian Parliamentary Crisis of 1897." *Canadian Slavonic Papers* 35, nos. 1-2 (March-June 1993): 103-120.

2919. Palairet, Michael. "The Habsburg Industrial Achievement in Bosnia-Hercegovina, 1878-1914: An Economic Spurt That Succeeded?" *Austrian History Yearbook*, no. 24 (1993): 133-152.

2920. Pulzer, Peter. "The Tradition of Austrian Antisemitism in the Nineteenth and Twentieth Centuries." *Patterns of Prejudice* 27, no. 1 (July 1993): 31-46.

2921. Stone, Daniel. "The First (and Only) Year of the May 3 Constitution." *Canadian Slavonic Papers* 35, nos. 1-2 (March-June 1993): 69-86.

2922. Vodopivec, Peter. "The Slovenes in the Habsburg Empire or Monarchy." *Nationalities Papers* 21, no. 1 (Spring 1993): 159-170.

2923. Wank, Solomon. "Some Reflections on Aristocrats and Nationalism in Bohemia (1861-1899)." *Canadian Review of Studies in Nationalism = Revue Canadienne des Etudes sur le Nationalisme* 20, nos. 1-2 (1993): 21-33.

2924. Wistrich, Robert S. "Jewish Intellectuals and Mass Politics in *Fin-de-Siècle* Vienna." *Partisan Review* 60, no. 1 (Winter 1993): 51-62.

The Baltics

2925. Kasekamp, Andreas. "The Estonian Veteran's League: A Fascist Movement?" *Journal of Baltic Studies* 24, no. 3 (Fall 1993): 263-268.

2926. Kukk, Mare. "Political Opposition in Soviet Estonia, 1940-1987." *Journal of Baltic Studies* 24, no. 4 (Winter 1993): 369-384.

2927. Laasi, Evald. "Finland's Winter War and Estonian Neutrality." *Journal of Baltic Studies* 24, no. 3 (Fall 1993): 269-282.

2928. Lieven, Anatol. *The Baltic Revolution: Estonia, Latvia, Lithuania and the Path to Independence.* New Haven, CT: Yale University Press, 1993. xxv, 454 pp. [Contents: 1. The Shape of the Land. Marsh and Forest. The Man-Made Landscape. The Baltic Cities. Peasant Peoples — 2. Surviving the Centuries. The Ancient Baltic Peoples. The Christian Conquest. The Lithuanian Empire and the Union with Poland. The Baltic Provinces under the Russian Empire — 3. Independence Won and Lost, 1918-40. The First Struggle for Independence. Economic and Social Consolidation. The Failure of Parliamentary Democracy, 1920-34. The Roots of Authoritarianism. Orphans of Versailles: Baltic Diplomacy, 1918-40 — 4. The Troglodyte International: The Soviet Impact on the Baltic. Conquest and "Revolution". The German Occupation. Resistance: The "Forest Brothers." Stalinism, Normalization, Stagnation. The Soviet Establishment: Past, Present and Future? The Dissidents — 5. Imagined Nations: Cycles of Cultural Rebirth. Folklore and Nationalism. The Creation of Language. Myth is History and History as Myth. Cultural Politics in the Reborn States — 6. Lost Atlantises: The Half-Forgotten Nationalities of the Baltic. An Area of Mixed Settlement. The Baltic Germans. The Jerusalem of Lithuania. The Frontier of Poland — 7. The Baltic Russians. A Question of Identity. The Baltic Russians through History. The Last Stand of the Soviet Union. Defending the Legacy of Peter: The Soviet and Russian Military Presence. Kaliningrad and the Kaliningrad Question — 8. The Independence Movements and their Successors, 1987-92. A Confusion of Terms. Rise of the National Movements, 1987-90. "Be Realistic: Ask the Impossible": The Declarations of Independence, 1990. The "Bloody Events": January to August 1991. The Fragmentation of Politics and the Difficulties of Government: Lithuania. Ethnic Estonian Politics, 1990-92. Ethnic Latvian Politics, 1990-92. The Baltic Independence Movements and the Baltic Russians — 9. Building on Ruins: The Recreation of the New States. The Baltic, Year Zero. Achieving Military Control. Industry and Energy. Privatization and Corruption. In the Scissors: Baltic Agriculture. The New Currencies. Banking on Chaos. The Church. Peoples Divided — Conclusion: The West and the Baltic States — Appendix 1: Historical Chronology, 3500 BC-1985 AD — Appendix 2: Contemporary Chronology 1985-92 — Appendix 3: Baltic Demography and Geography — Appendix 4: The Soviet Baltic Economies on the Eve of the National Revolutions (1989-90) — Appendix 5: Biographical Guide to Political Figures 1988-92.] REV: Liah Greenfeld, *New York Times Book Review* 98, no. 35 (August 29, 1993): 6. Robert Legvold, *Foreign Affairs* 72, no. 5 (November-December 1993): 173. Czeslaw Milosz, *New York Review of Books* 40, no. 18 (November 4, 1993): 12-16. Norman Stone, *National Interest*, no. 34 (Winter 1993-1994): 91-95. Theodore R. Weeks, *Journal of Baltic Studies* 24, no. 4 (Winter 1993): 404-405.

2929. Lopata, Raimundas. "Lithuanian-Polish Cooperation in 1918: the Ronikier-Voldemaras Treaty." *Journal of Baltic Studies* 24, no. 4 (Winter 1993): 349-358.

2930. ———. "The Second Spring of Nations and the Theory of Reconstruction of the Grand Duchy of Lithuania." *Lituanus* 39, no. 4 (Winter 1993): 68-78.

2931. Misiunas, Romuald J., and Rein Taagepera. *The Baltic States, Years of Dependence, 1940-1990.* Expanded and updated ed. Berkeley, CA: University of California Press, c1993. xvi, 400 pp. [Contents: Introduction: Historical Background —1. Before the Modern Age. The Road to the Modern Nation-States. The Years of Independence, 1918-1940 — 2. The War Years, 1940-1945. The Coming of the Soviets. The First Year of Soviet Occupation. War and Revolt. The German Occupation. The Return of the Soviets — 3. Postwar Stalinism, 1945-1953. Administration. Guerrilla Warfare and Collectivization. Economy and Culture. Normalization under New Norms, 1952-1953 — 4. The Re-emergence of National Cultures, 1954-1968.

The Vain Struggle for Political Autonomy. The Successful Struggle for Cultural Autonomy. Expansion of Contacts Abroad. Socio-Economic Trends. How the Baltic States Looked in 1968 — 5. Centralization and Westernization, 1968-1980. Politics and Ideology. Demographic and Social Trends. Economy and Ecology. Culture and the Expansion of Western Contacts. Dissent — 6. The Apogee of Stagnation, 1980-1986. Politics and Ideology. Society. Economy and Ecology. Culture: Continued Modernization and Russification. Dissent — 7. The National Renaissances, 1987-1990. 1987—the Latvian Phase: Ecological Protest and Beyond. 1988—the Estonian Phase: Striving for Autonomy. 1989—the Lithuanian Phase: Push for Independence. 1990—the First Stage towards Independence; Postscript. The Kaliningrad Oblast: A New Baltic Land? — App. A. Major Baltic Government Leaders and Administrators, 1938-1990 — App. B. Tables. 1. Population and Ethnicity of the Baltic Republics, 1939-1980. 2. Population Changes, 1939-1945. 3. War and Occupation Deaths, 1940-1945. 4. Lithuanian Guerrillas, 1944-1952: Armed Forces Involved. 5. Population Changes, 1945-1955. 6. Communist Party Size and Ethnicity, 1930-1980. 7. Industrial Employment and Index of Production, 1940-1980. 8. Agricultural Production and Efficiency, 1940-1978. 9. Rural Administrative Units, 1939-1980. 10. Urbanization and Living Space, 1940-1980. 11. Size, Relative Weight, and Ethnicity of Capitals, 1940-1979. 12. Marriage and Divorce Rates, 1940-1978. 13. Birth and Death Rates, 1940-1980. 14. Population Increase, 1950-1979. 15. The Share of Private Plots in Latvia's Agricultural Production, 1950-1977. 16. Average Yearly Growth Rates of Produced Income and Industrial Production, 1950-1980.]

2932. Racevskis, Karlis. "Voices from the Gulag: A Review Essay." *Journal of Baltic Studies* 24, no. 3 (Fall 1993): 299-306. [Review article on Anda Lice, ed., *Via Dolorosa: Stalinisma upuru liecibas* [The Testimony of Victims of Stalinism] (Riga: 1990).]

2933. Rowell, S. C. "Of Men and Monsters: Sources for the History of Lithuania in the Time of Gediminas (ca. 1315-1342)." *Journal of Baltic Studies* 24, no. 1 (Spring 1993): 73-112.

2934. Taagepera, Rein. *Estonia: Return to Independence.* Westview Series on the Post-Soviet Republics. Boulder, CO: Westview Press, 1993. xv, 268 pp. [Published in cooperation with the Harriman Institute. Contents: 1. Estonia's Role in the World. A Laboratory of Peaceful Methods of Political Struggle. A Model Cultural Autonomy for Minorities. The Importance of Being the Smallest. A Bridge Between Western and Eastern Europe. Estonia's Contribution to World Culture — 2. From Prehistory to World War I. Prehistory. Independent Estonia, A.D. 1200. German Rule, 1227-1561. Swedish Rule, 1561-1710. Early Russian Rule: The Peaking of Serfdom, 1710-1860. Estonian National Awakening Versus Russification, 1860-1917. How Estonia Was Prepared for Independence — 3. Independence and World War II. Achievement of Independence, 1917-1920. Years of Peace, 1920-1939. The Molotov-Ribbentrop Pact and the First Soviet Occupation, 1939-1941. German Occupation and Soviet Reoccupation 1941-1945. Why

Independence Did Not Last — 4. Soviet Occupation. Years of Genocide, 1945-1953. Years of Hope, 1954-1968. Years of Suffocation, 1968-1980. Why Sovietization Failed — 5. History Starts to Move. The False Start, 1980-1981. The Peak of Stagnation, 1982-1986. The Phosphate Spring and Hirvepark, 1987 — 6. The Quest for Autonomy. The Economic Autonomy Debate, September 1987-March 1988. The Spring of the Flag, April-October 1988. The Winter of Sovereignty, November 1988-April 1989. The Summer of the MRP Debate, May-September 1989. How Moscow Missed the Train on Autonomy — 7. The Quest for Independence. Estonian Congress and Supreme Council Elections, October 1989-March 1990. From ESSR to Occupied Republic of Estonia, April-December 1990. Independence Referendum, January-June 1991. Independence Regained, July-September 1991. Why Independence Was Recovered — 8. Independence in an Interdependent World. Economy. Ethnic Relations. Social Problems. Foreign and Military Relations. Domestic Politics. Estonia Looks to the Future; Appendix: Basic Data and Chronology.]

2935. Tereskinas, Arturas. "The King as Mirror: Autobiographies in 18th Century Poland-Lithuania." *Lituanus* 39, no. 4 (Winter 1993): 32-48. [Essay presented at the Conference of the Association for the Advancement of Baltic Studies, at Toronto, Canada, June 1992.]

2936. Vebers, Elmars. "Demography and Ethnic Politics in Independent Latvia: Some Basic Facts." *Nationalities Papers* 21, no. 2 (Fall 1993): 179-194.

Czechoslovakia

2937. Agnew, Hugh LeCaine. "The Emergence of Modern Czech National Consciousness: A Conceptual Approach." *Ethnic Groups* 10, nos. 1-3 (1993): 175-186. [Part of special issue devoted to "Pre-Modern and Modern National Identity in Russia and Eastern Europe."]

2938. Felak, James. "The Congress of the Young Slovak Intelligentsia, June, 1932: Its Context, Course and Consequences." *Nationalities Papers* 21, no. 2 (Fall 1993): 107-127.

2939. Huebner, Todd Wayne. "The Multinational 'Nation-State': The Origins and the Paradox of Czechoslovakia, 1914-1920." Ph.D. diss., Columbia University, 1993. [UMI order no: AAC 9333791.]

2940. Jelinek, Yeshayahu A. "Historical and Actual Minority Problems in Czechoslovakia." *Patterns of Prejudice* 27, no. 1 (July 1993): 93-105.

2941. Kramer, Mark. "The Prague Spring and the Soviet Invasion of Czechoslovakia: New Interpretations (Part 2 of 2)." *Cold War International History Project Bulletin*, no. 3 (Fall 1993): 2ff.

2942. Neudorfl, Marie L. "Czech History, Modern Nation-Building and Tomás G. Masaryk (1850-1937)." *Canadian Review of Studies in Nationalism = Revue Canadienne des Etudes sur le Nationalisme* 20, nos. 1-2 (1993): 13-20.

2943. Nolte, Claire E. " 'Every Czech a Sokol!' Feminism and Nationalism in the Czech Sokol Movement." *Austrian History Yearbook*, no. 24 (1993): 79-100.

2944. ———. "Our Brothers Across the Ocean: The Czech Sokol in America to 1914." *Czechoslovak and Central European Journal* 11, no. 2 (Winter 1993): 15-37. [On Czech nationalist gymnastic organization Sokol and its parallel body in the United States.]

2945. Obrman, Jan. "Havel Challenges Czech Historical Taboos." *RFE/RL Research Report* 2, no. 24 (June 11, 1993): 44-51.

2946. Von Teuber, Eugene, and Basil Entwistle. *Step Ahead of Disaster*. Salem, OR: Grosvenor USA, 1993. xiii, 162 pp. [A personal narrative of Czechoslovakia in World War II.]

East Germany

2947. Brenner, David. "Out of the Ghetto and into the Tiergarten: Redefining the Jewish Parvenu and His Origins in *Ost und Est*." *German Quarterly* 66, no. 2 (Spring 1993): 176-194. [Article is in German with an abstract in English.]

2948. Harrison, Hope Millard. "The Bargaining Power of Weaker Allies in Bipolarity and Crisis: The Dynamics of Soviet-East German Relations, 1953-1961." Ph.D. diss., Columbia University, 1993. [UMI order no: AAC 9412767.]

2949. Herf, Jeffrey. "Multiple Restorations: German Political Traditions and the Interpretation of Nazism, 1945-1946." *Central European History* 26, no. 1 (1993): 21-55.

2950. Kraemer, Dagmar. "Time Line: An Annotated Chronology of Events in Postwar Germany and the European Community." *Social Education* 57, no. 5 (September 1993): 251-255. [Part of special section entitled "The Case of Germany, Part 2," edited by Dagmar Kraemer and Manfred Stassen.]

2951. Large, David Clay. "Germany in Europe, 1945-92: A Historical Overview." *Social Education* 57, no. 5 (September 1993): 232-236. [Part of special section entitled "The Case of Germany, Part 2," edited by Dagmar Kraemer and Manfred Stassen.]

2952. Ostow, Robin. "From the Cold War Through the *Wende*: History Belonging, and the Self in East German Jewry." *Oral History Review* 21, no. 2 (Winter 1993): 59-72.

2953. Ryback, Timothy W. "Letters from the Dead." *New Yorker* 68, no. 50 (February 1, 1993): 58-71. ["On the fiftieth anniversary of their defeat at Stalingrad, the German people are contemplating their role as victims, as well as perpetrators, of Nazism."]

2954. Troska, Gea. "Entwicklungslinien der estnischen Dorfbesiedlung im 19. Jahrhundert." *Journal of Baltic Studies* 24, no. 1 (Spring 1993): 9-36.

Greece and Cyprus (Since 1821)

2955. Figueira, Thomas J. *Excursions in Epichoric History: Aiginetan Essays*. Greek Studies. Lanham, MD: Rowman & Littlefield, c1993. 433 pp.

2956. Mazower, Mark. *Inside Hitler's Greece: The Experience of Occupation, 1941-44*. New Haven, CT: Yale University Press, 1993. xxv, 437 pp.

2957. Molho, Rena. "Popular Antisemitism and State Policy in Salonika during the City's Annexation to Greece." *Jewish Social Studies* 50, nos. 3-4 (Summer-Fall 1988/1993): 253-264.

2958. Nachmani, Amikam. "Mirror Images: The Civil Wars in China and Greece." *Journal of the Hellenic Diaspora* 19, no. 1 (1993): 71-112.

Hungary

2959. Deme, Laszlo. "Pre-1848 Magyar Nationalism Revisited: Ethnic and Authoritarian or Political and Progressive?" *East European Quarterly* 27, no. 2 (Summer 1993): 141-169.

2960. Karaday, Victor. "Antisemitism in Twentieth-Century Hungary: A Socio-Historical Overview." *Patterns of Prejudice* 27, no. 1 (July 1993): 71-92.

2961. Katzburg, Nathaniel. "Louis Marshall and the White Terror in Hungary, 1919-1920." *American Jewish Archives* 45, no. 1 (Spring-Summer 1993): 1-12.

2962. Lengyel, György, ed. *Hungarian Economy and Society during World War II*. Translated from the Hungarian by Judit Pokoly. Contributions by György Lengyel, György Ránki, Lóránd Dombrády, Sándor Szakály, Károly Szabó, László Virágh, Ivan T. Berend, and Tamás Stark. Atlantic Studies on Society in Change, no. 74. East European Monographs, no. 362. War and Society in East Central Europe, vol. 29. Boulder, CO: Social Science Monographs; Highland Lakes, NJ: Atlantic Research and Publication; New York: Distributed by Columbia University Press, 1993. xvii, 284 pp. [Contents: I. Coordinates. György Lengyel, "Institutions, Elites, Ideologies: From Controlled Economy to War Economy," pp. 3-38; György Ránki, "The Economy of Occupied Europe," pp. 39-73. II. Army, Economy, Society. Lóránd Dombrády, "Financing the Hungarian Rearmament," pp. 77-101; Sándor Szakály, "The Composition of the Higher Military Elite," pp. 103-125; Károly Szabó and László Virágh, "Controlling the Agriculture and the Producers," pp. 127-149; Iván T. Berend, "The Composition and Position of the Working Class during the War," pp. 151-168. III. War Casualties. Tamás Stark, "Hungary's Casualties in World War II" [abridged and translated version of *Magyarország második világháborus embervesztesége* (Budapest, 1989)], pp. 171-260.]

2963. Montgomery, John Flournoy. *Hungary: The Unwilling Satellite*. Morristown, NJ: Vista Books, 1993. v, 281 pp. [Originally published: (New York: Devin-Adair, 1947). Reprint.]

2964. Peng, Yusheng. "Intergenerational Mobility of Class and Occupation in Mid-20th Century England and Post-War Hungary." Ph.D. diss., University of California, Los Angeles, 1993.

2965. Révész, Tamás. "Freedom of the Press: Its Idea and Realization in Pre-1914 Hungary." *Hungarian Studies Review* 20, nos. 1-2 (Spring-Fall 1993): 93-101.

Poland

2966. Batowski, Henryk. "17 September 1939: Before and After." *East European Quarterly* 27, no. 4 (Winter 1993): 523-534.

2967. Blanke, Richard. *Orphans of Versailles: The Germans in Western Poland, 1918-1939.* Lexington, KY: University Press of Kentucky, c1993. xii, 316 pp. REV: David Stefancic, *Canadian Slavonic Papers* 35, nos. 1-2 (March-June 1993): 197.

2968. Drozdowski, Piotr. "Echoes of the Polish Revolution in the Late Eighteenth and Early Nineteenth Century English Literature: A Selection of Works and Voices: Part One." *Polish Review* 38, no. 1 (1993): 3-24.

2969. Duzinkiewicz, Janusz. *Fateful Transformations: The Four Years' Parliament and the Constitution of May 3, 1791.* East European Monographs, no. 368. Boulder, CO: East European Monographs; New York: Distributed by Columbia University Press, 1993. xi, 334 pp.

2970. Engel, David. *Facing a Holocaust: The Polish Government-in-Exile and the Jews, 1943-1945.* Chapel Hill, NC: University of North Carolina Press, c1993. x, 317 pp. [Sequel to: *In the Shadow of Auschwitz: The Polish Government-in-Exile and the Jews, 1939-1942* (Chapel Hill, NC: University of North Carolina Press, 1987).] REV: Gershon David Hundert, *Central European History* 26, no. 2 (1993): 244-246.

2971. Fajfer, Luba. "The Polish Military and the Crisis of 1970." *Communist and Post-Communist Studies* 26, no. 2 (June 1993): 205-225.

2972. Górecki, Piotr. *Parishes, tithes, and society in earlier medieval Poland, c. 1100-c. 1250.* Transactions of the American Philosophical Society, v. 83, pt. 2. Philadelphia, PA: American Philosophical Society, 1993. 146 pp.

2973. Knoll, Paul W. "National Consciousness in Medieval Poland." *Ethnic Groups* 10, nos. 1-3 (1993): 65-84. [Part of special issue devoted to "Pre-Modern and Modern National Identity in Russia and Eastern Europe."]

2974. Koszyca, Kazimierz. *Opowiesci o turystach i zolnierzach gen. Wladyslawa Sikorskiego: Brygada Strzelców Karpackich, 1940-1942.* Wyd. 1. Chicago, IL: Kolo Karpatczyków w Chicago, 1993. 320 pp.

2975. Pogonowski, Iwo Cyprian. *Jews in Poland: A Documentary History: The Rise of Jews As a Nation from Congressus Judaicus in Poland to the Knesset in Israel.* New York: Hippocrene Books, c1993. 402 pp. [Contents: Pt. I. Text; Richard Pipes, "Foreword"; Jews in Poland, Synopsis of a 1000 Year History; 1264 Statute on Jewish Liberties in Poland; Jewish Autonomy in Poland 1264-1795; German Annihilation of the Jews — Pt. I. Appendixes. 1. Eastern Strategy, World War I. 2. H. Grynberg, "Is Polish Anti-Semitism Special?" 3. Reconciliation Appeal. 4. Polish Bishops on Anti-Semitism. 5. President Walesa's Speech to the Knesset. 6. Protest of an Open Slander and the "Genocide Libel" 7. Dr. R. Slovenko on Polish-Jewish Relations. 8. Bibliography and Recommended Reading — Pt. II. Illustrations. Jews in Polish Graphic Arts. Jewish Press in Poland — Pt. III. Atlas. Poland in Jewish History, A Perspective. Early Settlements in Poland, 966-1264. The Crucial 500 Years, 1264-1795. Under Foreign Rule, Competition, 1795-1918. The Last Blossoming of Jewish Culture in Poland, 1918-1939. Shoah, German Genocide of the Jews, 1940-1944. Briha, the Escape from Europe, 1945-.]

2976. Polonsky, Antony, Jakub Basista, and Andrzej Link-Lenczowski, eds. *The Jews in Old Poland, 1000-1795.* Contributions by Jerzy Wyrozumski, Zdislaw Pietrzyk, Andrzej Link-Lenczowski, Daniel Tollet, Krystyn Matwijowski, Shmul Ettinger, Israel Bartal, Altbauer Moshe, Anatol Leszczynski, Jacob Goldberg, Mordekhai Nadav, Gershon David Hundert, Chone Shmeruk, Stanislaw Grodziski, Shmuel Shilo, Jacek Sobczak, Maurycy Horn, Jan M. Malecki, Janina Bieniarzowna, Antoni Podraza, Zenon Guldon, and Karol Krzystanek. London; New York: I.B. Tauris; Oxford: Institute for Polish-Jewish Studies, 1993. viii, 361 pp. [Contents: Jerzy Wyrozumski, "Jews in medieval Poland"; Zdislaw Pietrzyk, "Judaizers in Poland in the second half of the sixteenth century"; Andrezej Link-Lenczowski, "The Jewish population in the light of the resolutions of the Dietines in the sixteenth to the eighteenth centuries"; Daniel Tollet, "The private life of Polish Jews in the Vasa Period"; Krystyn Matwijowski, "Jews and Armenians in the Polish-Lithuanian Commonwealth in the sixteenth and seventeenth centuries"; Shmul Ettinger, "The Four Years' Sejm and the Jews"; Artur Eisenbach, "The Council of the Four Lands"; Israel Bartal, "The pinkas of the Council of the Four Lands"; Moshe Altbauer, "The language of documents relating to Jewish autonomy in Poland"; Anatol Leszczynski, "The terminology of the bodies of Jewish self-government"; Jacob Goldberg, "The Jewish Sejm: its origins and functions"; Mordekhai Nadav, "Regional aspects of the autonomy of Polish Jews: the history of the Tykocin kehilla, 1670-1782"; Gershon David Hundert, "The kehilla and the municipality in private towns at the end of the early modern period"; Chone Shmeruk, "Hasidism and the kehilla"; Stanislaw Grodziski, "The Krakow voivode's jurisdiction over Jews: a study of the historical records of the Krakow's voivode's administration of justice to Jews"; Shmuel Shilo, "The individual versus the community in Jewish law in pre-eighteenth-century Poland"; Jacek Sobczak, "The condition of the Jewish population of Wschowa in the mid-eighteenth century"; Maurycy Horn, "The chronology and distribution of Jewish craft guilds in old Poland, 1613-1795"; Jan M. Malecki, "Jewish trade at the end of the sixteenth century and in the first half of the seventeenth century"; Janina Bieniarzowna, "Jewish trade in the century of Krakow's decline"; Antoni Podraza, "Jews and the village in the Polish commonwealth"; Zenon Guldon and Karol Krzystanek, "The Jewish population in the towns on the west bank of the Vistula in the Sandomierz Province from the sixteenth to the eighteenth centuries."]

2977. Sewerynski, Michal. "Development of the Collective Bargaining System in Poland after the Second World War." *Comparative Labor Law Journal* 14, no. 4 (Summer 1993): 441-477.

2978. Vinton, Louisa. "The Katyn Documents: Politics and History." *RFE/RL Research Report* 2, no. 4 (January 22, 1993): 19-31.

2979. Weinbaum, Laurence. *A Marriage of Convenience: The New Zionist Organization and the Polish Government 1936-1939.* East European Monographs, no. 369. Boulder, CO: East European Monographs; New York: Distributed by Columbia University Press, 1993. xiii, 295 pp. [Originally presented as the author's thesis (doctoral)— Warsaw University. Contents: A Note About Spelling; The Jewish Problem in Poland; Ideology; The New Zionist Organization; The Policy of Alliances and the Orientation Toward Poland; Reaction; Diplomacy and Economics; Military Aid; Emigration; The Zion-Sejm and Other Forms of Cooperation; The Marriage Breaks Down.]

2980. Wolff, Larry. "A Heating of the Blood: From Early Modern Patriotism to Modern Polish Nationalism in the Age of the Partitions." *Ethnic Groups* 10, nos. 1-3 (1993): 85-99. [Part of special issue devoted to "Pre-Modern and Modern National Identity in Russia and Eastern Europe."]

Romania

2981. Brucan, Silviu. *The Wasted Generation: Memoirs of the Romanian Journey from Capitalism to Socialism and Back.* Boulder, CO: Westview Press, 1993. xii, 227 pp. [Revised and expanded translation of: *Generatia irosita.* Contents: 1. What Made Him Flee; 2. The Origins of Social Revolt; 3. A Unique Historical Event: Conspiracy Between King and Communists; 4. The Stalinist Faith; 5. The National Backlash; 6. The Two Faces of Communist Society; 7. Red Diplomat in Washington; 8. The Illiterate Couple; 9. The Prelude of the Romanian Revolution; 10. The Inside Story of the Revolution; 11. The Day After...; Chronology of Events; International Perspectives: A Collection of Media and Policy Discussion; Index and List of Prominent Romanians.]

2982. Donath, Jaap. "The Hungarian Minority in Romania: Past, Present, and Future." *Ethnic Groups* 10, no. 4 (1993): 323-341.

2983. Kideckel, David A. *The Solitude of Collectivism: Romanian Villagers to the Revolution and Beyond.* Anthropology of Contemporary Issues. Ithaca, NY: Cornell University Press, 1993. xix, 255 pp. [Contents: A Note on Romanian Names and Pronunciation; 1. Labor, Culture, and the Long Romanian Night; 2. The Origins of Olt Land Culture, Class, and Consciousness; 3. Romanian Socialism as a Social and Cultural System; 4. Socialism Comes to the Olt Land; 5. Working for Self, Working for Socialism; 6.

Community and Conceit: Social Life and Change in the Socialist Village; 7. Meanings of Life in the Socialist Village; 8. The Revolution and Beyond.]

2984. Stahl, Henri H. "Théories des processus de 'modernisation' des Principautés Danubiennes et de l'ancien Royaume de Roumanie (1850-1920)." *Review* (Fernand Braudel Center) 16, no. 1 (Winter 1993): 85-111. [In French with English summary.]

2985. Torrey, Glenn. "Indifference and Mistrust: Russian-Romanian Collaboration in the Campaign of 1916." *Journal of Military History* 57, no. 2 (April 1993): 279-300.

2986. Totok, William. "Romania's Minorities: Reconcilable Conflicts? An Historical Perspective." *Uncaptive Minds* 6, no. 2 (23) (Summer 1993): 43-49. [Based on a paper delivered at a seminar on "The Promotion of Mutual Understanding and Inter-Cultural Coexistence in Romania" held in Tirgu Mures, October 30-November 1, 1992, and was published in the magazine *22.*]

2987. Watts, Larry L. *Romanian Cassandra: Ion Antonescu and the Struggle for Reform, 1916-1941.* East European Monographs, no. 358. Boulder, CO: East European Monographs; New York: Distributed by Columbia University Press, 1993. x, 390 pp. [Partial contents: When History Is Politics: In Lieu of an Introduction — 1. Antonescu as a Military Figure, 1918-1934. Professionalism Versus Traditionalism. The Separate Peace and Romanian Military Politics. The General Cihoski Affair. The Battle Against Corruption and Waste — 2. The General Staff, 1933-1934. The Skoda Scandal and Military Reform. The Reform of Defensive Strategy. The Clash over Military Reform. Antonescu's Resignation — 3. The King, the "Capitan," and the General, 1933-1937. The Reluctant Prince. Carol Reconsiders. The Monarchy and Balkan Political Conflict. Fascism, Anti-Semitism, and the Iron Guard. Carol and Fascism — 4. The Rise and Fall of the Iron Guard, 1933-1938. Antonescu and the Guard. The Case of Ion Gheorghe Duca. The Political Evolution of Corneliu Codreanu. The Elections of December 1937. The Goga-Cuza Government. The Reluctant General. The Campaign Against the Guard. The Trials of Codreanu. The Guard and Codreanu's Death: Transformation or Continuity? Antonescu, Germany, and the Military Threat to Romania — 5. The Collapse of Romania, 1939-1940. Carol and the German Alliance. Carol II, Mihail Moruzov, and German Intelligence. The Soviet Ultimatum. The Second Vienna Arbitration. Carol and Sima's Iron Guard. Royal Nazism and the Withdrawal from Bessarabia. From Prison to Presidency — 6. The National-Legionary State, September 1940-January 1941. Domestic Reform. Antonescu, Fascism, Nationalism, and Anti-Semitism. Romanian-German Cooperation. Social Reform Versus Revolutionary Fascism. The Jilava Massacre. Reform, the Guard, and the Great Powers. The Legionnaire's Rebellion; Epilogue: 1941-1944. Between Scylla and Charybdis. The Economic Legacy. The Political-Military Legacy. Antonescu and the Holocaust. The Iai Pogrom. The Deportations to Transnistria. The Final Solution. The Evacuation from Transnistria.]

Yugoslavia

2988. Antal, John F. "Operation 25: Yugoslavia Disintegrates." *Army* 43, no. 5 (May 1993): 28-35.

2989. Bebler, Anton. "Yugoslavia's Variety of Communist Federalism and Her Demise." *Communist and Post-Communist Studies* 26, no. 1 (March 1993): 72-86.

2990. Bucar, France. "Slovenia in Europe." *Nationalities Papers* 21, no. 1 (Spring 1993): 33-41.

2991. Cohen, Lenard J. *Broken Bonds: The Disintegration of Yugoslavia.* Boulder, CO: Westview Press, 1993. xvi, 299 pp. [Contents: 1. The Evolution of the Yugoslav idea: 1830-1980; 2. Socialist Reform in Crisis: The Post-Tito Debate; 3. Toward Postsocialism: The Emergence of Party Pluralism; 4. Sovereignty Asunder: The Fragmentation of State Authority; 5. Pluralism in the Southeast: Nationalism Triumphant; 6. Drifting Apart: "New" Elites and a Delegitimated Federation; 7. The Politics of Intransigence: Prelude to Civil War; 8. The Dissolution of the Second Yugoslavia: Balkan Violence and the International Response; 9. Yugoslavism's Failure and Future.]

2992. Cseres, Tibor. *Titoist Atrocities in Vojvodina, 1944-1945: Serbian Vendetta in Bacska.* Buffalo, NY: Hunyadi Pub., c1993. 166 pp.

2993. Djordjevic, Mihailo. "Mostar: A Serbian Cultural Center in the 1880s and 1890s." *Serbian Studies* 7, no. 2 (Fall 1993, published in 1995): 72-85.

2994. Dragnich, Alex N. "Serbia's Tragedies in the Twentieth Century: Some Reflections." *Serbian Studies* 7, no. 2 (Fall 1993, published in 1995): 1-15.

2995. Ferguson, Niall. "Europa Nervosa." *New Republic* 208, no. 22 (May 31, 1993): 22-24.

2996. Hayden, Robert M. "On Unbalanced Criticism." *East European Politics and Societies* 7, no. 3 (Fall 1993): 577-582. [Response to criticism by Anto Knezevic in vol. 7, no. 1 (Winter 1993): 155-166, of author's essay in vol. 6, no. 2 (Spring 1992): 207-212.]

2997. Huchthausen, Peter A. "Back to the Balkans." *U.S. Naval Institute Proceedings* 119, no. 6 (June 1993): 43-49.

2998. Huttenbach, Henry R. "Postscript: By Way of a Review." *Nationalities Papers* 21, no. 1 (Spring 1993): 197-200. [Review article on *Slovenski upor 1941* (Ljubljana: 1991) [Proceedings of the Conference on Slovene Resistance, held in Ljubljana, May 23-24, 1991].]

2999. International Commission to Inquire into the Causes and Conduct of the Balkan Wars. *The Other Balkan Wars: A 1913 Carnegie Endowment Inquiry in Retrospect.* With a new introduction by George F. Kennan. Washington, DC: Carnegie Endowment for International Peace: Brookings Institution Publications [distributor], c1993. ix, 413 pp. [Originally published: *Report of the International Commission to Inquire into the Causes and Conduct of the Balkan Wars* (The Endowment, 1914).] REV: Ivo Banac, *Foreign Policy,* no. 93 (December 1993-1994): 173-182.

Razvigor Bazala, *Foreign Service Journal* 70, no. 10 (October 1993): 44-48. William W. Finan, Jr., *Current History* 92, no. 577 (November 1993): 396.

3000. Irvine, Jill A. *The Croat Question: Partisan Politics in the Formation of the Yugoslav Socialist State.* Foreword by Ivo Banac. Boulder, CO: Westview Press, c1993. xviii, 318 pp. REV: James Beale, *Studies in Conflict and Terrorism* 16, no. 4 (October-December 1993): 333-335.

3001. Johnsen, William T. *Deciphering the Balkan Enigma: Using History to Inform Policy.* [Carlisle Barracks, PA]: Strategic Studies Institute, U.S. Army War College, 1993. ix, 97 pp. [Contents: The Balkans: Historical Battleground; The Origins of Conflict: Language, Religion, Ethnic Origin, and Culture; Political Fragmentation and Mistrust; Policy Insights and Assessments.]

3002. Kaplan, Robert D. *Balkan Ghosts: A Journey Through History.* 1st ed. New York: St. Martin's Press, 1993. xxvii, 307 pp. [Contents: Map of the Balkans; Prologue: Saints, Terrorists, Blood, and Holy Water — Pt. 1. Yugoslavia: Historical Overtures. 1. Croatia: "Just So They Could Go to Heaven"; 2. Old Serbia and Albania: Balkan "West Bank"; 3. Macedonia: "A Hand Thirsting Towards the Realm of the Stars"; 4. The White City and Its Prophet — Pt. 2. Romania: Latin Passion Play. 5. Athenee Palace, Bucharest; 6. The Danube's Bitter Kind; 7. Moldavia: "Conditioned to Hate"; 8. The Land Beyond Dracula's Castle: The Painted Monasteries of Bucovina; 9. Transylvanian Voices; 10. Transylvanian Tale: The Pied Piper's Children Go Back to Hamelin; 11. Last Glimpses: Timisoara and Bucharest — Pt. 3. Bulgaria: Tales from Communist Byzantium; 12. "The Warmth of Each Other's Bodies"; 13. The Price of Friendship; 14. The Bad and the Good — Pt. 4. Greece: Western Mistress, Eastern Bride; 15. Farewell to Salonika; 16. "Teach Me, Zorba. Teach Me to Dance!"; 17. The Secret History — Epilogue: The Road to Adrianople.] REV: Henry R. Cooper, Jr., *Slavic Review* 52, no. 3 (Fall 1993): 592-593. Van Coufoudakis, *Mediterranean Quarterly* 4, no. 4 (Fall 1993): 105-108. István Deák, *New York Times Book Review* 98, no. 13 (March 23, 1993): 3ff. W.W. F. [William W. Finan, Jr.], *Current History* 92, no. 577 (November 1993): 396. Jerry Kisslinger, *New Leader* (June 14, 1993): 17-19. Neil V. Lamont, *Military Review* 73, no. 12 (December 1993): 81. Noel Malcolm, *National Interest,* no. 32 (Summer 1993): 83-88. Tina Rosenberg, *Book World* 23, no. 13 (March 28, 1993): 1ff. *New York Times Book Review* 98, no. 49 (December 5, 1993): 3. *New Yorker* 68, no. 10 (April 26, 1993): 119. *Orbis* 37, no. 2 (Spring 1993).

3003. Knezevic, Anto. "Some Questions about a 'Balanced' Discussion." *East European Politics and Societies* 7, no. 1 (Winter 1993): 155-166. [Criticism of essay by Robert M. Hayden, "Balancing Discussion of Jasenovac and the Manipulation of History," in vol. 6, no. 2 (Spring 1992): 207-212.]

3004. Lencek, Rado L. "Preface." *Nationalities Papers* 21, no. 1 (Spring 1993): 5-10. [Introduction to the special issue "Voices from the Slovene Nation, 1990-1992."]

3005. Lindsay, Franklin. *Beacons in the Night: With the OSS and Tito's Partisans in Wartime Yugoslavia.* Stanford, CA: Stanford University Press, c1993. xxii, 383 pp. [Contents: 1. To Slovenia by Parachute; 2. Preparing for the Mission; 3. First Days with the Partisans; 4. Crossing the Border; 5. Inside the Third Reich; 6. Blowing Up Germany's Railroads; 7. Night Marches and Hidden Hospitals; 8. The Partisans Organize a Shadow Government; 9. Radios, Codes, and Codebreakers; 10. Liberation of a Mountain Valley; 11. The Lure of Austria; 12. Failure in Austria; 13. Revolution Comes into the Open; 14. The German Winter Offensive Begins; 15. Ethnic and Ideological Wars in Croatia; 16. Tito's Government Takes Control in Belgrade; 17. The Defeat of the Chetniks; 18. Communist Rule Becomes Absolute; 19. The Cold War Begins in Trieste; 20. In the Wake of the Hot War; 21. How It All Turned Out; Appendix: Political Boundaries and Ethnic Distribution in Postwar Yugoslavia.] REV: Thomas Barker, *Slovene Studies* 14, no. 1 (1992) [published March 1994]: 93-94.

3006. Lokar, Ales. "Modernization and Ethnic Problems in Carinthia." *Slovene Studies* 14, no. 1 (1992, published March 1994): 35-50.

3007. MacKenzie, David. "Democratic Russia and the Salonika Trial of 1917." *Serbian Studies* 7, no. 2 (Fall 1993, published in 1995): 16-27. [Presented at the 32nd Annual Meeting of the Southern Conference on Slavic Studies in Norfolk, VA, on March 18, 1994.]

3008. Magocsi, Paul Robert. *The Rusyns of Slovakia: An Historical Survey.* Classics of Carpatho-Rusyn Scholarship, 6. East European Monographs, no. 381. [Boulder, CO]: East European Monographs; New York: Distributed by Columbia University Press, 1993. xii, 185 pp. [*Rusyny na Slovens'ku.*]

3009. Mentzel, Peter. "The German Minority in Inter-War Yugoslavia." *Nationalities Papers* 21, no. 2 (Fall 1993): 129-143.

3010. Novakovich, Josip. "Witness: Shrapnel in the Liver: The Third Balkan War." *Massachusetts Review* 34, no. 1 (Spring 1993): 144-160. [Includes discussion of the Baptist Church in former Yugoslavia (especially in Daruvar, Croatia), the concentration camp in Yasenovac, and war crimes committed by Serbs and Croats during World War II.]

3011. Pirjevec, Joze. "Slovenes and Yugoslavia, 1918-1991." *Nationalities Papers* 21, no. 1 (Spring 1993): 109-118.

3012. Sekelj, Laslo. *Yugoslavia: The Process of Disintegration.* Translated from the Serbo-Croat by Vera Vukelic. Atlantic Studies on Society in Change, no. 76. East European Monographs, no. 359. Boulder, CO: Social Science Monographs; Highland Lakes, NJ: Atlantic Research and Publications; New York, NY: Distributed by Columbia University Press, 1993, c1992. xxiv, 324 pp. REV: Mark Biondich, *Canadian Slavonic Papers* 35, nos. 1-2 (March-June 1993): 187-188.

3013. Spencer, Christopher. "The Former Yugoslavia: Background to Crisis." *Behind the Headlines* 50, no. 4 (Summer 1993): 1-16.

3014. Strausz-Hupe, Robert. "Again, Rendezvous with History at Sarajevo." *Global Affairs* 8, no. 3 (Spring 1993): 49-57.

3015. Suster, Zeljan. "Serbia's Economic Relations with the West before World War I." *Serbian Studies* 7, no. 2 (Fall 1993, published in 1995): 28-48. [Presented at the annual convention of the AAASS in Honolulu, HI, November 17-21, 1993.]

9 International Relations

■ General

3016. Allen, William W., Antione D. Johnson, and John T. Nelsen, II. "Peacekeeping and Peace Enforcement Operations." *Military Review* 73, no. 10 (October 1993): 53-61.

3017. Becker, John D. "Combined and Coalition Warfighting: The American Experience." *Military Review* 73, no. 11 (November 1993): 25-29.

3018. Bowker, Mike, and Robin Brown, eds. *From Cold War to Collapse: Theory and World Politics in the 1980s*. Contributions by Robin Brown, Fred Halliday, Michael Cox, Richard Crockatt, Mike Bowker, Marysia Zalewski, and N. J. Rengger. Cambridge Studies in International Relations, 25. Cambridge; New York, NY: Cambridge University Press, 1993. xi, 183 pp. [Contents: Robin Brown, "Introduction: towards a new synthesis of international relations," pp. 1-20; Fred Halliday, "The Cold War as inter-systemic conflict—initial theses," pp. 21-34; Michael Cox, "Radical theory and the New Cold War," pp. 35-58; Richard Crockatt, "Theories of stability and the end of the Cold War," pp. 59-81; Mike Bowker, "Explaining Soviet foreign policy behaviour in the 1980s," pp. 82-114; Marysia Zalewski, "Feminist theory and international relations," pp. 115-144; N. J. Rengger, "No longer 'A Tournament of Distinctive Knights'? Systemic transition and the priority of international order," pp. 145-174; "Further reading," pp. 175-176.] REV: William B. Moul, *Canadian Journal of Political Science = Revue canadienne de science politique* 26, no. 3 (September 1993): 622-623.

3019. Brzezinski, Zbigniew. *Out of Control: Global Turmoil on the Eve of the Twenty-First Century*. New York: Scribner; Toronto: Maxwell Macmillan Canada; New York: Maxwell Macmillan International, 1993. xv, 240 pp. [Contents: Pt. I. The Politics of Organized Insanity. 1. The Century of Megadeath. 2. The Centrality of Metamyth. 3. Coercive Utopia — Pt. II. Beyond Political Awakening. 1. The Victory of Small Beliefs. 2. Permissive Cornucopia. 3. Philosophical Polarization — Pt. III. The Peerless Global Power. 1. The Paradox of Global Power. 2. The Dissonant Message. 3. The Faceless Rivals — Pt. IV. Dilemmas of Global Disorder. 1. The Geopolitical Vacuum. 2. The Vengeful Phoenix. 3. The Giant of Global Inequality — Pt. V. The Illusion of Control.] REV: Lee Edwards, *World & I* (August 1993): 302-308. Richard Lowry, *Freedom Review* 24, no. 3 (May-June 1993): 52-53. John Lukacs, *Book World* 23, no. 20 (May 16, 1993): 9. Walter Russell Mead, *New York Times Book Review* 98, no. 14 (April 4, 1993): 10. John W. Messer, *Military Review* 73, no. 9 (September 1993): 88. Joshua Muravchik, *Commentary* 96, no. 1 (July 1993): 64-66. Andrew J. Pierre, *Foreign Affairs* 72, no. 3 (Summer 1993): 195.

3020. Bungs, Dzintra. "Progress on Withdrawal from the Baltic States." *RFE/RL Research Report* 2, no. 25 (June 18, 1993): 50-59. [Part of special issue on "Post-Soviet Armies."]

3021. Caron, David D. "Toward an Arctic Environmental Regime." *Ocean Development and International Law* 24, no. 4 (October-December 1993): 377-392. [Article is based on remarks made at the Berkeley Conference on the Ocean Governance Study Group, held at Boalt Hall School of Law, University of California at Berkeley, January 11-13, 1993.]

3022. Chafetz, Glenn R. *Gorbachev, Reform, and the Brezhnev Doctrine: Soviet Policy toward Eastern Europe, 1985-1990*. Westport, CT: Praeger, 1993. 156 pp. [Contents: 1. Introduction; 2. Past as Prologue: Soviet Policy Toward Eastern Europe, 1945-1985; 3. Forces Impelling Change; 4. East European Policy as a Function of Domestic Reform and Politics; 5. Internal Ideological Change and Its External Implications; 6. The Rational Actor Revisited; 7. Conclusions.] REV: William Urban, *Journal of Baltic Studies* 24, no. 3 (Fall 1993): 311.

3023. Conference on Security and Cooperation in Europe. High Commissioner on National Minorities. "Documentation." *Human Rights Law Journal* 14, nos. 5-6 (June 30, 1993): 216-225. [March-April 1993: Recommendations by the CSCE High Commissioner, Max van der Stoel, upon his visits to Estonia, Latvia and Lithuania, with official government responses (pp. 216-222); Russian comments to the Recommendations concerning Estonia and Latvia (p. 223); Proposals by Commissioner van der Stoel upons his visits to Slovakia and Hungary, with official government responses (pp. 224-225).]

3024. Cortright, David. *Peace Works: The Citizen's Role in Ending the Cold War*. Boulder, CO: Westview Press, 1993. viii, 288 pp.

3025. Cullen, Robert. "Diplomacy: Cleansing Ethnic Hatred." *Atlantic* 272, no. 2 (August 1993): 30-36.

3026. De Weydenthal, Jan B. "Russia Mends Fences with Poland, the Czech Republic, and Slovakia." *RFE/RL Research Report* 2, no. 36 (September 10, 1993): 33-36.

3027. Edwards, Lee. "Confronting Democracy's Flaws." *World & I* 8, no. 8 (August 1993): 302-308. [Review article on Zbigniew Brzezinski, *Out of Control* (NY: Charles Scribner, 1993).]

3028. Enloe, Cynthia H. *The Morning After: Sexual Politics at the End of the Cold War*. Berkeley, CA: University of California Press, c1993. 326 pp. [Contents: 1. Are UN Peacekeepers Real Men? And Other Post-Cold War Puzzles; 2. Turning Artillery into Ambulances: Some

Feminist Caveats; 3. Beyond Steve Canyon and Rambo: Histories of Militarized Masculinity; 4. Bananas Militarized and Demilitarized; 5. It Takes More Than Two: The Prostitute, the Soldier, the State, and the Entrepreneur; 6. The Gendered Gulf: A Diary; 7. The Politics of Constructing the American Woman Soldier; 8. Feminism, Nationalism, and Militarism after the Cold War; 9. Conclusion: When Is Postwar Postpatriarchy?]

3029. Fasching, Darrell J. *The Ethical Challenge of Auschwitz and Hiroshima: Apocalypse or Utopia?* Albany, NY: State University of New York Press, c1993. xvi, 366 pp. [Partial contents: Prologue: The Challenge of Babel—From Alienation to Ethics after Auschwitz and Hiroshima. Pt. I. The Promise of Utopia and the Threat of Apocalypse — Pt. II. After Auschwitz and Hiroshima: Utopian Ethics for an Apocalyptic Age — Appendix: The United Nations Universal Declaration of Human Rights.]

3030. Hunter, Horace L., Jr. "Ethnic Conflict and Operations Other Than War." *Military Review* 73, no. 11 (November 1993): 18-24.

3031. Huntington, Samuel P. "The Clash of Civilizations?" *Foreign Affairs* 72, no. 3 (Summer 1993): 22-49.

3032. Iklé, Fred C. "The Enemy Within." *National Interest*, no. 32 (Summer 1993): 88-92. [Review article on Daniel Patrick Moynihan, *Pandaemonium: Ethnicity in International Politics* (NY: 1993).]

3033. Janowski, Ronald M. "Material Development in the New World Order." *Military Review* 73, no. 7 (July 1993): 38-44.

3034. Kipp, Jacob, ed. *Central European Security Concerns: Bridge, Buffer, Or Barrier?* Contributions by Jacob Kipp, László Valki, Theodor Winkler, Andrzej Korbonski, Iván Völgyes, Alexander Konovalov, Antoni Kaminski, Lech Kosciuk, Joshua Spero, Vasil Hudak, and Timothy Thomas. London; Portland, OR: F. Cass, 1993. 201 pp. [First appeared in a special issue of *European Security* 1, no. 4 (Winter 1992). Contents: László Valki, "Security Concerns in Central Europe," pp. 1-14; Theodor Winkler, "Central Europe and the Post-Cold War European Security Order," pp. 15-40; Andrzej Korbonski, "Facing the Legacy of Post-Stalinist Regimes," pp. 41-55; Iván Völgyes, "Military Security in the Post-Communist Age: Reflections on Myths and Misperceptions," pp. 56-64; Alexander Konovalov, "Central European Security: A View from Moscow," pp. 65-79; Antoni Kaminski and Lech Kosciuk, "Disintegration of the USSR and Central European Security: A Polish View," pp. 80-91; Joshua Spero, "Déja Vu All Over Again? Poland's Attempt to Avoid Entrapment Between Two Belligerents," pp. 92-117; Vasil Hudak, "East-Central Europe and the Czech and Slovak Republics in a New Security Environment," pp. 118-145; Jacob Kipp and Timothy Thomas, "International Ramifications of Yugoslavia's Serial Wars: The Challenge of Ethno-National Conflicts for a Post-Cold War European Order," pp. 146-193.]

3035. Kritz, Neil J. "The CSCE in the New Era." *Journal of Democracy* 4, no. 3 (July 1993): 17-28.

3036. Lampe, John R., and Daniel N. Nelson, eds. *East European Security Reconsidered*. Edited in collaboration with Roland Schonfeld. Contributions by John R. Lampe, Thomas W. Simons, Jr., Ronald H. Linden, Stephen F. Szabo, Dale R. Herspring, Ben Slay, Christoph Royen, Aurel Braun, Georg Brunner, Bennett Kovrig, and Daniel N. Nelson. Woodrow Wilson Center Special Studies. Washington, DC: Woodrow Wilson Center Press and Sudosteuropa-Gesellschaft; Baltimore, MD: Distributed by the Johns Hopkins University Press, c1993. viii, 217 pp. [Contents: John R. Lampe, "Acknowledgments"; Daniel N. Nelson, "Introduction"; Thomas W. Simons, Jr., "Can the West Afford the East?"; Ronald H. Linden, "Domestic Change and International Relations in the New Eastern Europe"; Stephen F. Szabo, "The New Germany and Central European Security"; Dale R. Herspring, "The Process of Change and Democratization in Eastern Europe: The Case of the Military"; Ben Slay, "Economic Disintegration and Reintegration in Eastern Europe: An Overview of Selected Issues"; Christoph Royen, "The Visegrad Triangle and the Western CIS: Potential Conflict Constellations"; Aurel Braun, "The Post-Soviet States' Security Concerns in East-Central Europe"; Georg Brunner, "Minority Problems and Policies in East-Central Europe"; Bennett Kovrig, "Creating Coherence: Collective Contributions to the Political Integration of Central and Eastern Europe"; Daniel N. Nelson, "Old Dogs, New Tricks: Paths to Security in Eastern Europe."]

3037. Moynihan, Daniel Patrick. *Pandaemonium: Ethnicity in International Politics*. Oxford; New York: Oxford University Press, 1993. xvii, 221 pp. [Expanded version of the 1991 Cyril Foster lecture delivered at Oxford, November 29, 1991.] REV: Henri J. Barkey, *Strategic Review* 21, no. 4 (Fall 1993): 60. Fred C. Iklé, *National Interest*, no. 32 (Summer 1993): 88-92. Richard Pipes, *Commentary* 96, no. 3 (September 1993): 55-58. Edward Said, *Book World* 23, no. 8 (February 21, 1993): 4. Daniel H. Simpson, *Parameters* 23, no. 3 (Autumn 1993): 114-115. Fritz Stern, *Foreign Affairs* 72, no. 3 (Summer 1993): 203. *Orbis* 37, no. 4 (Fall 1993). *Wilson Quarterly* 17, no. 3 (Summer 1993): 88-89.

3038. Neumann, Iver B. "Russia as Central Europe's Constituting Other." *East European Politics and Societies* 7, no. 2 (Spring 1993): 349-369.

3039. Nicholson, John Greer. "Russia and the Balkans." *Journal of the Hellenic Diaspora* 19, no. 2 (1993): 49-55. [Presented at a seminar on "Greece, the Balkans and the Eastern Mediterranean," at Dawson College in November 1992.]

3040. O'Donnell, Guillermo. *On the State, Democratization and Some Conceptual Problems: A Latin American View with Glances at Some Post-Communist Countries*. Working Paper (Helen Kellogg Institute for International Studies), 192. Notre Dame, IN: Helen Kellogg Institute for International Studies, University of Notre Dame, 1993. 23 pp. [Abstracts in English and Spanish.]

3041. Pfaff, William. *The Wrath of Nations: Civilization and the Furies of Nationalism.* New York: Simon & Schuster, 1993. 256 pp. REV: James Kurth, *National Interest,* no. 34 (Winter 1993-1994): 96-101. Walter Russell Mead, *New York Times Book Review* 98, no. 46 (November 7, 1993): 25. Karl E. Meyer, *New Leader* 76 (December 1993): 5-6. Conor Cruise O'Brien, *Foreign Affairs* 72, no. 5 (November-December 1993): 142-149. Ivan Sanders, *Commonweal* 120 (November 5, 1993): 26-29. Donald Zagoria, *Foreign Affairs* 72, no. 5 (November-December 1993): 180-181.

3042. Reisch, Alfred A. "Hungarian-Russian Relations Enter a New Era." *RFE/RL Research Report* 2, no. 2 (January 8, 1993): 5-10.

3043. Ross, Robert S., ed. *China, the United States, and the Soviet Union: Tripolarity and Policy Making in the Cold War.* Contributions by Robert S. Ross, Herbert J. Ellison, Michael B. Yahuda, Chi Su, Robert Legvold, and Stephen Sestanovich. Studies on Contemporary China. Armonk, NY: M.E. Sharpe, c1993. x, 204 pp. [Based on a conference held in Beijing in June 1990. Contents: Robert S. Ross and Herbert J. Ellison, "Introduction," pp. 3-8; Part I: China. Michael B. Yahuda, "The Significance of Tripolarity in China's Policy toward the United States Since 1972," pp. 11-37; Chi Su, "The Strategic Triangle and China's Soviet Policy," pp. 39-61. Part II: The Soviet Union. Robert Legvold, "Sino-Soviet Relations: The American Factor," pp. 65-92; Herbert J. Ellison, "Soviet-Chinese Relations: The Experience of Two Decades," pp. 93-121. Part III: The United States. Stephen Sestanovich, "U.S. Policy Toward the Soviet Union, 1970-1990: The Impact of China," pp. 125-147; Robert S. Ross, "U.S. Policy Toward China: The Strategic Context and the Policy-Making Process," pp. 149-177; Robert S. Ross, "Conclusion: Tripolarity and Policy Making," pp. 179-195.]

3044. Singer, Max, and Aaron Wildavsky. *The Real World Order: Zones of Peace, Zones of Turmoil.* Chatham, NJ: Chatham House Publishers, c1993. xv, 212 pp. [Contents: Pt. I. The Real World Order. 1. A Tale of Two Worlds; 2. Democracy and Modern Wealth Are New in the World Democracy and Peace; 3. Zones of Turmoil and Development; 4. What Difference Do Nuclear Weapons Make? 5. What the Last World Order Left Behind — Pt. II. New Policy Thinking for the Real World Order. 6. Supranations and Subnations—Rebirth of Federalisms; 7. Policy for the Zones of Turmoil; 8. American Foreign Policy in the Real World Order.] REV: Patrick Glynn, *Commentary* 96, no. 4 (October 1993): 57-60.

3045. Skelton, Ike. "Joint and Combined Operations in the Post-Cold War Era." *Military Review* 73, no. 9 (September 1993): 2-12.

3046. United States. Congress. House. Committee on Foreign Affairs. Subcommittee on Europe and the Middle East. *Developments in Europe and the Former Yugoslavia: Hearing before the Subcommittee on Europe and the Middle East of the Committee on Foreign Affairs, House of Representatives, One Hundred Third Congress, First Session, Septem-* ber 15, 1993. Washington: U.S. G.P.O., 1993. iii, 47 pp.

3047. ———. *Developments in Europe, September 1992: Hearing before the Subcommittee on Europe and the Middle East of the Committee on Foreign Affairs, House of Representatives, One Hundred Second Congress, Second Session, September 29, 1992.* Washington: U.S. G.P.O., 1993. iii, 116 pp.

3048. ———. *Developments in Europe—June 1992: Hearing before the Subcommittee on Europe and the Middle East of the Committee on Foreign Affairs, House of Representatives, One Hundred Second Congress, Second Session, June 23, 1992.* Washington: U.S. G.P.O., 1993. iii, 58 pp.

3049. ———. *Developments in Yugoslavia and Europe—August 1992: Hearing before the Subcommittee on Europe and the Middle East of the Committee on Foreign Affairs, House of Representatives, One Hundred Second Congress, Second Session, August 4, 1992.* Washington: U.S. G.P.O., 1993. iii, 84 pp.

3050. Valdez, Jonathan C. *Internationalism and the Ideology of Soviet Influence in Eastern Europe.* Soviet and East European Studies, 89. Cambridge; New York: Cambridge University Press, 1993. x, 214 pp.

3051. Waller, J. Michael. " 'Be Not Afraid.' " *World & I* 8, no. 5 (May 1993): 310-315. [Review article on George Weigel, *The Final Revolution: The Resistance Church and the Collapse of Communism* (NY: 1992); and Hélène Carrère d'Encausse, *The End of the Soviet Empire: The Triumph of the Nations* (NY: 1993).]

3052. Walters, E. Garrison. "Out of the Soviet Shadow: The United States and Eastern Europe." *Diplomatic History* 17, no. 1 (Winter 1993): 153-157. [Review article on Bennett Kovrig, *Of Walls and Bridges: The United States and Eastern Europe* (NY: 1991).]

3053. Wilson, Frank L. *The Failure of West European Communism: Implications for the Future.* 1st ed. New York: Paragon House, 1993. x, 137 pp.

3054. [omitted]

■ Diplomatic History

3055. Aga-Rossi, Elena. *Origins of the Bipolar World: Roosevelt's Policy towards Europe and the Soviet Union: A Reevaluation.* Working Paper (University of California, Berkeley. Center for German and European Studies), 2.8. Berkeley, CA: Center for German and European Studies, University of California, [1993]. 36 pp.

3056. ———. "Roosevelt's European Policy and the Origins of the Cold War: A Reevaluation." *Telos,* no. 96 (Summer 1993): 65-85. [Earlier version of this essay was published as "Origins of the Bipolar World. Roosevelt's Policy Towards Europe and the Soviet Union: A Reevaluation" in Working Papers, International and Area Studies (Berkeley, CA: 1993).]

3057. Arens, Ilmar. " 'Mene-Mene-Tekel-Ufarsin': Öselian Superintendent Oldekop Against the Swedish Government." *Journal of Baltic Studies* 24, no. 1 (Spring 1993): 3-8.

3058. Armstrong, David. *Revolution and World Order: The Revolutionary State in International Society.* Oxford: Clarendon Press; New York: Oxford University Press, 1993. viii, 328 pp. [Partial contents: "State and Class: The Russian Revolution," pp. 112-157.] REV: Roger Epp, *International Journal* 49, no. 1 (Winter 1993-1994): 163-164. Francis Fukuyama, *Foreign Affairs* 72, no. 5 (November-December 1993): 158.

3059. Blight, James G., Bruce J. Allyn, David A. Welch, and David Lewis. *Cuba on the Brink: Castro, the Missile Crisis, and the Soviet Collapse.* Foreword by Jorge I. Dominguez. 1st ed. New York: Pantheon Books, c1993. xxvii, 509 pp. [Text concerns the crisis itself and the January 1992 conference held in Havana. Contents: Jorge I. Dominguez, "Foreword"; Introduction: Toward the Brink; 1. Cuba on the Brink, 1962: The October Crisis; 2. Uses of the Brink: Cuban, American, and Russian Motives at the Havana Conference; 3. Cuba on the Brink, Then and Now: The Havana Conference on the Cuban Missile Crisis; 4. Cuba and the Brink: Fidel Castro v. History; 5. The Legacy of the Brink: Unfinished Business of the Havana Conference; Appendix 1: Chronology; Appendix 2: Letters Between Fidel Castro and Nikita Khrushchev.]

3060. Boia, Eugene. *Romania's Diplomatic Relations with Yugoslavia in the Interwar Period, 1919-1941.* East European Monographs, no. 356. Boulder, CO: East European Monographs; New York: Distributed by Columbia University Press, 1993, c1992. xiii, 501 pp. [Originally published as a thesis (Ph.D.)—Kent State University, 1992.]

3061. Boyd, Carl. *Hitler's Japanese Confidant: General Oshima Hiroshi and MAGIC Intelligence, 1941-1945.* Foreword by Peter Paret. Modern War Studies. Lawrence, KS: University Press of Kansas, c1993. xviii, 271 pp. [Partial contents: "MAGIC and the Enigma of the Eastern Front," pp. 75-95; "MAGIC and the Question of a German-Soviet Separate Peace," pp. 140-161.]

3062. Butkus, Zenonas. "Great Britain's Mediation in Establishing the Lithuanian-Latvian Frontier, 1920-1921." *Journal of Baltic Studies* 24, no. 4 (Winter 1993): 359-368.

3063. Chisholm, Anne, and Michael Davie. *Lord Beaverbrook: A Life.* 1st American ed. New York: Alfred A. Knopf; Distributed by Random House, 1993. ix, 589 pp. [Includes Beaverbrook's travel to the Soviet Union.] REV: Gerard J. De Groot, *International History Review* 15, no. 4 (November 1993): 832.

3064. Cisek, Janusz. "The Beginnings of Joseph Beck's Diplomatic Career: The Origins of His Mission to Admiral Horthy in October 1920." *East European Quarterly* 27, no. 1 (Spring 1993): 129-140.

3065. Clifford, J. Garry. "Juggling Balls of Dynamite." *Diplomatic History* 17, no. 4 (Fall 1993): 633-636.

[Review article on Warren F. Kimball, *The Juggler: Franklin Roosevelt as Wartime Statesman* (Princeton, NJ: 1991).]

3066. De Zayas, Alfred Maurice. *The German Expellees: Victims in War and Peace.* [Original German version translated by] John A. Koehler. New York: St. Martin's Press, 1993. xlii, 177 pp. [Translation of *Anmerkungen zur Vertreibung der Deutschen aus dem Osten.* Contents: "Official Map of the American Delegation to the Yalta Conference; Charles Barber, "Foreword"; 1. The Germans of East Central Europe; 2. The Expulsion Prehistory: Interbellum Years and World War II; 3. War and Flight; 4. Allied Decisions on Resettlement; 5. Expulsion and Deportation; 6. The Expellees in Germany—Yesterday and Today.] REV: Fritz Stern, *Foreign Affairs* 72, no. 4 (September-October 1993): 164.

3067. Divine, Robert A. *The Sputnik Challenge.* New York: Oxford University Press, 1993. xviii, 245 pp. REV: Stephen E. Ambrose, *Foreign Affairs* 72, no. 3 (Summer 1993): 199.

3068. Eden, Lynn. "The End of U.S. Cold War History? A Review Essay." *International Security* 18, no. 1 (Summer 1993): 174-207. [Review article on Melvyn P. Leffler, *A Preponderance of Power: National Security, the Truman Administration, and the Cold War* (Stanford, CA: Stanford University Press, 1992).]

3069. Elleman, Bruce A. "Secret Sino-Soviet Negotiations on Outer Mongolia, 1918-1925." *Pacific Affairs* 66, no. 4 (Winter 1993-1994): 539-563.

3070. Elleman, Bruce Allen. "The Soviet Union's Secret Diplomacy in China, 1919-1925." Ph.D. diss., Columbia University, 1993. [UMI order no: AAC 9412749.]

3071. Fink, Carole. *The Genoa Conference: European Diplomacy, 1921-1922.* Syracuse Studies on Peace and Conflict Resolution. Syracuse, NY: Syracuse University Press, 1993. xxx, 365 pp. [Originally published: (Chapel Hill: University of North Carolina Press, c1984).]

3072. Gaddis, John Lewis. "The Tragedy of Cold War History." *Diplomatic History* 17, no. 1 (Winter 1993): 1-16.

3073. Gallicchio, Marc. "Before History Had an End: Soviet-American Relations, 1941-1947." *Diplomatic History* 17, no. 3 (Summer 1993): 483-488. [Review article on Edward M. Bennett, *Franklin D. Roosevelt and the Search for Victory: American-Soviet Relations, 1939-1945* (Wilmington, DE: 1990); and James L. Gormly, *From Potsdam to the Cold War: Big Three Diplomacy, 1945-1947* (Wilmington, DE: 1990).]

3074. Gardner, Lloyd C. *Spheres of Influence: The Great Powers Partition Europe, from Munich to Yalta.* Chicago, IL: Ivan R. Dee, 1993. xvi, 302 pp. REV: Stephen E. Ambrose, *Foreign Affairs* 72, no. 5 (November-December 1993): 165. Joseph S. Nye, Jr., *New York Times Book Review* 98, no. 40 (October 3, 1993): 27.

3075. Goldberg, Harold J., ed. *Documents of Soviet-American Relations.* Gulf Breeze, FL: Academic International Press, 1993-. vols. [Contents: Vol. 1. Intervention, famine relief, international affairs, 1917-1933.]

3076. Harrison, Hope M. *Ulbricht and the Concrete "Rose": New Archival Evidence on the Dynamics of Soviet-East German Relations and the Berlin Crisis, 1958-1961.* Working Paper (Cold War International History Project), No. 5. Washington, DC: Woodrow Wilson International Center for Scholars, 1993. [119 pp]. [Appendices: A. Record of Khrushchev-Ulbricht Meeting, 30 November 1960; B. Letter from Ulbricht to Khrushchev, 18 January 1961; C. Letter from Khrushchev to Ulbricht, 30 January 1961; D. Letter from Ambassador Pervukhin to Foreign Minister Gromyko, 19 May 1961; E. Letter from Ulbricht to Khrushchev, June 1961; F. Letter from Ambassador Pervukhin to Foreign Minister Gromyko sent to the Central Committee on 4 July 1961; G. Khrushchev's Opening Speech to the 3-5 August 1961 Moscow Conference of Secretaries of the Central Committees of Communist and Workers' Parties of Socialist Countries for the Exchange of Opinions on Questions Concerning the Preparation and Conclusion of a German Peace Treaty; H. Ulbricht's Speech to 3-5 August 1961 Moscow Conference of Secretaries of the Central Committees of Communist and Workers' Parties of Socialist Countries for the Exchange of Opinions on Questions Concerning the Preparation and Conclusion of a German Peace Treaty; I. Letter from Ulbricht to Khrushchev, 15 September 1961; J. Letter from Khrushchev to Ulbricht, 28 September 1961; K. Letter from Ulbricht and the SED CC delegation to the CPSU 22nd Congress in Moscow to Khrushchev, 30 October 1961.]

3077. Hixson, Walter L. "Inside a Cold War Insider." *Diplomatic History* 17, no. 3 (Summer 1993): 477-481. [Review article on H.W. Brands, *Inside the Cold War: Loy Henderson and the Rise of the American Empire, 1918-1961* (NY: 1991).]

3078. Ingimundarson, Valur. "East Germany, West Germany, and U.S. Cold War Strategy, 1950-1954." Ph.D. diss., Columbia University, 1993. [UMI order no: AAC 9412775.]

3079. Jensen, Kenneth M., ed. *Origins of the Cold War: The Novikov, Kennan, and Roberts 'Long Telegrams' of 1946.* Contributions by Nikolai Novikov, George F. Kennan, Frank Roberts, Viktor L. Mal'kov, Melvyn P. Leffler, and Steven Merritt Miner. Rev. ed. with three new commentaries. Washington, DC: United States Institute of Peace Press, 1993. xx, 95 pp. [Contents: Richard H. Solomon, "Preface to the Revised Edition," pp. vii-x; Samuel W. Lewis, "Preface," pp. xi-xvii. The Telegrams. Nikolai Novikov, "The Novikov Telegram: Washington, September 27, 1946," pp. 3-16; George Kennan, "The Kennan 'Long Telegram': Moscow, February 22, 1946," pp. 17-31; Frank Roberts, "The Roberts Cables," pp. 33-67. The Commentaries. Viktor L. Mal'kov, "Commentary," pp. 73-79; Melvyn P. Leffler, "Commentary," pp. 81-88; Steven Merritt Miner, "Commentary," pp. 89-95.] REV: Albert Resis, *Russian History = Histoire russe* 20, nos. 1-4 (1993): 403-405.

3080. Jones, Howard, and Randall B. Woods. "Origins of the Cold War in Europe and the Near East: Recent Historiography and the National Security Imperative." *Diplomatic History* 17, no. 2 (Spring 1993): 251-310. [Essay by Jones and Woods (pp. 215-276) with the following commentaries: Emily S. Rosenberg, "The Cold War and the Discourse of National Security," pp. 277-284; Anders Stephanson, "Ideology and Neorealist Mirrors," pp. 285-295; and Barton J. Bernstein, "The Challenge of 'National Security'—A Skeptical View," pp. 296-310.]

3081. Kaminski, Andrzej Sulima. *Republic vs. Autocracy: Poland-Lithuania and Russia, 1686-1697.* Harvard Series in Ukrainian Studies. Cambridge, MA: Distributed by Harvard University Press for the Harvard Ukrainian Research Institute, c1993. 312 pp.

3082. Kaufman, Burton I. "John F. Kennedy as World Leader: A Perspective on the Literature." *Diplomatic History* 17, no. 3 (Summer 1993): 447-469.

3082b. Kennan, George F. *Around the Cragged Hill: A Personal and Political Philosophy.* 1st ed. New York: W.W. Norton, 1993. 272 pp. [Includes two chapters on international relations.] REV: David P. Calleo, *Book World* 23, no. 8 (February 21, 1993): 11. David Grann, *Fletcher Forum of World Affairs* 17, no. 2 (Summer 1993): 218-220. Vladimir Petrov, *Mediterranean Quarterly* 4, no. 3 (Summer 1993): 117-122. Arthur Schlesinger, *New York Review of Books* 40 (February 1, 1993): 3ff. John D. Stempel, *Foreign Service Journal* 70, no. 10 (October 1993): 49-51. Anders Stephanson, *Political Science Quarterly* 108, no. 4 (Winter 1993-1994): 758-760. George F. Will, *New York Times Book Review* 98, no. 1 (January 3, 1993): 7. *New Yorker* 68, no. 51 (February 8, 1993): 113.

3083. Kent, John. *British Imperial Strategy and the Origins of the Cold War, 1944-49.* Leicester; New York: Leicester University Press; New York: Distributed exclusively in the USA and Canada by St. Martin's Press, 1993. xi, 224 pp.

3084. Kingseed, Cole C., Brooks E. Kleber, Kevin L. Jamison, and Bryon E. Greenwald. "American POWs: A Debt Still Owed." *Military Review* 73, no. 10 (October 1993): 66-69. [Review article on Günter Bischof and Stephen E. Ambrose, *Eisenhower and the German POWs* (Baton Rouge, LA: Louisiana State University Press, 1992); James D. Sanders, Mark A. Sauter, and R. Cort Kirkwood, *Soldiers of Misfortune: Washington's Secret Betrayal of American POWs in the Soviet Union* (Bethesda, MD: National Press Books, 1992); Ernest Walker, *The Price of Surrender, 1941: The War in Crete* (New York: Sterling, 1992); Tom Bird, *American POWs of World War II: Forgotten Men Tell Their Stories* (Westport, CT: Praeger, 1992).]

3085. Kramer, Mark. "Tactical Nuclear Weapons, Soviet Command Authority, and the Cuban Missile Crisis." *Cold War International History Project Bulletin*, no. 3 (Fall 1993): 40ff.

3086. Lamb, Margaret. "Writing Up the Eastern Question in 1835-1836." *International History Review* 15, no. 2 (May 1993): 239-268.

3087. Lambakis, Steven. "Churchill versus Gorbachev: The Bout of the Century?" *Comparative Strategy* 12, no. 2 (April/June 1993): 225-232. [Compares the speeches at Fulton, Missouri, by Churchill ("The Sinews of Peace," 1946) and Gorbachev ("The River of Time and the Imperative of Action," 1992).]

3088. Lambakis, Steven James. *Winston Churchill, Architect of Peace: A Study of Statesmanship and the Cold War*. Contributions in Political Science, no. 322. Westport, CT: Greenwood Press, 1993. xii, 186 pp.

3089. Larch, William. "W. Averell Harriman and the Polish Question, December 1943-August 1944." *East European Politics and Societies* 7, no. 3 (Fall 1993): 513-554.

3090. Lehman, David E. "Arbitrary European Borders and Population Transfers: International Law and the Oder-Neisse Line." *Loyola of Los Angeles International and Comparative Law Journal* 15, no. 2 (February 1993): 485-519.

3091. Liu, Xuecheng. "The Sino-Indian Border Dispute and Sino-Indian Relations." Ph.D. diss., University of Texas at Austin, 1993. [Includes discussion of Central Asia. UMI order no: AAC 9413545.]

3092. Lombardi, Robert. "Embedded Containment: Creation of the COCOM Regime, 1947-1954." Ph.D. diss., University of Toronto, 1993. [UMI order no: AAC NN86226.]

3093. Lukes, Igor. "Stalin and Benes at the End of September 1938: New Evidence from the Prague Archives." *Slavic Review* 52, no. 1 (Spring 1993): 28-48.

3094. Marks, Frederick W., III. *Power and Peace: The Diplomacy of John Foster Dulles*. Westport, CT: Praeger, 1993. xiv, 266 pp. [Contents: 1. Dulles in Context; 2. The New Team; 3. The Arc of Negotiation; 4. The Man and the Myth; 5. The Challenge of International Communism; 6. The Mind of the Secretary; 7. In the Final Analysis.]

3095. May, Ernest R., ed. *American Cold War Strategy: Interpreting NSC 68*. Contributions by Ernest R. May, George F. Kennan, Dean Acheson, Paul H. Nitze, Robert R. Bowie, Carl Kaysen, Robert D. Blackwill, Georgi M. Kornienko, Paul Y. Hammond, William Appleman Williams, Samuel F. Wells, Jr., John Lewis Gaddis, Lloyd Gardner, Alonzo L. Hamby, Bruce Kuklick, Emily S. Rosenberg, Walter McDougall, Deborah Welch Larson, Zara Steiner, Helga Haftendorn, Geir Lundestad, Vladislav Zubok, and Shu Guang Zhang. Bedford Books in American History. Boston: Bedford Books of St. Martin's Press, c1993. xi, 228 pp. [Contents: Ernest R. May, "Introduction: NSC 68: The Theory and Politics of Strategy," pp. 1-19. Pt. 1. The Document; NSC 68: United States Objectives and Programs for National Security (April 14, 1950), pp. 23-82. Pt. 2. Commentaries; "Biases, Official and Scholarly," pp. 85-93; "Eyewitness Testimony," [George F. Kennan, pp. 94-96; Dean Acheson, pp. 96-99; Paul H. Nitze, pp. 99-107];

"Later Officials' Retrospects" [Robert R. Bowie, pp. 109-116; Carl Kaysen, pp. 116-120; Robert D. Blackwill, pp. 120-124; Georgi M. Kornienko, pp. 124-129]; "Interpreters of U.S. Foreign Policy" [Paul Y. Hammond, pp. 130-132; William Appleman Williams, pp. 133-135; Samuel F. Wells, Jr., pp. 135-140; John Lewis Gaddis, pp. 140-146; Lloyd Gardner, pp. 146-151]; "American Interpreters of American History" [Alonzo L. Hamby, pp. 152-156; Bruce Kuklick, pp. 156-159; Emily S. Rosenberg, pp. 160-164]; "A World Historian and a Social Scientist" [Walter McDougall, pp. 165-171; Deborah Welch Larson, pp. 172-177]; "Foreign Scholars" [Zara Steiner, pp. 178-181; Helga Haftendorn, pp. 182-184; Geir Lundestad, pp. 184-189; Vladislav Zubok, pp. 189-193; Shu Guang Zhang, pp. 193-198]; "Afterword," pp. 199-201; "Appendix A. Chronology of the Cold War, 1944-1954," pp. 202-205; "Appendix B. Some Public Opinion Polls, 1948-1951," pp. 206-208; "Suggestions for Further Reading," pp. 209-211; "The Postwar Division of Europe" [map], pp. 224-225; "The Spread of Communism in China and Korea" [maps], pp. 226-227.]

3096. McFadden, David W. *Alternative Paths: Soviets and Americans, 1917-1920*. New York: Oxford University Press, 1993. x, 448 pp. [Contents: Pt. 1. The Soviet-American Context. 1. Lenin's American Policy. 2. Many Actors in Search of a Policy: U.S. Discussions About the Bolsheviks, 1917-1919. Pt. 2. Interactions in Russia, 1917-1918. 3. Judson, Trotsky, and Bolshevik-American Military Collaboration, 1917-1918. 4. Raymond Robins and Discussions on Political and Economic Cooperation, 1917-1918. 5. Chicherin-Poole Discussions, May to August, 1918. Pt. 3. Isolation and the Search for Peace, 1918-1919. 6. Isolation and the Struggle for Contact. 7. Maksim Litvinov and the Bolshevik Opening to the West. 8. Paris I: The Prinkipo Failure. 9. Paris II: Bullitt's Mission to Lenin. 10. Paris III: Hoover-Nansen—The Politics of Food Relief. Pt. 4. Economic Overtures and Response, 1919-1920. 11. The Bolsheviks and Economic Diplomacy, 1919-1920. 12. The United States Responds: Red Scare and Definitive Policy, 1919-1920.] REV: Robert Legvold, *Foreign Affairs* 72, no. 4 (September-October 1993): 168. Neil Salzman, *Russian History = Histoire russe* 20, nos. 1-4 (1993): 343-345.

3097. ———. "Soviet Negotiating Behavior: A Research Design. Part One: Origins, 1917-1922." *Canadian Slavonic Papers* 35, nos. 1-2 (March-June 1993): 87-102.

3098. Mee, Charles L., Jr. *Playing God: Seven Fateful Moments When Great Men Met to Change the World*. New York: Simon & Schuster, c1993. 269 pp. [Includes chapters: "The Problem of Knowing: Pope Leo the Great and Attila the Hun"; "The Rule of Unintended Consequences: Roosevelt, Churchill, and Stalin."] REV: Edwin M. Yoder, Jr., *Book World* 23, no. 52 (December 26, 1993): 6.

3099. Melamed, E. I., comp. *Dzhordzh Kennan v russkoi pechati, 1871-1991: annotirovannyi bibliograficheskii ukazatl' = George Kennan (The Elder) in the Russian Press, 1871-1991: An Annotated Bibliographical Index in the Russian Language*. Occasional Paper (Kennan Institute for Advanced Russian Studies), no. 251. Washington, DC: Kennan Institute for Advanced Russian Studies, The Wilson

Center, [c1993]. 73 pp.

3100. Perlmutter, Amos. *FDR & Stalin: A Not So Grand Alliance, 1943-1945*. Columbia, MO: University of Missouri Press, c1993. xiv, 331 pp. [Contents: Why Another Book on FDR? — Pt. I. Roosevelt's Style and Strategy; The President's Style and World View; Roosevelt and His War Strategy — Pt. II. Roosevelt and Stalin, 1941-1943; Surrogate Diplomacy: Roosevelt's Informal Government; The Second Front; Stalin — Pt. III. Roosevelt and Stalin, 1943-1945; Teheran: The Road to Yalta; Yalta: The Epitome of a Rooseveltian Utopia; Roosevelt and the Balance of Power in Europe; President Roosevelt as a Diplomatic Failure — Appendix 1. Characteristics of Wendell Willkie; Appendix 2. U.S. Policies; Appendix 3. USSR Foreign Affairs; Appendix 4. Soviet-American Relations.]

3101. Plotke, A. J. *Imperial Spies Invade Russia: The British Intelligence Interventions, 1918*. Contributions in Military Studies, no. 131. Westport, CT: Greenwood Press, 1993. xiv, 283 pp. [Contents: 1. The Empire and the Interventions; 2. Intelligence Formation: DMI, MI2, MIO, MO5, MIR; 3. The Consolidation of Civilian Intelligence Oversight; 4. Convenient Fictions: Intervention and the Senior Dominion; 5. Trade and Intelligence in North Russia; 6. Into the North: January-March 1918; 7. Putting the Pieces Together: Intelligence-Operations in the South, 1917-1918; 8. The Third Option: Intelligence-Operations and Imperial Hegemony; 9. Dunsterforce: The Underestimated Case in Point, January-June 1918; 10. Agents in the Field and Men on the Spot; 11. Endings and Beginnings.]

3102. Reeves, Richard. *President Kennedy: Profile of Power*. New York: Simon & Schuster, 1993. 798 pp. [Includes the Cuban Missile Crisis.] REV: Stephen E. Ambrose, *Foreign Affairs* 72, no. 5 (November-December 1993): 164.

3103. Schroeder, Paul W. " 'System' and Systematic Thinking in International History." *International History Review* 15, no. 1 (February 1993): 116-134. [Review article on Ian W. Roberts, *Nicholas I and the Russian Intervention in Hungary* (London: 1991); Anselm Doering-Manteuffel, *Vom wiener Kongress zur pariser Konferenz. England, die deutsche Frage und das Mächtesystem 1815-1856: Vol. 28: Veröffentlichungen des deutschen historischen Instituts London*, ed. Adolf M. Birke (Göttingen: 1991); F.R. Bridge, *The Habsburg Monarchy among the Great Powers, 1815-1918* (NY: 1991); Norman Rich, *Great Power Diplomacy, 1814-1914* (NY: 1992); Evan Luard, *The Balance of Power: The System of International Relations, 1648-1815* (London: 1992); and Peter Krüger, ed., *Kontinuität und Wandel in der Staatenordnung der Neuzeit. Beiträge zur Geschichte des internationalen Systems: Vol. 1: Marburger Studien zur Neueren Geschichte* (Marburg: 1991).]

3104. Senarclens, Pierre de. *De Yalta au Rideau de fer: Les grandes puissances et les origines de la guerre froide*. Questions internationales = International Issues. [Paris]: Presses de la Fondation nationale des sciences politiques; [New York]: Berg, c1993. 382 pp.

3105. Sondhaus, Lawrence. "Austria-Hungary's Italian Policy under Count Beust, 1866-1871." *Historian* 56, no. 1 (Autumn 1993): 41-54.

3106. "Soviet Foreign Policy During the Cold War: A Documentary Sampler." *Cold War International History Project Bulletin*, no. 3 (Fall 1993): 1ff. [Translations of documents on Sino-Soviet relations, the Berlin Crisis of 1961, the Soviet role in the U.S.-North Vietnamese peace talks, conversations between Anatolii Dobrynin and Henry Kissinger in 1969, and Soviet policy in Afghanistan in 1979.]

3107. Spaulding, Robert Mark, Jr. " 'A Gradual and Moderate Relaxation': Eisenhower and the Revision of American Export Control Policy, 1953-1955." *Diplomatic History* 17, no. 2 (Spring 1993): 223-249.

3108. United States. Congress. Senate. Select Committee on POW/MIA Affairs. *Hearings on Cold War, Korea, WWII POWs: Hearings before the Select Committee on POW/MIA Affairs, United States Senate, One Hundred Second Congress, Second Session ... November 10 and 11, 1992*. United States. Congress. Senate S. hrg., 102-1130. Washington, DC: U.S. G.P.O., 1993. iv, 1044 pp.

3109. Wank, Solomon. "Desperate Counsel in Vienna in July 1914: Berthold Molden's Unpublished Memorandum." *Central European History* 26, no. 3 (1993): 281-310. [Includes Molden's "Promemoria" in the original German text (pp. 295-303) and in English translation (pp. 303-310).]

3110. Weathersby, Kathryn. "New Findings on the Korean War." *Cold War International History Project Bulletin*, no. 3 (Fall 1993): 1ff. [Analysis of a 1966 memorandum prepared by staff of the Soviet Foreign Ministry archive on Soviet relations with North Korea before and during the Korean War; translation by Weathersby.]

3111. ———. *Soviet Aims in Korea and the Origins of the Korean War, 1945-1950: New Evidence from Russian Archives*. Working Paper (Cold War International History Project), no. 8. Washington, DC: Woodrow Wilson International Center for Scholars, November 1993. 33 pp.

3112. Yoon, Mi Yung. "Explaining U.S. Intervention in Third World Internal Wars, 1945-1989." Ph.D. diss., Florida State University, 1993. [UMI order no: AAC 9332319.]

3113. Young, Harvey Leroy. "Franklin D. Roosevelt and Big Three Diplomacy, 1941-1945." Ph.D. diss., Washington State University, 1993. [UMI order no: AAC 9402932.]

3114. Zubok, Vladislav M. *Khrushchev and the Berlin Crisis (1958-1962)*. Working Paper (Cold War International History Project), No. 6. Washington, DC: Woodrow Wilson Center for Scholars, 1993. 4, 27 pp.

3115. Zurowski, Michael. "British Policy Towards the Polish Second Corps." *East European Quarterly* 27, no. 3 (Fall 1993): 271-300.

3116. ———. "Two Documents: The Polish Government-in-Exile and Territorial Revision." *Ukrainian Quarterly* 49, no. 4 (Winter 1993): 406-410.

■ East-West Relations

General

3117. Asmus, Ronald D., Richard L. Kugler, and F. Stephen Larrabee. "Building a New NATO." *Foreign Affairs* 72, no. 4 (September-October 1993): 28-40.

3118. Bowermaster, Jon. "Foreign Affairs: The Last Front of the Cold War." *Atlantic Monthly* 272, no. 5 (November 1993): 36-45. ["East-West tensions may have diminished in Europe, but not, it seems, above the Arctic Circle."]

3119. Brands, H. W. *The Devil We Knew: Americans and the Cold War*. New York: Oxford University Press, 1993. viii, 243 pp. [Contents: 1. The Last Days of American Internationalism: 1945-1950; 2. The National Insecurity State: 1950-1955; 3. The Immoral Equivalent of War: 1955-1962; 4. The Wages of Hubris: 1962-1968; 5. What Did We Know and When Did We Know It?: 1969-1977; 6. Old Verities Die Hardest: 1977-1984; 7. Who Won the Cold War?: 1984-1991.] REV: Kai Bird, *Book World* 23, no. 39 (September 26, 1993): 1ff.

3120. Clarke, Jonathan. "Replacing NATO." *Foreign Policy*, no. 93 (Winter 1993-1994): 22-40.

3121. Cowen Karp, Regina, ed. *Central and Eastern Europe: The Challenge of Transition*. Contributions by Regina Cowen Karp, Adam Bromke, Jennone Walker, Hieronim Kubiak, Jan Urban, Pál Dunay, Daniel N. Nelson, F. Stephen Larrabee, Alexander Konovalov, Kathleen Mihalisko, Caroline Kennedy-Pipe, Peter Vares, and Mare Haab. Solna, Sweden: SIPRI; Oxford; New York: Oxford University Press, 1993. xiv, 322 pp. [Contents: Part I. Introduction. Regina Cowen Karp, "The challenge of transition," pp. 3-14 — Part II. Central and Eastern Europe: old legacies, new conflicts. Adam Bromke, "Post-communist countries: challenges and problems," pp. 17-44; Jennone Walker, "Regional organizations and ethnic conflict," pp. 45-66 — Part III. The regional debate. Hieronim Kubiak, "Poland: national security in a changing environment," pp. 69-100; Jan Urban, "The Czech and Slovak republics: security consequences of the breakup of the CSFR," pp. 101-121; Pál Dunay, "Hungary: defining the boundaries of security," pp. 122-154; Daniel N. Nelson, "Creating security in the Balkans," pp. 155-176; F. Stephen Larrabee, "The former Yugoslavia: emerging security orientations," pp. 177-195; Alexander Konovalov, "Russia: security in transition," pp. 196-224; Kathleen Mihalisko, "Security issues in Ukraine and Belarus," pp. 225-257; Caroline Kennedy-Pipe, "The CIS: sources of stability and instability," pp. 258-282; Peter Vares and Mare Haab, "The Baltic states; *quo vadis*?" pp. 283-306.]

3122. Crow, Suzanne. "Russian Views on an Eastward Expansion of NATO." *RFE/RL Research Report* 2, no. 41 (October 15, 1993): 21-24.

3123. Doxey, Margaret. "New States, New Problems in the Post-Cold War World." *Behind the Headlines* 51, no. 1 (Autumn 1993): 14-20.

3124. Griffiths, Stephen Iwan. *Nationalism and Ethnic Conflict: Threats to European Security*. SIPRI Research Report, no. 5. Oxford; New York: Oxford University Press, c1993. 136 pp. [Partial contents: Nationalism and Ethnic Conflict in Central Europe; Nationalism and Ethnic Conflict in the Balkan States; Nationalism and Ethnic Conflict in Eastern Europe and Central Asia; The Response: The Principle Powers and the European Security Institutions; Conclusion.]

3125. Hayes, Geoffrey. "Middle Powers in the New World Order." *Behind the Headlines* 51, no. 2 (Winter 1993-1994): 1-14.

3126. Huber, Konrad J. "The CSCE and Ethnic Conflict in the East." *RFE/RL Research Report* 2, no. 31 (July 30, 1993): 30-36. [Includes sidebar: Milada Vachudova, "The CSCE Institutional Framework," pp. 33-35.]

3127. Joenniemi, Pertti, ed. *Cooperation in the Baltic Sea Region*. Contributions by Ole Wæver, Peter Vares, Olga Zurjari, Carl-Einer Stålvant, Alan Sweedler, Unto Vesa, Axel Krohn, Alexei Izyumov, Christian Wellman, Nikolaj Petersen, and Pertti Joenniemi. Washington, DC: Taylor & Francis, c1993. xiii, 185 pp. [Contents: Pertti Joenniemi and Ole Wæver, "By Way of Introduction: Why Regionalization?" pp. 1-8; Peter Vares and Olga Zurjari, "The Sharp Angles of Baltic Independence: Actors in International Politics," pp. 9-21; Ole Wæver, "Culture and Identity in the Baltic Sea Region," pp. 23-48; Carl-Einer Stålvant, "The Baltic Sea Area: An International Resource Region and a Test Case for Regionalism?" pp. 49-71; Alan Sweedler, "Prospects for Energy Cooperation Around the Baltic Rim," pp. 73-85; Unto Vesa, "Environmental Security and the Baltic Sea Region," pp. 87-98; Axel Krohn, "Naval Arms Control and Disarmament in the Baltic Sea Region," pp. 99-123; Alexei Izyumov, "Disarmament and Conversion in the Baltic Sea Region: Problems and Prospects," pp. 125-136; Christian Wellman, "Conversion, Peace Research, and Cooperation in the Baltic Sea Region: What the Links Might Be," pp. 137-147; Nikolaj Petersen, "Regional Cooperation and Regimes Around the Baltic Rim," pp. 149-159; Pertti Joenniemi, "Regionalization in the Baltic Sea Area: Actors and Policies," pp. 161-178.]

3128. Keating, Tom. "The Future of Multilateralism." *Behind the Headlines* 51, no. 1 (Autumn 1993): 8-13.

3129. Korey, William. *The Promises We Keep: Human Rights, the Helsinki Process, and American Foreign Policy*. Foreword by Daniel Patrick Moynihan. New York: St. Martin's Press in association with the Institute for EastWest Studies, New York, 1993. xxxvi, 529 pp. REV: Andrew J. Pierre, *Foreign Affairs* 72, no. 4 (September-

October 1993): 152.

3130. Kugler, Richard L. *Commitment to Purpose: How Alliance Partnership Won the Cold War*. RAND Library Collection, MR-190-RC/FF. Santa Monica, CA: RAND, 1993. xvii, 565 pp. [Supported by the Ford Foundation.]

3131. Lieber, Robert J. "Existential Realism After the Cold War." *Washington Quarterly* 16, no. 1 (Winter 1993): 155-168.

3132. Lugar, Richard. "NATO: Out of Area or Out of Business." *Foreign Policy Bulletin* 4, no. 2 (September-October 1993): 25-29. [Speech given by Senator Lugar on June 24, 1993.]

3133. Lundestad, Geir, and Odd Arne Westad, eds. *Beyond the Cold War: New Dimensions in International Relations*. Includes contributions by Willy Brandt, John Lewis Gaddis, Vladimir V. Shustov, and Jerzy Tomaszewski. Oslo: Scandinavian University Press; New York: Oxford University Press, c1993. xi, 257 pp. [Essays presented at the Nobel Jubilee Symposium, 1991, in Goteborg, Sweden. Partial contents: Willy Brandt, "Introduction: The Aftermath of the Cold War," pp. 1-5; John Lewis Gaddis, "The Cold War, the Long Peace, and the Future," pp. 7-22; Vladimir V. Shustov, "A View on the Origins of the Cold War and Some Lessons Thereof," pp. 23-37; Jerzy Tomaszewski, "Regional Conflicts in East and Central Europe," pp. 145-156.]

3134. Maguire, Matthew W. "Defining the New World Order." *Current History* 92, no. 573 (April 1993): 186-187. [Review article on Allen Lynch, *The Cold War is Over—Again* (Boulder, CO: 1992); Henry Brandon, ed., *In Search of a New World Order: The Future of U.S.-European Relations* (Washington, DC: 1992); and Janna Thompson, *Justice and World Order* (London: 1992).]

3135. McCarthy, James P. "Strengthening Security in Central and Eastern Europe: New Opportunities for NATO." *Strategic Review* 21, no. 1 (Winter 1993): 54-60.

3136. Meyerhofer, Nicholas J. *Germany and the United States Facing the Post-Communist World*. [Flagstaff, AZ]: Northern Arizona University, [1993?]. vi, 171 pp. [Papers from an international conference held September 24-27, 1990, at Northern Arizona University in Flagstaff, AZ, and sponsored by the Studiengesellschaft für Fragen Mittel- und Osteuropäischer Partnerschaft and the Conference on European Problems.]

3137. "NATO Foreign Ministers and North Atlantic Cooperation Council Hold Semi-Annual Meeting in Athens." *Foreign Policy Bulletin* 4, no. 2 (September-October 1993): 52-59. [Final Communiqué of the NATO Foreign Ministers Meeting, Athens, June 10. Includes addresses made by Secretary Christopher, Ambassador-at-Large Strobe Talbott, Ambassador to the U.N. Madeleine Albright, and Ambassador John J. Maresca (negotiator for Nagorno-Karabakh).]

3138. O'Boyle, Michael. "Right to Speak and Associate Under Strasbourg Case-Law with Reference to Eastern and Central Europe." *Connecticut Journal of International Law* 8, no. 2 (Spring 1993): 263-287. [Paper from the symposium, "Human Rights in Theory and Practice: A Time of Change and Development in Central and Eastern Europe," held in Budapest, March 19-20, 1993.]

3139. Schermers, Henricus G. "International Human Rights in the European Community and in the Nations of Central and Eastern Europe: An Overview." *Connecticut Journal of International Law* 8, no. 2 (Spring 1993): 313-322. [Paper from the symposium, "Human Rights in Theory and Practice: A Time of Change and Development in Central and Eastern Europe," held in Budapest, March 19-20, 1993.]

3140. Schifter, Richard. "The Conference on Security and Cooperation in Europe: Ancient History or New Opportunities?" *Washington Quarterly* 16, no. 4 (Autumn 1993): 121-129.

3141. Sens, Allen G. "NATO's Small Powers and Alliance Change after the Cold War." Ph.D. diss., Queen's University at Kingston, 1993. [UMI order no: AAC NN80689.]

3142. Sestanovich, Stephen. "Did the West Undo the East?" *National Interest*, no. 31 (Spring 1993): 26-34.

3143. Seymour, David. "The Extension of the European Convention on Human Rights to Central and Eastern Europe: Prospects and Risks." *Connecticut Journal of International Law* 8, no. 2 (Spring 1993): 243-261. [Paper from the symposium, "Human Rights in Theory and Practice: A Time of Change and Development in Central and Eastern Europe," held in Budapest, March 19-20, 1993.]

3144. Sikorski, Radek. "The New Shape of Europe." *National Review* 45, no. 25 (December 27, 1993): 26-27. ["Is the West losing Central Europe?"]

3145. Simon, Jeffrey. "Does Eastern Europe Belong in NATO?" *Orbis* 37, no. 1 (Winter 1993): 21-35. [Followed with response from Elliot A. Cohen, in vol. 37, no. 3 (Summer 1993): 459, and Simon's reply, pp. 460-461.]

3146. Stock, William Bradley. "Strategy and Ethics in Foreign Policy: Building a Stable Peace." Ph.D. diss., Fletcher School of Law and Diplomacy, 1993. [UMI order no: AAC 9322889.]

3147. United States. *An Act for Reform in Emerging New Democracies and Support and Help for Improved Partnership with Russia, Ukraine, and Other New Independent States of the Former Soviet Union*. [Washington, DC?: U.S. G.P.O., 1993]. [16] pp.

3148. United States. Congress. House. Committee on Foreign Affairs. *Act For Reform in Emerging New Democracies and Support and Help for Improved Partnership with Russia, Ukraine, and Other New Independent States or the "Friendship Act: Report together with Dissenting View (To Accompany H.R. 3000 ... Was Referred Jointly to the Committee on Foreign Affairs ...) (Including Cost Estimate of the Congressional Budget Office)*. United States. Congress. House Report, 103-297. [Washington, DC?: U.S.

G.P.O., 1993-. vols.

3149. United States. General Accounting Office. *Foreign Assistance: Meeting the Training Needs of Police in New Democracies: Report to Congressional Requesters.* Washington, DC: Gaithersburg, MD: The Office, 1993. 10 pp.

3150. ———. *Foreign Assistance: Promoting Judicial Reform to Strengthen Democracies: Report to Congressional Requesters.* Washington, DC: GAO, [1993]. 49 pp.

3151. Urquhart, Brian. "For a UN Volunteer Military Force." *New York Review of Books* 40, no. 11 (June 10, 1993): 3-4.

3152. Wagner, Harrison R. "What Was Bipolarity?" *International Organization* 47, no. 1 (Winter 1993): 77-106.

3153. Wohlforth, William Curtis. *The Elusive Balance: Power and Perceptions during the Cold War.* Cornell Studies in Security Affairs. Ithaca, NY: Cornell University Press, 1993. x, 317 pp. [Contents: 1. Power, Theory, and Hindsight; 2. Balance-of-Power Theory and Soviet Foreign Policy; 3. The Origins of Old Thinking; 4. Confronting the Postwar System, 1945-1953; 5. War, Power, and the Postwar Hierarchy, 1945-1953; 6. Perceived Power and the Crisis Years, 1956-1962; 7. Detente and the Correlation of Forces in the 1970s; 8. Lessons from the Cold War's Last Battle, 1980-1985; 9. Power, Ideas, and the Cold War's End; 10. The Elusive Balance of Power.]

3154. Young, John W. *The Longman Companion to Cold War and Detente, 1941-91.* Longman Companions to History. London; New York: Longman, 1993. xv, 355 pp.

Arms Control and Disarmament

3155. Abbott, Kenneth W. " 'Trust but Verify': The Production of Information in Arms Control Treaties and Other International Agreements." *Cornell International Law Journal* 26, no. 1 (Winter 1993): 1-58.

3156. Arbatov, Alexei. "START II, red ink, and Boris Yeltsin." *Bulletin of the Atomic Scientists* 49, no. 3 (April 1993): 16-21.

3157. Bundy, McGeorge, William J. Crowe, Jr., and Sidney Drell. "Reducing Nuclear Danger." *Foreign Affairs* 72, no. 2 (Spring 1993): 140-155.

3158. Bundy, McGeorge, William J. Crowe, Jr., and Sidney D. Drell. *Reducing Nuclear Danger: The Road Away from the Brink.* New York: Council on Foreign Relations Press, c1993. ix, 107 pp. [Contents: Ch. 1. The Big Two—and Warheads in Successor States — Ch. 2. The Case of Saddam and Other Dangers — Ch. 3. Putting It Together in Washington.] REV: Len Ackland, *New York Times Book Review* 98, no. 48 (November 28, 1993): 7.

3159. Bunn, George, and John B. Rhinelander. "The Arms Control Obligations of the Former Soviet Union." *Virginia Journal of International Law* 33, no. 2 (Winter 1993): 323-350.

3160. Burns, Richard Dean, editor-in-chief. *Encyclopedia of Arms Control and Disarmament.* New York: Scribner's; Toronto: Maxwell Macmillan Canada; New York: Maxwell Macmillan International, c1993. 3 vols. (xi, 1692 pp.). [Contents: Vol. 1, pt. 1. National and regional dimensions — v. 1, pt. 2. Themes and institutions — v. 2, pt. 3. Historical dimensions to 1945 — v. 2, pt. 4. Arms control activities since 1945 — v. 3, pt. 5. Treaties.] REV: Eliot A. Cohen, *Foreign Affairs* 72, no. 4 (September-October 1993): 154-155. Lavina Orlando, *International Social Science Review* 68, no. 3 (Summer 1993): 134-135. *Booklist* 90, no. 2 (September 15, 1993): 187.

3161. Clarke, Douglas L. "The Impact of START-2 on the Russian Strategic Forces." *RFE/RL Research Report* 2, no. 8 (February 19, 1993): 65-70.

3162. ———. "The Russian Military and the CFE Treaty." *RFE/RL Research Report* 2, no. 42 (October 22, 1993): 38-43.

3163. Crow, Suzanne. "START II: Prospects for Implementation." *RFE/RL Research Report* 2, no. 3 (January 15, 1993): 14-18.

3164. Gaffney, Frank J., Jr. "Star Wars II." *New Republic* 208, no. 6 (February 8, 1993): 10-11.

3165. Gusterson, Hugh. "Realism and the International Order after the Cold War." *Social Research* 60, no. 2 (Summer 1993): 279-300. [Article grew out of a paper given at the meetings of the Northeastern International Studies Association in 1989. Largely a critique of the concluding chapter of Albert Carnesale and Richard Haass, *Superpower Arms Control: Setting the Record Straight* (Cambridge, MA: 1987).]

3166. Kamp, Karl-Heinz. "Managing Nuclear Reductions in the CIS: A German View." *Strategic Review* 21, no. 4 (Fall 1993): 31-38.

3167. Kelley, Joseph E. *Soviet Nuclear Weapons: U.S. Efforts to Help Former Soviet Republics Secure and Destroy Weapons: Statement of Joseph E. Kelley, Director-in-Charge, International Affairs Issues, National Security and International Affairs Division, before the Committee on Governmental Affairs, U.S. Senate.* Testimony, GAO/T-NSIAD-93-5. [Washington, DC]: U.S. General Accounting Office, [1993]. 1 vol.

3168. Kiselyov, Sergei. "Our Man in Missouri." *Bulletin of the Atomic Scientists* 49, no. 2 (March 1993): 34-38. [Ukrainian journalist visits Whiteman Air Force Base in Missouri.]

3169. ———. "Ukraine: Stuck with the Goods." *Bulletin of the Atomic Scientists* 49, no. 2 (March 1993): 33-38.

3170. Knopf, Jeffrey W. "Beyond two-level games: domestic-international interaction in the intermediate-range nuclear forces negotiations." *International Organization* 47, no. 4 (Autumn 1993): 599-628.

3171. Koubi, Vally. "International Tensions and Arms Control Agreements." *American Journal of Political Science* 37, no. 1 (February 1993): 148-164.

3172. Lanier-Graham, Susan D. *The Ecology of War: Environmental Impacts of Weaponry and Warfare.* New York: Walker, 1993. xxx, 185 p. REV: Harry Crumpacker, *Army* 43, no. 9 (September 1993): 66.

3173. Lee, William T. "US-USSR Strategic Arms Control Agreements: Expectations and Reality." *Comparative Strategy* 12, no. 4 (October-December 1993): 415-436.

3174. Lenorovitz, Jeffrey M. "U.S./Russian team bids for ICBM demilitarization." *Aviation Week & Space Technology* 139, no. 18 (November 1, 1993): 89-90.

3175. Lepingwell, John W. R. "Beyond START: Ukrainian-Russian Negotiations." *RFE/RL Research Report* 2, no. 8 (February 19, 1993): 46-58.

3176. ———. "The Control of Former Soviet Nuclear Weapons: A Chronology." *RFE/RL Research Report* 2, no. 8 (February 19, 1993): 71-73.

3177. ———. "How Much Is a Warhead Worth?" *RFE/RL Research Report* 2, no. 8 (February 19, 1993): 62-64.

3178. ———. "Introduction: The Problem of Former Soviet Nuclear Weapons." *RFE/RL Research Report* 2, no. 8 (February 19, 1993): 1-3.

3179. ———. "Kazakhstan and Nuclear Weapons." *RFE/RL Research Report* 2, no. 8 (February 19, 1993): 59-61.

3180. ———. "Ukraine, Russia, and the Control of Nuclear Weapons." *RFE/RL Research Report* 2, no. 8 (February 19, 1993): 4-20.

3181. Lifton, Robert Jay. "Memo to Bill—V: Beware the 'Realists.'" *Nation* 256, no. 4 (February 1, 1993): 126-127.

3182. Lockwood, Dunbar. "Dribbling aid to Russia." *Bulletin of the Atomic Scientists* 49, no. 6 (July-August 1993): 39-42.

3183. Merrill, Philip. "Old World Order: Not All Yanks in Europe Should Come Home." *Policy Review*, no. 64 (Spring 1993): 44-48.

3184. Morrison, David C. "After the Race." *National Journal* 25, no. 48 (November 27, 1993): 2837-2841.

3185. Morrocco, John D. "START 2 verification to require more checks." *Aviation Week & Space Technology* 138, no. 2 (January 11, 1993): 27-28.

3186. Nahaylo, Bohdan. "The Shaping of Ukrainian Attitudes toward Nuclear Arms." *RFE/RL Research Report* 2, no. 8 (February 19, 1993): 21-45.

3187. Neuman, Stephanie G. "Controlling the Arms Trade: Idealistic Dream or Realpolitik?" *Washington Quarterly* 16, no. 3 (Summer 1993): 53-75.

3188. Nye, Joseph S., Jr. "A Cloud that Lingers." *World Monitor* 6, no. 2 (February 1993): 30-33.

3189. Payne, Keith B., Linda H. Vlahos, and Willis A. Stanley. "Evolving Russian Views on Defense: An Opportunity for Cooperation." *Strategic Review* 21, no. 1 (Winter 1993): 61-77.

3190. "Pertinent Documents." *Ukrainian Quarterly* 49, no. 1 (Spring 1993): 87-92. ["Statement by President Leonid Kravchuk on the Signing of the START II Treaty by the United States and Russia," p. 87; "Joint Communiqué on the Meeting between Presidents Yeltsin and Kravchuk," pp. 88-90; "Joint Statement on Chornobyl," p. 90; and "Ukrainian Statement on Nuclear Weapons," pp. 90-92.]

3191. Roberts, Brad. "From Nonproliferation to Antiproliferation." *International Security* 18, no. 1 (Summer 1993): 139-173.

3192. Savelyev, Aleksandr G., and Nikolay N. Detinov. "View from Russia: The Krasnoyarsk Affair." *Comparative Strategy* 12, no. 3 (July/September 1993): 343-350.

3193. Savelyev, Alexander. "A View from Russia: The ABM Treaty: Should We Keep It?" *Comparative Strategy* 12, no. 1 (January/March 1993): 103-107.

3194. Ukraine. Supreme Rada. "Supreme Rada Resolution on the Ratification of the Start I Treaty." *Ukrainian Quarterly* 49, no. 4 (Winter 1993): 422-424.

3195. United States. General Accounting Office. *Soviet Nuclear Weapons: Priorities and Costs Associated with U.S. Dismantlement Assistance: Report to the Honorable Hank Brown, U.S. Senate.* Washington, DC: Gaithersburg, MD: The Office, [1993]. 10 pp.

3196. "U.S. frees funds for Ukraine." *Aviation Week & Space Technology* 139, no. 5 (August 2, 1993): 29. [On U.S. support for nuclear disarmament.]

3197. Zuckerman, Lord. "The New Nuclear Menace." *New York Review of Books* 40, no. 12 (June 24, 1993): 14-19. [Review article on Joseph Rotblat et al., *A Nuclear-Weapon-Free World: Desirable? Feasible?* (Boulder, CO: 1993).]

Cultural and Scientific Relations

3198. Baker, John F. "Russia: Seeking to Enter the World Marketplace." *Publishers Weekly* 240, no. 16 (April 19, 1993): 10ff. [On a U.S. publisher delegation's visit to Moscow and Kiev.]

3199. Bollag, Burton. "Fulbright Alumni Seek Ways to Assist Countries of Former Eastern Bloc." *Chronicle of Higher Education* 39, no. 39 (June 2, 1993): A30-A31.

3200. ———. "Hundreds of American Academics Are Drawn to the Czech Republic." *Chronicle of Higher Education* 39, no. 21 (January 27, 1993): A40ff.

3201. Desruisseaux, Paul. "International Alliance of Universities Formed to Advance Exchanges with Former Soviet States." *Chronicle of Higher Education* 40, no. 13 (November 17, 1993): A49.

3202. ———. "Project Is Preparing Hundreds of Texts for Russian Students." *Chronicle of Higher Education* 39, no. 24 (February 17, 1993): A31ff.

3203. ———. "Scholar's Remark Leads to Journal Donations for Eastern Europe." *Chronicle of Higher Education* 39, no. 42 (June 23, 1993): A28.

3204. Kolb, Adrienne, and Lillian Hoddeson. "The mirage of the 'world accelerator for world peace' and the origins of the SSC, 1953-1983." *Historical Studies in the Physical and Biological Sciences* 24, no. 1 (1993): 101-124.

3205. McDonald, Kim A. "Communism's Collapse Brings New Role for International Exchanges Board." *Chronicle of Higher Education* 39, no. 28 (March 17, 1993): A42ff.

3206. ———. "U.S. and Russian Nuclear-Weapons Labs Plan Joint Experiments." *Chronicle of Higher Education* 39, no. 35 (May 5, 1993): A42.

3207. Monaghan, Peter. "In Armenia, an American University Takes Root Amid Hardship and Rubble." *Chronicle of Higher Education* 39, no. 48 (August 4, 1993): A31-A32.

3208. O'Donnell, Susannah Cassedy. "MNote: Glasnost in Alaska." *Museum News* 72, no. 4 (July-August 1993): 7-8. [On the Russian-Alaskan Northern Crossroads Discovery Center project.]

3209. Recknagel, Charles. "Students in Former Soviet Republics Will Compete for Scholarships to Study in U.S." *Chronicle of Higher Education* 40, no. 17 (December 15, 1993): A35-A36.

3210. "Russian Managers Coming to U. of Tulsa to Study Western Business and Marketing." *Chronicle of Higher Education* 39, no. 27 (March 10, 1993): A35.

3211. Silcox, Harry C. "Experiential Environmental Education in Russia: A Study in Community Service Learning." *Phi Delta Kappan* 74, no. 9 (May 1993): 706-709.

3212. Silcox, Harry C., and Shawn Sweeney. "A People-to-People Environmental Program in Russia: Experiential Service Learning in Novgorod, Russia." *Journal of Experiential Education* 16, no. 1 (May 1993): 25-27.

3213. Soros, George. *Nationalist Dictatorships versus Open Society.* New York: Soros Foundation, 1993. 20 pp. REV: Gundar J. King, *Journal of Baltic Studies* 24, no. 4 (Winter 1993): 395-402.

3214. Sterner, Eric R. "International Competition and Cooperation: Civil Space Programs in Transistion." *Washington Quarterly* 16, no. 3 (Summer 1993): 129-148.

3215. Treat, William. "East meets West in fair trial study: U.S. and Soviet Sub-Commission members work together for first time." *Human Rights Tribune* 1, no. 4 (Winter 1993): 12-13. [Members of United Nations Sub-Commission on the Prevention of Discrimination and the Protection of Minorities study the right to a fair trial.]

3216. Wagner, Matthew. "CDC Volunteers Helping to Build Democracies." *PS: Political Science & Politics* 26, no. 2 (June 1993): 304-305.

3217. Watzman, Herbert M. "7,000 Central Asian Students Enroll at Turkish Institutions." *Chronicle of Higher Education* 39, no. 42 (June 23, 1993): A29.

3218. Wildau, Susan T., Christopher W. Moore, and Bernard S. Mayer. "Developing Democratic Decision-Making and Dispute Resolution Procedures Abroad." *Mediation Quarterly* 10, no. 3 (Spring 1993): 303-320.

3219. Woodard, Colin. "Universities in Russia's Far-Flung Regions Strive to Set Up International Links." *Chronicle of Higher Education* 39, no. 47 (July 28, 1993): A35-A37.

3220. Zybert, Elzbieta Barbara, and Marcin Drzewiecki. "The European Community's Activities for Education and TEMPUS (Trans-European Mobility Scheme for University Studies)." *Ethnic Forum* 13, no. 1 (1993): 5-11.

■ International Communist Party Relations

3221. Bell, David S., ed. *Western European Communists and the Collapse of Communism.* Contributions by Stephen Gundle, David Arter, David S. Bell, Maria Teresa Patricio, Alan Stoleroff, Ole L. Smith, Jose Amodia, John Callaghan, Heinrich Bortfeldt, Wayne C. Thompson, and Gerrit Voerman. Oxford; Providence RI: Berg, 1993. xi, 202 pp. [Contents: Stephen Gundle, "The Italian Communist Party: Gorbachev and the End of 'Really Existing Socialism'"; David Arter, "Post-Communist Parties in Finland and Scandinavia: A Red-Green Road to the Twenty-first Century"; David S. Bell, "French Communism's Final Struggle"; Maria Teresa Patricio and Alan Stoleroff, "The Portuguese Communist Party: Loyalty to the 'Communist Ideal'"; Ole L. Smith, "The Greek Communist Party in the Post-Gorbachev Era"; Jose Amodia, "Requiem for the Spanish Communist Party"; John Callaghan, "Endgame: The Communist Party of Great Britain"; Heinrich Bortfeldt and Wayne C. Thompson, "The German Communists"; Gerrit Voerman, "Premature Perestroika: The Dutch Communist Party and Gorbachev"; "Conclusion: The Communist International and the Future of Communism"; Appendix: Statistical Information on Western European Communism.]

3222. Bellow, Saul. "Writers, Intellectuals, Politics: Mainly Reminiscence." *National Interest*, no. 31 (Spring 1993): 124-134.

3223. Finn, James. "Giving Intellectuals a Bad Name, or, An Obscenity of the Mind." *Freedom Review* 24, no. 2 (March-April 1993): 48.

3224. James, C. L. R. *World Revolution, 1917-1936: The Rise and Fall of the Communist International.* 1st paperback ed. Revolutionary Studies. Atlantic Highlands, NJ: Humanities Press, 1993. xxvi, 9-446 pp. [Originally published: (London: M. Secker and Warburg, 1937). With new introd.]

3225. Mesa-Lago, Carmelo, ed. *Cuba after the Cold War.* Includes contributions by Ronald H. Linden, Cole Blasier, Jorge I. Domínguez, Carmelo Mesa-Lago, Silvia Borzutzky, Aldo Vacs, Jan Svejnar, Jorge Pérez-López, and Horst Fabian. Pitt Latin American Series. Pittsburgh, PA: University of Pittsburgh Press, c1993. ix, 383 pp. [Partial contents: Carmelo Mesa-Lago, "Introduction: Cuba, the Last Communist Warrior," pp. 3-16; Ronald H. Linden, "Analogies and the Loss of Community: Cuba and East Europe in the 1990s," pp. 17-58; Cole Blasier, "The End of the Soviet-Cuban Partnership," pp. 59-97; Jorge I. Domínguez, "The Political Impact on Cuba of the Reform and Collapse of Communist Regimes," pp. 99-132; Carmelo Mesa-Lago, "The Economic Effects on Cuba of the Downfall of Socialism in the USSR and Eastern Europe," pp. 133-196; Silvia Borzutzky and Aldo Vacs, "The Impact of the Collapse of Communism and the Cuban Crisis on the South American Left," pp. 291-322; Jan Svejnar and Jorge Pérez-López, "A Strategy for the Economic Transformation of Cuba Based on the East European Experience," pp. 323-351; Carmelo Mesa-Lago and Horst Fabian, "Analogies Between East European Socialist Regimes and Cuba: Scenarios for the Future," pp. 353-380.] REV: *Wilson Quarterly* 17, no. 4 (Autumn 1993): 136-137.

3226. Meyer, Gerald. "Howard Fast: An American Leftist Reinterprets His Life." *Science & Society* 57, no. 1 (Spring 1993): 86-91. [Review article on Howard Fast, *Being Red* (NY: 1990).]

3227. Pedersen, Vernon Lee. "Red, White and Blue: The Communist Party of Maryland 1919-1949." Ph.D. diss., Georgetown University, 1993. [UMI order no: AAC 9413408.]

3228. Phelps, Christopher. "*Science & Society* and the *Marxist Quarterly*." *Science & Society* 57, no. 3 (Fall 1993): 359-362.

3229. Pike, David Wingeate. *In the Service of Stalin: The Spanish Communists in Exile, 1939-1945.* Oxford: Clarendon Press; New York: Oxford University Press, 1993. xix, 453 pp.

3230. S"ezd narodov Vostoka (1st: 1920: Baku, Azerbaijan). *To See the Dawn: Baku, 1920—First Congress of the Peoples of the East.* Edited by John Riddell. 1st ed. The Communist International in Lenin's Time. New York: Pathfinder, 1993. 344 pp.

3231. Wald, Alan. "Literary 'Leftism' Reconsidered." *Science & Society* 57, no. 2 (Summer 1993): 214-222. [Review article on James F. Murphy, *The Proletarian Moment: The Controversy Over Leftism in Literature* (Urbana, IL: 1991).]

■ U.S.S.R.

General

3232. Anderson, Richard D., Jr. *Public Politics in an Authoritarian State: Making Foreign Policy during the Brezhnev Years.* Ithaca, NY: Cornell University Press, 1993. xvi, 266 pp. [Contents: Going Public in Soviet Politics; Constituencies in Soviet Politics; Political Competition and Foreign Policy; Contrasting Visions of Socialism, 1964-1967; Brezhnev and Eastern Europe, October 1964-April 1966; Suslov and International Communism, October 1964-April 1966; Kosygin and the Capitalist World, October 1964-April 1966; Podgorny and the Third World, October 1964-April 1966; Shelepin and Sectarianism, May 1966-November 1967; Brezhnev Turns to Detente, 1970-1972; Bargaining for Detente, May 1971 and May 1972; Going Public, Foreign Policy, and Political Change.]

3233. Bradley, Mark, and Robert K. Brigham. *Vietnamese Archives and Scholarship on the Cold War Period: Two Reports.* Working Paper (Cold War International History Project), no. 7. Washington, DC: Woodrow Wilson International Center for Scholars, 1993. 27 pp. [Includes Soviet-Vietnamese relations. Contents: Mark Bradley, "Vietnamese archives and scholarship on the Cold War period"; Robert K. Brigham, "The archives of Vietnam and the Indochina Wars."]

3234. Checkel, Jeff. "Ideas, Institutions, and the Gorbachev Foreign Policy Revolution." *World Politics* 45, no. 2 (January 1993): 271-300.

3235. Clemens, Walter C., Jr. "Gorbachev's Role in International Detente: True Grit?" *Soviet and Post-Soviet Review* 20, no. 1 (1993): 51-76.

3236. Hallenberg, Jan. *The Political Transformation of Europe: The Analysis of Gorbachev's Foreign Policy in the U.S. and Sweden, 1985-1988.* Working Paper (University of California, Berkeley. Institute of Governmental Studies), 93-2. [Berkeley, CA]: Institute of Governmental Studies, University of California at Berkeley, [1993]. 35 pp.

3237. Kinsella, David Todd. "In the Shadow of Giants: Superpower Arms Transfers and Third World Conflict during the Cold War." Ph.D. diss., Yale University, 1993. [UMI order no: AAC 9331550.]

3238. Light, Margot, ed. *Troubled Friendships: Moscow's Third World Ventures.* London; New York: British Academic Press; London: Royal Institute of International Affairs, 1993. vii, 225 pp.

3239. Parrish, Scott David. "The USSR and the Security Dilemma: Explaining Soviet Self-Encirclement, 1945-1985." Ph.D. diss., Columbia University, 1993. [UMI order no: AAC 9318272.]

Covert Operations, Espionage, Terrorism

3240. Andrew, Christopher, and Oleg Gordievsky, eds. *Comrade Kryuchkov's Instructions: Top Secret Files on KGB Foreign Operations, 1975-1985.* Stanford, CA: Stanford

University Press, 1993. xv, 240 pp. [Updated ed. of: Instructions from the Centre (1991).]

3241. Carmichael, Virginia. *Framing History: The Rosenberg Story and the Cold War*. American Culture (Minneapolis, MN), 6. Minneapolis, MN: University of Minnesota Press, c1993. xxv, 299 pp.

3242. Cohen, Jacob. "Innocent After All?" *National Review* 45, no. 1 (January 18, 1993): 26-33. [On the Alger Hiss case.]

3243. ———. "The Rosenberg File." *National Review* 45, no. 14 (July 18, 1993): 48-52.

3244. Costello, John, and Oleg Tsarev. *Deadly Illusions*. 1st American ed. New York: Crown, c1993. xxii, 538 pp. REV: David Binder, *New York Times Book Review* 98, no. 38 (September 19, 1993): 16. Adam B. Ulam, *Book World* 23, no. 29 (July 18, 1993): 9ff.

3245. Glazer, Nathan. "Did We Go Too Far?" *National Interest*, no. 31 (Spring 1993): 135-140.

3246. Howe, Russell Warren. *Sleeping with the FBI: Sex, Booze, Russians, and the Saga of an American Counterspy Who Couldn't*. Washington, DC: National Press Books, c1993. 394 pp.

3247. Klingsberg, Ethan. "The Noel Field Dossier: Case Closed on Alger Hiss?" *Nation* 257, no. 15 (November 8, 1993): 528-532.

3248. Meyerson, Adam, and Alger Hiss. "Letters: To Tell the Truth: State of Denial." *Policy Review*, no. 63 (Winter 1993): 86-87. [Exchange of letters between Meyerson and Hiss, concerning Hiss' alleged espionage for the Soviet Union, and the possibility of proving or disproving this through documents in newly-opened Soviet archives.]

3249. Moss, Norman. "'Sonya' explains." *Bulletin of the Atomic Scientists* 49, no. 6 (July-August 1993): 9-11. ["A grandmother and ex-Soviet agent looks back."]

3250. Odom, William E. [Book Review]. *Book World (Washington Post)* 23, no. 39 (September 26, 1993): 1ff. [Review article on Victor Sheymov, *Tower of Secrets: A Real Life Spy Thriller* (Annapolis, MD: Naval Institute Press, 1993).]

3251. Onwudiwe, Ihekwoaba Declan. "Terrorism and the World System." Ph.D. diss., Florida State University, 1993. [UMI order no: AAC 9402510.]

3252. Ott, Marvin. "Shaking Up the CIA." *Foreign Policy*, no. 93 (Winter 1993-1994): 132-151.

3253. Park, Mun Su. "The International Dimensions of the Korean War: Geopolitical Realism, Misperception, and Postrevisionism." Ph.D. diss., State University of New York at Buffalo, 1993. [UMI order no: AAC 9420202.]

3254. Perlmutter, Amos. "Soviet Historiography, Western Journalism." *National Review* 45, no. 1 (January 18, 1993): 30-31. [On Dmitri Volkogonov's statements about Alger Hiss.]

3255. Powers, Thomas. "The Truth About the CIA." *New York Review of Books* 40, no. 9 (May 13, 1993): 49-55. [Review article on Mark Perry, *Eclipse: The Last Days of the CIA* (NY: 1992); Joseph Persico, *Casey: From the OSS to the CIA* (NY: 1990); Mark Adkin, *The Bear Trap: Afghanistan's Untold Story* (London: 1992); Tom Bower, *The Red Web: MI6 and the KGB Master Coup* (London: 1989); Robert J. Lamphere and Tom Schactman, *The FBI-KGB War: A Special Agent's Story* (NY: 1986); Tom Mangold, *Cold Warrior: James Jesus Angleton: The CIA's Master Spy Hunter* (London and NY: 1991); David Wise, *Molehunt: The Secret Search for Traitors that Shattered the CIA* (NY: 1992); George Blake, *No Other Choice: The Cold War Memories of the Ultimate Spy* (NY: 1990); Verne W. Newton, *The Cambridge Spies: The Untold Story of Maclean, Philby, and Burgess in America* (Lanham, MD: 1991); Jerrold L. Schecter and Peter S. Deriabin, *The Spy Who Saved the World: How a Soviet Colonel Changed the Course of the Cold War* (NY: 1992); Arthur B. Darling, *The Central Intelligence Agency: An Instrument of Government, to 1950* (University Park, PA: 1990); Ludwell Lee Montague, *General Walter Bedell Smith as Director of Central Intelligence, October 1950-February 1953* (University Park, PA: 1992); Ronald Kessler, *Moscow Station: How the KGB Penetrated the American Embassy* (NY: 1989); Burton Hersh, *The Old Boys: The American Elite and the Origins of the CIA* (NY: 1992); Jeffrey T. Richelson, *America's Secret Eyes in Space: The U.S. Spy Satellite Program* (NY: 1990); and Jeffrey T. Richelson, *American Espionage and the Soviet Target* (NY: 1987).]

3256. Schmidt, Maria. "The Hiss Dossier." *New Republic* 209, no. 19 (November 8, 1993): 17-20. ["A Hungarian scholar unearths secret files concerning the confessed spy Noel Field. The documents may clinch the argument that Alger Hiss really was a Communist agent."]

3257. Sheymov, Victor. *Tower of Secrets: A Real Life Spy Thriller*. Annapolis, MD: Naval Institute Press, c1993. xiii, 420 pp. REV: William E. Odom, *Book World* 23, no. 39 (September 26, 1993): 1ff.

3258. Tanenhaus, Sam. "Hiss: Guilty as Charged." *Commentary* 95, no. 4 (April 1993): 32-37.

3259. Ulam, Adam B. [Book Review]. *Book World (Washington Post)* 23, no. 29 (July 18, 1993): 9ff. [Review article on John Costello and Oleg Tsarev, *Deadly Illusions* (NY: Crown, 1993).]

U.S.S.R. and Asia/Pacific

3260. Arnold, Anthony. *The Fateful Pebble: Afghanistan's Role in the Fall of the Soviet Empire*. With a foreword by Theodore L. Eliot, Jr. Novato, CA: Presidio, c1993. xiv, 225 pp.

3261. Borer, Douglas Anthony. "Superpowers Defeated: A Comparison of Vietnam and Afghanistan." Ph.D. diss., Boston University, 1993. [UMI order no: AAC 9309790.]

3262. Cogan, Charles G. "Partners in Time: The CIA and Afghanistan since 1979." *World Policy Journal* 10, no. 2 (Summer 1993): 73-82.

3263. Denker, Debra. *Sisters on the Bridge of Fire: Journeys in the Crucible of High Asia.* Los Angeles, CA: Burning Gate Press, c1993. 332 pp.

3264. Fein, Helen. "Discriminating Genocide From War Crimes: Vietnam and Afghanistan Reexamined." *Denver Journal of International Law and Policy* 22, no. 1 (Fall 1993): 29-62.

3265. Hasegawa, Tsuyoshi, Jonathan Haslam, and Andrew Kuchins, eds. *Russia and Japan: An Unresolved Dilemma between Distant Neighbors.* Contributions by Gail W. Lapidus, Jonathan Haslam, Tsuyoshi Hasegawa, Igor Tyshetskii, Gilbert Rozman, Mike M. Mochizuki, Tsuneo Akaha, Takashi Murakami, Robert A. Scalapino, Bonnie S. Glaser, Amy Rauenhorst Goldman, John J. Stephan, Judith Thornton, Alexander Temkin, Andrew Kuchins, Sergei Goncharov, and Alexei Zagorskii. Research Series (University of California, Berkeley. International and Area Studies), no. 87. Berkeley, CA: International and Area Studies, University of California at Berkeley, c1993. xii, 456 pp. [Collection of essays by U.S., Japanese and Russian academics on Soviet- and Russo-Japanese relations. Contents: Gail W. Lapidus, "Foreword," pp. vii-x. The Soviet Union, Russia, and Japan. Jonathan Haslam, "The Pattern of Soviet-Japanese Relations since World War II," pp. 3-48; Tsuyoshi Hasegawa, "The Gorbachev-Kaifu Summit: Domestic and Foreign Policy Linkages," pp. 49-82; Igor Tyshetskii, "The Gorbachev-Kaifu Summit: The View from Moscow," pp. 83-99; Gilbert Rozman, "Japanese Images of the Soviet and Russian Role in the Asia-Pacific Region," pp. 101-123; Mike M. Mochizuki, "The Soviet/Russian Factor in Japanese Security Policy," pp. 125-160; Tsuneo Akaha and Takashi Murakami, "Soviet/Russian-Japanese Economic Relations," pp. 161-186. Russia and Japan from an Asian Perspective. Robert A. Scalapino, "Russia's Role in Asia: Trends and Prospects," pp. 189-212; Bonnie S. Glaser, "The Chinese Security Perspective on Soviet/Russian-Japanese Relations," pp. 213-242; Amy Rauenhorst Goldman, "The Dynamics of a New Asia: The Politics of Russian-Korean Relations," pp. 243-275. The Russian Far East. John J. Stephan, "The Political and Economic Landscape of the Russian Far East," pp. 279-298; Judith Thornton and Alexander Temkin, "The Consequences of Crisis for the Russian Far East Economy and for the Russo-Japanese Economic Relationship," pp. 299-339. The Domestic Sources of Soviet and Russian Foreign Policy. Andrew Kuchins, "The Soviet 'Sick Man' of Asia: The Sources and Legacy of the New Poltical Thinking," pp. 343-361; Sergei Goncharov and Andrew Kuchins, "The Domestic Sources of Russian Foreign Policy," pp. 363-397; Alexei Zagorskii, "Russian Security Policy Toward the Asia-Pacific Region: From USSR to CIS," pp. 399-416; Tsuyoshi Hasegawa, "Conclusion: Russo-Japanese Relations in the New Environment—Implications of Continuing Stalemate," pp. 417-453.] REV: Robert Legvold, *Foreign Affairs* 72, no. 4 (September-October 1993): 169-170. Donald Zagoria, *Foreign Affairs* 72,

no. 5 (November-December 1993): 180-181.

3266. Hussain, Farhat. "Determinants of Soviet Foreign Policy: A Study of Soviet Policy toward Pakistan, 1960-1971." Ph.D. diss., American University, 1993. [UMI order no: AAC 9407439.]

3267. Hussain, Syed Rifaat. "From Dependence to Intervention: Soviet-Afghan Relations during the Brezhnev Era (1964-1982)." Ph.D. diss., University of Denver, 1993. [UMI order no: AAC 9419261.]

3268. Joo, Seung-Ho. "Gorbachev's Foreign Policy Toward the Two Koreas, 1985-1991: Power and the New Political Thinking." Ph.D. diss., Pennsylvania State University, 1993. [UMI order no: AAC 9414307.]

3269. Kim, Hyung Kook. "Internalization of International Conflict: The Alliance-Making Process and the Division of Korea, 1945-1948." Ph.D. diss., Johns Hopkins University, 1993. [UMI order no: AAC 9327622.]

3270. Lohbeck, Kurt. *Holy War, Unholy Victory: Eyewitness to the CIA's Secret War in Afghanistan.* Foreword by Dan Rather. Washington, DC: Regnery Gateway, c1993. xiv, 306 pp.

3271. Lourie, Richard. [Book Review]. *Book World (Washington Post)* 23, no. 28 (July 11, 1993): 5. [Review article on Oleg Yermakov, *Afghan Tales: Stories from Russia's Vietnam* (NY: W. Morrow, 1993).]

3272. Mendelson, Sarah E. "Internal Battles and External Wars: Politics, Learning, and the Soviet Withdrawal from Afghanistan." *World Politics* 45, no. 3 (April 1993): 327-360.

3273. Mendelson, Sarah Elizabeth. "Explaining Change in Foreign Policy: The Soviet Withdrawal from Afghanistan." Ph.D. diss., Columbia University, 1993. [UMI order no: AAC 9412814.]

3274. Mostafa, Golam. "National Interest and Foreign Policy: A Case Study of Bangladesh-Soviet Relations, 1980-1990." Ph.D. diss., Carleton University, 1993. [UMI order no: AAC NN84035.]

3275. O'Ballance, Edgar. *Afghan Wars, 1839-1992: What Britain Gave Up and the Soviet Union Lost.* 1st English ed. New York: Brassey's, 1993. xix, 259 pp.

3276. ———. "Contingency Forces." *Military Review* 73, no. 6 (June 1993): 12-19.

3277. Oberg, James. "KAL 007: The Real Story." *American Spectator* 26, no. 10 (October 1993): 37-42.

3278. Overby, Paul. *Holy Blood: An Inside View of the Afghan War.* Westport, CT: Praeger, 1993. x, 230 pp.

3279. Price, Glen W. "Legal Analysis of the Kurile Island Dispute." *Temple International and Comparative Law Journal* 7, no. 2 (Fall 1993): 395-422.

3280. Quillen, Amy B. "The 'Kuril Islands' or the 'Northern Territories': Who Owns Them? Island Territorial Dispute Continues to Hinder Relations Between Russia and

Japan." *North Carolina Journal of International Law and Commercial Regulation* 18, no. 3 (Summer 1993): 633-661.

3281. Rais, Rasul Bakhsh. "Afghanistan and the Regional Powers." *Asian Survey* 33, no. 9 (September 1993): 905-922.

3282. Rubin, Barnett R. "Post-Cold War State Disintegration: The Failure of International Conflict Resolution in Afghanistan." *Journal of International Affairs* 46, no. 2 (Winter 1993): 469-492.

3283. Sarin, Oleg, and Lev Dvoretsky. *The Afghan Syndrome: The Soviet Union's Vietnam.* Novato, CA: Presidio, c1993. xiii, 195 pp. [Contents: From Monarchy to Republic; Holy War Against the Unfaithful; In the Combat Area; After the Soviet Troops Were Gone; Conclusion; Appendix A: Geography; Appendix B: Documentation and Research; Appendix C: War's Impact on Soldiers and Families; Appendix D: Supreme Soviet Decree; Appendix E: Summary of Najibullah Speech; Appendix F: Soviet Casualties.]

3284. Sayle, Murray. "Closing the File on Flight 007." *New Yorker* 69, no. 42 (December 13, 1993): 90-101.

3285. Wachter, Johannes. *Die Krise Afghanistans, 1978-1980: Ein Beitrag zur Geschichte der regionalen Ursachen der sowjetischen Interventionsentscheidung.* Europäische Hochschulschriften. Reihe III, Geschichte und ihre Hilfswissenschaften = European University Studies. Series III, History and Allied Studies, Bd. 327. Frankfurt am Main; New York: P. Lang, c1993. 284 pp.

3286. Yermakov, Oleg. *Afghan Tales: Stories From Russia's Vietnam.* Translated by Marc Romano. New York: W. Morrow and Co., c1993. 205 pp. [Translation of: *Afganskie rasskazy.* Contents: Baptism; Unit N Carried Out Exercises; Mars and the Soldier; Winter in Afghanistan; The Belles; The Snow-Covered House; A Springtime Walk; A Feast on the Bank of a Violet River; Safe Return; The Yellow Mountain; Glossary of Russian and Afghan Terms.] REV: Richard Lourie, *Book World* 23, no. 28 (July 11, 1993): 5.

3287. Ziegler, Charles E. *Foreign Policy and East Asia: Learning and Adaption in the Gorbachev Era.* Cambridge Soviet Paperbacks, 10. Cambridge; New York, NY: Cambridge University Press, 1993. xii, 197 pp.

U.S.S.R. and Latin America

3288. Cross, Sharyl. "Gorbachev's Policy in Latin America: Origins, Impact, and the Future." *Communist and Post-Communist Studies* 26, no. 3 (September 1993): 315-334.

3289. Draschner, Eugenio Armando. "The Evolution of Soviet Perceptions of and Policy towards Latin America, 1941-1990: A Learning Theory Perspective." Ph.D. diss., Columbia University, 1993. [UMI order no: AAC 9333754.]

3290. Hager, Robert Peter, Jr. "Moscow and the Central American Conflict, 1979-1991." Ph.D. diss., University of California, Los Angeles, 1993. [UMI order no: AAC 9420464.]

3291. "Officials Discuss Revolutionary Movements' Future." *World Affairs* 155, no. 4 (Spring 1993): 177-179. [Roundtable with Jacinto Suarez, first Nicaraguan ambassador to the USSR; Isidro Tellez, secretary general of the Marxist-Leninist People's Action Movement, MAP-ML; Onofre Guevara, delegate of the Sandinista National Liberation Front, FSLN: and unidentified reporter. From Managua Radio Sandino, 29 December 1991. Reprinted from *Foreign Broadcast Information Service, Latin America* (7 January 1992).]

U.S.S.R. and the Middle East

3292. Ginat, Rami. *The Soviet Union and Egypt, 1945-1955.* London; Portland, OR: Frank Cass, 1993. xii, 268 pp. [Originally presented as the author's thesis (doctoral)—University of London.]

3293. Hollis, Rosemary, ed. *The Soviets, Their Successors and the Middle East: Turning Point.* Foreword by Harold Walker. Contributions by Rosemary Hollis, Amnon Sella, Shahram Chubin, Carolyn Ekedahl, Melvin Goodman, Mark Smith, and Shirin Akiner. RUSI Defence Studies Series. New York, NY: St. Martin's Press, 1993. xiii, 206 pp. [Contents: Rosemary Hollis, "Introduction: Sliding into a New Era," pp. 1-15; Amnon Sella, "The Soviet Union, Israel and the PLO: Policy Shift in the 1980s," pp. 19-54; Shahram Chubin, "The Soviets and the Gulf: Changing Priorities in the 1980s," pp. 55-80; Carolyn Ekedahl and Melvin Goodman, "The Soviet Union and Iraq's Invasion of Kuwait," pp. 83-114; Mark Smith, "Russia's New Priorities and the Middle East," pp. 117-141; Shirin Akiner, "Whither Central Asia?" pp. 143-178.]

3294. Wehling, Fred. "Three Scenarios for Russia's Middle East Policy." *Communist and Post-Communist Studies* 26, no. 2 (June 1993): 182-204. [Paper adapted from a chapter in the author's Ph.D. dissertation, "The Dilemma of Superpower: Soviet Decision Making in Middle East Crises, 1967-1973" (University of California, Los Angeles, Political Science, 1992).]

U.S.S.R. and North America

3295. Aceves, William J. "Diplomacy at Sea: U.S. Freedom of Navigation Operations in the Black Sea." *Naval War College Review* 46, no. 2 (Spring 1993): 59-79.

3296. Amodio, Richard Ralph. "The Relationship of Projection, Nationalism, and Empathy to the Phenomenon of 'Enemy Images.'" Ph.D. diss., University of Cincinnati, 1993. [UMI order no: AAC 9329886.]

3297. Bacon, Jon Lance. *Flannery O'Connor and Cold War Culture.* Cambridge Studies in American Literature and Culture. Cambridge; New York: Cambridge University Press, 1993. ix, 174 pp. [Contents: 1. The Invaded Pastoral; 2. The Domesticated Intellectual; 3. Jesus Fanatics and Communist Foreigners; 4. The Segregated Pastoral; 5. The Invisible Country.]

3298. Bathurst, Robert B. *Intelligence and the Mirror: On Creating an Enemy.* Oslo: PRIO, International Peace Research Institute; London: Newbury Park: Sage Publications, 1993. ix, 131 pp.

3299. Beschloss, Michael R., and Strobe Talbott. *At the Highest Levels: The Inside Story of the End of the Cold War.* 1st ed. Boston, MA: Little, Brown, 1993. xiv, 498 pp. REV: Stephen E. Ambrose, *Foreign Affairs* 72, no. 3 (Summer 1993): 200. Angelo M. Codevilla, *Commentary* 95, no. 3 (March 1993): 63-64. Roger Draper, *New Leader* 76, no. 5 (April 5-19, 1993): 15-16. Godfrey Hodgson, *New York Times Book Review*, 98, no. 7 (February 14, 1993): 9. Stanley Hoffman, *Book World* 23, no. 9 (February 28, 1993): 1ff. Michael Johns, *Freedom Review* 24, no. 4 (July-August 1993): 45-47. Joseph Lepgold, *Political Science Quarterly* 108, no. 3 (Fall 1993): 544-545. Michael Mandelbaum, *World Policy Journal* 10, no. 3 (Fall 1993): 97-109. Vladimir O. Pechatnov, *Mediterranean Quarterly* 4, no. 3 (Summer 1993): 123-127. Arch Puddington, *American Spectator* 26, no. 5 (May 1993): 64-66. David Remnick, *New Yorker* 68, no. 49 (January 25, 1993): 105-108. B.S.V., *Lituanus* 39, no. 3 (Fall 1993): 85-86. Paul D. Wolfowitz, *National Review* 45 (September 1993): 62-65. *Harvard International Review* 16, no. 1 (Fall 1993): 80.

3300. Bird, Kai. [Book Review]. *Book World (Washington Post)* 23, no. 39 (September 26, 1993): 1ff. [Review article on H.W. Brands, *The Devil We Knew: Americans and the Cold War* (NY: Oxford University Press, 1993).]

3301. Blight, James G., Bryce J. Allyn, and David A. Welch. "Kramer vs. Kramer: Or, How Can You Have Revisionism in the Absence of Orthodoxy?" *Cold War International History Project Bulletin*, no. 3 (Fall 1993): 41ff. [Response to Mark Kramer's article in the same issue.]

3302. Bogumil, David Daniel. "Models of Conflict and Cooperation: Interaction Patterns of International Actors." Ph.D. diss., Purdue University, 1993. [UMI order no: AAC 9420786.]

3303. Boyle, Peter G. *American-Soviet Relations: From the Russian Revolution to the Fall of Communism.* London; New York: Routledge, 1993. xiv, 321 pp.

3304. Busch, Andrew E., and Elizabeth Edwards Spalding. "1983: Awakening from Orwell's Nightmare." *Policy Review*, no. 66 (Fall 1993): 71-75.

3305. Fried, Richard M. "Springtime for Stalin: Mosinee's 'Day Under Communism' As Cold War Pageantry." *Wisconsin Magazine of History* 77, no. 2 (Winter 1993-1994): 83-108. [Describes mock takeover of Mosinee, Wisconsin, on May Day 1950.]

3306. Gillon, Steven M., and Diane B. Kunz. *America during the Cold War.* Fort Worth, TX: Harcourt Brace Jovanovich, c1993. x, 414 pp.

3307. Hill, Kenneth L. *Cold War Chronology: Soviet-American Relations, 1945-1991.* Washington, DC: Congressional Quarterly, c1993. xiii, 362 pp.

3308. Hirshberg, Matthew S. *Perpetuating Patriotic Perceptions: The Cognitive Funtion of the Cold War.* Westport, CT: Praeger, 1993. xi, 227 pp. [Contents: 1. "America Won the Cold War!": An Introduction. Pt. I. The Cold War Schema in America; 2. Cognition, Culture, and the Cold War Schema; 3. Cold War Opinion in America; 4. Cold War Themes in American Culture; 5. Central American Elections on Network News: Cases of Cold War Framing. Pt. II. Cognitive Effects of the Cold War Schema. 6. Common Meanings for Cold War Concepts; 7. Balance, Stability, and Change in the Cold War Schema; 8. Attributions for Superpower Interventions; 9. Cold War Goals in American Foreign Policy: Nicaragua and the World; 10. Choosing Sides with the Cold War Schema; 11. Recalling Information Consistent with the Cold War Schema; 12. Conclusion.]

3309. Hite, Molly. " 'A Parody of Martyrdom': The Rosenbergs, Cold War Theology, and Robert Coover's *The Public Burning*." *Novel* 27, no. 1 (Fall 1993): 85-101. [Review article on Robert Coover, *The Public Burning* (New York: 1993).]

3310. Hixson, Walter L. " 'Red Storm Rising': Tom Clancy Novels and the Cult of National Security." *Diplomatic History* 17, no. 4 (Fall 1993): 599-613.

3311. Hofmann, George F. *Cold War Casualty: The Court-Martial of Major General Robert W. Grow.* Kent, OH: Kent State University Press, c1993. xiii, 251 p. REV: Nicholas Sellers, *Army* 43, no. 11 (November 1993): 60-61.

3312. Huard, Victor. "Canadian Ideological Responses to the Second World War." *Peace Research* 25, no. 2 (May 1993): 67-81.

3313. Huntley, Wade. "Point of View: The United States Was the Loser in the Cold War." *Chronicle of Higher Education* 39, no. 30 (March 31, 1993): A40.

3314. Kofsky, Frank. *Harry S Truman and the War Scare of 1948: A Successful Campaign to Deceive the Nation.* New York: St. Martin's Press, 1993. xi, 420 pp. [Contents: 1. Introduction: The Truth Was Expendable; 2. Crash Landing; 3. Takeoff Aborted; 4. War Games (I): Setting the Stage; 5. War Games (II): Attacking the Foe; 6. The Fruits of Victory; 7. A Worm in the Apple: The Peace Scare of May 1948; 8. Conclusions: Of Presidents and Precedents; Appendix A: Estimating Soviet Intentions and Capabilities, 1947-1948; Appendix B: On "Conspiracy Theories" in Fact and Fancy.]

3315. Kramer, Mark. "Tactical Nuclear Weapons, Soviet Command Authority, and the Cuban Missile Crisis: A Note." *International History Review* 15, no. 4 (November 1993): 740-751.

3316. Kristol, Irving. "My Cold War." *National Interest*, no. 31 (Spring 1993): 141-144.

3317. LaFeber, Walter. *America, Russia, and the Cold War, 1945-1992.* 7th ed. America in Crisis. New York: McGraw-Hill, c1993. x, 394 pp. [Rev. ed. of: *America, Russia, and the Cold War, 1945-1990.* 6th ed. (c1991).]

Contents: Introduction: The Burden of History (to 1941); 1. Open Doors, Iron Curtains (1941-1945); 2. Only Two Declarations of Cold War (1946); 3. Two Halves of the Same Walnut (1947-1948); 4. The "Different World" of NSC-68 (1948-1950); 5. Korea: The War for Both Asia and Europe (1950-1951); 6. New Issues, New Faces (1951-1953); 7. A Different Cold War (1953-1955); 8. East and West of Suez (1954-1957); 9. New Frontiers and Old Dilemmas (1957-1962); 10. Southeast Asia—and Elsewhere (1962-1966); 11. A New Containment: The Rise and Fall of Detente (1966-1976); 12. From Cold War to Old War: Reagan and Gorbachev (1977-1989); 13. A New World Order? (1989-).]

3318. Leeper, Karla Kay. "Criticism of Public Argument: The Strategic Balance and the Rhetoric of American Foreign Policy." Ph.D. diss., University of Kansas, 1993. [UMI order no: AAC 9405759.]

3319. Lowery, Daniel. [Book Review]. *Human Rights Quarterly* 15, no. 1 (February 1993): 197-204. [Review article on Natalie Hevener Kaufman, *Human Rights Treaties and the Senate: A History of Opposition* (Chapel Hill, NC: 1990); and Lawrence J. LeBlanc, *The United States and the Genocide Convention* (Durham, NC: 1991).]

3320. Mendelowitz, Allan I., and United States. General Accounting Office. *U.S. Food Aid Exports: The Role of Cargo Preference: Statement of Allan I. Mendelowitz, Before the Subcommittee on Foreign Agriculture and Hunger, Committee on Agriculture, House of Representatives*. Testimony, GAO/T-GGD-93-34. Washington, DC: Gaithersburg, MD: The Office, 1993. 15 pp.

3321. Murphey, Dwight D. "The 'Hollywood Blacklist' in Historical Perspective." *Journal of Social, Political and Economic Studies* 18, no. 3 (Fall 1993): 327-349.

3322. Murray, Shoon Kathleen. "American Elites' Reaction to the End of the Cold War: A 1988-1992 Panel Study." Ph.D. diss., Yale University, 1993. [UMI order no: AAC 9418540.]

3323. Nolan, Cathal J. *Principled Diplomacy: Security and Rights in U.S. Foreign Policy*. Contributions in Political Science, no. 313. Westport, CT: Greenwood Press, 1993. xiv, 292 pp. [Contents: Pt. I. The Soviet Union. 1. Responding to Revolution; 2. From Recognition to Alliance; 3. The Great Divide; 4. Rhetoric and Realism; 5. Human Rights and Detente; 6. Beyond Containment — Pt. II. The United Nations. 7. Active at the Creation; 8. An End to Leadership; 9. Congress vs. the President.]

3324. Ollapally, Deepa Mary. *Confronting Conflict: Domestic Factors and U.S. Policymaking in the Third World*. Contributions in Political Science, no. 324. Westport, CT: Greenwood Press, 1993. x, 217 pp. [Contents: 1. Introduction; 2. Contending Theoretical Frameworks: The Case for a Domestic Structures Approach; 3. Pre-1974 State Structure: The Formation of the Strong State; 4. Disarticulation of the Strong State; 5. Regional Conflicts Under a Strong State; 6. Regional Conflicts Under a Weaker State; 7. Conclusion.]

3325. "Our Common Home: World Prospects for Peace, Human Rights, and the Rule of Law: A Discussion with Mikhail Gorbachev." *Peace Magazine* 9, no. 3 (May-June 1993): 14-19. [Gorbachev's answers to questions from a panel of scholars at the University of Toronto, March 31, 1993.]

3326. Pessen, Edward. *Losing Our Souls: The American Experience in the Cold War*. Chicago: Ivan R. Dee, 1993. 255 pp.

3327. Petersen, Eric F. "The End of the Cold War: A Review of Recent Literature." *History Teacher* 26, no. 4 (August 1993): 471-485.

3328. Posner, Gerald. *Case Closed: Lee Harvey Oswald and the Assassination of JFK*. 1st ed. New York: Random House, 1993. xv, 607 pp.

3329. Pruessen, Ronald W. "Beyond the Cold War—Again: 1955 and the 1990s." *Political Science Quarterly* 108, no. 1 (Spring 1993): 59-84.

3330. Puddington, Arch. [Book Review]. *American Spectator* 26, no. 5 (May 1993): 64-66. [Review article on Michael R. Beschloss and Strobe Talbott, *At the Highest Levels* (Boston, MA: Little, Brown, 1993).]

3331. Rearden, Steven L. "Paul H. Nitze: Last of the Cold Warriors." *Diplomatic History* 17, no. 1 (Winter 1993): 143-151. [Review article on David Callahan, *Dangerous Capabilities: Paul Nitze and the Cold War* (NY: 1990).]

3332. Robins, Natalie. *Alien Ink: The FBI's War on Freedom of Expression*. New Brunswick, NJ: Rutgers University Press, 1993. 495 pp.

3333. Robinson, James. "Reason of State: The Origins of NSC 68." Ph.D. diss., Johns Hopkins University, 1993. [UMI order no: AAC 9327656.]

3334. Rostow, Eugene V. *Toward Managed Peace: The National Security Interests of the United States, 1759 to the Present*. New Haven, CT: Yale University Press, c1993. xii, 401 pp. [Includes section: Part III. The Age of Truman and Acheson, 1945 to the Present. Introduction, pp. 277-282; The Soviet Union Reaches for Hegemony: The Stalin Years, pp. 283-308; The Nuclear Dimension: A Case Study, pp. 309-336; The Gorbachev Era and Beyond, pp. 337-361; Epilogue: United States Foreign Policy after the Soviet Collapse, pp. 362-384.] REV: Fred Halliday, *Book World* 23, no. 33 (August 15, 1993): 4.

3335. Shapley, Deborah. *Promise and Power: The Life and Times of Robert McNamara*. 1st ed. Boston, MA: Little, Brown, c1993. xvii, 734 pp. REV: John J. Mearsheimer, *Bulletin of the Atomic Scientists* 49, no. 6 (July-August 1993): 49. Evan Thomas, *Book World* 23, no. 1 (January 3, 1993): 1.

3336. Shavit, David. *United States Relations with Russia and the Soviet Union: A Historical Dictionary*. Westport, CT: Greenwood, 1993. xviii, 256 pp.

3337. Shultz, George P. *Turmoil and Triumph: My Years as Secretary of State.* New York: Scribner's; Toronto: Maxwell Macmillan Canada; New York: Maxwell Macmillan International, c1993. xiii, 1184 pp. REV: Theodore Draper, *New York Review of Books* 40, no. 11 (June 10, 1993): 53. James Schlesinger, *National Interest*, no. 33 (Fall 1993): 79-85. Ronald Steel, *New York Review of Books* 40, no. 15 (September 23, 1993): 34.

3338. Shuster, Gerald Richard. "Ronald Reagan's Use of Rhetoric to Establish a New Consensus in Foreign Policy During His First Term in Office: An Analysis." Ph.D. diss., University of Pittsburgh, 1993. [UMI order no: AAC 9426699.]

3339. Soviet Union, and United States. Dept. of State. *Cultural Relations, Exchanges for 1989-1991: Program of Cooperation between the United States of America and the Union of Soviet Socialist Republics, Signed at Moscow May 31, 1988.* United States Treaties, etc. (Treaties and Other International Acts Series), 11454. Washington, DC: Dept. of State, [1993?]. 54 pp.

3340. ———. *Postal, Express Mail Service: Agreement, with Detailed Regulations, between the United States of America and Union of Soviet Socialist Republics, Signed at Moscow March 31, 1988.* United States Treaties, etc. (Treaties and Other International Acts Series), 11439. Washington, DC: Dept. of State, [1993?]. 20 pp.

3341. Struik, Dirk. "The Struik Case of 1951." *Monthly Review* 44, no. 8 (January 1993): 31-47.

3342. Thornton, Richard C. "Mikhail Gorbachev: A Preliminary Strategic Assessment." *World & I* 8, no. 1 (January 1993): 582-593.

3343. United States. Congress. Senate. Committee on Armed Services. *Current Developments in the Former Soviet Union: Hearings before the Committee on Armed Services, United States Senate, One Hundred Third Congress, First Session, February 3, 17, 24; March 3, 1993.* United States. Congress. Senate S. hrg., 103-242. Washington: U.S. G.P.O., 1993. iii, 216 pp.

3344. Wardinski, Michael Leon. "Truman's and Eisenhower's Perceptions of the Soviet Military Threat: A Learning Process?" Ph.D. diss., Catholic University of America, 1993. [UMI order no: AAC 9320175.]

3345. Winter, David G. "Power, Affiliation, and War: Three Tests of a Motivational Model." *Journal of Personality and Social Psychology* 65, no. 3 (September 1993): 532-545. [Includes discussion of the Cuban Missile Crisis.]

U.S.S.R. and Western Europe

3346. Doerr, Paul William. "Caution in the Card Room: The British Foreign Office Northern Department and the USSR, 1934-1940." Ph.D. diss., University of Waterloo, 1993. [UMI order no: AAC NN84615.]

3347. Pearlman, Michael D. "World War II Almanac: The Tehran Allied Summit Conference." *Military Review* 73, no. 12 (December 1993): 73-75.

3348. Shumaker, David Henry. "Gorbachev and German Unification: Moscow's German Policy, 1985-1990." Ph.D. diss., University of Virginia, 1993. [UMI order no: AAC 9402650.]

■ C.I.S.

General

3349. Adams, Jan S. *Will the Post-Soviet Commonwealth Survive?* Occasional Paper (Ohio State University. Mershon Center). Columbus, OH: Mershon Center, Ohio State University, [1993]. 19 pp. [An occasional paper from the Mershon Center project entitled "Assessing Alternative Futures for the United States and Post-Soviet Relations."]

3350. Almond, Mark. "Dawn of an Old Order." *National Review* 45, no. 19 (October 4, 1993): 47-49.

3351. Arbatov, Alexei G., ed. *The Security Watershed: Russians Debating Defense and Foreign Policy after the Cold War: Disarmament and Security Yearbook 1991/ 1992.* Foreword by Eduard A. Shevardnadze. Science & Global Security Monograph Series, v. 2. Yverdon, Switzerland; Langhorne, PA: Gordon and Breach Science Publishers, c1993. xvi, 623 pp.

3352. Armstrong, John A. "The Art of the Possible." *Soviet and Post-Soviet Review* 20, nos. 2-3 (1993): 129-134. [Response to Rex A. Wade, "The United States, Russia and the Republics" (pp. 115-128).]

3353. Bodie, William C. "Anarchy and Cold War in Moscow's 'Near Abroad.' " *Strategic Review* 21, no. 1 (Winter 1993): 40-53.

3354. ———. "The Threat to America from the Former USSR." *Orbis* 37, no. 4 (Fall 1993): 509-525.

3355. Brown, Bess. "Central Asian States Seek Russian Help." *RFE/RL Research Report* 2, no. 25 (June 18, 1993): 83-88. [Part of special issue on "Post-Soviet Armies."]

3356. Cox, Caroline, and John Eibner. *Ethnic Cleansing in Progress: War in Nagorno Karabakh.* Preface by Elena Bonner. Zurich; Washington, DC: Institute for Religious Minorities in the Islamic World, 1993. 68 pp.

3357. Crow, Suzanne. "Russian Parliament Asserts Control over Sevastopol." *RFE/RL Research Report* 2, no. 31 (July 30, 1993): 37-41. [Includes sidebar: "The 1954 Transfer of Crimea to the Ukrainian SSR," p. 38.]

3358. Daniels, Robert V. "Yel'tsin, Reform and the West." *Soviet and Post-Soviet Review* 20, nos. 2-3 (1993): 135-138. [Response to Rex A. Wade, "The United States, Russia and the Republics" (pp. 115-128).]

3359. Dombrowski, Peter. "Problems Facing US Assistance for the Post-Soviet Republics." *Soviet and Post-Soviet Review* 20, no. 2-3 (1993): 139-143. [Response to Rex A. Wade, "The United States, Russia and the Republics" (pp. 115-128).]

3360. Foye, Stephen. "Civilian-Military Tension in Ukraine." *RFE/RL Research Report* 2, no. 25 (June 18, 1993): 60-66. [Part of special issue on "Post-Soviet Armies."]

3361. Freedman, Robert O. "Israel and the Successor States of the Soviet Union: A Preliminary Analysis." *Mediterranean Quarterly* 4, no. 2 (Spring 1993): 64-89.

3362. Fuller, Elizabeth. "Russia's Diplomatic Offensive in the Transcaucasus." *RFE/RL Research Report* 2, no. 39 (October 1, 1993): 30-34.

3363. Goble, Paul A. "Ten Issues in Search of a Policy: America's Failed Approach to the Post-Soviet States." *Current History* 92, no. 576 (October 1993): 305-308.

3364. Graebner, Norman A. "The Dream and the Reality." *Soviet and Post-Soviet Review* 20, nos. 2-3 (1993): 145-148. [Response to Rex A. Wade, "The United States, Russia and the Republics" (pp. 115-128).]

3365. Kaufman, Burton I. "The Need for Priorities in American Relations with Russia." *Soviet and Post-Soviet Review* 20, nos. 2-3 (1993): 149-151. [Response to Rex A. Wade, "The United States, Russia and the Republics" (pp. 115-128).]

3366. Kiselyov, Sergei. "The view from Kiev." *Bulletin of the Atomic Scientists* 49, no. 9 (November 1993): 6-8. [On the Black Sea Fleet dispute between Russia and Ukraine.]

3367. Kravchuk, Leonid. "President Kravchuk's Statement on the Decision of the Russian Supreme Soviet Regarding Sevastopol." *Ukrainian Quarterly* 49, no. 2 (Summer 1993): 214-215.

3368. Leskov, Sergei. "The view from Moscow." *Bulletin of the Atomic Scientists* 49, no. 9 (November 1993): 8-9. [On the Black Sea Fleet dispute between Russia and Ukraine.]

3369. Lough, John. "The Place of the 'Near Abroad' in Russian Foreign Policy." *RFE/RL Research Report* 2, no. 11 (March 12, 1993): 21-29.

3370. Love, Lucinda. "International Agreement Obligations after the Soviet Union's Break-up: Current United States Practice and Its Consistency with International Law." *Vanderbilt Journal of Transnational Law* 26, no. 2 (May 1993): 373-415.

3371. Maggs, William Ward. "Armenia and Azerbaijan: Looking toward the Middle East." *Current History* 92, no. 570 (January 1993): 6-11.

3372. Mansbach, Richard W. "US Responsibilities to Russia in a Changing World, or Are We Knitting Socks for Uncle Joe Again?" *Soviet and Post-Soviet Review* 20, nos. 2-3 (1993): 153-156. [Response to Rex A. Wade, "The United States, Russia and the Republics" (pp. 115-128).]

3373. Rosefielde, Steven. "What is Wrong with Plans to Aid the CIS." *Orbis* 37, no. 3 (Summer 1993): 353-363.

3374. Saunders, Harold H. *The Concept of Relationship: A Perspective on the Future Between the United States and the Successor States to the Soviet Union*. Occasional Paper (Ohio State University. Mershon Center). Columbus, OH: Mershon Center, Ohio State University, 1993. 36 pp. [From the project "Assessing Alternative Futures for the United States and Post-Soviet Relations."]

3375. Sneider, Daniel, and Igor Torbakov. "Crimea—The Next Bosnia?" *National Review* 45, no. 15 (August 9, 1993): 26-28. [On Russian-Ukrainian relations.]

3376. Stefan, Charles G. "American Relations with the Former Soviet Union." *Mediterranean Quarterly* 4, no. 1 (Winter 1993): 71-91.

3377. United Nations. Security Council. "UN Security Council Statement on the Status of Sevastopol." *Ukrainian Quarterly* 49, no. 2 (Summer 1993): 215.

3378. Von Laue, Theodore H. "A Pessimist's Comment." *Soviet and Post-Soviet Review* 20, nos. 2-3 (1993): 157-160. [Response to Rex A. Wade, "The United States, Russia and the Republics" (pp. 115-128).]

3379. Wade, Rex A. "Professor Wade's Reply: Optimism and Pessimism, Democracy and Economics, the United States and Russia." *Soviet and Post-Soviet Review* 20, nos. 2-3 (1993): 161-168. [Reply to Armstrong, Daniels, Dombrowski, Graebner, Kaufman, Mansbach, and Von Laue, on their responses to author's "The United States, Russia and the Republics" (pp. 115-128).]

3380. ———. "The United States, Russia and the Republics." *Soviet and Post-Soviet Review* 20, nos. 2-3 (1993): 115-128. [Followed with responses from Armstrong, Daniels, Dombrowski, Graebner, Kaufman, Mansbach, and Von Laue, and a reply by Wade.]

Armenia

3381. Fuller, Elizabeth. "The Thorny Path to an Armenian-Turkish Rapprochement." *RFE/RL Research Report* 2, no. 12 (March 19, 1993): 47-51.

3382. United States. Congress. House. Select Committee on Hunger. *Humanitarian Crisis in Armenia: A Round Table Discussion: Informal Hearing before the Select Committee on Hunger, House of Representatives, One Hundred Third Congress, First Session, Hearing Held in Washington, DC, March 11, 1993*. Washington, DC: U.S. G.P.O., 1993. iii, 48 pp. [Serial no. 103-2.]

Azerbaijan

3383. Amnesty International. *Azerbaydzhan: Hostages in the Karabakh Conflict: Civilians Continue to Pay the Price*. New York, NY: Amnesty International, [1993]. 13 pp.

Central Asia

3384. Blank, Stephen J., Stephen C. Pelletiere, and William T. Johnsen. *Turkey's Strategic Position at the Crossroads of World Affairs*. Carlisle Barracks, PA: Strategic Studies Institute, U.S. Army War College, 1993. xi, 133 pp. [Authors examine Turkey's policies towards Europe, the Middle East, and the former Soviet Union's Muslim republics, and their impact on U.S. policy.]

3385. Cashel, Jim, and Christopher Kedzie. "Kazakhstan: Programs and Prospects." *Central Asia Monitor*, no. 2 (1993): 5-11.

3386. ———. "Uzbekistan: Programs and Prognosis." *Central Asia Monitor*, no. 1 (1993): 19-23. [Uzbekistan and U.S. aid.]

3387. Cranston, Alan. "Out of Focus: U.S. Policy Toward Central Asia." *Harvard International Review* 15, no. 3 (Spring 1993): 30ff.

3388. Eickelman, Dale F., ed. *Russia's Muslim Frontiers: New Directions in Cross-Cultural Analysis*. Contributions by Richard W. Cottam, George M. Korniyenko, Martha Brill Olcott, Alexei V. Malashenko, Abdujabar Abduvakhitov, Victor G. Korgun, David B. Edwards, Gene R. Garthwaite, Vyacheslav Ya. Belokrenisky, and Dimitri B. Novossyolov. Indiana Series in Arab and Islamic Studies. Bloomington, IN: Indiana University Press, c1993. ix, 206 pp. [Originated in workshops held in Moscow and Leningrad in August 1990 and in a conference held in Hanover, NH, and Washington, DC, in April 1991. Contents: Dale F. Eickelman, "Introduction: The Other 'Orientalist' Crisis"; Richard W. Cottam, "United States Middle East Policy in the Cold War Era"; Georgy M. Korniyenko, "Soviet Policy in the Middle East: A Practitioner's Interpretation"; Martha Brill Olcott, "Central Asia's Political Crisis"; Alexei V. Malashenko, "Islam versus Communism: The Experience of Coexistence"; Abdujabar Abduvakhitov, "Islamic Revivalism in Uzbekistan"; Victor G. Korgun, "The Afghan Revolution: A Failed Experiment"; David B. Edwards, "Words in the Balance: The Poetics of Political Dissent in Afghanistan"; Gene R. Garthwaite, "Reimagined Internal Frontiers: Tribes and Nationalism— Bakhtiyari and Kurds"; Vyacheslav Ya. Belokrenitsky, "Islam and the State in Pakistan"; Dimitri B. Novossyolov, "The Islamization of Welfare in Pakistan"; Richard Kurin, "Islamization in Pakistan: The *Sayyid* and the Dancer"; Muhammad Khalid Masud, "Conclusion: The Limits of 'Expert' Knowledge."] REV: Robert Legvold, *Foreign Affairs* 72, no. 5 (November-December 1993): 175. David Nalle, *Central Asia Monitor*, no. 5 (1993): 38.

3389. "Forum on Tajikistan." *Central Asia Monitor*, no. 4 (1993): 24-27. [Report of a Citizen Democracy Corps forum, held July 27, 1993. Includes summaries of comments by Lakim Kayumovich Kayumov, Donald Krumm, Barnett Rubin, Gustavo Toro, Thomas Greene, Tom Baker, and a report from Médecins sans Frontières.]

3390. Freedman, Robert O. "Israel and Central Asia: A Preliminary Analysis." *Central Asia Monitor*, no. 2 (1993): 16-20.

3390a. Greene, Ernest Thomas. "Aid to Tajikistan." *Central Asia Monitor*, no. 4 (1993): 21-24.

3391. "IRS Approves Crediting Taxes for Kazakhstan Venture." *Journal of International Taxation* 4, no. 9 (September 1993): 414-415.

3392. Kirschten, Dick. "Kirgizstan's Go-Getting Ambassador." *National Journal* 25, no. 41 (October 9, 1993): 2442. [On Ambassador Roza I. Otunbayeva.]

3393. Lange, Keely. "Perspectives across the Pamirs." *Swords and Ploughshares* 7, no. 3 (Spring 1993): 13-15. [On relations between Central Asia and Pakistan and between Central Asia and India.]

3394. Lubin, Nancy. "Dangers and Dilemmas: The Need for Prudent Policy toward Central Asia." *Harvard International Review* 15, no. 3 (Spring 1993): 6-9.

3395. Panico, Christopher J. "Uzbekistan's Southern Diplomacy." *RFE/RL Research Report* 2, no. 13 (March 26, 1993): 39-45.

3396. Reetz, Deitrich. "Pakistan and the Central Asia Hinterland Option: The Race for Regional Security and Development." *Journal of South Asian and Middle Eastern Studies* 17, no. 1 (Fall 1993): 28-56.

3397. Rubin, Barnett R. "Contradictory Trends in the International Relations of Central Asia." *Central Asia Monitor*, no. 6 (1993): 11-15.

3398. Walsh, J. Richard. "China and the New Geopolitics of Central Asia." *Asian Survey* 33, no. 3 (March 1993): 272-284.

Russian Federation

General

3399. Adams, Jan S. "Legislature Asserts Its Role in Russian Foreign Policy." *RFE/RL Research Report* 2, no. 4 (January 22, 1993): 32-36.

3400. Arbatov, Alexei G. "Russia's Foreign Policy Alternatives." *International Security* 18, no. 2 (Fall 1993): 5-43.

3401. Crow, Suzanne. "Russia Asserts Its Strategic Agenda." *RFE/RL Research Report* 2, no. 50 (December 17, 1993): 1-8.

3402. ———. "Russia Seeks Leadership in Regional Peacekeeping." *RFE/RL Research Report* 2, no. 15 (April 9, 1993): 28-32.

3403. Franckx, Erik. *Maritime Claims in the Arctic: Canadian and Russian Perspectives*. Dordrecht; Boston: M. Nijhoff, c1993. xxviii, 330 pp.

3404. Goltz, Thomas. "Letter from Eurasia: The Hidden Russian Hand." *Foreign Policy*, no. 92 (Fall 1993): 92-116.

3405. Halliday, Fred. "Russian Foreign Policy: Who's Driving the Troika?" *Nation* 256, no. 9 (March 8, 1993): 308-309.

3406. Kanet, Roger E. *Coping with Conflict: The Role of the Russian Federation.* ACDIS Occasional Paper. Urbana, IL: University of Illinois at Urbana-Champaign, 1993. 14 pp.

3407. Kanet, Roger E., and Brian V. Souders. "The Russian Federation and Its Western Neighbors: Developments in Russian Policy toward Central and Eastern Europe." *Democratizatsiya* 1, no. 3 (1993): 33-57.

3408. Konovalov, Alexander, Sergei Oznobistchev, and Dmitri Evstafiev. "Saying *da*, saying *nyet*." *Bulletin of the Atomic Scientists* 49, no. 9 (November 1993): 28-31.

3409. Kovner, Milton. "Russia in Search of a Foreign Policy." *Comparative Strategy* 12, no. 3 (July/ September 1993): 307-320.

3410. Long, Jennifer. "Redefining Russia's Foreign Policy." *Eurasian Reports* 3, no. 2 (Winter 1993): 87-104. [Part of special issue devoted to "What Is Russia?"]

3411. Nosenko, Tatiana. "The Emerging Security Environment in the Black Sea Region." *Mediterranean Quarterly* 4, no. 4 (Fall 1993): 48-59.

3412. Pavilionis, Peter. "Lukin on Russia's New Foreign Policy: An Interview with Ambassador Vladimir Lukin." *Eurasian Reports* 3, no. 2 (Winter 1993): 105-108. [Part of special issue devoted to "What Is Russia?"]

3413. Sorokin, Konstantin E. "Redefining Moscow's Security Policy in the Mediterranean." *Mediterranean Quarterly* 4, no. 2 (Spring 1993): 26-45.

3414. Sudarev, Vladimir P. "Russia and Latin America." *Hemisphere* 5, no. 2 (Winter-Spring 1993): 12-14.

3415. Webber, Mark. "The Emergence of the Foreign Policy of the Russian Federation." *Communist and Post-Communist Studies* 26, no. 3 (September 1993): 243-263.

3416. Yergin, Daniel, and Thane Gustafson. *Russia 2010—And What It Means for the World: The CERA Report.* 1st ed. New York: Random House, c1993. xiii, 300 p. [Cambridge Energy Research Associates.] REV: Serge Schmemann, *New York Times Book Review* 98, no. 52 (December 26, 1993): 2.

3417. Downes, Richard, ed. *Russian Views of Russian-Latin American Relations in the Post-Cold War World.* North-South Agenda Papers, no. 5. Coral Gables, FL: North-South Center, University of Miami, 1993. 15 pp.

Russian Federation and Asia/Pacific

3418. Batbayar, Tsedendambyn. "Mongolia in 1992: Back to One-Party Rule." *Asian Survey* 33, no. 1 (January 1993): 61-66.

3419. Bazhanov, Eugene, and Natasha Bazhanov. "Russia and Asia in 1992: A Balancing Act." *Asian Survey* 33, no. 1 (January 1993): 91-102.

3420. Blank, Stephen. "We Can Live Without You: Rivalry and Dialogue in Russo-Japanese Relations."

Comparative Strategy 12, no. 2 (April/June 1993): 173-198.

3421. Bogaturov, Alexei D. "The Yeltsin Adminstration's Policy in the Far East: In Search of a Concept." *Harriman Institute Forum* 6, no. 12 (August 1993): 1-9.

3422. DeVillafranca, Richard. "Japan and the Northern Territories Dispute: Past, Present, Future." *Asian Survey* 33, no. 6 (June 1993): 610-624.

3423. Foye, Stephen. "Russo-Japanese Relations: Still Traveling a Rocky Road." *RFE/RL Research Report* 2, no. 44 (November 5, 1993): 27-34.

3424. Hasegawa, Tsuyoshi. "The Eurasian Dimension of Russian Studies." *AAASS NewsNet* 33, no. 5 (November 1993): 1-2.

3425. Meyer, Peggy Falkenheim. "Moscow's Relations with Tokyo: Domestic Obstacles to a Territorial Agreement." *Asian Survey* 33, no. 10 (October 1993): 953-967.

3426. Nguyen, Hung P. "Russia and China: The Genesis of an Eastern Rapallo." *Asian Survey* 33, no. 3 (March 1993): 285-301.

3427. Thakur, Ramesh, and Carlyle A. Thayer, eds. *Reshaping Regional Relations: Asia-Pacific and the Former Soviet Union.* Contributions by Graeme Gill, Peter Shearman, Gerald Segal, Charles E. Ziegler, Tsuyoshi Hasegawa, Gary Klintworth, Ramesh Thakur, William Maley, Carlyle A. Thayer, Pushpa Thambipillai, R. A. Herr, D. J. McDougall, and William T. Tow. Boulder, CO: Westview Press, 1993. xiii, 299 pp. [Contents: Ramesh Thakur, "Asia-Pacific After the Cold War"; Graeme Gill, "The Agenda for Reform in Russia: Linkages between Domestic and Foreign Policies"; Peter Shearman, "Russia's Three Circles of Interests"; Gerald Segal, "Russia as an Asian-Pacific Power"; Charles E. Ziegler, "Russia and the Emerging Asian-Pacific Economic Order"; Tsuyoshi Hasegawa, "Japan"; Gary Klintworth, "China and East Asia"; Ramesh Thakur, "South Asia"; William Maley, "Regional Conflicts: Afghanistan and Cambodia"; Carlyle A. Thayer, "Indochina"; Pushpa Thambipillai, "Southeast Asia"; R. A. Herr and D. J. McDougall, "The South Pacific: Retreat from Vladivostok"; William T. Tow, "Regional Order in Asia-Pacific."]

3428. Yu, Bin. "Sino-Russian Military Relations: Implications for Asian-Pacific Security." *Asian Survey* 33, no. 3 (March 1993): 302-316.

Russian Federation and North America

3429. America and the Russian Future (1993: Washington, DC). *America and the Russian Future: Transcript of a Conference.* Occasional Paper (Kennan Institute for Advanced Russian Studies), no. 252. Washington, DC: Kennan Institute for Advanced Russian Studies, c1993. 85 pp. [Conference held on January 15, 1993, cosponsored by the Kennan Institute for Advanced Russian Studies and the Embassy of the Russian Federation in the U.S. Transcribed by Cynthia Lewis and Amy Smith.]

3430. Barnes, Fred. "White House Watch: Bill and Boris." *New Republic* 208, no. 17 (April 26, 1993): 11-12. ["A Clinton coup in Vancouver."]

3431. Barnet, Richard J. "Still Putting Arms First." *Harper's* 286, no. 1713 (February 1993): 59-65. ["The Cold War legacy confronting Clinton, abroad and at home."]

3432. Callahan, David. "Strobe the Great? The Russia-Policy Tsar." *Foreign Service Journal* 70, no. 7 (July 1993): 30-35.

3433. Canfield, Jeffrey L. "Recent Developments in Bering Sea Fisheries Conservation and Management." *Ocean Development and International Law* 24, no. 3 (July-September 1993): 257-289.

3434. Center for Strategic and International Studies (Washington, DC), and Council on Foreign and Defense Policy (Moscow, Russia). *Harmonizing the Evolution of U.S. and Russian Defense Policies.* Steering group cochairmen Fred Charles Iklé and Sergei A. Karaganov. Steering group members Alexei G. Arbatov et al. CSIS Panel Reports. Washington, DC: CSIS, c1993. vi, 46 p.

3435. Clarke, Jonathan. "The Conceptual Poverty of U.S. Foreign Policy." *Atlantic* 272, no. 3 (September 1993): 54-66.

3436. Clinton, Bill. "Tapping Grassroots Activism." *Surviving Together* 11, no. 2 (Summer 1993): 3-4. [Excerpt from a speech presented to the National Association of Newspaper Editors and reprinted from *U.S. Department of State Dispatch* (April 5, 1993).]

3437. Cohen, Stephen F. "Illusions and Realities: American Policy and Russia's Future." *Nation* 256, no. 14 (April 12, 1993): 476-485.

3438. Gann, L. H. *The United States and the New Russia.* Hoover Essays, no. 2. Stanford, CA: Hoover Institution, Stanford University, 1993. 47 pp.

3439. Ginsburgs, George, Alvin Z. Rubinstein, and Oles M. Smolansky, eds. *Russia and America: From Rivalry to Reconciliation.* Includes contributions by Viktor L. Israelyan, Donald D. Barry, Nicolai N. Petro, Robert J. Osborn, Nina Belyaeva, William C. Bodie, Martha Brill Olcott, Leonid Rudnytzky, Oleg G. Pocheptsov, Dilbar Turabekoya, Sergo A. Mikoyan, George Ginsburgs, David T. Twining, Igor Ivanovich Lukashuk, Yaroslav Bilinsky, Rajan Menon, Oles M. Smolansky, Alvin Z. Rubinstein, and Henry Trofimenko. Armonk, NY: M.E. Sharpe, c1993. xi, 353 pp. [Partial contents: Viktor L. Israelyan, "New Russia and the United States"; Donald D. Barry, "Constitutional Politics: The Russian Constitutional Court as a New Kind of Institution"; Nicolai N. Petro, "Conservative Politics in Russia: Implications for U.S.-Russian Relations"; Robert J. Osborn, "Russia: Federalism, Regionalism, and Nationality Claims"; Nina Belyaeva, "Comment: The American Vision of 'What's Wrong with Russia' and How Cooperation Can Help"; William C. Bodie, "Ukraine and Russian-American

Relations"; Martha Brill Olcott, "Central Asia and the New Russian-American Rapprochement"; Leonid Rudnytzky and Oleg G. Pocheptsov, "Comment: On 'Ukraine and Russian-American Relations'"; Dilbar Turabekoya, "Comment: On 'Central Asia and the New Russian-American Rapprochement'"; Sergo A. Mikoyan, "Comment: Understanding Ukraine"; George Ginsburgs, "Russian-American Cooperation in Policing Crime"; David T. Twining, "The New Nuclear Equation"; Igor Ivanovich Lukashuk, "Comment: The Context of Russian-American Cooperation in the Fight Against Crime"; Yaroslav Bilinsky, "Germany as a Factor in U.S.-Russian Relations: An Essay on a Growing 'Invisible' Challenge"; Rajan Menon, "Russia, America, and Northeast Asia After the Cold War"; Oles M. Smolansky, "The Russian Federation and the Middle East: An Evolving Relationship"; Alvin Z. Rubinstein, "Russia and America in Strategic Perspective"; Henry Trofimenko, "International Politics and U.S.-Russian Relations."]

3440. Goldberg, Andrew C. "America's Russian Conundrum." *World & I* 8, no. 8 (August 1993): 40-45. [Part of the special report "Russia: Is Reform Still Possible?"]

3441. Goodby, James E., and Benoit Morel, eds. *The Limited Partnership: Building a Russian-US Security Community.* Contributions by Edward B. Atkeson, Mikhail E. Bezrukov, Daria Fane, James E. Goodby, Fred Charles Iklé, David Kaiser, Steven Kull, Irving Lachow, Steven E. Miller, Benoit Morel, William W. Newmann, Sergey Rogov, and Judyth L. Twigg. Solna, Sweden: SIPRI, Stockholm International Peace Research Institute; Oxford; New York: Oxford University Press, 1993. xvii, 317 pp. [Contents: Part I. Introduction; James E. Goodby, "Introduction," pp. 3-8; Fred Charles Iklé, "The case for a Russian-US security community," pp. 9-22. Pt. II. Regime transition: from Cold war to co-operative security; William W. Newmann, "History accelerates: the diplomacy of co-operation and fragmentation," pp. 25-54; Daria Fane, "Moscow's nationalities problem: the collapse of empire and the challenges ahead," pp. 55-74; Sergey Rogov, "A national security policy for Russia," pp. 75-80; Mikhail E. Bezrukov, "The creation of a Russian foreign policy," pp. 81-93; David Kaiser, "Issues and images: Washington and Moscow in great power politics," pp. 94-110. Pt. III. Military power and international stability; Edward B. Atkeson, "Theatre forces in the Commonwealth of Independent States," pp. 113-149; Edward B. Atkeson, "US theatre forces in the year 2000," pp. 150-168; Benoit Morel, "High technology after the cold war," pp. 169-184; Irving Lachow, "The metastable peace: a catastrophe theory model of US-Russian relations," pp. 185-206. Pt. IV. Building a new security relationship; Steven Kull, "Co-operation or competition: the battle of ideas in Russia and the USA," pp. 209-223; William W. Newmann and Judyth L. Twigg, "Building a Eurasian-Atlantic security community: co-operative management of the military transition," pp. 224-248; Steven E. Miller, "Russian-US security co-operation on the high seas," pp. 249-271; Judyth L. Twigg, "Defence planning: the potential for transparency and co-operation," pp. 272-288; William W. Newmann, "Some limits on co-operation and transparency: operational security and the use of force," pp. 289-305.]

3442. Gray, John. "The Left's Last Utopia." *National Review* 45, no. 14 (July 18, 1993): 30-35. [Includes discussion of Russian perceptions of the United States.]

3443. Hosey, Walter J. "Economics, National Policy, and Military Strategy: The Growing Linkage in the 1990s." *Naval War College Review* 46, no. 2 (Spring 1993): 7-23.

3444. Janco, Gerard J. "Brzezinski on Russia's Regional Politics: An Interview with Zbigniew Brzezinski." *Eurasian Reports* 3, no. 2 (Winter 1993): 83-86. [Part of special issue devoted to "What Is Russia?"]

3445. Kovalyov, Sergei. "Open Letter to the U.S. Ambassador." *RCDA* 32, no. 4 (1993-1994): 75-77.

3446. Kullberg, Judith S. *The End of New Thinking? Elite Ideologies and the Future of Russian Foreign Policy.* Occasional Paper (Ohio State University. Mershon Center). Columbus, OH: Mershon Center at the Ohio State University, [1993]. 32 pp. [An Occasional Paper from the Mershon Center project entitled "Assessing Alternative Futures for the United States and Post-Soviet Relations". Prepared for the panel on "Russian Foreign and Security Policy," The Midwest Slavic Conference, East Lansing, Michigan, April 30-May 2, 1993.]

3447. Masters, Ian. "Russia in Crisis." *Contention: Debates in Society, Culture, and Science* 2, no. 3 (Spring 1993): 1-7. [Interview with Peter Reddaway, January 17, 1993, on "Background Briefing" on KPFK, Los Angeles, California.]

3448. Pushkov, Alexei K. "Letter from Eurasia: Russia and America: The Honeymoon's Over." *Foreign Policy*, no. 93 (Winter 1993-1994): 76-90.

3449. "Russia & Its Struggle Toward Democracy: An AJ Congress Statement." *Congress Monthly* 60, no. 4 (May-June 1993): 5.

3450. Toon, Malcolm. "Mission to Moscow." *Foreign Service Journal* 70, no. 5 (May 1993): 39-40. ["Searching for MIAs and POWs."]

3451. United States. Congress. House. Committee on Foreign Affairs. Subcommittee on Europe and the Middle East, and United States. Congress. House. Committee on Foreign Affairs. Subcommittee on International Security, International Organizations and Human Rights. *U.S. Stake in a Democratic Russia: Joint Hearing before the Subcommittees on Europe and the Middle East and International Security, International Organizations, and Human Rights of the Committee on Foreign Affairs, House of Representatives, One Hundred Third Congress, First Session, March 24, 1993.* Washington: U.S. G.P.O., 1993. v, 67 pp.

3452. [omitted]

Ukraine

3453. [omitted]

3454. Markus, Ustina. "Ukrainian-Chinese Relations: Slow but Steady Progress." *RFE/RL Research Report* 2, no. 45 (November 12, 1993): 19-23.

3455. Matiaszek, Petro. "International Legal Aspects of Ukraine's Claim to the Soviet Nuclear Legacy." *Ukrainian Quarterly* 49, no. 3 (Fall 1993): 252-293.

3456. "Pertinent Documents." *Ukrainian Quarterly* 49, no. 2 (Summer 1993): 209-215. ["Joint UCCA-UACC Letter to President Clinton on US Policy Towards Ukraine," pp. 209-210; "President Clinton's Response on US Policy Towards Ukraine," pp. 211-212; "President Clinton's Statement on the Sixtieth Anniversary of the Ukrainian Famine-Genocide," p. 213; "President Kravchuk's Statement on the Decision of the Russian Supreme Soviet Regarding Sevastopol," pp. 214-215; and "UN Security Council Statement on the Status of Sevastopol," p. 215.]

3457. Solchanyk, Roman. "The Ukrainian-Russian Summit: Problems and Prospects." *RFE/RL Research Report* 2, no. 27 (July 2, 1993): 27-30.

3458. United States. Congress. Senate. Committee on Foreign Relations. Subcommittee on European Affairs. *U.S. Policy on Ukrainian Security: Hearing before the Subcommittee on European Affairs of the Committee on Foreign Relations, United States Senate, One Hundred Third Congress, First Session, June 24, 1993.* United States. Congress. Senate. S. hrg., 103-214. Washington: U.S. G.P.O., 1993. iii, 62 pp.

■ Eastern Europe

General

3459. Academy of Political Science (U.S.), and Columbia University Institute of East Central Europe. *Ethno-Violence & Nationalism in Eastern Europe and U.S. Foreign Policy Responses: Special Proceedings.* New York, NY: Benjamin N. Cardozo School of Law, Yeshiva University and The Academy of Political Science, 1993. xiv, 76 pp. [Jointly published by the *New Europe Law Review* and *Political Science Quarterly.* Papers and other remarks originally presented at a conference organized by Political Science Quarterly and the Academy of Political Science with the cooperation of the Institute on Eastern Central Europe of Columbia University.]

3460. Austin, Robert. "Albanian-Greek Relations: The Confrontation Continues." *RFE/RL Research Report* 2, no. 33 (August 20, 1993): 30-35.

3461. ———. "Albanian-Macedonian Relations: Confrontation or Cooperation?" *RFE/RL Research Report* 2, no. 42 (October 22, 1993): 21-25.

3462. Basora, Adrian A. "Central and Eastern Europe: Imperative for Active U.S. Engagement." *Washington Quarterly* 16, no. 1 (Winter 1993): 67-78.

3463. Brzezinski, Zbigniew. "The Great Transformation." *National Interest*, no. 33 (Fall 1993): 3-13.

3464. Burant, Stephen R., and Voytek Zubek. "Eastern Europe's Old Memories and New Realities: Resurrecting the Polish-Lithuanian Union." *East European Politics and Societies* 7, no. 2 (Spring 1993): 370-393.

3465. Canfield, Jeffrey Lee. "Independent Baltic States: Maritime Law and Resource Management Implications." *Ocean Development and International Law* 24, no. 1 (January-March 1993): 1-39.

3466. Conference on Security and Cooperation in Europe. High Commissioner on National Minorities. "Documentation." *Human Rights Law Journal* 14, nos. 11-12 (December 31, 1993): 432-434. [Conclusions and recommendations by the CSCE High Commissioner, Max van der Stoel, together with official government responses.]

3467. Council of Europe. Parliamentary Assembly. "Documentation." *Human Rights Law Journal* 14, nos. 11-12 (December 31, 1993): 437-454. [Franz Matscher and Basil Hall, "Report on the legislation of the Republic of Slovenia," pp. 437-442; Franz Matscher and Jane Liddy, "Report on the legislation of the Czech Republic," pp. 442-446; Basil Hall and Louis-Edmound Pettiti, "Report on Human Rights in Slovakia," pp. 446-454.]

3468. De Weydenthal, Jan B. "EC Keeps Central Europe at Arm's Length." *RFE/RL Research Report* 2, no. 5 (January 29, 1993): 29-31.

3469. Földesi, Tamás. "The Right to Move and its Achilles' Heel, the Right to Asylum." *Connecticut Journal of International Law* 8, no. 2 (Spring 1993): 289-312. [Paper from the symposium, "Human Rights in Theory and Practice: A Time of Change and Development in Central and Eastern Europe," held in Budapest, March 19-20, 1993.]

3470. Frost, Howard E. "Eastern Europe's Search for Security." *Orbis* 37, no. 1 (Winter 1993): 37-53. [Includes "Appendix: Sample, by Country, of Cooperation Agreements Completed or Under Negotiation, August 1990 to July 1992," pp. 50-53.]

3471. Gerolymatos, André. "Introduction." *Journal of the Hellenic Diaspora* 19, no. 2 (1993): 5-10. [Introduces articles in the journal which were presented at a November 1992 seminar on "Greece, the Balkans and the Eastern Mediterranean," organized by the Hellenic Studies Center at Dawson College.]

3472. Harris, Scott A., and James B. Steinberg. *European Defense and the Future of Transatlantic Cooperation.* Santa Monica, CA: RAND, 1993. xiii, 65 pp. [Partial contents: The Franco-German Corps and the Eastern European Union.]

3473. Jensen, Kurt B. "The Baltic Sea in the Post-Cold War World." *Naval War College Review* 46, no. 4 (Autumn 1993): 29-41.

3474. Lutz, Robert E. "Enforcement of Foreign Judgments, Part II: A Selected Bibliography on Enforcement of U.S. Judgments in Foreign Countries." *International Lawyer* 27, no. 4 (Winter 1993): 1029-1059.

3475. Nikolaou, Ioannis. "Nations' Rebirth and States' Destruction in the Balkans: Anatomy of the Crisis in Southeastern Europe." *Journal of the Hellenic Diaspora* 19, no. 2 (1993): 31-48. [Presented at a seminar on "Greece, the Balkans and the Eastern Mediterranean," at Dawson College in November 1992.]

3476. Quigley, Kevin F. F. "Philanthropy's Role in East Europe." *Orbis* 37, no. 4 (Fall 1993): 581-598.

3477. Reisch, Alfred A. "Central and Eastern Europe's Quest for NATO Membership." *RFE/RL Research Report* 2, no. 28 (July 9, 1993): 33-47.

3478. ———. "The Central European Initiative: To Be or Not to Be?" *RFE/RL Research Report* 2, no. 34 (August 27, 1993): 30-37.

3479. ———. "Hungarian-Slovak Relations: A Difficult First Year." *RFE/RL Research Report* 2, no. 50 (December 17, 1993): 16-23.

3480. Shafir, Michael, and Alfred A. Reisch. "Roundtable: Transylvania's Past and Future." *RFE/RL Research Report* 2, no. 24 (June 11, 1993): 26-34. Gyorgy Tokay, George Schöpflin, Gustav Molnar, Tom Gallagher, Matei Cazacu, and Andrei Marga, participants.

3481. Shumaker, David. "The Origins and Development of Central European Cooperation: 1989-1992." *East European Quarterly* 27, no. 3 (Fall 1993): 351-373.

3482. Simon, Jeffrey. "Central Europe: 'Return to Europe' or Descent to Chaos?" *Strategic Review* 21, no. 1 (Winter 1993): 18-25.

3483. Stavrou, Christodoulos. *Die griechische Minderheit in Albanien.* Europäische Hochschulschriften. Reihe XXII, Soziologie = European University Studies. Series XXII, Sociology, 238. Frankfurt am Main; New York: P. Lang, c1993. vii, 254 p. [Originally presented as the author's thesis (doctoral)—Universität Münster, 1992.]

3484. Turack, Daniel C. "The Movement of Persons: The Practice of States in Central and Eastern Europe Since the 1989 Vienna CSCE." *Denver Journal of International Law and Policy* 21, no. 2 (Winter 1993): 289-309.

3485. United States. Congress. House. Committee on Foreign Affairs. Subcommittee on Europe and the Middle East. *U.S. Assistance to Central and Eastern Europe: Hearing before the Subcommittee on Europe and the Middle East of the Committee on Foreign Affairs, House of Representatives, One Hundred Second Congress, Second Session, June 3, 1992.* Washington: U.S. G.P.O., 1993. iii, 177 pp.

3486. Vachudova, Milada Anna. "The Visegrad Four: No Alternative to Cooperation?" *RFE/RL Research Report* 2, no. 34 (August 27, 1993): 38-47.

3487. Walker, George K. "Integration and Disintegration in Europe: Reordering the Treaty Map of the Continent." *Transnational Lawyer* 6, no. 1 (Spring 1993): 1-79. [Includes section "Disintegration and Union in Central and Eastern Europe: Legal Consequences," pp. 25-57.]

Albania

3488. Zanga, Louis. "Albania and Turkey Forge Closer Ties." *RFE/RL Research Report* 2, no. 11 (March 12, 1993): 30-33.

3489. ———. "Albania Moves Closer to the Islamic World." *RFE/RL Research Report* 2, no. 7 (February 12, 1993): 28-31.

The Baltics

3490. Crowe, David M. *The Baltic States and the Great Powers: Foreign Relations, 1938-1940*. Boulder, CO: Westview Press, c1993. xv, 264 pp.

3491. Estonia, and United States. Dept. of State. *Postal, Express Mail Service: Agreement with Detailed Regulations, between the United States of America and Estonia, Signed at Tallin and Washington, December 31, 1991 and February 10, 1992*. United States Treaties, etc. (Treaties and Other International Acts Series), 11852. Washington, DC: Dept. of State, [1993?]. 13 pp.

3492. Girnius, Saulius. "Lithuania's Foreign Policy." *RFE/RL Research Report* 2, no. 35 (September 3, 1993): 23-33.

3493. Latvia, and United States. Dept. of State. *Postal, Express Mail Service: Agreement with Detailed Regulations, between the United States of America and Latvia, Signed at Washington April 17, 1992*. United States Treaties, etc. (Treaties and Other International Acts Series), 11860. Washington, DC: Dept. of State, [1993?]. 13 pp.

3494. ———. *Postal, Money Orders: Agreement between the United States of America and Latvia, Signed at Washington April 17, 1992*. United States Treaties, etc. (Treaties and Other International Acts Series), 11859. Washington, DC: Dept. of State, [1993?]. 6 pp.

3495. Lithuania, and United States. Dept. of State. *Postal, Express Mail Service: Agreement, with Detailed Regulations, between the United States of America and Lithuania, Signed at Vilnius and Washington, September 21 and October 29, 1992*. United States Treaties, etc. (Treaties and Other International Acts Series), 11905. Washington, DC: Dept. of State, [1993?]. 13 pp.

Bulgaria

3496. Bulgaria, and United States. Dept. of State. *Postal, Express Mail Service: Agreement, with Detailed Regulations, between the United States of America and Bulgaria, Signed at Sofia and Washington, April 5 and May 20, 1991*. United States Treaties, etc. (Treaties and Other International Acts Series), 11811. Washington, DC: Dept. of State, [1993?]. 13 pp.

3497. Bulgaria, and United States. Dept. of State. *Postal, Intelpost Service: Memorandum of Understanding, with Details of Implementation, between the United States of America and the People's Republic of Bulgaria, Signed at Sofia and Washington, April 20 and June 13, 1990*. United States Treaties, etc. (Treaties and Other International Acts Series), 11763. Washington, DC: Dept. of State, [1993?]. 10 pp.

3498. Bulgaria, United States. President (1989-1993: Bush), and United States. Congress. Senate. Committee on Foreign Relations. *Treaty with Bulgaria Concerning the Encouragement and Reciprocal Protection of Investment: Message from the President of the United States Transmitting the Treaty between the United States of America and the Republic of Bulgaria Concerning the Encouragement and Reciprocal Protection of Investment, with Protocol and Related Exchange of Letters, Signed at Washington on September 23, 1992*. Treaty doc., 103-3. Washington, DC: U.S. G.P.O., 1993. vii, 27 pp. [103d Congress, 1st Session. Senate.]

3499. Engelbrekt, Kjell. "A Vulnerable Bulgaria Fears a Wider War." *RFE/RL Research Report* 2, no. 12 (March 19, 1993): 7-12.

3500. Haramiev-Drezov, Kyril. "Bulgarian-Russian Relations on a New Footing." *RFE/RL Research Report* 2, no. 15 (April 9, 1993): 33-38.

3501. United States. President (1993- : Clinton), and United States. Congress. House. Committee on Ways and Means. *Emigration Laws and Policies of the Republic of Bulgaria: Communication from the President of the United States Transmitting His Determination That Bulgaria Meets the Emigration Criteria of the Jackson-Vanik Amendment to the Trade Act of 1974, Pursuant to 19 U.S.C. 2432(B) and 2439(B)*. House Document (United States. Congress. House), 103-96. Washington: U.S. G.P.O., 1993. 4 pp.

(Former) Czechoslovakia

3502. Gibbons, Earl Francis, Jr. "Return to Europe: Czechoslovak Foreign Policy Since the Velvet Revolution." Ph.D. diss., University of Pittsburgh, 1993. [UMI order no: AAC 9406372.]

3503. Meisler, Stanley. " '...All they are saying is Give Prague a chance.' " *Smithsonian* 24, no. 3 (June 1993): 66-75. ["American twentysomethings are flocking to the city of Vaclav Havel, Franz Kafka, old Beatles tunes and booming new business."]

3504. Osterland, Holly A. "National Self-Determination and Secession: The Slovak Model." *Case Western Reserve Journal of International Law* 25, no. 3 (Summer 1993): 655-702.

3505. Pehe, Jiri. "Czech-Slovak Relations Deteriorate." *RFE/RL Research Report* 2, no. 18 (April 30, 1993): 1-5.

3506. Rosenberger, Chandler. "Independent Slovakia: A New Country's Old Habits." *World Policy Journal* 10, no. 3 (Fall 1993): 73-80.

Germany

3507. Armstrong, Tony. *Breaking the Ice: Rapproachment between East and West Germany, the United States and China, and Israel and Egypt.* Washington, DC: United States Institute of Peace Press, 1993. ix, 187 pp.

3508. East Germany, and United States. Dept. of State. *Cultural Relations: Exchanges for 1988-1989: Agreement between the United States of America and the German Democratic Republic, Signed at Berlin June 22, 1988.* United States Treaties, etc. (Treaties and Other International Acts Series), 11581. Washington, DC: Dept. of State, [1993?]. 12 pp.

3509. Ehlers, Dirk. "The German Unification: Background and Prospects." *Loyola of Los Angeles International and Comparative Law Journal* 15, no. 4 (June 1993): 771-811.

3510. Fisher, Marc. [Book Review]. *Book World (Washington Post)* 23, no. 50 (December 12, 1993): 5. [Review article on Timothy Garton Ash, *In Europe's Name: Germany and the Divided Continent* (NY: Random House, 1993).]

3511. Garton Ash, Timothy. *In Europe's Name: Germany and the Divided Continent.* 1st U.S. ed. New York: Random House, c1993. 680 pp. [Contents: Prologue: European Question; German Answers; Ostpolitik; Bonn-Moscow-Berlin; Germany and Germany; Beyond the Oder; A Second Ostpolitik; German Unification; Findings.] REV: Rolf Berghahn-Volker, *New York Times Book Review* 98, no. 51 (December 26, 1993): 1ff. Marc Fisher, *Book World* 23, no. 50 (December 12, 1993): 5. Richard C. Hottelet, *New Leader* 76 (December 27, 1993): 6-8. Tony Judt, *New York Review of Books* 40, no. 21 (December 16, 1993): 52ff. Radek Sikorski, *National Review* 45, no. 15 (December 13, 1993): 60-61.

3512. Gedmin, Jeffrey. [Book Review]. *American Spectator* 26, no. 1 (January 1993): 87-89. [Review article on Willy Brandt, *My Life in Politics* (NY: Viking, 1992).]

3513. Greenwald, G. Jonathan. *Berlin Witness: An American Diplomat's Chronicle of East Germany's Revolution.* University Park, PA: Pennsylvania State University Press, c1993. xviii, 347 pp. REV: Kenneth J. Dillon, *Foreign Service Journal* 70, no. 10 (October 1993): 51-53. Fritz Stern, *Foreign Affairs* 72, no. 5 (November-December 1993): 167.

3514. Iserman, Peter A. [Book Review]. *Book World (Washington Post)* 23, no. 31 (August 1, 1993): 7ff. [Review article on Craig R. Whitney, *Spy Trader: Germany's Devil's*

Advocate and the Darkest Secrets of the Cold War (NY: Times Books, 1993).]

3515. Johnson, Hazel J. "The Troubled Reunification of Korea." *PS: Political Science & Politics* 26, no. 1 (March 1993): 59-63. [Compares the possible reunification of North and South Korea to the reunification of East and West Germany.]

3516. Judt, Tony. "How the East Was Won." *New York Review of Books* 40, no. 21 (December 16, 1993): 52ff. [Review article on Timothy Garton Ash, *In Europe's Name: Germany and the Divided Continent* (NY: Random House, 1993).]

3517. Koch, Burkhard. "American and German Approaches to East Central Europe: A Comparison." *World Affairs* 156, no. 2 (Fall 1993): 86-96.

3518. Kretschmer, Stephan D. "Germany's Reunification and Its Implications for US Strategy." *Parameters* 23, no. 3 (Autumn 1993): 24-38.

3519. Lasky, Melvin J. "The Pacifist and the General." *National Interest*, no. 34 (Winter 1993-1994): 66-78. [Surveillance of Petra Kelly by the East German political police ("Stasi").]

3520. McAdams, A. James. *Germany Divided: From the Wall to Reunification.* Princeton Studies in International History and Politics. Princeton, NJ: Princeton University Press, c1993. xvii, 250 pp. REV: Peter H. Merkl, *Political Science Quarterly* 108, no. 4 (Winter 1993-1994): 764-765. *Orbis* 37, no. 4 (Fall 1993).

3521. McKinnon, Mike. "Impressions of Germany: A Personal Vignette." *Social Education* 57, no. 5 (September 1993): 248-249. [Part of special section entitled "The Case of Germany, Part 2," edited by Dagmar Kraemer and Manfred Stassen.]

3522. Philipsen, Dirk. *We Were the People: Voices from East Germany's Revolutionary Autumn of 1989.* Durham, NC: Duke University Press, 1993. x, 417 pp. [Contents: Pt. I. A Long Time Coming: Roots of Dissent and Opposition in the German Democratic Republic. 1. The Troubled Emergence of an Idea. Frank Eigenfeld, No Forum, and Harald Wagner, Democracy Now. Rainer Eppelmann, Protestant pastor, prominent oppositionist. Cornelia Matzke, Independent Women's Alliance. Ludwig Mehlhorn, Opposition theorist. Hans Modrow, Last communist prime minister. 2. The Party, the Workers, and Opposition Intellectuals. Werner Bramke, Party academic. East German Workers, Joint interview. Barbel Bohley, "Mother of the revolution". 3. The Many Meanings of "Reform". Klaus Kaden, Church emissary to the opposition. Sebastian Pflugbeil, Democratic strategist. Gerhard Ruden, Environmental activist. Andre Brie, Party vice-chairman. Ingrid Koppe, Opposition representative at the Central Round Table — Pt. II. Democracy—Now or Never. 4. Struggles with Self-Censorship: Deciding How Much to Seek. Ludwig Mehlhorn. Klaus Kaden. Frank Eigenfeld. Harald Wagner. Rainer Eppelmann. Cornelia Matzke. 5. The Constraints of a Party-Centered Perspective. Hans Modrow. Werner

Bramke. Andre Brie. 6. Workers in the "Workers' State"
East German Workers, Joint interview. Wolfgang K., Newly
elected union secretary. 7. Democratic Visions: A Question
of Scope, A Question of Possibility. Barbel Bohley. Sebastian
Pflugbeil. Ingrid Koppe — Pt. III. Taking Stock: The Search
for a Historical Perspective. 8. Between Opportunity and
Failure. Sebastian Pflugbeil. Klaus Kaden. Frank Eigenfeld,
Harald Wagner. Barbel Bohley. Hans Modrow. Werner
Bramke. Andre Brie. Ludwig Mehlhorn. Wolfgang K. —
Chronology of East German History, 1945-1990.] REV:
William I. Shorrock, *History: Reviews of New Books* 21, no. 4
(Summer 1993): 173. *Orbis* 37, no. 2 (Spring 1993).

3523. Plock, Ernest D. *East German-West German
Relations and the Fall of the GDR.* Boulder: Westview Press,
1993. viii, 220 pp.

3524. Pond, Elizabeth. *Beyond the Wall: Germany's
Road to Unification.* Washington, DC: Brookings Institution, 1993. xv, 367 pp. REV: Fritz Stern, *Foreign Affairs* 72,
no. 5 (November-December 1993): 167.

3525. ———. "Germany and Its European Environment." *Washington Quarterly* 16, no. 4 (Autumn 1993): 131-
140. ["Europe in the 1990s."]

3526. Rhee, Kang Suk. "Korea's Unification: The
Applicability of the German Experience." *Asian Survey* 33,
no. 4 (April 1993): 360-375.

3527. Thomsen, Horst, and Frauke Siefkes, comps.
*Bibliographie zur deutschen Einigung: Wirtschaftliche und
soziale Entwicklung in den neuen Bundesländern, November
1989 bis Juni 1992 = Bibliography on German Unification:
Economic and Social Developments in Eastern Germany,
November 1989 to June 1992.* München; New York: K.G.
Saur, 1993. xvii, 345 pp. [Bibliothek des Instituts für
Weltwirtschaft an der Universität Kiel, Zentralbibliothek
der Wirtschaftswissenschaften in der Bundesrepublik
Deutschland.]

3528. Whitney, Craig R. *Spy Trader: Germany's
Devil's Advocate and the Darkest Secrets of the Cold War.*
1st ed. New York: Times Books, c1993. xl, 375 pp. REV:
Fritz Stern, *Foreign Affairs* 72, no. 5 (November-December
1993): 167. David Wise, *New York Times Book Review* 98,
no. 24 (June 13, 1993): 9.

Greece and Cyprus (Since 1821)

3529. Iatrides, John O. "Greece in the Cold War,
and Beyond." *Journal of the Hellenic Diaspora* 19, no. 2
(1993): 11-30. [Presented at a seminar on "Greece, the
Balkans and the Eastern Mediterranean," at Dawson
College in November 1992.]

3530. Mitsotakis, Constantine. "The United States,
Greece, and Turkey: Problems and Opportunities in the
New International System." *Mediterranean Quarterly* 4, no.
4 (Fall 1993): 1-9.

3531. Redmond, John. *The Next Mediterranean
Enlargement of the European Community: Turkey, Cyprus,
and Malta?* Aldershot, Hants; Brookfield, VT: Dartmouth,

c1993. viii, 157 p.

3532. Rizopoulos, Nicholas X. "Pride, Prejudice,
and Myopia: Greek Foreign Policy in a Time Warp." *World
Policy Journal* 10, no. 3 (Fall 1993): 17-28.

3533. Stearns, Monteagle. "The Greek-American-
Turkish Triangle: What Shape after the Cold War?" *Mediterranean Quarterly* 4, no. 4 (Fall 1993): 16-29.

3534. Tsouderos, Virginia. "Greek Policy and the
Yugoslav Turmoil." *Mediterranean Quarterly* 4, no. 2
(Spring 1993): 1-13.

Hungary

3535. Hungary, and United States. Dept. of State.
*Scientific and Technical Cooperation: Earth Sciences:
Agreement between the United States of America and the
Hungarian People's Republic, Extending the Memorandum
of Understanding of January 6 and 20, 1984, As Extended,
Signed at Reston and Budapest, January 26 and February
9, 1988.* United States Treaties, etc. (Treaties and Other
International Acts Series), 11575. Washington, DC: Dept. of
State, [1993?]. 2 pp.

3536. ———. *Scientific and Technical Cooperation
in the Earth Sciences: Memorandum of Understanding
between the United States of America and the Hungarian
People's Republic, Signed at Reston and Budapest, January
6 and 20, 1984 and Extending Agreement, Signed at Reston
and Budapest, March 17 and April 21, 1986.* United States
Treaties, etc. (Treaties and Other International Acts Series),
11388. Washington, DC: Dept. of State, [1993?]. 7 pp.

3537. ———. *Scientific and Technological Coopera-
tion: Agreement between the United States of America and
the Hungarian People's Republic, Signed at Washington
March 23, 1987.* United States Treaties, etc. (Treaties and
Other International Acts Series), 11520. Washington, DC:
Dept. of State, [1993?]. 11 pp.

3538. Ionescu, Dan, and Alfred A. Reisch. "Still No
Breakthrough in Romanian-Hungarian Relations." *RFE/RL
Research Report* 2, no. 42 (October 22, 1993): 26-32.

3539. Kun, Joseph C. *Hungarian Foreign Policy:
The Experience of a New Democracy.* Foreword by Tom
Lantos. The Washington Papers, 160. Westport, CT:
Praeger, 1993. xxi, 168 pp. [Published with the Center for
Strategic and International Studies, Washington, DC.
Contents: 1. Foreign Policy before 1945. The Legacy of
Trianon. Life in Germany's Shadow. Hungary Enters the
War; 2. Years of Darkness. Winds of Change. The New
Diplomats. The Warsaw Pact Is Born. 1956—A Nation
Rebels. The Nagy Program: Independence and Neutrality.
The UN Debate. Betrayal. Foreign Policy Initiatives.
Unhappy Neighbors; 3. Light at the End of the Tunnel: The
1980s. The Balancing Act. Guidelines for the 1980s. Win-
dows to the West. Disagreements among Neighbors. Where
Diplomacy Failed. Conflicts with Prague. The Dam Contro-
versy; 4. Transition Regime. Foreign Policies of the Nemeth
Government. The Borders Open. Bold Initiatives, Far-

Reaching Consequences. Israel, South Korea, and the Vatican. Unchanging Bucharest. The Prague Connection. United We Stand: The Regional Approach; 5. The Antall Government. Words Followed by Action. The Changing of the (Diplomatic) Guard. Antall in Charge: Problems and Successes in 1990. Progress in Europe. The Growth of Regionalism. The Soviet Connection. Exit from the Pact: The Problem of Breaking Ranks. What Follows the Pact? The Security Debate Begins; 6. Sovereignty Restored. New Relations with Moscow. The Basic Treaty: The Talks Get Bogged Down. Communist Secret: Nuclear Warheads in Hungary. The Pact Ends. Security Concerns: How Far Away Is NATO? Visegrad: Triangular Progress. From Pentagonale to Hexagonale. The European Community: Great Expectations; 7. The Coup of August 1991 and Its Aftermath. The Basic Treaty Concluded. Approaches toward the Republics. Where Problems Prevail. The Triangle Gains Strength. The Spread of Regionalism. NATO Says No. Relations with the European Community: The First Opening. The Foreign Ministry: The November Housecleaning; 8. A Mid-Term Report. A Concept of Security. Problem Areas. The Antall Factor; Epilogue: Expectations vs. Realities; Appendix: Chronology 1867-1992.] REV: *Orbis* 37, no. 4 (Fall 1993).

3540. Pataki, Judith. "Hungary Copes with Refugee Influx." *RFE/RL Research Report* 2, no. 18 (April 30, 1993): 35-38.

3541. Reisch, Alfred A. "Hungarian-Ukrainian Relations Continue to Develop." *RFE/RL Research Report* 2, no. 16 (April 16, 1993): 22-28.

3542. ———. "Hungary Pursues Integration with the West." *RFE/RL Research Report* 2, no. 13 (March 26, 1993): 32-38.

3543. ———. "Hungary's Foreign Policy toward the East." *RFE/RL Research Report* 2, no. 15 (April 9, 1993): 39-48.

Poland

3544. Banasinski, Cezary. "Regional Developments: Poland." *International Lawyer* 27, no. 1 (Spring 1993): 228-232.

3545. De Weydenthal, Jan B. "Economic Issues Dominate Poland's Eastern Policy." *RFE/RL Research Report* 2, no. 10 (March 5, 1993): 23-26.

3546. ———. "Poland on Its Own: The Conduct of Foreign Policy." *RFE/RL Research Report* 2, no. 2 (January 8, 1993): 1-4.

3547. Elliot, T. Lynn. "Poland, Germany, and the End of the Cold War." *East European Quarterly* 27, no. 4 (Winter 1993): 535-551.

3548. Wolf-Rodda, Howard A. "The Support for Eastern European Democracy Act of 1989: A Description and Assessment of Its Responsiveness to the Needs of Poland." *Maryland Journal of International Law and Trade* 17, no. 1 (Spring 1993): 107-134.

Romania

3549. Falls, Donald R. "Soviet Decision-Making and the Withdrawal of Soviet Troops from Romania." *East European Quarterly* 27, no. 4 (Winter 1993): 489-502.

3550. Ionescu, Dan. "Romania Signs Association Accord with the EC." *RFE/RL Research Report* 2, no. 10 (March 5, 1993): 33-37.

3551. ———. "Romania's Quandary." *RFE/RL Research Report* 2, no. 12 (March 19, 1993): 13-17.

3552. Romania, and United States. Dept. of State. *Postal, Express Mail Service: Agreement, with Detailed Regulations, between the United States of America and the Socialist Republic of Romania, Signed at Washington December 14, 1989.* United States Treaties, etc. (Treaties and Other International Acts Series), 11718. Washington, DC: Dept. of State, [1993?]. 13 pp.

3553. Zidaru-Barbulescu, Aurel. "Romania Seeks Admission to the Council of Europe." *RFE/RL Research Report* 2, no. 2 (January 8, 1993): 11-16.

(Former) Yugoslavia

3554. "AJ Congress Resolution on Bosnia." *Congress Monthly* 60, no. 1 (January 1993): 10. [Resolution adopted by the Governing Council of the American Jewish Congress on October 18, 1992.]

3555. Akhavan, Payam. "Punishing War Crimes in the Former Yugoslavia: A Critical Juncture for the New World Order." *Human Rights Quarterly* 15, no. 2 (May 1993): 262-289.

3556. Ali, Rabia, and Lawrence Lifschultz, eds. *Why Bosnia? Writings on the Balkan War.* Stony Creek, CT: Pamphleteer's Press, c1993. lix, 353 pp.

3557. American Bar Association. Section of International Law and Practice. Task Force on War Crimes in Former Yugoslavia. *Report on the International Tribunal to Adjudicate War Crimes Committed in the Former Yugoslavia.* Chair Monroe Leigh. Washington, DC: Section of International Law and Practice, American Bar Association, c1993. x, 71 pp.

3558. Amnesty International. *Bosnia-Herzegovina: Rape and Sexual Abuse by Armed Forces.* New York, NY: Amnesty International U.S.A., [1993]. 14 pp.

3559. ———. *Federal Republic of Yugoslavia: International Monitoring in Kosovo and Beyond: Appeal to Governments from Secretary General of Amnesty International.* New York, NY: Amnesty International, [1993]. 7 pp.

3560. Anderson, Kenneth. "Illiberal Tolerance: An Essay on the Fall of Yugoslavia and the Rise of Multiculturalism in the United States." *Virginia Journal of International Law* 33, no. 2 (Winter 1993): 385-431.

3561. Andrejevich, Milan. "Serbia's Bosnian Dilemma." *RFE/RL Research Report* 2, no. 23 (June 4, 1993): 14-21.

3562. Atkeson, Edward B. "Who Will Sweep Up the Augean Stables?" *Army* 43, no. 5 (May 1993): 16-26. [Followed by letters to editor: Jeff Stein, "The Balkans: A Formidable Task," vol. 43, no. 6 (June 1993): 3; and Stuart Wilkes, "No Slavic Hercules," vol. 43, no. 8 (August 1993): 3.]

3563. Aydelott, Danise. "Mass Rape During War: Prosecuting Bosnian Rapists Under International Law." *Emory International Law Review* 7, no. 2 (Fall 1993): 585-631.

3564. Banac, Ivo. "Book Review: Misreading the Balkans." *Foreign Policy*, no. 93 (Winter 1993-1994): 173-182. [Review article on Slavenka Drakulic, *The Balkan Express: Fragments from the Other Side of War* (NY: 1993); Misha Glenny, *The Fall of Yugoslavia: The Third Balkan War* (NY: 1993); Roy Gutman, *A Witness to Genocide: The 1993 Pulitzer Prize-Winning Dispatches on the "Ethnic Cleansing" of Bosnia* (NY: 1993); Branka Magas, *The Destruction of Yugoslavia: Tracking the Break-up 1980-92* (NY: 1993); Mirko Grmek, Marc Gjidara, and Neven Simac, *Le nettoyage ethnique: Documents historiques sur une idéologie serbe* (Paris: 1993); and *The Other Balkan Wars: A 1913 Carnegie Endowment Inquiry in Retrospect*, with a new introduction by George Kennan (Washington, DC: 1993).]

3565. ———. "Croatianism." *New Republic* 209, no. 17 (October 25, 1993): 20-22. ["How Franjo Tudjman led his country into the abyss."]

3566. Barkey, Brett D. "Bosnia: A Question of Intervention." *Strategic Review* 21, no. 4 (Fall 1993): 48-59.

3567. Barnes, Fred. "White House Watch: Safe Haven." *New Republic* 208, no. 24 (June 14, 1993): 12-14.

3568. Barnes, James A. "Polling Deficit." *National Journal* 25, no. 20 (May 15, 1993): 1178ff.

3569. Bass, Gary J. "Courting Disaster." *New Republic* 209, no. 10 (September 6, 1993): 12-14.

3570. Begoun, David. "Tinderbox of the Balkans." *World & I* 8, no. 9 (September 1993): 90-95.

3571. Beljo, Ante, editor-in-chief. *Croatia and Bosnia-Herzegovina: Sacral Institutions on Target: Deliberate Military Destruction of Sacral Institutions in Croatia and Bosnia-Herzegovina.* Edited by Vladimir Pavlinic. Authors Mijo Gabric et al. Zagreb; New York: Croatian Information Center, 1993. 121 pp.

3572. Biden, Joseph R., Jr., and United States. Congress. Senate. Committee on Foreign Relations. *To Stand Against Aggression: Milosevic, the Bosnian Republic, and the Conscience of the West: A Report to the Committee on Foreign Relations, United States Senate.* S. Prt., 103-33. Washington, DC: U.S. G.P.O., 1993. vi, 98 pp.

3573. Block, Robert. "Killers." *New York Review of Books* 40 (November 18, 1993): 9-10.

3574. Blumenthal, Sidney. "Lonesome Hawk." *New Yorker* 69, no. 15 (May 31, 1993): 35-40. [Discusses Clinton administration policy on the war in the former Yugoslavia.]

3575. Bogdanovic, Bogdan. "The Murder of the City." *New York Review of Books* 40, no. 10 (May 27, 1993): 20.

3576. "Bosnia and the Future of Ethnic Cleansing." *World Affairs* 156, no. 2 (Fall 1993): 104-106. [Documentation Section: "An Open Letter to President Clinton and Other Western Heads of State". Signatories include: Margaret Thatcher, George Schultz, Sadruddin Aga Khan, Frank Carlucci, François Heisbourg, Jeanne J. Kirkpatrick, Zbigniew Brzezinski, William Clark, Paul H. Nitze, Eugene V. Rostow, Max M. Kampelman, Hanan Mikhail-Ashrawi, Natan Scharansky, Teddy Kollek, Murat Karayalcin, George Soros, Elie Wiesel, Czeslaw Milosz, Joseph Brodsky, Karl Popper, Albert Wohlstetter, and 90 others.]

3577. "Bosnian Bordello Camps." *Peace Magazine* 9, no. 1 (January-February 1993): 31.

3578. "Bosnian Quandary." *Nation* 256, no. 16 (April 26, 1993): 543-544.

3579. Breslow, Aimee. "Missed Opportunities." *Uncaptive Minds* 6, no. 3 (24) (Fall 1993): 65-70. [Interview with Jazez Jansa, defense minister for the Republic of Slovenia, on the Balkan war.]

3580. Brock, Peter. "Dateline Yugoslavia." *Foreign Policy*, no. 93 (Winter 1993-1994): 152-172.

3581. Bruun, Lori Lyman. "Beyond the 1948 Convention: Emerging Principles of Genocide in Customary International Law." *Maryland Journal of International Law and Trade* 17, no. 2 (Fall 1993): 193-226.

3582. Bugajski, Janusz. "The Lessons of Bosnia: Death, Destruction, and Desperation." *Ripon Forum* 29, no. 2 (April-May 1993): 21-25.

3583. Byrnes, Mark Stephen. "Shedding the 'Garb of Idealism': Truman Administration Policy Toward Spain and Yugoslavia." Ph.D. diss., University of Texas at Austin, 1993. [UMI order no: AAC 9400858.]

3584. Cerovic, Stanko. "Bosnia, Year Zero." *Freedom Review* 24, no. 3 (May-June 1993): 39-41.

3585. ———. "In Capitulation, Wisdom? Western Diplomacy." *Freedom Review* 24, no. 4 (July-August 1993): 19-21.

3586. Christopher, William. "Excerpts from Christopher's Press Conference After NATO Foreign Ministers Meeting, June 10, 1993." *Foreign Policy Bulletin* 4, no. 2 (September-October 1993): 23-24.

3587. ———. "Secretary Christopher Proposes Five-Point Agenda to Adapt NATO to Post-Cold War Circumstances." *Foreign Policy Bulletin* 4, no. 2 (September-October 1993): 20-23. [Speech given on June 8, 1993 at NATO Foreign Ministers Meeting in Athens.]

3588. Clemens, Walter C., Jr. "Can outsiders help? Lessons for third-party intervention in Bosnia." *International Journal* 48, no. 4 (Autumn 1993): 687-719.

3589. "Clinton and Milosevic." *New Republic* 208, no. 5 (February 1, 1993): 9.

3590. "Congress Takes Action Against Massive Rape of Women." *New Directions for Women* 22, no. 2 (March-April 1993): W1.

3591. Costa, Nicholas J. "A Balkan Danse Macabre." *East European Quarterly* 27, no. 4 (Winter 1993): 479-487.

3592. Covault, Craig. "NATO Air Power Focused on Bosnia." *Aviation Week & Space Technology* 139, no. 10 (September 6, 1993): 46-47.

3593. "A Crime Against the World." *New Directions for Women* 22, no. 2 (March-April 1993): W1.

3594. Crow, Suzanne. "Russia Adopts a More Active Policy." *RFE/RL Research Report* 2, no. 12 (March 19, 1993): 1-6.

3595. Cviic, Christopher. "A Culture of Humiliation." *National Interest*, no. 32 (Summer 1993): 79-82.

3596. ———. "Who's to Blame for the War in ex-Yugoslavia?" *World Affairs* 156, no. 2 (Fall 1993): 72-79.

3597. Degan, Vladimir-Djuro, Ove E. Bring, M. Kelly Malone, and Yehuda Z. Blum. "Correspondents' Agora: UN Membership of the Former Yugoslavia." *American Journal of International Law* 87, no. 2 (April 1993): 240-251. [Letters by Degan (pp. 240-244), Bring (pp. 244-246), and Malone (pp. 246-248) concerning Blum's article "Current Developments Note" (October 1992), with a reply by Blum (pp. 248-251).]

3598. Denitch, Bogdan. "Balkan Tragedy." *Dissent* 40, no. 4 (Fall 1993): 569-571. [Review article on Robert D. Kaplan, *Balkan Ghosts: A Journey through History* (NY: St. Martin's Press, 1993); Branka Magas, *The Destruction of Yugoslavia: Tracking the Break-Up, 1980-92* (London; NY: Verso, 1993); Misha Glenny, *The Fall of Yugoslavia: The Third Balkan War* (NY: Penguin Books, 1992); Mark Thompson, *A Paper House: The Ending of Yugoslavia* (NY: Pantheon Books, 1992); James Seroka and Vukasin Pavlovic, eds., *The Tragedy of Yugoslavia* (NY: M.E. Sharpe, 1992); *War Crimes in Bosnia-Hercegovina*, vols. 1 and 2 (NY: Helsinki Watch, 1992-1993).]

3599. ———. "Stop the Genocide in Bosnia." *Dissent* 40, no. 3 (Summer 1993): 283-287.

3600. ———. "Tragedy in Former Yugoslavia." *Dissent* 40, no. 1 (Winter 1993): 26-34.

3601. Detling, Karen J. "Eternal Silence: The Destruction of Cultural Property in Yugoslavia." *Maryland Journal of International Law and Trade* 17, no. 1 (Spring 1993): 41-75.

3602. Dialogues on Conflict Resolution: Bridging Theory and Practices (1992: Washington, DC). *Conflict and Conflict Resolution in Yugoslavia: A Conference Report "Discussions from Dialogues on Conflict Resolution: Bridging Theory and Practices: July 13-15, 1992*. Washington,
DC: U.S. Institute of Peace, 1993. vi, 40 pp.

3603. Dizdarevic, Zlatko. *Sarajevo: A War Journal.* Preface by Joseph Brodsky. Introduction by Robert Jay Lifton. 1st U.S. ed. New York: Fromm International, 1993. xxvi, 193 pp. [Translation of *Journal de guerre*; translated from the French by Anselm Hollo; edited from the original Serbo-Croatian by Ammiel Alcalay.] REV: Stephen Dobyns, *New York Times Book Review* 98, no. 51 (December 19, 1993): 1ff. H. Wayne Elliott, *Military Law Review* 142 (Fall 1993): 188-191. David Rieff, *Book World* 23, no. 47 (November 21, 1993): 1ff.

3604. Doder, Dusko. "Bosnian Dilemma." *Nation* 256, no. 9 (March 8, 1993): 293.

3605. ———. "Eurotroubles: Yugoslavia: New War, Old Hatreds." *Foreign Policy*, no. 91 (Summer 1993): 3-23.

3606. ———. "U.N. Sanctions on Serbia Devastate Its Colleges." *Chronicle of Higher Education* 39, no. 40 (June 9, 1993): A33.

3607. Dominis, Iva, and Ivo Bicanic. "Refugees and Displaced Persons in the Former Yugoslavia." *RFE/RL Research Report* 2, no. 3 (January 15, 1993): 1-4.

3608. Dragnich, Alex N. "The West's Mismanagement of the Yugoslav Crisis." *World Affairs* 156, no. 2 (Fall 1993): 63-71.

3609. Drakulic, Slavenka. *The Balkan Express: Fragments from the Other Side of War.* 1st American ed. New York: W.W. Norton & Co., 1993. 146 pp. REV: Ivo Banac, *Foreign Policy*, no. 93 (December 1993-1994): 173-182. Anthony Borden, *Nation* 256, no. 19 (May 17, 1993): 672-674. Michael Ignatieff, *New York Review of Books* 40, no. 9 (May 13, 1993): 3-5. Jerry Kisslinger, *New Leader* (June 14, 1993): 17-19. Robert Legvold, *Foreign Affairs* 72, no. 4 (September-October 1993): 170-171. Francine Prose, *New York Times Book Review* 98, no. 21 (May 23, 1993): 9-10.

3610. ———. "Death, Live." *New Republic* 208, no. 25 (June 21, 1993): 12-14. ["The Balkans on cable."]

3611. ———. "Love Story." *New Republic* 209, no. 17 (October 25, 1993): 14-16. ["A true tale from Sarajevo's horror."]

3612. ———. "Mass Rape in Bosnia: Women Hide Behind a Wall of Silence." *Nation* 256, no. 8 (March 1, 1993): 253ff.

3613. ———. "Zagreb: A Letter to My Daughter." *Harper's* 286, no. 1716 (May 1993): 13-16. [Excerpt from author's *Balkan Express: Fragments from the Other Side of War* (NY: 1994).]

3614. Drakulic, Slobodan. "Peacekeepers as Warmongers and Peacemakers as Warkeepers." *Peace Magazine* 9, no. 6 (November-December 1993): 16-19.

3615. Durham, Roger Joel. "Post-Cold War Relations Between the North and South: Studying the Effects of International Regimes on Less-Developed Countries." Ph.D.

diss., University of Oregon, 1993. [UMI order no: AAC 9415124.]

3616. Dyker, David, and Vesna Bojicic. "The Impact of Sanctions on the Serbian Economy." *RFE/RL Research Report* 2, no. 21 (May 21, 1993): 50-54.

3617. "Election of Judges of the International Tribunal for Violations of Humanitarian Law in the Former Yugoslavia." *American Journal of International Law* 87, no. 4 (October 1993): 668.

3618. Elliott, H. Wayne. "Sarajevo: A War Journal [Book Review]." *Military Law Review*, no. 142 (Fall 1993): 188-191. [Review article on Zlatko Dizdarevic, *Sarajevo: A War Journal* (New York: Fromm International, 1993).]

3619. "Embargo Against Federal Republic of Yugoslavia Tightened: War Crimes Investigative Body Created." *UN Chronicle* 30, no. 1 (March 1993): 4-12.

3620. Falk, Richard. "Intervention Revisited: Hard Choices and Tragic Dilemmas." *Nation* 257, no. 21 (December 20, 1993): 755-764. [On U.S. foreign policy toward Bosnia-Herzegovina.]

3621. Fenske, John. "The West and the 'Problem from Hell.'" *Current History* 92, no. 577 (November 1993): 353-356.

3622. "The Future of the Balkans: Interview with David Owen." *Foreign Affairs* 72, no. 2 (Spring 1993): 1-9. [Interview conducted on February 16, 1993.]

3623. Fyson, George, ed. *The Truth About Yugoslavia: Why Working People Should Oppose Intervention.* 1st ed. New York: Pathfinder, 1993. 89 pp. [Chiefly written by George Fyson, Jonathan Silberman and Argiris Malapanis.]

3624. Garton Ash, Timothy, Ivo Banac et al. "An Appeal for Yugoslavia." *New York Review of Books* 40, no. 4 (February 11, 1993): 8.

3625. Gedmin, Jeffrey. "Comrade Slobo." *American Spectator* 26, no. 4 (April 1993): 28-33.

3626. Gerlach, Jeffrey R. *Providing a Haven for Refugees: An Alternative to U.S. Military Intervention in the Balkans.* Foreign Policy Briefing, no. 23 (Apr. 12, 1993). Washington, DC: Cato Institute, 1993. 12 pp.

3627. Gerson, Allan. "Trying War Crimes." *Foreign Service Journal* 70, no. 5 (May 1993): 34-38.

3628. Gjelten, Tom. "Blaming the Victim." *New Republic* 209, no. 25 (December 20, 1993): 14-16.

3629. Glenny, Misha. "Bosnia R.I.P." *Nation* 257, no. 2 (July 12, 1993): 52-53.

3630. ———. "Bosnia: The Last Chance?" *New York Review of Books* 40, no. 3 (January 28, 1993): 5-8.

3631. ———. "Bosnia: The Tragic Prospect." *New York Review of Books* 40, no. 18 (November 4, 1993): 38ff.

3632. ———. "What Is To Be Done?" *New York Review of Books* 40, no. 10 (May 27, 1993): 14-16.

3633. Glynn, Patrick. "Not Bush." *New Republic* 208, no. 11 (March 15, 1993): 10. ["A defense of Clinton's emerging Balkan policy."]

3634. ———. "See No Evil." *New Republic* 209, no. 17 (October 25, 1993): 23ff.

3635. "Good Cop, Good Cop." *New Republic* 208, no. 23 (June 7, 1993): 7. ["The U.N.'s Balkan fallacy."]

3636. Goodby, James E. "Collective Security in Europe After the Cold War." *Journal of International Affairs* 46, no. 2 (Winter 1993): 299-321.

3637. Gottfried, Joseph. "Fair and unfair on Yugoslavia." *Freedom Review* 24, no. 5 (September-October 1993): 3. [Letter to the editor in response to the articles "In Capitulation, Wisdom?" and "His Brothers' Keeper" in vol. 24, no. 4 (July-August 1993): 19-23.]

3638. Gow, James. "One Year of War in Bosnia and Herzegovina." *RFE/RL Research Report* 2, no. 23 (June 4, 1993): 1-13.

3639. Goytisolo, Juan. "Sarajevo 1993." *Salmagundi*, no. 100 (Fall 1993): 166-178.

3640. Guicherd, Catherine. "The Hour of Europe: Lessons from the Yugoslav Conflict." *Fletcher Forum of World Affairs* 17, no. 2 (Summer 1993): 159-181.

3641. Gutman, Roy. *A Witness to Genocide: The 1993 Pulitzer Prize-Winning Dispatches on the "Ethnic Cleansing" of Bosnia.* New York: Macmillan Pub. Co.; Toronto: Maxwell Macmillan Canada; New York: Maxwell Macmillan International, c1993. xlii, 180 pp. REV: Ivo Banac, *Foreign Policy*, no. 93 (December 1993-1994): 173-182.

3642. Hagman, Hans-Christian. "The Balkan Conflicts: Prevention Is Better Than Cure." *Global Affairs* 8, no. 2 (Summer 1993): 18-37.

3643. Harrison, Thomas. "In Solidarity with Bosnia." *New Politics* 4, no. 3 (Summer 1993): 149-160.

3644. Hayden, Robert M. "The Partition of Bosnia and Herzegovina, 1990-1993." *RFE/RL Research Report* 2, no. 22 (May 28, 1993): 1-17. With commentaries by A. Ross Johnson and Patrick Moore. [Article is followed by commentaries: A. Ross Johnson, "Was Partition the Lesser Evil?" and Patrick Moore, "The Serbian and Croatian Factors."]

3645. Hehir, J. Brayan. "The 'state' of 'defense.'" *Commonweal* 120, no. 6 (March 26, 1993): 9-10. [On U.S. policies toward Bosnia.]

3646. Hobbs, Heidi H. "Whither Yugoslavia? The Death of a Nation." *Studies in Conflict and Terrorism* 16, no. 3 (July-September 1993): 187-199.

3647. Horwitz, Tony. "Balkan Death Trap." *Harper's* 286, no. 1714 (March 1993): 35-45. ["Scenes from a futile war."]

3648. Human Rights Watch. *The Lost Agenda: Human Rights and UN Field Operations.* Edited by Cynthia

Brown. New York: Human Rights Watch, c1993. 173 pp. [Examines five of the largest UN field operations in recent years, in Cambodia, El Salvador, Iraq, Somalia, and the former Yugoslavia.]

3649. "Human Rights II—Cherif Bassiouni Condemns 'Psychology' of Balkan Crimes." *JAMA: Journal of the American Medical Association* 270, no. 5 (1993): 643-644.

3650. Husarska, Anna. "Bihac Postcard: Pocket Change." *New Republic* 209, nos. 3 & 4 (July 19 & 26, 1993): 9-10. ["Life in the besieged enclave."]

3651. ———. "Pristina Postcard: The Next Bosnia." *New Republic* 209, no. 20 (November 15, 1993): 16-17.

3652. ———. "Sarajevo Diarist: Pure Wind." *New Republic* 209, no. 6 (August 9, 1993): 42.

3653. ———. "Unsafe Zone." *New Yorker* 69, no. 21 (July 12, 1993): 29-37. ["The Serbs may have the upper hand in the war in Bosnia, but they're still paranoid and defensive."]

3654. Ignatieff, Michael. "The Balkan Tragedy." *New York Review of Books* 40, no. 9 (May 13, 1993): 3-5. [Review article on Misha Glenny, *The Fall of Yugoslavia: The Third Balkan War* (NY: 1992); Branka Magas, *The Destruction of Yugoslavia: Tracking the Break-up, 1980-92* (London and NY: 1993); and Slavenka Drakulic, *The Balkan Express: Fragments from the Other Side* (NY: 1993).]

3655. Inoue, Yoshiko. "United Nations' Peacekeeping Role in the Post-Cold War Era: The Conflict in Bosnia-Herzegovina." *Loyola of Los Angeles International and Comparative Law Journal* 16, no. 1 (November 1993): 245-274.

3656. International Court of Justice. "Case Concerning Application of the Convention on the Prevention and Punishment of the Crime of Genocide." *American Journal of International Law* 87, no. 3 (July 1993): 505-521. [Consists of "Order of April 8, 1993" (pp. 505-520) and "Declaration of Judge Tarassov" (pp. 520-521).]

3657. Jackson, Robert H. "Armed humanitarianism." *International Journal* 48, no. 4 (Autumn 1993): 579-606. [Includes section "Humanitarian tragedy in Bosnia" (pp. 597-604).]

3658. Jansa, Janez. "Missed Opportunities." *Uncaptive Minds* 6, no. 3 (24) (Fall 1993): 65-70.

3659. Jeffords, James M., Hank Brown, and United States. Congress. Senate. Committee on Foreign Relations. *Trip to Croatia, Syria, Jordan, Israel, and Egypt: A Report to the Committee on Foreign Relations, United States Senate.* S. Prt., 103-57. Washington, DC: U.S. G.P.O., 1993. viii, 24 pp. [103d Congress, 1st session.]

3660. Job, Cvijeto. "Yugoslavia's Ethnic Furies." *Foreign Policy*, no. 92 (Fall 1993): 52-74.

3661. Jordan, June. "Bosnia betrayed." *Progressive* 57, no. 9 (September 1993): 15-16.

3662. Kaldor, Mary. "Protect Bosnia." *Nation* 256, no. 11 (March 22, 1993): 364-365.

3663. ———. "Sarajevo's reproach." *Progressive* 57, no. 9 (September 1993): 21-23.

3664. Kalogjera, Damir. "The Destruction of Dubrovnik." *Cross Currents: A Yearbook of Central European Culture*, no. 12 (1993): 160-165.

3665. Kaminski, Piotr. "Who Started the War?" *Uncaptive Minds* 6, no. 1 (22) (Winter-Spring 1993): 9-13. [Essay is in response to the interview with Aleksa Djilas (Summer 1992): 25-31.]

3666. Kaplan, Robert D. "Ground Zero." *New Republic* 209, no. 5 (August 2, 1993): 15-16. ["Is Macedonia the next Christian-Muslim war?"]

3667. Karaosmanoglu, Ali L. *Crisis in the Balkans.* Research Paper (United Nations Institute for Disarmament Research), no. 22. New York, NY: United Nations, 1993. v, 22 pp.

3668. Katzarova, Mariana. "Kosovo Waits." *Nation* 256, no. 3 (January 25, 1993): 77.

3669. ———. "Sarajevo Diary: H(e)aven Can Wait." *Nation* 257, no. 5 (August 9/16, 1993): 172-174.

3670. Kayal, Alya Z., Penny L. Parker, and David Weissbrodt. "The Forty-Fourth Session of the UN Sub-Commission on Prevention of Discrimination and Protection of Minorities and the Special Session of the Commission on Human Rights on the Situation in the Former Yugoslavia." *Human Rights Quarterly* 15, no. 2 (May 1993): 410-458.

3671. Kennan, George F. "The Balkan Crisis: 1913 and 1993." *New York Review of Books* 40, no. 13 (July 15, 1993): 3-7.

3672. Kenney, George, Marshall Harris, and Stephen Walker. "The Agony of Dissent." *Foreign Service Journal* 70, no. 11 (November 1993): 36-40.

3673. King, Amy Lou. "Bosnia-Herzegovina: Vance-Owen Agenda for a Peaceful Settlement: Did the U.N. Do Too Little, Too Late, to Support this Endeavor?" *Georgia Journal of International and Comparative Law* 23, no. 2 (Summer 1993): 347-375.

3674. Knoll, Erwin. "The uses of the Holocaust." *Progressive* 57, no. 7 (July 1993): 15-16. [On U.S. military help to Bosnia-Herzegovina.]

3675. Laber, Jeri. "Bosnia: Questions About Rape." *New York Review of Books* 40, no. 6 (March 25, 1993): 3-6.

3676. Lane, Charles. "Bosnia Postcard: Beyond Pale." *New Republic* 208, no. 22 (May 31, 1993): 16-18. ["Among the recalcitrant Serbs."]

3677. ———. "Croatia Postcard: Survivors." *New Republic* 208, no. 4 (January 25, 1993): 9-10.

3678. "A Last Chance." *New Yorker* 69, no. 23 (July 26, 1993): 4-6. ["The partition of Bosnia will bring apartheid to Europe."]

3679. Lewis, Samuel. "The Most Dangerous Game." *Foreign Service Journal* 70, no. 3 (March 1993): 33-35. ["Mediating international conflict."]

3680. Luttwak, Edward N. "If Bosnians Were Dolphins..." *Commentary* 96, no. 4 (October 1993): 27-32.

3681. Lynch, Allen, and Reneo Lukic. "Russian Foreign Policy and the Wars in the Former Yugoslavia." *RFE/RL Research Report* 2, no. 41 (October 15, 1993): 25-32.

3682. MacKenzie, Lewis. *Peacekeepers: The Road to Sarajevo.* Vancouver: Douglas & McIntyre, 1993. 334 pp. [Excerpted in *MacLean's* 106 (Sept. 6, 1993): 24-29.] REV: Metta Spencer, *Peace Magazine* 9, no. 6 (November-December 1993): 14.

3683. MacKinnon, Catharine A. "Crimes of War, Crimes of Peace." *UCLA Women's Law Journal* 4, no. 1 (Fall 1993): 59-86.

3684. Malcolm, Noel. "Is There A Doctor in the House?" *National Review* 45, no. 13 (July 5, 1993): 39-41. [On the European Community and the Yugoslav War.]

3685. Markotich, Stan. "Croatia's Krajina Serbs." *RFE/RL Research Report* 2, no. 41 (October 15, 1993): 5-10.

3686. ———. "Ethnic Serbs in Tudjman's Croatia." *RFE/RL Research Report* 2, no. 38 (September 24, 1993): 28-33.

3687. Markovich, Stephen C. "Introduction." *North Dakota Quarterly* 61, no. 1 (Winter 1993): 1-3. [Introduction to special issue entitled "Out of Yugoslavia."]

3688. Mearsheimer, John J., and Robert A. Pape. "The Answer." *New Republic* 208, no. 24 (June 14, 1993): 22ff. [Proposed solution for the Yugoslav War.]

3689. Mennard, Michael, Horace G. Lunt, and Dusko Doder. "Letters." *Foreign Policy*, no. 93 (Winter 1993-1994): 183-187. [Letters from Mennard (pp. 183-185) and Lunt (pp. 185-186) written in response to essay by Doder ("Yugoslavia: New War, Old Hatreds," no. 91); with reply from Doder (pp. 186-187).]

3690. Mercer, Jonathan Loveridge. "Broken Promises and Unfulfilled Threats: Resolve, Reputation, and Deterrence." Ph.D. diss., Columbia University, 1993. [UMI order no: AAC 9318263.]

3691. Meron, Theodor. "The Case for War Crimes Trials in Yugoslavia." *Foreign Affairs* 72, no. 3 (Summer 1993): 122-135.

3692. ———. "Editorial Comment: Rape as a Crime under International Humanitarian Law." *American Journal of International Law* 87, no. 3 (July 1993): 424-428.

3693. Mertus, Julie, and Vlatka Mihelic. *Open Wounds: Human Rights Abuses in Kosovo.* Edited by Jeri Laber. New York: Human Rights Watch, c1993. vxii, 148 pp.

3694. Mey, Holger H. "View from Germany: Germany, NATO, and the War in the Former Yugoslavia." *Comparative Strategy* 12, no. 2 (April/June 1993): 239-245.

3695. Moore, Patrick. "Bosnian Impasse Poses Dilemmas for Diplomacy." *RFE/RL Research Report* 2, no. 14 (April 2, 1993): 28-30.

3696. ———. "Endgame in Bosnia and Herzegovina?" *RFE/RL Research Report* 2, no. 32 (August 13, 1993): 17-23. [Includes sidebar: Milan Andrejevich, "The Presidency of Bosnia and Herzegovina: A Profile," p. 21.]

3697. ———. "A Return of the Serbian-Croatian Conflict?" *RFE/RL Research Report* 2, no. 42 (October 22, 1993): 16-20.

3698. ———. "The Shaky Truce in Croatia." *RFE/RL Research Report* 2, no. 21 (May 21, 1993): 46-49.

3699. ———. "War Returns to Croatia." *RFE/RL Research Report* 2, no. 9 (February 26, 1993): 40-43.

3700. ———. "The Widening Warfare in the Former Yugoslavia." *RFE/RL Research Report* 2, no. 1 (January 1, 1993): 1-11.

3701. Moore, W. John. "Soldiers for the Lord?" *National Journal* 25, no. 40 (October 2, 1993): 2361-2365.

3702. Morrison, David C. "Blue Helmet Blues." *National Journal* 25, no. 8 (February 20, 1993): 483.

3703. Nairn, Tom. "All Bosnians Now?" *Dissent* 40, no. 4 (Fall 1993): 403-410.

3704. Nash, Marian (Leich). "Contemporary Practice of the United States Relating to International Law." *American Journal of International Law* 87, no. 3 (July 1993): 433-441.

3705. "Nationalism & War Break Feminist Hearts & Solidarity." *New Directions for Women* 22, no. 2 (March-April 1993): 14.

3706. Nelson, Daniel N. "A Balkan Perspective." *Strategic Review* 21, no. 1 (Winter 1993): 26-39.

3707. Newhouse, John. "No Exit, No Entrance." *New Yorker* 69, no. 19 (June 28, 1993): 44-51. ["The NATO allies' lack of resolve on the Balkans could be the catalyst for a worse war to come."]

3708. O'Brien, James C. "Current Developments: The International Tribunal for Violations of International Humanitarian Law in the Former Yugoslavia." *American Journal of International Law* 87, no. 4 (October 1993): 639-659.

3709. Palairet, M. R. "How Long Can the Milosevic Regime Withstand Sanctions?" *RFE/RL Research Report* 2, no. 34 (August 27, 1993): 21-25.

3710. Pearl, Elizabeth L. "Punishing Balkan War Criminals: Could the End of Yugoslavia Provide an End to Victor's Justice?" *American Criminal Law Review* 30, no. 4 (Summer 1993): 1373-1414.

3711. Pesic, Vesna. "The Cruel Face of Nationalism." *Journal of Democracy* 4, no. 4 (October 1993): 100-103.

3712. Pfaff, William. "The Complacent Democracies." *New York Review of Books* 40, no. 13 (July 15, 1993): 17.

3713. ———. "Invitation to War." *Foreign Affairs* 72, no. 3 (Summer 1993): 97-109.

3714. ———. "Is Liberal Internationalism Dead?" *World Policy Journal* 10, no. 3 (Fall 1993): 5-15.

3715. Pitter, Laura, and Alexandra Stiglmayer. "Will the World Remember? Can the Women Forget?" *Ms.* 3, no. 5 (March-April 1993): 19-22.

3716. Polsby, Daniel D. "Equal Protection." *Reason* 25, no. 5 (October 1993): 34-38. ["In Bosnia or our own backyards, the good guys need guns too."]

3717. "Provisional Chronological List of States Which Have Recognized the Independence and Sovereignty of the Republic of Slovenia." *Nationalities Papers* 21, no. 1 (Spring 1993): 193-195.

3718. "Quiet Voices from the Balkans." *New Yorker* 69, no. 4 (March 15, 1993): 4-6.

3719. RAND Corporation, United States. Air Force, and Lessor Regional Crises/Peace Enforcement (1st: 1993: Santa Monica, CA). *Lessons from Bosnia.* Edited by Zalmay M. Khalilzad. CF-113-AF. Santa Monica, CA: RAND, 1993. ix, 34 pp. [Prepared for the United States Air Force. Proceedings of a meeting that took place at RAND in Santa Monica, CA, August 5, 1993.]

3720. Rieff, David. [Book Review]. *Book World (Washington Post)* 23, no. 47 (November 21, 1993): 1ff. [Review article on Zlatko Dizdarevic, *Sarajevo: A War Journal* (NY: Fromm International, 1993).]

3721. ———. "Homelands: Notes on the Ottoman Legacy Written in a Time of War." *Salmagundi*, no. 100 (Fall 1993): 3-15.

3722. Rizopoulos, Nicholas X. "A Third Balkan War?" *World Policy Journal* 10, no. 2 (Summer 1993): 1-5.

3723. Rosenberger, Chandler. "The Bridge on the Drina." *National Review* 45, no. 11 (June 7, 1993): 21-22.

3724. ———. "The Next Balkan War." *National Review* 45, no. 17 (September 6, 1993): 22ff. [On Serbian-Croatian relations and the future of Krajina.]

3725. Rosin, Hanna. "Speak No Evil." *New Republic* 209, no. 17 (October 25, 1993): 28.

3726. Rubenstein, Richard L. "Silent Partners in Ethnic Cleansing: the UN, the EC, and NATO." *In Depth* 3, no. 2 (Spring 1993): 35-57.

3727. Ruggie, John Gerard. "The U.N.: Wandering in the Void." *Foreign Affairs* 72, no. 5 (November-December 1993): 26-31.

3728. Ryback, Timothy W. "The Mission of Dr. Chaos." *New Yorker* 69, no. 25 (August 9, 1993): 48-57. [On a western relief mission.]

3729. Samuels, Gertrude. "Putting War Crimes on the UN Agenda: Nuremburg Reaffirmed." *New Leader* 76, no. 4 (March 8, 1993): 7-9.

3730. "Saving Sarajevo, From Below." *New Yorker* 69, no. 39 (November 22, 1993): 45-46.

3731. Scharf, Michael P., and Joshua L. Dorosin. "Interpreting UN Sanctions: The Rulings and Role of the Yugoslavia Sanctions Committee." *Brooklyn Journal of International Law* 19, no. 3 (1993): 771-827.

3732. Schmidt, Fabian. "Has the Kosovo Crisis Been Internationalized?" *RFE/RL Research Report* 2, no. 44 (November 5, 1993): 35-39.

3733. Schneider, Troy K. "In Person." *National Journal* 25, no. 45 (November 6, 1993): 2673. [On Victor Jackovich, U.S. Ambassador to Bosnia-Herzegovina.]

3734. Schneider, William. "Diplomatic Lessons, Real and False." *National Journal* 25, no. 21 (May 22, 1993): 1266.

3735. Schwartz, Stephen. "In Defense of the Bosnian Republic." *World Affairs* 156, no. 2 (Fall 1993): 80-85.

3736. Sears, David. "Save the Children." *World & I* 8, no. 6 (June 1993): 153-161.

3737. Sersic, Maja. "The Crisis in the Eastern Adriatic and the Law of the Sea." *Ocean Development and International Law* 24, no. 3 (July-September 1993): 291-299.

3738. Siegman, Henry. "Bosnia & the Lesson of Memory." *Congress Monthly* 60, no. 1 (January 1993): 9-11. [Text of an address delivered at an international conference in Lyons in 1992, "Résistance et Mémoire," commemorating the French resistance and the Nazi deportation of the Jews of France during World War II.]

3739. Siegman, Henry, Robert K. Lifton, and Ann F. Lewis. "AJ Congress Heads Broad Coalition Against Rape in Former Yugoslavia." *Congress Monthly* 60, no. 3 (March/April 1993): 5. [Letter to U.S. Ambassador to the United Nations Madeleine Albright from the American Jewish Congress and a coalition of organizations.]

3740. Sinclair, Clive. "Huck in Belgrade." *North Dakota Quarterly* 61, no. 1 (Winter 1993): 175-181. [Author's description of the "October Meeting of Writers" in Belgrade, Serbia.]

3741. Slapsak, Svetlana. "When words kill." *Uncaptive Minds* 6, no. 1 (22) (Winter-Spring 1993): 15-22. [Version of this essay published in *Republika* (December 1-15, 1992) and reprinted in *Puls* no. 59 (November-December 1992).]

3742. "Slouching Towards Bosnia." *New Yorker* 69, no. 37 (November 8, 1993): 8-10.

3743. Soros, George. "Bosnia and Beyond." *New York Review of Books* 40, no. 16 (October 7, 1993): 15-16.

3744. ———. "The Stakes in Bosnia." *Freedom Review* 24, no. 6 (November-December 1993): 4. [Originally published in *New York Review of Books* (October 7, 1993).]

3745. Spring, Baker. *Assessing America's Military Options in Bosnia*. Backgrounder, no. 939. Washington, DC: Heritage Foundation, 1993. 7 pp.

3746. Stavrou, Nikolaos A. "The Balkan Quagmire and the West's Response." *Mediterranean Quarterly* 4, no. 1 (Winter 1993): 24-45.

3747. Steinfels, Margaret O'Brien. "Notebook: The Virtues of Sarajevo: Reflections of a City Dweller." *Commonweal* 120, no. 12 (June 18, 1993): 4-5.

3748. "Stop Serbia Now." *New Republic* 208, no. 19 (May 10, 1993): 7.

3749. Swiss, Shana, and Joan E. Giller. "Rape as a Crime of War: A Medical Perspective." *JAMA: Journal of the American Medical Association* 270, no. 5 (August 4, 1993): 612-615.

3750. Swissler, John. "The Transformations of American Cold War Policy Toward Yugoslavia, 1948-1951." Ph.D. diss., University of Hawaii, 1993. [UMI order no: AAC 9416078.]

3751. Szasz, Paul C. "The Proposed War Crimes Tribunal for Ex-Yugoslavia." *New York University Journal of International Law and Politics* 25, no. 2 (Winter 1993): 405-435. ["Address delivered at the annual dinner of the *Journal of International Law and Politics* on April 19, 1993" pp. 405-488; "Appendix A: A Statute of the International Tribunal (Yugoslav War Crimes Tribunal) with cross-reference table to the ILC Draft Statute for an International Criminal Tribunal" pp. 436-452; and "Appendix B: ILC Draft Statute for an International Criminal Tribunal with cross-reference to the Statute of the International Tribunal" pp. 453-488.]

3752. Trnka, Kasim. "The Bosnian Case." *New York Review of Books* 40, no. 15 (September 23, 1993): 65-66. [Author is the former chief justice of the Constitutional Court of Bosnia.]

3753. Tucker, Robert W., and David C. Hendrickson. "America and Bosnia." *National Interest*, no. 33 (Fall 1993): 14-27.

3754. Tyrrell, R. Emmett, Jr. "Editorial: Botching Bosnia." *American Spectator* 26, no. 7 (July 1993): 14.

3755. United Nations. *The United Nations and the Situation in the Former Yugoslavia*. Reference Paper (United Nations. Dept. of Public Information). [New York?]: United Nations Dept. of Public Information, [1993]. 107 pp.

3756. United Nations. Security Council. "Documentation." *Human Rights Law Journal* 14, nos. 5-6 (June 30, 1993): 197-214. [On the establishment of an International Tribunal to prosecute violations of international humanitarian law committed in the former Yugoslavia since 1991.]

3757. United Nations Security Council. "Resolution 820 (1993) on Strengthening the Measures Regarding the Former Yugoslavia." *American Journal of International Law* 87, no. 3 (July 1993): 521-525.

3758. United States. Congress. Commission on Security and Cooperation in Europe. *Implementation of the Helsinki Accords: Hearing before the Commission on Security and Cooperation in Europe, One Hundred Third Congress, First Session: The Yugoslav Conflict, Potential for Spillover in the Balkans, July 21, 1993*. Washington: U.S. G.P.O., 1993. iii, 92 pp.

3759. ———. *Implementation of the Helsinki Accords: Hearing before the Commission on Security and Cooperation in Europe, One Hundred Third Congress, First Session, European Perspective on Bosnian Conflict, February 22, 1993*. Washington: U.S. G.P.O., 1993. iii, 263 pp.

3760. ———. *Implementation of the Helsinki Accords: Hearing before the Commission on Security and Cooperation in Europe, One Hundred Third Congress, First Session: War Crimes and the Humanitarian Crisis in the Former Yugoslavia, January 25, 1993*. Washington: U.S. G.P.O., 1993. iii, 189 pp. [CSCE 103-1-1.]

3761. ———. *Implementation of the Helsinki Accords: Hearing before the Commission on Security and Cooperation in Europe, One Hundred Third Congress, First Session: Crisis in Bosnia-Herzegovina, February 4, 1993*. Washington: U.S. G.P.O., 1993. iii, 28 pp.

3762. United States. Congress. House. Committee on Foreign Affairs. *The Crisis in Former Yugoslavia and the U.S. Role: Hearing before the Committee on Foreign Affairs, House of Representatives, One Hundred Third Congress, First Session, September 29, 1993*. Washington, DC: U.S. G.P.O., 1993, iii, 56 pp.

3763. ———. *Trip Report on the Baltic States, Slovakia, and Negotiations Concerning Former Yugoslavia: Report of a Study Mission to the Baltic States, Slovakia, Austria, Switzerland, and the United Kingdom, November 8-18, 1992, to the Committee on Foreign Affairs, U.S. House of Representatives*. Washington: U.S. G.P.O., 1993. vii, 21 pp. [102d Congress, 2d session. Committee print.]

3764. United States. Congress. Senate. Committee on Armed Services. *Joint Chiefs of Staff Briefing on Current Military Operations in Somalia, Iraq, and Yugoslavia: Hearing before the Committee on Armed Services, United States Senate, One Hundred Third Congress, First Session, January 29, 1993*. United States. Congress. Senate S. hrg., 103-176. Washington: U.S. G.P.O., 1993. iii, 118 pp.

3765. United States. General Accounting Office. *Serbia-Montenegro: Implementation of U.N. Economic Sanctions: Report to the Honorable Edward M. Kennedy, U.S. Senate*. Washington, DC: Gaithersburg, MD: The Office; The Office [distributor, 1993]. 32 pp.

3766. United States. President (1989-1993: Bush), and United States. Congress. House. Committee on Foreign Affairs. *Additional Measures with Respect to the Federal Republic of Yugoslavia (Serbia and Montenegro): Communication from the President of the United States Transmitting a Copy of an Executive Order with Respect to Additional Measures with the Federal Republic of Yugoslavia (Serbia and Montenegro), Pursuant to 50 U.S.C. 1701 et Seq. and 1601 et Seq. and 22 U.S.C. 287C.* House Document (United States. Congress. House), 103-40. Washington: U.S. G.P.O., 1993. iv, 2 pp.

3767. ———. *Developments Concerning the National Emergency with Respect to Serbia and Montenegro: Communication from the President of the United States Transmitting a Report on Developments Since His Last Report of May 30, 1992, Concerning the National Emergency with Respect to Serbia and Montenegro, Pursuant to 50 U.S.C. 1641(C).* House Document (United States. Congress. House), 103-14. Washington: U.S. G.P.O., 1993. 20 pp.

3768. United States. President (1993- : Clinton), and United States. Congress. House. Committee on Foreign Affairs. *Additional Measures with Respect to the Federal Republic of Yugoslavia (Serbia and Montenegro): Message from the President of the United States Transmitting His Executive Order Taking Additional Steps with Respect to the Actions and Policies of the Federal Republic of Yugoslavia (Serbia and Montenegro), Pursuant to 50 U.S.C. 1706(D) and 1641(B).* House Document (United States. Congress. House), 103-77. Washington: U.S. G.P.O., 1993. iv, 2 pp.

3769. ———. *Continuation of National Emergency with Respect to the Federal Republic of Yugoslavia (Serbia and Montenegro): Message from the President of the United States Transmitting Notification That the Federal Republic of Yugoslavia (Serbia and Montenegro) Emergency Is to Continue in Effect Beyond May 30, 1993, Pursuant to 50 U.S.C. 1622(D).* House Document (United States. Congress. House), 103-91. Washington: U.S. G.P.O., 1993. 2 pp.

3770. ———. *Developments Concerning the National Emergency with Respect to the Federal Republic of Yugoslavia (Serbia and Montenegro): Message from the President of the United States Transmitting a Report on Developments Since His Last Report of May 30, 1992, Concerning the National Emergency with Respect to the Federal Republic of Yugoslavia (Serbia and Montenegro), Pursuant to 50 U.S.C. 1641(C).* House Document (United States. Congress. House), 103-92. Washington: U.S. G.P.O., 1993. 49 pp.

3771. ———. *Support of the United Nations Efforts in Bosnia-Herzegovina: Communication from the President of the United States Transmitting His Actions in Support of the United Nations Efforts in Bosnia-Herzegovina.* House Document (United States. Congress. House), 103-67. Washington: U.S. G.P.O., 1993. 2 pp

3772. ———. *U.S. Efforts towards Peace and Stability in the Vital Balkan Region: Communication from the President of the United States Transmitting a Report on Progress of U.S. Efforts towards Peace and Stability in the Vital Balkan Region.* House Document (United States. Congress. House), 103-111. Washington: U.S. G.P.O., 1993. 2 pp.

3773. U.S. Congress. House. Committee on Foreign Affairs. *Trip Report on the Baltic States, Slovakia, and Negotiations Concerning Former Yugoslavia; Report of a Study Mission to the Baltic States, Slovakia, Austria, Switzerland and the United Kingdom, November 8-18, 1992, to the Committee on Foreign Affairs, U.S. House of Representatives.* Washington, DC: U.S. Government Printing Office, 1993. 21 pp. [102nd Congress, 2nd session.]

3774. Vagman, Vilim. "A Still, Small Voice from Sarajevo." *Congress Monthly* 60, no. 6 (September-October 1993): 2.

3775. Van Heuven, Marten. *Yugoslavia—What Issues? What Policies?* RAND note, P-7808. Santa Monica, CA: RAND, 1993. 16 pp. [Address given to the Washington Institute of Foreign Affairs, Washington, DC on February 4, 1993.]

3776. Vassilev, Rossen. "The Third Balkan War." *National Review* 45, no. 4 (March 1, 1993): 46-49.

3777. Vermaat, Emerson. "His Brothers' Keeper: In Conversation with Franjo Komarica." *Freedom Review* 24, no. 4 (July-August 1993): 21-23. ["Yugoslavia: Triumph of the Extremists."]

3778. Wajsman, Patrick. "Bosnia, whose responsibility?" *Freedom Review* 24, no. 4 (July-August 1993): 20. [Originally published in *Le Figaro* (Paris), June 1, 1993.]

3779. Walker, Stephen S. "Genocide: We Are Responsible." *Tikkun* 8, no. 6 (November-December 1993): 19-22.

3780. "War Rape: Letters from Ex-Yugoslavia." *Peace Magazine* 9, no. 2 (March/April 1993): 24-25.

3781. Webb, John. "Genocide Treaty-Ethnic Cleansing—Substantive and Procedural Hurdles in the Application of the Genocide Convention to Alleged Crimes in the Former Yugoslavia." *Georgia Journal of International and Comparative Law* 23, no. 2 (Summer 1993): 377-408.

3782. Weber, Vin. "Bosnia: Strange Alliances." *National Review* 45, no. 11 (June 7, 1993): 22-25.

3783. Wilsnack, Dorie. "Speaking Out Carefully." *New Directions for Women* 22, no. 2 (March-April 1993): 13.

3784. Wing, Adrien Katherine, and Sylke Merchán. "Rape, Ethnicity, and Culture: Spirit Injury from Bosnia to Black America." *Columbia Human Rights Law Review* 25, no. 1 (Fall 1993): 1-48.

3785. Woodward, Susan L. "Yugoslavia: Divide and fail." *Bulletin of the Atomic Scientists* 49, no. 9 (November 1993): 24-27.

3786. Wu, Yolanda S. "Genocidal Rape in Bosnia: Redress in United States Courts Under the Alien Tort Claims Act." *UCLA Women's Law Journal* 4, no. 1 (Fall 1993): 101-111.

3787. "Yugoslavia: Triumph of the Extremists." *Freedom Review* 24, no. 4 (July-August 1993): 19.

3788. Yugoslavia, and United States. Dept. of State. *Postal, Express Mail Service: Agreement, with Detailed Regulations, between the United States of America and Yugoslavia, Signed at Belgrade and Washington, January 22 and March 1, 1990.* United States Treaties, etc. (Treaties and Other International Acts Series), 11713. Washington, DC: Dept. of State, [1993?]. 13 pp.

3789. ———. *Scientific and Technical Cooperation: Agreement between the United States of America and the Socialist Federal Republic of Yugoslavia, Extending the Agreement of April 2, 1980, Effected by Exchange of Notes Dated at Belgrade June 21 and August 1, 1985.* United States Treaties, etc. (Treaties and Other International Acts Series), 11331. Washington, DC: Dept. of State, [1993?]. 3 pp.

3790. Zarycky, George. "Bosnia's Agony Shames the World." *Freedom Review* 24, no. 5 (September-October 1993): 42-43. [Article published in *Washington Post* (July 25, 1993).]

10 Language and Linguistics

■ General

3791. Archibald, John. *Language Learnability and L2 Phonology: The Acquisition of Metrical Parameters.* Studies in Theoretical PsychoLinguistics, v. 19. Dordrecht; Boston: Kluwer Academic Publishers, c1993. xviii, 199 pp.

3792. Extra, Guus, and Ludo Verhoeven, eds. *Immigrant Languages in Europe.* Includes contributions by Andrina Pavlinic and Donald Kenrick. Clevedon, UK; Phildelphia, PA: Multilingual Matters, c1993. vi, 326 pp. [Revised papers originally presented at an international colloquium held in December 1990 in Gilze-Rijen, Netherlands. Partial contents: Andrina Pavlinic, "Croatian or Serbian as a Diaspora Language in Western Europe," pp. 101-116; Donald Kenrick, "Romani at the Crossroads."] REV: Carol A. Blackshire-Belay, *Modern Language Journal* 77, no. 3 (Autumn 1993): 398-399.

3793. Fraenkel, Eran, and Christina Kramer, eds. *Language Contact—Language Conflict.* Balkan Studies (New York, NY), vol. 1. New York: P. Lang, c1993. 187 pp.

3794. Janda, Laura A. "The Shape of the Indirect Object in Central and Eastern Europe." *Slavic and East European Journal* 37, no. 4 (Winter 1993): 533-563.

3795. Jones, Sara Su. "Power of Babel: The Struggle to Balance Linguistic Unity and Diversity." *Harvard International Review* 15, no. 4 (Summer 1993): 46ff.

3796. Kostomarov, V. G. *My Genius, My Language: Reflections on Language in Society = Mon génie, ma langue: réflexions sur la question des langues dans la societe.* Translated by John Woodsworth and Marie Lamothe. Bilingual ed. Ottawa; New York: LEGAS, 1993. x, 57, x, 62 pp. [Partial contents: Language is Language; The Constant Cry of One's Native Language; My Friend, My Enemy— Another Language; Can a Bilingual Be Happy?; Ethnocentrism and Universalism in Language Development; Woe to a Language, Once It Is Out of Favor; Neither Publicity-Shy Nor Glory-Seeking.] REV: Frank Nuessel, *Language Problems & Language Planning* 17, no. 3 (Fall 1993): 290-292.

3797. Mayer, Harvey E. "Slavic, a Balticized Albanian?" *Lituanus* 39, no. 2 (Summer 1993): 78-83. [Response to Eric P. Hamp, "On Myths and Accuracy," *General Linguistics* 24, no. 4 (1984): 238-239, which criticized Mayer, "Two Linguistic Myths: Balto-Slavic and Common Baltic," *Lituanus* 27, no. 1 (1981): 63-68].]

3798. Oltean, Stefan. "A Survey of the Pragmatic and Referential Functions of Free Indirect Discourse." *Poetics Today* 14, no. 4 (Winter 1993): 691-714. [Article

deals with issues in English syntax and linguistics in general.]

3799. Popov, Vladimir. "De-Russifying Turkestan." *Wilson Quarterly* 17, no. 1 (Winter 1993): 158. [Letter to the editor in response to "Land of the Great Silk Road" in vol. 16, no. 3 (Summer 1992).]

3800. Walters, Frank D. "Taxonomy and the Undoing of Language: Dialogic Form in the Universal Languages of the Seventeenth Century." *Style* 27, no. 1 (Spring 1993): 1-16.

3801. Zlateva, Palma, ed. and trans. *Translation as Social Action: Russian and Bulgarian Perspectives.* Chapter introductions by André Lefevere. Contributions by Anna Lilova, Iliana Vladova, Jakob Retsker, Vladimir Gak, Leonid Barkhudarov, Alexander Shveitser, Andrei Danchev, Vilen Komissarov, Margarita Brandes, Irina Zimnyaya, Bistra Alexieva, Leonora Chernyakhovskaya, and Sider Florin. Translation Studies (London, England). London; New York: Routledge, 1993. viii, 132 pp. [Contents: Anna Lilova, "Categories for the study of translation," pp. 5-10; Iliana Vladova, "Essential features and specific manifestations of historical distance in original texts and their translations," pp. 11-17; Jakob Retsker, "The theory and practice of translation," pp. 18-31; Vladimir Gak, "Interlanguage asymmetry and the pronostication of transformations in translation," pp. 32-38; Leonid Barkhudarov, "The problem of the unit of translations," pp. 39-46; Alexander Shveitser, "Equivalence and adequacy," pp. 47-56; Andrei Danchev, "A note on phrasemic calquing," pp. 57-62; Vilen Komissarov, "Norms in translation," pp. 63-75; Margarita Brandes, "Comprehension, style, translation, and their interaction," pp. 76-86; Irina Zimnyaya, "A psychological analysis of translation as a type of speech activity," pp. 87-100; Bistra Alexieva, "A cognitive approach to translation equivalence," pp. 101-109; Leonora Chernyakhovskaya, "Sense and its expression through language," pp. 110-121; Sider Florin, "Realia in translation," pp. 122-128.]

■ Albanian

3802. Stefanllari, Ilo. *English-Albanian Dictionary.* Paperback ed. Hippocrene Standard Dictionary. New York: Hippocrene Books, 1993. 441 pp. [Originally published: (Tirane: 8 Nentori, 1986).]

■ Armenian

3803. Aroutunian, Diana, and Susanna Aroutunian. *Armenian-English, English-Armenian.* Hippocrene Concise Dictionary. New York, NY: Hippocrene books, c1993. 378 pp.

3804. Jungmann, Paul, and J. J. S. Weitenberg. *A Reverse Analytical Dictionary of Classical Armenian.* Trends in Linguistics. Documentation, 9. Berlin; New York: Mouton de Gruyter, 1993. viii, 836 pp.

3805. Samuelian, Thomas J. *Armenian Dictionary in Transliteration: Western Pronunciation: Armenian-English, English-Armenian.* New York: Armenian National Education Committee, c1993. xiii, 139 pp. [English and Modern West Armenian in roman transliteration; Armenian script forms also added.]

3806. Shields, Kenneth. "The Origin of the Armenian Locative Plural." *Journal of Indo-European Studies* 21, nos. 1 & 2 (Spring-Summer 1993): 55-62.

■ Baltic Languages

General

3807. Karaliunas, Simas. "Reflexes of IE *$h_2$rtko- 'bear' in Baltic." *Journal of Indo-European Studies* 21, nos. 3 & 4 (Fall/Winter 1993): 367-372.

3808. Mayer, Harvey E. "West Baltic Latvian/East Baltic Lithuanian." *Lituanus* 39, no. 3 (Fall 1993): 57-62.

3809. Vanagas, Aleksandras. "Three Lithuanian City Names: Priekule, Rietavas, Subacius." *Lituanus* 39, no. 1 (Spring 1993): 77-85.

Latvian

3810. Sosare, M., and I. Birzvalka. *Latvian-English, English-Latvian Dictionary.* Hippocrene Practical Dictionary. New York: Hippocrene Books, c1993. 205, 286 pp. [Compiler's name misprinted on title page as I. Borzvalka.]

Lithuanian

3811. Blevins, Juliette. "A tonal analysis of Lithuanian nominal accent." *Language: Journal of the Linguistic Society of America* 69, no. 2 (June 1993): 237-73.

3812. Klimas, Antanas. "The Two Kinds of Passive Voice in Lithuanian." *Lituanus* 39, no. 3 (Fall 1993): 63-71.

3813. Martsinkyavitshute, Victoria. *Lithuanian-English/English-Lithuanian.* Hippocrene Concise Dictionary. New York: Hippocrene Books, c1993. 382 pp.

■ Finno-Ugric Languages

3814. Ritter, Ralf-Peter. *Studien zu den Ältesten Germanischen Entlehnungen im Ostseefinnischen.* Opuscula Fenno-Ugrica Gottingensia, Bd. 5. Frankfurt am Main; New York: P. Lang, c1993. 286 pp.

■ German

3815. Kronenberg, Stephan. *Wirtschaftliche Entwicklung und die Sprache der Wirtschaftpolitik in der DDR (1949-1990).* Europäische Hochschulschriften. Reihe I, Deutsche Sprache und Literatur = European University Studies. Series I, German Language and Literature, 1396. Frankfurt am Main; New York: P. Lang, c1993. 324, xx pp. [Originally presented as the author's thesis (doctoral)—Universitat Frankfurt (Main), 1993.]

3816. Schmitt, Dieter. *Doktrin und Sprache in der Ehemaligen DDR Bis 1989: Eine Politikwissenschaftliche Analyse Unter Berucksichtigung Sprachwissenschaftlicher Gesichtspunkte.* Saarbrucker Politikwissenschaft, Bd. 14. Frankfurt am Main; New York: P. Lang, c1993. 174 pp.

■ Romanian

3817. Petrucci, Peter Ralph. "Slavic Features in the History of Rumanian." Ph.D. diss., University of Southern California, 1993.

■ Slavic Languages

General

3818. Bethin, Christina Y. "Neo-Acute Length in the North Central Dialects of Late Common Slavic." *Journal of Slavic Linguistics* 1, no. 2 (Summer-Fall 1993): 219-250.

3819. Birnbaum, Henrik. "On the Ethnogenesis and Protohome of the Slavs: The Linguistic Evidence." *Journal of Slavic Linguistics* 1, no. 2 (Summer-Fall 1993): 352-374. [Review article on Z. Golab, *The Origin of the Slavs* (Ohio: 1992).]

3820. Franks, Steven, and Katarzyna Dziwirek. "Negated Adjunct Phrases Are Really Partitive." *Journal of Slavic Linguistics* 1, no. 2 (Summer-Fall 1993): 280-305. [Versions of this paper were presented at the annual meetings of the American Association of Teachers of Slavic and East European Languages (New York, December 1992), the Formal Linguistics Society of Mid-America (Iowa City, April 1993), the Midwest Slavic Conference (East Lansing, May 1993) and the Canadian Linguistic Association (Ottawa, June 1993).]

3821. Hannan, Kevin. "The Language Question in Nineteenth-Century Moravia." *Czechoslovak and Central European Journal* 11, no. 2 (Winter 1993): 116-125.

3822. Janda, Laura A. *A Geography of Case Semantics: The Czech Dative and the Russian Instrumental.* Cognitive Linguistics Research, 4. Berlin; New York: Mouton de Gruyter, 1993. xiii, 225 pp.

3823. Kantor, Marvin. "On the 'Desire' to Hunt." *Journal of Slavic Linguistics* 1, no. 1 (Winter-Spring 1993): 83-91.

3824. Stankiewicz, Edward. *The Accentual Patterns of the Slavic Languages.* Stanford, CA: Stanford University Press, c1993. xxvi, 351 pp. REV: Tom Priestly, *Canadian*

Slavonic Papers 35, nos. 1-2 (March-June 1993): 198-200.

3825. Stoffel, Hans-Peter. "Slav migrant languages in the 'New World': cases of *Migranto-before-death?*" *Australian Slavonic and East European Studies* 7, no. 1 (1993): 75-89.

3826. Townsend, Charles E. [Review Article]. *Slavic and East European Journal* 37, no. 3 (Fall 1993): 363-369. [Review article on Karel Horálek, *Uvod do studia slovanskych jazyku* (Nottingham, England: 1992), translated by Peter Herrity.]

3827. Comrie, Bernard, and Greville G. Corbett, eds. *The Slavonic Languages*. Routledge Reference. Routledge Language Family Descriptions. London; New York: Routledge, 1993. xiii, 1078 pp.

East Slavic

General

3828. Mahota, William. "The Genitive Plural Endings in the East Slavic Languages." *Journal of Slavic Linguistics* 1, no. 2 (Summer-Fall 1993): 325-342.

Russian

3829. Andrews, David R. "American Intonational Interference in Emigre Russian: A Comparative Analysis of Elicited Speech Samples." *Slavic and East European Journal* 37, no. 2 (Summer 1993): 162-177.

3830. Andrews, Edna. "Interpretants and Linguistic Change: The Case of *-x* in Contemporary Standard Colloquial Russian." *Journal of Slavic Linguistics* 1, no. 2 (Summer-Fall 1993): 199-218.

3831. Babby, Leonard. "A Theta-Theoretic Analysis of *-en-* Suffixation in Russian." *Journal of Slavic Linguistics* 1, no. 1 (Winter-Spring 1993): 3-43.

3832. Beniukh, Oleg, and Ksana Beniukh. *Russian-English, English-Russian Dictionary*. Hippocrene Concise Dictionary. New York: Hippocrene Books, c1993. xi, 198, xix, iv, 209 pp.

3833. ———. *Russian-English, English-Russian Dictionary with Complete Phonetics*. New, rev. ed. Hippocrene Standard Dictionary. New York: Hippocrene Books, 1993. xi, 198, xx, iv, 209 pp. REV: James E. Bernhardt, *Modern Language Journal* 77, no. 4 (Winter 1993): 560.

3834. Beniukh, O. P., and G. V. Chernov. *Harrap's Pocket Russian*. New York: Prentice Hall, 1993. 576 pp.

3835. Benson, Morton. "A Proposal for the Simplification of Russian Orthography." *Slavic and East European Journal* 37, no. 4 (Winter 1993): 530-532.

3836. Benson, Morton, and Evelyn Benson. *Russian-English Dictionary of Verbal Collocations*. Amsterdam; Philadelphia, PA: J. Benjamins, 1993. xxii, 269 pp.

3837. Cooper, Brian. "Euphemism and Taboo of Language (With Particular Reference to Russian)." *Australian Slavonic and East European Studies* 7, no. 2 (1993): 61-84.

3838. Cubberley, Paul. "The phonological dynamics of foreign borrowings in Russian." *Australian Slavonic and East European Studies* 7, no. 1 (1993): 49-74.

3839. Dingley, John. "A New Grammar of Russian." *Canadian Slavonic Papers* 35, nos. 3-4 (September-December 1993): 385-394. [Review article on Terence Wade, *A Comprehensive Russian Grammar* (Oxford: 1992).]

3840. Feldstein, Ronald. "The Nature and Use of the Accentual Paradigm as Applied to Russian." *Journal of Slavic Linguistics* 1, no. 1 (Winter-Spring 1993): 44-60.

3841. Fowler, George, and Michael Yadroff. "The Argument Status of Accusative Measure Nominals in Russian." *Journal of Slavic Linguistics* 1, no. 2 (Summer-Fall 1993): 251-279.

3842. Gladney, Frank. "Russian *stanóvitsja* 'stands up' and *+i* Imperfective." *Journal of Slavic Linguistics* 1, no. 1 (Winter-Spring 1993): 61-79.

3843. Helden, W. Andries van. *Case and Gender: Concept Formation between Morphology and Syntax*. Studies in Slavic and General Linguistics, v. 20-21. Amsterdam; Atlanta, GA: Rodopi, 1993. 2 vols.

3844. Klapper, John. "Fleeting Prepositional *O* in the Contemporary Russian Language." *Russian Language Journal* 47, nos. 156-158 (Winter-Spring-Fall 1993): 17-33.

3845. Levine, James S. "Review Article." *Slavic and East European Journal* 37, no. 4 (Winter 1993): 564-563. [Review article on Nelleke Gerritsen, *Russian Reflexive Verbs. In Search of Unity in Diversity* (Atlanta, GA: 1990).]

3846. Mahota, William J. "Romance *re-* and Russian *voz-*." *Canadian Slavonic Papers* 35, nos. 3-4 (September-December 1993): 291-304.

3847. Mayer, Gerald L. "Teaching Russian Verb Conjugation: A Reappraisal." *Slavic and East European Journal* 37, no. 1 (Spring 1993): 85-97.

3848. Menlove, Darin Leo. "Teaching Russian Verbal Aspect: A Survey of Materials for Proficiency-Oriented Curricula." D.A. diss., State University of New York at Stony Brook, 1993. [UMI order no: AAC 9328156.]

3849. Mills, Margaret. "On Russian and English Pragmalinguistic Requestive Strategies." *Journal of Slavic Linguistics* 1, no. 1 (Winter-Spring 1993): 92-115.

3850. Morris, George W., Mark N. Vyatyutnev, and Lilia L. Vokhmina. *Russian Face to Face: A Communicative Program in Contemporary Russian: Level One*. Project director Dan E. Davidson. Lincolnwood, IL: National Textbook in cooperation with ACTR, 1993. 495 pp. REV: Benjamin Rifkin, *Modern Language Journal* 77, no. 4 (Winter 1993): 560-561.

3851. Pols, Adriana. *Varianty pristavochnykh glagolov nesovershennogo vida v russkom iazyke*. Studies in Slavic and General Linguistics, v. 19. Amsterdam; Atlanta, GA: Rodopi, 1993. 507 pp.

3852. Pugh, Stefan M. "More on Glides in Contemporary Standard Russian: The Loss of Intervocalic /j/ and /v/." *Journal of Slavic Linguistics* 1, no. 2 (Summer-Fall 1993): 343-351.

3853. Robblee, Karen E. "Individuation and Russian Agreement." *Slavic and East European Journal* 37, no. 4 (Winter 1993): 423-441.

3854. Williams, Adger. "The Argument Structure of *sja-* Predicates." *Journal of Slavic Linguistics* 1, no. 1 (Winter-Spring 1993): 167-190.

3855. Williams, E. Adger. "The So-Called Reflexive Marker *-sja* in Russian: Semantically Motivated Syntax and Cognitively Motivated Semantics." Ph.D. diss., University of California, Los Angeles, 1993.

3856. Windle, Kevin. [Review Article]. *Australian Slavonic and East European Studies* 7, no. 1 (1993): 123-135. [Review article on David Adshead, *Intermediate Russian Language Program: Contemporary Social Issues* (Melbourne: 1992).]

3857. Wu, YiYi. "Nekotorye voprosy o vremennykh predlozheniiakh s soiuzom poka." *Russian Language Journal* 47, nos. 156-158 (Winter-Spring-Fall 1993): 43-49.

3858. ———. "O valentnostiakh glagola i predikata." *Russian Language Journal* 47, nos. 156-158 (Winter-Spring-Fall 1993): 51-61.

Ruthenian

3859. Magocsi, Paul Robert. "Scholarly Seminar on the Codification of the Rusyn Language." *Canadian Review of Studies in Nationalism = Revue Canadienne des Etudes sur le Nationalisme* 20, nos. 1-2 (1993): 193-195. [Describes the First Congress of the Rusyn Language, organized by the Rusyn Renaissance Society (Presov, Slovakia) in cooperation with the Carpatho-Rusyn Research Center (United States), held November 6-7, 1992, in Bardejovské Kúpele, Slovakia.]

South Slavic

General

3860. Kabalin, Margaret Mary. "Vjekoslav Babukic: His Role As Linguist during the Illyrian Movement." Ph.D. diss., University of California, Berkeley, 1993. [UMI order no: AAC 9408022.]

Bulgarian

3861. Dyer, Donald L. "Determinedness and the Pragmatics of Bulgarian Sentence Structure." *Slavic and East European Journal* 37, no. 3 (Fall 1993): 273-292.

3862. Fielder, Grace E. *The Semantics and Pragmatics of Verbal Categories in Bulgarian*. Lewiston: Edwin Mellen Press, 1993. v, 441 pp. REV: Jane Hacking, *Canadian Slavonic Papers* 35, nos. 3-4 (September-December 1993): 417-418.

Macedonian

3863. Elson, Mark J. "Collocational Stress in Contemporary Standard Macedonian." *Slavic and East European Journal* 37, no. 2 (Summer 1993): 149-161.

Old Church Slavonic

3864. Hamp, Eric P. "OCS *Velii-velik'ii* and *-ok'*." *Journal of Slavic Linguistics* 1, no. 1 (Winter-Spring 1993): 80-82.

Serbo-Croatian

3865. Progovac, Ljiljana. "Locality and Subjunctive-Like Complements in Serbo-Croatian." *Journal of Slavic Linguistics* 1, no. 1 (Winter-Spring 1993): 116-144.

Slovene

3866. Gadányi, Károly. "From the History of Slovene 19th-Century Lexicography." *Slovene Studies* 14, no. 1 (1992, published March 1994): 3-8.

3867. Greenberg, Marc L. "Circumflex Advancement in Prekmurje and Beyond." *Slovene Studies* 14, no. 1 (1992, published March 1994): 69-91. [Preliminary version of this paper was presented at the Biennial Conference on Balkan and South Slavic Linguistics, Literatures and Folklore at the University of Chicago, April 9-11, 1992.]

West Slavic

General

3868. Hannan, Kevin. "Analogical Change in West Slavic *Be*." *Journal of Slavic Linguistics* 1, no. 2 (Summer-Fall 1993): 306-324.

3869. Pogonowski, Iwo C. *Polish-English, English-Polish Dictionary*. expanded 4th ed. Hippocrene Concise Dictionary. New York: Hippocrene Books, 1993. 239 pp.

Czech

3870. Chloupek, Jan, and Jiri Nekvapil, eds. *Studies in Functional Stylistics*. Contributions by Oldrich Leska, Jiri Nekvapil, Jan Chloupek, Karel Hausenblas, Otakar Soltys, Jiri Nekvapil, Frantisek Danes, Jiri Zeman, Alexandr Stich, and Jiri Kraus. Linguistic & Literary Studies in Eastern Europe, v. 36. Amsterdam; Philadelphia: J. Benjamins, 1993. 293 pp. [Contents: Oldrich Leska, Jiri Nekvapil and Otakar Soltys, "Prologue: Ferdinand de Saussure and the Prague Linguistic Circle"; Karel Hausenblas, "The Position of Style in Verbal Communication"; Jan Chloupek, "Language Varieties and Styles in Communication"; Alexandr Stich, "On the Beginnings of Modern Standard Czech"; Jiri Nekvapil, "Slang and Some Related Problems in Czech Linguistics"; Jan Chloupek, "Publicist Style"; Karel Hausenblas, "Semantic Contexts in a Poetical Work"; Frantisek Danes, "On the Stylistic Aspect of Coreferential Naming Chains"; Otakar Soltys, "The Position of Verbless Clauses in the System of Means of Czech Functional Styles"; Jiri Nekvapil, "On the Asymmetry between Syntactic and Elementary Textual Units"; Frantisek Danes, "The Language and Style of Hasek's Novel *The Good Soldier Svejk* from the Viewpoint of Translation"; Jiri Nekvapil and Jiri Zeman, "Conversion of 'Key Words' of English Song Lyrics into Czech"; Alexandr Stich, "On the Concept of Language Culture"; Jiri Kraus, "Rhetoric, Functional Stylistics and Theory of Language Culture"; Jiri Nekvapil, "Epilogue: On the Way to a General Stylistics of Human Activity."]

3871. Filip, Hana. "Aspect, Situation Types and Nominal Reference." Ph.D. diss., University of California, Berkeley, 1993. [UMI order no: AAC 9430470.]

3872. Rakusan, Jaromira. "Code Mixing as a Vehicle of Register: A Case of 'Old Chicago Czech.'" *Canadian Slavonic Papers* 35, nos. 3-4 (September-December 1993): 275-290.

Polish

3873. Mazur, Jan. *Geschichte der Polnischen Sprache.* Europäische Hochschulschriften. Reihe XVI, Slawische Sprachen und Literaturen = European University Studies. Series XVI, Slavonic Languages and Literatures, 44. Frankfurt am Main; New York: P. Lang, c1993. xi, 490 pp.

3874. Swan, Oscar E. "Notionality, Referentiality, and the Polish Verb 'BE.'" *Journal of Slavic Linguistics* 1, no. 1 (Winter-Spring 1993): 145-166.

Slovak

3875. Trnka, Nina. *Slovak-English, English-Slovak Dictionary.* Hippocrene Concise Dictionary. New York: Hippocrene Books, 1993. 359 pp.

■ Yiddish

3876. Goldberg, David, ed. *The Field of Yiddish: Studies in Language, Folklore, and Literature: Fifth Collection.* Contributions by Edward Stankiewicz, Christopher Hutton, Ellen F. Prince, Robert D. King, Neil G. Jacobs, Jean Baumgarten, David Goldberg, Daniela Mantovan, Dahlia Kaufman, Robert A. Rothstein, and Jeffrey Shandler. Evanston, IL: Northwestern University Press; New York: YIVO Institute for Jewish Research, c1993. viii, 327 pp. [Contents: Edward Stankiewicz, "The Yiddish Thematic Verbs," pp. 1-10; Christopher Hutton, "Normativism and the Notion of Authenticity in Yiddish Linguistics," pp. 11-57; Ellen F. Prince, "On the Discourse Functions of Syntactic Form in Yiddish; Expletive ES and Subject Positioning," pp. 59-86; Robert D. King, "Early Yiddish Vowel Systems: A Contribution by William G. Moulton to the Debate on the Origins of Yiddish," pp. 87-98; Neil G. Jacobs, "Central Yiddish Breaking and Drawl: The Implications of Fusion for a Phonological Rule," pp. 99-119; Jean Baumgarten, "Les Manuscrits Yidich de la Bibliothèque Nationale de Paris," pp. 121-151; David Goldberg, "Fantasy, Realism, and National Identity in Soviet Yiddish Juvenile Literature: Itsik Kipnis's Books for Children," pp. 153-202; Daniela Mantovan, "Der Nister's 'In vayn-keler': A Study in Metaphor," pp. 203-217; Dahlia Kaufman, "The First Yiddish Translation of *Julius Caesar*," pp. 219-242; Robert A. Rothstein, " 'Geyt a yid in shenkl arayn': Yiddish songs of Drunkenness," pp. 243-262; Jeffrey Shandler, " 'We Can Read and Understand': A Semiotic Analysis of the American Yiddish Primer and the Transformation of Literacy," pp. 263-301.]

3877. Schaechter, Mordkhe. *Yiddish II: An Intermediate and Advanced Textbook.* New York: Yiddish Language Resource Center, 1993. xxiii, 561 pp.

3878. ———. *Yidish tsevy: a lernbukh far mitndike un vaythalters.* Mit der redaktsyoneler hilf fun Avraham-Ya'akov Zaks. Nyu-York: Yidish-shprakhiker resursn-tsentr, Yidish-lige, 1993. 561, xxiii pp.

11 Literature

■ General

3879. Ari, Mark. *The Shoemaker's Tale*. 1st ed. Boston, MA: Zephyr Press, c1993. 245 pp.

3880. Batchelor, John Calvin. *Peter Nevsky and the True Story of the Russian Moon Landing: A Novel*. 1st ed. New York, NY: H. Holt and Co., 1993. 499 pp. REV: Terry Bisson, *Book World* 23, no. 17 (April 25, 1993): 3ff.

3881. Bayley, John. "Night Mail." *New York Review of Books* 40, no. 12 (June 24, 1993): 20-22. [Review article on Carolyn Forché, ed., *Against Forgetting: Twentieth-Century Poetry of Witness* (NY: 1993); includes Paul Celan and Miklós Radnoti.]

3882. Belentschikow, Valentin. *Russland und die Deutschen Expressionisten 1910-1925: Zur Geschichte der Deutsch-Russischen Literaturbeziehungen*. Europäische Hochschulschriften. Reihe XVIII, Vergleichende Literaturwissenschaft = European University Studies. Series XVIII, Comparative Literature, 73. Frankfurt am Main; New York: P. Lang, c1993-. vols. [A revision of the 1st pt. of the author's Habilitationsschrift—Universitat Potsdam, 1990.]

3883. Bell, Pearl K. "Fiction Chronicle." *Partisan Review* 60, no. 1 (Winter 1993): 63-77. [On Günter Grass, *The Call of the Toad* (NY: 1992) and Julian Barnes, *The Porcupine* (NY: 1992).]

3884. Bennett, Guy. "A Study in Avant-Garde Experimentalism: The Poetic Theory and Praxis of the Futurist, Cubo-Futurist, Dada, and Surrealist Groups." Ph.D. diss., University of California at Los Angeles, 1993. [UMI order no: AAC 9332638.]

3885. Boone, Troy. " 'He is English and Therefore Adventurous': Politics, Decadence, and Dracula." *Studies in the Novel* 25, no. 1 (Spring 1993): 76-91.

3886. Bushnell, Kristine. "Language As Activity. Formalism, the Bakhtin Circle, and the Debt to Humboldt and Potebnia." Ph.D. diss., Indiana University, 1993. [UMI order no: AAC 9410405.]

3887. Crnkovic, Gordana P. "American, English, and Eastern European Literature Against Closure: A Dialogical Perspective." Ph.D. diss., Stanford University, 1993. [UMI order no: AAC 9403925.]

3888. Croxen, Kevin Lee. "Slavic Neo-Latin Literature and the Vernaculars During the First Stage of the Slavic Baroque." Ph.D. diss., Harvard University, 1993. [UMI order no: AAC 9330890.]

3889. Cummins, Walter, comp. and ed. *Shifting Borders: East European Poetries of the Eighties*. Section editors Doris Kareva, Aina Kraujiete, Rimvydas Silbajoris, Ludmila Popova-Wightman, E. J. Czerwinski, Stana Dolezal, Bruce Berlind, Daniel Bourne, Stravros Deligioris, Larissa M. L. Z. Onyshkevych, and Ales Debeljak. Rutherford, NJ: Fairleigh Dickinson University Press; London; Toronto: Associated University Presses, c1993. 481 pp. [Partial contents: Poetry of the Baltic Republics; Poetry of the Central European States; Poetry of the South Slavs.]

3890. Dorovsky, Ivan. "The European Literary Process and Writers' Dual Residence." *Czechoslovak and Central European Journal* 11, no. 2 (Winter 1993): 71-80.

3891. Drozdowski, Piotr J. "Echoes of the Polish Revolution in Late Eighteenth and Early Nineteenth Century English Literature, Part II." *Polish Review* 38, no. 2 (1993): 131-148.

3892. Fallows, Randall. "Dramatic Realities: The Creation and Reception of American Political and Fictional Dramas of the Late 1940's and Their Influence on Gender Role Construction." Ph.D. diss., University of California, San Diego, Department of Literature, 1993.

3893. Filbin, Thomas. "Eurofiction, Interest Rates, and the Balance of Trade Problem." *Hudson Review* 46, no. 3 (Autumn 1993): 587-592. [Review article on Jaan Kross, *The Czar's Madman*, trans. Anselm Hollo (Pantheon Books); Ewa Kuryluk, *Century 21* (Dalkey Archive); and works by Colm Tóibín, Alan Lightman, and others.]

3894. Fleming, Juliet. [Book Review]. *Book World (Washington Post)* 23, no. 40 (October 3, 1993): 5. [Review article on D.M. Thomas, *Pictures at an Exhibition* (NY: Scribner's, 1993).]

3895. Forché, Carolyn, ed. *Against Forgetting: Twentieth-Century Poetry of Witness*. 1st ed. New York: W.W. Norton, c1993. 812 pp. [Includes Anna Akhmatova, Joseph Brodsky, Paul Celan, Langston Hughes, Osip Mandelshtam, Siamento, and Vahan Tekeyan.] REV: John Bayley, *New York Review of Books* 50, no. 12 (June 24, 1993): 20-22. Matthew Rothschild, *Progressive* 57, no. 10 (October 1993): 45-46.

3896. George, Emery. "Brilliance at Midnight: Arthur Koestler (1905-1983)." *Cross Currents: A Yearbook of Central European Culture*, no. 12 (1993): 42-53.

3897. Kennedy, Thomas E. "Introduction: Baltic Literature After Communism: Contemporary Prose and Poetry from Lithuania, Latvia, and Estonia." *Cimarron Review*, no. 104 (July 1993): 9-10. [Introduction to special feature section.]

3898. Longinovic, Tomislav Z. *Borderline Culture: The Politics of Identity in Four Twentieth-Century Slavic Novels.* Fayetteville, AR: University of Arkansas Press, 1993. xiii, 197 pp. [Contents: Introduction: Origins of Borderline Poetics in Slavic Culture; Gnosis, Power, and Writing in *The Master and Margarita*; Modernity, Gender, and Identity in *Ferdydurke*; History, Performance, and Horror in *The Tomb for Boris Davidovich*; Lyricism, Motherhood and Abjection in *Life Is Elsewhere*; The Rise of the Nation: From the Margin to the Center.]

3899. Lorme, Anna. *A Traitor's Daughter: A Novel.* Translated by Robert Bononno. French Expressions Series. New York: Holmes & Meier, 1993. 197 pp. [Translation of: *Une fille de traitre.*]

3900. Marx, Bill. "Gurus and Gadflies." *Parnassus* 18, no. 2 & 19, no. 1 (1993-1994): 100-120. [Review article on Adam Zagajewski, *Canvas* (New York: Farrar Straus Giroux, 1991); Czeslaw Milosz, *Provinces* (New York: Ecco Press, 1991); Miroslav Holub, *Vanishing Lung Syndrome* (Oberlin, OH: Oberlin College Press, 1990); Tadeusz Rózewicz, *They Came to See a Poet* (London: Anvil Press Poetry, 1991); Piotr Sommer, *Things to Translate & Other Poems* (Bloodaxe Books, 1991).]

3901. Okenfuss, Max J. "The Ages of Man on the Seventeenth-Century Muscovite Frontier." *Historian* 56, no. 1 (Autumn 1993): 87-104.

3902. Peroomian, Rubina. *Literary Responses to Catastrophe: A Comparison of the Armenian and the Jewish Experience.* Studies in Near Eastern Culture and Society, 8. Atlanta, GA: Scholars Press, c1993. x, 238 pp. [Contents: 1. Armenian and Jewish Traditional Responses to Catastrophe. The Concept of Sin and Punishment. The Sense of Shame and Humiliation. The Concept of Martyrdom. Perception and Treatment of Martyrdom. Secularization of Martyrdom; 2. Impact of the Renaissance on the Paradigm of Responses. New Response in Armenian Renaissance Literature. Jewish Cantonist Literature. The Armenian Vernacular. The 1880s; 3. Rehearsal For Genocide; 4. Zapel Esayan (1878-1942?). Amid the Ruins. Imagery. Characters. Revival as a Response. The Genocide; 5. Suren Partevian (1876-1921). The Cilician Catastrophe. The Armenian Woman. The Book of Blood. Literature of the 1915 Genocide; 6. Aram Antonian (1875-1951). Realistic Portrayal of the Armenian Tragedy. What Price Survival? Class Differences: A New Motif; 7. Hakob Oshakan (1883-1948). Biographical Sketch. Imperial Song of Triumph. Remnants. The Character of the Turk. The Character of the Armenian. Foreign Influence in Armeno-Turkish Relations. The Monotony of Genocide Literature. Conclusion.]

3903. Pynsent, Robert B., and S. I. Kanikova, ed. *Reader's Encyclopedia of Eastern European Literature.* 1st ed. New York, NY: HarperCollins, 1993. xiv, 605 pp. [Published in the U.K. in 1993 under the title: *The Everyman Companion to East European Literature.*] REV: Anna Otten, *Antioch Review* 51, no. 4 (Fall 1993): 649.

3904. Rhodes, Chip. "Education as Liberation: The Case of Anzia Yezierska's *Bread Givers.*" *Science & Society* 57, no. 3 (Fall 1993): 294-312.

3905. Rothschild, Matthew. "Words of Defiance." *Progressive* 57, no. 10 (October 1993): 45-46. [Review article on Carolyn Forché, ed., *Against Forgetting: Twentieth Century Poetry of Witness* (W.W. Norton).]

3906. Siebers, Tobin. *Cold War Criticism and the Politics of Skepticism.* Odeon. New York: Oxford University Press, 1993. xi, 163 pp. [Contents: 1. Introduction: The Politics of Skepticism; 2. Cold War Criticism; 3. Ethics or Politics? Comparative Literature, Multiculturalism, and Cultural Literacy; 4. Mourning Becomes Paul de Man; 5. The Politics of the Politics of Interpretation; 6. The Politics of Storytelling: Hannah Arendt's Eichmann in Jerusalem; 7. Conclusion: Toward a Post-Cold War Criticism.]

3907. Tempest, Snejana Jane. "Water: Folk Belief, Ritual and the East Slavic Wondertale." Ph.D. diss., Yale University, 1993. [UMI order no: AAC 9400375.]

3908. Thomas, D. M. *Pictures at an Exhibition.* 1st American ed. New York: Scribner's; Toronto: Maxwell Macmillan Canada; New York: Maxwell Macmillan International, 1993. 278 pp. REV: Frederick Busch, *New York Times Book Review* 98, no. 44 (October 31, 1993): 13-14. Juliet Fleming, *Book World* 23, no. 40 (October 3, 1993): 5.

Literary Figures

Conrad

3909. Bivona, Daniel. "Conrad's Bureaucrats: Agency, Bureaucracy and the Problem of Intention." *Novel* 26, no. 2 (Winter 1993): 151-169.

3910. Carabine, Keith, Owen Knowles, and Wieslaw Krajka, eds. *Contexts for Conrad.* Contributions by Wieslaw Krajka, Katarzyna Sokolowska, Eloise Knapp Hay, Ernest W. Sullivan III, Alex Kurczaba, G. W. Stephen Brodsky, Heliéna M. Krenn, Gail Fraser, Padmini Mongia, Paul B. Armstrong, Richard Ruppel, Peter L. Caracciolo, William Bonney, Paul Hollywood, and Ivo Vidan. Conrad, Eastern and Western Perspectives, v. 2. East European Monographs, no. 370. Boulder, CO: East European Monographs; Lublin: Maria Curie-Sklodowska University; New York: Distributed by Columbia University Press, 1993. 285 pp. [Contents: Wieslaw Krajka and Katarzyna Sokolowska, "Conrad's Polish Footprints," pp. 3-20; Eloise Knapp Hay, "Reconstructing 'East' and 'West' in Conrad's Eyes," pp. 21-40; Wieslaw Krajka, "Conrad and Poland: Under the Eyes of My Generation," pp. 41-56; Ernest W. Sullivan III, "Joseph Conrad Tries to Prove Who He Is: Life Insurance Form as Autobiography," pp. 57-71; Alex Kurczaba, "Gombrowicz and Conrad: The Question of Autobiography," pp. 73-86; G.W. Stephen Brodsky, "The Conrad Harlequinade: Bakhtin, Rabelais, and Conrad's Comic Spirit," pp. 87-101; Heliéna M. Krenn, "The 'Beautiful' World of Women: Women as Reflections of Colonial Issues in Conrad's Malay Novels," pp. 105-119; Gail Fraser, "Empire of the Senses: Miscegenation in *An Outcast of the Islands*," pp. 121-133; Padmini Mongia, "Empire, Narrative and the Feminine in

Lord Jim and *Heart of Darkness*," pp. 135-150; Paul B. Armstrong, "Misogyny and the Ethics of Reading: The Problem of Conrad's *Chance*," pp. 151-174; Richard Ruppel, "The Lagoon and the Popular Exotic Tradition," pp. 177-187; Peter L. Caracciolo, "The Use of the Expatrial Allusion in Conrad's Fiction," pp. 189-205; William Bonney, "Conrad's *Nostromo*: Money and Mystification on the Frontier," pp. 207-242; Paul Hollywood, "Conrad and Anarchist Theories of Language," pp. 243-264; Ivo Vidan, "Conrad and Thomas Mann," pp. 265-285.]

3911. Livingston, Robert Eric. "Seeing Through Reading: Class, Race and Literary Authority in Joseph Conrad's *The Nigger of the 'Narcissus.'*" *Novel* 26, no. 2 (Winter 1993): 133-150.

3912. Said, Edward W. *Culture and Imperialism*. New York: Alfred A. Knopf, 1993. xxviii, 380 pp. [Includes discussion of *Heart of Darkness* and other novels by Conrad.] REV: Camille Paglia, *Book World* 23, no. 10 (March 7, 1993): 1. Andrew J. Pierre, *Foreign Affairs* 72, no. 3 (Summer 1993): 194-195.

3913. Schwarz, Daniel R. [Book Review]. *Studies in the Novel* 25, no. 1 (Spring 1993): 108-111. [Review article on Daphna Erdinast-Vulcan, *Joseph Conrad and the Modern Temper* (Oxford: 1991).]

3914. Shaffer, Brian W. " 'Rebarbarizing Civilization': Conrad's African Fiction and Spencerian Sociology." *PMLA: Publications of the Modern Language Association of America* 108, no. 1 (January 1993): 45-58.

Simic

3915. Matthias, John. "The Singer of Tales." *North Dakota Quarterly* 61, no. 1 (Winter 1993): 110-111. ["For Charles Simic."]

3916. Simic, Charles. "Leaves." *Grand Street* 12, no. 1 (45) (1993): 45.

3917. ———. "On Not Thinking About Nature." *Harper's* 287, no. 1719 (August 1993): 28-29. [From "Fried Sausage," an essay by the author in *Ohio Review* (Winter).]

Wiesel

3918. Cargas, Harry James, ed. *Telling the Tale: A Tribute to Elie Wiesel on the Occasion of his 65th Birthday: Essays, Reflections, and Poems*. Contributions by Gail M. Gendler, Louis Daniel Brodsky, Franklin H. Littell, Dorothy Soelle, John K. Roth, William Heyden, Leo Eitinger, Harry J. Cargas, Elie Wiesel, Emil L. Fackenheim, Paul Braunstein, Alan L. Berger, and Bob Costas. 1st ed. St. Louis, MO: Time Being Books, c1993. 169 pp. [Contents: Harry J. Cargas, "Interview with Elie Wiesel"; Gail M. Gendler, "Elie Wiesel: a biographical overview"; E. Wiesel, "Marginal thoughts on Yiddish"; Harry J. Cargas, "Can we bring the Messiah? An interview..."; Louis Daniel Brodsky, "Twelve poems of the Holocaust"; Franklin H. Littell, "Proclaiming the silence"; Dorothy Soelle, "Re-remembering: in honor of Elie Wiesel"; John K. Roth, "From Night to Twilight: A philosopher's reading of E. Wiesel"; E. Wiesel,

"When an eye says Kaddish"; William Heyden, "To bring hope and help"; Leo Eitinger, "Trees"; Harry J. Cargas, "Night as autobiobiography"; E. Wiesel, "Three poems"; Emil L. Fackenheim, "Jew of fidelity"; Paul Braunstein, "E. Wiesel: a lasting impression"; Alan L. Berger, "E. Wiesel's second-generation witness: passing the torch of remembrance"; Bob Costas, "A wound that will never be healed: an interview..."; E. Wiesel, "Memories of Jerusalem."]

■ Albanian

3919. Elsie, Robert, ed. and trans. *Anthology of Modern Albanian Poetry: An Elusive Eagle Soars*. London; Boston, MA: Forest Books, 1993. xx, 213 pp. [Authorized by the Albanian National Commission for UNESCO.]

3920. Kadare, Ismail. *The Palace of Dreams*. Translated by Barbara Bray. 1st ed. New York, NY: William Morrow and Company, 1993. 205 pp. [Translation of: *Nepunesi i pallatit te endrrave*. Novel written in Albanian and translated from the French of Jusuf Vrioni by Bray.]

■ Armenian

3921. Davtian, Vahakn. "Lament for Charents." *Ararat* 34, no. 2 (no. 134) (Spring 1993): 12-13.

3922. Harutiunyan, Artem. [Two Poems]. *Ararat* 34, no. 3 (no. 135) (Summer 1993): 32-33. Translated by Tatul Sonentz. ["I'm Still Returning," p. 32, and "Warning," p. 34.]

3923. Russell, James. "A Lament for Charents." *Ararat* 34, no. 2 (no. 134) (Spring 1993): 12.

■ Bulgarian

3924. Bagryana, Elisaveta. [Poems]. *Cimarron Review*, no. 102 (January 1993): 18-20.

3925. Barnes, Julian. *The Porcupine*. 1st Vintage International ed. New York: Vintage International, 1993. 138 pp. [First published in Bulgarian, under the title *Bodlivo svinche*.]

3926. Karageorge, Yuri Vidov. "Three Bulgarian Poets." *Cimarron Review*, no. 102 (January 1993): 7-17. [On Elisaveta Bagryana, Nevena Stefanova, and Snezhina Slavova.]

3927. Slavova, Snezhina. [Poems]. *Cimarron Review*, no. 102 (January 1993): 23-24.

3928. Stefanova, Nevena. [Poems]. *Cimarron Review*, no. 102 (January 1993): 21-22.

3929. Stoianova, Danila. "From *Memory of a Dream*." *Literary Review* 37, no. 1 (Fall 1993): 85. Translated from the Bulgarian by Ludmilla Popova-Wightman. ["When the hills swell" and "On the marble terrace."]

■ Czech and Slovak

General

3930. Drabelle, Dennis. "The Engineer As Novelist." *Atlantic* 271, no. 5 (May 1993): 122-124. [Review article on Vladimír Páral, *Catapult: A Timetable of Rail, Sea, and Air Ways to Paradise,* William Harkins, trans. (Highland Park, NJ: 1989); and Vladimír Páral, *The Four Sonyas,* William Harkins, trans. (North Haven, CT: 1993).]

3931. Hodrová, Daniela. "Inner Place." *Czechoslovak and Central European Journal* 11, no. 2 (Winter 1993): 60-70. Translated from the Czech by Charles Townsend. [Article based on a paper presented at the World Congress of SVU, Prague, June 1992.]

3932. Hrabal, Bohumil. *The Little Town Where Time Stood Still; and, Cutting It Short.* Translated from the Czech by James Naughton. Introduction by Josef Skvorecky. 1st American ed. New York: Pantheon Books, c1993. xviii, 302 pp. [Translation of *Mestecko, kde se zastavil cas*; and, *Postriziny*.] REV: Miklós Vámos, *Nation* 257, no. 14 (November 1, 1993): 508-510.

3933. Kuehn, Heinz R. "Max Brod." *American Scholar* 62, no. 2 (Spring 1993): 269-276.

3934. Páral, Vladimír. *The Four Sonyas.* Translated from the Czech by William Harkins. 1st English-Language ed. Highland Park, NJ: Catbird Press, 1993. 391 pp. REV: Dennis Drabelle, *Atlantic* 271, no. 5 (May 1993): 122-124. Richard Lourie, *Book World* 23, no. 10 (March 7, 1993): 11. Karen von Kunes, *World Literature Today* 67, no. 3 (Summer 1993): 631-632.

3935. Polacek, Karel. *What Ownership's All About.* Translated from the Czech and introduced by Peter Kussi. 1st English-language ed. North Haven, CT: Catbird Press, 1993. 238 pp. REV: *New Yorker* 69, no. 36 (November 1, 1993): 131.

3936. Simecka, Martin M. *The Year of the Frog: A Novel.* Translated by Peter Petro. Foreword by Václav Havel. Pegasus Prize for Literature. Baton Rouge, LA: Louisiana State University, 1993. viii, 247 pp. REV: Elizabeth Gaffney, *New York Times Book Review* 98, no. 44 (October 31, 1993): 40.

Literary Figures

Holub

3937. Holub, Miroslav. "The Autumn Orchard." *Partisan Review* 60, no. 3 (Summer 1993): 419. Translated by Dana Habova and David Young.

3938. ———. "The Journey." *Partisan Review* 60, no. 3 (Summer 1993): 418-419. Translated by David Young and Miroslav Holub.

3939. ———. "Nature, Green in Tooth and Claw." *Harper's* 286, no. 1716 (May 1993): 26-27. [Excerpt from author's *Symbolic Tranquility* (forthcoming).]

Klíma

3940. Banville, John. "Living in the Shadows." *New York Review of Books* 40, no. 13 (July 15, 1993): 23-24. [Review article on Ivan Klíma, *Judge on Trial* (NY: 1993).]

3941. Goetz-Stankiewicz, M. "*Love and Garbage*: Can Ivan Klíma Do without an Adjective?" *Czechoslovak and Central European Journal* 11, no. 2 (Winter 1993): 91-102.

3942. Klíma, Ivan. *Judge on Trial.* Translated from the Czech by A. G. Brain. 1st American ed. New York: Alfred A. Knopf, 1993. 549 pp. [Translation of *Soudce z milosti*.] REV: John Banville, *New York Review of Books* 40, no. 13 (July 15, 1993): 23-24. Malcolm Bradbury, *New York Times Book Review* 98, no. 16 (April 18, 1993): 1ff. Dennis Drabelle, *Book World* 23, no. 16 (April 18, 1993): 6. John Updike, *New Yorker* 69, no. 19 (June 28, 1993): 99-102.

Kundera

3943. Drozd, Andrew M. "Polyphony in Kundera's *The Joke*." *Czechoslovak and Central European Journal* 11, no. 2 (Winter 1993): 81-90.

3944. Kundera, Milan. "Three Contexts of Art: From Nation to World." *Cross Currents: A Yearbook of Central European Culture*, no. 12 (1993): 5-14. Translated from the Czech by Peter Kussi.

3945. Misurella, Fred. *Understanding Milan Kundera: Public Events, Private Affairs.* Columbia, SC: University of South Carolina Press, c1993. xv, 216 pp. REV: Howard Eiland, *South Atlantic Review* 58, no. 4 (November 1993): 167-169.

3946. Thorpe, Michael. "Kundera's 'Black Flower.'" *Dalhousie Review* 73, no. 4 (Winter 1993-1994): 545.

3947. Wilhelmus, Tom. "Time and Distance." *Hudson Review* 46, no. 1 (Spring 1993): 247-255. [Review article on Milan Kundera, *The Joke* (HarperCollins) and works by Doris Lessing, Susan Sontag, and others.]

■ Estonian

3948. Ilmet, Peep. [Poems]. *Cimarron Review*, no. 104 (July 1993): 58-60. Translated by Krista Kaer. ["The Present is Like Sailcloth," p. 58; "The Oak Screams Out," p. 58; and "In Retreat," p. 59.]

3949. Kareva, Doris. [Poems]. *Cimarron Review*, no. 104 (July 1993): 60-61. Translated by Thomas H. Ilves. ["The Night Left A Scent," p. 60; "Her Quiet Words Let Loose," p. 60; "There Shall Come No Other and Better World," p. 61.]

3950. Kross, Jaan. *The Czar's Madman: A Novel.* Translated by Anselm Hollo. New York: Pantheon, c1993. 362 pp. [Translation of *Keisri hull*.] REV: Thomas Filbin, *Hudson Review* 46, no. 3 (Autumn 1993): 587-592. W. S. Kuniczak, *New York Times Book Review* 98, no. 4 (January 24, 1993): 12.

3951. Kuik, Valentin. "A Message." *Cimarron Review*, no. 104 (July 1993): 65-69. Translated by Krista Kaer.

3952. Langemets, Andres. "Estonia: East of the West, West of the East." *Cimarron Review*, no. 104 (July 1993): 53-54.

3953. Mutt, Mikael. "My Florakin, My Faunakin." *Cimarron Review*, no. 104 (July 1993): 62-64. Translated by Elmar Maripuu.

3954. Rummo, Paul-Eerik. [Poems]. *Cimarron Review*, no. 104 (July 1993): 55-57. Translated by Krista Kaer. ["An Ordinary Madman," p. 55; "A Quiet Madman," pp. 55-56; "A Raving Madman," pp. 56-57; "Normal People," p. 57.]

3955. Unt, Mati. "Via Regia." *Literary Review* 36, no. 2 (Winter 1993): 191-237. Translated from the Estonian by Mardi Valgemäe.

3956. Valgemäe, Mardi. "The Antic Disposition of a Finno-Ugric Novelist." *Journal of Baltic Studies* 24, no. 4 (Winter 1993): 389-394. [Jaan Kross.]

■ German

General

3957. Anderson, Susan C. "Walls and Other Obstacles: Peter Schneider's Critique of Unity in *Der Mauerspringer*." *German Quarterly* 66, no. 3 (Summer 1993): 362-371.

3958. Bangerter, Lowell A. "Anna Seghers and Christa Wolf." *Germanic Review* 68, no. 3 (Summer 1993): 127-132.

3959. Brockmann, Stephen. "A Literary Civil War." *Germanic Review* 68, no. 2 (Spring 1993): 69-78.

3960. Felstiner, John. " 'Clawed into Each Other': Jewish vs. Christian Memory in Paul Celan's 'Tenebrae.' " *TriQuarterly*, no. 87 (Spring-Summer 1993): 193-208.

3961. Fox, Thomas C. *Border Crossings: An Introduction to East German Prose*. Ann Arbor, MI: University of Michigan Press, c1993. xiv, 335 pp. [Contents: 1. Remembering the Past; 2. Forms of Protest: Early Experiments or the Politics of Epistemology; 3. Adjustment to the Quotidian: The Literature of Reform; 4. Beyond the Limits of the Permissible: The Literature of Dissent; 5. Socialist Feminism: The Example of Christa Wolf; 6. The Artist as Hero: The German-American Writer Stefan Heym; 7. Erasing Borders: The Literature of Convergence; Chronology of Cultural/Political Events.]

3962. Geulen, Eva. "The End of Art—Again: Afterthoughts on the German *Literaturstreit*." *Telos* 26, no. 1 (no. 95) (Spring 1993): 171-180.

3963. Ghossein, Mirene. "The Problematic of the Fragment in Twentieth Century Poetry: A Reader's Response." Ph.D. diss., Columbia University, 1993. [UMI order no: AAC 9412756.]

3964. Hawes, J. M. *Nietzsche and the End of Freedom: The Neo-Romantic Dilemma in Kafka, the Brothers Mann, Rilke and Musil, 1904-1914*. Historisch-Kritische Arbeiten zur Deutschen Literatur, Bd. 13. Frankfurt am Main; New York: Lang, c1993. 196 pp.

3965. Ibsch, Elrud, Ferdinand van Ingen, and Anthonya Visser. *Literatur und Politische Aktualitat*. Amsterdamer Beitrage zur Neueren Germanistik, Bd. 36. Amsterdam; Atlanta GA: Rodopi, 1993. 457 pp.

3966. Lewis, Alison. " 'Foiling the Censor': Reading and Transference as Feminist Strategies in the Works of Christa Wolf, Irmtraud Morgner, and Christa Moog." *German Quarterly* 66, no. 3 (Summer 1993): 372-386. [Article is in German and English.]

3967. Lorenz, Dagmar C. G. "The Unspoken Bond: Else Lasker-Schüler and Gertrud Kolmar in their Historical and Cultural Context." *Seminar: A Journal of Germanic Studies* 29, no. 4 (November 1993): 349-369.

3968. Ludde, Marie-Elisabeth. *Die Rezeption, Interpretation und Transformation Biblischer Motive und Mythen in Der DDR-Literatur und Ihre Bedeutung fur die Theologie*. Arbeiten zur Praktischen Theologie, Bd. 4. Berlin; New York: W. de Gruyter, 1993. vi, 178 pp. [Originally presented as the author's thesis (doctoral)— Greifswald, 1990.]

3969. Lukens, Nancy, and Dorothy Rosenberg, trans. and eds. *Daughters of Eve: Women's Writing from the German Democratic Republic*. Contributions by Dorothy Rosenberg, Gerti Tetzner, Renate Apitz, Maxie Wander, Charlotte Worgitzky, Christa Müller, Christine Wolter, Helga Schütz, Christa Wolf, Irmtraud Morgner, Helga Königsdorf, Rosemarie Zeplin, Daniela Dahn, Irene Böhme, Christiane Grosz, Monika Helmecke, Helga Schubert, Beate Morgenstern, Maria Seidemann, Angela Stachowa, Angela Krauss, Gabriele Eckart, Petra Werner, Maja Wiens, Katja Lange-Müller, and Doris Paschiller. European Women Writers Series. Lincoln, NE: University of Nebraska Press, c1993. xi, 329 pp. [Contents: Dorothy Rosenberg, "Introduction: Women, Social Policy, and Literature in the German Democratic Republic," pp. 1-22; Gerti Tetzner, "Karen W.," pp. 23-29; Renate Apitz, "Harmonious Elsa," pp. 31-38; Maxie Wander, "Ute G., 24, Skilled Worker, Single, One Child," pp. 39-48; Charlotte Worgitzky, "I Quit," pp. 49-60; Christa Müller, "Candida," pp. 61-94; Christine Wolter, "Early Summer," pp. 95-102; Helga Schütz, "In Anna's Name," pp. 103-109; Christa Wolf, "Revised Philosophy of a Tomcat," pp. 111-133; Irmtraud Morgner, "Third Fruit of Bitterfeld: The Tightrope," pp. 135-142; Helga Königsdorf, "The Surefire Tip," pp. 143-150; Rosemarie Zeplin, "The Shadow of a Lover," pp. 151-163; Daniela Dahn, "The Contemporary Feminine," pp. 165-168; Irene Böhme, "Women and Socialism: Four Interviews," pp. 169-177; Christiane Grosz, "The Trick," pp. 179-183; Monika Helmecke, "September 30th," pp. 185-191; Helga Schubert, "Breathing Room," pp. 193-199; Beate Morgenstern, "The Other Side of the Boulevard," pp. 201-214; Maria

Seidemann, "The Bridge Builder," pp. 215-224; Angela
Stachowa, "Talking about My Girlfriend Resa," pp. 225-233;
Angela Krauss, "Work," pp. 235-247; Gabriele Eckart, "Ilse,
56, Chairperson of an Agricultural Cooperative," pp. 249-
262; Petra Werner, "Lies Have Bright Wings," pp. 263-282;
Maja Wiens, "Dream Limits," pp. 283-291; Katja Lange-
Müller, "Sometimes Death Comes in Slippers," pp. 293-302;
Doris Paschiller, "Dignity," pp. 303-312.]

3970. Maron, Monika. *Silent close no. 6.* Translated
by David Newton Marinelli. Columbia, LA: Readers International, c1993. 184 pp. [Translation of *Stille Zeile sechs.*]
REV: Rand Richards Cooper, *New York Times Book Review*
98, no. 26 (June 27, 1993): 11.

3971. Mews, Siegfried. "After the Fall of the Berlin
Wall: German Writers and Unification." *South Atlantic
Review* 58, no. 2 (May 1993): 1-19.

3972. Miron, Susan. "On Joseph Roth." *Salmagundi*, nos. 98-99 (Spring-Summer 1993): 198-206.

3973. Pape, Walter. *1870/71-1989/90: German
Unifications and the Change of Literary Discourse.* European Cultures, v. 1. Berlin; New York: W. de Gruyter,
1993. iv, 382 pp.

3974. Peters, Peter. *Ich Wer Ist Das: Aspekte Der
Subjektdiskussion in Prosa und Drama der DDR (1976-
1989).* Literarhistorische Untersuchungen, Bd. 22. Frankfurt am Main; New York: P. Lang, c1993. x, 310 pp.

3975. Petersen, Vibeke Rützou. "Zillich's End: The
Formation of a Fascist Character in Anna Seghers's *Das
Ende.*" *Seminar: A Journal of Germanic Studies* 29, no. 4
(November 1993): 370-381.

3976. Robinson, David W. "Abortion as Repression
in Christoph Hein's *The Distant Lover.*" *New German
Critique*, no. 58 (Winter 1993): 65-78.

3977. Sonntag, Martina. "German Exile Literature,
1933-1945 in the College Curriculum." D.A. diss., State
University of New York at Stony Brook, 1993. [UMI order
no: AAC 9331980.]

3978. Spengler, Tilman. *Lenin's Brain.* Translated
by Shaun Whiteside. 1st ed. New York: Farrar, Straus,
Giroux, 1993. 266 pp. [Translation of: *Lenins Hirn* (Reinbek
bei Hamburg: Rowohlt, 1991).] REV: John Vernon, *New
York Times Book Review* 98, no. 35 (August 29, 1993): 22.

3979. Vogt, Jochen. "Have the Intellectuals Failed?
On the Sociopolitical Claims and the Influence of Literary
Intellectuals in West Germany." *New German Critique*, no.
58 (Winter 1993): 3-23.

3980. Zweig, Stefan. "The Tower of Babel." *Cross
Currents: A Yearbook of Central European Culture*, no. 12
(1993): 1-4. Translated and presented by Harry Zohn.

Literary Figures

Grass

3981. Frye, Lawrence O. "Günter Grass, *Katz und
Maus*, and Gastro-narratology." *Germanic Review* 68, no. 4
(Fall 1993): 176-184.

3982. Nemoto, Reiko Tachibana. "Günter Grass's
The Tin Drum and Oe Kenzaburo's *My Tears*: A Study in
Convergence." *Contemporary Literature* 34, no. 4 (Winter
1993): 740-766.

3983. ———. "On Two Interviews between Günter
Grass and Oe Kenzaburo." *World Literature Today* 67, no. 2
(Spring 1993): 301-305.

3984. Shafi, Monika. "Günter Grass' Zunge zeigen
als postmoderner Reisebericht." *German Quarterly* 66, no. 3
(Summer 1993): 339-349.

Johnson

3985. Baker, Gary Lee. "(Anti-)Utopian Elements
in Uwe Johnson's *Jahrestage:* Traces of Ernst Bloch."
Germanic Review 68, no. 1 (Winter 1993): 32-45.

3986. ———. "The Influence of Walter Benjamin's
Notion of Allegory on Uwe Johnson's *Jahrestage:* Form and
Approach to History." *German Quarterly* 66, no. 3 (Summer
1993): 318-329.

3987. Bond, D. G. *German History and German
Identity: Uwe Johnson's Jahrestage.* Amsterdamer
Publikationen zur Sprache und Literatur, Bd. 104.
Amsterdam; Atlanta, GA: Rodopi, 1993. 232 pp.

3988. Fickert, Kurt. "The Reunification Theme in
Johnson's *Das dritte Buch über Achim.*" *German Studies
Review* 16, no. 2 (May 1993): 225-233.

Kafka

3989. Alter, Robert. "Kafka as Kabbalist." *Salmagundi*, nos. 98-99 (Spring-Summer 1993): 86-99.

3990. Benson, Peter. "Entering *The Castle.*"
Journal of Narrative Technique 23, no. 2 (Spring 1993): 80-
91.

3991. Fickert, Kurt. "Kafka's Addenda to 'In der
Strafkolonie.'" *University of Dayton Review* 22, no. 1
(Spring 1993): 115-121.

3992. Goebel, Rolf J. "Constructing Chinese
History: Kafka's and Dittmar's Orientalist Discourse."
*PMLA: Publications of the Modern Language Association of
America* 108, no. 1 (January 1993): 59-71.

3993. Megged, Matti. "The Waiter." *Translation*,
no. 28 (Spring 1993): 70-82. Translated from the Hebrew by
Matti Megged.

3994. Weninger, Robert. "Sounding out the Silence
of Gregor Samsa: Kafka's Rhetoric of Dys-Communication."
Studies in Twentieth-Century Literature 17, no. 2 (Summer
1993): 263-286.

Wolf

3995. Ankum, Katharina von. "The Difficulty of Saying 'I': Translation and Censorship of Christa Wolf's *Der geteilte Himmel*." *Studies in Twentieth-Century Literature* 17, no. 2 (Summer 1993): 223-241.

3996. Wiesehan, Gretchen. "Christa Wolf Reconsidered: National Stereotypes in *Kindheitsmuster*." *Germanic Review* 68, no. 2 (Spring 1993): 79-87.

3997. Wilke, Sabine. "Between Female Dialogics and Traces of Essentialism: Gender and Warfare in Christa Wolf's Major Writings." *Studies in Twentieth-Century Literature* 17, no. 2 (Summer 1993): 243-262.

3998. Wolf, Christa. *The Author's Dimension: Selected Essays*. Edited by Alexander Stephan. Translated by Jan van Heurck. 1st ed. New York: Farrar, Straus, and Giroux, 1993. xii, 335 pp. [Translation of selections from *Die Dimension des Autors...*; *Ansprachen...*; and *Im Dialog*. Introduction by Grace Paley.] REV: Peter Demetz, *New York Times Book Review* 98, no. 14 (April 4, 1993): 1ff. *Wilson Quarterly* 17, no. 3 (Summer 1993): 90-91.

3999. ———. *What Remains and Other Stories*. Translated by Heike Schwarzbauer, and Rick Takvorian. 1st ed. New York: Farrar, Straus, and Giroux, 1993. 295 pp. REV: Peter Demetz, *New York Times Book Review* 98, no. 14 (April 4, 1993): 1ff. *Wilson Quarterly* 17, no. 3 (Summer 1993): 90-91.

■ **Greek**

4000. Ritsos, Yannis. "From 'Second Series'; From 'Third Series.'" *Literary Review* 36, no. 2 (Winter 1993): 247-248. Translated from the Greek by José García and Adamantia García-Baltatzi. [Poems from Ritsos' book *3 x 111 Tristychs* (Athens: 1982).]

4001. Savvas, Minas. "Remembering Yannis Ritsos." *Literary Review* 36, no. 2 (Winter 1993): 239-246.

■ **Hungarian**

4002. Basa, Eniko Molnár, special ed. *Hungarian Literature*. Contributions by Anne Paolucci, Eniko Molnár Basa, György Endre Szonyi, George F. Cushing, Laszló Rónay, Béla Pomogáts, Péter Dávidházi and Henry Paolucci. Review of National Literatures, v. 17. New York: Published for the Council on National Literatures by Griffon House Publications, c1993. 190 pp. [Contents: Anne Paolucci, "Hungary's "Neglected" National Literature," pp. 11-19; Eniko Molnár Basa, "Hungarian Literature: An Introductory Survey," pp. 20-31; György Endre Szonyi, "The Emergence of Major Trends and Themes in Hungarian Literature," pp. 32-58; George F. Cushing, "The Role of the National Poet," pp. 59-80; Laszló Rónay, "New Directions in Hungarian Literature," pp. 81-98; Béla Pomogáts, "Hungarian Literatures Beyond the Borders," pp. 99-118; Péter Dávidházi, "The Ideal of Literature in Hungarian Criticism," pp. 119-135; Eniko Molnár Basa, "Hungarian Literary/Critical Survey; Bibliographical Spectrum," pp. 136-154;

Anne Paolucci, Henry Paolucci, "Review Article: Hungary in Dante's *De Vulgari Eloquentia* and *Divina Commedia*," pp. 155-190.]

4003. Brody, Ervin C. "Felix Glück." *Literary Review* 37, no. 1 (Fall 1993): 63-71.

4004. Gergely, Agnes. "Three Poems." *Grand Street* 12, no. 1 (1993): 96-100. Translated by Nathaniel Tarn.

4005. Gombocz, István. "Miklós Györffy Novel *A ferfikor Nyara* [The Summertime of My Manhood], A Documentary of the Hungarian Sixties." *East European Quarterly* 27, no. 2 (Summer 1993): 213-222.

4006. Kosztolanyi, Dezso. *Anna Edes*. Translated and introduction by George Szirtes. Revived Modern Classic. New York: New Directions, 1993. xi, 220 pp. [Originally published: (London: Quartet Books, c1991).]

4007. Lewis, Virginia L. "The Price of Emancipation: Peasant-Noble Relations as Depicted by Novelists József Eötvös and Marie von Ebner-Eschenbach." *Hungarian Studies Review* 20, nos. 1-2 (Spring-Fall 1993): 3-23.

4008. Orbán, Ottó. [Poems]. *International Poetry Review* 19, no. 2 (Fall 1993): 38-49.

■ **Latvian**

4009. Aizpuriete, Amanda. "This Eventide Seems Split." *Cimarron Review*, no. 104 (July 1993): 31-38. Translated by Inguna Jansone.

4010. Bels, Albert. "The Official's Resurrection." *Cimarron Review*, no. 104 (July 1993): 46-50. Translated by Ieva Celle.

4011. Belsevica, Vizma. "Burbekisa." *Cimarron Review*, no. 104 (July 1993): 40-45. Translated by Ieva Celle.

4012. Berzins, Uldis. [Poems]. *Cimarron Review*, no. 104 (July 1993): 39. Translated by Ingus Josts. ["First Snow," p. 39; and "Moralizing Prose," p. 39.]

4013. Erzergailis, Inta. "Two Songs: the Poetry of Austra Skujina." *Journal of Baltic Studies* 24, no. 4 (Winter 1993): 327-348.

4014. Josts, Ingus. "Latvian Literature: 'It's Them Bad Russians / Them Russians.'" *Cimarron Review*, no. 104 (July 1993): 29-30.

4015. Ziedonis, Imants. "The Black Tale." *Cimarron Review*, no. 104 (July 1993): 51-52. Translated by Ieva Celle.

■ **Lithuanian**

4016. Balbierius, Alis. [Poems]. *Cimarron Review*, no. 104 (July 1993): 22. ["The Nemunas River Today," pp. 22; and "xxx," p. 22.]

4017. Kajokas, Donaldas. [Poems]. *Cimarron Review*, no. 104 (July 1993): 21. Translated by Jonas Zdanys. ["The Well," p. 21; and "Gates," p. 21.]

4018. Martinaitis, Marcelijus. [Poems from Kukutis's *Ballads*]. *Cimarron Review*, no. 104 (July 1993): 15-18. Translated by Laima Sruoginyte. ["How Kukutis Regained His Senses," pp. 15-16; "Kukutis' Sermon To The Pigs," pp. 16-17; and "Kukutis Wants To See His Homeland," pp. 17-18.]

4019. Ramonas, Antanas. "The Tramp." *Cimarron Review*, no. 104 (July 1993): 25-28. Translated by Daina Miniotaite.

4020. Rubavicius, Vytautas. [Poems]. *Cimarron Review*, no. 104 (July 1993): 19-20. Translated by Almantas Samalavicius. ["Winter Ideology, 1986," p. 19; and "Accident Not Yet Understood," p. 20.]

4021. Samalavicius, Almantas. "Lithuanian Prose and Poetry After the Soviets." *Cimarron Review*, no. 104 (July 1993): 11-14.

4022. Silbajoris, Rimvydas. "Existential Root Concepts of Lithuania in the Poetry of Sigitas Geda." *Lituanus* 39, no. 4 (Winter 1993): 5-12.

4023. Vaiciunaitè, Judita. "April in Dzukija." *Prism International* 31, no. 2 (Winter 1993): 64. Translated from the Lithuanian by Viktoria Skrupskelis and Stuart Friebert.

4024. ———. " 'In the Hospital' and 'Dragonflies.' " *Literary Review* 37, no. 1 (Fall 1993): 86. Translated from the Lithuanian by Viktoria Skrupskelis and Stuart Friebert.

4025. Vilimaite, Bite. "Destroyed by Moths." *Cimarron Review*, no. 104 (July 1993): 23-24. Translated by Daina Miniotaite.

■ Polish

General

4026. Baer, Joachim T. "Nietzsche and Polish Modernism." *Polish Review* 38, no. 1 (1993): 69-84.

4027. Blonski, Jan. "On the Jewish Sources of Bruno Schulz." *Cross Currents: A Yearbook of Central European Culture*, no. 12 (1993): 54-68. Translated from the Polish by Michael C. Steinlauf.

4028. Czaykowski, Bogdan. "Witold Gombrowicz's *Trans-Atlantyk*: A Novel for the New Europe?" *Cross Currents: A Yearbook of Central European Culture*, no. 12 (1993): 69-77.

4029. Czerwinski, E. J. "Polish Poetry Observed: Coming of Age." *Slavic and East European Journal* 37, no. 2 (Summer 1993): 231-234. [Review article on Stanislaw Baranczak and Clare Cavanagh, eds. and trans., *Polish Poetry of the Last Two Decades of Communist Rule: Spoiling Cannibals' Fun* (Evanston, IL: 1991); Leonard Nathan and Arthur Quinn, *The Poet's Work: An Introduction to Czeslaw Milosz* (Cambridge, MA: 1991); and Adam Czerniawski, ed., *The Mature Laurel: Essays on Modern Polish Poetry* (Chester Springs, PA: 1991).]

4030. Delbrück, Hansgerd. "Antiker und Moderner Helden-Mythos in Dürrenmatts 'ungeschichtlicher historischer Komödie' *Romulus der Grose*." *German Quarterly* 66, no. 3 (Summer 1993): 291-317. [Article is in German with an abstract in English.]

4031. Dickson, Jean. "Maria Dabrowska and the Politics of Translation." *Polish Review* 38, no. 3 (1993): 299-310. [Text and translations of correspondence between Dabrowska and Stankiewicz, pp. 303-310.]

4032. Gömöri, George. "Polish Authors in Ben Jonson's Library." *Polish Review* 38, no. 2 (1993): 187-190.

4033. Grynberg, Henryk. *The Victory*. Translated by Richard Lourie. Writings from an Unbound Europe. Evanston, IL: Northwestern University Press, 1993. xi, 107 pp. [Translation of *Zwyciestwo*.]

4034. Herling, Gustaw. *The Island: Three Tales*. Translated by Ronald Strom. New York: Viking, 1993. 151 pp. ["The Island" and "The Tower" were published in Polish under the title *Skrzydla oltarza*. "The Second Coming" was published under the title *Drugie przyjscie*. Contents: The Island; The Tower; The Second Coming.] REV: Louis Begley, *New York Times Book Review* 97 (December 27, 1992): 1ff. *New York Times Book Review* 98, no. 49 (December 5, 1993): 82.

4035. Keily, David. "The Socialist Realist Panegyric in the Polish Poetry of the Stalinist Era: The Case of Jaroslaw Iwaszkiewicz's 'List do Prezydenta.' " *Polish Review* 38, no. 1 (1993): 57-67.

4036. Kujawinski, Frank. "About Tymoteusz Karpowicz." *Lituanus* 39, no. 4 (Winter 1993): 13-15.

4037. ———. "Przybos and the Second Avant-Garde." *Polish Review* 38, no. 1 (1993): 25-39.

4038. ———. "A Selection from the Poetry of Tymoteusz Karpowicz." *Lituanus* 39, no. 4 (Winter 1993): 16-31. Translated by Frank Kujawinski and Ewa Zak. ["Musical Evening Stroll," p. 16; "Lupine Cantata," p. 17; "Fish," p. 18; "Voyage of a Branch," p. 19; "Circle of the Dance of Love," p. 20; "A Tombstone Showing Two Angels," p. 21; "A Moment in the Side Aisle," p. 22; "Morning Dialogue," pp. 23-24; "Reversed Light," p. 25; "Incomprehensible Cry," pp. 26-27; "A Lesson with the Magic Rabbit," pp. 28-29; and "In This Instant," pp. 30-31.]

4039. Maj, Bronislaw. "Selected Poems." *Cross Currents: A Yearbook of Central European Culture*, no. 12 (1993): 89-94. Introduced by Stanislaw Baranczak. ["September, Noon," p. 90; "No One Recognizes It As His Own," p. 90; "This Life Doubled," p. 91; "What They Say Today Is Not True," pp. 91-92; "I See a Gray House," p. 92; "Today," pp. 92-93; "Still," p. 93; "No One, Everyone," p. 93; "How," p. 93; "No More," p. 94.]

4040. Mikos, Michael J. "The Reception of Prus' *The Pharoah* in the United States." *Polish Review* 38, no. 1 (1993): 41-55.

4041. Parma, Ewa. [Poems]. *International Poetry Review* 19, no. 2 (Fall 1993): 63-67. Translated by Linda N. Foster and Beata Kane.

4042. Peretz, Maya. "In Search of the First Polish Woman Author." *Polish Review* 38, no. 4 (1993): 469-486.

4043. Perlinska, Agnieszka. "Cyprian Kamil Norwid: Letters as Literature." *Polish Review* 38, no. 2 (1993): 203-211.

4044. Szaruga, Leszek. "Two Poems." *Salmagundi*, no. 97 (Winter 1993): 110-111. Translated by W. D. Snodgrass, K. B. Snodgrass, Justyna Kostkowska, and Peter Lengyel. ["Watchman (for Zbigniew Herbert)," p. 110; and "An Evening with the Author," p. 111.]

4045. Szczypiorski, Andrzej. *A Mass for Arras.* Translated from the Polish by Richard Lourie. 1st English-language ed. New York: Grove Press, 1993. 188 pp. REV: David Sacks, *New York Times Book Review* 98, no. 41 (October 10, 1993): 28. Miklós Vámos, *Nation* 257, no. 9 (September 27, 1993): 325-326.

4046. Szymborska, Wislawa. "Parting with a View." *TriQuarterly*, no. 89 (Winter 1993): 178-179. Translated by Stanislaw Baranczak and Clare Cavanagh. [Part of the author's *The End and the Beginning* (Poland: 1993); it will also be included in *View with a Grain of Sand*, translated by Baranczak and Cavanagh.]

4047. Warwick, Ioanna-Veronika. "Civilization." *Poet Lore* 88, no. 1 (Spring 1993): 43.

Literary Figures

Herbert

4048. Gömöri, George. "The Faces of Mr. Cogito." *Canadian Slavonic Papers* 35, nos. 1-2 (March-June 1993): 1-12.

4049. Herbert, Zbigniew. "Achilles. Penthesilea." *New York Review of Books* 40, no. 17 (October 21, 1993): 22. Translated from the Polish by Joseph Brodsky.

4050. ———. "The Death of Lev." *New Yorker* 69, no. 4 (March 15, 1993): 78. Translation by Bogdana Carpenter and John Carpenter.

4051. ———. "Poetry." *Wilson Quarterly* 17, no. 1 (Winter 1993): 112-117. Translated by Czeslaw Milosz and Peter Dale Scott. [Poems from Zbigniew Herbert, *Selected Poems* (NY: 1986); selected and introduced by Joseph Brodsky. "Pebble," p. 114; "Elegy of Fortinbras," p. 115; "From Mythology," p. 115; "Why the Classics," p. 116; and "The Return of the Proconsul," p. 117.]

Kosinski

4052. Hawthorne, Mark D. "Disguise in Jerzy Kosinski's Novels." *Polish Review* 38, no. 3 (1993): 311-329.

4053. Straus, Dorothea. "Remembering Jerzy Kosinski." *Partisan Review* 60, no. 1 (Winter 1993): 138-142.

Milosz

4054. Milosz, Czeslaw. "Lithuania, After Fifty-two Years." *New Yorker* 69, no. 25 (August 9, 1993): 70-71. Translated by Czeslaw Milosz and Robert Hass.

4055. ———. "The Lithuanian Option and Oscar Vladislas de L. Milosz." *Cross Currents: A Yearbook of Central European Culture*, no. 12 (1993): 95-124. Translated by John Carpenter and Bogdana Carpenter.

4056. ———. "A Man-Fly." *New Yorker* 69, no. 6 (March 29, 1993): 60. Translated by Czeslaw Milosz and Robert Hass.

4057. ———. "Sarajevo." *New Republic* 209, no. 17 (October 25, 1993): 16. Translated by Czeslaw Milosz and Robert Hass. [Poem.]

4058. ———. "Woe!" *New Yorker* 69, no. 14 (May 24, 1993): 74. Translated by Czeslaw Milosz and Robert Hass.

Szymborska

4059. Szymborska, Wislawa. "Brueghel's Two Monkeys." *New Yorker* 69, no. 5 (March 22, 1993): 61. Translated from the Polish by Stanislaw Baranczak and Clare Cavanagh.

4060. ———. "Cat in an Empty Apartment." *New York Review of Books* 40, no. 17 (October 21, 1993): 42. Translated from the Polish by Stanislaw Baranczak and Clare Cavanagh.

4061. ———. "The End and the Beginning." *New Republic* 208, no. 3 (January 18, 1993): 40. Translated from the Polish by Stanislaw Baranczak and Clare Cavanagh. [Poem.]

4062. ———. "Reality Demands." *New Yorker* 69, no. 2 (March 1, 1993): 86-87. Translated by Stanislaw Baranczak and Clare Cavanagh.

Witkiewicz

4063. Kiebuzinska, Christine. "Witkacy's Theory of Pure Form: Change, Dissolution, and Uncertainty." *South Atlantic Review* 58, no. 4 (November 1993): 59-83.

Wyspianski

4064. Kraszewski, Charles S. "Stanislaw Wyspianski as Proselytising Translator: National Directioning in his Polonisations of *Hamlet* and *Le Cid*." *Canadian Slavonic Papers* 35, nos. 3-4 (September-December 1993): 305-328.

■ Romanian

General

4065. Cassian, Nina. "Notes on Romanian Poetry." *Parnassus* 18, no. 2 & 19, no. 1 (1993): 58-80. [Discussion of ideological control and political interference of Romanian authorities into creative poetic writing under the Ceausescu regime.]

4066. Manea, Norman. *Compulsory Happiness.* Translated from the French by Linda Coverdale. New York: Farrar, Straus & Giroux, c1993. 259 pp. [Four novellas written in Romanian, collected in French under title: *Le bonheur obligatoire.*] REV: Susan Miron, *Congress Monthly* 60, no. 7 (November-December 1993): 17-18. Lore Segal, *New York Times Book Review* 98, no. 22 (May 30, 1993): 7-8.

4067. Mazilescu, Virgil. [Poems]. *International Poetry Review* 19, no. 2 (Fall 1993): 53-61. Translated by Thomas C. Carlson and D. Radu Popa.

4068. Miron, Susan. "Norman Manea: Hot Heart, Cool Mind: Review Essay." *Congress Monthly* 60, no. 7 (November-December 1993): 17-18. [Review article on Norman Manea, *On Clowns: The Dictator and the Artist* (NY: 1992); Norman Manea, *October, Eight O'Clock*, trans. Cornelia Golna, Anselm Hollo, Mara Soceanu Vamos, Max Bleyleben, Marguerite Dorian, and Elliott B. Urdang (NY: 1992); and Norman Manea, *Compulsory Happiness*, trans. Linda Coverdale (NY: 1993).]

4069. Sorescu, Marin. "Three Poems." *Salmagundi*, no. 98-99 (Spring-Summer 1993): 81-83. Translated by W. D. Snodgrass, Dona Rosu, and Luciana Costea. ["The Convicted," p. 81; "Fortress," p. 82; and "Frames," p. 83.]

4070. Winkler, Manfred. [Poems]. *International Poetry Review* 19, no. 1 (Spring 1993): 6-7. Trans. by Bernhard Frank.

Literary Figures

Dumbrăveanu

4071. Carlson, T. C. [Book Review]. *Translation Review*, no. 41 (1993): 51. [Review article on Anghel Dumbrăveanu, *Love and Winter*, ed. and trans. A. J. Sorkin and I. G. Pana.]

■ Russian

General

4072. Efimov, Igor'. *Bremia dobra: russkii pisatel' kak vlastitel' dum.* Tenafly, NJ: Ermitazh, 1993. 203 pp.

4073. Gifford, April Elaine. "The Narrative Technique of *Skaz*." Ph.D. diss., Stanford University, 1993. [UMI order no: AAC 9317768.]

4074. Morris, Marcia A. *Saints and Revolutionaries: The Ascetic Hero in Russian Literature.* Studies of the Harriman Institute. Albany, NY: State University of New York Press, c1993. x, 256 pp. REV: David Kirk Prestel, *Slavic Review* 52, no. 4 (Winter 1993): 849-850.

4075. Perkins, Pamela, and Albert Cook. *The Burden Of Sufferance: Women Poets of Russia.* World Literature in Translation, 19. New York: Garland Publishing, 1993. xi, 206 pp.

4076. Polukhina, Valentina, Joe Andrew, and Robert Reid, eds. *Literary Tradition and Practice in Russian Culture: Papers from an International Conference on the Occasion of the Seventieth Birthday of Yury Mikhailovich Lotman: Russian Culture: Structure and Tradition, 2-6 July 1992, Keele University, United Kingdom.* Contributions by IU. M. Lotman, V. N. Toporov, M. L. Gasparov, Evgeny Permiakov, Roman Leibov, Anna Lisa Crone, Justin Doherty, Mikhail Lotman, Aminadav Dykman, Liudmila Zubova, Alexander Zholkovsky, Igor Pilshchikov, Valentina Polukhina, Tomas Venclova, Joe Andrew, Nina Perlina, Barbara Lönnqvist, Rosanna Casari, Joost van Baak, Pekka Pesonen, Chris Jones, Andrea Sillis, and Dobrochna Dyrcz-Freeman. Studies in Slavic Literature and Poetics, v. 20. Amsterdam; Atlanta, GA: Rodopi, 1993. xii, 341 pp. [The first of a projected three volumes of papers, to be published in 1993 and 1994, from the International Conference on Russian Culture, Structure and Tradition (1992: University of Keele). Contents: IU. M. Lotman, "Smert' kak problem siuzheta" ["Death as a Problem of Plot"], pp. 1-15; V.N. Toporov, "O 'rezonantnom' prostranstve literatury" ["On the Resonant Space of Literature"], pp. 16-60; M.L. Gasparov, "Nesostoiavshiisia russkii parnas" ["The Failed Parnassus in Russian Poetry"], pp. 61-66; Evgeny Permiakov, translated by Chris Jones, "On the 'Notebooks' of Viazemsky," pp. 67-76; Roman Leibov, translated by Andrea Sillis, "Tiutchev's Unnoticed Cycle," pp. 77-92; Anna Lisa Crone, "Tituchev and Identification of Self with Space in Petersburg Poetics of the Twentieth Century," pp. 93-105; Justin Doherty, "Acmeist Perceptions of Italy," pp. 106-122; Mikhail Lotman, "Mandel'shtam i Pasternak (opyt kontrastivnoi poetiki)," pp. 123-162; Aminadav Dykman, "Poetical Poppies: Some Thoughts on Classical Elements in the Poetry of Marina Tsvetaeva," pp. 163-176; Liudmila Zubova, " 'Mesto pusto' v poezii Tsvetaevoi," [title on p. 177: " 'Mesto pusto' v poezii Mariny Tsvetaevoi,"] pp. 177-191; Alexander Zholkovsky, "Six Easy Pieces on Grammar of Poetry, Grammar of Love," pp. 192-213; Igor Pilshchikov, "Brodsky and Baratynsky," pp. 214-228; Valentina Polukhina, "Landshaft liricheskoi lichnosti v poezii Brodskogo" ["The Landscape of the Self in Brodsky's Poetry"], pp. 229-245; Tomas Venclova, "Aleksander Wat: Three Futurist Poems," pp. 246-263; Joe Andrew, "Resurrection and Rebirth: Elena Gan's Society's Judgement," pp. 264-277; Nina Perlina, translated by Dobrochna Dyrcz-Freeman, "The Unfinished Episodes of Gogol's Plan for Dead Souls and their Fate in Russian Literature of the Second Half of the Nineteenth Century," pp. 278-289; Barbara Lönnqvist, "A Yurodivyi in the Drawing-Room— Hippolyte at Anna Schere's in *War and Peace*," pp. 290-303; Rosanna Casari, translated by Chris Jones, "Turgenev and the Myth of Psyche," pp. 304-311; Joost van Baak, translated by Chris Jones, "Leskov and Zamyatin: Stylizers of Russia," pp. 312-324; Pekka Pesonen, "Bitov's Text as Text: The Petersburg Text as a Context in Andrey Bitov's Prose," pp. 325-341.]

4077. Rice, James L. *Freud's Russia: National Identity in the Evolution of Psychoanalysis.* History of Ideas Series (New Brunswick, NJ). New Brunswick, NJ: Transaction Publishers, 1993. x, 288 pp. REV: Anna Makolkin, *Canadian Slavonic Papers* 35, nos. 3-4 (September-December 1993): 428-429.

4078. Woodward, James B. *Form and Meaning: Essays on Russian Literature*. Columbus, Ohio: Slavica Publishers, c1993. 368 pp.

Pre-Revolutionary Period (1700-1917)

4079. Andrew, Joe. *Narrative and Desire in Russian Literature, 1822-49: The Feminine and the Masculine*. New York: St. Martin's Press, 1993. vii, 257 pp. [Contents: 1. Introduction — 2. Pushkin's Southern Poems — 3. V.F. Odoevsky and the Two Princesses — 4. Elena Gan and A Futile Gift — 5. Mariya Zhukova and Patriarchal Power — 6. Alexander Herzen: Who Is To Blame? — 7. The Law of the Father and Netochka Nezvanova.]

4080. Anikin, Andrei V. "Money and the Russian Classics." *Diogenes* 41, no. 2 (no. 162) (1993): 99-109.

4081. Armstrong, Todd Patrick. "Innokentij Annenskij's 'The Cypress Chest': Contexts, Structures and Themes." Ph.D. diss., Ohio State University, 1993. [UMI order no: AAC 9411899.]

4082. Beaudoin, Luc Jean. "Evgenij Baratynskij's Narrative Poems and 'Evgenij Onegin': The Transformation of the Romantic Poema." Ph.D. diss., University of Toronto, 1993. [UMI order no: AAC NN86251.]

4083. Carlson, Paul Erik. "Some Functions of Poetic Diction in A.K. Tolstoy's 'Smert' Ioanna Groznogo.' " Ph.D. diss., University of California at Berkeley, 1993. [UMI order no: AAC 9407900.]

4084. Christensen, Peter G. "The Critique of Terrorism in the Novels of Boris Savinkov." *Australian Slavonic and East European Studies* 7, no. 2 (1993): 1-14.

4085. Comer, William John. "The Russian Religious Dissenters and the Literary Culture of the Symbolist Generation." Ph.D. diss., University of California, Berkeley, 1993. [UMI order no: AAC 9330505.]

4086. Franke, Ellen Mary. "A.P. Sumarkov's 'Dimitrij Samozvanic': Imitation or Innovation?" Ph.D. diss., University of Pittsburgh, 1993. [UMI order no: AAC 9333139.]

4087. Frierson, Cathy A. *Peasant Icons: Representations of Rural People in Late Nineteenth-Century Russia*. New York: Oxford University Press, 1993. x, 248 pp. REV: Barbara Alpern Engel, *Russian History = Histoire russe* 20, nos. 1-4 (1993): 305-306.

4088. Gasperetti, David. "The Carnivalesque Spirit of the Eighteenth-Century Russian Novel." *Russian Review* 52, no. 2 (April 1993): 166-183.

4089. Gibian, George, ed. *The Portable Nineteenth-Century Russian Reader*. The Viking Portable Library. New York, NY: Penguin Books, 1993. xxii, 641 pp. [Includes translations of works by Aleksandr Pushkin, Aleksandr Griboyedov, Mikhail Lermontov, Nikolay Gogol, Sergey Aksakov, Fyodor Tyutchev, Karolina Pavlova, Ivan Goncharov, Ivan Turgenev, Aleksandr Herzen, Kozma Prutkov, Fyodor Dostoyevsky, Leo Tolstoy, Anton Chekhov, Mikhail Saltykov-Shchedrin, Maxim Gorky, and Vladimir Solovyov. Includes translations by Walter Arndt, Vladimir Nabokov, Gillon R. Aitken, Frank R. Reeve, George Gibian, Dmitri Nabokov, Bernard Guilbert Guerney, Jesse Zeldin, M.C. Beverley, Barbara Heldt, David Magarshack, Ivy Litvinov, Tatiana Litvinov, Leo Navrozov, Richard Pevear, Larissa Volokhonsky, Aylmer Maude, S. Rapoport, John C. Kenworthy, Bernard Isaacs, and George L. Kline. "Suggestions for further reading," pp. 639-641.]

4090. Gribble, Lyubomira Parpulova. "*The Life of Peter and Fevroniia*: Transformations and Interpretations in Modern Russian Literature and Music." *Russian Review* 52, no. 2 (April 1993): 184-197.

4091. Hellebust, Rolf Eric. "The Pushkinian Tradition As Narrative and Intertext." Ph.D. diss., University of Toronto, 1993. [UMI order no: AAC NN82804.]

4092. Herman, David Benjamin Lyle. "Representing Otherness: Urban Poverty in Russian Literature from Karamzin to Nekrasov." Ph.D. diss., University of California at Berkeley, 1993. [UMI order no: AAC 9430530.]

4093. Hurych, Jitka. [Book Review]. *Style* 27, no. 1 (Spring 1993): 145-149. [Review article on Elizabeth Cheresh Allen, *Beyond Realism: Turgenev's Poetics of Secular Salvation* (Stanford, CA: Stanford University Press, 1992).]

4094. Hutchings, Stephen C. "Breaking the Circle of the Self: Domestication, Alienation and the Question of Discourse Type in Rozanov's Late Writings." *Slavic Review* 52, no. 1 (Spring 1993): 67-86.

4095. Kahn, Andrew. "Readings of Imperial Rome from Lomonosov to Pushkin." *Slavic Review* 52, no. 4 (Winter 1993): 745-768.

4096. Kaplan, Richard Edward. "Dostoevsky, Melville and the Conventions of the Novel: Fictional Alliances." Ph.D. diss., University of California, Los Angeles, 1993. [UMI order no: AAC 9418870.]

4097. Kuchar, Martha. " 'Kto vinovat?': Composition and Rhetorical Structure." Ph.D. diss., Cornell University, 1993. [UMI order no: AAC 9318908.]

4098. Mansour, Lawrence Kevin. "A.V. Druzhinin and the Origins of Russian Estheticist Criticism." Ph.D. diss., Brown University, 1993. [UMI order no: AAC 9406985.]

4099. Peterson, Ronald E. *A History of Russian Symbolism*. Linguistic & Literary Studies in Eastern Europe, v. 29. Amsterdam; Philadelphia: J. Benjamins Pub. Co., 1993. xiii, 254 pp. [Contents: Introduction; The Beginnings of Symbolism in Russia, 1892-1895. Merezhkovsky and Hippius. Sologub. Balmont. Bryusov and The Russian Symbolists; Individualism and Decadence, 1896-1898. The First Wave Continues. Decadence. Scorpio

Rising: Modernism in Art and Literature, 1899-1903.
Solovyov and Nietzsche. Anthologies at the Turn of the
Century. The World of Art. Religious-Philosophical Meet-
ings and Novyi Put. Skorpion. Severnye Tsvety. Grif.
Annensky. The Second Wave: Bely, Ivanov, Blok. The
Symbolists in 1902-1903. October, 1903; Symbolism as a
Unified Movement, 1904-April, 1906. Mir Iskussiva, Novyi
Put, and Voprosy Zhizni. Vesy. Anthologies. Symbolist
Verse in 1904. Fiction in 1904-1905. The Petty Demon. War
with Japan and Revolution in 1905. Intellectual Activity.
Zolotoe Runo. Bryusov, Bely, and Nina Petrovskaya. Essays.
April, 1906; Proliferation, Polemics, and Mystical Anar-
chism, May, 1906-1908. Polemics and Mystical Anarchism.
Pereval. Symbolist Verse in 1906-1907. Prose. 1907.
Drama. Anthologies. Factions. Younger Authors. Prose in
1907. The Fiery Angel. 1908. Anthologies. The
Merezhkovskys Return to Russia. Symbolist Verse and
Prose. Years of Crisis and Transition: Art vs. World View,
1909-1910. Vesy and Apollon. Musaget and Other Circles.
Collections, Essays. Verse. The Silver Dove. Sologub. The
Gogol Anniversary. Deaths. The Polemic about Symbolism;
The Beginning of the Decline, 1911-1914. Acmeism. Futur-
ism. Second Wave Revival. Summations. Comings and
Goings. Prose. Petersburg. Poetry. Drama. "Dispute";
Symbolism in the Past Tense, War, and Revolution, 1915-
1917. Formalism and Futurism. War. Prose. Kotik Letaev.
Poetry. Drama. Revolution; Epilogue: The Symbolists' Fates
and Their Influence. Zapiski Mechtateley. The Symbolists
after the Revolution. Bryusov, Blok, Bely. Sologub and
Annensky. Balmont and Ivanov. Merezhkovsky and
Hippius. Significant Others. Symbolism's Influence.]

4100. Pozefsky, Peter C. "Dmitrii Pisarev and the
Nihilistic Imagination: Social and Psychological Sources of
Russian Radicalism (1860-1868)." Ph.D. diss., University of
California, Los Angeles, 1993. [UMI order no: AAC
9411372.]

4101. Rancour-Laferriere, Daniel. "Lermontov's
Farewell to Unwashed Russia: A Study in Narcissistic
Rage." *Slavic and East European Journal* 37, no. 3 (Fall
1993): 293-304.

4102. Valentino, Russell Scott. "The Rise of the
Russian Tendentious Novel: Generic Hybridization and
Literary Change." Ph.D. diss., University of California, Los
Angeles, 1993. [UMI order no: AAC 9318725.]

4103. Wanner, Adrian. "Populism and Romantic
Agony: A Russian Terrorist's Discovery of Baudelaire."
Slavic Review 52, no. 2 (Summer 1993): 298-317.

4104. Zirin, Mary F. [Book Review]. *Translation
Review*, nos. 42-43 (1993): 50-53. [Review article on
Aleksandr Druzhinin, *Polinka Saks and The Story of Aleksei
Dmitrich*, trans. Michael R. Katz (Evanston, IL: Northwest-
ern University Press, 1992).]

Soviet Period (1917-1991, including Emigre Literature)

4105. Balasubramanian, Radha. "Spatial Form and
Character Revelations: Korolenko's Siberian Stories."

Canadian Slavonic Papers 35, nos. 3-4 (September-December 1993): 249-260.

4106. Banjanin, Milica. "Between Symbolism and
Futurism: Impressions By Day and By Night in Elena
Guro's City Series." *Slavic and East European Journal* 37,
no. 1 (Spring 1993): 67-84.

4107. Beraha, Laura. "The Last Rogue of History:
Picaresque Elements in Sasha Sokolov's *Palisandriia*."
Canadian Slavonic Papers 35, nos. 3-4 (September-Decem-
ber 1993): 201-220.

4108. Birden, Lorene Mae. "Ella/Elsa: The Making
of Triolet." Ph.D. diss., University of Massachusetts, 1993.
[UMI order no: AAC 9316622. Born Ella Jurievna Kagana
in Moscow in 1896, Elsa Triolet brought into her French
works ideas absorbed during her contact with Russian
Futurist poets and theoreticians. This study traces these
influences in her prose.]

4109. Borenstein, Eliot. "Men without Women:
Masculinity and Revolution in Early Soviet Literature."
Ph.D. diss., University of Wisconsin-Madison, 1993. [UMI
order no: AAC 9404718.]

4110. Briker, Boris. "The Notion of the Road in *The
Twelve Chairs* and *The Golden Calf* by I. Ilf and E. Petrov."
Canadian Slavonic Papers 35, nos. 1-2 (March-June 1993):
13-28.

4111. Brougher, Valentina G. "Myth in Vsevolod
Ivanov's *The Kremlin*." *Canadian Slavonic Papers* 35, nos.
3-4 (September-December 1993): 221-234.

4112. Brown, Clarence, ed. *The Portable Twentieth-
Century Russian Reader*. Rev. and updated ed. The Viking
Portable Library. New York: Penguin Books, 1993, c1985.
xviii, 615 pp. [Includes works by Leo Tolstoy, Anton
Chekhov, Maxim Gorky, Ivan Bunin, Nadezhda Teffi,
Alexander Blok, Andrei Bely, Evgeni Zamyatin, Velmir
Khlebnikov, Anna Akhmatova, Andrei Platonov, Boris
Pasternak, Osip Mandelstam, Mikhail Bulgakov, Isaac
Babel, Mikhail Zoshchenko, Yuri Olesha, Vladimir Nabokov,
Nadezhda Mandelstam, Daniil Kharms, Varlam Shalamov,
Alexander Solzhenitsyn, Andrei Sinyavsky, Yuri Kazakov,
Georgi Vladimov, Vladimir Voinovich, Sasha Sokolov.
Includes translations by Clarence Brown, Marian Fell,
Edythe C. Haber, Jon Stallworthy, Peter France, Robert A.
Maguire, John E. Malmstad, Avrahm Yarmolinsky, Joseph
Barnes, Max Hayward, Manya Harari, W.S. Merwin,
Michael Glenny, Andrew R. MacAndrew, Dmitri Nabokov,
Simon Karlinsky, George Gibian, John Glad, H.T. Willetts,
Richard Lourie, and Carl R. Proffer.]

4113. Bulgakov, Valentin. *Slovar' russkikh
zarubezhnykh pisatelei*. Edited by G. Vanecková. Introduction by Richard J. Kneeley. New York: Norman Ross Pub,
c1993. xxxvi, 241 pp.

4114. Carlisle, Olga Andreyev. *Under a New Sky: A
Reunion with Russia*. New York: Ticknor & Fields, 1993. xix,
248 pp. [Contents: Pt. I. Remembering the Sixties.
Pasternak's Mission; The Thaw; Alexander Solzhenitsyn's

Mission; Return to Russia; Aliosha; To Peredelkino; Kornei Ivanovich Chukovsky; Chukovsky's Granddaughter; Tulips for Pasternak; Pasternak: A Russian Poet. Pt. II. 1989. Sakharov's Hopes; Apartment 13; A Memorable Spring; Alexander Askoldov; A Conversation with Oleg; The Master and Margarita Revisited; Daniel Andreyev; My Aunt Alla; Slavophiles Old and New; A Slavophile Shrine; Lydia Korneevna Chukovskaya; Russia's Muse; Two Friends; Anna Akhmatova's Museum; In Search of the Constituent Assembly; Remembering the Emigres. Pt. III. 1990. Return to Moscow; A Spring Slow in Coming; Fear in Moscow; Farewell to the Soviet Union.] REV: John A. C. Greppin, *New York Times Book Review* 98, no. 12 (March 21, 1993): 1ff. Richard Lourie, *Book World* 23, no. 26 (June 27, 1993): 4.

4115. Cavanagh, Clare. "Pseudo-revolution in Poetic Language: Julia Kristeva and the Russian Avant-Garde." *Slavic Review* 52, no. 2 (Summer 1993): 283-297.

4116. Chances, Ellen. " 'In the Middle of the Contrast': Andrei Bitov and the Act of Writing." *World Literature Today* 67, no. 1 (Winter 1993): 65-68.

4117. Clardy, Jesse, and Betty Shalom. "Andrei Sinyavsky and Aleksandr Solzhenitsyn: Two Halves of One Brain." *Australian Slavonic and East European Studies* 7, no. 2 (1993): 15-29.

4118. Clowes, Edith W. *Russian Experimental Fiction: Resisting Ideology after Utopia.* Princeton, NJ: Princeton University Press, c1993. xvi, 236 pp. REV: Serafima Roll, *Canadian Slavonic Papers* 35, nos. 3-4 (September-December 1993): 414.

4119. Diment, Galya. "English as Sanctuary: Nabokov's and Brodsky's Autobiographical Writings." *Slavic and East European Journal* 37, no. 3 (Fall 1993): 346-361.

4120. Doroshenko, Nikolai. "The Living and the Dead." *World Literature Today* 67, no. 1 (Winter 1993): 28-30. Translated by Yuri Azarov and William Riggan.

4121. Dovlatov, Sergei. "Superfluous Man." *Partisan Review* 60, no. 1 (Winter 1993): 108-128. Translated from the Russian by Donald M. Fiene. [Short story.]

4122. Eshelman, Raoul. *Nikolaj Gumilev and Neoclassical Modernism: The Metaphysics of Style.* Slavische Literaturen, Bd. 3. Frankfurt am Main; New York: Peter Lang, c1993. 160 pp.

4123. Evtuhov, Catherine. "On Neo-Romanticism and Christianity: Some 'Spots of Time' in the Russian Silver Age." *Russian History* 20, nos. 1-4 (1993): 197-212.

4124. Gillespie, David. "Russian Writers Confront the Past: History, Memory, and Literature, 1953-1991." *World Literature Today* 67, no. 1 (Winter 1993): 74-79.

4125. Givens, John Rex. "Provincial Polemics: Folk Discourse in the Life and Novels of Vasilii Shukshin." Ph.D. diss., University of Washington, 1993. [UMI order no: AAC 9401426.]

4126. Glad, John, ed. *Conversations in Exile: Russian Writers Abroad.* Interviews translated by Richard Robin and Joanna Robin. Durham, NC: Duke University Press, 1993. 315 pp. [Translated from the Russian. Contents: "Introduction," pp. 1-28 — 1: The Older Generation; "Igor Chinnov," pp. 31-38; "Yury Ivask," pp. 39-49; "Roman Goul," pp. 50-65 — 2: Makers of Fantasy and Humor; "Vasily Aksyonov," pp. 69-84; "Vladimir Voinovich," pp. 85-97 — 3: The Aesthetes; "Joseph Brodsky," pp. 101-113; "Boris Khazanov," pp. 114-140; "Andrei Siniavsky and Maria Rozanova," pp. 141-173; "Sasha Sokolov," pp. 174-185 — 4: The Moralists; "Fridrikh Gorenstein," pp. 189-203; "Aleksandr Zinoviev," pp. 204-221; "Natalya Gorbanevskaya," pp. 222-235 — 5: The Realists; "Vladimir Maksimov," pp. 239-257; "Edward Limonov," pp. 258-269 — "A Chronology," pp. 271-294; "Glossary of Names," pp. 295-315.] REV: D. Barton Johnson, *Slavic and East European Journal* 37, no. 4 (Winter 1993): 586-587.

4127. Goldstein, Darra. *Nikolai Zabolotsky: Play for Mortal Stakes.* Cambridge Studies in Russian Literature. Cambridge; New York, NY: Cambridge University Press, 1993. xiii, 306 pp.

4128. Goscilo, Helena, ed. *Fruits of Her Plume: Essays on Contemporary Russian Women's Culture.* Contributions by Helena Goscilo, Caryl Emerson, Natal'ia Ivanova, Nicholas Zekulin, Svetlana Boym, Beth Holmgren, Stephanie Sandler, Nadya L. Peterson, Richard Chapple, Thomas Lahusen, Jerzy Kolodziej, Darra Goldstein, and John R. Givens. Armonk, NY: M.E. Sharpe, c1993. xxiii, 278 pp. [Contents: Helena Goscilo, "Introduction," pp. xvii-xxiii; Caryl Emerson, "Bakhtin and Women: A Nontopic with Immense Implications," pp. 3-20; Natal'ia Ivanova, "Bakhtin's Concept of the Grotesque and the Art of Petrushevskaia and Tolstaia," translated by Helena Goscilo, pp. 21-32; Nicholas Zekulin, "Soviet Russian Women's Literature in the Early 1980s," pp. 33-58; Svetlana Boym, "The Poetics of Banality: Tat'iana Tolstaia, Lana Gogoberidze, and Larisa Zvezdochetova," pp. 59-83; Beth Holmgren, "The Creation of Nadezhda Iakovlevna Mandel'shtam," pp. 85-111; Stephanie Sandler, "The Canon and the Backward Glance: Akhmatova, Lisnianskaia, Petrovykh, Nikolaeva," pp. 113-133; Helena Goscilo, "Speaking Bodies: Erotic Zones Rhetoricized," pp. 135-163; Nadya L. Peterson, "Games Women Play: The 'Erotic' Prose of Valeriia Narbikova," pp. 165-183; Richard Chapple, "Happy Never After: The Work of Viktoriia Tokareva and Glasnost'," pp. 185-204; Thomas Lahusen, " 'Leaving Paradise' and Perestroika: *A Week Like Any Other* and *Memorial Day* by Natal'ia Baranskaia," pp. 205-224; Jerzy Kolodziej, "Iuliia Voznesenskaia's Women: With Love and Squalor," pp. 225-238; Darra Goldstein, "The Heartfelt Poetry of Elena Shvarts," pp. 239-250; John R. Givens, "Reflections, Crooked Mirrors, Magic Theaters: Tat'iana Tolstaia's 'Peters,' " pp. 251-270.]

4129. Haber, Erika. "Fantastic Realism of Sinjavskij-Terc." Ph.D. diss., University of Michigan, 1993. [UMI order no: AAC 9332075.]

4130. Henry, Kathryn. "Russian Emigre Literature: Resisting Erasure." *Canadian-American Slavic Studies* 27, nos. 1-4 (1993): 107-120.

4131. Holmgren, Beth. *Women's Works in Stalin's Time: On Lidiia Chukovskaia and Nadezhda Mandelstam.* Bloomington, IN: Indiana University Press, c1993. x, 225 pp. [Contents: Women's Works in Stalin's Time. Lidiia Chukovskaia. Father and Daughter; Alternative Scripts and Novel Therapies; Notes on Anna Akhmatova. Nadezhda Mandelstam. Husband and Wife; *Hope against Hope*; *Hope Abandoned*. The Post-Stalin Legacy. The Widows' Might.] REV: Susan Ingram, *Canadian Slavonic Papers* 35, nos. 3-4 (September-December 1993): 420-421.

4132. Horowitz, Brian J. "The First Wave of Russian Emigration: New Perspectives Following the Fall of the Berlin Wall." *Slavic and East European Journal* 37, no. 3 (Fall 1993): 371-379. [Review article on A. Afanas'ev, ed., *Literatura russkogo zarubezh'ia: antologiia v shesti tomakh* [Literature of the Russian Emigration: An Anthology] Vol. 1, Book 1 (Moscow: 1990); D. Urnov, ed., *Serebrianyi vek: memuary* [The Silver Age: Memories] (Moscow: 1990); M.A. Maslin, ed., *O Rossii i russkoi filosofskoi kul'ture; filosofy russkogo posleoktiabr'skogo zarubezh'ia* [About Russia and Russian Philosophical Culture: Philosophers of Russia's Post-October Emigration] (Moscow: 1990); and Marc Raeff, *Russia Abroad: A Cultural History of the Russian Emigration 1919-1939* (NY: 1990).]

4133. Kalb, Judith E. "The Politics of an Esoteric Plot: Mikhail Kuzmin's *Death of Nero*." *Soviet and Post-Soviet Review* 20, no. 1 (1993): 35-50.

4134. Kates, Jim. [Book Review]. *Translation Review*, nos. 42-43 (1993): 53-55. [Review article on John Glad and Daniel Weissbort, eds., *Twentieth-Century Russian Poetry* (Iowa City, IA: University of Iowa Press, 1992).]

4135. Kolesnikoff, Nina. "The Generic Structure of Ljudmila Petrusevskaja's *Pesni vostocnyx slavjan*." *Slavic and East European Journal* 37, no. 2 (Summer 1993): 220-230.

4136. Kossman, Nina. [Poems]. *International Poetry Review* 19, no. 1 (Spring 1993): 43-57. Translated by Nina Kossman.

4137. Kozhinov, Vadim. "The Magazine *Nash Sovremennik* (Our Contemporary) and Russian Literature." *World Literature Today* 67, no. 1 (Winter 1993): 34-36. Translated by Yuri Azarov and William Riggan.

4138. Kreps, Mikhail. "Evropeiskaia noch': poeticheskoe mirooshchushchenie Vladislava Khodasevicha." *Canadian-American Slavic Studies* 27, nos. 1-4 (1993): 121-147.

4139. Ledger, Joanne. "Boris Ravenskikh's Staging of L.N. Tolstoi's *The Power of Darkness*: Some Echoes of the Avant-Garde During the Thaw." *Canadian Slavonic Papers* 35, nos. 3-4 (September-December 1993): 261-274.

4140. Ledkovsky, Marina. "Paradise Lost to Paradise Regained: Galina Kuznetsova's 'Olive Orchard.'" *Canadian-American Slavic Studies* 27, nos. 1-4 (1993): 148-156b.

4141. Mai, Birgit. *Satire im Sowjetsozialismus: Michail Soschtschenko, Michail Bulgakow, Ilja Ilf, Jewgeni Petrow.* Bern; New York: P. Lang, c1993. 206 pp.

4142. Manouelian, Edward. "Remizov's Judas: Aprocryphal Legend Into Symbolist Drama." *Slavic and East European Journal* 37, no. 1 (Spring 1993): 46-66.

4143. Marinov, Samuel G. "The Dramaturgy of Alexander Volodin." Ph.D. diss., University of Kansas, 1993. [UMI order no: AAC 9425942.]

4144. Mechik, Donat. "Pisateli Matveevy." *Canadian-American Slavic Studies* 27, nos. 1-4 (1993): 256-258.

4145. Murav, Harriet. "A Curse on Russia: Gorenshtein's *Anti-Psalom* and the Critics." *Russian Review* 52, no. 2 (April 1993): 213-227.

4146. Parthé, Kathleen. "The Righteous Brothers (and Sisters) of Contemporary Russian Literature." *World Literature Today* 67, no. 1 (Winter 1993): 91-99.

4147. Patera, Tatiana. "Roman *Ischeznovenie*: 'Oprokinutyi dom' na naberezhnoi, ili dolgoe proshchanie Iuriia Trifonova s detstvom." *Russian Language Journal* 47, nos. 156-158 (Winter-Spring-Fall 1993): 107-122.

4148. Popov, Konstantin G. "Khudozhestvennoe vremia v poezii L'va Ozerova." *Russian Language Journal* 47, nos. 156-158 (Winter-Spring-Fall 1993): 123-135.

4149. Rifkin, Benjamin. "The Christian Subtext in Bykov's *Cucelo*." *Slavic and East European Journal* 37, no. 2 (Summer 1993): 178-193.

4150. Rollberg, Peter. "Between Beast and God: Anatoly Kim's Apocalyptic Vision." *World Literature Today* 67, no. 1 (Winter 1993): 100-106.

4151. ———. *Invisible Transcendence: Vladimir Makanin's Outsiders.* Occasional Paper (Kennan Institute for Advanced Russian Studies), no. 253. Washington, DC: Kennan Institute for Advanced Russian Studies, [c1993]. 63 pp. [Study is based on a lecture presented at the Kennan Institute on December 4, 1992.]

4152. Ryan-Hayes, Karen. *Limonov's "It's Me, Eddie" and the Autobiographical Mode.* The Carl Beck Papers in Russian and East European Studies, no. 1004. Pittsburgh, PA: REES, Center for Russian & East European Studies, University of Pittsburgh, c1993. 37 pp. [Part of a book-length study entitled *Contemporary Russian Satire: a Genre Study*.]

4153. Rytman, Dora. "Russian-Jewish Literature as a Mirror of the Fate of Russian Jewry: The Special Case of Ilya Ehrenburg." Ph.D. diss., Brown University, 1993. [UMI order no: AAC 9407020.]

4154. Selivanova, Svetlana. "From the Seventies to the Nineties." *World Literature Today* 67, no. 1 (Winter

1993): 44-48. Yuri Azarov and William Riggan, trans.

4155. Shtein, Emanuil. *Literaturno-shakhmatnye kollizii: ot Nabokova i Talia do Solzhenitsyna i Fishera.* Orange, CT: Antiquary, 1993. 101 pp.

4156. Simmons, Cynthia. *Their Fathers' Voice: Vassily Aksyonov, Venedikt Erofeev, Eduard Limonov, and Sasha Sokolov.* Middlebury Studies in Russian Language and Literature, vol. 4. New York: P. Lang, c1993. 218 pp.

4157. Sivorinovsky, Alina. "Mother Tongue." *Lilith* 18, no. 3 (Summer 1993): 21-23.

4158. Smith, Vassar Williams. "Fyodor Sologub (1863-1927): A Critical Biography." Ph.D. diss., Stanford University, 1993. [UMI order no: AAC 9317820.]

4159. Smith, Viveca. "Profile: Ardis Publishers." *Translation Review,* no. 41 (1993): 47-50.

4160. Sosnora, Victor. [Poems]. *International Poetry Review* 19, no. 1 (Spring 1993): 27-41. Dean Furbish, trans.

4161. Sutton, Dana. "Reviews: *The Bedbug,* Lehman College, New York." *Slavic and East European Performance* 13, no. 3 (Fall 1993): 49-50. [Review of production which was part of Lehman College-CUNY's commemoration of the 100th anniversary of Mayakovsky's birth.]

4162. Todd, Albert C., and Max Hayward, eds. *Twentieth-Century Russian Poetry: Silver and Steel: An Anthology.* Edited with Daniel Weissbort. Selected, with an introduction by Yevgeny Yevtushenko. 1st ed. New York, NY: Doubleday, c1993. lxxxvi, 1078 pp. [Partial contents: Yevgeny Yevtushenko, "Compiler's Introduction"; Albert C. Todd, "Editor's Introduction"; Glossary; Children of the Golden Age: Poets Born Before 1900; Children of the Silver Age: Poets Born Before the Revolution; Children of the Steel Age: Poets Born Before World War II; Children of Omega and Alpha: Poets Born After World War II.]

4163. Tumanov, Vladimir A. "Unframed Direct Interior Monologue in European Fiction: A Study of Four Authors." Ph.D. diss., University of Alberta, 1993. [UMI order no: AAC NN81972. Examines interior monologue as a literary genre in relation to narrative theory and findings from psychology.]

4164. Vanchu, Anthony J. "Cross(-Dress)ing One's Way to Crisis: Popov, Petrushevskaya and the Crisis of Category in Contemporary Russian Culture." *World Literature Today* 67, no. 1 (Winter 1993): 107-118.

4165. Vishevskii, Anatolii. "Kak sdelan 'Zoo' Viktora Shklovskogo." *Canadian-American Slavic Studies* 27, nos. 1-4 (1993): 165-180.

4166. Vishevsky, Anatoly. "Creating a Shattered World: Toward the Poetics of Yevgeny Popov." *World Literature Today* 67, no. 1 (Winter 1993): 119-124.

4167. ———. *Soviet Literary Culture in the 1970s: The Politics of Irony.* Anthology of ironic prose translated by Michael Biggins and Anatoly Vishevsky. Gainesville, FL: University Press of Florida, c1993. x, 326 pp. [Partial contents: Pt. 1. Irony as the Leading Mode in Soviet Literature and Culture of the 1970s. 1. Irony in Siberian Literature. 2. Irony in Soviet Culture. 3. Ironic Prose as a Subgenre of the Humorous Short Story. Pt. 2. Anthology of Ironic Prose. E. Abramov, "The Sun Was Shining..."; V. Aksyonov, "A Cabdriver's Dream"; V. Aksyonov, "A Vulnerable Ego"; S. Altov, "A Tube of Ultramarine"; A. Arkanov, "Nightingales in September"; A. Arkanov, "Peaches"; A. Arkanov, "Cross Country"; A. Arkanov, "Before You Go"; V. Bakhchanian, "Man"; V. Bakhnov, "The Sleep Walker"; A. Bitov, "Someone Else's Dog"; B. Briker and A. Vishevsky, "Made in Heaven"; H. Drobiz, "A Lamppost and the Tower"; N. Elin and V. Kashaev, "In the Woods"; A. Gladilin, "The Double"; V. Gonik, "A Malady"; G. Gorin, "Cut! Let's Call It a Day"; G. Gorin, "Kurentsov Unclad"; G. Gorin, "Stop Potapov!"; G. Gorin, "The Dream"; A. Inin and L. Osadchuk, "On the Same Day Every Month"; D. Ivanov and V. Trifonov, "Sugar, Sugar"; D. Ivanov and V. Trifonov, "My Second Self"; L. Kaminsky, "Hack Writer"; F. Kamov, "The Bald Angel"; N. Katerli, "Victory"; H. Kemoklidze, "The Truth"; A. Khait, "When I Look in the Mirror"; R. Kireev, "My Strength of Character"; V. Klimovich, "In the Nick of Time"; N. Konyaev, "Nastenka the Tree"; V. Korotich, "Something about Astronomy"; F. Krivin, "If Such a Thing Should Happen..."; A. Kuchaev, "What Happened to Sergeev"; A. Kuchaev, "Nothing Special"; A. Kuchaev, "Happiness"; A. Kurlyandsky, "Cheating"; A. Kurlyandsky and A. Khait, "The Sixth Sense"; M. Mishin, "What Didn't Happen to Nenasbev"; L. Novozhenov, "One Fifty Four"; G. Pruslin, "Purple-Colored Camel"; N. Shakhbazov, "My Circle of Friends"; E. Shatko, "The Wheel of Fortune"; V. Slavkin, "Soyev's Masterpiece"; V. Tokareva, "One, Two, Three..."; V. Tokareva, "A Ruble Sixty Isn't Much"; M. Zadornov, "Still Young"; M. Zakharov, "One Life to Live...or a Tavern Story"; A. Zhitinsky, "Fantastic Miniatures."] REV: Munir Sendich, *Russian Language Journal = Russkii iazyk* 47, nos. 156-158 (Winter-Spring-Fall 1993): 369-370.

4168. Westphalen, Timothy C. "The Carnival-Grotesque and Blok's *The Puppet Show*." *Slavic Review* 52, no. 1 (Spring 1993): 49-66.

4169. Woll, Josephine. "The Minotaur in the Maze: Remarks on Lyudmila Petrushevskaya." *World Literature Today* 67, no. 1 (Winter 1993): 125-130.

4170. Yanishevsky, Arkady, and Inna Broude. *The Times of Turmoil: A Collection of Stories.* Translated from the Russian by Arkady Yanishevsky. Compiled by Inna Broude. Tenafly, NJ: Hermitage, 1993. 175 pp.

4171. Zalygin, Sergei Pavlovich. *The Commission.* Translated by David Gordon Wilson. DeKalb, IL: Northern Illinois University Press, 1993. xix, 358 pp. [Translation of *Komissiia.*]

4172. Zhukov, Anatoly. "Kolkhozniks and Writers." *World Literature Today* 67, no. 1 (Winter 1993): 54-56. Yuri Azarov and William Riggan, trans.

4173. Ziolkowski, Margaret. "The Figure of Saint Sebastian in Vladimir Dudintsev's *Belye odezhdy*." *World Literature Today* 67, no. 1 (Winter 1993): 131-135.

Post-Soviet Period (1992-)

4174. Aksyonov, Vassily. "Dystrophy of the 'Thick' and Bespredel of the 'Thin' (Literary Notes)." *World Literature Today* 67, no. 1 (Winter 1993): 18-23.

4175. Baklanov, Grigory. "Our Moral Duty." *World Literature Today* 67, no. 1 (Winter 1993): 25-27. Yuri Azarov and William Riggan, trans.

4176. Beshenkovskaya, Olga. [Poems]. *World Literature Today* 67, no. 1 (Winter 1993): 64. Translated by Anatoly Liberman and Vera Dunham. ["In a Land Whose..." and "Old Russia's Slavery Rights." From a special section entitled "Younger Russian Poets."]

4177. Chukhontsev, Oleg. [Poems]. *World Literature Today* 67, no. 1 (Winter 1993): 57. Henry Taylor, trans. ["The Road" and "I Woke." From a special section entitled "New Poetry from Russia."]

4178. Erofeev, Viktor. *Russian Beauty*. Translated by Andrew Reynolds. New York: Viking, 1993. vi, 343 pp. [Translation of *Russkaia krasavitsa*.] REV: David Plante, *New York Times Book Review* 98, no. 18 (May 2, 1993): 16. Elisabeth Rich, *Nation* 256, no. 24 (June 21, 1993): 875-878.

4179. Esin, Sergei. "Fantasies of Life." *World Literature Today* 67, no. 1 (Winter 1993): 31-33. Yuri Azarov and William Riggan, trans.

4180. Goscilo, Helena, and Byron Lindsey, eds. *The Wild Beach & Other Stories: An Anthology of Contemporary Russian Stories*. Contributions by Yury Trifonov, Vitaly Moskalenko, Leonid Shorokhov, Boris Ekimov, Natalya Sukhanova, Nikolai Shmelyov, Vladimir Tendryakov, Lyudmila Ulitskaya, Vyacheslav Kondratiev, Daniil Granin, Vyacheslav Pyetsukh, and Alexander Ivanchenko. Ardis Russian Literature Series. Ann Arbor, MI: Ardis; Distributed by Vintage Books, 1993. xxi, 352 pp. [Translated from Russian. Contents: Byron Lindsey and Helena Goscilo, "From the Editors"; Byron Lindsey, "Introduction"; Yury Trifonov, "A Short Stay in the Torture Chamber"; Vitaly Moskalenko, "The Wild Beach"; Leonid Shorokhov, "The Lifeguard"; Boris Ekimov, "The Chelyadins' Son-in-Law"; Natalya Sukhanova, "Delos"; Nikolai Shmelyov, "The Fur Coat Incident"; Vladimir Tendryakov, "Donna Anna"; Lyudmila Ulitskaya, "Lucky"; Vyacheslav Kondratiev, "At Freedom Station"; Daniil Granin, "The Forbidden Chapter"; Vyacheslav Pyetsukh, "The Ticket" and "Novy Zavod"; Alexander Ivanchenko, "Safety Procedure I."]

4181. Grachova, Nina. "Of What Use to Me." *World Literature Today* 67, no. 1 (Winter 1993): 63. Nina Kossman, trans. [From a special section entitled "Younger Russian Poets."]

4182. Kadir, Djelal. "Russian Literature at a Crossroads." *World Literature Today* 67, no. 1 (Winter 1993): 7-10.

4183. Kazantsev, Vassily. [Poems]. *World Literature Today* 67, no. 1 (Winter 1993): 59. Henry Taylor, trans. ["The Sounds" and "Who Has Been Exalted." From a special section entitled "New Poetry from Russia."]

4184. Krichensky, Ilya. [Poems]. *World Literature Today* 67, no. 1 (Winter 1993): 62. Albert C. Todd, trans. ["Refugees" and "Exhausted from Depression." From a special section entitled "Younger Russian Poets."]

4185. Kudimova, Marina. [Poems]. *World Literature Today* 67, no. 1 (Winter 1993): 63. Translated by Albert C. Todd and Simon Franklin. ["The Outing" and "When Still I Barely Rose." From a special section entitled "Younger Russian Poets."]

4186. Kustanovich, Konstantin. "Erotic Glasnost: Sexuality in Recent Russian Literature." *World Literature Today* 67, no. 1 (Winter 1993): 136-144.

4187. Kuznetsov, Yuri. [Poems]. *World Literature Today* 67, no. 1 (Winter 1993): 58. Henry Taylor, trans. ["I Know a Land," "To My Native Land." From a special section entitled "New Poetry from Russia."]

4188. Malashenko, Aleksei. *The Last Red August: A Russian Mystery*. Translated by Anthony Olcott. New York: Scribner's; Toronto: Maxwell Macmillan Canada; New York: Maxwell Macmillan International, c1993. 250 pp. [Translated from Russian. Fiction based on the attempted coup (1991).]

4189. Milman, Nyusya. "One Woman's Theme and Variations: The Prose of Lyudmila Petrushevskaya." Ph.D. diss., University of Michigan, 1993. [UMI order no: AAC 9409767.]

4190. Popov, Yevgeny. "The Silhouette of Truth." *World Literature Today* 67, no. 1 (Winter 1993): 37-39. Michael Finke and Anatoly Vishevsky, trans.

4191. Shcherbina, Tatyana. "No need for bullets, the heart explodes on its own." *Literary Review* 37, no. 1 (Fall 1993): 84. Translated from the Russian by J. Kates.

4192. Shklarevsky, Igor. "Instead of a Last Will and Testament." *World Literature Today* 67, no. 1 (Winter 1993): 60. Henry Taylor, trans. [From a special section entitled "New Poetry from Russia."]

4193. Sokolov, Vladimir. [Poems]. *World Literature Today* 67, no. 1 (Winter 1993): 61. Henry Taylor, trans. ["The Writing Life" and "Poetry." From a special section entitled "New Poetry from Russia."]

4194. Zekulin, Nicholas. "Changing Perspectives: The Prose of Natal'ia Baranskaia." *Canadian Slavonic Papers* 35, nos. 3-4 (September-December 1993): 235-247.

Literary Figures

Aitmatov

4195. Aitmatov, Chingiz. "The Intellectual Crisis, the End of Totalitarianism, and the Fate of Literature." *World Literature Today* 67, no. 1 (Winter 1993): 11-17.

Alexandra Heidi Karriker, trans.

4196. Kolesnikoff, Nina. "The Compositional and Temporal Structure of Ajtmatov's *Plaxa*." *Russian Language Journal* 47, nos. 156-158 (Winter-Spring-Fall 1993): 137-145.

Akhmatova

4197. Akhmatova, Anna. *A Stranger to Heaven and Earth: Poems of Anna Akhmatova.* Selected and translated by Judith Hemschemeyer. 1st Shambhala ed. Shambhala Centaur Editions. Boston, MA: Shambhala; [New York]: Distributed in the U.S. by Random House, 1993. xxiii, 115 pp. [Contents: Something in the World Called Love — I Am Not With Those Who Abandoned Their Land — The Lord Has Taught Us to Forgive.]

4198. Bayley, John. " 'Anna of All the Russias.' " *New York Review of Books* 40, no. 9 (May 13, 1993): 25-27. [Review article on Judith Hemschemeyer and Roberta Reeder, ed. and trans., *The Complete Poems of Anna Akhmatova* (Somerville, MA: 1990); Anatoly Nayman, *Remembering Anna Akhmatova*, trans. Wendy Rosslyn (NY: 1991); and Susan Amert, *In a Shattered Mirror: The Later Poetry of Anna Akhmatova* (Stanford, CA: 1992).]

4199. Hughes, Robert P. [Book Review]. *Book World (Washington Post)* 23, no. 17 (April 25, 1993): 5. [Review article on Ronald Meyer, *Anna Akhmatova: My Half Century, Selected Prose* (NY: 1992) and Roberta Reeder, *The Complete Poems of Anna Akhmatova*, translated by Judith Hemschemeyer (NY: 1992).]

4200. Ketchian, Sonia I., ed. *Anna Akhmatova, 1889-1989: Papers from the Akhmatova Centennial Conference, Bellagio Study and Conference Center, June 1989.* Contributions by Susan Amert, Inna Chechelnitsky, Anna Lisa Crone, Sam Norman Driver, M. L. Gasparov, Kamsar N. Grigorian, Sonia I. Ketchian, Anna Ljunggren, Maro Markarian, Leslie O'Bell, F. D. Reeve, Wendy Rosslyn, Nikita Struve, V. N. Toporov, T. V. Tsiv'ian, Vitalii Vilenkin, David Wells, T. Skulavcheva, and I. K. Grigorian. Modern Russian Literature and Culture, Studies and Texts, v. 28. Oakland, CA: Berkeley Slavic Specialties, c1993. 281 pp. [Contents: Sonia I. Ketchian, "Preface," pp. 9-10; Susan Amert, " 'Predystoriia': Akhmatova's Aetiological Myth," pp. 13-28; Inna Chechelnitsky, "Akhmatova and Pushkin: Apologia Pro Vita Sua," pp. 29-42; Anna Lisa Crone, "Genre Allusions in Poèma bez geroi: Masking Tragedy and Satyric Drama," pp. 43-59; Sam Norman Driver, "Anna Akhmatova and the Poetic Sequence," pp. 60-67; M. L. Gasparov, translated by T. Skulavcheva, "The Evolution of Akhmatova's Verse," pp. 68-74; Kamsar N. Grigorian (Ter-Grigorian), translated by I. K. Grigorian, "Anna Akhmatova's Poetic Translations of Some Poems by Vahan Terian," pp. 75-85; Sonia I. Ketchian, "Anna Akhmatova and W. B. Yeats: Points of Juncture," pp. 86-109; Anna Ljunggren, "Anna Akhmatova's Requiem: A Retrospective of the Love Lyric and Epos," pp. 110-126; Maro Markarian, translated by Sonia I. Ketchian, "The Lessons of Anna Akhmatova," pp. 127-135; Leslie O'Bell, "Akhmatova and Pushkin's Secret Writing," pp. 136-148; F. D. Reeve, "The

Inconstant Translation: Life into Art," pp. 149-169; Wendy Rosslyn, "Painters and Painting in the Poetry of Anna Akhmatova: The Relation between the Poetry and Painting," pp. 170-185; Nikita Struve, "O 'Polnochnykh stikakh,' " pp. 186-193; V. N. Toporov, "Ob istorizme Akhmatovoi (dve glavy iz knigi)," pp. 194-237; T. V. Tsiv'ian, " 'Poema bez geroia' Anny Akhmatovoi: Nekotorye itogi izucheniia v sviazi s problemoi 'tekst-chitatel'," pp. 238-248; Vitalii Vilenkin, translated by Anna Lisa Crone, "On A Poem Without a Hero," pp. 249-265; David Wells, "The Function of the Epigraph in Akhmatova's Poetry," pp. 266-281.]

4201. ———. "Axmatova's Civic Poem 'Stansy' and Its Puskinian Antecedent." *Slavic and East European Journal* 37, no. 2 (Summer 1993): 194-210.

4202. Loseff, Lev, and Barry Scherr, eds. *A Sense of Place: Tsarskoe Selo and its Poets: Papers from the 1989 Dartmouth Conference Dedicated to the Centennial of Anna Akhmatova.* Columbus, OH: Slavica Publishers, c1993. 368 pp.

4203. Shrayer, Maxim D. "Two Poems on the Death of Akhmatova: Dialogues, Private Codes, and the Myth of Akhmatova's Orphans." *Canadian Slavonic Papers* 35, nos. 1-2 (March-June 1993): 45-68.

Bakhtin

4204. Bakhtin, M. M. *Toward a Philosophy of the Act.* Translation and notes by Vadim Liapunov. Edited by Michael Holquist and Vadim Liapunov. 1st ed. University of Texas Press Slavic Series, no. 10. Austin, TX: University of Texas Press, 1993. xxiv, 106 pp.

4205. Gorman, David. "Bakhtin and His Circle: A Checklist of English Translations." *Style* 27, no. 4 (Winter 1993): 515-520. [Bibliography of publications by Bakhtin, Medvedev, and Voloshinov.]

4206. Mihailovic, Alexandar. "M.M. Bakhtin and the Theology of Discourse." Ph.D. diss., Yale University, 1993. [UMI order no: AAC 9400362.]

4207. Miller-Pogacar, Anesa. "Transculture and Culturology: Post-Structuralist Theory in Late and Post-Soviet Russia." Ph.D. diss., University of Kansas, 1993. [UMI order no: AAC 9405768.]

4208. Morace, Robert A. "Dialogues and Dialogics." *Modern Language Studies* 23, no. 3 (Summer 1993): 73-91.

4209. Morson, Gary Saul. "Strange Synchronies and Surplus Possibilities: Bakhtin on Time." *Slavic Review* 52, no. 3 (Fall 1993): 477-493. [Essay is adapted from the third chapter of author's book *Narrative and Freedom: The Shadows of Time* (New Haven, CT: forthcoming).]

4210. Wesling, Donald. "Mikhail Bakhtin and the Social Poetics of Dialect." *Papers On Language & Literature* 29, no. 3 (Summer 1993): 303-322. [Discusses Bakhtin's concept of social heteroglossia in its relation to dialect.]

Bely

4211. Bely, Andrei. "Kharakteristika sovremennikov (Podgotovka teksta, kommentarii M. Mironovoi)." *Australian Slavonic and East European Studies* 7, no. 1 (1993): 18-23.

4212. Mironova, Maria. "Andrei Belyi: memuarist." *Australian Slavonic and East European Studies* 7, no. 1 (1993): 1-17.

Brodsky

4213. Bethea, David. "Joseph Brodsky as Russian Metaphysical: A Reading of *Bol'shaia elegiia Dzhonu Donnu*." *Canadian-American Slavic Studies* 27, nos. 1-4 (1993): 69-89.

4214. Brodsky, Joseph. "Daedalus in Sicily." *New York Review of Books* 40, no. 16 (October 7, 1993): 14. Translated by Joseph Brodsky. [Poem.]

4215. ———. "Democracy!" *Partisan Review* 60, no. 2 (Spring 1993): 184ff. [Act Two.]

4216. ———. "Lullaby." *New Yorker* 69, no. 43 (December 20, 1993): 104. Translated by Joseph Brodsky.

4217. ———. "New Life." *New Yorker* 69, no. 10 (April 26, 1993): 86. [Poem.]

4218. ———. "Profile of Clio." *New Republic* 208, no. 5 (February 1, 1993): 60-67.

4219. Lilly, Ian K. "The Metrical Context of Brodsky's Centenary Poem for Axmatova." *Slavic and East European Journal* 37, no. 2 (Summer 1993): 211-219.

4220. Patterson, David. "From Exile to Affirmation: The Poetry of Joseph Brodsky." *Studies in Twentieth-Century Literature* 17, no. 2 (Summer 1993): 365-383.

4221. Ryan, Dennis. "Joseph Brodsky and the Fictions of Poetry, Including *Vers Libre*." *Lituanus* 39, no. 2 (Summer 1993): 70-77. [Response to Brodsky's essay on Venclova, "Poetry as a Form of Resistance to Reality," *Publications of the Modern Language Association* 107 (March 1992): 220-225.]

4222. Whedon, Tony. "A Ramble on Joseph Brodsky." *Salmagundi*, no. 97 (Winter 1993): 152-168.

Bulgakov

4223. Haber, Edythe C. "Dwellings and Devils in Early Bulgakov." *Slavic and East European Journal* 37, no. 3 (Fall 1993): 326-338.

4224. Larsen, Susan Kirsten. "The Poetics of Performance in the Works of Mixail Bulgakov." Ph.D. diss., Yale University, 1993. [UMI order no: AAC 9426199.]

4225. LeBlanc, Ronald D. "Feeding a Poor Dog a Bone: The Quest for Nourishment in Bulgakov's *Sobach'e serdtse*." *Russian Review* 52, no. 1 (January 1993): 58-78.

Bunin

4226. Lee, Sang Ryong. "An Analysis of Thematics, Poetics, and Aesthetics in Ivan Bunin's Prose Narratives." Ph.D. diss., University of Illinois at Urbana-Champaign, 1993. [UMI order no: AAC 9411685.]

4227. Marullo, Thomas Gaiton, ed. *Ivan Bunin: Russian Requiem, 1885-1920: A Portrait from Letters, Diaries, and Fiction*. Chicago, IL: Ivan R. Dee, 1993. x, 400 pp. [Contents: Pt. 1. Grey Dawn, 1885-1900 — Pt. 2. Gathering Clouds, 1901-1905 — Pt. 3. First Blood, 1906-1910 — Pt. 4. False Hopes, 1911-1913 — Pt. 5. Toward the Abyss, 1914-1916 — Pt. 6. In the Eye of the Hurricane, 1917-1918 — Pt. 7. Tidal Wave, 1919-1920 — Index of Prominent Russians Mentioned in the Text.]

Chekhov

4228. Brady, Owen E. [Performance Review]. *Theatre Journal* 45, no. 2 (May 1993): 242-244. [Review of director Joe Dowling's production of "Uncle Vanya" by Anton Chekhov at the Stratford Festival, Stratford, Ontario, Canada, June 23-27, 1992.]

4229. Brietzke, Alexander Kendrick. "Nothing Is But What Is Not: Chekhovian Drama and the Crisis of Representation." Ph.D. diss., Stanford University, 1993. [UMI order no: AAC 9309574. Re-evaluates the assumption that nothing happens in Chekhov's plays.]

4230. Jackson, Robert Louis, ed. *Reading Chekhov's Text*. Contributions by Anton P. Chekhov, Ivan Bunin, Marena Senderovich, Michael C. Finke, Vladimir Golstein, Nils Ake Nilsson, Willa Chamberlain Axelrod, Alexandar Mihailovic, Julie W. de Sherbinin, Robert Louis Jackson, Richard Peace, Liza Knapp, Joseph L. Conrad, Andrew R. Durkin, Paul Debreczeny, Svetlana Evdokimova, Laurence Senlick, and Gary Saul Morson. Series in Russian Literature and Theory. Evanston, IL: Northwestern University Press, 1993. vi, 258 pp. [Contents: Robert Louis Jackson, "Introduction"; Anton P. Chekhov, "Do You Need My Biography?"; Ivan Bunin, "In Memory of Chekhov"; Marena Senderovich, "Chekhov's Name Drama"; Michael C. Finke, " 'At Sea': A Psychoanalytic Approach to Chekhov's First Signed Work"; Robert Louis Jackson, " 'The Enemies': A Story at War with Itself?"; Vladimir Golstein, " 'Doma': At Home and Not at Home"; Nils Ake Nilsson, " 'The Bishop': Its Theme"; Willa Chamberlain Axelrod, "Passage from Great Saturday to Easter Day in 'Holy Night' "; Alexandar Mihailovic, "Eschatology and Entombment in 'Ionych' "; Julie W. de Sherbinin, "Life beyond Text: The Nature of Illusion in 'The Teacher of Literature' "; Robert Louis Jackson, "Chekhov's 'The Student' "; Richard Peace, " 'In Exile' and Russian Fatalism"; Liza Knapp, "Fear and Pity in 'Ward Six': Chekhovian Catharsis"; Joseph L. Conrad, "Chekhov's 'Volodya': Transformations of Turgenev's 'First Love' "; Andrew R. Durkin, "Allusion and Dialogue in 'The Duel' "; Paul Debreczeny, " 'The Black Monk': Chekhov's Version of Symbolism"; Svetlana Evdokimova, " 'The Darling': Femininity Scorned and Desired"; Laurence Senlick, "Offenbach and Chekhov; or, La Belle Elena"; Gary

Saul Morson, "Uncle Vanya as Prosaic Metadrama."] REV: M. D. Fowler, *Canadian Slavonic Papers* 35, nos. 3-4 (September-December 1993): 421-422.

4231. Johnson, Ronald L. *Anton Chekhov: A Study of the Short Fiction.* New York: Twayne Publishers, 1993. 164 pp. REV: George Pahomov, *Slavic Review* 52, no. 4 (Winter 1993): 870-872.

4232. May, Charles E. "Reality in the Modern Short Story." *Style* 27, no. 3 (Fall 1993): 369-379.

4233. Pahomov, George. "Cexov's 'The Grasshopper': A Secular Saint's Life." *Slavic and East European Journal* 37, no. 1 (Spring 1993): 33-45.

4234. Pervukhina, Natalia. "Chekhov's 'Easter Night' and the Ornate Style." *Canadian Slavonic Papers* 35, nos. 1-2 (March-June 1993): 29-44.

4235. Stanion, Charles. "Oafish Behavior in 'The Lady with the Pet Dog.' " *Studies in Short Fiction* 30, no. 3 (Summer 1993): 402-403.

4236. Turner, C. J. G. "Chekhov's Story without a Title: Chronotope and Genre." *Canadian Slavonic Papers* 35, nos. 3-4 (September-December 1993): 329-334.

Dostoevsky

4237. Biron, Rebecca Elizabeth. "Murder: Narrative Experiments in Subjectivity." Ph.D. diss., University of Iowa, 1993. [UMI order no: AAC 9404478. Chapter 1 outlines and critiques definitions of subjectivity within philosophy and psychoanalysis, using Fyodor Dostoevsky's *Crime and Punishment* as a model.]

4238. Bzhoza, Khalina. "Tragicheskoe v dukhovnoi zhizni romannogo slova (mezhdu Bakhtinym i Dostoevskim)." *Dostoevsky Studies = Dostoevskii: stat'i i materialy* 1, no. 2 (1993): 191-205.

4238a. Dostoevsky, Fyodor. *The Brothers Karamazov: A Novel in Four Parts and an Epilogue.* Translated and with an introduction and notes by David McDuff. Penguin Classics. New York, NY: Penguin, 1993. xxix, 920 pp.

4239. ———. *Crime and Punishment.* Translated from the Russian by Richard Pevear and Larissa Volokhonsky. Introduction by W. J. Leatherbarrow. Everyman's Library, 35. New York: Alfred A. Knopf, 1993. xxxv, 564 pp. [Translation of *Prestuplenie i nakazanie.*]

4239a. ———. *Crime and Punishment: A Novel in Six Parts with Epilogue.* Translated and annotated by Richard Pevear and Larissa Volokhonsky. 1st Vintage classics ed. Vintage Classics. New York: Vintage Books, 1993. xx, 564 pp. [Translation of *Prestuplenie i nakazanie.*]

4240. ———. *The Grand Inquisitor: With Related Chapters from The Brothers Karamazov.* Edited and with an introduction by Charles Guignon. Translated by Constance Garnett. Indianapolis, IN: Hackett Pub. Co., 1993. xliii, 80 pp. [Contents: Grand Inquisitor; Russian Monk.]

4241. ———. *Notes from Underground.* Translated and annotated by Richard Pevear and Larissa Volokhonsky. 1st ed. New York: Alfred A. Knopf, 1993. xxiii, 136 pp.

4242. ———. *A Writer's Diary.* Translated and annotated by Kenneth Lantz. With an introductory study by Gary Saul Morson. Series in Russian Literature and Theory. Evanston, IL: Northwestern University Press, 1993-1994. 2 vols. [Translation of *Dnevnik pisatelia.* Contents: Vol. 1. 1873-1876 — vol. 2. 1877-1881.]

4243. [omitted]

4244. [omitted]

4245. Farris, June Pachuta. "Current Bibliography." *Dostoevsky Studies = Dostoevskii: Stat'i i materialy* 1, no. 1 (1993): 39-102.

4246. ———. "Current Bibliography." *Dostoevsky Studies = Dostoevskii: stat'i i materialy* 1, no. 2 (1993): 221-243.

4247. Fitzgerald, Gene. "At Last: A Complete Edition of Dostoevsky's Letters." *Dostoevsky Studies = Dostoevskii: Stat'i i materialy* 1, no. 1 (1993): 105-115. [Review article on Fyodor Dostoevsky, *Complete Letters*, ed. and trans. David Lowe, 5 vol. (Ann Arbor, MI: 1988-1991).]

4248. Flath, Carol A. "Fear of Faith: The Hidden Religious Message of *Notes from Underground.*" *Slavic and East European Journal* 37, no. 4 (Winter 1993): 510-529.

4249. Frank, Joseph. "The Gambler: A Study in Ethnopsychology." *Hudson Review* 46, no. 2 (Summer 1993): 301-322.

4250. Fridlender, G. "Dostoevskii i Ibsen." *Dostoevsky Studies = Dostoevskii: stat'i i materialy* 1, no. 2 (1993): 209-217.

4251. Genet, Jean. "A Reading of *The Brothers Karamazov.*" *Grand Street* 12, no. 3 (1993): 172-176. Arthur Goldhammer, trans.

4252. Iliev, Stefan. "Who Is Stavrogin: An Aesthetic Interpretation." Ph.D. diss., University of Illinois at Urbana-Champaign, 1993. [UMI order no: AAC 9314882.]

4253. Jackson, Robert Louis. *Dialogues with Dostoevsky: The Overwhelming Questions.* Stanford, CA: Stanford University Press, 1993. 346 pp. [Contents: Introduction: Dostoevsky in Movement; 1. The Ethics of Vision I: Turgenev's "Execution of Tropmann" and Dostoevsky's View of the Matter; 2. The Ethics of Vision II: The Tolstoyan Synthesis; 3. The Ethics of Vision III: The Punishment of the Tramp Prokhorov in Chekhov's The Island of Sakhalin; 4. Dostoevsky in Chekhov's Garden of Eden: "Because of Little Apples"; 5. A View from the Underground: On Nikolai Nikolaevich Strakhov's Letter About His Good Friend Fyodor Mikhailovich Dostoevsky and on Leo Nikolaevich Tolstoy's Cautious Response to It; 6. In the Interests of Social Pedagogy: Gorky's Polemic Against the Staging of *The Devils* in 1913 and the *Aftermath* in 1917; 7. Chateaubriand and Dostoevsky: Elective Affinities; 8. Dostoevsky and the Marquis de

Sade: The Final Encounter; 9. The Root and the Flower: Dostoevsky and Turgenev, a Comparative Aesthetic; 10. Unbearable Questions: Two Views of Gogol and the Critical Synthesis. In the Darkness of the Night: Tolstoy's *Kreutzer Sonata* and Dostoevsky's *Notes from the Underground*; 12. States of Ambiguity: Early Shakespeare and Late Dostoevsky, the Two Ivans; 13. Counterpoint: Nietzsche and Dostoevsky; 14. Vision in His Soul: Vyacheslav I. Ivanov's Dostoevsky; 15. Bakhtin's Poetics of Dostoevsky and Dostoevsky's "Declaration of Religious Faith"; 16. Last Stop: Virtue and Immortality in *The Brothers Karamazov*.]

4254. Katz, Michael R. "The Nihilism of Sonia Marmeladova." *Dostoevsky Studies = Dostoevskii: Stat'i i materialy* 1, no. 1 (1993): 25-36.

4255. Lynch, Richard A. "Bakhtin's Ethical Vision." *Philosophy and Literature* 17, no. 1 (April 1993): 98-109. [Revised version of a paper read at the University of Illinois Graduate Philosophy Conference, May 1992.]

4256. Murav, Harriet. "Legal Fiction in Dostoevsky's *Diary of a Writer*." *Dostoevsky Studies = Dostoevskii: stat'i i materialy* 1, no. 2 (1993): 155-173.

4257. Natov, Nadine. "Report on the Seventh Dostoevsky Symposium." *Dostoevsky Studies = Dostoevskii: Stat'i i materialy* 1, no. 1 (1993): 139-143.

4258. Neuhäuser, Rudolf. "*The Dream of a Ridiculous Man*: Topicality as a Literary Device." *Dostoevsky Studies = Dostoevskii: stat'i i materialy* 1, no. 2 (1993): 175-190.

4259. Pope, Richard, and Nikita Lary. "G.M. Fridlender and the Academy Edition of Dostoevskij." *Slavic and East European Journal* 37, no. 1 (Spring 1993): 23-32.

4260. Repin, Natalie Vladimir. "The Eschatological Tendency in the Works of F. Dostoevsky (An Essay in Literary Exegesis)." Ph.D. diss., University of Illinois at Urbana-Champaign, 1993.

4261. Rosen, Steven J. "Homoerotic Body Language in Dostoevsky." *Psychoanalytic Review* 80, no. 3 (Fall 1993): 405-432.

4262. Selten, Jean-Paul C. J. "Freud and Dostoevsky." *Psychoanalytic Review* 80, no. 3 (Fall 1993): 441-455.

4263. Slattery, Dennis Patrick. "Corrupting Corpse vs. Reasoned Abstraction: The Play of Evil in *The Brothers Karamazov*." *Dostoevsky Studies = Dostoevskii: Stat'i i materialy* 1, no. 1 (1993): 3-23.

4264. White, Harry. "Dostoevsky's Christian Despot." *Russian Language Journal* 47, nos. 156-158 (Winter-Spring-Fall 1993): 65-79.

Elagin

4265. Baker, Robert L. "Ivan Elagin: An Appreciation." *Canadian-American Slavic Studies* 27, nos. 1-4 (1993): 217-218.

4266. Betaki, Vasilii. "Sonet Ivanu Elaginu." *Canadian-American Slavic Studies* 27, nos. 1-4 (1993): 294. [Poem.]

4267. Bogachinskaia-Perlina, Nina. "Ivanu Elaginu: Apologeticheskoe." *Canadian-American Slavic Studies* 27, nos. 1-4 (1993): 296-297. [Poem.]

4268. ———. "Pamiati Ivana Elagina." *Canadian-American Slavic Studies* 27, nos. 1-4 (1993): 295. [Poem.]

4269. Bongart, Sergei. "Stikhi Ivanu Elaginu." *Canadian-American Slavic Studies* 27, nos. 1-4 (1993): 298. [Poem.]

4270. D'iachenko, Boris. "Klan Matveevykh." *Canadian-American Slavic Studies* 27, nos. 1-4 (1993): 219-229.

4271. Dimer, Evgeniia. "Velikan." *Canadian-American Slavic Studies* 27, nos. 1-4 (1993): 230-233.

4272. Elagin, Ivan. "Certain Difficulties in Translating Poetry." *Canadian-American Slavic Studies* 27, nos. 1-4 (1993): 181-191. [Speech given at a conference sponsored by PEN in 1970.]

4273. ———. "Pis'mo Mikhailu Krepsu." *Canadian-American Slavic Studies* 27, nos. 1-4 (1993): 279.

4274. Etkind, Efim. "Metafory izgnaniia." *Canadian-American Slavic Studies* 27, nos. 1-4 (1993): 1-8.

4275. Fesenko, Tat'iana. "Sorok shest' let druzhby s Ivanom Elaginym: vospominaniia." *Canadian-American Slavic Studies* 27, nos. 1-4 (1993): 234-244. [Excerpt from the book *Sorok shest' let druzhby s Ivanom Elaginym* (Paris: 1991).]

4276. Hollerbakh, Sergei. "Vospriiatie khudozhnika." *Canadian-American Slavic Studies* 27, nos. 1-4 (1993): 245-249.

4277. Lipska, Grazhina. "Neskol'ko izrechenii Ivana Elagina." *Canadian-American Slavic Studies* 27, nos. 1-4 (1993): 289-291. [Elagin's anecdotes compiled by his students.]

4278. Liubin, Evgenii. "V fevral'skuiu metel'." *Canadian-American Slavic Studies* 27, nos. 1-4 (1993): 250-252.

4279. Markov, Vladimir, and Ivan Elagin. "Sostiazanie v perevode." *Canadian-American Slavic Studies* 27, nos. 1-4 (1993): 192-194. [Two translations, one by Markov and one by Elagin, of "To His Coy Mistress" by Andrew Marvell.]

4280. Matveyeff, Helen. "Knight of the Spirit." *Canadian-American Slavic Studies* 27, nos. 1-4 (1993): 253-255.

4281. Matveyeff, Helen, and Ivan Elagin. "Muza v domashnikh tapochkakh." *Canadian-American Slavic Studies* 27, nos. 1-4 (1993): 280-288.

4282. Moseshvili, Georgii. " 'Poema bez nazvaniia' Ivana Elagina (Opyt razvernutogo kommentariia)." *Cana-*

dian-American Slavic Studies 27, nos. 1-4 (1993): 9-19.

4283. Nollan, Valerie Z. "My Life: In Memoriam Ivan Elagin." *Canadian-American Slavic Studies* 27, nos. 1-4 (1993): 301. [Poem.]

4284. Osipovich, Alexander. "Za Shakhmatami." *Canadian-American Slavic Studies* 27, nos. 1-4 (1993): 259-260.

4285. Pahomov, George. "Ivan Elagin: A Retrospective." *Canadian-American Slavic Studies* 27, nos. 1-4 (1993): 20-30.

4286. Petrochenkov, V. "Pamiati ushedshikh." *Canadian-American Slavic Studies* 27, nos. 1-4 (1993): 302. [Poem.]

4287. Pruner, Liudmila. "Ivan Elagin: Slavianskii fakul'tet, satira i poeziia (Bagateli)." *Canadian-American Slavic Studies* 27, nos. 1-4 (1993): 261-269.

4288. Shtein, Eduard. "Ivan Elagin: Akrostishist." *Canadian-American Slavic Studies* 27, nos. 1-4 (1993): 270-273.

4289. Sinkevich, Valentina. "Ivanu Elaginu, Elene Dubrovinoi." *Canadian-American Slavic Studies* 27, nos. 1-4 (1993): 303-305. [Poem.]

4290. ———. "Poslednie dni i poslednie knigi Ivana Elagina." *Canadian-American Slavic Studies* 27, nos. 1-4 (1993): 31-46.

4291. Slavina, Kira. "Pamiati Ivana Elagina." *Canadian-American Slavic Studies* 27, nos. 1-4 (1993): 306. [Poem.]

4292. Smith, Melissa T., and Miroslaw Kukielka. "Selected Bibliography of Ivan Elagin." *Canadian-American Slavic Studies* 27, nos. 1-4 (1993): 309-315.

4293. Tolmachev, Vasilii. "Khristianskie motivy v russkoi poezii i tvorchestvo Ivana Elagina." *Canadian-American Slavic Studies* 27, nos. 1-4 (1993): 47-63.

4294. Vitkovskii, Evgenii. "I list mel'kaet." *Canadian-American Slavic Studies* 27, nos. 1-4 (1993): 307-308. [Poem.]

4295. Wallace, Charlotte. "An Evening with Ivan Elagin." *Canadian-American Slavic Studies* 27, nos. 1-4 (1993): 274-275.

4296. Wilt, Ning Wan. "Ivan Elagin v Kitae." *Canadian-American Slavic Studies* 27, nos. 1-4 (1993): 64-67.

4297. ———. "Moi uchitel' Ivan Venediktovich Elagin." *Canadian-American Slavic Studies* 27, nos. 1-4 (1993): 276-278.

Gogol'

4298. Ernst, Charles A. S. " 'I Am That King': Disordered History and Delusional Writing: The Artful Derangements of Gogol's 'Diary.' " *Cithara* 32, no. 2 (May 1993): 39-48.

4299. Fusso, Susanne. *Designing Dead Souls: An Anatomy of Disorder in Gogol*. Stanford, CA: Stanford University Press, 1993. 195 pp.

4300. Seifrid, Thomas. "Suspicion toward Narrative: The Nose and the Problem of Autonomy in Gogol's 'Nos.' " *Russian Review* 52, no. 3 (July 1993): 382-396. [Shorter version of this paper was delivered at the Twenty-Third National Convention of the AAASS in Miami, FL, in November 1991.]

4301. Shapiro, Gavriel. *Nikolai Gogol and the Baroque Cultural Heritage*. University Park, PA: Pennsylvania State University Press, c1993. xiii, 259 pp. [Originally presented as the author's thesis (doctoral)—University of Illinois at Urbana-Champaign, 1984.]

4302. Swensen, Andrew J. "Vampirism in Gogol's Short Fiction." *Slavic and East European Journal* 37, no. 4 (Winter 1993): 490-509.

Kharms

4303. Carrick, Neil Peter. "Daniil Kharms and a Theology of the Absurd." Ph.D. diss., Northwestern University, 1993. [UMI order no: AAC 9327166.]

4304. Kharms, Daniil. *Incidences*. Edited and translated by Neil Cornwell. Extraordinary Classics. London; New York: Serpent's Tail, 1993. vii, 227 pp. [Translated from the Russian. Contents: Incidents — Assorted stories — Yelizaveta Bam: A Dramatic Work — Non-fiction and assorted writings, theoretical pieces.]

Mandel'shtam

4305. Cixous, Hélène. "We Who Are Free, Are We Free?" *Critical Inquiry* 19, no. 2 (Winter 1993): 201-219.

4306. Harris, Jane Gary. "Sources, Echoes, and Transformations: Mandelshtam's Armenian Myth in the Lyrics of the 1930s." *Canadian-American Slavic Studies* 27, nos. 1-4 (1993): 90-106.

4307. Mandelstam, Osip. *The Noise of Time: The Prose of Osip Mandelstam*. Edited and translated with critical essays by Clarence Brown. New York, NY: Penguin Books, 1993. 249 pp.

Nabokov

4308. Barabtarlo, Gennady. "Nabokov's Reliquary Poem." *Russian Review* 52, no. 4 (October 1993): 540-546.

4309. Bloom, Barbara. "A Collection (portfolio)." *Grand Street* 12, no. 3 (1993): 177-193. With commentary by Howard Halle. [Article contains reproductions of art work by Bloom based on Vladimir Nabokov's books.]

4310. Boyd, Brian. "Annotation to *Ada*: 1. Part 1, Chapter 1." *Nabokovian*, no. 30 (Spring 1993): 9-48.

4311. ———. "Annotation to *Ada*: 2. Part 1, Chapter 2." *Nabokovian*, no. 31 (Fall 1993): 8-40.

4312. Flower, Dean. "Nabokov and Nastiness." *Hudson Review* 45, no. 4 (Winter 1993): 573-582.

4313. Foster, John Burt, Jr. *Nabokov's Art of Memory and European Modernism.* Princeton, NJ: Princeton University Press, c1993. xviii, 260 pp. [Contents: Pt. 1. Points of Departure. 1. The European Nabokov, the Modernist Moment, and Cultural Biography. 2. The Self-Defined Origins of an Artist of Memory. From Synesthesia to the Two Master Narratives. Nietzsche, Baudelaire, and the Discourse of Modernity. 3. The Rejection of Anticipatory Memory: From Mary to *The Defense* and Glory (1925-1930). Pt. 2. Toward France. 4. Encountering French Modernism: Kamera Obskura (1931-1932). 5. From the Personal to the Intertextual: Dostoevsky and the Two-Tiered Mnemonic System in Despair (1932-1933). 6. Narrative between Art and Memory: Writing and Rewriting "Mademoiselle O" (1936-1967). 7. Memory Modernism, and the Fictive Autobiographies. Recollected Emotion in "Spring in Fialta" (1936-1947). The Covert Modernism of *The Gift* (1934-1937). Pt. 3. In English. 8. Cultural Mobility and British Modernism: *The Real Life of Sebastian Knight* and *Bend Sinister* (1938-1946). 9. Autobiographical Images: The Shaping of *Speak, Memory* (1946-1967). 10. The Cultural Self-Consciousness of *Speak, Memory.* Epilogue: Proust over T. S. Eliot in *Pale Fire* (1962).] REV: Galya Diment, *Slavic Review* 52, no. 3 (Fall 1993): 634-635.

4314. Goldpaugh, Tom. "A Persistent Snore in the Next Room: Nabokov and *Finnegans Wake.*" *Nabokovian,* no. 30 (Spring 1993): 58-60. [Abstract of a paper delivered at the Annual MLA Convention, New York City, December 1992.]

4315. Nester, Robbi L. Kellman. "Doubling and Discovery: Vladimir Nabokov's Literary Games." Ph.D. diss., University of California at Irvine, 1993. [UMI order no: AAC 9402430.]

4316. Nicol, Charles. "Annotations & Queries." *Nabokovian,* no. 30 (Spring 1993): 49-57. Contributions by Jake Pultorak, Jason Merrill, and D. Barton Johnson. [Includes analysis of *Lolita, Pnin* and *Ada.*]

4317. ———. "Annotations & Queries." *Nabokovian,* no. 31 (Fall 1993): 41-54. Contributions by Gerard De Vries, Earl Sampson, and Galya Diment. [Includes analysis of Nabokov's poetry and *Pnin.*]

4318. Parker, Stephen Jan. "1992 Nabokov Bibliography." *Nabokovian,* no. 31 (Fall 1993): 55-68.

4319. ———. "News." *Nabokovian,* no. 30 (Spring 1993): 3-8.

4320. ———. "News." *Nabokovian,* no. 31 (Fall 1993): 3-7.

4321. Shapiro, Gavriel. "On Nabokov's Pen Name Sirin." *Nabokovian,* no. 30 (Spring 1993): 62. [Abstract of a paper delivered at the Annual AATSEEL Convention, New York City, December 1992.]

4322. ———. "The Salome Motif in Nabokov's *Invitation to a Beheading.*" *Nabokovian,* no. 30 (Spring 1993): 61. [Abstract of a paper delivered at the Annual MLA Convention, New York City, December 1992.]

4323. Toker, Leona. "Liberal Ironists and the 'Gaudily Painted Savage': On Richard Rorty's Reading of Vladimir Nabokov." *Nabokovian,* no. 30 (Spring 1993): 60. [Abstract of a paper delivered at the Annual MLA Convention, New York City, December 1992.]

4324. Wickliff, Gregory. "The Politics of Perception: Vladimir Nabokov's Images of the 1940s." *Nabokovian,* no. 30 (Spring 1993): 62-63. [Abstract of Ph.D. dissertation, Purdue University, December 1991.]

Pasternak

4325. Dryzhakova, Elena. "Stoit li perevodit' stikhi?" *Canadian-American Slavic Studies* 27, nos. 1-4 (1993): 199-216. [Compares the translations of Brown, Argus, and Elagin to the Pasternak poem.]

4326. Kostalevsky, Marina. "Olitsetvorennye dostovernosti (Poetiko-muzykal'nyi kliuch k stikhotvoreniiu Pasternaka 'Opiat Shopen ne ishchet vygod...')." *Russian Language Journal* 47, nos. 156-158 (Winter-Spring-Fall 1993): 81-93.

4327. Smoliakova, Nelly. "Ob odnom perevode Ivana Elagina." *Canadian-American Slavic Studies* 27, nos. 1-4 (1993): 195-198.

4328. Vaserstein, Tamara. "K voprosu o prototipe glavnogo geroia 'Doktora Zhivago.'" *Russian Language Journal* 47, nos. 156-158 (Winter-Spring-Fall 1993): 95-105.

Pushkin

4329. Bethea, David M., ed. *Puskin Today.* Contributions by William Mills Todd, III, Caryl Emerson, Sergej Davydov, Simon Karlinsky, Daniel Rancour-Laferriere, William E. Harkins, David M. Bethea, J. Thomas Shaw, Walter Vickery, Leslie O'Bell, Stephanie Sandler, Geroge J. Gutsche, Paul Debreczeny, and Victor Terras. Bloomington, IN: Indiana University Press, c1993. vi, 258 pp. [Contents: David M. Bethea, "Introduction," pp. 1-10; William Mills Todd, III, "'The Russian Terpsichore's Soul-Filled Flight': Dance Themes in *Eugene Onegin,*" pp. 13-30; Caryl Emerson, "'The Queen of Spades' and the Open End," pp. 31-37; Sergej Davydov, "Puskin's Easter Triptych; 'Hermit fathers and immaculate women,' 'Imitation of the Italian,' and 'Secular Power,'" pp. 38-58; Simon Karlinsky, "Bestuzev-Marlinskij's Journey to Revel' and Puskin," pp. 59-72; Daniel Rancour-Laferriere, "The Couvade of Peter the Great: A Psychoanalytic Aspect of *The Bronze Horseman,*" pp. 73-85; William E. Harkins, "The Rejected Image: Puskin's Use of Antenantiosis," pp. 86-98; David M. Bethea, "The Role of the Eques in Puskin's *Bronze Horseman,*" pp. 99-118; J. Thomas Shaw, "Puskin on His African Heritage: Publications during His Lifetime," pp. 121-135; Walter Vickery, "Odessa—Watershed Year: Patterns in Puskin's Love Lyrics," pp. 136-151; Leslie O'Bell, "Through the Magic Crystal to *Eugene Onegin,*" pp. 152-170; Stephanie Sandler, "Solitude and Soliloquy in *Boris Gudunov,*" pp. 171-184;

Geroge J. Gutsche, "Puskin and Nicholas: The Problem of 'Stanzas,'" pp. 185-200; Paul Debreczeny, "Puskin's Reputation in Nineteenth-Century Russia; A Statistical Approach," pp. 201-213; Victor Terras, "Puskin's Prose Fiction in a Historical Context," pp. 214-219.] REV: John McNair, *Australian Slavonic and East European Studies* 7, no. 1 (1993): 137-139.

4330. Frazier, Melissa. *"Kapitanskaia dochka* and the Creativity of Borrowing." *Slavic and East European Journal* 37, no. 4 (Winter 1993): 472-489.

4331. Shaw, J. Thomas. "Parts of Speech in Puskin's Rhymewords and Nonrhymed Endwords." *Slavic and East European Journal* 37, no. 1 (Spring 1993): 1-22.

4332. Tracy, Lewis. "Decoding Puskin: Resurrecting Some Readers' Responses to *Egyptian Nights.*" *Slavic and East European Journal* 37, no. 4 (Winter 1993): 456-471.

Rasputin

4333. Diment, Galya. "Valentin Rasputin and Siberian Nationalism." *World Literature Today* 67, no. 1 (Winter 1993): 69-73.

4334. Laychuk, Julian. "Conflicts in the Soviet Countryside in the Novellas of Valentin Rasputin." *Rocky Mountain Review of Language and Literature* 47, nos. 1-2 (1993): 11-30.

4335. Rasputin, Valentin. " 'Motherland' Is Not an Abstract Notion." *World Literature Today* 67, no. 1 (Winter 1993): 40-43. Yuri Azarov and William Riggan, trans.

Rybakov

4336. Rybakov, Anatoli. *Fear.* Translated by Antonina W. Bouis. New York, NY: Laurel, 1993, c1992. viii, 689 pp. [Translation of: *Tridtsat' piatyi i drugie gody.* First published: (Boston, MA: Little, Brown, 1992).]

4337. Schultze, Sydney. "The Moral Dimension of Rybakov's *Deti Arbata.*" *Russian Language Journal* 47, nos. 156-158 (Winter-Spring-Fall 1993): 147-155.

Solzhenitsyn

4338. Dunlop, John B. "Solzhenitsyn Delays His Return to Russia." *RFE/RL Research Report* 2, no. 3 (January 15, 1993): 5-7.

4339. Solzhenitsyn, Aleksandr. "Pis'mo Ivanu Elaginu." *Canadian-American Slavic Studies* 27, nos. 1-4 (1993): 292.

Tolstaya

4340. Alagova, Tamara, and Nina Efimov. "Interview with Tatyana Tolstaya." *World Literature Today* 67, no. 1 (Winter 1993): 49-53. Michael A. Aguirre, trans.

4341. Goscilo, Helena. "Perspective in Tatyana Tolstaya's Wonderland of Art." *World Literature Today* 67, no. 1 (Winter 1993): 80-90.

Tolstoy

4342. Mandelker, Amy. *Framing Anna Karenina: Tolstoy, The Woman Question, and the Victorian Novel.* Theory and Interpretation of Narrative Series. Columbus, OH: Ohio State University Press, c1993. xv, 241 pp.

4343. Orwin, Donna Tussing. *Tolstoy's Art and Thought, 1847-1880.* Princeton, NJ: Princeton University Press, c1993. viii, 269 pp. [Contents: Pt. 1. The 1850s. 1. Analysis and Synthesis. The Hegelian Atmosphere of the 1850s. Chernyshevsky. The Contemporary Reception of Tolstoy's Work. Tolstoy and Chernyshevshy. Subjective Reality for the Early Tolstoy. Tolstoy's Goethean Realism. 2. The Young Tolstoy's Understanding of the Human Soul. Tolstoy, the Psychological Analyst. Synthesis and the Influence of Rousseau. 3. The First Synthesis: Nature and the Young Tolstoy. Tolstoy's Understanding of Nature in the Early 1850s. A Maturing Philosophy of Nature (Tolstoy and Fet). Botkin and the Exploration of the Feelings. Sterne. N. V. Stankevich. Nature, Reason, and the Feelings ("Lucerne"). Objective and Subjective Poetry. The Metaphysics of Opposites and Goethe Again. Pt. 2. The 1860s. 4. Nature and Civilization in *The Cossacks*. Natural Necessity in The Cossacks. The Morality of Self-Sacrifice in the Stag's Lair. The Cossack as Savage Man. 5. The Unity of Man and Nature in *War and Peace*. Nature and History in *War and Peace*. Circular versus Faustian Reason in *War and Peace*. The Morality of Nature in *War and Peace*. The Importance of Spirit in Wartime. Reason, Morality, and Nature in the Human Soul. The Rostovs and "Living Life" The Bolkonskys. Pierre. "Lyrical Daring" in *War and Peace*. Pt. 3. The 1870s. 6. From Nature to Culture in the 1870s. Schopenhauer. Schopenhauer and Arzamas. Nature after Schopenhauer. Linking Happiness and Morality in Anna Karenina. 7. Drama in *Anna Karenina*. The Symposium in the Restaurant. Anna as Heroine of a Novel. Anna's Radical Individualism. To Judge or Not Judge Anna. 8. Science, Philosophy and Synthesis in the 1870s. The Enduring Importance of Unity for Tolstoy. Atomism. Kantian Epistemology. The Attack on the Individual. The Denigration of the "Personality" The Morally Free Individual in *Anna Karenina*. Synthesis and Lyrical Daring Once Again.] REV: Andrew Donskov, *Canadian Slavonic Papers* 35, nos. 3-4 (September-December 1993): 423-424.

4344. Rojas, Carlos. "Picasso and Tolstoy: On Life, Love and Death." *Comparatist* 17 (May 1993): 1-17.

4345. Tolstoy, Lev. *Anna Karenina.* Edited and introduced by Leonard J. Kent and Nina Berberova. New York: Modern Library, 1993. xxvii, 927 pp. [Revised version of the Constance Garnett translation.]

4346. Woodworth, Marc. "Sophia Tolstoy at Yasnaya Polyana." *Salmagundi,* no. 100 (Fall 1993): 147-149.

Tsvetaeva

4347. Mamonova, Tatyana. "Feminizm Mariny Tsvetaevoi = Feminism of Marina Tsvetaeva." *Woman and Earth* 2, no. 1 (December 10, 1993): 24-27.

4348. Osipovich, Tat'iana. "Mif detstva v avtobiograficheskoi proze Mariny Tsvetaevoi." *Canadian-American Slavic Studies* 27, nos. 1-4 (1993): 157-164.

4349. Schweitzer, Viktoria. *Tsvetaeva.* Translated from the Russian by Robert Chandler and H. T. Willetts. Edited and annotated by Angela Livingstone. 1st American ed. New York: Farrar, Straus & Giroux, 1993. xv, 413 p. [Translation of *Byt i bytie Mariny TSvetaevoi.* Poetry translated by Peter Norman.] REV: David M. Bethea, *New York Times Book Review* 98, no. 27 (July 4, 1993): 2ff. Mary Oliver, *Book World* 23, no. 26 (June 27, 1993): 4.

4350. Sinitsky, T. "Her Road: Tribute to Marina Tsvetaeva." *Woman and Earth* 2, no. 1 (December 10, 1993): 20-21.

4351. Tavis, Anna A. "Russia in Rilke: Rainer Maria Rilke's Correspondence with Marina Tsvetaeva." *Slavic Review* 52, no. 3 (Fall 1993): 494-511.

Yevtushenko

4352. Yevtushenko, Yevgeny. "The Loss." *World Literature Today* 67, no. 1 (Winter 1993): 5. Yevgeny Yevtushenko and James Reagan, trans. [Followed by a critical article by Yevgeny Yevtushenko (p. 5).]

4353. ———. *Ne umirai prezhde smerti: Russkaia skazka = Don't Die Before Your Death.* New York: Liberty Pub. House, 1993. 537 pp.

4354. ———. "What is Lost in the Poem 'The Loss'?" *World Literature Today* 67, no. 1 (Winter 1993): 5. Joseph Mozur, trans.

■ Ukrainian

4355. Black, Helen. " 'Blood-remembering': Notes on Oles Honchar's *The Cathedral.*" *Ukrainian Quarterly* 49, no. 2 (Summer 1993): 195-200.

4356. Fizer, John. "Ukrainian Criticism in the Post-Socialist Realism Period." *Ukrainian Quarterly* 49, no. 1 (Spring 1993): 14-22.

4357. Makaryk, Irena R. "Ophelia as Poet: Lesja Ukrainka and the Woman as Artist." *Canadian Review of Comparative Literature = Revue Canadienne de Littérature Comparée* 20, nos. 3-4 (September-December 1993): 337-354.

4358. Miller, Irina. "Creating the Dramatic Space: *Blind Sight* by the Yara Arts Group." *Slavic and East European Performance* 13, no. 3 (Fall 1993): 40-43. [Review of a Yara Arts Group (New York) production based on the life and work of Yeroshenko.]

4359. Rudnytzky, Leonid. "Unfettered by History: The Imaginative Writings of Mykhaylo Hrushevsky." *Ukrainian Quarterly* 49, no. 1 (Spring 1993): 23-34.

4360. Windle, Kevin. "Shevchenko's narrative poem *Maria* in three Russian translations: a comparative study." *Australian Slavonic and East European Studies* 7, no. 1 (1993): 25-47.

■ Yiddish and Hebrew

4361. Alter, Robert. "Fogel and the Forging of a Hebrew Self." *Prooftexts* 13, no. 1 (January 1993): 3-13.

4362. Fogel, David. "Language and Style in Our Young Literature (1931)." *Prooftexts* 13, no. 1 (January 1993): 15-20. Translated from the Hebrew by Yeal Meroz and Eric Zakim.

4363. Glatstein, Jacob. *I Keep Recalling: The Holocaust Poems of Jacob Glatstein.* Translated from the Yiddish by Barnett Zumoff. Introduction by Emanuel S. Goldsmith. [Hoboken, NJ]: Ktav Pub. House, c1993. xxvi, 289 pp. [Illustrations by Yonia Fain.]

4364. Glick, Hirsh. "Partisan Hymn." *Tikkun* 8, no. 2 (March/April 1993): 31. Translated from the Yiddish by Aaron Kramer.

4365. Gluzman, Michael. "Unmasking the Politics of Simplicity in Modernist Hebrew Poetry: Rereading David Fogel." *Prooftexts* 13, no. 1 (January 1993): 21-43.

4366. Hoffman, Yoel. "Kätzchen." *Translation*, no. 28 (Spring 1993): 13-65. Translated from the Hebrew by David Kriss and Eddie Levenston.

4367. Kronfeld, Chana. "Fogel and Modernism: A Liminal Moment in Hebrew Literary History." *Prooftexts* 13, no. 1 (January 1993): 45-63.

4368. Mantovan, Daniela. "Der Nister and His Symbolist Short Stories (1913-1929): Patterns of Imagination." Ph.D. diss., Columbia University, 1993. [UMI order no: AAC 9412809.]

4369. Nachmias, Simon. "I Don't Understand Russian and I Translate." *Translation*, no. 28 (Spring 1993): 106. Translated from the Hebrew by Robert Friend and Michel Konstantyn.

4370. Seidman, Naomi. " 'It Is You I Speak from within Me': David Fogel's Poetics of the Feminine Voice." *Prooftexts* 13, no. 1 (January 1993): 87-102.

4371. Seidman, Naomi Sheindel. " 'A Marriage Made in Heaven?': The Sexual Politics of Hebrew-Yiddish Diglossia." Ph.D. diss., University of California, Berkeley, 1993.

4372. Shavit, Uzi. "David Fogel and Hebrew Free Verse: Is There a Fogelian *Nusah* in Hebrew Poetry?" *Prooftexts* 13, no. 1 (January 1993): 65-86.

4373. Yudkin, Leon I., ed. *Hebrew Literature in the Wake of the Holocaust.* Contributions by Leon I. Yudkin, Abraham Marthan, William D. Brierley, Livia Bitton Jackson, Zilla Jane Goodman, Avraham Balaban, Rachel Feldhay Brenner, and Savyon Liebrecht. Rutherford: Fairleigh Dickinson University Press; London; Toronto: Associated University Presses, c1993. 131 pp. [Published in conjunction with the International Center for University Teaching of Jewish Civilization. Contents: Leon I. Yudkin, "Introduction," pp. 9-10; Leon I. Yudkin, "Narrative Perspectives in Holocaust Literature," pp. 13-32; Abraham

Marthan, "The Ivory Tower and the Gas Chamber: On the Nature and Teaching of Holocaust Literature," pp. 33-51; William D. Brierley, "Memory in the Work of Yehiel Dinur (Ka-Tzetnik 135633)," pp. 52-74; Livia Bitton-Jackson, "Miriam Akavia: Redeeming the Past," pp. 75-84; Zilla Jane Goodman, "Aharon Appelfeld's *The Immortal Bartfuss*: The Holocaust, the Body, and Repression," pp. 85-96; Avraham Balaban, "Aharon Appelfeld's *For Every Sin*: The Jewish Legacy after the Holocaust," pp. 97-107; Rachel Feldhay Brenner, "The Reception of Holocaust Testimony in Israeli Literature: Shulamit Hareven's 'The Witness' and 'Twilight,' " pp. 108-124; Savyon Liebrecht, "The Influence of the Holocaust on My Work," pp. 125-130.]

4374. Zakim, Eric. "Between Fragment and Authority in David Fogel's (Re)Presentation of Subjectivity." *Prooftexts* 13, no. 1 (January 1993): 103-124.

■ (Former) Yugoslav

General

4375. Balantic, France. [Poems]. *North Dakota Quarterly* 61, no. 1 (Winter 1993): 28-30. Translated by Frank F. Bukvic. ["The Marked Ones," p. 28; "The Whiteness of Death," p. 28; "A Mouth Filled with Earth," p. 29; Autumn Fires," p. 29; "At the Crossroads," p. 30; "The Evening is Red," p. 30.]

4376. Bankovic, Jelena S. "*Sumatraism* and Expressionist Firmament of Crnjanski's Literary Creation." *Serbian Studies* 7, no. 1 (Spring 1993): 19-32.

4377. Bankovic, Jelena Stanoje. "Metamorphoses of Descent in Crnjanski's Literary Creation: A Psychoanalytical and Psycholinguistic Study." Ph.D. diss., University of Illinois at Chicago, 1993. [UMI order no: AAC 9335112.]

4378. Beckovic, Matija. [Poems]. *North Dakota Quarterly* 61, no. 1 (Winter 1993): 31-33. Translated by Peter Russell. ["False Tracks," p. 31; "Matija Beckovic," p. 32; "A Lament for Myself—A Fragment," p. 33.]

4379. Bernik, France. "The National and the Universal in Slovene Literature." *Slovene Studies* 14, no. 2 (1992, published September 1994): 125-131. [Paper presented at a special session of the Society for Slovene Studies at the 1993 annual meeting of the American Association of Teachers of Slavic and East European Languages in Toronto, Ontario, Canada, December 27-30, 1993, on the occasion of the 20th Anniversary of Activities of the Society for Slovene Studies.]

4380. Burns, Richard. "Song of a Survivor." *North Dakota Quarterly* 61, no. 1 (Winter 1993): 34-35. ["For Oskar Davico."]

4381. Butler, Francis. "Mechanical Borrowing or Conscious Adaptation? The Monk Domentijan's Use of the East Slavic *Sermon on Law and Grace*." *Slavic and East European Journal* 37, no. 4 (Winter 1993): 442-455.

4382. Butler, Thomas. "Muslim Singers of Tales in the Balkans: The Clue to Homer." *Cross Currents: A Yearbook of Central European Culture*, no. 12 (1993): 166-171. [Includes text of "Hasan Aga's Wife" (pp. 169-171).]

4383. Crnjanski, Milos. "Apotheosis." *Serbian Studies* 7, no. 2 (Fall 1993, published in 1995): 123-128. Translated by Bogdan Rakic.

4384. Davico, Oskar. "Poems from Hana (1939)." *North Dakota Quarterly* 61, no. 1 (Winter 1993): 55-57. Translated by Richard Burns and Dasa Maric.

4385. Debeljak, Ales. "Fearful Moments." *North Dakota Quarterly* 61, no. 1 (Winter 1993): 58. Translated by Ales Debeljak and Kelly Hawkins.

4386. Dizdar, Mak. "From *The Stone Sleeper*." *North Dakota Quarterly* 61, no. 1 (Winter 1993): 59-62. Introduced and translated by Francis R. Jones. ["Introduction," pp. 59-60; "Testament on the Hunt," pp. 60-61; "Sun," p. 62.]

4387. Djordjevic, Milan. [Poems]. *North Dakota Quarterly* 61, no. 1 (Winter 1993): 63-64. Translated by Milan Djordjevic. ["Orange," p. 63; "Pure Colors," pp. 63-64.]

4388. Gadjanski, Ivan. [Poems]. *North Dakota Quarterly* 61, no. 1 (Winter 1993): 73-77. Translated by Karolina Udovicki. ["Balkan Street," pp. 73-76; "Summing Up," p. 77.]

4389. Gavrilovic, Manojle. [Poems]. *North Dakota Quarterly* 61, no. 1 (Winter 1993): 78. Translated by Vasa D. Mihailovich. ["Building a City," p. 78; "The Master of Bees," p. 78.]

4390. Gorup, Radmila Jovanovic. "Pavic's *The Inner Side of the Wind*: A Postmodern Novel." *Serbian Studies* 7, no. 1 (Spring 1993): 57-68.

4391. Herman-Sekulic, Maja. "Gumbo." *North Dakota Quarterly* 61, no. 1 (Winter 1993): 79. ["In memoriam Milan Milisic."]

4392. Hristic, Jovan. [Poems]. *North Dakota Quarterly* 61, no. 1 (Winter 1993): 80-82. Translated by Bernard Johnson. ["Who Still Needs Fine Stories?" p. 80; "Socrates on the Battlefield," p. 80; "Barbarians," p. 81; "Orators Makes Speechs on the Squares," p. 82.]

4393. Jovanovski, Meto. "Journey." *North Dakota Quarterly* 61, no. 1 (Winter 1993): 89-94. Translated by Jeffrey J. Folks and Meto Jovanovski.

4394. Juraga, Dubravka, and M. Keith Booker. "Literature, Power, and Oppression in Stalinist Russia and Catholic Ireland: Danilo Kis's Use of Joyce in *A Tomb for Boris Davidovich*." *South Atlantic Review* 58, no. 4 (November 1993): 39-58.

4395. Jurak, Mirko. "Jack Tomsic's Poetry: The Spiritual, Ethnic, Acculturational and Social Functions of Literature." *Slovene Studies* 14, no. 2 (1992, published September 1994): 139-148. [Paper presented at a panel entitled "Slovene Emigrant Literature after World War II" held at the AAASS Convention in Honolulu, HI, November 1993.]

4396. Kisevic, Enes. [Poems]. *North Dakota Quarterly* 61, no. 1 (Winter 1993): 95-97. Translated by Ellen Elias-Bursac. ["An Exiled Child's Letter," pp. 95-96; "Dear Birch," p. 97; "Forgive Them, O Lord," p. 97.]

4397. Koneski, Blaze. "Prayer." *North Dakota Quarterly* 61, no. 1 (Winter 1993): 98. Translated by Dragana Marinkovic and Richard Burns.

4398. Kos, Janko. "Contemporary Slovene Literature." *Nationalities Papers* 21, no. 1 (Spring 1993): 119-126.

4399. Kuic, Gordana. "From *A Scent of Balkan Rain*." *North Dakota Quarterly* 61, no. 1 (Winter 1993): 99. Translated by Richard Burns. ["Salamon Ruben ben Israel of Salonika, 1688."]

4400. Lalic, Ivan V. [Poems]. *North Dakota Quarterly* 61, no. 1 (Winter 1993): 100-102. Translated by Francis R. Jones. ["The Voice Singing in the Gardens," pp. 100-101; "Byzantium," pp. 101-102.]

4401. ———. "Some Notes on Yugoslav Literature: A Historical Approach." *North Dakota Quarterly* 61, no. 1 (Winter 1993): 12-17. Translated by Richard Burns and Jadrana Velickovic. [Presented at the Wheatland Conference on Literature, Lisbon, Portugal, May 4-8, 1988.]

4402. Lengold, Jelena. "A Suburban Hotel." *North Dakota Quarterly* 61, no. 1 (Winter 1993): 103. Translated by Veno Taufer.

4403. Maksimovic, Desanka. [Poems]. *North Dakota Quarterly* 61, no. 1 (Winter 1993): 104-107. Translated by Richard Burns, Jasna B. Misic, and Marie Schulte. ["I Have No More Time," p. 104; "Anticipation," p. 105; "Speak Softly," p. 105; "Nobody Knows," p. 105; "Morana," p. 106; "Morana's Lullaby," p. 107.]

4404. Markovic, Vito. "From *Analects*." *North Dakota Quarterly* 61, no. 1 (Winter 1993): 108-109. Translated by Richard Burns and Vera Radojevic.

4405. Maver, Igor. "The Art of Janko N. Rogelj's Fiction and Poetry." *Slovene Studies* 14, no. 2 (1992, published September 1994): 161-167. [Paper presented at a panel entitled "Slovene Emigrant Literature after World War II" held at the AAASS Convention in Honolulu, HI, November 1993.]

4406. Meyer, Priscilla. "Scholarship and Art: An Interview with Dubravka Ugresic." *Cross Currents: A Yearbook of Central European Culture*, no. 12 (1993): 189-203.

4407. Mihajlovic, Jasmina. "Elements of Milorad Pavic's Postmodern Poetics." *Serbian Studies* 7, no. 1 (Spring 1993): 33-38.

4408. Milisic, Milan. [Poems]. *North Dakota Quarterly* 61, no. 1 (Winter 1993): 112-113. Translated by

Maja Herman-Sekulic. ["Treacherously, from Behind," p. 112; "Flaubert," p. 113.]

4409. Milivojevic, Dragan. "*Fantasy* and *Fantastic* in Contemporary and Recent Serbian, Croatian and Macedonian Literature." *Serbian Studies* 7, no. 2 (Fall 1993, published in 1995): 86-95.

4410. Miljkovic, Branko. [Poems]. *North Dakota Quarterly* 61, no. 1 (Winter 1993): 114-115. Translated by John Matthias and Vladeta Vuckovic. ["An Orphic Legacy," p. 114; "To the Earth Right Now," p. 115.]

4411. Motola, Gabriel. "Danilo Kis: Death and the Mirror." *Antioch Review* 51, no. 4 (Fall 1993): 605-621.

4412. Novakovich, Josip. "On Becoming a Prophet: A Tale." *North Dakota Quarterly* 61, no. 1 (Winter 1993): 116-118.

4413. Otrzan, Durda. "The Angel." *North Dakota Quarterly* 61, no. 1 (Winter 1993): 119-120. Translated by Ellen Elias-Bursac.

4414. Pavlich, Walter. "Sarajevo Bear." *Atlantic* 271, no. 3 (March 1993): 55. [Poem.]

4415. Pavlovic, Miodrag. [Poems]. *North Dakota Quarterly* 61, no. 1 (Winter 1993): 121-123. Translated by Bernard Johnson. ["Scout," pp. 121-122; "Again Kosovo," pp. 122-123.]

4416. Petric, Jerneja. "A Poet in Search of Her Roots: Rose Mary Prosen's *Apples*." *Slovene Studies* 14, no. 2 (1992, published September 1994): 133-137. [Paper presented at a panel entitled "Slovene Emigrant Literature after World War II" held at the AAASS Convention in Honolulu, HI, November 1993.]

4417. Petrov, Aleksandar. [Poems]. *North Dakota Quarterly* 61, no. 1 (Winter 1993): 124-128. Translated by Richard Burns. ["Poetry Visits an Old Lady," pp. 124-125; "Dinner by Candlelight," pp. 125-126; "Heavenly Firebird," pp. 126-128.]

4418. Raickovic, Stevan. "Open the Door Into Night." *Serbian Studies* 7, no. 2 (Fall 1993, published in 1995): 130.

4419. ———. "September." *Serbian Studies* 7, no. 2 (Fall 1993, published in 1995): 129. Translated by Dejan B. Markovich.

4420. Rajic, Negovan. "Crossing the Border." *North Dakota Quarterly* 61, no. 1 (Winter 1993): 132-143. Translated by Judith Cowan.

4421. Rakic, Bogdan. "From Fact to Fiction: An Early English Version of Milos Crnjanski's *The Novel of London*." *Serbian Studies* 7, no. 1 (Spring 1993): 39-55.

4422. Rames, Clifford N. "Kornat." *North Dakota Quarterly* 61, no. 1 (Winter 1993): 144-154.

4423. Russell, Peter. [Poems]. *North Dakota Quarterly* 61, no. 1 (Winter 1993): 155-156. ["The Death of a Swift," pp. 155-156; "Sarajevo," p. 156.]

4424. Selenic, Slobodan. "Two Excerpts from *Fathers and Forefathers*." *North Dakota Quarterly* 61, no. 1 (Winter 1993): 157-170. Introduced and translated by Ellen Elias-Bursac.

4425. Seraphinoff, Michael John. "The Works of Kiril Pejchinovich in the 19th Century Macedonian Awakening." Ph.D. diss., University of Washington, 1993. [UMI order no: AAC 9409365.]

4426. Simic, A. B. "Poets." *North Dakota Quarterly* 61, no. 1 (Winter 1993): 174. Translated by Richard Burns and Dasa Maric.

4427. Simic, Goran. "Sarajevo Sorrow: Five Poems." *Salmagundi*, no. 100 (Fall 1993): 98-101. Translated by Amela Simic. ["The Face of Sorrow," p. 99; "At the Beginning, After Everything," p. 99; "Lejla's Secret," p. 100; "Love Story" pp. 100-101; "Ruza and the Trams," p. 101.]

4428. Sljivic-Simsic, Biljana. "Women in Life and Fiction at the Turn of the Century (1884-1914)." *Serbian Studies* 7, no. 2 (Fall 1993, published in 1995): 106-122.

4429. Tadijanovic, Dragutin. [Poems]. *North Dakota Quarterly* 61, no. 1 (Winter 1993): 186-187. Translated by E. D. Goy. ["My Sister Takes the Milk to Town," p. 186; "Moonlight on the Sea," p. 187.]

4430. Tax, Meredith. "Croatia's 'Witches': Five Women Who Won't Be Silenced." *Nation* 256, no. 18 (May 10, 1993): 624-627.

4431. Tisma, Aleksandar. *Kapo*. Translated from the Serbo-Croatian by Richard Williams. 1st ed. New York: Harcourt Brace & Co., c1993. 294 pp. [Translation of: *Kapo* (Beograd: Nolit, 1987).] REV: Bruce Allen, *New York Times Book Review* 98 (November 14, 1993): 67.

4432. Tomcic, Goran. "Fluorescent Sorrow." *Poet Lore* 88, no. 1 (Spring 1993): 49. Translated by Ines Modrcin, Goran Tomcic, and Tali Makell.

4433. ———. "Here." *Poet Lore* 88, no. 1 (Spring 1993): 50. Translated by Ines Modrcin, Goran Tomcic, and Tali Makell.

4434. Ugresic, Dubravka. *Fording the Stream of Consciousness*. Translated by Michael Henry Heim. Writings from an Unbound Europe. Literature in Translation, 5. Evanston, IL: Northwestern University Press, 1993. 225 pp. [Translation of *Forsiranje romana reke*. Originally published (London: Virago Press, 1991).]

4435. ———. *In the Jaws of Life*. Translated by Celia Hawkesworth and Michael Henry Heim. Foreword by Andrew Wachtel. Writings from an Unbound Europe. Literature in Translation, 4. Evanston, IL: Northwestern University Press, 1993. xii, 252 pp. [Originally published (London: Virago Press, 1992).]

4436. Ujevic, Tin. [Poems]. *North Dakota Quarterly* 61, no. 1 (Winter 1993): 188-192. Translated by Richard Burns and Dasa Maric. ["Daily Lament," pp. 188-189; From *The Necklace* "XXXII," "XXV," and "XXXI," p. 190-191; "Frailty," p. 191; "Star on High," p. 192.]

4437. Velmar-Jankovic, Svetlana. "From *Dungeon*." *North Dakota Quarterly* 61, no. 1 (Winter 1993): 193-204. Translated by Celia Hawkesworth.

4438. Vrhovac, Duska. [Poems]. *North Dakota Quarterly* 61, no. 1 (Winter 1993): 205-208. Translated by Richard Burns and Vera Radojevic. ["Visitation," p. 205; "Dugout—I," p. 206; "Dugout—II," p. 206; "Dugout—III," p. 207; "Ring-a-by," p. 207; "It Doesn't Matter Why," p. 208; "Between Bed and Table," p. 208.]

4439. Vuckovic, Vladeta. "The First Dimension (First Half)." *North Dakota Quarterly* 61, no. 1 (Winter 1993): 209-211. Translated by John Matthias and Vladeta Vuckovic. [From *The Dimensions*.]

4440. Zagoricnik, Franci. [Poems]. *North Dakota Quarterly* 61, no. 1 (Winter 1993): 212-220. Translated by Tone Percic and Bridget Peet. ["starting up," pp. 212-213; "Mordana," p. 214; "under three," p. 215; "under four," pp. 216-217; "striptease," pp. 217-218; "the flood," pp. 219-220.]

4441. Zagoricnik-Simonovic, Ifigenija. [Poems]. *North Dakota Quarterly* 61, no. 1 (Winter 1993): 221-223. Translated by Anthony Rudolf and Ifigenija Zagoricnik-Simonovic. ["Under the Same Roof," p. 221; "Long-Term Misunderstanding," p. 222; "Love Poem," p. 223.]

4442. Zitnik, Janja. "The American Reception of Louis Adamic's Last Book on Yugoslavia." *Slovene Studies* 14, no. 2 (1992, published September 1994): 149-159. [Paper presented at a panel entitled "Slovene Emigrant Literature after World War II" held at the AAASS Convention in Honolulu, HI, November 1993.]

4443. Zivancevic, Nina. [Poems]. *North Dakota Quarterly* 61, no. 1 (Winter 1993): 224-226. Translated by Nina Zivancevic. ["If You Just Imagine," p. 224; "Transparency," p. 225; "Love," p. 226.]

Literary Figures

Andric

4444. Andric, Ivo. "Selections from *Signs by the Roadside*." *North Dakota Quarterly* 61, no. 1 (Winter 1993): 18-27. Introduced and translated by Celia Hawkesworth.

4445. Essex, Ruth. "De-framed." *North Dakota Quarterly* 61, no. 1 (Winter 1993): 65-72.

Pavic

4446. Disch, Thomas M. [Book Review]. *Book World (Washington Post)* 23, no. 28 (July 11, 1993): 5. [Review article on Milorad Pavic, *The Inner Side of the Wind: Or the Novel of Hero and Leander* (NY: Knopf, 1993).]

4447. Pavic, Milorad. *The Inner Side of the Wind, Or, The Novel of Hero and Leander*. Translated from the Serbo-Croatian by Christina Pribicevic-Zoric. 1st American ed. New York: Alfred A. Knopf; Distributed by Random House, 1993. 77, 97 pp. ["Hero" and "Leander" are bound back-to-back inverted. Translation of *Unutrasnja strana vetra, ili, Roman o Heri i Leandru*. "So that the reader is afforded the opportunity to read the novel from either lover's point of view, it is approachable [by reading] from either the front cover (Hero's story) or the back (Leander's).") REV: W. S. Di Piero, *New York Times Book Review* 98, no. 24 (June 13, 1993): 11-12. Thomas M. Disch, *Book World* 23, no. 28 (July 11, 1993): 5.

Popa

4448. Jones, Francis R. "The Stargazer's Legacy: Vasko Popa." *North Dakota Quarterly* 61, no. 1 (Winter 1993): 83-88. [Includes quotes from Popa's poems, translated by Francis R. Jones and Anne Pennington.]

4449. Lekic, Anita. *The Quest for Roots: The Poetry of Vasko Popa.* Preface by Charles Simic. Balkan Studies (New York, NY), v. 2. New York: P. Lang, c1993. xiv, 178 pp. [Based on the author's dissertation.]

4450. Popa, Vasko. [Poems]. *North Dakota Quarterly* 61, no. 1 (Winter 1993): 129-131. Translated by Francis R. Jones. ["The Little Box," p. 129; "The Little Box's Admirers," pp. 129-130; "The Little Box's Prisoners," p. 130; "Last News of the Little Box," p. 131.]

4451. Vladiv-Glover, Slobodanka. "Vasko Popa's *Thing* Poetry and the American Poet Charles Simic." *Serbian Studies* 7, no. 2 (Fall 1993, published in 1995): 96-105.

12 Military Affairs

■ General

4452. Brauer, Jürgen, and Manas Chatterji, eds. *Economic Issues of Disarmament: Contributions from Peace Economics and Peace Science.* Foreword by Kenneth J. Arrow. Includes contribution by John Tepper Marlin. New York, NY: New York University Press, 1993. xvi, 372 pp. [Papers from a conference held at the University of Notre Dame (Notre Dame, IN), November 30-December 1, 1990. Partial contents: John Tepper Marlin, "US and Soviet Conversion," pp. 152-171.] REV: Richard Cooper, *Foreign Affairs* 72, no. 4 (September-October 1993): 159.

4453. Dupuy, Trevor N. *Future Wars: The World's Most Dangerous Flashpoints.* New York, NY: Warner Books, c1993. xvi, 334 pp. REV: David R. Hogg, *Military Review* 73, no. 9 (September 1993): 87-88.

4454. Foye, Stephen. "The Soviet Legacy." *RFE/RL Research Report* 2, no. 25 (June 18, 1993): 1-8. [Includes sidebars: "Treaty on CIS Collective Security," pp. 4-5; and "CIS Joint Command Abolished," p. 8.]

4455. Heuser, Beatrice. "Warsaw Pact Military Doctrines in the 1970s and 1980s: Findings in the East German Archives." *Comparative Strategy* 12, no. 4 (October-December 1993): 437-457.

4456. Lockwood, Jonathan Samuel, and Kathleen O'Brien Lockwood. *The Russian View of U.S. Strategy: Its Past, Its Future.* New Brunswick, NJ: Transaction Publishers, c1993. 233 pp. [Rev. ed. of: *The Soviet View of U.S. Strategic Doctrine* (c1983). Contents: Pt. I. Doctrinal Overview. 1. The Development of U.S. Strategic Doctrine. 2. The Evolution of Soviet Strategic Doctrine. Pt. II. Massive Retaliation Period (1954-1960). 3. The Soviet View of Massive Retaliation. 4. Limited War: Can U.S. Imperialism Restrain Itself?. Pt. III. Flexible Response Period (1961-1968). 5. Flexible Response and Soviet Reaction. 6. Soviet Reaction to the McNamara Concepts. Pt. IV. Realistic Deterrence Period (1969-1982). 7. The Crisis of Capitalism: Soviet Views of the Nixon Doctrine. 8. Dangerous Reversal: Soviet Reaction to the Limited Nuclear Options Strategy. 9. Toward Nuclear Warfighting: The Soviet View of Presidential Directive 59. Pt. V. From Strategic Defense Initiative to the Collapse of Communism (1983-1991). 10. Nightmare Becomes Reality: The Soviet View of SDI. 11. The Future of U.S. and Russian Strategy; Appendix A: Comparison of US/USSR ICBM/SLBM/Bomber Deployments, 1960-1991. Appendix B: Chronology of Major Events Involving Use of Soviet Military Power 1954-1991; Appendix C: The Impact of Ballistic Missile Defense on Operational Warfare.]

4457. Nelson, Daniel N. "Ancient enmities, modern guns." *Bulletin of the Atomic Scientists* 49, no. 10 (December 1993): 21-27. ["Leaking armories in the old Warsaw Pact are not the cause of the wars in Eastern Europe, but they've made them a good deal bloodier."]

4458. Wettig, Gerhard. "Warsaw Pact Planning in Central Europe: The Current Stage of Research." *Cold War International History Project Bulletin,* no. 3 (Fall 1993): 51. [Comment on "Warsaw Pact Military Planning in Central Europe: Revelations from the East German Archives", a translation of a report by the West German Defense Ministry that appeared in no. 2 (1992).]

4459. Wulf, Herbert, ed. *Arms Industry Limited.* Includes contributions by Julian Cooper, Alexei Izyumov, Herbert Wulf, Maciej Perczynski, Pawel Wieczorek, Oldreich Cechak, Jan Selesovsky, and Milan Stembera. Solna, Sweden: Sipri: New York: Oxford University Press, 1993. xviii, 415 pp. [Partial contents: Julian Cooper, "The Soviet Union and the successor republics: defense industries coming to terms with disunion"; Alexei Izyumov, "The Soviet Union: arms control and conversion, plan and reality"; Herbert Wulf, "The Soviet Union and the successor republics: arms exports and the strugle with the heritage of the military-industrial complex"; Maciej Perczynski and Pawel Wieczorek, "Poland: declining industry in a period of difficult economic transformation"; Oldreich Cechak, Jan Selesovsky and Milan Stembera, "Czechoslovakia: reduction in arms production in a time of economic and political transformation."]

■ East-West Balance of Forces

4460. Chodakewitz, Susan B., and Jill L. Jermano. "Proliferation, the Former Soviet Union and the Post-Cold War Chill." *Strategic Review* 21, no. 4 (Fall 1993): 78-80.

4461. "Documentation." *Comparative Strategy* 12, no. 1 (January/March 1993): 109-113. [Five documents: Excerpt of Speech to the United Nations Security Council by Yeltsin (January 31, 1992); Joint U.S.-Russian Statement on a Global Protection System, Bush and Yeltsin (June 7, 1992); Joint Statement, U.S.-Russian High-Level Group (July 14, 1992); Excerpt of Statement of Berdennikov on Russian-American Consultations on Global Anti-ballistic Defense (July 17, 1992); Joint Statement on Global Protection System Consultations (September 22, 1992).]

4462. Flournoy, Michele A., ed. *Nuclear Weapons after the Cold War: Guidelines for U.S. Policy.* Foreword by Ashton B. Carter. New York, NY: HarperCollins College Publishers, c1993. xviii, 314 pp. REV: Andrew J. Pierre, *Foreign Affairs* 72, no. 2 (Spring 1993): 166.

4463. Fulgham, David A. "Pentagon pushes air-to-air upgrades." *Aviation Week & Space Technology* 139, no. 3

(July 19, 1993): 20-21. ["Russian, Israeli missiles superior at close ranges."]

4464. Hadley, Stephen. "Global Protection System: Concept and Progress." *Comparative Strategy* 12, no. 1 (January/March 1993): 3-6.

4465. Harries, Owen. "The Collapse of 'The West.'" *Foreign Affairs* 72, no. 4 (September-October 1993): 41-53.

4466. Hughes, David. "Arms experts fear nuclear blackmail." *Aviation Week & Space Technology* 138, no. 1 (January 4, 1993): 61-62.

4467. Lehman, Ronald F., III. "Changing Realities." *Comparative Strategy* 12, no. 1 (January/March 1993): 47-51.

4468. McIntosh, Daniel. "Working with the Bomb: Soviet and American Planning for the Use of Intercontinental Nuclear Forces, 1945-1968." Ph.D. diss., University of Denver, 1993. [UMI order no: AAC 9412602.]

4469. Nash, Marian (Leich). "Contemporary Practice of the United States Relating to International Law." *American Journal of International Law* 87, no. 1 (January 1993): 103-111. ["Arms Control and Disarmament," pp. 108-111.]

4470. ———. "Contemporary Practice of the United States Relating to International Law." *American Journal of International Law* 87, no. 2 (April 1993): 258-281.

4471. Payne, Keith B. "Editor's Introduction: Special Issue: Defense Against Ballistic Missiles: The Emerging Consensus for SDI?" *Comparative Strategy* 12, no. 1 (January/March 1993): iii-iv. [Articles in this issue derived from presentations at an international conference on the future of missile defense, held September 23-25, 1992, and sponsored by the National Institute for Public Policy and the American Astronautical Society.]

4472. United States Congress Senate Committee on Armed Services. *Military Implications of START I and START II: Hearings before the Committee on Armed Services, United States Senate, One Hundred Second Congress, Second Session, July 28 and August 4, 1992.* United States. Congress. Senate S. hrg., 102-953. Washington: U.S. G.P.O., 1992 [i.e. 1993]. iii, 272 pp.

■ Russia/U.S.S.R.

General

4473. Colby, Gale. "Fabricating guilt." *Bulletin of the Atomic Scientists* 49, no. 8 (October 1993): 12-13. [On a *Moscow News* article on chemical weapons tests in the Soviet Union.]

4474. Crowe, William J., Jr., and David Chanoff. *The Line of Fire: From Washington to the Gulf, the Politics and Battles of the New Military.* New York: Simon &

Schuster, c1993. 367 pp. [Includes descriptions of Crowe's visits to the Soviet Union (in 1989 and 1990), and Akhromeyev's visits to the U.S. (1988 and 1990). Partial contents: "Russians," pp. 271-298.] REV: Eliot A. Cohen, *Foreign Affairs* 72, no. 3 (Summer 1993): 196.

4475. Kianitsa, Victor. "Test Anxiety." *Bulletin of the Atomic Scientists* 49, no. 8 (October 1993): 37-39. [On Soviet Union nuclear testing in Kazakhstan.]

History

4476. Aksan, Virginia. "The One-Eyed Fighting the Blind: Mobilization, Supply, and Command in the Russo-Turkish War of 1768-1774." *International History Review* 15, no. 2 (May 1993): 221-238.

4477. Armstrong, Richard N. "World War II Almanac: Prokhorovka: The Great Tank Battle." *Military Review* 73, no. 7 (July 1993): 64-67.

4478. Baumann, Robert F. *Russian-Soviet Unconventional Wars in the Caucasus, Central Asia, and Afghanistan.* Leavenworth Papers, no. 20. Fort Leavenworth, KS: Combat Studies Institute, U.S. Army Command and General Staff College, [1993]. ix, 219 pp.

4479. Campbell, D'Ann. "Women in Combat: The World War II Experience in the United States, Great Britain, Germany, and the Soviet Union." *Journal of Military History* 57, no. 2 (April 1993): 301-323.

4480. Dmytryshyn, Basil. "The SS Division 'Galicia': Its Genesis, Training, Deployment." *Nationalities Papers* 21, no. 2 (Fall 1993): 53-73.

4481. Holloway, David. "Soviet scientists speak out." *Bulletin of the Atomic Scientists* 49, no. 4 (May 1993): 18-19. [Part of special issue on the Soviet bomb.]

4482. Julian, Thomas A. "Operations at the Margin: Soviet Bases and Shuttle-Bombing." *Journal of Military History* 57, no. 4 (October 1993): 627-652. [On U.S. Army Air Force use of Soviet bases for bombing raids against the Axis powers during World War II.]

4483. Khariton, Yuli, and Yuri Smirnov. "The Khariton version." *Bulletin of the Atomic Scientists* 49, no. 4 (May 1993): 20-31. [Part of special issue on the Soviet bomb.]

4484. Leskov, Sergei. "Dividing the glory of the fathers." *Bulletin of the Atomic Scientists* 49, no. 4 (May 1993): 37-39. [Part of special issue on the Soviet bomb.]

4485. Malbon, Kenneth Wayne. "Admiral Gorshkov and Russia's Naval Heritage: A Quest for Strategic Mobility." Ph.D. diss., Fletcher School of Law and Diplomacy, 1993. [UMI order no: AAC 9322885.]

4486. Neilson, Keith. " 'Pursued by a Bear': British Estimates of Soviet Military Strength and Anglo-Soviet Relations, 1922-1939." *Canadian Journal of History* =

Annales canadiennes d'histoire 28, no. 2 (August 1993): 189-221.

4487. Sagdeev, Roald. "Russian scientists save American secrets." *Bulletin of the Atomic Scientists* 49, no. 4 (May 1993): 32-36. [Part of special issue on the Soviet bomb.]

4488. Shukman, Harold, ed. *Stalin's Generals.* Contributions by Richard Woff, Geoffrey Jukes, David Glantz, Gabriel Gorodetsky, John Erickson, Oleg Rzheshevsky, Viktor Anfilov, Shimon Navch, Catherine Andreyev, Dmitri Volkogonov, and Viktor Anfilov. 1st Grove Press ed. New York: Grove Press, 1993. xix, 394 pp. [Contents: Richard Woff, "Antonov"; Geoffrey Jukes, "Bagramyan"; David Glantz, "Batov"; David Glantz, "Boldin"; Viktor Anfilov, "Budenny"; Richard Woff, "Chuikov"; Gabriel Gorodetsky, "Golikov"; Oleg Rzheshevsky, "Konev"; Geoffrey Jukes, "Kuznetsov"; John Erickson, "Malinovsky"; Geoffrey Jukes, "Meretskov"; John Erickson, "Moskalenko"; John Erickson, "Novikov"; Richard Woff, "Rokossovsky"; Richard Woff, "Rudenko"; Richard Woff, "Rybalko"; Oleg Rzheshevsky, "Shaposhnikov"; Geoffrey Jukes, "Shtemenko"; Viktor Anfilov, "Timoshenko"; Shimon Navch, "Tukhachevsky"; Geoffrey Jukes, "Vasilevsky"; David Glantz, "Vatutin"; Catherine Andreyev, "Vlasov"; Dmitri Volkogonov, "Voroshilov"; Richard Woff, "Zakharov"; Viktor Anfilov, "Zhukov"; Richard Woff, "Stalin's ghosts."]

4489. Soutor, Kevin. "To Stem the Red Tide: The German Report Series and Its Effect on American Defense Doctrine, 1948-1954." *Journal of Military History* 57, no. 4 (October 1993): 653-688.

Organization

4490. Davenport, Brian Andrew. "Soviet Civil-Military Relations, 1977-1991: The Persistence and Transformation of Authority." Ph.D. diss., University of Southern California, 1993.

4491. Partan, Matthew Alexander. "The Military Fails to Act: Explaining Soviet Ministry of Defense Responses to Domestic Challenges, 1985 to 1991." Ph.D. diss., Massachusetts Institute of Technology, 1993.

Theory and Doctrine

4492. Green, William C., and W. Robert Reeves, eds. and trans. *Soviet Military Encyclopedia.* Abridged English language ed. Boulder, CO: Westview, 1993. 4 vols. REV: Eliot A. Cohen, *Foreign Affairs* 72, no. 5 (November-December 1993): 163.

4493. Swita, Bogdan. "The OMG in the Offense." *Military Review* 73, no. 11 (November 1993): 30-40.

4494. Zisk, Kimberly Marten. *Engaging the Enemy: Organization Theory and Soviet Military Innovation, 1955-1991.* Princeton, NJ: Princeton University Press, 1993. x, 286 pp.

■ C.I.S.

General

4495. Almquist, Peter. "Arms Producers Struggle to Survive as Defense Orders Shrink." *RFE/RL Research Report* 2, no. 25 (June 18, 1993): 33-41. [Part of special issue on "Post-Soviet Armies."]

4496. Clarke, Douglas L. "Rusting Fleet Renews Debate on Navy's Mission." *RFE/RL Research Report* 2, no. 25 (June 18, 1993): 25-32. [Part of special issue on "Post-Soviet Armies."]

4497. Coleman, Kevin T. "The Rise of Militias in the Former Soviet Union." *Eurasian Reports* 3, no. 2 (Winter 1993): 109-124. [Part of special issue devoted to "What Is Russia?"]

4498. Foye, Stephen. "The CIS Armed Forces." *RFE/RL Research Report* 2, no. 1 (January 1, 1993): 41-45.

4499. ———. "End of CIS Command Heralds New Russian Defense Policy?" *RFE/RL Research Report* 2, no. 27 (July 2, 1993): 45-49.

4500. Fuller, Elizabeth. "Paramilitary Forces Dominate Fighting in Transcaucasus." *RFE/RL Research Report* 2, no. 25 (June 18, 1993): 74-82. [Part of special issue on "Post-Soviet Armies."]

4501. Gorman, Patrick. "The Emerging Army in Azerbaijan." *Central Asia Monitor*, no. 1 (1993): 31-36.

4502. Hinckley, Steedman, RAND Corporation, and United States. Army. *Department of Defense Assistance to the Former Soviet Republics: Potential Applications of Existing Army Capabilities.* Santa Monica, CA: RAND, 1993. xxii, 62 pp. [Report no. MR-245-A. Prepared for the United States Army.]

4503. Isby, David C., and Thomas H. Johnson. "Post-Soviet Nuclear Forces and the Risk of Accidental or Unauthorized Limited Nuclear Strikes." *Strategic Review* 21, no. 4 (Fall 1993): 7-21.

4504. Janco, Gerard J., and Andrei Kortunov. "The Birth of the Russian Army in the New Eurasia." *Eurasian Reports* 3, no. 2 (Winter 1993): 125-132. [Part of special issue devoted to "What Is Russia?"]

4505. "Leadership Update." *RFE/RL Research Report* 2, no. 25 (June 18, 1993): 96-105. [Part of special issue on "Post-Soviet Armies". "Defense and Security Officials in the Post-Soviet States," pp. 96-103; "Key Officials of the CIS and Russian Armed Forces," pp. 104-105.]

4506. Lockwood, Jonathan Samuel. "The View from Ukraine: The Aspiring Nuclear Power." *Strategic Review* 21, no. 4 (Fall 1993): 22-30.

4507. Markus, Ustina. "Belarus Debates Security Pacts as a Cure for Military Woes." *RFE/RL Research Report* 2, no. 25 (June 18, 1993): 67-73. [Part of special issue on "Post-Soviet Armies."]

4508. "Profiles of the CIS Defense Ministers." *RFE/RL Research Report* 2, no. 25 (June 18, 1993): 89-93. [Part of special issue on "Post-Soviet Armies."]

4509. Socor, Vladimir. "The Fourteenth Army in Moldova: There to Stay?" *RFE/RL Research Report* 2, no. 25 (June 18, 1993): 42-49. [Part of special issue on "Post-Soviet Armies". Title on p. 42 "Russia's Army in Moldova: There to Stay?"]

4510. Ustiugov, Mikhail. "An Embarrassment Of Weapons." *Bulletin of the Atomic Scientists* 49, no. 8 (October 1993): 48-50.

4511. Wolf, Charles, Jr., United States. Office of the Under Secretary of Defense for Policy, RAND Corporation, and Biennial Rand-Hoover Symposium (3rd: 1992: Santa Monica, CA). *The Role of the Military Sector in the Economies of Russia and Ukraine: Proceedings of the RAND-Hoover Symposium, November 1992.* Santa Monica, CA: RAND, 1993. xiv, 286 pp. [Meeting was the third in a series of biennial conferences organized by RAND and the Hoover Institution.]

Russian Federation

General

4512. Bukharin, Oleg. "Soft landing for bomb uranium." *Bulletin of the Atomic Scientists* 49, no. 7 (September 1993): 44-49.

4513. Clarke, Douglas L. "Chemical Weapons in Russia." *RFE/RL Research Report* 2, no. 2 (January 8, 1993): 47-53.

4514. Fedorenko, Sergei. "Russia and Arms Control: The Trials of Transition to a Post-Soviet Era." *Naval War College Review* 46, no. 2 (Spring 1993): 45-58.

4515. Foye, Stephen. "Russian Arms Exports after the Cold War." *RFE/RL Research Report* 2, no. 13 (March 26, 1993): 58-66.

4516. ———. "Russia's Defense Establishment in Disarray." *RFE/RL Research Report* 2, no. 36 (September 10, 1993): 49-54.

4517. ———. "Russia's Fragmented Army Drawn into the Political Fray." *RFE/RL Research Report* 2, no. 15 (April 9, 1993): 1-7.

4518. Gaddy, Clifford, and Melanie Allen. "Dreams of a Salesman." *Brookings Review* 11, no. 4 (Fall 1993): 36-41. ["The Russian drive to increase arms exports."]

4519. Goldanskii, Vitalii I. "Russia's 'red-brown' hawks." *Bulletin of the Atomic Scientists* 49, no. 5 (June 1993): 24-27. [On military reform in Russia and the Russian nationalist position on disarmament.]

4520. Handler, Joshua. "No sleep in the deep for Russian subs." *Bulletin of the Atomic Scientists* 49, no. 3 (April 1993): 7-9.

4521. Lenorovitz, Jeffrey M. "Russian maker of SLBMs seeks civilian spin-offs." *Aviation Week & Space Technology* 139, no. 6 (August 9, 1993): 48-49.

4522. ———. "U.S. entrepreneurs seek Russian SLBMs." *Aviation Week & Space Technology* 138, no. 16 (April 19, 1993): 22-23.

4523. ———. "U.S.-Russian SLBM venture plans initial test for 1994." *Aviation Week & Space Technology* 138, no. 18 (May 3, 1993): 60-61. [On sea-launched ballistic missile program.]

4524. Leskov, Sergey. "The Plague and the Bomb." *RCDA* 32, no. 3 (1993-1994): 48-50.

4525. Meyer, Stephen M. "Troopers." *New Republic* 209, no. 17 (October 25, 1993): 10. ["Why the Russian military backed Yeltsin."]

4526. Morrocco, John D. "Russia to cut R&D, boost procurement." *Aviation Week & Space Technology* 138, no. 26 (June 28, 1993): 55.

4527. "The Myths and Legends of Chemical Disarmament." *RCDA* 32, no. 3 (1993-1994): 43-47. [Translation of article from *Izvestiia* (December 2, 1992).]

4528. Popova, Lydia. "Russia's nuclear elite on rampage." *Bulletin of the Atomic Scientists* 49, no. 3 (April 1993): 14ff.

4529. "Russian (C.I.S.) Strategic Nuclear Forces, End of 1992." *Bulletin of the Atomic Scientists* 49, no. 2 (March 1993): 49. [Table.]

4530. Shilin, Valerii N. *Russian Small Arms Manufacture and Export Patterns: "IZHMASH" Production Association.* [Alexandria, VA: Global Consultants, c1993]. v, 119 leaves. [Published in cooperation with the Institute for Research on Small Arms in International Security.]

4531. Stulberg, Adam N. "The High Politics of Arming Russia." *RFE/RL Research Report* 2, no. 49 (December 10, 1993): 1-8.

4532. Zisk, Kimberly Marten. *Civil-Military Relations in the New Russia.* Occasional Paper (Ohio State University. Mershon Center). Columbus, OH: Mershon Center, Ohio State University, 1993. 26 pp. [Revised version of a paper prepared for the Mershon Center 25th Anniversary Conference on Civil-Military Relations, December 4 and 5, 1992.]

Aerospace and Air Force

4533. Covault, Craig. "Russia debates doctrine, bomber, fighter decisions." *Aviation Week & Space Technology* 138, no. 22 (May 31, 1993): 23.

4534. ———. "Russian bomber force seeks tactical role." *Aviation Week & Space Technology* 139, no. 20 (November 15, 1993): 44-49.

4535. ———. "Russian helicopters spark controversy." *Aviation Week & Space Technology* 138, no. 25 (June 21, 1993): 52-55.

4536. ———. "Russian SA-12 missiles eyed for European ABM." *Aviation Week & Space Technology* 139, no. 11 (September 13, 1993): 99.

4537. ———. "Russians rejuvenate military space assets." *Aviation Week & Space Technology* 138, no. 1 (January 4, 1993): 54-55.

4538. ———. "Sukhoi may seek U.S. partner for new fighter." *Aviation Week & Space Technology* 139, no. 13 (September 27, 1993): 47-48.

4539. Mecham, Michael. "Malaysia buys MiG-29s, F/A-18Ds." *Aviation Week & Space Technology* 139, no. 1 (July 5, 1993): 24-25.

4540. Nguyen, Hung P. "Russia's Continuing Work on Space Forces." *Orbis* 37, no. 3 (Summer 1993): 413-423.

4541. ———. *Submarine Detection from Space: A Study of Russian Capabilities.* Studies in Military Science and Strategy. Annapolis, MD: Naval Institute Press, c1993. 79 pp.

Organization

4542. Erickson, John. "Fallen From Grace: The New Russian Military." *World Policy Journal* 10, no. 2 (Summer 1993): 19-24.

4543. Foye, Stephen. "Updating Russian Civil-Military Relations." *RFE/RL Research Report* 2, no. 46 (November 19, 1993): 44-50.

4544. Lepingwell, John W. R. "Is the Military Disintegrating from Within?" *RFE/RL Research Report* 2, no. 25 (June 18, 1993): 9-16. [Part of special issue on "Post-Soviet Armies."]

4545. ———. "Restructuring the Russian Military." *RFE/RL Research Report* 2, no. 25 (June 18, 1993): 17-24. [Part of special issue on "Post-Soviet Armies."]

Theory and Doctrine

4546. Atkeson, Edward B. "*Glasnost*-Generated 'Windows' Offer Glimpses into Kremlin: Clues to Military Thinking." *Army* 43, no. 4 (April 1993): 12-14.

4547. ———. "Russia Revamps Machinery to Grind Out a New Doctrine: Nuclear Capabilities at Forefront." *Army* 43, no. 8 (August 1993): 9-11.

4548. Cohen, Elliot A. "A Visit to the General Staff." *National Review* 45, no. 4 (March 1, 1993): 25-26.

4549. FitzGerald, Mary C. "Chief of Russia's General Staff Academy Speaks Out on Moscow's New Military Doctrine." *Orbis* 37, no. 2 (Spring 1993): 281-288.

4550. ———. "Russia's New Military Doctrine." *Naval War College Review* 46, no. 2 (Spring 1993): 24-44.

Ukraine

4551. Blair, Bruce G. "World Watch: Ukraine's Nuclear Backlash." *Brookings Review* 11, no. 3 (Summer 1993): 46.

4552. "An Interview with Ukrainian Defense Minister Kostyantyn Morozov." *Ukrainian Quarterly* 49, no. 3 (Fall 1993): 245-251. Translated by R. K. Stojko-Lozynskyj.

4553. Kuzio, Taras. "Nuclear Weapons and Military Policy in Independent Ukraine." *Harriman Institute Forum* 6, no. 9 (May 1993): 1-14.

4554. Markus, Ustina. "Ukraine Restructures Its Air Forces: New Role, New Problems." *RFE/RL Research Report* 2, no. 42 (October 22, 1993): 48-53.

4555. Mearsheimer, John J. "The Case for a Ukrainian Nuclear Deterrent." *Foreign Affairs* 72, no. 3 (Summer 1993): 50-66.

4556. Miller, Steven E. "The Case Against a Ukrainian Nuclear Deterrent." *Foreign Affairs* 72, no. 3 (Summer 1993): 67-80.

4557. Morrison, David C. "Uke Nukes." *National Journal* 25, nos. 51-52 (December 18, 1993): 3026.

4558. Ukraine. Supreme Rada. "Supreme Rada's Resolution on Ukraine's Military Doctrine." *Ukrainian Quarterly* 49, no. 4 (Winter 1993): 416-422.

■ Eastern Europe

General

4559. Barany, Zoltan D. *Soldiers and Politics in Eastern Europe, 1945-90: The Case of Hungary.* New York, NY: St. Martin's Press, 1993. xi, 243 pp.

4560. Cupitt, Richard T. "The Political Economy of Arms Exports in Post-Communist Societies: The Cases of Poland and the CSFR." *Communist and Post-Communist Studies* 26, no. 1 (March 1993): 87-103.

4561. Dimitrova, Antoaneta. "The Plight of the Bulgarian Arms Industry." *RFE/RL Research Report* 2, no. 7 (February 12, 1993): 48-53.

4562. Engelbrekt, Kjell. "Bulgaria and the Arms Trade." *RFE/RL Research Report* 2, no. 7 (February 12, 1993): 44-47.

4563. Gent, C. J. van, and J. K. A. Bontje. *East German Air Force: Final Flightline.* Osceola, WI: Motorbooks International, 1993. 1 vol. [Originally published: (Shrewsbury, England: Airlife Pub., 1993).]

4564. Girnius, Saulius. "Problems in the Lithuanian Military." *RFE/RL Research Report* 2, no. 42 (October 22, 1993): 44-47.

4565. Obrman, Jan. "Military Reform in the Czech Republic." *RFE/RL Research Report* 2, no. 41 (October 15, 1993): 37-42.

4566. Reisch, Alfred A. "The Hungarian Army in Transition." *RFE/RL Research Report* 2, no. 10 (March 5, 1993): 38-52.

4567. ———. "Hungary Acquires MiG-29s from Russia." *RFE/RL Research Report* 2, no. 33 (August 20, 1993): 49-56.

4568. Sabbat-Swidlicka, Anna. "Poland's Arms Trade Faces New Conditions." *RFE/RL Research Report* 2, no. 6 (February 5, 1993): 49-53.

4569. Tunstall, Graydon A., Jr. *Planning For War Against Russia and Serbia: Austro-Hungarian and German Military Strategies, 1871-1914.* Atlantic Studies on Society in Change, no. 78. East European Monographs, no. 374. War and Society in East Central Europe, vol. 31. Boulder, CO: Social Science Monographs; Highland Lakes, NJ: Atlantic Research and Publications; New York: Distributed by Columbia University Press, 1993. viii, 373 pp. [Contents: I. Elder Moltke 1871-1888; II. Military Planning 1888-1905; III. The Bosnian Crisis, 1908-1909; IV. Strategic Planning and Military Agreements 1909-1914; V. The Balkan Wars, 1912-1913; VI. The July 1914 Crisis; VII. Mobilization; VIII. The Historiography of Mobilization, the Railroad Bureau, the Creation of a Habsburg Command Conspiracy and its Critics; IX. The War: Failure of the Schlieffen Plan; X. Epilogue: The Battles of Lemberg.]

Former Yugoslavia

4570. Bebler, Anton A. "The Yugoslav People's Army and the Fragmentation of a Nation." *Military Review* 73, no. 8 (August 1993): 38-51.

4571. Cancian, Mark F. "The *Wehrmacht* in Yugoslavia: Lessons of the Past?" *Parameters* 23, no. 3 (Autumn 1993): 75-84.

4572. Covault, Craig. "Bosnian air ops test NATO/ U.N." *Aviation Week & Space Technology* 139, no. 9 (August 30, 1993): 49-51.

4573. Gow, James. "Rump Yugoslavia: Perisic Replaces Panic as Chief of Staff." *RFE/RL Research Report* 2, no. 43 (October 29, 1993): 54-59.

4574. Henckaerts, Jean-Marie. "Deportation and Transfer of Civilians in Time of War." *Vanderbilt Journal of Transnational Law* 26, no. 3 (October 1993): 469-519. [Includes section "The Yugoslav War of Dismemberment," pp. 496-500.]

13 Philosophy, Political Theory, Ideology

■ General

4575. Arato, Andrew. *From Neo-Marxism to Democratic Theory: Essays on the Critical Theory of Soviet-Type Societies.* Armonk, NY: M.E. Sharpe, c1993. xiv, 342 pp. [Contents: Pt. I. Western Marxism and Soviet-Type Societies. 1. Authoritarian Socialism and the Frankfurt School. 2. Between Apology and Critique: Marcuse's Soviet Marxism. 3. Critical Sociology and Authoritarian State Socialism. 4. From Western to Eastern Marxism: Rudolf Bahro. 5. Immanent Critique and Authoritarian Socialism: On Konrad and Szelenyi's Intellectuals. 6. The Budapest School and Actually Existing Socialism. 7. Facing Russia: Castoriadis and the Problem of Soviet-Type Societies. Pt. II. The Rise of Civil Society and Democratic Theory. 8. Civil Society vs. the State: Poland 1980-81. 9. Empire vs. Civil Society: Poland 1981-82. 10. The Democratic Theory of the Polish Opposition: Normative Intentions and Strategic Ambiguities. 11. Some Perspectives of Democratization in East Central Europe. 12. Social Theory, Civil Society, and the Transformation of Authoritarian Socialism. 13. Revolution, Civil Society, and Democracy. 14. Social Movements and Civil Society in the Soviet Union.]

4576. Bunce, Valerie. "Leaving Socialism: A 'Transition to Democracy'?" *Contention: Debates in Society, Culture and Science* 3, no. 1 (Fall 1993): 35-47.

4577. Donald, Moira. *Marxism and Revolution: Karl Kautsky and the Russian Marxists, 1900-1924.* New Haven, CT: Yale University Press, 1993. xii, 324 pp. [List of Kautsky's works: pp. 290-307.]

4578. Gottlieb, Roger S., ed. *Radical Philosophy: Tradition, Counter-Tradition, Politics.* Philadelphia, PA: Temple University Press, 1993. xi, 288 pp. REV: Nino Langiulli, *Telos* nos. 98-99 (Winter 1993-Fall 1994): 271-286.

4579. Heilbroner, Robert. "Looking Forward: Does Socialism Have a Future?" *Nation* 257, no. 9 (September 27, 1993): 312-316.

4580. Korchak, A. A. "Contemporary Totalitarianism: A Systems Approach." *East European Quarterly* 27, no. 1 (Spring 1993): 1-46.

4581. Maxwell, William Joseph. "Dialectical Engagements: The 'New Negro' and the 'Old Left', 1918-1940." Ph.D. diss., Duke University, 1993. [UMI order no: AAC 9420406.]

4582. Skidmore, Dan. "Theorizing the Fall of Communism and the Future of Socialism: Rational Choice Theory, Ideology, and Labor Process." *Journal of Political and Military Sociology* 21, no. 2 (Winter 1993): 135-162.

4583. Smith, Barry, ed. *Philosophy and Political Change in Eastern Europe.* Contributions by J. C. Nyiri, Tibor Hajdu, G. M. Tamas, E. Gellner, Wojciech Zelaniec, Jan Wolenski, Jan Pavlik, William McBride, Ivanka Raynova, Edward M. Swiderski, and Barry Smith. 1st ed. Monist Library of Philosophy. LaSalle, IL: Hegeler Institute, 1993. 192 pp. [Papers presented at a conference in the Hungarian Academy of Sciences, Budapest, March 1992. Contents: J.C. Nyiri, "Tradition and Bureaucratic Lore: Lessons from Hungary"; Tibor Hajdu, "Ideology and Technology: A Comment on Nyiri"; G.M. Tamas, "Conservatism, Philosophy and Eastern Europe"; E. Gellner, "An Ideological Might-Have-Been"; Wojciech Zelaniec, "Philosophy and Ideology: The Case of Poland"; Jan Wolenski, "Marxism and the Professionalisation of Philosophy"; Jan Pavlik, "Philosophy, 'Parallel Polis' and Revolution: The Case of Czechoslovakia"; William McBride and Ivanka Raynova, "Visions from the Ashes: Philosophical Life in Bulgaria from 1945 to 1992"; Edward M. Swiderski, "The Crisis of Continuity in Post-Soviet Russian Philosophy"; Barry Smith, "The New European Philosophy."]

4584. Verdery, Katherine. "What Was Socialism and Why Did It Fail?" *Contention: Debates in Society, Culture and Science* 3, no. 1 (Fall 1993): 1-23.

4585. Zelnik, Reginald E. "Not the Juice but the Juicer: On No-Longer Existing Socialism and Lemonade." *Contention: Debates in Society, Culture and Science* 3, no. 1 (Fall 1993): 25-34. [Reply to Katherine Verdery, "What Was Socialism and Why Did It Fail?" pp. 1-23.]

■ Russia/U.S.S.R./C.I.S.

4586. Blakely, Allison. "American Influences on Russian Reformist Thought in the Era of the French Revolution." *Russian Review* 52, no. 4 (October 1993): 451-471.

4587. Bobrov, Sergei. *Neizvestnaia kniga Sergeia Bobrova: Iz Sobraniia Biblioteki Stenfordskogo Universiteta.* Edited by M. L. Gasparov. Stanford Slavic Studies, v. 6. Oakland, CA: Berkeley Slavic Specialties, 1993. xii, 95 p. [Includes facsim. of: *Kritika zhiteiskoi filosofii* (Moskva: Kn-vo "TSentrifuga," 1918). Contents: M.L. Gasparov, "Ob odnoi futuristicheskoi shutke"; K. Bubera, "Kritika zhiteiskoi filosofii" redaktsiia, predislovie i primiechaniia Sergieia Bobrova; M.L. Gasparov, "Vospominaniia o Sergee Bobrove."]

4588. Copp, John Walter. "The Role of the Anarchists in the Russian Revolution and Civil War, 1917-1921: A Case Study in Conspiratorial Party Behavior during Revolution." Ph.D. diss., Columbia University, 1993. [UMI order no: AAC 9318229.]

4589. Emerson, Caryl. " 'And the Demons Entered into the Swine': The Russian Intelligentsia and Post-Soviet Religious Thought." *Cross Currents* 43, no. 2 (Summer 1993): 184-202. [Followed by letter to the editor by G. Robina Quale, vol. 43, no. 3 (Fall 1993): 428.]

4590. Evans, Alfred B., Jr. *Soviet Marxism-Leninism: The Decline of an Ideology.* Westport, CT: Praeger, 1993. 237 pp. [Contents: 1. Marx and the Stages of Communism — 2. Lenin on Socialist Construction — 3. The Consolidation of Stalinism — 4. Mature Stalinism: Continuity within Transition — 5. Khrushchev: The Full-Scale Construction of Communism — 6. Khrushchev: Social and Political Change — 7. Brezhnev: The Stage of Developed Socialism — 8. Social Structure and Social Transformation in Developed Socialism — 9. The Socialist Way of Life — 10. Gorbachev on Stagnation and Restructuring — 11. The Hope of Reform: Socialist Pluralism — 12. The Collapse of the Dream — 13. Conclusion: The Revenge of Politics.]

4591. Fortescue, Stephen. "Institutions vs. personalities in the USSR and Russia: a response to Graeme Gill." *Australian Slavonic and East European Studies* 7, no. 1 (1993): 111-122. [Response to article by Gill, "From the USSR to the CIS: *plus ça change...?*" in vol. 6, no. 2 (1992): 97-106.]

4592. Gellner, Ernest. "Homeland of the Unrevolution." *Daedalus* 122, no. 3 (Summer 1993): 141-153.

4593. Groth, Alexander J., and Stuart Britton. "Gorbachev and Lenin: Psychological Walls of the Soviet 'Garrison State.' " *Political Psychology* 14, no. 4 (December 1993): 627-650.

4594. Horowitz, Brian Jay. "M.O. Gershenzon and Intellectual Life of Russia's Silver Age." Ph.D. diss., University of California, Berkeley, 1993. [UMI order no: AAC 9408010.]

4595. Jordan, Bradley Owen. "Subject(s) to Change: Revolution As Pedagogy, or Representations of Education and the Formation of the Russian Revolutionary." Ph.D. diss., University of Pennsylvania, 1993. [UMI order no: AAC 9331793.]

4596. Kljamkin, I. M. " 'To Overcome, Not to Reject....' " *Studies in East European Thought* 45, nos. 1-2 (June 1993): 71-73.

4597. Masters, Roger D. "Evolutionary Biology and the New Russia." *Journal of Social and Evolutionary Systems* 16, no. 3 (1993): 243-249.

4598. Mészáros, István. "Marxism, Politics, Morality." *Monthly Review* 45, no. 2 (June 1993): 28-36.

4599. Müller, Eberhard. "Fragen zur Rezeption der russischen religiösen Philosophie heute." *Studies in East European Thought* 45, no. 4 (December 1993): 235-253.

4600. Nemeth, Thomas. "Debol'skij and Lesevic on Kant: Two Russian Philosophies in the 1870s." *Studies in East European Thought* 45, no. 4 (December 1993): 281-311.

4601. Peet, Richard. "Reinventing Marxist Geography: A Critique of Bassin." *Annals of the Association of American Geographers* 83, no. 1 (March 1993): 156-160. [Commentary on the article by Mark Bassin, "Geographical Determinism in *Fin-de-siècle* Marxism: Georgii Plekhanov and the Environmental Basis of Russian History," in vol. 82, no. 1 (March 1992): 3-22.]

4602. Quale, G. Robina. "The Meaning of *Sobornost'*." *Cross Currents* 43, no. 3 (Fall 1993): 428. [Letter in response to Caryl Emerson's article " 'And the Demons Entered into the Swine': The Russian Intelligentsia and Post-Soviet Religious Thought" in vol. 43, no. 2 (Summer 1993): 184-202.]

4603. Romano, Carlin. "The Dispossessed: Russian Philosophy Awaits Its Revolution." *Lingua Franca* 4, no. 1 (November-December 1993): 33-41. [Observations on the 19th World Congress of Philosophy, held in Moscow.]

4604. Rosenthal, Bernice Glatzer. "Lofty Ideals and Worldly Consequences: Visions of *Sobornost'* in Early Twentieth-Century Russia." *Russian History* 20, nos. 1-4 (1993): 179-195.

4605. Swiderski, E. M. "Notes and Comments." *Studies in East European Thought* 45, nos. 1-2 (June 1993): 135-142. [Describes *Put'*, a new philosophical journal published in Russia; includes introduction to *Put'*, "Transforming the Tradition," by editor Anatoly Jakovlĕv (pp. 135-141).]

4606. Tolstykh, V. I. "Introduction." *Studies in East European Thought* 45, nos. 1-2 (June 1993): 3-5. [Introduction to special issue on "Marxism and the Socialist Idea in Russia Today."]

4607. Yakovlev, Alexander. *The Fate of Marxism in Russia.* Translated from the Russian by Catherine A. Fitzpatrick. New Haven, CT: Yale University Press, c1993. xxi, 250 pp. [Translation of *Predislovie—obval—posleslovie*. Contents: Introduction; Thomas F. Remington, "Alexander Yakovlev and the Limits of Reform"; Alexander Tsipko, "Foreword to the Russian Edition: The Truth is Never Late"; Prelude; The Collapse; Aftermath; Appendix 1: Social Alternatives of the Twentieth Century. Lecture delivered at Columbia University, November 15, 1991; Appendix 2: Bolshevism as a Phenomenon. Lecture delivered at Harvard University, November 17, 1991; Appendix 3: Democracy, Russia, the Third Way. Lecture delivered at Princeton University, November 21, 1991; Appendix 4: Ethics and Reformation. Speech delivered at the International Conference "After 1991: Capitalism and Ethics," at the Vatican, January 14, 1992; Appendix 5: Monopoly, Morality, and Common Sense. Speech delivered at Oxford University, January 29, 1992.]

4608. Zviglyanich, Vladimir A. *The Morphology of Russian Mentality: A Philosophical Inquiry into Conservatism and Pragmatism.* Lewiston: E. Mellen Press, c1993. v, 318 pp. REV: Peter Reddaway, *New York Review of Books* 40, no. 20 (December 2, 1993): 16ff.

■ Eastern Europe

4609. Arthur, Chris, and Joseph McCarney. "Marxism Today: An Interview with István Mészáros." *Monthly Review* 44, no. 11 (April 1993): 9-24. [Abbreviated version of an interview published in the British journal *Radical Philosophy*, no. 62 (Fall 1992): 27ff.]

4610. Brzezinski, Jerzy, ed. *Creativity and Consciousness: Philosophical and Psychological Dimensions.* Poznan Studies in the Philosophy of the Sciences and the Humanities, v. 31. Amsterdam; Atlanta, GA: Rodopi, 1993. 412 pp.

4611. Cave, David. *Mircea Eliade's Vision for a New Humanism.* New York: Oxford University Press, 1993. x, 218 pp. REV: Adriana Berger, *Society* 30, no. 5 (July-August 1993): 84-87.

4612. Dobryninas, Aleksandras. "The Paradoxes of Freedom: In Search of Their Roots and Fruits." *Lituanus* 39, no. 4 (Winter 1993): 49-67. [On nationalism and communism in the Baltic states.]

4613. Elshtain, Jean Bethke. "Politics Without Cliché." *Social Research* 60, no. 3 (Fall 1993): 433-444.

4614. Gyáni, Gábor. "Political Uses of Tradition in Postcommunist East Central Europe." *Social Research* 60, no. 4 (Winter 1993): 893-913. Translated by Ronald Radzai.

4615. Haman, Ales. "Václav Cerny and Existentialism: *The First Notebook on Existentialism.*" *Czechoslovak and Central European Journal* 11, no. 2 (Winter 1993): 103-109.

4616. Hundt, Martin. *Geschichte des Bundes der Kommunisten, 1836-1852.* Philosophie und Geschichte der Wissenschaften, Bd. 3. Frankfurt am Main; New York: P. Lang, c1993. 812 pp.

4617. Kohák, Erazim. "Truth and the humanities." *Human Studies* 16, no. 3 (July 1993): 239-253.

4618. Krabbe, Erik C. W., Renee Jose Dalitz, and Pier A. Smit. *Empirical Logic and Public Debate: Essays in Honour of Else M. Barth.* Poznan Studies in the Philosophy of the Sciences and the Humanities, v. 35. Amsterdam; Atlanta, GA: Rodopi, 1993. 337 pp.

4619. Krasnodebski, Zdzislaw. "Longing for Community: Phenomenological Philosophy of Politics and the Dilemmas of European Culture." *International Sociology* 8, no. 3 (September 1993): 339-353.

4620. Król, Marcin. "Being a Conservative in a Postcommunist Country." *Social Research* 60, no. 3 (Fall 1993): 589-607.

4621. Matustik, Martin J. *Postnational Identity: Critical Theory and Existential Philosophy in Habermas, Kierkegaard, and Havel.* Critical Perspectives (New York, NY). New York: Guilford Press, 1993. xxii, 329 pp. REV: Aviezer Tucker, *Telos* nos. 98-99 (Winter 1993-Fall 1994): 287-293.

4622. Nowak, Leszek, and Marcin Paprzycki, eds. *Social System, Rationality and Revolution.* Poznan Studies in the Philosophy of the Sciences and the Humanities, v. 33. Amsterdam; Atlanta, GA: Rodopi, 1993. 456 pp.

4623. Page, Benjamin B. "Conversations with Bondy." *Monthly Review* 44, no. 11 (April 1993): 25-38.

4624. Pavkovic, Aleksandar. *Slobodan Jovanovic: An Unsentimental Approach to Politics.* East European Monographs, no. 371. Boulder, CO: East European Monographs; New York: Distributed by Columbia University Press, 1993. xiv, 231 pp.

4625. Phillips, William. "Communism and the Graying of Character." *Partisan Review* 60, no. 2 (Spring 1993): 179-181. [On the effects of communism and anticommunism on intellectual discourse in Eastern Europe and the West, with Jan Kavan as an example.]

4626. Radnitzky, Gerard, and Hardy Bouillon. *Government: Servant or Master?* Poznan Studies in the Philosophy of the Sciences and the Humanities, v. 30. Amsterdam; Atlanta, GA: Rodopi, 1993. xlvii, 322 pp. [Papers from a colloquium held in Vienna, Austria in the fall of 1988. A publication of the Professors World Peace Academy in Europe.]

4627. Rose, Gillian. *Judaism and Modernity: Philosophical Essays.* Oxford, UK; Cambridge, MA: Basil Blackwell, 1993. xii, 297 pp. REV: Willi Goetschel, *Telos* nos. 98-99 (Winter 1993-Fall 1994): 295-297.

4628. Tucker, Aviezer. "No Czechs or Dogs Allowed: The Former *Praxis International* in Prague." *Telos*, no. 98-99 (Winter 1993-Fall 1994): 255-258.

4629. Urbancic, Ivan. "Philosophy with the Slovenes." *Nationalities Papers* 21, no. 1 (Spring 1993): 127-137.

■ Philosophers and Theorists

Arendt

4630. Berghahn, Klaus L. "Jewish Identity and Modern Politics." *Telos* 26, no. 3 (no. 97) (Fall 1993): 178-182. [Review article on Dagmar Barnouw, *Visible Spaces: Hannah Arendt and the German Jewish Experience* (Baltimore, MD: 1990).]

4631. Biskowski, Lawrence J. "Practical Foundations for Political Judgment: Arendt on Action and World." *Journal of Politics* 55, no. 4 (November 1993): 867-887.

4632. Burke, John Francis. "Voegelin, Heidegger, and Arendt: Two's Company and Three's a Crowd?" *Social Science Journal* 30, no. 1 (1993): 83-97.

4633. Canovan, Margaret. "Arendt and the Politics of Plurality." *Telos* 26, no. 3 (no. 97) (Fall 1993): 172-177. [Review article on Ursula Ludz, ed., *Hannah Arendt, Was ist Politik? Fragmente aus dem Nachlass* (Munich: 1993).]

4634. Cutting-Gray, Joanne. "Hannah Arendt, Feminism and the Politics of Alterity: 'What Will We Lose If We Win?'" *Hypatia* 8, no. 1 (Winter 1993): 35-54.

4635. Disch, Lisa J. "More Truth Than Fact: Storytelling as Critical Understanding in the Writings of Hannah Arendt." *Political Theory* 21, no. 4 (November 1993): 665-694.

4636. Hinchman, Sandra K. "Re-reading Arendt." *Telos* 26, no. 3 (no. 97) (Fall 1993): 164-172. [Review article on Margaret Canovan, *Hannah Arendt: A Reinterpretation of Her Political Thought* (Cambridge: 1993).]

4637. Honig, Bonnie. "The Politics of Agonism." *Political Theory* 21, no. 3 (August 1993): 528-533. [Response to Dana R. Villa, "Beyond Good and Evil: Arendt, Nietzsche, and the Aestheticization of Political Action," no. 20 (May 1992): 274-308.]

4638. Isaac, Jeffrey C. "Situating Hannah Arendt on Action and Politics." *Political Theory* 21, no. 3 (August 1993): 534-540. [Response to Dana R. Villa, "Beyond Good and Evil: Arendt, Nietzsche, and the Aestheticization of Political Action," no. 20 (May 1992): 274-308.]

Marx

4639. Best, Stephen. [Review Article]. *New Political Science*, no. 27 (Winter 1993): 129-136. [Review article on Stephen Eric Bronner, *Socialism Unbound* (NY: 1990).]

4640. Gelman, A. I. "'A Drama That Should Be Studied.'" *Studies in East European Thought* 45, nos. 1-2 (June 1993): 63-65.

4641. Gusejnov, A. A. "Is Theory Responsible for Practice?" *Studies in East European Thought* 45, nos. 1-2 (June 1993): 51-61.

4642. Gusejnov, A. A., and V. I. Tolstykh. "Preface: 'Is Marxism Dead?'" *Studies in East European Thought* 45, nos. 1-2 (June 1993): 1-2. [Articles in this issue orginated at the discussion "Is Marxism Dead?" organized by Svobodnoye slovo (Moscow), held in early 1990.]

4643. Kantor, K. M. "A Quick and Unjust Trial." *Studies in East European Thought* 45, nos. 1-2 (June 1993): 75-88.

4644. Lebedev, V. P. "Marx Was Right in Details and Great in His Errors." *Studies in East European Thought* 45, nos. 1-2 (June 1993): 7-18.

4645. Marot, John Eric. "Marxism, Science, Materialism: Toward a Deeper Appreciation of the 1908-1909 Philosophical Debate in Russian Social Democracy." *Studies in East European Thought* 45, no. 3 (September 1993): 147-167.

4646. Matizen, V. E. "Marxist Postulates and Concentration Camp Practices." *Studies in East European Thought* 45, nos. 1-2 (June 1993): 19-22.

4647. Mayer, Robert. "The Dictatorship of the Proletariat from Plekhanov to Lenin." *Studies in East European Thought* 45, no. 4 (December 1993): 255-280. [Author contests Hal Draper's analysis of Plekhanov's and Lenin's interpretation of Marx's phrase "dictatorship of the proletariat."]

4648. Mezhujev, V. M. "Marxism in the Context of the History of Civilization and Culture." *Studies in East European Thought* 45, nos. 1-2 (June 1993): 23-35.

4649. Podoroga, V. A. "Can Marxian Thought Be Separated from Totalitarian Ideology?" *Studies in East European Thought* 45, nos. 1-2 (June 1993): 67-69.

4650. Solov'ëv, E. Ju. "Not a Forecast, But a Social Prophesy." *Studies in East European Thought* 45, nos. 1-2 (June 1993): 37-49.

4651. Stepin, V. S. "The Fate of Marxism and the Future of Civilization." *Studies in East European Thought* 45, nos. 1-2 (June 1993): 117-133.

4652. Tolstykh, V. I. "The Heart of the Matter, or What Must Not Be Simplified." *Studies in East European Thought* 45, nos. 1-2 (June 1993): 103-115.

4653. Tsipko, A. S. "Intellectual Hypocrisy of the 'Orthodoxes' or a Long Way to Common Sense." *Studies in East European Thought* 45, nos. 1-2 (June 1993): 89-101.

Solovyov

4654. Poulin, Frances. "Vladimir Solov'ev's *Rossiia i vselenskaia tserkov'*, Early Slavophilism's Pneumatic Spirit, and the Pauline Prophet." *Russian Review* 52, no. 4 (October 1993): 528-539.

Stalin

4655. Ree, Erik van. "Stalin's Organic Theory of the Party." *Russian Review* 52, no. 1 (January 1993): 43-57.

Trotsky

4656. Braun, Eileen. "The Prophet Reconsidered: Trotsky on the Soviet Failure to Achieve Socialism." Ph.D. diss., George Washington University, 1993. [UMI order no: AAC 9403348.]

4657. Trotskii, Leon. *Permanentnaia revolutsiia.* [Edited and with introduction by] Felix J. Kreisel. Cambridge, MA: Izd-vo Iskra Research, c1993. xx, 372 pp.

14 Psychology

■ Russia/U.S.S.R./C.I.S

4658. Asherian, Armen. "Managerial Leadership and Effectiveness, and Their Relationship to Personality in the Former USSR." Ph.D. diss., University of Michigan, 1993.

4659. Barron, Ruth A., Jennifer Leaning, and Barry H. Rumack. "The Catastrophe Reaction Syndrome: Trauma in Tbilisi." *International Journal of Law & Psychiatry* 16, no. 3/4 (1993): 403-426. [Outlines the violent events in Tbilisi, Georgia, in April and May 1989, and psychological reaction of the citizens.]

4660. Bodunov, Mikhail V. "Factor structure of the Pavlovian Temperament Survey in a Russian population: Comparison and preliminary findings." *Personality and Individual Differences* 14, no. 4 (April 1993): 557-563. [Paper presented at the International Workshop "Cross-Cultural Research on Temperament" of the European Association for Personality, Nieborow, Poland, September 1991.]

4661. Coalson, Bob. "The Trauma of War: Homecoming After Afghanistan." *Journal of Humanistic Psychology* 33, no. 4 (Fall 1993): 48-62.

4662. Ginzburg, Harold M. "The Psychological Consequences of the Chernobyl Accident—Findings from the International Atomic Energy Agency Study." *Public Health Reports* 108, no. 2 (March-April 1993): 184-192.

4663. Holowinsky, Ivan Z. "Psychological Science in Ukraine, Past Legacy, Future Challenges and Opportunities." *Ukrainian Quarterly* 49, no. 1 (Spring 1993): 35-43.

4664. Hood, Albert B. "A Fulbright Counseling Psychologist in a Rebellious Soviet Republic." *Counseling Psychologist* 21, no. 4 (October 1993): 635-642.

4665. Kon, Igor S. "Identity Crisis and Postcommunist Psychology." *Symbolic Interaction* 16, no. 4 (Winter 1993): 395-410. [Revised version of a paper presented at the 1992 Stone Symposium, Las Vegas, Nevada. A version was read as a lecture at the 1992 meeting of the East-West Conference of the European Association of Experimental Social Psychology, Munster, Germany.]

4666. Miller, Thomas W., Robert F. Kraus, Adel Semyonova Tatevosyan, and Peter Kamenchenko. "Post-Traumatic Stress Disorder in Children and Adolescents of the Armenian Earthquake." *Child Psychiatry and Human Development* 24, no. 2 (Winter 1993): 115-123.

4667. O'Neil, James M. "A Counseling Psychologist in Russia as a Fulbright Scholar: 'James in Wonderland.'"

Counseling Psychologist 21, no. 4 (October 1993): 643-652. [Manuscript was presented at the convention of the American Psychological Association, Washington, DC, August 18, 1992 as part of the symposium "The Soviet Union Fulbright Program and Counseling Psychology: International Implications."]

4668. Thompson, Angela M. "Vasily Vasilyevich Nalimov: Russian Visionary." *Journal of Humanistic Psychology* 33, no. 3 (Summer 1993): 82-98.

4669. Voren, Robert van. "Ukrainian Psychiatry: Back to Basics." *RFE/RL Research Report* 2, no. 3 (January 15, 1993): 38-41.

4670. Wight, Randall D. "The Pavlov-Yerkes Connection: What Was Its Origin?" *Psychological Record* 43, no. 3 (Summer 1993): 351-360.

4671. Winer, Chana. "On the Cutting Edge: Family Therapy Training in Russia." *Contemporary Family Therapy* 15, no. 1 (February 1993): 93-99.

■ Eastern Europe

4672. Adler, Nanci, Gerard O. W. Mueller, and Mohammed Ayat. "Psychiatry Under Tyranny: A Report on the Political Abuse of Romanian Psychiatry During the Ceausescu Years." *Current Psychology* 12, no. 1 (Spring 1993): 3-17.

4673. Bauer, Michael, Stefan Priebe, Bettina Häring, and Kerstin Adamczak. "Long-Term Mental Sequelae of Political Imprisonment in East Germany." *Journal of Nervous and Mental Disease* 181, no. 4 (April 1993): 257-262.

4674. Brozek, Josef, and Jiří Hoskovec. "Contributions to the History of Psychology: XCVI: Psychology in Communist and Postcommunist Czechoslovakia: Toward a Synthesis." *Psychological Reports* 73, no. 1 (August 1993): 239-248.

4675. Füredi, János, Magda Barcy, Gyula Kapusi, and Judit Novák. "Family Therapy in a Transitional Society." *Psychiatry* 56, no. 4 (November 1993): 328-337.

4676. Rolde, Alexandra K. "Notes: Meeting of the Psychoanalytic Society of New England, East, October 28, 1991: Psychoanalysis in Czechoslovakia, Michael Sebek, Ph.D." *Psychoanalytic Quarterly* 62, no. 2 (April 1993): 348-350.

4677. Sebek, Michael. "Psychoanalysis in Czechoslovakia." *Psychoanalytic Review* 80, no. 3 (Fall 1993): 433-439.

■ Psychologists and Theorists

Freud

4678. Freud, Sigmund. *The Correspondence of Sigmund Freud and Sandor Ferenczi*. Edited by Eva Brabant, Ernst Falzeder, and Patrizia Giampieri-Deutsch. Cambridge, MA: Belknap Press of Harvard University Press, 1993-. vols. [Edited under the supervision of Andre Haynal; transcribed by Ingeborg Meyer-Palmedo; translated by Peter T. Hoffer; introduction by Andre Haynal. Contents: Vol. 1. 1908-1914.]

Vygotsky

4679. Newman, Fred, and Lois Holzman. *Lev Vygotsky: Revolutionary Scientist*. Critical Psychology. London; New York: Routledge, 1993. x, 240 pp.

15 Religion

■ General

4680. Ablamowicz-Borri, Malgorzata. "Buddhist 'Protestantism' in Poland." *Religion in Eastern Europe* 13, no. 2 (April 1993): 34-40. [Article is a summary of the author's master thesis: *The Social and Economic Aspects of Modern Implantation of Buddhism in Poland*, submitted in 1991 at Nanterre University-Paris.]

4681. Baturin, Andrei, and Sergey Gryzunov. "Bosnia: Mosques and Churches Are Burning." *RCDA* 32, no. 4 (1993-1994): 70-71. [Translation of article from *Izvestiia* (July 31, 1993).]

4682. Burke, Justin. "Buddhist Prayer Wheels Turn Again in Ulan-Ude." *Surviving Together* 11, no. 3 (Fall 1993): 36-37.

4683. Chrostowski, Waldemar. "The Catholic-Jewish and Polish-Jewish Dialogue in the New Poland." *Religion in Eastern Europe* 13, no. 6 (December 1993): 36-43.

4684. *Gnosis on the Silk Road: Gnostic Texts from Central Asia.* Translated by Hans-Joachim Klimkeit. 1st ed. [San Francisco, CA]: HarperSanFrancisco, c1993. xx, 405 pp. [Translations from Iranian and Turkish.]

4685. Ioannides, Anastasios. "The Balkans Today and after the War." *RCDA* 32, no. 4 (1993-1994): 69-70. [Excerpt from *Review of International Affairs* (Belgrade), English-language edition (1993).]

4686. Klingenstein, Grete. "Modes of Religious Tolerance and Intolerance in Eighteenth-Century Habsburg Politics." *Austrian History Yearbook*, no. 24 (1993): 1-16.

4687. Levine, Irving B. "Kirchentag-1993." *Journal of Ecumenical Studies* 30, no. 2 (Spring 1993): 306-307.

4688. Linn, Gerhard. "The Power of the Powerless." *Religion in Eastern Europe* 13, no. 5 (October 1993): 1-9.

4689. Martin, Luther H., ed. *Religious Transformations and Socio-Political Change: Eastern Europe and Latin America.* Includes contributions by Luther H. Martin, Leonid J. Smolyakov, Vladimir Zotz, Dalibor Papousek, Bretislav Horyna, Jan Szmyd, Iren Lovasz, Dimitry Mickulsky, Janusz Danecki, Gary Lease, Ivan Strenski, Armin W. Geertz, and Ugo Bianchi. Religion and Society (Hague, Netherlands), 33. Berlin; New York: Mouton de Gruyter, 1993. xiv, 457 pp. [Papers presented at a conference of the International Association for the History of Religions, August 5-9, 1991. Partial contents: Luther H. Martin, "Introduction"; Leonid J. Smolyakov, "The intelligentsia between secular and religious culture"; Vladimir Zotz, "Personal spiritual orientations and religiousness in (former) Soviet society"; Dalibor Papousek, "John Paul II and Mikhail Gorbachev: The process of globalization in multidimensional comparison"; Bretislav Horyna, "The analogy of the proportionalitas: The coherence between socio-political development and the development of religion in the new socio-cultural reality of Czechoslovakia"; Jan Szmyd, "National history, culture and the process of religious change"; Iren Lovasz, "Religion and revolution: A Hungarian pilgrimage in Rumania"; Dimitry Mickulsky, "Muslim fundamentalism in Soviet Central Asia: A social perspective"; Janusz Danecki, "The Muslims of Poland: A religious minority in transition"; Gary Lease, "Delusion and illusion, false hopes and failed dreams: religion, the churches and East Germany's 1989 'November revolution'"; Ivan Strenski, "Political culture, religious culture and sacrifice"; Armin W. Geertz, "Theories on tradition and change in sociology, anthropology, history, and the history of religions"; Ugo Bianchi, "Method, theory, and the subject matter"; Jeppe Sinding Jensen, "What sort of 'reality' is religion?"; E. Thomas Lawson, "Methodological conceits and theoretical opportunities: Reflections on the level of analysis appropriate for explaining socio-cultural phenomena."]

4690. Mojzes, Paul. [Book Review]. *Religion in Eastern Europe* 13, no. 4 (August 1993): 48. [Review article on Igor Troyanovsky, ed., *Religion in the Soviet Republics: A Guide to Christianity, Judaism, Islam, Buddhism, and Other Religions* (San Francisco, CA: HarperSanFrancisco, 1991).]

4691. Muray, Leslie A. "Central and Eastern European Cultural and Religious Resources for the Creation of World Peace." *Religion in Eastern Europe* 13, no. 5 (October 1993): 10-22.

4692. Parsons, Howard L. "Moral and Spiritual Changes in the Last Years of the Soviet Union: Part II." *Religion in Eastern Europe* 13, no. 1 (February 1993): 1-18. [Continued from the previous issue.]

4693. Petrovic, Ranko. "Security in the Balkans: A Possibility or a Utopia." *RCDA* 32, no. 4 (1993-1994): 68-69. [Excerpt from *Review of International Affairs* (Belgrade), English-language edition (1993).]

4694. Ramet, Sabrina Petra, ed. *Religious Policy in the Soviet Union.* Contributions by Philip Walters, Sabrina Petra Ramet, Otto Luchterhandt, Jane Ellis, J. A. Hebly, Larry E. Holmes, John Dunstan, Samuel A. Kliger, Paul H. De Vries, John Anderson, Marjorie Mandelstam Balzer, Oxana Antic, Anatolii Levitin-Krasnov, Myroslaw Tataryn, and Walter Sawatsky. Cambridge; New York, NY: Cambridge University Press, 1993. xix, 361 pp. [Contents: Philip Walters, "A Survey of Soviet Religious Policy," pp. 3-30; Sabrina Petra Ramet, "Religious policy in the era of Gorbachev," pp. 31-52; Otto Luchterhandt, "The Council for

Religious Affairs," pp. 55-83; Jane Ellis, "Some reflections about religious policy under Kharchev," pp. 84-104; J.A. Hebly, "The State, the church, and the *oikumene*: the Russian Orthodox Church and the World Council of Churches, 1948-1985," pp. 105-122; Larry E. Holmes, "Fear no evil: schools and religion in Soviet Russia, 1917-1941," pp. 125-157; John Dunstan, "Soviet schools, atheism and religion," pp. 158-186; Samuel A. Kliger and Paul H. De Vries, "The Ten Commandments as values in Soviet people's consciousness," pp. 187-205; John Anderson, "Out of the kitchen, out of the temple: religion, atheism and women in the Soviet Union," pp. 206-228; Marjorie Mandelstam Balzer, "Dilemmas of the spirit: religion and atheism in the Yakut-Sakha Republic," pp. 231-251; Oxana Antic, "The Spread of modern cults in the USSR," pp. 252-270; Anatolii Levitin-Krasnov, "The Russian Orthodox Renovationist Movement and its Russian historiography during the Soviet period," pp. 273-291; Myroslaw Tataryn, "The Re-emergence of the Ukrainian (Greek) Catholic Church in the USSR," pp. 292-318; Walter Sawatsky, "Protestantism in the USSR," pp. 319-349; Sabrina Petra Ramet, "Epilogue: Religion after the collapse," pp. 350-354.] REV: Serhii Plokhy, *Canadian Slavonic Papers* 35, nos. 3-4 (September-December 1993): pp. 425-427.

4695. Ruebner, Ralph, Mary L. Martin, and Carolyn H. Gasey. "Religion and the Law in the Commonwealth of Independent States and the Baltic Nations." *Touro Journal of Transnational Law*, no. 4 (Spring 1993): 103-148.

4696. Snelling, John. *Buddhism in Russia: The Story of Agvan Dorzhiev, Lhasa's Emissary to the Tzar.* Shaftesbury, Dorset; Rockport, MA: Element, 1993. xiv, 320 pp.

4697. Solomon, Norman. "International Interfaith Conferences Held in Europe." *Journal of Ecumenical Studies* 30, no. 2 (Spring 1993): 302-303.

4698. Volf, Miroslav. "Exclusion and Embrace: Theological Reflections in the Wake of 'Ethnic Cleansing.'" *Religion in Eastern Europe* 13, no. 6 (December 1993): 1-20.

4699. White, William Luther. [Book Review]. *Religion in Eastern Europe* 13, no. 2 (April 1993): 41-46. [Review article on Paul Mojzes, *Religious Liberty in Eastern Europe and the USSR: Before and After the Great Transformation* (New York: Columbia University Press, 1992).]

■ Christianity

General

4700. Bonta, Bruce D. *Peaceful Peoples: An Annotated Bibliography.* Metuchen, NJ: Scarecrow Press, 1993. xi, 288 pp. [Includes chapters on the Anabaptists, Brethren, Doukhobors, Hutterites, Mennonites, and Moravians.]

4701. Gasparov, Boris, and Olga Raevsky-Hughes, eds. *Christianity and the Eastern Slavs: Volume I: Slavic Cultures in the Middle Ages.* Contributions by John Meyendorff, Aleksandr Panchenko, Henrik Birnbaum, Fairy

von Lilienfeld, John Fennell, Donald Ostrowski, Jaroslaw Pelenski, Paul Robert Magocsi, Dean S. Worth, Harvey Goldblatt, Francis J. Thomson, Pavel Sigalov, Boris Uspenskii, Gail Lenhoff, Priscilla Hunt, Maria Pliukhanova, and Guy Picarda. California Slavic Studies, vol. 16. Berkeley, CA: University of California Press, c1993. 374 pp. [English and Russian; summaries in English. Based on papers delivered at two international conferences held in May 1988, at the University of California, Berkeley, and the Kennan Institute for Advanced Russian Studies (Washington, DC) to commemorate the millennium of the Christianization of Kievan Rus'. Contents: Boris Gasparov, "Introduction," pp. 1-8; I. History of Christianity. John Meyendorff, "Universal Witness and Local Identity in Russian Orthodoxy (988-1988)," pp. 11-29; Aleksandr Panchenko, "Kreshchenie Rusi: mirovozzrencheskie i esteticheskie aspekty = The Baptism of Rus': Ideological and Aesthetic Aspects," pp. 30-40; Henrik Birnbaum, "Christianity before Christianization: Christians and Christian Activity in Pre-988 Rus'," pp. 42-62; Fairy von Lilienfeld, "The Spirituality of the Early Kievan Caves Monastery," pp. 63-76; John Fennell, "When Was Olga Canonized?" pp. 77-82; Donald Ostrowski, "Why Did the Metropolitan Move from Kiev to Vladimir in the Thirteenth Century?" pp. 83-101; Jaroslaw Pelenski, "The Origins of the Muscovite Ecclesiastical Claims to the Kievan Inheritance (Early Fourteenth Century to 1458/1461)," pp. 102-115; Paul Robert Magocsi, "Religion and Identity in the Carpathians: East Christians in Poland and Czechoslovakia," pp. 116-138; II. Church Slavonic and the Medieval Literary Tradition. Dean S. Worth, "([Church] Slavonic) Writing in Kievan Rus'," pp. 141-153; Harvey Goldblatt, "On the Place of the Cyrillo-Methodian Tradition in Epiphanius's *Life of Saint Stephen of Perm*," pp. 154-178; Francis J. Thomson, "The Corpus of Slavonic Translations Available in Muscovy: The Cause of Old Russia's Intellectual Silence and a Contributory Factor to Muscovite Cultural Autarky," pp. 179-214; Pavel Sigalov, "Tserkovnoslavianizmy v ukrainskom iazyke = Church Slavonicisms in Ukrainian," pp. 215-237; III. Christianity and Medieval Cultural Paradigms. Boris Uspenskii, "Soliarno-lunarnaia simvolika v oblike russkogo khrama = Solar and Lunar Symbolism in the Exterior of the Russian Church," pp. 241-250; Gail Lenhoff, "The Notion of 'Uncorrupted Relics' in Early Russian Culture," pp. 252-275; Priscilla Hunt, "Justice in Avvakum's Fifth Petition to Tsar Aleksei Mikhailovich," pp. 276-296; Maria Pliukhanova, "Traditsionnost' i unikal'nost' sochinenii protopopa = Tradition and Originality: Archpriest Avvakum's Works in the Light of the 'Third Rome' Tradition," pp. 297-326; Guy Picarda, "The Evolution of Church Music in Belorussia," pp. 328-355.]

4702. Kurth, James. "The Vatican's Foreign Policy." *National Interest*, no. 32 (Summer 1993): 40-52.

4703. Lavelle, Michael. "The Pope Who Could." *Commonweal* 120, no. 7 (April 9, 1993): 39-40. [Review article on George Weigel, *The Final Revolution* (NY: Oxford University Press, 1992) and Owen Chadwick, *The Christian Church in the Cold War* (London: Allen Lane; Penguin Press, 1992).]

4704. Ledeen, Michael. "This Political Pope." *American Enterprise* 4, no. 4 (July-August 1993): 40-43.

4705. Mojzes, Paul. [Book Review]. *Religion in Eastern Europe* 13, no. 1 (February 1993): 45-46. [Review article on George Weigel, *The Final Revolution: The Resistance Chuch and the Collapse of Communism* (New York: Oxford University Press, 1992).]

4706. Nemeth, Thomas. "Karpov and Jurkevic on Kant: Philosophy in Service to Orthodoxy?" *Studies in East European Thought* 45, no. 3 (September 1993): 169-211.

4707. Novak, Michael. *The Catholic Ethic and the Spirit of Capitalism.* New York: Free Press; Toronto: Maxwell Macmillan Canada; New York: Maxwell Macmillan International, c1993. xvii, 334 pp. [Includes discussion of the fall of socialism in Eastern Europe and John Paul II. Contents: Introduction: More Than the Protestant Ethic — Max Weber's Limits — The Human Spirit — Toward a Catholic Ethic — Pt. 1. Which System? Leo XIII to Pius XI (1891-1931). 1. Catholics Against Capitalism. Fanfani's Italy. Mean, Petty, Selfish, and Materialistic. Wealth Is a Means, Not an End. The Catholic Spirit Slowly Awakens. 2. Socialism, No! Capitalism? Maybe: Leo XIII. Why Did Socialism Fail? Workers, Yes! Capitalism? Maybe. Toward the Future. 3. Social Justice Redefined: Pius XI. Rescuing a Virtue. Conceptual Fog. A Brief Historical Overview. A Way Out. The Civil Society: Five Further Steps. From 1931 to 1991 — Pt. 2. A New Birth of Freedom: John Paul II (1978-). 4. The Second Liberty. Two Concepts of Liberty. Order in the Ancien Regime. A Great Year, 1989. The Anticapitalist Bias of Intellectuals. Reconciling Economics and Religion. Convergence on Choice. Dynamic Order. In the Direction of Mind. The Three Spheres of Liberty. One Root, Two Liberties. 5. Capitalism Rightly Understood. Background Reflections. Outline of *Centesimus Annus*. A Christian Social Anthropology. Capitalism, Yes. The Limits of Capitalism. Toward a More Civil Debate — Pt. 3. Next? Poverty, Race, Ethnicity, and Other Perplexities of the 21st Century. 6. War on Poverty: "Created Goods Should Abound" The Universal Destination and the Way. Reconstructing the World Order. International Poverty. Domestic Poverty. Social Invention. 7. Ethnicity, Race, and Social Justice. International Perspectives. The "Civil Society" Project. 8. Against the Adversary Culture. Against Nihilism. Culture and Character. American Founding Principles, Current Practice. The Pope's Challenge to the U.S. Protecting the Moral Ecology. The Institutional Task — Epilogue: The Creative Person — Seven Moral Themes — The Right Stuff — Latin America — The New Virtues Required — The Heart of the Matter: Creativity.] REV: Fred Barnes, *Book World* 23, no. 11 (March 14, 1993): 2. Richard C. Bayer, *Theological Studies* 54 (September 1993): 592-593. Henry J. Ferry, *Mediterranean Quarterly* 4, no. 4 (Fall 1993): 108. Thomas A. Hemphill, *Business and Society Review* no. 87 (Fall 1993): 67-68. John P. Tiemstra, *Cross Currents* 43, no. 4 (Winter 1993-1994): 545-549. Kenneth L. Woodward, *New York Times Book Review* 98, no. 12 (March 21, 1993): 11.

4708. Oikonomou, Elias. "Foundations, Doctrine, and Politics of the Eastern Orthodox Church." *Mediterra-*

nean Quarterly 4, no. 1 (Winter 1993): 57-70.

4709. Pryor, Frederic L. "The Roman Catholic Church and the Economic System: A Review Essay." *Journal of Comparative Economics* 17, no. 1 (March 1993): 129-150. [Includes discussion of Pope John Paul II, *Centesimus Annus* (Boston, MA: 1991).]

4710. Pulcini, Theodore. "Recent Strides toward Reunion of the Eastern and Oriental Orthodox Churches: Healing the Chalcedonian Breach." *Journal of Ecumenical Studies* 30, no. 1 (Winter 1993): 34-50.

4711. Slater, Wendy, and Kjell Engelbrekt. "Eastern Orthodoxy Defends Its Position." *RFE/RL Research Report* 2, no. 35 (September 3, 1993): 48-58.

4712. Toews, J. B. *A Pilgrimage of Faith: The Mennonite Brethren Church in Russia and North America, 1860-1990.* Perspectives on Mennonite Life and Thought, 8. Winnipeg, MB; Hillsboro, KS: Kindred Press, c1993. vii, 376 pp.

4713. Weigel, George. "The Collapse of Communism: Recovering the Transcendent Order." *World & I* 8, no. 5 (May 1993): 368-378.

4714. Wood, Marina. "An Orthodox Handbook." *Vox Benedictina* 10, no. 1 (Summer 1993): 123-148. [Glossary of Greek and Russian terms used in Orthodox Christianity. Reprinted from *An Orthodox Handbook* (Kettering, Northants.: 1991).]

Russia/U.S.S.R./C.I.S.

4715. Aldridge, James Francis. "The Cross and Its Cult in an Age of Iconoclasm." Ph.D. diss., Ohio State University, 1993. [UMI order no: AAC 9316128.]

4716. Avdoyan, Levon. *Pseudo-Yovhannes Mamikonean, The History of Taron (Patmut'iwn Taronoy): Historical Investigation, Critical Translation, and Historical and Textual Commentaries.* Occasional Papers and Proceedings (Scholars Press). Suren D. Fesjian Academic Publications, no. 6. Atlanta, GA: Scholars Press, c1993. xxxix, 279 pp.

4717. Bablumian, Sergei. "Armenia After Vazgen." *RCDA* 32, no. 3 (1993-1994): 53. [Translation of article from *Izvestiia* (August 20, 1994).]

4718. Batalden, Stephen K., ed. *Seeking God: The Recovery of Religious Identity in Orthodox Russia, Ukraine, and Georgia.* Contributions by Stephen K. Batalden, Michael A. Meerson, Eve Levin, Gregory L. Freeze, Brenda Meehan, Boris A. Uspensky, Robert O. Crummey, Roy R. Robson, Frank E. Sysyn, Fairy von Lilienfeld, Michael D. Palma, and Charles Frazee. DeKalb, IL: Northern Illinois University Press, 1993. 299 pp. [Earlier versions of all except one essay were presented at the symposium on "The Recovery of Religious Identity in the Soviet Union" held at Arizona State University in March 1991. Contents: Stephen K. Batalden, "Introduction"; Michael A. Meerson, "The Life and Work of Father Aleksandr Men'"; Eve Levin, "Dvoeverie and Popular Religion"; Gregory L. Freeze, "The Wages of

Sin: The Decline of Public Penance in Imperial Russia";
Brenda Meehan, "Popular Piety, Local Initiative, and the
Founding of Women's Religious Communities in Russia,
1764-1907"; Boris A. Uspensky, "The Schism and Cultural
Conflict in the Seventeenth Century"; Robert O. Crummey,
"Interpreting the Fate of Old Believer Communities in the
Eighteenth and Nineteenth Centuries"; Roy R. Robson,"An
Architecture of Change: Old Believer Liturgical Spaces in
Late Imperial Russia"; Frank E. Sysyn, "The Third Rebirth
of the Ukrainian Autocephalous Orthodox Church and the
Religious Ukraine, 1989-1991"; Fairy von Lilienfeld,
"Reflections on the Current State of the Georgian Church
and Nation"; Stephen K. Batalden, "The Contemporary
Politics of the Russian Bible: Religious Publication in a
Period of Glasnost"; Stephen K. Batalden and Michael D.
Palma, "Orthodox Pilgrimage and Russian Landholding in
Jerusalem: The British Colonial Record"; Charles Frazee,
"Using Vatican Archives in the Study of Eastern Christian-
ity."]

4719. Bovkalo, A., and A. Galkin. "Church Life in
the Novgorod Diocese." *Religion in Eastern Europe* 13, no. 6
(December 1993): 44-45.

4720. Burchard, Christoph, ed. *Armenia and the
Bible: Papers Presented to the International Symposium
Held at Heidelberg, July 16-19, 1990.* Contributions by
Rouben P. Adalian, Shahe Ajamian, Aïda-Aznive K.
Boudjikanian, Claude E. Cox, Armenuhi Drost-Abgarjan,
Michel van Esbroeck, Christian Hannick, Friedrich Heyer,
Manuel M. Jinbachian, Dickran Kouymjian, Louis Leloir,
Barbara J. Merguerian, Parouïr Mouradian, Bernard
Outtier, Avedis K. Sanjian, Gaguik Sarkissian, Folker
Siegert, Abraham Terian, Joseph J. S. Weitenberg, and
Andranik Zeitounian. University of Pennsylvania Armenian
Texts and Studies, 12. Atlanta, GA: Scholars Press, c1993.
x, 251 pp. [Published under the auspices of the Association
Internationale des Etudes Arméniennes. Contents: Rouben
P. Adalian, "From Scripture to Text to Icon: The Armenian
Bible in View of Modern Technology and Scholarship," pp. 1-
14; Shahe Ajamian, "An Introduction to the Book of Psalms
by David Anhaght," pp. 15-21; Aïda Boudjikanian, "Valeurs
morales et religieuses dans la vie pratique des Arméniens
du Liban. Résultats comparatifs d'une enquête menée
parmi la population Chrétienne libanaise en 1987," pp. 23-
33; Claude Cox, "The Translations of Aquila, Symmachus
and Theodotion Found in the Margins of Armenian Manuscripts," pp. 35-45; Armenuhi Drost-Abgarjan, "Biblisches in
moderner armenischer Literatur am Beispiel von Parujr
Sewaks 'Nimmerverstummender Glockenturm,' " pp. 47-71;
Michel van Esbroeck, "Une exégèse rare d'Isaïse 29, 11-12
conservée en arménien," pp. 73-78; Christian Hannick,
"Bibelexegese in armenischen Handschriftenkolophonen,"
pp. 79-86; Friedrich Heyer, "Biblische Bezüge in den 95
Elegien des Gregor von Nareg," pp. 87-96; Manuel M.
Jinbachian, "Modern Armenian Translations of the Bible,"
pp. 97-123; Dickran Kouymjian, "The Evolution of Arme-
nian Gospel Illumination: The Formative Period (9th-11th
Centuries)," pp. 125-142; Louis Leloir, "Comment les
premiers moines arméniens ont-ils lu la Bible?" pp. 143-152;
Barbara J. Merguerian, "The Armenian Bible and the

American Missionaries: The First Four Decades (1820-
1860)," pp. 153-169; Parouïr Mouradian, "Importance des
citations bibliques rencontrées dans les documents
littéraires et épigraphiques mediévaux arméniens," pp. 171-
179; Bernard Outtier, "Réponses oraculaires dans des
manuscrits bibliques caucasiens," pp. 181-184; Avedis K.
Sanjian, "Esayi Nceci and Biblical Exegesis," pp. 185-193;
Gaguik Sarkissian, "Les phases préliminaires de la langue
littéraire arménienne vues par un historien," pp. 195-206;
Folker Siegert, "Dir rhetorische Qualität der armenischen
Bibel," pp. 207-211; Abraham Terian, "The Bible in Verse by
Gregory Magistros," pp. 213-219; Joseph J.S. Weitenberg,
"The Language of Mesrop: L'Arménien pour lui-même?" pp.
221-231; Andranik Zeitounian, "Les divergences des
manuscrits grecs et arméniens du 'Livre de la Genèse'," pp.
233-243.]

4721. Crummey, Robert O. "Old Belief as Popular
Religion: New Approaches." *Slavic Review* 52, no. 4 (Winter
1993): 700-712.

4722. Gaffney, Edward McGlynn, Jr. "Pray for it."
Commonweal 120, no. 9 (May 7, 1993): 5-7. [On religious
freedom in Russia.]

4723. Krakhmalnikova, Zoya. "The Ideology of
Schism: The Danger of the Government's Political Games
with Orthodoxy." *RCDA* 32, no. 2 (1993-1994): 24-29.
[Abridged from *Izvestiia* (April 19, 19940.]

4724. Lefevere, Patricia. "Ecumenical Tensions in
Russia." *Religion in Eastern Europe* 13, no. 4 (August 1993):
42-44.

4725. Lorgus, Andrei. "Render Unto Caesar: A
Historical Apology." *RCDA* 32, no. 1 (1993-1994): 4-7.
[Abridged translation of an article in *Journal of the Moscow
Patriarchate* (November 12, 1992).]

4726. Loya, Joseph A. [Book Review]. *Religion in
Eastern Europe* 13, no. 3 (June 1993): 42-43. [Review article
on David Little, *Ukraine: The Legacy of Intolerance* (Washington, DC: United States Institute of Peace Press, 1991).]

4727. Martyniuk, Jaroslaw. "Religious Preferences
in Five Urban Areas of Ukraine." *RFE/RL Research Report*
2, no. 15 (April 9, 1993): 52-55.

4728. Meehan, Brenda. *Holy Women of Russia: The
Lives of Five Orthodox Women Offer Spiritual Guidance for
Today.* 1st ed. [San Francisco, CA]: HarperSanFrancisco,
c1993. x, 182 pp.

4729. Moss, James. "Russian Orthodox Episcopacy:
1990-1993." *RCDA* 32, no. 3 (1993-1994): 51-53.

4730. Oller, Thomas Hilary. "The Nikol'skij
Apocalypse Codex and Its Place in the Textual History of
Medieval Slavic Apocalypse Manuscripts." Ph.D. diss.,
Brown University, 1993. [UMI order no: AAC 9407003.]

4731. Peachey, Paul. "Rethinking Nationalism and
Democracy in the Light of Post-Communist Experience."
Religion in Eastern Europe 13, no. 1 (February 1993): 26-37.
[Report on symposium, held May 15-16, 1992, co-sponored

by the Council for Research in Philosophy and Values at Catholic University, and the Rolling Ridge Study Retreat Community. The participants focussed on the work of Ghia Nodia of the Institute of Philosophy in the Georgian Academy of Sciences in Tbilisi.]

4732. Renik, Krzysztof. "Faith and Freedom in the New Russia: Interview with Father Stanislaw Opiela." *Uncaptive Minds* 6, no. 1 (22) (Winter-Spring 1993): 87-94. [Interview published in *Tygodnik Powszechny* (December 27, 1992).]

4733. Robson, Roy R. "Liturgy and Community among Old Believers, 1905-1917." *Slavic Review* 52, no. 4 (Winter 1993): 713-724.

4734. Slater, Wendy. "The Russian Orthodox Church." *RFE/RL Research Report* 2, no. 20 (May 14, 1993): 92-95.

4735. Warhola, James W. *Russian Orthodoxy and Political Culture in Transformation*. Carl Beck Papers in Russian and East European Studies, no. 1006. Pittsburgh, PA: Center for Russian & East European Studies, University of Pittsburgh, 1993. 53 pp.

4736. Wolkovich-Valkavicius, William L. "A Chronicle about Ireland, Lithuania, and a Marian Statue." *Lituanus* 39, no. 2 (Summer 1993): 51-69.

4737. Wood, James E., Jr. "Editorial: The Battle Over Religious Freedom in Russia." *Journal of Church and State* 35, no. 3 (Summer 1993): 491-502.

4738. Wright, J. Robert, ed. *On Being a Bishop: Papers on Episcopacy from the Moscow Consultation, 1992.* New York: Church Hymnal Corporation, 1993. ix, 230 pp. [Contains the contributions of American Anglican participants of the meeting held in Moscow in June, 1992. Papers by the Russian Orthodox participants are given in summaries.] REV: John Jay Hughes, *Journal of Ecumenical Studies* 30, nos. 3-4 (Summer-Fall 1993): 445.

4739. Yakunin, Gleb. "Now It Is Time for Clergy to Repent." *RCDA* 32, no. 1 (1993-1994): 8-9. [Translation of an article published in *Izvestiia* (January 15, 1993).]

Eastern Europe

4740. Althausen, Johannes. "The Church in the GDR Between Accomodation and Resistance." *Religion in Eastern Europe* 13, no. 6 (December 1993): 21-35.

4741. Brock, Peter. "Faustus Socinus as a Pacifist." *Polish Review* 38, no. 4 (1993): 441-446.

4742. ———. "Marcin Czechowic on the *Via Crucis*, Self-Defense, and Government (1575)." *Mennonite Quarterly Review* 67, no. 4 (October 1993): 451-468.

4743. Broun, Janice. "The Bulgarian Orthodox Church Schism." *Religion in Eastern Europe* 13, no. 3 (June 1993): 1-5.

4744. ———. "Slovakia embraces the past." *Commonweal* 120, no. 16 (September 24, 1993): 15.

4745. Byrnes, Timothy A. "What's a Catholic country to do?" *Commonweal* 120, no. 16 (September 24, 1993): 11-13.

4746. Carlson, Maria. *'No Religion Higher Than Truth': A History of the Theosophical Movement in Russia, 1875-1922.* Princeton, NJ: Princeton University Press, c1993. vi, 298 pp. REV: Donald P. Gray, *Ukrainian Quarterly* 49, no. 3 (Fall 1993): 327-332. James West, *Slavic Review* 52, no. 4 (Winter 1993): 872-873.

4747. Chadwick, Owen. *The Christian Church in the Cold War*. Penguin History of the Church, 7. London; New York, NY: Penguin Books, c1993. viii, 240 pp. [First published (London: A. Lane, 1992).] REV: Michael Lavelle, *Commonweal* 120, no. 7 (April 9, 1993): 39-40.

4748. Conway, John S. "*Kirche im Sozialismus*: East German Protestantism's Political and Theological Witness, 1945-1990." *Religion in Eastern Europe* 13, no. 4 (August 1993): 1-21.

4749. Dartel, Geert van, Jure Kristo, and Paul Mojzes. "Responses to the Article 'The Role of the Religious Communities in the War in Former Yugoslavia.'" *Religion in Eastern Europe* 13, no. 5 (October 1993): 45ff. [Van Dartel and Kristo respond to article by Mojzes in vol. 13, no. 3 (June 1993); followed with reply by Mojzes.]

4750. Dykema, Peter A., and Heiko A. Oberman, eds. *Anticlericalism in Late Medieval and Early Modern Europe*. Studies in Medieval and Reformation Thought, v. 51. Leiden; New York: E.J. Brill, 1993. xi, 704 pp. [Proceedings of an international colloquium held September 20-22, 1990, at the University of Arizona (Tucson, AZ), convened by the Division for Late Medieval and Reformation Studies.] REV: E. J. Furcha, *Mennonite Quarterly Review* 67, no. 4 (October 1993): 489.

4751. Gagnere, Nathalie. "The Return of God and the Challenge of Democracy: The Catholic Church in Central Eastern Europe." *Journal of Church and State* 35, no. 4 (Autumn 1993): 859-884.

4752. Girnius, Saulius. "The Catholic Church in Post-Soviet Lithuania." *RFE/RL Research Report* 2, no. 41 (October 15, 1993): 43-46.

4753. Grzymala-Moszczynska, Halina. "Factors Affecting Unconditional Acceptance of the Institution of the Church in Poland." *Religion in Eastern Europe* 13, no. 4 (August 1993): 22-27.

4754. Hann, Chris M. "Religion and Nationality in Central Europe: The Case of the Uniates." *Ethnic Groups* 10, nos. 1-3 (1993): 201-213. [Part of special issue devoted to "Pre-Modern and Modern National Identity in Russia and Eastern Europe."]

4755. Hart, Andrew R. "The Role of the Lutheran Church in Estonian Nationalism." *Religion in Eastern Europe* 13, no. 3 (June 1993): 6-12.

4756. Hegedüs, Loránt. "In the Eleventh Hour: The Immediate Past, the Present, and the Future of the Reformed Church in Hungary." *Religion in Eastern Europe* 13, no. 4 (August 1993): 28-41.

4757. Hillar, Marian. "Poland's Contribution to the Reformation: Socinians and Their Ideas on Religious Freedom." *Polish Review* 38, no. 4 (1993): 447-468.

4758. Himka, John-Paul, James T. Flynn, and James Niessen, eds. *Religious Compromise, Political Salvation: The Greek Catholic Church and Nation-Building in Eastern Europe.* Contributions by John-Paul Himka, James T. Flynn, and James Niessen. The Carl Beck Papers in Russian and East European Studies, no. 1003. Pittsburgh, PA: Center for Russian & East European Studies, University of Pittsburgh, 1993. 68 pp. [Presented at the annual convention of the American Association for the Advancement of Slavic Studies in 1990. Contents: John-Paul Himka, "The Greek Catholic Church and the Ukrainian nation in Galicia"; James T. Flynn, "The Uniate Church in Belorussia: a case of nation-building?"; James Niessen, "The Greek Catholic Church and the Romanian nation in Transylvania."]

4759. Hupchick, Dennis P. "Orthodoxy and Bulgarian Ethnic Awareness Under Ottoman Rule, 1396-1762." *Nationalities Papers* 21, no. 2 (Fall 1993): 75-93.

4760. Kornilov, Leonid. "Polish Government and Church Are Mutually Independent." *RCDA* 32, no. 4 (1993-1994): 71. [Translation of article from *Izvestiia* (July 31, 1993).]

4761. Kosztolnyik, Zoltan J. "In the European Mainstream: Hungarian Churchmen and Thirteenth-Century Synods." *Catholic Historical Review* 79, no. 3 (July 1993): 413-433.

4762. Liechty, Daniel. *Sabbatarianism in the Sixteenth Century: A Page in the History of the Radical Reformation.* Berrien Springs, MI: Andrews University Press, c1993. x, 94 pp. [Contents: Pt. I. Anabaptist Sabbatarianism in Silesia and Moravia. The Anabaptist Movement. Hans Denck and Hans Hut. Hut's Missionary Journey. Oswald Glaidt. Chiliastic Influences. Oswald Glaidt's Defense of Sabbatarianism. Oswald Glaidt's Later Years. Andreas Fischer's Defense of Sabbatarianism. Andreas Fischer's Later Years — Pt. II. Unitarian Sabbatarianism in Transylvania. Hungary at the Time of the Reformation. The Rise of Unitarianism. Francis David and Unitarian Radicalism. Theological Foundation of Sabbatarianism. Sabbatarians in the First Generation. Sabbatarians in the Second Generation. Sabbatarian Ideology Under Simon Pechi. The Great Persecution of 1638. Sabbatarians in Later Generations.]

4763. Lopatkiewicz, Tadeusz, and Malgorzata Lopatkiewicz. *Mala sakral'na arkhitektura na lemkivshchyni = Small Sacral Architecture in Lemkivshchyna.* Translated by Zoia Verbova. Niu Iork: Fundatsiia doslidzhennia Lemkivshchyny, 1993. 490 pp.

4764. "Message of Church Leaders on the Situation in the Former Yugoslavia." *Religion in Eastern Europe* 13, no. 3 (June 1993): 38-41.

4765. "Methodological Guidelines for the Election of Clergy." *RCDA* 32, no. 3 (1993-1994): 54-55. ["From Secret Archives." Prepared by Bodlak.]

4766. Michnik, Adam. *The Church and the Left.* Edited, translated, and introduction by David Ost. Chicago, IL: University of Chicago Press, 1993. xvii, 301 pp. [Translation of *Kosciol, lewica, dialog.*] REV: Jaroslaw Anders, *New Republic* 208 (May 17, 1993): 42ff. Kenneth W. Banta, *Book World* 23, no. 17 (April 25, 1993): 7. Robert Legvold, *Foreign Affairs* 72, no. 3 (Summer 1993): 205 Larry Wolff, *New York Times Book Review* 98, no. 12 (March 21 1993): 11-12. *Orbis* 37, no. 2 (Spring 1993).

4767. Mojzes, Paul. "The Role of the Religious Communities in the War in Former Yugoslavia." *Religion in Eastern Europe* 13, no. 3 (June 1993): 13-31. [Followed with responses by Geert van Dartel and Jure Kristo in vol. 13, no. 5 (October 1993).]

4768. Obrman, Jan, and Pavel Mates. "Czech Republic Debates Return of Church Property." *RFE/RL Research Report* 2, no. 19 (May 7, 1993): 46-50.

4769. Pawlikowski, John T. "The Holocaust: Its Implications for Contemporary Church-State Relations in Poland." *Religion in Eastern Europe* 13, no. 2 (April 1993): 1-13. [Paper was presented to the International Congress of Polish Scholars, sponsored by the Polish Institute of Arts and Sciences (USA), Yale University, June 19, 1992.]

4770. Peachey, Paul. "European Renewal: A Christian Contribution?" *Religion in Eastern Europe* 13, no. 1 (February 1993): 41-44. [Report on the symposium "The Political and Cultural Renewal of Europe: The Contribution of the Christian Social Teaching," held August 30-September 3, 1992, in Augsburg, Germany.]

4771. Pollis, Adamantia. "Eastern Orthodoxy and Human Rights." *Human Rights Quarterly* 15, no. 2 (May 1993): 339-356.

4772. Raikin, Spas T. "Schism in the Bulgarian Orthodox Church." *Religion in Eastern Europe* 13, no. 1 (February 1993): 19-25.

4773. Rejchrt, Milos. "Christian Peace Conference: A Posthumous Creature of Brezhnevian Stalinism." *RCDA* 32, no. 2 (1993-1994): 34-36.

4774. Robertson, Charles G., Jr. "The Evangelical Reformed Church in the New Polish Context." *Religion in Eastern Europe* 13, no. 2 (April 1993): 14-28.

4775. Roter, Zdenko. "The Church and Contemporary Slovene History." *Nationalities Papers* 21, no. 1 (Spring 1993): 71-80.

4776. Ruml, Joel. "East German Disenchantment: Interview with Heiko Krebs." *RCDA* 32, no. 1 (1993-1994): 11-14. [Translation of article published in *Protestant*, no. 2 (1994).]

4777. Sabbat-Swidlicka, Anna. "Church and State in Poland." *RFE/RL Research Report* 2, no. 14 (April 2, 1993): 45-57.

4778. "Slovak Lutherans Find Themselves in a New Country." *Religion in Eastern Europe* 13, no. 4 (August 1993): 45-47.

4779. "Songs of Praise in Latvia." *War Cry* 113, no. 13 (June 19, 1993): 17-19. [Includes "Interview with Captain and Mrs. Bjorn (Mona) Stockman, Salvation Army officers stationed in Riga, Latvia," p. 19.]

4780. Tos, Niko. "(Non)Religiousness in Slovenia." *Religion in Eastern Europe* 13, no. 5 (October 1993): 23-44.

4781. Tranda, Bogdan. "The Great Change and the Protestants." *Religion in Eastern Europe* 13, no. 2 (April 1993): 29-33.

4782. Yoder, Bill. "Protestant Adjustments After the Break-up of Yugoslavia." *Religion in Eastern Europe* 13, no. 3 (June 1993): 32-37.

4783. ———. "Protestants in (Former) Yugoslavia." *Religion in Eastern Europe* 13, no. 1 (February 1993): 38-40.

■ Judaism

4784. "Another First: Jewish Women Gather in Kiev." *Lilith* 18, no. 4 (Fall 1993): 5. [International conference of Jewish women, titled "Reconnecting for the First Time" scheduled for May 23-27, 1994.]

4785. "A First: Female Rabbi Serving in Ukraine." *Lilith* 18, no. 4 (Fall 1993): 5.

4786. Katz, Steven T., ed. *Interpreters of Judaism in the Late Twentieth Century.* B'nai B'rith History of the Jewish People. Washington, DC: B'nai B'rith Books, c1993. xv, 423 pp.

4787. Klagsbrun, Francine. "Legends & Lessons." *Congress Monthly* 60, no. 7 (November-December 1993): 7-9.

4788. Nalder, Allan. "Soloveitchik's Halakhic Man: Not a *Mithnagged*." *Modern Judaism* 13, no. 2 (May 1993): 119-147.

4789. Schwartzman, Arnold. *Graven Images: Graphic Motifs of the Jewish Grave Stone.* Foreword by Chaim Potok. New York, NY: H.H. Abrams, 1993. 144 pp. [Discusses European Jewish grave markers from the Middle Ages to the 20th Century.] REV: Eric J. Brock, *Newsletter of the Association for Gravestone Studies* 17, no. 3 (Summer 1993): 19.

4790. Solomon, Norman. *The Analytic Movement: Hayyim Soloveitchik and His Circle.* South Florida Studies in the History of Judaism, no. 58. Atlanta, GA: Scholars Press, c1993. xvi, 268 pp. [Based on the author's thesis (Ph.D.)—University of Manchester, 1966.]

4791. Zipperstein, Steven J. "Between Tribalism and Utopia: Ahad Ha'am and the Making of Jewish Cultural Politics." *Modern Judaism* 13, no. 3 (October 1993): 231-247.

■ Islam

4792. Akiner, Shirin. "On Its Own: Islam in Post-Soviet Central Asia." *Harvard International Review* 15, no. 3 (Spring 1993): 18-27.

4793. Al-Khathllan, Saleh Mohammed Farhan. "Uzbeks and Islam: Their Contemporary Political Culture. An Empirical Study." Ph.D. diss., University of Kansas, 1993. [UMI order no: AAC 9405709.]

4794. Hadar, Leon T. "What Green Peril?" *Foreign Affairs* 72, no. 2 (Spring 1993): 27-42.

4795. Norris, H. T. *Islam in the Balkans: Religion and Society between Europe and the Arab World.* Columbia, SC: University of South Carolina Press, c1993. xxii, 304 pp. [Contents: 1. The Arabs, the Slavs, the Hungarian Saracens and the Arnauts. The Arabs enter Balkan history. Middle Eastern beliefs among the Slavs. The Arab threat to Byzantium. Arabs and Bulgarians at the beginning of the tenth century. Dubrovnik and the Arab East. Pecheneg and Khwarizmian Muslims in medieval Hungary. Al-Idrisi (548/1154) describes the Yugoslav coast, Albania and the Macedonian interior. The Arnauts. Balkan regions, the 'Chanson de Roland' and medieval Arabic folk epics — 2. Oriental influences on Islamic and non-Islamic life and literature in Bosnia, in Macedonia and among the Albanians. The Bogomil and Christian background. Islam and the Balkan city. Mosque, tekke and library. Arabic and Persian scholarship. Early Islamic poets in Albania. Islamic popular literature. Early nineteenth-century poets — 3. Sufi movements and orders in the Balkans and their historical links with the Sufism of Central Asia. The Baktashiyya. Non-Shiite Sufi orders in the Balkans. The Qadiriyya. The Mawlawiyya. The Khalwatiyya. The Naqshabandiyya. The Malamiyya. Shaykh al-Ta'ifa al-Bayramiyya. The origins of the Baktashiyya in Albania. When were the first tekkes built in the heart of Albania? Kruje — 4. Muslim heroes of the Bulgars, the Tatars of the Dobrudja, the Albanians and the Bosnians. Oriental legends about the Arabian and Central Asian ancestry of the Bulgars and Arnauts. The folk epic, religious mission, miracles and many tombs of Sari Saltik. Kruje, Sari Saltik and Gjerg Elez Alia in Albania and Bosnia — 5. Albanian Sufi poets of the nineteenth and twentieth centuries and their impact on contemporary Albanian thought. The writings of Naim Frasheri. Naim Frasheri's poem on Skanderbeg. Naim Frasheri's Baktashi works. The historical background to Naim's 'Qerbelaja'. The tekkes of Iraq. The epic of Fuduli and his influences on later Albanian literature. 'Qerbelaja'. Twentieth-century Sufi poets of Kosovo. The Baktashi legacy in the verse of Baba Ali Tomori. The neo-mysticism of Hamid Gjylbegaj. — 6. Balkan Muslims in the history of the Maghrib, Egypt and Syria and the influence of the Arab East in the courtly life of Ali Pasha of Tepelene. Albanians and Bosnians in Algeria and Tunisia. Albanians in Egypt. Albanians and the Cairene Baktashi tekkes. The history of Shaykh Muhammad Lutfi Baba and Shaykh Ahmad Sirri Baba. al-Hajj Umar Lutfi Bashanzi. Ali Pasha of Tepelene. The Albanians in Syria — 7. Bridges and barriers of Islamic faith and culture within Balkan Muslim and non-Muslim societies. The battle of Kosovo and the Serb crusade against Islam. Syncretic movements and religious bridge-building in the late Middle Ages. Romanian monasteries and mosques and links with the Arab East. Islam in Kosovo. The Future — Appendix: The Serbian view of Islam in the 1980s.]

4796. Vasilyev, Aleksey. "Russia and the Islamic World: Partners or Adversaries?" *RCDA* 32, no. 4 (1993-1994): 63-66. [Translation of article from *Izvestiia* (March 10, 1992).]

16 Science and Technology

■ General

4797. Akhundov, Murad. "Soviet Science under the Pressure of Ideology." *Soviet and Post-Soviet Review* 20, no. 2-3 (1993): 183-193.

4798. Birkhoff, Garrett. "Oscar Zariski (24 April 1899-4 July 1986)." *Proceedings of American Philosophical Society* 137, no. 2 (June 1993): 305-320.

4799. Boggio, G., and R. Thomas. "Cooperation with Eastern European Countries in Science and Research: A New Initiative of the European Community." *Technology in Society* 15, no. 1 (1993): 149-154. [Part of special issue on science and technology in Eastern Europe.]

4800. Bollag, Burton. "Czech Academy of Sciences to Close a Quarter of Its Institutes and Dismiss 2,000 Employees." *Chronicle of Higher Education* 39, no. 28 (March 17, 1993): A42.

4801. Crowe, Gregory D. "Science and Technology with a Human Face: Russian-American Perspectives." *Slavic Review* 52, no. 2 (Summer 1993): 318-332. [Summarizes the first three of six two-day workshops, alternately held in Russia and the U.S., sponsored by MIT's Science, Technology, and Society Program.]

4802. Denchev, Stoyan. "Science and Technology in the New Bulgaria." *Technology in Society* 15, no. 1 (1993): 57-63. [Part of special issue on science and technology in Eastern Europe.]

4803. Frackowiak, Jan Krzystof. "Addendum: New Methods of Financing Science in Poland." *Technology in Society* 15, no. 1 (1993): 71-73. [Part of special issue on science and technology in Eastern Europe.]

4804. Greenstein, George. "The Ladies of Observatory Hill: Annie Jump Cannon and Cecilia Payne-Gaposchkin." *American Scholar* 62, no. 3 (Summer 1993): 437-446. [Includes the marriage of Anglo-American astronomer Cecilia Payne to Russian émigré astronomer Sergei Gaposchkin.]

4805. Hughes, David. "U.S., Russia bargain for enriched uranium." *Aviation Week & Space Technology* 138, no. 2 (January 11, 1993): 28-29.

4806. Karczewski, Witold. "The New Approach to Science and Technology in Poland." *Technology in Society* 15, no. 1 (1993): 65-69. [Part of special issue on science and technology in Eastern Europe.]

4807. Kerekes, Sandor. "Economics, Technology, and Environment in Hungary." *Technology in Society* 15, no. 1 (1993): 137-147. [Part of special issue on science and technology in Eastern Europe.]

4808. Lenorovitz, Jeffrey M., and Boris Rybak. "Engineers flee low-paying CIS jobs." *Aviation Week & Space Technology* 139, no. 13 (September 27, 1993): 53-55.

4809. McDonald, Kim A. "Russian Science Still Threatened Despite Reforms." *Chronicle of Higher Education* 39, no. 34 (April 28, 1993): A37-A38.

4810. Medvedev, Zhores. "The Death of Science in Russia." *Dissent* 40, no. 4 (Fall 1993): 423-426.

4811. Muczyk, Jan P. "The Polish School of Mathematics." *East European Quarterly* 27, no. 2 (Summer 1993): 231-242.

4812. Oborne, Michael. "OECD Science and Technology Policy Reviews in Hungary and Czechoslovakia." *Technology in Society* 15, no. 1 (1993): 155-159. [Part of special issue on science and technology in Eastern Europe.]

4813. Pavlenko, Vladimir. "Commentary: Arctic Research in Russia." *Arctic* 46, no. 3 (September 1993): iii-iv.

4814. Pungor, Ernö, and Lajos Nyiri. "The Reconstruction of Science and Technology in Hungary." *Technology in Society* 15, no. 1 (1993): 25-39. [Part of special issue on science and technology in Eastern Europe.]

4815. Read, Piers Paul. *Ablaze: The Story of the Heroes and Victims of Chernobyl.* 1st ed. New York: Random House, c1993. xxxi, 362 pp. [Also published (London: Secker & Warburg, 1993).] REV: David Holloway, *New York Review of Books* 40, no. 11 (June 10, 1993): 36-38. Dan Kurzman, *Book World* 23, no. 17 (April 25, 1993): 6. Linda M. Perney, *Audubon* 95, no. 2 (March-April 1993): 120ff. *New Yorker* 68, no. 13 (May 17, 1993): 107.

4816. Solingen, Etel. "Between Markets and the State: Scientists in Comparative Perspective." *Comparative Politics* 26, no. 1 (October 1993): 31-51.

4817. Ullschmeid, Jirí. "Addendum: Financing R&D Systems in OECD Countries and Czechoslovakia—A Comparison." *Technology in Society* 15, no. 1 (1993): 53-56. [Part of special issue on science and technology in Eastern Europe.]

4818. Vizi, Sylvester E. "Reversing the Brain Drain from Eastern European Countries: The 'Push' and 'Pull' Factors." *Technology in Society* 15, no. 1 (1993): 101-109. [Part of special issue on science and technology in Eastern Europe.]

4819. Weiss, Charles, Jr. "The Re-Emergence of Eastern European Science and Technology." *Technology in Society* 15, no. 1 (1993): 3-23. [Part of special issue on science and technology in Eastern Europe.]

4820. ———. "Scientific and Technological Responses to Structural Adjustment: Human Resources and Research Issues in Hungary, Turkey, and Yugoslavia." *Technology in Society* 15, no. 3 (1993): 281-299.

4821. Zahradnik, Rudolf. "Research and Education in Czechoslovakia: A Few Remarks." *Technology in Society* 15, no. 1 (1993): 41-52. [Part of special issue on science and technology in Eastern Europe.]

4822. Zviglyanich, Vladimir A. *Scientific Knowledge as a Culture and Historical Process: The Cultural Prospects of Science*. Lewiston: E. Mellen Press, 1993. 280 pp. [Translation of *Nauchnoe poznanie kak kul'turno istoricheskii protsess*.]

■ Computer Science

4823. Bati, Ferenc. "Technological Strategic Alliance: Digital Equipment Corporation in Hungary—As a Case in Point." *Technology in Society* 15, no. 1 (1993): 159-163. [Part of special issue on science and technology in Eastern Europe.]

4824. "DEC exploits Russian aerospace niche." *Aviation Week & Space Technology* 138, no. 26 (June 28, 1993): 52.

4825. Dyker, David A., and George Stein. "Russian Software: Adjusting to the World Market." *RFE/RL Research Report* 2, no. 44 (November 5, 1993): 50-53.

4826. Hughes, David. "New planning software aids Bosnian airdrops." *Aviation Week & Space Technology* 138, no. 17 (April 26, 1993): 59-61.

4827. Richards, Lynn. "Greening the Globe: The Magic of Electronic Mail." *Surviving Together* 11, no. 4 (Winter 1993): 20-21.

■ Engineering and Technology

4828. Del Tredici, Robert. "First, puzzlement; then action." *Bulletin of the Atomic Scientists* 49, no. 2 (March 1993): 24-29.

4829. Graham, Loren R. *The Ghost of the Executed Engineer: Technology and the Fall of the Soviet Union*. Russian Research Center Studies, 87. Cambridge, MA: Harvard University Press, 1993. xiv, 128 pp. [Contents: The Radical Engineer; From Political Prisoner to Soviet Consultant; Early Soviet Industrialization; Technocracy, Soviet Style; Contemporary Engineering Failures; Epilogue: The Ghost of Peter Palchinsky.] REV: Susan Gross Solomon, *New York Times Book Review* 98, no. 48 (November 28, 1993): 7-8. S. Frederick Starr, *New Republic* 209, no. 23 (December 6, 1993): 47-49.

4830. ———. *Science in Russia and the Soviet Union: A Short History*. Cambridge History of Science. Cambridge; New York: Cambridge University Press, 1993. x, 321 pp. REV: Charles Coulston Gillispie, *New York Times Book Review* 98, no. 12 (March 21, 1993): 25. Alexei

Kojevnikov, *Science* 261, no. 5126 (September 3, 1993): 1336-1338. Robert Legvold, *Foreign Affairs* 72, no. 2 (Spring 1993): 178.

4831. Halverson, Thomas. "Tickling time bombs: East bloc reactors." *Bulletin of the Atomic Scientists* 49, no. 6 (July-August 1993): 43-48.

4832. Hare, Paul, and Ray Oakey. *The Diffusion of New Process Technologies in Hungary: Eastern European Innovation in Perspective*. London: Pinter Publishers; New York: Distributed in the USA and Canada by St. Martin's Press, 1993. xii, 185 pp.

4833. Hippel, Frank von. "The National Interest." *Technology Review* 96, no. 6 (August-September 1993): 70. [On the disposal of bomb-grade plutonium extracted from reactor-fuel reprocessing plants and dismantled nuclear weapons.]

4834. Hopkins, Arthur T. *Unchained Reactions: Chernobyl, Glasnost, and Nuclear Deterrence*. Washington, DC: National Defense University Press, 1993. xviii, 153 pp.

4835. International Council of Scientific Unions. Scientific Committee on Problems of the Environment. *Radioecology After Chernobyl: Biogeochemical Pathways of Artificial Radionuclides*. Edited by Frederick Warner and Roy M. Harrison. SCOPE Report, 50. Chichester; New York: Published on behalf of the Scientific Committee on Problems of the Environment (SCOPE) of the International Council of Scientific Unions (ICSU) by Wiley, c1993. xxxii, 367 pp.

4836. Kapitza, Sergei P. "Lessons of Chernobyl." *Foreign Affairs* 72, no. 3 (Summer 1993): 7-11.

4837. Lenorovitz, Jeffrey M. "Antonov expands role in freighter leasing." *Aviation Week & Space Technology* 139, no. 11 (September 13, 1993): 43.

4838. ———. "Ex-Soviet crash rates surprisingly steady." *Aviation Week & Space Technology* 139, no. 23 (December 6, 1993): 22-23.

4839. ———. "Ukrainian engine enters ground tests." *Aviation Week & Space Technology* 139, no. 17 (October 25, 1993): 32.

4840. Leskov, Sergei. "Lies and incompetence." *Bulletin of the Atomic Scientists* 49, no. 5 (June 1993): 13ff. [On the hazards of radioactive waste in the former Soviet Union.]

4841. Mabe, William. "Retrofit Russian research reactors." *Bulletin of the Atomic Scientists* 49, no. 3 (April 1993): 9-11.

4842. Machlis, Sharon. "Promising Technologies from Eurasia." *Surviving Together* 11, no. 4 (Winter 1993): 46-47. [Excerpt from *Design News* (March 22, 1993).]

4843. Merwin, S. E., and Michail I. Balonov. *The Chernobyl Papers*. Richland, WA: Research Enterprises, c1993-. vols.

4844. Ponomarev, Vitalii. "The Nuclear Industry in Kazakhstan and Kyrgyzstan." *Central Asia Monitor*, no. 2 (1993): 29-34.

4845. Symposium on Nuclear Accidents: Liabilities and Guarantees (1992: Helsinki, Finland), OECD. Nuclear Energy Agency, and International Atomic Energy Agency. *Nuclear Accidents: Liabilities and Guarantees: Proceedings of the Helsinki Symposium, 31 August-3 September 1992 = Accidents nucleaires: Responsabilites et garanties: Compte rendu du symposium d'Helsinki.* Paris: The Agency; Washington, DC: OECD Publications and Information Centre, [distributor], 1993. 600 pp.

■ Life Sciences, Medicine, Public Health

4846. Babcock, Glenys A. "Perceptions of peril." *Bulletin of the Atomic Scientists* 49, no. 5 (June 1993): 11-12. [On Chernobyl's aftereffects.]

4847. Baer, Karl Ernst von, and Anton Dohrn. *Correspondence, Karl Ernst Von Baer (1792-1876), Anton Dohrn (1840-1909).* Edited by Christiane Groeben. Introduction by Jane M. Oppenheimer. Transactions of the American Philosophical Society, v. 83, pt. 3. Philadelphia, PA: American Philosophical Society, 1993. 156 pp. [Translations from the German by Christiane Groeben and Jane M. Oppenheimer.]

4848. Balodis, Valdis, Karlis Kalviskis, Kamils Ramans, Imants Liepa, Guntis Brumelis, Ilze Magone, and Olgerts Nikodemus. "Environmental Assessment in Latvia: Overview of Past Research and Future Perspectives." *Journal of Baltic Studies* 24, no. 3 (Fall 1993): 223-232.

4849. Browning, Graeme. "How Moscow's looking for a quick cure." *National Journal* 25, no. 29 (July 17, 1993): 1816-1819. [On visits by Russian scientists to the U.S. Food and Drug Administration, Environmental Protection Agency, and other regulatory agencies.]

4850. Carter, Michelle, and Michael J. Christensen. *Children of Chernobyl: Raising Hope from the Ashes.* Introduction by Olga Korbut. Minneapolis, MN: Augsburg, c1993. xxii, 214 pp.

4851. Dadian, Susan. "Mending Broken Lives at the Plastic and Reconstructive Surgery Center in Armenia." *Surviving Together* 11, no. 4 (Winter 1993): 59-60.

4852. Davis, Christopher M. "Eastern Europe and the Former USSR: An Overview." *RFE/RL Research Report* 2, no. 40 (October 8, 1993): 31-34. [Part of special section on the health care crisis in Eastern Europe and the former Soviet Union.]

4853. ———. "The Former Soviet Union." *RFE/RL Research Report* 2, no. 40 (October 8, 1993): 35-43. [Part of special section on the health care crisis in Eastern Europe and the former Soviet Union.]

4854. DeBardeleben, Joan. [Book Review]. *Slavic Review* 52, no. 3 (Fall 1993): 593-596. [Review article on Murray Feshbach and Alfred Friendly, Jr., *Ecocide in the USSR: Health and Nature under Siege* (NY: 1992); M. Turnbull, *Soviet Environmental Practices: The Most Critical Investment* (Brookfield, VT: 1991); and Philip R. Pryde, *Environmental Management in the Soviet Union* (NY: 1991).]

4855. Dekaris, D., A. Sabionicello, and R. Mazuran. "Multiple Changes of Immunologic Parameters in Prisoners of War: Assessments after Release from a Camp in Manjaca, Bosnia." *JAMA: Journal of the American Medical Association* 270, no. 5 (August 4, 1993): 595-599.

4856. Farmer, Richard G. "What American Physicians Can Learn from Their NIS Partners." *Surviving Together* 11, no. 4 (Winter 1993): 60-61. [Reprinted from *Common Health.* 1, no. 6.]

4857. Gascoigne-Frain, Claire. "Who Will Care For Russia's Children?" *Surviving Together* 11, no. 3 (Fall 1993): 43-44.

4858. Girnius, Saulius. "Lithuania." *RFE/RL Research Report* 2, no. 40 (October 8, 1993): 53-55. [Part of special section on the health care crisis in Eastern Europe and the former Soviet Union.]

4859. Gofman, John W. "Beware the data diddlers." *Bulletin of the Atomic Scientists* 49, no. 4 (May 1993): 40-44. [On Chernobyl's aftereffects.]

4860. Gould, Jay M. "The Sickening of a Society: Chernobyl—The Hidden Tragedy." *Nation* 256, no. 10 (March 15, 1993): 331-334. [Review article on Vladimir Chernousenko, *Chernobyl: Insight from the Inside* (Berlin and NY: 1991).]

4861. Green, Eric. "Poisoned Legacy." *Environmental Science & Technology* 27, no. 4 (April 1993): 590-595. [Outlines the environmental problems facing the independent states of the former Soviet Union.]

4862. Holloway, David. "The Politics of Catastrophe." *New York Review of Books* 40, no. 11 (June 10, 1993): 36-38. [Review article on Murray Feshbach and Alfred Friendly, Jr., *Ecocide in the USSR: Health and Nature Under Siege* (NY: 1992); Grigorii Medvedev, *The Truth About Chernobyl*, trans. Evelyn Rossiter (NY: 1991); Grigorii Medvedev, *No Breathing Room: The Aftermath of Chernobyl*, trans. Evelyn Rossiter (NY: 1993); and Piers Paul Read, *Ablaze: The Story of the Heroes and Victims of Chernobyl* (NY: 1993).]

4863. Ionescu, Dan. "Romania." *RFE/RL Research Report* 2, no. 40 (October 8, 1993): 60-62. [Part of special section on the health care crisis in Eastern Europe and the former Soviet Union.]

4864. Konon, Natasha. "Protecting a Citizen's Right to Clean Water in St. Petersburg." *Surviving Together* 11, no. 4 (Winter 1993): 22-24.

4865. Kuzman, M. "Fatalities in the War in Croatia, 1991 and 1992: Underlying and External Causes of Death." *JAMA: Journal of the American Medical Association* 270, no. 5 (August 4, 1993): 626-628.

4866. Marples, David. "Chernobyl's lengthening shadow." *Bulletin of the Atomic Scientists* 49, no. 7 (September 1993): 38-43.

4867. Marples, David R. "A Correlation between Radiation and Health Problems in Belarus?" *Post-Soviet Geography* 34, no. 5 (May 1993): 281-292.

4868. ———. "The Legacy of the Chernobyl Disaster in Belarus." *RFE/RL Research Report* 2, no. 5 (January 29, 1993): 46-50.

4869. "Natural Healing In Chelyabinsk." *Surviving Together* 11, no. 2 (Summer 1993): 57-58. [Adapted from an interview with Lidia Yamchuk and Hanif Shaimardanov, reprinted from *Spectrum* (November-December 1992).]

4870. Navarro, Vicente. "Has Socialism Failed? An Analysis of Health Indicators Under Capitalism and Socialism." *Science & Society* 57, no. 1 (Spring 1993): 6-30.

4871. Neuber, Joanne, and Uldine Netzer. "Nursing: A Meeting of Two Worlds." *Surviving Together* 11, no. 2 (Summer 1993): 58-59. [Reprinted from *Common Health* (February 1993).]

4872. Neuber, Joanne, and Mark Storey. "US-Ukraine Partnership Improves Patient and Hospital Health." *Surviving Together* 11, no. 4 (Winter 1993): 61-62. [Excerpt from *Common Health* (August-September 1993).]

4873. Padgett, Deborah K. "Sociodemographic and Disease-Related Correlates of Depressive Morbidity Among Diabetic Patients in Zagreb, Croatia." *Journal of Nervous and Mental Disease* 181, no. 2 (February 1993): 123-129.

4874. Pataki, Judith. "Hungary." *RFE/RL Research Report* 2, no. 40 (October 8, 1993): 50-52. [Part of special section on the health care crisis in Eastern Europe and the former Soviet Union.]

4875. Potrykowska, Alina. "Mortality and Environmental Pollution in Poland." *Research & Exploration* 9, no. 2 (Spring 1993): 255-256.

4876. Rossianov, Kirill O. "Editing Nature: Joseph Stalin and the 'New' Soviet Biology." *Isis* 84, no. 4 (December 1993): 728-745.

4877. Rothman, David J., and Sheila M. Rothman. "The New Romania." *New York Review of Books* 40, no. 15 (September 23, 1993): 56-57.

4878. Schreiber, Vratislav. "The Medical Sciences in Czechoslovakia." *Technology in Society* 15, no. 1 (1993): 131-136. [Part of special issue on science and technology in Eastern Europe.]

4879. "Shot Therapy." *Nation* 256, no. 11 (March 22, 1993): 364. [On the Russian health-care system.]

4880. Shulman, Seth. "A Treasure Trove of Data from East Germany." *Technology Review* 96, no. 2 (February-March 1993): 14-15. [On ecological disasters in Eastern Germany and their impact on public health.]

4881. Solomon, Susan Gross. "The Soviet-German Syphilis Expedition to Buriat Mongolia, 1928: Scientific Research on National Minorities." *Slavic Review* 52, no. 2 (Summer 1993): 204-232.

4882. Stanecki, Karen, Anatoly Monisov, Marina Savelyeva, and Murray Feshbach. "AIDS in Eurasia: A Call to Action." *Surviving Together* 11, no. 3 (Fall 1993): 40-43. [Excerpts from the proceedings of a conference on HIV/AIDS in Central and Eastern Europe and the former Soviet Union (FSU) held in April 1993.]

4883. Stassen, Manfred. "The German Statutory Health Insurance System." *Social Education* 57, no. 5 (September 1993): 247-248. [Part of special section entitled "The Case of Germany, Part 2," edited by Dagmar Kraemer and Manfred Stassen.]

4884. Stepanov, Dmitri, and V. Shumilkin. "Letter from St. Petersburg: What Ails Russian Medicine?" *Freedom Review* 24, no. 6 (November-December 1993): 18-19. Translated by Cathy Young.

4885. "Toxic Nightmare: Mendeleyev's Table Frolics in Petersburg's Drinking Water." *Surviving Together* 11, no. 4 (Winter 1993): 23. [Adapted from Tatyana Beloshchutska, "Poisoned Peter: All of Mendeleyev's Table Frolics in a Glass of Drinking Water from the Neva," *Komsomolskaya Pravda* (July 17, 1993), reprinted in *JPRS* (September 20, 1993).]

4886. Vachudova, Milada, and Sharon Fisher. "The Czech and Slovak Republics." *RFE/RL Research Report* 2, no. 40 (October 8, 1993): 44-49. [Part of special section on the health care crisis in Eastern Europe and the former Soviet Union.]

4887. Vanden Heuvel, Katrina. "Eastward, Christian Soldiers!: Right-to-Lifers Hit Russia." *Nation* 257, no. 14 (November 1, 1993): 489-492.

4888. Vinton, Louisa. "Poland." *RFE/RL Research Report* 2, no. 40 (October 8, 1993): 56-59. [Part of special section on the health care crisis in Eastern Europe and the former Soviet Union.]

4889. Watson, Amanda. "Primary Immunization in Eurasia." *Surviving Together* 11, no. 2 (Summer 1993): 59-61. [Reprinted from *Common Health* (April 1993).]

4890. Weiner, Douglas R. "Essay review." *Isis* 84, no. 1 (March 1993): 124-127. [Review article on Daniel Philip Todes, *Darwin with Malthus: The Struggle for Existence in Russian Evolutionary Thought* (New York: 1989); and Alexander Vucinich, *Darwin in Russian Thought* (Berkeley, CA: 1988).]

4891. Zielinska, Eleonora. "Recent Trends in Abortion Legislation in Eastern Europe, with Particular Reference to Poland." *Criminal Law Forum* 4, no. 1 (1993): 47-93. Translated by Regina A. Gorzkowska.

4892. Zimov, S. A., I. P. Semiletov, S. P. Daviodov, Yu V. Voropaev, S. F. Prosyannikov, C. S. Wong, and Y. -H

Chan. "Wintertime CO2 Emission from Soils of Northeastern Siberia." *Arctic* 46, no. 3 (September 1993): 197-204.

■ Space Sciences

4893. Asker, James R. "New station plan unveiled; Russia vows to contribute." *Aviation Week & Space Technology* 139, no. 19 (November 8, 1993): 25-26.

4894. ———. "Russian role key in station debate." *Aviation Week & Space Technology* 139, no. 13 (September 27, 1993): 22-23.

4895. ———. "U.S./Russian station plan raises doubts in Congress." *Aviation Week & Space Technology* 139, no. 15 (October 11, 1993): 23.

4896. Covault, Craig. "Aerospace eyes Tupolev production." *Aviation Week & Space Technology* 139, no. 10 (September 6, 1993): 59.

4897. ———. "Russia forges ahead on Mir 2." *Aviation Week & Space Technology* 138, no. 11 (March 15, 1993): 26-27.

4898. ———. "Russia launches three spy satellites." *Aviation Week & Space Technology* 139, no. 13 (September 27, 1993): 24.

4899. ———. "Russians locked in struggle for space program control." *Aviation Week & Space Technology* 138, no. 5 (February 1, 1993): 57-59.

4900. ———. "U.S., Russia draft historic space pact." *Aviation Week & Space Technology* 139, no. 10 (September 6, 1993): 22-23.

4901. Johnson, Nicholas L., and David M. Rodvold. *Europe and Asia in Space, 1991-1992.* Kirkland AFB, NM: USAF Phillips Laboratory, 1993. vi, 313 pp. [Includes discussion of the space program of the former Soviet Union.]

4902. "Klimov to assemble PT6A, PW200 engines." *Aviation Week & Space Technology* 139, no. 12 (September 20, 1993): 41.

4903. Lenorovitz, Jeffrey M. "ARPA team to visit Russia for WIG vechicle study." *Aviation Week & Space Technology* 138, no. 21 (May 24, 1993): 25.

4904. ———. "Control of Kazakh launch base disputed." *Aviation Week & Space Technology* 139, no. 4 (July 26, 1993): 26. [Russia and Kazakhstan fail to agree upon Baikonur space-base.]

4905. ———. "Joint flight to gather ICBM tracking data." *Aviation Week & Space Technology* 139, no. 16 (October 18, 1993): 96-97.

4906. ———. "Lockheed, Krunichev to market Proton launcher." *Aviation Week & Space Technology* 138, no. 1 (January 4, 1993): 24.

4907. ———. "Russia may hold space station key." *Aviation Week & Space Technology* 139, no. 8 (August 23, 1993): 22-24. [On cooperation between NASA and the Mir project.]

4908. ———. "Russia nears entry into launch market." *Aviation Week & Space Technology* 138, no. 21 (May 24, 1993): 26.

4909. ———. "Russia to expand role in manned space flight." *Aviation Week & Space Technology* 139, no. 5 (August 2, 1993): 62-63.

4910. ———. "Russian capsule returns data from Mir space station." *Aviation Week & Space Technology* 139, no. 2 (July 12, 1993): 25-28.

4911. ———. "Russian cost estimates due on U.S. station modules." *Aviation Week & Space Technology* 138, no. 20 (May 17, 1993): 33-34.

4912. ———. "Russian Proton booster offered for Indonesian launch." *Aviation Week & Space Technology* 138, no. 15 (April 12, 1993): 61-62.

4913. ———. "Russian role complicates joint flight." *Aviation Week & Space Technology* 139, no. 7 (August 16, 1993): 71.

4914. ———. "Russians completing new ground-effect vehicle." *Aviation Week & Space Technology* 138, no. 17 (April 26, 1993): 62-63.

4915. Leskov, Sergei. "Notes from a Dying Spaceport." *Bulletin of the Atomic Scientists* 49, no. 8 (October 1993): 40-43. [On the potential for commercial launches from Baikonur.]

4916. Manca, Marie Antoinette. "The Political Economy of United States Space Policy: National and Transnational Dimensions." Ph.D. diss., City University of New York, 1993. [UMI order no: AAC 9325128.]

4917. "Russians adapt military technology for comsats." *Aviation Week & Space Technology* 139, no. 9 (August 30, 1993): 58-59.

4918. "Russians consider winged booster." *Aviation Week & Space Technology* 139, no. 10 (September 6, 1993): 60.

4919. Rybak, Boris. "Russia pledges support for Ulyanovsk factory." *Aviation Week & Space Technology* 139, no. 2 (July 12, 1993): 34.

4920. Shifrin, Carole A., and Raf Fairford. "Russian MiG-29s collide at British Air show." *Aviation Week & Space Technology* 139, no. 5 (August 2, 1993): 28-29.

4921. Tarasenko, Maxim. "Twinkle, twinkle little Topaz." *Bulletin of the Atomic Scientists* 49, no. 6 (July-August 1993): 11-13. ["Orbiting nuclear reactor shot down—for now—by astronomers."]

4922. Willits, C. A. "A better way to build the U.S.-Russian station." *Aviation Week & Space Technology* 139, no. 16 (October 18, 1993): 75-79.

17 Sociology

■ General

4923. Wasburn, Philo C., ed. *Research in Political Sociology*. Includes contributions by Richard G. Braungart, Margaret M. Braungart, and Eva Etzioni-Halevy. Greenwich, CT: JAI Press, 1993. xxi, 386 pp. [Partial contents: Richard G. Braungart and Margaret M. Braungart, "Historical Generations and Citizenship: 200 Years of Youth Movements," pp. 139-174; Eva Etzioni-Halevy, "The Autonomy of Elites and Transitions from Non-Democratic Regimes: The Cases of the Former Soviet Union and Poland," pp. 257-276.]

■ Russia/U.S.S.R./C.I.S.

4924. Adams, Will. "Soviet Youth Speaks Out." *AAASS Newsletter* 33, no. 1 (January 1993): 11. [Results of questionnaire administered to students at an economics institute in Irkutsk.]

4925. Bahry, Donna. "Society Transformed? Rethinking the Social Roots of Perestroika." *Slavic Review* 52, no. 3 (Fall 1993): 512-554.

4926. Buckley, Mary. *Redefining Russian Society and Polity*. Boulder, CO: Westview Press, 1993. xviii, 346 pp. [Partial contents: Introduction: Ideas in Historical Context. Glasnost as Prerequisite. Emotions and Methodology. Makers of History and Objects of Research. Sources and Approach. Organization — 1. Reactions to Perestroika. What Was Perestroika? Reactions to the Failures of Economic Reform. Political Chaos, Confusion, and Conflict. Glasnost, Democratization, Media, and Theater. New Movements and New Agendas. Newspapers, Movements, and Conceptual Frameworks. Concepts and Definitions — 2. Interpretations of Glasnost. Glasnost: The Means to Perestroika. Glasnost Outstripping Perestroika. Glasnost Under Attack. The Uses of Glasnost. Glasnost as Leninist and Positive. Glasnost as Unfettered Inquiry. Glasnost as Disorienting and Destabilizing — 3. Social Deviance and Social Collapse. Crime. Drug Abuse. Prostitution. AIDS. Rape. Child Abuse. Suicide. Limits to the "New" Social Issues — 4. "New" Failures in Housing and Health Care. Housing Conditions. Contraception. Abortion. Infant Mortality. The Shame of Social Policy. 5. Pluralism Redefined. Pluralism Condemned or Ignored. Democratic Socialism—Enemy of Socialism. Democratic Socialism and the Laws of History. Democratic Centralism, Not Pluralism. Dissident Defense of Democratic Socialism. Pluralist Society in Contemporary Ideological Struggles. Socialist Pluralism on Public Agendas. Gorbachev's Changing View of Pluralism. From Socialist Monopoly to Socialist Pluralism. From Totalitarianism to Socialist Pluralism and a Multi-party System. Pluralism and Choice. Pluralism as Objective Necessity. A Renewal of Socialism Through Pluralism. Democrats Enthusiastic for Pluralism. Leninists Against Pluralism. Anarchists Against the State and Pluralism. Pluralism in the Social Sciences. Pluralism and Transition — 6. Democracy and Civil Society. Divisions over Democratization. Gorbachev: Democratization and Leninism. Democrats and Mass Parties. Leninists and Democratizing the CPSU. Anarchists and Democracy as Manipulation. Strong Leadership and Authoritarian Solutions. Civil Society. Parties and Citizenship. Preconditions for and Consequences of Civil Society. State, Citizen, and Representation — 7. Learning Democracy. Ideas and Context; Practical Problems for Democracy. A Weak Congress of People's Deputies. Imprecise Powers. The Rush for Sovereignty, Ungovernability, Fragmentation, and Anarchy. The Tyranny of the Nomenklatura and the Persisting Power of the Apparat. Ineffective Representation. Nihilism in the Soviets. Factions Before Parties. Unstable New Parties. The New Soviets: Achievements and Weaknesses — 8. Crisis. Consensus and Disagreement. Crisis and Myth. Gorbachev: Contradictions of the Transition Period. Popov: State, Nationality, and Economic Crises. Afanasyev: Self-destructive Drift and the Crisis of Power. Yeltsin: Coordinated Persecution and CPSU Resistance. The Democratic Union: Gorbachev Propping Up Totalitarianism. Miners: Partocracy, Shortages, and Price Increases. The United Labor Front: Crisis as Counter-revolution. Leninists: Crisis and the Loss of Leninism. Leaders of the August Coup: Crisis and the State of Emergency. Polity Divided — 9. Alternative Crises. Pamiat: Genocide of the Russian People. Patriots: The Secularization of Culture and Discrimination. Monarchists: The Virus of Bolshevism. Christians: The Evil of Atheism. Greens: Ecological Catastrophe. Feminists: Discrimination Against Women. Anarchists: Bonapartism of the Party-State Apparat — 10. Conclusion. The End of State Socialism. Redefining Society and Polity. Redefinition Continued. New Agendas.]

4927. Carbaugh, Donal. " 'Soul' and 'Self': Soviet and American Cultures in Conversation." *Quarterly Journal of Speech* 79, no. 2 (May 1993): 182-200. [Analysis of discussion on the "Donahue in Russia" program taped in Moscow and broadcast in the U.S. the week of February 9, 1987.]

4928. Connell, Rachel A. "Juvenile Justice Reform in Kazakhstan." *Surviving Together* 11, no. 3 (Fall 1993): 47-48.

4929. Conway, J. F. "An uncertain future: Life after glasnost and perestroika." *Canadian Journal of Sociology = Cahiers canadiens de sociologie* 18, no. 2 (Spring 1993): 197-206. [Review article on Jeffrey C. Goldfarb, *Beyond Glasnost: The Post-Totalitarian Mind* (Chicago, IL: University of Chicago Press, 1991); and David Mandel, *Perestroika and the Soviet People: Rebirth of the Labor Movement* (Montreal: Black Rose, 1991).]

4930. Filippov, Alexander F. "A Final Look Back at Soviet Sociology." *International Sociology* 8, no. 3 (September 1993): 355-373. Translated by Philip Grathoff.

4931. Gibson, James L. "Perceived Political Freedom in the Soviet Union." *Journal of Politics* 55, no. 4 (November 1993): 936-974.

4932. Gibson, James L., and Raymond M. Duch. "Political Intolerance in the USSR: The Distribution and Etiology of Mass Opinion." *Comparative Political Studies* 26, no. 3 (October 1993): 286-329. [Revised version of a paper delivered at the 1991 Annual Meeting of the Western Political Science Association, Seattle, WA, March 21-23, 1991.]

4933. Groark, Christina, Kathryn Rudy, and Christine Donnorummo. "Opening the Door to Youth in St. Petersburg." *Surviving Together* 11, no. 2 (Summer 1993): 37-38.

4934. Lemke, Jürgen. "Gay and Lesbian Life in East Germany Society Before and After 1989." *Oral History Review* 21, no. 2 (Winter 1993): 31-39. Translated by Judith Orban.

4935. Mikhailovskaya, Inga. "Why the Russian Public Will Support Reform." *East European Constitutional Review* 2, no. 4/vol. 3, no. 1 (Fall 1993-Winter 1994): 28-32. Translated by Catherine Fitzpatrick. [Results of survey conducted in the Russian Federation in July 1993 by the Human Rights Project Group.]

4936. Powell, David E. "Social Problems in Russia." *Current History* 92, no. 576 (October 1993): 325-330.

4937. Remnick, David. "America: Love It or Loathe It." *New York Times Magazine* (June 6, 1993): 26ff. ["Russians are more obsessed with the United States now than they were during the cold war, and the obsession is much more complicated." Article adapted from author's *Lenin's Tomb: The Last Days of the Soviet Empire*.]

4938. Rhodes, Mark. "The Former Soviet Union and the Future: Facing Uncertainty." *RFE/RL Research Report* 2, no. 24 (June 11, 1993): 52-55.

4939. ———. "Political Attitudes in Russia." *RFE/ RL Research Report* 2, no. 3 (January 15, 1993): 42-44.

4940. ———. "Russians Say Peter Was Greater than Lenin." *RFE/RL Research Report* 2, no. 7 (February 12, 1993): 54-55.

4941. Ries, Nancy Virginia. "Mystical Poverty and the Rewards of Loss: Russian Culture and Conversation during Perestroika." Ph.D. diss., Cornell University, 1993.

4942. Robinson, John P., Ted Robert Gurr, Erjan Kurbanov, Stephen McHale, and Ivan Slepenkov. "Ethnonationalist and Political Attitudes Among Post-Soviet Youth: The Case of Russia and Ukraine." *PS:*

Political Science & Politics 26, no. 3 (September 1993): 516-521.

4943. Rouse, Timothy P., and N. Prabha Unnithan. "Comparative Ideologies and Alcoholism: The Protestant and Proletarian Ethics." *Social Problems* 40, no. 2 (May 1993): 213-227.

4944. Ryan, Michael, comp. and trans. *Social Trends in Contemporary Russia: A Statistical Source-Book*. New York, NY: St. Martin's Press, 1993. xiii, 249 pp.

4945. Schillinger, Liesl. "Moscow Postcard: Barbski." *New Republic* 209, nos. 12 & 13 (September 20 & 27, 1993): 10-11.

4946. ———. "Moscow Postcard: May Day." *New Republic* 208, no. 21 (May 24, 1993): 13-15. [On politics and popular culture in Moscow.]

4947. ———. "Moscow Postcard: Uneasy Rider." *New Republic* 208, no. 16 (April 19, 1993): 9-11. [On a frightening experience in a Moscow taxi.]

4948. Sloutsky, Vladimir M., and Joshua Searle-White. "Psychological Responses of Russians to Rapid Social Change in the Former U.S.S.R." *Political Psychology* 14, no. 3 (September 1993): 511-526.

4949. Solomon, Andrew. "Young Russia's Defiant Decadence." *New York Times Magazine* (July 18, 1993): 16ff.

4950. Speiser, Tertia A. "Changing the System, One Child at a Time." *Surviving Together* 11, no. 4 (Winter 1993): 52-53.

4951. Stepanov, Dmitri. "The Choice of a New Generation." *Freedom Review* 24, no. 3 (May-June 1993): 3-6. Translated by Cathy Young.

4952. Stephan, Walter G., Vladimir Ageyev, Cookie White Stephan, Marina Abalakina, Tatyana Stefanenko, and Lisa Coates-Shrider. "Measuring Stereotypes: A Comparison of Methods Using Russian and American Samples." *Social Psychology Quarterly* 56, no. 1 (March 1993): 54-64.

4953. Zabelina, Tatyana, and Yevgeni Israelyan. "Crisis Centers Assist Victims of Violence." *Surviving Together* 11, no. 4 (Winter 1993): 29-31. Translated by Andrew Reese. [Excerpt from *Vy i my* (Fall 1993).]

■ Eastern Europe

4954. Agócs, Peter, and Sándor Agócs. "Hungary's Aged: Social Policy in a Post-Communist State." *University of Dayton Review* 22, no. 2 (Winter 1993-1994): 45-59.

4955. Alisauskiene, Rasa, Rita Bajaruniene, and Birute Sersniova. "Policy Mood and Socio-political Attitudes in Lithuania." *Journal of Baltic Studies* 24, no. 2 (Summer 1993): 135-148.

4956. Borneman, John. "Time-Space Compression and the Continental Divide in German Subjectivity." *Oral History Review* 21, no. 2 (Winter 1993): 41-57.

4957. Csepeli, György, Tamás Kolosi, Mária Neményi, and Antal Örkény. "Our Futureless Values: The Forms of Justice and Injustice Perception in Hungary in 1991." *Social Research* 60, no. 4 (Winter 1993): 865-892.

4958. Dobratz, Betty A. "Changing Value Orientations and Attitudes Toward the European Community: A Comparison of Greeks with Citizens of Other European Community Nations." *East European Quarterly* 27, no. 1 (Spring 1993): 97-127.

4959. Ershova, Elena. "The Draft Russian Family Law: A Step Backward for Women." *Surviving Together* 11, no. 2 (Summer 1993): 46-49. Translated by Andrew Reese. [Excerpts from an analysis by Elena Ershova.]

4960. Haderka, F. Jiri. "Czechoslovakia: Decline and Fall of the Federation and its Family Law." *University of Louisville Journal of Family Law* 32, no. 2 (Spring 1993): 281-292.

4961. Johnson, Alice K., Richard L. Edwards, and Hildegard Puwak. "Foster Care and Adoption Policy in Romania: Suggestions for International Intervention." *Child Welfare* 72, no. 5 (September-October 1993): 489-506.

4962. Kabele, Jiri. "The Dynamics of Social Problems and Czechoslovak Transition." *Social Research* 60, no. 4 (Winter 1993): 763-785. Translated by Ronald Radzai.

4963. Khazova, Olga. "Commonwealth of Independent States: Family Law in the Former Soviet Republics: A Year Without the Union." *University of Louisville Journal of Family Law* 32, no. 2 (Spring 1993): 445-454.

4964. Kivirahk, Juhan, Rain Rosimannus, and Indrek Pajumaa. "The Premises for Democracy: A Study of Political Values in Post-Independent Estonia." *Journal of Baltic Studies* 24, no. 2 (Summer 1993): 149-160.

4965. Kourvetaris, George A. "Greek Attitudes Toward Political and Economic Integration into the EEC." *East European Quarterly* 27, no. 3 (Fall 1993): 375-415.

4966. Leviatin, David. "Listening to the New World: Voices from the Velvet Revolution." *Oral History Review* 21, no. 1 (Spring 1993): 9-22.

4967. Liepins, Valdis. "Baltic Attitudes to Economic Recovery: A Survey of Public Opinion in the Baltic Countries." *Journal of Baltic Studies* 24, no. 2 (Summer 1993): 189-200.

4968. Motivans, Albert. "Social and Public Opinion Research in the Baltic Countries." *Journal of Baltic Studies* 24, no. 2 (Summer 1993): 127-134.

4969. Offe, Claus. "The Politics of Social Policy in East European Transitions: Antecedents, Agents, and Agenda of Reform." *Social Research* 60, no. 4 (Winter 1993): 649-684.

4970. Okolicsanyi, Károly. "Hungary's Misused and Costly Social Security System." *RFE/RL Research Report* 2, no. 17 (April 23, 1993): 12-16.

4971. Ostow, Robin. "Restructuring Our Lives: National Unification and German Biographies: Introduction." *Oral History Review* 21, no. 2 (Winter 1993): 1-8.

4972. Plato, Alexander von. "The Consensus Against the Victors: 1945 and 1990." *Oral History Review* 21, no. 2 (Winter 1993): 73-79.

4973. "Romania's Unwanted Children." *Foreign Service Journal* 70, no. 9 (September 1993): 35-39. [Interview with Virginia Carson Young.]

4974. Schafer, Robert B., Elisabeth A. Schafer, and Signe Dobelniece. "Latvia in Transition: A Study of Change in a Former Republic of the USSR." *Journal of Baltic Studies* 24, no. 2 (Summer 1993): 161-172.

4975. Siklová, Jirina. "Backlash." *Social Research* 60, no. 4 (Winter 1993): 737-749. Translated by Ronald Radzai.

4976. Szmatka, Jacek, Zdzislaw Mach, and Janusz Mucha, eds. *Eastern European Societies on the Threshold of Change*. Contributions by Jacek Szmatka, Zdzislaw Mach, Janusz Mucha, Dragoslav Slejska, Jan Kubik, Miroslawa Marody, Vojko Antoncic, Veljko Rus, Krzysztof Nowak, Edmund Wnuk-Lipinski, Lena Kolarska-Bobinska, Krzysztof Gorlach, Imre Kovach, Tamás Kolosi, Marek Ziolkowski, Mikk Titma, Nancy Brandon Tuma, Jane L. Curry, Marian Niezgoda, and Anna Kosiarz-Stolarska. Lewiston, NY: E. Mellen Press, c1993. 313 pp. [Contents: Jacek Szmatka, Zdzislaw Mach, Janusz Mucha, "Introduction: In Search of the Syndrome of Threshold Situation," pp. 1-13; Dragoslav Slejska, "Attitudes Toward Restructuring in Czechslovakia: Disjunction Between Social Criticism and Social Activity," pp. 15-21; Jan Kubik, "Social and Political Instability in Poland: A Theoretical Reconsideration," pp. 23-64; Miroslawa Marody, "Basic Dimensions of Social Consciousness of Polish Society," pp. 65-81; Vojko Antoncic and Veljko Rus, "Conceptions and Perceptions of Justice in Yugoslavia," pp. 83-109; Krzysztof Nowak, "Three Models of Legitimization Crisis: Poland 1970-1985," pp. 111-124; Edmund Wnuk-Lipinski, "Peculiarities of the Structure of the Monocentric Mass Society," pp. 125-138; Lena Kolarska-Bobinska, "Socialist Welfare State in Transition," pp. 139-159; Krzysztof Gorlach, "The Embourgeoisement Trajectory: How It Works in Polish Society," pp. 161-174; Imre Kovach, "Part-Time Small-Scale Farming As a Major Form of Economic Pluractivity in Hungary," pp. 175-191; Tamas Kolosi, "The Reproduction of Life-Style: Comparison of Czechoslovakian, Hungarian and Dutch Data," pp. 193-206; Marek Ziolkowski, "Individuals and the Social System: The Types of Individuality and Varieties of its Contribution to Society," pp. 207-224; Mikk Titma and Nancy Brandon Tuma, "Stratification Research in a Changing World," pp. 225-254; Jane L. Curry, "How Democracy Has Not Created Democracy: The Polish Case," pp. 255-275; Marian Niezgoda and Anna Kosiarz-Stolarska, "Education in Poland at the Crossroads," pp. 277-293; Zdzislaw Mach, "The Construction of National Identity and Nationalistic Ideology in a Socialist State: The Case of Poland," pp. 295-305.]

4977. Torpey, John. "Growing Together, Coming Apart: German Society since Unification." *Social Education* 57, no. 5 (September 1993): 236-239. [Part of special section entitled "The Case of Germany, Part 2," edited by Dagmar Kraemer and Manfred Stassen.]

4978. Varga, Laszlo. "The Image of the Jews in Hungarian Public Opinion." *Patterns of Prejudice* 27, no. 2 (October 1993): 103-118.

4979. Williams, John Alexander. "Unpacking Pinckney in Poland." *Appalachian Journal* 20, no. 2 (Winter 1993): 162-175.

■ Sports

4980. Allison, Lincoln, ed. *The Changing Politics of Sport.* Manchester; New York: Manchester University Press; New York, NY: Distributed in the USA and Canada by St. Martin's Press, c1993. viii, 238 pp. [Introductory chapter cites the effect on international sports events of the collapse of East European communist regimes.] REV: Barrie Houlihan, *Journal of Sport History* 20, no. 3 (Winter 1993): 297-299.

4981. Edelman, Robert. *Serious Fun: A History of Spectator Sports in the USSR.* New York: Oxford University Press, 1993. xvi, 286 pp. REV: Steven G. Marks, *Journal of Sport History* 20, no. 3 (Winter 1993): 305-307.

4982. Lane, Charles. "Sarajevo Postcard: Tennis Anyone?" *New Republic* 208, no. 14 (April 5, 1993): 11-12. ["Bosnia's oddest magazine."]

4983. Monaghan, Peter. "Historian Uses 'Serious Fun' of Sports as a Window on Life in the Soviet Union." *Chronicle of Higher Education* 39, no. 44 (July 7, 1993): A10-A11.

4984. Peppard, Victor, and James Riordan. *Playing Politics: Soviet Sport Diplomacy to 1992.* Russian and East European Studies (Greenwich, Conn.), v. 3. Greenwich, CT: JAI Press, 1993. x, 184 pp.

4985. Riordan, Jim. "Rewriting Soviet Sports History." *Journal of Sport History* 20, no. 3 (Winter 1993): 247-258.

4986. ———. "Sidney Jackson: An American in Russia's Boxing Hall of Fame." *Journal of Sport History* 20, no. 1 (Spring 1993): 49-56.

■ Women's Studies

4987. Adler, Leonore Loeb, ed. *International Handbook on Gender Roles.* Foreword by Nancy Felipe Russo. Includes contributions by Nancy Felipe Russo, Diomedes C. Markoulis, Maria Dikaiou, Halina Grzymala-Moszczynska, Harold Takooshian, Anie Sanentz Kalayjian, and Edward Melkonian. Westport, CT: Greenwood, 1993. xxii, 525 pp. [Partial contents: Nancy Felipe Russo, "Foreword"; Leonore Loeb Adler, "Introduction"; Diomedes C. Markoulis and Maria Dikaiou, "Greece"; Halina Grzymala-Moszczynska, "Poland"; Harold Takooshian, Anie Sanentz

Kalayjian and Edward Melkonian, "The Soviet Union and Post-Soviet Era."]

4988. "Anastasia Posadskaya on the Russian Women's Movement." *Surviving Together* 11, no. 3 (Fall 1993): 26-27. [Adapted from an interview with Posadskaya by the Postfactum News Agency, "Women's Discussion Club," *Interlegal* (May 1993).]

4989. Azhgikhina, Nadezhda. "Not A Word About Feminism." *Surviving Together* 11, no. 2 (Summer 1993): 49-50. Translated by Andrew Reese. [Excerpt from an article in *Vy i my* (Spring 1993).]

4990. "Building Bridges: Guide to Feminist Solidarity." *Woman and Earth* 2, no. 1 (December 10, 1993): 42-43. ["Transfiguration," by Bonnie Marshall; "Ukrainian Centre of Women's Studies," by Solomeya Pavlychko; "Women's Studies Initiative," by Dasa Duhacek; and "Journals of the East and the West."]

4991. "Businesswomen Resolve to Address Russian Government." *Surviving Together* 11, no. 1 (Spring 1993): 60. Translated by Diane Schlipper.

4992. Chester, Pamela. "Teaching Slavic Studies: Teaching about Gender in Russian Literature." *AAASS Newsletter* 33, no. 3 (May 1993): 15.

4993. DeSilva, Lalith. "Women's Emancipation Under Communism: A Re-evaluation." *East European Quarterly* 27, no. 3 (Fall 1993): 301-316.

4994. Einhorn, Barbara. *Cinderella Goes to Market: Citizenship, Gender, and Women's Movements in East Central Europe.* London; New York: Verso, 1993. viii, 280 pp.

4995. Emadi, Hafizullah. "Development Strategies and Women in Albania." *East European Quarterly* 27, no. 1 (Spring 1993): 79-96.

4996. Ferree, Myra Marx, and Brigitte Young. "Three Steps Back for Women: German Unification, Gender and University 'Reform.'" *PS: Political Science & Politics* 26, no. 2 (June 1993): 199-205.

4997. Fong, Monica S. *The Role of Women in Rebuilding the Russian Economy.* Studies of Economies in Transformation, Paper No. 10. Washington, DC: World Bank, 1993. viii, 50 pp.

4998. Funk, Nanette. "Feminism and Post-Communism." *Hypatia* 8, no. 4 (Fall 1993): 85-88. [Introduction to articles by feminists from Eastern Europe and the former Soviet Union.]

4999. Funk, Nanette, and Magda Mueller, eds. *Gender Politics and Post-Communism: Reflections from Eastern Europe and the Former Soviet Union.* Introduction by Nanette Funk. Contributions by Nanette Funk, Rossica Panova, Raina Gavrilova, Cornelia Merdzanska, Dimitrina Petrova, Maria Todorova, Doina Pasca Harsanyi, Mariana Hausleitner, Hana Havelková, Jirina Siklová, Zuzana Kiczková, Etela Farkasová, Alena Heitlinger, Andjelka Milic, Slavenka Drakulic, Dasa Duhacek, Hildegard Maria

Nickel, Tatiana Böhm, Christina Schenk, Irene Dölling, Anne Hampele, Enikö Bollobás, Maria Adamik, Olga Tóth, Joanna Goven, Malgorzata Fuszara, Anna Titkow, Ewa Hauser, Barbara Heyns, Jane Mansbridge, Larissa Lissyutkina, Elizabeth Waters, and Zillah Eisenstein. Thinking Gender. New York: Routledge, 1993. x, 349 pp. [Contents: Nanette Funk, "Introduction: Women and Post-Communism," pp. 1-14. Bulgaria. Rossica Panova, Raina Gavrilova, and Cornelia Merdzanska, "Thinking Gender: Bulgarian Women's Im/possibilities," pp. 15-21; Dimitrina Petrova, "The Winding Road to Emancipation in Bulgaria," pp. 22-29; Maria Todorova, "The Bulgarian Case: Women's Issues or Feminist Issues?" pp. 30-38. Romania. Doina Pasca Harsanyi, "Women in Romania," pp. 39-52; Mariana Hausleitner, "Women in Romania: Before and After the Collapse," pp. 53-61. Czech and Slovak Republics. Hana Havelková, "A Few Prefeminist Thoughts," pp. 62-73; Jirina Siklová, "Are Women in Central and Eastern Europe Conservative?" pp. 74-83; Zuzana Kiczková and Etela Farkasová, "The Emancipation of Women: A Concept that Failed," pp. 84-94; Alena Heitlinger, "The Impact of the Transition from Communism on the Status of Women in the Czech and Slovak Republics," pp. 95-108. Former Yugoslavia. Andjelka Milic, "Women and Nationalism in the Former Yugoslavia," pp. 109-122; Slavenka Drakulic, "Women and the New Democracy in the Former Yugoslavia," pp. 123-130; Dasa Duhacek, "Women's Time in the Former Yugoslavia," pp. 131-137. Former German Democratic Republic. Hildegard Maria Nickel, "Women in the German Democratic Republic and in the New Federal States: Looking Backward and Forward (Five Theses)," pp. 138-150; Tatiana Böhm, "The Women's Question as a Democratic Question: In Search of Civil Society," pp. 151-159; Christina Schenk, "Lesbians and Their Emancipation in the Former German Democratic Republic: Past and Future," pp. 160-167; Irene Dölling, " 'But the Pictures Stay the Same...' The Image of Women in the Journal Für Dich Before and After the 'Turning Point,' " pp. 168-179; Anne Hampele, "The Organized Women's Movement in the Collapse of the GDR: The Independent Women's Association (UFV)," pp. 180-193; Nanette Funk, "Abortion and German Unification," pp. 194-200. Hungary. Enikö Bollobás, " 'Totalitarian Lib': The Legacy of Communism for Hungarian Women," pp. 201-206; Maria Adamik, "Feminism and Hungary," pp. 207-212; Olga Tóth, "No Envy, No Pity," pp. 213-223; Joanna Goven, "Gender Politics in Hungary: Autonomy and Antifeminism," pp. 224-240. Poland. Malgorzata Fuszara, "Abortion and the Formation of the Public Sphere in Poland," pp. 241-252; Anna Titkow, "Political Change in Poland: Cause, Modifier, or Barrier to Gender Equality?" pp. 253-256; Ewa Hauser, Barbara Heyns, and Jane Mansbridge, "Feminism in the Interstices of Politics and Culture: Poland in Transition," pp. 257-273. Former USSR-Commonwealth of Independent States. Larissa Lissyutkina, "Soviet Women at the Crossroads of Perestroika," pp. 274-286; Elizabeth Waters, "Finding a Voice: The Emergence of a Women's Movement," pp. 287-302; Zillah Eisenstein, "Eastern European Male Democracies: A Problem of Unequal Equality," pp. 303-317; Nanette Funk, "Feminism East and West," pp. 318-330.] REV: Lori

Gruen and Lisa A. Mulholland, Hypatia 8, no. 4 (Fall 1993): 160-164. Mariana Katzarova, Nation 257, no. 4 (July 26, 1993-August 2, 1993): 148-150.

5000. Goldman, Wendy Z. Women, the State, and Revolution: Soviet Family Policy and Social Life, 1917-1936. Cambridge Russian, Soviet, and Post-Soviet Studies, Soviet Law and Social Change, 1917-1936. Cambridge; New York, NY: Cambridge University Press, 1993. xi, 351 pp. [Contents: The origins of the Bolshevik vision: Love unfettered, Women free; The first retreat: Besprizornost and socialized child rearing; Law and life collide: Free union and the wage-earning population; Stirring the sea of peasant stagnation; Pruning the "bourgeois thicket": Drafting a new Family Code; Sexual freedom or social chaos: The debate on the 1926 Code; Controlling reproduction: Women versus the state; Recasting the vision: The resurrection of the family; Conclusion: Stalin's oxymorons: Socialist state, law, and family.]

5001. Goscilo, Helena. New Members and Organs: The Politics of Porn. The Carl Beck Papers in Russian and East European Studies, no. 1007. Pittsburgh, PA: Center for Russian & East European Studies, University of Pittsburgh, c1993. 44 pp.

5002. Havelková, Hana. " 'Patriarchy' in Czech Society." Hypatia 8, no. 4 (Fall 1993): 89-96.

5003. Herzog, Dagmar. "New Developments in German Women's History." Journal of Women's History 4, no. 3 (Winter 1993): 180-189. [Review article on Ute Frevert, Women in German History: From Bourgeois Emancipation to Sexual Liberation (Oxford: 1988); Ann Taylor, Feminism and Motherhood in Germany, 1800-1914 (New Brunswick, NJ: 1991); and Marion A. Kaplan, The Making of the Jewish Middle Class: Women, Family and Identity in Imperial Germany (NY: 1991).]

5004. Hoffman, Merle. "Sex After the Fall: Starting a Birth Control Revolution in Russia." On the Issues, no. 26 (Spring 1993): 24-29.

5005. Isaak, Jo Anna. "Writing and Righting: The Language of Gender." Surviving Together 11, no. 4 (Winter 1993): 31-34. [Excerpt from "Reflections of Resistance: Women Artists on Both Sides of the Mir," Heresies 7, no. 2 (1992): 8-37.]

5006. Jankowska, Hanna. "The Reproductive Rights Campaign in Poland." Women's Studies International Forum 16, no. 3 (May-June 1993): 291-296. [On women's organizations in Poland.]

5007. Kauppinen-Toropainen, Kaisa, and James E. Gruber. "Antecedents and Outcomes of Woman-Unfriendly Experiences: A Study of Scandinavian, Former Soviet, and American Women." Psychology of Women Quarterly 17, no. 4 (December 1993): 431-456.

5008. Kerig, Patricia K., Yulya Y. Alyoshina, and Alla S. Volovich. "Gender-Role Socialization in Contemporary Russia: Implications for Cross-Cultural Research."

Psychology of Women Quarterly 17, no. 4 (December 1993): 389-408.

5009. Khudyakova, Tatiana. "Businesswomen Are Uniting." *Surviving Together* 11, no. 1 (Spring 1993): 60. [Reprinted from *Izvestiia* (September 18, 1992). Translated by ISAR staff.]

5010. Kon, Igor, and James Riordan, eds. *Sex and Russian Society.* Contributions by Igor Kon, Larissa I. Remennick, Lynne Attwood, Igor Kon, Elizabeth Waters, Sergei Golod, and Lev Shcheglov. Bloomington, IN: Indiana University Press, 1993. viii, 168 pp. [Contents: James Riordan, "Introduction," pp. 1-13; Igor Kon, "Sexuality and Culture," pp. 15-44; Larissa I. Remennick, "Patterns of Birth Control," pp. 45-63; Lynne Attwood, "Sex and the Cinema," pp. 64-88; Igor Kon, "Sexual Minorities," pp. 89-115; Elizabeth Waters, "Soviet Beauty Contests," pp. 116-134; Sergei Golod, "Sex and Young People," pp. 135-151; Lev Shcheglov, "Medical Sexology," pp. 152-164.] REV: Katrina vanden Heuvel, *Nation* 256, no. 24 (June 21, 1993): 870-874.

5011. Kulagina, Alla. "Obraz zhenshchiny v chastushke = Image of Women in the Chastushka." *Woman and Earth* 2, no. 1 (December 10, 1993): 31-34.

5012. Kupriashkina, Svetlana. "First Feminist Seminar in Ukraine." *Surviving Together* 11, no. 4 (Winter 1993): 34.

5013. Kupryashkina, Svetlana. "Women Seek New Roles, Rights in Ukraine." *Surviving Together* 11, no. 1 (Spring 1993): 55-56.

5014. Lenton, Rhonda L. "Home versus career: Attitudes towards women's work among Russian women and men, 1992." *Canadian Journal of Sociology = Cahiers canadiens de sociologie* 18, no. 3 (Summer 1993): 325-331.

5015. Marody, Mira. "Why I Am Not a Feminist: Some Remarks on the Problem of Gender Identity in the United States and Poland." *Social Research* 60, no. 4 (Winter 1993): 853-864.

5016. Marshall, Bonnie. "Long of Hair and Short of Wit: Women in Russian Satirical Anecdotes." *Woman and Earth* 2, no. 1 (December 10, 1993): 28-30.

5017. Mayhall, Stacey L. "Gendered Nationalism and 'New' Nation-States: 'Democratic Progress' in Eastern Europe." *Fletcher Forum of World Affairs* 17, no. 2 (Summer 1993): 91-99.

5018. Mirovitskaya, Natalia. "The Double Burden Weighs Heavier on Rural Russian Women." *Surviving Together* 11, no. 3 (Fall 1993): 27-30. [Second of three articles.]

5019. ———. "Women and the Post-Socialist Reversion to Patriarchy." *Surviving Together* 11, no. 2 (Summer 1993): 44-46.

5020. ———. "Women, Nature and Society: Changing the Soviet Paradigm." *Surviving Together* 11, no. 4 (Winter 1993): 26-29.

5021. Moghadam, Valentine M., ed. *Democratic Reform and the Position of Women in Transitional Economies.* Contributions by Sharon L. Wolchik, Barbara Einhorn, Marilyn Rueschemeyer, Dobrinka Kostova, Ireneusz Bialecki, Barbara Heyns, Gail Warshofsky Lapidus, Anastasia Posadskaya, Valentina Bodrova, Kaisa Kauppinen-Toropainen, Monica Fong, Gillian Paull, Liba Paukert, Gordon Weil, Maria Ciechocinska, and Valentine M. Moghadam. Studies in Developmental Economics. Oxford: Clarendon Press: New York; Oxford University Press, 1993. viii, 366 pp. [Discussions and findings of a research conference that took place at the World Institute for Development Economics Research (WIDER) in September 1991. Contents: Valentine M. Moghadam, "Introduction: Gender Dynamics of Economic and Political Change: Efficiency, Equality, and Women," pp. 1-25. Part I: Democratization and Women in Central and Eastern Europe. Sharon L. Wolchik, "Women and the Politics of Transition in Central and Eastern Europe," pp. 29-47; Barbara Einhorn, "Democratization and Women's Movements in Central and Eastern Europe: Concepts of Women's Rights," pp. 48-74; Marilyn Rueschemeyer, "Women in East Germany: From State Socialism to Capitalist Welfare State," pp. 75-91; Dobrinka Kostova, "The Transition to Democracy in Bulgaria: Challenges and Risks for Women," pp. 92-109; Ireneusz Bialecki and Barbara Heyns, "Educational Attainment, the Status of Women, and the Private School Movement in Poland," pp. 110-134. Part II: Perestroika and Women in the Soviet Union. Gail Warshofsky Lapidus, "Gender and Restructuring: The Impact of Perestroika and its Aftermath on Soviet Women," pp. 137-161; Anastasia Posadskaya, "Changes in Gender Discourses and Policies in the Former Soviet Union," pp. 162-179; Valentina Bodrova, "Glasnost and 'the Woman Question' in the Mirror of Public Opinion: Attitudes towards Women, Work, and the Family," pp. 180-196; Kaisa Kauppinen-Toropainen, "Comparative Study of Women's Work Satisfaction and Work Commitment: Research Findings from Estonia, Moscow, and Scandinavia," pp. 197-214. Part III: Economic Reform and Women's Employment. Monica Fong and Gillian Paull, "Women's Economic Status in the Restructuring of Eastern Europe," pp. 217-247; Liba Paukert, "The Changing Economic Status of Women in the Period of Transition to a Market Economy System: The Case of the Czech and Slovak Republics after 1989," pp. 248-279; Gordon Weil, "Economic Reform and Women: A General Framework with Specific Reference to Hungary," pp. 280-301; Maria Ciechocinska, "Gender Aspects of Dismantling the Command Economy in Eastern Europe: The Case of Poland," pp. 302-326; Valentine M. Moghadam, "Bringing the Third World In: A Comparative Analysis of Gender and Restructuring," pp. 327-352.]

5022. Morinaga, Yasuko, Irene Hanson Frieze, and Anuska Ferligoj. "Career Plans and Gender-Role Attitudes of College Students in the United States, Japan and Slovenia." *Sex Roles* 29, nos. 5/6 (September 1993): 317-334.

5023. Naiman, Eric. "Revolutionary Anorexia (NEP as Female Complaint)." *Slavic and East European Journal* 37, no. 3 (Fall 1993): 305-325.

5024. Oinas, Felix J. "Couvade in Estonia." *Slavic and East European Journal* 37, no. 3 (Fall 1993): 339-345.

5025. Radford-Ruether, Rosemary. "Women, First and Last Colony: Female Status and Roles Within Race and Class Hierarchy." *Humboldt Journal of Social Relations* 19, no. 2 (1993): 391-416. [Includes section "Women in Eastern European Socialism," pp. 403-407.]

5026. Rassweiler, Anne D. "Siberian Women Today." *Surviving Together* 11, no. 3 (Fall 1993): 23-24.

5027. Robbins, Sonia Jaffe. "Prawa Wyboru Polskim Kobietom: Polish Women Fight for Choice." *New Directions for Women* 22, no. 2 (March-April 1993): 26.

5028. Ruthchild, Rochelle Goldberg. *Women in Russia and the Soviet Union: An Annotated Bibliography.* New York: G.K. Hall; Toronto: Maxwell Macmillan Canada; New York: Maxwell Macmillan International, c1993. xiv, 203 pp. [Contents: "References and General Bibliographies," pp. 1-3; "General Works," pp. 4-8; "Folk and Peasant Culture," pp. 9-13; "The Ancient and Medieval Periods to 1682," pp. 14-18; "Sophia, Peter the Great, and the Era of the Empresses, 1682-1796," pp. 19-23; "Catherine the Great, 1762-1796," pp. 24-36; "Return of the Emperors, 1796-1855," pp. 37-41; "Reform, Reaction, and Revolutions, 1855-1917," pp. 42-95; "The Soviet Period, 1918-1991," pp. 96-169.]

5029. Sauer, Birgit. "Political Culture and the Participation of Women in the German Democratic Republic after the 'Wende.'" *New Political Science*, no. 24/25 (Spring-Summer 1993): 19-37.

5030. Schillinger, Liesl. "Moscow Postcard: *Devushki!*" *New Republic* 209, no. 6 (August 9, 1993): 9-10. [On the sexual harrasment of women in Moscow.]

5031. Schultz, Debra. "At Independent Forum, Women's Groups Move from Problems to Strategy." *Surviving Together* 11, no. 1 (Spring 1993): 57-58.

5032. Silbey, Jessica, Wendy Jagerson, and Millie Didio. "The First and Second Independent Women's Forums." *Woman and Earth* 2, no. 1 (December 10, 1993): 38-39. [First Independent Women's Forum, held March 1991 in Soviet Union; Second Forum held November 1992 in Dubna.]

5033. Simpson, Patricia Anne. "Feminisms in the Fatherland." *Cross Currents: A Yearbook of Central European Culture*, no. 12 (1993): 204-217. [On Germany.]

5034. Snitow, Ann. "Poland's Abortion Law: The Church Wins, Women Lose." *Nation* 256, no. 16 (April 26, 1993): 556-559.

5035. Stent, Angela. "Women in the Post-Communist World: The Politics of Identity and Ethnicity." *World Policy Journal* 10, no. 4 (Winter 1993-1994): 65-71.

5036. Tedin, Kent L., and Oi-Kuan Fiona Yap. "The Gender Factor in Soviet Mass Politics: Survey Evidence from Greater Moscow." *Political Research Quarterly* 46, no. 1 (March 1993): 179-211.

5037. United Nations. Centre for Social Development and Humanitarian Affairs. *Women in Decision-making: Case-study on Hungary.* New York: United Nations, 1993. iv, 50 pp.

5038. Voronina, Olga. "Soviet Patriarchy: Past and Present." *Hypatia* 8, no. 4 (Fall 1993): 97-112.

5039. Wierling, Dorothée. "Three Generations of East German Women: Four Decades of the GDR and After." *Oral History Review* 21, no. 2 (Winter 1993): 19-29.

5040. "Women's Studies Centers and Programs in Eastern Europe and the Former Soviet Union." *Hypatia* 8, no. 4 (Fall 1993): 127-128.

5041. "Yeltsin's Decree: A Step Forward for Women." *Surviving Together* 11, no. 2 (Summer 1993): 48. [Reprinted from "Women's Discussion Club" in *Interlegal* (March 1993).]

5042. Yulina, Nina S. "Women and Patriarchy." *Women's Studies International Forum* 16, no. 1 (January-February 1993): 57-63. Translated from Russian by John Ryder. [On women in post-Soviet Russia.]

18 Obituaries

5043. "Literary Necrology 1992." *World Literature Today* 67, no. 2 (Spring 1993): 320. [Notes the deaths of Martin Camaj, Albanian poet and novelist in exile; Ivar Ivask, Estonian poet and artist and former editor of *World Literature Today*; and Raimond Kolk, Estonian poet and prose writer.]

Arban

5044. Natov, Nadine. "In Memoriam: Dominique Arban." *Dostoevsky Studies = Dostoevskii: Stat'i i materialy* 1, no. 1 (1993): 144-146. [Noted French authority on Dostoevsky.]

Berberova

5045. Buck, Joan Juliet, and Richard Avedon. "Nina Berberova." *New Yorker* 69, no. 35 (October 25, 1993): 94.

Beershtain/Birshtein

5046. Crookall, David. "Editorial: Marie Beershtain." *Simulation & Gaming* 24, no. 1 (March 1993): 5.

5047. Dzhukov, R. F., and A. I. Mikhaylushkin. "In Memoriam: Marie Mironovna Beershtain/Marie M. Birshtein, 1902-1992." *Simulation & Gaming* 24, no. 1 (March 1993): 6.

5048. Gagnon, John H. "In Memoriam: Marie Mironovna Beershtain/Marie M. Birshtein, 1902-1992." *Simulation & Gaming* 24, no. 1 (March 1993): 7.

5049. Wolfe, Joseph, and David Crookall. "In Memoriam: Marie Mironovna Beershtain/Marie M. Birshtein, 1902-1992." *Simulation & Gaming* 24, no. 1 (March 1993): 7-8.

Brandt

5050. Birnbaum, Norm. "In Memoriam: Willy Brandt, 1913-1992." *Dissent* 40, no. 1 (Winter 1993): 125-126.

Bykovsky

5051. Bloch, Marie, and Lubomyr R. Wynar. "Lew Bykovsky, 1895-1992." *Ethnic Forum* 13, no. 1 (1993): 65-68.

Deutsch

5052. Merritt, Richard L. "In Memoriam [Karl W. Deutsch]." *PS: Political Science & Politics* 26, no. 1 (March 1993): 100-101.

Elagin

5053. Aleshkovskii, Iuz, Iosif Brodskii, and Lev Losev. "Pamiati poeta [Ivan Elagin]." *Canadian-American Slavic Studies* 27, nos. 1-4 (1993): 293. [Obituary composed for *Russkaia mysl'*, *Novoe russkoe slovo*, and *Kontinent*.]

Gedroitsa

5054. Natova, Nadezhda. "Pamiati kniazia Alekseia Nikolaevicha Gedroitsa (In memoriam: Prince Aleksei Nikolaevich Gedroits)." *Dostoevsky Studies = Dostoevskii: Stat'i i materialy* 1, no. 1 (1993): 147-151. [Russian emigré musician, literary scholar, historian, stage director.]

Grigorenko

5055. "In Memoriam: Zinaida Grigorenko." *RCDA* 32, no. 4 (1993-1994): 78. [Exiled Russian dissident and human rights activist.]

Heien

5056. Jarvis, Donald K. "In Memoriam: Larry G. Heien." *Slavic and East European Journal* 37, no. 2 (Summer 1993): 273-274.

Hewett

5057. Brada, Josef C. "In Memoriam: Ed A. Hewett (1942-1993)." *Journal of Comparative Economics* 17, no. 4 (December 1993): 711-714.

5058. Hunter, Holland. "In Memoriam: Ed A. Hewett." *Comparative Economic Studies* 35, no. 1 (Spring 1993): iii-iv.

Hordynsky

5059. Tytla, Bohdan. "Ad Memoriam: Svyatoslav Hordynsky (1906-1993)." *Ukrainian Quarterly* 49, no. 3 (Fall 1993): 350-352. [Ukrainian poet, translator, artist, art theorist, critic and editor.]

Horszowki

5060. "Passages: Mieczyslaw Horszowki (1892-1993)." *Clavier* 32, no. 6 (July-August 1993): 50.

Kerze

5061. [Obituary for Frank Kerze (1876-1961)]. *Slovene Studies* 14, no. 2 (1992, published September 1994): [123]. [Publisher and editor of Slovene-language immigrant newspapers and writer.]

Klaniczay

5062. Kushner, Eva. "Tibor Klaniczay: In Memoriam." *Canadian Review of Comparative Literature = Revue Canadienne de Littérature Comparée* 20, nos. 1-2 (March-June 1993): 283-284. [Hungarian scholar of comparative literature and Renaissance literary critic.]

Labedz

5063. Gershman, Carl, Leszek Kolakowski, Zbigniew Brzezinski, and Edward Shils. "Leopold Labedz (1920-1993)." *Journal of Democracy* 4, no. 4 (October 1993): 141-142. [Excerpts of memorial service speeches.]

5064. "Leo Labedz (1920-1993)." *Journal of Democracy* 4, no. 3 (July 1993): 141.

Lachs

5065. Chopra, Sudhir K. "The Teacher: Lachs at the Hague Academy." *American Journal of International Law* 87, no. 3 (July 1993): 420-423. [Part of special section "In Memoriam: Judge Manfred Lachs (1914-1993)."]

5066. Franck, Thomas M. "The Private Lachs: Life as Art." *American Journal of International Law* 87, no. 3 (July 1993): 419-420. [Part of special section "In Memoriam: Judge Manfred Lachs (1914-1993)."]

5067. Gorove, Stephen. "In Memoriam: Judge Manfred H. Lachs (1914-1993)." *Journal of Space Law* 21, no. 1 (1993): i. [Polish diplomat and judge; President of the International Court of Justice; and President of the International Institute of Space Law.]

5068. "In Memoriam: Manfred Lachs." *Emory International Law Review* 7, no. 1 (Spring 1993): xi-xii.

5069. Schachter, Oscar. "The UN Years: Lachs the Diplomat." *American Journal of International Law* 87, no. 3 (July 1993): 414-416. [Part of special section "In Memoriam: Judge Manfred Lachs (1914-1993)."]

5070. Schwebel, Stephen M. "On the Bench: Lachs the Judge." *American Journal of International Law* 87, no. 3 (July 1993): 416-419. [Part of special section "In Memoriam: Judge Manfred Lachs (1914-1993)."]

Meyendorff

5071. Majeska, George P. "John Meyendorff, 1926-1992." *Dumbarton Oak Papers*, no. 47 (1993): ix-xi.

Mladenov

5072. Scatton, Ernest. "In Memoriam: Maksim Sl. Mladenov, 1930-1992." *Slavic and East European Journal* 37, no. 1 (Spring 1993): 146-147.

Mouriki

5073. Maguire, Henry, and Nancy Sevcenko. "Doula Mouriki, 1934-1991." *Dumbarton Oak Papers*, no. 47 (1993): xiii-xvi.

Mstyslav I

5074. "Ad Memoriam: Patriarch Mstyslav I (1898-1993)." *Ukrainian Quarterly* 49, no. 2 (Summer 1993): 236-238. [Mstyslav I was Patriarch of Kiev and All Ukraine and Metropolitan of the Ukrainian Orthodox Church of the USA.]

Nureyev

5075. Barnes, Clive. "Rudolf Nureyev: Fugitive Glimpses." *Dance Magazine* 67, no. 4 (April 1993): 34ff.

5076. Carlson, Richard W. "Nureyev-Fonteyn, RIP." *American Spectator* 26, no. 5 (May 1993): 29-33.

5077. Croce, Arlene, and Richard Avedon. "Rudolf Nureyev." *New Yorker* 68, no. 48 (January 18, 1993): 80-83.

Pervushin

5078. Zekulin, Gleb. "In Memoriam: Nikolai V. Pervushin (1899-1993)." *Canadian Slavonic Papers* 35, nos. 3-4 (September-December 1993): [199-200]. [Russian emigre journalist, literary critic, translator, professor, and United Nations interpreter.]

Pribic

5079. Wukasch, Charles. "In Memoriam: Nikola Pribic (1913-1992)." *Slavic and East European Journal* 37, no. 3 (Fall 1993): 421.

Renkiewicz

5080. "Frank Renkiewicz." *Polish American Studies* 50, no. 2 (Autumn 1993): p. 2 of cover.

Ridgway

5081. Nadein, Vladimir. "Ridgway, Great General, Dies." *Military Review* 73, no. 10 (October 1993): 64. Translated by William M. Connor, and Robert R. Love. [Eighth US Army commander in the Korean War; NATO Supreme Allied Commander; and Chief of Staff of the US Army. From *Izvestiia* (July 29, 1993): 7.]

Schoonmaker

5082. Fleer, Jack D. "In Memoriam [Donald O. Schoonmaker]." *PS: Political Science & Politics* 26, no. 4 (December 1993): 819.

Shklar

5083. Hoffman, Stanley. "In Memoriam [Judith Shklar]." *PS: Political Science & Politics* 26, no. 2 (June 1993): 275-276.

Taranovsky

5084. Bailey, James, and Henryk Baran. "In Memoriam: Kiril Fedorovich Taranovsky (1911-1993)." *Slavic and East European Journal* 37, no. 3 (Fall 1993): 417-420.

Trager

5085. Hockett, Charles F. "Obituary: George Leonard Trager." *Language: Journal of the Linguistic Society of America* 69, no. 4 (December 1993): 778-788.

Weitzmann

5086. Kessler, Herbert L. "Kurt Weitzmann, 1904-1993." *Dumbarton Oak Papers*, no. 47 (1993): xix-xxiii.

Wildenmann

5087. Sigel, Robert S. "In Memoriam [Rudolf Wildenmann]." *PS: Political Science & Politics* 26, no. 4 (December 1993): 821.

Zawacki

5088. Marquess, Harlan E. "In Memoriam: Edmund Ignace Zawacki." *Slavic and East European Journal* 37, no. 4 (Winter 1993): 611-612.

19 Reviews of Books Published in Previous Years

■ General

General Collections, Festschrifts, Symposia

5089. Adam, Jan, ed. *Economic Reforms and Welfare Systems in the USSR, Poland, and Hungary: Social Contract in Transformation.* Contributions by Jan Adam, Janet G. Chapman, Elizabeth Clayton, Murray Feshbach, Ann Rubin, Henryk Flakierski, Zbigniew M. Fallenbuchl, Zsuzsa Ferge, and Janos Timar. New York: St. Martin's Press, 1991. xv, 182 pp. [Contents: Jan Adam, "Social Contract"; Janet G. Chapman, "Drastic Changes in the Soviet Social Contract"; Elizabeth Clayton, "The Social Contract: Soviet Price and Housing Policy"; Murray Feshbach and Ann Rubin, "Health Care in the USSR"; Henryk Flakierski, "Social Policies in the 1980s in Poland: A Discussion of New Approaches"; Zbigniew M. Fallenbuchl, "Economic Reform and Changes in the Welfare System in Poland"; Zsuzsa Ferge, "Recent Trends in Social Policy in Hungary"; Janos Timar, "Economic Reform and New Employment Problems in Hungary".] REV: Alastair McAuley, *Slavic Review* 52, no. 2 (Summer 1993): 385-386.

5090. Allcock, John B., John J. Horton, and Marko Milivojevic, eds. *Yugoslavia in Transition: Choices and Constraints: Essays in Honour of Fred Singleton.* New York: Berg; Distributed by St. Martin's Press, 1992. xi, 461 pp. REV: Gale Stokes, *Slavic Review* 52, no. 4 (Winter 1993): 886-887.

5091. Bukowski, Charles, and J. Richard Walsh, eds. *Glasnost, Perestroika, and the Socialist Community.* New York: Praeger, 1990. xi, 176 pp. REV: John A. Armstrong, *Journal of Baltic Studies* 22, no. 4 (Winter 1991): 374-376. Roger Hamburg, *Perspectives on Political Science* 20, no. 1 (Winter 1991): 42. John Riser, *Studies in East European Thought* 45, no. 3 (September 1993): 219-225.

5092. Michta, Andrew A., and Ilya Prizel, eds. *Postcommunist Eastern Europe: Crisis and Reform.* New York: St. Martin's Press, c1992. x, 205 pp. [In association with the Johns Hopkins Foreign Policy Institute.] REV: John A. Armstrong, *Journal of Baltic Studies* 24, no. 3 (Fall 1993): 310-311. Paul G. Lewis, *Soviet and Post-Soviet Review* 20, nos. 2-3 (1993): 249-250. *Orbis* 37, no. 2 (Spring 1993).

5093. Parker, Andrew, Mary Russo, Doris Sommer, and Patricia Yeager, eds. *Nationalisms and Sexualities.* New York: Routledge, c1992. xi, 451 pp. [Includes essay by Greta N. Slobin on V. Aksenov's *Island of Crimea*; Sander L. Gilman on two German novels; Catherine Portuges on Hungarian filmmaker Martás Méstzáros.] REV: Aparajita Sagar, *College Literature* 19, no. 3/20, no. 1 (October 1992-

Feburary 1993): 240-242.

5094. Pavlyshyn, Marko, ed. *Glasnost' in Context: On the Recurrence of Liberalizations in Central and East European Literatures and Cultures.* Berg European Studies Series, New York: Berg; Distributed by St. Martin's Press, 1990. xi, 206 pp. [Selected papers from an interdisciplinary conference held at Monash University in February 1988.] REV: Anita Shelton, *Nationalities Papers* 21, no. 2 (Fall 1993): 234-236.

5095. Shtromas, Alexander S., and Morton A. Kaplan, eds. *The Soviet Union and the Challenge of the Future.* 1st ed. New York: Paragon House, 1988-1989. 4 vols. [Contents: Vol. 1. Stasis and Change — v. 2. Economy and Society — v. 3. Ideology, Culture and Nationality — v. 4. Russia and the World.] REV: Donald W. Treadgold, *Russian Review* 49, no. 3 (July 1990): 358-360. Henry R. Huttenbach, *Nationalities Papers* 21, no. 2 (Fall 1993): 208-210. Timothy E. O'Connor, *Studies in East European Thought* 45, no. 3 (September 1993): 214-217.

5096. Simmie, James, and Joze Dekleva, eds. *Yugoslavia in Turmoil: After Self-Management?* London; New York: Pinter, 1991. xviii, 167 pp. REV: Thomas Palm, *Journal of Baltic Studies* 24, no. 4 (Winter 1993): 406-408.

5097. Timberlake, Charles E., ed. *Religious and Secular Forces in Late Tsarist Russia: Essays in Honor of Donald W. Treadgold.* Contributions by Charles E. Timberlake, David M. Goldfrank, William A. James, John M. McErlean, John Basil, Alan Kimball, Thomas C. Sorenson, Robert L. Nichols, Joseph Schiebel, Edward J. Lazzerini, David Davies, Tsuyoshi Hasegawa, Nicholas V. Riasanovsky, and Robert F. Byrnes. Seattle, WA: University of Washington Press, c1992. x, 366 pp. [Contents: Charles E. Timberlake, "Introduction: Religious Pluralism, the Spread of Revolutionary Ideas, and the Church-State Relationship in Tsarist Russia"; David M. Goldfrank, "Theocratic Imperatives, the Transcendent, the Worldly, and Political Justice in Russia's Early Inquisitions"; William A. James, "The Jesuits' Role in Founding Schools in Late Tsarist Russia"; John M. McErlean, "Catholic, Liberal, European: A Critic of Orthodox Russia, the Diplomat Prince P.B. Kozlovskii (1783-1840)"; John Basil, "The Russian Theological Academies and the Old Catholics, 1870-1905"; Alan Kimball, "Alexander Herzen and the Native Lineage of the Russian Revolution"; Charles E. Timberlake, "Tver Zemstvo's Technical School in Rzhev: A Case Study in the Dissemination of Revolutionary and Secular Ideas"; Joseph Schiebel, "Marxism and Aziatchina: Secular Religion, the Nature of Russian Society, and the Organization of the Bolshevik Party"; David Davies, "Mikhail Gershenzon's 'Secret Voice': The Making of a Cultural Nihilist"; Thomas C. Sorenson, "Pobedonostsev's Parish Schools: A Bastion

Against Secularism"; Robert L. Nichols, "The Friends of God: Nicholas II and Alexandra at the Canonization of Serafim of Sarov, July 1903"; Edward J. Lazzerini, "The Debate over Instruction of Muslims in Post-1905 Russia: A Local Perspective"; Tsuyoshi Hasegawa, "Crime, Police, and Mob Justice in Petrograd during the Russian Revolutions of 1917"; Nicholas V. Riasanovsky, "Donald Warren Treadgold, Historian in Our Midst: A Brief Appreciation"; Robert F. Byrnes, "Don Treadgold: A Builder of Slavic Studies".] REV: Gregory L. Freeze., *Catholic Historical Review* 79, no. 4 (October 1993): 764-766. Charles A. Ruud, *Canadian Slavonic Papers* 35, nos. 3-4 (September-December 1993): 413.

5098. Wedel, Janine R., ed. *The Unplanned Society: Poland During and After Communism*. NY: Columbia University Press, 1992. 271 pp. REV: Robert Legvold, *Foreign Affairs* 71, no. 4 (Fall 1992): 212-213. Andrzej W. Tymowski, *Telos*, no. 92 (Summer 1992): 187-191. Bronislaw Misztal, *Contemporary Sociology* 22, no. 6 (November 1993): 834-836.

Bibliographies, Reference Works, Sources

5099. Anderson, Karen, and Jonathan J. Halperin. *Through a Glass Clearly: Finding, Evaluating and Using Business Information from the Soviet Region*. SLA Occasional Papers Series, no. 3. Washington, DC: Special Libraries Association, c1992. 1 vol. [Prepared by FYI Information Resources.] REV: Elin B. Christianson, *Library Quarterly* 63, no. 3 (July 1993): 397-398.

5100. Balch Institute for Ethnic Studies. Research Library. *A Guide to the Manuscript and Microfilm Collections of the Research Library of the Balch Institute for Ethnic Studies*. Compiled and edited by Monique Bourque and R. Joseph Anderson. Philadelphia, PA: Balch Institute for Ethnic Studies, c1992. ix, 129 pp. REV: Alexandra S. Gressitt, *American Archivist* 56, no. 2 (Spring 1993): 377-378. Mark Kulikowski, *Polish American Studies* 50, no. 2 (Autumn 1993): 114-115.

5101. Fortunoff Video Archive for Holocaust Testimonies. *Guide to Yale University Library Holocaust Video Testimonies*. Garland Reference Library of Social Science, v. 604, etc. New York: Garland, 1990-. vols. REV: Samuel Totten, *Holocaust and Genocide Studies* 7, no. 1 (Spring 1993): 140.

5102. Frankel, Benjamin, ed. *The Cold War, 1945-1991*. Foreword by Townsend Hoopes. Detroit, MI: Gale Research, c1992. 3 vols. [Contents: Vol. 1. Leaders and Other Important Figures in the United States and Western Europe — v. 2. Leaders and Other Important Figures in the Soviet Union, Eastern Europe, China, and the Third World — v. 3. Resources: Chronology, History, Concepts, Events, Organizations, Bibliography, Archives.] REV: *Booklist* 89, no. 22 (August 1993): 2086.

5103. Karlowich, Robert A., comp. *A Guide to Scholarly Resources on the Russian Empire and the Soviet Union in the New York Metropolitan Area*. Armonk, NY: M.E. Sharpe, c1990. xxii, 312 pp. [Sponsored by the Bibliography, Information Retrieval and Documentation Subcommittee of the Joint Committee on Soviet Studies of the Social Science Research Council and the American Council of Learned Societies.] REV: G.J. [Gerald Janecek], *Slavic and East European Journal* 37, no. 1 (Spring 1993): 141.

5104. Multicultural History Society of Ontario. *A Guide to the Collections of the Multicultural History Society of Ontario*. Compiled by Nick G. Forte. Edited and with an introduction by Gabriele Scardellato. [Toronto]: Multicultural History Society of Ontario, 1992. xx, 695 pp. REV: Lubomyr R. Wynar, *Ethnic Forum* 13, no. 1 (1993): 69-73.

5105. Parrish, Michael. *Soviet Security and Intelligence Organizations, 1917-1990: A Biographical Dictionary and Review of Literature in English*. New York: Greenwood Press, 1992. xxv, 669 pp. REV: Amy Knight, *Slavic Review* 52, no. 2 (Summer 1993): 390. Walter C. Uhler, *Russian History = Histoire russe* 20, nos. 1-4 (1993): 375-377.

5106. Pockney, B. P. *Soviet Statistics since 1950*. New York: St. Martin's Press, 1991. 333 pp. REV: Beth A. Mitchneck, *Soviet and Post-Soviet Review* 19, nos. 1-3 (1992): 330-331. Barry Mendel Cohen, *History: Reviews of New Books* 21, no. 3 (Spring 1993): 127.

5107. Sokol, Stanley S., and Sharon F. Mrotek Kissane. *The Polish Biographical Dictionary: Profiles of Nearly 900 Poles Who Have Made Lasting Contributions to World Civilization*. With a brief history of Poland by Alfred L. Abramowicz. Wauconda, IL: Bolchazy-Carducci Publishers, c1992. 477 pp. REV: Mark Kulikowski, *Polish Review* 37, no. 3 (1992): 371-372. James S. Pula, *Polish American Studies* 50, no. 1 (Spring 1993): 88-91.

5108. University of Minnesota. Immigration History Research Center. *The Immigration History Research Center: A Guide to the Collections*. Compiled and edited by Suzanna Moody and Joel Wurl. Foreword by Rudolph J. Vecoli. Bibliographies and Indexes in American History, no. 20. New York: Greenwood Press, 1991. xxiii, 446 pp. REV: Lubomyr R. Wynar, *Ethnic Forum* 13, no. 1 (1993): 69-73.

5109. Vargas, Mark A., ed. *A Guide to the Polish-American Holdings in the Milwaukee Urban Archives*. Milwaukee, WI: Golda Meir Library, University of Wisconsin, Milwaukee, 1991. 30 pp. REV: Mark Kulikowski, *Polish American Studies* 50, no. 2 (Autumn 1993): 114-115.

5110. Wilson, Andrew, and Nina Bachkatov. *Russia and the Commonwealth A to Z*. 1st ed. New York: HarperPerennial, c1992. xii, 258 pp. [British edition has title: *Russia Revised*. English edition enlarged from the French edition. Translation of *Nouveaux Sovietiques de A a Z*.] REV: *Booklist* 89, no. 11 (February 1, 1993): 1005.

Bibliology and the History of Printing

5111. Mathews, Thomas F., and Avedis K. Sanjian. *Armenian Gospel Iconography: The Tradition of the Glajor Gospel*. Edited by Thomas F. Mathews. Includes contributions by Mary Virginia Orna, and James R. Russell. Dumbarton Oaks Studies, 29. Washington, DC: Dumbarton Oaks Research Library and Collection, c1991. 246 pp. REV: Robert S. Nelson, *Speculum* 68, no. 3 (July 1993): 837-839.

5112. McReynolds, Louise. *The News Under Russia's Old Regime: The Development of a Mass-Circulation Press*. Princeton, NJ: Princeton University Press, c1991. xii, 313 pp. REV: Alfred J. Rieber, *Slavic Review* 51, no. 4 (Winter 1992): 818-820. Charles A. Ruud, *American Historical Review* 97, no. 5 (December 1992): 1567-1568. James H. Krukones, *Russian History = Histoire russe* 20, nos. 1-4 (1993): 309-310. Gary Marker, *Russian Review* 52, no. 1 (January 1993): 110-112. Robert C. Williams, *Historian* 55, no. 2 (Winter 1993): 355.

5113. Ruud, Charles A. *Russian Entrepreneur: Publisher Ivan Sytin of Moscow, 1851-1934*. Kingston, Ontario; Buffalo: McGill-Queen's University Press, c1990. x, 270 pp. REV: James H. Krukones, *Russian History* 17, no. 3 (Fall 1990): 354-355. Thomas C. Owen, *Canadian Slavonic Papers* 32, no. 2 (June 1990): 183-184. Joseph Bradley, *American Historical Review* 96, no. 5 (December 1991): 1579-1580. Marianna Tax Choldin, *Library Quarterly* 61, no. 4 (October 1991): 449-450. Ben Eklof, *Canadian-American Slavic Studies* 25, nos. 1-4 (1991): 277-280. Elizabeth K. Valkenier, *History: Reviews of New Books* 20, no. 1 (Fall 1991): 34. Louise McReynolds, *Journal of Modern History* 64, no. 4 (December 1992): 855-856. Mary P. Stuart, *Slavic Review* 51, no. 1 (Spring 1992): 172-173. David Das, *Nationalities Papers* 21, no. 2 (Fall 1993): 197. Leo A. LaDell, *East/West Education* 14, no. 1 (Spring 1993): 76-79.

5114. Steinberg, Mark D. *Moral Communities: The Culture of Class Relations in the Russian Printing Industry, 1867-1907*. Studies on the History of Society and Culture, 14. Berkeley, CA: University of California Press, c1992. x, 289 pp. REV: Heather Hogan, *Russian History = Histoire russe* 20, nos. 1-4 (1993): 310-311. William G. Rosenberg, *Slavic Review* 52, no. 2 (Summer 1993): 361-362. David Stefancic, *History: Reviews of New Books* 22, no. 1 (Fall 1993): 39.

5115. Studemeister, Marguerite. *Bookplates and Their Owners in Imperial Russia: An Illustrated Survey of the Holdings at Stanford University*. Tenafly, NJ: Hermitage Publishers, 1991. 220 pp. REV: G.J. [Gerald Janecek], *Slavic and East European Journal* 37, no. 1 (Spring 1993): 142.

Biography and Autobiography

5116. Alexander, John T. *Catherine the Great: Life and Legend*. New York: Oxford University Press, 1989. xii, 418 pp. REV: James G. Hart, *Historian* 52, no. 3 (May 1990): 494-495. Robert E. Jones, *Russian History* 17, no. 1 (Spring 1990): 87-88. Cynthia H. Whittaker, *Russian Review* 49, no. 1 (January 1990): 92-93. Wilson R. Augustine, *Canadian-American Slavic Studies* 25, nos. 1-4 (1991): 261-262. Edward C. Thaden, *Journal of Modern History* 63, no. 3 (September 1991): 614-616. James Cracraft, *Slavic*

Review 52, no. 1 (Spring 1993): 107-115. Marc Raeff, *American Historical Review* 98, no. 4 (October 1993): 1143-1155.

5117. Andreas-Salomé, Lou. *Looking Back: Memoirs*. Edited by Ernst Pfeiffer. Translated by Breon Mitchell. 1st American ed. European Sources, New York: Paragon House, 1991. 226 pp. [Translation of *Lebensruckblick*. Includes chapter "Russian Experience," on the political and cultural issues of the 1930s, and discussion of "old Russia".] REV: Gwyneth Cravens, *Nation* 254 (March 2, 1992): 279-281. Peter F. Ostwald, *American Journal of Psychiatry* 149 (September 1992): 1262. Robert M. Chalfin, *Psychoanalytic Quarterly* 62, no. 4 (October 1993): 683-687.

5118. Arbatov, Georgi. *The System: An Insider's Life in Soviet Politics*. 1st U.S. ed. New York: Time Books, c1992. xix, 380 pp. [Based on: *Zatianuvsheesia vyzdorovlenie, 1953-1985 gg*. Originally published (Moscow: Mezhdunar. otnosheniia, 1991).] REV: Stephen F. Cohen, *New York Times Book Review* (August 16, 1992): 13-14. Robert Legvold, *Foreign Affairs* 71, no. 5 (Winter 1992-1993): 211. Richard Pipes, *New Republic* 207, no. 17 (October 19, 1992): 40-43. George J. Neimanis, *Journal of Baltic Studies* 24, no. 2 (Summer 1993): 201-206. Arch Puddington, *American Spectator* 26, no. 1 (January 1993): 89-90.

5119. Bonner, Elena. *Mothers and Daughters*. Translated by Antonina W. Bouis. 1st American ed. New York: A.A. Knopf, 1992. xi, 349 pp. [Translation of *Dochki-materi*.] REV: Andrea Lee, *New York Times Book Review* (March 22, 1992): 9. *Publishers Weekly* 239, no. 2 (January 6, 1992): 58. Edward Alexander, *Ararat* 34, no. 2 (Spring 1993): 60-61.

5120. Brandt, Willy. *My Life in Politics*. New York: Viking, 1992. xxv, 498 pp. [Translated, abridged edition of *Erinnerungen*.] REV: Jeffrey Gedmen, *American Spectator* 26, no. 1 (January 1993): 87-89. Paul Weissman, *New York Times Book Review* 98, no. 3 (January 17, 1993): 24.

5121. Buber, Martin. *The Letters of Martin Buber: A Life of Dialogue*. Edited by Nahum N. Glatzer and Paul Mendes-Flohr. Translated by Richard Winston, Clara Winston, and Harry Zohn. New York: Schocken Books, c1991. xiii, 722 pp. REV: Martin S. Jaffee, *Congress Monthly* 60, no. 3 (March-April 1993): 16-18. Avishai Margalit, *New York Review of Books* 40, no. 18 (November 4, 1993): 66-71.

5122. Bullock, Alan. *Hitler and Stalin: Parallel Lives*. 1st American ed. New York: Knopf; Distributed by Random House, 1992. xviii, 1081 pp. [Originally published (London: HarperCollins, 1991).] REV: Lee Congdon, *History: Reviews of New Books* 21, no. 1 (Fall 1992): 41-42. Gordon A. Craig, *New York Review of Books* 39, no. 7 (April 9, 1992): 3-5. Norman Davies, *New York Times Book Review* (March 22, 1992): 3ff. William G. Hyland, *Commentary* 94, no. 2 (August 1992): 62-64. Charles S. Maier, *New Republic* 206, no. 24 (June 15, 1992): 42-45. Fritz Stern, *Foreign Affairs* 71, no. 3 (Summer 1992): 165-166. Gilbert Taylor, *Booklist* 88, no. 9 (January 1, 1992): 793. *Publishers Weekly*

239, no. 3 (January 13, 1992): 39. Joseph Shattan, *American Spectator* 26, no. 1 (January 1993): 85-87. Walter C. Uhler, *Naval War College Review* 46, no. 3, Sequence 343 (Summer 1993): 136-167. Ken Wolf, *Historian* 55, no. 2 (Winter 1993): 332.

5123. Conquest, Robert. *Stalin: Breaker of Nations.* 1st American ed. New York: Viking, 1991. xvii, 346 pp. REV: Richard Pipes, *New York Times Book Review* (November 10, 1991): 14-15. John Pearson Roche, *New Leader* 74, no. 14 (December 30, 1991): 25-26. John H. Stanhope, *Journal of Social, Political and Economic Studies* 16, no. 4 (Winter 1991): 509-510. Stephen J. Blank, *Parameters* 22, no. 4 (Winter 1992-1993): 118-119. Roman Brachman, *Midstream* 38, no. 1 (January 1992): 42-44. Terence Emmons, *New Republic* 206, no. 10 (March 9, 1992): 33-41. Charles H. Fairbanks, Jr., *National Review* 44, no. 3 (February 17, 1992): 45-48. Jacob E. Heilbrunn, *Global Affairs*, 7, no. 2 (Spring 1992): 186-202. Robert Legvold, *Foreign Affairs* 71, no. 2 (Spring 1992): 205. Vladimir Tismaneanu, *Orbis* 36, no. 3 (Summer 1992): 473-474. J. Arch Getty, *Slavic Review* 52, no. 4 (Winter 1993): 914-915. T. R. Ravindranathan, *Canadian Journal of History = Annales canadienne d'histoire* 28, no. 3 (December 1993): 545-559.

5124. Elwood, R. C. *Inessa Armand: Revolutionary and Feminist.* Cambridge; New York, NY: Cambridge University Press, 1992. xi, 304 pp. REV: Barbara Evans Clements, *Slavic Review* 52, no. 2 (Summer 1993): 366-367. Ruth A. Dudgeon, *Russian History = Histoire russe* 20, nos. 1-4 (1993): 327-328. Beatrice Farnsworth, *American Historical Review* 98, no. 3 (June 1993): 915. Lynne Viola, *Historian* 56, no. 1 (Autumn 1993): 120-121. Adam Ulam, *New York Times Book Review* 98, no. 4 (January 24, 1993): 12ff.

5125. Friedman, Maurice. *Encounter on the Narrow Ridge: A Life of Martin Buber.* 1st ed. New York: Paragon House, 1991. xi, 496 pp. REV: Avishai Margalit, *New York Review of Books* 40, no. 18 (November 4, 1993): 66-71.

5126. Giroud, Francoise. *Alma Mahler, or The Art of Being Loved.* Translated by R. M. Stock. Oxford; New York: Oxford University Press, 1991. 162 pp. [Translation of *Alma Mahler, ou, L'art d'etre aimee.*] REV: *Publishers Weekly* 239, no. 4 (January 20, 1992): 55. Julia Moore, *Notes* 49, no. 3 (March 1993): 972-977.

5127. Gromyko, Andrei. *Memoirs.* Translated by Harold Shukman. Foreword by Henry A. Kissinger. New York: Doubleday, 1990. 414 pp. REV: George Ball, *New York Times Book Review* (April 1, 1990): 7. John C. Campbell, *Foreign Affairs* 69, no. 3 (Summer 1990): 185. Cullen Murphy, *New Republic* 202, no. 20 (May 14, 1990): 9-12. Robert Tucker, *New Republic* 202, no. 20 (May 14, 1990): 45-50. Adam B. Ulam, *National Review* 42, no. 8 (April 30, 1990): 42-43. Charles E. Ziegler, *Russian History* 17, no. 4 (Winter 1990): 482-484. Walter C. Clemens, Jr., *Soviet and Post-Soviet Review* 20, nos. 2-3 (1993): 233-239.

5128. Hughes, Lindsey. *Sophia, Regent of Russia, 1657-1704.* New Haven, CT: Yale University Press, 1990.

xvii, 345 pp. REV: David M. Goldfrank, *Canadian-American Slavic Studies* 25, nos. 1-4 (1991): 256-258. Helen S. Hundley, *Historian* 54, no. 1 (Autumn 1991): 126-127. Margaret Patoski, *History: Reviews of New Books* 20, no. 1 (Fall 1991): 34-35. Susan Groag Bell, *Women's Review of Books* 9, no. 8 (May 1992): 28-29. Robert O. Crummey, *American Historical Review* 97, no. 1 (February 1992): 250-251. Charles A. Ruud, *Canadian Journal of History = Annales canadienne d'histoire* 27, no. 2 (August 1992): 400-402. Chester Dunning, *Journal of Modern History* 65, no. 1 (March 1993): 234-235. Nancy Shields Kollmann, *Russian Review* 52, no. 2 (April 1993): 270-271. J. Eric Myles, *Canadian Slavonic Papers* 35, nos. 3-4 (September-December 1993): 397-398.

5129. Khrushchev, Sergei. *Khrushchev on Khrushchev: An Inside Account of the Man and His Era.* Edited and translated by William Taubman. 1st ed. Boston, MA: Little, Brown & Co., c1990. xiii, 423 pp. REV: Paul J. Best, *Russian History* 17, no. 4 (Winter 1990): 477-478. George W. Breslauer, *New York Times Book Review* (July 29, 1990): 10. John C. Campbell, *Foreign Affairs* 69, no. 5 (Winter 1990-1991): 198-199. Richard Ned Lebow, *Bulletin of the Atomic Scientists* 47, no. 4 (May 1991): 43-45. David Remnick, *New York Review of Books* 38, no. 21 (December 19, 1991): 72-81. Vladimir Tismaneanu, *Orbis* 35, no. 1 (Winter 1991): 146. Walter C. Clemens, Jr., *Soviet and Post-Soviet Review* 20, nos. 2-3 (1993): 233-239.

5130. Lanouette, William, and Bela Silard. *Genius in the Shadows: A Biography of Leo Szilard: The Man Behind the Bomb.* Foreword by Jonas Salk. New York: Scribner's, c1992. 587 pp. REV: Hans Bethe, *Physics Today* 46 (September 1993): 63-64. David Hafemeister, *American Journal of Physics* 61 (September 1993): 862-863. Gregg Herken, *Nature* 362, (April 15, 1993): 661. Wil Lepkowski, *Chemical & Engineering News* 71 (November 1, 1993): 42-43. Rebecca Lowen, *Bulletin of the Atomic Scientists* 49 (June 1993): 51-52. Max Perutz, *New York Review of Books* 40 (October 7, 1993): 17-20. V. V. Raman, *Physics Teacher* 31 (May 1993): 318. Silvan Schweber, *Science* 261 (September 10, 1993): 1461-1462. Dick Teresi, *New York Times Book Review* 98, no. 4 (January 24, 1993): 1ff.

5131. Laqueur, Walter. *Stalin: The Glasnost Revelations.* New York: Scribner's, c1990. xi, 382 pp. REV: David K. Shipler, *New York Times Book Review* (November 18, 1990): 3ff. Adam B. Ulam, *National Review* 42, no. 23 (December 3, 1990): 48-49. Leon Aron, *Commentary* 91, no. 4 (April 1991): 60-64. John C. Campbell, *Foreign Affairs* 70, no. 2 (Spring 1991): 192. Roger Draper, *New Leader* 74, no. 1 (January 14, 1991): 16-17. Leo Gruliow, *Antioch Review* 49, no. 2 (Spring 1991): 288-295. Harvey Klehr, *Congress Monthly* 58, no. 6 (September-October 1991): 21-23. Vladimir Tismaneanu, *Orbis* 35, no. 4 (Fall 1991): 627. Mark Von Hagen, *Nation* 252, no. 11 (March 25, 1991): 382ff. Arthur E. Adams, *Russian Review* 51, no. 2 (April 1992): 281-282. Terence Emmons, *New Republic* 206, no. 10 (March 9, 1992): 33-41. Vladimir Brovkin, *Russian History = Histoire russe* 20, nos. 1-4 (1993): 378-380.

5132. Larina, Anna. *This I Cannot Forget: The Memoirs of Nikolai Bukharin's Widow.* Introduction by Stephen F. Cohen. Translated from the Russian by Gary Kern. New York: W.W. Norton & Co., 1991. 384 pp. [Translation of: *Nezabyvaemoe.*] REV: Abraham Brumberg, *Nation* 256, no. 15 (April 19, 1993): 526-528. Robert Conquest, *New York Review of Books,* 40, no. 15 (September 23, 1993): 24-27. Irving Howe, *Dissent* 40, no. 3 (Summer 1993): 385-386. Robert Legvold, *Foreign Affairs* 72, no. 3 (Summer 1993): 206-207. W. Bruce Lincoln, *Book World* 23, no. 14 (April 4, 1993): 6ff. Harlow Loomis Robinson, *New York Times Book Review* 98, no. 12 (March 21, 1993): 1ff. Anatole Shub, *New Leader,* 76 (May 17-31, 1993): 5-6. *New Yorker* 69, no. 8 (April 12, 1993): 121. *Orbis* 37, no. 4 (Fall 1993).

5133. Macrae, Norman. *John von Neumann.* New York: Pantheon Books, 1992. x, 405 p. REV: Albert B. Stewart, *Antioch Review* 51, no. 2 (Spring 1993): 302.

5134. Morton, Marian J. *Emma Goldman and the American Left: "Nowhere at Home."* Twayne's Twentieth-Century American Biography Series, no. 14. New York: Twayne Publishers, 1992. xi, 183 pp. REV: Joyce Antler, *American Jewish Archives* 45, no. 2 (Fall-Winter 1993): 219-228.

5135. O'Connor, Timothy Edward. *The Engineer of Revolution: L.B. Krasin and the Bolsheviks, 1870-1926.* Boulder, CO: Westview Press, 1992. xix, 322 pp. REV: E. R. Zimmermann, *Canadian Journal of History = Annales canadienne d'histoire* 27, no. 3 (December 1992): 565-566. Alex G. Cummins, *Russian History = Histoire russe* 20, nos. 1-4 (1993): 348-349. Daniel Orlovsky, *American Historical Review* 98, no. 4 (October 1993): 1292. Anne Rassweiler, *Russian Review* 52, no. 3 (July 1993): 429-430. George E. Snow, *Historian* 55, no. 4 (Summer 1993): 756. Lee J. Williames, *History: Reviews of New Books* 21, no. 3 (Spring 1993): 136.

5136. Phillips, Hugh D. *Between the Revolution and the West: A Political Biography of Maxim M. Litvinov.* Boulder, CO: Westview Press, 1992. xii, 244 pp. REV: Robert H. Johnston, *Canadian Slavonic Papers* 35, nos. 1-2 (March-June 1993): 181-182. James K. Libbey, *Russian History = Histoire russe* 20, nos. 1-4 (1993): 384. Timothy E. O'Connor, *Russian Review* 52, no. 4 (October 1993): 567-568. Christine A. White, *American Historical Review* 98, no. 5 (December 1993): 1648.

5137. Pomper, Philip. *Lenin, Trotsky, and Stalin: The Intelligentsia and Power.* New York: Columbia University Press, 1990. 446 pp. REV: Barbara Evans Clements, *American Historical Review* 97, no. 2 (April 1992): 583-584. Priscilla Johnson McMillan, *Journal of Interdisciplinary History* 23, no. 1 (Summer 1992): 187-189. Vladimir Brovkin, *Slavic Review* 52, no. 3 (Fall 1993): 596-598.

5138. Radzinsky, Edvard. *The Last Tsar: The Life and Death of Nicholas II.* Translated from the Russian by Marian Schwartz. New York: Doubleday, c1992. 462 pp. [Translation of *Zhizn i smert Nikolaia II.*] REV: David Pryce-Jones, *National Review* 44, no. 21 (November 2,

1992): 58-60. S. Frederick Starr, *New York Times Book Review* (July 19, 1992): 1ff. Tatyana Tolstaya, *New York Review of Books* 39, no. 21 (December 17, 1992): 3-10. Mark Kulikowski, *Russian History = Histoire russe* 20, nos. 1-4 (1993): 320-322.

5139. Rezzori, Gregor von. *The Snows of Yesteryear: Portraits for an Autobiography.* Translated from the German by H. F. Broch de Rotherman. 1st American ed. New York: Knopf; Distributed by Random House, 1989. 290 pp. [Translation of *Blumen im Schnee.*] REV: Anne Bernays, *New York Times Book Review* 94 (November 26, 1989): 10-11. Michael Ignatieff, *New York Review of Books* 36, nos. 21-22 (January 18, 1990): 3-4. Donald G. Daviau, *World Literature Today* 65, no. 1 (Winter 1991): 112. André A. Aciman, *Salmagundi,* nos. 90-91 (Spring-Summer 1991): 33-44. Robert Dassanowsky-Harris, *Modern Austrian Literature* 26, no. 2 (1993): 190-191.

5140. Service, Robert. *Lenin, A Political Life.* Bloomington, IN: Indiana University Press, c1985-c1991. 2 vols. [Contents: Vol. 1. The Strengths of Contradiction — v. 2. Worlds in Collision.] REV: John W. McDonald, *Perspectives on Political Science* 22, no. 2 (Spring 1993): 95.

5141. Spence, Richard B. *Boris Savinkov: Renegade on the Left.* East European Monographs, no. 316. Boulder, CO: East European Monographs; New York: Distributed by Columbia University Press, 1991. v, 540 pp. REV: Michael Melancon, *Slavic Review* 51, no. 4 (Winter 1992): 813-814. Kai von Jena, *Journal of Baltic Studies* 23, no. 4 (Winter 1992): 417-419. Donald Senese, *Russian History = Histoire russe* 20, nos. 1-4 (1993): 329-330.

5142. Tucker, Robert C. *Stalin in Power: The Revolution from Above, 1929-1941.* New York: W.W. Norton, c1990. 707 pp. REV: Peter Kenez, *New Leader* 73, no. 16 (December 10-24, 1990): 23-24. David K. Shipler, *New York Times Book Review* (November 18, 1990): 3ff. John C. Campbell, *Foreign Affairs* 70, no. 3 (Summer 1991): 173-174. Vladimir Tismaneanu, *Orbis* 35, no. 3 (Summer 1991): 469. Mark Von Hagen, *Nation* 252, no. 11 (March 25, 1991): 382ff. Terence Emmons, *New Republic* 206, no. 10 (March 9, 1992): 33-41. T. R. Ravindranathan, *Canadian Journal of History = Annales canadienne d'histoire* 28, no. 3 (December 1993): 545-559.

5143. Vaksberg, Arkady. *Stalin's Prosecutor: The Life of Andrei Vyshinsky.* Translated from the Russian by Jan Butler. 1st American ed. New York: Grove Weidenfeld, 1991. xi, 374 pp. [Also published under the title *The Prosecutor and the Prey: Vyshinsky and the 1930s' Moscow Show Trials* (London: Weidenfeld and Nicolson, 1990).] REV: Arnold Beichman, *New York Times Book Review* (July 7, 1991): 25. John C. Campbell, *Foreign Affairs* 70, no. 3 (Summer 1991): 174. Jacob E. Heilbrunn, *Global Affairs,* 7, no. 2 (Spring 1992): 186-202. Vladimir Tismaneanu, *Orbis* 36, no. 1 (Winter 1992): 146-147. Eugene Huskey, *Russian History = Histoire russe* 20, nos. 1-4 (1993): 381-382.

5144. Vardy, Steven Bela. *Attila the Hun.* World Leaders Past & Present. New York: Chelsea House Publishers, 1991. 111 pp. REV: Timothy Goodwin, *Ethnic Forum*

13, no. 2/vol. 14, no. 2 (1993-1994): 161-162.

5145. Volkogonov, Dmitri. *Stalin: Triumph and Tragedy*. Edited and translated from the Russian by Harold Shukman. 1st American ed. New York: Grove Weidenfeld, 1991. xxvii, 642 pp. [Translation of *Triumfi tragediia*.] REV: Ronald Hingley, *New York Times Book Review* 96 (September 29, 1991): 9. Robert V. Legvold, *Foreign Affairs* 70, no. 5 (Winter 1991-1992): 199. Stephen J. Blank, *Parameters* 22, no. 4 (Winter 1992-1993): 118-119. Roman Brachman, *Midstream* 38, no. 1 (January 1992): 42-44. Terence Emmons, *New Republic* 206, no. 10 (March 9, 1992): 33ff. Leo Gruliow, *Antioch Review* 50, no. 3 (Summer 1992): 591. David Remnick, *New York Review of Books* 39, no. 18 (November 5, 1992): 12-17. T. R. Ravindranathan, *Canadian Journal of History = Annales canadienne d'histoire* 28, no. 3 (December 1993): 545-559. *Orbis* 37, no. 3 (Summer 1993).

5146. Walesa, Lech, and Arkadiusz Rybicki. *The Struggle and the Triumph: An Autobiography*. Translated by Franklin Philip, and Helen Mahut. 1st English-language ed. New York: Arcade, c1992. 330 pp. [Translation of *Les chemins de la democratie*; original title: *Droga do wolnoscie*.] REV: Stanislaw Baranczak, *New York Times Book Review* (November 15, 1992): 3. *Orbis* 37, no. 1 (Winter 1993).

5147. Winkler, Gershon. *They Called Her Rebbe: The Maiden of Ludomir*. New York: Judaica Press, 1991. xv, 235 pp. REV: Naomi Danis, *Lilith* 18, no. 1 (Winter 1993): 25.

Communications and the Media

5148. Goetz-Stankiewicz, Marketa, ed. *Good-bye, Samizdat: Twenty Years of Czechoslovak Underground Writing*. Foreword by Timothy Garton Ash. Evanston, IL: Northwestern University Press, 1992. xxxi, 309 pp. REV: Edward J. Czerwinski, *World Literature Today* 67, no. 3 (Summer 1993): 632-633.

5149. Taylor, Sally J. *Stalin's Apologist: Walter Duranty, The New York Times's Man in Moscow*. New York: Oxford University Press, 1990. 404 pp. REV: Francine du Plessix Gray, *New York Times Book Review* (June 24, 1990): 3. Jacob Heilbrunn, *New Leader* 73, no. 7 (April 30, 1990): 19-20. Richard Krolik, *Washington Journalism Review* 12, no. 5 (June 1990): 51. John P. Roche, *Strategic Review* 18, no. 4 (Fall 1990): 59-61. David Satter, *Orbis* 35, no. 1 (Winter 1991): 148-149. Raymond H. Anderson, *Journalism Quarterly* 69, no. 1 (Spring 1992): 218-219. Fred W. Viehe, *Ukrainian Quarterly* 49, no. 2 (Summer 1993): 204-205.

5150. Wasburn, Philo C. *Broadcasting Propaganda: International Radio Broadcasting and the Construction of Political Reality*. Praeger Series in Political Communication. Westport, CT: Praeger, 1992. xxiv, 178 pp. REV: Doris A Graber, *Political Science Quarterly* 108, no. 3 (Fall 1993): 563-565. Manfred K. Wolfram, *Journalism Quarterly* 70 (Autumn 1993): 713-714.

Emigres, Refugees, Diaspora

General

5151. Augustinos, Gerasimos. *The Greeks of Asia Minor: Confession, Community, and Ethnicity in the Nineteenth Century*. Kent, OH: Kent State University Press, c1992. x, 270 pp. REV: Charles A. Frazee, *American Historical Review* 98, no. 3 (June 1993): 904.

5152. Bedrosian, Margaret. *The Magical Pine Ring: Culture and the Imagination in Armenian-American Literature*. Detroit, MI: Wayne State University Press, c1991. 249 pp. [Includes discussion of prose writers Emmanuel Varandyan, Peter Sourian, Peter Najarian, Michael J. Arlen, Richard Hagopian, William Saroyan, and poets Diana Der Hovanessian, David Kherdian, Harold Bond, and Peter Balakian.] REV: David Stephen Calonne, *Ararat* 34, no. 2 (Spring 1993): 61-64.

5153. Bedrosian, Margaret, and Leo Hamalian, eds. *Crossroads: Short Fiction by Armenian-American Writers*. 1st ed. New York: Ashod Press, 1992. 176 pp. [Contents: W. Saroyan, "Madness in the family"; L. Surmelian, "America in my blood"; R. Hagopian, "Dove brings peace"; J. Barsamian, "Ashod's boarding house"; H. Barba, "Armenian Cowboy"; K. Kalfaian, "Juno in the pine ring"; K. Manoogian, "Everyone's got to die sometime"; L. Alishan, "Two stories"; P. Sourian, "Secret tournament"; R. Neresian, "Solstice"; A. Calin, "Green house"; M. Casey, "HHQ driver"; R. Hewsen, "Von Lievendorf papers"; P. Najarian, "Daughters of memory"; M. Krekorian, "Corridor".] REV: Diana Magarian Brown, *Ararat* 34, no. 2 (Spring 1993): 55-56.

5154. Bottomley, Gillian. *From Another Place: Migration and the Politics of Culture*. New York: Cambridge University Press, 1992. 183 pp. [Includes Greece.] REV: Katherine Betts, *International Migration Review* 27, no. 4 (Winter 1993): 899.

5155. Buenker, John D., and Lorman A. Ratner, eds. *Multiculturalism in the United States: A Comparative Guide to Acculturation and Ethnicity*. New York: Greenwood Press, c1992. vi, 271 pp. [Partial contents: Edward R. Kantowicz, "Polish-Americans," pp. 131-147; Edward Shapiro, "Jewish-Americans," pp. 149-172; John D. Buenker and Lorman A. Ratner, "Bibliographical Essay," pp. 231-258.] REV: Diana Duerler, *Ethnic Forum* 13, no. 1 (1993): 94-95. Harriet Ottenheimer, *Explorations in Sights and Sounds* 13 (Summer 1993): 15-16. Andrew Rolle, *History: Reviews of New Books* 21, no. 3 (Spring 1993): 112.

5156. Cohen, David Steven, ed. *America, the Dream of My Life: Selections from the Federal Writers' Project's New Jersey Ethnic Survey*. New Brunswick, NJ: Rutgers University Press, 1990. xvi, 295 pp. [Includes notes from interviews with Polish, Jewish, Lithuanian, Russian and Ukrainian emigres.] REV: Betty Boyd Caroli, *Journal of American Ethnic History* 12, no. 2 (Winter 1993): 66-67.

5157. Crowe, David, and John Kolsti, eds. *The Gypsies of Eastern Europe*. Introduction by Ian Hancock. Armonk, NY: M.E. Sharpe, c1991. vi, 194 pp. REV: Jiri

Lipa, *Canadian-American Slavic Studies* 26, nos. 1-4 (1992): 452-454. James Niessen, *Slavic Review* 51, no. 3 (Fall 1992): 592-594. Irina Livezeanu, *Canadian Review of Studies in Nationalism = Revue Canadienne des Etudes sur le Nationalisme* 20, nos. 1-2 (1993): 138-139. William G. Lockwood, *Contemporary Sociology* 22, no. 1 (January 1993): 49.

5158. Fainhauz, David. *Lithuanians in the USA: Aspects of Ethnic Identity*. Chicago, IL: Lithuanian Library Press, 1991. 246 pp. REV: Aleksandras Gedmintas, *Lituanus* 38, no. 2 (Summer 1992): 79-81. Stanislaus A. Blejwas, *Polish American Studies* 50, no. 2 (Autumn 1993): 111-113. William Wolkovich-Valkavicius, *Lituanus* 39, no. 4 (Winter 1993): 89-91.

5159. Foster, Edward Halsey. *William Saroyan: A Study of the Short Fiction*. Twayne's Studies in Short Fiction Series, no. 26. New York: Twayne; Toronto: Maxwell Macmillan Canada; New York: Maxwell Macmillan International, c1991. xvii, 174 pp. REV: Gerald Locklin, *Studies in Short Fiction* 30, no. 2 (Spring 1993): 199-200.

5160. Janzen, William. *Limits on Liberty: The Experience of Mennonite, Hutterite, and Doukhobor Communities in Canada*. Toronto; Buffalo, NY: University of Toronto Press, 1990. viii, 375 pp. REV: Ellen Baar, *Canadian Journal of Political Science = Revue canadienne de science politique* 24 (September 1991): 635-636. John W. Friesen, *Canadian Historical Review* 72 (June 1991): 260-261. Leo Driedger, *Mennonite Quarterly Review* 67, no. 1 (January 1993): 120-122.

5161. Karlowich, Robert A. *We Fall and Rise: Russian-Language Newspapers in New York City, 1889-1914*. Metuchen, NJ: Scarecrow Press, 1991. 332 pp. REV: Brent O. Peterson, *International Migration Review* 27, no. 1 (Spring 1993): 212.

5162. Klaassen, Walter. *The Days of Our Years: A History of the Eigenheim Mennonite Church Community: 1892-1992*. Rosthern, Sask.: Eigenheim Mennonite Church, 1992. 312 pp. [Story of a community which came from two primary colonies in the Ukraine and was later joined by others from Prussia, Minnesota and Oklahoma.] REV: Cornelius J. Dyck, *Mennonite Quarterly Review* 67, no. 1 (January 1993): 125-126. Paul Friesen, *Saskatchewan History* 45, no. 1 (Spring 1993): 42-43.

5163. Krause, Corinne Azen. *Grandmothers, Mothers and Daughters: Oral Histories of Three Generations of Ethnic American Women*. Twayne's Oral History Series, no. 6. Boston, MA: Twayne Publishers, 1991. xiv, 231 pp. REV: Donna Gabaccia, *American Jewish History* 81, no. 1 (Autumn 1993): 117-120. Virginia R. Mitchell, *Polish American Studies* 50, no. 1 (Spring 1993): 98-99.

5164. Nielsen, George R. *In Search of a Home: Nineteenth-Century Wendish Immigration*. 1st ed. College Station, TX: Texas A&M University Press, 1989. xiv, 213 pp. [An earlier version of this book was published as *In Search of a Home: The Wends (Sorbs) on the Australian and Texas Frontier*.] REV: James S. Pula, *Journal of American Ethnic History* 12, no. 2 (Winter 1993): 86.

5165. Noble, Allen G., ed. *To Build in a New Land: Ethnic Landscapes in North America*. Creating the North American Landscape. Baltimore, MD: Johns Hopkins University Press, c1992. x, 455 pp. [Partial contents: Allen G. Noble, "Migration to North America: Before, During and After the Nineteenth Century," pp. 3-25; Allen G. Noble, "German-Russian Mennonites in Manitoba," pp. 268-284; John E. Rau, "Czechs in South Dakota," pp. 285-306; John C. Lehr, "Ukrainians in Western Canada," pp. 309-330.] REV: James P. Allen, *Geographical Review* 83, no. 3 (July 1993): 345-346. Tyrel G. Moore, *Professional Geographer* 45, no. 3 (August 1993): 378.

5166. Organisation for Economic Co-operation and Development. *Trends in International Migration: Continuous Reporting System on Migration*. Paris: OECD, 1992. 157 pp. [Part I includes case study of Germany and the former Yugoslavia; Part III concerns East-West and intraregional migration, including Hungary, Poland, and the former Czechoslovakia.] REV: M.P.T., *Population and Development Review* 19, no. 2 (June 1993): 394-395.

5167. Reimers, David M. *Still the Golden Door: The Third World Comes to America*. 2nd ed. New York: Columbia University Press, 1992. xii, 362 pp. REV: Stephen J. Valone, *Polish American Studies* 50, no. 2 (Autumn 1993): 120-121.

5168. Salo, Matt T., ed. *100 Years of Gypsy Studies: Papers from the 10th Annual Meeting of the Gypsy Lore Society, North American Chapter, March 25-27, 1988, Wagner College, Staten Island, New York, Commemorating the Centennial of the Gypsy Lore Society*. Section editors Victor A. Friedman, Carol Silverman, and Anita Volland. Publication, no. 5. Cheverly, MD: The Society, 1990. 286 pp. REV: Katherine Livingston, *Science* 249 (August 17, 1990): 809. Ruth E. Andersen, *Journal of American Folklore* 106, no. 422 (Fall 1993): 508-510.

5169. Saroyan, William. *Armenian Trilogy*. Edited with an introductory essay and glossary by Dickran Kouymjian. Fresno, CA: Press at California State University, 1986. ix, 195 pp. REV: H. Aram Veeser, *Ararat* 34, no. 2 (Spring 1993): 67-72.

5170. ———. *The Man with the Heart in the Highlands & Other Early Stories*. New York: New Directions, 1989. x, 144 pp. REV: Gerald Locklin, *Studies in Short Fiction* 30, no. 2 (Spring 1993): 199-200.

5171. ———. *Warsaw Visitor; Tales from the Vienna Streets: The Last Two Plays of William Saroyan*. Edited and introduction by Dickran Kouymjian. Fresno, CA: Press at California State University, Fresno, 1991. ix, 213 pp. REV: H. Aram Veeser, *Ararat* 34, no. 2 (Spring 1993): 67-72.

5172. Scheffel, David. *In the Shadow of the Antichrist: The Old Believers in Alberta*. Peterborough, Ontario; Lewiston, NY: Broadview Press, 1991. xvii, 252 pp. REV: Peter Holquist, *Slavic Review* 52, no. 4 (Winter 1993): 915-

916. Thomas Robbins, *Journal for the Scientific Study of Religion* 32, no. 4 (December 1993): 420-421.

5173. Sigel, Roberta S., ed. *Political Learning in Adulthood: A Sourcebook of Theory and Research.* Chicago, IL: University of Chicago Press, 1989. xvi, 483 pp. REV: James M. Carlson, *Political Psychology* 14, no. 2 (June 1993): 374-378.

5174. Sigel, Roberta S., and Marilyn Hoskin, eds. *Education for Democratic Citizenship: A Challenge for Multi-Ethnic Societies.* Hillsdale, NJ: Erlbaum Associates, 1991. vi, 226 pp. [Papers presented at a conference sponsored by the Spencer Foundation of Chicago.] REV: James M. Carlson, *Political Psychology* 14, no. 2 (June 1993): 374-378.

5175. Wolkovich-Valkavicius, William. *Lithuanian Fraternalism: 75 Years of U.S. Knights of Lithuania.* Brooklyn, NY: The Knights, c1988. xix, 303 pp. REV: Karel D. Bicha, *Journal of American Ethnic History* 10, nos. 1-2 (Fall 1990-Winter 1991): 134-135. Alfred Erich Senn, *Catholic Historical Review* 79, no. 2 (April 1993): 368-369.

5176. ———. *Lithuanian Religious Life in America: A Compendium of 150 Roman Catholic Parishes and Institutions.* Norwood, MA: Lithuanian Religious Life in America; W. Bridgewater, MA: Distributed by Corporate Fulfillment Systems, 1991-. vols. [Partial contents: Vol. 1 Eastern United States.] REV: Stanislaus A. Blejwas, *Polish American Studies* 50, no. 1 (Spring 1993): 91-96. Alfred Erich Senn, *Catholic Historical Review* 79, no. 2 (April 1993): 368-369.

Jews

5177. Avni, Haim. *Argentina & the Jews: A History of Jewish Immigration.* Translated from the Hebrew by Gila Brand. Judaic Studies Series. Tuscaloosa, AL: University of Alabama Press, c1991. xvii, 267 pp. [Translation of *Mi-bitul ha-Inkvizitsyah ve-'ad "Hok ha shevut".* Published in cooperation with the American Jewish Archives.] REV: David Sheinin, *American Jewish History* 81, no. 1 (Autumn 1993): 128-130.

5178. Baumel, Judith Tydor. *Unfulfilled Promise: Rescue and Resettlement of Jewish Refugee Children in the United States, 1934-1945.* Juneau, AK: Denali Press, c1990. x, 228 pp. [Discusses Holocaust-era refugees in the United States.] REV: Rafael Medoff, *American Jewish History* 81, no. 1 (Autumn 1993): 120-124. Marianne Sanua, *Journal of American Ethnic History* 12, no. 2 (Winter 1993): 83-84.

5179. Boyarin, Jonathan. *Polish Jews in Paris: The Ethnography of Memory.* The Modern Jewish Experience. Bloomington, IN: Indiana University Press, c1991. x, 195 pp. REV: Kenneth Brown, *American Anthropologist* 95, no. 1 (March 1993): 239-240. Iwona Irwin-Zarecka, *Contemporary Sociology* 22, no. 4 (July 1993): 600.

5180. Brecher, Frank W. *Reluctant Ally: United States Foreign Policy toward the Jews from Wilson to Roosevelt.* Contributions in Political Science, Global Perspectives in History and Politics, no. 278. New York: Greenwood Press, 1991. xvii, 168 pp. REV: Monty Noam Penkower, *American Jewish History* 81, no. 1 (Autumn 1993): 124-127.

5181. Eisenstadt, S. N. *Jewish Civilization: The Jewish Historical Experience in a Comparative Perspective.* SUNY Series in Israeli Studies. Albany, NY: State University of New York Press, c1992. ix, 314 pp. [Includes chapters "Modern Jewish Historical Experience in Eastern Europe" and "The Two Poles: The Holocaust and Heterogeneity of Jewish Experience".] REV: Leah R. Baer, *Middle East Studies Association Bulletin* 27, no. 2 (December 1993): 256. M. Herbert Danzger, *Contemporary Sociology* 22, no. 6 (November 1993): 827.

5182. Feingold, Henry L., general ed. *The Jewish People in America.* Authors: Eli Faber, Hasia R. Diner, Gerald Sorin, and Edward S. Shapiro. Baltimore, MD: The Johns Hopkins University Press, [1992]. 5 vols. [Contents: Vol. 1. A time for planting: the first migration, 1654-1820, by Eli Faber — v. 2. A time for gathering: the second migration, 1820-1880, by Hasia R. Diner — v. 3. A time for building: the third migration, 1880-1920, by Gerald Sorin — v. 4. A time for searching: entering mainstream, 1920-1945 — v. 5. A time for healing: American Jewry since World War II, by Edward S. Shapiro.] REV: Scott Heller, *Chronicle of Higher Education* 39, no. 13 (November 18, 1992): A8-A10. Beth Levine, *Publishers Weekly* 239, no. 35 (August 3, 1992): 20. Naomi W. Cohen, *Congress Monthly* 60, no. 1 (January 1993): 18-19. Jonathan Hartman, *Ethnic Forum* 13, no. 2/ vol. 14, no. 2 (1993-1994): 148. Gershon David Hundert, *Canadian Journal of History = Annales canadienne d'histoire* 28, no. 3 (December 1993): 620.

5183. Fishman, Sylvia Barack, ed. *Follow My Footprints: Changing Images of Women in American Jewish Fiction.* Brandeis Series in American Jewish History, Culture, and Life. Hanover, NH: University Press of New England for Brandeis University Press, c1992. xv, 506 pp. [Begins with section entitled "The Eastern European Milieu".] REV: R.K. [Rachel Kadish], *Lilith* 18, no. 2 (Spring 1993): 34-35.

5184. Friesel, Evyatar. *Atlas of Modern Jewish History.* Rev. from the Hebrew ed. Studies in Jewish History. New York: Oxford University Press, 1990. 1 atlas. [Rev. and translated ed. of *Atlas Karta le-toldot 'Am Yisra'el ba-zeman he-hadash.*] REV: Paul Robert Magocsi, *Studies in Contemporary Jewry* 11 (1993): 265-267.

5185. Gay, Ruth. *The Jews of Germany: A Historical Portrait.* Introduction by Peter Gay. New Haven, CT: Yale University Press, 1992. xiii, 297 pp. REV: Jerry Z.Muller, *Commentary* 95, no. 3 (March 1993): 61-62. Pamela Spence Richards, *Library Quarterly* 63, no. 3 (July 1993): 396. Irwin M. Wall, *Central European History* 26, no. 2 (1993): 238.

5186. Glenn, Susan A. *Daughters of the Shtetl: Life and Labor in the Immigrant Generation.* Ithaca, NY: Cornell University Press, 1990. 312 pp. REV: Neil M. Cowan, *American Jewish History* 80, no. 3 (Spring 1991): 425-427. Hasia R. Diner, *Journal of American History* 78, no. 2

(September 1991): 706. Sonya Michel, *American Historical Review* 96, no. 5 (December 1991): 1624-1625. Alison Gardy, *Lilith* 17, no. 1 (Winter 1992): 28ff. Noel J. Kent, *Explorations in Sights and Sounds* (annual review supplement to *Explorations in Ethnic Studies*), no. 12 (Summer 1992): 25-26. Deborah Dash Moore, *International Migration Review* 26, no. 3 (Fall 1992): 1018. Joyce Antler, *American Jewish Archives* 45, no. 2 (Fall-Winter 1993): 219-228. Ruth Schwartz Cowan, *Journal of American Ethnic History* 12, no. 2 (Winter 1993): 81-83. Ruth Milkman, *Signs* 18, no. 2 (Winter 1993): 376-388.

5187. Gold, Steven J. *Refugee Communities: A Comparative Field Study.* Sage Series on Race and Ethnic Relations, v. 4. Newbury Park, CA: Sage Publications, c1992. xiv, 256 pp. [Comparative study of Vietnamese and Soviet Jewish refugees.] REV: Janet E. Benson, *Explorations in Sights and Sounds* 13 (Summer 1993): 29-30. Madeleine Tress, *International Migration Review* 27, no. 2 (Summer 1993): 431. Mary C. Waters, *Social Forces* 71, no. 3 (March 1993): 829.

5188. Helmreich, William B. *Against All Odds: Holocaust Survivors and the Successful Lives They Made in America.* New York, NY: Simon & Schuster, c1992. 348 pp. REV: Stephen J. Whitfield, *New Leader* 75, no. 16 (December 14-28, 1992): 15-16. Deborah E. Lipstadt, *American Historical Review* 98, no. 5 (December 1993): 1701. Edward S. Shapiro, *Congress Monthly* 60, no. 4 (May-June 1993): 21-22.

5189. Hyman, Harold M. *Oleander Odyssey: The Kempners of Galveston, Texas, 1854-1980s.* Kenneth E. Montague Series in Oil and Business History, no. 6. College Station, TX: Texas A&M University Press, 1990. xxi, 486. [Story of five generations of Kempner family begins with H. Kempner, who emigrated to America from Poland to avoid service in the Russian army.] REV: Natalie Ornish, *American Jewish Archives* 45, no. 1 (Spring-Summer 1993): 116-188.

5190. *Jewish Hometown Associations and Family Circles in New York: The WPA Yiddish Writers' Group Study.* Edited with an introduction and afterword by Hannah Kliger. The Modern Jewish Experience. Bloomington: Indiana University Press, c1992. 164 pp. ["The WPA's 'Jewish *landsmanshaftn* and family circles in New York' ".] REV: Benny Kraut, *History: Reviews of New Books* 21, no. 4 (Summer 1993): 155.

5191. Perlman, Robert. *Bridging Three Worlds: Hungarian-Jewish Americans, 1848-1914.* Amherst: University of Massachusetts Press, c1991. 302 pp. REV: Donna Gabaccia, *Journal of American History* 79, no. 1 (June 1992): 268-269. Sydney Stahl Weinberg, *American Historical Review* 98, no. 1 (February 1993): 258-259.

5192. Robinson, Ira, Pierre Anctil, and Mervin Butovsky, eds. *An Everyday Miracle: Yiddish Culture in Montreal.* [Montreal]: Vehicule Press; St. Paul, MN: U.S. Distributor, Bookslinger, c1990. 169 pp. REV: David Rome, *American Jewish Archives* 45, no. 1 (Spring-Summer 1993): 109-111.

5193. Ro'i, Yaacov. *The Struggle for Soviet Jewish Emigration, 1948-1967.* Soviet and East European Studies, 75. Cambridge; New York: Cambridge University Press, 1991. xvii, 458 pp. REV: David L. Williams, *History: Reviews of New Books* 21, no. 1 (Fall 1992): 31. Alexandra S. Korros, *Russian Review* 52, no. 3 (July 1993): 434-435. Robert Weinberg, *American Historical Review* 98, no. 3 (June 1993): 911.

5194. Sachar, Howard M. *A History of the Jews in America.* New York: Knopf, c1992. xiv, 1051 pp. REV: William L. O'Neill, *New York Times Book Review* 97 (June 28, 1992): 29. *Publishers Weekly* 239, no. 14 (March 16, 1992): 68. Egal Feldman, *Journal of American History* 80, no. 1 (June 1993): 236. Jeffrey S. Gurock, *American Historical Review* 98, no. 3 (June 1993): 934. John Livingston, *History: Reviews of New Books* 21, no. 3 (Spring 1993): 111. Glenn Sharfman, *Historian* 56, no. 1 (Autumn 1993): 178-179. Gerald Sorin, *Reviews in American History* 21 (June 1993): 190-194.

5195. Salitan, Laurie P. *Politics and Nationality in Contemporary Soviet Jewish Emigration, 1968-89.* New York: St. Martin's Press, 1992. 180 pp. REV: Zvi Gitelman, *Political Science Quarterly* 107, no. 4 (Winter 1992-1993): 781. Robert O. Freedman, *Slavic Review* 52, no. 1 (Spring 1993): 150-151.

5196. Sanders, Ronald. *Shores of Refuge: A Hundred Years of Jewish Emigration.* 1st ed. New York, NY: Holt, c1988. xiii, 673 pp. REV: John D. Klier, *Nationalities Papers* 21, no. 2 (Fall 1993): 252-253.

5197. Schwartz, Laurens R. *Jews and the American Revolution: Haym Salomon and Others.* Foreword by Arno Penzias. Jefferson, NC: McFarland, 1987. xiii, 172 pp. REV: Christopher Neil Fritsch, *Polish American Studies* 50, no. 1 (Spring 1993): 98.

5198. Wertheimer, Jack. *Unwelcome Strangers: East European Jews in Imperial Germany.* Studies in Jewish History. New York: Oxford University Press, 1987. ix, 275 pp. REV: Michael Berkowitz, *Nationalities Papers* 21, no. 2 (Fall 1993): 247-249.

Poles

5199. Galazka, Jacek, and Albert Juszczak. *Polish Heritage Travel Guide to U.S.A. & Canada.* Cornwell Bridge, CT: Polish Heritage Publications; New York, NY: Distributed by Hippocrene Books, 1992. xvi, 246 pp. REV: James S. Pula, *Polish American Studies* 50, no. 1 (Spring 1993): 97.

5200. Gladsky, Thomas S. *Princes, Peasants, and Other Polish Selves: Ethnicity in American Literature.* Amherst, MA: University of Massachusetts Press, c1992. ix, 313 pp. REV: Barbara Tepa Lupack, *American Literature* (June 1993): 392-393.

5201. Nowakowski, Jacek, ed. *Polish-American Ways.* 1st ed. New York: Perennial Library, c1989. 156 pp. REV: Michael A. Guzik, *Polish American Studies* 50, no. 2 (Autumn 1993): 120.

5202. Pacyga, Dominic A. *Polish Immigrants and Industrial Chicago: Workers on the South Side, 1880-1922.* Urban Life and Urban Landscape Series. Columbus, OH: Ohio State University Press, 1991. xiv, 298 pp. REV: Victor Greene, *Journal of American History* 80, no. 1 (June 1993): 288. Joseph J. Parot, *American Historical Review* 98, no. 1 (February 1993): 263-264.

5203. Pienkos, Donald E. *For Your Freedom through Ours: Polish-American Efforts on Poland's Behalf, 1863-1991.* East European Monographs, no. 311. Boulder, CO: East European Monographs; NY: Distributed by Columbia University Press, 1991. 620 pp. REV: Dominic A. Pacyga, *Journal of American Ethnic History* (June 1993): 97-98.

5204. Pula, James S., and Eugene E. Dziedzic. *United We Stand: The Role of Polish Workers in the New York Mills Textile Strikes, 1912 and 1916.* East European Monographs, no. 286. Boulder, CO: East European Monographs; NY: Distributed by Columbia University Press, 1990. 296 pp. REV: William G. Falkowski, Jr., *Journal of American History* 78, no. 2 (September 1991): 712. Stanislaus A. Blejwas, *Polish Review* 37, no. 1 (1992): 111-113. Dominic Pacyga, *Polish American Studies* 49, no. 1 (1992): 87-88. Joseph J. Parot, *International Migration Review* 27, no. 1 (Spring 1993): 211-212.

5205. Radzilowski, John, and Jennifer Mahal. *Out on the Wind: Poles and Danes in Lincoln County, Minnesota, 1880-1905.* Marshall, MN: Crossings Press, c1992. x, 126 pp. REV: Maureen A. Harp, *Agricultural History* 347, no. 1 (Winter 1993): 92-94. Dennis Kolinski, *Polish American Studies* 50, no. 1 (Spring 1993): 85-88. David L. Smith, *Polish Review* 38, no. 3 (1993): 335-337.

5206. Wytrwal, Joseph A. *The Polish Experience in Detroit.* 1st ed. Detroit, MI: Endurance Press, 1992. x, 538 pp. REV: Earl Boyea, *Catholic Historical Review* (April 1993): 367-368. Frank Renkiewicz, *International Migration Review* 27, no. 3 (Fall 1993): 651-652.

Russians

5207. Hassell, James E. *Russian Refugees in France and the United States Between the World Wars.* Transactions of the American Philosophical Society, v. 81, pt. 7. Philadelphia, PA: American Philosophical Society, 1991. vii, 96 pp. REV: Robert H. Johnson, *Canadian-American Slavic Studies* 25, nos. 1-4 (1991): 330-331. Wayne S. Vucinich, *Russian History = Histoire russe* 20, nos. 1-4 (1993): 353-354.

5208. Raeff, Marc. *Russia Abroad: A Cultural History of the Russian Emigration, 1919-1939.* New York: Oxford University Press, 1990. viii, 239 pp. REV: Josephine Woll, *New York Times Book Review* (April 29, 1990): 21. William Richardson, *Historian* 54, no. 1 (Autumn 1991): 136-137. Alfred Erich Senn, *American Historical Review* 96, no. 5 (December 1991): 1586. Robert C. Williams, *Russian Review* 50, no. 1 (January 1991): 112-113. T. R. Ravindranathan, *International History Review* 14, no. 2

(May 1992): 397-399. Brian J. Horowitz, *Slavic and East European Journal* 37, no. 3 (Fall 1993): 371-379. Donald Senese, *Canadian American Slavic Studies = Revue Canadienne Américaine d'Etudes Slaves* 27, nos. 1-4 (1993): 404-406.

5209. Swerdlow, Max. *Brother Max: Labour Organizer and Educator.* Edited by Gregory S. Kealey. St. John's Nfld.: Committee on Canadian Labour History, c1990. xv, 128 pp. REV: Gordon Hak, *Canadian Historical Review* 74, no. 1 (March 1993): 134-135.

Ukrainians

5210. Goa, David J., ed. *The Ukrainian Religious Experience: Traditions and the Canadian Cultural Context.* Edmonton: Canadian Institute of Ukrainian Studies, 1989. xiv, 243 pp. [Based on a conference held March, 1986, at the University of Alberta.] REV: Charles Frazee, *Church History* 62, no. 1 (March 1993).

5211. Hryniuk, Stella, and Lubomyr Luciuk, eds. *Canada's Ukrainians: Negotiating an Identity.* Toronto, Ontario; Buffalo, NY: published in association with the Ukrainian Canadian Centennial Committee by University of Toronto Press, c1991. 510 pp. REV: Jean Burnet, *Canadian Historical Review* 74, no. 4 (December 1993): 646-649.

5212. Kuropas, Myron B. *The Ukrainian Americans: Roots and Aspirations, 1884-1954.* Toronto, Ontario; Buffalo, NY: University of Toronto Press, c1991. xxvii, 534 pp. REV: June Granatir Alexander, *American Historical Review* 97, no. 2 (April 1992): 629. Ralph S. Clem, *Contemporary Sociology* 21, no. 3 (May 1992): 339-340. James E. Mace, *International Migration Review* 26, no. 3 (Fall 1992): 1017. Bohdan C. Procko, *Journal of American History* 79, no. 2 (September 1992): 681. Lubomyr R. Wynar, *Ethnic Forum* 12, no. 2 (1992): 94-96. Patricia A. Krafcik, *Pacific Northwest Quarterly* 84, no. 1 (January 1993): 37. Lubomyr Luciuk, *Canadian Review of Studies in Nationalism = Revue Canadienne des Etudes sur le Nationalisme* 20, nos. 1-2 (1993): 167-168. Frances Swyripa, *Canadian Historical Review* 74, no. 1 (March 1993): 151-153.

5213. Martynowych, Orest T. *Ukrainians in Canada: The Formative Period, 1891-1924.* Edmonton, Alberta: Canadian Institute of Ukrainian Studies Press, University of Alberta, 1991. xxvi, 562 pp. REV: M. Mark Stolarik, *Histoire sociale = Social History* 25, no. 50 (November 1992): 425-426. Lubomyr Luciuk, *Canadian Historical Review* 74, no. 1 (March 1993): 153-155. Bohdan P. Procko, *American Historical Review* 98, no. 3 (June 1993): 982.

5214. Subtelny, Orest. *Ukrainians in North America: An Illustrated History.* Toronto, Ontario; Buffalo, NY: University of Toronto Press, c1991. xii, 283 pp. REV: Jars Balan, *Canadian Literature*, no. 136 (Spring 1993): 129-130. Jean Burnet, *Canadian Historical Review* 74, no. 4 (December 1993): 646-649. Lubomyr R. Wynar, *Ethnic Forum* 13, no. 2/vol. 14, no. 2 (1993-1994): 143-148.

Libraries and Library Science

5215. Kimmage, Dennis, comp. and ed. *Russian Libraries in Transition: An Anthology of Glasnost Literature*. Jefferson, NC: McFarland, c1992. 214 pp. REV: Marianna Tax Choldin, *Slavic Review* 51, no. 4 (Winter 1992): 840-842. Robert H. Burger, *College & Research Libraries* 54, no. 2 (March 1993): 184-185. Tatjana Lorkovic, *Libraries & Culture* 28, no. 4 (Fall 1993): 484-486.

Numismatics and Philately

5216. Julian, R. W. *Russian Silver Coinage, 1795-1917*. [Logansport, IN]: [R.W. Julian], n.a. REV: *Numismatist* 106, no. 11 (November 1993): 1591.

Slavic and East European Studies in the West

5217. Diamond, Sigmund. *Compromised Campus: The Collaboration of Universities with the Intelligence Community, 1945-1955*. New York: Oxford University Press, 1992. ix, 371 pp. [Includes Russian studies programs at Harvard and Yale.] REV: Richard Gid Powers, *New York Times Book Review* (June 21, 1992): 9-10. Ellen Schrecker, *Nation* 255, no. 1 (July 6, 1992): 22-24. Maurice Isserman, *American Historical Review* 98, no. 3 (June 1993): 977. Jordan E. Kurland, *Slavic Review* 52, no. 1 (Spring 1993): 116-121. John S. Whitehead, *Journal of American History* 80, no. 1 (June 1993): 333.

5218. Laqueur, Walter. *Thursday's Child Has Far to Go: A Memoir of the Journeying Years*. New York: Charles Scribner's Sons; Toronto: Maxwell Macmillan Canada; New York: Maxwell Macmillan International, c1992. xiv, 418 pp. REV: Edith Kurzweil, *Partisan Review* 60, no. 2 (Spring 1993): 289. Ernst Pawel, *Book World* 23, no. 5 (January 31, 1993): 4-5. Irwin Wall, *Central European History* 26, no. 3 (1993): 359-361.

Travel and Description

5219. Akchurin, Marat. *Red Odyssey: A Journey through the Soviet Republics*. 1st ed. New York: HarperCollins, c1992. viii, 406 pp. REV: Robert Legvold, *Foreign Affairs* 71, no. 4 (Fall 1992): 211. *Orbis* 37, no. 2 (Spring 1993).

5220. Anderson, Marian. *My Lord, What a Morning: An Autobiography*. Introduction by Nellie Y. McKay. Wisconsin Studies in American Autobiography, Madison, WI: University of Wisconsin Press, c1992. xxxiii, 314 pp. [Originally published (New York: Viking, 1956). Includes author's concert trip to the Soviet Union.] REV: Catherine Udall Turley, *Explorations in Sights and Sounds* 13 (Summer 1993): 14.

5221. Freeman, John, photographer. *Moscow Revealed*. Text by Kathleen Berton. 1st ed. New York: Abbeville Press, c1991. 221 pp. REV: William C. Brumfield, *Journal of the Society of Architectural Historians* 52, no. 1 (March 1993): 107-109.

5222. Grudzinska Gross, Irena. *The Scar of Revolution: Custine, Tocqueville, and the Romantic Imagi-

nation*. Berkeley, CA: University of California Press, c1991. xv, 191 pp. REV: Harvey Mitchell, *Canadian-American Slavic Studies* 27, nos. 1-4 (1993): 335-337. Norman E. Saul, *Russian History = Histoire russe* 20, nos. 1-4 (1993): 289-290. James T. Schleifer, *American Historical Review* (February 1993): 154-155. Andrzej W. Tymowski, *Polish Review* 37, no. 3 (1992): 366-369. Judith Zimmerman, *Russian Review* 52, no. 1 (January 1993): 113.

5223. Leighton, Ralph. *Tuva or Bust! Richard Feynman's Last Journey*. New York: W.W. Norton, c1991. 254 pp. REV: Ruth I. Meserve, *Mongolian Studies* 16 (1993): 99-100.

5224. MacLean, Rory. *Stalin's Nose: Travels Around the Bloc*. 1st U.S. ed. Boston, MA: Little, Brown & Co., c1992. 233 pp. REV: Jonathan Yardley, *Book World* 23, no. 4 (January 24, 1993): 3.

5225. Magris, Claudio. *Danube: A Journey through the Landscape, History and Culture of Central Europe*. Translated from the Italian by Patrick Creagh. 1st American ed. New York: Farrar, Straus & Giroux, 1989. 416 pp. [Translation of *Danubio*.] REV: Michael Ignatieff, *New York Review of Books* 36, no. 21-22 (January 18, 1990): 3-4. John P. Spielman, *Germanic Review* 67, no. 4 (Fall 1992): 189. Karl A. Roider, Jr., *Austrian History Yearbook* 24 (1993): 228-229.

5226. Neiman, Susan. *Slow Fire: Jewish Notes from Berlin*. New York: Schocken Books, c1992. x, 306 pp. REV: *Publishers Weekly* 239, no. 4 (January 20, 1992): 55. Kathy Sillman, *Lilith* 18, no. 2 (Spring 1993): 32.

5227. Richards, Susan. *Epics of Everyday Life: Encounters in a Changing Russia*. New York: Viking, 1991. xiv, 366 pp. REV: David Gurevich, *New York Times Book Review* (July 14, 1991): 13. Ben Eklof, *Slavic Review* 52, no. 3 (Fall 1993): 624-626.

5228. Sourian, Peter. *At the French Embassy in Sofia: Essays & Criticism*. 1st ed. New York: Ashod Press, c1992. 253 pp. REV: Hagop Missak Merjian, *Ararat* 34, no. 2 (Spring 1993): 58-60.

■ Anthropology, Ethnology, Archaeology

5229. Balzer, Marjorie Mandelstam, ed. *Shamanism: Soviet Studies of Traditional Religion in Siberia and Central Asia*. Armonk, NY: M.E. Sharpe, c1990. xviii, 197 pp. REV: Bruce Grant, *Canadian Slavonic Papers* 33, no. 1 (March 1991): 89-90. Demitri B. Shimkin, *Anthropological Quarterly* 64, no. 1 (January 1991): 45-47. Helen S. Hundley, *Russian Review* 51, no. 2 (April 1992): 293-294. Henry N. Michael, *Canadian American Slavic Studies = Revue Canadienne Américaine d'Etudes Slaves* 27, nos. 1-4 (1993): 409-412.

5230. Chernykh, E. N. *Ancient Metallurgy in the USSR: The Early Metal Age*. Translated from the Russian by Sarah Wright. New Studies in Archaeology. New York: Cambridge University Press, 1992. xxiii, 335 pp. REV:

Robert Maddin, *Slavic Review* 52, no. 4 (Winter 1993): 902-904.

5231. Dexter, Miriam Robbins. *Whence the Goddesses: A Source Book.* 1st ed. Athene Series, New York: Pergamon Press, 1990. xi, 280 pp. [Partial contents: "Latvian and Lithuanian goddesses," pp. 53-59; "Ancient Slavic goddesses," pp. 61-67.] REV: Deborah Ann Light, *Ms.* 1 (September-October 1990): 27. Edgar C. Polomé, *Journal of Indo-European Studies* 21, nos. 1-2 (Spring-Summer 1993): 175-176.

5232. Hubbs, Joanna. *Mother Russia: The Feminism Myth in Russian Culture.* Bloomington, IN: Indiana University Press, c1988. 302 pp. REV: Nancy Shields Kollmann, *Slavic Review* 49, no. 4 (Winter 1990): 648-649. Eve Levin, *American Historical Review* 95, no. 5 (December 1990): 1585-1586. Richard Morris, *American Anthropologist* 92, no. 2 (June 1990): 529-530. Maureen Perrie, *Russian Review* 49, no. 3 (July 1990): 334-335. Dianne E. Farrell, *Signs* 17, no. 1 (Autumn 1991): 236ff. Adele Barker, *Canadian American Slavic Studies = Revue Canadienne Américaine d'Etudes Slaves* 27, nos. 1-4 (1993): 341-343.

5233. Ivanits, Linda J. *Russian Folk Belief.* Foreword by Felix J. Oinas. Designed and illustrated by Sophie Schiller. Armonk, NY: M.E. Sharpe, c1989. 257 pp. REV: J. Gregg, *Choice* (January 1990): 806. Robert B. Klymasz, *Canadian Slavonic Papers* 32, no. 1 (March 1990): 101-102. Natalie K. Moyle, *Slavic and East European Journal* 34, no. 1 (Spring 1990): 127-128. Joanna Hubbs, *Slavic Review* 50, no. 1 (Spring 1991): 206-207. Stephen C. Hutchings, *Russian Review* 50, no. 1 (January 1991): 90-91. Richard A. Morris, *American Anthropologist* 93, no. 2 (June 1991): 467. Adele Barker, *Canadian American Slavic Studies = Revue Canadienne Américaine d'Etudes Slaves* 27, nos. 1-4 (1993): 346-348.

5234. Miller, Frank J. *Folklore for Stalin: Russian Folklore and Pseudofolklore of the Stalin Era.* Studies of the Harriman Institute, Armonk, NY: M.E. Sharpe, c1990. xiv, 192 pp. REV: Joseph L. Conrad, *Russian History* 18, no. 2 (Summer 1991): 245-247. Joanna Hubbs, *Harvard Ukrainian Studies* 16, nos. 1-2 (June 1992): 211-212. Natalie Kononenko, *Canadian American Slavic Studies = Revue Canadienne Américaine d'Etudes Slaves* 27, nos. 1-4 (1993): 397-398. Kathleen Parthé, *Russian Review* 52, no. 1 (January 1993): 116-117.

5235. Molokhovets, Elena. *Classic Russian Cooking: Elena Molokhovets' A Gift to Young Housewives.* Translated, introduced and annotated by Joyce Toomre. Indiana-Michigan Series in Russian and East European Studies, Bloomington, IN: Indiana University Press, c1992. xiii, 680 pp. REV: Eve Levin, *Russian History = Histoire russe* 20, nos. 1-4 (1993): 268-269. Tatyana Tolstaya, trans. Jamey Gambrell, *New York Review of Books* 40, no. 17 (October 21, 1993): 24-26.

5236. Okely, Judith, and Helen Callaway, eds. *Anthropology and Autobiography.* London; New York: Routledge, 1992. xiv, 252 pp. [Articles from a 1989 Conference on Anthropology and Autobiography, held at the University of York, England. Includes Okely's account of fieldwork among Gypsies and Margaret Kenna's studies from her research on a Greek island.] REV: Daniel M. Schores, *International Social Science Review* 68, no. 2 (Spring 1993): 83-84.

5237. Tringham, Ruth, and Dusan Krstic, eds. *Selevac: A Neolithic Village in Yugoslavia.* Monumenta Archaeologica (University of California, Los Angeles. Institute of Archaeology), v. 15. Los Angeles, CA: Institute of Archaeology, University of California, 1990. xii, 712 pp. REV: Brad Bartel, *American Antiquity* 58, no. 3 (July 1993): 590.

■ Culture and the Arts

General

5238. Anderson, Mark M. *Kafka's Clothes: Ornament and Aestheticism in the Habsburg Fin de Siècle.* Oxford: Clarendon Press; New York: Oxford University Press, 1992. 231 pp. REV: John D. Barlow, *American Scholar* 62, no. 4 (Autumn 1993): 614-616.

5239. Borisova, Elena A., and Grigory Sternin. *Russian Art Nouveau.* New York: Rizzoli, 1988. 400 pp. [Translation of *Art nouveau russe* (Paris: Editions du Regard, c1987).] REV: Mary Ann Szporluk, *Russian Literature Triquarterly*, no. 23 (1990): 425. William C. Brumfield, *Journal of the Society of Architectural Historians* 52 (March 1993): 107-109.

5240. Brumfield, William C., and Milos M. Velimirovich, eds. *Christianity and the Arts in Russia.* Cambridge; New York: Cambridge University Press, 1991. xv, 172, 95 pp. [Volume is based on essays presented at a symposium, held in May 1988 at the Library of Congress. Contents: Edward V. Williams, "Aural icons of Orthodoxy: the sonic typology of Russian bells"; Tatiana Vladyshevskaia, "On the links between music and icon painting in medieval Rus"; Natalia Teteriatnikov, "The role of the devotional image in the religious life of pre-Mongol Rus"; Kenneth Levy, "The Slavic reception of Byzantine Chant"; Alison Hilton, "Piety and pragmatism: Orthodox saints and Slavic nature gods in Russian folk art"; Margarita Mazo, "'We don't summon spring in the summer': traditional music and beliefs of the contemporary Russian village"; Richard F. Taruskin, "Christian themes in Russian opera"; William C. Brumfield, "The 'New style' and the revival of Orthodox Church architecture"; Vladimir Morosan, "Liturgical singing or sacred music? : understanding the aesthetic of the New Russian choral school"; Robert L. Nichols, "The icon and the machine in Russia's religious renaissance, 1900-1909"; John E. Bowlt, "Orthodoxy and the avant-garde: sacred images in the work of Goncharova, Malevich, and their contemporaries"; Anna Lawton, "Art and religion in the films of Andrei Tarkovskii".] REV: James Cracraft, *Slavic Review* 51, no. 3 (Fall 1992): 626. Brian Bennett, *Journal of Religion* 73, no. 1 (January 1993): 146-147. David J. Goa, *Canadian Slavonic Papers* 35, nos. 3-4 (September-December 1993): 396-397. Daniel Rowland,

Russian History = Histoire russe 20, nos. 1-4 (1993): 270-271.

5241. Friedberg, Maurice. *How Things Were Done in Odessa: Cultural and Intellectual Pursuits in a Soviet City.* Boulder, CO: Westview Press, 1991. 145 pp. REV: Barbara Sciacchitano, *Canadian-American Slavic Studies* 26, nos. 1-4 (1992): 397-399. Robert Weinberg, *Slavic Review* 51, no. 3 (Fall 1992): 633-634. Patricia Herlihy, *Russian Review* 52, no. 1 (January 1993): 133.

5242. Likhachev, Dmitrii S. *Reflections on Russia.* Edited by Nicolai N. Petro. Translated by Christine Sever. CCRS Series on Change in Contemporary Soviet Society. Boulder, CO: Westview Press, 1991. xxii, 191 pp. [With a foreword by S. Frederick Starr.] REV: Henrik Birnbaum, *Canadian-American Slavic Studies* 25, nos. 1-4 (1991): 247-248. David Remnick, *New York Review of Books* 39, no. 9 (May 14, 1992): 44-51. Frank E. Sysyn, *Canadian Slavonic Papers* 34, nos. 1-2 (March-June 1992): 143-152. Edward L. Keenan, *Russian History = Histoire russe* 20, nos. 1-4 (1993): 274-277. Nancy Shields Kollmann, *Slavic Review* 52, no. 4 (Winter 1993): 904-905.

5243. Milojkovic-Djuric, Jelena. *Tradition and Avant-Garde: The Arts in Serbian Culture between the Two World Wars.* Boulder, CO: East European Monographs; New York: Distributed by Columbia University Press, 1984. vii, 175 pp. REV: Vladimir Milicic, *Canadian American Slavic Studies = Revue Canadienne Américaine d'Etudes Slaves* 27, nos. 1-4 (1993): 354-356.

5244. Roman, Gail Harrison, and Virginia Hagelstein Marquardt, eds. *The Avant-Garde Frontier: Russia Meets the West, 1910-1930.* Gainesville, FL: University of Florida Press, c1992. xvi, 291 pp. [Contents: Charles S. Mayer, "The Impact of the Ballets Russes on Design in the West, 1909-1914"; Gail Harrison Roman, "Tatlin's Tower: Revolutionary Symbol and Aesthetic"; Myroslava M. Mudrak and Virginia Hagelstein Marquardt, "Environments of Propaganda: Russian and Soviet Expositions and Pavilions in the West"; K. Paul Zygas, "OSA's 1927 Exhibition of Contemporary Architecture: Russia and the West Meet in Moscow"; Magdalena Dabrowski, "Malevich and Mondrian: Nonobjective Form as the Expression of the 'Absolute' "; K. Michael Hays, "Photomontage and Its Audience: El Lissitzky Meets Berlin Dada"; Christina Lodder, "The VKhKUTEMAS and the Bauhaus"; Virginia Hagelstein Marquardt, "Louis Lozowick: An American's Assimilation of Russian Avant-Garde Art of the 1920s".] REV: Janet Kennedy, *Slavic Review* 52, no. 4 (Winter 1993): 874-875.

5245. Stites, Richard. *Russian Popular Culture: Entertainment and Society Since 1900.* Cambridge Soviet Paperbacks, 7. Cambridge; New York: Cambridge University Press, 1992. xvii, 269 pp. [Discography: pp. 246-249; filmography: pp. 250-256; videography: pp. 257-258.] REV: Robert Edelman, *Slavic Review* 52, no. 3 (Fall 1993): 568-578. James von Geldern, *Soviet and Post-Soviet Review* 20, nos. 2-3 (1993): 250-252. Theodore Taranovski, *Russian History = Histoire russe* 20, nos. 1-4 (1993): 358-359.

Katrina Vanden Heuvel, *Book World* 23, no. 2 (January 10, 1993): 6-7.

5246. Valkenier, Elizabeth. *Russian Realist Art: The State and Society: The Peredvizhniki and Their Tradition.* Morningside ed. Studies of the Harriman Institute. New York: Columbia University Press, 1989. xix, 255 pp. REV: Gail Harrison Roman, *Russian History* 17, no. 1 (Spring 1990): 119-120. Stephen C. Feinstein, *Canadian American Slavic Studies = Revue Canadienne Américaine d'Etudes Slaves* 27, nos. 1-4 (1993): 350-351.

5247. Wardropper, Ian et al. *News from a Radiant Future: Soviet Porcelain from the Collection of Craig H. and Kay A. Tuber.* Chicago, IL: Art Institute of Chicago, c1992. 92 pp. [Catalog of an exhibition held at the Art Institute of Chicago, October 25, 1992-January 31, 1993, and travelling to other institutions during 1993.] REV: Janet Kennedy, *Russian History = Histoire russe* 20, nos. 1-4 (1993): 354-355.

Culture and Politics

5248. Fleishman, Lazar'. *Materialy po istorii russkoi i sovetskoi kul'tury: iz arkhiva Guverovskogo Instituta.* Stanford Slavic Studies, vol. 5. Stanford, CA: Stanford University, 1992. 273 pp. [Contents: I. Iz Gor'kovskoi biografii: M. Gor'kii i V. L. Burtsev; Pis'ma Gor'kogo k Burtsevu; Pis'ma k Zhitlovskomu i Volkhovskomu; II. Epizody iz istorii amerikansko-sovetskikh kul'turnykh otnoshenii: Vstuplenie; Dzhozeff Frimen i Boris Pil'niak; V polemike c Maksom Istmenom; K istorii meksikanskogo fil'ma Eizenshteina.] REV: Henry Elbaum, *Canadian Slavonic Papers* 35, nos. 1-2 (March-June 1993): 170-172.

5249. Goldfarb, Jeffrey C. *Beyond Glasnost: The Post-Totalitarian Mind.* Foreword by Jan Jozef Szczepanski. with a new preface. Chicago, IL: University of Chicago Press, 1991. xliii, 248 pp. REV: John Downing, *Journal of Communication* 42, no. 2 (Spring 1992): 153-162. Ronen Palan, *Sociological Inquiry* 62 (Spring 1992): 275-278. J. F. Conway, *Canadian Journal of Sociology* 18, no. 2 (Spring 1993): 197-206.

5250. Groys, Boris. *The Total Art of Stalinism: Avant-Garde, Aesthetic Dictatorship, and Beyond.* Translated by Charles Rougle. Princeton, NJ: Princeton University Press, c1992. 126 pp. [Translation of *Gesamtkunstwerk Stalin.*] REV: Darra Goldstein, *Russian History = Histoire russe* 20, nos. 1-4 (1993): 367-368. Vyacheslav Ivanov, *Slavic Review* 52, no. 3 (Fall 1993): 600-604. Mary A. Nicholas, *Slavic and East European Journal* 37, no. 4 (Winter 1993): 602-604.

5251. Günther, Hans, ed. *The Culture of the Stalin Period.* New York: St. Martin's Press, 1990. xxi, 291 pp. [Published in association with the School of Slavonic and East European Studies, University of London. Papers from a conference held October 20-23, 1986 at the Centre for Interdisciplinary Research of the University of Bielefeld.] REV: Sherman D. Spector, *History: Reviews of New Books* 19, no. 4 (Summer 1991): 178. James G. Hart, *Historian* 54, no. 2 (Winter 1992): 332-333. Denise J. Youngblood, *Canadian American Slavic Studies = Revue Canadienne Américaine d'Etudes Slaves* 27, nos. 1-4 (1993): 408-409.

5252. Nove, Alec. *Glasnost' in Action: Cultural Renaissance in Russia*. Rev. ed. Boston, MA: Unwin Hyman, 1990. xi, 259 pp. REV: James E. Hassell, *Soviet and Post-Soviet Review* 20, no. 1 (1993): 83.

5253. Read, Christopher. *Culture and Power in Revolutionary Russia: The Intelligentsia and the Transition from Tsarism to Communism*. New York: St. Martin's Press, 1990. xii, 266 pp. REV: Lynn Mally, *Slavic Review* 50, no. 4 (Winter 1991): 1018. Timothy E. O'Connor, *American Historical Review* 96, no. 5 (December 1991): 1584. Stephen Vlychenko, *History: Reviews of New Books* 20, no. 1 (Fall 1991): 27-28. Edith W. Clowes, *Russian History = Histoire russe* 20, nos. 1-4 (1993): 330-332.

5254. Stites, Richard. *Revolutionary Dreams: Utopian Vision and Experimental Life in the Russian Revolution*. New York: Oxford University Press, 1989. xii, 307 pp. REV: Barbara Evans Clements, *American Historical Review* 95, no. 4 (October 1990): 1251-1252. Aileen Kelly, *New York Review of Books* 37, no. 19 (December 6, 1990): 60-67. Richard Pipes, *Orbis* 34, no. 2 (Spring 1990): 296-297. Richard Wortman, *Russian Review* 49, no. 2 (April 1990): 183-187. Donald J. Raleigh, *Canadian-American Slavic Studies* 25, nos. 1-4 (1991): 322-323. J. Thomas Sanders, *Problems of Communism* 40, no. 6 (November-December 1991): 115-123. Robert Edelman, *Slavic Review* 52, no. 3 (Fall 1993): 568-578.

5255. Tolstoy, Vladimir, Irina Bibikova, and Catherine Cooke, eds. *Street Art of the Revolution: Festivals and Celebrations in Russia, 1918-33*. Translated from the Russian by Frances Longman, Felicity O'Dell, and Vladimir Vnukov. New York: Vendome Press; Distributed by Rizzoli International, 1990. 240 pp. [Also published (London: Thames and Hudson, 1990); originally published (Moscow: Iskusstvo, c1984).] REV: Jamey Gambrell, *New York Review of Books* 40, no. 8 (April 22, 1993): 52-59.

5256. Verdery, Katherine. *National Ideology under Socialism: Identity and Cultural Politics in Ceausescu's Romania*. Societies and Culture in East-Central Europe, 7. Berkeley, CA: University of California Press, c1991. xvi, 406 pp. REV: Mary Ellen Fischer, *Canadian-American Slavic Studies* 25, nos. 1-4 (1991): 448-450. Mabel Berezin, *Contemporary Sociology* 21, no. 3 (May 1992): 306-308. István Deák, *New York Review of Books* 39, no. 5 (March 5, 1992): 43-51. Richard Handler, *American Anthropologist* 94, no. 4 (December 1992): 967. John R. Lampe, *Annals of the American Academy of Political and Social Science*, no. 523 (September 1992): 231-232. Alexander C. Pacek, *Journal of Politics* 54, no. 4 (November 1992): 1223-1226. Vladimir Tismaneanu, *Orbis* 36, no. 4 (Fall 1992): 625. John Borneman, *American Ethnologist* 20, no. 3 (August 1993): 649-650. Marcel Cornis-Pope, *Slavic Review* 52, no. 4 (Winter 1993): 853-855.

5257. White, Steven. *The Bolshevik Poster*. New Haven, CT: Yale University Press, 1988. vii, 152 pp. REV:

Lynn Mally, *Canadian American Slavic Studies = Revue Canadienne Américaine d'Etudes Slaves* 27, nos. 1-4 (1993): 430-431.

Architecture

5258. Brumfield, William C., ed. *Reshaping Russian Architecture: Western Technology, Utopian Dreams*. Woodrow Wilson Center Series, Washington, DC: Woodrow Wilson International Center for Scholars; Cambridge; New York: Cambridge University Press, 1990. xvii, 222 pp. REV: James H. Bater, *Canadian Slavonic Papers* 32, no. 2 (June 1990): 192-193. Mikaella Kagan, *Post-Soviet Geography* 33, no. 2 (February 1992): 116-118. William Richardson, *Russian Review* 51, no. 2 (April 1992): 271-272. Elizabeth Klosty Beaujour, *Slavic and East European Journal* 37, no. 3 (Fall 1993): 408-409. Elizabeth Kridl Valkenier, *Canadian American Slavic Studies = Revue Canadienne Américaine d'Etudes Slaves* 27, nos. 1-4 (1993): 391-392.

5259. Brumfield, William Craft. *The Origins of Modernism in Russian Architecture*. Berkeley, CA: University of California Press, c1991. xxv, 343 pp. REV: Albert J. Schmidt, *American Historical Review* 97, no. 2 (April 1992): 584. Roann Barris, *Canadian American Slavic Studies = Revue Canadienne Américaine d'Etudes Slaves* 27, nos. 1-4 (1993): 398-400. Hugh D. Hudson, Jr., *Russian Review* 52, no. 1 (January 1993): 99-100. Pavel Ilyin, *Russian History = Histoire russe* 20, nos. 1-4 (1993): 303-305. Janet Kennedy, *Slavic and East European Journal* 37, no. 2 (Summer 1993): 263-264. Anatole Senkevitch, *Progressive Architecture* 74 (June 1993): 132ff.

5260. Burkhardt, Francois, Claude Eveno, and Boris Podrecca, eds. *Joze Plecnik, Architect, 1872-1957*. Translated by Carol Volk. Contributions by Francois Burkhardt, Claude Eveno, Boris Podrecca, Carol Volk, Joze Plecnik, Friedrich Achleitner, Petr Krecic, Edo Ravnikar, Alain Arvois, Cristina C. von Eybesfeld, Damjan Prelovsek, Vladimir Slapeta, Alena Kubova, Guy Ballange, Lucius Burckhardt, and Linde Burkhardt. Cambridge, MA: MIT Press, 1992. ix, 216 pp. [Including Ljubljana Museum of Architecture, work in Prague, Vienna, and Slovenia, "Czech modernity".] REV: Charles S. Mayer, *Slavic Review* 52, no. 3 (Fall 1993): 587-588.

5261. Cohen, Jean-Louis. *Le Corbusier and the Mystique of the USSR: Theories and Projects for Moscow, 1928-1936*. Translated by Kenneth Hylton. Princeton, NJ: Princeton University Press, c1992. xvi, 254 pp. [Translation of *Le Corbusier et la mystique de l'URSS*.] REV: Martin Filler, *New York Times Book Review* (December 6, 1992): 46. William C. Brumfield, *American Historical Review* 98, no. 2 (April 1993): 535. Joseph D. McCadden, *Russian History = Histoire russe* 20, nos. 1-4 (1993): 366-367. Anatole Senkevitch, *Progressive Architecture* 74, no. 6 (June 1993): 132ff.

5262. Schmidt, Albert J. *The Architecture and Planning of Classical Moscow: A Cultural History*. Memoirs of the American Philosophical Society, v. 181. Philadelphia,

PA: American Philosophical Society, 1989. xiii, 218 pp. REV: James Cracraft, *Russian Review* 49, no. 3 (July 1990): 337-338. Thomas W. Gaehtgens, *Journal of Modern History* 62, no. 4 (December 1990): 891-894. Robert E. Jones, *Journal of Interdisciplinary History* 21, no. 1 (Summer 1990): 155-156. Michael F. Hamm, *American Historical Review* 96, no. 3 (June 1991): 914. George E. Munro, *Canadian American Slavic Studies = Revue Canadienne Américaine d'Etudes Slaves* 27, nos. 1-4 (1993): 356-358.

5263. Tarkhanov, Alexei, and Sergei Kavtaradze. *Architecture of the Stalin Era.* Designed and compiled by Mikhail Anikst. Translated by Robin Whitby, Julia Whitby, and James Paver. New York: Rizzoli International, 1992. 192 pp. REV: Hugh D. Hudson, Jr., *Slavic Review* 52, no. 2 (Summer 1993): 397-398.

5264. Vale, Lawrence J. *Architecture, Power and National Identity.* New Haven, CT: Yale University Press, c1992. x, 338 pp. REV: Larry R. Ford, *Geographical Review* 83, no. 3 (July 1993): 348-351.

Dance

5265. Nijinska, Bronislava. *Bronislava Nijinska: Early Memoirs.* Translated and edited by Irina Nijinska, and Jean Rawlinson. Introduction by Anna Kisselgoff. Durham, NC: Duke University Press, 1992. xxv, 546 pp. [Originally published (New York: Rinehart and Winston, c1981).] REV: Tim Scholl, *Slavic Review* 52, no. 4 (Winter 1993): 848-849.

5266. Volkov, Solomon. *Balanchine's Tchaikovsky: Conversations with Balachine on His Life, Ballet and Music.* Translated by Antonina Bouis. New York: Doubleday, 1992. xxvii, 202 pp. REV: Alexander Poznansky, *Slavic Review* 52, no. 4 (Winter 1993): 864-865.

Music

General

5267. Greene, Victor. *A Passion for Polka: Old-Time Ethnic Music in America.* Berkeley, CA: University of California Press, c1992. vi, 355 pp. REV: Robert P. Pula, *Polish American Studies* 50, no. 2 (Autumn 1993): 115-117.

5268. Herndon, Marcia, and Susanne Ziegler, eds. *Music Gender and Culture.* Senior Editor Max Peter Baumann. West Germany: Florian Noetzel Verlag Wilhelmshaven; New York: C.F. Peters, 1990. 307 pp. [Includes essay by Anna Czekanowska on Slavic women's music.] REV: Virginia Giglio, *Ethnomusicology* 37, no. 1 (Winter 1993): 115-117.

5269. Messing, Scott. *Neoclassicism in Music: From the Genesis of the Concept through the Schoenberg/Stravinsky Polemic.* Studies in Musicology, no. 101. Ann Arbor, MI: UMI Research Press, 1988. xvi, 215 pp. REV: Richard Taruskin, *19th Century Music* 16, no. 3 (Spring 1993): 286-302.

Russia/U.S.S.R.

5270. Dubinsky, Rostislav. *Stormy Applause: Making Music in a Worker's State.* Boston, MA: Northeastern University Press, 1991. x, 291 pp. REV: Elizabeth Bishop, *Slavic Review* 52, no. 3 (Fall 1993): 643-644.

5271. MacDonald, Ian. *The New Shostakovich.* Boston, MA: Northeastern University Press, 1990. 339 pp. REV: Malcolm Hamrick Brown, *Notes* 49, no. 3 (March 1993): 955-961. Richard F. Taruskin, *Slavic Review* 52, no. 2 (Summer 1993): 396-397.

5272. Orlova, Alexandra, comp. and ed. *Musorgsky Remembered.* Translated by Veronique Zaytzeff, and Frederick Morrison. Russian Music Studies, Bloomington, IN: Indiana University Press, c1991. xiii, 186 pp. REV: Caryl Emerson, *Slavic Review* 51, no. 3 (Fall 1992): 544-556. Robert W. Oldani, *Russian History = Histoire russe* 20, nos. 1-4 (1993): 300-301.

5273. ——, comp. *Tchaikovsky: A Self-Portrait.* Translated by R. M. Davison. Foreword by David Brown. Oxford; New York: Oxford University Press, c1991. xxiv, 436 pp. REV: Gerald R. Seaman, *Notes* 49, no. 3 (March 1993): 1013-1016.

5274. Poznansky, Alexander. *Tchaikovsky: The Quest for the Inner Man.* New York: Schirmer; Maxwell Macmillan International, c1991. xix, 679 pp. REV: Paul Griffins, *New York Times Book Review* (January 5, 1992): 24. Algis Valiunas, *American Spectator* 25, no. 5 (May 1992): 74-76. Gerald R. Seaman, *Notes* 49, no. 3 (March 1993): 1013-1016.

5275. Prokofiev, Sergei. *Soviet Diary, 1927, and Other Writings.* Translated and edited by Oleg Prokofiev. Associate editor Christopher Palmer. Boston, MA: Northeastern University Press, 1992. xvi, 315 pp. [Also published: (London: Faber and Faber, 1991).] REV: *Publishers Weekly* 239, no. 6 (January 27, 1992): 80. Laurel E. Fay, *Notes* 49, no. 4 (June 1993): 1417-1419.

5276. Schonberg, Harold C. *Horowitz: His Life and Music.* New York: Simon & Schuster, c1992. 427 pp. [Russian-born pianist.] REV: David Blum, *New York Times Book Review* (November 29, 1992): 28. Hugh McGinnis, *Clavier* 32, no. 4 (April 1993): 11.

Eastern Europe

5277. Bartók, Bela. *Bela Bartók Essays.* Selected and edited by Benjamin Suchoff. Lincoln, NB: University of Nebraska Press, 1992. xvi, 567 pp. [Originally published: (New York: St. Martin's Press, 1976).] REV: Wilfrid Mellers, *American Scholar* 62, no. 3 (Summer 1993): 474-477.

5278. Czekanowska, Anna. *Polish Folk Music: Slavonic Heritage, Polish Tradition, Contemporary Trends.* Cambridge Studies in Ethnomusicology. Cambridge; New York: Cambridge University Press, 1990. xii, 226 pp. REV: Anne Swartz, *Slavic Review* 51, no. 2 (Summer 1992): 366-

367. Barbara Krader, *Notes* 49, no. 3 (March 1993): 1060-1061.

5279. Fowler, Kenneth. *Received Truths: Bertolt Brecht and the Problem of Gestus and Musical Meaning.* AMS Studies in German Literature and Culture, 1. New York: AMS Press, c1991. xi, 88 pp. [Based on the author's M.A. thesis (McGill University).] REV: Jean M. Snook, *Seminar* 29, no. 2 (May 1993): 206-208.

5280. Freibergs, Imants. *Saules dainu indekss = Lativan Sun Song Index.* Montreal: Helios, 1990. vii, 299 pp. REV: Valdis J. Zeps, *Journal of Baltic Studies* 24, no. 2 (Summer 1993): 207-208.

5281. Gillies, Malcolm. *Bartók Remembered.* 1st American ed. New York: Norton, 1990. 238 pp. REV: Damjana Bratuz, *Notes* 49, no. 3 (March 1993): 1031-1033.

5282. Manuel, Peter. *Popular Musics of the Non-Western World: An Introductory Survey.* New York: Oxford University Press, 1988. xii, 287 pp. [Includes discussion of popular music in Greece and Yugoslavia.] REV: Stephen H. Martin, *Notes* 49, no. 4 (June 1993): 1511-1513.

5283. Matossian, Nouritza. *Xenakis.* London: Kahn & Averill; White Plains, NY Pro/Am Music Resources, 1991. 271 pp. [Includes Xenakis' childhood in Romania and participation in the Greek Resistance during World War II.] REV: Charles Shere, *Notes* 50, no. 1 (September 1993): 96-100.

5284. Payzant, Geoffrey. *Eduard Hanslick and Ritter Berlioz in Prague: A Documentary Narrative.* Calgary, Alta.: University of Calgary, 1991. xiv, 139 pp. REV: Kenneth DeLong, *Notes* 49, no. 3 (March 1993): 1007.

5285. Rappoport-Gelfand, Lidia. *Musical Life in Poland: The Post-War Years 1945-1977.* Translated by Irina Lasoff, and James Walker. Introduction by Jennifer M. Goheen. Musicology, v. 10. New York: Gordon and Breach Science Publishers, c1991. 248 pp. REV: Cindy Bylander, *Notes* 49, no. 4 (June 1993): 1471-1473.

5286. Smialek, William. *Ignacy Feliks Dobrzynski and Musical Life in Nineteenth-Century Poland.* Lewiston, NY: Edwin Mellen Press, c1991. xvii, 195 pp. REV: Jim Samson, *Music and Letters* (May 1993): 306-307.

5287. Xenakis, Iannis. *Arts / Sciences: Alloys. The Thesis Defense of Iannis Xenakis.* Translated by Sharon Kanach. Monographs in Musicology, 3. New York: Pendragon Press, 1985. x, 133 pp. [Transcription of Xenakis' thesis defense which took place May 18, 1976, at the Sorbonne (Paris).] REV: Charles Shere, *Notes* 50, no. 1 (September 1993): 96-100.

5288. ———. *Formalized Music: Through and Mathematics in Composition.* rev. ed. Harmonologia Series, no. 6. Stuyvesant, NY: Pendragon Press, c1992. xiv, 387 pp. REV: Charles Shere, *Notes* 50, no. 1 (September 1993): 96-100.

Painting, Sculpture, Graphic Arts

5289. Barooshian, Vahan. *The Art of Liberation: Alexander A. Ivanov.* Lanham, MD: University Press of America, 1987. x, 105 pp. REV: John O. Norman, *Slavic and East European Journal* 35 (Spring 1991): 170-171. John E. Bowlt, *Canadian American Slavic Studies = Revue Canadienne Américaine d'Etudes Slaves* 27, nos. 1-4 (1993): 351-352.

5290. Cantor, Jay. *On Giving Birth to One's Mother: Essays on Art and Society.* 1st ed. New York: Knopf: Distributed by Random House, 1991. 177 pp. [Title essay discusses Arshile Gorky's 1934 painting "The Artist & His Mother"] REV: Ara Baliozian, *Ararat* 34, no. 2 (Spring 1993): 61-64.

5291. Crone, Rainer, and David Moos. *Kazimir Malevich: The Climax of Disclosure.* Chicago, IL: University of Chicago Press, 1991. viii, 230 pp. REV: Darra Goldstein, *Slavic Review* 51, no. 4 (Winter 1992): 853-854. John E. Bowlt, *Russian Review* 52, no. 3 (July 1993): 424-425. Charlotte Douglas, *Russian History = Histoire russe* 20, nos. 1-4 (1993): 355-357.

5292. D'Andrea, Jeanne, ed. *Kazimir Malevich, 1878-1935: National Gallery of Art, Washington, D.C., 16 September 1990-4 November 1990, the Armand Hammer Museum of Art and Cultural Center, Los Angeles, 28 November 1990-13 January 1991, the Metropolitan Museum of Art, New York, 7 February 1991-24 March 1991.* Los Angeles, CA: Armand Hammer Museum of Art and Cultural Center, c1990. 230 pp. REV: John Golding, *New York Review of Books* 38, nos. 1-2 (January 17, 1991): 16ff. John F. Martin, *Russian History* 18, no. 2 (Summer 1991): 224-225. Myroslava M. Mudrak, *Slavic and East European Journal* 36, no. 4 (Winter 1992): 525-527. Milka Bliznakov, *Russian Review* 52, no. 1 (January 1993): 98. Robert C. Williams, *Studies in East European Thought* 45, no. 3 (September 1993): 225-226.

5293. Kornetchuk, Elena. *The Quest for Self-Expression: Painting in Moscow and Leningrad, 1965-1990.* Introduction by John E. Bowlt. Columbus, OH: Columbus Museum of Art; Seattle, WA: Distributed by University of Washington Press, 1990. 191 pp. [Exhibit organized by Columbus Museum of Art; E. Jane Connell, curator; Elena Kornetchuk, guest curator.] REV: John O. Norman, *Russian Review* 52, no. 1 (January 1993): 101-102.

5294. Lissitzky, El. *About Two Squares: In Six Constructions: A Suprematist Tale.* 1st MIT Press ed. [Cambridge, MA]: MIT Press, 1991. 1 vol. [Translation of *Pro dva kvadrata.* Accompanied by Patricia Railing, "More About Two Squares" 52 pp.] REV: Margaret B. Betz, *Slavic and East European Journal* 37, no. 2 (Summer 1993): 262-263.

5295. Roberts, Norma, ed. *The Quest for Self-Expression: Painting in Moscow and Leningrad, 1965-1990.* Introduction by John E. Bowlt. Essay by Elena Kornetchuk. Columbus, OH: Columbus Museum of Art; Seattle, WA: Distributed by the University of Washington Press, 1990.

191 pp. [Exhibition organized by the Columbus Museum of Art, Jane Connell, curator, and Elena Kornetchuk, guest curator. Edited by Norma Roberts.] REV: Alison L. Hilton, *Soviet and Post-Soviet Review* 19, nos. 1-3 (1992): 312-314. Wendy Salmond, *Slavic and East European Journal* 36, no. 3 (Fall 1992): 388-389. John O. Norman, *Russian Review* 52, no. 1 (January 1993): 101-102.

5296. Roskill, Mark. *Klee, Kandinsky, and the Thought of Their Time: A Critical Perspective.* Urbana, IL: University of Illinois Press, c1992. xix, 279 pp. REV: Lucian Krukowski, *Journal of Aesthetics and Art Criticism* 51, no. 3 (Summer 1993): 517-518.

5297. Ross, David A., ed. *Between Spring and Summer: Soviet Conceptual Art in the Era of Late Communism.* 1st MIT Press ed. Tacoma, WA: Tacoma Art Museum; Boston, MA: Institute of Contemporary Art; Cambridge, MA: MIT Press, c1990. x, 206 pp. [Catalogue of exhibition held June 15-September 9, 1990, at the Tacoma Art Museum; November 1, 1990-January 6, 1991 at the Institute of Contemporary Art, Boston; February 16-March 31, 1991 at the Des Moines Art Center.] REV: John Loughery, *Hudson Review* 44, no. 1 (Spring 1991): 118-124. Wendy R. Salmond, *Russian Review* 52, no. 1 (January 1993): 100-101.

5298. Solomon R. Guggenheim Museum et al. *The Great Utopia: The Russian and Soviet Avant-Garde, 1915-1932.* New York: Guggenheim Museum; Distributed by Rizzoli International, c1992. xv, 732 pp. [Contributions translated from Russian and German. Catalog of an exhibition held at the Schirn Kunsthalle Frankfurt, March 1-May 10, 1992; Stedelijk Museum Amsterdam, June 5-August 23, 1992; and the Solomon R. Guggenheim Museum, September 25-December 15, 1992.] REV: Nicoletta Misler, *Structurist.* nos. 33-34 (1993-1994): 113-115.

5299. Stupples, Peter. *Pavel Kuznetsov: His Life and Art.* Cambridge Studies in the History of Art, Cambridge; New York: Cambridge University Press, 1989. xix, 370 pp. REV: Alison Hilton, *Soviet Union = Union Soviétique* 17, nos. 1-2 (1990): 118-121. John F. Martin, *Russian History* 17, no. 1 (Spring 1990): 120-122. Janet Kennedy, *Slavic and East European Journal* 35, no. 1 (Spring 1991): 168-169. John E. Bowlt, *Russian Review* 51, no. 1 (January 1992): 111-112. Martina Roudabush Norelli, *Canadian American Slavic Studies = Revue Canadienne Américaine d'Etudes Slaves* 27, nos. 1-4 (1993): 381-382.

5300. Valkenier, Elizabeth Kridl. *Ilya Repin and the World of Russian Art.* New York: Columbia University Press, c1990. xiv, 248 pp. REV: Wendy Salmond, *Russian History* 17, no. 3 (Fall 1990): 368-369. John O. Norman, *History: Reviews of New Books* 20, no. 1 (Fall 1991): 35. Richard R. Brettell, *Slavic Review* 51, no. 2 (Summer 1992): 369-370. Sarah P. Burke, *Russian Review* 51, no. 1 (January 1992): 115-116. Jamey Gambrell, *New York Review of Books* 40, no. 8 (April 22, 1993): 52-59. Alison Hilton, *Canadian American Slavic Studies = Revue Canadienne Américaine d'Etudes Slaves* 27, nos. 1-4 (1993): 409-412.

5301. ———, ed. *The Wanderers: Masters of 19th-Century Russian Painting: An Exhibition from the Soviet Union.* Dallas, TX: Dallas Museum of Art, c1990. x, 204 pp. [Exhibition organized by InterCultura, Fort Worth, the Dallas Museum of Art, in cooperation with the Ministry of Culture of the USSR.] REV: Alison Hilton, *Russian Review* 52, no. 1 (January 1993): 106-107.

Theater and Cinema

General

5302. Cole, Susan Letzler. *The Absent One: Mourning Ritual, Tragedy, and the Performance of Ambivalence.* University Park: Pennsylvania State University Press, 1985. 183 pp. [Includes discussion of Ionesco's *Exit the King* and Chaikin's *Trespassing.*] REV: C.M. [Carol Martin], *TDR The Drama Review* 37, no. 1 (Spring 1993): 178-179.

5303. Donskov, Andrew, and Richard Sokoloski, eds. *Slavic Drama: The Question of Innovation: Proceedings.* Edited with Roman Weretelnyk and John Woodsworth. Ottawa, Ontario: University of Ottawa Press, c1991. 359 pp. [Proceedings of the Slavic Drama Symposium, held at the University of Ottawa, May 2-4, 1991.] REV: Halina Stephan, *Slavic and East European Journal* 36, no. 4 (Winter 1992): 495-496. Thomas Eekman, *Slavic Review* 52, no. 1 (Spring 1993): 135-136. Melissa T. Smith, *Canadian American Slavic Studies = Revue Canadienne Américaine d'Etudes Slaves* 27, nos. 1-4 (1993): 322-324.

5304. Klaic, Dragan. *The Plot of the Future: Utopia and Dystopia in Modern Drama.* Theater: Theory/Text/Performance. Ann Arbor, MI: University of Michigan Press, 1991. vi, 258 pp. REV: Peter P. Müller, *Theatre Journal* 45, no. 4 (December 1993): 566-568.

5305. Londré, Felicia Hardison. *The History of World Theater: From the English Restoration to the Present.* New York: Continuum, 1991. xii, 644 pp. [Companion volume to Margot Berthold, ed., *The History of World Theater: From the Beginnings to the Baroque.* Includes discussion of Russian and Polish theater.] REV: Robert Findlay, *Theatre Journal* 44 (December 1992): 554-555. Thomas Postlewait, *Theater History Studies* 13 (1993): 243-247.

5306. Senelick, Laurence, ed. *National Theatre in Northern and Eastern Europe, 1746-1900.* Associate editors, Peter Bilton et al. Theatre in Europe. Cambridge; New York: Cambridge University Press, 1991. xxx, 480 pp. [Includes Chapters on Poland, 1765-1830; the Czech Lands (Bohemia and Moravia), 1784-1881; Hungary, 1810-1838; Rumania, 1818-1852; and Russia, 1812-1898.] REV: Harold B. Segel, *Slavic and East European Journal* 37, no. 3 (Fall 1993): 393-395.

Russia/U.S.S.R.

5307. Baer, Nancy Van Norman. *Theatre in Revolution: Russian Avant-Garde Stage Design, 1913-1935.* Contributions by John E. Bowlt et al. New York: Thames & Hudson; San Francisco, CA: Fine Arts Museums of San Francisco, c1991. 207 pp. REV: Robert Johnson, *Dance Chronicle* 16, no. 1 (1993): 121-127.

5308. Benedetti, Jean, ed. and trans. *The Moscow Art Theatre Letters.* New York: Routledge, c1991. xv, 377 pp. REV: Laurence Senelick, *Russian History* 18, no. 3 (Fall 1991): 370-371. Burnet M. Hobgood, *Theatre Survey* 34, no. 2 (November 1993): 113-115.

5309. Carnicke, Sharon Marie. *The Theatrical Instinct: Nikolai Evreinov and the Russian Theatre of the Early Twentieth Century.* American University Studies. Series XXVI, Theatre Arts, vol. 2. New York: P. Lang, c1989. xii, 247 pp. REV: Daniel Gerould, *Soviet and East European Performance* 10, no. 3 (Winter 1990): 59-60. Cheyanne Boyd, *Slavic and East European Journal* 35, no. 2 (Summer 1991): 282-283. Katherine Eaton, *Slavic Review* 50, no. 3 (Fall 1991): 731. George Kalbouss, *Russian Review* 50, no. 4 (October 1991): 495-496. Martha Manheim, *Comparative Drama* 25, no. 4 (Winter 1991-92): 393-396. J. Douglas Clayton, *Canadian Slavonic Papers* 34, no. 3 (September 1992): 319. Catherine Schuler, *Modern Drama* 36, no. 4 (December 1993): 585-588.

5310. Horton, Andrew, and Michael Brashinsky. *The Zero Hour: Glasnost and Soviet Cinema in Transition.* Princeton, NJ: Princeton University Press, c1992. 287 pp. [Filmography: pp. 251-261.] REV: Josephine Woll, *Russian Review* 52, no. 4 (October 1993): 550.

5311. Kelly, Catriona. *Petrushka: The Russian Carnival Puppet Theatre.* Cambridge Studies in Russian Literature. Cambridge; New York: Cambridge University Press, 1990. xv, 292 pp. REV: J. Douglas Clayton, *Canadian Slavonic Papers* 32, no. 4 (December 1990): 505-507. Milica Banjanin, *Russian Review* 51, no. 2 (April 1992): 270-271. Sharon Marie Carnicke, *Slavic Review* 51, no. 1 (Spring 1992): 186-187. Roberta Reeder, *Slavic and East European Journal* 36, no. 3 (Fall 1992): 383-385. Marjorie L. Hoover, *Canadian American Slavic Studies = Revue Canadienne Américaine d'Etudes Slaves* 27, nos. 1-4 (1993): 382-384.

5312. Kenez, Peter. *Cinema and Soviet Society, 1917-1953.* Cambridge Studies in the History of Mass Communications. Cambridge; New York: Cambridge University Press, 1992. ix, 281 pp. REV: Jeffrey Brooks, *Slavic Review* 51, no. 4 (Winter 1992): 842-843. Vance Kepley, Jr., *Film Quarterly* 47, no. 1 (Fall 1993): 42-43. Lynn Mally, *American Historical Review* 98, no. 4 (October 1993): 1298. William Richardson, *Historian* 55, no. 3 (Spring 1993): 546-547. Denise J. Youngblood, *Russian History = Histoire russe* 20, nos. 1-4 (1993): 360-361.

5313. Taylor, Richard, and Ian Christie, eds. *Inside the Film Factory: New Approaches to Russian and Soviet Cinema.* Soviet Cinema, London; New York: Routledge, 1991. xviii, 256 pp. [Contents: Richard Taylor and Ian Christie, "Introduction: Entering the film factory"; Yuri Tsivian, "Early Russian cinema: some observations"; Mikhail Yampolsky, "Kuleshov's experiments and the new anthropology of the actor"; Vance Kepley, Jr., "Intolerance and the Soviets: a historical investigation"; Vance Kepley, Jr., "The origins of Soviet cinema: a study in industrial development"; Ian Christie, "Down to earth: *Aelita* relo-

cated"; Denise J. Youngblood, "The return of the native: Yakov Protazanov and Soviet cinema"; J. Hoberman, "A face to the *shtetl*: Soviet Yiddish cinema, 1924-36"; Bernard Eisenschitz, "A fickle man, or portrait of Boris Barnet as a Soviet director"; "Interview with Alexander Medvedkin"; Ian Christie, "Making sense of early Soviet sound"; Richard Taylor, "Ideology as mass entertainment: Boris Shumyatsky and Soviet cinema in the 1930s".] REV: Kevin Moss, *Slavic Review* 51, no. 4 (Winter 1992): 843-844. Benjamin Rifkin, *Slavic and East European Journal* 36, no. 3 (Fall 1992): 387-388. Steven P. Hill, *Film Quarterly* 46, no. 4 (Summer 1993): 43-44. Vladimir Padunov, *Russian History = Histoire russe* 20, nos. 1-4 (1993): 361-363.

5314. Youngblood, Denise J. *Movies for the Masses: Popular Cinema and Soviet Society in the 1920s.* Cambridge; New York, NY: Cambridge University Press, 1992. xix, 259 pp. REV: B. Y. Nebesio, *Canadian Slavonic Papers* 35, nos. 1-2 (March-June 1993): 194-195. Andrew Horton, *Film Quarterly* 47, no. 2 (Winter 1993-1994): 56-57.

Eastern Europe

5315. Elsom, John. *Cold War Theatre.* London; New York: Routledge, 1992. ix, 198 pp. REV: Loren Kruger, *Theatre Journal* 45, no. 4 (December 1993): 555-557.

5316. Filipowicz, Halina. *A Laboratory of Impure Forms: The Plays of Tadeusz Różewicz.* Contributions in Drama and Theatre Studies, no. 35. New York: Greenwood Press, 1991. xxii, 171 pp. REV: E. J. Czerwinski, *Slavic and East European Journal* 36, no. 2 (Summer 1992): 258-260. Stephen Grecco, *World Literature Today* 66, no. 3 (Summer 1992): 546-547. Michal Kobialka, *Theatre Journal* 45, no. 1 (March 1993): 131-133.

5317. Hubner, Zygmunt. *Theater & Politics.* Edited and translated by Jadwiga Kosicka. Foreword by Daniel Gerould. Afterword by Andrzej Wajda. Evanston, IL: Northwestern University Press, 1992. xvi, 222 pp. [Translation of *Polityka i teatr*.] REV: Edward J. Czerwinski, *Polish Review* 38, no. 2 (1993): 247-248.

5318. Kantor, Tadeusz. *Wielopole / Wielopole: An Exercise in Theatre.* Translated from the Polish by Mariusz Tchorek and G. M. Hyde. London; New York: Marion Boyars: New York: Distributed in the U.S. and Canada by Rizzoli International, 1990. 159 pp. REV: Christine Kiebuzinska, *Theatre Journal* 45, no. 1 (March 1993): 130-131.

5319. Karpinski, Maciej. *The Theatre of Andrzej Wajda.* Translated by Christiana Paul. Directors in Perspective. Cambridge; New York: Cambridge University Press, 1989. xviii, 135 pp. [Translation of *Andrzej Wajda—teatr*.] REV: E. J. Czerwinski, *World Literature Today* 64, no. 3 (Summer 1990): 489-490. Halina Filipowicz, *Slavic Review* 49, no. 4 (Winter 1990): 687-688. Andrew B. Harris, *Theatre Journal* 42, no. 1 (March 1990): 131-132. David Bradby, *Modern Drama* 35, no. 3 (September 1992): 486-487. Daniel J. Goulding, *Canadian American Slavic Studies = Revue Canadienne Américaine d'Etudes Slaves* 27, nos. 1-4 (1993): 376-377.

5320. Kott, Jan. *The Gender of Rosalind: Interpretations: Shakespeare, Buchner, Gautier*. Translated by Jadwiga Kosicka and Mark Rosenzweig. Evanston, IL: Northwestern University Press, c1992. 88 pp. [Collection of essays by the author, translated from Polish.] REV: David Malcolm, *Polish Review* 38, no. 2 (1993): 228-230.

5321. ———. *The Memory of the Body: Essays on Theater and Death*. Translations by Jadwiga Kosicka, Lillian Vallee et al. Evanston, IL: Northwestern University Press, 1992. ix, 153 pp. [Translated from the Polish.] REV: A.D. [Ann Daly], *TDR: The Drama Review* 37, no. 2 (Summer 1993): 189-190. E. J. Czerwinski, *World Literature Today* 67, no. 2 (Spring 1993): 408.

5322. Madach, Imre. *The Tragedy of Man*. Translated from the Hungarian by Thomas R. Mark. Includes essay by Mihaly Szegedy-Maszak. East European Monographs, no. 272. Boulder, CO: East European Monographs; New York: Distributed by Columbia University Press, 1989. ix, 148 pp. [Translation of *Az ember tragediaja*.] REV: Lee Congdon, *Canadian American Slavic Studies = Revue Canadienne Américaine d'Etudes Slaves* 27, nos. 1-4 (1993): 362-364.

5323. Michalek, Boleslaw, and Frank Turaj. *The Modern Cinema of Poland*. Bloomington, IN: Indiana University Press, c1988. xvi, 205 pp. REV: Daniel Goulding, *Film Quarterly* 45, no. 1 (Fall 1991): 48-49, Daniel J. Goulding, *Canadian American Slavic Studies = Revue Canadienne Américaine d'Etudes Slaves* 27, nos. 1-4 (1993): 343-345.

5324. Yarrow, Ralph, ed. *European Theatre, 1960-1990: Cross-Cultural Perspectives*. London; New York: Routledge, 1992. x, 255 pp. [Partial contents: George Hyde, "Poland," pp. 182-219.] REV: A.D. [Ann Daly], *TDR The Drama Review* 37, no. 2 (Summer 1993): 189. Felicia Hardison Londré, *Comparative Drama* 27, no. 2 (Summer 1993): 254-256.

■ Economics and Foreign Trade

General

5325. Åslund, Anders, ed. *Market Socialism or the Restoration of Capitalism?* Cambridge; New York: Cambridge University Press, 1992. x, 215 pp. [Selected papers from the World Congress for Soviet and East European Studies (4th: 1990: Harrogate, England).] REV: Peter Rutland, *Soviet and Post-Soviet Review* 20, nos. 2-3 (1993): 259-260.

5326. ———. *Post-Communist Economic Revolutions: How Big a Bang?* Foreword by Stephen Sestanovich. Significant Issues Series. Creating the Post-Communist Order, v. 14, no. 9. Washington, DC: Center for Strategic and International Studies, c1992. xi, 106 pp. REV: *Wilson Quarterly* 17, no. 2 (Spring 1993): 150-151.

5327. Bertsch, Gary, and Steven Elliott-Gower, eds. *The Impact of Governments on East-West Economic Relations*. East-West European Economic Interaction, vol. 12.

New York: New York University Press, 1991. 407 pp. [Contents: Gary K. Bertsch and Steven Elliott-Gower, "Editors' Introduction"; Nikolai Shmelev, "Perestroika and East-West economic interaction"; Jerry F. Hough, "The Soviet attitude toward integration in the World economy"; Wladimir Andreff, "Soviet foreign trade reforms and the challenge to East European economic relations With the West"; Richard F. Kaufman, "U.S.-Soviet trade policy in the 1980s"; Carol Rae Hansen, "U.S. East-West trade policy"; Urszula Plowiec, "U.S. foreign economic policy towards Eastern Europe"; Nikolai Shmelev, "U.S. East-West economic policy: a Soviet view"; Friedrich Levcik, "Comments on Part II"; Paul Marer, "Foreign trade strategies in Eastern Europe: determinants, outcomes, prospects"; Tamás Bácskai, "The role of governments in fostering East-West economic cooperation"; Laszlo Lang, "The role of the Hungarian government in East-West economic relations"; Aleksander Lukaszewicz, "The impact of governments on East-West economic relations: the case of Poland"; Peter Sydow, "East-West economic relations and national interests: the case of the GDR"; Váltr Komárek, "East European governments and East-West economic relations: the case of Czechoslovakia"; Dragomir Vojnic, "The reform of socialism and East-West relations: the Yugoslav experience"; Christopher Saunders, Andrzej Rudka, Jean Tesche, and Jozef M. van Brabant, "Comments on Part III"; Klaus Schneider, "The role of the EC in East-West economic relations"; Irène Commeau-Rufin, "EC-CMEA economic relations: realities and prospects"; Joachim Jahnke, "The role of the government of the Federal Republic of Germany in East-West economic relations"; Issei Nomura, "The role of Japan in East-West economic relations"; Fritz Gehart, "The role of the Austrian government in East-West economic relations"; Leah Haus, "The Western politics of East-West trade negotiations: East European countries and the GATT"; Dariusz K. Rosati, "The role of the West European and Japanese governments in East-West economic relations: the view from Eastern Europe"; Karel Dyba and John McIntyre, "Comments on Part IV"; Allen J. Lenz, "Global adjustment problems of the 1990s: the effects on East-West trade policies"; John P. Hardt, "East-West economic interdependence and the rise of foreign trade constituencies"; Wolfgang Heinrichs, "East-West economic relations in the 1990s: the demand on politics"; Oleg Bogomolov, "New thinking and the role of governments in the World economy"; Norbert Kloten, Jozef M. van Brabant, and Henry Nau, "Comments on Part V"; Philipp Rieger, "Annex: Introductory remarks to the 12th Workshop".] REV: William Diebold, Jr., *Foreign Affairs* 70, no. 4 (Fall 1991): 173-174. Henri J. Warmenhoven, *Perspectives on Political Science* 22, no. 4 (Fall 1993): 185.

5328. Brabant, Jozef M. van. *The Planned Economies and International Economic Organizations*. Soviet and East European Studies, 77. Cambridge; New York: Cambridge University Press, 1991. xv, 318 pp. REV: William Diebold, Jr., *Foreign Affairs* 70, no. 5 (Winter 1991-92): 188. Robert W. Campbell, *Slavic Review* 51, no. 2 (Summer 1992): 332-336. Tracy Murray, *Journal of Comparative Economics* 17, no. 1 (March 1993): 156-157.

5329. Campbell, Robert W. *The Socialist Economies in Transition: A Primer on Semi-Reformed Systems.* Bloomington, IN: Indiana University Press, c1991. x, 241 pp. REV: Robert V. Legvold, *Foreign Affairs* 70, no. 5 (Winter 1991-92): 198-199. John M. Litwack, *Slavic Review* 51, no. 4 (Winter 1992): 854-855. J. Michael Montias, *Journal of Comparative Economics* 17, no. 4 (December 1993): 786-789.

5330. Committee on Science, Engineering, and Public Policy (U.S.). Panel on the Future Design and Implementation of U.S. National Security Export Controls. *Finding Common Ground: U.S. Export Controls in a Changed Global Environment.* Washington, DC: National Academy Press, 1991. xviii, 390 pp. REV: J. David Richardson, *Journal of Economic Literature* 30. no. 4 (December 1992): 2153-2154. *Orbis* 37, no. 1 (Winter 1993).

5331. Csaba, László. *Eastern Europe in the World Economy.* Soviet and East European Studies, 68. Cambridge; New York: Cambridge University Press, c1990. 403 pp. [Revised and enlarged edition of *Kelet-Europa a vilaggazdasagban.*] REV: William Diebold, Jr., *Foreign Affairs* 70, no. 2 (Spring 1991): 180; *Foreign Affairs* 70, no. 5 (Winter 1991-92): 188. Jan Prybyla, *Orbis* 36, no. 4 (Fall 1992): 589-596. Ryszard Rapacki, *Comparative Economic Studies* 34, nos. 3-4 (Fall-Winter 1992): 107-109. Pekka Sutela, *Journal of Comparative Economics* 17, no. 1 (March 1993): 165-166.

5332. Haus, Leah A. *Globalizing the GATT: The Soviet Union's Successor States, Eastern Europe, and the International Trading System.* Washington, DC: Brookings Institution, c1992. 141 pp. REV: *George Washington Journal of International Law and Economics* 26, no. 1 (1992): 223-224. Patrick Clawson, *Orbis* 36, no. 3 (Summer 1992): 465. William Diebold, Jr., *Foreign Affairs* 71, no. 3 (Summer 1992): 172. John E. Osborn, *SAIS Review* 12, no. 2 (Summer-Fall 1992): 158-160. Jean Kinsey, *Journal of Consumer Affairs* 27, no. 2 (December 1993): 424-427. Frances H. Oneal, *Soviet and Post-Soviet Review* 20, no. 1 (1993): 95. Kendall Stiles, *American Political Science Review* 87, no. 2 (June 1993): 541-542.

5333. Hillman, Arye L., ed. *Markets and Politicians: Politicized Economic Choice.* World Bank Regional and Sectoral Studies. Boston, MA: Kluwer, c1991. xvi, 368 pp. [Second section on markets and socialism; includes Schnytzer's discussion of the transitional stage between centralized and market systems.] REV: Ben T. Yu, *Journal of Comparative Economics* 17, no. 1 (March 1993): 170-172.

5334. Keren, Michael, and Gur Ofer, eds. *Trials of Transition: Economic Reform in the Former Communist Bloc.* Boulder, CO: Westview Press, 1992. xx, 308 pp. REV: Christine Rider, *Slavic Review* 52, no. 4 (Winter 1993): 895-896.

5335. Los, Maria, ed. *The Second Economy in Marxist States.* New York: St. Martin's Press, 1990. xiv, 240 pp. REV: Lynn Turgeon, *Comparative Economic Studies* 32, no. 4 (Winter, 1990): 114-116. William Moskoff, *Russian Review* 50, no. 2 (April 1991): 239-240. Stuart Henry, *Canadian Journal of Criminology* 35, no. 1 (January 1993): 75-79.

5336. Mastanduno, Michael. *Economic Containment: CoCom and the Politics of East-West Trade.* Cornell Studies in Political Economy. Ithaca, NY: Cornell University Press, 1992. xiv, 353 pp. REV: Beverly Crawford, *American Political Science Review* 87, no. 4 (December 1993): 1057-1059. William Diebold, Jr., *Foreign Affairs* 72, no. 2 (Spring 1993): 170-171. *Orbis* 37, no. 2 (Spring 1993).

5337. Milanovic, Branko. *Liberalization and Entrepreneurship: Dynamics of Reform in Socialism and Capitalism.* Armonk, NY: M.E. Sharpe, c1989. 183 pp. REV: Susan J. Linz, *Comparative Economic Studies* 32, no. 4 (Winter 1990): 117-118. Kazimierz Poznanski, *Journal of Comparative Economics* 15, no. 4 (December 1991): 720-722. John W. Murphy, *Studies in Soviet Thought* 43, no. 1 (January 1992): 61-63. Ben Slay, *Slavic Review* 52, no. 2 (Summer 1993): 374-375.

5338. Noyes, Richard, ed. *Now the Synthesis: Capitalism, Socialism, and the New Social Contract.* London: Shepheard-Walryn; New York: Holmes & Meier, 1991. vi, 241 pp. REV: Laurence S. Moss, *Southern Economic Journal* 60, no. 1 (July 1993): 263-265.

5339. Peebles, Gavin. *A Short History of Socialist Money.* Sydney; Boston, MA: Allen & Unwin; Concord, MA: U.S. Distribution, Paul and Co., 1991. xiii, 170 pp. REV: Paul Evans, *Journal of Economic Literature* 31, no. 2 (June 1993): 937.

5340. Poznanski, Kazimierz Z., ed. *Constructing Capitalism: The Reemergence of Civil Society and Liberal Economy in the Post-Communist World.* Boulder, CO: Westview Press, 1992. vii, 230 pp. [Product of an international political economy colloquium series held at the Henry M. Jackson School of International Studies.] REV: Dmitri Shalin, *Contemporary Sociology* 22, no. 3 (May 1993): 398-399. *Orbis* 37, no. 3 (Summer 1993).

5341. Prybyla, Jan S. *Reform in China and Other Socialist Economies.* AEI Studies, 505. Washington, DC: AEI Press for the American Enterprise Institute; Lanham, MD: Distributed by University Press of America, 1990. xiii, 357 pp. REV: Peter M. Lichtenstein, *Southern Economic Journal* 60, no. 1 (July 1993): 260-261.

5342. Pryor, Frederic L. *The Red and the Green: The Rise and Fall of Collectivized Agriculture in Marxist Regimes.* Princeton, NJ: Princeton University Press, c1992. x, 550 pp. REV: Forrest D. Colburn, *American Political Science Review* 87, no. 2 (June 1993): 533-534. Nicholas Eberstadt, *Annals of the American Academy of Political and Social Science*, no. 529 (September 1993): 186-187. Roy D. Laird, *Slavic Review* 52, no. 1 (Spring 1993): 141-142. Zeno Carl C. Mabbs, *American Journal of Agricultural Economics* 75, no. 3 (August 1993): 866-867. Louis Putterman, *Journal of Economic Literature* 31, no. 3 (September 1993): 1486-1488.

5343. Reisinger, William M. *Energy and the Soviet Bloc: Alliance Politics after Stalin.* Ithaca, NY: Cornell

University Press, 1992. xiii, 184 pp. REV: Robert Legvold, *Foreign Affairs* 71, no. 4 (Fall 1992): 211-212. Karen Dawisha, *American Political Science Review* 87, no. 2 (June 1993): 544. Bradley R. Gitz, *Journal of Politics* 55, no. 4 (November 1993): 1215-1217. John M. Kramer, *Slavic Review* 52, no. 1 (Spring 1993): 152-154.

5344. Richter, Sandor, ed. *The Transition from Command to Market Economies in East-Central Europe.* Westview Special Studies in International Economics. The Vienna Institute for Comparative Economic Studies Yearbook, 4. Boulder, CO: Westview Press in cooperation with the Vienna Institute for Comparative Economic Studies, 1992. x, 321 pp. [Contents: Amit Bhaduri, "The Economics of Transition: Conventional Stabilization and the East European Transition"; Kazimierz Laski, "Transition from Command to Market Economies in Central and Eastern Europe: First Experiences and Questions"; Friedrich Levcik, "The Thorny Path of Transition from Command to Market Economy"; Raimund Dietz, "Ten Propositions towards a Theory of Transformation: From Command to Exchange Communication"; Gabor Hunya, "Specific Issues of Transition: Privatization of Big Enterprises in Central and Eastern Europe: General Concepts and the Hungarian Experience"; Zdenek Lukas, "Czechoslovakia's Agriculture at the Crossroads"; Ilse Grosser, "Economic Transition in Bulgaria"; Peter Havlik, "Internal and External Environment of Transition: The Soviet Economy on the Brink of Confrontation"; Franjo Stiblar, "External Indebtedness of Yugoslavia and Its Federal Units"; Peter Havlik, "East-West GDP Comparisons: Problems, Methods and Results"; Hubert Gabrisch, "International Aspects of the Economic Transformation in Central and Eastern Europe"; Waltraut Urban, "Economic Lessons from Two Newly Industrializing Countries in the Far East?".] REV: John P. Bonin, *Comparative Economic Studies* 35, no. 3 (Fall 1993): 61-63.

5345. World Congress for Soviet and East European Studies (4th: 1990: Harrogate, England). *The Soviet Union and Eastern Europe in the Global Economy: Selected Papers from the Fourth World Congress for Soviet and East European Studies, Harrogate, 1990.* Edited by Marie Lavigne. Cambridge; New York: Cambridge University Press, 1992. xv, 219 pp. REV: Martin C. Spechler, *Comparative Economic Studies* 35, no. 2 (Summer 1993): 59-60.

Russia/U.S.S.R.

5346. Åslund, Anders. *Gorbachev's Struggle for Economic Reform.* Updated and expanded ed. Studies in Soviet History and Society. Ithaca, NY: Cornell University Press, 1991. 262 pp. REV: Peter Reddaway, *New York Review of Books* 38, no. 18 (November 7, 1991): 53-59. Jan Prybyla, *Orbis* 36, no. 4 (Fall 1992): 589-596. Anthony Jones, *Contemporary Sociology* 22, no. 1 (January 1993): 47.

5347. Brada, Josef C., and Michael P. Claudon, eds. *The Emerging Russian Bear: Integrating the Soviet Union into the World Economy.* Includes contributions by Josef C. Brada, Vladimir T. Musatov, Peter J. Pettibone, Francis A. Scotland, John A. Bohn, Jr., David H. Levey, Keith A. Rosten, Viktor P. Mozolin, Peter B. Maggs, Alexander L.

Katkov, Michail A. Portnoy, and Keith A. Rosten. Geonomics Institute for International Economic Advancement Series, New York: New York University Press, c1991. xiii, 228 pp. [Proceedings of Geonomics Institute seminar "Financial Markets, Joint Ventures, and Business Opportunities in the Soviet Union," held in May 1990.] REV: Guido Biessen, *Journal of Comparative Economics* 17, no. 1 (March 1993): 158-161.

5348. Burandt, Gary, and Nancy Giges. *Moscow Meets Madison Avenue: The Adventures of the First American Adman in the U.S.S.R.* 1st ed. New York: HarperBusiness, c1992. xiv, 222 pp. REV: Stuart Elliott, *New York Times Book Review* (December 27, 1992): 15. Deroy Murdock, *Freedom Review* 24, no. 2 (March-April 1993): 42-43.

5349. Campbell, Robert W. *The Failure of Soviet Economic Planning: System, Performance, Reform.* Bloomington, IN: Indiana University Press, c1992. xii, 185 pp. REV: Gary Krueger, *Comparative Economic Studies* 35, no. 2 (Summer 1993): 70-71.

5350. Claudon, Michael P., and Tamar L. Gutner, eds. *Investing in Reform: Doing Business in a Changing Soviet Union.* Geonomics Institute for International Economic Advancement Series. New York: New York University Press, c1991. xix, 279 pp. REV: John E. Tedstrom, *Journal of Comparative Economics* 17, no. 1 (March 1993): 162-164.

5351. Connor, Walter D. *The Accidental Proletariat: Workers, Politics, and Crisis in Gorbachev's Russia.* Princeton, NJ: Princeton University Press, c1991. xv, 374 pp. REV: Michael Burawoy, *Contemporary Sociology* 21, no. 6 (November 1992): 774-785. Jeffrey W. Hahn, *American Political Science Review* 86, no. 3 (September 1992): 824-825. Robert Legvold, *Foreign Affairs* 71, no. 2 (Spring 1992): 206. Linda J. Cook, *Journal of Politics* 55, no. 4 (November 1993): 1212-1215. Michael D. Kennedy, *American Journal of Sociology* 98, no. 5 (March 1993): 1244-1247. Silvana Malle, *Slavic Review* 52, no. 2 (Summer 1993): 387-388. Mervyn Matthews, *Annals of the American Academy of Political and Social Science*, no. 528 (July 1993): 182-183. Lewis H. Siegelbaum, *International Labor and Working-Class History*, no. 43 (Spring 1993): 135-138.

5352. Coopersmith, Jonathan. *The Electrification of Russia, 1880-1926.* Ithaca, NY: Cornell University Press, 1992. xii, 274 pp. REV: Daniel Brower, *American Historical Review* 98, no. 4 (October 1993): 1294. Alex G. Cummins, *Russian History = Histoire russe* 20, nos. 1-4 (1993): 350-351. Clifford M. Foust, *Business History Review* 67, no. 2 (Summer 1993): 361-363. Thomas C. Owen, *Slavic Review* 52, no. 3 (Fall 1993): 645-646.

5353. Davies, R. W., ed. *From Tsarism to the New Economic Policy: Continuity and Change in the Economy of the USSR.* Ithaca, NY: Cornell University Press, 1991. 417 pp. [Includes tables of social and economic statistics, pp. 249-337.] REV: Carol S. Leonard, *Journal of Economic History* 52, no. 3 (September 1992): 719-720. Lars T. Lih, *Slavic Review* 51, no. 4 (Winter 1992): 814-815. James H.

Bater, *American Historical Review* 98, no. 4 (October 1993): 1296-1297. Thomas C. Owen, *Russian Review* 52, no. 3 (July 1993): 431-432.

5354. Dowlah, A. F. *Soviet Political Economy in Transition: From Lenin to Gorbachev.* Contributions in Economics and Economic History, no. 130. New York: Greenwood Press, 1992. vi, 287 pp. REV: *Comparative Economic Studies* 35, no. 2 (Summer 1993): 68-70.

5355. Dyker, David A. *Restructuring the Soviet Economy.* London; New York: Routledge, 1992. viii, 231 pp. REV: Christine White, *Business History Review* 67, no. 3 (Autumn 1993): 527-528.

5356. Ellman, Michael, and Vladimir Kontorovich, eds. *The Disintegration of the Soviet Economic System.* London; New York: Routledge, 1992. 281 pp. [Ten of the chapters are revised versions of papers submitted at the World Congress for Soviet and East European Studies (4th: 1990: Harrogate, England).] REV: William B. Husband, *Business History Review* 67, no. 3 (Autumn 1993): 524-526.

5357. Enthoven, Adolf J. H., Jaroslav V. Sokolov, and Alexander M. Petrachkov. *Doing Business in Russia and the Other Former Soviet Republics: Accounting and Joint Venture Issues.* Bold Step Research Series. Montvale, NJ: Institute of Management Accountants, c1992. 259 pp. REV: Timothy S. Doupnik, *Accounting Review* 68, no. 2 (April 1993): 427-428.

5358. Filtzer, Donald. *Soviet Workers and De-Stalinization: The Consolidation of the Modern System of Soviet Production Relations, 1953-1964.* Soviet and East European Studies, 87. Cambridge; New York: Cambridge University Press, 1992. xv, 318 pp. REV: Simon Clarke, *Sociology* (November 1993): 717-719. Henry Reichman, *Russian History = Histoire russe* 20, nos. 1-4 (1993): 400-401.

5359. Galenson, Walter. *New Trends in Employment Practices: An International Survey.* Contributions in Labor Studies, no. 34. New York: Greenwood Press, 1991. ix, 159 pp. [Includes chapter on the Soviet model of employment.] REV: Oliver Clarke, *Industrial and Labor Relations Review* 46, no. 3 (April 1993): 596-597.

5360. Geron, Leonard. *Soviet Foreign Economic Policy under Perestroika.* Chatham House Papers, NY: Council on Foreign Relations Press, c1990. 126 pp. REV: John C. Campbell, *Foreign Affairs* 70, no. 3 (Summer 1991): 175. Perry L. Patterson, *Russian Review* 52, no. 1 (January 1993): 135-136.

5361. Gregory, Paul R. *Restructuring the Soviet Economic Bureaucracy.* Soviet Interview Project Series, New York: Cambridge University Press, 1990. xii, 181 pp. REV: F.I. Kushnirsky, *Russian Review* 50, no. 4 (October 1991): 503. Don K. Rowney, *Slavic Review* 50, no. 4 (Winter 1991): 1034-1035. Leland G. Stauber, *Soviet and Post-Soviet Review* 20, no. 1 (1993): 99.

5362. Hewett, Ed A., and Clifford G. Gaddy. *Open for Business: Russia's Return to the Global Economy.*

Washington, DC: Brookings Institution, c1992. xii, 164 pp. REV: Adam Banker, *Fletcher Forum of World Affairs* 17, no. 2 (Summer 1993): 225-227. William Diebold, Jr., *Foreign Affairs* 72, no. 2 (Spring 1993): 171.

5363. Hewett, Ed A., and Victor H. Winston, eds. *Milestones in Glasnost and Perestroyka.* Washington, DC: Brookings Institution, c1991-. 2 vols. [Readings based on contributions to Soviet Economy, 1985-1991. Contents: Vol. 1. The Economy (522 pp.) — v. 2. Politics and People (568 pp.).] REV: William W. Finan, Jr., *Current History* 90, no. 558 (October 1991): 346. John Downing, *Journal of Communication* 42, no. 2 (Spring 1992): 153-162. Jan Prybyla, *Orbis* 36, no. 4 (Fall 1992): 589-596. Joseph Pelzman, *Russian Review* 52, no. 3 (July 1993): 439-441.

5364. Hunter, Holland, and Janusz M. Szyrmer. *Faulty Foundations: Soviet Economic Policies, 1928-1940.* Princeton, NJ: Princeton University Press, c1992. 339 pp. REV: Robert Legvold, *Foreign Affairs* 71, no. 5 (Winter 1992-1993): 212. Mark Harrison, *Economic History Review* (November 1993): 830-831.

5365. International Monetary Fund, World Bank, Organisation for Economic Co-operation and Development, and EBRD. *The Economy of the USSR: Summary and Recommendations.* Washington, DC: The World Bank, c1990. iv, 51 pp. [Follows *A Study of the Soviet Economy* (Paris: International Monetary Fund et al., 1991), vols. 1-3.] REV: Abram Bergson, *Journal of Comparative Economics* 17, no. 1 (March 1993): 177-180.

5366. Jones, Anthony, and William Moskoff, eds. *The Great Market Debate in Soviet Economics: An Anthology.* Armonk, NY: M.E. Sharpe, 1991. 408 pp. [Translations of articles from Soviet periodicals. Contents: Nikolai Shmelev, "New anxieties"; V. Koreetseva, L. Perepelkin, and O. Shkaratan, "From bureaucratic centralism to economic integration of sovereign republics"; Leonid Abalkin, "The market in a socialist economy"; "The creation of a market" (an *EKO* roundtable); Vladimir P. Shkredov, "Socialism and property"; L. Nikiforov and V. Rutgaizer, "Leasing relations in the economic system of socialism"; "You can't outsmart life: a discussion of the proposed law on property in the USSR" (a *Kommunist* roundtable); "What path should we take?" (an *EKO* roundtable); V. M. Rutgaizer, A. I. Shmarov, and N. V. Kirichenko, "Reform of retail prices, the mechanism of compensation, and development of the consumer goods market"; "The anatomy of prices" (an interview on a topic of the day); S. M. Ignatev, "The banking system: paths of reform"; "Channeling personal savings into production" (a discussion among the editors of *Voprosy economiki*); "How can unemployment be avoided?" (a *Voprosy ekonomiki* roundtable); R. V. Ryvkina, "Economic culture as society's memory"; Nikolai Shmelev, "On urgent measures to prevent the collapse of the soviet economy"; "The 'Ryzhkov plan': economic report of Premier Nikolai Ryzhkov to the supreme soviet; "The 'Shatalin plan': transition to a market economy; "The 'Gorbachev plan': basic guidelines for the stabilization of the national economy and the transition to a market economy".] REV: Joseph Pelzman, *Southern Economic Journal* 59, no. 4 (April 1993): 849-851.

5367. ———. *Ko-ops: The Rebirth of Entrepreneurship in the Soviet Union.* Bloomington, IN: Indiana University Press, c1991. xvii, 153 pp. REV: Debra E. Soled, *Current History* 90, no. 558 (October 1991): 345. Michael Burawoy, *Contemporary Sociology* 21, no. 6 (November 1992): 774-785. Robert W. Campbell, *Slavic Review* 51, no. 2 (Summer 1992): 332-336. Jane I. Dawson, *Political Science Quarterly* 107, no. 4 (Winter 1992-1993): 756-757. David A. Dyker, *Harvard Ukrainian Studies* 16, nos. 1-2 (June 1992): 222-223. Michael A. Murphy, *Journal of Comparative Economics* 16, no. 4 (December 1992): 785-788. Holland Hunter, *Annals of the American Academy of Political and Social Science*, no. 526 (March 1993): 216-217. Peter Rutland, *Russian Review* 52, no. 2 (April 1993): 289-290.

5368. Koropeckyj, I. S., ed. *The Ukrainian Economy: Achievements, Problems, Challenges.* Harvard Series in Ukrainian Studies, Cambridge, MA: Harvard Ukrainian Research Institute; Distributed by Harvard University Press, c1992. xxvi, 436 pp. [Contents: I. S. Koropeckyj, "Introduction"; Ivan Lukinov, "Radical Reconstruction of the Ukrainian Economy: Reasons, Reforms, Outlook"; Ralph S. Clem, "Demographic Trends in Ukraine in the Late Twentieth Century"; Stephen Rapawy, "Labor Force and Employment in Ukraine"; Leslie Dienes, "Energy, Minerals, and Economic Policy"; David A. Dyker, "Capital Formation, Capital Stock, and Capital Productivity"; Serhii Pyrozhkov, "Discussion"; Andrii Revenko, "Gross Social Product and Net Material Product and Their Sectoral Structures"; F. I. Kushnirsky, "National Income of Ukraine: Estimation and Analysis"; Blaine McCants, "Ukrainian Industrial Productivity: A Republic-Comparative Analysis"; Elizabeth Clayton, "Ukrainian Agriculture"; Holland Hunter, "Discussion"; Gertrude E. Schroeder, "Living Standards in Ukraine: Retrospect and Prospect"; Mariian Dolishnii, "Regional Aspects of Ukraine's Economic Development"; Craig ZumBrunnen, "Environmental Conditions"; Alan Abouchar, "Discussion"; Tetiana Pakhomova and Serhii Mischenko, "Ukraine's External Trade"; Volodimir N. Bandera, "Income Transfers and Macroeconomic Accountability from the Republic Standpoint"; I. S. Koropeckyj, "Discussion".] REV: Martin C. Spechler, *Slavic Review* 52, no. 4 (Winter 1993): 896-898.

5369. Malle, Silvana. *Employment Planning in the Soviet Union: Continuity and Change.* Studies in Soviet History and Society. New York: St. Martin's Press in association with the Centre for Russian and East European Studies, University of Birmingham, 1990. 334 pp. REV: Peter Rutland, *Slavic Review* 51, no. 1 (Spring 1992): 145-146. Michael Ellman, *Russian Review* 52, no. 1 (January 1993): 142-143.

5370. Mandel, David. *Perestroika and the Soviet People: Rebirth of the Labour Movement.* Montreal, Quebec; New York: Black Rose Books, c1991. vi, 207 pp. REV: Alan Silverman, *Peace Magazine* 8, no. 2 (March-April 1992): 26-27. J. F. Conway, *Canadian Journal of Sociology* 18, no. 2 (Spring 1993): 197-206. Joan DeBardeleben, *Canadian Journal of Political Science = Revue canadienne de science*

politique 26, no. 3 (September 1993): 584-585.

5371. Mehrotra, Santosh. *India and the Soviet Union: Trade and Technology Transfer.* Soviet and East European Studies, 73. New York: Cambridge University Press, 1990. 242 pp. REV: Sumit Ganguly, *Journal of Asian Studies* 51, no. 2 (May 1992): 434-435. Colin Lawson, *International History Review* 14, no. 3 (August 1992): 631-633. Brigitte H. Schulz, *Canadian-American Slavic Studies* 26, nos. 1-4 (1992): 428-430. Kanti Bajpai, *Slavic Review* 52, no. 2 (Summer 1993): 392-393.

5372. Millar, James R. *The Soviet Economic Experiment.* Edited and introduction by Susan J. Linz. Urbana: University of Illinois Press, c1990. 297 pp. REV: Earl Brubaker, *Comparative Economic Studies* 33, no. 4 (Winter 1991): 130-132. Tracey Johnstone, *Canadian Slavonic Papers* 33, no. 1 (March 1991): 91. Paul R. Gregory, *Russian Review* 52, no. 4 (October 1993): 579-580.

5373. Nove, Alec. *Studies in Economics and Russia.* New York: St. Martin's Press, 1990. 375 pp. REV: Holland Hunter, *Slavic Review* 51, no. 3 (Fall 1992): 571-572. Josef C. Brada, *Russian Review* 52, no. 1 (January 1993): 135.

5374. Ofer, Gur, and Aaron Vinokur. *The Soviet Household under the Old Regime: Economic Conditions and Behavior in the 1970s.* Cambridge; New York: Cambridge University Press, 1992. xviii, 396 pp. REV: Jarmila L.A. Horna, *Canadian Slavonic Papers* 34, no. 4 (December 1992): 511-513. Holland Hunter, *Journal of Economic Literature* 31, no. 4 (December 1993): 2010-2011. James R. Millar, *Slavic Review* 52, no. 2 (Summer 1993): 386-387. Joseph M. Nowakowski, *Southern Economic Journal* 60, no. 2 (October 1993): 527-528.

5375. Peck, Merton J., and Thomas J. Richardson, eds. *What Is to Be Done? Proposals for the Soviet Transition to the Market.* Foreword by Stanislav Shatalin. Includes contributions by Wil Albeda et al. A Yale Fastback, New Haven, CT: Yale University Press, c1991. xviii, 220 pp. [Study of the International Institute for Applied Systems Analysis.] REV: Padma Desai, *New York Times Book Review* (April 12, 1992): 20. William Diebold, Jr., *Foreign Affairs* 71, no. 2 (Spring 1992): 196. John Feffer, *Commonweal* 119, no. 6 (March 27, 1992): 27-28. Abram Bergson, *Journal of Economic Literature*, 31, no. 1 (March 1993): 280-282. Thomas Cushman, *American Journal of Sociology* 98, no. 5 (March 1993): 1247-1249. David Gleicher, *Science & Society* 57, no. 3 (Fall 1993): 369-372.

5376. Pokhlebkin, William. *A History of Vodka.* Translated from the Russian by Renfrey Clarke. London; New York: Verson, 1992. xvi, 222 pp. [Translation of *Istoriia vodki*.] REV: George E. Snow, *Russian History = Histoire russe* 20, nos. 1-4 (1993): 265-266. *New Yorker* 68, no. 51 (February 8, 1993): 113.

5377. Puffer, Sheila M., ed. *The Russian Management Revolution: Preparing Managers for the Market Economy.* Foreword by Lawrence McKibbin. Armonk, NY: M.E. Sharpe, c1992. 290 pp. REV: Sheryl B. Ball, *Slavic Review* 52, no. 4 (Winter 1993): 899.

5378. Silverman, Bertram, Robert Vogt, and Murray Yanowitch, eds. *Labor and Democracy in the Transition to a Market System: A U.S.-Post Soviet Dialogue.* U.S.-Post-Soviet Dialogues. Armonk, NY: M.E. Sharpe, c1992. xxii, 228 pp. [Contents: Vera Kabalina and Alla K. Nazimova, "Labor Conflict Today"; Anna A. Temkina, "The Social Base of Economic Reforms"; Leonid A. Gordon and Eduard V. Klopov, "The Workers' Movement in a Postsocialist Perspective"; Iurii Volkov, "The Transition to a Mixed Economy and the Prospects for the Labor and Trade-Union Movement"; Boris Rakitskii, "The Struggle for the Interests of Working People in the Transition from a Totalitarian to a Democratic (Market) Economy"; Galina Ia. Rakitskaia, "Hired Labor or Self-Management?"; Emil N. Rudyk, "The Western Experience of Industrial Democracy and Its Significance"; Tatiana I. Zaslavskaia and Vladimir L. Kosmarskii, "The Labor Market Phenomena and Public Opinion"; Evgenii G. Antosenkov, "Current Employment Problems in the Soviet Economy and Means of Resolving Them"; Anatolii D. Shkira, "The Employment Problem During the Transition to a Market Economy"; Richard B. Freeman, "Getting Here from There"; Samuel Bowles, "Markets: Indispensable Servants, Cruel Masters"; Michael J. Piore, "The Limits of the Market and the Transformation of Socialism"; Benjamin Ward, "Marketization and the Defense of Labor's Interests"; Joseph S. Berliner, "The Workers State in Denationalization".] REV: William Diebold, Jr., *Foreign Affairs* 72, no. 2 (Spring 1993): 171.

5379. Solo, Robert A. *Opportunity Knocks: American Economic Policy after Gorbachev.* Armonk, NY: M.E. Sharpe, c1991. 207 pp. REV: Henry R. Nau, *Annals of the American Academy of Political and Social Science,* no. 523 (September 1992): 224-226. Paul D. Bush, *Journal of Economic Issues* 27, no. 3 (September 1993): 996-999.

5380. Spulber, Nicholas. *Restructuring the Soviet Economy: In Search of the Market.* Ann Arbor, MI: University of Michigan Press, c1991. 315 pp. REV: Robert V. Legvold, *Foreign Affairs* 70, no. 5 (Winter 1991-92): 199. Debra E. Soled, *Current History* 90, no. 558 (October 1991): 345. Jan Prybyla, *Orbis* 36, no. 4 (Fall 1992): 589-596. Jan Adam, *Slavic Review* 52, no. 1 (Spring 1993): 145-146. Holland Hunter, *Annals of the American Academy of Political and Social Science,* no. 526 (March 1993): 216-217.

5381. Sutela, Pekka. *Economic Thought and Economic Reform in the Soviet Union.* Cambridge Soviet Paperbacks, 5. New York: Cambridge University Press, 1991. x, 197 pp. REV: Robert W. Campbell, *Slavic Review* 51, no. 2 (Summer 1992): 332-336. Doug Brown, *Journal of Economic Issues* 27, no. 1 (March 1993): 271-274. Gertrude Schroeder, *Russian Review* 52, no. 1 (January 1993): 134.

5382. Ticktin, Hillel. *Origins of the Crisis in the USSR: Essays on the Political Economy of a Disintegrating System.* Armonk, NY: M.E. Sharpe, c1992. ix, 192 pp. REV: Colin M. White, *Australian Slavonic and East European Studies* 6, no. 2 (1992): 127-128. Michael Cox, *Russian Review* 52, no. 3 (July 1993): 436-437.

Eastern Europe

5383. Alogoskoufis, George, Lucas Papademos, and Richard Portes, eds. *The External Constraints on Macroeconomic Policy: The European Experience.* Cambridge; New York: Cambridge University Press, 1991. xvii, 384 pp. [Selected papers presented at a conference on Macroeconomic Policy and the External Constraint, held in Athens, May 24-26, 1990, and sponsored by the Centre for Economic Policy Research and the Bank of Greece. Includes chapter on Greece, chapter on Germany, and two chapters on global economic integration.] REV: John T. Cuddington, *Journal of Economic Literature* 31, no. 2 (June 1993): 897-899.

5384. Atkinson, Anthony B., and John Micklewright. *Economic Transformation in Eastern Europe and the Distribution of Income.* Cambridge; New York, NY: Cambridge University Press, 1992. xvi, 448 pp. [Contents: 1: Introduction and summary — 2: Why study the distribution pre-1990? — 3: Data: availability, quality and comparability — 4: The distribution of earnings — 5: The distribution of household incomes — 6: Interpreting income data — 7: Measuring poverty — 8: Poverty and the safety net — Sources and methods.] REV: Abram Bergson, *Journal of Economic Literature,* 31, no. 2 (June 1993): 892-893. Branko Milanovic, *Finance & Development* 30, no. 3 (September 1993): 49-50. *Orbis* 37, no. 4 (Fall 1993).

5385. Bird, Graham R., ed. *Economic Reform in Eastern Europe.* Aldershot; Brookfield, VT: E. Elgar, c1992. xvii, 187 pp. [Based on a conference held by the Department of Economics at the University of Surrey, in February 1991.] REV: Robert Campbell, *Comparative Economic Studies* 35, no. 2 (Summer 1993): 65-66.

5386. Blanchard, Olivier, Rudiger Dornbusch, Paul Krugman, Richard Layard, and Lawrence Summers. *Reform in Eastern Europe.* Cambridge, MA: MIT Press, c1991. xxiii, 98 pp. REV: John C. Campbell, *Foreign Affairs* 70, no. 4 (Fall 1991): 183. Ronald I. McKinnon, *Journal of Economic Literature* 30, no. 2 (June 1992): 936-937. Jan Prybyla, *Orbis* 36, no. 4 (Fall 1992): 589-596. Perry L. Patterson, *Slavic Review* 52, no. 4 (Winter 1993): 885-886. Steven Pressman, *Southern Economic Journal* 59, no. 3 (January 1993): 563-565.

5387. Boyd, Michael L. *Organization, Performance and System Choice: East European Agricultural Development.* Boulder, CO: Westview Press, 1991. xiv, 181 pp. REV: Robert C. Stuart, *Journal of Economic Literature* 30, no. 2 (June 1992): 937-938. Michael L. Wyzan, *Journal of Comparative Economics* 16, no. 2 (June 1992): 340-343. Gregory J. Brock, *Comparative Economic Studies* 35, no. 1 (Spring 1993): 119-120.

5388. Burawoy, Michael, and János Lukács. *The Radiant Past: Ideology and Reality in Hungary's Road to Capitalism.* Chicago, IL: University of Chicago Press, c1992. xvi, 215 pp. REV: John Feffer, *Christianity and Crisis* 52, no. 18 (December 14, 1992): 412ff. Michael D. Kennedy, *Social Forces* 71, no. 1 (September 1992): 246-248. Robert Legvold, *Foreign Affairs* 71, no. 3 (Summer 1992): 179-180.

Ireneusz Bialecki, *Contemporary Sociology* 22, no. 1 (January 1993): 43. Elizabeth Kiss, *American Political Science Review* 87, no. 2 (June 1993): 514-515. Alexander J. Matejko, *Canadian Journal of Political Science = Revue canadienne de science politique* 26, no. 2 (June 1993): 411. Ákos Róna-Tas, *American Journal of Sociology* 99, no. 3 (November 1993): 770-771. Nigel Swain, *Social Science Quarterly* 74, no. 3 (September 1993): 688-689.

5389. Clague, Christopher, and Gordon C. Rausser, eds. *The Emergence of Market Economies in Eastern Europe*. Cambridge, MA: B. Blackwell, 1992. x, 352 pp. [Contents: Christopher Clague, "Introduction: The Journey to a Market Economy"; Lawrence Summers, "The Next Decade in Central and Eastern Europe"; Peter Murrell, "Evolution in Economics and in the Economic Reform of the Centrally Planned Economies"; Mancur Olson, "The Hidden Path to a Successful Economy"; Robert Cooter, "Organization as Property: Economic Analysis of Property Law Applied to Privatization"; Alan Walters, "The Transition to a Market Economy"; Ronald McKinnon, "Taxation, Money, and Credit in a Liberalizing Socialist Economy"; Sebastian Edwards, "Stabilization and Liberalization Policies for Economies in Transition: Latin American Lessons for Eastern Europe"; Joseph E. Stiglitz, "The Design of Financial Systems for the Newly Emerging Democracies in Eastern Europe"; Robert Willig, "Anti-Monopoly Policies and Institutions"; David Newbery, "The Safety Net During Transformation: Hungary"; Anne Krueger, "Institutions for the New Private Sector"; Stanley Fischer, "Privatization in East European Transformation"; Gordon Rausser and Leo Simon, "The Political Economy of Transition in Eastern Europe: Packaging Enterprises for Privatization"; Jan Winiecki, "Privatization in East-Central Europe: Avoiding Major Mistakes"; Scott Thomas, "The Political Economy of Privatization: Poland, Hungary, and Czechoslovakia"; Arnold Harberger, "Strategies for the Transition"; András Nagy, "Institutions and the Transition to a Market Economy"; Gordon Rausser, "Lessons for Emerging Market Economies in Eastern Europe".] REV: William Diebold, Jr., *Foreign Affairs* 71, no. 5 (Winter 1992-1993): 201-202. Maria Los, *Canadian Slavonic Papers* 34, no. 4 (December 1992): 498-499. George Viksnins, *Journal of Baltic Studies* 23, no. 2 (Summer 1992): 191-196. Robert Campbell, *Slavic Review* 52, no. 3 (Fall 1993): 620-621.

5390. Csaba, László, ed. *Systemic Change and Stabilization in Eastern Europe*. Contributions by Anders Åslund et al. Aldershot: Dartmouth; Brookfield, VT: Gower, c1991. x., 141 pp. [Papers originally presented at the European Association for Comparative Economic Studies' first international conference, held in Verona, Italy, September 27-29, 1990.] REV: David M. Kemme, *Slavic Review* 51, no. 4 (Winter 1992): 861-862. Xavier Richet, *Comparative Economic Studies* 35, no. 2 (Summer 1993): 63-65.

5391. Dobosiewicz, Zbigniew. *Foreign Investment in Eastern Europe*. London; New York: Routledge, 1992. xiv, 134 pp. REV: William Diebold, Jr., *Foreign Affairs* 72, no. 2 (Spring 1993): 171.

5392. Enderlyn, Allyn, and Oliver C. Dziggel. *Cracking Eastern Europe: Everything Marketers Must Know to Sell into the World's Newest Emerging Markets*. Chicago, IL: Probus, c1992. xxi, 385 pp. REV: *Booklist* 89, no. 15 (April 1, 1993): 1454.

5393. Katz, Bernard S., and Libby Rittenberg, eds. *The Economic Transformation of Eastern Europe: Views from Within*. Westport, CT: Praeger, 1992. xviii, 192 pp. [Contents: Jiri Hlavacek, "The Case for Privatization in Czechoslovakia and Other Centrally Planned Economies"; Zoltan Bara, "The Role of Property Rights in the Transition in Hungary"; Maciej Iwanek, "Poland's Property Rights Problem in the Transition"; Ivan Ribnikar, "Transition into a Market Economy: The Road to Privatization in Yugoslavia"; Jerzy Skuratowicz, "The Unexpected Consequences of Traditional Macro Stabilization Policy during Transition: The Case of Poland"; Ales Bulir, "Macroeconomic Policy and Institutions in the Czechoslovak Transition: The Starting Point and First Steps"; Milan Sojka, "The Transformation of the Czechoslovak Economy and Unemployment"; Andrzej Kondratowicz and Jan Michalek, "Polish Trade Adjustment under Convertibility"; Katalin Szabo, "Small is Also Beautiful in the East: The Boom of Small Ventures in Hungary"; Mieczyslaw W. Socha and Urszula Sztanderska, "Polish Firms in Transition"; Jerzy Wilkin, "The Role of Peasants in the Systemic Transformation of the Polish Economy, 1944-1990".] REV: Robert R. Ebert, *Comparative Economic Studies* 35, no. 2 (Summer 1993): 72-73. W. Eric McElwain, *Transnational Lawyer* 6, no. 2 (Fall 1993): 601-602.

5394. Lampe, John R., ed. *Creating Capital Markets in Eastern Europe*. Woodrow Wilson Center Special Studies. Washington, DC: Woodrow Wilson Center Press; Baltimore, MD: Johns Hopkins University Press, c1992. xi, 114 pp. [Contents: Alice Teichova, "Interwar Capital Markets in Central and Southeastern Europe"; Maurice E. May, "Current Capital Markets in the United States, Western Europe, and Japan"; Dirk W. Damrau, "The Role of Foreign Investment in East European Privatization: Hungary, Poland, and Czechoslovakia"; Jozsef Rotyis, "The Budapest Stock Exchange"; Marvin R. Jackson, "Company Management and Capital Market Development in the Transition"; Alfredo Thorne, "Reforming Financial Systems in Eastern Europe: The Case of Bulgaria".] REV: Jerry L. Petr, *Slavic Review* 52, no. 3 (Fall 1993): 607-609.

5395. Lampe, John R., Russell O. Prickett, and Ljubisa S. Adamovic. *Yugoslav-American Economic Relations Since World War II*. Durham, NC: Duke University Press, 1990. xi, 249 pp. REV: Robert V. Legvold, *Foreign Affairs* 70, no. 5 (Winter 1991-92): 200. Stephen N. Sestanovich, *Foreign Service Journal* 68, no. 12 (December 1991): 43-44. Ronald H. Linden, *American Historical Review* 98, no. 1 (February 1993): 273-274.

5396. McKinnon, Ronald I. *The Order of Economic Liberalization: Financial Control in the Transition to a Market Economy*. Johns Hopkins Studies in Development. Baltimore, MD: Johns Hopkins University Press, c1991. xii, 200 pp. [Includes Eastern Europe.] REV: Robert W. Campbell, *Slavic Review* 51, no. 2 (Summer 1992): 332-336.

William Diebold, Jr., *Foreign Affairs* 71, no. 2 (Spring 1992): 196. Anne O. Krueger, *Journal of Comparative Economics* 17, no. 1 (March 1993): 184-186.

5397. Nagengast, Carole. *Reluctant Socialists, Rural Entrepreneurs: Class, Culture, and the Polish State.* Studies in the Ethnographic Imagination. Boulder, CO: Westview Press, 1991. 239 pp. REV: Bronislaw Misztal, *Contemporary Sociology* 22, no. 1 (January 1993): 48. Michael Stewart, *Man* (December 1993): 847-848.

5398. Plestina, Dijana. *Regional Development in Communist Yugoslavia: Success, Failure, and Consequences.* Boulder, CO: Westview Press, 1992. xxix, 223 pp. REV: Francine Friedman, *American Political Science Review* 87, no. 4 (December 1993): 1047-1048. Evan Kraft, *Political Science Quarterly* 108, no. 4 (Winter 1993-1994): 764-765.

5399. Prychitko, David L. *Marxism and Workers' Self-Management: The Essential Tension.* Contributions in Economics and Economic History, no. 123. New York: Greenwood Press, c1991. xvii, 153 pp. [Especially Yugoslavia.] REV: Milan Vodopivec, *Journal of Comparative Economics* 17, no. 1 (March 1993): 187-189.

5400. Przeworski, Adam. *Democracy and the Market: Political and Economic Reforms in Eastern Europe and Latin America.* Studies in Rationality and Social Change. Cambridge; New York: Cambridge University Press, 1991. xii, 210 pp. REV: Ellen Comisso, *Contemporary Sociology* 21, no. 3 (May 1992): 317-320. Barbara Geddes, *American Political Science Review* 86, no. 4 (December 1992): 1093-1094. Michael Hechter, *American Journal of Sociology* 97, no. 6 (May 1992): 1761-1764. Gretchen Casper, *Comparative Political Studies* 26, no. 1 (April 1993): 136-140. John R. Freeman, *Journal of Politics* 55, no. 1 (February 1993): 283-285. Ian Shapiro, *World Politics* 46, no. 1 (October 1993): 121-150. Adam Török, *Slavic Review* 52, no. 3 (Fall 1993): 621-623.

5401. Siklos, Pierre L. *War Finance, Reconstruction, Hyperinflation, and Stabilization in Hungary, 1938-48.* New York: St. Martin's Press, 1991. xx, 281 pp. REV: Stephen T. Eaton, *Canadian Journal of Economics* 26, no. 1 (February 1993): 246-248. Alan S. Milward, *International History Review* 15, no. 2 (May 1993): 389.

5402. Sinn, Gerlinde, and Hans-Werner Sinn. *Jumpstart: The Economic Unification of Germany.* Translated by Juli Irving-Lessman. Cambridge, MA: MIT Press, c1992. xviii, 243 pp. REV: *Orbis* 37, no. 2 (Spring 1993).

5403. Szelenyi, Ivan, Robert Manchin, Pál Juhász, Bálint Magyar, and Bill Martin. *Socialist Entrepreneurs: Embourgeoisement in Rural Hungary.* Madison, WI: University of Wisconsin Press, 1988. xvi, 255 pp. [Class structure and social mobility, ethnographic observation focusing on officials, proletarians, entrepreneurs, and peasant workers. Concluding essay with G. Konrad on intellectuals in socialist societies. Awarded C. W. Mills award.] REV: Steven Brint, *American Journal of Sociology* 95, no. 1 (July 1989): 218-219. Ákos Róna-Tas, *Slavic Review* 52, no. 2 (Summer 1993): 377-379.

5404. Tsaliki, Persefoni V. *The Greek Economy: Sources of Growth in the Postwar Era.* New York: Praeger, 1991. xvi, 196 pp. REV: Nicholas C. Baltas, *Journal of Developing Areas* 27, no. 2 (January 1993): 273-274. George A. Jouganatos, *Review of Radical Political Economics* 25, no. 2 (June 1993): 145-147.

5405. Yunker, James A. *Socialism Revised and Modernized: The Case for Pragmatic Market Socialsm.* New York: Praeger, 1992. xiii, 337 pp. REV: Gladys Parker Foster, *Journal of Economic Issues* 27, no. 3 (September 1993): 964-966. Holland Hunter, *Comparative Economic Studies* 35, no. 1 (Spring 1993): 121-123. *Orbis* 37, no. 1 (Winter 1993).

■ Education and Scholarship

5406. Brickman, William W., and John T. Zepper, comps. *Russian and Soviet Education, 1731-1989: A Multilingual Annotated Bibliography.* Garland Reference Library of Social Science, v. 200. Reference Books in International Education, vol. 9. New York: Garland, 1992. xix, 538 pp. REV: Charles T. Evans, *East/West Education* 14, no. 2 (Fall 1993): 174-175.

5407. Evans, Karen, and Ian G. Haffenden, eds. *Education for Young Adults: International Perspectives.* International Perspectives on Adult and Continuing Education, London; New York: Routledge, 1991. xi, 157 pp. [Partial contents: Part I. East and West. Robert Cowen, "A comparative comment on youth and development: political ideology and change," pp. 15-27; David Marsland, "Trends in youth education and development, East and West," pp. 28-43; Pamela W. Fearey and Olga Lalor, "Youth and higher education in the USSR," pp. 67-73.] REV: John Snarey and Phyllis Curtis, *Comparative Education Review* 37, no. 1 (February 1993): 77-80.

5408. Fletcher, George. *The Compleat Handbook and Glossary of Soviet Education.* Foreword by Mario Caruso. New York: Globe Language Services, 1992. vi, 124 pp. REV: Charles T. Evans, *East/West Education* 14, no. 2 (Fall 1993): 174-175.

5409. Ginsburg, Mark B., ed. *Understanding Educational Reform in Global Context: Economy, Ideology, and the State.* Garland Reference Library of Social Science, v. 663. Reference Books in International Education, vol. 22. New York: Garland, 1991. xx, 403 pp. [Partial contents: Peter Darvas, "Perspectives of Educational Reform in Hungary".] REV: E. Mark Hanson, *Comparative Education Review* 37, no. 3 (August 1993): 329-332.

5410. Holmes, Larry E. *The Kremlin and the Schoolhouse: Reforming Education in Soviet Russia, 1917-1931.* Indiana-Michigan Series in Russian and East European Studies. Bloomington, IN: Indiana University Press, c1991. xv, 214 pp. REV: Sylvia Russell, *Canadian-American Slavic Studies* 25, nos. 1-4 (1991): 319-320. Peter Konecny, *Canadian Slavonic Papers* 34, no. 3 (September 1992): 331-332. N. Riasanovsky, *Historian* 54, no. 4 (Summer 1992): 712-713. Mary Schaeffer Conroy, *East/West Education* 14, no. 1 (Spring 1993): 74-76. Peter Kenez, *American Historical Review* 98, no. 1 (February 1993): 205-206. William B. Husband, *Russian Review* 52, no. 1 (January 1993): 119-20.

5411. Keeves, John, Malcom J. Rosier, T. Neville Postlethwaite, and David Wiley, eds. *IEA Study of Science.* 1st ed. International Studies in Educational Achievement, vols. 8-10. Oxford; New York: Published for the International Association for the Evaluation of Educational Achievement by Pergamon Press, 1991-1992. 3 vols. [Partial contents: Vol. I. Science Education and Curricula in Twenty-Three Countries — v. II. Science Achievement in Twenty-Three Countries — v. III. Changes in Science Education and Achievement: 1970 to 1984. Vol. I includes Zoltan Bathory and Peter Vari, "Hungary," pp. 136-145, and Krystyna Czupial, "Poland," pp. 223-231.] REV: Sandra Gottfried, *Comparative Education Review* 37, no. 3 (August 1993): 327-329.

5412. Leavitt, Howard B., ed. *Issues and Problems in Teacher Education: An International Handbook.* Foreword by Arthur W. Foshay. New York: Greenwood Press, 1992. xvi, 292 pp. [Partial contents: Christa Händle, "Germany," pp. 125-137; Joan B. Wilson, "Union of Soviet Socialist Republics," pp. 233-246.] REV: Delbert H. Long, *Educational Studies* 24, no. 4 (Winter 1993): 353-358. Yenbo Wu, *Comparative Education Review* 37, no. 4 (November 1993): 497-499.

5413. Lee, David Currie. *The People's Universities of the USSR.* Contributions to the Study of Education, no. 29. New York: Greenwood Press, 1988. xv, 264 pp. REV: John Dunstan, *Comparative Education Review* 36, no. 2 (May 1992): 239-241. Samuel Kassow, *Russian Review* 52, no. 2 (April 1993): 290-291.

5414. Muckle, James. *Portrait of a Soviet School under Glasnost.* New York: St. Martin's Press, 1990. ix, 205 pp. REV: Ben Eklof, *Slavic Review* 51, no. 1 (Spring 1992): 176-177. David Currie Lee, *Soviet and Post-Soviet Review* 19, nos. 1-3 (1992): 287-288. Anthony Jones, *Russian Review* 52, no. 3 (July 1993): 441.

5415. Santa Maria, Phillip. *The Question of Elementary Education in the Third Russian State Duma, 1907-1912.* Lewiston, NY: Mellen Press, c1990. 119 pp. REV: Ben Eklof, *Russian Review* 52, no. 1 (January 1993): 126-127.

5416. Thomas, R. Murray, ed. *Education's Role in National Development Plans: Ten Country Cases.* New York: Praeger, 1992. xii, 290 pp. [Papers from the 1990 Western Regional Conference of the Comparative and International Education Society. Partial contents: Part I: Socialism in the USSR and Eastern Europe. Rosalind Latiner Raby, "The Soviet Union," pp. 43-62; Susanne M. Shafer, "The German Democratic Republic," pp. 63-83.] REV: Patricia S. Weibust, *Comparative Education Review* 37, no. 3 (August 1993): 336-337.

5417. Wulff, Kenneth R. *Education in Poland: Past, Present, and Future.* Lanham, MD: University Press of America, c1992. 110 pp. REV: Andrew Kier Wise, *East/West Education* 14, no. 2 (Fall 1993): 175-176.

■ Geography and Demography

5418. Barratt, Glynn. *Russia and the South Pacific, 1696-1840.* University of British Columbia Press Pacific Maritime Studies Series, 5, 7-8, 10. Vancouver: University of British Columbia Press, 1988-1992. 4 vols. [Contents: Vol. 1. The Russians and Australia — v. 2. Southern and Eastern Polynesia — v. 3. Melanesia and the Western Polynesian Fringe — v. 4. The Tuamotu Islands and Tahiti.] REV: Barry Gough, *International History Review* 12, no. 2 (May 1990): 366-368. Barry Gough, *International History Review* 12, no.3 (August 1990): 580-581. T.B. Millar, *Canadian Journal of History = Annales canadienne d'histoire* 25, no. 2 (August 1990): 306-307. Norman E. Saul, *American Historical Review* 95, no. 4 (October 1990): 1249-1250. Martin Crouch, *Russian History* 18, no. 2 (Summer 1991): 204-205. James A. Boutilier, *Pacific Affairs* 65, no. 1 (Spring 1992): 134-136. Glyndwr Williams, *International History Review* 15, no. 4 (November 1993): 783.

5419. Bater, James H. *The Soviet Scene: A Geographical Perspective.* New York: E. Arnold, 1989. xv, 304 pp. [Historical and political background for students of Soviet geography; demography, urban planning, management of land and resources, industrialization, quality of life, Gorbachev's reforms.] REV: Ellen K. Cromley, *Economic Geography* 65, no. 3 (July 1989): 260-262. Kathleen Braden, *Geographical Review* 80, no. 4 (October 1990): 452-453. Ludmila Iliina and Zbigniew Mieczkowski, *Canadian Geographer* 36, no. 3 (Fall 1992): 297-299. Boris Mironov, *Slavic Review* 52, no. 3 (Fall 1993): 656-658.

5420. Komlos, John. *Nutrition and Economic Development in the Eighteenth-Century Habsburg Monarchy: An Anthropometric History.* Princeton, NJ: Princeton University Press, c1989. xvii, 325 pp. REV: Rose E. Frisch, *Population and Development Review* 16, no. 2 (June 1990): 370-371. Franz A.J. Szabo, *Canadian Journal of History = Annales canadienne d'histoire* 25, no. 3 (December 1990): 409-411. Andrew D. Foster, *Annals of the American Academy of Political and Social Science*, no. 518 (November 1991): 217-219. William W. Hagen, *Journal of Economic History* 51, no. 3 (September 1991): 717-719. Amy Thompson McCandless, *Southern Economic Journal* 57, no. 4 (April 1991): 1203-1204. Edgar Melton, *Journal of Social History* 24, no. 4 (Summer 1991): 900-901. James C. Riley, *American Historical Review* 96, no. 3 (June 1991): 909-911. Richard H. Steckel, *Journal of Economic Literature* 29, no. 3 (September 1991): 1208-1209. Paula Sutter Fichtner, *Histoire sociale = Social History* 25, no. 49 (May 1992): 194-196. Scott M. Eddie, *Slavic Review* 52, no. 1 (Spring 1993): 140-1.

5421. Lappo, G. M., N. V. Petrov, and John Adams. *Urban Geography in the Soviet Union and the United States.* Translated by Joel Quam and Craig ZumBrunnen. Edited by Craig ZumBrunnen. Savage, MD: Rowman & Littlefield, c1992. 317 pp. REV: Robert Gohstand, *Slavic Review* 52, no. 3 (Fall 1993): 653-656.

5422. Lewis, Robert A., ed. *Geographic Perspectives on Soviet Central Asia*. Cartography by Robert R. Churchill, and Amanda Tate. Studies of the Harriman Institute, New York: Routledge, 1992. xv, 323 pp. [Contents: Robert A. Lewis, "Introduction"; Ralph S. Clem, "The Frontier and Colonialism in Russian and Soviet Central Asia"; Lee Schwartz, "The Political Geography of Soviet Central Asia: Integrating the Central Asian Frontier"; Peter Sinnott, "The Physical Geography of Soviet Central Asia and the Aral Sea Problem"; Ronald D. Liebowitz, "Soviet Geographical Imbalances and Soviet Central Asia"; Peter R. Craumer, "Agricultural Change, Labor Supply, and Rural Out-Migration in Soviet Central Asia"; Michael Paul Sacks, "Work Force Composition, Patriarchy, and Social Change"; Ozod B. Ata-Mirzayev and Abdukhakim A. Kayumov, "The Demography of Soviet Central Asia and its Future"; Richard H. Rowland, "Demographic Trends in Soviet Central Asia and Southern Kazakhstan"; Robert J. Kaiser, "Social Mobilization in Soviet Central Asia"; Robert J. Kaiser, "Nations and Homelands in Soviet Central Asia".] REV: William Fierman, *Slavic Review* 52, no. 1 (Spring 1993): 159-160. Philip Micklin, *Professional Geographer* 45, no. 2 (May 1993): 238-239.

5423. Mather, John R., and Galina V. Sdasyuk, eds. *Global Change: Geographical Approaches*. Contributions by Roger G. Barry, Tatiana V. Bochkareva, Geroge J. Demko, Aleksandr V. Drozdov, Nikita F. Glazovsky, Sergei P. Gorshkov, Samuel N. Goward, David E. Greenland, Julia A. Jones, Aleksandr N. Krenke, John R. Mather, James K. Mitchell, Sergei M. Myagkov, William E. Riebsame, Tatiana G. Runova, Galina V. Sdasyuk, Vladimir N. Solntsev, Andrei A. Velitchko, Thompson Webb, III, and Cort J. Willmott. Geographical Dialogue, Tucson, AZ: University of Arizona Press, c1991. xix, 289 pp. ["A joint USSR-USA project under the scientific leadership of Vladimir M. Kotlyakov and Gilbert F. White".] REV: Ian Burton, *Annals of the Association of American Geographers* 83, no. 2 (June 1993): 385-387. John E. Oliver, *Geographical Review* 83, no. 1 (January 1993): 112-114.

5424. Mazurkiewicz, Ludwik. *Human Geography in Eastern Europe and the Former Soviet Union*. Foreword by R. J. Johnston. New York: Halsted Press, 1992. 163 pp. REV: Colin Thomas, *Geography* (April 1993): 232.

5425. Mezs, Ilmars. *Latviesi Latvija, etnodemografisks apskats*. Kalamzoo, MI: LSC Apgalds, 1992. 74 pp. REV: Aleksis Dreimanis, *Journal of Baltic Studies* 24, no. 2 (Summer 1993): 214-215.

5426. Ruble, Blair A. *Leningrad: Shaping a Soviet City*. Lane Studies in Regional Government. Berkeley, CA: Published for the Institute of Governmental Studies and the Institute of International Studies, University of California, Berkeley, by the University of California Press, c1990. xxvi, 328 pp. REV: Michael F. Hamm, *Russian History* 17, no. 4 (Winter 1990): 481-482. J. H. Bater, *Canadian-American Slavic Studies* 25, nos. 1-4 (1991): 370-372. Daniel R. Brower, *Russian Review* 50, no. 3 (July 1991): 366-367. David T. Cattell, *American Historical Review* 96, no. 4 (October 1991): 1242-1243. Pavel Ilyin, *Soviet Geography*

32, no. 1 (January 1991): 58-60. Peter Konecny, *Canadian Slavonic Papers* 33, no. 1 (March 1991): 93-95. R.B. McKean, *Social Science Quarterly* 72, no. 3 (September 1991): 632-633. James C. Clingermayer, *Policy Studies Journal* 21, no. 1 (1993): 144-148.

5427. Stern, Geoffrey, ed. *Atlas of Communism*. Contributions by Terrell Carver, David Childs, Margot Light, Geoffrey Roberts, George Schöpflin, Peter Shearman, Hazhir Teimourian, Richard Walker, Michael Williams, and Michael Yahuda. New York: Macmillan, c1991. 256 pp. REV: Gerald L. Ingalls, *Professional Geographer* 45, no. 1 (February 1993): 122-123.

5428. Zelinsky, Wilbur, and Leszek A. Kosinski. *The Emergency Evacuation of Cities: A Cross-National Historical and Geographical Study*. Savage, MD: Rowman & Littlefield, c1991. xvi, 345 pp. [Partial contents: "Skopje, 1963," pp. 57-61; "Warsaw, 1939-44," pp. 98-115; "USSR, 1941-44," pp. 140-152; "Leningrad, 1941-45," pp. 152-160; "Chernobyl," pp. 231-240.] REV: Donald J. Zeigler, *Geographical Review* 83, no. 3 (July 1993): 332-334.

■ Government, Law, Politics

General

5429. Brown, Charles J., and Armando M. Lago. *The Politics of Psychiatry in Revolutionary Cuba*. Washington, DC: Freedom House of Human Rights, 1991. xiii, 217 pp. [In preface, Soviet dissident Vladimir Bukovsky compares repression in Cuba to that in the Soviet Union.] REV: Jorge Carro, *Human Rights Quarterly* 15, no. 4 (November 1993): 779-782. Julie Hack, *New York University Journal of International Law and Politics* 25, no. 5 (Winter 1993): 529-530.

5430. Bushnell, P. Timothy, Vladimir Shlapentokh, Christopher K. Vanderpool, and Jeyaratnam Sundram, eds. *State Organized Terror: The Case of Violent Internal Repression*. Contributions by Alex P. Schmid, James McCamant, Charles D. Brocket, Rhoda E. Howard, Jonathan R. Adelman, William Manley, David Pion-Berlin, Bernd Weghner, Stanley K. Shernock, Ben Kiernan, Cahnthou Boua, William O. McCagg, Jr., Dmitry Shlapentokh, Helen Fine, Jan Jia-Jing Wu, and Robert A. Solo. Series on State Violence, State Terrorism, and Human Rights. Boulder, CO: Westview Press, 1991. x, 312 pp. [Includes chapters on political repression, show trials, and the political police in the Soviet Union, Hungary, and Afghanistan.] REV: Stephen Sloan, *Conflict Quarterly* 12, no. 4 (Fall 1992): 87-89. Donna M. Schlagheck, *Studies in Conflict and Terrorism* 16, no. 3 (July-September 1993): 233-234.

5431. Campeanu, Pavel. *Exit: Toward Post-Stalinism*. Translated by Michel Vale. Armonk, NY: M.E. Sharpe, c1990. xiii, 169 pp. [Translated from an unpublished French manuscript. Text also appeared in *International Journal of Sociology* 20, nos. 1-2.] REV: John C. Campbell, *Foreign Affairs* 70, no. 3 (Summer 1991): 175.

Józef Böröcz, *Slavic Review* 52, no. 2 (Summer 1993): 375-376.

5432. Chirot, Daniel, ed. *The Crisis of Leninism and the Decline of the Left: The Revolutions of 1989.* Contributions by W. W. Rostow, Daniel Chirot, Ken Jowitt, Stephen E. Hanson, Bruce Cummings, Elizabeth J. Perry, Nicholas R. Lardy, Seymour Martin Lipset, and David Calleo. Jackson School Publications in International Studies. Seattle, WA: University of Washington Press, c1991. xv, 245 pp. REV: Michael D. Kennedy, *Contemporary Sociology* 21, no. 3 (May 1992): 311-313. Barrett L. McCormick, *Journal of Asian Studies* 51, no. 2 (May 1992): 367-369. Vladimir Tismaneanu, *Orbis* 36, no. 1 (Winter 1992): 144-145. William W. Goetz, *Social Education* 57, no. 1 (January 1993): 48. Anthony Oberschall, *Social Forces* 72, no. 1 (September 1993): 266-268.

5433. Ferdinand, Peter. *Communist Regimes in Comparative Perspective: The Evolution of the Soviet, Chinese, and Yugoslav Systems.* Savage, MD: Barnes & Noble, 1991. xi, 352 pp. REV: Anita Shelton, *History: Reviews of New Books* 21, no. 2 (Winter 1993): 91.

5434. Frucht, Richard C., ed. *Labyrinth of Nationalism: Complexities of Diplomacy: Essays in Honor of Charles and Barbara Jelavich.* Columbus, OH: Slavica, c1992. 377 pp. REV: Carole Rogel, *Slavic Review* 52, no. 3 (Fall 1993): 605-606.

5435. Hobsbawm, E. J. *Nations and Nationalism Since 1780: Programme, Myth, Reality.* Wiles Lectures. Cambridge; New York: Cambridge University Press, 1990. viii, 191 pp. [Based on lectures presented at the Queen's University of Belfast, May 1985.] REV: György Csepeli, *Nationalities Papers* 21, no. 2 (Fall 1993): 255-257.

5436. Kappeler, Andreas, Fikret Adanir, and Alan O'Day, eds. *The Formation of National Elites: Comparative Studies on Governments and Non-Dominant Ethnic Groups in Europe, 1850-1940.* New York: New York University Press, 1992. xxii, 351 pp. [Includes essays on the Ukrainians in the Russian Empire, Poles in the Grand Duchy of Poznan, and Czechs.] REV: Theodore R. Weeks, *Slavic Review* 52, no. 3 (Fall 1993): 609-610.

5437. Paul, Ellen Frankel, ed. *Totalitarianism at the Crossroads.* Studies in Social Philosophy & Policy, no. 12. [Bowling Green, OH]: Social Philosophy & Policy Center; New Brunswick, NJ: Transaction, 1990. 217 pp. [Contents: Ellen Frankel Paul, "Introduction," pp. 1-7; Vladimir Bukovsky, "Totalitarianism in Crisis: Is There a Smooth Transition to Democracy?" pp. 9-30; Adam Ulam, "Perestroika and Ideology," pp. 31-49; Andrzej Walicki, "'The Captive Mind' Revisited: Intellectuals and Communist Totalitarianism in Poland," pp. 51-95; John Gray, "Totalitarianism, Reform and Civil Society," pp. 97-142; Zbigniew Rau, "Four Stages of One Path out of Socialism," pp. 143-169; Roger Scruton, "Totalitarianism and the Rule of Law," pp. 171-213.] REV: Lucy Despard, *Foreign Affairs* 69, no. 5 (Winter 1990-1991): 202. Tsuyoshi Hasegawa, *Slavic Review* 50, no. 4 (Winter 1991): 1026-1028. James P. Konzak, *Orbis* 35, no. 2 (Spring 1991): 310-311. Abbott

Gleason, *Nationalities Papers* 21, no. 2 (Fall 1993): 227-229.

5438. Rau, Zbigniew, ed. *The Reemergence of Civil Society in Eastern Europe and the Soviet Union.* Boulder, CO: Westview Press, 1991. 181 pp. REV: J. Guy Lalande, *Canadian Slavonic Papers* 34, no. 3 (September 1992): 339-340. John Bendix, *American Political Science Review* 87, no. 1 (March 1993): 248-249. José Casanova, *Slavic Review* 52, no. 3 (Fall 1993): 488-490. Ákos Róna-Tas, *Contemporary Sociology* 22, no. 1 (January 1993): 35-37. *Orbis* 37, no. 3 (Summer 1993).

5439. Snyder, Louis L. *Encyclopedia of Nationalism.* 1st ed. New York: Paragon House, 1990. xxii, 445 pp. REV: Peter F. Sugar, *Nationalities Papers* 21, no. 2 (Fall 1993): 195-196.

5440. Tismaneanu, Vladimir, ed. *In Search of Civil Society: Independent Peace Movements in the Soviet Bloc.* New York: Routledge, 1990. x, 193 pp. REV: Juliana Geran Pilon, *Reason* 22, no. 9 (February 1991): 50-51. Metta Spencer, *Canadian Slavonic Papers* 33, no. 1 (March 1991): 98-99. Patrice Dabrowski, *Fletcher Forum of World Affairs* 16, no. 1 (Winter 1992): 176-178. John B. Dunlop, *American Political Science Review* 86, no. 1 (March 1992): 262-264. Anita Shelton, *Nationalities Papers* 21, no. 2 (Fall 1993): 219-220.

5441. Vidal Sassoon International Center for the Study of Antisemitism (Universitah ha-'Ivrit bi-Yerushalayim). *Antisemitism: An Annotated Bibliography.* Edited by Susan Sarah Cohen. Garland Reference Library of Social Science, vols. 366, 895. New York: Garland, 1987-. vols. [The Felix Posen Bibliographic Project on Antisemitism in cooperation with the Jewish National and University Library. Includes material on Eastern Europe and Russia.] REV: Susannah Heschel, *Journal of Church and State* 35, no. 2 (Spring 1993): 432.

5442. Westoby, Adam. *The Evolution of Communism.* 1st American ed. New York: Free Press, 1989. 333 pp. [Frist published (Cambridge: Polity Press in association with Basil Blackwell, 1989).] REV: Herbert J. Ellison, *Nationalities Papers* 21, no. 2 (Fall 1993): 199-201.

5443. White, Stephen et al. *Communist and Post-Communist Political Systems: An Introduction.* 3rd ed. New York: St. Martin Press, 1990. xi, 357 pp. [Rev. ed. of *Communist Political Systems* 2nd ed. rev. (1987).] REV: Laurence Thorsen, *Nationalities Papers* 21, no. 2 (Fall 1993): 232-233.

5444. Wistrich, Robert S. *Anti-Semitism: The Longest Hatred.* 1st American ed. New York: Pantheon Books, c1991. xxvi, 341 pp. [Originally published (London: Methuen, 1991).] REV: Donald L. Niewyk, *Historian* 55, no. 4 (Summer 1993): 773. *Wilson Quarterly* 17, no. 2 (Spring 1993): 85-86.

U.S.S.R.

5445. Balzer, Harley D., ed. *Five Years that Shook the World: Gorbachev's Unfinished Revolution.* Contributions by Blair A. Ruble, Gertrude E. Schroeder, Murray Feshbach, Harley D. Balzer, Paul Goble, Josephine Woll, Helena Goscilo, Angela Stent, Robert T. Huber, Jerry F. Hough, and Galina V. Starovoitova. Boulder, CO: Westview Press, 1991. xi, 267 pp. REV: Robert V. Legvold, *Foreign Affairs* 70, no. 5 (Winter 1991-92): 199-200. John Bushnell, *Slavic Review* 51, no. 3 (Fall 1992): 557-563. R. Edward Glatfelter, *Perspectives on Political Science* 22, no. 4 (Fall 1993): 185. Minton F. Goldman, *Asian Thought and Society* 18, nos. 53-54 (May-December 1993): 201-202. Stephen White, *Russian Review* 52, no. 2 (April 1993): 282-283.

5446. Barry, Donald D., ed. *Toward the "Rule of Law" in Russia? Political and Legal Reform in the Transition Period.* Armonk, NY: M.E. Sharpe, c1992. xxv, 402 pp. [Revised papers from a conference held at Lehigh University, May 30-June 1, 1991. Contents: Donald D. Barry, "Introduction"; Gianmaria Ajani, "The Rise and Fall of the Law-Based State in the Experience of Russian Legal Scholarship: Foreign Scholarship and Domestic Style"; Eugene Huskey, "From Legal Nihilism to *Pravovoe Gosudarstvo*: Soviet Legal Development, 1917-1990"; Harold J. Berman, "The Rule of Law and the Law-Based State with Special Reference to the Soviet Union"; Louise I. Shelley, "Legal Consciousness and the *Pravovoe Gosudarstvo*"; Dietrich André Loeber, "Regional and National Variations: The Baltic Factor"; John N. Hazard, "The Evolution of the Soviet Constitution"; Frances Foster-Simons, "The Soviet Legislature: Gorbachev's School of Democracy"; Ger P. van den Berg, "Executive Power and the Concept of *Pravovoe Gosudarstvo*"; Hiroshi Oda, "The Law-Based State and the CPSU"; George Ginsburgs, "Domestic Law and International Law: Importing Superior Standards"; Robert Sharlet, "The Fate of Individual Rights in the Age of Perestroika"; Nicolai Petro, "Informal Politics and the Rule of Law"; Peter H. Solomon, Jr., "Reforming Criminal Law Under Gorbachev: Crime, Punishment, and the Rights of the Accused"; Donald D. Barry, "The Quest for Judicial Independence: Soviet Courts in a *Pravovoe Gosudarstvo*"; Peter B. Maggs, "Substantive and Procedural Protection of the Rights of Economic Entities and Their Owners"; William B. Simons, "Soviet Civil Law and the Emergence of a *Pravovoe Gosudarstvo*: Do Foreigners Figure in the Grand Scheme?"; Kathryn Hendley, "The Ideals of the *Pravovoe Gosudarstvo* and the Soviet Workplace: A Case Study of Layoffs"; Albert Schmidt, "Soviet Legal Developments 1917-1990: A Comment"; Egidijus Kuris, "The Baltic Case and the Problem of Creating a Law-Based Society"; Vladimir Entin, "Lawmaking Under Gorbachev Judged by the Standards of a Law-Based Society"; Avgust Mishin, "Constitutional Reform in the USSR"; Pranas Kuris, "Implementation of International Human Rights Standards in the Lithuanian Legal System and the Problem of the Law-Based State"; Yuri Feofanov, "Rejection of Justice"; Valery Savitsky, "What Kind of Court and Procuracy?"; Viktor P. Mozolin, "Enterprises on the Difficult Path to a Market Economy: Legal Aspects".] REV: Michael Goldstein, *Russian History = Histoire russe* 20, nos. 1-4 (1993): 413-414. Pam Jordan, *Canadian Slavonic Papers* 35, nos. 3-4 (September-December 1993): 401-402.

5447. Bennigsen, Alexandre, and Marie Broxup. *The Islamic Threat to the Soviet State.* New York: St. Martin's Press, 1983. 170 pp. REV: Muriel Atkin, *Contention: Debates in Society, Culture, and Science* 2, no. 2 (Winter 1993): 89-106.

5448. Billington, James H. *Russia Transformed: Breakthrough to Hope: Moscow, August 1991.* New York; Toronto: Maxwell Macmillan Canada; New York: Maxwell Macmillan International: Free Press, c1992. vi, 202 pp. REV: Bernard Gwertzman, *New York Times Book Review* (August 23, 1992): 5. Robert Legvold, *Foreign Affairs* 71, no. 5 (Winter 1992-1993): 211. Stephen N. Sestanovich, *Foreign Service Journal* 69, no. 11 (November 1992): 51-52. Otto P. Chaney, *Military Review* 73, no. 10 (October 1993): 76.

5449. Critchlow, James. *Nationalism in Uzbekistan: A Soviet Republic's Road to Sovereignty.* Boulder, CO: Westview Press, 1991. xviii, 231 pp. REV: Miron Rezun, *Conflict Quarterly* 12, no. 3 (Summer 1992): 64-70. Donald S. Carlisle, *Russian Review* 52, no. 3 (July 1993): 442-443. Nancy Lubin, *Central Asia Monitor*, no. 5 (1993): 35-37.

5450. Denber, Rachel, ed. *The Soviet Nationality Reader: The Disintegration in Context.* Contributions by Walker Connor, Richard Pipes, Hélène Carrère d'Encausse, Gregory Gleason, Grey Hodnett, Philip G. Roeder, John H. Miller, Mark Beissinger, John A. Armstrong, Gertrude E. Schroeder, Donna Bahry, Carol Nechemias, John Dunlop, Jonathan Pool, Barbara A. Anderson, Brian D. Silver, Teresa Rakowska-Harmstone, Gail Warshofsky Lapidus, V. Stanley Vardys, Ronald Grigor Suny, Roman Szporluk, Paul Goble, Alexander J. Motyl, and Stephan Kux. Boulder, CO: Westview Press, 1992. ix, 635 pp. [Reprinted from various publications. Contents: Walker Connor, "The Soviet Prototype"; Richard Pipes, "The Establishment of the Union of Soviet Socialist Republics"; Hélène Carrère d'Encausse, "When the 'Prison of Peoples' Was Opened"; Gregory Gleason, "The Evolution of the Soviet Federal System"; Grey Hodnett, "The Debate Over Soviet Federalism"; Philip G. Roeder, "Soviet Federalism and Ethnic Mobilization"; John H. Miller, "Cadres Policy in Nationality Areas: Recruitment of CPSU First and Second Secretaries in Non-Russian Republics of the USSR"; Mark Beissinger, "Ethnicity, the Personnel Weapon and Neoimperial Integration: Ukrainian and RSFSR Provincial Party Officials Compared"; John A. Armstrong, "The Ethnic Scene in the Soviet Union: The View of the Dictatorship"; Gertrude E. Schroeder, "Nationalities and the Soviet Economy"; Donna Bahry and Carol Nechemias, "Half Full or Half Empty? The Debate Over Soviet Regional Equality"; Donna Bahry, "The Evolution of Soviet Fiscal Federalism"; John Dunlop, "Language, Culture, Religion, and Cultural Awareness"; Jonathan Pool, "Soviet Language Planning: Goals, Results, Options"; Barbara A. Anderson and Brian D. Silver, "Equality, Efficiency, and Politics in Soviet Bilingual Education Policy, 1934-1980"; Teresa Rakowska-Harmstone, "The Dialectics of Nationalism in the USSR"; Gail Warshofsky Lapidus, "Ethnonationalism and Political Stability: The Soviet Case"; V. Stanley Vardys, "Lithuanian National Politics"; Ronald

Grigor Suny, "Nationalism and Democracy in Gorbachev's Soviet Union: The Case of Karabagh"; Roman Szporluk, "Dilemmas of Russian Nationalism"; Paul Goble, "Ethnic Politics in the USSR"; Alexander J. Motyl, "The Sobering of Gorbachev: Nationality, Restructuring, and the West"; Stephan Kux, "Soviet Federalism".] REV: James E. Beale, *Studies in Conflict and Terrorism* 16, no. 1 (January-March 1993): 75-77. Wlodzimierz Rozenbaum, *Soviet and Post-Soviet Review* 20, nos. 2-3 (1993): 257-258.

5451. Farmer, Kenneth C. *The Soviet Administrative Elite.* New York: Praeger, 1992. xii, 296 pp. REV: Scott Nichols, *Annals of the American Academy of Political and Social Science,* no. 529 (September 1993): 184-185. John Willerton, *Russian Review* 52, no. 4 (October 1993): 570.

5452. Felshman, Neil. *Gorbachev, Yeltsin, and the Last Days of the Soviet Empire.* New York: St. Martin's Press, 1992. 276 pp. REV: Robert Vincent Daniels, *New Leader* 76, no. 1 (January 11, 1993): 17-18.

5453. Fuller, Graham E. *Central Asia: The New Geopolitics.* Santa Monica, CA: RAND, 1992. xvi, 86 pp. REV: *Orbis* 37, no. 2 (Spring 1993).

5454. Ginsburgs, George, and William B. Simons. *The Soviet Union and International Cooperation in Legal Matters.* Law in Eastern Europe, no. 38. Dordrecht; Boston, MA: M. Nijhoff; Hingham, MA: Distributed by Kluwer Academic, 1988-c1994. 3 vols. [Contents: Pt. 1. Recognition of Arbitral Agreements and Execution of Foreign Commercial Arbitral Awards; Pt. 2. Civil Law; Pt. 3. Criminal Law.] REV: Peter B. Maggs, *American Journal of International Law* 83 (July 1989): 701-702. Paul B. Stephan, III, *Russian Review* 49, no. 3 (July 1990): 373-375. Charles T. Myers, *Russian Review* 52, no. 4 (October 1993): 576-577. *George Washington Journal of International Law and Economics* 26, no. 3 (1993): 695-697.

5455. Goldman, Marshall I. *What Went Wrong with Perestroika.* Updated ed. New York: W.W. Norton, c1992. 282 pp. [New chapter for this edition discusses Boris Yeltsin and what lies ahead for Russia and the other republics.] REV: Melor Sturua, *New York Times Book Review* (February 2, 1992): 15. Thomas F. Remington, *Russian Review* 52, no. 3 (July 1993): 438-439.

5456. Gorbachev, Mikhail. *The August Coup: The Truth and the Lessons.* 1st ed. New York: HarperCollins, c1991. 127 pp. REV: David Remnick, *New York Review of Books* 38, no. 21 (December 19, 1991): 72-81. Philip Taubman, *New York Times Book Review* (December 8, 1991): 3ff. Vladimir Bukovsky, *New Republic* 205, nos. 28-29 (January 6 & 13, 1992): 41-44. Theodore Draper, *New York Review of Books* 39, no. 11 (June 11, 1992): 7-14. Carl G. Jacobsen, *Bulletin of the Atomic Scientists* 48, no. 1 (January-February 1992): 41-42. Robert Legvold, *Foreign Affairs* 71, no. 2 (Spring 1992): 205. Daniel Singer, *Nation* 254, no. 6 (February 17, 1992): 202-205. Sharyl Cross, *Presidential Studies Quarterly* 23, no. 4 (Fall 1993): 814-816.

5457. Greenfeld, Liah. *Nationalism: Five Roads to Modernity.* Cambridge, MA: Harvard University Press,

1992. xii, 581 pp. [Includes Russia.] REV: John Gray, *New York Times Book Review* (December 27, 1992): 6-7. Alex Inkeles, *Society* 30, no. 6 (September-October 1993): 77-83. Fritz Stern, *Foreign Affairs* 72, no. 3 (Summer 1993): 203. *Wilson Quarterly* 17, no. 4 (Autumn 1993): 79-80.

5458. Holman, Paul et al. *The Soviet Union after Perestroika: Change and Continuity.* Includes contributions by Paul Holman, Paul Craig Roberts, Karen LaFollette, John J. Dziak, Andrew F. Krepinevich, Jr., Fred F. Littlepage, Sergei Fedorenko, and Robert L. Pfalzgraff, Jr. Special Report (Institute for Foreign Policy Analysis). Washington, DC: Brassey's, 1991. xvii, 117 pp. [Publication of the Institute for Foreign Policy Analysis (Cambridge, MA and Washington, DC).] REV: Russell W. Ramsey, *Military Review* 71, no. 12 (December 1991): 99-100. Lawrence E. Modisett, *Naval War College Review* 46, no. 3, Sequence 343 (Summer 1993): 134-136.

5459. Hosking, Geoffrey A. *The Awakening of the Soviet Union.* Enlarged ed. Cambridge, MA: Harvard University Press, 1991. 246 pp. REV: Peter Reddaway, *New York Review of Books* 38, no. 18 (November 7, 1991): 53-59. Hugh Ragsdale, *Slavic Review* 51, no. 2 (Summer 1992): 356-357. Linda J. Cook, *Russian Review* 52, no. 1 (January 1993): 139-140.

5460. Hosking, Geoffrey A., Jonathan Aves, and Peter J. S. Duncan. *The Road to Post-Communism: Independent Political Movements in the Former Soviet Union, 1985-1991.* New York: Pinter; Distributed by St. Martin's Press, 1992. vii, 236 pp. REV: Vera Tolz, *Slavic Review* 52, no. 2 (Summer 1993): 384-385. William Urban, *Journal of Baltic Studies* 24, no. 1 (Spring 1993): 123.

5461. Huber, Robert T., and Donald R. Kelley, eds. *Perestroika-Era Politics: The New Soviet Legislature and Gorbachev's Political Reforms.* Contemporary Soviet Politics. Armonk, NY: M.E. Sharpe, c1991. 246 pp. REV: Thomas Cushman, *American Journal of Sociology* 98, no. 1 (July 1992): 225-227. Stephen White, *Russian Review* 52, no. 4 (October 1993): 578.

5462. Huttenbach, Henry R., ed. *Soviet Nationality Policies: Ruling Ethnic Groups in the USSR.* Nationalities Papers. Monograph Series "Studies in Issues", no. 6. London; New York: Mansell, 1990. xiv, 302 pp. REV: David D. Laitin, *Russian History* 17, no. 4 (Winter 1990): 437-441. Marjorie Mandelstam Balzer, *Slavic Review* 50, no. 4 (Winter 1991): 1037-1038. John A. Armstrong, *Russian Review* 51, no. 2 (April 1992): 291-193. John Bushnell, *Canadian Review of Studies in Nationalism = Revue Canadienne des Etudes sur le Nationalisme* 20, nos. 1-2 (1993): 151-152. Ralph T. Fisher, Jr., *Nationalities Papers* 21, no. 2 (Fall 1993): 207-208.

5463. Johnston, R. J., David Knight, and Eleonore Kofman, eds. *Nationalism, Self-Determination & Political Geography.* London; New York: Croom Helm, 1988. 229 pp. [Papers from a conference held in Sebastian, Spain, in August 1986. Includes chapter by Graham Smith on the former USSR.] REV: Robert J. Kaiser, *Canadian Review of Studies in Nationalism = Revue Canadienne des Etudes sur* *le Nationalisme* 20, nos. 1-2 (1993): 119-120.

5464. Kagarlitsky, Boris. *The Disintegration of the Monolith*. Translated by Renfrey Clarke. London; New York: Verso, 1992. x, 169 pp. REV: Robert Legvold, *Foreign Affairs* 72, no. 3 (Summer 1993): 206.

5465. Krasnov, Vladislav. *Russia Beyond Communism: A Chronicle of National Rebirth*. CCRS Series on Change in Contemporary Soviet Society, Boulder, CO: Westview Press, 1991. xxi, 355 pp. [Published in cooperation with the Center for Contemporary Russian Studies, Monterey Institute of International Studies.] REV: Stephen Kotkin, *Political Science Quarterly* 107, no. 3 (Fall 1992): 581-582. Robert Legvold, *Foreign Affairs* 71, no. 2 (Spring 1992): 207-208. Robert F. Byrnes, *Perspectives on Political Science* 22, no. 3 (Summer 1993): 136. Alfred Evans, Jr., *Russian Review* 52, no. 2 (April 1993): 284-285.

5466. Levin, Nora. *The Jews in the Soviet Union since 1917: Paradox of Survival*. New York: New York University Press, c1988. 2 vols. REV: Michael F. Hamm, *Russian History* 17, no. 2 (Summer 1990): 244-246. Arthur A. Levin, *Canadian-American Slavic Studies* 24, no. 4 (Winter 1990): 488-489. William O. McCagg, Jr., *American Historical Review* 95, no. 5 (December 1990): 1593-1594. Morris Slavin, *Midstream* 36, no. 7 (October-November 1990): 46-47. Phillip D. Mikesell, *Journal of Baltic Studies* 23, no. 3 (Fall 1992): 318-319. Thomas E. Sawyer, *Russian Review* 52, no. 1 (January 1993): 117-118.

5467. Low, Alfred D. *Soviet Jewry and Soviet Policy*. East European Monographs, no. 281. Boulder, CO: East European Monographs; New York: Distributed by Columbia University Press, 1990. xv, 249 pp. REV: John C. Campbell, *Foreign Affairs* 69, no. 4 (Fall 1990): 190-191. Shlomo Lambroza, *Soviet Union = Union Soviétique* 17, nos. 1-2 (1990): 129-130. Zvi Gitelman, *Russian Review* 51, no. 1 (January 1992): 137-138. John A. Armstrong, *Canadian Review of Studies in Nationalism = Revue Canadienne des Etudes sur le Nationalisme* 20, nos. 1-2 (1993): 149-150. Henry R.Huttenbach, *Nationalities Papers* 21, no. 2 (Fall 1993): 249-250.

5468. Lowenhardt, John, James R. Ozinga, and Erik van Ree. *The Rise and Fall of the Soviet Politburo*. New York: St. Martin's Press, 1992. xix, 244 pp. REV: Anthony D'Agostino, *Soviet and Post-Soviet Review* 20, nos. 2-3 (1993): 255-257.

5469. Marples, David R. *Ukraine under Perestroika: Ecology, Economics, and the Workers' Revolt*. New York: St. Martin's Press, 1991. 243 pp. REV: Peter J. Potichnyj, *Canadian Journal of Political Science = Revue canadienne de science politique* 25, no. 2 (June 1992): 411-412. Zenovia A. Sochor, *Soviet and Post-Soviet Review* 20, no. 1 (1993): 80.

5470. McAuley, Alastair, ed. *Soviet Federalism: Nationalism and Economic Decentralisation*. Studies in Federalism, New York: St. Martin's Press, 1991. ix, 214 pp. REV: V. Stanley Vardys, *Slavic Review* 52, no. 1 (Spring 1993): 149-150.

5471. Melville, Andrei, and Gail W. Lapidus, eds. *The Glasnost Papers: Voices on Reform from Moscow*. Compiled and with a commentary by O. Aliakrinskii et al. Boulder, CO: Westview Press, 1990. 359 pp. REV: Brian Coleman, *SAIS Review* 11, no. 2 (Summer-Fall 1991): 215-216. T.H. Rigby, *Political Science Quarterly* 106, no. 3 (Fall 1991): 514-515. Robert V. Daniels, *Slavic Review* 51, no. 2 (Summer 1992): 339-342. John Downing, *Journal of Communication* 42, no. 2 (Spring 1992): 153-162. Jeffrey W. Hahn, *Russian Review* 51, no. 2 (April 1992): 287-288. Donald Schwartz, *Canadian Slavonic Papers* 34, nos. 1-2 (March-June 1992): 196. James E. Hassell, *Soviet and Post-Soviet Review* 20, no. 1 (1993): 83.

5472. Mitchell, R. Judson. *Getting to the Top in the USSR: Cyclical Patterns in the Leadership Succession Process*. Stanford, CA: Hoover Institution Press, c1990. 237 pp. REV: John C. Campbell, *Foreign Affairs* 70, no. 3 (Summer 1991): 174. Carl Linden, *Perspectives on Political Science* 21, no. 3 (Summer 1992): 166-167. Robert J. Osborn, *Slavic Review* 51, no. 1 (Spring 1992): 137-138. T.H. Rigby, *Russian Review* 52, no. 1 (January 1993): 136-137.

5473. Motyl, Alexander J., ed. *The Post-Soviet Nations: Perspectives on the Demise of the USSR*. Contributions by Gregory Gleason, Walker Connor, Ronald J. Hill, Neil Harding, John N. Hazard, Mark R. Beissinger, Amy Knight, Theodore H. Friedgut, Zvi Gitelman, Richard E. Ericson, Walter D. Connor, and Alexander J. Motyl. Studies of the Harriman Institute, New York: Columbia University Press, c1992. xi, 322 pp. [Contents: Gregory Gleason, "The 'National Factor' and the Logic of Sovietology"; Walker Connor, "Soviet Policies Toward the Non-Russian Peoples in Theoretic and Historic Perspective: What Gorbachev Inherited"; Ronald J. Hill, "Ideology and the Making of a Nationalities Policy"; Neil Harding, "Legitimations, Nationalities, and the Deep Structure of Ideology"; John N. Hazard, "Managing Nationalism: State, Law, and the National Question in the USSR"; Mark R. Beissinger, "Elites and Ethnic Identities in Soviet and Post-Soviet Politics"; Amy Knight, "The Political Police and the National Question in the Soviet Union"; Theodore H. Friedgut, "Nations of the USSR: From Mobilized Participation to Autonomous Diversity"; Zvi Gitelman, "Development and Ethnicity in the Soviet Union"; Richard E. Ericson, "Soviet Economic Structure and the National Question"; Walter D. Connor, "Class, Social Structure, Nationality"; Alexander J. Motyl, "The End of Sovietology: From Soviet Studies to Post-Soviet Studies".] REV: Roger Brubaker, *Contemporary Sociology* 22, no. 4 (July 1993): 514-517. Peter J.S. Duncan, *Canadian Slavonic Papers* 35, nos. 3-4 (September-December 1993): 408-409. William Fierman, *Slavic Review* 52, no. 3 (Fall 1993): 606-607. Robert Legvold, *Foreign Affairs* 72, no. 2 (Spring 1993): 180. William Urban, *Journal of Baltic Studies* 24, no. 1 (Spring 1993): 119-120.

5474. ———, ed. *Thinking Theoretically About Soviet Nationalities: History and Comparison in the Study of the USSR*. Contributions by Alexander J. Motyl, Donald L. Horowitz, John A. Armstrong, Anthony D. Smith, M.

Crawford Young, Paul R. Brass, David D. Laitin, Roger Petersen, John W. Slocum, Charles F. Furtado, Jr., Michael Hechter, S. N. Eisenstadt, Kenneth Minogue, Beryl Williams, and Ernest Gellner. Studies of the Harriman Institute, New York: Columbia University Press, c1992. vi, 284 pp. [Contents: Alexander J. Motyl, "Introduction: What This Book Is Not, and What It Is"; Donald L. Horowitz, "How to Begin Thinking Comparatively about Soviet Ethnic Problems"; John A. Armstrong, "The Autonomy of Ethnic Identity: Historic Cleavages and Nationality Relations in the USSR"; Anthony D. Smith, "Ethnic Identity and Territorial Nationalism in Comparative Perspective"; M. Crawford Young, "The National and Colonial Question and Marxism: A View from the South"; Paul R. Brass, "Language and National Identity in the Soviet Union and India"; David D. Laitin, Roger Petersen, and John W. Slocum, "Language and the State: Russia and the Soviet Union in Comparative Perspective"; Charles F. Furtado, Jr. and Michael Hechter, "The Emergence of Nationalist Politics in the USSR: A Comparison of Estonia and the Ukraine"; S.N. Eisenstadt, "Center-Periphery Relations in the Soviet Empire: Some Interpretive Observations"; Kenneth Minogue and Beryl Williams, "Ethnic Conflict in the Soviet Union: The Revenge of Particularism"; Ernest Gellner, "Nationalism in the Vacuum"; Alexander J. Motyl, "Building Bridges and Changing Landmarks: Theory and Concept in the Study of Soviet Nationalities".] REV: Michael D. Kennedy, *Slavic Review* 51, no. 4 (Winter 1992): 844-845. Hank Johnston, *Journal of Baltic Studies* 24, no. 2 (Summer 1993): 211-212. Tim McDaniel, *Contemporary Sociology* 22, no. 4 (July 1993): 512-514.

5475. Nahaylo, Bohdan, and Victor Swoboda. *Soviet Disunion: A History of the Nationalities Problem in the USSR.* 1st American Ed. New York: Free Press, c1990. xvi, 432 pp. REV: John A. Armstrong, *Problems of Communism* 39, no. 4 (July-August 1990): 78-83. John C. Campbell, *Foreign Affairs* 69, no. 5 (Winter 1990-1991): 201. Ernest Gellner, *New Republic* 202, no. 25 (June 18, 1990): 34-38. John Jaworsky, *Canadian Slavonic Papers* 32, no. 4 (December 1990): 497-499. Peter Keresztes, *American Spectator* 24, no. 3 (March 1991): 38-39. George Liber, *Political Science Quarterly* 106, no. 2 (Summer 1991): 339-340. Nancy Lubin, *New York Times Book Review* (July 15, 1990): 16. Rado Pribic, *Journal of Interdisciplinary History* 22, no. 2 (Autumn 1991): 330-331. Michael Rywkin, *Slavic Review* 50, no. 4 (Winter 1991): 1036-1037. David Satter, *Orbis* 35, no. 1 (Winter 1991): 148. Audrey L. Altstadt, *Russian Review* 51, no. 4 (October 1992): 590-591. Thomas Oleszczuk, *Nationalities Papers* 21, no. 2 (Fall 1993): 216-217.

5476. Olcott, Martha B., Lubomyr Hajda, and Anthony Olcott, eds. *The Soviet Multinational State: Readings and Documents.* The USSR in Transition, Armonk, NY: M.E. Sharpe, c1990. xii, 605 pp. REV: Edward J. Lazzerini, *Nationalities Papers* 21, no. 2 (Fall 1993): 216-217.

5477. Pinkus, Benjamin. *The Jews of the Soviet Union: The History of a National Minority.* New York:

Cambridge University Press, 1988. 397 pp. REV: Robert Weinberg, *Russian Review* 49, no. 2 (April 1990): 226-227. Gregory Gleason, *Canadian Review of Studies in Nationalism = Revue Canadienne des Etudes sur le Nationalisme* 18, nos. 1-2 (1991): 273-274. Arthur Levin, *Canadian Journal of History = Annales canadienne d'histoire* 26, no. 1 (April 1991): 136-137. Alexander Orbach, *Journal of Modern History* 63, no. 1 (March 1991): 206-209. Michael Rywkin, *Slavic Review* 50, no. 1 (Spring 1991): 198-199. Robert M. Seltzer, *American Historical Review* 98, no. 3 (June 1993): 911.

5478. Rees, E. A., ed. *The Soviet Communist Party in Disarray: The XXVIII Congress of the Communist Party of the Soviet Union.* Includes contribution by Stephen White, E. A. Rees, R. W. Davies, and Jonathan Haslam. Studies in Soviet History and Society, New York, NY: St. Martin's Press, 1992. vii, 226 pp. [Contents: Stephen White, "Background to the XXVIII Congress; The politics of the XXVII Congress"; E. A. Rees, "Economic policy; Nationalities policy"; R. W. Davies, "History and perestroika"; Jonathan Haslam, "Foreign policy"; E. A. Rees, "Party relations with the military and the KGB".] REV: John A. Armstrong, *Journal of Baltic Studies* 24, no. 3 (Fall 1993): 310-311. John Miller, *Australian Slavonic and East European Studies* 7, no. 1 (1993): 142-145.

5479. Rezun, Miron, ed. *Nationalism and the Breakup of an Empire: Russia and Its Periphery.* Westport, CT: Praeger, 1992. x, 197 pp. REV: Aileen A. Espiritu, *Canadian Slavonic Papers* 35, nos. 3-4 (September-December 1993): 412-413. William Urban, *Journal of Baltic Studies* 24, no. 1 (Spring 1993): 121-122.

5480. Rywkin, Michael. *Moscow's Muslim Challenge: Soviet Central Asia.* Revised ed. Armonk, NY: M.E. Sharpe, c1990. 181 pp. REV: Muriel Atkin, *Contention: Debates in Society, Culture, and Science* 2, no. 2 (Winter 1993): 89-106.

5481. Sedaitis, Judith B., and Jim Butterfield, eds. *Perestroika from Below: Social Movements in the Soviet Union.* Boulder, CO: Westview Press, 1991. 220 pp. REV: John F. Young, *Canadian Slavonic Papers* 33, nos. 3-4 (December 1991): 374. Elena Zdravomyslova, *Contemporary Sociology* 22, no. 1 (January 1993): 50.

5482. Sharlet, Robert. *Soviet Constitutional Crisis: From De-Stalinization to Disintegration.* Contemporary Soviet/Post-Soviet Politics, Armonk, NY: M.E. Sharpe, c1992. xii, 191 pp. [Contents: Introduction: Crisis and Constitutional Reform in Tsarist Russia and the Soviet Union. Understanding Constitutionalism. The Quest for a Constitution in the Russian and Soviet Past. The USSR in Crisis: From Constitutional Reform to Political Decline 1: Brezhnev and the Soviet Constitution of 1977: Codifying De-Stalinization. The Path of Constitutional Reform. Continuity and Change. A Soviet "Systems" Approach. The Citizen and the State. Participation and Public Discussion. Constitutional Revision and Ratification. The Constitution as "Magic Wall" Epilogue 2: The Andropov-Chernenko Interregnum: Juridicizing the System. The USSR at the

End of the Brezhnev Era: Diagnosing the Problems. Interim Remedies, 1980-82. Andropov Takes Charge: Campaigning for Discipline. Legislating for Discipline: The Andropov Record. Andropov's Legacy. The Chernenko Record. Demise of a Campaign: From "Discipline" to "Upbringing" Epilogue. 3: Gorbachev and the Soviet Constitutional Crisis: From De-Stalinization to Disintegration. The Transition to Constitutionalism. The Dimensions of Constitutional Reform. Constitutional Traditionalism. The Politics of Constitutionalism. The Limits of Constitutionalism in the USSR. A "Constitutional" Coup. Epilogue: Constitutional Futures.] REV: John N. Hazard, *Slavic Review* 52, no. 1 (Spring 1993): 154-155.

5483. Simon, Gerhard. *Nationalism and Policy toward the Nationalities in the Soviet Union: From Totalitarian Dictatorship to Post-Stalinist Society*. Translated from the German by Karen Forster, and Oswald Forster. Westview Special Studies on the Soviet Union and Eastern Europe, Boulder, CO: Westview Press, 1991. xvii, 483 pp. [Rev. and updated translation of *Nationalismus und Nationalitatenpolitik in der Sowjetunion*.] REV: Robert V. Legvold, *Foreign Affairs* 70, no. 5 (Winter 1991-1992): 197-198. William Fierman, *Slavic Review* 51, no. 3 (Fall 1992): 572-573. Michae Turner, *Orbis* 36, no. 2 (Spring 1992): 307-308. George Liber, *Russian Review* 52, no. 4 (October 1993): 572-573.

5484. Tarasulo, Isaac J., ed. *Perils of Perestroika: Viewpoints From the Soviet Press, 1989-1991*. Alexander Shchelkin, Yevgeny Yevtushchenko, Ivan Dzyuba, Oleg Moroz, Piatras Keidoshus, Vitautas Petkiavicius, Alexei II (Patriarch), R. Safarov, Alexei Kiva, Alexander Tsipko, Oleg Kalungin, Nina Andreyeva, and Ilya Zalavsky. Wilmington, DE: SR Books, 1992. xxi, 355 pp. [Translated from the Russian. Contents: Alexander Shchelkin, "The dynamics of freedom"; A. Kuznetsov, "Not all theaters are erotic"; Yevgeny Yevtushchenko, "A nation begins with its women"; Ivan Dzyuba, "A commonwealth of cultures"; Oleg Moroz, "Vilnius: a night in spring"; Piatras Keidoshus and Vitautas Petkiavicius, "Confessions of a 'renegade'"; Patriarch Alexei II, "Faith without action is dead"; "A letter from Russia's writers"; R. Safarov, "Looking around at the past"; Alexei Kiva, "Will the Party catch up with Perestroika?"; Alexander Tsipko, "Do we need yet another experiment?: Ideological paradoxes of reform"; Oleg Kalungin, "The KGB has not changed its principles...yet"; Nina Andreyeva, "The striving for truth has not yet been suppressed"; Ilya Zalavsky, "Enough talk!, let's get to work!".] REV: John Bushnell, *Slavic Review* 51, no. 3 (Fall 1992): 557-563. John Downing, *Journal of Communication* 42, no. 2 (Spring 1992): 153-162. Ira Smolensky, *Journal of Baltic Studies* 23, no. 4 (Winter 1992): 419. Max Mote, *Canadian Slavonic Papers* 35, nos. 1-2 (March-June 1993): 191-192.

5485. Timofeyev, Lev. *Russia's Secret Rulers*. Translated by Catherine A. Fitzpatrick. Afterword by Anton Koslov. 1st ed. New York: Knopf; Distributed by Random House, 1992. vi, 177 pp. REV: Celestine Bohlen, *New York Times Book Review* (December 13, 1992): 19. Abraham Brumberg, *Book World* 23, no. 8 (February 21, 1993): 6.

Orbis 37, no. 3 (Summer 1993).

5486. Tolz, Vera. *The USSR's Emerging Multiparty System*. Foreword by S. Frederick Starr. Washington Papers, 148. New York: Praeger; Washington, DC: Center for Strategic and International Studies, 1990. xvi, 123 pp. REV: Lucy Despard, *Foreign Affairs* 70, no. 2 (Spring 1991): 191-192. Douglas Nicoll, *Journal of Baltic Studies* 22, no. 4 (Winter 1991): 369. Peter Reddaway, *New York Review of Books* 38, no. 18 (November 7, 1991): 53-59. Ronald J. Hill, *Russian Review* 51, no. 3 (July 1992): 454-455. Jim Butterfield, *Soviet and Post-Soviet Review* 20, nos. 2-3 (1993): 247-248. Norma C. Noonan, *Perspectives on Political Science* 22, no. 3 (Summer 1993): 137.

5487. Urban, Michael E. *An Algebra of Soviet Power: Elite Circulation in the Belorussian Republic, 1966-86*. Cambridge; New York: Cambridge University Press, 1989. xvi, 183 pp. REV: William A. Clark, *Russian Review* 50, no. 3 (July 1991): 375-376. Linda J. Cook, *Journal of Politics* 53, no. 3 (August 1991): 912-914. John P. Willerton, *American Political Science Review* 85, no. 4 (December 1991): 1427-1433. Peter Rutland, *Slavic Review* 52, no. 1 (Spring 1993): 158-159.

5488. ———. *More Power to the Soviets: The Democratic Revolution in the USSR*. International Library of Studies in Communism, Aldershot, Hants: E. Elgar; Brookfield, VT: Gower, c1990. x, 167 pp. REV: Valerie Bunce, *American Political Science Review* 85, no. 3 (September 1991): 1066-1067. John F. Young, *Canadian Slavonic Papers* 33, nos. 3-4 (December 1991): 379-380. Jeffrey W. Hahn, *Slavic Review* 51, no. 1 (Spring 1992): 138-139. Theodore H. Friedgut, *Russian Review* 52, no. 2 (April 1993): 285-286.

5489. Vaksberg, Arkady. *The Soviet Mafia*. Translated from the Russian by John Roberts, and Elizabeth Roberts. New York: St. Martin's Press, 1991. x, 275 pp. [Also published (London: Weidenfeld and Nicolson, 1991).] REV: Jonas Bernstein, *American Spectator* 25, no. 7 (July 1992): 61ff. David Remnick, *New York Review of Books* 39, no. 13 (July 16, 1992): 45-50. Louise I. Shelley, *Slavic Review* 51, no. 3 (Fall 1992): 578-579. William A. Clark, *Soviet and Post-Soviet Review* 20, no. 1 (1993): 97. John Quigley, *Criminal Law Forum* 4, no. 3 (1993): 567-572.

5490. Willerton, John P. *Patronage and Politics in the USSR*. Soviet and East European Studies, 82. Cambridge; New York: Cambridge University Press, 1992. xv, 305 pp. REV: Bohdan Harasymiw, *Canadian Journal of Political Science = Revue canadienne de science politique* 25, no. 4 (December 1992): 792-793. Thomas F. Remington, *American Political Science Review* 87, no. 1 (March 1993): 252. Emanuela Todeva, *Sociology* (August 1993): 541-542. Michael E. Urban, *Russian Review* 52, no. 4 (October 1993): 577.

5491. Yin, John. *Government of the USSR under Perestroika*. 1st ed. Sudbury, Ontario: Northernmost View Press, 1991. viii, 328 pp. REV: David Marples, *Canadian Slavonic Papers* 34, nos. 1-2 (March-June 1992): 191-192.

Nathaniel Richmond, *Russian Review* 52, no. 2 (April 1993): 287.

5492. Zile, Zigurds L. *Ideas and Forces in Soviet Legal History: A Reader on the Soviet State and Law.* New York: Oxford University Press, 1992. xxxi, 551 pp. [Contains 400 documents in 16 chapters: 1. Wellsprings; 2. Seizure of Power; 3. Preservation of the Imperial Patrimony; 4. Implementation of Order and Repression; 5. Expansion of Dominion and Dependency; 6. Replacement of Market by Administration; 7. Restoration of Civil Law for a Mixed Economy; 8. Forced Collectivization of Agriculture; 9. Industrialization by the State; 10. Readjustment and Consolidation of Orthodoxy; 11. Perfection of Terror; 12. Escalation of Perfidy, Woe, and Vanity; 13. Selective Dissociation from the Past; 14. Attempt at Ideological Revival; 15. Management of Stagnation and Decay; 16. Dissolution of Structures and Myths.] REV: Eugene Huskey, *Russian History = Histoire russe* 20, nos. 1-4 (1993): 411-412.

Eastern Europe

5493. Ackerman, Bruce. *The Future of Liberal Revolution.* New Haven, CT: Yale University Press, c1992. viii, 152 pp. REV: Andrew J. Pierre, *Foreign Affairs* 71, no. 5 (Winter 1992-1993): 196-197. Richard A. Posner, *East European Constitutional Review* 1, no. 3 (Fall 1992): 35-37. Robert P. Beschel, Jr., *Political Science Quarterly* 108, no. 2 (Summer 1993): 342-344.

5494. Banac, Ivo, ed. *Eastern Europe in Revolution.* Ithaca, NY: Cornell University Press, 1992. 255 pp. [Partial proceedings of a conference held at Yale University on November 5, 1990.] REV: Robert Legvold, *Foreign Affairs* 71, no. 3 (Summer 1992): 179. Sabrina Petra Ramet, *Slavic Review* 51, no. 3 (Fall 1992): 598-599. Raymond Taras, *Canadian-American Slavic Studies* 26, nos. 1-4 (1992): 433-435. Joseph Held, *Canadian Slavonic Papers* 35, nos. 1-2 (March-June 1993): 158-159. Ferenc Miszlivetz, *Contemporary Sociology* 22, no. 1 (January 1993): 41. *Orbis* 37, no. 3 (Summer 1993).

5495. Berglund, Sten, and Jan Åke Dellenbrant, eds. *The New Democracies in Eastern Europe: Party Systems and Political Cleavages.* Contributions by Sten Berglund, Jan Åke Dellenbrant, Marian Grzybowski, and Marek Bankowicz. Studies of Communism in Transition, Brookfield, VT: E. Elgar, c1991. 237 pp. [Contents: Sten Berglund and Jan Ake Dellenbrant, "The Breakdown of Authoritarianism in Eastern Europe"; Sten Berglund and Jan Ake Dellenbrant, "The Failure of Popular Democracy"; Marian Grzybowski, "The Transition of the Polish Party System"; Jan Ake Dellenbrant, "The Re-Emergence of Multi-Partism in the Baltic States"; Sten Berglund, "The Breakdown of the German Democratic Republic"; Marek Bankowicz, "Czechoslovakia—from Masaryk to Havel"; Marian Grzybowski, "The Transition from One-Party Hegemony to Competitive Pluralism: The Case of Hungary"; Marek Bankowicz, "Bulgaria—The Limited Revolution"; Sten Berglund and Jan Åke Dellenbrant, "Prospects for the New Democracies in Eastern Europe".] REV: Stefania Szlek

Miller, *Canadian Slavonic Papers* 34, no. 3 (September 1992): 327-328. Krzysztof Jasiewicz, *Slavic Review* 52, no. 1 (Spring 1993): 143-144.

5496. Bradley, John F. N. *Czechoslovakia's Velvet Revolution: A Political Analysis.* East European Monographs, no. 345. Boulder, CO: East European Monographs; New York: Distributed by Columbia University Press, 1992. xxiii, 140, [56] pp. [Appended: 22 annexes [56 pp.] in Czech.] REV: Stanislav Kirschbaum, *Canadian Slavonic Papers* 35, nos. 1-2 (March-June 1993): 188-189.

5497. Brewer, Bob, general ed. *My Albania: Ground Zero.* Interviews by Remzi Lani and Briseida Mema. Translations by Ilir Ikonomi. New York: Lion of Tepelena Press, c1992. [86] pp. [Includes poetry by Azem Shkreli, photography by Bob Brewer, cartoons by Enrik Veizi. Translated from Albanian.] REV: Kay Downey, *Ethnic Forum* 13, no. 1 (1993): 83-84. Thomas Emmert, *Slavic Review* 52, no. 3 (Fall 1993): 617-618.

5498. Brown, J. F. *Nationalism, Democracy, and Security in the Balkans.* RAND Research Study, Aldershot, Hants; Brookfield, VT: Dartmouth, c1992. x, 205 pp. REV: James L. Marketos, *Mediterranean Quarterly* 4, no. 4 (Fall 1993): 112-115.

5499. ———. *Surge to Freedom: The End of Communist Rule in Eastern Europe.* Soviet & East European Studies, Durham, NC: Duke University Press, 1991. x, 338 pp. REV: John C. Campbell, *Foreign Affairs* 70, no. 4 (Fall 1991): 182. Michael Bernhard, *Political Science Quarterly* 107, no. 2 (Summer 1992): 377-378. Joseph Held, *Perspectives on Political Science* 21, no. 3 (Summer 1992): 167. Heidi H. Hobbs, *Studies in Conflict and Terrorism* 15, no. 2 (April-June 1992): 160-162. Vladimir Tismaneanu, *Orbis* 36, no. 1 (Winter 1992): 147. Joel M. Jenswold, *Social Science Quarterly* 74, no. 3 (March 1993): 224.

5500. Cohen, Renae, and Jennifer L. Golub. *Attitudes towards Jews in Poland, Hungary, and Czechoslovakia: A Comparative Survey.* Working Papers on Contemporary Anti-Semitism, New York, NY: American Jewish Committee, Institute of Human Relations, c1991. 44 pp. REV: Arthur Hertzberg, *New York Review of Books* 50, no. 12 (June 24, 1993): 51-57.

5501. Cviic, Christopher. *Remaking the Balkans.* Chatham House Papers, New York: Council on Foreign Relations Press, c1991. viii, 113 pp. REV: Ronald M. Bonesteel, *Military Review* 72, no. 6 (June 1992): 90-91. Charles Jelavich, *Slavic Review* 51, no. 3 (Fall 1992): 591-592. Robert D. Kaplan, *Orbis* 36, no. 2 (Spring 1992): 308. Robert Legvold, *Foreign Affairs* 71, no. 2 (Spring 1992): 207. Dennis Reinhartz, *Canadian Review of Studies in Nationalism = Revue Canadienne des Etudes sur le Nationalisme* 20, nos. 1-2 (1993): 134.

5502. Dahrendorf, Ralf. *Reflections on the Revolution in Europe: In a Letter Intended to Have Been Sent to a Gentleman in Warsaw.* 1st ed. New York: Times Books, c1990. 163 pp. [Translation of *Betrachtungen uber die Revolution in Europa in einem Brief, der an einen Herrn in*

Warschau gerichtet ist (Stuttgart: Deutsche Berlags-Anstalt, 1990). A portion of this work was originally published in different form in *Marxism Today* (May 1990).] REV: Kenneth Minogue, *National Review* 42, no. 20 (October 15, 1990): 84-85. John C. Campbell, *Foreign Affairs* 70, no. 2 (Spring 1991): 193-194. Dankwart A. Rustow, *Political Science Quarterly* 106, no. 3 (Fall 1991): 564-565. E.P. Thompson, *Dissent* 38, no. 3 (Summer 1991): 426-428. Vladimir Tismaneanu, *Orbis* 35, no. 3 (Summer 1991): 467-468. Anita Shelton, *Nationalities Papers* 21, no. 2 (Fall 1993): 237.

5503. Danopolous, Constantine P., ed. *The Decline of Military Regimes: The Civilian Influence.* Includes contribution by Alison Reminton. Westview Special Studies in Military Affairs, Boulder, CO: Westview Press, 1988. xiii, 282 pp. [Includes discussion of Greece and Poland. Partial contents: Alison Remington, "Polish Soldiers in Politics: The Party in Uniform?".] REV: Siobhan A. Handley, *New York University Journal of International Law and Politics* 25, no. 5 (Winter 1993): 512-514.

5504. Dragnich, Alex N. *Serbs and Croats: The Struggle in Yugoslavia.* New York: Harcourt Brace Jovanovich, 1992. xxi, 202 pp. REV: David Binder, *New York Times Book Review* (October 25, 1992): 19. Timothy L. Thomas, *Military Review* 72, no. 12 (December 1992): 96. Aleksa Djilas, *New Republic* 208, no. 4 (January 25, 1993): 38-42. Robert Legvold, *Foreign Affairs* 72, no. 3 (Summer 1993): 207. Michael Mennard, *Mediterranean Quarterly* 4, no. 2 (Spring 1993): 136-1397.

5505. Fitzmaurice, John. *The Baltic: A Regional Future?* New York, NY: St. Martin's Press, 1992. xi, 171 pp. REV: William Urban, *Journal of Baltic Studies* 24, no. 3 (Fall 1993): 309.

5506. Frankland, Mark. *The Patriots' Revolution: How Eastern Europe Toppled Communism and Won Its Freedom.* Chicago, IL: I.R. Dee, c1992. xxiv, 356 pp. REV: Robert Legvold, *Foreign Affairs* 71, no. 3 (Summer 1992): 179. Barbara Hicks, *Political Science Quarterly* 108, no. 1 (Spring 1993): 186-187.

5507. Gedmin, Jeffrey. *The Hidden Hand: Gorbachev and the Collapse of East Germany.* AEI Studies, 554. Washington, DC: AEI Press; Lanham, MD: Distributed by National Book Network, 1992. ix, 169 pp. REV: Robert Legvold, *Foreign Affairs* 71, no. 5 (Winter 1992-1993): 212-213. Gottfried Dietze, *Perspectives on Political Science* 22, no. 2 (Spring 1993): 95. Jacob Heibrunn, *History: Reviews of New Books* 21, no. 3 (Spring 1993): 128. *Orbis* 37, no. 1 (Winter 1993).

5508. Gilberg, Trond. *Nationalism and Communism in Romania: The Rise and Fall of Ceausescu's Personal Dictatorship.* Boulder, CO: Westview Press, 1990. x, 289 pp. REV: John C. Campbell, *Foreign Affairs* 69, no. 5 (Winter 1990-1991): 202. Christian Kirkpatrick, *Current History* 89, no. 551 (December 1990): 425ff. John C. Campbell, *Canadian-American Slavic Studies* 25, nos. 1-4 (1991): 446-448. Gary Hanson, *History: Reviews of New Books* 19, no. 3 (Spring 1991): 127-128. Louis L. Ortmayer, *Conflict* 11, no.

1 (January-March 1991): 96-98. Gabriel Topor, *Journal of International Affairs* 45, no. 1 (Summer 1991): 287-289. J. H. Jensen, *Nationalities Papers* 21, no. 2 (Fall 1993): 239-241. Ladis K. D. Kristof, *Slavic Review* 52, no. 4 (Winter 1993): 888-889.

5509. Glenny, Misha. *The Fall of Yugoslavia: The Third Balkan War.* London; New York: Penguin, 1992. x, 193 pp. REV: Ivo Banac, *Foreign Policy*, no. 93 (December 1993-1994): 173-182. Aleksa Djilas, *New Republic* 208, no. 4 (January 25, 1993): 38-42. Michael Ignatieff, *New York Review of Books* 40, no. 9 (May 13, 1993): 3-5.

5510. Goldfarb, Jeffrey C. *After the Fall: The Pursuit of Democracy in Central Europe.* New York, NY: Basic Books, c1992. xiv, 267 pp. REV: Abraham Brumberg, *New York Times Book Review* (June 14, 1992): 26. Robert Legvold, *Foreign Affairs* 71, no. 2 (Spring 1992): 207. Urs Leimbacher, *Harvard International Review* 14, no. 4 (Summer 1992): 50-51. Andrei S. Markovits, *Political Science Quarterly* 107, no. 3 (Fall 1992): 533-536. Stephen Miller, *Journal of Democracy* 3, no. 4 (October 1992): 125-129. Gale Stokes, *New Leader* 75, no. 8 (June 29, 1992): 18-19. *Publishers Weekly* 239, no. 6 (January 27, 1992): 85. Robert F. Forrest, *Social Science Quarterly* 74, no. 2 (June 1993): 460. Ken Jowitt, *Contemporary Sociology* 22, no. 1 (January 1993): 37.

5511. Goodwyn, Lawrence. *Breaking the Barrier: The Rise of Solidarity in Poland.* New York: Oxford University Press, 1991. xxx, 466 pp. REV: Michael Bernhard, *Studies in Comparative Communism* 24, no. 3 (September 1991): 313-330. John Patrick Diggins, *New York Times Book Review* (June 2, 1991): 12. Timothy Garton Ash, *New York Review of Books* 38, no. 11 (June 13, 1991): 46-58. Andrzej Tymowski, *Telos*, no. 90 (Winter 1991-92): 157-174. Andrzej Korbonski, *American Historical Review* 97, no. 3 (June 1992): 892-893. Raymond Taras, *Political Science Quarterly* 107, no. 2 (Summer 1992): 378-381. Jeff Manza, *Industrial and Labor Relations Review* 46, no. 3 (April 1993): 600-602.

5512. Hankiss, Elemér. *East European Alternatives.* Oxford: Clarendon Press; New York: Oxford University Press, 1990. xiv, 319 pp. REV: John Schiemann, *Journal of International Affairs* 45, no. 1 (Summer 1991): 304-306. Claus Offe, *Contemporary Sociology* 21, no. 3 (May 1992): 304-306. Paul Hollander, *Partisan Review* 60, no. 2 (Spring 1993): 296-301.

5513. Kaminski, Bartlomiej. *The Collapse of State Socialism: The Case of Poland.* Princeton, NJ: Princeton University Press, c1991. xiv, 264 pp. REV: Robert V. Legvold, *Foreign Affairs* 70, no. 5 (Winter 1991-92): 198. John R. Lampe, *Annals of the American Academy of Political and Social Science*, no. 523 (September 1992): 231-232. Vladimir Tismaneanu, *Orbis* 36, no. 1 (Winter 1992): 144. Padraic Kenney, *Slavic Review* 52, no. 4 (Winter 1993): 890-891.

5514. Lasky, Melvin J. *Voices in a Revolution: The Collapse of East German Communism.* New Brunswick, NJ: Transaction, c1992. 116 pp. REV: Fritz Stern, *Foreign*

Affairs 71, no. 5 (Winter 1992-1993): 208-209. *Orbis* 37, no. 1 (Winter 1993).

5515. Lemke, Christiane, and Gary Marks, eds. *The Crisis of Socialism in Europe.* Durham, NC: Duke University Press, 1992. x, 253 pp. REV: Valerie Bunce, *Political Science Quarterly* 108, no. 1 (Spring 1993): 194-195. Paul Hollander, *American Journal of Sociology* 98, no. 6 (May 1993): 1519.

5516. Mitten, Richard. *Politics of Antisemitic Prejudice: The Waldheim Phenomenon in Austria.* Boulder, CO: Westview Press, 1992. ix, 261 pp. REV: James Shedel, *Central European History* 26, no. 3 (1993): 370-371.

5517. Pilon, Juliana Geran, and Bowling Green State University. Social Philosophy & Policy Center. *The Bloody Flag: Post-Communist Nationalism in Eastern Europe: Spotlight on Romania.* Foreword by Robert Conquest. Studies in Social Philosophy & Policy, no. 16. New Brunswick, NJ: Transaction, 1992. 126 pp. REV: Robert Legvold, *Foreign Affairs* 71, no. 5 (Winter 1992-1993): 211-212. *Orbis* 37, no. 1 (Winter 1993).

5518. Rachwald, Arthur R. *In Search of Poland: The Superpowers' Response to Solidarity, 1980-1989.* Stanford, CA: Hoover Institution Press, 1990. xii, 149 pp. REV: Patrice M. Dabrowski, *Fletcher Forum of World Affairs* 15, no. 2 (Summer 1991): 218-220. Virginia L. Montijo, *Orbis* 35, no. 1 (Winter 1991): 143. Edward Platt, *Perspectives on Political Science* 22, no. 3 (Summer 1993): 136.

5519. Ramet, Sabrina P. *Nationalism and Federalism in Yugoslavia, 1962-1991.* 2nd ed. Bloomington, IN: Indiana University Press, c1992. xviii, 346 pp. [Revised edition of Nationalism and Federalism in Yugoslavia, 1963-1983 (Bloomington, IN: Indiana University Press, 1984).] REV: Carole Rogel, *Slovene Studies* 13, no. 2 (1991) [published July 1993]: 203-204. Mark Biondich, *Canadian Slavonic Papers* 35, nos. 1-2 (March-June 1993): 184. John C. Campbell, *American Historical Review* 98, no. 3 (June 1993): 907. Carole Rogel, *Canadian Review of Studies in Nationalism = Revue Canadienne des Etudes sur le Nationalisme* 20, nos. 1-2 (1993): 140-141.

5520. ———. *Social Currents in Eastern Europe: The Sources and Meaning of the Great Transformation.* Durham, NC: Duke University Press, 1991. xii, 434 pp. REV: Jarmila L.A. Horna, *Canadian Slavonic Papers* 33, nos. 3-4 (December 1991): 391-392. Alexander C. Pacek, *Journal of Politics* 54, no. 4 (November 1992): 1223-1226. Peter Rutland, *American Political Science Review* 86, no. 3 (September 1992): 833-834. Ivan Avakumovic, *Canadian Journal of Political Science = Revue canadienne de science politique* 26, no. 2 (June 1993): 409-410. Anthony Jones, *Annals of the American Academy of Political and Social Science*, no. 528 (July 1993): 185. Ákos Róna-Tas, *Contemporary Sociology* 22, no. 1 (January 1993): 35-37.

5521. Senn, Alfred Erich. *Lithuania Awakening.* Societies and Culture in East-Central Europe, Berkeley, CA:

University of California Press, c1990. 294 pp. REV: Sara Ginaite, *Canadian Slavonic Papers* 32, no. 4 (December 1990): 517-518. Danute S. Harmon, *Lituanus* 37, no. 3 (Fall 1991): 94-96. Richard J. Krickus, *Problems of Communism* 40, no. 6 (November-December 1991): 135-140. Hugi Olafsson, *Journal of International Affairs* 45, no. 1 (Summer 1991): 285-287. Robert A. Vitas, *Journal of Baltic Studies* 22, no. 2 (Summer 1991): 189-191. Lucy Cox, *Slavic Review* 51, no. 3 (Fall 1992): 586-587. Mari Firkatian-Wozniak, *History: Reviews of New Books* 20, no. 2 (Winter 1992): 69-70. Romuald J. Misiunas, *Canadian-American Slavic Studies* 26, nos. 1-4 (1992): 354-[357]. Alexander Shtromas, *Russian Review* 51, no. 2 (April 1992): 290-291. Mikk Titma, *Contemporary Sociology* 21, no. 3 (May 1992): 310-311. V. Stanley Vardys, *Nationalities Papers* 21, no. 2 (Fall 1993): 210-212.

5522. Staniszkis, Jadwiga. *The Dynamics of the Breakthrough in Eastern Europe: The Polish Experience.* Translated from the Polish by Chester A. Kisiel. Foreword by Ivan Szelenyi. Societies and Culture in East-Central Europe, 6. Berkeley, CA: University of California Press, c1991. xiii, 303 pp. REV: Valerie Bunce, *Contemporary Sociology* 21, no. 3 (May 1992): 308-309. Jan Kubik, *Slavic Review* 52, no. 4 (Winter 1993): 857-858.

5523. Swain, Nigel. *Hungary: The Rise and Fall of Feasible Socialism.* London; New York: Verso, c1992. vii, 264 pp. REV: Robert Legvold, *Foreign Affairs* 71, no. 5 (Winter 1992-1993): 212. Ákos Róna-Tas, *Slavic Review* 52, no. 3 (Fall 1993): 590-591.

5524. Thompson, Mark. *A Paper House: The Ending of Yugoslavia.* 1st American ed. New York: Pantheon, c1992. xi, 350 pp. ["Appendix: Danilo Kis on nationalism": pp. [337]-340.] REV: Carole Rogel, *Slovene Studies* 13, no. 2 (1991) [published July 1993]: 205-206. Aleksa Djilas, *New Republic* 208, no. 4 (January 25, 1993): 38-42. Robert Legvold, *Foreign Affairs* 72, no. 2 (Spring 1993): 178-179. Albert U. Mitchum, *Airpower Journal* 7, no. 2 (Summer 1993): 86. *Orbis* 37, no. 2 (Spring 1993).

5525. Van den Heuvel, Martin, and Jan G. Siccama, eds. *The Disintegration of Yugoslavia.* Contributions by Joep Leersen, Ivo Banac, Geert Van Dartel, Paul Shoup, Predrag Simic, Willem Vermeer, Robert Aspeslagh, Radovan Vukadinovic, Maarten Lak, and Koen Koch. Yearbook of European Studies = Annuaire d'études européennes, 5. Amsterdam; Atlanta, GA: Rodopi, 1992. xii, 218 pp. [Contents: Joep Leersen, "Preface"; "Introduction"; Ivo Banac, "The origins and development of the concept of Yugoslavia"; Geert van Dartel, "Nationalities and religion in Yugoslavia"; Paul Shoup, "Titoism and the national question in Yugoslavia: a reassessment"; Predrag Simic, "Civil War in Yugoslavia—the roots of disintegration"; Willem Vermeer, "Albanians and Serbs in Yugoslavia"; Robert Aspeslagh, "Trianon dissolved: the status of Vojvodina reconsidered?"; Radovan Vukadinovic, "Yugoslavia and the East: from non-alignment to disintegration"; Maarten Lak, "The involvement of the European Community in the Yugoslav crisis of 1991"; Koen Koch, "Conflicting visions of state and society in present-day Yugoslavia"; "Epilogue".] REV: John K. Cox, *Slavic Review* 52, no. 3 (Fall 1993): 616-617.

5526. Wheaton, Bernard, and Zdenek Kavan. *The Velvet Revolution: Czechoslovakia, 1988-1991*. Boulder, CO: Westview Press, 1992. xvi, 255 pp. REV: H. Gordon Skilling, *Czechoslovak and Central European Journal* 11, no. 2 (Winter 1993): 128-129.

5527. Wistrich, Robert S., ed. *Austrians and Jews in the Twentieth Century: From Franz Joseph to Waldheim*. New York, NY: St. Martin's Press, 1992. xviii, 280 pp. REV: Allan Janik, *Central European History* 26, no. 3 (1993): 356-357.

5528. Zuzowski, Robert. *Political Dissent and Opposition in Poland: The Workers' Defense Committee "KOR"*. Westport, CT: Praeger, 1992. 293 pp. REV: Robert Legvold, *Foreign Affairs* 72, no. 2 (Spring 1993): 179-180.

■ History

General

5529. Black, Cyril E., Jonathan E. Helmreich, Paul C. Helmreich, Charles P. Issawi, and A. James McAdams. *Rebirth: A History of Europe Since World War II*. Boulder, CO: Westview Press, 1992. xv, 565 pp. REV: Joe Amato, *Annals of the American Academy of Political and Social Science*, no. 530 (November 1993): 207. Stephen D. Carls, *Historian* 56, no. 1 (Autumn 1993): 107-108.

5530. Bonney, Richard. *The European Dynastic States, 1494-1660*. The Short Oxford History of the Modern World. Oxford; New York: Oxford University Press, 1991. xxxiv, 658 pp. [Partial contents: "Poland-Lithuania and Sweden: Imperial Conflict and Dynastic Struggle," pp. 256-272; "Muscovy and Poland-Lithuania: the Attempted 'Gathering of the Russian Lands'," pp. 272-285; "Ottoman Supremacy in South-East Europe and the Middle East," pp. 285-301.] REV: Thomas I. Crimando, *Historian* 56, no. 1 (Autumn 1993): 109-110.

5531. Carr, William. *The Origins of the Wars of German Unification*. Origins of Modern Wars, London; New York: Longman, 1991. xiv, 239 pp. REV: Bernard A. Cook, *Journal of Military History* 57, no. 1 (January 1993): 153-154.

5532. Chalk, Frank, and Kurt Jonassohn. *The History and Sociology of Genocide: Analyses and Case Studies*. New Haven, CT: Yale University Press, c1990. xviii, 461 pp. [Published in cooperation with the Montreal Institute for Genocide Studies.] REV: Raymond Pearson, *Nationalities Papers* 21, no. 2 (Fall 1993): 253-255.

5533. Churchill, Winston S. *The World Crisis*. New York: Charles Scribner's Sons, 1992. xii, 866 pp. [Reprint of 1931 abridgement of original four-volume work.] REV: Francis P. Sempa, *Strategic Review* 21, no. 3 (Summer 1993): 72-73.

5534. Dundes, Alan, ed. *The Blood Libel Legend: A Casebook in Anti-Semitic Folklore*. Includes contribution by Charlotte Klien. Madison, WI: University of Wisconsin Press, c1991. ix, 385 pp. [Partial contents: Charlotte Klien, "Damascus to Kiev: Civilta Cattolica on Ritual Murder".] REV: Haya Bar-Itzhak, *American Anthropologist* 95, no. 1 (March 1993): 176.

5535. Fein, Helen, ed. *Genocide Watch*. Includes contributions by James Mace and Walter K. Ezell. New Haven, CT: Yale University Press, c1992. x, 204 pp. REV: Benjamin B. Ferencz, *American Journal of International Law* 87, no. 3 (July 1993): 474-475. David P. Forsythe, *Contemporary Sociology* 22, no. 3 (May 1993): 360-362.

5536. Flayhart, William Henry III. *Counterpoint to Trafalgar: The Anglo-Russian Invasion of Naples, 1805-1806*. Columbia, SC: University of South Carolina Press, c1992. xi, 198 pp. REV: Jeremy Black, *History: Reviews of New Books* 21, no. 4 (Summer 1993): 170.

5537. Goldstone, Jack A., Ted Robert Gurr, and Farrokh Moshiri, eds. *Revolutions of the Late Twentieth Century*. Includes contributions by Farrokh Moshiri, Jaroslaw Piekalkiewicz, and Anwar-ul-Haq Ahady. Boulder, CO: Westview Press, 1991. xii, 395 pp. [Partial contents: Farrokh Moshiri, "Revolutionary Conflict Theory in an Evolutionary Perspective," pp. 4-36; Jaroslaw Piekalkiewicz, "Poland: Nonviolent Revolution in a Socialist State," pp. 136-161; Anwar-ul-Haq Ahady, "Afghanistan: State Break-down," pp. 162-193.] REV: Steve Breyman, *History: Reviews of New Books* 21, no. 4 (Summer 1993): 189. Ellis Goldberg, *Comparative Political Studies* 26, no. 1 (April 1993): 383-387.

5538. Hinds, Lynn Boyd, and Theodore Otto Windt, Jr. *The Cold War as Rhetoric: The Beginnings, 1945-1950*. Praeger Series in Political Communication. New York: Praeger, 1991. xxiv, 272 pp. REV: Barbie Zelizer, *Journal of Communication* 43, no. 1 (Winter 1993): 178-180.

5539. *The History and the Life of Chinggis Khan: The Secret History of the Mongols*. Translated and annotated by Urgunge Onon. Leiden; New York: E.J. Brill, 1990. xix, 183 pp. [Includes translation of *Yuan ch'ao pi shih*.] REV: Alan J. K Sanders, *Pacific Affairs* 66, no. 1 (Spring 1993): 108.

5540. International Conference of Historians (1988: Freiburg im Breisgau, Germany). *The Conduct of the Air War in the Second World War: An International Comparison: Proceedings of the International Conference of Historians in Freiburg im Briesgau, Federal Republic of Germany, from 29 August to 2 September 1988*. Edited by Horst Boog. Includes contribution by Von Hardesty. Studies in Military History. New York: Berg; Distributed by St. Martin's, 1992. xii, 763 pp. [Partial contents: I. Air Warfare and Modernity. II. The Air Forces and the Armaments Industry. III. The Military, Research, Technology. IV. Doctrine, Technology, Logistics. VI. Tactical and Strategic Air Warfare. VII. Intelligence and Air Warfare. VIII. Air Power, Air Policy, High Command. Includes Von Hardesty, "The Soviet Air Force: Doctrine, Organisation and Technology"; also includes debate between Olaf Groehler of East Germany and Horst Boog of West Germany on Nazi Germany bombing strategy.] REV: Richard R. Muller, *Journal of Military History* 57, no. 1 (January 1993): 172-173.

5541. Kahn, David. *Seizing the Enigma: The Race to Break the German U-Boat Codes, 1939-1943*. Boston, MA: Houghton Mifflin, 1991. xii, 336 pp. [Includes discussion of the Polish contributions to deciphering German Enigma communications.] REV: Marilyn Sarchfield, *Naval War College Review* 46, no. 1, Sequence 341 (Winter 1993): 124-125.

5542. Kertész, Imre. *Fateless*. Translated by Christopher C. Wilson and Katharina M. Wilson. Evanston, IL: Northwestern University Press, 1992. 191 pp. REV: Dean Flower, *Hudson Review* 46, no. 2 (Summer 1993): 395-396. Clara Györgyey, *World Literature Today* 67, no. 4 (Autumn 1993): 863.

5543. Kirsch, G. B., F. M. Schweitzer, W. Stojko, and G. L. Mahoney, eds. *The West in Global Context: A Documentary History*. Lido Beach: Whittier Pubs., 1992. REV: Lowell J. Satre, *Ukrainian Quarterly* 49, no. 3 (Fall 1993): 332.

5544. Naarden, Bruno. *Socialist Europe and Revolutionary Russia: Perception and Prejudice, 1848-1923*. Cambridge; New York, NY: Cambridge University Press, 1992. 595 pp. REV: Michael Confino, *Canadian Slavonic Papers* 35, nos. 1-2 (March-June 1993): 179-180.

5545. Rachnevsky, Paul. *Genghis Khan: His Life and Legacy*. translated and edited by Thomas Nivison Haining. Oxford; Cambridge: Blackwell, 1992. xvii, 313 pp. [Translation of *Cinggis-Khan, sein Leben und Wirken*.] REV: Reuven Amitai-Preiss, *International History Review* 15, no. 3 (August 1993): 558. Anatoly M. Khazanov, *Mongolian Studies* 16 (1993):106.

5546. Sevcenko, Ihor. *Byzantium and the Slavs in Letters and Culture*. Renovatio, 1. Cambridge, MA: Harvard Ukrainian Research Institute; Napoli: Instituto Universitario Orientale; Cambridge, MA: Distributed in the USA by Harvard University Press, c1991. xii, 740 pp. [Contains articles, reviews and other short pieces originally published between 1952 and 1984.] REV: David K. Prestel, *Slavic and East European Journal* 37, no. 2 (Summer 1993): 259-261.

5547. Subtelny, Orest. *Ukraine: A History*. Toronto, Ontario; Buffalo, NY: Published by the University of Toronto Press in association with the Canadian Institute of Ukrainian Studies, University of Alberta, c1988. 666 pp. [Kievan Rus', Polish-Lithuanian period, Cossack era, Russian and Austrian Imperial rule, twentieth century including Soviet rule and Ukrainian diaspora.] REV: Oleh W. Gerus, *Russian History* 17, no. 1 (Spring 1990): 109-110. John Switalski, *Polish Review* 35, nos. 3-4 (1990): 276-280. Frances Swyripa, *Canadian Historical Review* 71, no. 1 (March 1990): 134-135. Christine D. Worobec, *Soviet Union = Union Soviétique* 17, no. 3 (1990): 314-315. Martha Bohachevsky-Chomiak, *Canadian-American Slavic Studies*

25, nos. 1-4 (1991): 382-384. David D. Laitin, *World Politics* 44, no. 1 (October 1991): 139-177. Thomas M. Prymak, *Canadian Review of Studies in Nationalism = Revue Canadienne des Etudes sur le Nationalisme* 18, nos. 1-2 (1991): 259-260. Edward D. Wynot, Jr., *American Historical Review* 96, no. 1 (February 1991): 209-210. Arthur Levin, *Canadian Ethnic Studies* 24, no. 1 (1992): 166. Lubomyr R. Wynar, *Ethnic Forum* 13, no. 2/vol. 14, no. 2 (1993-1994): 143-148.

5548. Sword, Keith, ed. *The Soviet Takeover of the Polish Eastern Provinces, 1939-41*. Contributions by John Erickson, Ryszard Szawlowski, Jan T. Gross, Yosef Litvak, Jan Malanowski, Keith Sword, Bogdan Czaykowski, Mieczyslaw Inglot, and Tomasz Strzembosz. New York: St. Martin's Press, 1991. xxiii, 318 pp. [Result of a conference held at the School of Slavonic and East European Studies, University of London, in April 1989. Contents: John Erickson, "The Red Army's march into Poland, September 1939"; Ryszard Szawlowski, "The Polish-Soviet War of September 1939"; Jan T. Gross, "Polish POW camps in the Soviet-occupied western Ukraine"; Yosef Litvak, "The plight of refugees from the German-occupied territories"; Jan Malanowski, "Sociological aspects of the annexation of Poland's eastern provinces to the USSR in 1939-41"; Keith Sword, "Soviet economic policy in the annexed areas"; Bogdan Czaykowski, "Soviet policies in the literary sphere: their effects and implications"; Mieczyslaw Inglot, "The socio-political role of the Polish literary tradition in the cultural life of Lwoow: the example of Adam Mickiewicz's work"; Tomasz Strzembosz, "Armed resistance in the north-eastern provinces of the Polish republic, 1939-41"; Appendices: 1. The reactions of the world press to the Soviet invasion of Poland on 17 September 1939; 2. "A Historical Campaign" (Soviet account of the Red Army's campaign in Poland); 3. Documents relating to the mass deportations.] REV: Zvi Gitelman, *Slavic Review* 51, no. 3 (Fall 1992): 617-618. John Micgiel, *Polish Review* 37, no. 3 (1992): 358-359. Douglas A. Borer, *History: Reviews of New Books* 21, no. 2 (Winter 1993): 80. Peter Kenez, *Russian History = Histoire russe* 20, nos. 1-4 (1993): 391-392.

5549. Sylla, Richard, and Gianni Toniolo, eds. *Patterns of European Industrialization: The Nineteenth Century*. Includes contributions by Paul R. Gregory, David F. Good, and Olga Crisp. London; New York: Routledge; Rome: Fondazione Adriano Olivetti, 1991. xii, 276 pp. [Partial contents: Paul R. Gregory, "The Role of the State in Promoting Economic Development: The Russian Case and its General Implications"; David F. Good, "Austria-Hungary"; Olga Crisp, "Russia".] REV: John S. Lyons, *Journal of Economic Literature* 31, no. 2 (June 1993): 928-930.

5550. Ulam, Adam. *The Communists: The Story of Power and Lost Illusions, 1948-1991*. New York: Scribner's; Toronto: Maxwell MacMillan Canada; New York: Maxwell Macmillan International, c1992. xiii, 528 pp. REV: Roger Draper, *New Leader* 75, no. 3 (March 9, 1992): 17-18. Ernest Gellner, *New Republic* 206, no. 25 (June 22, 1992): 40-41. Walter Laqueur, *New York Times Book Review* (March 29, 1992): 13-14. Robert Legvold, *Foreign Affairs* 71, no. 3 (Summer 1992): 177. *Publishers Weekly* 239, no. 6 (January 27, 1992): 80. Wayne Dowler, *Journal of Church and State* 35, no. 2 (Spring 1993): 413-414. Stanley W. Page, *Historian* 55, no. 3 (Spring 1993): 564. Richard F. Staar, *Mediterranean Quarterly* 4, no. 1 (Winter 1993): 120-123.

5551. Weintraub, Stanley. *Long Day's Journey into War: December 7, 1941*. New York, NY: Dutton, c1991. 706 pp. REV: Bernard D. Williams, *Historian* 56, no. 1 (Autumn 1993): 182.

5552. Zemke, Hubert. *Zemke's Stalag: The Final Days of World War II*. As told to Roger A. Freeman. Washington, DC: Smithsonian Institution Press, 1991. xi, 148 pp. [Primarily about conditions for American prisoners of war in Nazi Germany's Stalag Luft I; includes some discussion of the arrival of the Soviets.] REV: Bruce A. Brant, *Military Review* 73, no. 2 (February 1993): 85.

Historiography

5553. Kellogg, Frederick. *A History of Romanian Historical Writing*. Bakersfield, CA: Charles Schlacks, Jr., c1990. 132 pp. REV: Paul E. Michelson, *American Historical Review* 96, no. 5 (December 1991): 1573-1574. George F. Jewsbury, *Austrian History Yearbook* 24 (1993): 227-228.

5554. Shelton, Anita Krystyna. *The Democratic Idea in Polish History and Historiography: Franciszek Bujak, 1875-1953*. East European Monographs, no. 267. Boulder, CO: East European Monographs, 1989. ix, 315 pp. REV: Norman M. Naimark, *Slavic Review* 51, no. 4 (Winter 1992): 826-831. Adam A. Hetnal, *Polish Review* 38, no. 1 (1993): 96-98.

Byzantine and Ottoman Empires

5555. Alexander, Edward. *A Crime of Vengeance: An Armenian Struggle for Justice*. New York: Free Press; Toronto: Collier Macmilland Canada; New York: Maxwell Macmillan International, c1991. v, 218 pp. [On the 1921 assassination in Berlin of Talaat Pasha by Soghomon Tehlirian.] REV: Levon A. Saryan, *Ararat* 32, no. 1 (Winter 1992): 66-67. István Deák, *New York Review of Books* 40 (October 7, 1993): 46ff.

5556. Andric, Ivo. *The Development of Spiritual Life in Bosnia under the Influence of Turkish Rule*. Edited and translated by Zelimir B. Juricic and John F. Loud. Durham, NC: Duke University Press, 1990. xxii, 125 pp. [Translation of *Die Entwicklung des geistigen Lebens in Bosnien unter der Einwirkung der türkischen Herrschaft* (Doctoral thesis, University of Graz, 1924).] REV: Bonnie Marshall, *World Literature Today* 65, no. 4 (Autumn 1991): 736. John V.A. Fine, Jr., *Slavic Review* 51, no. 4 (Winter 1992): 834-835. Peter F. Sugar, *Austrian History Yearbook* 24 (1993): 219-220.

5557. Melson, Robert. *Revolution and Genocide: On the Origins of the Armenian Genocide and the Holocaust*. Foreword by Leo Kuper. Chicago, IL: University of Chicago Press, 1992. 363 pp. REV: Irving Louis Horowitz, *American Political Science Review* 87, no. 2 (June 1993): 530-531.

George F. Jewsbury, *Historian* 55, no. 4 (Summer 1993): 753-754. Firuz Kazemzadeh, *New York Times Book Review* 98, no. 17 (April 25, 1993): 13-14.

5558. Shaw, Stanford J. *The Jews of the Ottoman Empire and the Turkish Republic*. New York: New York University Press, 1991. xiii, 380 pp. REV: Daniel J. Schroeter, *American Historical Review* 98, no. 3 (June 1993): 916.

5559. Vassilian, Hamo B., ed. *The Armenian Genocide: A Comprehensive Bibliography and Library Reference Guide*. 1st ed. Glendale, CA: Armenian Reference Books, 1992. 103 pp. REV: Fred Assadourian, *Ararat* 34, no. 2 (Spring 1993): 53-54.

5560. Vucinich, Wayne S., and Thomas A. Emmert, eds. *Kosovo: Legacy of a Medieval Battle*. Minnesota Mediterranean and East European Monographs, 1. Minneapolis, MN: University of Minnesota Press, 1991. 342 pp. REV: David MacKenzie, *Modern Greek Studies Yearbook*, no. 7 (1991): 558-561. Kemal H. Karpat, *Slavic Review* 52, no. 2 (Summer 1993): 383-384.

The Holocaust

5561. Adelson, Alan, and Robert Lapides, comps. and eds. *Lodz Ghetto: Inside a Community Under Siege*. Afterword by Geoffrey Hartman. Annotations and bibliographical notes by Marek Web. New York, NY: Viking, 1989. xxi, 526 pp. [Translated from German, Hebrew, Polish, and Yiddish.] REV: Walter Reich, *New York Times Book Review* (May 6, 1990): 41. Samuel Totten, *Holocaust and Genocide Studies* 7, no. 2 (Fall 1993): 281-287. Samuel Totten, *Social Education* 57, no. 7 (November-December 1993): 393.

5562. Amis, Martin. *Time's Arrow, or, The Nature of the Offense*. 1st American ed. New York: Harmony Books, c1991. 168 pp. REV: Jascha Kessler, *Contention: Debates in Society, Culture, and Science* 3, no. 1 (Fall 1993): 103-107.

5563. Bankier, David. *The Germans and the Final Solution: Public Opinion Under Nazism*. Jewish Society and Culture. Cambridge, MA: B. Blackwell, 1992. 206 pp. REV: Robert Gellately, *American Historical Review* 98, no. 4 (October 1993): 1280.

5564. Berger, Alan L., ed. *Bearing Witness to the Holocaust, 1939-1989*. Lewiston, NY: E. Mellon Press, c1991. xi, 355 pp. [Proceedings of the 19th Annual Scholar's Conference on the Holocaust and the Church Struggle, held in Philadelphia, March 5-7, 1989.] REV: Richard Libowitz, *Holocaust and Genocide Studies* 7, no. 3 (Winter 1993): 432.

5565. Blady Szwajger, Adina. *I Remember Nothing More: The Warsaw Children's Hospital and the Jewish Resistance*. Translated from the Polish by Tasja Darowska and Danusia Stok. 1st Touchstone ed. New York: Simon & Schuster, 1992. xv, 184 p. [Originally published: (London: Collins Harvill, 1990).] REV: Diane Cole, *Lilith* 18, no. 1 (Winter 1993): 26-28.

5566. Block, Gay, and Malka Drucker. *Rescuers: Portraits of Moral Courage in the Holocaust.* Prologue by Cynthia Ozick. Afterword by Harold M. Schulweis. 1st ed. New York: Holmes & Meier, 1992. xvi, 255 pp. REV: Susan Schnur, *Lilith* 17, no. 3 (Summer 1992): 35. *Publishers Weekly* 239, no. 10 (February 17, 1992): 60. W.H. Locke Anderson, *Monthly Review* 44, no. 10 (March 1993): 50-56.

5567. Breitman, Richard. *The Architect of Genocide: Himmler and the Final Solution.* 1st ed. New York: Knopf, 1991. 335 pp. [Includes Eastern Europe and the Soviet Union.] REV: Yehuda Bauer, *Holocaust and Genocide Studies* 6, no. 3 (1991): 307-312. Daniel Jonah Goldhagen, *New Republic* 205, no. 19 (November 4, 1991): 34-39. Michael H. Kater, *New York Times Book Review* (May 5, 1991): 7. Fritz Stern, *Foreign Affairs* 70, no. 3 (Summer 1991): 173. Jacob Heilbrunn, *New Leader* 75, no. 5 (April 6, 1992): 18-20. Lawrence D. Stokes, *Historian* 54, no. 2 (Winter 1992): 320-321. Otis C. Mitchell, *History: Reviews of New Books* 22, no. 2 (Winter 1993): 79.

5568. Browning, Christopher R. *Ordinary Men: Reserve Police Battalion 101 and the Final Solution in Poland.* 1st ed. New York: HarperCollins, c1992. xxii, 231 pp. REV: Daniel Jonah Goldhagen, *New Republic* 207, nos. 3-4 (July 13 & 20, 1992): 49-52. Walter Reich, *New York Times Book Review* (April 12, 1992): 1ff. Fritz Stern, *Foreign Affairs* 71, no. 4 (Fall 1992): 209. *Publishers Weekly* 239, no. 6 (January 27, 1992): 83. Edward Alexander, *Commentary* 95, no. 2 (February 1993): 32-36. Richard Breitman, *American Historical Review* 98, no. 5 (December 1993): 1637. Franklin H. Littell, *Holocaust and Genocide Studies* 7, no. 1 (Spring 1993): 121.

5569. ———. *The Path to Genocide: Essays on Launching the Final Solution.* Cambridge; New York: Cambridge University Press, 1992. xiii, 191 pp. REV: Lawrence D. Stokes, *Central European History* 26, no. 3 (1993): 361-363.

5570. Butnaru, I. C. *The Silent Holocaust: Romania and Its Jews.* Foreword by Elie Wiesel. Contributions to the Study of World History, no. 31. New York: Greenwood Press, 1992. xxv, 236 pp. REV: Paul E. Michelson, *Historian* 55, no. 2 (Winter 1993): 334-335.

5571. Cohen, Asher, Joav Gelber, and Charlotte Wardi, eds. *Comprehending the Holocaust: Historical and Literary Reseearch.* Frankfurt am Main; New York: P. Lang, c1988. 372 pp. [Papers prepared for a congress held June 1986 by the Strochlitz Institute at the University of Haifa.] REV: Lewis Fried, *Ethnic Forum* 13, no. 1 (1993): 86-87.

5572. Dawidowicz, Lucy S. *What Is the Use of Jewish History? Essays.* Edited and introduction by Neal Kozodoy. 1st ed. New York: Schocken Books, c1992. xxiii, 278 pp. REV: Edward Alexander, *Commentary* 95, no. 2 (February 1993): 32-36. Norma Rosen, *Congress Monthly* 60, no. 4 (May-June 1993): 20-21.

5573. Gilbert, Martin. *Auschwitz and the Allies.* 1st American ed. New York: Holt, Rinehard and Winston,

c1981. 368 pp. REV: Frederick M. Schweitzer, *Ukrainian Quarterly* 49, no. 3 (Fall 1993): 323-327.

5574. Hass, Aaron. *In the Shadow of the Holocaust: The Second Generation.* Ithaca, NY: Cornell University Press, 1990. 178 pp. [Interviews with children of Holocaust survivors.] REV: Aaron Berman, *Journal of American Ethnic History* 12, no. 2 (Winter 1993): 85-86. Samuel Totten, *Holocaust and Genocide Studies* 7, no. 2 (Fall 1993): 289.

5575. Headland, Ronald. *Messages of Murder: A Study of the Reports of the Einsatzgruppen of the Security Police and the Security Service, 1941-1943.* Rutherford, NJ: Fairleigh Dickinson University Press, c1992. 303 pp. [Includes Soviet Union.] REV: Richard Breitman, *American Historical Review* 98, no. 5 (December 1993): 1637. George C. Browder, *Central European History* 26, no. 3 (1993): 363-365. Jerome F. Brown, *History: Reviews of New Books* 21, no. 4 (Summer 1993): 171.

5576. Hilberg, Raul. *The Destruction of the European Jews.* Chicago, IL: Quadrangle Books, 1961. x, 788 pp. REV: Edward Alexander, *Commentary* 95, no. 2 (February 1993): 32-36.

5577. ———. *Perpetrators, Victims, Bystanders: The Jewish Catastrophe, 1933-1945.* 1st ed. New York, NY: Aaron Asher Books, c1992. xii, 340 pp. [Contents: Pt. 1. Perpetrators. 1. Adolf Hitler. 2. The Establishment. 3. Old Functionaries. 4. Newcomers. 5. Zealots, Vulgarians, and Bearers of Burdens. 6. Physicians and Lawyers. 7. Non-German Governments. 8. Non-German Volunteers — Pt. II. Victims. 9. The Jewish Leaders. 10. The Refugees. 11. Men and Women. 12. Mixed Marriages. 13. Children. 14. Christian Jews. 15. The Advantaged, the Strugglers, and the Dispossessed. 16. The Unadjusted. 17. The Survivors — Pt. III. Bystanders. 18. Nations in Adolf Hitler's Europe. 19. Helpers, Gainers, and Onlookers. 20. Messengers. 21. The Jewish Rescuers. 22. The Allies. 23. Neutral Countries. 24. The Churches.] REV: István Deák, *New York Review of Books* 39, no. 17 (October 22, 1992): 40-43. Michael Robert Marrus, *New York Times Book Review* 97 (September 20, 1992): 14-15. Edward Alexander, *Commentary* 95, no. 2 (February 1993): 32-36. Gerald M. Costello, *U.S. Catholic* 58 (February 1993): 48-51.

5578. Höss, Rudolf. *Death Dealer: The Memoirs of the SS Kommandant at Auschwitz.* Edited by Steven Paskuly. Translated by Andrew Pollinger. Buffalo, NY: Prometheus, 1992. 390 pp. REV: István Deák, *New York Review of Books* 39, no. 16 (October 8, 1992): 8-13. Lucy Despard, *Foreign Affairs* 71, no. 5 (Winter 1992-1993): 209. *Publishers Weekly* 239, no. 15 (March 23, 1992): 57. Kevin Lewis, *Journal of Church and State* 35, no. 3 (Summer 1993): 630.

5579. Isaacson, Judith Magyar. *Seed of Sarah: Memoirs of a Survivor.* Urbana, IL: University of Illinois Press, c1990. xi, 171 pp. [The Holocaust in Hungary.] REV: Richard J. Prystowsky, *Holocaust and Genocide Studies* 7, no. 1 (Spring 1993): 124.

5580. Jagendorf, Siegfried. *Jagendorf's Foundry: A Memoir of the Romanian Holocaust, 1941-1944*. Introduction and commentaries by Aron Hirt-Manheimer. Foreword by Elie Wiesel. 1st ed. New York: HarperCollins, c1991. 209 pp. REV: Irving Abrahamson, *Midstream* 37, no. 5 (June-July 1991): 42-43. Leon Rappoport, *Holocaust and Genocide Studies* 6, no. 4 (1991): 424-426. István Deák, *New York Review of Books* 39, no. 5 (March 5, 1992): 43-51. Haim Chertok, *Congress Monthly* 60, no. 5 (July-August 1993): 22.

5581. Klein, Cecilie. *Sentenced to Live: A Survivor's Memoir*. Preface by Samuel Pisar. New York: Holocaust Library, c1988. 146 pp. REV: Richard J. Prystowsky, *Holocaust and Genocide Studies* 7, no. 1 (Spring 1993): 124.

5582. Langer, Lawrence L. *Holocaust Testimonies: The Ruins of Memory*. New Haven, CT: Yale University Press, c1991. xix, 216 pp. REV: Lucy Edwards Despard, *Foreign Affairs* 70, no. 4 (Fall 1991): 179. Madeline Marget, *Commonweal* 118, no. 16 (September 27, 1991): 552-553. David G. Roskies, *Commentary* 92, no. 5 (November 1991): 57-59. Gordon R. Mork, *History: Reviews of New Books* 20, no. 3 (Spring 1992): 132. Gabriel Motola, *Congress Monthly* 60, no. 3 (March-April 1993): 20-21.

5583. Millu, Liana. *Smoke over Birkenau*. Translated from the Italian by Lynne Sharon Schwartz. 1st English-language ed. Philadelphia, PA: Jewish Publication Society, 1991. 202 pp. REV: Gabriel Motola, *Nation* 255, no. 11 (October 12, 1992): 401-403. Diane Cole, *Lilith* 18, no. 1 (Winter 1993): 26-28. Phyllis Raphael, *Congress Monthly* 60, no. 1 (January 1993): 20-22.

5584. Ofer, Dalia. *Escaping the Holocaust: Illegal Immigration to the Land of Israel, 1939-1944*. Studies in Jewish History. New York: Oxford University Press, 1990. 408 pp. [Includes Balkan States.] REV: Donald L. Niewyk, *Historian* 54, no. 1 (Autumn 1991): 135. Frank W. Brecher, *Middle East Journal* 46, no. 4 (Autumn 1992): 689-690. Jack Fischel, *Midstream* 38, no. 5 (June-July 1992): 45-46. Yaacov Shavit, *American Historical Review* 97, no. 3 (June 1992): 900-902. Morton J. Merowitz, *History: Reviews of New Books* 21, no. 3 (Spring 1993): 129.

5585. Polonsky, Antony, ed. *"My Brother's Keeper?" Recent Polish Debates on the Holocaust*. London; New York: Routledge in association with the Institute for Polish-Jewish Studies, c1990. 242 pp. REV: Abraham Rzepkowicz, *Congress Monthly* 58, no. 2 (February 1991): 22-23. István Deák, *New York Review of Books* 39, no. 18 (November 5, 1992): 22-26. Edward D. Wynot, Jr., *Nationalities Papers* 21, no. 2 (Fall 1993): 250-251.

5586. Pressac, Jean-Claude. *Auschwitz: Technique and Operation of the Gas Chambers*. Translated from the French by Peter Moss. New York, NY: Beate Klarsfeld Foundation, 1989. 564 pp. REV: Vera Laska, *International Social Science Review* 68, no. 3 (Summer 1993): 139-141.

5587. Rittner, Carol, and John K. Roth, eds. *Memory Offended: The Auschwitz Convent Controversy*. NY: Praeger, 1991. xiv, 289 pp. [Includes an appendix with key documents on the controversy, pp. 209-270.] REV: Sheila

Schwartz, *Holocaust and Genocide Studies* 7, no. 3 (Winter 1993): 422-425.

5588. Roland, Charles G. *Courage Under Siege: Starvation, Disease, and Death in the Warsaw Ghetto*. Studies in Jewish History. New York: Oxford University Press, 1992. viii, 310 pp. REV: Eugene V. Boisaubin, *JAMA* 270, no. 5 (August 4, 1993): 649-650. Howard Markel, *Bulletin of the History of Medicine* 67, no. 4 (Winter 1993): 741. Robert N. Proctor, *New England Journal of Medicine* 328, no. 19 (May 13, 1993): 1428.

5589. Schmidt, Elfriede. *1938—and the Consequences: Questions and Responses: Interviews*. Translated by Peter J. Lyth. Studies in Austrian Literature, Culture, and Thought. Riverside, CA: Ariadne Press, c1992. 381 pp. [Translation of *1938— und Was dann?*] REV: Bruce F. Pauley, *Modern Austrian Literature* 26, no. 2 (1993): 171-172.

5590. Shimoni, Gideon, ed. *The Holocaust in University Teaching*. 1st ed. New York: Pergamon Press, 1991. xiii, 279 pp. [Prepared in association with the International Center for University Teaching of Jewish Civilization, Jerusalem.] REV: Samuel Totten, *Educational Studies* 24, no. 4 (Winter 1993): 338-343.

5591. Spiegelman, Art. *Maus II: A Survivor's Tale: And Here My Troubles Began*. 1st ed. New York: Pantheon, c1991. 135 pp. REV: Lawrence L. Langer, *New York Times Book Review* (November 3, 1991): 1ff. Molly Finn, *Commonweal* 119, no. 4 (February 28, 1992): 23-24. Hillel Halkin, *Commentary* 93, no. 2 (February 1992): 55-56. Samuel Totten, *Social Education* 57, no. 6 (October 1993): 338.

5592. Taylor, Telford. *The Anatomy of the Nuremberg Trials: A Personal Memoir*. 1st ed. New York: Knopf, 1992. xii, 703 pp. [Contents: 1. Nuremberg and the Laws of War; 2. The Nuremberg Ideas; 3. Justice Jackson Takes Over; 4. Establishing the Court: The London Charter; 5. The Defendants and the Charges: Krupp and the German General Staff; 6. Berlin to Nuremberg; 7. Nuremberg: Pretrial Pains and Problems; 8. On Trial; 9. The Nuremberg War Crimes Community; 10. The SS and the General Staff-High Command; 11. Individual Defendants, Future Trials, and Criminal Organizations; 12. The French and Soviet Prosecutions; 13. The Defendants: Goering and Hess; 14. The Defendants: "Murderers' Row"; 15. The Defendants: Bankers and Admirals; 16. The Defendants: The Last Nine; 17. The Closing Arguments; 18. The Indicted Organizations; 19. The Defendants' Last Words; 20. The Judgments of Solomons; 21. Judgment: Law, Crime, and Punishment; 22. Epilogue and Assessment.] REV: Martin Gilbert, *New York Times Book Review* 97 (November 22, 1992): 15ff. Fred L. Borch, *Military Law Review* 142 (Fall 1993): 191-193. István Deák, *New York Review of Books* 40 (October 7, 1993): 46ff. Donald M. Douglas, *Historian* 56, no. 1 (Autumn 1993): 151-152. Erwin Knoll, *Progressive* 57, no. 1 (January 1993): 36-37. William L. O'Neill, *New Leader* 76 (January 11, 1993): 18-19.

5593. Vidal-Naquet, Pierre. *Assassins of Memory: Essays on the Denial of the Holocaust.* Translated and with a foreword by Jeffrey Mehlman. European Perspectives, New York: Columbia University Press, c1992. xxv, 205 pp. [Translation of *Assassins de la memoire.* Contents: "A paper Eichmann" (1980); "On Faurisson and Chomsky" (1981); "On the side of the persecuted" (1981); "Theses on revisionism" (1985); "Assassins of memory" (1987).] REV: Walter Reich, *New York Times Book Review* 98, no. 28 (July 11, 1993): 1ff.. Fritz Stern, *Foreign Affairs* 72, no. 3 (Summer 1993): 203.

5594. Wiesenthal, Simon. *Justice, Not Vengeance.* Translated from the German by Ewald Osers. 1st American ed. New York: Grove Weidenfeld, c1989. xi, 372 pp. [Translation of *Recht, night Rache.*] REV: Roger W. Smith, *Holocaust and Genocide Studies* 7, no. 3 (Winter 1993): 425-432.

Russia/U.S.S.R.

5595. Carrère d'Encausse, Hélène. *The Russian Syndrome: One Thousand Years of Political Murder.* Translated by Caroline Higgit. Foreword by Adam B. Ulam. New York: Holmes & Meier, 1992. xvii, 477 pp. [Translation of *Malheur russe.*] REV: Robert Legvold, *Foreign Affairs* 72, no. 5 (November-December 1993): 174.

5596. Crummey, Robert O., ed. *Reform in Russia and the U.S.S.R.: Past and Prospects.* Urbana, IL: University of Illinois Press, 1989. 318 pp. REV: John C. Campbell, *Foreign Affairs* 69, no. 2 (Spring 1990): 180-181. N.G.O. Pereira, *Canadian Journal of History = Annales canadienne d'histoire* 15, no. 1 (April 1990): 130. William G. Wagner, *Russian History* 17, no. 2 (Summer 1990): 251-253. Ben Eklof, *Russian Review* 50, no. 2 (April 1991): 229-230. Alfred J. Rieber, *Journal of Modern History* 65, no. 2 (June 1993): 435-436.

5597. Dukes, Paul. *A History of Russia: Medieval, Modern, Contemporary.* 2nd ed. Durham, NC: Duke University Press, 1990. xii, 425 pp. REV: R. M. Davidson, *Studies in East European Thought* 45, no. 3 (September 1993): 217-218.

5598. Trubetzkoy, Nikolai Sergeevich. *The Legacy of Genghis Khan and Other Essays on Russia's Identity.* Edited and with a postscript by Anatoly Liberman. Preface by Viacheslav V. Ivanov. Michigan Slavic Materials, no. 33. Ann Arbor, MI: Michigan Slavic Publications, 1991. xiv, 400 pp. REV: Marc Raeff, *Slavic Review* 51, no. 4 (Winter 1992): 806-807. Frank E. Sysyn, *Canadian Slavonic Papers* 34, nos. 1-2 (March-June 1992): 143-152. William E. Watson, *Canadian American Slavic Studies = Revue Canadienne Américaine d'Etudes Slaves* 27, nos. 1-4 (1993): 413-415.

5599. Wade, Rex A., and Scott J. Seregny, eds. *Politics and Society in Provincial Russia: Saratov, 1590-1917.* Columbus, OH: Ohio State University Press, c1989. x, 468 pp. [Based on papers presented at a conference held in the summer of 1985 in Urbana, IL, and sponsored by the Russian and East European Center at the University of

Illinois.] REV: Roberta T. Manning, *Russian Review* 52, no. 2 (April 1993): 274-275. Richard G. Robbins, Jr., *Slavic Review* 52, no. 4 (Winter 1993): 905-906.

5600. White, Stephen, ed. *New Directions in Soviet History: Selected Papers from the Fourth World Congress for Soviet and East European Studies, Harrogate, 1990.* Cambridge; New York: Cambridge University Press, 1992. xvi, 209 pp. REV: Lewis H. Siegelbaum, *Slavic Review* 51, no. 2 (Summer 1992): 355-356. William B. Husband, *Russian History = Histoire russe* 20, nos. 1-4 (1993): 370-372.

Imperial Period

5601. Aronson, I. Michael. *Troubled Waters: The Origins of the 1881 Anti-Jewish Pogroms in Russia.* Pitt Series in Russian and East European Studies, no. 13. Pittsburgh, PA: University of Pittsburgh Press, c1990. xii, 286 pp. REV: Henry J. Tobias, *Canadian-American Slavic Studies* 25, nos. 1-4 (1991): 280-281. Stephen M. Berk, *American Historical Review* 97, no. 1 (February 1992): 255-256. Erich E. Haberer, *Canadian Slavonic Papers* 34, no. 3 (September 1992): 321-322. Alexandra S. Korros, *Russian Review* 51, no. 4 (October 1992): 585-586. Robert Weinberg, *Journal of Social History* 26, no. 1 (Fall 1992): 159-161. Michael F. Hamm, *Russian History = Histoire russe* 20, nos. 1-4 (1993): 316-320.

5602. Bradley, Joseph. *Guns for the Tsar: American Technology and the Small Arms Industry in Nineteenth-Century Russia.* DeKalb, IL: Northern Illinois University Press, 1990. xi, 274 pp. REV: Robert F. Baumann, *International History Review* 15, no. 1 (February 1993): 170.

5603. Christian, David. *Living Water: Vodka and Russian Society on the Eve of Emancipation.* New York: Oxford University Press, c1990. 447 pp. REV: Colin White, *Australian Slavonic and East European Studies* 5, no. 1 (1991): 133-134. Steven Hoch, *American Historical Review* 97, no. 1 (February 1992): 253. Dan Usher, *Annals of the American Academy of Political and Social Science*, no. 524 (November 1992): 203-205. Christine D. Worobec, *Journal of Interdisciplinary History* 22, no. 4 (Spring 1992): 744-746. John F. Hutchinson, *Russian Review* 52, no. 1 (January 1993): 112-113.

5604. Clowes, Edith W., Samuel D. Kassow, and James L. West, eds. *Between Tsar and People: Educated Society and the Quest for Public Identity in Late Imperial Russia.* Princeton, NJ: Princeton University Press, 1991. 383 pp. REV: Gust Olson, *Canadian Slavonic Papers* 34, nos. 1-2 (March-June 1992): 181-182. G. M. Hamburg, *American Historical Review* 98, no. 4 (October 1993): 1291-1292. David A.J. Macey, *Slavic Review* 52, no. 1 (Spring 1993): 177-178.

5605. Daly, John C. K. *Russian Seapower and the "Eastern Question", 1827-41.* Annapolis, MD: Naval Institute Press, 1991. xvii, 314 pp. REV: Walter C. Uhler, *Russian History = Histoire russe* 20, nos. 1-4 (1993): 287-289.

5606. Daniel, Wallace L. *Grigorii Teplov: A States-man at the Court of Catherine the Great*. Russian Biography Series, no. 10. Newtonville, MA: Oriental Research Part-ners, 1991. ix, 194 pp. REV: Herbert H. Kaplan, *Slavic Review* 52, no. 2 (Summer 1993): 357.

5607. Foust, Clifford M. *Rhubarb: The Wondrous Drug*. Princeton, NJ: Princeton University Press, c1992. xxi, 371 pp. [Chapter 3 is a new analysis and an expansion of a few pages in author's Muscovite and Mandarin (1969). Preliminary versions were read at meetings of the Southern Conference on Slavic Studies (Atlanta, GA, 1983) and the American Association for the Advancement of Slavic Studies (New Orleans, LA, 1986). Partial contents: "The Russian Rhubarb Trade," pp. 46-78.] REV: Roderick E. McGrew, *American Historical Review* 98, no. 3 (June 1993): 840. Patricia P. Timberlake, *Russian History = Histoire russe* 20, nos. 1-4 (1993): 267-268.

5608. Hamburg, G. M. *Boris Chicherin & Early Russian Liberalism, 1828-1866*. Stanford, CA: Stanford University Press, 1992. ix, 443 pp. REV: Abbott Gleason, *Russian History = Histoire russe* 20, nos. 1-4 (1993): 292-293.

5609. Kassow, Samuel D. *Students, Professors, and the State in Tsarist Russia*. Berkeley: University of Califor-nia Press, c1989. 438 pp. REV: John P. LeDonne, *Social Science Quarterly* 71, no. 4 (December 1990): 872-873. Allen Sinel, *Canadian Slavonic Papers* 31, no. 1 (March 1990): 77-78. Daniel R. Brower, *American Historical Review* 96, no. 1 (February 1991): 214. Terence Emmons, *Journal of Modern History* 63, no. 3 (September 1991): 616-618. James C. McClelland, *Canadian-American Slavic Studies* 25, nos. 1-4 (1991): 293-297. Robert F. Byrnes, *Slavic Review* 51, no. 3 (Fall 1992): 611-613. James T. Flynn, *Russian Review* 52, no. 4 (October 1993): 557-558.

5610. Kingston-Mann, Esther, and Timothy Mixter, eds. *Peasant Economy, Culture, and Politics of European Russia, 1800-1921*. Edited with the assistance of Jeffrey Burds. Princeton, NJ: Princeton University Press, c1991. xviii, 443 pp. REV: David L. Ransel, *Peasant Studies* 18, no. 2 (Winter 1991): 117-129. Daniel Brower, *Agricultural History* 66, no. 1 (Winter 1992): 97-98. Mary Schaeffer Conroy, *East/West Education* 13, no. 1 (Spring 1992): 82-83. Steven L. Hoch, *Slavic Review* 51, no. 2 (Summer 1992): 358-359. W. M. Pintner, *Journal of Economic History* 52, no. 2 (June 1992): 486-487. Alfred J. Rieber, *Journal of Interdisciplinary History* 23, no. 2 (Autumn 1992): 377-379. Maureen Perrie, *Russian Review* 52, no. 1 (January 1993): 109-110.

5611. LeDonne, John P. *Absolutism and Ruling Class: The Formation of the Russian Political Order, 1700-1825*. New York: Oxford University Press, 1991. 376 pp. REV: John T. Alexander, *American Historical Review* 97, no. 5 (December 1992): 1565-1566. Walter M. Pinter, *Russian Review* 52, no. 1 (January 1993): 108-109.

5612. Lincoln, W. Bruce. *The Great Reforms: Autocracy, Bureaucracy, and the Politics of Change in Imperial Russia*. DeKalb, IL: Northern Illinois University Press, 1990. xxi, 281 pp. REV: Charles A. Ruud, *Canadian Slavonic Papers* 33, nos. 3-4 (December 1991): 369-370. Richard C. Sutton, *Russian History* 18, no. 2 (Summer 1991): 209-211. Theodore Taranovski, *American Historical Review* 96, no. 5 (December 1991): 1578-1579. Thomas S. Pearson, *Russian Review* 51, no. 2 (April 1992): 273-274. Daniel Brower, *Slavic Review* 52, no. 1 (Spring 1993): 175-176. David Moon, *Journal of Modern History* 65, no. 1 (March 1993): 235-237.

5613. Marks, Steven G. *Road to Power: The Trans-Siberian Railroad and the Colonization of Asian Russia, 1850-1917*. Ithaca, NY: Cornell University Press, 1991. xxiii, 240 pp. REV: Gary Hansen, *Canadian-American Slavic Studies* 25, nos. 1-4 (1991): 275-276. J.L. Black, *International History Review* 14, no. 4 (November 1992): 787-788. J. Kenneth Kreider, *History: Reviews of New Books* 20, no. 3 (Spring 1992): 119. Thomas C. Owen, *Journal of Asian Studies* 51, no. 1 (February 1992): 130. Alfred J. Rieber, *American Historical Review* 97, no. 3 (June 1992): 896-897. David A.J. Macey, *Slavic Review* 52, no. 2 (Summer 1993): 364-366. Benjamin D. Rhodes, *Technology and Culture* 34, no. 2 (April 1993): 434.

5614. McGrew, Roderick E. *Paul I of Russia, 1754-1801*. Oxford: Clarendon Press; New York: Oxford Univer-sity Press, 1992. xi, 405 pp. REV: Jack M. Lauber, *Histo-rian* 56, no. 1 (Autumn 1993): 140. Marc Raeff, *American Historical Review* 98, no. 4 (October 1993): 1143-1155. Hugh Ragsdale, *Slavic Review* 52, no. 2 (Summer 1993): 358-359.

5615. McKean, Robert B., ed. *New Perspectives in Modern Russian History: Selected Papers from the Fourth World Congress for Soviet and East European Studies, Harrogate, 1990*. New York: St. Martin's Press, 1992. xii, 287 pp. [World Congress for Soviet and East European Studies (4th: 1990: Harrogate, England).] REV: Steven G. Marks, *Russian History = Histoire russe* 20, nos. 1-4 (1993): 307-308. Donald W. Treadgold, *Slavic Review* 52, no. 3 (Fall 1993): 648-649.

5616. Mosse, Werner Eugen. *Perestroika under the Tsars*. New York: I.B. Tauris; Distributed by St. Martin's Press, 1992. xii, 298 pp. REV: David A.J. Macey, *Slavic Review* 52, no. 4 (Winter 1993): 909-910.

5617. Owen, Thomas C. *The Corporation under Russian Law, 1800-1917: A Study in Tsarist Economic Policy*. Studies of the Harriman Institute. New York: Cambridge University Press, 1991. 234 pp. REV: Alfred J. Rieber, *Canadian-American Slavic Studies* 25, nos. 1-4 (1991): 266-268. Jo Ann Ruckman, *Russian History* 18, no. 3 (Fall 1991): 365-367. Walter J. Gleason, *History: Reviews of New Books* 21, no. 1 (Fall 1992): 30. Steven G. Marks, *American Historical Review* 97, no. 4 (October 1992): 1250-1251. John P. McKay, *Business History Review* 66, no. 2 (Summer 1992): 426-428. Albert J. Schmidt, *Slavic Review* 51, no. 1 (Spring 1992): 170-171. William G. Wagner, *Russian Review* 52, no. 3 (July 1993): 425-426.

5618. Roberts, Ian W. *Nicholas I and the Russian Intervention in Hungary*. New York: St. Martin's Press,

1991. xi, 301 pp. REV: Barbara Jelavich, *Austrian History Yearbook*, no. 23 (1992): 261-263. Peter Pastor, *Slavic Review* 51, no. 3 (Fall 1992): 603-604. Thomas Pearson, *Historian* 55, no. 1 (Autumn 1992): 134-135. Dennis Reinhartz, *History: Reviews of New Books* 20, no. 3 (Spring 1992): 120. George F. Jewsbury, *Russian History = Histoire russe* 20, nos. 1-4 (1993): 290-292. Michael M. Luther, *Russian Review* 52, no. 4 (October 1993): 561-562. Paul Schroder, *International History Review* 15, no. 1 (February 1993): 116-134.

5619. Saunders, David. *Russia in the Age of Reaction and Reform, 1801-1881.* Longman History of Russia, London; New York: Longman, 1992. xii, 386 pp. REV: Jack M. Lauber, *History: Reviews of New Books* 22, no. 1 (Fall 1993): 40. Gregory L. Freeze, *American Historical Review* 98, no. 3 (June 1993): 910. Franklin A. Walker, *Slavic Review* 52, no. 2 (Summer 1993): 361. Frank Wcislo, *Russian History = Histoire russe* 20, nos. 1-4 (1993): 284-285.

5620. Wcislo, Francis William. *Reforming Rural Russia: State, Local Society, and National Politics, 1855-1914.* Studies of the Harriman Institute. Princeton, NJ: Princeton University Press, c1990. xviii, 347 pp. REV: Lynne Viola, *Canadian Slavonic Papers* 32, no. 4 (December 1990): 490-492. Thomas S. Pearson, *American Historical Review* 96, no. 4 (October 1991): 1245. David Christian, *Annals of the American Academy of Political and Social Science*, no. 520 (March 1992): 196-197. David A.J. Macey, *Russian Review* 51, no. 2 (April 1992): 274-276. Neil B. Weissman, *Slavic Review* 51, no. 1 (Spring 1992): 171-172. Roberta T. Manning, *Journal of Modern History* 65, no. 4 (December 1993): 909-910. Samuel C. Ramer, *Russian History = Histoire russe* 20, nos. 1-4 (1993): 296-298.

5621. Worobec, Christine D. *Peasant Russia: Family and Community in the Post-Emancipation Period.* Princeton, NJ: Princeton University Press, c1991. xiv, 257 pp. [Based on the author's thesis (Ph.D.)—University of Toronto.] REV: David L. Ransel, *Peasant Studies* 18, no. 2 (Winter 1991): 117-129. Beatrice Farnsworth, *American Historical Review* 97, no. 1 (February 1992): 254. Steven L. Hoch, *Journal of Interdisciplinary History* 23, no. 1 (Summer 1992): 183-185. Lynne Viola, *Canadian Slavonic Papers* 34, nos. 1-2 (March-June 1992): 190-191. Scott J. Seregny, *Russian Review* 52, no. 1 (January 1993): 131-133.

Late Empire, War, Revolution (1894-1917)

5622. Ascher, Abraham. *The Revolution of 1905.* Stanford, CA: Stanford University Press, 1988-1992. 2 vols. [Contents: Vol. 1. Russia in Disarray — v. 2. Authority Restored.] REV: Deborah Hardy, *Annals of the American Academy of Political and Social Science* no. 502 (March 1989): 166-167. L. Engelstein, *Slavic Review* 48, no. 4 (Winter 1989): 659-660. Scott J. Seregny, *Russian Review* 48, no. 2 (April 1989): 192-194. E. R. Zimmermann, *Canadian Journal of History = Annales canadienne d'histoire* 24, no. 1 (April 1989): 129-130. Victoria E. Bonnell, *American Historical Review* 95, no. 2 (April 1990): 550-551. John Bushnell, *Historian* 52, no. 4 (August 1990): 653-654. John

Bushnell, *Russian Review* 52, no. 4 (October 1993): 559-560. Erich E. Haberer, *Canadian Slavonic Papers* 35, nos. 1-2 (March-June 1993): 156-158. David MacKenzie, *Historian* 55, no. 4 (Summer 1993): 727. David McDonald, *Canadian Journal of History = Annales canadienne d'histoire* 28, no. 1 (April 1993): 131. J. Lee Schneidman, *History: Reviews of New Books* 21, no. 4 (Summer 1993): 186.

5623. Bonner, Thomas Neville. *To the Ends of the Earth: Women's Search for Education in Medicine.* Cambridge, MA: Harvard University Press, 1992. xiv, 232 pp. [Includes some history on Russian women who studied medicine in Switzerland.] REV: Stanley Bernstein, *Antioch Review* 51, no. 1 (Winter 1993): 145. Hughes Evans, *Isis* 84, no. 2 (June 1993): 399. Penina Midgal Glazer, *Journal of the History of the Behavioral Sciences* 29, no. 3 (July 1993): 231. Dorothy Rudy, *Annals of the American Academy of Political and Social Science* no. 528 (July 1993): 196. Pamela J. Walker, *Canadian Journal of History = Annales canadienne d'histoire* 28, no. 2 (August 1993): 390.

5624. Brovkin, Vladimir N., ed. and trans. *Dear Comrades: Menshevik Reports on the Bolshevik Revolution and the Civil War.* Hoover Archival Documentaries, Hoover Institution Press Publication, 398. Stanford, CA: Hoover Institution Press, c1991. xxii, 275 pp. REV: Frederick Corney, *Russian Review* 52, no. 1 (January 1993): 115-116. Lee J. Williames, *History: Reviews of New Books* 21, no. 2 (Winter 1993): 80.

5625. Desind, Philip. *Jewish and Russian Revolutionaries Exiled to Siberia, 1901-1917.* Jewish Studies, v. 6. Lewiston, ME: Edwin Mellen Press, c1990. xx, 494, 204 pp. ["Part I: From the Shtetl to Siberia" is a partial translation of "Der durkhgegangener Veg" by Israel Pressman; Parts II, III, and IV are by Philip Desind.] REV: Anna Geifman, *Russian Review* 52, no. 3 (July 1993): 428-429.

5626. Frankel, Edith Rogovin, Jonathan Frankel, and Baruch Knei-Paz, eds. *Revolution in Russia: Reassessments of 1917.* Contributions by Jonathan Frankel, Israel Getzler, Donald J. Raleigh, Rex A. Wade, Allan Wildman, John Channon, Diane P. Koenker, William G. Rosenberg, David Mandel, Ziva Galili, Ronald Grigor Suny, Stephen F. Jones, Ingeborg Fleischhauer, Neil Harding, Robert Service, John Keep, D. A. Longley, Edward Acton, and Baruch Knei-Paz. Cambridge; New York: Cambridge University Press, 1992. xx, 434 pp. [Essays first presented in preliminary form at a conference held in Jerusalem in January 1988 as a tribute to Israel Getzler. Contents: Jonathan Frankel, "1917: the problem of alternatives"; Israel Getzler, "Soviets as agents of democratisation"; Donald J. Raleigh, "Political power in the Russian revolution: a case study of Saratov"; Rex A. Wade, "The Red Guards: spontaneity and the October revolution"; Allan Wildman, "Officers of the general staff and the Kornilov movement"; John Channon, "The peasantry in the revolutions of 1917"; Diane P. Koenker and William G. Rosenberg, "Perceptions and reality of labour protest, March to October 1917"; David Mandel, "October in the Ivanovo-Kineshma industrial region"; Ziva Galili, "Commercial-industrial circles in revolution: the failure of 'industrial progressivism'"; Ronald Grigor Suny, "Nationalism and class in the Russian revolution: a comparative discussion"; Stephen F. Jones, "Georgian social democracy in 1917"; Ingeborg Fleischhauer, "The ethnic Germans in the Russian revolution"; Neil Harding, "Lenin, socialism and the state in 1917"; Robert Service, "The Bolsheviks on political campaign in 1917: a case study of the war question"; John Keep, "Lenin's time budget: the Smolny period"; D.A. Longley, "Iakovlev's question, or the historiography of the problem of spontaneity and leadership in the Russian revolution of February 1917"; Edward Acton, "The libertarians vindicated? The libertarian view of the revolution in the light of recent Western research"; Baruch Knei-Paz, "Russian Marxism: theory, action and outcome".] REV: N.G.O. Pereira, *Canadian Journal of History = Annales canadienne d'histoire* 27, no. 3 (December 1992): 567-570. Vladimir Brovkin, *American Historical Review* 98, no. 4 (October 1993): 1297-1298. John Bushnell, *Russian History = Histoire russe* 20, nos. 1-4 (1993): 334-336. Scott H. Nichols, *Historian* 55, no. 3 (Spring 1993): 538-539.

5627. Golder, Frank Alfred. *War, Revolution, and Peace in Russia: The Passages of Frank Golder, 1914-1927.* Compiled, edited, and introduced by Terence Emmons and Bertrand M. Patenaude. Hoover Archival Documentaries. Hoover Institution Press Publication, 411. Stanford, CA: Hoover Institution Press, Stanford University, c1992. xxvi, 369 pp. [Contents: Journey I: 1914: Russia goes to war — Journey II: 1917: The revolution begins — Journey III: 1921-1923: Victors and victims (September 1921-April 1922); Between war and peace (June-November 1922); Bolshevism at a crossroads (November 1922-May 1923) — Journey IV: 1925: Reds and Whites — Journey V: 1927: How the mighty have fallen!] REV: Ralph T. Fisher, Jr., *Russian Review* 52, no. 4 (October 1993): 565-566. Neil Salzman, *Russian History = Histoire russe* 20, nos. 1-4 (1993): 339-340.

5628. Heresch, Elisabeth. *Blood on the Snow: Eyewitness Accounts of the Russian Revolution.* 1st American ed. New York: Paragon House, 1990. xiii, 250 pp. [Translation of *Blutiger Schnee*.] REV: W. Bruce Lincoln, *Slavic Review* 50, no. 4 (Winter 1991): 1020-1021. Dennis Reinhartz, *History: Reviews of New Books* 19, no. 4 (Summer 1991): 177. Charles E. Clark, *History Teacher* 27, no. 1 (November 1993): 93-94.

5629. Jackson, George, editor-in-chief. *Dictionary of the Russian Revolution.* Assistant editor Robert Devlin. New York: Greenwood Press, 1989. xviii, 704 pp. REV: John Hatch, *Russian Review* 49, no. 4 (October 1990): 503-504. R.E. Johnson, *Canadian Slavonic Papers* 32, no. 4 (December 1990): 525. Evan Mawdsley, *Soviet Union = Union Soviétique* 17, nos. 1-2 (1990): 171-173. Terence Emmons, *Slavic Review* 50, no. 3 (Fall 1991): 701-702. John W. Long, *Russian History = Histoire russe* 20, nos. 1-4 (1993): 332-333.

5630. Judge, Edward H., and James Y., Jr. Simms, eds. *Modernization and Revolution: Dilemmas of Progress in Late Imperial Russia: Essays in Honor of Arthur P. Mendel.* Foreword by William G. Rosenberg. Contributions by James

Y., Jr. Simms, Edward H. Judge, Scott J. Seregny, Thad Radzilowski, Robert W. Thurston, Mark Kulikowski, and Diane P. Koenker. East European Monographs, no. 336. Boulder, CO: East European Monographs; New York: Distributed by Columbia University Press, 1992. xviii, 206 pp. [Contents: James Y. Simms, Jr., "The Famine and the Radicals"; Edward H. Judge, "Urban Growth and Anti-Semitism in Russian Moldavia"; Scott J. Seregny, "Russian Teachers and Peasant Revolution, 1895-1917"; Edward H. Judge, "Peasant Resettlement and Social Control in Late Imperial Russia"; Thad Radzilowski, "Unscrambling the Jumbled Catalog: Feudalism and the Revolution of 1905 in the Writings of N.P. Pavlov-Silvanskii"; Robert W. Thurston, "New Thoughts on the Old Regime and the Revolution of 1917 in Russia: A Review of Recent Western Literature"; Mark Kulikowski, "Rethinking the Origins of the Rasputin Legend"; Diane P. Koenker, "Moscow, 1917: Workers' Revolution, Worker Control".] REV: Abraham Ascher, *Russian History = Histoire russe* 20, nos. 1-4 (1993): 314-316. Anders Henriksson, *Canadian Slavonic Papers* 35, nos. 1-2 (March-June 1993): 175-176. Theodore Taranovski, *Slavic Review* 52, no. 4 (Winter 1993): 908-909.

5631. Klier, John D., and Shlomo Lambroza, eds. *Pogroms: Anti-Jewish Violence in Modern Russian History.* Contributions by John D. Klier, I. Michael Aronson, Moshe Mishkinsky, Erich Haberer, Alexander Orbach, Michael Ochs, Shlomo Lambroza, Robert Weinberg, Peter Kenez, Hans Rogger, and Avraham Greenbaum. Cambridge; New York: Cambridge University Press, 1992. xx, 393 pp. [Contents: John D. Klier, "Russian Jewry on the Eve of the Pogroms"; John D. Klier, "The Pogrom Paradigm in Russian History"; I. Michael Aronson, "The Anti-Jewish Pogroms in Russia in 1881"; Moshe Mishkinsky, "'Black Repartition' and the Pogroms of 1881-1882"; Erich Haberer, "Cosmopolitanism, Antisemitism, and Populism: A Reappraisal of the Russian and Jewish Socialist Response to the Pogroms of 1881-1882"; Alexander Orbach, "The Development of the Russian Jewish Community, 1881-1903"; Michael Ochs, "Tsarist Officialdom and Anti-Jewish Pogroms in Poland"; Shlomo Lambroza, "The Pogroms of 1903-1906"; Robert Weinberg, "The Pogrom of 1905 in Odessa: A Case Study"; Peter Kenez, "Pogroms and White Ideology in the Russian Civil War"; Hans Rogger, "Conclusion and Overview"; Avraham Greenbaum, "Bibliographical Essay".] REV: David Engel, *Slavic Review* 52, no. 2 (Summer 1993): 270-271. Michael F. Hamm, *Russian History = Histoire russe* 20, nos. 1-4 (1993): 316-320. Patricia Herlihy, *Russian Review* 52, no. 4 (October 1993): 563-564.

5632. Koenker, Diane P., and William G. Rosenberg. *Strikes and Revolution in Russia, 1917.* Princeton, NJ: Princeton University Press, c1989. xix, 393 pp. REV: Rose L. Glickman, *Russian History* 17, no. 4 (Winter 1990): 443-444. John Keep, *American Historical Review* 96, no. 3 (June 1991): 918. Jean-Guy Lalande, *Histoire sociale—Social History* 24, no. 48 (November 1991): 406-408. S.A. Smith, *Russian Review* 50, no. 1 (January 1991): 102-103. Charters Wynn, *Slavic Review* 51, no. 3 (Fall 1992): 614-615. Chris Ward, *Journal of Modern History* 65, no. 1 (March 1993): 241-243.

5633. Kowalski, Ronald I. *The Bolshevik Party in Conflict: The Left Communist Opposition of 1918*. Pitt Series in Russian and East European Studies, no. 14. Pittsburgh, PA: University of Pittsburgh Press, c1991. x, 244 pp. REV: James C. McClelland, *Russian Review* 51, no. 3 (July 1992): 440-441. Michael Melançon, *Slavic Review* 52, no. 2 (Summer 1993): 368-369. Zenovia A. Sochor, *American Historical Review* 98, no. 1 (February 1993): 205.

5634. Lindemann, Albert S. *The Jew Accused: Three Anti-Semitic Affairs (Dreyfus, Beilis, Frank), 1894-1915*. Cambridge; New York: Cambridge University Press, 1991. x, 301 pp. [Includes trial of Mendel Beilis, 1913.] REV: Lawrence Fleischer, *Criminal Law Forum* 3, no. 2 (Winter 1992): 317-325. Nancy MacLean, *Journal of American History* 79, no. 2 (September 1992): 685-686. Hans Rogger, *Slavic Review* 52, no. 2 (Summer 1993): 362-364. Stephen Wilson, *American Historical Review* 98, no. 3 (June 1993): 836.

5635. McDaniel, Tim. *Autocracy, Modernization, and Revolution in Russia and Iran*. Princeton, NJ: Princeton University Press, c1991. 239 pp. REV: John Foran, *Contemporary Sociology* 21, no. 2 (March 1992): 197-198. Jeff Goodwin, *American Journal of Sociology* 97, no. 4 (January 1992): 1141-1142. Charles Tilly, *American Political Science Review* 86, no. 4 (December 1992): 1084-1085. Theodore H. Von Laue, *Slavic Review* 51, no. 1 (Spring 1992): 174-175. John Foran, *Contention: Debates in Society, Culture, and Science* 2, no. 2 (Winter 1993): 65-88. Lewis H. Siegelbaum, *Russian Review* 52, no. 2 (April 1993): 278-279.

5636. McDonald, David MacLaren. *United Government and Foreign Policy in Russia, 1900-1914*. Cambridge, MA: Harvard University Press, 1992. 276 pp. REV: Abraham Ascher, *Slavic Review* 52, no. 3 (Fall 1993): 647-648. Melissa K. Bokovoy, *Russian History = Histoire russe* 20, nos. 1-4 (1993): 324-326. W. Bruce Lincoln, *American Historical Review* 98, no. 3 (June 1993): 912. Keith Neilson, *Historian* 55, no. 3 (Spring 1993): 550-551.

5637. McKean, Robert B. *St. Petersburg Between the Revolutions: Workers and Revolutionaries, June 1907-February 1917*. New Haven, CT: Yale University Press, 1990. xv, 606 pp. REV: Richard K. Debo, *Canadian Slavonic Papers* 33, no. 2 (June 1991): 201-203. Forest L. Grieves, *Perspectives on Political Science* 20, no. 3 (Summer 1991): 179. Blair A. Ruble, *Social Science Quarterly* 72, no. 2 (June 1991): 395. Norman E. Saul, *History: Reviews of New Books* 20, no. 1 (Fall 1991): 27. Patricia Herlihy, *Historian* 54, no. 2 (Winter 1992): 351-352. Michael Melancon, *Southern Humanities Review* 26 (Fall 1992): 363-365. Deborah L. Pearl, *Russian Review* 51, no. 3 (July 1992): 442-443. Reginald E. Zelnik, *American Historical Review* 97, no. 1 (February 1992): 256. Jean-Guy Lalande, *Histoire sociale = Social History* 26, no. 51 (May 1993): 176-177.

5638. Melançon, Michael. *The Socialist Revolutionaries and the Russian Anti-War Movement, 1914-1917*. Columbus, OH: Ohio State University Press, c1990. 368 pp.

REV: Paul Avrich, *American Historical Review* 97, no. 2 (April 1992): 585-586. Lutz Häfner, *Russian Review* 52, no. 2 (April 1993): 276-277.

5639. Rabinowitch, Alexander. *Prelude to Revolution: The Petrograd Bolsheviks and the July 1917 Uprising*. 1st Midland Book ed. A Midland Book, MB 661. Bloomington: Indiana University Press, 1991. 299 pp. REV: George E. Snow, *Soviet and Post-Soviet Review* 20, no. 1 (1993): 78.

5640. Radkey, Oliver H. *Russia Goes to the Polls: The Election to the All-Russian Constituent Assembly, 1917*. Foreword by Sheila Fitzpatrick. Studies in Soviet History and Society. Ithaca, NY: Cornell University Press, 1989. 171 pp. [Enlarged edition of *The Election to the Russian Constituent Assembly of 1917* (1950).] REV: J. Eugene Clay, *Russian History* 17, no. 3 (Fall 1990): 376-378. Bruce F. Adams, *Canadian-American Slavic Studies* 25, nos. 1-4 (1991): 309-310. Donald J. Raleigh, *Slavic Review* 51, no. 1 (Spring 1992): 168. Vladimir Brovkin, *Journal of Modern History* 65, no. 1 (March 1993): 240-241. Michael Melançon, *Russian Review* 52, no. 1 (January 1993): 125-126.

5641. Reed, John. *John Reed and the Russian Revolution: Uncollected Articles, Letters, and Speeches on Russia, 1917-1920*. Edited by Eric Homberger and John Biggart. New York: St. Martin's Press, 1992. xxiv, 320 pp. REV: Ronald J. Jensen, *Russian History = Histoire russe* 20, nos. 1-4 (1993): 341-343, Kenneth Straus, *Slavic Review* 52, no. 1 (Spring 1993): 168-169. Rex A. Wade, *Russian Review* 52, no. 4 (October 1993): 566-567.

5642. Thurston, Robert W. *Liberal City, Conservative State: Moscow and Russia's Urban Crisis, 1906-1914*. New York: Oxford University Press, 1987. viii, 266 pp. REV: Stephen D. Corrsin, *Russian Review* 52, no. 4 (October 1993): 564-565.

5643. Wynn, Charters. *Workers, Strikes, and Pogroms: The Donbass-Dnepr Bend in Late Imperial Russia, 1870-1905*. Princeton, NJ: Princeton University Press, c1992. 289 pp. REV: Jan L. Feldman, *Slavic Review* 52, no. 1 (Spring 1993): 169-171 Theodore H. Friedgut, *Russian Review* 52, no. 4 (October 1993): 558-559. Patricia Herlihy, *Russian History = Histoire russe* 20, nos. 1-4 (1993): 323-324, Diane P. Koenker, *American Historical Review* 98, no. 4 (October 1993): 1293.

U.S.S.R. (1917-1991)

5644. Ammende, Ewald. *Human Life in Russia*. Introduction by Lord Dickinson. Historical introduction by James E. Mace. Cleveland, OH: Zubal, 1984. ix, 319 pp. REV: [Fred W. Viehe, on table of contents; George Kulchytsky, on p. 202], *Ukrainian Quarterly* 49, no. 2 (Summer 1993): 201-202.

5645. Barber, John, and Mark Harrison. *The Soviet Home Front, 1941-1945: A Social and Economic History of the USSR in World War II*. New York: Longman, 1991. 252 pp. REV: Richard Bidlack, *Slavic Review* 51, no. 3 (Fall

1992): 616-617. M. K. Dziewanowski, *Russian History = Histoire russe* 20, nos. 1-4 (1993): 392-394.

5646. Boffa, Giuseppe. *The Stalin Phenomenon.* Translated by Nicholas Fersen. Ithaca, NY: Cornell University Press, 1992. xii, 205 pp. [Translation of *Il fenomeno Stalin nella storia del XX secolo.*] REV: Robert V. Daniels, *Slavic Review* 51, no. 4 (Winter 1992): 809-810. Lewis H. Siegelbaum, *Russian Review* 52, no. 3 (July 1993): 433-434.

5647. Burlatsky, Fedor. *Khrushchev and the First Russian Spring: The Era of Khrushchev through the Eyes of His Advisor.* Translated from the Russian by Daphne Skillen. New York: Scribner's; Maxwell Macmillan International, c1991. 286 pp. REV: George W. Breslauer, *New York Times Book Review* (May 10, 1992): 10-11. Anatole Shub, *New Leader* 75, no. 7 (June 1-15, 1992): 15-16. *Publishers Weekly* 239, no. 8 (February 10, 1992): 66-67. Ronald J. Jensen, *History: Reviews of New Books* 22, no. 1 (Fall 1993): 39. *Orbis* 37, no. 1 (Winter 1993).

5648. Carrère d'Encausse, Hélène. *The Great Challenge: Nationalities and the Bolshevik State, 1917-1930.* Translated by Nancy Festinger. Foreword by Richard Pipes. New York: Holmes & Meier, 1992. xiv, 262 pp. [Translation of *Le grand defi.*] REV: Robert Legvold, *Foreign Affairs* 71, no. 2 (Spring 1992): 207. James Mace, *Canadian Slavonic Papers* 34, no. 4 (December 1992): 493-494. Ira Smolensky, *Journal of Baltic Studies* 23, no. 2 (Summer 1992): 200. Gregory Gleason, *Russian Review* 52, no. 2 (April 1993): 275-276. Tim McDaniel, *Contemporary Sociology* 22, no. 4 (July 1993): 512-514. Mark Saroyan, *Canadian Review of Studies in Nationalism = Revue Canadienne des Etudes sur le Nationalisme* 20, nos. 1-2 (1993): 148-149. *Orbis* 37, no. 1 (Winter 1993).

5649. Colton, Timothy J., and Robert Legvold, eds. *After the Soviet Union: From Empire to Nations.* Contributions by Timothy J. Colton, Richard E. Ericson, Roman Szporluk, Stephen M. Meyer, and Robert Legvold. 1st ed. New York: W.W. Norton, c1992. 208 pp. [Contents: Timothy J. Colton, "Politics"; Richard E. Ericson, "Economics"; Roman Szporluk, "The National Question"; Stephen M. Meyer, "The Military"; Robert Legvold, "Foreign Policy".] REV: Francis P. Sempa, *Presidential Studies Quarterly* 23, no. 2 (Fall 1993): 797-799. David L. Williams, *Political Science Quarterly* 108, no. 1 (Spring 1993): 166-167.

5650. Conquest, Robert. *The Great Terror: A Reassessment.* New York: Oxford University Press, 1990. 570 pp. REV: Norman Davies, *New York Times Book Review* (May 13, 1990): 20-21. Tatyana Tolstaya, *New York Review of Books* 38, no. 7 (April 11, 1991): 3ff. T. R. Ravindranathan, *Canadian Journal of History = Annales canadienne d'histoire* 28, no. 3 (December 1993): 545-559.

5651. ———. *The Harvest of Sorrow: Soviet Collectivization and the Terror-Famine.* New York: Oxford University Press, 1986. 412 pp. REV: [Martin Barger, on table on contents; Martin Berger, on p. 204], *Ukrainian Quarterly* 49, no. 2 (Summer 1993): 202-204.

5652. Daniels, Robert V. *Trotsky, Stalin, and Socialism.* Boulder, CO: Westview Press, 1991. 208 pp. REV: Philip Pomper, *Slavic Review* 51, no. 3 (Fall 1992): 615-616. Michael Turner, *Orbis* 36, no. 4 (Fall 1992): 627-628. Elizabeth Kridl Valkenier, *History: Reviews of New Books* 21, no. 1 (Fall 1992): 31. Michael Cox, *Russian Review* 52, no. 4 (October 1993): 568-70. Michael Gelb, *Russian History = Histoire russe* 20, nos. 1-4 (1993): 384-385. Timothy E. O'Connor, *Historian* 55, no. 4 (Summer 1993): 733.

5653. Farber, Samuel. *Before Stalinism: The Rise and Fall of Soviet Democracy.* London; New York: Verso, 1990. xiii, 288 pp. REV: Richard Sakwa, *Russian History* 17, no. 4 (Winter 1990): 456-457. Irving H. Anellis, *Studies in Soviet Thought* 44, no. 3 (November 1992): 229-230. Ralph T. Fisher, Jr., *Nationalities Papers* 21, no. 2 (Fall 1993): 204-206.

5654. Fitzpatrick, Sheila, Alexander Rabinowitch, and Richard Stites, eds. *Russia in the Era of NEP: Explorations in Soviet Society and Culture.* Indiana-Michigan Series in Russian and East European Studies. Bloomington, IN: Indiana University Press, c1991. viii, 344 pp. REV: Daniel Brower, *Russian History* 18, no. 2 (Summer 1991): 241-243. T. Yedlin, *Canadian Slavonic Papers* 34, nos. 1-2 (March-June 1992): 184-185. James Hughes, *European History Quarterly* (April 1993): 298-299. Lynn Mally, *Journal of Interdisciplinary History* 24, no. 1 (Summer 1993): 150-151. Daniel Orlovsky, *Slavic Review* 52, no. 3 (Fall 1993): 598-599. *Economic History Review* (May 1993): 420.

5655. Hughes, James. *Stalin, Siberia, and the Crisis of the New Economic Policy.* Soviet and East European Studies, 81. Cambridge; New York: Cambridge University Press, 1991. xiii, 260 pp. REV: Nellie Hauke Ohr, *Canadian-American Slavic Studies* 25, nos. 1-4 (1991): 341-343. Neil B. Weissman, *Soviet and Post-Soviet Review* 19, nos. 1-3 (1992): 333-334. Victor L. Mote, *Journal of Comparative Economics* 17, no. 1 (March 1993): 173-176. Lynne Viola, *Russian Review* 52, no. 3 (July 1993): 432-433.

5656. Knappe, Siegfried, and Charles T. Brusaw. *Soldat: Reflections of a German Soldier, 1936-1949.* Assisted by Susan Davis McLaughlin. 1st ed. New York: Orion Books, 1992. xv, 384 p. REV: Scott R. McMeen, *Military Review* 73, no. 1 (January 1993): 94-95. Anna Otten, *Antioch Review* 51, no. 3 (Summer 1993): 455-456. *Orbis* 37, no. 4 (Fall 1993).

5657. Lampert, Nick, and Gábor T. Rittersporn, eds. *Stalinism: Its Nature and Aftermath: Essays in Honour of Moshe Lewin.* Armonk, NY: M.E. Sharpe, c1992. 291 pp. REV: J. Arch Getty, *Russian Review* 52, no. 1 (January 1993): 123-124. Holland Hunter, *Russian History = Histoire russe* 20, nos. 1-4 (1993): 384-385. Stephen Kotkin, *Slavic Review* 52, no. 1 (Spring 1993): 164-166.

5658. Lourie, Richard. *Russia Speaks: An Oral History from the Revolution to the Present.* 1st ed. New York: E. Burlingame, c1991. 396 pp. REV: Anatole Shub, *New York Times Book Review* (March 24, 1991): 19. David

McDonald, *Russian History = Histoire russe* 20, nos. 1-4 (1993): 372-373.

5659. McAuley, Mary. *Soviet Politics 1917-1991.* Oxford; New York: Oxford University Press, 1992. 132 pp. REV: William A. Clark, *Russian History = Histoire russe* 20, nos. 1-4 (1993): 374-375. Robert Vincent Daniels, *New Leader* 76, no. 1 (January 11, 1993): 17-18. John Erickson, *History Today* (January 1993): 58-60.

5660. Moskoff, William. *The Bread of Affliction: The Food Supply in the USSR during World War II.* Soviet and East European Studies, 76. Cambridge; New York: Cambridge University Press, 1990. xvi, 256 pp. REV: Thomas J. Greene, *Canadian Slavonic Papers* 33, no. 2 (June 1991): 205-206. Patrick R. Taylor, *Canadian-American Slavic Studies* 25, nos. 1-4 (1991): 354-356. Richard Bidlack, *Russian Review* 51, no. 3 (July 1992): 443-444. W. Bruce Lincoln, *Annals of the American Academy of Political and Social Science*, no. 521 (May 1992): 199-200. George Yaney, *American Historical Review* 97, no. 2 (April 1992): 587-588. James R. Millar, *Journal of Economic History*, 53, no. 1 (March 1993): 176-178.

5661. Paul, Allen. *Katyn: The Untold Story of Stalin's Polish Massacre.* New York: Scribner's; Maxwell Macmillan International, c1991. 390 pp. REV: Robert Conquest, *New York Times Book Review* (September 1, 1991): 11-12. David Remnick, *New York Review of Books* 38, no. 21 (December 19, 1991): 72-81. Lawrence C. Allin, *History: Reviews of New Books* 21, no. 1 (Fall 1992): 29-30. Neil N. Franklin, *Military Review* 72, no. 3 (March 1992): 91-92. Robert Legvold, *Foreign Affairs* 71, no. 2 (Spring 1992): 205. Alice-Catherine Carls, *Polish Review* 38, no. 4 (1993): 486-490.

5662. Pethybridge, Roger. *One Step Backwards, Two Steps Forward: Soviet Society and Politics in the New Economic Policy.* Oxford: Clarendon Press; New York: Oxford University Press, 1990. xi, 453 pp. REV: Peter Kenez, *American Historical Review* 97, no. 4 (October 1992): 1253. Stephen Kotkin, *Russian History = Histoire russe* 20, nos. 1-4 (1993): 369-370.

5663. Rapoport, Yakov. *The Doctors' Plot of 1953: A Survivor's Memoir of Stalin's Last Act of Terror Against Jews and Science.* Cambridge, MA: Harvard University Press, 1991. 280 pp. REV: Paul Goldberg, *New York Times Book Review* (March 24, 1991): 25. Lynne Viola, *Canadian Slavonic Papers* 33, no. 2 (June 1991): 213-214. William McCagg, *Slavic Review* 51, no. 3 (Fall 1992): 619-620. Joseph L. Wieczynski, *History: Reviews of New Books* 20, no. 3 (Spring 1992): 119-120. Arthur Adams, *Russian History = Histoire russe* 20, nos. 1-4 (1993): 399-400.

5664. Rittersporn, Gábor Tamás. *Stalinist Simplifications and Soviet Complications: Social Tensions and Political Conflicts in the USSR, 1933-1953.* Social Orders, v. 5. Chur, Switzerland; New York: Harwood Academic, c1991. xii, 334 pp. REV: Eugene Huskey, *American Historical Review* 97, no. 4 (October 1992): 1253-1254. Robert Thurston, *Slavic Review* 52, no. 3 (Fall 1993): 599-600.

5665. Shimotomai, Nobuo. *Moscow under Stalinist Rule, 1931-34.* New York: St. Martin's Press, 1991. 179 pp. REV: Catherine Merridale, *Slavic Review* 51, no. 4 (Winter 1992): 867-868. Larry E. Holmes, *Russian Review* 52, no. 1 (January 1993): 128-129.

5666. Siegelbaum, Lewis H. *Soviet State and Society Between Revolutions, 1918-1929.* Cambridge Soviet Paperbacks, 8. Cambridge; New York: Cambridge University Press, 1992. xiii, 284 pp. REV: Wendy Goldman, *Slavic Review* 52, no. 2 (Summer 1993): 369-730.

5667. Wade, Rex A., ed. *Documents of Soviet History.* Gulf Breeze, FL: Academic International Press, 1991-. vols. [Contents: Vol. 1. The Triumph of Bolshevism, 1917-1919 — v. 2. Triumph and Retreat, 1920-1922 — v. 3. Lenin's Heirs, 1923-1925.] REV: Gregory L. Freeze, *Russian History = Histoire russe* 20, nos. 1-4 (1993): 333-334. Peter Kenez, *Russian Review* 52, no. 4 (October 1993): 567.

5668. White, Christine A. *British and American Commercial Relations with Soviet Russia, 1918-1924.* Chapel Hill, NC: University of North Carolina Press, c1992. xii, 345 pp. REV: Robert Cole, *History: Reviews of New Books* 21, no. 4 (Summer 1993): 165. Timothy E. O'Connor, *American Historical Review* 98, no. 5 (December 1993): 1575. Stephen White, *Slavic Review* 52, no. 3 (Fall 1993): 644.

5669. Witkin, Zara. *An American Engineer in Stalin's Russia: The Memoirs of Zara Witkin, 1932-1934.* Edited introduction by Michael Gelb. Berkeley, CA: University of California Press, c1991. ix, 363 pp. REV: Loren R. Graham, *New York Times Book Review* (December 29, 1991): 9. David W. McFadden, *International History Review* 14, no. 4 (November 1992): 821-823. Fraser Ottanelli, *Journal of American History* 79, no. 2 (September 1992): 711. Christine A. White, *Business History Review* 66, no. 3 (Autumn 1992): 632-633. David L. Hoffman, *Russian History = Histoire russe* 20, nos. 1-4 (1993): 386-387. Robert McCutcheon, *Technology and Culture* 34, no. 2 (April 1993): 435-436.

Territories and Adjacent States

5670. Allworth, Edward. *The Modern Uzbeks: From the Fourteenth Century to the Present: A Cultural History.* Studies of Nationalities in the USSR, Stanford, CA: Hoover Institution Press, Stanford University, 1990. xiv, 410 pp. REV: Alton S. Donnelly, *Canadian-American Slavic Studies* 25, nos. 1-4 (1991): 375-378. David D. Laitin, *World Politics* 44, no. 1 (October 1991): 139-177. David Nalle, *Middle East Journal* 45, no. 1 (Winter 1991): 131. William Fierman, *Russian Review* 51, no. 2 (April 1992): 272-273. Khalid Yahya Blankinship, *Muslim World* 83, nos. 3-4 (July-October 1993): 347-349.

5671. Broxup, Marie Bennigsen, ed. *The North Caucasus Barrier: The Russian Advance towards the Muslim World.* Contributions by Abdurahman Avtorkhanov, Marie Bennigsen Broxup, Fanny E. B. Bryan, Moshe Gammer, Paul B. Henze, and Chantal Lemercier-

Quelquejay. New York: St. Martin's Press, 1992. 252 pp. [Contents: Marie Bennigsen Broxup, "Introduction: Russia and the North Caucasus"; Chantal Lemercier-Quelquejay, "Cooptation of the Elites of Kabarda and Daghestan in the sixteenth century"; Moshe Gammer, "Russian Strategies in the Conquest of Chechnia and Daghestan, 1825-1859"; Paul B. Henze, "Circassian Resistance to Russia"; Marie Bennigsen Broxup, "The Last *Ghazawat*: The 1920-1921 Uprising"; Abdurahman Avtorkhanov, "The Chechens and the Ingush during the Soviet Period and its Antecedents"; Fanny E.B. Bryan, "Internationalism, Nationalism, and Islam before 1990"; Marie Bennigsen Broxup, "After the Putsch, 1991".] REV: Paul A. Goble, *Middle East Studies Association Bulletin* 27, no. 2 (December 1993): 213.

5672. Chance, Norman A. *The Inupiat and Arctic Alaska: An Ethnography of Modern Development.* Case Studies in Cultural Anthropology. Fort Worth, TX: Holt, Rinehart and Winston, c1990. xxx, 241 pp. [Chapter 2 "The Colonial Encounter," includes discussion of Russian economic aspirations for North America.] REV: Margaret B. Blackman, *American Indian Quarterly* 17, no. 1 (Winter 1993): 121-123.

5673. Emmons, George Thornton. *The Tlingit Indians.* Edited with additions by Frederica De Laguna. Bibliography by Jean Low. Anthropological Papers of the American Museum of Natural History, v. 70. Seattle, WA: University of Washington Press; New York: American Museum of Natural History, c1991. xl, 488 pp. [Author served in U.S. Navy in Alaska, 1880-1890.] REV: James R. Moriarty, III, *Western Historical Quarterly* 24, no. 1 (February 1993): 83-84.

5674. Forsyth, James. *A History of the Peoples of Siberia: Russia's North Asian Colony, 1581-1990.* Cambridge; New York: Cambridge University Press, 1992. 455 pp. REV: Greg Poelzer, *Canadian Slavonic Papers* 34, no. 4 (December 1992): 500-501. Gary Hanson, *Canadian Journal of History = Annales canadienne d'histoire* 28, no. 2 (August 1993): 379-381. Helen S. Hundley, *Historian* 55, no. 3 (Spring 1993): 537-538. Richard A. Pierce, *American Historical Review* 98, no. 4 (October 1993): 1290. Denis J. B. Shaw, *Journal of Historical Geography* 19, no. 1 (January 1993): 88-89. Donald W. Treadgold, *Russian History = Histoire russe* 20, nos. 1-4 (1993): 279-281.

5675. Himka, John-Paul. *Galician Villagers and the Ukrainian National Movement in the Nineteenth Century.* New York: St. Martin's Press, 1988. xxxvi, 358 pp. REV: Martha Bohachevsky-Chomiak, *American Historical Review* 95, no. 2 (April 1990): 545-546. Stella Hryniuk, *Russian Review* 49. no. 1 (January 1990): 93-96. Stefan Kienkiewicz, *Harvard Ukrainian Studies* 14, nos. 1-2 (June 1990): 167-170. Frank E. Sysyn, *Slavic Review* 49, no. 4 (Winter 1990): 655-666. John A. Armstrong, *Canadian Review of Studies in Nationalism = Revue Canadienne des Etudes sur le Nationalisme* 18, nos. 1-2 (1991): 261-262. Victor O. Buyniak, *Canadian Ethnic Studies* 24, no. 1 (1992): 164-165. Anthony J. Amato, *Slavic Review* 52, no. 4 (Winter 1993): 892-893. Wolfdieter Bihl, *Austrian History Yearbook* 24 (1993): 239-240.

5676. Hopkirk, Peter. *The Great Game: The Struggle for Empire in Central Asia.* New York: Kodansha International, 1992. 565 pp. REV: Phoebe-Lou Adams, *Atlantic* 270, no. 5 (November 1992): 161-162. Byron Farwell, *New York Times Book Review* (September 13, 1992): 11. Keith Neilson, *Conflict Quarterly* 12, no. 1 (Winter 1992): 92-93. Ray Alan, *New Leader* 76, no. 4 (March 8, 1993): 13-14.

5677. Hrushevs'kyi, Mykhailo. *Na poroze novoi Ukrainy: Statti i dzherel'ni materiialy.* Edited by Lubomyr Wynar. New York: Ukrainian Historical Association, 1992. xx, 278 pp. REV: Thomas M. Prymak, *Slavic Review* 52, no. 2 (Summer 1993): 379-380.

5678. Hryniuk, Stella. *Peasants with Promise: Ukrainians in Southeastern Galicia, 1880-1900.* Edmonton, Alberta: Canadian Institute of Ukrainian Studies Press, University of Alberta, 1991. 299 pp. REV: Martha Bohchevsky-Chomiak, *Harvard Ukrainian Studies* 16, nos. 1-2 (June 1992): 216-217. J.-Guy Lalande, *Canadian Journal of History = Annales canadienne d'histoire* 27, no. 2 (August 1992): 398-400. Steven L. Hoch, *American Historical Review* 98, no. 2 (April 1993): 528.

5679. Kamenetsky, Ihor, ed. *The Tragedy of Vinnytsia: Materials on Stalin's Policy of Extermination in Ukraine during the Great Purge, 1936-1938.* Toronto, Ontario; New York: Ukrainian Historical Association in cooperation with Bahriany Foundation and Ukrainian Research and Documentation Center, 1989. xviii, 265 pp. REV: John-Paul Himka, *Canadian Slavonic Papers* 32, no. 4 (December 1990): 516-517. Mark B. Tauger, *Slavic Review* 51, no. 4 (Winter 1992): 812-813. Lubomyr Luciuk, *Ukrainian Quarterly* 49, no. 1 (Spring 1993): 82-83.

5680. Khodarkovsky, Michael. *Where Two Worlds Met: The Russian State and the Kalmyk Nomads, 1600-1771.* Ithaca, NY: Cornell University Press, 1992. xiv, 278 pp. REV: Yuri Bregel, *Slavic Review* 52, no. 4 (Winter 1993): 901-902.

5681. Kohut, Zenon E. *Russian Centralism and Ukrainian Autonomy: Imperial Absorption of the Hetmanate, 1760s-1830s.* Monograph Series (Harvard Ukrainian Research Institute). Cambridge, MA: Distributed by Harvard University Press for the Harvard Ukrainian Research Institute, c1988. xv, 363 pp. [Revision of thesis (Ph.D.)—University of Pennsylvania, 1975, under the title The Abolition of Ukrainian Autonomy.] REV: Walter Hanchett, *Russian History* 17, no. 1 (Spring 1990): 110-111. John-Paul Himka, *East European Quarterly* 24, no. 3 (Fall 1990): 408. Jacek Jedruch, *Polish Review* 35, nos. 3-4 (1990): 273. Michael Klimenko, *Journal of Baltic Studies* 21, no. 2 (Summer 1990): 167-170. John LeDonne, *American Historical Review* 95, no. 5 (December 1990): 1584-1585. Thomas M. Prymak, *Canadian Slavonic Papers* 32, no. 1 (March 1990): 104-105. Herbert Kaplan, *Canadian-American Slavic Studies* 25, nos. 1-4 (1991): 385-386. Theophilus C. Prousis, *Historian* 53, no. 2 (Winter 1991): 332-333. Hans J. Torke, *Harvard Ukrainian Studies* 15, nos. 1-2 (June 1991): 221-223. Stephen D. Corrsin, *Cana-*

dian Review of Studies in Nationalism = Revue Canadienne des Etudes sur le Nationalisme 19, nos. 1-2 (1992): 209-211. Frank E. Sysyn, *Russian Review* 52, no. 1 (January 1993): 120-121.

5682. Koropeckyj, I. S., ed. *Ukrainian Economic History: Interpretive Essays*. Harvard Ukrainian Research Institute Sources and Documents Series. Cambridge, MA: Distributed by Harvard University Press for the Harvard Ukrainian Research Institute, c1991. xiv, 390 pp. [Contains papers presented at a conference at the Harvard Ukrainian Research Institute in 1985. Covers the period ca. 1100-1914.] REV: Stella Hryniuk, *Russian Review* 52, no. 1 (January 1993): 121-122.

5683. Liber, George O. *Soviet Nationality Policy, Urban Growth, and Identity Change in the Ukrainian SSR, 1923-1934*. Soviet and East European Studies, 84. Cambridge; New York, NY: Cambridge University Press, 1992. xvii, 289 pp. REV: Andrea Chandler, *Canadian Slavonic Papers* 34, no. 4 (December 1992): 506-507. James E. Mace, *Ukrainian Quarterly* 49, no. 1 (Spring 1993): 68-69.

5684. Marples, David R. *Stalinism in Ukraine in the 1940s*. New York: St. Martin's Press, 1992. xix, 228 pp. REV: Alan Ball, *Slavic Review* 52, no. 4 (Winter 1993): 911-912. David Saunders, *International History Review* 15, no. 3 (August 1993): 609.

5685. Oregon Historical Society. *Soft Gold: The Fur Trade and Cultural Exchange on the Northwest Coast of America*. Historical introduction and annotation by Thomas Vaughan. Ethnographic annotation by Bill Holm. 2nd ed., rev. Portland, OR: Oregon Historical Society, 1990. xi, 297 pp. [Includes discussion of Russian fur trade.] REV: Robert Coutts, *American Indian Quarterly* 17 no. 1 (Winter 1993): 125-126.

5686. Potichnyj, Peter J. et al., ed. *Ukraine and Russia in Their Historical Encounter*. Edmonton: Canadian Institute of Ukrainian Studies Press, University of Alberta, 1992. xiv, 346 pp. ["Papers from the first Conference on Ukrainian-Russian Relations held October 8-9, 1981 in Hamilton, Ontario".] REV: Mikhail V. Dmitriev, translated from the Russian by Eva DeMarco, *Canadian Slavonic Papers* 35, nos. 1-2 (March-June 1993): 131-147.

5687. Suny, Ronald Grigor. *The Making of the Georgian Nation*. Studies of Nationalities in the USSR, Bloomington, IN: Indiana University Press in association with the Hoover Institution Press, Stanford University, c1988. xviii, 395 pp. REV: Keith Hitchins, *American Historical Review* 95, no. 2 (April 1990): 548-549. Stephen F. Jones, *Russian Review* 49, no. 4 (October 1990): 501-503. David D. Laitin, *World Politics* 44, no. 1 (October 1991): 139-177. Dennis Ogden, *Canadian-American Slavic Studies* 25, nos. 1-4 (1991): 431-432. Charles A. Ruud, *Canadian Review of Studies in Nationalism = Revue Canadienne des Etudes sur le Nationalisme* 19, nos. 1-2 (1992): 208-209. Abraham Rzepkowicz, *Ararat* 33, no. 132 (Autumn 1992): 70-71. Charles A. Ruud, *Canadian Review of Studies in Nationalism = Revue Canadienne des Etudes sur le Nationalisme* 20, nos. 1-2 (1993): 152-153.

5688. Velichkovsii, Paisii (Saint). *The Life of Paisij Velyckovs'kyj*. Translated by J. M. E. Featherstone. With an introduction by Anthony-Emil N. Tachiaos. Harvard Library of Early Ukrainian Literature. English Translations, v. 4. Cambridge, MA: distributed by Harvard University Press for the Harvard Ukrainian Research Institute, 1990. 172 pp. REV: David K. Prestel, *Canadian American Slavic Studies = Revue Canadienne Américaine d'Etudes Slaves* 27, nos. 1-4 (1993): 426-428.

5689. Wood, Alan, ed. *The History of Siberia: From Russian Conquest to Revolution*. New York: Routledge, 1991. xiv, 192 pp. [Volume results from the activities of the British Universities Siberian Studies Seminar.] REV: Raymond H. Fisher, *Russian History* 18, no. 3 (Fall 1991): 363-365. Nicole L. Young, *Canadian-American Slavic Studies* 25, nos. 1-4 (1991): 255-256. Helen S. Hundley, *Historian* 54, no. 3 (Spring 1992): 536-537. David Stefancic, *History: Reviews of New Books* 21, no. 1 (Fall 1992): 30-31. N.G.O. Pereira, *Studies in East European Thought* 45, no. 3 (September 1993): 226-228.

5690. Wood, Alan, and French R.A., eds. *The Development of Siberia: People and Resources*. New York: St. Martin's Press, 1989. xviii, 266 pp. [Papers from the Fourth British Universities Siberian Studies Seminar held at the School of Slavonic and East European Studies, University of London, April 1986.] REV: W. Bruce Lincoln, *Slavic Review* 52, no. 1 (Spring 1993): 161-162.

Eastern Europe

5691. Banac, Ivo. *The National Question in Yugoslavia: Origins, History, Politics*. Ithaca, NY: Cornell University Press, 1988. 452 pp. REV: Susan L. Woodward, *World Politics* 41, no. 2 (January 1989): 267-305. Elinor Murray Despalatovic, *Canadian Review of Studies in Nationalism = Revue Canadienne des Etudes sur le Nationalisme* 20, nos. 1-2 (1993): 141-142.

5692. Bering, Dietz. *The Stigma of Names: Antisemitism in German Daily Life, 1812-1933*. Ann Arbor, MI: University of Michigan Press, 1992. xii, 345 pp. REV: Jerry Z. Muller, *Commentary* 95, no. 3 (March 1993): 61-62.

5693. Bíró, Sándor. *The Nationalities Problem in Transylvania, 1867-1940: A Social History of the Romanian Minority Under Hungarian Rule, 1867-1918 and the Hungarian Minority Under Romanian Rule, 1918-1940*. Translated from the Hungarian original by Mario D. Fenyo. Atlantic Studies on Society in Change, no. 66. East European Monographs, no. 333. Boulder, CO: Social Science Monographs; Highland Lakes, NJ: Atlantic Research and Publications; New York: Distributed by Columbia University Press, 1991. xix, 744 pp. [Originally published as *Kisebbsegben es tobbsegben, romanok es magyarok 1867-1949* (Bern, Switzerland: 1989).] REV: Paul E. Michelson, *Slavic Review* 52, no. 3 (Fall 1993): 611-612.

5694. Borsi-Kálmán, Bela. *Hungarian Exiles and the Romanian National Movement, 1849-1867*. Translated by Eva Pálmai. Atlantic Studies on Society in Change, no. 67. East European Monographs, no. 331. Boulder, CO:

Social Science Monographs; Highland Lakes, NJ: Atlantic Research and Publications; New York: Distributed by Columbia University Press, 1991. xvi, 333 pp. [Translated from Hungarian.] REV: James Niessen, *Slavic Review* 52, no. 3 (Fall 1993): 615-616.

5695. Bracewell, Catherine Wendy. *The Uskoks of Senj: Piracy, Banditry, and Holy War in the Sixteenth-Century Adriatic.* Ithaca, NY: Cornell University Press, 1992. xiv, 329 pp. REV: Nicholas I. Novosel, *Slavic Review* 51, no. 4 (Winter 1992): 835-836. Thomas M. Barker, *Journal of Military History* 57, no. 1 (January 1993): 139-140. Gunther E. Rothenberg, *Journal of Interdisciplinary History* 24, no. 1 (Summer 1993): 148. Traian Stoianovich, *American Historical Review* 98, no. 3 (June 1993): 903.

5696. Bradley, John F. N. *The Czechoslovak Legion in Russia, 1914-1920.* East European Monographs, no. 321. Boulder, CO: East European Monographs; New York: Distributed by Columbia University Press, 1991. iii, 156 pp. [Rev. ed. of author's thesis (doctoral—Sorbonne, 1963), entitled *Le Legion tchecoslovaque en Russie, 1914-1920.*] REV: Richard B. Spence, *Canadian-American Slavic Studies* 25, nos. 1-4 (1991): 304-306. Victor M. Fic, *Czechoslovak and Central European Journal* 11, no. 1 (Summer 1992): 107-108. Evan Mawdsley, *Slavic Review* 52, no. 3 (Fall 1993): 619-620. John A. White, *Russian History = Histoire russe* 20, nos. 1-4 (1993): 337-338.

5697. Breuilly, John, ed. *The State of Germany: The National Idea in the Making, Unmaking, and Remaking of a Modern Nation-State.* London; New York: Longman, 1992. xiii, 243 pp. REV: James C. Albisetti, *History: Reviews of New Books* 21, no. 3 (Spring 1993): 123.

5698. Bridge, F. R. *The Habsburg Monarchy among the Great Powers, 1815-1918.* New York: Berg; Distributed by St. Martin's Press, 1990. viii, 417 pp. [Rev. ed. of From Sadowa to Sarajevo (1972).] REV: Lawrence J. Flockerzie, *East-Central Europe* 18, no. 1 (1991): 102-105. Robert J. Gentry, *Historian* 54, no. 3 (Spring 1992): 504-505. Ralph Menning, *History: Reviews of New Books* 20, no. 3 (Spring 1992): 117-118. Norman Rich, *American Historical Review* 97, no. 1 (February 1992): 247-249. Paul Schroder, *International History Review* 15, no. 1 (February 1993): 116-134. Solomon Wank, *Central European History* 26, no. 1 (1993): 123-127. Samuel R. Williamson, Jr., *Austrian History Yearbook* 24 (1993): 243-245.

5699. Brock, Peter. *Folk Cultures and Little Peoples: Aspects of National Awakening in East Central Europe.* East European Monographs, no. 346. Boulder, CO: East European Monographs; New York: Distributed by Columbia University Press, 1992. vi, 210 pp. REV: David J. Goa, *Canadian Slavonic Papers* 35, nos. 3-4 (September-December 1993): 402. Yuri Slezkine, *Slavic Review* 52, no. 4 (Winter 1993): 893.

5700. Bucholz, Arden. *Moltke, Schlieffen, and Prussian War Planning.* New York: Berg; Distributed by St. Martin's, 1991. xi, 352 pp. REV: Dennis Showalter, *Journal of Military History* 57, no. 1 (January 1993): 154-156.

5701. Cassia, Paul Sant, and Constantina Bada. *The Making of the Modern Greek Family: Marriage and Exchange in Nineteenth Century Athens.* Cambridge; New York: Cambridge University Press, 1992. xv, 282 pp. REV: Ernestine Friedl, *American Historical Review* 98, no. 3 (June 1993): 904.

5702. Castellan, Georges. *History of the Balkans: From Mohammed the Conqueror to Stalin.* Translated by Nicholas Bradley. East European Monographs, no. 325. Boulder, CO: East European Monographs; New York: Distributed by Columbia University Press, 1992. 493 pp. [Translation of *Histoire des Balkans: XIVe-XXe siècle* (Paris: 1991).] REV: Mark Biondich, *Canadian Slavonic Papers* 35, nos. 1-2 (March-June 1993): 163.

5703. Crane, John O., and Sylvia E. Crane. *Czechoslovakia: Anvil of the Cold War.* Foreword by Corliss Lamont. New York: Praeger, 1991. xxvi, 352 pp. REV: Vratislav Pechota, *Czechoslovak and Central European Journal* 10, no. 2 (Winter 1991): 143-146. Douglas A. Borer, *Perspectives on Political Science* 21, no. 1 (Winter 1992): 45-46. Radomir V. Luza, *International History Review* 14, no. 2 (May 1992): 423-425. Stanley B. Winters, *American Historical Review* 97, no. 3 (June 1992): 890-891. Igor Lukes, *Slavic Review* 52, no. 4 (Winter 1993): 889-890.

5704. Deák, István. *Beyond Nationalism: A Social and Political History of the Habsburg Officer Corps, 1848-1918.* New York: Oxford University Press, 1990. xiii, 273 pp. REV: John Bushnell, *Slavic Review* 50, no. 4 (Winter 1991): 1041. William C. Fuller, Jr., *Canadian-American Slavic Studies* 25, nos. 1-4 (1991): 425-427. Martin Kitchen, *Canadian Journal of History = Annales canadienne d'histoire* 26, no. 1 (April 1991): 117-119. Kenneth W. Rock, *Historian* 54, no. 1 (Autumn 1991): 117-118. Ivan Sanders, *Commonweal* 118, no. 1 (January 11, 1991): 25-28. Lawrence Sondhaus, *Journal of Military History* 55, no. 2 (April 1991): 253-254. Sandor Agocs, *Hungarian Studies Review* 19, nos. 1-2 (Spring-Fall 1992): 77-85. Johann Christoph Allmayer-Beck, *Austrian History Yearbook*, no. 23 (1992): 254-256. Roy A. Austensen, *German Studies Review* 15, no. 2 (May 1992): 404-405. Michael Burleigh, *American Historical Review* 97, no. 2 (April 1992): 578. N. F. Dreisziger, *Canadian Slavonic Papers* 34, nos. 1-2 (March-June 1992): 162-163. Holger H. Herwig, *Naval War College Review* 45, no. 1 (Winter 1992): 118-119. Béla K. Király, *Canadian Review of Studies in Nationalism = Revue Canadienne des Etudes sur le Nationalisme* 19, nos. 1-2 (1992): 190-191. Leonard V. Smith, *Polish Review* 37, no. 2 (1992): 237-239. Samuel R. Williamson, Jr., *Journal of Modern History* 64, no. 4 (December 1992): 839-841. Larry Wolff, *Harvard Ukrainian Studies* 16, nos. 1-2 (June 1992): 217-219. Peter Sugar, *Nationalities Papers* 21, no. 2 (Fall 1993): 238-239.

5705. Dedijer, Vladimir, comp. and ed. *The Yugoslav Auschwitz and the Vatican: The Croatian Massacre of the Serbs During World War II.* Translated by Harvey L. Kendall. Buffalo, NY: Prometheus, 1992. 444 pp. [Revised translation of the German version which was translated from the Serbo-Croatian (Roman) original: *Vatikan i*

Jasenovac.] REV: István Deák, *New York Review of Books* 39, no. 18 (November 5, 1992): 22-26. George J. Prpic, *Catholic Historical Review* 79, no. 3 (July 1993): 560-562. Sabrina Petra Ramet, *Journal of Church and State* 35, no. 4 (Autumn 1993): 900-902.

5706. Eisenbach, Artur. *The Emancipation of the Jews in Poland, 1780-1870.* Edited by Antony Polonsky. Translated by Janina Dorosz. Cambridge, MA: B. Blackwell, 1991. 632 pp. REV: Gershon David Hundert, *American Historical Review* 98, no. 3 (June 1993): 905.

5707. Evans, R. J. W., and T. V. Thomas, eds. *Crown, Church and Estates: Central European Politics in the Sixteenth and Seventeenth Centuries.* Contributions by R. J. W. Evans, Volker Press, Winfried Eberhard, Alfred Kohler, Günther R. Burkert, Sergij Vilfan, László Makkai, Gernot Heiss, István Bitskey, Kálmán Benda, Jaroslav Pánek, Josef Válka, Winfried Schulze, Gottfried Schramm, Inge Auerbach, Robert Bireley, Georg Heilingsetzer, Katalin Péter, Antoni Maczak, Orest Subtelny, and H. G. Koenigsberger. New York: St. Martin's Press, 1991. 321 pp. [Contents: R.J.W. Evans, "Introduction"; Volker Press, "The System of Estates in the Austrian Hereditary Lands and in the Holy Roman Empire: A Comparison"; Winfried Eberhard, "The Political System and the Intellectual Traditions of the Bohemian *Ständestaat* from the Thirteenth to the Sixteenth Century"; Alfred Kohler, "Ferdinand I and the Estates: Between Confrontation and Co-operation, 1521-64"; Günther R. Burkert, "Protestantism and Defence of Liberties in the Austrian Lands under Ferdinand I"; Sergij Vilfan, "Crown, Estates, and the Financing of Defence in Inner Austria, 1500-1630"; László Makkai, "The Crown and the Diets of Hungary and Transylvania in the Sixteenth Century"; Gernot Heiss, "Princes, Jesuits, and the Origins of Counter-Reformation in the Habsburg Lands"; István Bitskey, "The Collegium Germanicum Hungaricum in Rome and the Beginning of Counter-Reformation in Hungary"; Kálmán Benda, "Habsburg Absolutism and the Resistance of the Hungarian Estates in the Sixteenth and Seventeenth Centuries"; Jaroslav Pánek, "The Religious Question and the Political System of Bohemia before and after the Battle of the White Mountain"; Josef Válka, "Moravia and the Crisis of the Estates' System in the Lands of the Bohemian Crown"; Winfried Schulze, "Estates and the Problem of Resistance in Theory and Practice in the Sixteenth and Seventeenth Centuries"; Gottfried Schramm, "Armed Conflict in East-Central Europe: Protestant Noble Opposition and Catholic Royalist Factions, 1604-20"; Inge Auerbach, "The Bohemian Opposition, Poland-Lithuania, and the Outbreak of the Thirty Years War"; Robert Bireley, "Ferdinand II: Founder of the Habsburg Monarchy"; Georg Heilingsetzer, "The Austrian Nobility, 1600-50: Between Court and Estates"; Katalin Péter, "The Struggle for Protestant Religious Liberty at the 1646-47 Diet in Hungary"; Antoni Maczak, "Confessions, Freedoms, and the Unity of Poland-Lithuania"; Orest Subtelny, "The Contractual Principle and Right of Resistance in the Ukraine and Moldavia"; H.G. Koenigsberger, "Epilogue: Central and Western Europe".] REV: Karin J. MacHardy, *Central European History* 26, no. 1 (1993): 119.

5708. Fulbrook, Mary. *The Divided Nation: A History of Germany, 1918-1990.* New York: Oxford University Press, 1992. 405 pp. [Originally published in United Kingdom in 1991 by Fontana Press with title: *The Fontana History of Germany, 1918-1990.*] REV: John M. Block, *History: Reviews of New Books* 21, no. 4 (Summer 1993): 171.

5709. Garlinski, Józef. *The Survival of Love: Memoirs of a Resistance Officer.* Cambridge, MA: B. Blackwell, 1991. x, 231 pp. REV: Judith Burnley, *New York Times Book Review* (August 4, 1991): 19. István Deák, *New York Review of Books* 39, no. 18 (November 5, 1992): 22-26. Adam A. Hetnal, *Polish Review* 38, no. 1 (1993): 93-95.

5710. Georgescu, Vlad. *The Romanians: A History.* Edited by Matei Calinescu. Translated by Alexandra Bley-Vroman. Romanian Literature and Thought in Translation Series. Columbus, OH: Ohio State University Press, c1991. xiv, 357 pp. [Translation of: *Istoria romanilor de la origini pina in zilele noastre.*] REV: István Deák, *New York Review of Books* 39, no. 5 (March 5, 1992): 43-51. Richard Frucht, *Slavic Review* 51, no. 2 (Summer 1992): 352-353. Paul E. Michelson, *American Historical Review* 97, no. 4 (October 1992): 1246-1247. Keith Hitchins, *Austrian History Yearbook* 24 (1993): 224-225.

5711. Gruber, Helmut. *Red Vienna: Experiment in Working-Class Culture, 1919-1934.* New York: Oxford University Press, 1991. x, 270 pp. REV: Alfred Diamant, *American Historical Review* 98, no. 1 (February 1993): 201-202. Albert Lindemann, *International Labor and Working-Class History*, no. 43 (Spring 1993): 134. James J. Ward, *Journal of Interdisciplinary History* 24, no. 1 (Summer 1993): 147. J. Robert Wegs, *Austrian History Yearbook* 24 (1993): 263-265.

5712. Halecki, Oscar. *Jadwiga of Anjou and the Rise of East Central Europe.* Edited with a foreword by Thaddeus V. Gromada. Atlantic Studies on Society in Change, no. 73. East European Monographs, no. 308. Boulder, CO: Social Science Monographs; Highland Lakes, NJ: Atlantic Research and Publications; New York: Distributed by Columbia University Press, 1991. xvi, 400 pp. [A Polish Institute of Arts and Sciences of America book.] REV: John W. Barker, *International History Review* 15, no. 1 (February 1993): 145. Paul W. Knoll, *Polish Review* 38, no. 2 (1993): 221-225.

5713. Hammond, Nicholas G. L. *The Miracle That Was Macedonia.* Sidgwick & Jackson Great Civilization Series. New York: St. Martin's Press, 1991. ix, 229 pp. REV: Thomas W. Gallant, *Historian* 55, no. 2 (Winter 1993): 345.

5714. Held, Joseph, ed. *The Columbia History of Eastern Europe in the Twentieth Century.* New York: Columbia University Press, c1992. lxix, 435 pp. [Volume originated in a conference held at Rutgers University's Camden Campus in February 1990.] REV: Sabrina Petra Ramet, *Slavic Review* 52, no. 3 (Fall 1993): 607. Peter Wozniak, *History: Reviews of New Books* 21, no. 3 (Spring 1993): 127.

5715. Hiden, John, and Patrick Salmon. *The Baltic Nations and Europe: Estonia, Latvia, and Lithuania in the Twentieth Century.* London; New York: Longman, 1991. x, 224 pp. REV: Jeffrey Canfield, *Naval War College Review* 46, no. 1, Sequence 341 (Winter 1993): 142-144. Andres Kasekamp, *European History Quarterly* (April 1993): 296-298. Romuald J. Misiunas, *American Historical Review* 98, no. 1 (February 1993): 202-203.

5716. Jelavich, Charles. *South Slav Nationalisms— Textbooks and Yugoslav Union before 1914.* Columbus, OH: Ohio State University Press, c1990. xvii, 359 pp. REV: Keith Hitchins, *American Historical Review* 97, no. 4 (October 1992): 1247-1248. James Niessen, *Libraries & Culture* 28, no. 4 (Fall 1993): 486-487. Jim Seroka, *Canadian Review of Studies in Nationalism = Revue Canadienne des Etudes sur le Nationalisme* 20, nos. 1-2 (1993): 139-140.

5717. Kann, Robert A. *Dynasty, Politics, and Culture: Selected Essays.* Edited by Stanley B. Winters. Foreword by Carl E. Schorske. Atlantic Studies on Society in Change, no. 72. East European Monographs, no. 317. Boulder, CO: Social Science Monographs; Highland Lakes, NJ: Atlantic Research and Publications; New York: Distributed by Columbia University Press, 1991. xvi, 444 pp. [Contents: Carl E. Schorske, "Foreword"; Introduction; Stanley B. Winters, "The Forging of a Historian: Robert A. Kann in America, 1939-1976"; "The Dynasty and the Imperial Idea"; "Dynastic Relations and European Power Politics (1848-1918)"; Archduke Franz Ferdinand and Count Berchtold During His Term as Foreign Minister, 1912-1914"; "Heir Apparent Archduke Franz Ferdinand and His Stance on the Bohemian Question"; "The Austro-Hungarian Compromise of 1867 in Retrospect: Causes and Effect"; "The Social Prestige of the Officer Corps in the Habsburg Empire from the Eighteenth Century to 1918"; "The German Empire and the Habsburg Monarchy, 1871-1918"; "Emperor Franz Joseph and the Outbreak of World War I: A Reflection on Dr. Heinrich Kanner's Notes as a Source"; "Higher Education and Politics in the Austrian Constitutional Monarchy (1867-1918)"; "Imperial Hangovers: The Case of Austria"; "Forty Years After the Anschluss"; "Reflections on the Relevance Problem in Modern Historiography"; "Hermann Broch and the Philosophy of History"; Comprehensive Bibliography of Publications by Robert A. Kann.] REV: Peter F. Sugar, *Slavic Review* 52, no. 3 (Fall 1993): 618-619. Samuel R. Williamson, Jr, *Austrian History Yearbook* 24 (1993): 225-227.

5718. Kersten, Krystyna. *The Establishment of Communist Rule in Poland, 1943-1948.* Translated and annotated by John Micgiel, and Michael H. Bernhard. Foreword by Jan T. Gross. Societies and Culture in East-Central Europe, Berkeley: University of California Press, c1991. 535 pp. REV: Jaroslaw Piekalkiewicz, *Canadian-American Slavic Studies* 25, nos. 1-4 (1991): 415-417. Robert Legvold, *Foreign Affairs* 71, no. 3 (Summer 1992): 178-179. Vladimir Tismaneanu, *Orbis* 36, no. 4 (Fall 1992): 623-624. M. K. Dziewanowski, *American Historical Review* 98, no. 2 (April 1993): 530-531. Norman M. Naimark, *Polish Review* 38, no. 2 (1993): 244-247. William J. Woolley,

History: Reviews of New Books 21, no. 2 (Winter 1993): 80.

5719. Latawski, Paul, ed. *The Reconstruction of Poland, 1914-23.* Contributions by Paul Latawski, Eugene C. Black, Roman Szporluk, Józef Garlinski, Anna M. Cienciala, Kay Lundgreen-Nielsen, Piotr Wandycz, Andrzej Ajnenkiel, Zbigniew Landau, Wojciech Roszkowski, and Janusz Sibora. New York: St. Martin's Press, 1992. 217 pp. [Contents: Paul Latawski, "Roman Dmowski, the Polish Question, and Western Opinion, 1915-18: The Case of Britain"; Eugene C. Black, "Squaring a Minorities Triangle: Lucien Wolf, Jewish Nationalists and Polish Nationalists"; Roman Szporluk, "Polish-Ukrainian Relations in 1918: Notes for Discussion"; Józef Garlinski, "The Polish-Ukrainian Agreement, 1920"; Anna M. Cienciala, "The Battle of Danzig and the Polish Corridor at the Paris Peace Conference of 1919"; Kay Lundgreen-Nielsen, "Aspects of American Policy towards Poland at the Paris Peace Conference and the Role of Isaiah Bowman"; Piotr Wandycz, "Dmowski's Policy at the Paris Peace Conference: Success or Failure?"; Andrzej Ajnenkiel, "The Establishment of a National Government in Poland, 1918"; Zbigniew Landau, "The Economic Integration of Poland, 1918-23"; Wojciech Roszkowski, "The Reconstruction of the Government and State Apparatus in the Second Polish Republic"; Janusz Sibora, "The Origins of the Polish Foreign Ministry: 11 November 1918-January 1919"; Appendix: Documents Relating to the Reconstruction of Poland. 1. Proclamation Grand Duke Nicholas, 14 August 1914; 2. Proclamation 5 November 1916; 3. Dmowski's "Memorandum on the Territory of the Polish State" 26 March 1917; 4. Wilson's Fourteenth Point 8 January 1919; 5. Pilsudski Decree 18 November 1918; 6. Paton Memorandum "Polish Claims to Danzig and West Prussia" 27 February 1919; 7. Minorities Treaty 28 June 1919; 8. Polish-Ukrainian Agreement 21 April 1920.] REV: Paul Latawski, *International History Review* 15, no. 3 (August 1993): 596. Neal Pease, *Polish Review* 38, no. 2 (1993): 230-232.

5720. *The Laws of the Medieval Kingdom of Hungary.* Translated and edited by János M. Bak et al. Laws of East Central Europe. Laws of Hungary. Series I, v. 1-. Bakersfield, CA: C. Schlacks, c1989-. vols. [Contents: Vol. 1. 1000-1301 — v. 2. 1301-1457. With a critical essay on the previous editions by Andor Csizmadia.] REV: Steven Bela Vardy, *Speculum* 68, no. 1 (January 1993): 102-104.

5721. Levine, Hillel. *Economic Origins of Antisemitism: Poland and Its Jews in the Early Modern Period.* New Haven, CT: Yale University Press, c1991. xiii, 271 pp. REV: Y. Michal Bodemann, *Contemporary Sociology* 21, no. 4 (July 1992): 455-456. Gershon David Hundert, *American Historical Review* 97, no. 4 (October 1992): 1246. Eli Lederhendler, *Slavic Review* 51, no. 4 (Winter 1992): 833-834. Albert S. Lindemann, *Journal of Interdisciplinary History* 23, no. 2 (Autumn 1992): 342-344. John K. Roth, *Annals of the American Academy of Political and Social Science*, no. 523 (September 1992): 232-234. Magdalena M. Opalski, *Polish Review* 38, no. 4 (1993): 494-496.

5722. Lewin, Isaac, and Nahum Michael Gelber. *A History of Polish Jewry During the Renewal of Poland.* New

York: Shengold Publishers, c1990. 332 pp. [Contents: Isaac Lewin, "The Political History of Polish Jewry, 1918-1919"; Nahum Michael Gelber, "The National Autonomy of Eastern-Galician Jewry in the West-Ukrainian Republic, 1918-1919".] REV: Celia Stopnicka Heller, *Polish Review* 38, no. 3 (1993): 337-342.

5723. Longworth, Philip. *The Making of Eastern Europe.* New York: St. Martin's Press, 1992. xii, 320 pp. REV: Antoni Maczak, *American Historical Review* 98, no. 4 (October 1993): 1288-1289.

5724. Lucas, Franz D., and Margret Heitmann. *Stadt des Glaubens: Geschichte und Kultur der Juden in Glogau.* Wissenschaftliche Abhandlungen des Salomon Ludwig Steinheim-Instituts fur Deutsch-Judische Geschichte, Bd. 3. Beitrage zur Geschichter der Juden in Schlesien, 1. Hildesheim; New York: G. Olms, 1991. viii, 582 pp. REV: Peter Pulzer, *Central European History* 26, no. 3 (1993): 351-353.

5725. Ludwikowski, Rett R. *Continuity and Change in Poland: Conservatism in Polish Political Thought of the Nineteenth and Twentieth Centuries.* Washington, DC: Catholic University of America Press, c1991. xv, 313 pp. REV: Brian A. Porter, *Slavic Review* 52, no. 2 (Summer 1993): 380-381. Joan S. Skurnowicz, *American Historical Review* 98, no. 1 (February 1993): 199-200.

5726. Mazower, Mark. *Greece and the Inter-War Economic Crisis.* Oxford Historical Monographs, New York: Clarendon Press, 1991. 334 pp. REV: Dimitri Kitsikis, *International History Review* 15, no. 3 (August 1993): 606. John A. Koumoulides, *History: Reviews of New Books* 21, no. 2 (Winter 1993): 76. Thanos Veremis, *European History Quarterly* (July 1993): 406-407.

5727. McCagg, William O., Jr. *A History of Habsburg Jews, 1670-1918.* Bloomington, IN: Indiana University Press, c1989. xi, 289 pp. REV: Erich Haberer, *Canadian Slavonic Papers* 32, no. 1 (March 1990): 108-109. Donald L. Niewyk, *Historian* 52, no. 1 (Autumn 1990): 109-110. Bruce F. Pauley, *German Studies Review* 13, no. 1 (February 1990): 140. Peter F. Sugar, *American Historical Review* 96, no. 2 (April 1991): 553. Peter Pulzer, *Journal of Modern History* 64, no. 1 (March 1992): 172-173. Marsha L. Rozenblit, *Austrian History Yearbook*, no. 23 (1992): 160-180. Leonard V. Smith, *Polish Review* 38, no. 1 (1993): 101-103.

5728. Mikus, Joseph A. *La Slovaquie, la vérité sur son histoire.* Translated from the English by Renée Mikus-Perréal. Toronto, Ontario: Institut Culturel Slovaque, 1991. 109 pp. REV: Guy Héraud, *Language Problems & Language Planning* 17, no. 2 (Summer 1993): 162.

5729. Molnár, Miklós. *From Béla Kun to János Kádár: Seventy Years of Hungarian Communism.* Translated by Arnold J. Pomerans. New York: Berg; Distributed by St. Martin's Press, 1990. xii, 281 pp. REV: John C. Campbell, *Foreign Affairs* 70, no. 3 (Summer 1991): 177. Peter Pastor, *Slavic Review* 52, no. 4 (Winter 1993): 887-888.

5730. Oldson, William O. *A Providential Anti-Semitism: Nationalism and Polity in Nineteenth Century Romania.* Memoirs of the American Philosophical Society, v. 193. Philadelphia, PA: American Philosophical Society, c1991. ix, 177 pp. REV: R.V. Burks, *American Historical Review* 97, no. 2 (April 1992): 579-580. Dov B. Lungu, *Canadian Slavonic Papers* 35, nos. 3-4 (September-December 1993): 398-399.

5731. Pauley, Bruce F. *From Prejudice to Persecution: A History of Austrian Anti-Semitism.* Chapel Hill, NC: University of North Carolina Press, c1992. xxix, 426 pp. REV: Lionel B. Steiman, *Modern Austrian Literature* 26, no. 2 (1993): 173-176. Michael J. Zeps, *Catholic Historical Review* 79, no. 1 (January 1993): 125.

5732. Pleshoyano, Dan V. *Colonel Nicolae Plesoianu and the National Regeneration Movement in Walachia.* Translated from the French by Kathe Lieber. East European Monographs, no. 310. Boulder, CO: East European Monographs; New York: Distributed by Columbia University Press, 1991. x, 176 pp. REV: Robert F. Forrest, *Canadian Review of Studies in Nationalism = Revue Canadienne des Etudes sur le Nationalisme* 20, nos. 1-2 (1993): 145-147.

5733. Rady, Martyn C. *Romania in Turmoil: A Contemporary History.* London; New York: I.B. Tauris, 1992. vii, 216 pp. REV: Richard Frucht, *Slavic Review* 52, no. 3 (Fall 1993): 613-14. Robert Legvold, *Foreign Affairs* 72, no. 2 (Spring 1993): 180.

5734. Raun, Toivo U. *Estonia and the Estonians.* 2nd ed. Studies of Nationalities in the USSR, Stanford, CA: Hoover Institution Press, Stanford University, 1991. xix, 336 pp. REV: Tiina Kurman, *Journal of Baltic Studies* 23, no. 1 (Spring 1992): 81. David Crowe, *Russian Review* 52, no. 3 (July 1993): 443.

5735. Rees, H. Louis. *The Czechs During World War I: The Path to Independence.* East European Monographs, no. 339. Boulder, CO: East European Monographs; New York: Distributed by Columbia University Press, 1992. vii, 170 pp. REV: Bruce Garver, *Czechoslovak and Central European Journal* 11, no. 2 (Winter 1993): 126-128.

5736. Roesdahl, Else, and David M. Wilson, eds. *From Viking to Crusader: The Scandinavians and Europe 800-1200.* New York: Rizzoli, 1992. 429 pp. REV: William Urban, *Journal of Baltic Studies* 24, no. 3 (Fall 1993): 311-312.

5737. Rosen, F. *Bentham, Byron, and Greece: Constitutionalism, Nationalism, and Early Liberal Political Thought.* Oxford: Clarendon Press; New York: Oxford University Press, 1992. xii, 332 pp. REV: Allison Dube, *Canadian Journal of Political Science = Revue canadienne de science politique* 26, no. 3 (September 1993): 611-612. D.L. LeMahieu, *American Historical Review* 98, no. 5 (December 1993): 1607.

5738. Saab, Ann Pottinger. *Reluctant Icon: Gladstone, Bulgaria, and the Working Classes, 1856-1878.* Harvard Historical Studies, 109. Cambridge, MA: Harvard

University Press, 1991. 257 pp. REV: Mari Firkatian-
Wozniak, *History: Reviews of New Books* 21, no. 1 (Fall
1992): 17-18. P.R. Ghosh, *International History Review* 14,
no. 4 (November 1992): 788-790. Phillip E. Myers, *Historian*
54, no. 4 (Summer 1992): 730-731. Marvin Swartz, *American Historical Review* 97, no. 4 (October 1992): 1218-1219.
J.P. Parry, *History* (February 1993): 136-137.

5739. Sabaliunas, Leonas. *Lithuanian Social
Democracy in Perspective, 1893-1914.* Duke Press Policy
Studies. Durham, NC: Duke University Press, 1990. viii,
205 pp. REV: David Crowe, *Russian History* 17, no. 3 (Fall
1990): 359-361. Debra E. Soled, *Current History* 89, no. 549
(October 1990): 333. Toivo U. Raun, *American Historical
Review* 96, no. 4 (October 1991): 1245-1246. Alfred Erich
Senn, *Slavic Review* 50, no. 4 (Winter 1991): 1049. Robert
A. Vitas, *Journal of Baltic Studies* 22, no. 4 (Winter 1991):
365-367. Andrew Ezergailis, *Russian Review* 51, no. 1
(January 1992): 121-122. Joseph L. Harmon, *Lituanus* 39,
no. 2 (Summer 1993): 84-87.

5740. Schatz, Jaff. *The Generation: The Rise and
Fall of the Jewish Communists of Poland.* Societies and
Culture in East-Central Europe, 5. Berkeley, CA: Univer-
sity of California Press, c1991. x, 408 pp. REV: Troy Judt,
Canadian-American Slavic Studies 25, nos. 1-4 (1991): 410-
412. Martin Berger, *History: Reviews of New Books* 21, no. 1
(Fall 1992): 26. Vladimir Tismaneanu, *Orbis* 36, no. 2
(Spring 1992): 306-307. Edward D. Wynot, Jr., *American
Historical Review* 98, no. 1 (February 1993): 200.

5741. Schollgen, Gregor. *A Conservative Against
Hitler: Ulrich von Hassell, Diplomat in Imperial Germany,
the Weimar Republic, and the Third Reich, 1881-1944.*
Translated by Louise Willmot. Foreword by Michael
Balfour. New York: St. Martin's Press, 1991. xiii, 188 pp.
[Translation of *Ulrich von Hassell, 1881-1944: ein
Konservativer in der Opposition* (Munchen: Beck, c1990).
Hassell was minister to Yugoslavia.] REV: Ralph R.
Menning, *History: Reviews of New Books* 21, no. 3 (Spring
1993): 122.

5742. Sked, Alan. *The Decline and Fall of the
Habsburg Empire, 1815-1918.* NY: Longman, 1989. 295 pp.
REV: Gregory C. Ference, *East Central Europe* 18, no. 1
(1991): 101-102. Solomon Wank, *Central European History*
26, no. 1 (1993): 123-127.

5743. Skilling, H. Gordon, ed. *Czechoslovakia,
1918-88: Seventy Years from Independence.* Contributions by
H. Gordon Skilling, George J. Kovtun, Jaroslav Opat,
Walter Ullmann, Edita Bosak, Ronald M. Smelser, Paul
Robert Magocsi, Frederick M. Barnard, Radoslav Selucky,
Igor Hajek, Peter Petro, and Václav Havel. New York: St.
Martin's Press, 1991. xv, 232 pp. [Proceedings of a confer-
ence held October 1988 in Toronto. Contents: H. Gordon
Skilling, "Lions or Foxes: Heroes or Lackeys?"; George J.
Kovtun, "T.G. Masaryk: The Problem of a Small Nation";
Jaroslav Opat, "On the Emergence of Czechoslovakia";
Walter Ullmann, "Benes Between East and West"; Edita
Bosak, "Slovaks and Czechs: An Uneasy Coexistence";
Ronald M. Smelser, "Castles On the Landscape: Czech-

German Relations"; Paul Robert Magocsi, "Magyars and
Carpatho-Rusyns"; Frederick M. Barnard, "Political Cul-
ture: Continuity and Discontinuity"; Radoslav Selucky,
"From Capitalism to Socialism"; Igor Hajek, "Traditions of
Czech Literature: Curses and Blessings"; Peter Petro,
"Slovak Literature: Loyal, Dissident and Emigre"; Václav
Havel, "A Neglected Generation".] REV: Joseph F. Zacek,
Czechoslovak and Central European Journal 11, no. 1
(Summer 1992): 106-107. Stanislav Kirschbaum, *Canadian
Slavonic Papers* 35, nos. 1-2 (March-June 1993): 188-189.

5744. Spence, Richard B., and Linda L. Nelson, eds.
*Scholar, Patriot, Mentor: Historical Essays in Honor of
Dimitrije Djordjevic.* East European Monographs, no. 320.
Boulder, CO: East European Monographs; New York:
Distributed by Columbia University Press, 1992. xi, 422 pp.
REV: Sava Bosnitch, *Canadian Slavonic Papers* 35, nos. 1-2
(March-June 1993): 189.

5745. Steenson, Gary P. *After Marx, Before Lenin:
Marxism and Socialist Working-Class Parties in Europe,
1884-1914.* Pittsburgh, PA: University of Pittsburgh Press,
c1991. xi, 353 pp. REV: Ellen Furlough, *Labor History* 34,
nos. 2-3 (Spring-Summer 1993): 415-416. Wolf Ken Fones,
Labor Studies Journal 18, no. 3 (Fall 1993): 75-77.

5746. Stokes, Gale. *Politics as Development: The
Emergence of Political Parties in Nineteenth Century Serbia.*
Durham, NC: Duke University Press, 1990. xiv, 400 pp.
REV: Thomas A. Emmert, *Modern Greek Studies Yearbook*,
no. 7 (1991): 570-572. Andrew Rossos, *Canadian Slavonic
Papers* 33, no. 1 (March 1991): 95-96. Jim Seroka, *Cana-
dian Review of Studies in Nationalism = Revue Canadienne
des Etudes sur le Nationalisme* 19, nos. 1-2 (1992): 175-176.
John D. Treadway, *American Historical Review* 97, no. 5
(December 1992): 1564-1565. Karl Kaser, *Nationalities
Papers* 21, no. 2 (Fall 1993): 243-245.

5747. Sully, Melanie A. *A Contemporary History of
Austria.* London; New York: Routledge, 1990. xiii, 179 pp.
REV: Peter Wozniak, *East European Quarterly* 27, no. 4
(Winter 1993): 557-559.

5748. Tismaneanu, Vladimir. *Reinventing Politics:
Eastern Europe from Stalin to Havel.* New York: Free Press;
Toronto: Maxwell Macmillan Canada; New York: Maxwell
Macmillan International, c1992. xvii, 312 pp. REV: Robert
Legvold, *Foreign Affairs* 71, no. 3 (Summer 1992): 179.
Stephen Miller, *Journal of Democracy* 3, no. 4 (October
1992): 125-129. Gale Stokes, *New Leader* 75, no. 8 (June 29,
1992): 18-19. *Publishers Weekly* 239, no. 8 (February 10,
1992): 64. Jeffrey C. Goldfarb, *Bulletin of the Atomic
Scientists* 49, no. 2 (March 1993): 44. Sabrina Petra Ramet,
American Political Science Review 87, no. 2 (June 1993):
526-527.

5749. Wandycz, Piotr S. *The Price of Freedom: A
History of East Central Europe from the Middle Ages to the
Present.* New York: Routledge, 1992. 330 pp. REV: Lee
Congdon, *History: Reviews of New Books* 22, no. 1 (Fall
1993): 37.

5750. Weitz, John. *Hitler's Diplomat: The Life and Times of Joachim von Ribbentrop.* New York: Ticknor & Fields, 1992. xv, 376. REV: George O. Kent, *History: Reviews of New Books* 21, no. 3 (Spring 1993): 134.

5751. Wiles, Timothy, ed. *Poland Between the Wars, 1918-1939.* Bloomington, IN: Indiana University Polish Studies Center, 1989. xvi, 319 pp. [A collection of papers and discussions from the conference "Poland Between the Wars: 1918-1939", held in Bloomington, Indiana, February 21-23, 1985.] REV: Neal Pease, *Polish Review* 37, no. 1 (1992): 123-124. Samuel D. Kassow, *Slavic Review* 52, no. 1 (Spring 1993): 136-137.

5752. Williamson, Samuel R., Jr. *Austria-Hungary and the Origins of the First World War.* The Making of the 20th Century, New York: St. Martin's Press, 1991. xviii,.272 pp. REV: Lawrence J. Flockerzie, *East-Central Europe* 18, no. 1 (1991): 102-105. F. R. Bridge, *International History Review* 14, no. 2 (May 1992): 384-385. E. D. Brose, *Historian* 54, no. 4 (Summer 1992): 743-744. Holger H. Herwig, *Naval War College Review* 45, no. 3 (Summer 1992): 139-141. Ralph Menning, *History: Reviews of New Books* 20, no. 3 (Spring 1992): 117-118. Norman Rich, *American Historical Review* 97, no. 1 (February 1992): 247-249. George Strong, *Journal of Military History* 56, no. 1 (January 1992): 133-134. Glenn Torrey, *Slavic Review* 51, no. 1 (Spring 1992): 159-160. Zbynek A. B. Zeman, *Austrian History Yearbook* 24 (1993): 256-257.

5753. Zlatar, Zdenko. *Our Kingdom Come: The Counter-Reformation, the Republic of Dubrovnik, and the Liberation of the Balkan Slavs.* East European Monographs, no. 342. Boulder, CO: East European Monographs; New York: Distributed by Columbia University Press, 1992. xxi, 464 pp. REV: Mark Biondich, *Canadian Slavonic Papers* 35, nos. 1-2 (March-June 1993): 195-197.

■ International Relations

General

5754. Baranovsky, Vladimir, and Hans-Joachim Spanger, eds. *In from the Cold: Germany, Russia, and the Future of Europe.* Foreword by Eduard Shevardnadze. Boulder, CO: Westview Press, 1992. xxv, 321 pp. REV: Robert Legvold, *Foreign Affairs* 72, no. 4 (September-October 1993): 170.

5755. Braun, Aurel, ed. *The Soviet-East European Relationship in the Gorbachev Era: The Prospects for Adaptation.* Westview Special Studies on the Soviet Union and Eastern Europe, Boulder, CO: Westview Press, 1990. xi, 249 pp. REV: John C. Campbell, *Foreign Affairs* 69, no. 4 (Fall 1990): 192-193. Louis Furmanski, *Perspectives on Political Science* 20, no. 3 (Summer 1991): 180. Joshua B. Spero, *Problems of Communism* 40, no. 6 (November-December 1991): 141-151. Vladimir Wozniuk, *Canadian-American Slavic Studies* 26, nos. 1-4 (1992): 353-354. Roger E. Kanet, *Nationalities Papers* 21, no. 2 (Fall 1993): 259-260.

5756. Carter, April. *Peace Movements: International Protest and World Politics Since 1945.* The Postwar World. London; New York: Longman, c1992. xv, 283 pp. REV: Peter Brock, *American Historical Review* 98, no. 2 (April 1993): 474.

5757. Chazan, Naomi, ed. *Irredentism and International Politics.* Includes contributions by Donald L. Horowitz, Shalom Reichman, Arnon Golan, Richard Stoess, and Brian Weinstein. Studies in International Politics. Boulder, CO: Lynne Rienner Publishers; London: Adamantine Press, 1991. ix, 161 pp. [Most of the contributions to this book were originally presented at a workshop held at the Center for International Studes at the Massachusetts Institute of Technology in April 1986, sponsored by the Leonard Davis Institute of International Relations of the Hebrew University of Jerusalem. Partial contents: Shalom Reichman and Arnon Golan, "Irrendentism and Boundary Adjustments in Post-World War I Europe," pp. 51-68; Richard Stoess, "Irredentism in Germany since 1945," pp. 69-79; Brian Weinstein, "Language Planning as an Aid and a Barrier to Irredentism," pp. 111-138.] REV: Thomas A. Hopkins, *American Political Science Review* 86, no. 2 (June 1992): 575-576. Laura Murray, *Journal of International Affairs* 45, no. 2 (Winter 1992): 648-652. William Safran, *Canadian Review of Studies in Nationalism = Revue Canadienne des Etudes sur le Nationalisme* 20, nos. 1-2 (1993): 120-122.

5758. Claude, Richard Pierre, and Weston Burns H., eds. *Human Rights in the World Community: Issues and Action.* 2nd ed. Philadelphia, PA: University of Pennsylvania Press, 1992. xiii, 463 pp. REV: Morton Sklar, *American Journal of International Law* 87, no. 3 (July 1993): 475-476.

5759. Dalby, Simon. *Creating the Second Cold War: The Discourse of Politics.* Geography and International Relations Series. London: Pinter; New York: Guilford Press, 1990. xi, 211 pp. REV: David B. Knight, *Canadian Geographer = Géographe Canadien* 37, no. 2 (Summer 1993): 187.

5760. Damrosch, Lori Fisler, and David Scheffer, eds. *Law and Force in the New International Order.* Boulder, CO: Westview Press, 1991. xviii, 326 pp. REV: Robert F. Drinan, *American Journal of International Law* 87, no. 3 (July 1993): 484-485.

5761. Dinstein, Yoram, ed. *The Protection of Minorities and Human Rights.* Associate editor Mala Tabory. Includes contributions by Mala Tabory, Vladmir A. Kartashkin, Zvi Magen, Vojin Dimitrijevic, and László Valki. Dordrecht; Boston, MA: M. Nijhoff; Norwell, MA: Kluwer Academic, 1992. xii, 537 pp. [Partial contents: Mala Tabory, "Minority Rights in the CSCE Context," pp. 187-211; Vladmir A. Kartashkin, "International Protection of Minorities: The Soviet Perspective," pp. 377-385; Zvi Magen, "Jews in the USSR: A Minority at Crossroads," pp. 387-418; Vojin Dimitrijevic, "Nationalities and Minorites in the Yugoslav Federation," pp. 419-433; László Valki, "Minority Protection in Hungary—Hungarian Minorities Abroad," pp. 435-461.] REV: *George Washington Journal of International Law and Economics* 26, no. 3 (1993): 693-695.

5762. Francioni, Francesco, and Tullio Scovazzi, eds. *International Responsibility for Environmental Harm.* International Environmental Law and Policy Series. London; Boston: Graham & Trotman; Norwell, MA: Kluwer Academic, 1991. xv, 499 pp. [Includes essay on Chernobyl.] REV: Louise de La Fayette, *American Journal of International Law* 87, no. 3 (July 1993): 488-489.

5763. Hampson, Fen Osler, and Christopher Maule, eds. *Canada among Nations, 1992-93: A New World Order?* Includes contribution by Lenard Cohen. Carleton Public Policy Series, 8. Ottawa: Carleton University Press; Don Mills, Ont.: Oxford University Press, 1992. xx, 301 pp. [Includes essay by Lenard Cohen on the evolving situation in Eastern Europe.] REV: Tom Keating, *International Journal* 49, no. 1 (Winter 1993-1994): 156-158.

5764. Henkin, Louis et al. *Right v. Might: International Law and the Use of Force.* Foreword by John Temple Swing. New York: Council on Foreign Relations Press, 1989. xii, 124 pp. REV: Amy B. Dickinson and David L.Green, *Emory International Law Review* 7, no. 1 (Spring 1993): 233-248.

5765. Jones, Robert A. *The Soviet Concept of "Limited Sovereignty" from Lenin to Gorbachev: The Brezhnev Doctrine.* New York: St. Martin's Press, c1990. viii, 337 pp. REV: John C. Campbell, *Foreign Affairs* 69, no. 3 (Summer 1990): 185-186. Daniel McIntosh, *American Political Science Review* 85, no. 2 (June 1991): 666-667. Ronald H. Linden, *Slavic Review* 52, no. 2 (Summer 1993): 390-391. Sarah M. Terry, *Russian Review* 52, no. 2 (April 1993): 283-284. *Studies in East European Thought* 45, no. 3 (September 1993): 213-214.

5766. Kim, Young C., and Gaston J. Sigur, eds. *Asia and the Decline of Communism.* New Brunswick, NJ: Transaction, c1992. 296 pp. REV: Gilbert Rozman, *Slavic Review* 52, no. 1 (Spring 1993): 162-163.

5767. Kimball, Warren F., ed. *American Unbound: World War II and the Making of a Superpower.* Includes contribution by Hayden B. Peake. Franklin and Eleanor Roosevelt Institute Series on Diplomatic and Economic History. New York: St. Martin's Press, 1992. 188 pp. [Partial contents: Hayden B. Peake, "Soviet Espionage and the Office of Strategic Services".] REV: Gary B. Ostrower, *History: Reviews of New Books* 22, no. 1 (Fall 1993): 201.

5768. Maier, Charles S., ed. *The Cold War in Europe: Era of a Divided Continent.* New York: M. Wiener, 1991. viii, 358 pp. REV: Darlene L. Boroviak, *Perspectives on Political Science* 22, no. 4 (Fall 1993): 192-193.

5769. Menges, Constantine C. *The Future of Germany and the Atlantic Alliance.* Washington, DC: AEI Press; Lanham, MD: Distributed by National Book Network, 1991. xiii, 284 pp. REV: Thomas Risse-Kappen, *Bulletin of the Atomic Scientists* 49, no. 1 (January-February 1993): 48-49.

5770. Newman, Frank, and David Weissbrodt. *International Human Rights: Law, Policy, and Process.* Cincinnati: Anderson Pub. Co., 1990. xxiv, 812 pp. [In-

cludes chapter on CSCE.] REV: Mark W. Janis, *American Journal of International Law* 87, no. 1 (January 1993): 196.

5771. Plischke, Elmer, comp. and ed. *Contemporary U.S. Foreign Policy: Documents and Commentary.* New York: Greenwood Press, 1991. xlv, 846 pp. REV: Marian (Leich) Nash, *American Journal of International Law* 87, no. 3 (July 1993): 497-500.

5772. Quaye, Christopher O. *Liberation Struggles in International Law.* Philadelphia, PA: Temple University Press, 1991. vii, 382 pp. REV: Mark H. Bricker, *New York University Journal of International Law and Politics* 25, no. 5 (Winter 1993): 523-525.

5773. Simon, Jeffrey, ed. *European Security Policy after the Revolutions of 1989.* Washington, DC: National Defense University Press, 1991. xvi, 640 pp. [Papers from a conferences held at the National Defense University in June 1990, sponsored by Strategic Capabilities Assessment Center, Institute for National Strategic Studies.] REV: Paul Dotson, *Perspectives on Political Science* 22, no. 4 (Fall 1993): 191. Russell W. Ramsey, *Naval War College Review* 46, no. 3, Sequence 343 (Summer 1993): 159.

5774. Snyder, Jack L. *Myths of Empire: Domestic Politics and International Ambition.* Cornell Studies in Security Affairs, Ithaca, NY: Cornell University Press, 1991. viii, 330 pp. [Includes discussion of the Soviet Union after World War II and the United States in the Cold War.] REV: Theodore H. Von Laue, *Slavic Review* 51, no. 2 (Summer 1992): 338-339. Michael E. Long, *Military Review* 73, no. 10 (October 1993): 80. Tony Smith, *American Historical Review* 98, no. 2 (April 1993): 473.

5775. Tamnes, Rolf. *The United States and the Cold War in the High North.* Aldershot, Hants; Brookfield, VT: Dartmouth, c1991. 384 pp. REV: Wayne S. Cole, *American Historical Review* 98, no. 1 (February 1993): 274.

5776. Thompson, Kenneth W. *Traditions and Values in Politics and Diplomacy: Theory and Practice.* Political Traditions in Foreign Policy Series. Baton Rouge, LA: Louisiana State University Press, c1992. xii, 353 pp. REV: Greg Russell, *Journal of Politics* 55, no. 3 (August 1993): 862. Robert A. Strong, *Review of Politics* 55, no. 4 (Fall 1993): 738-739.

5777. Ullman, Richard H. *Securing Europe.* Princeton, NJ: Princeton University Press, c1991. xv, 183 pp. REV: Jonathan Dean, *New York Times Book Review* 96 (May 19, 1991): 11-12. Robert Jervis, *American Political Science Review* 86 (September 1992): 853-854. Michael Baun, *Annals of the American Academy of Political and Social Science*, no. 527 (May 1993): 188-189. John W. Outland, *Perspectives on Political Science* 22, no. 3 (Summer 1993): 139.

5778. Wettig, Gerhard. *Changes in Soviet Policy towards the West.* Boulder, CO: Westview Press, 1991. 193 pp. REV: John C. Campbell, *Foreign Affairs* 70, no. 4 (Fall 1991): 181. Valerie Bunce, *International Journal* 47, no. 4 (Autumn 1992): 858-859. Paul Buteux, *Canadian-American Slavic Studies* 26, nos. 1-4 (1992): 400-402 Tsuyoshi

Hasegawa, *Russian Review* 52, no. 1 (January 1993): 130-131.

Diplomatic History

5779. Abramson, Rudy. *Spanning the Century: The Life of W. Averell Harriman, 1891-1986*. New York: W. Morrow, 1992. 779 pp. [Includes Harriman's tour as ambassador in Moscow during World War II, discussion of U.S.-Soviet relations.] REV: Roger Draper, *New Leader* 75, no. 10 (August 10-24, 1992): 15-16. Jacob Heilbrunn, *New Republic* 207, no. 5 (July 27, 1992): 53-59. William G. Hyland, *Foreign Affairs* 71, no. 4 (Fall 1992): 194-197. Harold Jablon, *Historian* 55, no. 3 (Spring 1993): 571. Warren F. Kimball, *American Historical Review* 98, no. 2 (April 1993): 589.

5780. Bell, P. M. H. *John Bull and the Bear: British Public Opinion, Foreign Policy, and the Soviet Union, 1941-1945*. London; New York: E. Arnold; New York: Distributed in the USA by Routledge, Chapman and Hall, 1990. x, 214 pp. REV: Robert Cole, *American Historical Review* 97, no. 2 (April 1992): 559. Trevor Lloyd, *Historian* 54, no. 3 (Spring 1992): 500-501. Gordon W. Morrell, *International History Review* 14, no. 3 (August 1992): 607-609. William D. Muller, *History: Reviews of New Books* 21, no. 1 (Fall 1992): 17. Randall Bennett Woods, *Journal of Modern History* 65, no. 3 (September 1993): 611-615.

5781. Bennett, Edward M. *Franklin D. Roosevelt and the Search for Victory: American-Soviet Relations, 1939-1945*. America in the Modern World. Wilmington, DE: SR Books, 1990. xxvii, 207 pp. REV: John M. Carroll, *Historian* 54, no. 1 (Autumn 1991): 144-145. Thomas R. Maddux, *Pacific Historical Review* 60, no. 4 (November 1991): 573-574. Melvin Small, *American Historical Review* 96, no. 5 (December 1991): 1641-1642. Sean Dennis Cashman, *International History Review* 14, no. 3 (August 1992): 592-595. Marc Gallicchio, *Diplomatic History* 17, no. 3 (Summer 1993): 483-488.

5782. Berger, Graenum. *A Not So Silent Envoy: A Biography of Ambassador Samuel David Berger*. 1st ed. New Rochelle, NY: J.W.B. Hampton, c1992. viii, 221 pp. [Berger served with the Lend-Lease mission in Britian in World War II; fought communists in post-war Europe; later served in Greece.] REV: Stephen E. Ambrose, *Foreign Affairs* 72, no. 3 (Summer 1993): 201-202.

5783. Beschloss, Michael R. *The Crisis Years: Kennedy and Khrushchev, 1960-1963*. New York: E. Burlingame, c1991. 816 pp. REV: Michael Krepon, *New York Times Book Review* (June 16, 1991): 3. Richard Ned Lebow, *Bulletin of the Atomic Scientists* 47, no. 10 (December 1991): 41-42. Gaddis Smith, *Foreign Affairs* 70, no. 4 (Fall 1991): 174. George W. Ball, *New York Review of Books* 39, no. 4 (February 13, 1992): 16-20. James D. Blundell, *Military Review* 72, no. 2 (February 1992): 96. James N. Giglio, *Journal of American History* 79, no. 3 (December 1992): 1246-1248. Fred I. Greenstein, *Reviews in American History* 20, no. 1 (March 1992): 96-104. Carl Kaysen, *Political Science Quarterly* 107, no. 1 (Spring 1992): 157-158. Toby Zanin, *International Journal* 48, no. 1 (Winter

1992-1993): 178-180. Robert H. Ferrell, *Review of Politics* 55, no. 2 (Spring 1993): 367-369.

5784. Brands, H. W. *Inside the Cold War: Loy Henderson and the Rise of the American Empire, 1918-1961*. New York: Oxford University Press, 1991. 337 pp. REV: Adam Garfinkle, *Orbis* 35, no. 3 (Summer 1991): 465. Gaddis Smith, *Foreign Affairs* 70, no. 4 (Fall 1991): 174. David Mayers, *International History Review* 14, no. 3 (August 1992): 579-581. Robert J. McMahon, *Journal of American History* 79, no. 1 (June 1992): 314-316. Walter L. Hixson, *Diplomatic History* 17, no. 3 (Summer 1993): 477-481.

5785. Brinkley, Douglas. *Dean Acheson: The Cold War Years, 1953-71*. New Haven, CT: Yale University Press, c1992. xiv, 429 pp. [Includes U.S.-Soviet relations in the 1950s and 1960s, the Berlin crises of 1958-1962, the Cuban Missile Crisis, and NATO.] REV: George Ball, *New York Review of Books* 39, no. 21 (December 17, 1992): 11-15. Gregory F. Treverton, *Foreign Affairs* 71, no. 5 (Winter 1992-1993): 204. H.W. Brands, *American Historical Review* 98, no. 5 (December 1993): 1705. Jacob Heilbrunn, *Perspectives on Political Science* 22, no. 4 (Fall 1993): 165-166. Walter LaFeber, *Political Science Quarterly* 108, no. 2 (Summer 1993): 333-334. J. C. Livingston, *Historian* 56, no. 1 (Autumn 1993): 155-156. Jeffrey Salmon, *Commentary* 95, no. 2 (February 1993): 64-66.

5786. Brugioni, Dino A. *Eyeball to Eyeball: The Inside Story of the Cuban Missile Crisis*. Edited by Robert F. McCort. 1st ed. New York: Random House, c1991. xvi, 622 pp. REV: Graham T. Allison, *New York Times Book Review* (February 9, 1992): 12. George W. Ball, *New York Review of Books* 39, no. 4 (February 13, 1992): 16-20. Jules R. Benjamin, *Historian* 55, no. 1 (Autumn 1992): 157-158. James N. Giglio, *Journal of American History* 79, no. 3 (December 1992): 1246-1248. Walter Pforzheimer, *Strategic Review* 20, no. 2 (Spring 1992): 56-59. Russell W. Ramsey, *Army* 42, no. 11 (November 1992): 60-61. William F. Furr, *Airpower Journal* 7, no. 1 (Spring 1993): 75-76.

5787. Clarke, Joseph Calvitt III. *Russia and Italy against Hitler: The Bolshevik-Fascist Rapprochement of the 1930s*. Foreword by Clifford Foust. Contributions to the Study of World History, no. 21. New York: Greenwood Press, 1991. 218 pp. REV: David MacKenzie, *Historian* 54, no. 1 (Autumn 1991): 115-116. Alan Cassels, *International History Review* 14, no. 1 (February 1992): 175-177. Anna M. Cienciala, *Soviet and Post-Soviet Review* 19, nos. 1-3 (1992): 310-312. Timothy E. O'Connor, *American Historical Review* 97, no. 1 (February 1992): 187. William R. Rock, *History: Reviews of New Books* 20, no. 3 (Spring 1992): 116. Jonathan Haslam, *Russian History = Histoire russe* 20, nos. 1-4 (1993): 390-391. T.R. Ravindranathan, *Russian Review* 52, no. 1 (January 1993): 118-119. Sergio Romano, *Journal of Modern History* 65, no. 2 (June 1993): 382-384.

5788. Corum, James S. *The Roots of Blitzkrieg: Hans von Seeckt and the German Military Reform*. Modern War Studies. Lawrence, KS: University Press of Kansas,

1992. xvii, 274 pp. [Includes discussion of Soviet-German cooperation in the 1920s.] REV: Larry H. Addington, *Journal of Military History* 57, no. 3 (July 1993): 561-562. Martin Blumenson, *Army* 43, no. 2 (February 1993): 61. Robert Citino, *American Historical Review* 98, no. 5 (December 1993): 1635. Eliot A. Cohen, *Foreign Affairs* 72, no. 5 (November-December 1993): 162-163. Peter J. Schifferle, *Military Review* 73, no. 11 (November 1993): 80.

5789. Debo, Richard K. *Survival and Consolidation: The Foreign Policy of Soviet Russia, 1918-1921.* Montreal, Quebec; Buffalo: McGill-Queen's University Press, c1992. xiii, 502 pp. REV: N.G.O. Pereira, *Canadian Slavonic Papers* 34, no. 4 (December 1992): 499-500. Stephen Blank, *American Historical Review* 98, no. 3 (June 1993): 915. David W. McFadden, *International History Review* 15, no. 4 (November 1993): 822. Keith Neilson, *Canadian Journal of History = Annales canadienne d'histoire* 28, no. 2 (August 1993): 364-366. Timothy E. O'Connor, *Russian History = Histoire russe* 20, nos. 1-4 (1993): 348-349.

5790. Dima, Nicholas. *From Moldavia to Moldova: The Soviet-Romanian Territorial Dispute.* [2nd ed.]. East European Monographs, no. 309. Boulder, CO: East European Monographs; New York: Distributed by Columbia University Press, 1991. v, 194 pp. [Revised edition of *Bessarabia and Bukovina* (1982).] REV: Richard Frucht, *Canadian Review of Studies in Nationalism = Revue Canadienne des Etudes sur le Nationalisme* 20, nos. 1-2 (1993): 145-147. Irina Livezeanu, *Slavic Review* 52, no. 3 (Fall 1993): 614-615.

5791. Fawcett, Louise L'Estrange. *Iran and the Cold War: The Azerbaijan Crisis of 1946.* Cambridge Middle East Library, 26. Cambridge; New York: Cambridge University Press, 1992. xii, 227 pp. REV: Fred H. Lawson, *International History Review* 14, no. 4 (November 1992): 840-842. Cosroe Chaqueri, *Middle East Studies Association Bulletin* 27, no. 1 (July 1993): 52. William B. Quandt, *Foreign Affairs* 72, no. 4 (September-October 1993): 173.

5792. Feste, Karen A. *Expanding the Frontiers: Superpower Intervention in the Cold War.* New York: Praeger, 1992. 211 pp. REV: Andrew J. Pierre, *Foreign Affairs* 71, no. 4 (Fall 1992): 198. *Orbis* 37, no. 1 (Winter 1993).

5793. Frazier, Robert. *Anglo-American Relations with Greece: The Coming of the Cold War, 1942-47.* New York: St. Martin's Press, 1991. 233 pp. REV: Lawrence S. Wittner, *Journal of American History* 79, no. 2 (September 1992): 722. Howard Jones, *American Historical Review* 98, no. 2 (April 1993): 475. Bruce R. Kuniholm, *International History Review* 15, no. 1 (February 1993): 200.

5794. Gormly, James L. *From Potsdam to the Cold War: Big Three Diplomacy, 1945-1947.* Wilmington, DE: SR Books, 1990. xviii, 242 pp. REV: Keith Eubank, *Journal of American History* 78, no. 3 (December 1991): 1140-1141. T. Michael Ruddy, *Historian* 54, no. 1 (Autumn 1991): 122-123. Fraser Harbutt, *Pacific Historical Review* 61, no. 4 (November

1992): 583-584. Marc Gallicchio, *Diplomatic History* 17, no. 3 (Summer 1993): 483-488.

5795. Haslam, Jonathan. *The Soviet Union and the Threat from the East, 1933-41: Moscow, Tokyo, and the Prelude to the Pacific War.* Pitt Series in Russian and East European Studies, no. 16. Pittsburgh, PA: University of Pittsburgh Press, c1992. 208 pp. REV: Paul Dukes, *International History Review* 15, no. 3 (August 1993): 608. Dale R. Herspring, *Russian History = Histoire russe* 20, nos. 1-4 (1993): 388-390.

5796. Hiden, John, and Thomas Lane, eds. *The Baltic and the Outbreak of the Second World War.* Contributions by John Hiden, Mieczyslaw Nurek, Rolf Ahmann, Anita Prazmowska, Patrick Salmon, Bogdan Koszel, Thomas Lane, and Alfonsas Eidintas. Cambridge; New York: Cambridge University Press, 1992. xiii, 177 pp. [Contents: John Hiden, "Introduction: Baltic security problems between the two World Wars"; Mieczyslaw Nurek, "Great Britain and the Baltic in the last months of peace, March-August 1939"; Rolf Ahmann, "Nazi German policy towards the Baltic states on the eve of the Second World War"; Anita Prazmowska, "The role of Danzig in Polish-German relations on the eve of the Second World War"; Patrick Salmon, "Great Britain, the Soviet Union and Finland at the beginning of the Second World War"; Bogdan Koszel, "The attitude of the Scandinavian countries to Nazi Germany's war preparations and its aggression on Poland"; Thomas Lane, "The Soviet occupation of Poland through British eyes"; Alfonsas Eidintas, "The meeting of the Lithuanian Cabinet, 15 June 1940".] REV: Anna M. Cienciala, *Journal of Military History* 57, no. 2 (April 1993): 342-343. David M. Crowe, *Slavic Review* 52, no. 1 (Spring 1993): 138-139. Ruth Henig, *European History Quarterly* no. 4 (October 1993): 629-632. Anders Henriksson, *Soviet and Post-Soviet Review* 20, no. 1 (1993): 77. Loyd E. Lee, *Historian* 55, no. 4 (Summer 1993): 747-748. Scott Hughes Myerly, *Russian History = Histoire russe* 20, nos. 1-4 (1993): 395-397.

5797. Hilton, Stanley E. *Brazil and the Soviet Challenge, 1917-1947.* Austin, TX: University of Texas Press, c1991. 287 pp. REV: William Richardson, *American Historical Review* 97, no. 5 (December 1992): 1634-1635. John W. F. Dulles, *Americas* 49, no. 3 (January 1993): 417-418.

5798. Hoopes, Townsend, and Douglas Brinkley. *Driven Patriot: The Life and Times of James Forrestal.* New York: Knopf, 1992. 597 pp. REV: David Callahan, *New York Times Book Review* (May 3, 1992): 11. Jacob Heilbrunn, *New Republic* 207, no. 15 (October 5, 1992): 38-43. William G. Hyland, *Foreign Affairs* 71, no. 4 (Fall 1992): 194-197. Ronald Steel, *New York Review of Books* 39, no. 14 (August 13, 1992): 33-36. Robert Strausz-Hupé, *Orbis* 36, no. 4 (Fall 1992): 622. Robert Cuff, *Canadian Journal of History = Annales canadienne d'histoire* 28, no. 1 (April 1993): 142. Jeffrey M. Dorwart, *American Historical Review* 98, no. 3 (June 1993): 972. Wilson D. Miscamble, *Journal of American History* 80, no. 1 (June 1993): 335.

5799. Inglis, Fred. *The Cruel Peace: Everyday Life and the Cold War*. New York: Basic Books, c1991. 492 pp. REV: Adam Garfinkle, *Orbis* 36, no. 2 (Spring 1992): 288. Elaine Tyler May, *Reviews in American History* 20, no. 3 (September 1992): 416-420. Stephen J. Whitfield, *Journal of American History* 79, no. 2 (September 1992): 730. Lester R. Kurtz, *Contemporary Sociology* 22, no. 3 (May 1993): 439-440.

5800. International Conference on International Relations (2nd: 1989: American University of Paris). *The Opening of the Second World War: Proceedings of the Second International Conference on International Relations, Held at the American University of Paris, September 26-30, 1989.* Edited by David Wingeate Pike. Includes contributions by Doron Kiesel, George Urbaniak, Gerhard Krebs, Elizabeth de Reau, Keith Sword, Alexander Nekrich, Yutaka Akino, and Sumio Yatano. American University Studies. Series IX, History, vol. 105. New York: P. Lang, 1991. xl, 385 pp. [Includes: essay on the German Polish campaign; essay by George Urbaniak on the Soviet occupation of eastern Poland in 1939; Gerhard Kreb on Polish-Japanese relations; Alexander Nekrich on the Nazi-Soviet pacts of 1939; Yataka Akino and Sumio Yatano on Soviet-Japanese relations; and essay on the Winter War.] REV: Gerhard L. Weinberg, *Journal of Military History* 57, no. 2 (April 1993): 341.

5801. Jelavich, Barbara. *Russia's Balkan Entanglements, 1806-1914*. Cambridge; New York, NY: Cambridge University Press, 1991. xi, 291 pp. REV: Nick Ceh and Edward Thaden, *Canadian Review of Studies in Nationalism = Revue Canadienne des Etudes sur le Nationalisme* 20, nos. 1-2 (1993): 147-148. Richard C. Hall, *Russian Review* 52, no. 2 (April 1993): 273-274. George F. Jewsbury, *Russian History = Histoire russe* 20, nos. 1-4 (1993): 286-287. T.A. Meininger, *American Historical Review* 98, no. 2 (April 1993): 534. Timothy E. O'Connor, *Historian* 55, no. 2 (Winter 1993): 350. Ann Pottinger Saab, *International History Review* 15, no. 2 (May 1993): 357.

5802. Jones, Howard. *"A New Kind of War": America's Global Strategy and the Truman Doctrine in Greece*. New York: Oxford University Press, 1989. 327 pp. REV: Lawrence S. Wittner, *American Historical Review* 95, no. 4 (October 1990): 1314-1315. Wilson D. Miscamble, *Historian* 53, no. 3 (Spring 1991): 593-594. Bruce R. Kuniholm, *International History Review* 15, no. 1 (February 1993): 204.

5803. Jordan, Nicole. *The Popular Front & Central Europe: The Dilemmas of French Impotence, 1918-1945*. Cambridge; New York: Cambridge University Press, 1992. xvi, 348 pp. REV: John C. Cairns, *Journal of Military History* 57, no. 1 (January 1993): 163-165.

5804. Kaiser, Philip M. *Journeying Far and Wide: A Political and Diplomatic Memoir*. New York: Charles Scribner's Sons; Toronto: Maxwell Macmillan Canada; New York: Maxwell Macmillan International, c1992. xiv, 352 pp. [Contents: The Brooklyn Years; The Wisconsin Years; Oxford Before World War II: An American Perspective; The Truman Years: Labor and International Affairs; Albany After Washington: Averell Harriman, Governor of New York; The Kennedy Years: Ambassador in Africa; The United Kingdom in the 1960s: American Minister; Carter's Ambassador to Communist-Controlled Hungary; Austria's Postwar Democracy: Ambassador to Vienna; Reflections on the End of the Century.] REV: Douglas Brinkley, *Book World* 23, no. 3 (January 17, 1993): 9.

5805. Kettle, Michael. *Russia and the Allies 1917-1920*. London; New York: Routledge & Kegan Paul, 1988. 401 pp. REV: Peter Kenez, *American Historical Review* 95, no. 3 (June 1990): 785-786. Richard H. Ullman, *Slavic Review* 49, no. 2 (Summer 1990): 288. Timothy E. O'Connor, *Canadian-American Slavic Studies* 25, nos. 1-4 (1991): 310-312. James W. Hulse, *Historian* 54, no. 2 (Winter 1992): 347-348. John W. Long, *Russian History = Histoire russe* 20, nos. 1-4 (1993): 345-346.

5806. Kimball, Warren F. *The Juggler: Franklin Roosevelt as Wartime Statesman*. Princeton, NJ: Princeton University Press, c1991. xii, 304 pp. REV: D. K. Adams, *International History Review* 15, no. 1 (February 1993): 201.

5807. Leffler, Melvyn P. *A Preponderance of Power: National Security, the Truman Administration, and the Cold War*. Stanford Nuclear Age Series. Stanford, CA: Stanford University Press, c1992. xvii, 689 pp. REV: Carolyn Eisenberg, *Nation* 254, no. 20 (May 25, 1992): 700-704. John Lewis Gaddis, *Atlantic* 269, no. 2 (February 1992): 100-103. Lawrence S. Kaplan, *Reviews in American History* 20, no. 3 (September 1992): 411-415. Stephen J. Randall, *International Journal* 48, no. 1 (Winter 1992-1993): 176-178. Albert Resis, *Journal of Political and Military Sociology* 20, no. 1 (Summer 1992): 175-177. Michael S. Sherry, *Journal of American History* 79, no. 2 (September 1992): 725-726. Gaddis Smith, *Foreign Affairs* 71, no. 2 (Spring 1992): 198. Ronald Steel, *New York Review of Books* 39, no. 14 (August 13, 1992): 33-36. George F. Botjer, *History: Reviews of New Books* 21, no. 2 (Winter 1993): 64. H.W. Brands, *American Historical Review* 98, no. 2 (April 1993): 604. Lynn Eden, *International Security* 18, no. 1 (Summer 1993): 174-207. R.C. Grogin, *Canadian Journal of History = Annales canadienne d'histoire* 28, no. 1 (April 1993): 144-146. Benjamin T. Harrison, *Russian History = Histoire russe* 20, nos. 1-4 (1993): 402. Johnston, *Perspectives on Political Science* 22, no. 3 (Summer 1993): 124. Manfred Jonas, *Historian* 55, no. 4 (Summer 1993): 790. Stephen J. Lofgren, *Military Review* 73, no. 4 (April 1993): 83-84. Wilson D. Miscamble, *Review of Politics* 55, no. 2 (Spring 1993): 363-367. William Safran, *Annals of the American Academy of Political and Social Science* no. 526 (March 1993): 197.

5808. MacLean, Elizabeth Kimball. *Joseph E. Davies: Envoy to the Soviets*. New York: Praeger, 1992. 247 pp. REV: James K. Libbey, *Russian History = Histoire russe* 20, nos. 1-4 (1993): 387-388.

5809. McCalla, Robert B. *Uncertain Perceptions: U.S. Cold War Crisis Decision-Making*. Ann Arbor, MI: University of Michigan Press, c1992. 226 pp. [U.S.-Soviet relations.] REV: Eileen M. Crumm, *Journal of Politics* 55, no. 4 (November 1993): 1217. Robert Jervis, *Political Science Quarterly* 108, no. 1 (Spring 1993): 160-161.

5810. McCullough, David. *Truman*. New York: Simon & Schuster, 1992. 1117 pp. [Includes U.S.-Soviet relations during and immediately after World War II, the Potsdam conference of July 1945, the atomic bomb, the origins of the Cold War, the Truman Doctrine and the Marshall Plan, the Berlin airlift of 1948-1949, and the Korean War.] REV: Alan Brinkley, *New York Times Book Review* (June 21, 1992): 1ff. Alonzo L. Hamby, *World & I* 7, no. 8 (August 1992): 338-349. Gregory F. Treverton, *Foreign Affairs* 71, no. 5 (Winter 1992-1993): 202. C. Vann Woodward, *New York Review of Books* 39, no. 13 (July 16, 1992): 26-30. Donald R. McCoy, *American Historical Review* 98, no. 3 (June 1993): 973. Franklin D. Mitchell, *Journal of American History* 80, no. 1 (June 1993): 334.

5811. Miscamble, Wilson D. *George F. Kennan and the Making of American Foreign Policy, 1947-1950*. Princeton Studies in International History and Politics. Princeton, NJ: Princeton University Press, c1992. xvii, 419 pp. [Focus on Kennan's role as head of the U.S. State Department's Policy Planning Staff in the late 1940s.] REV: William G. Hyland, *Foreign Affairs* 71, no. 4 (Fall 1992): 197. *Publishers Weekly* 239, no. 15 (March 23, 1992): 54-55. H.W. Brands, *Journal of American History* 80, no. 1 (June 1993): 336. Walter L. Hixson, *Pacific Historical Review* 62, no. 4 (November 1993): 521. Melvyn P. Leffler, *International History Review* 15, no. 2 (May 1993): 397. Anders Stephanson, *Annals of the American Academy of Political and Social Science*, no. 529 (September 1993): 201. Mark A. Stoler, *American Historical Review* 98, no. 3 (June 1993): 975.

5812. Morison, John, ed. *Eastern Europe and the West: Selected Papers from the Fourth World Congress for Soviet and East European Studies, Harrogate, 1990*. New York: St. Martin's Press, 1992. xix, 271 pp. REV: Kay Lundgreen-Nielsen, *International History Review* 15, no. 3 (August 1993): 604.

5813. Nadeau, Remi. *Stalin, Churchill, and Roosevelt Divide Europe*. New York: Praeger, 1990. xii, 259 pp. REV: Honore Catudal, *Historian* 54, no. 1 (Autumn 1991): 134. Robert C. Hilderbrand, *Journal of American History* 78, no. 4 (March 1992): 1506-1507. Betty Miller Unterberger, *Political Science Quarterly* 107, no. 1 (Spring 1992): 164-165. A. Reza Vahabzadeh, *Annals of the American Academy of Political and Social Science*, no. 520 (March 1992): 195-196. D. K. Adams, *International History Review* 15, no. 1 (February 1993): 201. Roger Hamburg, *Perspectives on Political Science* 22, no. 3 (Summer 1993): 138-139.

5814. Nathan, James A., ed. *The Cuban Missile Crisis Revisited*. New York: St. Martin's Press, 1992. xii, 302 pp. REV: Stephen E. Ambrose, *Foreign Affairs* 72, no. 3 (Summer 1993): 201. Gregory F. Treverton, *Foreign Affairs* 72, no. 2 (Spring 1993): 174-175.

5815. Neilson, Keith, and B. J. C. McKercher, eds. *Go Spy the Land: Military Intelligence in History*. Includes contributions by Christopher Andrew and John Ferris.

Westport, CT: Praeger, 1992. xiv, 205 pp. [Partial contents: Christopher Andrew, "The Nature of Military Intelligence," pp. 1-16; John Ferris, "Lord Salisbury, Secret Intelligence, and British Policy toward Russia and Central Asia, 1874-1878," pp. 115-152.] REV: James W. McKenney, *Historian* 56, no. 1 (Autumn 1993): 146-147.

5816. Petkov, Petro M. *The United States and Bulgaria in World War I*. East European Monographs, no. 306. Boulder, CO: East European Monographs, 1991. 252 pp. REV: Betty Miller Unterberger, *International History Review* 15, no. 2 (May 1993): 379.

5817. Romsics, Ignác, ed. *Wartime American Plans for a New Hungary: Documents from the U.S. Department of State, 1942-1944*. Atlantic Studies on Society in Change, no. 77. East European Monographs, no. 354. War and Society in East Central Europe, v. 30. Boulder, CO: Social Science Monographs; Highland Lakes, NJ: Atlantic Research and Publications; New York, NY: Distributed by Columbia University Press, 1992. xvii, 328 pp. REV: N. F. Dreisziger, *Hungarian Studies Review* 20, nos. 1-2 (Spring-Fall 1993): 122-125.

5818. Saiu, Liliana. *The Great Powers and Rumania, 1944-1946: A Study of the Early Cold War Era*. East European Monographs, no. 335. Boulder, CO: East European Monographs; New York: Distributed by Columbia University Press, 1992. xiii, 290 pp. REV: Frederick Kellogg, *Slavic Review* 52, no. 3 (Fall 1993): 612-613. Paul E. Michelson, *American Historical Review* 98, no. 5 (December 1993): 1577. William Urban, *Journal of Baltic Studies* 24, no. 3 (Fall 1993): 315.

5819. Salzman, Neil V. *Reform and Revolution: The Life and Times of Raymond Robins*. Kent, OH: Kent State University Press, c1991. xiv, 472 pp. [Includes Russian Revolution of 1917.] REV: Bruce S. Greenawalt, *International History Review* 14, no. 3 (August 1992): 590-592. Robert James Maddox, *Journal of American History* 79, no. 1 (June 1992): 706. Timothy E. O'Connor, *Soviet and Post-Soviet Review* 19, nos. 1-3 (1992): 294-295. Bertrand M. Patenaude, *Slavic Review* 51, no. 4 (Winter 1992): 817-818. John A. White, *Russian History = Histoire russe* 20, nos. 1-4 (1993): 340-341.

5820. Saul, Norman E. *Distant Friends: The United States and Russia, 1763-1867*. Lawrence, KS: University Press of Kansas, c1991. xvi, 448 pp. REV: Helen S. Hundley, *Historian* 54, no. 2 (Winter 1992): 388. Ronald J. Jensen, *American Historical Review* 97, no. 2 (April 1992): 638-639. Irby C. Nichols, Jr., *Pacific Historical Review* 61, no. 3 (August 1992): 443-444. Frederick F. Travis, *Journal of American History* 79, no. 1 (June 1992): 243. William Earl Weeks, *Journal of the Early Republic* 12, no. 2 (Summer 1992): 250-251. Ivan Avakumovic, *Russian History = Histoire russe* 20, nos. 1-4 (1993): 283-284. Joseph A. Fry, *International History Review* 15, no. 2 (May 1993): 350. Betty Miller Unterberger, *Russian Review* 52, no. 1 (January 1993): 127-128.

5821. Sharp, Alan. *The Versailles Settlement: Peacemaking in Paris, 1919*. The Making of the 20th

Century, New York: St. Martin's Press, 1991. xi, 243 pp. [Includes chapter on Eastern Europe.] REV: Hines H. Hall, *History: Reviews of New Books* 21, no. 3 (Spring 1993): 124. R. D. Zehnder, *Austrian History Yearbook* 24 (1993): 271-272.

5822. Thompson, Robert Smith. *The Missiles of October: The Declassified Story of John F. Kennedy and the Cuban Missile Crisis.* New York: Simon & Schuster, c1992. 395 pp. REV: Gregory F. Treverton, *Foreign Affairs* 71, no. 5 (Winter 1992-1993): 205. James N. Giglio, *American Historical Review* 98, no. 4 (October 1993): 1351. *Antioch Review* 51, no. 1 (Winter 1993): 154.

5823. United States. Central Intelligence Agency. *CIA Documents on the Cuban Missile Crisis, 1962.* Edited by Mary S. McAuliffe. Washington, DC: History Staff, Central Intelligence Agency, [1992]. xxii, 376 pp. REV: Gregory F. Treverton, *Foreign Affairs* 72, no. 2 (Spring 1993): 174-175.

5824. Van Oudenaren, John. *Détente in Europe: The Soviet Union and the West since 1953.* Durham, NC: Duke University Press, 1991. xi, 490 pp. REV: Herbert J. Ellison, *Slavic Review* 51, no. 4 (Winter 1992): 868-869. Raymond L. Garthoff, *Political Science Quarterly* 107, no. 3 (Fall 1992): 538. Norma Noonan, *History: Reviews of New Books* 21, no. 1 (Fall 1992): 44. Allen Lynch, *Russian History = Histoire russe* 20, nos. 1-4 (1993): 405-406. Carl H. McMillan, *Canadian Slavonic Papers* 35, nos. 3-4 (September-December 1993): 399-400.

5825. Vitas, Robert A. *The United States and Lithuania: The Stimson Doctrine of Nonrecognition.* New York: Praeger, 1990. 175 pp. REV: Cal Clark, *Perspectives on Political Science* 21, no. 2 (Spring 1992): 109. David M. Crowe, *Russian Review* 51, no. 1 (January 1992): 138-139. Alfred Erich Senn, *Nationalities Papers* 21, no. 2 (Fall 1993): 212-213.

East-West Relations

General

5826. Ekins, Paul. *A New World Order: Grassroots Movements for Global Change.* New York: Routledge, 1992. 248 pp. REV: Wendell Gordon, *Journal of Economic Issues* 27, no. 3 (September 1993): 974.

5827. Gaddis, John Lewis. *The United States and the End of the Cold War: Implications, Reconsiderations, Provocations.* New York: Oxford University Press, 1992. 301 pp. REV: William G. Hyland, *Foreign Affairs* 71, no. 4 (Fall 1992): 197. Gaddis Smith, *Foreign Affairs* 71, no. 2 (Spring 1992): 198-199. Alan Tonelson, *New York Times Book Review* (May 17, 1992): 15-16. Norman A. Graebner, *American Historical Review* 98, no. 3 (June 1993): 975. Robert James Maddox, *History: Reviews of New Books* 21, no. 3 (Spring 1993): 116.

5828. Layard, Richard. *East-West Migration: The Alternatives.* Cambridge, MA: MIT Press, c1992. ix, 94 pp. REV: William Diebold, Jr., *Foreign Affairs* 72, no. 2 (Spring 1993): 170.

5829. Lynch, Allen. *The Cold War Is Over—Again.* Boulder, CO: Westview Press, 1992. xv, 208 pp. REV: Gregory F. Treverton, *Foreign Affairs* 71, no. 5 (Winter 1992-1993): 204. Matthew W. Maguire, *Current History* 92, no. 573 (April 1993): 186-187. Matthew Rendall, *Journal of International Affairs* 46, no. 2 (Winter 1993): 557-562.

5830. Soros, George. *Underwriting Democracy.* New York: Free Press, c1991. 258 pp. REV: Vladimir Tismaneanu, *Orbis* 36, no. 3 (Summer 1992): 474-475. David P. Forsythe, *History: Reviews of New Books* 21, no. 2 (Winter 1993): 90-91.

5831. Treverton, Gregory F. *America, Germany, and the Future of Europe.* Princeton, NJ: Princeton University Press, c1992. xii, 240 pp. REV: Wolfgang Dreschsler, *Perspectives on Political Science* 22, no. 3 (Summer 1993): 139-140.

5832. Verheyen, Dirk. *The German Question: A Cultural, Historical, and Geopolitical Exploration.* Boulder, CO: Westview Press, 1991. 228 pp. REV: Richard M. Hunt, *Annals of the American Academy of Political and Social Science* no. 528 (July 1993): 186.

5833. Zoppo, Ciro Elliott, ed. *Nordic Security at the Turn of the Twentieth-First Century.* Foreword by Rodney Kennedy-Minott. Contributions by Rodney Kennedy-Minott, Ciro Elliott Zoppo, Tomas H. Ries, Rene Nyberg, Krister Wahlback, Kari Mottola, Pauli O. Jarvenpaa, Crister S. Garrett, Ingemar N. Dorfer, Richard A. Bitzinger, Burkhard Auffermann, and Robert C. Hall. Contributions in Military Studies, no. 117. Westport, CT: Greenwood Press, 1992. xix, 247 pp. [Prepared under the auspices of the Center for International and Strategic Affairs, University of California, Los Angeles. Contents: Rodney Kennedy-Minott, "Foreword" — Pt. I. The Policy Agenda. Ciro Elliott Zoppo, "The Issues of Nordic Security: The Dynamics of East-West Politics, Emerging Technologies, and Definitions of National Defense"; Tomas H. Ries, "Developments in East-West Security and Northern Europe" — Pt. II. The Scandinavian Context of Nordic Security. Rene Nyberg and Krister Wahlback, "Security and Neutrality in the North of Europe and Changing East-West Relations"; Kari Mottola, "Finland's Foreign Policy and Defense in a Changing East-West Security Environment"; Pauli O. Jarvenpaa, "Technology and Military Doctrine in the Future of Finnish Defense"; Crister S. Garrett, "Sweden and the Nordic Security Equation"; Ingemar N. Dorfer, "Technology and Military Doctrine in the Future of Swedish Defense"; Richard A. Bitzinger, "The Politics of Defense in NATO's Northern Flank: Denmark, Norway, and Iceland" — Pt. III. The Soviet and American Superpowers and Nordic Security. Burkhard Auffermann, "New Thinking in Soviet Foreign Policy and Nordic Security; Robert C. Hall, "Soviet Deployments, Potentials in Soviet Military Doctrine, and Nordic Security"; Rodney Kennedy-Minott, "The Forward Maritime Strategy and Nordic Security" — Pt. IV. Policy Challenges. Ciro Elliott Zoppo, "Problems and Prospects for Nordic Security by the Year 2000".] REV: John W. Messer, *Military Review* 73, no. 6 (June 1993): 85.

Arms Control and Disarmament

5834. Adler, Emanuel, ed. *The International Practice of Arms Control*. Contributions by Emanuel Adler, Thomas C. Schelling, Paul Doty, Robert R. Bowie, Lawrence Freedman, Johan Jorgen Holst, Catherine M. Kelleher, A. A. Kokoshin, Joseph S. Nye, Jr., Robert Jervis, Steve Weber, Marc Trachtenberg, Barry R. Posen, Ashton B. Carter, and Jennifer E. Sims. Baltimore, MD: Johns Hopkins University Press, 1992. xiv, 287 pp. [Contents: Emanuel Adler, "Arms Control, Disarmament, and National Security: A Thirty Year Retrospective and a New Set of Anticipations"; Thomas C. Schelling, "The Thirtieth Year"; Paul Doty, "Arms Control: 1960, 1990, 2020"; Robert R. Bowie, "Arms Control in the 1990s"; Lawrence Freedman, "The End of Formal Arms Control"; Johan Jorgen Holst, "Arms Control in the Nineties: A European Perspective"; Catherine M. Kelleher, "Arms Control in a Revolutionary Future: Europe"; A.A. Kokoshin, "Arms Control: A View from Moscow"; Joseph S. Nye, Jr., "Arms Control and International Politics"; Robert Jervis, "Arms Control, Stability, and Causes of War"; Steve Weber, "Cooperation and Interdependence"; Marc Trachtenberg, "The Past and Future of Arms Control"; Barry R. Posen, "Crisis Stability and Conventional Arms Control"; Ashton B. Carter, "Emerging Themes in Nuclear Arms Control"; Jennifer E. Sims, "The American Approach to Nuclear Arms Control: A Retrospective".] REV: Tariq Rauf, *International Journal* 48, no. 3 (Summer 1993): 567-568.

5835. Blechman, Barry M. et al. *Naval Arms Control: A Strategic Assessement*. New York: St. Martins Press in association with the Henry L. Stimson Center, 1991. xii, 268 pp. REV: Albert M. Bottoms, *Naval War College Review* 46, no. 4 (Autumn 1993): 148-150.

5836. Gray, Colin S. *House of Cards: Why Arms Control Must Fail*. Cornell Studies in Security Affairs, Ithaca, NY: Cornell University Press, 1992. xii, 242 pp. REV: Gideon Rose, *National Interest*, no. 30 (Winter 1992-1993): 93-100. Bernard L. McNamee, *Emory International Law Review* 7, no. 1 (Spring 1993): 249-257.

5837. Kartchner, Kerry M. *Negotiating START: Strategic Arms Reduction Talks and the Quest for Strategic Stability*. With a foreword by Edward L. Rowny. New Brunswick, NJ: Transaction, c1992. 329 pp. REV: Brian Murray, *Slavic Review* 52, no. 1 (Spring 1993): 155-156.

5838. Mandelbaum, Michael, ed. *The Other Side of the Table: The Soviet Approach to Arms Control*. Contributions by Michael Mandelbaum, Rebecca Strode, Coit D. Blacker, Andrew C. Goldberg, and Cynthia Roberts. New York: Council on Foreign Relations Press, c1990. vi, 209 pp. REV: Gregory F. Treverton, *Foreign Affairs* 69, no. 2 (Spring 1990): 169. Joyce P. Kaufman, *Perspectives on Political Science* 20, no. 3 (Summer 1991): 182-183. William H. Kincade, *Russian Review* 52, no. 1 (January 1993): 143.

5839. Rowny, Edward L. *It Takes One to Tango*. Washington, DC: Brassey's, c1992. xiv, 273 pp. REV: James J. Dunphy, *Military Review* 73, no. 6 (June 1993): 86. Emily O. Goldman, *Strategic Review* 21, no. 2 (Spring 1993): 68-70.

Andrew J. Pierre, *Foreign Affairs* 72, no. 2 (Spring 1993): 164.

5840. Tower, John G., James Brown, and William K. Cheek, eds. *Verification: The Key to Arms Control in the 1990s*. Washington, DC: Brassey's, c1992. 243 pp. REV: Gregory F. Treverton, *Foreign Affairs* 71, no. 3 (Summer 1992): 171. Albert M. Bottoms, *Naval War College Review* 46, no. 4 (Autumn 1993): 148-150.

5841. Wittner, Lawrence S. *The Struggle Against the Bomb*. Stanford, CA: Stanford University Press, 1993-. 3 vols. [projected]. REV: Joseph Levitt, *International Journal* 49, no. 1 (Winter 1993-1994): 165-167.

International Communist Party Relations

5842. Bugajski, Janusz. *Fourth World Conflicts: Communism and Rural Societies*. Boulder, CO: Westview Press, 1991. xi, 308 pp. REV: Krishna K. Tummala, *Perspectives on Political Science* 22, no. 3 (Summer 1993): 1401.

5843. Diggins, John Patrick. *The Rise and Fall of the American Left*. New York: W.W. Norton, c1992. 432 pp. [Expanded version of The American Left in the Twentieth Century. Contents: The Left as a theoretical problem — The new intellectuals — Strangers in the land : the proletariat and Marxism — The lyrical left — The Old Left — The New Left — The academic left — Poetry of the past : the rewriting of American history — Power, freedom, and the failure of theory.] REV: Nick Salvatore, *American Historical Review* 98, no. 1 (February 1993): 264-265.

5844. Katz, Mark N., ed. *The USSR and Marxist Revolutions in the Third World*. Woodrow Wilson Center Series. Washington, DC: Woodrow Wilson International Center for Scholars; NY: Cambridge University Press, 1990. 153 pp. REV: Robert V. Legvold, *Foreign Affairs* 70, no. 5 (Winter 1991-92): 200. Roger Hamburg, *Slavic Review* 51, no. 3 (Fall 1992): 574-575. Daniel R. Kempton, *Soviet and Post-Soviet Review* 19, nos. 1-3 (1992): 309-310. Roger E. Kanet, *International History Review* 15, no. 1 (February 1993): 213.

5845. Kheng, Cheah Boon, ed. *From PKI to the Comintern, 1924-1941: The Apprenticeship of the Malayan Communist Party: Selected Documents and Discussion*. Southeast Asia Program Series, no. 8. Ithaca, NY: Southeast Asia Program, Cornell University, 1992. 143 pp. REV: Anthony Short, *Pacific Affairs* 66, no. 1 (Spring 1993): 131.

5846. Klehr, Harvey, and John Earl Haynes. *The American Communist Movement: Storming Heaven Itself*. Social Movements Past and Present. New York: Twayne; Toronto: Maxwell Macmillan Canada; New York: Maxwell Macmillan International, c1992. xiii, 210 pp. REV: Thomas Armstrong, *Historian* 55, no. 2 (Winter 1993): 390. Annette T. Rubinstein, *Science & Society* 57, no. 4 (Winter 1993-1994): 468. Robert W. Sellen, *History: Reviews of New Books* 21, no. 3 (Spring 1993): 116.

5847. Ottanelli, Fraser M. *The Communist Party of the United States: From the Depression to World War II*.

New Brunswick, NJ: Rutgers University Press, c1991. xii, 307 pp. REV: Maurice Isserman, *Reviews in American History* 20, no. 4 (December 1992): 536-542. Robin D.G. Kelley, *American Historical Review* 97, no. 1 (February 1992): 305. Harvey Klehr, *Journal of American History* 78, no. 4 (March 1992): 1497-1498. Norman Penner, *Canadian Historical Review* 74, no. 1 (March 1993): 135-137.

5848. Scalapino, Robert A. *The Last Leninists: The Uncertain Future of Asia's Communist States*. Foreword by Stephen Sestanovich. Significant Issues Series. Creating the Post-Communist Order, v. 14, no. 3. Washington, DC: Center for Strategic and International Studies, c1992. xvii, 104 pp. REV: Nicholas Eberstadt, *Annals of the American Academy of Political and Social Science*, no. 529 (September 1993): 186-187. *Orbis* 37, no. 1 (Winter 1993).

5849. Urban, Joan Barth, ed. *Moscow and the Global Left in the Gorbachev Era*. Ithaca, NY: Cornell University Press, 1992. xii, 204 pp. [Contains papers from a panel at the World Congress for Soviet and East European Studies (4th: 1990: Harrogate, England).] REV: Gaye Christoffersen, *Journal of Asian Studies* 51, no. 4 (November 1992): 875-877. Robert Legvold, *Foreign Affairs* 71, no. 4 (Fall 1992): 212. Kimberly Marten Zisk, *American Political Science Review* 87, no. 1 (March 1993): 245-246.

U.S.S.R.

General

5850. Amundsen, Kirsten. *Soviet Strategic Interests in the North*. New York: St. Martin's Press, 1990. xii, 153 pp. REV: William F. Hickman, *Naval War College Review* 46, no. 1, Sequence 341 (Winter 1993): 139-142.

5851. Goodman, Melvin A. *Gorbachev's Retreat: The Third World*. New York: Praeger, 1991. xii, 206 pp. REV: Robert V. Legvold, *Foreign Affairs* 70, no. 5 (Winter 1991-92): 200. Amy E. Kezerian, *SAIS Review* 12, no. 1 (Winter-Spring 1992): 178-180. Kenneth L. Privratsky, *Military Review* 72, no. 2 (February 1992): 95-96. Alvin Z. Rubinstein, *Orbis* 36, no. 1 (Winter 1992): 146. Elizabeth Kridl Valkenier, *Journal of Asian Studies* 51, no. 1 (February 1992): 121-122. Elizabeth Kridl Valkenier, *Russian Review* 52, no. 2 (April 1993): 287-288.

5852. Kanet, Roger E., Deborah Nutter Miner, and Tamara J. Resler, eds. *Soviet Foreign Policy in Transition*. Cambridge; New York: Cambridge University Press, 1992. xvi, 308 pp. [Selected papers from the World Congress for Soviet and East European Studies (4th: 1990: Harrogate, England); edited for the International Committee for Soviet and East European Studies.] REV: Elizabeth Kridl Valkenier, *Journal of Developing Areas* 28, no. 1 (October 1993): 124-125.

5853. Kull, Steven. *Burying Lenin: The Revolution in Soviet Ideology and Foreign Policy*. Boulder, CO: Westview Press, 1992. xvi, 219 pp. REV: Robert Legvold, *Foreign Affairs* 71, no. 4 (Fall 1992): 211. Sean Patrick Murphy, *Current History* 91, no. 567 (October 1992): 347. Stephen Page, *Canadian Slavonic Papers* 34, no. 4 (Decem-

ber 1992): 504-505. O.M. Smolansky, *Canadian-American Slavic Studies* 26, nos. 1-4 (1992): 402-404. S. N. MacFarlane, *Russian Review* 52, no. 4 (October 1993): 578-579. Kimberly Marten Zisk, *American Political Science Review* 87, no. 1 (March 1993): 245-246.

5854. MccGwire, Michael. *Perestroika and Soviet National Security*. Washington, DC: Brookings Institution, c1991. 481 pp. REV: Sonja S. Moyer, *Military Review* 71, no. 7 (July 1991): 92. Gregory F. Treverton, *Foreign Affairs* 70, no. 2 (Spring 1991): 176-177. Rose Gottemoeller, *Soviet and Post-Soviet Review* 19, nos. 1-3 (1992): 285-287. William F. Hickman, *Naval War College Review* 45, no. 1 (Winter 1992): 118-120. Robert A. Vitas, *Armed Forces & Society* 19, no. 1 (Fall 1992): 157-159. Kimberly Marten Zisk, *Russian Review* 51, no. 3 (July 1992): 451-452. R. Judson Mitchell, *Perspectives on Political Science* 22, no. 4 (Fall 1993): 184-185.

5855. Odom, William E. *On Internal War: American and Soviet Approaches to Third World Clients and Insurgents*. Durham, NC: Duke University Press, 1992. 271 pp. REV: Steven R. David, *American Political Science Review* 86, no. 3 (September 1992): 845-846. Alvin Z. Rubinstein, *Orbis* 36, no. 3 (Summer 1992): 463-464. Gregory F. Treverton, *Foreign Affairs* 71, no. 4 (Fall 1992): 200. Richard J. Payne, *Annals of the American Academy of Political and Social Science*, no. 526 (March 1993): 198-200.

5856. Saivetz, Carol R., ed. *The Soviet Union and the Third World*. John M. Olin Critical Issues Series. Boulder, CO: Westview Press, 1989. ix, 230 pp. REV: Lawrence B. Stollar, *Studies in Comparative Communism* 23, no. 1 (Spring 1990): 89-99. Arthur J. Klinghoffer, *Canadian-American Slavic Studies* 26, nos. 1-4 (1992): 417-419. Bruce R. Kuniholm, *Russian Review* 52, no. 2 (April 1993): 288-289.

5857. Sodaro, Michael J. *Moscow, Germany, and the West from Khrushchev to Gorbachev*. Studies of the Harriman Institute. Ithaca, NY: Cornell University Press, 1990. xiv, 423 pp. REV: John C. Campbell, *Foreign Affairs* 70, no. 4 (Fall 1991): 181-182. Leigh Sarty, *Canadian Slavonic Papers* 33, nos. 3-4 (December 1991): 375-376. Joshua B. Spero, *Problems of Communism* 40, no. 6 (November-December 1991): 141-151. Jack Dukes, *American Historical Review* 97, no. 3 (June 1992): 844-845. Richard F. Staar, *Russian Review* 51, no. 3 (July 1992): 446-447. Angela Stent, *Slavic Review* 51, no. 3 (Fall 1992): 575-576. Celeste A. Wallander, *American Political Science Review* 86, no. 3 (September 1992): 852-853. Matthew D. Lyon, *Russian History = Histoire russe* 20, nos. 1-4 (1993): 406-408.

Covert Operations, Espionage, Terrorism

5858. Blake, George. *No Other Choice: An Autobiography*. New York: Simon & Schuster, c1990. xi, 286 pp. REV: Michael Herman, *Conflict Quarterly* 12, no. 3 (Summer 1992): 75-78. Thomas Powers, *New York Review of Books* 40, no. 9 (May 13, 1993): 49-55.

5859. Douglass, Joseph D., Jr. *Red Cocaine: The Drugging of America.* Introduction by Ray S. Cline. 1st ed. Atlanta, GA: Clarion House, c1990. xxii, 277 pp. REV: Richard B. Craig, *Orbis* 37, no. 1 (Winter 1993): 135-147.

5860. Kessler, Ronald. *Moscow Station: How the KGB Penetrated the American Embassy.* New York: Scribner's, c1989. 305 pp. REV: David Wise, *New York Times Book Review,* 19 Mar 1989, 12. Denis Dirscherl, *Ukrainian Quarterly* 46, no. 1 (Spring 1990): 84-85. Thomas Powers, *New York Review of Books* 40, no. 9 (May 13, 1993): 49-55.

5861. Lamphere, Robert J. *The FBI-KGB War: A Special Agent's Story.* 1st ed. New York: Random House, 1986. 320 pp. REV: Thomas Powers, *New York Review of Books* 40, no. 9 (May 13, 1993): 49-55.

5862. Mangold, Tom. *Cold Warrior: James Jesus Angleton: The CIA's Master Spy Hunter.* New York: Touchstone: Simon & Schuster, 1991. 462 pp. REV: Murray Kempton, *New York Review of Books* 38, no. 14 (August 15, 1991): 16. Walter Laqueur, *New Republic* 205, no. 6 (August 5, 1991): 40-41. Gregory F. Treverton, *Foreign Affairs* 70, no. 5 (Winter 1991-92): 183. Ray Alan, *New Leader* 75, no. 7 (June 1-15, 1992): 13-14. Bruce D. Berkowitz, *Orbis* 36, no. 3 (Summer 1992): 462. John B. Haseman, *Military Review* 72, no. 12 (December 1992): 98-99. Erwin Knoll, *Progressive* 56, no. 1 (January 1992): 36-40. F.W. Parkinson, *Conflict Quarterly* 12, no. 4 (Fall 1992): 80-82. Paul B. Davis, *History: Reviews of New Books* 21, no. 2 (Winter 1993): 68. Raymond L. Garthoff, *Political Science Quarterly* 108, no. 1 (Spring 1993): 161-163. Thomas Powers, *New York Review of Books* 40, no. 9 (May 13, 1993): 49-55.

5863. Newton, Verne W. *The Cambridge Spies: The Untold Story of Maclean, Philby, and Burgess in America.* Lanham, MD: Madison Books; Distributed by National Book Network, c1991. xx, 448 pp. REV: James Bamford, *New York Times Book Review* (June 30, 1991): 13-14. Ronald Radosh, *American Spectator* 24, no. 10 (October 1991): 46-47. Thomas Powers, *New York Review of Books* 40, no. 9 (May 13, 1993): 49-55.

5864. Richelson, Jeffrey. *American Espionage and the Soviet Target.* New York: W. Morrow, 1987. 383 pp. REV: Thomas Powers, *New York Review of Books* 40, no. 9 (May 13, 1993): 49-55.

5865. Schecter, Jerrold L., and Peter S. Deriabin. *The Spy Who Saved the World: How a Soviet Colonel Changed the Course of the Cold War.* New York: Scribner's; Toronto: Maxwell Macmillan Canada; New York: Maxmillan International, c1992. xvi, 488 pp. REV: Richard N. Armstrong, *Military Review* 72, no. 12 (December 1992): 97. Ralph de Tolendano, *National Review* 44 (August 3, 1992): 40-42. Tim Weiner, *Washington Monthly* 24 (May 1992): 45ff. *Publishers Weekly* 239, no. 6 (January 27, 1992): 84. Thomas G. Paterson, *Journal of American History* 80, no. 1 (June 1993): 344. Thomas Powers, *New York Review of Books* 40, no. 9 (May 13, 1993): 49-55. *Orbis* 37, no. 1 (Winter 1993).

5866. Wise, David. *Molehunt: The Secret Search for Traitors that Shattered the CIA.* 1st ed. New York: Random House, c1992. 325 pp. REV: Michael R. Beschloss, *New York Times Book Review* (March 15, 1992): 11. *Publishers Weekly* 239, no. 6 (January 27, 1992): 81. Thomas Powers, *New York Review of Books* 40, no. 9 (May 13, 1993): 49-55.

U.S.S.R. and Asia/Pacific

5867. Cordesman, Anthony H., and Abraham R. Wagner. *The Lessons of Modern War.* Boulder, CO: Westview Press; London: Mansell, 1990. 3 vols. [Contents: Vol. 1. The Arab-Israeli Conflicts 1973-1989 — v. 2. The Iran-Iraq War — v. 3. The Afghan and Falklands Conflicts.] REV: Theodore L. Gatchel, *Naval War College Review* 46, no. 2 (Spring 1993): 149-151.

5868. Dittmer, Lowell. *Sino-Soviet Normalization and Its International Implications, 1945-1990.* Jackson School Publications in International Studies, Seattle, WA: University of Washington Press, c1992. viii, 373 pp. REV: Donald S. Zagoria, *Foreign Affairs* 71, no. 5 (Winter 1992-1993): 216. Dennis J. Dunn, *International History Review* 15, no. 3 (August 1993): 627. Gilbert Rozman, *Russian Review* 52, no. 4 (October 1993): 574-575. Richard C. Thornton, *American Historical Review* 98, no. 4 (October 1993): 1211.

5869. Khan, Riaz M. *Untying the Afghan Knot: Negotiating Soviet Withdrawal.* Durham, NC: Duke University Press, 1991. 402 pp. REV: Douglas A. Borer, *Political Science Quarterly* 107, no. 4 (Winter 1992-1993): 760-762. Thomas T. Hammond, *Slavic Review* 51, no. 3 (Fall 1992): 573. Sarah E. Mendelsohn, *Bulletin of the Atomic Scientists* 48, no. 9 (November 1992): 43-44. Alvin Z. Rubinstein, *Orbis* 36, no. 4 (Fall 1992): 628. Marvin G. Weinbaum, *Journal of Asian Studies* 52, no. 3 (August 1993): 757-758.

5870. Maley, William, and Fazel Haq Saikal. *Political Order in Post-Communist Afghanistan.* Boulder, CO: Lynne Rienner, 1992. 80 pp. REV: Marvin G. Weinbaum, *Middle East Studies Association Bulletin* 27, no. 1 (July 1993): 64.

5871. Rozman, Gilbert. *Japan's Response to the Gorbachev Era, 1985-1991: A Rising Superpower Views a Declining One.* Princeton, NJ: Princeton University Press, c1992. xi, 376 pp. REV: Donald S. Zagoria, *Foreign Affairs* 71, no. 3 (Summer 1992): 183. Tsuneo Akaha, *Journal of Asian Studies* 52, no. 3 (August 1993): 734-736. Tsuyoshi Hasegawa, *Journal of Japanese Studies* 19, no. 2 (Summer 1993): 537-543. Eiko Ikegami, *Contemporary Sociology* 22, no. 2 (March 1993): 206. Donald W. Klein, *Pacific Affairs* 66, no. 2 (Summer 1993): 279-280. Rajan Menon, *Slavic Review* 52, no. 4 (Winter 1993): 852-853. William Nester, *Asian Thought and Society* 18, no. 52 (January-April 1993): 75-77. *Orbis* 37, no. 3 (Summer 1993).

5872. Saikal, Amin, and William Maley. *Regime Change in Afghanistan: Foreign Intervention and the Politics of Legitimacy.* Boulder, CO: Westview Press, 1991. 190 pp. [Includes Soviet occupation (1979-1989).] REV: Thomas J. Barfield, *Middle East Studies Association*

Bulletin 26, no. 2 (December 1992): 216-217. Max L. Gross, *Middle East Journal* 46, no. 4 (Autumn 1992): 693-694. Richard S. Newell, *Annals of the American Academy of Political and Social Science* no. 525 (January 1993): 176.

5873. Sicker, Martin. *The Strategy of Soviet Imperialism: Expansion in Eurasia.* New York: Praeger, 1988. 172 pp. REV: Stephen Blank, *Nationalities Papers* 21, no. 2 (Fall 1993): 203-204.

5874. Tamarov, Vladislav. *Afghanistan: Soviet Vietnam.* Translated by Naomi Marcus, Marianne Clarke Trangen, and Vladislav Tamarov. San Francisco, CA: Mercury House, c1992. 183 pp. [Translated from Russian.] REV: Phoebe-Lou Adams, *Atlantic* 270, no. 3 (September 1992): 121. Linda Rocawich, *Progressive* 56, no. 6 (June 1992): 39-42. *Publishers Weekly* 239, no. 16 (March 30, 1992): 94. John F. Murphy, Jr., *Journal of Military History* 57, no. 2 (April 1993): 359-360.

5875. Thakur, Ramesh, and Carlyle A. Thayer. *Soviet Relations with India and Vietnam.* New York: St. Martin's Press, 1992. 315 pp. REV: D.R. SarDesai, *Journal of Asian Studies* 51, no. 4 (November 1992): 872-874. Rajan Menon, *International History Review* 15, no. 3 (August 1993): 640.

U.S.S.R. and Latin America

5876. Adams, Jan S. *A Foreign Policy in Transition: Moscow's Retreat from Central America and the Caribbean, 1985-1992.* Durham, NC: Duke University Press, c1992. 248 pp. REV: Sharyl Cross, *Soviet and Post-Soviet Review* 20, nos. 2-3 (1993): 260-262. Elizabeth Kridl Valkenier, *American Political Science Review* 87, no. 4 (December 1993): 1049. Deborah J. Yashar, *Political Science Quarterly* 108, no. 4 (Winter 1993-1994): 739-740.

5877. Miller, Nicola. *Soviet Relations with Latin America, 1959-1987.* New York: Cambridge University Press, 1989. 252 pp. REV: Roger Hamburg, *Problems of Communism* 39, no. 5 (September-October 1990): 99-107. William M. LeoGrande, *American Political Science Review* 84, no. 4 (December 1990): 1346-1347. Abraham F. Lowenthal, *Foreign Affairs* 69, no. 2 (Spring 1990): 177. Roderick J. Barman, *International History Review* 13, no. 1 (February 1991): 206-208. Stephen G. Rabe, *Slavic Review* 50, no. 2 (Summer 1991): 447. William Richardson, *Canadian-American Slavic Studies* 25, nos. 1-4 (1991): 363-364. Aldo C. Vacs, *Journal of Interamerican Studies and World Affairs* 33, no. 1 (Spring 1991): 189-192. Cole Blasier, *Russian Review* 51, no. 1 (January 1992): 140-141. Marina Oborotova, *Latin American Research Review* 28 no. 3 (1993): 183-188.

5878. Prizel, Ilya. *Latin America through Soviet Eyes: The Evolution of Soviet Perceptions during the Brezhnev Era, 1964-1982.* Soviet and East European Studies, 72. Cambridge; New York: Cambridge University Press, 1990. xiii, 253 pp. REV: Michael Radu, *Orbis* 34, no. 4 (Fall 1990): 629. Linda Greenow, *Current History* 90, no. 553 (February 1991): 77. Roger Hamburg, *Russian Review* 50, no. 3 (July 1991): 378-379. William Richardson, *Ameri-*

can Historical Review 96, no. 3 (June 1991): 921-922. Aldo C. Vacs, *Journal of Interamerican Studies and World Affairs* 33, no. 1 (Spring 1991): 189-192. Ronald C. Newton, *International History Review* 14, no. 1 (February 1992): 203-205. Harold Dana Sims, *Americas* 49 (July 1992): 112-114. Robert K. Evanson, *Soviet and Post-Soviet Review* 20, nos. 2-3 (1993): 252-254. Marina Oborotova, *Latin American Research Review* 28, no. 3 (1993): 183-188.

5879. Smith, Wayne S., ed. *The Russians Aren't Coming: New Soviet Policy in Latin America.* Boulder, CO: L. Rienner, 1992. xii, 196 pp. REV: Abraham F. Lowenthal, *Foreign Affairs* 71, no. 3 (Summer 1992): 176. Michael Radu, *Orbis* 36, no. 4 (Fall 1992): 643. Marina Oborotova, *Latin American Research Review* 28, no. 3 (1993): 183-188.

U.S.S.R. and the Middle East

5880. Freedman, Robert O. *Moscow and the Middle East: Soviet Policy Since the Invasion of Afghanistan.* Cambridge; New York: Cambridge University Press, 1991. xii, 426 pp. [Contents: On the eve, Soviet policy toward the Middle East from World War II until the invasion of Afghanistan — Soviet policy from the invasion of Afghanistan until the death of Brezhnev — The interregnum, Moscow and the Middle East under Andropov and Chernenko — Moscow and the Middle East under Gorbachev, new thinking in theory and practice — Conclusion, continuity and change in Soviet policy toward the Middle East.] REV: John C. Campbell, *Foreign Affairs* 70, no. 4 (Fall 1991): 184. Galia Golan, *Slavic Review* 51, no. 4 (Winter 1992): 866. Roger E. Kanet, *American Political Science Review* 86, no. 3 (September 1992): 840-841. Mark N. Katz, *Soviet and Post-Soviet Review* 19, nos. 1-3 (1992): 318. Joseph A. Kechichian, *Middle East Studies Association Bulletin* 26, no. 1 (July 1992): 84-85. John C. Campbell, *Russian Review* 52, no. 3 (July 1993): 437-438.

5881. Fuller, Graham E. *Turkey Faces East: New Orientations toward the Middle East and the Old Soviet Union.* Santa Monica, CA: RAND, 1992. xi, 70 pp. REV: *Orbis* 37, no. 4 (Fall 1993).

5882. Golan, Galia. *Moscow and the Middle East: New Thinking on Regional Conflict.* Chatham House Papers. New York: Published in North America for the Royal Institute of International Affairs by the Council on Foreign Relations Press, c1992. 102 pp. REV: Robert Legvold, *Foreign Affairs* 72, no. 2 (Spring 1993): 180.

5883. Karsh, Efraim. *Soviet Policy towards Syria since 1970.* New York: St. Martin's Press, c1991. 235 pp. REV: Roger E. Kanet, *American Political Science Review* 86, no. 3 (September 1992): 840-841. Robert O. Freedman, *Slavic Review* 52, no. 3 (Fall 1993): 652-653. Michael Graham Fry and Tamara Bitar, *International History Review* 15, no. 3 (August 1993): 642.

5884. Kriesberg, Louis. *International Conflict Resolution: The U.S.-USSR and Middle East Cases.* New Haven, CT: Yale University Press, c1992. xii, 275 pp. REV: Andrew J. Pierre, *Foreign Affairs* 71, no. 4 (Fall 1992): 198. K. J. Holsti, *American Political Science Review* 87, no. 4

(December 1993): 1054-1055. David S. Meyer, *Contemporary Sociology* 22, no. 5 (September 1993): 691. William J. Weida, *Annals of the American Academy of Political and Social Science*, no. 530 (November 1993): 208.

5885. Shemesh, Haim. *Soviet-Iraqi Relations, 1968-1988: In the Shadow of the Iraq-Iran Conflict.* Boulder, CO: Lynne Rienner, 1992. x, 285 pp. REV: William B. Quandt, *Foreign Affairs* 71, no. 3 (Summer 1992): 182. O.M. Smolansky, *American Historical Review* 98, no. 4 (October 1993): 1300.

5886. Smolansky, Oles M., and Bettie M. Smolansky. *The USSR and Iraq: The Soviet Quest for Influence.* Durham, NC: Duke University Press, c1991. xi, 346 pp. REV: John C. Campbell, *Foreign Affairs* 70, no. 4 (Fall 1991): 184. W.D. Bushnell, *Military Review* 72, no. 2 (February 1992): 95. Shafiga Daulet, *Annals of the American Academy of Political and Social Science*, no. 520 (March 1992): 189-190. Roger E. Kanet, *American Political Science Review* 86, no. 3 (September 1992): 840-841. Mark N. Katz, *Russian Review* 51, no. 4 (October 1992): 591-592. Carol R. Saivetz, *Middle East Journal* 46, no. 1 (Winter 1992): 109-110. David L. Williams, *Social Science Quarterly* 73, no. 3 (September 1992): 713-714. Michael Graham Fry and Tamara Bitar, *International History Review* 15, no. 3 (August 1993): 642. Vladimir Petrov, *Perspectives on Political Science* 22, no. 3 (Summer 1993): 137.

U.S.S.R. and North America

5887. Brement, Marshall. *Reaching Out to Moscow: From Confrontation to Cooperation.* Foreword by Claiborne Pell. New York: Praeger, 1991. ix, 191 pp. REV: Robert Legvold, *Foreign Affairs* 71, no. 3 (Summer 1992): 178. G. Douglas Nicoll, *Journal of Baltic Studies* 23, no. 2 (Summer 1992): 199. Alvin Z. Rubinstein, *Orbis* 36, no. 4 (Fall 1992): 626-627. William J. Weida, *Annals of the American Academy of Political and Social Science*, no. 530 (November 1993): 207-208.

5888. Breslauer, George W., and Philip E. Tetlock, eds. *Learning in U.S. and Soviet Foreign Policy.* Boulder, CO: Westview Press, 1991. xiv, 881 pp. REV: Lloyd S. Etheredge, *American Political Science Review* 86, no. 3 (September 1992): 838-839. Adam Garfinkle, *Orbis* 36, no. 2 (Spring 1992): 291. Leigh Sarty, *Canadian Slavonic Papers* 34, nos. 1-2 (March-June 1992): 180-181. David D. Finley, *Soviet and Post-Soviet Review* 20, no. 1 (1993): 82.

5889. Broadwater, Jeff. *Eisenhower & the Anti-Communist Crusade.* Chapel Hill, NC: University of North Carolina Press, c1992. xiii, 291 pp. REV: Roger Biles, *History: Reviews of New Books* 21, no. 2 (Winter 1993): 63.

5890. Callahan, David. *Dangerous Capabilities: Paul Nitze and the Cold War.* New York: HarperCollins, 1990. 572 pp. REV: Debra E. Soled, *Current History* 89, no. 551 (December 1990): 438. Charles M. Dobbs, *Journal of American History* 78, no. 2 (September 1991): 736-737. Lawrence J. Korb, *Naval War College Review* 44, no. 4 (Autumn 1991): 139-140. Scott R. McMichael, *Military Review* 71, no. 2 (February 1991): 92. Gaddis Smith,

Foreign Affairs 70, no. 2 (Spring 1991): 183. Colin S. Gray, *Parameters* 22, no. 3 (Autumn 1992): 113-114. Geoffrey S. Smith, *Conflict Quarterly* 12, no. 2 (Spring 1992): 87-89. Steven L. Rearden, *Diplomatic History* 17, no. 1 (Winter 1993): 143-151.

5891. Debs, Eugene V. *Letters of Eugene V. Debs.* Edited by J. Robert Constantine. Urbana, IL: University of Illinois Press, 1991. 3 vols. REV: Sean Wilentz, *Dissent* 40, no. 1 (Winter 1993): 111-115.

5892. Isaacson, Walter. *Kissinger: A Biography.* New York: Simon & Schuster, c1992. 893 pp. REV: Kai Bird, *Nation* 255 (November 16, 1992): 584ff. Theodore Draper, *New York Times Book Review*, 97 (September 6, 1992): 1ff. Stephen Richards Graubard, *New York Times Book Review*, 97 (October 25, 1992): 30-31. Anthony Hartley, *National Review* 44 (December 14, 1992): 49-50. Jacob Heilbrunn, *New Republic* 207 (November 16, 1992): 32-40. Jim Hoagland, *Times Literary Supplement* no. 4671 (October 9, 1992): 4. Josef Joffe, *Commentary* 94 (December 1992): 49-52. Kenneth L. Adelman, *Parameters* 23, no. 1 (Spring 1993): 106-108. Steve Brzezinski, *Antioch Review* 51, no. 2 (Spring 1993): 304. Walter LaFeber, *Political Science Quarterly* 108 (Spring 1993): 157-158. George Szamuely, *American Spectator* 26 (January 1993): 82-85. *Wilson Quarterly* 17, no. 2 (Spring 1993): 77-79.

5893. Mandelbaum, Michael, ed. *The Rise of Nations in the Soviet Union: American Foreign Policy and the Disintegration of the USSR.* New York: Council on Foreign Relations Press, 1991. 120 pp. REV: Richard J. Krickus, *Problems of Communism* 40, no. 6 (November-December 1991): 135-140. Robert V. Legvold, *Foreign Affairs* 70, no. 5 (Winter 1991-92): 198. Ira Smolensky, *Journal of Baltic Studies* 22, no. 4 (Winter 1991): 369-370. J. L. Black, *Conflict Quarterly* 12, no. 1 (Winter 1992): 77-78. Ellsworth Raymond, *Perspectives on Political Science* 22, no. 4 (Fall 1993): 184-185.

5894. Nixon, Richard. *Seize the Moment: America's Challenge in a One-Superpower World.* New York: Simon & Schuster, 1992. 322 pp. [Includes discussion of U.S. policy toward the former Soviet Union.] REV: Elliott Abrams, *Commentary* 93, no. 3 (March 1992): 62-64. Adam Garfinkle, *Orbis* 36, no. 3 (Summer 1992): 460-461. William G. Hyland, *Foreign Affairs* 71, no. 3 (Summer 1992): 173-174. John O'Sullivan, *National Review* 44, no. 7 (April 13, 1992): 46-48. Richard Perle, *New York Times Book Review* (January 19, 1992): 3. Mansbach, *Perspectives on Political Science* 22, no. 4 (Fall 1993): 182. Sam C. Sarkesian, *Annals of the American Academy of Political and Social Science*, no. 527 (May 1993): 174. Jan van Tol, *Naval War College Review* 46, no. 3, Sequence 343 (Summer 1993): 158-159.

5895. Oberdorfer, Don. *The Turn: From the Cold War to a New Era: The United States and the Soviet Union, 1983-1990.* New York: Poseidon Press, c1991. 514 pp. REV: Michael R. Beschloss, *New York Times Book Review* (October 27, 1991): 11-12. Lester W. Grau, *Military Review* 71, no. 12 (December 1991): 98. Fred Barnes, *American*

Spectator 25, no. 1 (January 1992): 67-68. David Callahan, *Commonweal* 119, no. 4 (February 28, 1992): 24-25. Bruce Fein, *History: Reviews of New Books* 20, no. 4 (Summer 1992): 145. Adam Garfinkle, *Orbis* 36, no. 2 (Spring 1992): 289-290. Nathan Glazer, *National Interest*, no. 28 (Summer 1992): 102-108. Robert Legvold, *Foreign Affairs* 71, no. 2 (Spring 1992): 206. Joseph L. Nogee, *Slavic Review* 51, no. 4 (Winter 1992): 860-861. Donald M. Snow, *Annals of the American Academy of Political and Social Science*, no. 524 (November 1992): 192-193. Michael Mandelbaum, *World Policy Journal* 10, no. 3 (Fall 1993): 97-109.

5896. Robins, Natalie. *Alien Ink: The FBI's War on Freedom of Expression*. New York: William Morrow, 1992. 495 pp. REV: T. Michael Ruddy, *History: Reviews of New Books* 21, no. 3 (Spring 1993): 117. Jon Weiner, *Journal of American History* 80, no. 1 (June 1993): 316.

5897. Sanders, James D., Mark Sauter, and R. Cort Kirkwood. *Soldiers of Misfortune: Washington's Secret Betrayal of America's POWs in the Soviet Union*. Washington, DC: National Press Books, c1992. 352 pp. REV: Brooks E. Kleber, *Military Review* 73, no. 10 (October 1993): 66-67.

5898. Shimko, Keith L. *Images and Arms Control: Perceptions of the Soviet Union in the Reagan Administration*. Ann Arbor, MI: University of Michigan Press, c1991. 277 pp. REV: Martha Cottam, *American Political Science Review* 86, no. 3 (September 1992): 849. Adam Garfinkle, *Orbis* 36, no. 4 (Fall 1992): 622-623. Robert Jervis, *Political Science Quarterly* 107, no. 2 (Summer 1992): 331-332. Thomas B. Trout, *Journal of Politics* 55, no. 3 (August 1993): 858-860.

5899. Sirgiovanni, George. *An Undercurrent of Suspicion: Anti-Communism in America during World War II*. New Brunswick, NJ: Transaction Publishers, c1989. ix, 209 pp. REV: Robert J. Goldstein, *History: Reviews of New Books* 21, no. 2 (Winter 1993): 69.

5900. Stephan, Paul B., III, and Boris M. Klimenko, eds. *International Law and International Security: Military and Political Dimensions: A U.S.-Soviet Dialogue*. Contributions by Paul B. Stephan, III, B. M. Klimenko, William D. Jackson, V. N. Fedorov, Oscar Schachter, S. A. Yegorov, Thomas Graham, Jr., S. N. Kiselev, A. Yu. Meshkov, B. R. Tuzmukhamedov, E. T. Agayev, N. P. Smidovich, M. I. Ul'yanov, John B. Rhinelander, John H. McNeill, S. V. Kortunov, A. L. Semeyko, P. G. Litavrin, Harold G. Maier, V. I. Kuznetsov, Louis B. Sohn, John N. Moore, Robert F. Turner, and A. V. Zmeyevskii. Armonk, NY: M.E. Sharpe, c1991. xxii, 362 pp. [Contents: Paul B. Stephan III and B. M. Klimenko, "Introduction"; William D. Jackson and V. N. Fedorov, "Renunciation of Military Aggression"; Oscar Schachter and V. N. Fedorov, "The Scope of Legitimate Self-Defense"; Oscar Schachter and S. A. Yegorov, "Internal Conflicts and International Law"; Thomas Graham, Jr., S. N. Kiselev, A. Yu. Meshkov, B. R. Tuzmukhamedov, and E. T. Agayev, "Limitations on Nuclear Weapons"; Thomas Graham, Jr., and N. P. Smidovich, "Limitations on Chemical and Biological Weapons"; Thomas Graham, Jr., and M. I. Ul'yanov,

"Limitation on the Development and Use of New Systems and Weapons of Mass Destruction and the Question of a Total Ban"; John B. Rhinelander and E. T. Agayev, "Limitations on the Military Use of Space"; John H. McNeill, S. V. Kortunov, B. R. Tuzmukhamedov, A.L. Semeyko, and P. G. Litavrin, "Reduction on the Overall Level of Military Forces"; John B. Rhinelander and B. R. Tuzmukhamedov, "Verification of Arms Control Agreements and the Rights of Domestic Sovereignty"; Harold G. Maier and V. I. Kuznetsov, "The Principles of Sovereignty, Sovereign Equality and National Self-Determination"; Louis B. Sohn and S. A. Yegorov, "Prevention and Peaceful Resolution of International Conflicts, Crises, and Disputes"; William D. Jackson, John N. Moore, Robert F. Turner, and V. I. Kuznetsov, "The Principles of Cooperation and Good Faith Fulfillment of International Obligations"; John H. McNeill, B. M. Klimenko, and B. R. Tuzmukhamedov, "Measures for Strengthening Mutual Guarantees of Non-Aggression Among States"; Paul B. Stephan, III, and A. V. Zmeyevskii, "Prevention and Control of International Terrorism".] REV: Andrew Y. Piatnicia, *New York University Journal of International Law and Politics* 25, no. 5 (Winter 1993): 522-523. Nicholas Rostow, *American Journal of International Law* 87, no. 4 (October 1993): 682-684.

5901. United States. Dept. of State. *Foreign Relations of the United States, 1955-1957. Volume XXIV, Soviet Union; Eastern Mediterranean*. Editor in chief John P. Glennon. Editors Ronald D. Landa et al. Department of State Publication, 9699. Washington, DC: Dept. of State, 1989. xxvi, 768 pp. REV: Manfred Jonas, *Journal of American History* 80, no. 1 (June 1993): 343.

5902. Zimmerman, William, ed. *Beyond the Soviet Threat: Rethinking American Security Policy in a New Era*. Contributions by William Zimmerman, Deborah Yarsike, Allen Lynch, Richard Hyland Phillips, Philip G. Roeder, Andrew Bennett, Miroslav Nincic, Charles L. Glaser, Ted Hopf, and Paul Huth. Ann Arbor, MI: University of Michigan Press, c1992. xi, 223 pp. [Contents: William Zimmerman and Deborah Yarsike, "Mass Publics and New Thinking in Soviet and Russian Foreign Policy"; Allen Lynch, "Changing Elite Views on the International System"; Richard Hyland Phillips, "Reasonable Sufficiency and Defensive Defense in Soviet Conventional Military Policy"; Philip G. Roeder, "Dialectics of Doctrine: Politics of Resource Allocation and the Development of Soviet Military Thought"; Andrew Bennett, "Patterns of Soviet Military Interventionism, 1975-1990: Alternative Explanations and their Implications"; Miroslav Nincic, "America's Soviet Policy: Patterns of Incentives"; Charles L. Glaser and Ted Hopf, "Models of Soviet-American Relations and their Implications for Future Russian-American Relations"; Paul Huth, "The European Security Implications of the Dissolution of the Soviet Empire".] REV: Robert Legvold, *Foreign Affairs* 72, no. 2 (Spring 1993): 179.

U.S.S.R. and Western Europe

5903. Penttila, Risto E. J. *Finland's Search for Security through Defence, 1944-89*. New York: St. Martin's

Press, 1991. 209 pp. REV: Bo Petersson, *International History Review* 15, no. 2 (May 1993): 394.

5904. Pittman, Avril. *From Ostpolitik to Reunification: West German-Soviet Political Relations Since 1974.* Soviet and East European Studies, 85. New York: Cambridge University Press, 1992. 226 pp. REV: Fritz Stern, *Foreign Affairs* 71, no. 5 (Winter 1992-1993): 209. Jonathan Sperber, *Historian* 55, no. 3 (Spring 1993): 555-556.

5905. Pravda, Alex, and Peter J. S. Duncan, eds. *Soviet-British Relations since the 1970s.* Cambridge; New York: Cambridge University Press, 1990. xii, 263 pp. [Published in association with the Royal Institute of International Affairs.] REV: Jacques Levesque, *Canadian Slavonic Papers* 32, no. 4 (December 1990): 495-496. Stephen Shenfield, *Slavic Review* 50, no. 4 (Winter 1991): 1025. S.T. MacKenzie, *Canadian-American Slavic Studies* 26, nos. 1-4 (1992): 409-411. N. H. Gaworek, *Soviet and Post-Soviet Review* 20, no. 1 (1993): 86.

Eastern Europe

5906. Alexander, Yonah, and Dennis A. Pluchinsky, eds. *European Terrorism Today & Tomorrow.* Brassey's Terrorism Library, Washington, DC: Brassey's (US), c1992. xv, 208 pp. [Includes discussion of West Germany's Red Army Faction, Italy's Red Brigades and Greece's revolutionary organization 17 November.] REV: Todd E. Pierce, *Military Review* 73, no. 3 (March 1993): 92-94.

5907. Borneman, John. *After the Wall: East Meets West in the New Berlin.* New York, NY: Basic Books, c1991. x, 258 pp. REV: Anthony Bailey, *New York Times Book Review* (July 14, 1991): 15-16. Lucy Despard, *Foreign Affairs* 70, no. 3 (Summer 1991): 178. Michael Klees, *Fletcher Forum of World Affairs* 16, no. 1 (Winter 1992): 160-162. Andrei S. Markovits, *Contemporary Sociology* 21, no. 3 (May 1992): 314-315. Eric Scheye, *Political Psychology* 14, no. 4 (December 1993): 749-752.

5908. Kovrig, Bennett. *Of Walls and Bridges: The United States and Eastern Europe.* New York: New York University Press, c1991. xiii, 425 pp. REV: John C. Campbell, *Foreign Affairs* 70, no. 4 (Fall 1991): 182-183. A. Paul Kubricht, *East-Central Europe* 18, no. 2 (1991): 257-258. John C. Campbell, *American Historical Review* 97, no. 3 (June 1992): 961-962. Stanislav Kirschbaum, *Canadian Journal of Political Science = Revue canadienne de science politique* 25, no. 4 (December 1992): 807-808. Norman E. Saul, *History: Reviews of New Books* 20, no. 3 (Spring 1992): 96-97. E. Garrison Walters, *Diplomatic History* 17, no. 1 (Winter 1993): 153-157.

5909. Stiller, Werner, and Jefferson Adams. *Beyond the Wall: Memoirs of an East and West German Spy.* Brassey's Intelligence & National Security Library, Washington, DC: Brassey's, c1992. xvii, 240 pp. [Translation of *Im Zentrum der Spionage*.] REV: Kristie Macrakis, *Science* 262, no. 5141 (December 17, 1993): 1908-1910.

5910. United States. Dept. of State. *Foreign Relations of the United States, 1955-1957. Volume XXVI,*

Central and Southeastern Europe. Editor in chief John P. Glennon. Editors Roberta L. DiGangi et al. Department of State Publication, 9930. Washington, DC: Dept. of State, 1990. xxiv, 838 pp. REV: Manfred Jonas, *Journal of American History* 80, no. 1 (June 1993): 343.

■ Language and Linguistics

General

5911. Carlton, Terence R. *Introduction to the Phonological History of the Slavic Languages.* Columbus, OH: Slavica, 1991. 461 pp. REV: Marc Greenberg, *Slovene Studies* 13, no. 2 (1991) [published July 1993]: 223-229. Horace G. Lunt, *Slavic Review* 51, no. 3 (Fall 1992): 629-631. Frank Y. Gladney, *Slavic and East European Journal* 37, no. 1 (Spring 1993): 127-129. Mark R. Lauersdorf, *Language: Journal of the Linguisitc Society of America* 69, no. 4 (December 1993): 848-849.

5912. Dow, James R., ed. *Language and Ethnicity.* Includes contributions by Rakhmiel Pletz and Marion Lois Huffines. Focusschrift in Honor of Joshua A. Fishman on the Occasion of His 65th Birthday, v. 2. Amsterdam; Philadelphia, PA: Benjamins, 1991. 255 pp. [Includes essay by Rakhmiel Pletz on the use of Yiddish by offspring of Jewish immigrants in Philadelphia and essay by Marion Lois Huffines on the use of Pennsylvania German among the Mennonite and Amish.] REV: N. C. Dorian, *Language* 69, no. 1 (March 1993): 199. Joan M. Fayer, *Modern Language Journal* 77, no. 1 (Spring 1993): 124.

5913. Fierman, William. *Language Planning and National Development: The Uzbek Experience.* Contributions to the Sociology of Language, 60. Berlin; New York: Mouton de Gruyter, 1991. xiii, 358 pp. REV: Seran Dogancay, *Language Problems & Language Planning* 17, no. 3 (Fall 1993): 288-290.

5914. Fishman, Joshua A. *Yiddish: Turning to Life.* Amsterdam; Philadelphia, PA: J. Benjamins, 1991. xii, 522 pp. REV: Robert D. King, *Language: Journal of the Linguistic Society of America* 68, no. 4 (December 1992): 831-833. Manfred Klarberg, *Language Problems & Language Planning* 17, no. 2 (Summer 1993): 160-161.

5915. Golab, Zbigniew. *The Origins of the Slavs: A Linguist's View.* Columbus, OH: Slavica, 1992. 454 pp. REV: Henrik Birnbaum, *Journal of Slavic Linguistics* 1, no. 2 (Summer-Fall 1993): 352-374. E.C.P. [Edgar C. Polomé], *Journal of Indo-European Studies* 21, nos. 1 & 2 (Spring-Summer 1993): 179-181.

5916. Ivir, Vladimir, and Damir Kalogjera, ed. *Languages in Contact and Contrast: Essays in Contact Linguistics.* Trends in Linguistics. Studies and Monographs, 54. Berlin; New York: Mouton de Gruyter, 1991. xi, 502 pp. [Includes forty-two papers; one is on translating a short story by Anton Chekhov; one is on native language retention in Croatian and Serbian Church communities in Milwaukee, WI.] REV: Kendall A. King, *Language: Journal* *of the Linguisitc Society of America* 69, no. 2 (June 1993): 423-424.

5917. Kolupaila-Masiokas, Evelyn, and Bruno Masiokas. *Zodziai—zodziai: lietuviski-angliski (su paaiskinimais): tarimas, kalbos dalys, linksniuotes, asmenuotes, kirciai, atitikmenys, issireiskimai = Words— Words. Lithuanian-English (With Explanations). Pronunciation. Parts of Lanugage. Declensions. Conjugations. Accent Groups. Synonyms. Expressions.* Aurora, CO (13902 E. Marina Dr. #404, Aurora, CO 80014-3756): Raguva Press, 1992. 1 vol. REV: Antanas Klimas, *Lituanus* 39, no. 1 (Spring 1993): 91-93.

5918. Laponce, J. A. *Languages and their Territories.* Translated from the French by Anthony Martin-Sperry. Toronto; Buffalo: University of Toronto Press, c1987. x, 265 pp. [Translation of *Langue et territoire.* Includes discussion of languages in the Soviet Union.] REV: Jesse Levitt, *Language Problems & Language Planning* 17, no. 1 (Spring 1993): 66-67.

5919. Lehmann, Winfred P., and Helen-Jo Jakusz Hewitt, eds. *Language typology 1988: Typological models in reconstruction.* Amsterdam Studies in the Theory and History of Linguistic Science. Series IV, Current Issues in Linguistic Theory, v. 81. Amsterdam; Philadelphia, PA: J. Benjamins, 1991. 182 pp. [Based on a meeting held in Leningrad, June 13-15, 1988, the last in the serioes of linguistic conferences inaugurated by IREX (International Research and Exchanges Board) in 1984.] REV: B. Comrie, *Language* 69, no. 1 (March 1993): 210.

5920. *Perspectives on Indo-European Language, Culture and Religion: Studies in Honor of Edgar C. Polome.* Journal of Indo-European Studies. Monograph, nos. 7, 9. McLean, VA: Institute for the Study of Man, c1991-c1992. 2 vols. [Includes chapter on languages of the Caucausus. Partial contents: Homer Thomas, "Indo-European: From the Paleolithic to the Neolithic," pp. 12-37; G. A. Klimov, "The Kartvelian Analogue of Proto-Indo-European *suomb(h)o- 'spongy, porous'," pp. 111-116; Pierre Swiggers, "The Indo-European Origin of the Greek Meters: Antoine Meillet's Views and Their Reception by Emile Benveniste and Nikolai Trubetzkoy," pp. 199-215.] REV: Winfred P. Lehmann, *Journal of Indo-European Studies* 21, nos. 1 & 2 (Spring-Summer 1993): 185-186.

5921. Thelin, Nils B., ed. *Verbal Aspect in Discourse: Contributions to the Semantics of Time and Temporal Perspective in Slavic and Non-Slavic Languages.* Contributions by Nils B. Thelin, Kyril T. Holden, Linda R. Waugh, Boris Gasparov, Catherine V. Chvany, Jean-Pierre Desclés, Zlatka Guentchéva, Grace E. Fielder, Patricia R. Chaput, Peter T. Merrill, Alan Timberlake, Hannu Tommola, André G. F. van Holk, and Peter Alberg Jensen. Pragmatics & Beyond: New Series, 5. Amsterdam; Philadelphia, PA: J. Benjamins, 1990. xviii, 460 pp. [Some papers presented at the World Congress for Soviet and East European Studies (3rd: 1985: Washington, DC). Contents: Nils B. Thelin, "Verbal Aspect in Discourse: On the State of the Art"; Nils B. Thelin, "On the Concept of Time:

Prolegomena to A Theory of Aspect and Tense in Narrative Discourse"; Kyril T. Holden, "The Functional Evolution of Aspect in Russian"; Linda R. Waugh, "Discourse Functions of Tense-Aspect in French: Dynamic Synchrony"; Boris Gasparov, "Notes on the 'Metaphysics' of Russian Aspect"; Catherine V. Chvany, "Verbal Aspect, Discourse Saliency, and the So-Called 'Perfect of Result' in Modern Russian"; Jean-Pierre Desclés and Zlatka Guentchéva, "Discourse Analysis of Aorist and Imperfect in Bulgarian and French"; Grace E. Fielder, "Narrative Context and Russian Aspect"; Patricia R. Chaput, "Temporal and Semantic Factors Affecting Russian Aspect Choice in Questions"; Peter R. Merrill, "Russian Aspect in Questions: Information and Invariance in Discourse"; Alan Timberlake, "The Aspectual Case of Predicative Nouns in Lithuanian Texts"; Hannu Tommola, "On Finnish 'Aspect' in Discourse"; André G.F. van Holk, "Aspect in Textual Deep Structure: On the Message Theme of Puskin's The Bronze Horseman"; Peter Alberg Jensen, "Narrative Description or Descriptive Narration: Problems of Aspectuality in Cechov".] REV: Frank Y. Gladney, *Slavic and East European Journal* 36, no. 1 (Spring 1992): 128-131. Victor A. Friedman, *Language: Journal of the Linguisitc Society of America* 69, no. 2 (June 1993): 436-437.

5922. Torikashvili, John J. *Georgian-English, English-Georgian Dictionary.* 1st ed. Hippocrene Concise Dictionary. New York: Hippocrene Books, 1992. 347 pp. REV: Howard I. Aronson, *Modern Language Journal* 77, no. 4 (Winter 1993): 547-548.

5923. Young, John Wesley. *Totalitarian Language: Orwell's Newspeak and Its Nazi and Communist Antecedents.* Charlottesville, VA: University Press of Virginia, c1991. xi, 3354 pp. REV: John D. Hartman, *History: Reviews of New Books* 21, no. 2 (Winter 1993): 91.

East Slavic

5924. Beniukh, Oleg, and Ksana Beniukh. *Russian-English Dictionary with Phonetics.* Hippocrene Standard Dictionary. New York: Hippocrene Books, c1991. xi, 198 pp. REV: G.J. [Gerald Janecek], *Slavic and East European Journal* 37, no. 1 (Spring 1993): 141.

5925. Cioran, Samuel D. *Russian Alive! An Introduction to Russian.* Illustrated by Gennadi Kalinin. Ann Arbor, MI: Ardis, c1992. 428 pp. REV: Olga Kagan and Zita Dabars, *Slavic and East European Journal* 37, no. 3 (Fall 1993): 405-407. Maurice I. Levin, *Russian Language Journal = Russkii iazyk* 47, nos. 156-158 (Winter-Spring-Fall 1993): 333-337. Monika A. Lozinska, *Canadian Slavonic Papers* 35, nos. 1-2 (March-June 1993): 164-166.

5926. Cioran, Samuel D., and Gennadi Kalinin. *Welcome to Divnograd: An Illustrated Workbook for Students of Russian.* Ann Arbor, MI: Ardis, c1992. vi, 180 pp. REV: Olga Kagan, *Slavic and East European Journal* 37, no. 3 (Fall 1993): 405-407. Monika A. Lozinska, *Canadian Slavonic Papers* 35, nos. 1-2 (March-June 1993): 164-166.

5927. Corten, Irina H. *Vocabulary of Soviet Society and Culture: A Selected Guide to Russian Words, Idioms, and*

Expressions of the Post-Stalin Era, 1953-1991. Durham, NC: Duke University Press, 1992. xvi, 176 pp. REV: Colin Patridge, *Modern Fiction Studies* 37 (Winter 1991): 801-802. Mark J. Elson, *Modern Language Journal* 77, no. 2 (Summer 1993): 263-264. Donna Farina, *Canadian Slavonic Papers* 35, nos. 1-2 (March-June 1993): 166-167. Eugene Kozlowski, *East/West Education* 14, no. 1 (Spring 1993): 79-82.

5928. Hrabovsky, Leonid. *Ukrainian-English, English-Ukrainian Dictionary.* 1st ed. New York: Hippocrene, c1991. 431 pp. REV: Robert A. DeLossa, *Harvard Ukrainian Studies* 16, nos. 1-2 (June 1992): 199-200. Victoria A. Babenko-Woodbury, *Modern Language Journal* 77, no. 2 (Summer 1993): 274-275.

5929. Leighton, Lauren G. *Two Worlds, One Art: Literary Translation in Russia and America.* DeKalb, IL: Northern Illinois University Press, 1991. xix, 272 pp. REV: Rainer Schulte, *World Literature Today* 66, no. 3 (Summer 1992): 589. John M. Kopper, *Canadian American Slavic Studies = Revue Canadienne Américaine d'Etudes Slaves* 27, nos. 1-4 (1993): 377-379. Sidney Monas, *Russian Review* 52, no. 3 (July 1993): 423-424. Anthony Olcott, *Slavic Review* 52, no. 2 (Summer 1993): 398-400.

5930. Lusin, Natalia. *Russian Grammar.* Hauppauge, NY: Barron's Educational Series, c1992. viii, 280 pp. REV: Maurice I. Levin, *Russian Language Journal = Russkii iazyk* 47, nos. 156-158 (Winter-Spring-Fall 1993): 329-332.

5931. Marder, Stephen. *A Supplementary Russian-English Dictionary.* Columbus, OH: Slavica, 1992. 522 pp. [Supplement to A. Smirnitsky's Russian-English dictionary and M. Wheeler's The Oxford Russian-English dictionary.] REV: Morton Benson, *Slavic and East European Journal* 37, no. 4 (Winter 1993): 592-594. Charles E. Townsend, *Russian Language Journal = Russkii iazyk* 47, nos. 156-158 (Winter-Spring-Fall 1993): 325-327.

5932. Mills, Margaret, ed. *Topics in Colloquial Russian.* Contributions by Margaret H. Mills, O. A. Lapteva, Olga T. Yokoyama, Curt Woolhiser, Jan Eames Schallert, Karen Ryan-Hayes, Eva Eckert, Lenore A. Grenoble, Frederick R. Patton, David R. Andrews, Paula Goodman Finedore, James F. Cradler, Michael K. Launer, Galina Barinova, and Vitalij Shevoroshkin. American University Studies. Series XII, Slavic Languages and Literature, vol. 11. New York: P. Lang, c1990. 203 pp. [Contents: Margaret H. Mills, "Preface"; O.A. Lapteva, "Introduction"; Olga T. Yokoyama, "Responding with a Question in Colloquial Russian"; Curt Woolhiser, "'Missing Prepositions' in Colloquial Russian Relative Clauses"; Margaret H. Mills, "Perceived Stress and Utterance Organization in Colloquial Russian"; Jan Eames Schallert, "Intontation Beyond the Utterance: A Distributional Analysis of Rising and Falling Contours"; O.A. Lapteva, "Diskussionnye voprosy izucheniia ustnoi literaturnoi rechi v aspekte teorii normy"; Karen Ryan-Hayes, "Psychological Characterization in Russian Satire: *razgovornaja rec'* and *nesobstvenno-prjamaja rec'*"; Eva Eckert, "Expressing Motion in Russian and Czech";

Lenore A. Grenoble, "Variation in Colloquial Speech: Russian and Polish Verbs of Motion"; Frederick R. Patton, "Soviet Research on Substandard Speech"; David R. Andrews, "A Semantic Categorization of Some Borrowings from English in Third-Wave Emigré Russian"; Paula Goodman Finedore, "Context, Cohesion, and Colloquial Russian"; James F. Cradler and Michael K. Launer, "Teaching Aural Comprehension of Colloquial Russian"; Galina Barinova and Vitalij Shevoroshkin, "Observations on the Role of Oslyshki in Linguistic Research".] REV: Charles E. Gribble, *Modern Language Journal* 76, no. 3 (Autumn 1992): 429. Gerard L. Ervin, *Slavic and East European Journal* 37, no. 4 (Winter 1993): 594-595.

5933. Norgård-Sørensen, Jens. *Coherence Theory: The Case of Russian.* Trends in Linguistics. Studies and Monographs, 63. Berlin; New York: Mouton de Gruyter, 1992. ix, 222 pp. REV: Valentina Zaitseva, *Russian Language Journal = Russkii iazyk* 47, nos. 156-158 (Winter-Spring-Fall 1993): 343-350.

5934. Simes, Natasha. *Years of Change: Reading the Soviet Press.* Dubuque, IA: Kendall/Hunt, c1992. xi, 317 pp. REV: Marina Gorelikova, *Russian Language Journal = Russkii iazyk* 47, nos. 156-158 (Winter-Spring-Fall 1993): 351-359.

5935. Ushekevich, Alexander, and Alexandra Zezuling. *Byelorussian-English, English-Byelorussian Dictionary: With Complete Phonetics.* New York: Hippocrene Books, 1992. REV: Wayles Browne, *Slavic and East European Journal* 37, no. 4 (Winter 1993): 595-596.

5936. Wade, Terence. *A Comprehensive Russian Grammar.* Cambridge, MA: B. Blackwell, 1992. xxvi, 582 pp. REV: Maurice I. Levin, *Russian Language Journal* 46, nos. 153-155 (Winter-Spring-Fall 1992): 306-310; Emil Vrabie, *Slavic and East European Journal* 37, no. 1 (Spring 1993): 131-133.

South Slavic

5937. Bugarski, Ranko, and Celia Hawkesworth, eds. *Language Planning in Yugoslavia.* Contributions by Ranko Bugarski, Dubravko Skiljan, August Kovacec, Melanie Mikes, Dalibor Brozovic, Kenneth E. Naylor, Milorad Radovanovic, Pavle Ivic, Joze Toporisic, Olga Miseska Tomic, Isa Zymberti, Darko Tanaskovic, Peter Herrity, George Thomas, Thomas F. Magner, Dunja Jutronic-Tihomirovic, Damir Kalogjera, and Sven Gustavsson. Columbus, OH: Slavica, 1992. 233 pp. [Contents: I. Language Situation and General Policy. Ranko Bugarski, "Language in Yugoslavia: Situation, Policy, Planning," pp. 9-26; Dubravko Skiljan, "Standard Languages in Yugoslvia," pp. 27-42; August Kovacec, "Languages of National Minorities and Ethnic Groups in Yugoslavia," pp. 43-58; Melanie Mikes, "Languages of National Minorities in Vojvodina," pp. 59-71; Dalibor Brozovic, "The Yugoslav Model of Language Planning: A Confrontation with Other Multilingual Models," pp. 72-79; II. Planning of Individual Languages. Kenneth E. Naylor, "The Sociolinguistic Situation in Yugoslavia, with Special

Empahsis on Serbo-Croatian," pp. 80-92; Milorad Radovanovic, "Standard Serbo-Croatian and the Theory of Language Planning," pp. 93-100; Pavle Ivic, "Language Planning in Serbia Today," pp. 101-110; Joze Toporisic, "The Status of Slovene in Yugoslavia," pp. 111-116; Olga Miseska Tomic, "Standard, Dialect and Register in Macedonian," pp. 117-129; Isa Zymberi, "Albanian in Yugoslavia," pp. 130-139; Darko Tanaskovic, "The Planning of Turkish as a Minority Language," pp. 140-161; III. Aspects of Change and Variation. Peter Herrity, "The Problematic Nature of the Standardisation of the Serbo-Croatian Literary Language in the Second Half of the Nineteenth Century," pp. 162-175; George Thomas, "Lexical Purism as an Aspect of Language Cultivation in Yugoslavia," pp. 176-188; Thomas F. Magner, "Urban Vernaculars and the Standard Language in Yugoslavia," pp. 189-199; Dunja Jutronic-Tihomirovic, "Standard Language and Dialects in Contact," pp. 200-211; Damir Kalogjera, "Attitudes to Dialects in Language Planning," pp. 212-222; Appendix I. Sven Gustavsson, "Between East, West and South Slavic: Rusyn Language Planning," pp. 223-225; Appendix II. Map of Yugoslavia.] REV: Rasia Dunatov, *Slavic Review* 52, no. 2 (Summer 1993): 382-383. Victor A. Friedman, *Modern Language Journal* 77, no. 2 (Summer 1993): 396-397. Marc L. Greenberg, *Slavic and East European Journal* 37, no. 4 (Winter 1993): 596-597. Zoran Starcevic, *Canadian Slavonic Papers* 35, nos. 1-2 (March-June 1993): 162.

5938. Hill, Peter. *The Dialect of Gorno Kalenik.* Columbus, OH: Slavica, c1990. 255 pp. [Macedonian dialect in the Phlorina region of Greece.] REV: Tom Priestly, *Canadian Slavonic Papers* 34, nos. 1-2 (March-June 1992): 168-169. Joseph Schallert, *Slavic and East European Journal* 37, no. 3 (Fall 1993): 400-402.

5939. Milivojevic, Dragan, and Vasa D. Mihailovich, eds. *Yugoslav Linguistics in English, 1900-1980: A Bibliography.* Columbus, OH: Slavica, 1990. 122 pp. REV: Tom Priestly, *Canadian Slavonic Papers* 34, nos. 1-2 (March-June 1992): 171-172. G.J. [Gerald Janecek], *Slavic and East European Journal* 37, no. 1 (Spring 1993): 141-142.

5940. Steenwijk, Han. *The Slovene Dialect of Resia: San Giorgio.* Studies in Slavic and General Linguistics, v. 18. Amsterdam; Atlanta, GA: Rodopi, 1992. xxiii, 352 pp. REV: Tom Priestly, *Canadian Slavonic Papers* 35, nos. 1-2 (March-June 1993): 190.

West Slavic

5941. Bethin, Christina Y. *Polish Syllables: The Role of Prosody in Phonology and Morphology.* Columbus, OH: Slavica, 1992. 278 pp. REV: Magda Stroinska, *Canadian Slavonic Papers* 35, nos. 1-2 (March-June 1993): 160-161.

5942. Sgall, Petr, Jirí Hronek, Alexandr Stich, and Ján Horecky. *Variation in Language: Code Switching in Czech as a Challenge for Sociolinguistics.* Linguistic & Literary Studies in Eastern Europe, v. 39. Amsterdam; Philadelphia, PA: J. Benjamins, c1992. xii, 368 pp. REV:

Zdenek Salzmann, *Language: Journal of the Linguisitc Society of America* 69, no. 4 (December 1993): 875-876.

5943. Walczynski, Waldemar. *Reading Authentic Polish.* Washington, DC: Center for Applied Linguistics; U.S. Dept. of Education, Office of Educational Research and Improvement, Educational Resources Information Center, 1991. v, 463 pp. REV: Madeline G. Levine, *Modern Language Journal* 77, no. 1 (Spring 1993): 124-125.

■ Literature

General

5944. Appelfeld, Aharon. *Katerina.* Translated from the Hebrew by Jeffrey M. Green. 1st U.S. ed. New York: Random House, c1992. 212 pp. [Translation of: *Katerinah.*] REV: John Bayley, *New York Review of Books* 39, no. 18 (November 5, 1992): 18-20. Judith Grossman, *New York Times Book Review* (September 27, 1992): 9. Elie Wiesel, *New Leader* 75, no. 16 (December 14-28, 1992): 24. Susan Miron, *Congress Monthly* 60, no. 3 (March-April 1993): 21-23. Juliana G. Pilon, *World & I* (March 1993): 310-314.

5945. Barnes, Julian. *The Porcupine.* 1st American ed. New York: Knopf; Distributed by Random House, 1992. 138 pp. [First published in Bulgarian, under the title *Bodlivo svinche.*] REV: John Bayley, *New York Review of Books* 39, no. 21 (December 17, 1992): 30-32. Anthony Lejeune, *National Review* 44, no. 24 (December 14, 1992): 51-52. Robert Stone, *New York Times Book Review* (December 13, 1992): 3. Dean Flower, *Hudson Review* 46, no. 2 (Summer 1993): 395-396. Maureen Howard, *Yale Review* 81, no. 2 (April 1993): 134-136. Catherine Kord, *Antioch Review* 51, no. 3 (Summer 1993): 458-459. Arch Puddington, *Commentary* 95, no. 5 (May 1993): 62-64.

5946. Costa, Luis, Richard Critchfield, Richard Golsan, and Wulf Koepke, eds. *German and International Perspectives on the Spanish Civil War: The Aesthetics of Partisanship.* 1st ed. Columbia, SC: Camden House, c1992. 503 pp. [Includes Arthur Koestler.] REV: Caroline Molina, *South Atlantic Review* 58, no. 3 (September 1993): 141-142.

5947. Davie, Donald. *Slavic Excursions: Essays on Russian and Polish Literature.* Chicago, IL: University of Chicago Press, 1990. 312 pp. REV: Walter Fred Smith, III, *Slavic and East European Journal* 37, no. 3 (Spring 1993): 100-101.

5948. Dodd, W. J. *Kafka and Dostoevsky: The Shaping of Influence.* New York: St. Martin's Press, 1992. xii, 237 pp. REV: Thomas Hollweck, *Seminar* 29, no. 4 (November 1993): 430-432.

5949. Heier, Edmund. *Studies on Johan Caspar Lavater (1741-1801) in Russia.* Slavica Helvetica, Bd. 37. Bern; New York: P. Lang, c1991. 179 pp. REV: Thomas Salumets, *Seminar* 29, no. 2 (May 1993): 183-184.

5950. Sendich, Munir, ed. *Studies in Slavic Literatures and Culture in Honor of Zoya Yurieff.* East Lansing, MI: Russian Language Journal, 1988. iii, 357 pp.

REV: Nancy L. Cooper, *Slavic and East European Journal* 37, no. 2 (Summer 1993): 237.

5951. Sollors, Werner, ed. *The Invention of Ethnicity.* Includes contribution by Mary Dearborn. New York: Oxford University Press, 1989. xx, 294 pp. [Includes a study of Anzia Yezierska by Mary Dearborn.] REV: K. D. Milobar, *Canadian Review of Studies in Nationalism = Revue Canadienne des Etudes sur le Nationalisme* 20, nos. 1-2 (1993): 161-162.

5952. Walker, Scott, ed. *Graywolf Annual Nine: Stories from the New Europe.* Includes contributions by Danilo Kis, Dubravka Ugresic, Ladislav Dvorak, Ivan Klíma, Teet Kallas, Regina Ezera, Juozas Aputis, William J. Hannaher, Michael Henry Heim, Suzanne Rappaport, George Theiner, Tono Onu, Tamara Zalite, and Angus Roxburgh. Graywolf Annual, 9. Saint Paul, MN: Graywolf Press, c1992. xiv, 205 pp. [Partial contents: Scott Walker, "Introduction," pp. ix-xiv; Danilo Kis, "From *Garden, Ashes,*" trans. William J. Hannaher, pp. 1-13; Dubravka Ugresic, "A Hot Dog in a Warm Bun," trans. Michael Henry Heim, pp. 14-33; Ladislav Dvorak, "Swords 'n' Sabers," trans. Suzanne Rappaport, pp. 34-48; Ivan Klíma, "Monday Morning: A Black Market Tale," trans. George Theiner, pp. 49-68; Teet Kallas, "Back to the Rocks," trans. Tono Onu, pp. 69-79; Regina Ezera, "Man Needs Dog," trans. Tamara Zalite, pp. 80-102; Juozas Aputis, "The Glade with Life-Giving Water," trans. Angus Roxburgh, pp. 103-110.] REV: Maureen Howard, *Yale Review* 81, no. 2 (April 1993): 141-143.

5953. Weissbort, Daniel, ed. *The Poetry of Survival: Post-War Poets of Central and Eastern Europe.* New York: St. Martin's Press, c1991. 384 pp. [Partial contents: Bertolt Brecht; Vladimír Holan; Peter Huchel; Edvard Kocbek; Czeslaw Milosz; Nelly Sachs; Leopold Staff; Anna Swirszczynska; Yehuda Amichai; Ingeborg Bachmann; Johannes Bobrowski; Nina Cassian; Paul Celan; Hans Magnus Enzensberger; Jerzy Ficowski; Zbigniew Herbert; Miroslav Holub; Tymoteusz Karpowicz; Artur Miedzyrzecki; Slavko Mihalic; Agnes Nemes Nagy; Dan Pagis; Janos Pilinszky; Vasko Popa; Tadeusz Rozewicz; Wislawa Szymborska; Natan Zach; Reiner Kunze.] REV: E. J. Czerwinski, *World Literature Today* 66, no. 3 (Summer 1992): 590. David Malcolm, *Polish Review* 38, no. 1 (1993): 112-114. Bronislava Volková, *Slavic Review* 52, no. 4 (Winter 1993): 880-881.

Baltic

5954. Belsevica, Vizma. *Bille.* Ithaca, NY: Mezabele, 1992. 253 pp. REV: Juris Silenieks, *World Literature Today* 67, no. 2 (Spring 1993): 414.

5955. Kaplinski, Jaan. *I Am the Spring in Tartu: and Other Poems Written in English.* Edited and introduced by Laurence P. A. Kitching. Vancouver, B.C.: Laurel Press, 1991. xxiv, 76 pp. REV: Billy Collins, *Journal of Baltic Studies* 24, no. 2 (Summer 1993): 208-210. Ilmar Mikiver, *World Literature Today* 67, no. 3 (Summer 1993): 639.

5956. Kelertas, Violeta, ed. *"Come into My Time": Lithuania in Prose Fiction, 1970-90.* Urbana, IL: University of Illinois Press, 1992. vii, 251 pp. [Collection of short stories translated from Lithuanian.] REV: Viktoria Skrupskelis, *World Literature Today* 67, no. 2 (Spring 1993): 415. Audrone B. Willeke, *Journal of Baltic Studies* 24, no. 2 (Summer 1993): 213-214.

5957. Sutema, Liune. *Graffiti.* Chicago, IL: AM & M Publications, 1992. 52 pp. REV: Rimvydas Silbajoris, *World Literature Today* 67, no. 4 (Autumn 1993): 865.

Bulgarian

5958. Dubarova, Petya. *Here I Am, in Perfect Leaf Today: The Poetic Will of Petya Dubarova.* Translated by Don D. Wilson. Canton, CT: Singular Speech, c1992. 64 pp. REV: Yuri Vidov Karageorge, *World Literature Today* 67, no. 2 (Spring 1993): 405-406.

5959. Kristeva, Julia. *The Samurai: A Novel.* Translated by Barbara Bray. New York: Columbia University Press, c1992. 341 pp. REV: Wendy Steiner, *New York Times Book Review* (November 15, 1992): 9ff. Maureen Howard, *Yale Review* 81, no. 2 (April 1993): 139.

5960. ——. *Strangers to Ourselves.* Translated by Leon S. Roudiez. European Perspectives. New York: Columbia University Press, c1991. 230 pp. [Includes discussion of Nabokov's *The Real Life of Sebastian Knight.*] REV: Michael McClintick, *Philosophy and Literature* 16, no. 2 (October 1992): 418-419. Linda Myrsiades, *College Literature* 20, no. 3 (October 1993): 174-176.

5961. Walker, Brenda, and Belin Tonchev, trans. *The Devil's Dozen: Thirteen Bulgarian Women Poets.* Translated in collaboration with Svetoslav Piperov. London; Boston: Forest Books; Sofia: Svyat, [1990]. xiii, 174 pp. REV: Yuri Vidov Karageorge, *World Literature Today* 67, no. 1 (Winter 1993): 208-209.

Czech and Slovak

5962. Havel, Václav. *Open Letters: Selected Writings, 1965-1990.* Selected and edited by Paul Wilson. 1st American ed. New York: Knopf; Distributed by Random House, 1991. 415 pp. REV: Josef Anderle, *Czechoslovak and Central European Journal* 10, no. 2 (Winter 1991): 150-154. John C. Campbell, *Foreign Affairs* 70, no. 4 (Fall 1991): 184. Erwin Knoll, *Progressive* 57, no. 4 (April 1993): 40-43.

5963. ——. *Summer Meditations.* Translated from the Czech by Paul Wilson. 1st American ed. New York: Knopf, 1992. 151 pp. [Translation of *Letni premitani.*] REV: Ralf Dahrendorf, *New York Times Book Review* (June 7, 1992): 1ff. George F. Kennan, *New York Review of Books* 39, no. 15 (September 24, 1992): 3-4. Aviezer Tucker, *Telos,* no. 91 (Spring 1992): 179-184. Erwin Knoll, *Progressive* 57, no. 4 (April 1993): 40-43. *Orbis* 37, no. 3 (Summer 1993).

5964. Hruby, Peter. *Daydreams and Nightmares: Czech Communist and Ex-Communist Literature 1917-1987.* East European Monographs, no. 290. Boulder, CO: East European Monographs; New York: Distributed by Columbia University Press, 1990. 362 pp. REV: Paul I. Trensky, *Czechoslovak and Central European Journal* 9, nos. 1-2

(Summer-Winter 1990): 154-157. V. Ambros, *Canadian Slavonic Papers* 33, no. 2 (June 1991): 195-196. Karen von Kunes, *Canadian American Slavic Studies = Revue Canadienne Américaine d'Etudes Slaves* 27, nos. 1-4 (1993): 412-413.

5965. Klíma, Ivan. *Love and Garbage*. Translated from the Czech by Ewald Osers. 1st American ed. New York: Knopf, 1991. 223 pp. [Translation of *Laska a smeti*.] REV: Philip Roth, *New York Review of Books* 37, no. 6 (April 12, 1990): 14-22. Stanislaw Baranczak, *New Republic* 205, no. 5 (July 29, 1991): 36-39. Eva Hoffman, *New York Times Book Review* (May 12, 1991): 9. Peter Z. Schubert, *World Literature Today* 65, no. 2 (Spring 1991): 325. Peter Filkins, *Partisan Review* 60, no. 3 (Summer 1993): 487-493.

5966. Kundera, Milan. *The Joke: Definitive Version*. 1st ed. New York, NY: HarperCollins, c1992. xi, 317 pp. [Fully revised by the author. Translation of *Zert*.] REV: Tom Wilhelmus, *Hudson Review* 46, no. 1 (Spring 1993): 247-255.

5967. Páral, Vladimír. *Catapult: A Timetable of Rail, Sea, and Air Ways to Paradise*. Translated by William Harkins. 1st English-language ed. Highland Park, NJ: Catbird Press; Distributed by Independent Publishers Group, c1989. 226 pp. REV: Peter Z. Schubert, *Slavic and East European Journal* 34, no. 3 (Fall 1990): 398-399. Dennis Drabelle, *Atlantic* 271, no. 5 (May 1993): 122-124. Richard Lourie, *Book World* 23, no. 10 (March 7, 1993): 11.

5968. Pekarkova, Iva. *Truck Stop Rainbows*. Translated by David Powelstock. 1st ed. New York: Farrar, Straus & Giroux, 1992. 279 pp. [Translation of *Pera a perute*.] REV: Danielle Crittenden, *National Review* 45, no. 7 (April 12, 1993): 69.

5969. Rudinsky, Norma L. *Incipient Feminists: Women Writers in the Slovak National Revival*. Appendix of Slovak women poets 1798-1875 by Marianna Pridavková-Mináriková. Slovak Language and Literature, 3. Columbus, OH: Slavica, c1991. 285 pp. REV: Ján Simko, *Czechoslovak and Central European Journal* 11, no. 1 (Summer 1992): 110-114. M. Mark Stolarik, *Slavic Review* 51, no. 3 (Fall 1992): 621. Míla Sasková-Pierce, *Slavic and East European Journal* 37, no. 4 (Winter 1993): 590-592.

5970. Schamschula, Walter, ed. *An Anthology of Czech Literature*. Westslavische Beitrage = West Slavic Contributions, 2. Frankfurt am Main; New York: P. Lang, c1990. 2 vols. [Partial contents: Vol. 1 1st Period: From the Beginnings until 1410.] REV: William E. Harkins, *Czechoslovak and Central European Journal* 11, no. 2 (Winter 1993): 129-131.

5971. Skvorecky, Josef. *The Miracle Game*. Translated by Paul Wilson. 1st American ed. New York: Knopf, 1991. 436 pp. [Translation of *Mirakl*.] REV: John Bemrose, *MacLean's* 103 (December 31, 1990): 47. John Bayley, *New York Review of Books* 38, no. 7 (April 11, 1991): 45-46. Angela Carter, *New York Times Book Review* (February 10, 1991): 1ff. John Clute, *Nation* no. 252 (March 25, 1991): 381-382. Arnost Lustig, *World & I* 6, no. 4 (April 1991):

390-396. E. J. Czerwinski, *World Literature Today* 66, no. 1 (Winter 1992): 162-163. Peter Filkins, *Partisan Review* 60, no. 3 (Summer 1993): 487-493.

5972. Timrava. *That Alluring Land: Slovak Stories*. Edited and translated by Norma L. Rudinsky. Pitt Series in Russian and East European Studies, no. 15. Pittsburgh, PA: University of Pittsburgh Press, c1992. xvi, 324 pp. [Translation of *Ta zem vabna*. Contents: Battle; That alluring land; No joy at all; The Tapak clan; Great War heros.] REV: Gale Harris, *Belles Lettres* 8, no. 1 (Fall 1992): 24-25. Hilda Scott, *Women's Review of Books* 9, nos. 10-11 (July 1992): 41-42. Peter Z. Schubert, *World Literature Today* 67, no. 4 (Autumn 1993): 858.

5973. Urbánek, Zdenek. *On the Sky's Clayey Bottom: Sketches and Happenings from the Years of Silence*. Translated from the Czech by William Harkins. Foreword by Václav Havel. 1st ed. New York: Four Walls Eight Windows, c1992. vii, 232 pp. REV: Stanislaw Baranczak, *New Republic* 207, no. 18 (October 26, 1992): 43-45. Ann Morrissett Davidon, *New York Times Book Review* (November 29, 1992): 20. Veronika Ambros, *World Literature Today* 67, no. 4 (Autumn 1993): 855.

German

5974. Calabro, Tony. *Bertolt Brecht's Art of Dissemblance*. Wakefield, NH: Longwood Academic, 1990. xv, 158 pp. REV: David Krasner, *Modern Drama* 36, no. 4 (December 1993): 587-588.

5975. Colin, Amy. *Paul Celan: Holograms of Darkness*. Jewish Literature and Culture, Bloomington: Indiana University Press, 1991. 211 pp. REV: Jerry Glenn, *World Literature Today* 66, no. 3 (Summer 1992): 512. Gilya Gerda Schmidt, *Modern Judaism* 12, no. 3 (October 1992): 299-302. John Felstiner, *Comparative Literature* 45 (Summer 1993): 303-304.

5976. Karl, Frederick R. *Franz Kafka: Representative Man*. New York: Ticknor & Fields, 1991. xix, 810 pp. REV: Leigh Hafrey, *New York Times Book Review* (February 23, 1992): 16. Marvin Thompson, *World Literature Today* 66, no. 2 (Spring 1992): 339-340. Peter Wolfe, *Studies in Short Fiction* 30, no. 1 (Winter 1993): 110-111.

5977. Martin, Biddy. *Woman and Modernity: The (Life)Styles of Lou Andreas-Salomé*. Ithaca, NY: Cornell University Press, 1991. xiv, 250 pp. REV: Peter Gölz, *Seminar* 29, no. 2 (May 1993): 194-195.

5978. Mueller, Roswitha. *Bertolt Brecht and the Theory of Media*. Lincoln, NE: University of Nebraska Press, c1989. xiii, 149 pp. REV: Robert C. Conard, *German Studies Review* 13, no. 3 (October 1990): 573-575. Deborah Linderman, *Film Quarterly* 46, no. 4 (Summer 1993): 28-29.

5979. Murray, Jack. *The Landscapes of Alienation: Ideological Subversion in Kafka, Céline, and Onetti*. Stanford, CA: Stanford University Press, 1991. 364 pp. REV: Mary Ann Witt, *Comparatist* 17 (May 1993): 166.

5980. Ören, Aras. *Please, No Police*. Translated from the Turkish by Teoman Sipahigil. Introduction by Akile Gursay Tezcan. Modern Middle East Literature in Translation Series. Austin, TX: Center for MIddle Eastern Studies. University of Texas at Austin, 1992. xxxvii, 136 pp. [First written in Turkish and translated from the Turkish; orginally published in German as *Bitte nix Polizei* (1980). Novel about guest workers in Germany; includes treatment of refugees from the Soviet sector.] REV: Alice H. G. Phillips, *Current History* 92, no. 570 (January 1993): 43.

5981. Reshetylo-Rothe, Daria A. *Rilke and Russia: A Re-Evaluation*. Studies in Modern German Literature, vol. 18. New York: P. Lang, 1990. xiv, 357 pp. REV: Susanne Kimball, *Seminar* 29, no. 3 (September 1993): 333-334.

Hungarian

5982. Konrád, György. *A Feast in the Garden*. Translated from the Hungarian by Imre Goldstein. 1st ed. New York: Harcourt Brace Jovanovich, 1992. 394 pp. [Translation of *Kerti mulatsag*. Excerpt published in *Harper's* 284, no. 1703 (April 1992): 32ff.] REV: Stanislaw Baranczak, *New Republic* 207, no. 10 (August 31, 1992): 42-45. Ian Buruma, *New York Review of Books* 39, no. 13 (July 16, 1992): 11-12. Betty Falkenberg, *New Leader* 75, no. 8 (June 29, 1992): 17-18. *Publishers Weekly* 239, no. 7 (February 3, 1992): 61. Peter Filkins, *Partisan Review* 60, no. 3 (Summer 1993): 487-493. *Orbis* 37, no. 2 (Spring 1993).

5983. Várkonyi, István. *Ferenc Molnar and the Austro-Hungarian "Fin de Siècle"*. Austrian Culture, vol. 15. New York: P. Lang, 1992. xiii, 136 pp. REV: Lee Congdon, *Slavic Review* 52, no. 4 (Winter 1993): 858-859.

5984. Zend, Robert. *Daymares: Selected Fictions on Dreams and Time*. Edited by Brian Wyatt. Foreword by John Robert Colombo. Vancouver: Cacanadadada, 1991. xiii, 186 pp. [Afterword by Northrop Frye.] REV: Richard Stevenson, *Dalhousie Review* 73, no. 1 (Spring 1993): 100-102.

Polish

5985. Baranczak, Stanislaw. *Breathing under Water and Other East European Essays*. Cambridge, MA: Harvard University Press, 1990. 258 pp. REV: E. J. Czerwinski, *World Literature Today* 65, no. 3 (Summer 1991): 512-513. Norman M. Naimark, *Slavic Review* 51, no. 1 (Spring 1992): 179-180. Halina Stephan, *Slavic and East European Journal* 36, no. 1 (Spring 1992): 140-142. Theodosia S. Robertson, *Canadian American Slavic Studies = Revue Canadienne Américaine d'Etudes Slaves* 27, nos. 1-4 (1993): 440-442. Anita Shelton, *Nationalities Papers* 21, no. 2 (Fall 1993): 257-259.

5986. Baranczak, Stanislaw, and Clare Cavanagh, eds. and trans. *Spoiling Cannibals' Fun: Polish Poetry of the Last Two Decades of Communist Rule*. Foreword by Helen Vendler. Evanston, IL: Northwestern University Press, c1991. xxi, 196 pp. REV: Bogdana Carpenter, *World Literature Today* 66, no. 4 (Autumn 1992): 745-746. Maya Peretz, *Polish Review* 37, no. 3 (1992): 345-353. Bogdana Carpenter, *World Literature Today* 66, no. 4 (Autumn 1992): 745-746. Maya Peretz, *Polish Review* 37, no. 3 (1992): 345-353. E. J. Czerwinski, *Slavic and East European Journal* 37, no. 2 (Summer 1993): 231-234.

5987. Carpenter, Bogdana, ed. *Monumenta Polonica: The First Four Centuries of Polish Poetry: A Bilingual Anthology*. Michigan Slavic Publications, no. 31. Ann Arbor, MI: Michigan Slavic Publications, c1989. 567 pp. REV: Stanislaw Baranczak, *Polish Review* 35, nos. 3-4 (1990): 261-262. David A. Frick, *Slavic and East European Journal* 34, no. 4 (Winter 1990): 551-552. Harold B. Segel, *Slavic Review* 52, no. 2 (Summer 1993): 393-395.

5988. Czerniawski, Adam, ed. *The Mature Laurel: Essays on Modern Polish Poetry*. Bridgend, Mid Glamorgan: Seren Books; Chester Springs, PA: Dufour Editions, c1991. xii, 325 pp. REV: Joachim T. Baer, *World Literature Today* 66, no. 2 (Spring 1992): 371. George Gömöri, *Polish Review* 37, no. 3 (1992): 373-375. E. J. Czerwinski, *Slavic and East European Journal* 37, no. 2 (Summer 1993): 231-234.

5989. Erdinast-Vulcan, Daphna. *Joseph Conrad and the Modern Temper*. Oxford English Monographs. Oxford: Clarendon Press; New York: Oxford University Press, 1991. vi, 218 pp. REV: Brian W. Shaffer, *Modern Fiction Studies* 38, no. 4 (Winter 1992): 957-958. Daniel R. Schwarz, *Studies in the Novel* 25, no. 1 (Spring 1993): 108-111.

5990. Fiut, Aleksander. *The Eternal Moment: The Poetry of Czeslaw Milosz*. Translated by Theodosia S. Robertson. Berkeley, CA: University of California Press, c1990. xiv, 226 pp. [Translation of *Moment wieczny*.] REV: Stanislaw Baranczak, *Slavic and East European Journal* 35, no. 1 (Spring 1991): 164-165. Harold B. Segel, *Harvard Ukrainian Studies* 16, nos. 1-2 (June 1992): 193-198. Bozena Karwowska, *Canadian American Slavic Studies = Revue Canadienne Américaine d'Etudes Slaves* 27, nos. 1-4 (1993): 387-388.

5991. Kott, Jan, ed. *Four Decades of Polish Essays*. Evanston, IL: Northwestern University Press, c1990. xi, 403 pp. REV: Vladimir Tismaneanu, *Orbis* 35, no. 2 (Spring 1991): 306-307. Norman M. Naimark, *Slavic Review* 51, no. 1 (Spring 1992): 179-180. Anita Shelton, *Nationalities Papers* 21, no. 2 (Fall 1993): 257-259.

5992. Krasicki, Ignacy. *The Adventures of Mr. Nicholas Wisdom*. Translated by Thomas H. Hoisington. Introduction by Helena Goscilo. Evanston, IL: Northwestern University Press, 1992. xxvii, 148 pp. REV: Gerard T. Kapolka, *Polish Review* 38, no. 4 (1993): 505-508.

5993. Kuryluk, Ewa. *Century 21*. Normal, IL: Dalkey Archive Press, 1992. 340 pp. REV: Thomas Filbin, *Hudson Review* 46, no. 3 (Autumn 1993): 587-592.

5994. Mikos, Michael J., trans. *Medieval Literature of Poland: An Anthology*. Garland Library of Medieval Literature, v. 82. New York: Garland, 1992. xxxvi, 223 pp.

REV: Samuel Fiszman, *Slavic and East European Journal* 37, no. 3 (Fall 1993): 395-396.

5995. Nathan, Leonard, and Arthur Quinn. *The Poet's Work: An Introduction to Czeslaw Milosz.* Cambridge, MA: Harvard University Press, 1991. 178 pp. REV: Bogdana Carpenter, *World Literature Today* 66, no. 2 (Spring 1992): 371-372. Donald Davie, *New Republic* 206, no. 11 (March 16, 1992): 34-37. Harold B. Segel, *Harvard Ukrainian Studies* 16, nos. 1-2 (June 1992): 193-198. Helen Vendler, *New York Review of Books* 39, no. 14 (August 13, 1992): 44-46. E. J. Czerwinski, *Slavic and East European Journal* 37, no. 2 (Summer 1993): 231-234. Madeline G. Levine, *Slavic Review* 52, no. 1 (Spring 1993): 134.

5996. Szymborska, Wislawa. *People on a Bridge: Poems.* Introduced and translated by Adam Czerniawski. London; Boston, MA: Forest Books, 1990. xvi, 78 pp. REV: Bogdana Carpenter, *World Literature Today* 66, no. 1 (Winter 1992): 163-164. Maya Peretz, *Polish Review* 38, no. 1 (1993): 114-118.

5997. Witkiewicz, Stanislaw. *The Witkiewicz Reader.* Edited, translated, and introduction by Daniel Gerould. Evanston, IL: Northwestern University Press, c1992. xiii, 359 pp. REV: Edward J. Czerwinski, *Polish Review* 38, no. 4 (1993): 485-486.

Romanian

5998. Cosma, Flavia. *47 Poems.* Translated by Don D. Wilson. Lubbock, TX: Texas Tech University Press, c1992. viii, 99 pp. [English and Romanian.] REV: Marcel Cornis-Pope, *World Literature Today* 67, no. 4 (Autumn 1993): 806-807.

5999. Crasnaru, Daniela. *Letters from Darkness: Poems.* Translated by Fleur Adcock. Oxford; New York: Oxford University Press, 1991. x, 47 pp. REV: Marguerite Dorian, *World Literature Today* 67, no. 1 (Winter 1993): 172.

6000. Dumbrăveanu, Anghel. *Selected Poems: Love and Winter.* Edited by Adam J. Sorkin. Translated by Adam J. Sorkin and Irian Grigorescu Pana. Lewiston, NY: Mellen, 1992. xiv, 205 pp. REV: Marguerite Dorian, *World Literature Today* 67, no. 4 (Autumn 1993): 807.

6001. Manea, Norman. *October, Eight O'Clock.* Translated from the Romanian by Cornelia Golna, Anselm Hollo, Mara Soceanu Vamos, Max Bleyleben, Marguerite Dorian, and Elliott B. Urdang. New York: Grove Weidenfeld, 1992. v, 216 pp. [Contents: The sweater — Death — We might have been four — The balls of faded yarn — Proust's tea — Weddings — The exact hour — Tale of the enchanted pig — The instructor — Summer — The turning point — Portrait of the yellow apricot tree — The partition — Seascape with birds — October, eight o'clock.] REV: Stanislaw Baranczak, *New Republic* 206, no. 22 (June 1,1992): 44-49. John Bayley, *New York Times Book Review* (June 21, 1992): 3ff. Louis Begley, *New York Review of Books* 39, no. 15 (September 24, 1992): 6-8. Gabriel Motola, *Nation* 255, no. 11 (October 12, 1992): 401-403. John Updike, *New Yorker* 68, no. 39 (November 16, 1992): 134-

142. *Publishers Weekly* 239, no. 15 (March 23, 1992): 59. Maria Green, *World Literature Today* 67, no. 2 (Spring 1993): 363. Susan Miron, *Congress Monthly* 60, no. 7 (November-December 1993): 17-18.

6002. ———. *On Clowns: The Dictator and the Artist: Essays.* 1st ed. New York: Grove Weidenfeld, 1992. 178 pp. [Translated from the Romanian.] REV: Stanislaw Baranczak, *New Republic* 206, no. 22 (June 1, 1992): 44-49. John Bayley, *New York Times Book Review* (June 21, 1992): 3ff. John Updike, *New Yorker* 68, no. 39 (November 16, 1992): 134-142. Susan Miron, *Congress Monthly* 60, no. 7 (November-December 1993): 17-18.

Russian

General

6003. Barta, Peter I., and Ulrich Goebel, eds. *The European Foundations of Russian Modernism.* Studies in Russian and German, no. 4. Studies in Slavic Language and Literature, v. 7. Lewiston, NY: Edwin Mellen Press, c1991. 328 pp. REV: Greta N. Slobin, *Slavic and East European Journal* 37, no. 2 (Summer 1993): 247-248.

6004. Bethea, David M. *The Shape of Apocalypse in Modern Russian Fiction.* Princeton, NJ: Princeton University Press, c1989. xix, 307 pp. REV: Laura D. Weeks, *Russian Review* 49, no. 2 (April 1990): 217-218. Nadya Peterson, *Slavic Review* 51, no. 3 (Fall 1992): 625-626. Peter I. Barta, *Canadian American Slavic Studies = Revue Canadienne Américaine d'Etudes Slaves* 27, nos. 1-4 (1993): 373-374.

6005. Briggs, A. D. P. *A Comparative Study of Pushkin's The Bronze Horseman, Nekrasov's Red-Nosed Frost, and Blok's The Twelve: The Wild World.* Studies in Slavic Language and Literature, vol. 5. Lewiston, NY: Edwin Mellen Press, c1990. 276 pp. REV: Carol Ueland, *Russian Review* 52, no. 2 (April 1993): 266-267.

6006. Bristol, Evelyn. *A History of Russian Poetry.* New York: Oxford University Press, 1991. ix, 354 pp. REV: John A. Barnstead, *Dalhousie Review* 72 (Summer 1992): 251-255; Elena Siemens, *Canadian Slavonic Papers* 34, no. 3 (September 1992): 328-329. Victor Terras, *World Literature Today* 66, no. 3 (Summer 1992): 543. Barry P. Scherr, *Slavic and East European Journal* 37, no. 2 (Summer 1993): 239-241.

6007. Dmitriev, Viktor. *Serebriannyi gost: O liricheskom geroe Bal'monta.* Tenafly, NJ: Ermitazh, c1992. 185 pp. REV: Mark Al'tshuller, *Russian Language Journal* 46, no. 153-155 (Winter-Spring-Fall 1992): 317-319. Evelyn Bristol, *Slavic and East European Journal* 37, no. 4 (Winter 1993): 579-80.

6008. Gaiser-Shnitman, Svetlana. *Venedikt Erofeev: "Moskva-Petushki" ili "The Rest is Silence".* Slavica Helvetica, Bd. 30. Bern; New York: P. Lang, c1987. 307 pp. REV: Diana Lewis Burgin, *Canadian American Slavic*

Studies = Revue Canadienne Américaine d'Etudes Slaves 27, nos. 1-4 (1993): 371-373.

6009. Gasparov, Boris, Robert P. Hughes, and Irina Paperno, eds. *Cultural Mythologies of Russian Modernism: From the Golden Age to the Silver Age.* California Slavic Studies, vol. 15. Berkeley, CA: University of California Press, c1992. 494 pp. [In English and Russian. Papers delivered at a conference held at the University of California, Berkeley, in May 1987, sponsored by the Center for Slavic and East European Studies.] REV: Irina Gutkin, *Slavic Review* 52, no. 2 (Summer 1993): 400-401.

6010. Nemec Ignashev, Diane M., and Sarah Krive. *Women and Writing in Russia and the USSR: A Bibliography of English-Language Sources.* Garland Reference Library of the Humanities, vol. 1280. New York: Garland, 1992. xiii, 328 pp. REV: June Pachuta Farris, *Russian Review* 52, no. 4 (October 1993): 582. Lyubomira Parpulova Gribble, *Russian Language Journal = Russkii iazyk* 47, nos. 156-158 (Winter-Spring-Fall 1993): 361-364. Mary F. Zirin, *Slavic Review* 52, no. 2 (Summer 1993): 410-411.

6011. Pomorska, Krystyna. *Jakobsonian Poetics and Slavic Narrative: From Pushkin to Solzhenitsyn.* Edited by Henryk Baran. Sound and Meaning: The Roman Jakobson Series in Linguistics and Poetics, Durham, NC: Duke University Press, 1992. xxvi, 323 pp. [Twenty essays by Krystyna Pomorska. Contents: "The Structure of Prose"; "The Segmentation of Narrative Prose"; "Toward a Typology of the Roman-fleuve"; "Alexander Solzhenitsyn: The Overcoded Word"; "Tolstoi: Contra Semiosis"; "Tolstoi's Triplets: An Approach to Biography and Creativity"; "Tolstoi's Rotary System (On Symbolism in War and Peace)" [with Mark Drazen]; "Pasternak and Futurism"; "Music as Theme and Structure"; "The Fate of the Artist"; "Doctor Zhivago"; "Maiakovskii and the Myth of Immortality in the Russian Avant-garde"; "A Note on Tat'iana's Letter: 'Tu' and 'Vous'"; "Semiotic Implications of Pushkin's Rhymes"; "Observations on Ukrainian Erotic Folk Songs"; "Problems of Parallelism in Gogol's Prose"; "Polish Culture in Jakobson's Research"; "The Autobiography of a Scholar: Jakobson's Generation"; "The Drama of Science: Trubetzkoy's Correspondence With Jakobson"; "Postscript to Dialogues: Roman Jakobson, His Poet Friends and Collaborators".] REV: Galya Diment, *Slavic Review* 52, no. 4 (Winter 1993): 879-880. Charles Lock, *Canadian Slavonic Papers* 35, nos. 3-4 (September-December 1993): 410-412. Denis Mickiewicz, *Russian Language Journal = Russkii iazyk* 47, nos. 156-158 (Winter-Spring-Fall 1993): 371-372.

6012. Terras, Victor. *A History of Russian Literature.* New Haven, CT: Yale University Press, c1991. x, 654 pp. REV: William E. Harkins, *Slavic Review* 51, no. 4 (Winter 1992): 846-847. Allan Reid, *International Fiction Review* 19, no. 2 (1992): 128-129. Michael Katz, *Russian Review* 52, no. 3 (July 1993): 415-416. Ewa M. Thompson, *World Literature Today* 67, no. 3 (Summer 1993): 626.

6013. Thompson, Ewa M., ed. *The Search for Self-Definition in Russian Literature.* 1st ed. Houston, TX: Rice University Press, 1991. xiii, 216 pp. [Selected papers from a conference held at Rice University, September 22-23, 1989.] REV: Elena Siemens, *Canadian Slavonic Papers* 33, nos. 3-4 (December 1991): 396-398. Kathleen Parthé, *Slavic Review* 51, no. 2 (Summer 1992): 379-380. Alex E. Alexander, *Polish Review* 38, no. 3 (1993): 331-332.

6014. Wachtel, Andrew Baruch. *The Battle for Childhood: Creation of a Russian Myth.* Stanford, CA: Stanford University Press, 1990. 262 pp. REV: Andrew R. Durkin, *Slavic Review* 50, no. 4 (Winter 1991): 1059-1060. Milton Ehre, *Slavic and East European Journal* 35, no. 3 (Fall 1991): 433-434. David L. Ransel, *Russian Review* 50, no. 3 (July 1991): 354-355. Donna Orwin, *Canadian Slavonic Papers* 34, nos. 1-2 (March-June 1992): 175-176. Gary Cox, *Canadian American Slavic Studies = Revue Canadienne Américaine d'Etudes Slaves* 27, nos. 1-4 (1993): 425.

Pre-Revolutionary Period (1700-1917)

6015. Allen, Elizabeth Cheresh. *Beyond Realism: Turgenev's Poetics of Secular Salvation.* Stanford, CA: Stanford University Press, 1992. viii, 255 pp. REV: Jitka Hurych, *Style* 27, no. 1 (Spring 1993): 145-149. Richard Kaplan, *Philosophy and Literature* 17, no. 2 (October 1993): 359-360. Ruele K. Wilson, *Canadian Slavonic Papers* 35, nos. 1-2 (March-June 1993).

6016. Baehr, Stephen Lessing. *The Paradise Myth in Eighteenth-Century Russia: Utopian Patterns in Early Secular Russian Literature and Culture.* Studies of the Harriman Institute. Stanford, CA: Stanford University Press, c1991. xiv, 308 pp. REV: Marcus C. Levitt, *Canadian Slavonic Papers* 33, nos. 3-4 (December 1991): 382-383. Irina Reyfman, *Eighteenth Century Studies* 26 (Fall 1992): 191-194. Il'ia Serman, *Slavic Review* 51, no. 4 (Winter 1992): 847-848. James Cracraft, *American Historical Review* 98, no. 2 (April 1993): 532. Yvonne Howell, *Science-Fiction Studies* 20, no. 1 (March 1993): 125-127. Thomas Newlin, *Russian Review* 52, no. 4 (October 1993): 551. I. R. Titunik, *Slavic and East European Journal* 37, no. 3 (Fall 1993): 381-383.

6017. Boss, Valentin. *Milton and the Rise of Russian Satanism.* Toronto, Ontario; Buffalo, NY: University of Toronto Press, c1991. xxvi, 276 pp. REV: Nicholas V. Riasanovsky, *American Historical Review* 97, no. 3 (June 1992): 894-895. Gerald J. Schiffhorst, *South Atlantic Review* 57, no. 2 (May 1992): 126-127. Stephen L. Baehr, *Slavic and East European Journal* 37, no. 2 (Summer 1993): 241-243. Bernice Glatzer Rosenthal, *Russian Review* 52, no. 3 (July 1993): 416-417.

6018. Breger, Louis. *Dostoevsky: The Author as Psychoanalyst.* New York: New York University Press, c1989. xiv, 295 pp. REV: Daniel Rancour-Laferriere, *Slavic and East European Journal* 36, no. 3 (Fall 1992): 366-367. Gary Rosenshield, *Dostoevsky Studies = Dostoevskii: Stat'i i materialy* 1, no. 2 (1993): 247-250.

6019. Briggs, A. D. P. *Alexander Pushkin, Eugene Onegin.* Landmarks of World Literature. Cambridge; New York: Cambridge University Press, 1992. viii, 116 pp.

[Contents: 1: The poetry of Eugene Onegin. The Russian language. Problems of translation. The Onegin stanza. A close look at two stanzas — 2: Shades of unreality. The story. The presence of Pushkin. Inherited perceptions of Eugene Onegin. Morning into midnight — 3: The unreal reputations of Eugene Onegin and Tatyana Larina. Eugene Onegin. Guilty or not guilty? Imaginary superiority. The Byronic background. In and out of character. Tatyana Larina. The two Tatyanas and two Eugenes. The two rejection scenes. The earlier Tatyana — 4: Olga, Lensky and the duel. The younger sister. Vladimir Lensky. The duel. Why did he do it? — 5: It is in verse, but is it a novel? 'The careless fruit of my amusements'. An educated pen. In search of the serious content. Privacy of conscience and moral awareness. History and fate. The possibility and closeness of happiness. Dealing with death. Knowledge of human nature. Eugene Onegin as a landmark.] REV: Richard Gregg, *Slavic Review* 52, no. 4 (Winter 1993): 869-870.

6020. Catteau, Jacques. *Dostoyevsky and the Process of Literary Creation*. Translated by Audrey Littlewood. Cambridge Studies in Russian Literature. Cambridge; New York: Cambridge University Press, 1989. xiv, 553 pp. [Translation of *Le creation litteraire Chez Dostoievski*.] REV: Gary R. Jahn, *Modern Fiction Studies* 36, no. 2 (Summer 1990): 294-295. Charles Lock, *Canadian Slavonic Papers* 32, no. 1 (March 1990): 92-94. Gary Rosenshield, *Slavic Review* 50, no. 3 (Fall 1991): 724-725. Joseph Frank, *Common Knowledge* 1, no. 2 (Fall 1992): 129. Robin Feuer Miller, *Russian Review* 51, no. 3 (July 1992): 427-428. Roger Anderson, *Dostoevsky Studies = Dostoevskii: Stat'i i materialy* 1, no. 1 (1993): 128-130.

6021. Danow, David K. *The Dialogic Sign: Essays on the Major Novels of Dostoevsky*. Middlebury Studies in Russian Language and Literature, vol. 2. New York: P. Lang, c1991. ix, 219 pp. REV: C. J. G. Turner, *Canadian Slavonic Papers* 35, nos. 1-2 (March-June 1993): 152-153.

6022. Dostoevsky, Fyodor. *Fyodor Dostoevsky: Complete Letters*. Edited and translated by David A. Lowe and Ronald Meyer. Ann Arbor, MI: Ardis, c1988-c1991. 5 vols. [Vols. 2-5 edited and translated by David A. Lowe. Contents: Vol. 1. 1832-1859 — v. 2. 1860-1867 — v. 3. 1868-1871 — v. 4. 1872-1877 — v. 5. 1878-1881.] REV: Gary R. Jahn, *Modern Fiction Studies* 36, no. 2 (Summer 1990): 294-295. A.T. Netick, *Choice* (January 1990): 806. Victor Terras, *Slavic and East European Journal* 34, no. 3 (Fall 1990): 379-380. Ellen Chances, *Slavic Review* 52, no. 3 (Fall 1993): 631-632. Gene Fitzgerald, *Dostoevsky Studies* 1, no. 1 (1993): 105-115.

6023. Druzhinin, Aleksandr. *Polinka Saks; and, The Story of Aleksei Dmitrich*. Translated and introduction by Michael R. Katz. Evanston, IL: Northwestern University Press, 1992. 245 pp. [Translation of *Polin'ka Saks* and *Rasskaz Alekseia Dmitricha*.] REV: Barbara Heldt, *Canadian Slavonic Papers* 35, nos. 1-2 (March-June 1993): 167-168. Mary F. Zirin, *Translation Review*, nos. 42-43 (1993): 50-53.

6024. Fusso, Susanne, and Priscilla Meyer, eds. *Essays on Gogol: Logos and the Russian Word*. Series in Russian Literature and Theory, Evanston, IL: Northwestern University Press, c1992. xiii, 291 pp. [Papers presented at a conference held at Wesleyan University, April 9-10, 1988.] REV: Milton Ehre, *Slavic and East European Journal* 37, no. 3 (Fall 1993): 383-384. Andrew Wachtel, *Slavic Review* 52, no. 1 (Spring 1993): 124-125.

6025. Gordin, IAkov. *Lev Tolstoi i russkaia istoriia*. Tenafly, NJ: Ermitazh, 1992. 151 pp. REV: Patricia Carden, *Slavic Review* 52, no. 3 (Fall 1993): 638-639.

6026. Gunn, Judith. *Dostoyevsky: Dreamer and Prophet*. 1st ed. Oxford; Batavia, IL: Lion Pub., 1990. 175 pp. REV: John M. Ellison, *Dostoevsky Studies = Dostoevskii: Stat'i i materialy* 1, no. 2 (1993): 262.

6027. Hammarberg, Gitta. *From the Idyll to the Novel: Karamzin's Sentimentalist Prose*. Cambridge Studies in Russian Literature. Cambridge; New York: Cambridge University Press, 1991. xiii, 334 pp. REV: Marcus C. Levitt, *Canadian Slavonic Papers* 33, nos. 3-4 (December 1991): 388-389. Maria Pavlovszky, *Russian Review* 52, no. 2 (April 1993): 267-268.

6028. Herdman, John. *The Double in Nineteenth-Century Fiction: The Shadow Life*. New York: St. Martin's Press, 1991. xi, 174 pp. [Includes discussion of Gogol', Dostoevsky and Chekhov.] REV: Mathew David Fisher, *Studies in Short Fiction* 30, no. 2 (Spring 1993): 205-206.

6029. Jones, Malcolm V. *Dostoyevsky after Bakhtin: Readings in Dostoyevsky's Fantastic Realism*. Cambridge; New York, NY: Cambridge University Press, 1990. xvii, 221 pp. REV: R.L. Busch, *Canadian Slavonic Papers* 33, no. 2 (June 1991): 198-200. Roger Anderson, *Russian Review* 51, no. 1 (January 1992): 110-111. Anna Tavis, *Slavic and East European Journal* 36, no. 1 (Spring 1992): 101-106. Caryl Emerson, *Dostoevsky Studies = Dostoevskii: Stat'i i materialy* 1, no. 2 (1993): 251-255. Andrew Wachtel, *Canadian American Slavic Studies = Revue Canadienne Américaine d'Etudes Slaves* 27, nos. 1-4 (1993): 380-381.

6030. Kohn, Martin, Carol Donley, and Delese Wear. *Literature and Aging: An Anthology*. Kent, OH: Kent State University Press, 1992. xviii, 424 pp. [Includes Chekhov's "Misery".] REV: Ute Carson, *Social Science & Medicine* 37, no. 8 (October 1993): 1087-1088.

6031. Lary, N. M. *Dostoevsky and Soviet Film: Visions of Demonic Realism*. Ithaca, NY: Cornell University Press, 1986. 279 pp. REV: Jerome H. Katsell, *Dostoevsky Studies = Dostoevskii: Stat'i i materialy* 1, no. 2 (1993): 259-261.

6032. Leatherbarrow, W. J. *Fyodor Dostoyevsky— The Brothers Karamazov*. Landmarks of World Literature. Cambridge; New York: Cambridge University Press, 1992. ix, 115 pp. [Contents: 1: The background to the novel — 2: The novel. The family. The fragmented hero. The quest for harmony. Pro and contra. 'A realist in a higher sense' — 3: The critical reception.] REV: Deborah Martinsen, *Dostoevsky Studies = Dostoevskii: Stat'i i materialy* 1, no. 2

(1993): 255-257. Victor Terras, *Slavic Review* 52, no. 3 (Fall 1993): 632-633.

6033. Levitt, Marcus C. *Russian Literary Politics and the Pushkin Celebration of 1880.* Studies of the Harriman Institute. Ithaca, NY: Cornell University Press, 1989. x, 233 pp. REV: Gary Cox, *Russian Review* 49, no. 4 (October 1990): 489-490. Sona Stephan Hoisington, *Slavic and East European Journal* 34, no. 2 (Summer 1990): 257-258. Michael R. Katz, *Slavic Review* 49, no. 4 (Winter 1990): 676. Bernice Glatzer Rosenthal, *American Historical Review* 96, no. 3 (June 1991): 914-915. Linda Gerstein, *Canadian American Slavic Studies = Revue Canadienne Américaine d'Etudes Slaves* 27, nos. 1-4 (1993): 345-346.

6034. Lynch, Michael F. *Creative Revolt: A Study of Wright, Ellison, and Dostoevsky.* American University Studies. Series XXIV, American Literature, vol. 12. New York: P. Lang, c1990. 194 pp. REV: Byron Lindsey, *Slavic and East European Journal* 37, no. 4 (Winter 1993): 577.

6035. Marmeladov, Yuri I. *Dostoevsky's Secret Code: The Allegory of Elijah the Prophet.* Translated by Jay MacPherson. Lawrence, KS: Coronado Press, 1987. ix, 125 pp. [Based on the author's uncompleted manuscript.] REV: Curt Whitcomb, *Dostoevsky Studies = Dostoevskii: Stat'i i materialy* 1, no. 1 (1993): 134-136.

6036. McLean, Hugh, ed. *In the Shade of the Giant: Essays on Tolstoy.* Contributions by Hugh McLean, Ruth Rischin, John Weeks, Irina Gutkin, Andrew Wachtel, Joan Grossman, and John Kopper. California Slavic Studies, vol. 13. Berkeley, CA: University of California Press, c1989. viii, 193 pp. REV: Michael R. Katz, *Slavic Review* 49, no. 4 (Winter 1990): 678-679. Nicholas O. Warner, *Russian Review* 49, no. 4 (October 1990): 488-489. Sydney Schultze, *Slavic and East European Journal* 35, no. 2 (Summer 1991): 279-280. C. J. G. Turner, *Canadian American Slavic Studies = Revue Canadienne Américaine d'Etudes Slaves* 27, nos. 1-4 (1993): 368-369.

6037. Murav, Harriet. *Holy Foolishness: Dostoevsky's Novels & the Poetics of Cultural Critique.* Stanford, CA: Stanford University Press, 1992. 213 pp. REV: Dennis Patrick Slattery, *Dostoevsky Studies = Dostoevskii: Stat'i i materialy* 1, no. 2 (1993): 257-259. Diane Oenning Thompson, *Slavic Review* 52, no. 3 (Fall 1993): 630-631.

6038. Pachmuss, Temira. *D.S. Merezhkovsky in Exile: The Master of the Genre of Biographie Romancée.* American University Studies. Series XII, Slavic Languages and Literature, v. 12. New York: P. Lang, c1990. xvi, 338 pp. REV: Victor Terras, *World Literature Today* 65, no. 3 (Summer 1991): 508. George Cheron, *Slavic and East European Journal* 36, no. 3 (Fall 1992): 369-371. Bernice Glatzer Rosenthal, *Canadian American Slavic Studies = Revue Canadienne Américaine d'Etudes Slaves* 27, nos. 1-4 (1993): 392-395.

6039. Ponomareff, Constantin V. *On the Dark Side of Russian Literature, 1709-1910.* American University Studies. Series XII, Slavic Languages and Literature, v. 2.

New York: P. Lang, 1987. x, 261 pp. REV: Uliana Gabara, *Canadian American Slavic Studies = Revue Canadienne Américaine d'Etudes Slaves* 27, nos. 1-4 (1993): 415-416.

6040. Reyfman, Irina. *Vasilii Trediakovsky: The Fool of the "New" Russian Literature.* Studies of the Harriman Institute. Stanford, CA: Stanford University Press, 1991. 316 pp. REV: I.R. Titunik, *Slavic and East European Journal* 35, no. 4 (Winter 1991): 574-576. Margareta O. Thompson, *Russian Review* 51, no. 3 (July 1992): 426. Il'ia Serman, trans. by Vitaly Chernetsky, *Slavic Review* 52, no. 4 (Winter 1993): 866-868.

6041. *Russian Views of Pushkin's Evgenii Onegin.* Translated and with an introduction and notes by Sona Stephan Hoisington. Bloomington, IN: Indiana University Press, c1988. xvii, 199 pp. [Verse passages translated by Walter Arndt; foreword by Caryl Emerson.] REV: Stephanie Sandler, *Slavic Review* 49, no. 4 (Winter 1990): 677-678. Victor Terras, *Russian Review* 49, no. 2 (April 1990): 211-212. Brett Cooke, *Slavic and East European Journal* 37, no. 2 (Summer 1993): 246-247. William Mills Todd, III, *Canadian American Slavic Studies = Revue Canadienne Américaine d'Etudes Slaves* 27, nos. 1-4 (1993): 401-402.

6042. Seeley, Frank Friedeberg. *Turgenev: A Reading of His Fiction.* Cambridge Studies in Russian Literature. Cambridge; New York: Cambridge University Press, 1991. xiv, 380 pp. REV: Reuel K. Wilson, *Canadian Slavonic Papers* 33, nos. 3-4 (December 1991): 394-396. Andrew R. Durkin, *Slavic and East European Journal* 36, no. 3 (Fall 1992): 365-366. Dale E. Peterson, *Russian Review* 52, no. 3 (July 1993): 418-419.

6043. Silbajoris, Rimvydas. *Tolstoy's Aesthetics and His Art.* Columbus, OH: Slavica, 1991. 319 pp. REV: Amy Mandelker, *Slavic Review* 51, no. 2 (Summer 1992): 384-385. Donna Orwin, *Canadian Slavonic Papers* 34, no. 3 (September 1992): 340-341. Patricia Carden, *Slavic and East European Journal* 37, no. 4 (Winter 1993): 574-576. John M. Kopper, *Canadian-American Slavic Studies* 27, nos. 1-4 (1993): 326-328. Joseph Troncale, *Russian Review* 52, no. 1 (January 1993): 105-106.

6044. Sologub, Fyodor. *Melkii bes: Drama v piati deistviiakh (shesti kartinakh).* Edited and with an afterword by Stanley J. Rabinowitz. Modern Russian Literature and Culture, Studies and Texts, v. 26. Berkeley, CA: Berkeley Slavic Specialities, 1988. 156 pp. REV: George Kalbouss, *Slavic and East European Journal* 37, no. 3 (Fall 1993): 386.

6045. Terras, Victor. *The Idiot: An Interpretation.* Twayne's Masterwork Studies, no. 57. Boston, MA: Twayne, 1990. xii, 106 pp. REV: Gary Cox, *International Fiction Review* 18, no. 1 (1991): 58-59. Charles A. Moser, *Russian Review* 51, no. 2 (April 1992): 266. Gary Rosenshield, *Slavic and East European Journal* 36, no. 1 (Spring 1992): 110-111. Richard Chapple, *Dostoevsky Studies = Dostoevskii: Stat'i i materialy* 1, no. 2 (1993): 261-262.

6046. Trace, Arther S. *Furnace of Doubt: Dostoevsky and "The Brothers Karamazov".* 1st ed. Peru, IL: Sherwood Sugden, c1988. 178 pp. REV: Roger Anderson, *Russian Review* 49, no. 4 (October 1990): 486-487. Curt Whitcomb, *Russian Language Journal* 44, no. 147-149 (Winter-Spring-Fall 1990): 370-372. Donald M. Fiene, *Dostoevsky Studies = Dostoevskii: Stat'i i materialy* 1, no. 1 (1993): 125-128.

6047. Wachter, Thomas. *Die künstlerische Welt in späten Erzählungen Cechovs.* Slavische Literaturen, Bd. 1. Frankfurt am Main; New York: P. Lang, c1992. 324 pp. [Revision of the author's thesis (doctoral)—Universität Hamburg, 1990.] REV: C. J. G. Turner, *Canadian Slavonic Papers* 35, nos. 1-2 (March-June 1993): 192.

6048. Wes, Marinus A. *Classics in Russia 1700-1855: Between Two Bronze Horsemen.* Brill's Studies in Intellectual History, v. 33. Leiden; New York: E.J. Brill, 1992. viii, 366 pp. [Translation of *Tussen twee bronzen ruiters.*] REV: Arthur Dolsen, *Canadian Slavonic Papers* 35, nos. 1-2 (March-June 1993): 193. Andrew Kahn, *Slavic and East European Journal* 37, no. 4 (Winter 1993): 571-573. Marc Raeff, *American Historical Review* 98, no. 3 (June 1993): 909-910.

Soviet-Period (1917-1991, includes Emigre Literature)

6049. Akhmatova, Anna. *The Complete Poems of Anna Akhmatova.* Edited by Roberta Reeder. Translated by Judith Hemschemeyer. Updated & expanded ed., 2nd. Boston, MA: Zephyr Press; Edinburgh: Canongate Press, 1992. 908 pp. REV: John Bayley, *New York Review of Books* 40, no. 9 (May 13, 1993): 25-27. Robert P. Hughes, *Book World* 23, no. 17 (April 25, 1993): 5. Sonia I. Ketchian, *Slavic Review* 52, no. 3 (Fall 1993): 642-643.

6050. ———. *My Half Century: Selected Prose.* Edited by Ronald Meyer. Ann Arbor, MI: Ardis, c1992. xlvi, 439 pp. REV: Robert P. Hughes, *Book World* 23, no. 17 (April 25, 1993): 5. Rosette C. Lamont, *World Literature Today* 67, no. 3 (Summer 1993): 628-629.

6051. Alexandrov, Vladimir E. *Nabokov's Otherworld.* Princeton, NJ: Princeton University Press, c1991. 270 pp. REV: Charles Lock, *Canadian Slavonic Papers* 33, nos. 3-4 (December 1991): 383-385. Brian Boyd, *Modern Fiction Studies* 38, no. 2 (Summer 1992): 477-478. Stephen Jan Parker, *Slavic and East European Journal* 36, no. 1 (Spring 1992): 124-125. Richard Rorty, *Common Knowledge* 1, no. 2 (Fall 1992): 126. Pekka Tammi, *Russian Review* 51, no. 4 (October 1992): 582-583. Dale E. Peterson, *Studies in Twentieth-Century Literature* 17, no. 2 (Summer 1993): 412-415.

6052. Amert, Susan. *In a Shattered Mirror: The Later Poetry of Anna Akhmatova.* Stanford, CA: Stanford University Press, 1992. xii, 274 pp. [Based on the author's doctoral dissertation.] REV: John Bayley, *New York Review of Books* 40, no. 9 (May 13, 1993): 25-27.

6053. Beaujour, Elizabeth K. *Alien Tongues: Bilingual Russian Writers of the "First" Emigration.* Ithaca,

NY: Cornell University Press, 1989. xiv, 263 pp. [Especially Nabokov.] REV: Teresa Polowy, *Canadian Slavonic Papers* 32, no. 2 (June 1990): 205-207. Maurice Friedberg, *Russian Review* 50, no. 1 (January 1991): 86-88. Julian W. Connolly, *Canadian American Slavic Studies = Revue Canadienne Américaine d'Etudes Slaves* 27, nos. 1-4 (1993): 369-371.

6054. Berberova, Nina. *The Tattered Cloak and Other Novels.* Translated from the Russian by Marian Schwartz. 1st ed. New York: Knopf; Distributed by Random House, 1991. 307 pp. [Contents: The Resurrection of Mozart; The Waiter and the Slut; Astashev in Paris; The Tattered Cloak; The Black Pestilence; In Memory of Schliemann.] REV: Gabriele Annan, *New York Review of Books* 38, no. 15 (September 26, 1991): 3-4. Penelope Lively, *New York Times Book Review* 96 (June 23, 1991): 6. Anne Tyler, *New Republic* 204, no. 24 (June 17, 1991): 48-49. Tom Wilhelmus, *Hudson Review* 45 (Spring 1992): 133-135. Peter Filkins, *Partisan Review* 60, no. 3 (Summer 1993): 487-493.

6055. Boyd, Brian. *Vladimir Nabokov: The American Years.* Princeton, NJ: Princeton University Press, c1991. xiv, 783 pp. REV: Walter Kendrick, *New York Times Book Review* (September 22, 1991): 1ff. Charles Lock, *Canadian Slavonic Papers* 33, nos. 3-4 (December 1991): 383-385. Kenneth S. Lynn, *American Spectator* 24, no. 10 (October 1991): 36-37. Anne Tyler, *Atlantic* 268, no. 4 (October 1991): 128-130. Robert M. Adams, *New York Review of Books* 39, no. 3 (January 30, 1992): 3-5. Vladimir E. Alexandrov, *Slavic Review* 51, no. 4 (Winter 1992): 838-840. Julian W. Connolly, *Slavic and East European Journal* 36, no. 4 (Winter 1992): 514-516. Charles Ross, *Modern Fiction Studies* 38, no. 2 (Summer 1992): 479. Lee Siegel, *Commonweal* 119, no. 11 (June 5, 1992): 23-25. Michael Wood, *New Republic* 205, no. 30 (January 20, 1992): 38-41. Pekka Tammi, *Russian Review* 52, no. 2 (April 1993): 265-266.

6056. Boym, Svetlana. *Death in Quotation Marks: Cultural Myths of the Modern Poet.* Harvard Studies in Comparative Literature, 41. Cambridge, MA: Harvard University Press, 1991. viii, 291 pp. [Includes discussion of Vladimir Mayakovsky and Marina Tsvetaeva.] REV: Wallace Fowlie, *Sewanee Review* 100 (Spring 1992): xxx-xxxii. Nadya Peterson, *Slavic Review* 51, no. 1 (Spring 1992): 190-191. Caryl Emerson, *Comparative Literature Studies* 30, no. 3 (1993): 321-324. Ronald D. LeBlanc, *Slavic and East European Journal* 37, no. 1 (Spring 1993): 119-121.

6057. Brodsky, Joseph. *Watermark.* 1st ed. New York: Farrar, Straus & Giroux, 1992. vii, 135 pp. REV: James Marcus, *New York Times Book Review* (May 31, 1992): 32. Philippe D. Radley, *World Literature Today* 67, no. 1 (Winter 1993): 204.

6058. Broude, Inna. *Ot Khodasevicha do Nabokova: Nostal'gicheskaia tema v poezii pervoi russkoi emigratsii.* Tenafly, NJ: Ermitazh, 1990. 160 pp. REV: Galya Diment, *Russian Review* 52, no. 1 (January 1993): 97. Temira

Pachmuss, *Slavic and East European Journal* 37, no. 3 (Fall 1993): 387-388.

6059. Connolly, Julian W. *Nabokov's Early Fiction: Patterns of Self and Other*. New York: Cambridge University Press, 1992. pp. REV: Priscilla Meyer, *Slavic Review* 52, no. 3 (Fall 1993): 635-636.

6060. Cornwell, Neil, ed. *Daniil Kharms and the Poetics of the Absurd: Essays and Materials*. Contributions by Neil Cornwell, Iakov Druskin, Anatolii Aleksandrov, Jean-Philippe Jaccard, Anthony Anemone, Robin Aizlewood, Milena Michalski, Rosanna Giaquinta, Aleksandr Kobrinsky, Lazar Fleishman, Daniil Kharms, Jerzy Faryno, Nina Perlina, Tat'iana Nikol'skaia, Mikhail Meilakh, Robin Milner-Gulland, and Julian Graffy. New York: St. Martin's Press, 1991. xvi, 282 pp. [Most of the essays translated from Russian. Contents: Neil Cornwell, "Daniil Kharms, Black miniaturist"; Iakov Druskin, "On Daniil Kharms"; Anatolii Aleksandrov, "A Kharms chronology"; Jean-Philippe Jaccard, "Daniil Kharms in the context of Russian and European literature of the absurd"; Anthony Amemone, "The anti-world of Danill Kharms: on the significance of the absurd"; Robin Azelwood, "Towards an interpretation of Kharms's Sluchai"; Milena Michalski, "Slobodan Pesic's file Slucaj harms and Kharms's Sluchai"; Rosanna Giaquinta, "Elements of the fantastic in Daniil Kharms's Starukha"; Aleksandr Kobrinsky, "Some features of the poetics of Kharms's prose: the story Upadanie ('The Falling')"; Lazar Fleishman, "On one enigmatic poem by Daniil Kharms"; Daniil Kharms, "I Razrushenie"; Jerzy Faryno, "Kharms's '1st Destruction'"; Nina Perlina, "Daniil Kharms's poetic system: Text, context, intertext"; Tat'iana Nikol'skaia, "The oberiuty and the theatricalisation of life"; Mikhail Meilakh, "Kharms's play Elizaveta Bam"; Daniil Kharms, "Yelizaveta Bam: A dramatic work: a new translation from the definitive text by Neil Cornwell"; Robin Milner-Gulland, "Beyond the turning-point: an afterword"; Neil Cornwell and Julian Graffy, "Selected bibliography".] REV: George Gibian, *Slavic Review* 51, no. 2 (Summer 1992): 380-381. Larissa Tumanov, *Canadian Slavonic Papers* 34, nos. 1-2 (March-June 1992): 183-184. Alice Nakhimovsky, *Slavic and East European Journal* 37, no. 3 (Fall 1993): 388-389.

6061. Curtis, J. A. E. *Manuscripts Don't Burn: Mikhail Bulgakov, A Life in Letters and Diaries*. 1st ed. Woodstock, NY: Overlook Press, 1992. xiv, 306 pp. REV: David M. Bethea, *New York Times Book Review* 98, no. 1 (January 3, 1993): 3ff. Olga Andreyev Carlisle, *Book World* 23, no. 5 (January 31, 1993): 6ff. Richard L. Chapple, *Canadian American Slavic Studies = Revue Canadienne Américaine d'Etudes Slaves* 27, nos. 1-4 (1993): 386-387. Laura D. Weeks, *Russian Review* 52, no. 3 (July 1993): 419-420.

6062. Danow, David K. *The Thought of Mikhail Bakhtin: From Word to Culture*. New York: St. Martin's Press, 1991. 158 pp. REV: Larissa Rudova, *Slavic Review* 51, no. 2 (Summer 1992): 375-378. Caryl Emerson, *Slavic and East European Journal* 37, no. 4 (Winter 1993): 581-584.

6063. Davidson, Pamela. *The Poetic Imagination of Vyacheslav Ivanov: A Russian Symbolist's Perception of Dante*. Cambridge Studies in Russian Literature. Cambridge; New York: Cambridge University Press, 1989. xv, 319 pp. REV: R.D.B. Thomson, *Canadian Slavonic Papers* 32, no. 1 (March 1990): 95-96. Clarence Brown, *Slavic Review* 50, no. 1 (Spring 1991): 211-212. Anna Frajlich-Zajac, *Slavic and East European Journal* 35, no. 2 (Summer 1991): 287-288. Virginia H. Bennett, *Slavic Review* 51, no. 4 (Winter 1992): 852-853. Maria Carlson, *Canadian American Slavic Studies = Revue Canadienne Américaine d'Etudes Slaves* 27, nos. 1-4 (1993): 338-339.

6064. Davidson, Pamela, and Isia Tlusty, comps. *Posviashchaetsia Akhmatovoi: Stikhi raznykh poetov, posviashchennye Akhmatovoi*. Edited with introduction by Pamela Davidson. Foreword by Evgenii Rein. Tenafly, NJ: Ermitazh, 1991. xi, 170 pp. [Anthology of poems dedicated to or inspired by Akhmatova.] REV: Victor Terras, *World Literature Today* 65, no. 3 (Summer 1991): 509. Sonia I. Ketchian, *Slavic and East European Journal* 37, no. 2 (Summer 1993): 255.

6065. Ehlers, Klaas-Hinrich. *Das dynamische System: Zur Entwicklung von Begriff und Metaphorik des Systems bei Jurij N. Tynjanov*. New York: Peter Lang, 1992. 287 pp. REV: Peter Rollberg, *Slavic Review* 52, no. 4 (Winter 1993): 874-875.

6066. Fleishman, Lazar. *Boris Pasternak: The Poet and His Politics*. Cambridge, MA: Harvard University Press, 1990. xi, 359 pp. REV: George Cheron, *Russian History* 17, no. 4 (Winter 1990): 471-472. Henry Gifford, *New York Review of Books* 37, no. 9 (May 31, 1990): 26-31. Julian L. Laychuk, *Canadian Slavonic Papers* 32, no. 4 (December 1990): 510-511. E. Yarwood, *Choice* (December 1990): 634-635. Clare Cavanagh, *Slavic Review* 50, no. 4 (Winter 1991): 1061-1063. Irene Masing-Delic, *World Literature Today* 65, no. 3 (Summer 1991): 507-508. Christopher J. Barnes, *Russian Review* 51, no. 1 (January 1992): 113-114. Margareta O. Thompson, *Canadian American Slavic Studies = Revue Canadienne Américaine d'Etudes Slaves* 27, nos. 1-4 (1993): 317-318.

6067. Garrard, John, and Carol Garrard. *Inside the Soviet Writers' Union*. New York: Free Press, c1990. xv, 303 pp. REV: Clarence Brown, *Russian History* 17, no. 4 (Winter 1990): 489-490. John C. Campbell, *Foreign Affairs* 69, no. 3 (Summer 1990): 184. Jeffrey C. Goldfarb, *New York Times Book Review* (March 18, 1990): 15. D.B. Johnson, *Choice* (October 1990): 315. Tomas Venclova, *New Republic* 203, no. 10 (September 3, 1990): 34-38. Carol Any, *Slavic and East European Journal* 35, no. 2 (Summer 1991): 296-298. Russell Bova, *Perspectives on Political Science* 20, no. 2 (Spring 1991): 121. Lev Loseff, *Russian Review* 50, no. 3 (July 1991): 385-387. Joseph Mozur, *World Literature Today* 65, no. 1 (Winter 1991): 137-138. Marianna Tax Choldin, *Libraries & Culture* 27, no. 1 (Winter 1992): 89. N. N. Shneidman, *Canadian American Slavic Studies = Revue Canadienne Américaine d'Etudes Slaves* 27, nos. 1-4 (1993): 402-404. Anna A. Tavis, *Slavic Review* 52, no. 2 (Summer 1993): 401-402.

6068. Gillespie, David C. *Iurii Trifonov: Unity through Time*. Cambridge Studies in Russian Literature. Cambridge; New York: Cambridge University Press, 1992. x, 248 pp. [Based on work done for the author's doctoral thesis in 1984-1985.] REV: Rolf Hellebust, *Canadian Slavonic Papers* 35, nos. 3-4 (September-December 1993): 405.

6069. Gimpilevich-Shvartsman, Zina. *Intelligent v romanakh "Doktor Zhivago" i "Master i Margarita"*. Orange, CT: Antiquary, 1988. 194 pp. REV: Margareta O. Thompson, *Canadian American Slavic Studies = Revue Canadienne Américaine d'Etudes Slaves* 27, nos. 1-4 (1993): 353-354.

6070. Ginzburg, Lydia. *On Psychological Prose*. Edited and translated by Judson Rosengrant. Foreword by Edward J. Brown. Princeton, NJ: Princeton University Press, c1991. xxi, 398 pp. [Translation of *O psikhologicheskoi proze*.] REV: Jane Gary Harris, *Slavic Review* 51, no. 2 (Summer 1992): 385-387. Thomas Gaiton Marullo, *Slavic and East European Journal* 37, no. 2 (Summer 1993): 235-236.

6071. Glad, John, ed. *Literature in Exile*. Contributions by William Gass, Nuruddin Farah, Jan Vladislav. Jorge Edwards, Yurii Miloslavsky, Antonin Liehm, Virgil Tanase, Jiri Grusa, Guillermo Cabrera Infante, Horst Bienek, Libuse Moníková, Edward Limonov, Nedim Gürsel, Jan Novak, Richard Kim, Jaroslav Vejvoda, Dennis Brutus, Anton Shamas, Lev Kopelev, Vladimir Voinovich, Georgii Vladimov, Sergei Dovlatov, Joseph Brodsky, Raissa Orlova, Adam Zagajewski, Wojciech Karpinski, Tomas Venclova, and Yurii Druzhnikov. Durham, NC: Duke University Press, 1990. xii, 175 pp. [Papers and discussion from a conference held in Vienna, December 2-5, 1987, under the auspices of the Wheatland Foundation of New York.] REV: Rimvydas Silbajoris, *Journal of Baltic Studies* 21, no. 4 (Winter 1990): 369-374. Victoria A. Babenko-Woodbury, *Slavic and East European Journal* 35, no. 1 (Spring 1991): 149-150. Reinhold Grimm, *Comparative Literature Studies* 30, no.1 (1993): 106.

6072. Glad, John, and Daniel Weissbort, eds. *Twentieth-Century Russian Poetry*. Iowa City, IA: University of Iowa Press, c1992. xxxviii, 384 pp. [Expanded edition of *Russian Poetry: The Modern Period* (c1978).] REV: Jim Kates, *Translation Review*, nos. 42-43 (1993): 53-54. Victor Terras, *World Literature Today* 67, no. 1 (Winter 1993): 204.

6073. Harris, Jane Gary, ed. *Autobiographical Statements in Twentieth-century Russian Literature*. Contributions by Jane Gary Harris, Anna Lisa Crone, Olga Raevsky-Hughes, Charlene Castellano, Krystyna Pomorska, Elizabeth Klosty Beaujour, Krista Hanson, John Pilling, Fiona Björling, Charles Isenberg, Sarah Pratt, Patricia Carden, and Andrew J. Nussbaum. Studies of the Harriman Institute. Princeton, NJ: Princeton University Press, c1990. 287 pp. [Contents: Jane Gary Harris, "Introduction: The Diversity of Discourse: Autobiographical Statements in Theory and Praxis"; Anna Lisa Crone, "Rozanov and Autobiography: The Case of Vasily Vasilievich"; Olga Raevsky-Hughes, "Alexey Remizov's Later Autobiographical Prose"; Charles Castellano, "Andrey Bely's Memories of Fiction"; Jane Gary Harris, "Autobiography and History: Osip Mandelstam's *Noise of Time*"; Krystyna Pomorska, "Boris Pasternak's *Safe Conduct*"; Elizabeth Klosty Beaujour, "The Imagination of Failure: Fiction and Autobiography in the Work of Yury Olesha"; Krista Hanson, "Autobiography and Conversion: Zoshchenko's *Before Sunrise*"; John Pilling, "A Tremulous Prism: Nabokov's *Speak, Memory*"; Fiona Björling, "Yury Trifonov's *The House on the Embankment*: Fiction or Autobiography?"; Charles Isenberg, "The Rhetoric of Nadezhda Mandelstam's *Hope Against Hope*"; Sarah Pratt, "Lydia Ginzburg and the Fluidity of Genre"; Krystyna Pomorska, "Roman Jakobson: The Autobiography of a Scholar"; Patricia Carden, "In Search of the Right Milieu: Eduard Limonov's Kharkov Cycle"; Andrew J. Nussbaum, "Literary Selves: The Tertz-Sinyavsky Dialogue".] REV: Patricia Pollock Brodsky, *World Literature Today* 65, no. 2 (Spring 1991): 320-321. Robin Feuer Miller, *Slavic Review* 50, no. 4 (Winter 1991): 1061-1063. Mary A. Nicholas, *Slavic and East European Journal* 35, no. 3 (Fall 1991): 438-439. A.F. Zweers, *Germano-Slavica* 7, no. 1 (1991): 66-68. Robin Feuer Miller, *Slavic Review* 50, no. 4 (Winter 1991): 1061-1063. Cynthia Simmons, *Russian Review* 52, no. 3 (July 1993): 421-423.

6074. Holquist, Michael. *Dialogism: Bakhtin and His World*. New Accents, New York: Routledge, 1990. 204 pp. REV: Larissa Rudova, *Slavic Review* 51, no. 2 (Summer 1992): 375-378. Anne Nesbet, *Slavic and East European Journal* 37, no. 1 (Spring 1993): 122-124.

6075. Iossel, Mikhail. *Every Hunter Wants to Know: A Leningrad Life*. New York: W.W. Norton, 1991. 244 pp. REV: Howard Mittelmark, *New York Times Book Review* (November 17, 1991): 20. Josip Novakovich, *Prairie Schooner* 67, no. 2 (Summer 1993): 154-159. Robbie Clipper Sethi, *Studies in Short Fiction* 30, no. 1 (Winter 1993): 100-102.

6076. Kasack, Wolfgang. *Dictionary of Russian Literature Since 1917*. Translated by Maria Carlson and Jane T. Hedges. Bibliographical revision by Rebecca Atack. New York: Columbia University Press, 1988. xvi, 502 pp. REV: Kathleen Parthé, *Slavic Review* 49, no. 3 (Fall 1990): 504-505. Mary Stuart, *Canadian American Slavic Studies = Revue Canadienne Américaine d'Etudes Slaves* 27, nos. 1-4 (1993): 435-436.

6077. Klimenko, Michael. *Ehrenburg: An Attempt at a Literary Portrait*. American University Studies. Series XII, Slavic Languages and Literature, vol. 7. New York: P. Lang, c1990. 273 pp. REV: C. Nicholas Lee, *Russian Review* 52, no. 4 (October 1993): 552.

6078. Kustanovich, Konstantin. *The Artist and the Tyrant: Vassily Aksenov's Works in the Brezhnev Era*. Columbus, OH: Slavica, c1992. 219 pp. REV: Elena Krasnostchekova, *Canadian Slavonic Papers* 35, nos. 1-2 (March-June 1993): 176-177. Kathleen Parthé, *Slavic Review* 52, no. 4 (Winter 1993): 877-878.

6079. Laychuk, Julian L. *Ilya Ehrenburg: An Idealist in an Age of Realism*. Bern; New York: Lang, c1991.

x, 486 pp. REV: Peter G. Christensen, *Canadian Slavonic Papers* 35, nos. 1-2 (March-June 1993): 153.

6080. Ledkovskaia-Astman, Marina, ed. *Rossiia glazami zhenshchin: literaturnaia antologiia.* Tenafly, NJ: Ermitazh, 1989. 189 pp. REV: Mary A. Nicholas, *Slavic and East European Journal* 35, no. 2 (Summer 1991): 304-305. Adele Barker, *Slavic Review* 52, no. 2 (Summer 1993): 409-410.

6081. Ledkovsky, Marina, comp. *Russia According to Women: Literary Anthology.* Tenafly, NJ: Hermitage, 1991. 175 pp. [Translation of *Rossiia glazami zhenshchin.*] REV: Mary A. Nicholas, *Slavic and East European Journal* 36, no. 2 (Summer 1992): 244-245. Bonnie Marshall, *World Literature Today* 67, no. 1 (Winter 1993): 203-204.

6082. Loseff, Lev, ed. *Boris Pasternak: 1890-1990.* Contributions by Boris Paramonov, Barry Scherr, Feliks Roziner, Alexander Zholkovsky, Ilya Serman, Igor Efimov, Efim Etkind, John M. Kopper, Elena Gessen, Walter Arndt, Leonid Dolgopolov, Yurii Shcheglov, Lev Loseff, Fazil Iskander, Nina Tabidze, Yunna Morits, Leonid Vinogradov, and Vladimir Uflyand. Norvichskie simpoziumy po russkoi Literature i kul'ture, v. 1. Northfield, VT: Russkaia shkola Norvichskogo Universiteta = Norwich University Russian School, 1991. 299 pp. REV: Kathleen E. Dillon, *Slavic and East European Journal* 37, no. 1 (Spring 1993): 109-110.

6083. Mandelstam, Osip. *Poems from Mandelstam.* Translated by R. H. Morrison. Introduction by Ervin C. Brody. Rutherford, NJ: Fairleigh Dickinson University Press, c1990. 118 pp. REV: Jane Gray Harris, *Canadian American Slavic Studies = Revue Canadienne Américaine d'Etudes Slaves* 27, nos. 1-4 (1993): 422-424.

6084. Masing-Delic, Irene. *Abolishing Death: A Salvation Myth of Russian Twentieth-Century Literature.* Stanford, CA: Stanford University Press, 1992. 363 pp. REV: Milton Ehre, *Russian Language Journal = Russkii iazyk* 47, nos. 156-158 (Winter-Spring-Fall 1993): 365-367.

6085. Milne, Lesley. *Mikhail Bulgakov: A Critical Biography.* Cambridge; New York: Cambridge University Press, 1990. xiv, 324 pp. REV: Zina Gimpelevich-Schwartzman, *Canadian American Slavic Studies = Revue Canadienne Américaine d'Etudes Slaves* 27, nos. 1-4 (1993): 417-419.

6086. Morson, Gary Saul, and Caryl Emerson. *Mikhail Bakhtin: Creation of a Prosaics.* Stanford, CA: Stanford University Press, 1990. xx, 530 pp. REV: Don Bialostosky, *Novel* 26, no. 1 (Fall 1992): 109-111. Aileen Kelly, *New York Review of Books* 39, no. 15 (September 24, 1992): 44-48. Eric Naiman, *Modern Fiction Studies* 38, no. 2 (Summer 1992): 531-534. Anna Tavis, *Slavic and East European Journal* 36, no. 1 (Spring 1992): 101-106. Gary Rosenshield, *Russian Review* 52, no. 1 (January 1993): 102-103.

6087. Muravina, Nina. *Vstrechi s Pasternakom.* Tenafly, NJ: Ermitazh, 1990. 223 pp. REV: Walter F. Kolonosky, *Slavic and East European Journal* 37, no. 4 (Winter 1993): 584-585.

6088. Naiman, Anatoly. *Remembering Anna Akhmatova.* Introduction by Joseph Brodsky. Translated by Wendy Rosslyn. New York: Henry Holt, c1991. xiii, 240 p. [Translation of: *Rasskazy o Anne Akhmatovoi.*] REV: Elizabeth Tucker, *Nation* 254, no. 9 (March 9, 1992): 309-311. John Bayley, *New York Review of Books* 40 (May 13, 1993): 25-27.

6089. Nakhimovsky, Alice Stone. *Russian-Jewish Literature and Identity: Jabotinsky, Babel, Grossman, Galich, Roziner, Markish.* Johns Hopkins Jewish Studies. Baltimore, MD: Johns Hopkins University Press, c1991. xiv, 251 pp. REV: Judith Deutsch Kornblatt, *Slavic Review* 51, no. 2 (Summer 1992): 368-369. Milton Ehre, *Russian Review* 52, no. 4 (October 1993): 554-555. Haim Gamburg, *Canadian American Slavic Studies = Revue Canadienne Américaine d'Etudes Slaves* 27, nos. 1-4 (1993): 320-322. Rosette C. Lamont, *World Literature Today* 67, no. 1 (Winter 1993): 205. Michael Stanislawski, *Judaism* 42 (Summer 1993): 376-377.

6090. Parthé, Kathleen F. *Russian Village Prose: The Radiant Past.* Princeton, NJ: Princeton University Press, c1992. xiv, 194 pp. REV: Dragan Milivojevic, *World Literature Today* 67, no. 3 (Summer 1993): 626-627. Harriet Murav, *Slavic Review* 52, no. 4 (Winter 1993): 878-879.

6091. Pittman, Riitta H. *The Writer's Divided Self in Bulgakov's The Master and Margarita.* New York: St. Martin's Press, 1991. x, 211 pp. REV: Kevin Moss, *Russian Review* 52, no. 3 (July 1993): 420-421.

6092. Polukhina, Valentina. *Brodsky Through the Eyes of His Contemporaries.* New York: St. Martin's Press, 1992. xi, 348 pp. [Includes interviews with Roy Fisher, Yakov Gordin, Iurii Kublanovskii, Aleksandr Kushner, Lev Loseff, Czeslaw Milosz, Anatolii Naiman, Aleksei Parshchikov, Ol'ga Sedakova, Evgenii Rein, Elena Shvarts, Tomas Venclova, and Derek Walcott.] REV: Joachim T. Baer, *World Literature Today* 67, no. 3 (Summer 1993): 627-628. Galya Diment, *Slavic Review* 52, no. 4 (Winter 1993): 879-880. Bozena Karwowska, *Canadian Slavonic Papers* 35, nos. 1-2 (March-June 1993): 182-184.

6093. ———. *Joseph Brodsky: A Poet for Our Time.* Cambridge Studies in Russian Literature. Cambridge; New York: Cambridge University Press, 1989. xx, 324 pp. REV: David M. Bethea, *Slavic and East European Journal* 35, no. 3 (Fall 1991): 447-448. Michael B. Kreps, *Russian Review* 50, no. 3 (July 1991): 358-359. Galya Diment, *Canadian American Slavic Studies = Revue Canadienne Américaine d'Etudes Slaves* 27, nos. 1-4 (1993): 3384-386.

6094. Rancour-Laferriere, Daniel, ed. *Russian Literature and Psychoanalysis.* Linguistic & Literary Studies in Eastern Europe, v. 31. Amsterdam; Philadelphia, PA: J. Benjamins, 1989. x, 485 pp. [Part II is the proceedings of the Conference on Russian Literature and Psychoanalysis which was held at the University of California, Davis, February 20-22, 1987.] REV: Rimvydas Silbajoris, *Slavic and East European Journal* 35, no. 3 (Fall 1991): 429-430. Mary Lucia W. Bun, *Russian Review* 52, no. 1 (January 1993): 104-105. Caryl Emerson, *Canadian*

American Slavic Studies = Revue Canadienne Américaine d'Etudes Slaves 27, nos. 1-4 (1993): 358-362.

6095. Robin, Régine. *Socialist Realism: An Impossible Aesthetic.* Translated by Catherine Porter. Foreword by Leon Robel. Stanford, CA: Stanford University Press, 1992. xxxvii, 345 pp. [Translation of *Le realisme socialiste: une esthetique impossible.*] REV: Paul Morris, *Canadian Slavonic Papers* 35, nos. 1-2 (March-June 1993): 186-187.

6096. Seifrid, Thomas. *Andrei Platonov: Uncertainites of Spirit.* Cambridge; New York: Cambridge University Press, 1992. xii, 273 pp. REV: Galya Diment, *Russian Review* 52, no. 4 (October 1993): 555-556. Sona S. Hoisington, *Slavic and East European Journal* 37, no. 4 (Winter 1993): 585-586.

6097. Seyffert, Peter. *Soviet Literary Structuralism: Background, Debate, Issues.* Columbus, OH: Slavica, 1985, c1983. 378 pp. REV: Catherine V. Chvany, *Russian Language Journal = Russkii iazyk* 47, nos. 156-158 (Winter-Spring-Fall 1993): 339-342.

6098. Shmelyov, Ivan. *The Hidden Face and Other Stories.* Translated by Olga Sorokin. Oakland, CA: Barbary Coast, 1991. 206 pp. REV: Ludmila Prednewa, *World Literature Today* 67, no. 1 (Winter 1993): 206.

6099. Shneidman, N. N. *Soviet Literature in the 1980s: Decade of Transition.* Toronto, Ontario; Buffalo: University of Toronto Press, c1989. 250 pp. REV: D.B. Johnson, *Choice* (January 1990): 806. Natasha Kolchevska, *Slavic and East European Journal* 34, no. 3 (Fall 1990): 385-387. John Garrard, *Russian Review* 50, no. 3 (July 1991): 352-353. Walter F. Kolonosky, *Modern Fiction Studies* 37, no. 2 (Summer 1991): 325-328. Nadya Peterson, *Slavic Review* 50, no. 2 (Summer 1991): 463-464. Anna Bronstein, *Canadian American Slavic Studies = Revue Canadienne Américaine d'Etudes Slaves* 27, nos. 1-4 (1993): 366-367.

6100. Shraer-Petrov, David. *Villa Borgeze: Stikhotvoreniia.* Holyoke, MA: New England Publishing, 1992. 69 pp. REV: Victor Terras, *World Literature Today* 67, no. 1 (Winter 1993): 207.

6101. Sinkevich, Valentina, ed. *Berega: stikhi poetov vtoroi emigratsii = Berega: An Anthology of Second Wave Poets.* Compiled by Valentina Sinkevich and Vladimir Shatalov. Philadelphia, PA: Encounters, 1992. 290 pp. REV: Oleg Il'inskii, *Zapiski Russkoi akademicheskoi gruppy v SShA = Transactions of the Association of Russian-American Schlolars in the U.S.A.* 25 (1992-1993): 320-323. Victoria A. Babenko-Woodbury, *World Literature Today* 67, no. 3 (Summer 1993): 625-626. Anatoly Liberman, *Slavic and East European Journal* 37, no. 2 (Summer 1993): 257-258.

6102. Sklodowska, Elzbieta. *La Parodia en la nueva novela hispanoamerica (1960-1985).* Purdue University Monographs in Romance Languages, v. 34. Amsterdam; Philadelphia, PA: J. Benjamins, 1991. xix, 219 pp. [Includes critical theory of Mikhail Bakhtin and the Russian formalists.] REV: Brian Evenson, *World Literature*

Today 67, no. 1 (Winter 1993): 161.

6103. Slobin, Greta N. *Remizov's Fictions, 1900-1921.* DeKalb, IL: Northern Illinois University Press, 1991. xxi, 203 pp. REV: Walter F. Kolonosky, *Modern Fiction Studies* 38, no. 4 (Winter 1992): 971-972. Sarah P. Burke, *Slavic and East European Journal* 37, no. 2 (Summer 1993): 251-252. Stephen C. Hutchings, *Slavic Review* 52, no. 2 (Summer 1993): 407-409. Edward Manouelian, *Canadian American Slavic Studies = Revue Canadienne Américaine d'Etudes Slaves* 27, nos. 1-4 (1993): 333-334.

6104. Tertz, Abram [Andrei Siniavskii]. *Little Jinx.* Translated by Larry P. Joseph and Rachel May. Foreword by Edward J. Brown. Evanston, IL: Northwestern University Press, c1992. xvi, 80 pp. [Translation of *Kroshka tsores.*] REV: Jodi Daynard, *New York Times Book Review* (September 20, 1992): 46. Bill Marx, *Nation* 255, no. 14 (November 2, 1992): 511-513. Philippe D. Radley, *World Literature Today* 67, no. 3 (Summer 1993): 629.

6105. Tolstaya, Tatyana. *Sleepwalker in a Fog.* Translated from the Russian by Jamey Gambrell. 1st ed. New York: Knopf; Distributed by Random House, 1992. 192 pp. REV: Anita Desai, *New Republic* 206, no. 14 (April 6, 1992): 36-38. Richard Lourie, *World & I* 7, no. 8 (August 1992): 332-337. David Plante, *New York Times Book Review* (January 12, 1992): 7-8. David Remnick, *New York Review of Books* 39, no. 9 (May 14, 1992): 44-51. Susanna Sloat, *Belles Lettres* 7, no. 3 (Spring 1992): 30-31. Margaret Ziolkowski, *World Literature Today* 67, no. 1 (Winter 1993): 206-207.

6106. Tsvetaeva, Marina. *Art in the Light of Conscience: Eight Essays on Poetry.* Translated with introduction and notes by Angela Livingstone. Cambridge, MA: Harvard University Press, 1992. x, 214 pp. REV: Patricia Pollock Brodsky, *World Literature Today* 66, no. 3 (Summer 1992): 542-543. Sibelan E. S. Forrester, *Slavic and East European Journal* 37, no. 1 (Spring 1993): 116-117. Olga Peters Hasty, *Slavic Review* 52, no. 1 (Spring 1993): 123-124. Tomas Venclova, *New Republic* 208, no. 14 (April 5, 1993): 38-42.

6107. Vroon, Ronald. *Velimir Xlebnikov's Krysa: A Commentary.* Stanford Slavic Studies, v. 2. Stanford, CA: Stanford University, 1989. 200 pp. REV: Evelyn Bristol, *Russian Review* 51, no. 3 (July 1992): 435-436. Gerald Janecek, *Slavic and East European Journal* 37, no. 2 (Summer 1993): 254.

6108. Woll, Josephine. *Invented Truth: Soviet Reality and the Literary Imagination of Yurii Trifonov.* Durham, NC: Duke University Press, 1991. ix, 167 pp. REV: Richard Sheldon, *Soviet and Post-Soviet Review* 19, nos. 1-3 (1992): 335-336. Sigrid McLaughlin, *Slavic Review* 52, no. 2 (Summer 1993): 402-404.

Ukrainian

6109. Luckyj, George S. N., and Naukove tovarystvo imeny Shevchenka. *Ukrainian Literature in the Twentieth Century: A Reader's Guide.* Toronto, Ontario;

Buffalo, NY: published for the Shevchenko Scientific Society by the University of Toronto Press, 1992. 136 pp. REV: Michael M. Naydan, *Slavic and East European Journal* 37, no. 1 (Spring 1993): 124-125.

6110. Pavlyshyn, Marko, ed. *Stus as Text.* Melbourne: Monash University, 1992. 91 pp. REV: Natalia Burianyk, *Canadian Slavonic Papers* 35, nos. 1-2 (March-June 1993): 180.

6111. Slavutych, Iar. *Ukraiinska literatura v Kanadi: vybrani doslidzhenniia statti i retsenzii = Ukrainian Literature in Canada.* Edmonton, Alta.: Slavuta, 1992. 336 pp. REV: Wolodymyr T. Zyla, *World Literature Today* 67, no. 4 (Autumn 1993): 859-860.

6112. Slavutych, Yar. *Three Narratives and Six Poems.* Three Narratives translated by Roman Orest Tatchyn. Six Poems translated by Orysia Ferbey and Watson Kirkconnell. Edmonton, Alta.: Slavuta, 1992. 64 pp. REV: Wolodymyr T. Zyla, *World Literature Today* 67, no. 2 (Spring 1993): 409-410.

6113. Tarnawsky, Marta. *Ukrainian Literature in English: Articles in Journals and Collections, 1840-1965; An Annotated Bibliography.* Occasional Research Report (Canadian Institute of Ukrainian Studies), no. 51. Edmonton, Alberta: Canadian Institute of Ukrainian Studies. University of Alberta, 1992. xii, 176 pp. REV: Dmytro Shtohryn, *Ukrainian Quarterly* 49, no. 1 (Spring 1993): 75-79.

6114. ———. *Ukrainian Literature in English: Books and Pamphlets, 1890-1965: An Annotated Bibliography.* Occasional Research Report (Canadian Institute of Ukrainian Studies), no. 19. Edmonton, Alberta: Canadian Institute of Ukrainian Studies, University of Alberta, 1988. 127 pp. REV: Dmytro Shtohryn, *Ukrainian Quarterly* 49, no. 1 (Spring 1993): 75-79.

6115. Tarnawsky, Ostap. *Poems.* Philadephia, PA: Privately printed, 1992. 449 pp. REV: Wolodymyr T. Zyla, *Ukrainian Quarterly* 49, no. 1 (Spring 1993): 79-82. Wolodymyr T. Zyla, *World Literature Today* 67, no. 3 (Summer 1993): 637-368.

6116. Zaitsev, Pavlo. *Taras Shevchenko, a Life.* Edited and translated by George S. N. Luckyj. Toronto, Ontario; Buffalo, NY: published for the Shevchenko Scientific Society by the University of Toronto Press, c1988. xi, 284 pp. REV: Marko Pavlyshyn, *Russian Review* 49, no. 1 (January 1990): 108-109. Oleh S. Inytzkyj, *Canadian American Slavic Studies = Revue Canadienne Américaine d'Etudes Slaves* 27, nos. 1-4 (1993): 419-420.

Yiddish

6117. Fiedler, Leslie A. *Fiedler on the Roof: Essays on Literature and Jewish Identity.* 1st ed. Boston, MA: D.A. Godine, 1991. xviii, 184 pp. [Includes some discussion of Singer.] REV: Lawrence E. Mintz, *American Jewish History* 81, no. 1 (Autumn 1993): 113-115.

6118. Singer, Isaac Bashevis. *The Certificate.* Translated by Leonard Wolf. New York: Farrar, Straus & Giroux, 1992. 231 pp. [Translation of *Tsertifikat.*] REV: Lore Dickstein, *New York Times Book Review* 97 (November 22, 1992): 7. Dean Flower, *Hudson Review* 46, no. 2 (Summer 1993): 396-397. Ursula Hegi, *Book World* 23, no. 1 (January 3, 1993): 2. Rita D. Jacobs, *World Literature Today* 67, no. 2 (Spring 1993): 404.

6119. Wisse, Ruth R. *I.L. Peretz and the Making of Modern Jewish Culture.* Samuel and Althea Stroum Lectures in Jewish Studies. Seattle, WA: University of Washington Press, c1991. xvii, 128 pp. REV: Moshe D. Sherman, *Studies in Religion = Sciences Religieuses* 22, no. 3 (Summer 1993): 389-390.

(Former) Yugoslav

6120. *The Battle of Kosovo.* Translated from the Serbian by John Matthias and Vladeta Vuckovic. Preface by Charles Simic. Athens, OH: Swallow Press, 1987. 103 pp. REV: Robert W. Lewis, *North Dakota Quarterly* 61, no. 1 (Winter 1993): 229-232.

6121. Bogert, Ralph. *The Writer as Naysayer: Miroslav Krleza and the Aesthetic of Interwar Central Europe.* UCLA Slavic Studies, v. 20. Columbus, OH: Slavica, 1991. 266 pp. REV: Anto Knezevic, *Canadian Slavonic Papers* 34, nos. 1-2 (March-June 1992): 179-180. Vladislava Ribnikar, *Slavic Review* 51, no. 2 (Summer 1992): 367-368. Sibelan E.S. Forrester, *Slavic and East European Journal* 37, no. 3 (Fall 1993): 396-397.

6122. Foley, John Miles. *Traditional Oral Epic: The Odyssey, Beowulf, and the Serbo-Croatian Return Song.* Berkeley, CA: University of California Press, c1990. xi, 424 pp. REV: Jan Louis Perkowski, *Slavic and East European Journal* 36, no. 2 (Summer 1992): 266-267. William Bernard McCarthy, *Journal of American Folklore* 106, no. 420 (Spring 1993): 233-235. Jeff Opland, *Comparative Literature* 45, no. 4 (Fall 1993): 361-731. Karl Reichl, *Speculum* 68, no. 4 (October 1993): 1116-1118.

6123. Kocbek, Edvard. *Na vratih zvecer = At the Door of Evening.* Translated by Tom Lozar. Ljubljana; Dorion, Quebec: Muses' Co./Compagnie des Muses, 1990. 113 pp. [Poems in Slovene with English translations on facing pages.] REV: Ales Debeljak, *Slovene Studies* 13, no. 2 (1991, published July 1993): 217-218.

6124. Simic, Charles, ed. and trans. *The Horse Has Six Legs: An Anthology of Serbian Poetry.* Saint Paul, MN: Graywolf Press, 1992. 222 pp. [Translated from the Serbo-Croatian.] REV: Stanislaw Baranczak, *New Republic* 208, no. 9 (March 1, 1993): 28-32. Vasa D. Mihailovich, *World Literature Today* 67, no. 2 (Spring 1993): 409.

6125. Tadic, Novica. *Night Mail: Selected Poems.* Translated with an introduction by Charles Simic. Field Translation Series, 19. Oberlin, OH: Oberlin College Press, c1992. 119 pp. REV: Branko Mikasinovich, *World Literature Today* 67, no. 2 (Spring 1993): 409.

■ Military Affairs

General

6126. Almquist, Peter. *Red Forge: Soviet Military Industry Since 1965.* New York: Columbia University Press, c1990. xi, 227 pp. [Revised version of author's doctoral dissertation, Massachusetts Institute of Technology.] REV: Alex G. Cummins, *Russian History* 17, no. 4 (Winter 1990): 480-481. Matthew Evangelista, *American Political Science Review* 85, no. 4 (December 1991): 1433-1436. Dale R. Herspring, *Armed Forces & Society* 17, no. 4 (Summer 1991): 625-626. Mark Kramer, *Soviet and Post-Soviet Review* 20, no. 1 (1993): 91. *Orbis* 37, no. 2 (Spring 1993).

6127. Blank, Stephen J., and Jacob W. Kipp, eds. *The Soviet Military and the Future.* Contributions in Military Studies, no. 130. Westport, CT: Greenwood Press, 1992. viii, 318 pp. REV: William T. Lee, *Military Review* 73, no. 7 (July 1993): 78. William Urban, *Journal of Baltic Studies* 24, no. 2 (Summer 1993): 212-213.

6128. Brown, Neville. *The Strategic Revolution: Thoughts for the Twenty-First Century.* 1st English ed. London; Washington: Brassey's; New York, NY: Distributed by Macmillan, 1992. x, 248 pp. REV: Saul Z. Barr, *Airpower Journal* 7, no. 2 (Summer 1993): 85-86.

6129. Cooper, Julian. *The Soviet Defense Industry: Conversion and Economic Reform.* Chatham House Papers. New York: Council on Foreign Relations Press, c1991. 111 pp. REV: *George Washington Journal of International Law and Economics* 26, no. 1 (1992): 228-230. Robert W. Campbell, *Slavic Review* 51, no. 2 (Summer 1992): 332-336. Thomas J. Richardson, *Russian Review* 52, no. 4 (October 1993): 575-576. *Orbis* 37, no. 2 (Spring 1993).

6130. Dunay, Pál. *Military Doctrine: Change in the East?* Occasional Paper Series (Institute for East-West Security Studies), 15. New York: Institute for East-West Security Studies, 1990. 85 pp. REV: J. C. Granville, *Russian Review* 52, no. 1 (January 1993): 138-139.

6131. Fodor, Neil. *The Warsaw Treaty Organization: A Political and Organizational Analysis.* New York: St. Martin's Press, 1990. xv, 235 pp. REV: Wolfgang T. Schlauch, *Nationalities Papers* 21, no. 2 (Fall 1993): 206-207.

6132. Frank, Willard C., Jr., and Philip S. Gillette, eds. *Soviet Military Doctrine from Lenin to Gorbachev, 1915-1991.* Contributions by Robert B. Bathurst, Bruce W. Menning, Jacob W. Kipp, David M. Glantz, Harriet Fast Scott, Raymond L. Garthoff, Dale R. Herspring, Roy Allison, Kent D. Lee, Valentin V. Larionov, Lester W. Grau, Graham H. Turbiville, Jr., and Mary C. FitzGerald. Contributions in Military Studies, no. 125. Westport, CT: Greenwood Press, 1992. xiv, 427 pp. [Some papers derived from conference held at Old Dominion University in May 1989. Contents: "Introduction"; Robert B. Bathurst, "Soviet Military Doctrine: Form and Content"; Bruce W. Menning, "Bases of Soviet Military Doctrine"; Jacob W. Kipp, "Lenin and Clausewitz: The Militarization of Marxism, 1915-1921"; Jacob W. Kipp, "Soviet Military Doctrine and the Origins of Operational Art, 1917-1936"; David M. Glantz, "Developing Offensive Success: The Soviet Conduct of Operational Maneuver"; Harriet Fast Scott, "Soviet Military Doctrine in the Nuclear Age, 1945-1985"; Raymond L. Garthoff, "New Thinking and Soviet Military Doctrine"; Dale R. Herspring, "The Soviet Military and Change"; Roy Allison, "Reasonable Sufficiency and Changes in Soviet Security Thinking"; Kent D. Lee, "Implementing Defensive Doctrine: The Role of Soviet Military Science"; Valentin V. Larionov, "Soviet Military Doctrine: Past and Present (1989)"; Valentin V. Larionov, "Four Models of Force Counterpositioning"; Lester W. Grau, "An Interpretation of General Larionov's Diagram"; Graham H. Turbiville, Jr., and David M. Glantz, "Soviet Military Strategy: Context and Prospects (1990)"; Valentin V. Larionov, "Response"; Mary C. FitzGerald, "The Dilemma in Moscow's Defensive Force Posture"; Mary C. FitzGerald, "The Soviet Image of Future War: The Impact of Desert Storm"; "Appendix: Draft Statements on Military Reform (Excerpts) and Military Doctrine (Complete), November 1990"; "A Brief Bibliography of Writings in English Concerning Soviet Military Doctrine".] REV: Fred Clark Boli, *Comparative Strategy* 12, no. 4 (1993): 481-482. Ralph Peters, *Military Review* 73, no. 7 (July 1993): 77-78.

6133. Michta, Andrew A. *The Red Eagle: The Army in Polish Politics, 1944-1988.* Stanford, CA: Hoover Institution Press, 1990. 270 pp. REV: John C. Campbell, *Foreign Affairs* 69, no. 3 (Summer 1990): 186. Michal Chorosnicki, *Polish Review* 38, no. 2 (1993): 232-235.

6134. Nation, R. Craig. *Black Earth, Red Star: A History of Soviet Security Policy, 1917-1991.* Ithaca, NY: Cornell University Press, 1992. xvi, 341 pp. REV: Andrew J. Pierre, *Foreign Affairs* 71, no. 5 (Winter 1992-1993): 198-199. Robert Vincent Daniels, *New Leader* 76, no. 1 (January 11, 1993): 17-18. Herbert J. Ellison, *American Historical Review* 98, no. 4 (October 1993): 1299. Raymond L. Garthoff, *Political Science Quarterly* 108, no. 2 (Summer 1993): 350-351. Stuart Kaufman, *Russian History = Histoire russe* 20, nos. 1-4 (1993): 377-378.

6135. Swider, Raymond J., Jr. *Soviet Military Reform in the Twentieth Century: Three Case Studies.* Contributions in Military Studies, no. 129. New York: Greenwood Press, 1992. 177 pp. REV: William Urban, *Journal of Baltic Studies* 24, no. 2 (Summer 1993): 212-213.

6136. Twining, David Thomas. *Strategic Surprise in the Age of Glasnost.* New Brunswick, NJ: Transaction, c1992. vii, 309 pp. [Includes discussion of events within the Soviet Union and discussion of U.S.-Soviet relations.] REV: David M. Glantz, *Military Review* 72, no. 9 (September 1992): 94-96. Wayne A. Silkett, *Parameters* 22, no. 3 (Autumn 1992): 125-126. Saul Z. Barr, *Airpower Journal* 7, no. 2 (Summer 1993): 85-86. Sam C. Sarkesian, *Annals of the American Academy of Political and Social Science*, no. 527 (May 1993): 174-175.

East-West Balance of Forces

6137. Baucom, Donald R. *The Origins of SDI, 1944-1983*. Modern War Studies. Lawrence, KS: University of Kansas Press, c1992. xix, 276 pp. REV: Edward Rhodes, *International History Review* 15, no. 3 (August 1993): 622. Keith Shimko, *Political Science Quarterly* 108, no. 1 (Spring 1993): 185-186.

6138. Broad, William. *Teller's War: The Top-Secret Story Behind the Star Wars Deception*. New York: Simon & Schuster, 1992. 350 pp. REV: Bruce D. Berkowitz, *Orbis* 36, no. 4 (Fall 1992): 617. Daniel O. Graham, *Journal of Social, Political and Economic Studies* 17, no. 1 (Spring 1992): 123-125. Michael Krepon, *New York Times Book Review* (February 23, 1992): 2. Gregory F. Treverton, *Foreign Affairs* 71, no. 2 (Spring 1992): 192. *Publishers Weekly* 239, no. 3 (January 13, 1992): 44. Julian J. DelGaudio, *History: Reviews of New Books* 21, no. 3 (Spring 1993): 116.

6139. Grabbe, Crockett L. *Space Weapons and the Strategic Defense Initiative*. Ames, IA: Iowa State University Press, 1991. xii, 252 pp. [Includes Soviet Union.] REV: I.H.Ph. Diederiks-Verschoor, *Journal of Space Law* 20, no. 1 (1992): 92-93. Kenneth R. Mayer, *Annals of the American Academy of Political and Social Science*, no. 527 (May 1993): 193-194.

6140. Haslam, Jonathan. *The Soviet Union and the Politics of Nuclear Weapons in Europe, 1969-1987*. Ithaca, NY: Cornell University Press, 1990. 227 pp. REV: Gregory F. Treverton, *Foreign Affairs* 69, no. 4 (Fall 1990): 179. Wolfram F. Hanrieder, *American Political Science Review* 85, no. 3 (September 1991): 1073-1074. George E. Hudson, *Russian Review* 50, no. 3 (July 1991): 376-377. Paul Buteux, *International History Review* 14, no. 3 (August 1992): 648-651. Jonathan Adelman, *American Historical Review* 98, no. 5 (December 1993): 1649.

6141. Herf, Jeffrey. *War by Other Means: Soviet Power, West German Resistance, and the Battle of the Euromissiles*. New York: Free Press; Toronto: Collier; New York: Maxwell Macmillan International, c1991. xiii, 369 pp. REV: Adam Garfinkle, *Orbis* 35, no. 3 (Summer 1991): 459. Michael Lind, *Commentary* 91, no. 6 (June 1991): 59-61. Susanne Peters, *Telos*, no. 88 (Summer 1991): 205-210. Gregory F. Treverton, *Foreign Affairs* 70, no. 2 (Spring 1991): 178. Charles Burdick, *Annals of the American Academy of Political and Social Science*, no. 521 (May 1992): 189-190. Matthew Evangelista, *International History Review* 14, no. 4 (November 1992): 849. Forest L. Grieves, *Perspectives on Political Science* 22, no. 3 (Summer 1993): 140. Jerry Z. Muller, *Partisan Review* 60, no. 1 (Winter 1993): 164-167.

6142. Reiss, Edward. *The Strategic Defense Initiative*. Cambridge Studies in International Relations, 23. Cambridge; New York, NY: Cambridge University Press, 1992. xiv, 249 pp. REV: Andrew J. Pierre, *Foreign Affairs* 72, no. 2 (Spring 1993): 166.

Military History

6143. Bartov, Omer. *Hitler's Army: Soldiers, Nazis, and War in the Third Reich*. New York: Oxford University Press, 1991. 238 pp. [Especially the Eastern Front and campaigns in the Soviet Union.] REV: Richard Breitman, *Historian* 54, no. 4 (Summer 1992): 697-698. George H. Stein, *American Historical Review* 97, no. 4 (October 1992): 1242-1243. Lawrence D. Stokes, *International History Review* 15, no. 1 (February 1993): 194.

6144. Fuller, William C., Jr. *Strategy and Power in Russia, 1600-1914*. New York: Free Press, c1992. xx, 557 pp. REV: William C. Green, *Strategic Review* 20, no. 4 (Fall 1992): 61-63. Curtis S. King, *Military Review* 72, no. 12 (December 1992): 99-100. Alvin Z. Rubinstein, *Orbis* 36, no. 4 (Fall 1992): 627. Brian M. Downing, *Contemporary Sociology* 22, no. 2 (March 1993): 204. Robert S. Wood, *Naval War College Review* 46, no. 3, Sequence 343 (Summer 1993): 132-134.

6145. Menning, Bruce W. *Bayonets Before Bullets: The Imperial Russian Army, 1861-1914*. Indiana-Michigan Series in Russian and East European Studies. Bloomington, IN: Indiana University Press, c1992. x, 334 pp. REV: Robert Argenbright, *Russian History = Histoire russe* 20, nos. 1-4 (1993): 298-300. Daniel W. Graf, *Journal of Military History* 57, no. 3 (July 1993): 558. Ralph Peters, *Military Review* 73, no. 5 (May 1993): 84-85.

6146. Soviet Union. General Staff. *Soviet Documents on the Use of War Experience*. Translated by Harold S. Orenstein. Introduction by David M. Glantz. Cass Series on the Soviet Study of War, nos. 1-2. Portland, OR: F. Cass, c1991. 2 vols. [Contents: Vol. 1. The Initial Period of War, 1941 — v. 2. The Winter Campaign, 1941-1942.] REV: James F. Gebhardt, *Military Review* 72, no. 12 (December 1992): 91-93. Louis C. Rotundo, *Slavic Review* 52, no. 2 (Summer 1993): 372-373.

6147. Stolfi, R. H. S. *Hitler's Panzers East: World War II Reinterpreted*. Norman: University of Oklahoma Press, c1991. 272 pp. [Campaigns in the Soviet Union.] REV: Zoltan Kramar, *History: Reviews of New Books* 21, no. 2 (Winter 1993): 79. Lawrence D. Stokes, *International History Review* 15, no. 1 (February 1993): 194. Alan F. Wilt, *American Historical Review* 98, no. 3 (June 1993): 897.

6148. Svechin, Aleksandr A. *Strategy*. Edited by Kent D. Lee. Introductory essays by Andrei A. Kokoshin et al. Minneapolis, MN: East View Publications, 1992. viii, 374 pp. [Translation of *Strategiia*.] REV: John Erickson, *Journal of Military History* 57, no. 1 (January 1993): 160-162.

6149. Verona, Sergiu. *Military Occupation and Diplomacy: Soviet Troops in Romania, 1944-1958*. Foreword by J. F. Brown. Durham, NC: Duke University Press, 1992. xii, 211 pp. REV: John C. Campbell, *Foreign Affairs* 71, no. 3 (Summer 1992): Stephen Fischer-Galati, *Soviet and Post-Soviet Review* 19, nos. 1-3 (1992): 339-340. Vladimir Tismaneanu, *Orbis* 36, no. 4 (Fall 1992): 624-625. J. Calvitt Clarke, III, *Russian History = Histoire russe* 20, nos. 1-4

(1993): 397-398. Paul E. Michelson, *International History Review* 15, no. 4 (November 1993): 838. Sergiu Verona, *American Historical Review* 98, no. 3 (June 1993): 907.

6150. Von Hagen, Mark. *Soldiers in the Proletarian Dictatorship: The Red Army and the Soviet Socialist State, 1917-1930.* Studies of the Harriman Institute. Studies in Soviet History and Society. Ithaca, NY: Cornell University Press, 1990. xviii, 369 pp. REV: Thomas F. Remington, *Russian History* 17, no. 4 (Winter 1990): 450-451. John Bushnell, *American Historical Review* 96, no. 4 (October 1991): 1250-1251. Peter Kenez, *Slavic Review* 50, no. 3 (Fall 1991): 699-700. Lars T. Lih, *Canadian-American Slavic Studies* 25, nos. 1-4 (1991): 317-318. Elise Kimerling Wirtschafter, *Russian Review* 50, no. 3 (July 1991): 363-364. Lynn Mally, *International Labor and Working-Class History*, no. 42 (Fall 1992): 127-130. Allan Wildman, *Journal of Modern History* 64, no. 1 (March 1992): 188-190. Tsuyoshi Hasegawa, *Nationalities Papers* 21, no. 2 (Fall 1993): 201-203.

■ **Philosophy, Political Theory, Ideology**

General

6151. Brewer, Anthony. *Marxist Theories of Imperialism: A Critical Survey.* 2nd ed. London; New York: Routledge, 1990. xi, 300 pp. REV: Martin Bronfenbrenner, *History of Political Economy* 24, no. 3 (Fall 1992): 753-755. John Willoughby, *Science & Society* 57, no. 3 (Fall 1993): 378-380.

6152. Buchanan, Allen. *Secession: The Morality of Political Divorce from Fort Sumter to Lithuania and Quebec.* Boulder, CO: Westview Press, 1991. xviii, 174 pp. [Includes independence movements in Lithuania and the Baltic states.] REV: Avigail Eisenberg, *Canadian Journal of Political Science = Revue canadienne de science politique* 25, no. 2 (June 1992): 389-390. Will Kymlicka, *Political Theory* 20, no. 3 (August 1992): 527-532. Desmond Morton, *International Journal* 48, no. 1 (Winter 1992-1993): 189-190. Mary Ellen O'Connell, *International Lawyer* 26, no. 4 (Winter 1992): 1127-1131. Andrew J. Pierre, *Foreign Affairs* 71, no. 2 (Spring 1992): 190. Vivian Williams, *New York University Journal of International Law and Politics* 25, no. 1 (Fall 1992): 201-203. Charles R. Beitz, *Philosophical Review* 102, no. 4 (October 1993): 622-624. Crawford Young, *Review of Politics* 55, no. 2 (Spring 1993): 354-356.

6153. Gottlieb, Roger S. *Marxism, 1844-1990: Origins, Betrayal, Rebirth.* Revolutionary Thought/Radical Movements, New York: Routledge, 1992. xvii, 248 pp. REV: Harvey J. Kaye, *American Historical Review* 98, no. 5 (December 1993): 1563. *Orbis* 37, no. 2 (Spring 1993).

6154. Hamilton, Richard F. *The Bourgeois Epoch: Marx and Engels on Britain, France, and Germany.* Chapel Hill, NC: University of North Carolina Press, c1991. xii, 293 pp. REV: Robert M. Fishman, *Contemporary Sociology* 22, no. 5 (September 1993): 758.

6155. Heller, Agnes, and Ferenc Fehér. *The Grandeur and Twilight of Radical Universalism.* New Brunswick, NJ: Transaction Publishers, 1991. viii, 579 pp. REV: Vladimir Tismaneanu, *Partisan Review* 60, no. 3 (Summer 1993): 483-487.

6156. Huntington, Samuel P. *The Third Wave: Democratization in the Late Twentieth Century.* 1st ed. The Julian J. Rothbaum Distinguished Lecture Series, v. 4. Norman, OK: University of Oklahoma Press, c1991. 366 pp. [On the transition of thirty countries from nondemocratic to democratic political systems from 1974 to 1990. Includes Russia, the Soviet Union, and Eastern Europe (especially Czechoslovakia, Hungary, Poland, and Romania).] REV: Morton Kondracke, *National Interest*, no. 27 (Spring 1992): 98-99. Samuel C. Patterson, *Perspectives on Political Science* 21, no. 2 (Spring 1992): 100-101. Andrew J. Pierre, *Foreign Affairs* 71, no. 2 (Spring 1992): 190. Joshua Murarchik, *Orbis* 37, no. 4 (Fall 1993): 643-649. Philippe C. Schmitter, *Review of Politics* 55, no. 2 (Spring 1993): 348-351.

6157. Jowitt, Ken. *New World Disorder: The Leninist Extinction.* Berkeley, CA: University of California Press, 1992. 342 pp. [Collection of essays published between 1974 and 1992.] REV: Stephen Holmes, *East European Constitutional Review* 1, no. 2 (Summer 1992): 31-32. Robert Legvold, *Foreign Affairs* 71, no. 4 (Fall 1992): 213. Vladimir Tismaneanu, *Orbis* 36, no. 4 (Fall 1992): 613-614. Vladimir Tismaneanu, *Society* 30, no. 1 (November-December 1992): 113-115. Victor Zaslavsky, *Contemporary Sociology* 22, no. 1 (January 1993): 38.

6158. Kornai, János. *The Socialist System: The Political Economy of Communism.* Princeton, NJ: Princeton University Press, c1992. xxviii, 644 pp. REV: Daniel Chirot, *Slavic Review* 52, no. 4 (Winter 1993): 855-856. Chris Kuehl, *Social Science Journal* 30, no. 2 (1993): 213-215. Jean Tesche, *Southern Economic Journal* 60, no. 1 (July 1993): 270-271. Ivan Szelenyi, *Contemporary Sociology* 22, no. 1 (January 1993): 33.

6159. Krieger, Leonard. *Ideas and Events: Professing History.* Edited by M. L. Brick. Introduction by Michael Ermarth. Chicago, IL: University of Chicago Press, 1992. xxix, 409 pp. REV: Melvin Small, *Historian* 56, no. 1 (Autumn 1993): 135-136.

6160. Rigby, S. H. *Engels and the Formation of Marxism: History, Dialectics and Revolution.* Manchester, England; New York: Manchester University Press; New York: Distributed by St. Martin's Press, c1992. viii, 256 pp. REV: Donald M. Lowe, *American Historical Review* 98, no. 4 (October 1993): 1239.

6161. Rozman, Gilbert, Seizaburo Sato, and Gerald Segal, eds. *Dismantling Communism: Common Causes and Regional Variations.* Washington, DC: Woodrow Wilson Center Press; Baltimore, MD: Johns Hopkins University Press, 1992. x, 405 pp. [Chapters derived from papers presented at two workshops held at the Woodrow Wilson Center in Washington, DC, in October 1990 and January 1991.] REV: Roger E. Kanet, *Slavic Review* 52, no. 2

(Summer 1993): 373-374. Robert Legvold, *Foreign Affairs* 72, no. 2 (Spring 1993): 179. Stefania Szlek Miller, *Soviet and Post-Soviet Review* 20, nos. 2-3 (1993): 246-247.

6162. Steele, David Ramsay. *From Marx to Mises: Post-Capitalist Society and the Challenge of Economic Calculation.* La Salle, IL: Open Court, c1992. xviii, 440 pp. REV: Evan Kraft, *Comparative Economic Studies* 35, no. 3 (Fall 1993): 75-77.

6163. Walicki, Andrzej. *Russia, Poland, and Universal Regeneration: Studies on Russian and Polish Thought of the Romantic Epoch.* Notre Dame, IN: University of Notre Dame Press, c1991. x, 225 pp. REV: Lois S. Becker, *American Historical Review* 98, no. 2 (April 1993): 534. Abbott Gleason, *Canadian American Slavic Studies = Revue Canadienne Américaine d'Etudes Slaves* 27, nos. 1-4 (1993): 334-335. Irena Grudzinska Gross, *Polish Review* 38, no. 1 (1993): 110-112. Nicholas V. Riasanovsky, *Russian Review* 52, no. 3 (July 1993): 426-427.

6164. White, Dan S. *Lost Comrades: Socialists of the Front Generation, 1918-1945.* Cambridge, MA: Harvard University Press, 1992. viii, 255 pp. REV: Nathanael Greene, *History: Reviews of New Books* 21, no. 4 (Summer 1993): 173. Robert J. Young, *International History Review* 15, no. 2 (May 1993): 380.

Russia/U.S.S.R.

6165. Bakhurst, David. *Consciousness and Revolution in Soviet Philosophy: From the Bolsheviks to Evald Ilyenkov.* Modern European Philosophy. Cambridge; New York: Cambridge University Press, 1991. xi, 292 pp. REV: David G. Rowley, *Russian Review* 51, no. 4 (October 1992): 593-594. Sean Sayers, *Canadian Slavonic Papers* 34, nos. 1-2 (March-June 1992): 176-177. James P. Scanlan, *Canadian American Slavic Studies = Revue Canadienne Américaine d'Etudes Slaves* 27, nos. 1-4 (1993): 328-330.

6166. Chaadaev, Peter. *Philosophical Works of Peter Chaadaev.* Edited by Raymond McNally and Richard Tempest. Sovietica (Universite de Fribourg. Ost-Europa Institut), v. 56. Dordrecht; Boston: Kluwer Academic, c1991. 318 pp. [Translated from the French. Contents: The philosophical letters addressed to a lady — The apologia of a madman — Fragments and diverse thoughts.] REV: James Rogers, *Canadian American Slavic Studies = Revue Canadienne Américaine d'Etudes Slaves* 27, nos. 1-4 (1993): 324-325.

6167. Christoff, Peter K. *An Introduction to Nineteenth-Century Russian Slavophilism.* Boulder, CO: Westview Press, c1991. vii, 469 pp. REV: Theodore R. Weeks, *Slavic Review* 51, no. 2 (Summer 1992): 364-365. Walter J. Gleason, Jr., *American Historical Review* 98, no. 1 (February 1993): 203-205. G. M. Hamburg, *Russian Review* 52, no. 3 (July 1993): 417-418. Raymond T. McNally, *Russian History = Histoire russe* 20, nos. 1-4 (1993): 293-295.

6168. Graham, Loren R. *Science, Philosophy, and Human Behavior in the Soviet Union.* New York: Columbia University Press, 1987. xiii, 565 pp. [Expanded, updated, and revised version of *Science and Philosophy in the Soviet Union.*] REV: Eugene Lashchyk, *Physics Today* 42, no. 4 (April 1989): 63-65. Valery N. Soyfer, *Bulletin of the Atomic Scientists* 45, no. 7 (September 1989): 39-40. Paul R. Josephson, *Russian Review* 51, no. 1 (January 1992): 135-136. Nathan M. Brooks, *Soviet and Post-Soviet Review* 20, no. 1 (1993): 88.

6169. Howard, M. C., and J. E. King. *A History of Marxian Economics.* Princeton, NJ: Princeton University Press, 1989. 2 vols. [Contents: Vol. 1. 1883-1929 — v. 2. 1929-1990.] REV: Rondo Cameron, *American Historical Review* 98, no. 3 (June 1993): 836. David Gleicher, *Journal of Economic Literature* 31, no. 2 (June 1993): 887.

6170. Lotman, Yuri M. *Universe of the Mind: A Semiotic Theory of Culture.* Translated from the Russian by Ann Shukman. Introduction by Umberto Eco. Bloomington, IN: Indiana University Press, c1990. 288 pp. REV: Stephen Hutchings, *Slavic and East European Journal* 36, no. 2 (Summer 1992): 245-247. Amy Mandelker, *Russian Review* 52, no. 4 (October 1993): 552-553.

6171. Steila, Daniela. *Genesis and Development of Plekhanov's Theory of Knowledge: A Marxist Between Anthropological Materialism and Physiology.* Sovietica (Universite de Fribourg. Ost-Europa Institut), v. 55. Dordrecht; Boston: Kluwer Academic, c1991. ix, 246 pp. REV: James A. Rogers, *Canadian American Slavic Studies = Revue Canadienne Américaine d'Etudes Slaves* 27, nos. 1-4 (1993): 420-421. William G. Wagner, *Russian Review* 52, no. 1 (January 1993): 114.

6172. Vucinich, Alexander. *Darwin in Russian Thought.* Berkeley, CA: University of California Press, c1988. x, 468 pp. REV: Edith Clowes, *American Historical Review* 96, no. 2 (April 1991): 564-565. Abbott Gleason, *Russian Review* 50, no. 2 (April 1991): 223-224. James A. Rogers, *Canadian American Slavic Studies = Revue Canadienne Américaine d'Etudes Slaves* 27, nos. 1-4 (1993): 348-350.

Eastern Europe

6173. Cioran, E. M. *On the Heights of Despair.* Translated and introduction by Ilinca Zarifopol-Johnston. Chicago, IL: University of Chicago Press, 1992. xxi, 128 pp. [Translation of *Pe culmile disperarii.*] REV: *Orbis* 37, no. 2 (Spring 1993).

6174. Congdon, Lee. *Exile and Social Thought: Hungarian Intellectuals in Germany and Austria, 1919-1933.* Princeton, NJ: Princeton University Press, c1991. xvi, 376 pp. REV: István Deák, *International History Review* 14, no. 4 (November 1992): 808-810. Paul Gottfried, *Telos*, no. 92 (Summer 1992): 178-180. Peter Pastor, *American Historical Review* 97, no. 3 (June 1992): 843. William M. Johnson, *Austrian History Yearbook* 24 (1993): 258-260.

6175. Havel, Václav. *Václav Havel: Living in Truth: Twenty-two Essays Published on the Occasion of the Award of the Erasmus Prize to Václav Havel.* ed. Jan Vladislav.

London; Boston, MA: Faber & Faber, 1989. xix, 315 pp. [Includes texts by and about Havel. Originally published by Faber in 1987 under the title *Václav Havel, or, Living in Truth*.] REV: Erwin Knoll, *Progressive* 57, no. 4 (April 1993): 40-43.

6176. Kadarkay, Arpad. *Georg Lukács: Life, Thought, and Politics*. Cambridge, MA: B. Blackwell, 1991. 538 pp. REV: Marina Allemano, *Canadian Review of Comparative Literature* 19, no. 3 (September 1992): 423-426. Eva L. Corredor, *Philosophy and Literature* 16, no. 2 (October 1992): 382-383. Hans H. Rudnick, *World Literature Today* 66, no. 4 (Autumn 1992): 788-789. Zoltan Tarr, *Contemporary Sociology* 22, no. 5 (September 1993): 756.

6177. Kolakowski, Leszek. *Modernity on Endless Trial*. Chicago, IL: University of Chicago Press, 1990. vii, 261 pp. [Essays written between 1973 and 1986.] REV: Arthur Coleman Danto, *New York Times Book Review* 95 (December 1990): 1ff. Diogenes Allen, *Commonweal* 118, no. 5 (March 8, 1991): 165-166. Peter L. Berger, *Commentary* 91, no. 4 (April 1991): 56-58. Toby E. Huff, *Society* 28, no. 5 (July-August 1991): 94-95. Vladimir Tismaneanu, *Partisan Review* 60, no. 3 (Summer 1993): 483-487.

6178. Lukacs, Georg. *The Process of Democratization*. Translated from the German by Susanne Bernhardt, and Norman Levine. With an introduction by Norman Levine. SUNY Series in Contemporary Political Philosophy. Albany, NY: State University of New York Press, c1991. 179 pp. REV: Alfred G. Meyer, *Slavic Review* 51, no. 3 (Fall 1992): 596-597. James Lawler, *Science & Society* 57, no. 4 (Winter 1993-1994): 474. Zoltan Tarr, *Contemporary Sociology* 22, no. 5 (September 1993): 756.

6179. Mendell, Marguerite, and Daniel Salee, eds. *The Legacy of Karl Polanyi: Market, State and Society at the End of the Twentieth Century*. Contributions by Manfred Bienefeld, Alan Wolfe, Brent McClintock, James Ronald Stanfield, Trent Schroyer, Fred Block, Gérald Berthoud, Jacques Godbout, Björn Hettne, André Gunder Frank, Maria Fuentes, Kálman Miszei, Tadeusz Kowalik, Domenico Mario Nuti, Ivan Szelenyi, and Gyorgy Litvan. New York: St. Martin's Press, 1991. 276 pp. [Contents: Manfred Bienefeld, "Karl Polanyi and the Contradictions of the 1980s"; Alan Wolfe, "Market, State and Society as Codes of Moral Obligation"; Brent McClintock and James Ronald Stanfield, "The Crisis of the Welfare State: Lessons from Karl Polanyi"; Trent Schroyer, "Karl Polanyi's Post-Marxist Critical Theory"; Fred Block, "Contradictions of Self-Regulating Markets"; Gérald Berthoud, "The Human Body as a Commodity: Universal Values and Market Truths"; Jacques Godbout, "The Self-Regulating State"; Björn Hettne, "Europe and the Crisis: The Regionalist Scenario Revisited"; André Gunder Frank and Maria Fuentes, "Social Movements, the State and Transformation"; Kálman Miszei, "The "Small Transformation": The Historical Process of Economic Reforms in Eastern Europe"; Tadeusz Kowalik, "The Polish Postscript, 1989"; Domenico Mario Nuti, "Tibor Liska's Entrepreneurial Socialism"; Ivan Szelenyi, "Karl Polanyi and the Theory of a Socialist Mixed Economy"; Gyorgy Litvan, "Democratic and Socialist Values in Karl

Polanyi's Thought".] REV: Warren J. Samuels, *Comparative Economic Studies* 34, no. 2 (Summer 1992): 84-86. William C. Schaniel, *Journal of Economic Issues* 27, no. 3 (September 1993): 981.

6180. Staniszkis, Jadwiga. *The Ontology of Socialism*. Edited and translated by Peggy Watson. New York: Oxford University Press, 1992. 191 pp. [Translation of *Ontologia socjalizmu*.] REV: Peter Beilharz, *Contemporary Sociology* 22, no. 6 (November 1993): 838.

■ Psychology

6181. Freud, Sigmund. *The Diary of Sigmund Freud, 1929-1939: A Record of the Final Decade*. Translated, annotated, introduction by Michael Molnar. New York: Scribner's; Toronto: Maxwell Macmillan Canada; New York: Maxwell Macmillan International, c1992. xxvi, 326 pp. REV: Hannah S. Decker, *Isis* 84, no. 2 (June 1993): 410. Emanuel Rice, *Congress Monthly* 60, no. 2 (February 1993): 18-19.

6182. Van der Veer, René, and Jaan Valsiner. *Understanding Vygotsky: A Quest for Synthesis*. Cambridge, MA: B. Blackwell, 1991. 450 pp. REV: Carl Ratner, *Journal of the History of the Behavioral Sciences* 29, no. 3 (July 1993): 277.

6183. Wertsch, James V. *Voices of the Mind: A Sociocultural Approach to Mediated Action*. Cambridge, MA: Harvard University Press, 1991. viii, 169 pp. [Includes Bakhtin and Vygotsky.] REV: Alex Kozulin, *Russian Review* 52, no. 2 (April 1993): 291-292.

■ Religion

General

6184. Misztal, Bronislaw, and Anson Shupe, eds. *Religion and Politics in Comparative Perspective*. Westport, CT: Praeger, 1992. xii, 223 pp. [Papers from the 12th World Congress of Sociology, held in Madrid in 1990. Includes three essays on Poland, and Hank Johnston's "Religious Nationalism: Six Propositions from Eastern Europe and the Former Soviet Union".] REV: Jeffrey K. Hadden, *Journal for the Scientific Study of Religion* 32, no. 4 (December 1993): 416-417.

6185. Moen, Matthew C., and Lowell S. Gustafson, eds. *The Religious Challenge to the State*. Philadelphia, PA: Temple University Press, 1992. xi, 294 pp. [Includes discussion of Eastern Europe.] REV: Joseph Tamney, *Journal for the Scientific Study of Religion* 32, no. 2 (June 1993): 192-193.

6186. Mojzes, Paul. *Religious Liberty in Eastern Europe and the USSR: Before and after the Great Transformation*. East European Monographs, no. 337. Boulder, CO: East European Monographs; New York: Distributed by Columbia University Press, 1992. xviii, 473 pp. REV: D. Pospielovsky, *Canadian Slavonic Papers* 34, no. 4 (December 1992): 507-508. Dennis J. Dunn, *Catholic Historical*

Review 79, no. 2 (April 1993): 354-355. Joseph T. Hapak, *Journal of Baltic Studies* 24, no. 3 (Fall 1993): 308-309. Norman Pease, *American Historical Review* 98, no. 5 (December 1993): 1599. Jane B. Swan, *Journal of Ecumenical Studies* 30, nos. 3-4 (Summer-Fall 1993): 476-477. William Luther White, *Religion in Eastern Europe* 13, no. 2 (April 1993): 41-46.

6187. Stewart, Charles. *Demons and the Devil: Moral Imagination in Modern Greek Culture.* Princeton, NJ: Princeton University Press, c1991. xix, 330 pp. REV: K. E. Fleming, *Journal of Religion* 73, no. 1 (January 1993): 142-143. Sarah Iles Johnston, *History of Religions* 33, no. 2 (November 1993): 202-204. Edmund Keeley, *New York Review of Books* (July 15, 1993): 34-35.

6188. Troyanovsky, Igor, ed. *Religion in the Soviet Republics: A Guide to Christianity, Judaism, Islam, Buddhism, and Other Religions.* 1st ed. San Francisco, CA: HarperSanFrancisco, c1991. xiv, 210 pp. [Collection of essays, speeches, documents and information.] REV: Paul Mojzes, *Journal of Church and State* 35, no. 4 (Autumn 1993): 917-918. Paul Mojzes, *Religion in Eastern Europe* 13, no. 4 (August 1993): 48-49.

Christianity

6189. Brock, Peter. *Studies in Peace History.* York, England: W. Sessions; Syracuse, NY: Distributors, Syracuse University Press, 1991. vi, 103 pp. [Partial contents: A Polish Anabaptist in defence of conscientious objection, 1575; Socinian antimilitarism in Poland from 1605 to 1660; Pacifist witness in dualist Hungary; Conscientious objectors in Lenin's Russia: a report, 1924.] REV: J. R. Burkholder, *Mennonite Quarterly Review* 67, no. 2 (April 1993): 241-243.

6190. Bushkovitch, Paul. *Religion and Society in Russia: The Sixteenth and Seventeenth Centuries.* New York: Oxford University Press, 1992. vi, 278 pp. [Contents: Introduction: Russian History and Russian Orthodoxy — 1. Orthodoxy in the Sixteenth Century — 2. The Landholding Class and Its Religious World — 3. The Church in the Seventeenth Century — 4. Saints and Miracles in Church Policy — 5. The Era Of Miracles — 6. The Beginnings of Change — 7. The Rise of the Sermon — Appendix: The Manuscripts of Epifanii Slavinetskii's Sermons.] REV: James G. Hart, *Historian* 55, no. 3 (Spring 1993): 532-533. Valerie Kivelson, *Russian Review* 52, no. 4 (October 1993): 556-557. Eve Levin, *American Historical Review* 98, no. 3 (June 1993): 908. Samuel J. Nesdoly, *History: Reviews of New Books* 21, no. 4 (Summer 1993): 174.

6191. Calian, Carnegie Samuel. *Theology without Boundaries: Encounters of Eastern Orthodoxy and Western Tradition.* 1st ed. Louisville, KY: Westminster/John Knox Press, c1992. 130 pp. REV: John W. Barker, *Journal of Church and State* 35, no. 4 (Autumn 1993): 902-903. George D. Gregory, *Journal of Ecumenical Studies* 30, nos. 3-4 (Summer-Fall 1993): 447-448.

6192. Epp, Jacob D. *A Mennonite in Russia: The Diaries of Jacob D. Epp, 1851-1880.* Translated and edited, with an introduction and analysis, by Harvey L. Dyck.

Toronto, Ontario; Buffalo, NY: University of Toronto Press, c1991. x, 456 pp. REV: Roy R. Robson, *Harvard Ukrainian Studies* 16, nos. 1-2 (June 1992): 225-227. James Urry, *Mennonite Quarterly Review* 66, no. 2 (April 1992): 272-274. Winfred A. Kohls, *Russian History = Histoire russe* 20, nos. 1-4 (1993): 295-296. Michael Newton, *Studies in Religion = Sciences Religieuses* 22, no. 1 (Winter 1993): 140.

6193. Fleishcer, Manfred P., ed. *The Harvest of Humanism in Central Europe: Essays in Honor of Lewis W. Spitz.* St. Louis, MO: Concordia Pub. House, c1992. 389 pp. REV: Stephen Varvis, *Mennonite Quarterly Review* 67, no. 1 (January 1993): 123-125.

6194. *Hagiography of Kievan Rus.* Translated and introduction by Paul Hollingsworth. Harvard Library of Early Ukrainian Literature. English Translations, v. 2. [Boston, MA]: Distributed by Harvard University Press for the Ukrainian Research Institute of Harvard University, 1992. xcv, 267 pp. REV: George D. Knysh, *Ukrainian Quarterly* 49, no. 2 (Summer 1993): 205-208. T. Allan Smith, *Canadian Slavonic Papers* 35, nos. 1-2 (March-June 1993): 173-175.

6195. Hosking, Geoffrey A., ed. *Church, Nation and State in Russia and Ukraine.* New York: St. Martin's Press, 1991. xv, 357 pp. REV: Gregory L. Freeze, *Russian Review* 52, no. 1 (January 1993): 140-141. Wolfgang Heller, *Slavic Review* 52, no. 2 (Summer 1993): 395. Roy R. Robson, *Russian History = Histoire russe* 20, nos. 1-4 (1993): 270-271.

6196. Kantor, Marvin. *The Origins of Christianity in Bohemia: Sources and Commentary.* Evanston, IL: Northwestern University Press, c1990. viii, 299 pp. REV: Thomas J. Drobena, *Slavic Review* 51, no. 3 (Fall 1992): 599-600. David R. Holeton, *Czechoslovak and Central European Journal* 11, no. 1 (Summer 1992): 114-116. Walter K. Hanak, *Speculum* 68, no. 4 (October 1993): 1146-1148.

6197. Little, David. *Ukraine: The Legacy of Intolerance.* Series on Religion, Nationalism, and Intolerance. Washington, DC: United States Institute of Peace Press, 1991. xxii, 111 pp. [First of a six-part study.] REV: Joseph A. Loya, *Religion in Eastern Europe* 13, no. 3 (June 1993): 42-43.

6198. Nielsen, Niels C. *Revolutions in Eastern Europe: The Religious Roots.* Maryknoll, NY: Orbis Books, c1991. vii, 175 pp. REV: James Edward Wood, Jr., *Journal of Church and State* 35, no. 2 (Spring 1993): 411-412.

6199. Ramet, Pedro, ed. *Christianity Under Stress.* Durham, NC: Duke University Press, 1990. viii, 454 pp. REV: John C. Campbell, *Foreign Affairs* 70, no. 3 (Summer 1991): 162. Dennis J. Dunn, *Slavic Review* 50, no. 4 (Winter 1991): 1056. Joseph A. Loya, *Occasional Papers on Religion in Eastern Europe* 11, no. 1 (February 1991): 44-47. Gerard F. Rutan, *American Political Science Review* 85, no. 3 (September 1991): 1050-1051. Joseph L. Wieczynski, *Catholic Historical Review* 77, no. 2 (April 1991): 286. James T. Flynn, *Nationalities Papers* 21, no. 2 (Fall 1993): 213-215.

6200. ———, ed. *Christianity Under Stress.*
Durham, NC: Duke University Press, c1988. vi, 471 pp.
REV: John B. Dunlop, *Canadian-American Slavic Studies*
24, no. 3 (Fall 1990): 380-382. Henry Lane Hull, *Catholic
Historical Review* 79, no. 1 (January 1993): 126.

6201. ———. *Cross and Commissar: The Politics of
Religion in Eastern Europe and the USSR.* Bloomington, IN:
Indiana University Press, c1987. x, 244 pp. REV: Henry
Lane Hull, *Catholic Historical Review* 79, no. 1 (January
1993): 126.

6202. Ramet, Sabrina Petra, ed. *Christianity
under Stress.* Contributions by Sabrina Petra Ramet, Sape
A. Zylstra, Paul Bock, Joseph Pungur, Earl A. Pope, Paul
Mojzes, N. Gerald Shenk, Walter Sawatsky, Lawrence
Klippenstein, and Gerd Stricker. Durham, NC: Duke
University Press, 1992. 441 pp. [Contents: Sabrina Petra
Ramet, "Protestantism and communism: Patterns of
interaction in eastern Europe and the Soviet Union"; Sape
A. Zylstra, "Protestantism: theology and politics"; Sabrina
Petra Ramet, "Protestantism in East Germany, 1949-1989:
a summing up"; Paul Bock, "Protestantism in Czechoslova-
kia and Poland"; Joseph Pungur, "Protestantism in
Hungary: the communist era"; Earl A. Pope, "Protestant-
ism in Romania"; Paul Mojzes and N. Gerald Shenk,
"Protestantism in Bulgaria and Yugoslavia since 1945";
Walter Sawatsky, "Protestantism in the USSR"; Lawrence
Klippenstein, "Conscientious objectors in eastern Europe:
The quest for free choice and alternative service"; Sabrina
Petra Ramet, "The new church-state configuration in
eastern Europe".] REV: Robert Legvold, *Foreign Affairs*
72, no. 4 (September-October 1993): 168. Samuel J.
Nesdoly, *Canadian Slavonic Papers* 35, nos. 1-2 (March-
June 1993): 185.

6203. *Sermons and Rhetoric of Kievan Rus'.*
Translated and with an introduction by Simon Franklin.
Harvard Library of Early Ukrainian Literature, v. 5.
Cambridge, MA: Distributed by Harvard University Press
for the Harvard Ukrainian Research Institute, 1991. cxv,
213 pp. [English translations of documents originally
composed in Church Slavonic.] REV: Leonid S. Chekin,
Slavic Review 51, no. 2 (Summer 1992): 387-388. Marius L.
Cybulski, *Zapiski russkoi akademicheskoi gruppy v SShA =
Transactions of the Association of Russian-American
Schlolars in the U.S.A.*, no. 25 (1992-1993): 328-330. Gail
Lenhoff, *Slavic and East European Journal* 36, no. 3 (Fall
1992): 362-363. David K. Prestel, *Canadian American
Slavic Studies = Revue Canadienne Américaine d'Etudes
Slaves* 27, nos. 1-4 (1993): 330-332.

6204. Weigel, George. *The Final Revolution: The
Resistance Church and the Collapse of Communism.* New
York: Oxford University Press, 1992. xvi, 255 pp. REV:
Charles Gati, *New York Times Book Review* (November 15,
1992): 12. John Gray, *National Review* 44, no. 21 (Novem-
ber 2, 1992): 55-56. Jonathan Kwitny, *New Leader* 75, no.
16 (December 14-28, 1992): 7-9. Philip J. Costopoulos,
Journal of Democracy 4, no. 1 (January 1993): 126-129.
Michael Lavelle, *Commonweal* 120, no. 7 (April 9, 1993): 39-
40. Richard Lowry, *Freedom Review* 24, no. 2 (March-April

1993): 40-41. Colman McCarthy, *Book World* 23, no. 5
(January 31, 1993): 4. Paul Mojzes, *Religion in Eastern
Europe* 13, no. 1 (February 1993): 45-46. Arch Puddington,
Commentary 95, no. 3 (March 1993): 56-58. *Orbis* 37, no. 2
(Spring 1993).

6205. Wybrew, Hugh. *The Orthodox Liturgy: The
Development of the Eucharistic Liturgy in the Byzantine
Rite.* Crestwood, NY: St. Vladimir's Seminary Press, 1990.
xi, 189 pp. REV: David J. Goa, *Canadian Slavonic Papers*
35, nos. 3-4 (September-December 1993): 396-397.

Judaism

6206. Boyarin, Jonathan. *Storm from Paradise: The
Politics of Jewish Memory.* Minneapolis, MN: University of
Minnesota Press, c1992. xx, 161 pp. REV: Kurt Lang,
Contemporary Sociology 22, no. 4 (July 1993): 596-599.

6207. Frankel, Jonathan, and Steven J.
Zipperstein, eds. *Assimilation and Community: The Jews in
Nineteenth-Century Europe.* Contributions by Jonathan
Frankel, Israel Finestein, Todd M. Endelman, Phyllis Cohen
Albert, Paula E. Hyman, Richard I. Cohen, Michael Graetz,
David Sorkin, Marion A. Kaplan, Marsha L. Rozenblit,
Hillel J. Kieval, Michael K. Silber, Eli Lederhendler, and
Steven J. Zipperstein. New York: Cambridge University
Press, 1992. 384 pp. [Contents: Jonathan Frankel, "Assimi-
lation and the Jews in nineteenth-century Europe: towards
a new historiography?"; Israel Finestein, "Jewish emancipa-
tionists in Victorian England: self-imposed limits to assimi-
lation"; Todd M. Endelman, "German Jews in Victorian
England: a study in drift and defection"; Phyllis Cohen
Albert, "Israelite and Jew: how did nineteenth-century
French Jews understand assimilation?"; Paula E. Hyman,
"The social contexts of assimilation: village Jews and city
Jews in Alsace"; Richard I. Cohen, "Nostalgia and 'return to
the ghetto': a cultural phenomenon in Western and Central
Europe"; Michael Graetz, "Jewry in the modern period: the
role of the 'rising class' in the politicization of Jews in
Europe"; David Sorkin, "The impact of emancipation on
German Jewry: a reconsideration"; Marion A. Kaplan,
"Gender and Jewish history in Imperial Germany"; Marsha
L. Rozenblit, "Jewish assimilation in Habsburg Vienna";
Hillel J. Kieval, "The social vision of Bohemian Jews:
intellectuals and community in the 1840s"; Michael K.
Silber, "The entrance of Jews into Hungarian society in
Vormärz: the case of the 'casinos'"; Eli Lederhendler,
"Modernity without emancipation or assimilation? The case
of Russian Jewry"; Steven J. Zipperstein, "Ahad Ha'am and
the politics of assimilation".] REV: Michael A. Meyer,
Historian 54, no. 4 (Summer 1992): 708-709. Jack Jacobs,
Journal of Interdisciplinary History 24, no. 2 (Autumn
1993): 315.

6208. Hundert, Gershon David. *The Jews in a
Polish Private Town: The Case of Opatow in the Eighteenth
Century.* Johns Hopkins Jewish Studies. Baltimore, MD:
Johns Hopkins University Press, c1992. xvi, 242 pp. REV:
Hillel J. Kieval, *American Historical Review* 98, no. 4
(October 1993): 1289. Eli Lederhendler, *Slavic Review* 52,

no. 2 (Summer 1993): 376-377. Adam Teller, *Polish Review*
38, no. 1 (1993): 98-101.

■ Science and Technology

General

6209. Bailes, Kendall E. *Science and Russian
Culture in an Age of Revolutions: V.I. Vernadsky and His
Scientific School, 1863-1945.* Indiana-Michigan Series in
Russian and East European Studies. Bloomington, IN:
Indiana University Press, c1990. xii, 238 pp. REV: Yakob
M. Rabkin, *Canadian Slavonic Papers* 32, no. 2 (June 1990):
186-188. Terence Emmons, *Slavic Review* 50, no. 4 (Winter
1991): 1010-1011. Linda J. Lubrano, *Russian Review* 50, no.
2 (April 1991): 221-222. Alexander Vucinich, *American
Historical Review* 96, no. 2 (April 1991): 565-566. Marc
Raeff, *Journal of Modern History* 64, no. 1 (March 1992):
182-184. Nathan M. Brooks, *Soviet and Post-Soviet Review*
20, no. 1 (1993): 90. James C. McClelland, *Canadian
American Slavic Studies = Revue Canadienne Américaine
d'Etudes Slaves* 27, nos. 1-4 (1993): 432-433.

6210. Chernyak, Yuri B., and Joel L. Lebowitz, eds.
*Frontiers of Science: Reports from the Final International
Session of the Moscow Refusnik Seminar.* Annals of the New
York Academy of Sciences, v. 661. New York, NY: New
York Academy of Sciences, 1992. xxvi, 371 pp. [Contribu-
tions from the Final (Eighth) International Session of the
Moscow Sunday Refusnik Seminar.] REV: Katherine
Livingston, *Science* 262, no. 5130 (October 1, 1993): 125.

6211. Copernicus, Nicolaus. *Minor Works.* Transla-
tion and commentary by Edward Rosen and Erna Hilfstein.
Foundations of Natural History. Baltimore, MD: Johns
Hopkins University Press, 1992. xv, 373 pp. [Translated
from the Latin.] REV: William H. Donahue, *Isis* 84, no. 3
(September 1993): 570.

6212. ———. *On the Revolutions.* Translation and
commentary by Edward Rosen. Foundations of Natural
History. Baltimore, MD: Johns Hopkins University Press,
1992. xxi, 452 pp. [Translation of *De revolutionibus orbium
caelestium.*] REV: William H. Donahue, *Isis* 84, no. 3
(September 1993): 570.

6213. Jasentuliyana, Nandasiri, ed. *Space Law:
Development and Scope.* Foreword by Manfred Lachs.
Publication of the International Institute of Space Law,
Westport, CT: Praeger, 1992. xxiii, 281 pp. [Includes
chapter by Vladlen Vereshshetin on the former Soviet
Union.] REV: Katherine M. Gorove, *Journal of Space Law*
21, no. 1 (1993): 70-71. Milton L. Smith, *American Journal
of International Law* 87, no. 2 (April 1993): 357-360.

6214. Josephson, Paul R. *Physics and Politics in
Revolutionary Russia.* California Studies in the History of
Science, Berkeley, CA: University of California Press, 1991.
423 pp. REV: James T. Andrews, *Canadian-American
Slavic Studies* 25, nos. 1-4 (1991): 320-322. Julie V. Brown,
American Historical Review 98, no. 5 (December 1993):
1648. V. Paul Kenney, *Review of Politics* 55, no. 4 (Fall

1993): 745-749. Marshall S. Shatz, *Russian Review* 52, no. 3
(July 1993): 430.

Life Sciences, Medicine, Public Health

6215. Adams, Mark B., ed. *The Wellborn Science:
Eugenics in Germany, France, Brazil, and Russia.* Mono-
graphs on the History and Philosophy of Biology, New York:
Oxford University Press, 1990. x, 242 pp. REV: Bentley
Glass, *Quarterly Review of Biology* 68, no. 1 (March 1993):
61-67. Leila Zenderland, *Journal of the History of the
Behavioral Sciences* 29, no. 3 (July 1993): 164.

6216. British Medical Association. *Medicine
Betrayed: The Participation of Doctors in Human Rights
Abuses: Report of a Working Party, British Medical Associa-
tion.* London; Atlantic Highlands, NJ: Zed Books, c1992.
xvii, 234 pp. [Includes references to Soviet Union and
Eastern Europe.] REV: Michael A. Grodin, *Social Science &
Medicine* 37, no. 8 (October 1993): 277.

6217. Feshbach, Murray, and Alfred Friendly, Jr.
Ecocide in the USSR: Health and Nature under Siege.
Foreword by Lester Brown. New York, NY: BasicBooks,
c1992. xvii, 376 pp. REV: David E. Powell, *Natural History*
(August 1992): 73-75. Douglas R. Weiner, *New York Times
Book Review* 97 (June 7, 1992): 14. *Publishers Weekly* 239,
no. 13 (March 9, 1992): 44. *Wilson Quarterly* 16, no. 4
(Autumn 1992): 89-90. Brian Bonhomme, *Nationalities
Papers* 21, no. 2 (Fall 1993): 220-223. Francheska Chalidze,
Central Asia Monitor, no. 1 (1993): 36-38. Joan
DeBardeleben, *Slavic Review* 52, no. 3 (Fall 1993): 593-596.
David Holloway, *New York Review of Books* 40, no. 11 (June
10, 1993): 36-38. Michael McCally, *Bulletin of the Atomic
Scientists* 49, no. 1 (January-February 1993): 47-48.
Stanton S. Miller, *Environmental Science & Technology* 27,
no. 4 (April 1993): 610. Robert H. Randolph, *Isis* 84, no. 3
(September 1993): 602-604. Charles E. Ziegler, *Russian
History = Histoire russe* 20, nos. 1-4 (1993): 411-412. *Future
Survey Annual* 13 (1993): 23-24.

6218. Geptner, V. G., A. A. Nasimovich, and A. G.
Bannikov. *Mammals of the Soviet Union.* Scientific editor
Robert S. Hoffman. Washington, DC: Smithsonian Institu-
tion Libraries; National Science Foundation, 1988-. vols.
[Translation of *Mlekopitaiushchie Sovetskogo Soiuza.*] REV:
John L. Gittleman, *Journal of Mammalogy* 74, no. 2 (May
1993): 510-511.

6219. Gore, Albert. *Earth in the Balance: Ecology
and the Human Spirit.* Boston, MA: Houghton Mifflin,
c1992. 407 pp. [Includes discussion of the destruction of the
Aral Sea.] REV: Emily D. Pelton, *Foreign Affairs* 71, no. 2
(Spring 1992): 197-198. Tony Baltic, *Journal of Leisure
Research* 25, no. 2 (1993): 218-220.

6220. Gould, Peter. *Fire in the Rain: The Demo-
cratic Consequences of Chernobyl.* Baltimore, MD: Johns
Hopkins University Press, 1990. 163 pp. REV: John
Michael Carfora, *American Political Science Review* 86, no.
1 (March 1992): 267-268. Richard G. Kuhn, *Canadian
Geographer* 36, no. 3 (Fall 1992): 299-300. Ján Drdos,

Annals of the Association of American Geographers 83, no. 2 (June 1993): 379-380.

6221. Hu, Howard, Arjun Makhijani, and Katherine Yih. *Plutonium: Deadly Gold of the Nuclear Age.* Contributing authors Alexandra Brooks et al. Cambridge, MA: International Physicians Press, 1992. xiii, 178 pp. REV: Jonathan B. Tucker, *Technology Review* 96, no. 8 (November-December 1993): 72-74.

6222. Hutchinson, John F. *Politics and Public Health in Revolutionary Russia, 1890-1918.* Baltimore, MD: Johns Hopkins University Press, c1990. 253 pp. REV: John T. Alexander, *Bulletin of the History of Medicine* 65, no. 2 (Summer 1991): 281. Julie V. Brown, *Soviet Union = Union Soviétique* 18, nos. 1-3 (1991): 355-357. G. M. Hamburg, *Slavic Review* 50, no. 4 (Winter 1991): 1019-1020. Patricia Herlihy, *Journal of Interdisciplinary History* 22, no. 1 (Summer 1991): 131-133. Adele Lindenmeyr, *Canadian-American Slavic Studies* 25, nos. 1-4 (1991): 288-293. Lillian Liu, *Russian History* 18, no. 2 (Summer 1991): 225-229. David L. Ransel, *Canadian Slavonic Papers* 33, no. 2 (June 1991): 196-197. Scott J. Seregny, *American Historical Review* 96, no. 4 (October 1991): 1246-1247. Neil B. Weissman, *Russian Review* 50, no. 3 (July 1991): 359-360. John W. Long, *History: Reviews of New Books* 20, no. 4 (Summer 1992): 170-171. Laura Engelstein, *Journal of Modern History* 65, no. 1 (March 1993): 237-240.

6223. Medvedev, Grigori. *The Truth about Chernobyl.* Translated from the Russian by Evelyn Rossiter. Foreword by Andrei Sakharov. American ed. [New York]: Basic Books, [1991]. xi, 274 pp. [Translation of *Chernobylskaia khronika.*] REV: John C. Campbell, *Foreign Affairs* 70, no. 4 (Fall 1991): 180-181. Loren Graham, *New York Times Book Review* (April 7, 1991): 1ff. Jonathan King, *Society* 29, no. 1 (November-December 1991): 90-92. Lawrence M. Lidsky, *Technology Review* 94, no. 3 (April 1991): 73ff. David R. Marples, *Bulletin of the Atomic Scientists* 47, no. 5 (June 1991): 38-39. John Michael Carfora, *American Political Science Review* 86, no. 1 (March 1992): 267-268. Adam A. Hetnal, *Ukrainian Quarterly* 49, no. 1 (Spring 1993): 70-75. David Holloway, *New York Review of Books* 40, no. 11 (June 10, 1993): 36-38.

6224. Pryde, Philip R. *Environmental Management in the Soviet Union.* Cambridge Soviet Paperbacks, 4. Cambridge; New York: Cambridge University Press, 1991. xx, 314 pp. REV: Howard Lehman, *Policy Studies Review* 20, no. 4 (Winter 1992): 719-732. Victor L. Mote, *Soviet and Post-Soviet Review* 19, nos. 1-3 (1992): 336-339. Craig ZumBrunnen and Andrea Hagen, *Professional Geographer* 44, no. 3 (August 1992): 361-362. Joan DeBardeleben, *Slavic Review* 52, no. 3 (Fall 1993): 593-596. Andrea Hagan and Craig ZumBrunnen, *Russian Review* 52, no. 4 (October 1993): 580-582. Michael K. Launer and Marilyn J. Young, *Nationalities Papers* 21, no. 2 (Fall 1993): 223-227.

6225. Rosenthal, Marilynn M., and Marcel Frenkel, eds. *Health Care Systems and Their Patients: An International Perspective.* Boulder, CO: Westview Press, 1992. xix, 345 pp. [Includes discussion of the Soviet Union and

Hungary.] REV: Mary Ruggie, *American Journal of Sociology* 99, no. 1 (July 1993): 260-261.

6226. Solomon, Susan Gross, and John F. Hutchinson, eds. *Health and Society in Revolutionary Russia.* Indiana-Michigan Series in Russian and East European Studies. Bloomington, IN: Indiana University Press, c1990. xiv, 256 pp. [Published in cooperation with the Centre for Russian and East European Studies, University of Toronto.] REV: Patricia Herlihy, *Journal of Interdisciplinary History* 22, no. 1 (Summer 1991): 131-133. Adele Lindenmeyr, *Canadian-American Slavic Studies* 25, nos. 1-4 (1991): 288-293. Lillian Liu, *Russian History* 18, no. 2 (Summer 1991): 225-229. David L. Ransel, *Canadian Slavonic Papers* 33, no. 2 (June 1991): 196-197. Demitri B. Shimkin, *Soviet Union = Union Soviétique* 18, nos. 1-3 (1991): 342-344. Elizabeth Waters, *Australian Slavonic and East European Studies* 5, no. 1 (1991): 131-132. Jeffrey Brooks, *Russian Review* 51, no. 1 (January 1992): 126. Jean-Guy Lalande, *Histoire sociale = Social History* 25, no. 50 (November 1992): 441-443. Laura Engelstein, *Journal of Modern History* 65, no. 1 (March 1993): 237-240. Douglas Weiner, *Journal of the History of the Behavioral Sciences* 29, no. 3 (July 1993): 231.

6227. Turnbull, M. *Soviet Environmental Policies and Practices: The Most Critical Investment.* Aldershot, Hants; Brookfield, VT: Dartmouth, c1991. xiv, 215 pp. [S. Revell, consultant; A. Main, consultant; D. J .I. Matko, R. Berry, W. Joyce, translators; W. V. Wallace, project administrator.] REV: Joan DeBardeleben, *Slavic Review* 52, no. 3 (Fall 1993): 593-596.

6228. Weiner, Douglas R. *Models of Nature: Ecology, Conservation, and Cultural Revolution in Soviet Russia.* Indiana-Michigan Series in Russian and East European Studies. Bloomington, IN: Indiana University Press, c1988. xiv, 312 pp. REV: Alexander Vucinich, *American Historical Review* 95, no. 1 (February 1990): 212-213. Zigurds L. Zile, *Slavic Review* 49, no. 3 (Fall 1990): 457-458. Robert H. Randolph, *Isis* 84, no. 3 (September 1993): 602-604.

■ Sociology

General

6229. Altbach, Philip G. *Student Political Activism: An International Reference Handbook.* New York: Greenwood Press, 1989. xiv, 505 pp. [Includes chapter on Yugoslavia and chapter on the Soviet Union.] REV: John A. Nkinyangi, *Comparative Education Review* 37, no. 1 (February 1993): 72-73.

6230. Ferge, Zsuzsa, and Jon Eivind Kolberg, eds. *Social Policy in a Changing Europe.* Public Policy and Social Welfare, v. 10. Frankfurt am Main: Campus Verlag; Boulder, CO: Westview Press, c1992. viii, 318 pp. REV: Joakim Palme, *Contemporary Sociology* 22, no. 6 (November 1993): 788-789.

6231. Jones, Anthony, ed. *Professions and the State: Expertise and Autonomy in the Soviet Union and Eastern Europe.* Labor and Social Change, Philadelphia, PA: Temple University Press, 1991. 256 pp. REV: Eliot Friedson, *Contemporary Sociology* 20, no. 5 (September 1991): 569-570. Victor V. Golubchikov, *American Journal of Sociology* 98, no. 5 (March 1993): 1249-1251.

Russia/U.S.S.R./C.I.S.

6232. Adelman, Deborah. *The "Children of Perestroika": Moscow Teenagers Talk about Their Lives and the Future.* Narratives translated by Deborah Adelman, Fay Greenbaum, and Sharon McKee. Armonk, NY: M.E. Sharpe, c1991. xxiii, 256 pp. REV: Angene H. Wilson, *Social Education* 57, no. 2 (February 1993): 95.

6233. Engelstein, Laura. *The Keys to Happiness: Sex and the Search for Modernity in Fin-de-Siècle Russia.* Ithaca, NY: Cornell University Press, 1992. xiii, 461 pp. REV: Bruce F. Adams, *Russian History = Histoire russe* 20, nos. 1-4 (1993): 312-313. Mark D. Steinberg, *American Historical Review* 98, no. 3 (June 1993): 825-827. Katrina vanden Heuvel, *Nation* 256, no. 24 (June 21, 1993): 870-874.

6234. Gudkov, Lev, and Alex Levinson. *Attitudes Toward Jews in the Soviet Union: Public Opinion in Ten Republics.* New York: American Jewish Committee, 1992. 80 pp. REV: Arthur Hertzberg, *New York Review of Books* 50, no. 12 (June 24, 1993): 51-57.

6235. Jones, Anthony, Walter D. Connor, and David E. Powell, eds. *Soviet Social Problems.* The John M. Olin Critical Issues Series. Boulder, CO: Westview Press, 1991. 337 pp. REV: Debra E. Soled, *Current History* 90, no. 558 (October 1991): 346. Katrina vanden Heuvel, *New York Times Book Review* (February 17, 1991): 10. Theodore H. Friedgut, *Russian Review* 51, no. 3 (July 1992): 450-451. Stephen Kotkin, *Canadian-American Slavic Studies* 26, nos. 1-4 (1992): 390-392. Michael Paul Sacks, *Slavic Review* 51, no. 1 (Spring 1992): 151-152. Vladimir Shlapentokh, *Contemporary Sociology* 22, no. 1 (January 1993): 46.

6236. Joyce, Walter, ed. *Social Change and Social Issues in the Former USSR: Selected Papers from the Fourth World Congress for Soviet and East European Studies, Harrogate, 1990.* Contributions by Gregory Andrusz, Lars Ohlsson, John M. Kramer, Alain Blum, Walter Joyce, W. Ward Kingkade, Eduardo E. Arriaga, and Jim Riordan. New York: St. Martin's Press in association with the International Council for Soviet and East European Studies, 1992. xii, 162 pp. [Contents: Gregory Andrusz, "The Market as Distributor of Housing under Socialism: Its Virtues and Vices"; Lars Ohlsson, "The Soviet Union's New Co-operatives: Goals and Accomplishments"; John M. Kramer, "Drug Abuse in the USSR"; Alain Blum, "Mortality Patterns in the USSR and Causes of Death: Political Unity and Regional Differentials"; Walter Joyce, "The Battle Continues: Gorbachev's Anti-Alcohol Policies"; W. Ward Kingkade and Eduardo E. Arriaga, "Sex Differentials in Mortality in the Soviet Union"; Jim Riordan, "Disabled 'Afgantsy': Fighters

for a Better Deal".] REV: Paul Hollander, *Slavic Review* 52, no. 2 (Summer 1993): 389-390.

6237. Kotkin, Stephen. *Steeltown, USSR: Soviet Society in the Gorbachev Era.* Berkeley, CA: University of California Press, c1991. xxx, 269 pp. REV: John C. Campbell, *Foreign Affairs* 70, no. 4 (Fall 1991): 180. Leo Gruliow, *Antioch Review* 49, no. 4 (Fall 1991): 607-609. Peter Reddaway, *New York Review of Books* 38, no. 18 (November 7, 1991): 53-59. David Satter, *Orbis* 35, no. 4 (Fall 1991): 628. William Taubman, *New York Times Book Review* (April 14, 1991): 13. Michael Burawoy, *Contemporary Sociology* 21, no. 6 (November 1992): 774-785. Theodore H. Friedgut, *Slavic Review* 51, no. 1 (Spring 1992): 140-142. Kuo-Wei Lee, *Social Science Quarterly* 73, no. 3 (September 1992): 715-716. Hugh Ragsdale, *Soviet and Post-Soviet Review* 19, nos. 1-3 (1992): 316-318. John F. Young, *Canadian Slavonic Papers* 34, nos. 1-2 (March-June 1992): 187-188. William Moskoff, *Annals of the American Academy of Political and Social Science*, no. 525 (January 1993): 177-178. Lewis H. Siegelbaum, *International Labor and Working-Class History*, no. 43 (Spring 1993): 135-138.

6238. Lane, David. *Soviet Society Under Perestroika.* Rev. ed. New York: Routledge, 1992. 441 pp. REV: Ben Eklof, *Slavic Review* 52, no. 1 (Spring 1993): 156-157.

6239. Pearson, Landon. *Children of Glasnost: Growing Up Soviet.* Seattle, WA: University of Washington Press, c1990. 505 pp. REV: Stephen T. Kerr, *Comparative Education Review* 36, no. 4 (November 1992): 537-540. Delbert H. Long, *Soviet and Post-Soviet Review* 19, nos. 1-3 (1992): 295-297. Rosalind Latiner Raby, *Russian Review* 52, no. 1 (January 1993): 137-138.

6240. Shlapentokh, Vladimir. *Soviet Intellectuals and Political Power: The Post-Stalin Era.* Princeton, NJ: Princeton University Press, c1990. xiv, 330 pp. REV: John C. Campbell, *Foreign Affairs* 70, no. 3 (Summer 1991): 176. Evgeny Vodichev, *Slavic Review* 50, no. 4 (Winter 1991): 1028-1029. Mark Lupher, *Contemporary Sociology* 21, no. 2 (March 1992): 206-207. Michael E. Urban, *Russian Review* 52, no. 2 (April 1993): 281-282.

6241. Smith, Hedrick. *The New Russians.* rev. ed. New York: Random House, 1991. xxxi, 734 pp. REV: Ben Eklof, *Slavic Review* 52, no. 3 (Fall 1993): 624-626.

6242. Vallee, Jacques, and Martine Castello. *UFO Chronicles of the Soviet Union: A Cosmic Samizdat.* New York: Ballantine Books, 1992. xii, 212 pp. REV: *Publishers Weekly* 239, no. 6 (January 27, 1992): 83. Erik Vaughn, *Skeptical Inquirer* 18, no. 1 (Fall 1993): 82-85.

Eastern Europe

6243. Cornia, Giovanni Andrea, and Sándor Sipos, eds. *Children and the Transition to the Market Economy: Safety Nets and Social Policies in Central and Eastern Europe.* Brookfield, VT: Avebury, c1991. 251 pp. REV: William McGreevey, *Population and Development Review* 19, no. 4 (December 1993): 868-871.

6244. *Gay Voices from East Germany.* Interviews by Jürgen Lemke. Bloomington, IN: Indiana University Press, c1991. vi, 197 pp. [Translation of *Ganz normal anders.* English-language version edited and with an introduction by John Borneman; translations and introductions by Steven Stoltenberg, et al.] REV: Hugh Murray, *Journal of Social History* 27, no. 2 (Winter 1993): 427-430.

6245. Kennedy, Michael D. *Professionals, Power and Solidarity in Poland: A Critical Sociology of Soviet-Type Society.* Soviet and East European Studies, 79. New York: Cambridge University Press, 1991. 421 pp. REV: Michael Bernhard, *Slavic Review* 51, no. 4 (Winter 1992): 855-856. Bronislaw Misztal, *Contemporary Sociology* 22, no. 6 (November 1993): 834-836.

6246. Kohn, Melvin L., and Kazimierz M. Slomcynski. *Social Structure and Self-Direction: A Comparative Analysis of the United States and Poland.* Cambridge, MA: B. Blackwell, 1990. 301 pp. REV: Duane F. Alwin, *Contemporary Sociology* 22, no. 1 (January 1993): 58-61.

6247. Laba, Roman. *The Roots of Solidarity: A Political Sociology of Poland's Working-Class Democratization.* Princeton, NJ: Princeton University Press, c1991. xii, 247 pp. REV: Michael Bernhard, *Studies in Comparative Communism* 24, no. 3 (September 1991): 313-330. Timothy Garton Ash, *New York Review of Books* 38, no. 11 (June 13, 1991): 46-58. Andrzej Tymowski, *Telos*, no. 90 (Winter 1991-92): 157-174. Jane L. Curry, *Slavic Review* 51, no. 3 (Fall 1992): 582-583. Andrzej Korbonski, *American Historical Review* 97, no. 3 (June 1992): 892-893. Ewa Morawska, *American Journal of Sociology* 97, no. 4 (January 1992): 1143-1144. Jeff Manza, *Industrial and Labor Relations Review* 46, no. 3 (April 1993): 600-602. David Ost, *Contemporary Sociology* 22, no. 1 (January 1993): 44.

6248. Stern, Frank. *The Whitewashing of the Yellow Badge: Antisemitism and Philosemitism in Postwar Germany.* Translated by William Templer. Studies in Antisemitism, New York: Published for the Vidal Sassoon International Center for the Study of Antisemitism (SICSA), the Hebrew University of Jerusalem by Pergamon Press, 1992. 455 pp. REV: Lawrence Baron, *American Historical Review* 98, no. 5 (December 1993): 1639.

Women's Studies

6249. Adler, Leonore Loeb, ed. *Women in Cross-Cultural Perspective.* Foreword by Harriet P. Lefley. Includes contributions by Halina Grzymala-Moszczynska, Lena Zhernova, and Harold Takooshian. New York: Praeger, 1991. xxii, 270 pp. [Partial contents: Halina Grzymala-Moszczynska, "Women in Poland"; Lena Zhernova, "Women in the USSR"; Harold Takooshian, "Soviet Women".] REV: Norma C. Noonan, *Women & Politics* 13, nos. 3-4 (1993): 231-232.

6250. Attwood, Lynne. *The New Soviet Man and Woman: Sex-Role Socialization in the USSR.* Bloomington, IN: Indiana University Press, c1990. x, 263 pp. REV: Michael Paul Sacks, *Russian Review* 51, no. 3 (July 1992):

448-449. Elizabeth Waters, *Slavic Review* 52, no. 4 (Winter 1993): 916-917.

6251. Becher, Jeanne, ed. *Women, Religion and Sexuality: Studies on the Impact of Religious Teachings on Women.* Includes contribution by Ance-Lucia Manolache. 1st ed. Philadelphia, PA: Trinity Press International, 1991. xii, 265 pp. [Papers sponsored by the World Council of Churches, Sub-unit on Women in Church and Society. Partial contents: Ance-Lucia Manolache, "Orthodoxy and Women".] REV: Sonya A. Quistlund, *Journal of Ecumenical Studies* 30, no. 1 (Winter 1993): 131-132.

6252. Buckley, Mary, ed. *Perestroika and Soviet Women.* Cambridge; New York: Cambridge University Press, 1992. xiii, 183 pp. REV: Alena Heitlinger, *Canadian Slavonic Papers* 34, no. 4 (December 1992): 496-498. Ruth A. Dudgeon, *Soviet and Post-Soviet Review* 20, nos. 2-3 (1993): 245-246.

6253. Clements, Barbara Evans, Barbara Alpern Engel, and Christine D. Worobec, eds. *Russia's Women: Accommodation, Resistance, Transformation.* Berkeley, CA: University of California Press, c1991. xi, 300 pp. REV: Mary Allen, *Canadian Slavonic Papers* 33, nos. 3-4 (December 1991): 386-387. Debra E. Soled, *Current History* 90, no. 558 (October 1991): 345. Boris Mironov, *Slavic Review* 51, no. 2 (Summer 1992): 362-364. Elizabeth A. Wood, *Women's Review of Books* 9, no. 8 (May 1992): 26-27. Adele Lindenmeyr, *Journal of Interdisciplinary History* 23, no. 4 (Spring 1993): 808-809. Rochelle Ruthchild, *Russian Review* 52, no. 4 (October 1993): 562-563. Isabel A. Tirado, *American Historical Review* 98, no. 5 (December 1993): 1646-1648.

6254. Drakulic, Slavenka. *How We Survived Communism and Even Laughed.* New York: W.W. Norton, 1992. 197 pp. REV: Lucy Despard, *Foreign Affairs* 71, no. 2 (Spring 1992): 208. Erika Munk, *Women's Review of Books* 9, no. 8 (May 1992): 1ff. Linda Rocawich, *Progressive* 56, no. 12 (December 1992): 38-39. Loretta Stec, *National Women's Studies Association Journal* 4, no. 3 (Fall 1992): 398-400. Cathy Young, *New York Times Book Review* (April 19, 1992): 11. *Publishers Weekly* 239, no. 3 (January 13, 1992): 39. *Orbis* 37, no. 1 (Winter 1993).

6255. Edmondson, Linda, ed. *Women and Society in Russia and the Soviet Union.* Contributions by Catriona Kelly, Charlotte Rosenthal, Mary Schaeffer Conroy, Linda Edmondson, Barbara T. Norton, Richard Abraham, Marina Ledkovsky (Astman), Elizabeth Waters, Sue Bridger, and Mary Buckley. Cambridge; New York: Cambridge University Press, 1992. ix, 233 pp. [Contents: Catriona Kelly, " 'Better halves'?: representations of women in Russian urban popular entertainments, 1870-1910; Charlotte Rosenthal, "The Silver Age: highpoint for women?"; Mary Schaeffer Conroy, "Women pharmacists in Russia before World War I: women's emancipation, feminism, professionalization, nationalism and class conflict"; Linda Edmondson, "Women's rights, civil rights and the debate over citizenship in the 1905 Revolution"; Barbara T. Norton, "Laying the foundations of democracy in Russia: E.D. Kuskova's contribution, February-October 1917"; Richard Abraham, "Mariia L. Bochkareva and the Russian amazons of 1917"; Marina Ledkovsky (Astman), "Russian women writers: an overview: post-revolutionary dispersion and adjustment"; Elizabeth Waters, "Victim or villain?: prostitution in post-revolutionary Russia"; Sue Bridger, "Young women and perestroika"; Mary Buckley, "Glasnost and the woman question".] REV: Adele Lindenmeyr, *Russian History = Histoire russe* 20, nos. 1-4 (1993): 311-312. Richard Stites, *Slavic Review* 52, no. 2 (Summer 1993): 367-368.

6256. Farnsworth, Beatrice, and Lynne Viola, eds. *Russian Peasant Women.* Contributions by Mary Matossian, Christine D. Worobec, Rose L. Glickman, Cathy A. Frierson, Beatrice Farnsworth, Samuel C. Ramer, Brenda Meehan-Waters, Beatrice Farnsworth, Lynne Viola, Roberta T. Manning, Norton D. Dodge, Murray Feshbach, and Susan Bridger. New York: Oxford University Press, 1992. 304 pp. [Most items reprinted from various publications. Contents: Mary Matossian, "The Peasant Way of Life"; Christine D. Worobec, "Temptress or Virgin? The Precarious Sexual Position of Women in Postemancipation Ukrainian Peasant Society"; Rose L. Glickman, "Peasant Women and Their Work"; Cathy A. Frierson, "Razdel: The Peasant Family Divided"; Beatrice Farnsworth, "The Litigious Daughter-in-Law: Family Relations in Rural Russia in the Second Half of the Nineteenth Century"; Samuel C. Ramer, "Childbirth and Culture: Midwifery in the Nineteenth-Century Russian Countryside"; Brenda Meehan-Waters, "To Save Oneself: Russian Peasant Women and the Development of Women's Religious Communities in Prerevolutionary Russia"; Beatrice Farnsworth, "Village Women Experience the Revolution"; Beatrice Farnsworth, "Rural Women and the Law: Divorce and Property Rights in the 1920s"; Lynne Viola, "Bab'i Bunty and Peasant Women's Protest during Collectivization"; Roberta T. Manning, "Women in the Soviet Countryside on the Eve of World War II, 1935-1940"; Norton D. Dodge and Murray Feshbach, "The Role of Women in Soviet Agriculture"; Susan Bridger, "Soviet Rural Women"; Susan Bridger, "Rural Women and Glasnost".] REV: E.R. Zimmerman, *Canadian Journal of History = Annales canadienne d'histoire* 28, no. 2 (December 1993): 617.

6257. Jaworski, Rudolf, and Bianka Pietrow-Ennker, eds. *Women in Polish Society.* Contributions by Bianka Pietrow-Ennker, Bogna Lorence-Kot, Rudolf Jaworski, Irena Homola Skapska, Adam Winiarz, Malgorzata Czyszkowska-Peschler, Maria Nietyksza, and Anna Zarnowska. East European Monographs, no. 344. Boulder, CO: East European Monographs; New York: Distributed by Columbia University Press, 1992. 219 pp. [Contents: Bianka Pietrow-Ennker, "Women in Polish Society: A Historical Introduction"; Bogna Lorence-Kot, "Konspiracja: Probing the Topography of Women's Under-

ground Activities: The Kingdom of Poland in the Second Half of the Nineteenth Century"; Rudolf Jaworski, "Polish Women and the Nationality Conflict in the Province of Posen at the Turn of the Century"; Irena Homola Skapska, "Galicia: Initiatives for the Emancipation of Polish Women"; Adam Winiarz, "Girls' Education in the Kingdom of Poland (1815-1915)"; Malgorzata Czyszkowska-Peschler, "She Is—A Nobody Without Name: The Professional Situation of Polish Women-of-Letters in the Second Half of the Nineteenth Century"; Maria Nietyksza, "The Vocational Activities of Women in Warsaw at the Turn of the Nineteenth Century"; Anna Zarnowska, "Women in Working Class Families in the Congress Kingdom (the Russian Zone of Poland) at the Turn of the Nineteenth Century"; Adam Winiarz, "The Women Question in the Kingdom of Poland during the Nineteenth Century: A Bibliographical Essay".] REV: John J. Kulczycki, *Polish Review* 38, no. 4 (1993): 491-493.

6258. Loizos, Peter, and Evthymios Papataxiarchis, eds. *Contested Identities: Gender and Kinship in Modern Greece.* Princeton Modern Greek Studies. Princeton, NJ: Princeton University Press, c1991. vii, 259 pp. REV: Peter S. Allen, *Journal of the Hellenic Diaspora* 17, no. 2 (1991): 135-141. Roland S. Moore, *Journal of American Folklore* 105, no. 415 (Winter 1992): 105-107. C. Nadia Seremetakis, *American Ethnologist* (May 1993): 410-411.

6259. Offen, Karen, Ruth Roach Pierson, and Jane Rendall, eds. *Writing Women's History: International Perspectives.* Petra Rantzsch, Erika Uitz, Andrea Feldman, Efi Avdela, and Mary Zirin. Bloomington, IN: Indiana University Press for the International Federation for Research in Women's History, c1991. xli, 552 pp. [Most of the essays were prepared for the international conference on the history of women held in Bellagio, Italy, July 1989. Partial contents: Petra Rantzsch and Erika Uitz, "Historical Research on Women in the German Democratic Republic"; Andrea Feldman, "Women's History in Yugoslavia," pp. 417-421; Efi Avdela, "The 'History of Women' in Greece," pp. 423-427; Mary Zirin, "Women, Gender and Family in the Soviet Union and Central/East Europe: A Preliminary Bibliography," pp. 457-516.] REV: Margaret Strobel, *American Historical Review* 98, no. 1 (February 1993): 130-132.

6260. Rai, Shirin, Hilary Pilkington, and Annie Phizacklea, eds. *Women in the Face of Change: The Soviet Union, Eastern Europe and China.* Includes contribution by Chris Corrin. London; New York: Routledge, 1992. x, 227 pp. [Partial contents: Chris Corrin, "Gendered Identities: Women's Experience of Change in Hungary".] REV: Marlene Kadar, *Hungarian Studies Review* 20, nos. 1-2 (Spring-Fall 1993): 119-122.

Author Index

964, 983, 998, 1442, 1503, 3436, 3456, 3501, 3768, 3769, 3770, 3771, 3772
University of Minnesota. Immigration History Research Center 5108
University of Pittsburgh. School of Law 937
Unnithan, N. Prabha 4943
Unruh, Delbert 748
Unt, Mati 3955
Unterberger, Betty Miller 5816, 5820
Updike, John 3942
Urban, George R. 1730
Urban, Jan 3121
Urban, Joan Barth 5849
Urbán, László 775
Urban, Michael E. 1779, 5487, 5488, 5490, 6240
Urban, Rob 143
Urban, Waltraut 5344
Urban, William 321, 431, 2224, 3022, 5460, 5473, 5479, 5505, 5736, 5818, 6127, 6135
Urbancic, Ivan 4629
Urbánek, Zdenek 5973
Urbaniak, George 5800
Urdang, Elliott B. 4068, 6001
Uris, Leon 2705
Urnov, D. 4132
Urquhart, Brian 3151
Urtans, Juris 432
U.S. Holocaust Memorial Museum 2741, 2742, 2743, 2744, 2745, 2746
Ushekevich, Alexander 5935
Uspensky, Boris A. 4701, 4718
Uspensky, Gleb 113
Ustenko, Oleg 914
Ustinova, L. I. 384
Ustiugov, Mikhail 988, 989, 990, 1868, 4510
Utter, Derek 1288
Utter, Robert F. 2201
Vachou, Michael 518
Vachudova, Milada 3126, 3486, 4886
Vacs, Aldo 3225
Vagman, Vilim 3774
Vago, Raphael 2529
Vaiciunaitè, Judita 4023, 4024
Vaksberg, Arkady 1747, 5143, 5489
Valchev, Rumen 1354
Valdez, Jonathan C. 3050
Vale, Lawrence J. 5264
Vale, Michel 5431
Valentino, Russell Scott 4102
Valgemäe, Mardi 508, 3955, 3956
Válka, Josef 5707
Valkenier, Elizabeth Kridl 621, 1553, 2611, 5246, 5258, 5300, 5301, 5851, 5852, 5876
Valki, László 3034, 5761
Vallee, Jacques 6242
Vallee, Lillian 5321
Valone, Stephen J. 5167
Valsiner, Jaan 6182
Vamos, Mara Soceanu 4068, 6001
Vámos, Miklós 2416, 3932, 4045
Van Atta, Don 1048, 1049, 1050, 1189, 1220, 2013, 2014
Van Dartel, Geert 5525

Van den Berg, Ger P. 5446
Van den Heuvel, Martin 5525
Van der Veer, René 6182
Van Heuven, Marten 2236, 3775
Van Oudenaren, John 5824
Van Siclen, Sally J. 1255
Van Tol, Jan 5894
Vanagas, Aleksandras 3809
Vanatta, Marianne 1106
Vanchu, Anthony J. 4164
Vanden Heuvel, Katrina 1731, 2088, 4887, 5010, 5245, 6233
Vanderpool, Christopher K. 5430
Vanecková, G. 4113
Vanous, Jan 953
Varady, Tibor 2546
Varanese, James B 1224
Vardy, Steven Bela 216, 5144, 5720
Vardys, V. Stanley 5450, 5470, 5521
Vares, Peter 3121, 3127
Varga, Csaba 2202
Varga, Gyula 765
Varga, Laszlo 4978
Vargas, Mark A. 5109
Várhegyi, Éva 1435
Vari, Anna 836
Vari, Peter 5411
Várkonyi, István 5983
Varner, Michael C. 820
Varsbergs, Vilis 2423
Varvis, Stephen 6193
Vaserstein, Tamara 4328
Vasil'ev, Sergei A. 459, 460
Vasiliev, Sergei A. 876, 962
Vasilyev, Aleksey 4796
Vassilev, Rossen 3776
Vassilian, Hamo B. 201, 5559
Vaughan, Thomas 5685
Vaughn, Erik 6242
Vaughn, Gerald F. 1335
Vavilov, Andrey 962
Vebers, Elmars 2936
Vebra, Evaldas 1275
Vecoli, Rudolph J. 5108
Veduta, Elena 787
Veeser, H. Aram 5169, 5171
Vejvoda, Jaroslav 6071
Velichkovsii, Paisii (Saint) 5688
Velickovic, Jadrana 4401
Velimirovich, Milos M. 5240
Velitchko, Andrei A. 5423
Velkoff, Victoria A. 1605
Velmar-Jankovic, Svetlana 4437
Velychenko, Stephen 2612
Venclova, Tomas 4076, 6071, 6106
Vendler, Helen 5986
Venger, Alex 227
Verbova, Zoia 4763
Verdery, Katherine 2530, 4584, 5256
Verebélyi, Imre 788
Veremis, Thanos 5726
Verheyen, Dirk 5832
Verhoeven, Ludo 3792
Vermaat, Emerson 3777
Vermeer, Willem 5525
Verneuil, Henri 202
Vernon, John 3978

Verona, Sergiu 953, 6149
Vesa, Unto 3127
Vhay, Patricia K. 883
Vickers, John 758
Vickery, Walter 4329
Vidal Sassoon International Center for the Study of Antisemitism (Universitah ha-'Ivrit bi-Yerushalayim) 5441
Vidal-Naquet, Pierre 5593
Vidan, Ivo 3910
Vidláková, Olga 788, 1360, 2279
Viechtbauer, Volker 2015
Viehe, Fred W. 5149
Viehe, Karl William 1072
Viesulas, Romas Tauras 2440
Vikulov, Valerian 904
Vila, Benjamin Bastida 1322
Vile, Patricia 219
Vilenkin, Vitalii 4200
Vilfan, Sergij 5707
Vilimaite, Bite 4025
Villanueva, Delano 957
Vincentz, Volkhart 821
Vinogradov, Leonid 6082
Vinogradov, V. N. 2787
Vinogradov, Yuri G. 428
Vinokur, Aaron 5374
Vinton, Louisa 1326, 1481, 1482, 2488, 2489, 2490, 2491, 2492, 2493, 2494, 2495, 2496, 2497, 2978, 4888
Viola, Lynne 2846, 5124, 5655, 6256
Virágh, László 2962
Virshup, Amy 636
Vishevsky, Anatoly 4165, 4166, 4167, 4190
Vishnevskaya, Maria 876
Vishniac, Roman 657
Vishny, Robert 1006
Visser, Anthonya 3965
Vissi, Ferenc 1255
Vitas, Robert A. 1692, 2441, 5825
Vitkovskii, Evgenii 4294
Vizi, Sylvester E. 4818
Vjugin, Oleg 962
Vlachoutsicos, Charalambos 1093
Vladimirovitz, Boris 1660
Vladimov, Georgii 4112, 6071
Vladislav, Jan 2266, 6071, 6175
Vladiv-Glover, Slobodanka 4451
Vladova, Iliana 3801
Vladyshevskaia, Tatiana 5240
Vlahos, Linda H. 3189
Vlasihin, Vasily A. 1887, 2016
Vlasov, Slava 701
Vnukov, Vladimir 5255
Voaden, Denys J. 392
Vodopivec, Milan 968, 1505, 1513, 5399
Vodopivec, Peter 2922
Voerman, Gerrit 3221
Vogel, Heinrich 953
Vogt, Jochen 3979
Vogt, Robert 1136, 5378
Vogt-Downey, Marilyn 1732
Voinovich, Vladimir 509, 4112, 6071
Vojnic, Dragomir 830, 1225, 5327
Vokhmina, Lilia L. 3850
Volavkov, Hana 2747
Volf, Miroslav 4698

Title Index

Titles for journal articles, book chapters, and dissertations are given in quotation marks. Titles for journals and books are given in italics. Titles for monographic series are given in plain text.

Subject Index

560 SUBJECT INDEX

Poland—Bankruptcy **1296**
Poland—Banks and Banking **1234, 1303, 1476**
Poland—Belarus **3464, 3545**
Poland—Black Market **5098**
Poland—Boundaries **5719**
Poland—British Perceptions of **2968, 3887, 5812**
Poland—Buddhism **4680**
Poland—Bureaucracy **2451, 2462**
Poland—Business Law **1228, 1451, 2478, 2486**
Poland—Business Opportunities **1298, 1470, 1484**
Poland—Businessmen **1486**
Poland—Capitalism **1449, 1475, 1486**
Poland—Carpatho-Rusyns (Ruthenians) **155**
Poland—Catholic Church **124, 708, 2461, 2480, 2485, 3051, 4702,**
    4745, 4751, 4753, 4766, 4777, 4999, 5034, 5587, 6199
Poland—Censorship **128, 5317**
Poland—Central Planning **1297, 1464**
Poland—Christian-Jewish Relations **5585, 5587**
Poland—Christianity **4683, 4741, 4742, 4757, 4774, 4781**
Poland—Church and State **708, 2480, 2485, 4745, 4760, 4766,**
    4769, 4777, 5006, 5034
Poland—Church History **2972, 4766, 5098**
Poland—Cinema **661, 713, 714, 728, 5323**
Poland—Civil Society **2149, 2457, 2462, 2905, 4575, 4620**
Poland—Civil-Military Relations **2451, 2971, 5503, 5751, 6133**
Poland—Coal Mines and Mining **1480**
Poland—Coal Trade **1480**
Poland—Communism **2169, 2500, 4976, 5098, 5513, 5537, 5718,**
    5740
Poland—Communism and Christianity **4766**
Poland—Communism and Family **5015**
Poland—Communism and Society **6257**
Poland—Communist Party **2443, 2465, 2477, 2483, 2494, 2971,**
    5718
Poland—Communist Takeover (1943-1948) **5718**
Poland—Communists **5740**
Poland—Composers **570, 578, 5286**
Poland—Constitution **1636, 2454, 2473, 2478**
Poland—Constitutional History **2969**
Poland—Constitutional Law **1638, 2162, 2174, 2447, 2474**
Poland—Corruption **2475**
Poland—Criticism **5320, 5321**
Poland—Cryptography **5541**
Poland—Culture and Politics **124, 485, 708, 2454, 2455, 4035,**
    5437, 5986
Poland—Czechoslovakia **2906**
Poland—Daily Life **2452, 2471**
Poland—De-Communization **2445, 2478, 2496**
Poland—Debt, External **1464**
Poland—Defense Industries **4560**
Poland—Democratization **10, 1478, 1667, 1683, 2149, 2164, 2166,**
    2449, 2459, 2468, 2476, 2905, 4923, 4976, 5495, 6156
Poland—Demography **4875, 5397**
Poland—Description and Travel **415, 419**
Poland—Diplomatic History **5719, 5796**
Poland—Dissidents **128, 708, 2149, 2500, 4976, 5528, 5986, 6245**
Poland—Ecology **4875**
Poland—Economic Conditions (1945-1980) **1323, 1448**
Poland—Economic Conditions (1981-1990) **1323, 1457, 1471, 1475,**
    1486
Poland—Economic Conditions (To 1795) **2972, 2976**
Poland—Economic Conditions **817, 1248, 1255, 1259, 1323, 1450,**
    1452, 1457, 1458, 1464, 1469, 1475, 1487, 2489, 2977, 5522,
    5721
Poland—Economic Conversion **1, 10, 777, 780, 787, 792, 800, 817,**
    1228, 1241, 1294, 1296, 1326, 1452, 1456, 1458, 1460, 1462,
    1463, 1464, 1465, 1467, 1470, 1472, 1473, 1474, 1475, 1476,

1477, 1482, 2456, 2472, 2476, 2484, 2489, 4976, 5021, 5089,
    5719, 6179
Poland—Economic Management **1296, 1467, 1470, 1477**
Poland—Economic Performance **1324, 2478**
Poland—Economic Policy (1945-1981) **1459**
Poland—Economic Policy (1981-1990) **1295, 1297, 1320, 1323,**
    1457, 1459, 1461, 1473, 1475, 1486
Poland—Economic Policy **775, 777, 1248, 1259, 1275, 1295, 1323,**
    1449, 1461, 1468, 1471, 1476, 1481, 1485, 2444, 2486, 2977,
    5021
Poland—Economic Stabilization **1461, 1464, 1473, 2457**
Poland—Economic Theory **1462**
Poland—Economics **1464**
Poland—Education **1449, 2485, 4806, 4976, 5411, 5417, 6257**
Poland—Education and State **5417**
Poland—Election Law **2493**
Poland—Elections **1637, 1667, 2154, 2443, 2450, 2455, 2458, 2461,**
    2467, 2477, 2480, 2483, 2484, 2490, 2495, 2499
Poland—Electoral System **2467**
Poland—Emigration and Immigration **251, 5155, 5202**
Poland—Employment **1482**
Poland—Entrepreneurs **1477, 5337**
Poland—Entrepreneurship **1483**
Poland—Environment **1461**
Poland—Environmental Policy **1275, 1454**
Poland—Ethnic Identity **2973, 2980**
Poland—Ethnic Relations **2589, 2671, 2967, 2973, 2975, 2976,**
    2979, 5500, 5585, 5587, 5706, 5719, 5721, 5722, 5740, 5751,
    6257
Poland—European Community **1450, 1451, 1479, 3544**
Poland—European Union **3546**
Poland—Exports **1460**
Poland—Family and Gender Issues **5027, 5034**
Poland—Farmers **4976**
Poland—Feminism **4999, 5006, 5015**
Poland—Fiction **3879, 4033, 5944, 6118**
Poland—Finance **1296, 1470, 1484**
Poland—Fiscal Policy **833, 5393**
Poland—Folk Music **576, 5278**
Poland—Food Supply **827**
Poland—Foreign Economic Relations **811, 814**
Poland—Foreign Investments **757, 780, 837, 1293, 1467, 1482,**
    1484, 5394
Poland—Foreign Policy **1451, 2453, 2478, 3545, 3546, 5719**
Poland—Foreign Relations **10, 3081, 3481, 3544, 5719, 5751, 5796**
Poland—Foreign Trade **10, 1290, 1304, 1451, 1473, 1479, 3545,**
    4568, 5327, 5393
Poland—Formalism **464**
Poland—Free Enterprise **1464, 1483**
Poland—Freedom of the Press **72**
Poland—Genealogy **272, 275**
Poland—Geography **1604**
Poland—German Occupation (1914-1918) **5719**
Poland—Germans **2967, 5719**
Poland—Germany **2325, 2929, 3090, 3546**
Poland—Germany—Boundaries **5757**
Poland—Government Business Enterprises **1471**
Poland—Government-in-Exile (1939-1945) **2652, 2970, 3089, 3115**
Poland—Great Britain **3891**
Poland—Higher Education **1578, 1596**
Poland—Historiography **2611, 2612, 4976, 5554, 5812**
Poland—History **69, 155, 2169, 2588, 2589, 2905, 2967, 2968,**
    2969, 2970, 2972, 2973, 2976, 2978, 2979, 2980, 3464, 4976,
    5530, 5417, 5554, 5712, 5714, 5719, 5725, 5740, 5751, 5796,
    6257
Poland—History of Science **4811**
Poland—Hungary **3064**

Russia (Federation)—Central Asia 1777, 1778, 1803, 1807, 1810, 2055, 2097, 3355, 3395, 3397, 4796
Russia (Federation)—Central Europe 3407
Russia (Federation)—Checheno-Ingushetia 1824, 2053
Russia (Federation)—Chemical and Biological Weapons 114, 1899, 4473, 4513, 4524, 4527
Russia (Federation)—Children 106, 4945, 4950
Russia (Federation)—China (PRC) 1085, 3419, 3421, 3426, 3428
Russia (Federation)—Christianity 4719, 4723
Russia (Federation)—Church and State 1991, 4711 4732, 4734, 4735
Russia (Federation)—Church History 4735
Russia (Federation)—Cinema 664, 667, 668, 689, 701, 1911, 5010
Russia (Federation)—C.I.S. 1798, 1952, 1957, 2059, 3369, 3402, 4499
Russia (Federation)—Civil Aviation 1107, 1116, 1119
Russia (Federation)—Civil Rights 1870, 1887, 1936, 2134
Russia (Federation)—Civil Society 1916, 2066, 4999
Russia (Federation)—Civilization 470, 3031
Russia (Federation)—Civil-Military Relations 1913, 3369, 4514, 4525, 4532, 4543
Russia (Federation)—Class Structure 1139
Russia (Federation)—Clergy 4729
Russia (Federation)—College Students 1537
Russia (Federation)—Colleges and Universities 3219
Russia (Federation)—Commercial Crime 1001
Russia (Federation)—Commercial Law 891, 937, 1025, 1026
Russia (Federation)—Commercial Policy 5362
Russia (Federation)—Commodity Exchanges 1053, 1064, 1066
Russia (Federation)—Commodity Market 1077
Russia (Federation)—Communist Party 396, 1656, 1891, 2084, 2090, 2092
Russia (Federation)—Computer Networks 1115, 4827
Russia (Federation)—Computer Software 4825
Russia (Federation)—Computers 1010, 2026, 4825
Russia (Federation)—Conference on Security and Cooperation in Europe 3023
Russia (Federation)—Conservation of Natural Resources 1145
Russia (Federation)—Constitution 1898, 1900, 1922, 1923, 1924, 1933, 1938, 1942, 1944, 1973, 1979, 1980, 1990, 2006, 2008, 2009, 2017, 2019, 2023, 2063, 2081
Russia (Federation)—Constitutional Courts 1878, 1964, 1992, 2005
Russia (Federation)—Constitutional Law 1075, 1637, 1673, 1704, 1748, 1825, 1887, 1892, 1897, 1918, 1929, 1939, 1957, 1964, 1966, 1972, 1982, 1983, 2005, 2006, 2016, 2020, 2030, 2042, 2064, 2069
Russia (Federation)—Consumer Rights 1188
Russia (Federation)—Cooperative Societies 4172
Russia (Federation)—Copper Industry 1171
Russia (Federation)—Copyright Law 113, 1020, 1911, 2026
Russia (Federation)—Corruption 109, 116, 782, 1016, 2004, 2024, 2032
Russia (Federation)—Cossacks 2045, 4497
Russia (Federation)—Cost and Standard of Living 914, 1002, 1036, 1082, 1184, 1185, 1186, 1187, 1189, 1192
Russia (Federation)—Crime 400, 1016, 1036, 1742, 1920, 1929, 2028, 2032, 2036, 2076, 4936, 4949, 4953
Russia (Federation)—Criminal Law 1912, 2035
Russia (Federation)—Criminals 1742
Russia (Federation)—Culture and Politics 88, 472, 473, 496, 499, 533, 617, 1670, 2028, 4124, 4137, 4154, 4179, 4186, 4190, 4333, 4338, 4340, 4597, 4935, 4990
Russia (Federation)—Currency 1053, 1056, 1058, 1061, 1064, 1066, 1067, 1074
Russia (Federation)—Customs and Rituals 425
Russia (Federation)—Czech Republic 3026
Russia (Federation)—Dance 535

Russia (Federation)—De-Communization 538, 1006, 1656, 1878, 2089
Russia (Federation)—Defense Industries 877, 887, 4495, 4496, 4511, 4567
Russia (Federation)—Democracy 2072, 3451
Russia (Federation)—Democratization 499, 852, 1643, 1658, 1671, 1687, 1704, 1793, 1878, 1879, 1887, 1893, 1907, 1958, 1983, 2030, 2040, 2041, 2066, 2069, 2070, 2078, 2087, 3156, 3364, 3378, 3380, 3437, 3449, 4519
Russia (Federation)—Demography 953, 1609, 4882
Russia (Federation)—Description and Travel 396, 400, 401, 1011, 1031
Russia (Federation)—Directories 2011
Russia (Federation)—Disasters and Accidents 4920
Russia (Federation)—Dissidents 2021
Russia (Federation)—Dramatists 683
Russia (Federation)—Drug Abuse 4933
Russia (Federation)—Drugs 4936
Russia (Federation)—Eastern Europe 3026, 3042, 3407
Russia (Federation)—Eastern Europe—International Economic Relations 3026
Russia (Federation)—Ecology 913, 1039, 1141, 1143, 1146, 1154, 1155, 1164, 1165, 1167, 1168, 1172, 1693, 1997
Russia (Federation)—Economic Assistance 1045, 1095, 1174, 1183
Russia (Federation)—Economic Conditions 762, 817, 822, 844, 876, 953, 1001, 1008, 1013, 1017, 1022, 1047, 1074, 1194, 2029, 2030
Russia (Federation)—Economic Conversion 400, 766, 780, 781, 787, 792, 800, 802, 817, 819, 829, 833, 852, 876, 878, 887, 919, 928, 945, 962, 1001, 1003, 1005, 1006, 1008, 1010, 1011, 1013, 1014, 1015, 1016, 1018, 1019, 1021, 1023, 1024, 1027, 1031, 1034, 1035, 1036, 1037, 1044, 1050, 1051, 1056, 1059, 1060, 1061, 1063, 1065, 1068, 1072, 1077, 1078, 1082, 1084, 1093, 1094, 1095, 1100, 1101, 1109, 1110, 1112, 1116, 1117, 1124, 1127, 1128, 1139, 1176, 1185, 1187, 1188, 1190, 1191, 1193, 1194, 1195, 1196, 1197, 1199, 1200, 1202, 1537, 1538, 1876, 1889, 1891, 1892, 1928, 1942, 1945, 1946, 1957, 1969, 1970, 1974, 1987, 2001, 2027, 2032, 3416, 3437, 4511, 4528, 4849, 4879, 4899, 4919, 5021, 5326
Russia (Federation)—Economic Crime 628, 1016
Russia (Federation)—Economic Development 1155, 1179, 1183
Russia (Federation)—Economic Indicators 1008
Russia (Federation)—Economic Management 1093, 1197
Russia (Federation)—Economic Performance 1002, 1078, 1202, 2001
Russia (Federation)—Economic Policy 784, 792, 844, 885, 876, 962, 1017, 1022, 1054, 1063, 1075, 1077, 1102, 1127, 1129, 1131, 1150, 1190, 1191, 1192, 1193, 1196, 1198, 1202, 1887, 1999, 3446), 4511, 5021
Russia (Federation)—Economic Stabilization 1009, 1056, 1058, 1063, 1065, 1131
Russia (Federation)—Economic Theory 1193, 1201
Russia (Federation)—Education 530, 538, 1523, 1528, 1529, 1530, 1533, 1553
Russia (Federation)—Elections 1901, 1929, 1933, 1958, 1961, 1980, 1993, 2022, 2029, 2067, 2078, 2081, 2091
Russia (Federation)—Electoral System 2089
Russia (Federation)—Emigration and Immigration 400
Russia (Federation)—Employee Benefits 1130
Russia (Federation)—Employee Ownership 1117
Russia (Federation)—Employment 1029, 1135
Russia (Federation)—Energy 819, 1178
Russia (Federation)—Entrepreneurs 396, 400, 628, 701, 1033, 1093, 1876, 4951
Russia (Federation)—Entrepreneurship 1014, 1037, 1044, 1082, 1194
Russia (Federation)—Environment 1165

ÉDITIONS DE L'ÉCOLE DES HAUTES ÉTUDES EN SCIENCES SOCIALES

European Bibliography of Slavic and East European Studies

Bibliographie européenne des travaux sur l'ex-URSS et l'Europe de l'Est

Europäische Bibliographie zur Osteuropaforschung

The *European Bibliography of Slavic and East European Studies* is the result of cooperation between seven Western European countries. Its aim is to include works in the social sciences, literature, the arts and linguistics published in those countries on Central and Eastern Europe, Russia, and the Newly Independent States of the former Soviet Union. It comprises books, periodical articles, book reviews and dissertations published either in the languages of the cooperating countries to the Bibliography or in the languages of the subject area. Its main divisions are: geography, history, economy, law, politics, international relations, social problems, culture, literature and the arts, linguistics, and more.

The Bibliography includes a subject index to the classification, a name index and a list of periodicals searched (1,500 titles).

*

* *

Vol. III	1977	xxv-462 pages	5,930 references	260 FF
Vol. IV	1978	xxxviii-525 pages	5,841 references	290 FF
Vol. V	1979	xxviii-340 pages	5,827 references	260 FF
Vol. VI	1980	xxxiv-374 pages	6,274 references	300 FF
Vol. VII	1981	xxxii-384 pages	7,126 references	350 FF
Vol. VIII	1982	xxxii-309 pages	6,981 references	420 FF
Vol. IX-X	1983-1984	xxxii-512 pages	13,403 references	550 FF
Vol. XI	1985	xxxiii-277 pages	7,033 references	420 FF
Vol. XII	1986	xxxiii-278 pages	6,754 references	420 FF
Vol. XIII	1987	xxxiii-270 pages	6,699 references	420 FF
Vol. XIV	1988	xxxv-286 pages	7,222 references	420 FF
Vol. XV	1989	xxxv-324 pages	7,768 references	420 FF
Vol. XVI	1990	xxxv-396 pages	10,120 references	480 FF
Vol. XVII	1991	(in the press)	8,797 references	480 FF

Orders:

INSTITUT D'ÉTUDES SLAVES
9, rue Michelet, F - 75006 Paris

Payment to **INSTITUT D'ÉTUDES SLAVES**
— Post Office account
30041-00001-0120443 X020-94 Paris
— Banking account **Crédit lvonnais**
nº 30002-00498-00000 40321 N-79

Editorial address:

Bibliographie européenne
École des hautes études en sciences sociales
54, boulevard Raspail
F - 75006 Paris